Contents

Maori in the modern world colour section following p.264

Adrenalin heaven colour section following p.504

Protecting New Zealand's native wildlife colour section following p.616

◄◄ Lake Wakatipu ◄ SH6, near Punakaiki, the West Coast

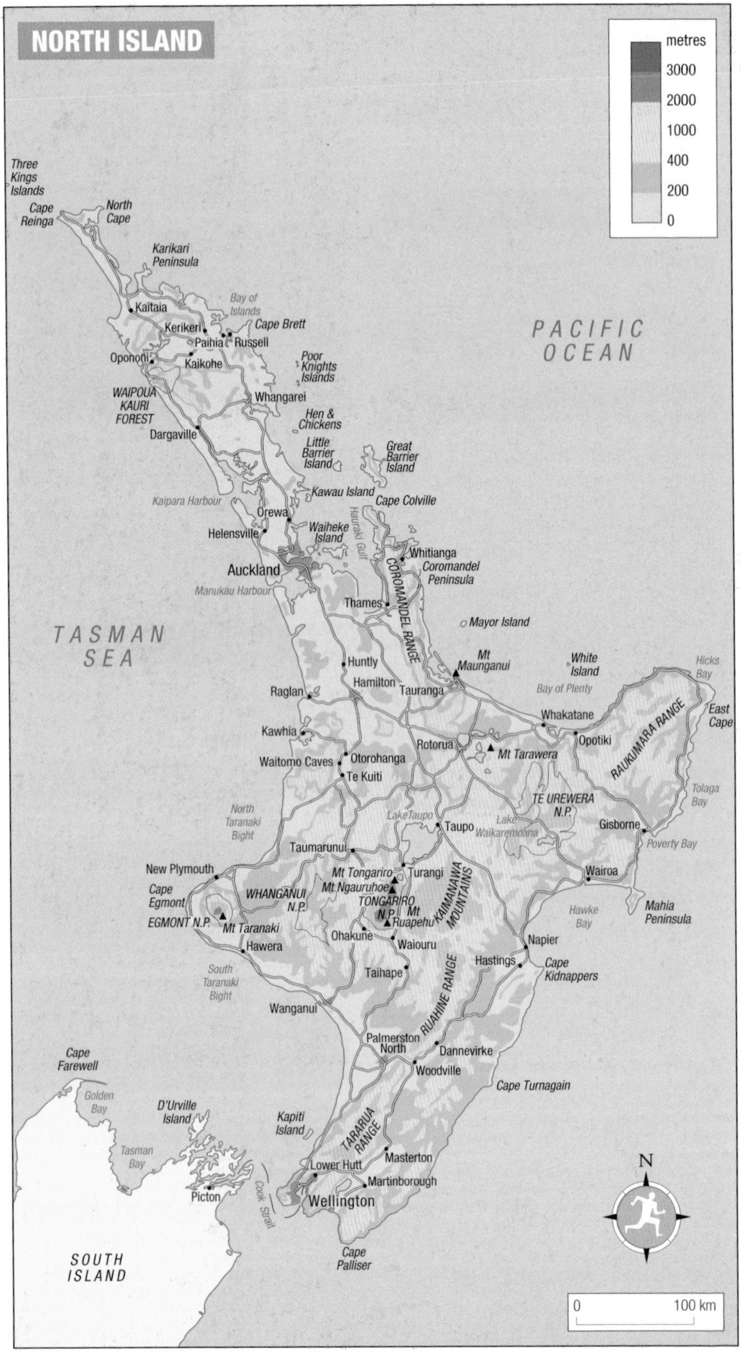

NORTH ISLAND

metres
3000
2000
1000
400
200
0

PACIFIC OCEAN
TASMAN SEA
Three Kings Islands
Cape Reinga
North Cape
Karikari Peninsula
Bay of Islands
Kaitaia
Kerikeri
Cape Brett
Paihia
Russell
Opononi
Kaikohe
Poor Knights Islands
WAIPOUA KAURI FOREST
Whangarei
Hen & Chickens
Dargaville
Little Barrier Island
Great Barrier Island
Kawau Island
Kaipara Harbour
Cape Colville
Orewa
Hauraki Gulf
Waiheke Island
Helensville
Whitianga
Auckland
COROMANDEL RANGE
Coromandel Peninsula
Manukau Harbour
Thames
Mayor Island
Mt Maunganui
White Island
Hicks Bay
Huntly
Hamilton
Tauranga
Bay of Plenty
Raglan
Whakatane
East Cape
Kawhia
Opotiki
Rotorua
Mt Tarawera
RAUKUMARA RANGE
Waitomo Caves
Otorohanga
Te Kuiti
TE UREWERA N.P.
Tolaga Bay
North Taranaki Bight
Lake Taupo
Taupo
Lake Waikaremoana
Gisborne
Poverty Bay
Taumarunui
New Plymouth
Mt Tongariro
Turangi
Mt Ngauruhoe
KAIMANAWA MOUNTAINS
Wairoa
Cape Egmont
WHANGANUI N.P.
TONGARIRO N.P.
Mt Ruapehu
Hawke Bay
Mahia Peninsula
EGMONT N.P.
Mt Taranaki
Ohakune
Waiouru
Napier
Hawera
Hastings
Cape Kidnappers
Taihape
RUAHINE RANGE
South Taranaki Bight
Wanganui
Palmerston North
Dannevirke
Woodville
Cape Farewell
Cape Turnagain
Golden Bay
D'Urville Island
Kapiti Island
TARARUA RANGE
Tasman Bay
Masterton
Lower Hutt
Martinborough
Picton
Cook Strait
Wellington
Cape Palliser
SOUTH ISLAND
N
0 100 km

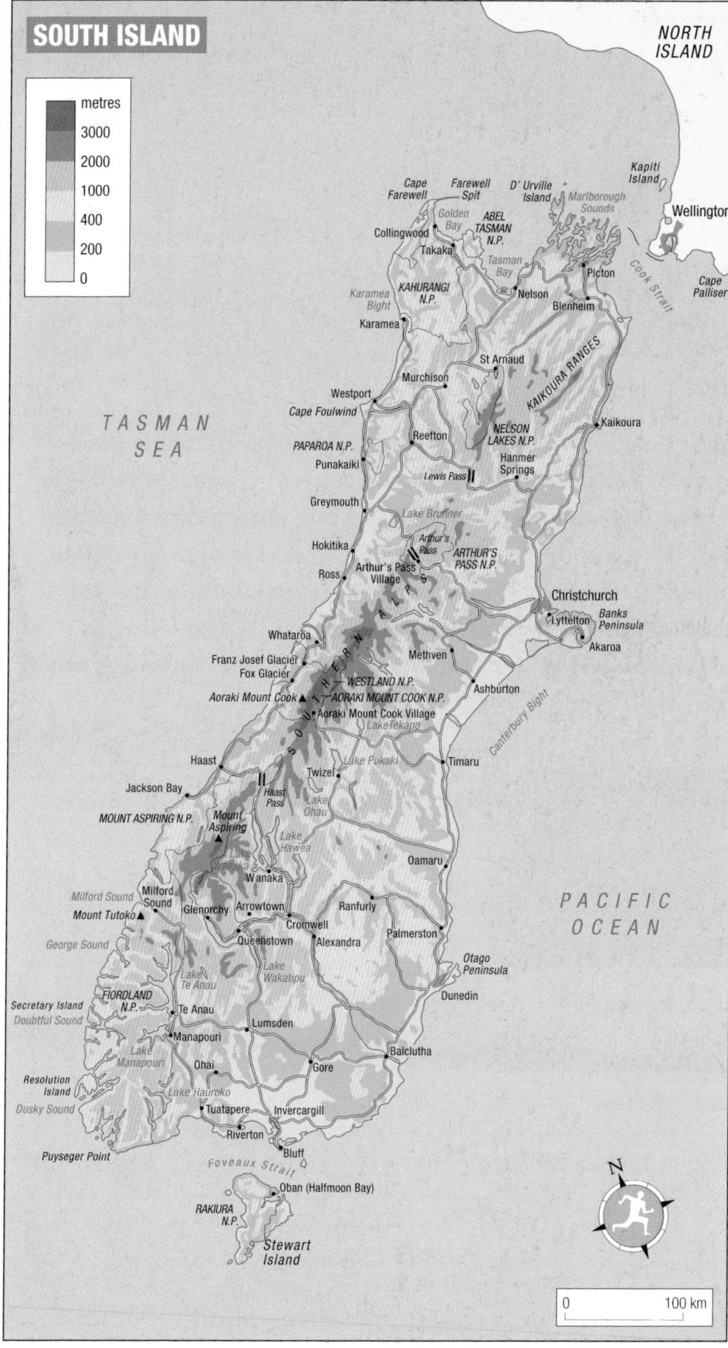
SOUTH ISLAND
metres
3000
2000
1000
400
200
0
NORTH ISLAND
Kapiti Island
Wellington
Cape Palliser
Cook Strait
Cape Farewell
Farewell Spit
D' Urville Island
Marlborough Sounds
Golden Bay
ABEL TASMAN N.P.
Collingwood
Takaka
Tasman Bay
Picton
Nelson
Blenheim
Karamea Bight
KAHURANGI N.P.
Karamea
St Arnaud
KAIKOURA RANGES
Murchison
Westport
Cape Foulwind
TASMAN SEA
NELSON LAKES N.P.
Kaikoura
Reefton
PAPAROA N.P.
Punakaiki
Hanmer Springs
Lewis Pass
Greymouth
Lake Brunner
Hokitika
Arthur's Pass
ARTHUR'S PASS N.P.
Ross
Arthur's Pass Village
Christchurch
Lyttelton
Banks Peninsula
Akaroa
SOUTHERN ALPS
Whataroa
Franz Josef Glacier
Fox Glacier
Methven
WESTLAND N.P.
Aoraki Mount Cook
AORAKI MOUNT COOK N.P.
Aoraki Mount Cook Village
Ashburton
Lake Tekapo
Canterbury Bight
Haast
Lake Pukaki
Timaru
Twizel
Jackson Bay
Haast Pass
Lake Ohau
MOUNT ASPIRING N.P.
Mount Aspiring
Lake Hawea
Lake Wanaka
Wanaka
Oamaru
Milford Sound
Milford Sound
Mount Tutoko
Glenorchy
Arrowtown
Ranfurly
PACIFIC OCEAN
Cromwell
Queenstown
Alexandra
Palmerston
George Sound
Lake Wakatipu
Otago Peninsula
Lake Te Anau
FIORDLAND N.P.
Dunedin
Secretary Island
Doubtful Sound
Te Anau
Lumsden
Manapouri
Lake Manapouri
Balclutha
Ohai
Gore
Resolution Island
Lake Hauroko
Dusky Sound
Tuatapere
Invercargill
Riverton
Bluff
Puysegur Point
Foveaux Strait
N
Oban (Halfmoon Bay)
RAKIURA N.P.
Stewart Island
0
100 km

Introduction to New Zealand

New Zealand comes with a reputation as a unique land packed with magnificent, raw scenery: craggy coastlines, sweeping beaches, primeval forests, snowcapped glacier-fed lakes and unparalleled wildlife, all beneath a brilliant blue sky. Even Kiwis – named after the odd flightless bird that has become the national emblem – are filled with astonishment at the stupendous vistas and variety of what they call "Godzone" (God's own country).

All this encourages boundless diversions, from moody strolls along windswept beaches and multi-day tramps over alpine passes to adrenalin-charged adventure activities like bungy jumping and whitewater rafting. In fact, some visitors treat the country as a kind of large-scale assault course, aiming to tackle as many challenges as possible in the time available. The one-time albatross of isolation (even Australia is two thousand kilometres away) has become a boon, bolstering New Zealand's clean, **green** image – in truth, more an accident of geography than the result of government policy.

Despite the country's popularity, it remains largely free of the crowds you might expect. Almost everything is easily accessible, packed into a land area little larger than Britain but with a population of only 4.3 million, over half of it tucked away in the three largest **cities**: Auckland, the capital Wellington, and Christchurch on the South Island. Elsewhere, you can travel miles through verdant steep-hilled farmland without seeing a soul, and there are even remote spots that, it's reliably contended, no human has yet visited.

Geologically, New Zealand split off from the super-continent of Gondwanaland early, developing a unique **ecosystem** in which birds adapted to fill the role normally held by mammals, many becoming flightless through lack of predators. That all changed around 800 years ago, when the arrival of Polynesian navigators made this the last major landmass to be settled by humans. On sighting the new land from their canoes, Maori named it **Aotearoa** – "the land of the long white cloud" – and proceeded to radically alter the fragile ecosystem, dispatching forever the giant ostrich-sized moa, which formed a major part of their diet. A delicate balance was achieved before the arrival of **Pakeha** – white Europeans, predominantly of British origin – who swarmed off their square-rigged ships full of colonial zeal.

▲ Arrowtown, near Queenstown

Fact file

- Adrift in the south Pacific some 2000km east of Australia, New Zealand was only peopled around 800 years ago.
- At 268,000 square kilometres, New Zealand is a little larger than the UK and about two-thirds the size of California. With 4.3 million people, most parts of the country are thinly populated, though Auckland has around 1.3 million inhabitants.
- For an instinctively conservative nation, New Zealand has often been socially progressive. It was the first country with votes for women and workers' pensions, and now pursues a bicultural approach to its race relations.
- New Zealand has almost 40 million sheep. That's nine for every inhabitant.
- New Zealand's economy has traditionally been agricultural, and dairy products, meat and wool remain central to its continued prosperity, with forestry and fishing also playing a part. There is a growing "knowledge economy" and, with over 2 million visitors a year, tourism is a big earner.
- New Zealand's flora and fauna developed independently, giving rise to a menagerie of exotica: tall tree ferns, the kea (an alpine parrot), the reptilian tuatara, the oddball kiwi, and many more.

The Lord of the Rings

When Peter Jackson chose to locate his *Lord of the Rings* trilogy in New Zealand the country rejoiced, even appointing a special minister for the project. However, few could have anticipated how completely it would take over the country. For thousands of visitors, no visit to Aotearoa is complete without a tour of film locations. Despite efforts to minimize the impact on the land and remove all sets, enterprising individuals have set up tours to show where it all happened. While this is a good way to see some of the country's magnificent scenery, be prepared for some disappointment. Scenes rarely look as they did in the films. Mountains from one part of the country were often used as a backdrop for plains hundreds of kilometres away, and digital manipulation has rendered many landscapes unrecognizable.

For more information see "Books", p.919.

North Island

Otaki Gorge p.299 Location for much of the Shire.
Tongariro National Park p.332 Mount Doom and Mordor were mainly shot here.
Putangirua Pinnacles p.452 Aragorn journeyed through on the Dimholt Road.
Wellington p.457 Helm's Deep was in the now-inaccessible Dry Creek Quarry, parts of the hobbits' flight from the Nazgûl were on Mount Victoria, and the Embassy Theatre saw the world premiere of *The Return of the King*.

South Island

Nelson p.515 Jens Hansen jewellers made the "One Ring To Rule Them All".
Mount Owen p.540 Near Nelson, this was the location for Dimrill Dale.
Mount Sunday p.646 The foothills of the Alps became Edoras, capital of Rohan.
Twizel p.659 Barren fields west of town were the location for the Battle of Pelennor Fields, though Queenstown's the Remarkables became the backdrop.
Arrowtown p.794 The Ford of Bruinen was shot here and in Skippers Canyon.
Queenstown p.774 The Pillars of the Kings were filmed on the Kawarau River near the bungy bridge; numerous scenes were shot at The Deer Park; and part of the Remarkables became Dimrill Dale.
Glenorchy p.800 Scenes of Isengard and Lothlórien were shot here and Saruman's tower, Orthanc, was digitally mapped onto the landscape.
Mavora Lakes p.810 The island of Nen Hithoel was shot here.
Wanaka p.810 The ride to Rivendell occurred near here.

The subsequent uneasy coexistence between **Maori** and **European** societies informs the current wrangles over cultural identity and land and resource rights. The British didn't invade as such, and were to some degree reluctant to enter into the 1840 **Treaty of Waitangi**, New Zealand's founding document, which effectively ceded New Zealand to the British Crown while guaranteeing Maori hegemony over their land and traditional gathering and fishing rights. As time wore on and increasing numbers of settlers demanded to buy ever larger parcels of land from Maori, antipathy soon surfaced, eventually escalating to hostility. Once Maori were subdued, a policy of partial integration all but destroyed **Maoritanga** – the Maori way of doing things. Maori, however, were left well outside the new European order, where difference was perceived as tantamount to a betrayal of the emergent sense of nationhood. Although elements of this still exist and Presbyterian and Anglican values have proved hard to shake off, the Kiwi psyche has become infused with Maori generosity and hospitality, coupled with a colonial mateyness and the unerring belief that whatever happens, "she'll be right".

However, an underlying inferiority complex lingers: you may well find yourself interrogated as to your opinions of the country almost before you leave the airport. Balancing this is an extraordinary enthusiasm for **sports** and **culture**, which generate a swelling pride in New Zealanders when they witness plucky Kiwis taking on the world.

▲ The All Blacks perform the haka

Paua

Paua is New Zealand's endemic species of abalone, and is found in shallow waters, encrusted in a lime scale. With vigorous polishing this can be removed to reveal a wonderfully iridescent shell, all swirls of silver, blue, green and purple. Early Maori used slivers as lures to catch the eye of fish and inlaid shaped pieces into carvings, especially as the eyes of tiki figures. Its later use in tourist trinkets has produced some wonderfully kitsch items, but you're more likely to appreciate its use in Maori crafts, perhaps incorporated into a brooch or inlaid in a mirror frame.

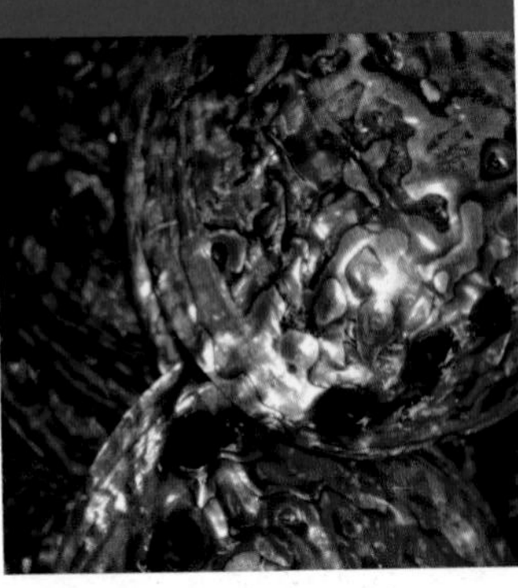

Only in the last thirty years has New Zealand come of age and developed a true national self-confidence, something partly forced on it by Britain severing the colonial apron strings in the early 1970s, and partly by the resurgence of Maori identity. Maori demands have been nurtured by a willingness on the part of most Pakeha to redress the wrongs perpetrated over the last century and a half, as long as it doesn't impinge on their high standard of living or overall feeling of control. More recently, integration has been replaced with a policy of **biculturalism** – promoting two cultures alongside each other, but with maximum interaction. The uncertainties of this future are further compounded by extensive recent **immigration** from China, Korea and South Asia.

Where to go

New Zealand packs a lot into the limited space available and is small enough that you can visit the main sights in a couple of weeks, but allow a month for a reasonable look around. Obviously, the scenery is the big draw, and most people only pop into the big cities on arrival and departure – something easily done with open-jaw air tickets allowing you to fly into Auckland and out of Christchurch.

Go-ahead **Auckland** is sprawled around the sparkling Waitemata Harbour, an arm of the island-studded Hauraki Gulf. From here, most people head south, missing out on **Northland**, the cradle of both Maori and Pakeha colonization, which is cloaked in wonderful sub-tropical forest harbouring New Zealand's largest kauri trees. East of Auckland the coast follows the isolated greenery and long, golden beaches of the **Coromandel Peninsula**, before running down to the beach towns of the **Bay of Plenty**. The lands immediately south are assailed by the ever-present sulphurous whiff of **Rotorua**, with its spurting geysers and bubbling pools of mud, and the volcanic plateau centred on the trout-filled waters of **Lake Taupo** and three snowcapped volcanoes. Cave fans will want to head west of Taupo to the eerie limestone caverns of **Waitomo**. From Taupo it's just a short hop to the delights of canoeing on the **Whanganui River**, a broad, emerald green waterway banked by virtually impenetrable bush and the almost perfect cone of **Mount Taranaki**, whose summit is accessible in a day. East of Taupo lie the ranges that form the North Island's backbone, and beyond them the **Hawke's Bay wine country**, centred on the Art Deco city of Napier. Further south, the up-and-coming wine region of Martinborough is just an hour or so away from the capital, **Wellington**, its centre squeezed onto reclaimed harbourside land and suburbs slung across steep hills overlooking glistening bays. Politicians and bureaucrats give it well-scrubbed and urbane sophistication, enlivened by a burgeoning café society and after-dark scene.

The **South Island** kicks off with the world-renowned wineries of **Marlborough** and appealing **Nelson**, a pretty and compact spot surrounded by lovely beaches and within easy reach of the hill country around the **Nelson Lakes National Park** and the fabulous sea kayaking of the **Abel Tasman National Park**. From the top of the South Island you've a choice of nipping around behind the 3000-metre summits of the Southern Alps and following the West Coast to the fabulous **glaciers** at Fox and Franz Josef, or sticking to the east, passing the whale-watching territory of **Kaikoura** en route to the South Island's

▲ Auckland and Rangitoto Island

largest centre, straight-laced Christchurch, a city with its roots firmly in the traditions of England. From here it's possible to head across country to the West Coast via Arthur's Pass on one of the country's most scenic train trips, or shoot southwest across the patchwork Canterbury Plains to the foothills of the **Southern Alps** and **Aoraki Mount Cook** with its distinctive drooping-tent summit.

Hot pools, geysers and boiling mud

One of the lasting memories of time spent in New Zealand is laying back in a bush-girt **natural hot pool** gazing up at the stars. New Zealand lies on the Pacific Ring of Fire, and earthquakes and volcanic activity are common. Superheated steam finds its way to the surface as **geysers** (only around Rotorua), **boiling mud pools** (Rotorua and Taupo) and **hot springs**. Blissfully, there are around eighty hot springs across the northern two-thirds of the North Island and another fifteen along a thin thread down the western side of the Southern Alps.

Over thirty are commercial **resorts** offering tepid swimming pools, near scalding baths, BBQ areas and perhaps mineral mud and hydrothermal pampering. The remainder are **natural pools**, either in the bush, beside a stream or welling up from below a sandy beach. A few are well known, but many more require a little sleuthing: locals like to keep the best spots to themselves. Check out **Ⓦwww.nzhotpools.co.nz**, which includes a hot pools' map of the country, links to resorts and details of how to get to some of the free natural hot pools. Also read our notes on **amoebic meningitis** on p.79.

To get you started, we've picked a handful of the best well-known spots (listed north to south).

Polynesian Spa Commercial resort right in Rotorua with something for everyone: mineral pools, family spa, adult-only open-air complex and all manner of body treatments. See p.305

Hot Water Beach Come at low tide, rent a spade and dig yourself a hot pool beside the cool surf. See p.376

Maruia Springs Small resort in the hills 200km north of Christchurch. Particularly magical in winter. See p.633

Welcome Flat Hot Springs Four natural pools gloriously sited amid mountain scenery just south of Fox Glacier. It is a six- to seven-hour walk in and you can stay at the adjacent DOC hut. See p.761

▶ Picnicking on Kapiti Island, Western North Island

The flatlands of Canterbury run down, via the grand architecture of **Oamaru**, to the unmistakably Scottish-influenced city of **Dunedin**, a base for exploring the teeming wildlife of the **Otago Peninsula** with its albatross colony and opportunities for penguin-watching. In the middle of the nineteenth century, prospectors arrived here and rushed inland to gold strikes throughout central Otago and around stunningly set **Queenstown**, now a highly commercialized activity centre where bungy jumping, rafting, jetboating and skiing hold sway. This is also the tramping heartland, with the **Routeburn Track** linking Queenstown to the rain-sodden fiords, lakes and mountains of **Fiordland**, and the famous **Milford Track**. The further south you travel, the more you'll feel the bite of the Antarctic winds, which reach their peak on New Zealand's third landmass, the tiny and isolated **Stewart Island**, covered mostly by dense coastal rainforest that offers one of your best chances of spotting a kiwi in the wild.

When to go

With over a thousand kilometres of ocean in every direction, it comes as no surprise that New Zealand has a maritime climate, warm through the southern summer months of December to March and never truly cold, even in winter.

▼ Little Kaiteriteri, Abel Tasman National Park

Weather patterns are strongly affected by the prevailing westerlies, which suck up moisture from the Tasman Sea and dump it on the western side of both islands. The South Island gets the lion's share, with the West Coast and Fiordland ranking among the world's wettest places. The mountain ranges running the length of both islands cast long rain shadows over the eastern lands, making them considerably drier, though the south is a few degrees cooler than elsewhere, and sub-tropical Auckland and Northland are appreciably more humid. In the North Island, warm, damp summers fade almost imperceptibly into cool, wet winters, but the further south you go the more the year divides into four distinct seasons.

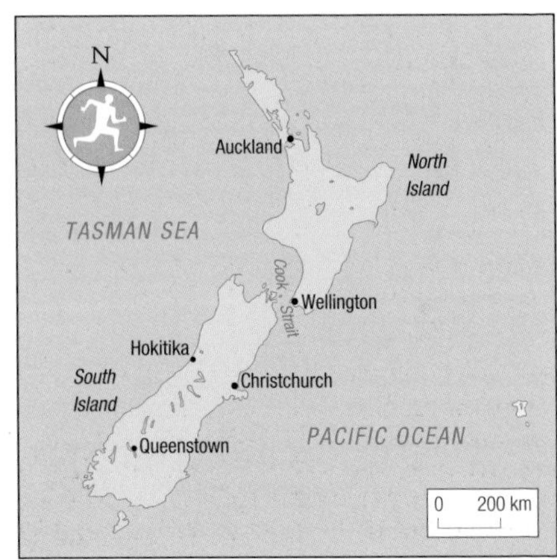

Such regional variation makes it viable to visit at any time of year, provided you pick your destinations. The **summer** months from December to March are the most popular and you'll find everything open, though often packed with holidaying Kiwis from Christmas to mid-January. Accommodation throughout summer is at a premium. In general, you're better off joining the bulk of foreign visitors during the **shoulder seasons** – October, November and April – when sights and attractions can be a shade quieter, and rooms easier to come by. **Winter** (May–Sept) is the wettest, coldest and consequently least popular time, though Northland can still be relatively balmy. The switch to prevailing southerly winds tends to bring periods of crisp, dry and cloudless weather to the West Coast and heavy snowfalls to the Southern Alps and Central North Island, allowing New Zealand to offer some of the most varied and least-populated **skiing and snowboarding** anywhere.

Average monthly temperatures and rainfall

	Jan	Feb	Mar	Apr	May	Jun	July	Aug	Sept	Oct	Nov	Dec
Auckland												
av. max. temp. (°C)	23	23	22	19	17	14	13	14	16	17	19	21
av. min. temp. (°C)	16	16	15	13	11	9	8	8	9	11	12	14
av. rainfall (mm)	79	94	81	97	112	137	145	117	102	102	89	79
av. max. temp. (°F)	73	73	72	66	63	57	55	57	61	63	66	70
av. min. temp. (°F)	61	61	59	55	52	48	46	46	48	52	54	57
av. rainfall (inches)	3.1	3.7	3.2	3.8	4.4	5.4	5.7	4.6	4.0	4.0	3.5	3.1
Wellington												
av. max. temp. (°C)	21	21	19	17	14	13	12	12	14	16	17	19
av. min. temp. (°C)	13	13	12	11	8	7	6	6	8	9	10	12
av. rainfall (mm)	81	81	81	97	117	117	137	117	97	102	89	89
av. max. temp. (°F)	70	70	66	63	57	55	54	54	57	61	63	66
av. min. temp. (°F)	55	55	54	52	46	45	43	43	46	48	50	54
av. rainfall (inches)	3.2	3.2	3.2	3.8	4.6	4.6	5.4	4.6	3.8	4.0	3.5	3.5
Christchurch												
av. max. temp. (°C)	21	21	19	17	13	11	10	11	14	17	19	21
av. min. temp. (°C)	12	12	10	7	4	2	2	2	4	7	8	11
av. rainfall (mm)	56	43	48	48	66	66	69	48	46	43	48	56
av. max. temp. (°F)	70	70	66	63	55	52	50	52	57	63	66	70
av. min. temp. (°F)	54	54	50	45	39	36	36	36	39	45	46	52
av. rainfall (inches)	2.2	1.7	1.9	1.9	2.6	2.6	2.7	1.9	1.8	1.7	1.9	2.2
Hokitika												
av. max. temp. (°C)	19	19	18	16	14	12	12	12	13	15	16	18
av. min. temp. (°C)	12	12	11	8	6	3	3	3	6	8	9	11
av. rainfall (mm)	262	191	239	236	244	231	218	239	226	292	267	262
av. max. temp. (°F)	66	66	64	61	57	54	54	54	55	59	61	64
av. min. temp. (°F)	54	54	52	46	43	37	37	37	43	46	48	52
av. rainfall (inches)	10.3	7.5	9.4	9.3	9.6	9.1	8.6	9.4	8.9	11.5	10.5	10.3
Queenstown												
av. max. temp. (°C)	21	21	20	15	11	9	9	11	14	18	19	20
av. min. temp. (°C)	10	10	9	7	3	1	0	1	3	5	7	10
av. rainfall (mm)	79	72	74	72	64	58	59	63	66	77	64	62
av. max. temp. (°F)	70	70	68	59	52	48	48	52	57	64	66	68
av. min. temp. (°F)	50	50	48	45	37	34	32	34	37	41	45	50
av. rainfall (inches)	3.1	2.8	2.9	2.8	2.5	2.3	2.3	2.5	2.6	3.0	2.5	2.4

things not to miss

It's not possible to see everything that New Zealand has to offer in one trip – and we don't suggest you try. What follows, in no particular order, is a selective taste of the islands' highlights: outstanding buildings and natural wonders, adventure activities and exotic wildlife. They're arranged in five colour-coded categories, which you can browse through to find the very best things to see and experience. All highlights have a page reference to take you straight into the Guide, where you can find out more.

01 Milford Sound Page **853** • Experience the grandeur and beauty of Fiordland on the area's most accessible fiord, especially atmospheric when the mist descends after heavy rainfall.

02 Abel Tasman National Park Page **522** • Kayaking the shoreline or hiking the Coast Track is a great way to see the Abel Tasman National Park.

03 Wai-O-Tapu Page **317** • The best of Rotorua's geothermal sites, Wai-O-Tapu offers beautiful, mineral-coloured lakes, plopping mud pools and a geyser that erupts on cue each morning.

04 Bungy jumping Page **65** • New Zealand's trademark adventure sport can be tried at Kawerau Bridge, the original commercial jump site, or some of the super-high mega jumps nearby.

05 Surfing at Raglan Page **243** • A left-hand break that's one of the world's longest, coupled with reliable swells, makes Raglan a prime surfing destination.

06 Christchurch Art Gallery Page **579** • The South Island's most extensive collection of New Zealand art is housed in a striking modern building in the heart of Christchurch.

07 Taieri Gorge Railway Page **682** • Dating back to 1859, the Taieri Gorge Railway penetrates otherwise inaccessible mountain landscapes and is a dramatic journey at any time of the year.

08 Farewell Spit Page **539** • This slender 25km arc of sand dunes and beaches is a nature reserve protecting a host of bird species including black swans, wrybills, curlews and dotterels.

09 Moeraki Boulders Page **620** • Don't pass through the Oamaru area without a visit to the these large, perfectly round, natural spheres with a honeycomb centre, just sitting in the surf.

11 Hangi Page **52** • Sample fall-off-the-bone pork and chicken along with sweet potatoes and pumpkin, disinterred after several hours' steaming in a Maori earth oven.

10 White Island Page **397** • Take an appealing boat trip out to New Zealand's most active volcano, and stroll through the sulphurous lunar landscape to peer into the steaming crater.

12 Otago Central Rail Trail Page **831** • Taking three leisurely days on a bike is the best way to tackle this 150km trail, which follows the route of a former rail line through some ruggedly barren country.

13 Wine Page **54** • New Zealand produces some world-beating wines, especially Sauvignon Blanc from the Marlborough region.

14 The Routeburn Track Page **806** • One of the country's finest walks, showcasing forested valleys, rich birdlife, thundering waterfalls, river flats, lakes and wonderful mountain scenery.

15 Tree ferns Page **906** • New Zealand has a unique ecosystem, its ubiquitous tree ferns sometimes reaching up to 10m in height and providing shade for more delicate specimens.

16 Whanganui River Journey Page **273** • This relaxing three-day canoe trip along a historic waterway takes you far away from roads through some of the North Island's loveliest scenery.

17 **Whale watching** Page **559** • Whale watching off the Kaikoura Peninsula is justifiably highly popular, and you don't have to stick to a boat trip to do it, with plane and helicopter rides on offer to up the adrenalin ante.

18 **Tongariro Alpine Crossing** Page **340** • A superb one-day hike through the volcanic badlands of the Tongariro National Park, passing the cinder cone of Mount Ngauruhoe, along the shores of turquoise lakes and with long views right across the North Island.

19 **Museum of New Zealand (Te Papa)** Page **468** • A celebration of the people, culture and art of New Zealand that's as appealing to kids as it is to adults, with an impressive use of state-of-the-art technology.

20 Hokianga Harbour Page **219** • As a low-key antidote to the commercialization of the Bay of Islands, the sand dunes, quiet retreats and crafts culture of the Hokianga Harbour are hard to beat.

21 Art Deco, Napier Page **431** • The world's most homogenous collection of small-scale Art Deco architecture owes its genesis to the devastating 1931 earthquake that flattened Napier.

22 Diving at the Poor Knights Islands Page **182** • Two-dive day-trips visit any of several dozen sites at one of the world's best diving destinations. A couple of nearby naval wrecks add to the possibilities.

23 The glaciers Page **752** • The steep and dramatic Fox and Franz Josef glaciers can be explored by glacier hike, ice climbing and helicopter flights landing on the snowfields above.

24 East Cape Page **402** • A varied coastline and the slow pace of life make the East Cape a place to linger.

25 Ninety Mile Beach Page **214** • This seemingly endless wave-lashed golden strand is a designated highway, plied by tour buses that regularly stop to let passengers toboggan down the steep dunes.

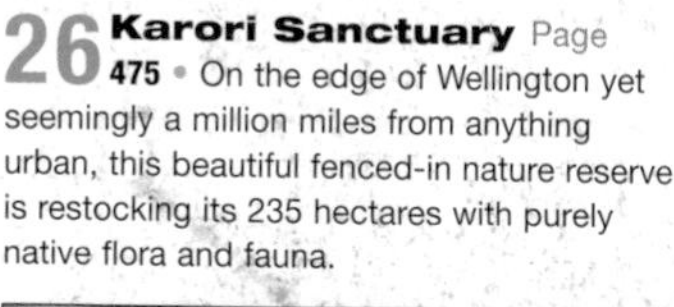

26 Karori Sanctuary Page **475** • On the edge of Wellington yet seemingly a million miles from anything urban, this beautiful fenced-in nature reserve is restocking its 235 hectares with purely native flora and fauna.

27 Jetboating Page **65** • This countrywide obsession finds its most iconic expression in Queenstown's Shotover River, but there are excellent jetboating opportunities all over the country.

28 The Catlins Coast Page **692** • Seals and dolphins and a slow pace of life make the Catlins a great place to unwind for a few days.

29 Penguin watching Page **688** • Penguin Place, on the Otago Peninsula, offers the rare chance to see a protected penguin nesting area close up from a unique system of hides and trenches.

30 Caving and cave rafting Page **248** • Enter Waitomo's labyrinthine netherworld on huge abseils and explore its glow-worm-filled cave systems while floating down streams on inner tubes.

Basics

Basics

Getting there

The quickest and easiest way to get to New Zealand is to fly. It is possible to arrive by sea, but unless you own a boat, this means joining a cruise, paying for your passage on a cargo ship or joining a private yacht as crew – all of which are expensive and time-consuming.

There are very few charter flights or all-in package deals to New Zealand, so flying there almost always involves **scheduled flights**. Fares depend on the season, with the highest prices during the New Zealand summer (Dec–Feb); fares drop during the shoulder seasons (Sept–Nov & March–May) and you'll get the cheapest prices during the low (ski) season (June–Aug).

If New Zealand is only one stop on a longer journey, you might want to consider buying a **Round-the-World** (RTW) ticket. Some travel agents can sell you an "off-the-shelf" RTW ticket that will have you touching down in about half a dozen cities (Auckland is on many itineraries); others will have to assemble one for you, which can be tailored to your needs, though this is liable to be more expensive.

Tourists and those on short-term working visas (see p.73) are generally required by New Zealand immigration to arrive with a ticket out of the country, so one-way tickets are really only viable for Australian and New Zealand residents. If you've purchased a return ticket and find you want to stay longer or head off on a totally different route, it's sometimes possible to cash in the return half of your ticket (though you'll make a loss on the deal) at the same travel agent where you bought it. Alternatively, you could try flogging it on the Internet – but don't hold your breath.

From the UK and Ireland

Over a dozen airlines compete to fly you from Britain to New Zealand for as little as £690, but prices depend upon the time of year, and can rocket up to around £1800 at Christmas. Going for the **cheapest flight** typically means sacrificing some comfort, which you may regret, given that your journey will last at least 24 hours, longer if your flight makes more than the obligatory refuelling stop. There are no direct flights to New Zealand from Ireland, and prices are proportionately higher, since the short hop to London (£80–100 return, cheaper with Internet deals) has to be added on to the fare.

No matter how keen you are to arrive in New Zealand, it makes sense, mostly from a health point of view, to break the journey, and most **scheduled flights** allow multiple **stopovers** either in North America and the Pacific, or Asia and Australia. The vast majority of direct scheduled flights depart from London Heathrow, though some services operate from London Gatwick and Manchester. Overseas flights into Wellington or Dunedin are rare, so the only real choice is between the main international airport at Auckland, in the north of the North Island, and the airport at Christchurch, midway down the South Island. Christchurch receives fewer direct flights but many scheduled airlines have a code-share shuttle from Auckland at no extra cost. The most desirable option, an **open-jaw ticket** (flying into one and out of the other), usually costs no more than an ordinary return and means not retracing your steps to leave.

The best deals along fixed **Round-the-World** (RTW; usually valid for 12 months) routes include London through Buenos

Departure tax

New Zealand's **departure tax** is never included in airline ticket prices. When you leave the country, each person aged 12 and over must pay $25 (in NZ dollars; credit cards accepted) after check-in.

Aires, Auckland, Sydney, Bangkok and Nairobi for £1350–1600, or Doha, Bangkok, Singapore, Sydney, Auckland and Los Angeles for £729–1100; Trailfinders (see p.31) will usually knock a little off using slightly amended routes. It is also possible to reduce your flight costs by incorporating an overland section into your RTW ticket: common land sectors include Delhi to Kathmandu, Brisbane or Sydney to Cairns, and Buenos Aires to São Paulo. Routes combining the resources of two or more airlines in a RTW ticket are more expensive and almost infinitely variable.

From the US and Canada

The only direct trans-Pacific flights to New Zealand are those from Los Angeles to Auckland (with Air New Zealand and Qantas), San Francisco to Auckland (with Air New Zealand), and Vancouver to Auckland (again with Air New Zealand), a flight of 12–16 hours. These are the only companies flying planes, but assorted code-share partners – Air Canada, American Airlines, British Airways, etc – will sell tickets to New Zealand, usually offering several connections a day to the two other major airports, Wellington and Christchurch.

From the US an LA-Auckland or San Francisco-Auckland round-trip Apex fare goes for around US$900 during the southern winter, rising to about US$1700 in peak southern summer season. Flights from all other US cities are routed via California. Off-peak you might expect to pay US$1400–1800 from New York or Chicago, but shopping around the discount agents or checking out the newspapers for special offers could save you more than a few bucks.

From Canada, Air New Zealand run direct Vancouver–Auckland flights and code-share with Air Canada for links to provincial capitals. Depending on the season, sample Apex midweek fares are in the following ranges: from Vancouver CAN$1200–1800; from Toronto CAN$2100–2600; from Montréal CAN$2200–2600. Substantial savings can sometimes be made through discount travel companies and websites.

An alternative approach is to fly **via Asia**. It isn't as much of a detour as it sounds, especially if you're flying from Canada or the east coast of the US, and may work out cheaper. Korean Airlines has flights from Anchorage, Atlanta, Chicago, Dallas, Las Vegas, Los Angeles, New York, San Francisco, Seattle, Toronto, Vancouver and Washington DC, all changing at Seoul (Incheon) before continuing on to Auckland.

If New Zealand is only one stop on a longer journey, you might consider a **Round-the-World (RTW)** ticket. A sample itinerary of LA–Samoa–Fiji–Auckland–Sydney–Kuala Lumpur–Istanbul–London–LA would cost US$3400 (low-season departure).

An equally exotic option is to stop off at a **Pacific island** or two along the way. Air New Zealand visits half a dozen islands and often charges less than US$100 per stopover.

Internal flights

If you are planning on doing a lot of travelling within New Zealand, especially between the North and South islands, book your tickets online well in advance – reductions can be as high as fifty percent. It may also be worth looking into the **air passes** offered by Air New Zealand. The airline markets a variety of cheap one-way flights from Auckland and Christchurch to various NZ destinations, if booked at the same time as an international flight. Alternatively, within the Domestic, Tasman and Pacific booking section of their website, you can buy one-way flights to a number of destinations at Smart Saver fares (the cheapest tickets, all recently reduced by up to 27 percent to try to see off competition from Qantas and to a lesser degree Pacific Blue), or use a **South Pacific Air Pass**, based on a zone system within New Zealand. Flying within zone one costs NZ$120, zone two NZ$210, three NZ$290, four NZ$340. Qantas's **Boomerang Pass** is available to all international travellers (not just Qantas ticket holders), and comprises zones dependent upon air miles – zone one costs £65 for anything up to 1200km, zone two £120 for anything up to 1840km and zone three £146 for anything, in Oz or NZ, above 1841km.

From Australia

Qantas, Jetstar, Air New Zealand and Pacific Blue all operate frequent flights between Australia and New Zealand, and the competition keeps **prices** reasonable. It may also be worth checking out the less frequent flights with Thai, Singapore, Emirates and Aerolineas Argentinas, especially if New Zealand is part of wider travels.

It's a relatively short hop across the Tasman Sea: **flying time** from Sydney or Melbourne to Auckland or Christchurch is around three hours. There's an ever-changing range of special offers, and your best bet is to check the latest with a specialist travel agent (see p.31) or visit the airlines' websites. Some of the **best deals** are with Qantas' budget wing, Jetstar, which flies to Christchurch from Brisbane, the Gold Coast, Melbourne and Sydney and offers fares as low as A$330 return if you're prepared to go for non-refundable JetSaver tickets.

Pacific Blue is equally competitive, with direct flights from Brisbane, Melbourne and Sydney to Auckland, Wellington and Christchurch.

Qantas and Air New Zealand each fly several daily trans-Tasman flights, and prices vary enormously depending on demand: book well in advance in summer. By shopping around you should be able to land a return flight from most eastern cities to Auckland, Wellington, Christchurch or Dunedin for A$500. Flights from Perth start at around A$1000.

Open-jaw tickets – which let you fly into one city and out of another, making your own way between – can save a lot of backtracking, and add little (if anything) to the total fare. There are also various **air passes** for internal flights available (see "Getting Around", p.28, for details).

There's a huge variety of holidays and tours to New Zealand available in Australia. For example, Air New Zealand's holiday subsidiary packages short **city-breaks** (flight and accommodation) and **fly-drive** deals for little more than the cost of the regular airfare. In winter, there are accommodation **skiing** packages to New Zealand's ski-fields; all-inclusive four-day trips to Queenstown start from A$800, rising to A$1000 for a seven-day trip.

From South Africa

Travelling to New Zealand from South Africa generally involves flying via Australia. Qantas flies Johannesburg–Sydney then on to Auckland, Wellington or Christchurch. South African Airlines (Ⓦwww.flyssa.com) operates the same route as a codeshare with Qantas and Air New Zealand. Expect to pay R15,000–24,000 depending on season.

Airlines, agents and tour operators

Many airlines and discount travel websites offer you the opportunity to book your tickets **online**, cutting out the costs of agents and middlemen. Good deals can often be found through discount or auction sites, as well as the airlines' own websites.

If time is limited and you have a clear idea of what it is you want to do, there are good deals going on tours. There are loads of companies, offering everything from flexible backpacker-oriented excursions through mainstream bus **tours** to no-expense-spared extravaganzas.

Full "see-it-all" packages can work out to be quite expensive but aren't bad value, considering what you'd be spending anyway. A number of companies operate flexible bus tours, which you can hop off whenever you like and rejoin a day or two later when the next bus comes through (see p.36 for details of these).

Pretty much all the major tour operators can also book you onto **tramping** trips, including some of the guided Great Walks (see p.66); you'll still need to book way in advance, though. For **skiing** trips, the cheapest option is usually to contact ski clubs at the fields directly: check out the contacts at Ⓦwww.snow.co.nz.

Even if an all-in package doesn't appeal, there may be some mileage in pre-booking some accommodation, tours or a rental vehicle through a travel agent.

Airlines

In the UK and Ireland

Aerolineas Argentinas UK Ⓣ020/7290 7887, Ⓦwww.aerolineas.com.ar. London Heathrow via Madrid and Buenos Aires to Auckland.

Air Canada UK Ⓣ0871/220 1111, Republic of Ireland Ⓣ01/679 3958; Ⓦwww.aircanada.ca.

Fly less – stay longer! Travel and Climate Change

Climate change is perhaps the single biggest issue facing our planet. It is caused by a build-up in the atmosphere of carbon dioxide and other greenhouse gases, which are emitted by many sources – including planes. Already, **flights** account for thre to four percent of human-induced global warming: that figure may sound small, but it is rising year on year and threatens to counteract the progress made by reducing greenhouse emissions in other areas.

Rough Guides regard travel as a **global benefit**, and feel strongly that the advantages to developing economies are important, as are the opportunities for greater contact and awareness among peoples. But we also believe in travelling responsibly, which includes giving thought to how often we fly and what we can do to redress any harm that our trips may create.

We can travel less or simply reduce the amount we travel by air (taking fewer trips and staying longer, or taking the train if there is one); we can avoid night flights (which are more damaging); and we can make the trips we do take "climate neutral" via a carbon offset scheme. **Offset schemes** run by climatecare.org, carbonneutral.com and others allow you to "neutralize" the greenhouse gases that you are responsible for releasing. Their websites have simple calculators that let you work out the impact of any flight – as does our own. Once that's done, you can pay to fund projects that will reduce future emissions by an equivalent amount. Please take the time to visit our website and make your trip climate neutral, or get a copy of the *Rough Guide to Climate Change* for more detail on the subject.

www.roughguides.com/climatechange

From London Heathrow to Auckland via Vancouver and Honolulu.

Air New Zealand UK ⓣ0800/028 4149, ⓦwww.airnewzealand.co.nz. To Auckland, via Los Angeles and the popular South Pacific route with a choice of stopovers in Honolulu, Fiji, Western Samoa, the Cook Islands, Tahiti and Tonga. There's also a daily service from London to Auckland via Hong Kong.

British Airways UK ⓣ0870/850 9850, Republic of Ireland ⓣ1890/626 747; ⓦwww.britishairways.com. From London Heathrow to Auckland and Christchurch, with stopovers in LA or Brisbane.

Cathay Pacific UK ⓣ020/8834 8888, ⓦwww.cathaypacific.com.

Garuda Indonesia UK ⓣ020/7467 8661, ⓦwww.garuda-indonesia.com. London Gatwick to Auckland via Bangkok and Bali.

Japan Airlines UK ⓣ0845/774 7700, ⓦwww.jal.co.jp. Heathrow to Auckland via Tokyo.

Korean Air UK ⓣ0800/413 000, Republic of Ireland ⓣ01/799 7990; ⓦwww.koreanair.com. Heathrow to Auckland and Christchurch via Seoul.

Malaysia Airlines (MAS) ⓦwww.malaysianairlines.com. From Heathrow to Auckland via Kuala Lumpur.

Qantas UK ⓣ020/8846 0466, Republic of Ireland ⓣ01/407 3278; ⓦwww.qantas.com.au. From Heathrow to Auckland and Christchurch, via LA, Bangkok, Singapore, Sydney and Melbourne.

Singapore Airlines UK ⓣ0844/800 2380, Republic of Ireland ⓣ01/671 0722; ⓦwww.singaporeair.com. Flights from Heathrow and Manchester to Auckland and Christchurch via Singapore, long wait at Singapore on Manchester flights.

Thai Airways International UK ⓣ0870/606 0911, ⓦwww.thaiair.com. From Heathrow to Auckland via Bangkok and Sydney.

In the US and Canada

Air Canada ⓣ1-888/247-2262, ⓦwww.aircanada.ca

Air New Zealand US ⓣ1-800/262-1234, Canada ⓣ1-800/663-5494; ⓦwww.airnewzealand.com

American Airlines ⓣ1-800/433-7300, ⓦwww.aa.com

British Airways ⓣ1-800/247-9297, ⓦwww.britishairways.com

Korean Airlines ⓣ1-800/438-5000, ⓦwww.koreanair.com

Qantas Airways ⓣ1-800/227-4500, ⓦwww.qantas.com

In Australia

Aerolineas Argentinas ⓣ02/9234 9000, ⓦwww.aerolineas.com.ar

Air New Zealand ⓣ13 2476, ⓦwww.airnz.com.au

Emirates Airline ⓣ1300/303 777, ⓦwww.emirates.com
Jetstar ⓣ13 1538, ⓦwww.jetstar.com
Pacific Blue ⓣ13 1645, ⓦwww.flypacificblue.com
Qantas ⓣ13 1313, ⓦwww.qantas.com.au
Singapore Airlines ⓣ13 1011, ⓦwww.singaporeair.com
Thai Airways ⓣ1300/651 960, ⓦwww.thaiair.com

Travel agents

In the UK

North South Travel UK ⓣ & ⓕ01245/608 291, ⓦwww.northsouthtravel.co.uk. Friendly, competitive travel agency, offering discounted fares worldwide – profits are used to support projects in the developing world, especially the promotion of sustainable tourism.
Quest Worldwide ⓣ0845/880 0248, ⓦwww.questtravel.com. Specialists in round-the-world and Australasian discount fares.
STA Travel UK ⓣ0871/230 0040, ⓦwww.statravel.co.uk. Worldwide specialists in low-cost flights and tours for students and under-26s, though other customers are welcome. Experts on New Zealand travel with branches in major Kiwi cities.
Trailfinders UK ⓣ020/7628 7628, ⓦwww.trailfinders.com, Republic of Ireland ⓣ021/464 8877, ⓦwww.trailfinders.ie. One of the best-informed and most efficient agents for independent travellers; produce a very useful quarterly magazine worth scrutinizing for round-the-world routes.

In Australia

Backpackers World Travel ⓣ1800/67 67 63, ⓦwww.backpackersworld.com.au.
STA Travel ⓣ13 4782, ⓦwww.statravel.com.au.
Trailfinders ⓣ1300/780 212, ⓦwww.trailfinders.com.au.

In the US and Canada

Educational Travel Center ⓣ1-800/747-5551 or 608/256-5551, ⓦwww.edtrav.com. Student/youth discount agent.
STA Travel US ⓣ1-800/781-4040, ⓦwww.statravel.com.
Travel Cuts Canada ⓣ1-866/246-9762, US ⓣ1-800/592-2887; ⓦwww.travelcuts.com. Canadian student-travel organization.

Online booking agents

ⓦ**www.cheapflights.co.uk** Bookings from the UK and Ireland only (for US, ⓦwww.cheapflight.com; for Canada, ⓦwww.cheapflights.ca; for Australia, ⓦwww.cheapflights.com.au). Flight deals, travel agents, plus links to other travel sites.
ⓦ**www.cheaptickets.com** Discount flight specialists (US only).
ⓦ**www.expedia.com** Discount airfares, all-airline search engine and daily deals (US only); for the UK ⓦwww.expedia.co.uk; for Canada ⓦwww.expedia.ca).
ⓦ**www.lastminute.com** Offers last-minute holiday packages and flight-only deals (UK only; for Australia, ⓦwww.lastminute.com.au).
ⓦ**www.opodo.co.uk** User-friendly, UK-only booking site – owned by major airlines such as BA and Air France – with good deals on flights and packages.
ⓦ**www.priceline.com** Name-your-own-price website that has deals at around forty percent off standard fares. You cannot specify flight times (although you do specify dates) and the tickets are non-refundable and non-transferable (US only; for the UK, ⓦwww.priceline.co.uk).
ⓦ**www.skyauction.com** Bookings from the US only. Auctions tickets and travel packages using a "second bid" scheme. The best strategy is to bid the maximum you're willing to pay, since if you win you'll pay just enough to beat the runner-up regardless of your maximum bid.
ⓦ**www.travelocity.com** Destination guides, hot web fares and best deals for car hire, accommodation

and lodging as well as fares. Provides access to the travel agent system, SABRE, the most comprehensive central reservations system in the US.

Specialist package and tour agents

For details of New Zealand-based tour operators see p.66.

In the UK

The Adventure Company ⓣ0845/450 5314, ⓦwww.primeadventures.co.uk. Fifty different itineraries for people wanting to see as much of the country as possible.

Contiki ⓣ020/8290 6422, ⓦwww.contiki.co.uk. Bus tours with itineraries ranging from 3 days around the Bay of Islands (£150) to a 15-day grand tour (around £690 from Auckland), with accommodation and most meals included.

Freedom Australia and New Zealand ⓣ0870/742 4000, ⓦwww.freedomnz.co.uk. Coach tours or self-drives with all the organizational headaches removed.

High Places ⓣ0114/275 7500, ⓦwww.highplaces.co.uk. Trips to NZ specializing in high-country hiking and cycling.

The Traveller ⓣ0800/091 1513, ⓦwww.thetravelleruk.com. Tour package specialists for both islands.

In the US

Adventures Abroad ⓣ1-800/665-3998, ⓦwww.adventures-abroad.com. Adventure specialists often combining NZ with Australia and Fiji.

Collette Vacations US ⓣ1-800/340-5158, Canada ⓣ1-800/468-5955; ⓦwww.collettevacations.com. Specialists in Australia and New Zealand travel. Their 19-day fully escorted tour of New Zealand, including trips to glaciers and rainforests, starts at US$2899, plus the cost of international flights.

Contiki Holidays ⓣ1-888/CONTIKI, ⓦwww.contiki.com. Specialists in travel for 18–35s. Their several land packages range from a 7-day South Island tour (NZ$949) to a 13-day Grand Adventurer (NZ$1765).

Elderhostel ⓣ1-800/454-5768, ⓦwww.elderhostel.org. Educational and activity programmes primarily for senior travellers. In addition to joint Australia/New Zealand packages, there are specialist month-long tours like Land of Geysers and Greenstone (US$6762, plus the cost of international flights), and Middle Earth Locations (13 nights; US$4116).

Holidaze Ski Tours ⓣ1-800/526-2827 or 732/280-1120, ⓦwww.holidaze.com. Short all-inclusive ski holidays to NZ.

Newmans South Pacific Vacations ⓣ1-800/342-1956, ⓦwww.newmansvacations.com. Specialists in New Zealand vacations, with around 25 package options in addition to fully independent tours.

REI Adventures ⓣ1-800/622-2236, ⓦwww.rei.com/adventures. REI offer an 11-day hiking and kayaking tour of NZ for around US$3800 (plus international flights).

Swain Tours ⓣ1-800/22-SWAIN, ⓦwww.swainaustralia.com. South Pacific specialists offering customized individual and group itineraries including a 12-day NZ highlights trip (US$2820 including domestic flights).

In Australia

Contiki Australia ⓣ02/9511 2200, ⓦwww.contiki.com. Frenetic tours for 18- to 35-year-old party animals.

Value Tours ⓣ1300/ 361 322, ⓦwww.valuetours.com.au. Skiing and snowboarding holidays throughout New Zealand, plus airfares, car and campervan rental and accommodation passes.

Getting around

New Zealand is a relatively small country and getting around is easy, with some form of public transport going to most destinations, though sometimes limited to one or two services per day. Most out-of-the-way places are accessible with will, flexibility and a little ingenuity.

Internal **flights** are reasonably priced if booked well in advance, but you'll appreciate the scenery better by travelling at ground level. The cheapest and easiest, though slowest, way to get around is by using **buses** (coaches or shuttle buses). The **rail service**, by contrast, is limited and expensive.

For getting off the beaten track having your own wheels is a boon. Rental **cars** and campervans can be remarkably good value for two or more people but if you are staying in the country for more than a couple of months, it's more economical to buy a vehicle. New Zealand is renowned for its green countryside and **cycling** is an excellent way to see the country.

Competition on the **ferries** connecting the North and South islands means passenger fares are good value, though transporting vehicles is pricey. Planes and boats give limited access to offshore islands and the parts of the mainland that remain stubbornly impenetrable by road, though an increase in specialist **tours** makes getting into the wilds ever easier.

Regular long-distance bus, train and plane services are found under "Travel details" at the end of each chapter, with local buses and trains covered in the main text.

By air

Many visitors fly into Auckland at the beginning of their trip and out from Christchurch at the end, so don't touch **domestic flights**. But those with a tight timetable wanting to hit a few key sights in a short time might be tempted by good-value internal fares, the product of competition. For more details on booking internal flights from your home country, see the box on p.28.

By far the biggest domestic operator is Air New Zealand, serving all the main centres and numerous minor ones (25 destinations in all). The main competition is from Qantas, which serves Auckland, Wellington, Christchurch, Rotorua and Queenstown.

Air New Zealand runs single-class planes with **fares** that come in three levels, offering lower fares for decreased flexibility: there are fewer low-cost fares at popular times. For example, a one-way flight between Auckland and Christchurch might cost $99 as a Smart Saver, $205 as a Flexi Saver or $333 Fully Flexible.

Qantas has a similar system, often with slightly cheaper fares, though it pays to check. Children (aged 2–11 inclusive) typically pay three-quarters of the adult fare, but don't expect backpacker or senior discounts: the best bet is to book early and be flexible enough to go for the budget options.

Other flights you might take are scenic jaunts from Auckland to Great Barrier Island, the hop over Cook Strait and the short trip from Invercargill to Stewart Island.

Air companies

Air New Zealand ⓣ0800/737 000, ⓦwww.airnz.co.nz.

Great Barrier Airlines & Air Coromandel ⓣ0800/900 600, ⓦwww.greatbarrierairlines.co.nz. Flights between Auckland, Coromandel and Great Barrier Island.

Great Barrier Xpress & Mountain Air ⓣ0800/222 123, ⓦwww.mountainair.co.nz. Flights between Auckland, Whangarei and Great Barrier Island.

Qantas ⓣ0800/808 767, ⓦwww.qantas.co.nz.

Soundsair ⓣ0800/505 005, ⓦwww.soundsair.co.nz. Small planes across Cook Strait.

Stewart Island Flights ⓣ03/218 9129, ⓦwww.stewartislandflights.com. Scheduled services between Invercargill and Stewart Island.

Mileage chart

All distances in km

Auckland	449	127	325	423	357	241
	Gisborne	394	823	216	585	739
		Hamilton	452	296	231	368
			Kaitaia	748	681	108
				Napier	412	661
Blenheim					New Plymouth	597
321	Christchurch					Pahia (Bay of Islands)
683	361	Dunedin				
520	408	570	Franz Josef			
331	255	565	189	Greymouth		
666	554	424	146	335	Haast	
899	578	217	542	731	396	Invercargill
1092	771	410	660	849	514	280
651	330	319	506	524	360	445
117	417	799	485	296	631	1016
29	350	711	549	360	695	928
808	487	281	365	554	219	189
971	650	289	539	728	393	159
749	428	276	294	483	148	248
265	336	670	294	105	440	836

By bus

You can get most places on long-distance **buses** (sometimes called "coaches") and smaller **shuttle buses**, which essentially offer the same service but are more likely to drop you off and pick up at hotels, hostels and the like. Services are generally reliable and reasonably comfortable, and stiff competition keeps prices competitive. The larger buses are usually air-conditioned, and some have toilets, though all services stop every couple of hours, at wayside tearooms and points of interest along the way. Most of your fellow passengers are likely to be visitors to New Zealand so drivers usually give a commentary, the quality of which varies enormously.

InterCity and Newmans

Easily the biggest operator, **InterCity** runs high-quality full-size buses all over the country. They operate closely with **Newmans**, who pitch themselves as slightly more luxurious and target sightseeing excursions. In practice, the two companies share a timetable and InterCity passes can often be used on Newmans buses: when we refer to InterCity we are generally referring to services run collectively by InterCity and Newmans.

Standard one-way **fares** are: Auckland to Rotorua $46, Auckland to Wellington $110, Picton to Christchurch $52, Christchurch to Queenstown $66, Queenstown to Fox Glacier $110 and Fox Glacier to Nelson $107. Prices often plummet during off-peak periods and a range of **discounted fares** is available, with an advance-purchase Saver fare yielding a twenty-five percent **discount** and a Super Saver fifty percent. Extreme Saver and Web Saver fares are also available: book early for the best prices. YHA, VIP and BBH cardholders get fifteen percent discounts off Standard rates but you'll often find cheaper deals by chasing down the various Saver fares.

InterCity also offers numerous fixed-route **passes** such as the Bay of Islands Pass around southern Northland ($105), the Pacific Coast Highway Pass between Auckland and Wellington ($209), the West Coast Passport from Picton to Queenstown ($169), and the Total NZ Experience, loosely covering both islands ($729).

Kids aged 2–11 travel for two-thirds the adult fare.

537	234	280	206	202	457	658	
394	287	332	298	445	468	538	
411	107	153	107	75	331	532	
861	558	602	531	524	779	983	
178	225	143	299	307	252	323	
234	299	296	308	173	160	355	
777	474	518	445	440	697	898	
Palmerston North	339	259	415	342	74	145	
	Rotorua	80	86	166	309	460	
		Taupo	156	163	229	380	
			Tauranga	151	439	545	
				Waitomo	273	473	
					Wanganui	195	
						Wellington	
Milford Sound							
578	Mount Cook						
1145	747	Nelson					
1121	680	113	Picton				
307	271	850	837	Queenstown			
121	426	1024	1000	166	Te Anau		
366	212	779	778	71	245	Wanaka	
954	629	230	294	659	823	588	Westport

Other buses

A host of **bus** and **shuttle bus** companies compete directly with InterCity/Newmans on the main routes and fill in the gaps around the country (especially in the South Island), often linking with the services of the major operators to take you off the beaten track. Generally they cost less (sometimes appreciably) and are often more obliging when it comes to drop-offs and pick-ups, though seldom as comfortable over long distances. We've listed a number of the major operators below, but there are many more mentioned in the appropriate sections of the Guide.

Official (i-SITE) visitor centres carry **timetables** of companies operating in their area, so you can compare frequencies and prices. **Fare structures** are generally straightforward, with fixed prices and no complicated Savers and discounts. Typical examples include: Auckland to Rotorua $50; Picton to Christchurch $40; Christchurch to Queenstown $50.

Main bus companies

Atomic Shuttles ⓣ03/349 0697, ⓦwww.atomictravel.co.nz. Major long-distance bus operator in the South Island.

Guthreys Express ⓣ0800/732 528, ⓦwww.guthreys.co.nz. Mostly covering the northern half of the North Island.

InterCity & Newmans Auckland ⓣ09/623 1503, Wellington ⓣ04/385 0520, Christchurch ⓣ03/365 1113, Dunedin ⓣ03/471 7143, Queenstown ⓣ03/441 1344, ⓦwww.intercitycoach.co.nz & www.newmanscoach.co.nz. Long-distance buses nationwide.

Naked Bus ⓣ0900/62533; ⓦwww.nakedbus.com. Cheap, frill-free trips on both islands.

Northliner Express ⓣ09/623 1503, ⓦwww.northliner.co.nz. Bus travel around Northland, owned by InterCity.

Southern Link/K Bus ⓣ03/358 8355, ⓦwww.southernlinkcoaches.co.nz. Routes all over the South Island.

Wanaka Connexions ⓣ0800/244 844, ⓦwww.time2.co.nz. Linking Dunedin, Queenstown and Wanaka.

By train

Not much is left of New Zealand's passenger train service besides **commuter train** services in Wellington and Auckland and a few intercity trains. The **long-distance services** that do exist are scenic runs, primarily used by tourists; trains are so slow that they have ceased to be practical transport for most New

Backpacker buses

One of the cheapest ways to cover a lot of ground is on a **backpacker bus**, which combines some of the flexibility of independent travel with the convenience of a tour. You typically purchase a ticket for a fixed route (usually valid for twelve months), and then take it at your own pace. You can either stick with the one bus for the entire journey with nights spent at various towns along the route, or stop off longer in places and hop on a later bus. During peak times, note that some buses may be full, so you'll need to plan onward travel several days in advance. Most companies operate year-round, though services are reduced in winter.

The emphasis is on **experiencing the country** rather than travelling from one town to the next, so you'll be stopping off to bungy jump, hike or somesuch. Being part of a group of forty rowdy backpackers arriving at some idyllic spot isn't everyone's idea of a good time and, by using assorted public transport, it is often just as cheap to make your own way around New Zealand. But if you want almost everything organized for you, and a ready-made bunch of like-minded fellow travellers this sort of travel has undeniable appeal.

It can be 5–10 percent cheaper to **book before you arrive** in New Zealand, as some deals are simply not available once you arrive: check the websites or with your travel agent. You might also save a few dollars by being a YHA, VIP, BBH or ISIC cardholder. Tickets don't generally cover accommodation, activities (although these are often discounted), side trips, food or travel between the North and South islands.

The best known are the **Kiwi Experience** (ⓣ09/366 9830, ⓦwww.kiwiexperience.com), who have a largely deserved reputation for attracting high-spirited revellers. They offer a huge array of passes, from a trip to Cape Reinga starting in Auckland (min 3 days; $178) to the Full Monty (min 31 days; $1480).

The prime contender for the backpacker bus crown is **Magic Travellers Network** (Auckland ⓣ09/358 5600, ⓦwww.magicbus.co.nz), whose magic buses offer a pretty comprehensive selection of trips and guarantee a seat if you book at least 24hr in advance. They work in with the YHA, offering substantial discounts to YHA cardholders, and target more independent-minded travellers. Their Spirit of New Zealand pass is valid for a year and covers the country in 23 travel days ($1035), while the Northern Discovery heads from Auckland to Rotorua, Taupo, Napier, Wellington and Waitomo before returning to Auckland for just $358.

Stray (NZ ⓣ09/309 8772; ⓦwww.straytravel.com), aims to get further off the beaten track with more stops away from the main tourist honeypots. Trips typically include: a South Island circuit (min 16 days; $835); a basic North Island circuit (min 7 days; $450); and the whole country (min 31 days; $1614).

There's an altogether more free-spirited approach to **Flying Kiwi Wilderness Expeditions** (ⓣ03/547 0171 & 0800/693 296, ⓦwww.flyingkiwi.com), which get off the beaten track and eschew city hostels in favour of camping out. Converted buses are equipped with bikes, canoes, windsurfers, kitchen, awning, fridge, beds, tents and hot shower, and everyone mucks in with the cooking and the dishes. Trips operate all year and once on board you stick with the same group. Options range from the Northern Express from Wellington to Auckland via Taupo (2 days; $168, plus $32 food and camp fund) to a full NZ tour (27 days; $1795, plus $768 food and camp fund).

For those interested in multi-day tours and adventure activities and not the flash-through, one-day-only approach of the backpacker buses check out "Outdoor activities" (p.66), where more intimate and specialized excursions are listed. Women-only tours are included in "Travel essentials" (see p.87).

Zealanders. Minimal investment in infrastructure and rolling stock is beginning to have an effect on standards, but railway travel remains a pleasant experience.

Trains have reclining seats, a buffet car with reasonable, good-value food, beer, panoramic windows, and occasionally a glass-backed observation carriage. You also get a sporadic and not particularly diverting commentary. A ticket guarantees a seat: passengers check in on the platform before boarding and bags are carried in a luggage van.

Long-distance trains are all run by **Tranz Scenic** (Ⓣ04/495 0775 & 0800/872 467, Ⓦwww.tranzscenic.co.nz), which operates three passenger routes. The longest is the *Overlander* **between Auckland and Wellington**, passing through some of the more rural areas of the North Island as well as the scenic Central Plateau with its volcanic peaks. Interesting stops along the way include Te Awamutu, Te Kuiti (where the train is met by a shuttle bus to Waitomo Caves) and National Park (with access to Mount Ruapehu and the Tongariro Alpine Crossing). The service leaves both Auckland and Wellington daily around 7.35am and reaches its destination around 7.20pm.

In the South Island, the *TranzCoastal* runs **between Christchurch and Picton**, a pretty run sometimes hugging the coast. It leaves Christchurch at 7am for the run up through Kaikoura (10am) and Blenheim (11.45pm) to Picton (12.15pm). It then returns from Picton (1pm) through Blenheim (1.30pm), and Kaikoura (3.30pm) to Christchurch (6.20pm).

The finest rail journey in New Zealand is the *TranzAlpine* **between Christchurch and Greymouth** on the West Coast – it is covered in detail on p.585.

Fares are higher than the comparable bus tickets but with discounts and the use of a travel pass (see below), travelling is still reasonably good value. Most people get the standard or **Flexi fare**, which gives a discount in return for advance booking, limited availability and only a fifty percent refund if cancelled after the departure time. Seniors (60 and over) can get a thirty percent discount on standard fares, though most folk do better by going for a Scenic Rail Pass (see box below) Blind and some disabled travellers (see p.86) are entitled to a forty percent discount on the standard fare.

Sample fares include: Auckland to Wellington (Flexi Fare $119, one way); Picton to Christchurch (Standard $104, one way); Christchurch to Greymouth (Standard $139 one way, $194 return).

Apart from a couple of short-run steam trains, the only other passenger trains are along the **Taieri Gorge Railway** (see p.682) between Dunedin and Middlemarch, again run almost entirely for the benefit of tourists.

Travel passes

If you're doing a lot of travelling by bus and train, there are savings to be made with travel passes. Tranz Scenic's **Scenic Rail Pass** (Ⓣ0800/872 467, Ⓦwww.transzscenic.co.nz) gives unlimited travel on Tranz Scenic trains for a week ($309, children $205). The pass also includes one *Interislander* ferry passage between the North and South islands.

InterCity/Newmans offer their own **Flexi-Pass**, allowing you buy bus travel by the hour – the more hours you buy the better the savings. You would typically need 45 hours ($454) to cover one of the main islands, more like 60 hours ($585) for a full tour, and if that's not enough you can top-up your pass with, say, 10 hours ($110). The Flexi-Pass is valid for 12 months and journeys can be booked online or by free-calling Ⓣ0800/222 146. Travellers wanting to move around pretty quickly might be better off with one of the **New Zealand Travel Passes** (Ⓣ0800/339966, Ⓦwww.travelpass.co.nz). The 2-in-One travel pass has various options from 5 days of travel in a year ($399) to 15 days in a year ($871) and includes a Cook Strait ferry crossing. Slightly more expensive variants also throw in a train journey and a domestic flight.

Finally, the backpacker tour buses (see p.36) offer lower prices in return for older buses and – in some cases – a more boisterous time.

By car

For maximum flexibility, it's hard to beat **driving** around New Zealand: you'll be able to get to places beyond the reach of public transport and to set your own timetable. With the freedom to camp or stay in cheaper places away from town centres this is a very economical option for two or more people, though it has a greater environmental cost.

In order to drive in New Zealand you need a valid **licence** from your home country or an International Driver's Licence (available from your national motoring organization). These are valid for up to a year in New Zealand and you must always carry your licence when driving.

In New Zealand you **drive on the left** and will find **road rules** similar to those in the UK, Australia and the US. The one variation peculiar to New Zealand is that you must give way to all traffic crossing or coming from your right; this means that if you are turning left and another car coming from the opposite direction wants to turn right into the same side road, you must let them go first. All occupants must wear **seatbelts** and drivers must park in the same direction as that in which they are travelling; **parking** facing oncoming traffic is illegal.

The **speed limit** for the open road is 100km per hr, reduced to 70km per hr or 50km per hr in built-up areas. Speeding fines start at $30 and rapidly increase as the degree of transgression (speed over the limit) increases. Some drivers flash their headlights at oncoming cars to warn of lurking police patrols but the advent of hidden cameras makes this pointless. **Drink driving** has traditionally been a problem in New Zealand: as part of a campaign to cut the death-toll, random breath tests have been introduced and offenders are dealt with severely.

Road conditions are generally good and **traffic** is relatively light except around Auckland and at rush hour in Wellington. Most roads are sealed (paved), although a few have a metalled surface composed of an aggregate of loose chippings. Clearly marked on most maps, these are slower to drive along, prone to wash-outs and landslides after heavy rain, and demand considerably more care and attention from the driver. Some rental companies prohibit the use of their cars on the worst metalled roads – typically those at Skippers Canyon and around the northern tip of Coromandel Peninsula. Always check conditions locally before setting off on these routes.

Other **hazards** include one-lane bridges: a sign before the bridge will indicate who has right of way, and on longer examples there'll be a passing place halfway across. Even on relatively major roads you might also come across **flocks of sheep**, slow-moving farm equipment and monstrous logging trucks, all made more of a nuisance by the paucity of passing lanes.

Unleaded and super unleaded **petrol** and diesel are available in New Zealand and in larger towns petrol stations are open 24hr. In smaller towns, they may close after 8pm, so be sure to fill up for long evening or night journeys. At publication, prices were hovering around $1.75 a litre for unleaded, $1.85 for super unleaded, and $1.25 for diesel, with higher prices in more out-of-the-way places.

If you're driving your own vehicle, check if the **New Zealand Automobile Association**

(Ⓦwww.nzaa.co.nz) has reciprocal rights with motoring organizations from your country to see if you qualify for their cover; otherwise, you can join as an overseas visitor. Apart from a free 24-hour **emergency breakdown service** (Ⓣ0800/500 222) – excluding vehicles bogged on beaches – membership entitles you to free maps, accommodation guides and legal assistance, discounts on some rental cars and accommodation, plus access to insurance and pre-purchase vehicle inspection services.

Car rental

Visitors driving around New Zealand typically pick up a car in Auckland, tour the North Island to Wellington where they leave the first vehicle, cross Cook Strait, pick up a second car in Picton, then drive around the South Island dropping off the car in Christchurch. The whole thing can be done in reverse, and may work out cheaper as there are savings in going against the flow.

New Zealand is awash with companies wanting to rent you a car. You'll even see deals for under $30 a day, though only for older, small cars rented for over a month in winter (June–Aug). Demand is high over the main summer season and prices rise accordingly.

Most of the **major international companies** – Avis, Budget, Hertz, National, Thrifty, etc – are represented here and offer good deals for virtually new cars. **Nationwide firms** offer cheaper rates partly by minimizing overheads and offering older (but perfectly serviceable) vehicles. You may find even cheaper deals with cut-rate local companies, which are fine for short stints, though for general touring nationwide companies are probably the best bet. Their infrastructure helps when it comes to crossing between the North and South islands (see p.460) and they typically offer free breakdown assistance.

In peak season it usually pays to have a car **booked in advance**. At quieter times you can often pick up something cheaper once you arrive; and in winter (except in ski areas) you can almost name your price. Provided your rental period is four days or more the deal will be for **unlimited kilometres**. The rates quoted below are for summer season assuming a two-week rental period, but don't be afraid to haggle at any time.

As a general rule, Ace, Apex, Omega and Pegasus offer reasonably new cars at moderate prices, while the rest of the NZ companies listed below try desperately to undercut each other and offer **low prices**.

Based on a two-week rental in summer, for two people a **small car** (1.3–1.8 litre) might cost $50–70 a day from the majors, $30–60 from national firms. For those requiring a little more comfort, or needing to fit in the kids, a **medium-sized car** (2–3 litre) would be more appropriate. This might cost $80–90 from the majors and $40–80 from national companies. Unless you're here in winter and want to get up to the ski-fields without tyre chains you don't really need a **4WD**, which generally costs $90–130 a day; you'll be better off renting one for short trips in specific areas.

If you are renting for several weeks, there is often no **drop-off fee** for leaving the vehicle somewhere other than where you picked it up. For shorter rental periods you may be charged $150–300, though if you're travelling south to north, you may be able to sweet-talk your way out of drop-off charges. At different times in the season Wellington, Picton, Christchurch and Queenstown have a glut of cars that are needed elsewhere, and companies will offer **relocation deals**. Look at hostel notice boards, call the firms listed below or phone around companies listed under "Rental Cars" in the Yellow Pages. Some companies want quick delivery, while others will allow you to spend a few more days en route for a reduced rental rate.

Before signing on the dotted line you must have a full, clean **driver's licence** and be over 21; drivers under 25 often pay more for insurance. In most cases insurance is included in the quoted cost but you are liable for any windscreen damage and the first $1000 of any damage. With some of the cheaper companies this excess can be as much as $3000 if the accident is your fault. This can usually be reduced to $250 or zero by paying an additional $10–20 a day Collision Damage Waiver. Usually before giving you a car rental companies take a credit-card imprint or a cash bond from you for $1000. If you have an accident, the bond is used to pay for any damage: in some cases you can pay anything up to the value of the bond; in others you pay the entire bond no matter how slight the damage. Read the small print, look around the car for any visible **defects**, so you won't end up being charged for someone else's mistakes, and check whether there are any restrictions on driving along certain roads.

New Zealand car rental agencies

A2B Rentals ⓣ0871/720 2035 & 0800/616 888, ⓦwww.a2b-car-rental.co.nz.
Ace Rental Cars ⓣ09/303 3112 & 0800/502 277, ⓦwww.acerentalcars.co.nz.
Apex ⓣ03/379 6897 & 0800/939 597, ⓦwww.apexrentals.co.nz.
Bargain Rental Cars ⓣ09/444 4573 & 0800/566 300 ⓦwww.bargainrentals.co.nz.
Omega ⓣ09/377 5573 & 0800/525 210, ⓦwww.omegarentals.com.
Pegasus ⓣ03/548 2852 & 0800/803 580, ⓦwww.rentalcars.co.nz.

Campervan rental

Throughout the summer, New Zealand roads seem clogged with **campervans** (small motor homes). Almost all are driven by foreign visitors who rent them for a few weeks and drive around the country staying in campsites and sneaking the odd free night in wayside rest areas. This is not strictly legal, but you're unlikely to be hassled in isolated spots – do, however, make an effort to be considerate with your waste.

A small campervan is generally suitable for two adults and perhaps a couple of kids and comes with a fold-down bed and compact kitchen. Larger models sleep four or more and often have a shower and toilet.

Medium to large **campervan rentals** (based on a 3-week rental) average about $140–280 a day during the high season (Dec–Feb), dropping a little for a couple of months either side and plummeting to $50–100 in winter. The two biggest rental firms are Maui and Britz (effectively the same company), but a few smaller firms (listed above) offer cheaper rates, saving 20–30 percent.

Small vans are often quite cramped and aimed at backpackers prepared to sacrifice comfort to save money. These typically cost $60–95 a day during summer, $60–75 in the shoulder season and $45–55 in the depths of winter. The current trend is for wildly painted vans, often with arcane or quirky comments graffitied on them: witness Escape Rentals and Wicked Campers. Other good bets are the distinctive orange Spaceships that have been imaginatively converted to suit two adults, possibly more if you're very friendly. For an affordable and slightly offbeat experience go for a restored, classic VW campervan (possibly with a pop-top), from Auckland-based Kiwi Kombis, who charge $130–230 a day, depending on dates and van.

For all campervans there's usually a minimum rental period of 5–7 days, but you get unlimited kilometres, a kitchen kit and perhaps airport transfer. Insurance is often included but you may be liable for the first $1000–5000 and you should seriously consider paying extra fees to get this liability reduced. Most companies have a supply of tents, camping kits, outdoor chairs and tables that can be rented for a few dollars.

No special **licence** is required to drive a campervan, but some caution is needed, especially in high winds and when climbing hills and going around tight corners. Finally, have some consideration for other road users and pull over to let folk pass wherever possible.

Campervan rentals: medium to large

Adventure NZ ⓣ09/276 7100, UK ⓣ0800/123 555; ⓦwww.nzmotorhomes.co.nz.
Backpacker Campervans ⓣ09/275 0200 & 0800/422 267, ⓦwww.backpackercampervans.com.
Britz ⓣ09/275 9090 & 0800/831 900, ⓦwww.britz.com.
Escape ⓣ0800/216 171, ⓦwww.escaperentals.co.nz.
Eurocampers ⓣ09/422 2571 & 0800/489 226, ⓦwww.eurocampers.co.nz.
Freedom Campers ⓣ03/259 4730 & 0800/325 939, ⓦwww.freedomcampers.co.nz.
Kea Campers ⓣ09/441 7833 & 0800/520 052, ⓦwww.keacampers.com.
Maui ⓣ09/275 3013 & 0800/651 080, ⓦwww.maui-rentals.com.

Small vans and conversions

Backpackers Transport ⓣ09/475 9870 & 0800/226 769, ⓦwww.backpackernz.co.nz.
Escape ⓣ021/288 8372 & 0800/216 171, ⓦwww.escaperentals.co.nz.
Ezy ⓣ09/734 4360 & 0800/399 736, ⓦwww.ezy.co.nz.
Kiwi Kombis ⓣ09/533 9335, ⓦwww.kiwikombis.com.
Spaceships ⓣ09/309 8777 & 0800/772 237, ⓦwww.spaceships.tv.
Wicked Campers ⓣ0800/246 870, ⓦwww.wickedcampers.com.au.

Buying a used vehicle

Buying a **used vehicle** can be cost-effective if you are staying in the country for more than a couple of months and may even be worthwhile for shorter periods. Reselling can recoup enough of the price to make it cheaper than using public transport or renting. Of course, if you buy cheap there's also a greater risk of breakdowns and expensive repairs. The majority of people buy cars in Auckland and then try to sell them in Christchurch, so there's something to be said for buying in Christchurch where you'll often have more choice and a better bargaining position.

Some of the best deals are found on backpacker **hostel noticeboards** where older cars and vans are typically offered for $500–4000. Realistically you can expect to pay upwards of $2500 for something half-decent. It may not look pretty and with a **private sale** there's no guarantee the vehicle will make yet another trip around the country, but you might get an added bonus like camping gear thrown in with the car (or offered at a snip). Alternatively, trawl the used car ads in local papers for likely candidates.

For a little more peace of mind, buy from a **dealership**. There are plenty all over the country, especially in Auckland, Christchurch and Wellington. Prices begin at around $5000 and some yards offer a **buy-back service**, usually paying about fifty percent of the purchase price. If you're confident of your ability to spot a lemon, you can try to pick up a cheap car at an **auction**; they're held weekly in Auckland (see listings p.135), and Christchurch and are advertised in the local press. Be aware that you'll usually be liable for the **buyer's premium** of ten percent over your bid.

Before you commit yourself, consult the vehicle ownership section of the NZ Land Transport Safety Authority website (ⓦwww.ltsa.govt.nz/vehicle-ownership), which has good advice on buying and the pitfalls. The *Buying a used car* fact sheet (ⓦwww.ltsa.govt.nz/factsheets/41.html) is particularly helpful.

Unless you really know your big end from your steering column you'll want to arrange a mobile **vehicle inspection**, either from the AA (ⓣ0800/500 333, ⓦwww.aa.co.nz; members $105, non-members $130 at an inspection centre or members $120, non-members $145 using the mobile service), or the equally competitive Car Inspection Services (ⓣ0800/500 800 in Auckland and Wellington, ⓦwww.carinspections.co.nz). The inspection may give you enough ammunition to negotiate a price reduction. Finally, before you close a private sale, call

AA LemonCheck (ⓣ0800/500 333, ⓦwww.aalemoncheck.co.nz), who will fill you in on registration history, possible odometer tampering and any debts on the vehicle ($20 for members, $25 for non-members).

Before they're allowed on the road, all vehicles must have a **Warrant of Fitness** (WOF), which is a test of its mechanical worthiness and safety. WOFs are carried out and issued by specified garages and testing stations and last for a year if the vehicle is less than six years old, or six months if older. Check the expiry date, as the test must have been carried out no more than one month before sale. The vehicle should also have a current **vehicle licence** which must be renewed before it expires (6 months $95, 12 months $184 for petrol driven, private vehicles): post offices and AA offices are the most convenient for this though you can also do it online at ⓦwww.transact.landtransport.govt.nz.

You **transfer ownership** with a form (filled in by buyer and seller) at the post office: the licence plates stay with the vehicle. Next you'll need **insurance**, either Comprehensive (which covers your vehicle and any other damaged vehicles) or Third Party, Fire & Theft (which covers your own vehicle against fire and theft, but only pays out on damage to other vehicles in case of an accident). There are dozens of companies listed under "Insurance Companies" in the Yellow Pages: shop around as prices vary widely, but expect to pay, a minimum of $400 for six months' Third Party, Fire & Theft cover.

By motorbike

Visitors from most countries can ride in New Zealand with their normal licence, though it (or your international licence) must specify motorbikes. Helmets are compulsory, and you'll need to be prepared to ride on gravel roads from time to time. Take it easy at first if you're not used to loose surfaces.

Few people bring their own bike but **bike rental** is available from the companies running guided bike tours (see p.67). It isn't cheap, and for a 650cc machine in summer you can expect to pay $160–200 a day. Bike Adventure New Zealand (ⓣ027/498 8287 & 0800/498 600, ⓦwww.banz.co.nz) offers 600cc enduro machines for $95 a day for short periods, dropping to $50 a day for ten weeks. Alternatively, try the same channels as for "Buying a used vehicle" on p.41.

Motorbike tours

The obvious alternative is an organized **tour**, self-guided or guided, usually incorporating top of the range accommodation, restaurants and bikes.

Adventure New Zealand Motorcycle Tours & Rentals ⓣ03/548 5787 & 0800/848 6337, ⓦwww.gotournz.com. Nelson-based company providing upmarket, small-group guided or self-guided tours around the South Island, with itineraries tweaked to suit and a luxury coach in your wake. Rates range from $10,200 for a standard ten-day trip on a relatively modest bike to $24,700 for a full 21-day tour on a luxury bike.

New Zealand Motorcycle Rentals & Tours ⓣ0800/692 453, UK freephone ⓣ0800/917 3941, US freephone ⓣ1-866/490-7940; ⓦwww.nzbike.com. Another specialist top-end company, offering guided all-inclusive tours staying in quality accommodation, semi-guided tours and bike rental. A fully guided 13-day tour will set you back $5975.

Te Waipounamu Motorcycle Hire & Tours ⓣ03/372 3537, ⓦwww.motorcycle-hire.co.nz. These folk do upscale tours round the bottom of the South Island and bike rentals from Harley to Beamer (7 days on a Harley will cost $290 per day).

Cycling

If you have bags of time, **cycling** is an excellent way of getting around. Distances aren't enormous, the weather is generally benign, traffic is usually light, and the countryside is gorgeous. Everywhere you go you'll find hostels and campsites well set up for campers but also equipped with rooms and cabins for when the weather really sucks.

But there are downsides. New Zealand's road network is skeletal, so in many places you'll find yourself riding on main roads or unsealed minor roads. You'll also experience a fair bit of rain and have to climb quite a lot of hills.

Contrary to what you might think, cycling the **South Island** is an easier proposition than the **North Island**. The South Island's alpine backbone presents virtually the only geographical barrier, while the eastern two-thirds of the island comprise a flat plain. In the North Island you can barely go 10km without encountering significant hills – and you have to contend with a great deal more traffic, including intimidating logging trucks.

New Zealand law requires all cyclists to wear a **helmet**. Some **fitness** is important, but distances don't have to be great and you can take things at your own pace. If you'd rather go with a **guided group**, see our recommendations on p.67.

For more **information** get the *Pedallers' Paradise* guides (Ⓦwww.paradise-press.co.nz) or Bruce Ringer's *New Zealand by Bike* (see Contexts, p.921).

The bike

Since the vast majority of riding will be on sealed roads with only relatively short sections of gravel, it is perfectly reasonable (and more efficient) to get around New Zealand on a touring bike. But fashion dictates most people use a **mountain bike** fitted with fat but relatively smooth tyres.

On long trips to New Zealand it's cheaper to **bring your own bike**, set up to your liking before you leave home. Most international airlines simply count bikes as a piece of luggage and don't incur any extra cost as long as you don't exceed your baggage limit. However, they do require you use a **bike bag** or box or at the very least remove pedals and handlebars and wrap the chain. Some airlines will sell you a cardboard bike box at the airport, though your friendly local bike dealer may give you one free. Soft bags are probably the most convenient (they're easy to carry on the bike once you arrive), but if you are flying out from the same city you arrive in you can often store hardshell containers (free or for a small fee) at the backpacker hostel where you spend your first and last nights: call around.

Renting bikes for more than the odd day can be an expensive option, costing anything from $25–45 a day, depending on whether you want a bike with little more than pedals and brakes, a tourer or a state-of-the-art mountain bike. Specialist cycle shops do economical monthly rental for around $200–250 for a touring bike and $300 or more for a full-suspension superbike.

For long-distance cycle touring, it's generally cheaper to **buy a bike**. You're probably looking at paying at least $1000 to get fully kitted out with new equipment, but it is worth checking hostel noticeboards for **secondhand bikes** (under $500 is a reasonable deal), often accompanied by extras like wet-weather gear, lights, a helmet and a pump. Some cycle shops offer **buy-back deals**, where you buy at full price and they guarantee to refund about fifty percent of the purchase price at the end of your trip. Contact Adventure Cycles, 1 Laurie Ave, Parnell (Ⓣ09/309 5566 & 0800/940 2453, Ⓦwww.adventure-auckland.co.nz/advcychm.html), in Auckland. If you're bringing your own bike, the same folk will let you store the bike box you transported your machine in, help you organize an emergency package of spare parts and extra clothing to be forwarded at your request, and give your bike a once-over before you set off, all for around $35. The best bet for servicing and spares in Christchurch is Laurie Dawe Cycles, 838 Colombo St (Ⓣ021/233 4405, Ⓦwww.lauriedawecycles.co.nz).

Transporting bikes

Lethargy, boredom, breakdowns or simply a need to shift your bike between islands mean you'll need to use **public transport** at some point. You can usually hoick your bike onto a bus (generally $10–15) or train ($10–20 per journey) though space is often limited so book well in advance. Crossing Cook Strait, the Interislander and Blue Bridge ferries charge $10–15.

Bikes usually travel free on buses, trains and ferries if packed in a bike bag and treated as ordinary luggage. Air New Zealand will fly your bike free if it is within your baggage allowance; Qantas will charge you at their normal excess baggage rate, though that doesn't cut into your free allowance.

Hitching and organized rides

Although many travellers enthuse about **hitching** in New Zealand – and it does enjoy a reputation of relative safety – the official advice is don't. Sadly, New Zealand has its share of unpleasant individuals and, with an extensive network of affordable transport and tours at your disposal, there's no reason to take unnecessary risks.

However, if you are determined to work those thumbs then follow a few **rules**: hitch in pairs (no guarantee of avoiding trouble but safer than going solo); trust your instincts – there will always be another car; ask the driver where they are going, rather than telling them where you're headed; and keep your gear with you so you can make a quick getaway.

Finding the best **hitching spots** around the country is generally a matter of common sense, or common knowledge on the travellers' grapevine. Some town and city hostels drop their guests at hitching spots as a matter of course. Pick a spot where you can be clearly seen and drivers can stop safely.

It is generally safer to organize a ride before you set off, though this still demands some trust on both sides. Hostel notice boards are the best bet, and if no one seems to be going where you want to go, stick up your own notice. Usually you'll be expected to share petrol costs.

By ferry

The **ferries** you're most likely to use are vehicle-carrying services plying Cook Strait between Wellington on the North Island and Picton on the South Island. Details are given in the "Crossing Cook Strait" box on p.460.

Passenger ferries link Bluff, in the south of the South Island, to Stewart Island, and both vehicle and passenger ferries connect Auckland with the Hauraki Gulf islands, principally Waiheke, Rangitoto and Great Barrier. Information about these short trips is included in our accounts of Invercargill and Auckland. Most visitors spend more boat time on cruises – whale watching, dolphin swimming, sightseeing – or **water taxis**.

Accommodation

Accommodation will take up a fair chunk of your money while in New Zealand, but the good news is that standards across all categories are excellent. Almost every town has a motel or hostel of some description, so finding accommodation is seldom a problem – though it's essential to book in advance during high summer (from Christmas through to the end of January) and advisable a month or two either side.

Kiwis travel widely at home, most choosing to self-cater at the country's huge number of well-equipped **campsites** (aka motor camps or holiday parks) and **motels**, shunning **hotels**, which cater mainly to package holidaymakers and the business community. The range of **B&Bs**, **homestays**, **farmstays** and **lodges** form an appealing alternative, covering the whole spectrum from a room in someone's suburban home to pampered luxury in a country mansion.

Since the mid-1980s, New Zealand has pioneered the **backpacker hostel**, a less-regimented alternative to traditional YHAs, which have transformed themselves dramatically to compete. Found all over the country, hostels offer superb value to budget travellers.

Wherever you stay, you can expect unstinting hospitality and a truckload of valuable advice on local activities and onward travel. We've included a wide selection of New Zealand's best accommodation throughout the book, and more detail can be gleaned from specialist accommodation guides.

Many places are now accredited using the nationwide **Qualmark** system (ⓦwww.qualmark.co.nz), which grades different

Accommodation price codes

Accommodation listed in this guide has been categorized into one of nine **price bands**. The rates quoted represent the cheapest available double or twin room in high season, though we have generally ignored the short spike in prices around Christmas and New Year. Single rooms usually cost only ten to twenty percent less than doubles or twins In hostels and campsites where individual dorm beds are available, we have given the full price assuming no discount cards. YHA members get a $3 discount at full YHAs, BBH members typically save $3 (sometimes more) at BBH-affiliated establishments and VIP cardholders save $1 a night. DOC hut and camping fees are also per person, unless otherwise stated.

Prices normally include Goods and Services Tax (GST), as do our codes.

❶ less than $50 per room
❷ $50–69
❸ $70–99
❹ $100–129
❺ $130–159
❻ $160–199
❼ $200–249
❽ $250–349
❾ over $350

types of accommodation – exclusive, hotel, self-contained, guest and hosted, holiday parks and backpackers – from one to five stars. Most fall between three stars (very good) and four plus (at the top end of excellent), but there is no way of knowing whether, for example, a 4-star backpacker is superior to rooms at a 5-star holiday park. Many places choose not to join the system, but may be just as good or better.

Useful accommodation guides and websites

AA Accommodation Guide ⓦwww.aatravel.co.nz. Annual advertising-based guide for the whole country; concentrates on motels and holiday parks but has some coverage of hotels and lodges. Available free from most motels and i-SITE offices.

The Bed & Breakfast Book ⓦwww.bnb.co.nz. Annually updated listing of member B&Bs, boutique lodges, homestays and farmstays, covering around 1000 places all over New Zealand. Entries are submitted by the owners, so it's a good idea to read between the lines. Available from bookshops, visitor centres and many of the places listed in the book; nominally $20 (plus $10 for international postage) but often much cheaper.

Charming Bed & Breakfast ⓦwww.bnbnz.com. Glossy B&B guide concentrating on mid-range places. Available through their website for the price of postage and can often be picked up free at B&Bs.

Friars' Guide ⓦwww.friars.co.nz. An advertising-based annual guide with fairly comprehensive coverage of the country's more upmarket B&Bs and boutique lodges. Available ($35) from NZ bookshops and vendors listed on their website.

House rental Many Kiwis own a holiday home (aka *bach* or *crib*) which they rent out when they're not using them. Many are in superb locations next to beaches but you'll often have to agree to a minimum stay (perhaps four nights). Rates vary enormously, peaking around Christmas (when availability is very low) and plummeting in winter. Sites to check out include ⓦwww.bookabach.co.nz and ⓦwww.holidayhouses.co.nz.

Hotels and motels

In New Zealand, **hotel** is a term frequently used to describe old-style pubs, which were once legally obliged to provide rooms for drinkers to recuperate from their excesses. Many no longer provide accommodation, but some have transformed themselves into backpacker hostels, while others are dedicated to preserving the tradition. At their best, such hotels (❸–❹) offer comfortable rooms in characterful, historic buildings, though just as often lodgings are rudimentary. Hotel bars are frequently at the centre of small-town life and, at weekends in particular, they can be pretty raucous; you may find a budget room at a hostel a better bet.

In the cities and major resorts, you'll also come across hotels in the conventional sense, predominantly business- or tour bus-oriented places (❻–❾) with all the trappings. Priced accordingly, they're seldom good value, though at quiet times and weekends there can be substantial discounts; it's always worth asking.

Most Kiwi families on the move prefer the astonishingly well-equipped **motels** (❹–❻), which congregate along the roads running into town, making them more convenient for drivers than for those using trains or buses. They come provided with bed linen, towels, Sky TV, bathroom, a full kitchen and tea and coffee, but are often fairly functional concrete-block places with little to distinguish one from another. Rooms range from all-in-one **studios**, with beds, kettle, toaster and a microwave, through **one-bedroom units**, usually with a full and separate kitchen, to two- and three-**bedroom suites**, sleeping six or eight. Suites generally go for the same basic price as a one-bedroom unit, with each additional adult paying $15–20, making them an economical choice for groups travelling together. Anything calling itself a **motor inn** (❺–❼) or similar will be quite luxurious, with a bar, restaurant, swimming pool and sauna but no cooking facilities.

B&Bs, lodges and boutique hotels

While families might prefer the freedom and adaptability of a motel, couples are generally better served by a **bed and breakfast** (B&B; ❸–❻). This might be a simple room with a bathroom down the hall and a modest continental breakfast included in the price. But the term also encompasses luxurious colonial homes with well-furnished en-suite rooms and sumptuous home-cooked breakfasts. Those at the top end are now fashioning themselves as lodges, boutique hotels and **"exclusive retreats"** (❼–❾), where standards of service and comfort are raised to extraordinary levels, with prices to match.

Rates drop in the low season, when these places can often be exceptionally good value. If you're travelling alone and don't fancy hostels, B&Bs can also be a viable alternative, usually charging **lone travellers** 60–80 percent of the double room rate, though some only ask fifty percent.

Homestays and farmstays

Homestays (❹–❻) usually offer a guest room or two in an ordinary house where you muck in with the owners and join them for breakfast the following morning. Staying in such places can be an excellent way to meet ordinary New Zealanders; you'll be well looked after, sometimes to the point of being overwhelmed by your hosts' generosity. It is courteous to **call in advance**, and bear in mind you'll usually have to **pay in cash**. Rural versions often operate as **farmstays** (❹–❻), where you're encouraged to stay a couple of nights and are welcome to spend the intervening day trying your hand at farm tasks: rounding up sheep, milking cows, fencing, whatever might need doing. Both homestays and farmstays charge for a double room, including breakfast; some cook dinner on request for $25–50 per person, and you may pay a small fee for lunch if you spend the day at the farm or for a packed lunch.

Hostels, backpackers and YHAs

New Zealand has over four hundred budget and self-catering places, pretty much interchangeably known as **hostels** or **backpackers** (❶–❸) and offering a dorm bed or bunk for around $17–27. They're often in superb locations – bang in the centre of town, beside the beach, close to a ski-field or amid magnificent scenery in a national or forest park – and are great places to meet other travellers and pick up local information, aided by genuinely helpful managers. Backpacker hostels range in size from as few as four beds up to huge premises accommodating several hundred travellers. Virtually wherever you stay you'll find a fully equipped kitchen, laundry, TV and games room, a travellers' noticeboard, and a stack of tourist information. Beds are generally fully made up with clean sheets; you should bring your own towel, though you can rent one for a few dollars. **Internet access** (typically a coin-op booth, and increasingly Wi-Fi) is now pretty standard, though a few rural places intentionally eschew such mod cons. Depending on the area, there may be a pool, barbecue, bike and/or canoe rental and information on local work opportunities. For **security**, many of the better places offer cupboards for your gear, though you'll usually need your own lock. Almost all hostels in New Zealand are affiliated with local and international organizations that offer **accommodation discounts** to members, along with an array of other travel- and activity-related savings.

Some hostels allow you to pitch a tent in the grounds and use the facilities for around $15 a person, but generally the most basic and cheapest accommodation is in a 6 to 12-bunk **dorm** ($17–25), with 3- and 4-bed rooms (also known as three-shares and four-shares) usually priced a couple of dollars higher. Most hostels also have **double**, **twin** and **family rooms** (❶–❷ for two), the more expensive ones with en-suite bathrooms. Lone travellers who don't fancy a dorm can sometimes get a **single room** for around $35, and many larger places (especially YHAs and Base backpackers) also offer **women-only dorms**.

Around 60 places are classified as **YHA hostels** or associate YHA hostels, which, unlike their European HI counterparts, have abandoned lock-outs, curfews and arcane opening hours, but maintain a predominance of single-sex dorms. Newer hostels have been purpose-built to reflect the YHA's environmental concerns, promoting recycling and energy conservation. YHA and associate YHA hostels are listed on the annual *YHA Backpacker Map* and in the eight regional

guides (all free to members and non-members from hostels and organization offices). You should obtain a **Hostelling International Card** in your own country (see p.48 for contact details), but you can buy a $40 annual membership in NZ, which includes a phonecard loaded with around $14 of free calling time. Non-members can pay the additional $3 rate per night. The rest of the hostels are affiliated **associate hostels**, where no membership card is required, though there is often a discount of a dollar or so for members. Most YHAs request that you don't use your own sleeping bag to avoid bed bugs and the like. You can book ahead either from another hostel or through the YHA National Reservations Centre (see p.48), and through Hostelling International offices in your home country.

YHAs are outnumbered by around six-to-one by other **backpacker hostels**, where the atmosphere is more variable; some are friendly and relaxed, others more party-oriented. Many are aligned with the NZ-based **Budget Backpacker Hostels**, and are listed (along with current prices) in the *BBH Accommodation Guide*, widely available from hostels and visitor centres. The entries are written by the hostels and don't pretend to be impartial but each hostel is given a **percentage rating** based on a survey of guests, an assessment that is usually a good indicator of quality, though city hostels seldom score as highly as the best rural places. Anyone can stay at BBH hostels, but savings can be made by buying a BBH Club Card ($45), which generally saves the holder $3–4 on each night's stay in either a dorm or a room. Cards are available from BBH and all participating hostels, and each card doubles as a rechargeable phonecard loaded with $20 worth of calling time.

Over seventy hostels are members of **VIP Backpacker Resorts**, an umbrella organization that offers a dollar off each night's stay to people who buy its annual VIP Discount Card ($43, valid in New Zealand, at VIP hostels worldwide).

For advice on backcountry camping and trampers' huts, see the "Outdoor Activities" section on p.61.

Hostel organizations

YHA offices

New Zealand ⓣ0800/278 299 or 03/379 9808, ⓦwww.yha.co.nz.
Australia ⓦwww.yha.com.au.
Canada ⓦwww.hihostels.ca.
England and Wales ⓦwww.yha.org.uk.
Ireland ⓦwww.anoige.ie.
Northern Ireland ⓦwww.hini.org.uk.
Scotland ⓦwww.syha.org.uk.
USA ⓦwww.hiusa.org.

Other backpacker organizations

BBH ⓦwww.bbh.co.nz.
VIP Backpacker Resorts ⓦwww.vip.co.nz.

Holiday parks, campsites and cabins

New Zealand has some of the world's best **camping** facilities, and even if you've never camped before, you may well find yourself using **holiday parks** (❶–❹; also known as **motor camps**), which are geared for families on holiday, with space to pitch tents, powered sites (or hook-ups) for campervans and usually a broad range of dorms, cabins and motel units. You'll find more down-to-earth camping at wonderfully located DOC sites.

Camping is largely a summer activity (Nov–May), especially in the South Island. At worst, New Zealand can be very wet, windy and plagued by voracious winged **insects**, so the first priority for tent campers is good-quality gear with a fly sheet which will repel the worst that the elements can dish out, and an inner tent with enough bug-proof ventilation for hot mornings.

Busy times at motor camps fall into line with the school holidays, making Easter and the summer period from Christmas to the end of January the most hectic. Make **reservations** as far in advance as possible at this time, and a day or two before you arrive through February and March. DOC sites are not generally bookable, and while this is no problem through most of the year, Christmas can be a mad free-for-all.

See p.40 for information about responsible overnight stops outside official areas.

Campsites and cabins

Campsites are typically located on the outskirts of towns and are invariably well equipped, with a communal kitchen, TV lounge, games area, laundry and sometimes a swimming pool; non-residents can often get showers for around $3–5. **Campers** usually get the quietest and most sylvan corner of the site and are charged around $10–15 per person; camping prices throughout the guide are per person unless followed by "per site". There is often no distinction between tent pitches and the **powered sites** set aside for campervans, but the latter usually cost an extra few dollars per person for the use of power hook-ups and dump stations.

In addition, most campsites have some form of on-site accommodation: the basic dorm-style **lodge** ($15–25 per person); **standard cabins** (❶–❷ for two, plus $10 for each extra person), often little more than a shed with bunks; larger, fully equipped cabins variously known as **kitchen cabins**, tourist cabins or self-contained (s/c) cabins (❷, plus $15 per extra person) have cooking facilities; and if you step up to **tourist flats** (❸ for two, plus $15 per extra person), you also get your own bathroom. The flasher places also have self-contained **motel units** (❹–❺ for two, plus $15–20 per extra person), usually with a separate bedroom and a TV. Cabins and units generally sleep two to four, but motor camps often have at least one place sleeping six or eight. **Sheets** and **towels** are rarely included, so bring a sleeping bag or be prepared to pay to rent bed linen (typically a one-off $5–10 fee). Sometimes pans and plates can be borrowed after handing over a small deposit, though for longer stays it is worth bringing your own.

Campsites are independently run but some have now aligned themselves with nation-wide organizations which set minimum standards. Look out for **Top 10** sites (Ⓦwww.top10.co.nz), which maintain a reliably high standard in return for slightly higher prices. By purchasing a $30 club card you save ten percent on each night's stay and get local discounts; the card (valid two years) is transferable to Australia.

DOC campsites

Few holiday parks can match the idyllic locations of the several hundred **campsites** operated by the **Department of Conservation** (DOC; Ⓦwww.doc.govt.nz) in national parks, reserves, maritime and forest parks, the majority beautifully set by sweeping beaches or deep in the bush. This is back-to-nature camping, low-cost and with simple **facilities**, though sites almost always have running water and toilets of some sort. Listed in DOC's free *Conservation Campsites* leaflet (available from DOC offices), the sites fall into one of three categories: **informal** (free), often with nothing but a water supply; the more common **standard** ($3–10, typically $5 or $6), all with vehicular access and many with barbecues, fireplaces, picnic tables and refuse collection; and rare **serviced** ($8–14 per person), which are similar in scope to the regular motor camps. Children aged 5–15 are charged 25–50 percent off the adult price, and only the serviced sites can be booked in advance.

Food and drink

Forget preconceptions about "slam in the lamb" Kiwi cuisine with pavlova for dessert. New Zealand's food scene is brilliant – in terms of the quality of the food, its cooking, presentation and the places where it's served.

Kiwi **gastronomy** has its roots in the British culinary tradition, an unfortunate heritage that still informs cooking patterns for older New Zealanders and occasionally rears its ugly head in some farmstays and guesthouses. Indeed, it is only in the last twenty years or so that New Zealand's chefs have really woken up to the possibilities presented by a fabulous larder of super-fresh, top-quality ingredients, formulating what might be termed **Modern Kiwi** cuisine. Taking its culinary cues from Californian and contemporary Australian cooking, it combines traditional elements such as steak, salmon and crayfish with flavours drawn from the **Mediterranean**, **Asia** and the **Pacific Rim**: sun-dried tomatoes, lemongrass, basil, ginger, coconut, and many more. Restaurateurs feel duty-bound to fill their menu with as broad a spectrum as possible, lining up seafood linguini, couscous, sushi, Thai venison meatballs and a chicken korma alongside the rack of lamb and gourmet pizza. Sometimes this causes gastronomic overload, but often it is simply mouth-watering.

Meat and fish

New Zealanders have a taste for **meat**, the quality of which is superb, with New Zealand lamb often at the head of the menu (due to traveller expectation) but matched in flavour by venison and beef.

With the country's extensive coastline, it's no surprise that **fish** and seafood loom large. The white, flaky flesh of the snapper is the most common saltwater fish, but you'll also come across tuna, John Dory, groper (often known by its Maori name of *hapuku*), flounder, blue cod, the firm and delicately flavoured *terakihi* and the moist-textured orange roughy. Salmon is common, but not trout, which cannot be bought or sold (an archaic law originally intended to protect sport fishing when trout were introduced to NZ in the nineteenth century), though most hotels and restaurants will cook one if you've caught it. All are also very tasty smoked, though *terakihi*, *hapuku*, blue cod, marlin and smoked eel take some beating.

One much-loved delicacy is whitebait, a tiny silvery fish mostly caught on the West Coast and eaten whole in fritters during the August to November season.

Shellfish are a real New Zealand speciality. The king of them all is the *toheroa*, a type of clam dug from the sands of Ninety Mile Beach on the rare occasions when numbers reach harvestable levels. They are usually made into soups and are sometimes replaced by the inferior and sweeter *tuatua*, also dug from Northland beaches. On menus you're more likely to come across the fabulous Bluff oysters, scallops and sensational green-lipped mussels, which have a flavour and texture that's hard to beat and are farmed in the cool clear waters of the Marlborough Sounds, especially around Havelock. Crayfish is also available round the coast and should be sought out, particularly when touring Kaikoura and the East Cape.

Fruit, vegetables and dairy produce

New Zealand's **fruit** is a winner, especially at harvest time when stalls line the roadsides selling apples, pears, citrus and stonefruits for next to nothing. Top-quality fruit and dairy products are the starting point for delicious desserts, traditionally variations on the themes of ice cream, cheesecake and pavlova, though today supplemented by rich cakes and modern twists on British-style steamed puddings.

Vegetables are generally fresh and delicious. British favourites such as potatoes, carrots, peas and cabbage, along with pumpkin and squash, are common in Kiwi homes but on restaurant menus you're far more likely to encounter aubergines (eggplant), capsicums (bell peppers) and tomatoes. Pacific staples to look out for are *kumara* (sweet potato), which crops up in *hangi* and deep-fried as *kumara* chips. A delicious crossover point between fruit and vegetables is carrot cake, which comes in many variations; Kiwis have a passion for it and most cafés and restaurants offer up their own special take on it.

New Zealanders eat a lot of **dairy**. Small producers, particularly around the Kapiti Coast (north of Wellington), Blenheim and Banks Peninsula (east of Christchurch), turn out some gorgeous, if expensive cheeses, from traditional hard cheddar styles to creamy blues, via spicy pepper bries. Basic supermarket cheeses tend to be bland so head for the deli counter and get cheese from local specialists. Delicious ice cream of the firm, scooped variety is something of a New Zealand institution, and is available in a vast range of flavours, including intensely fruity ones and the indulgent hokey pokey – vanilla ice cream riddled with chunks of caramel.

Vegetarian food

The abundance of fresh vegetables and dairy food means that self-catering **vegetarians** will eat well, though in restaurants they are less well served. Outside the major centres you'll find hardly any dedicated vegetarian restaurants and will have to rely on the token meat-free dishes served in most cafés. Salad, sandwiches, vegetarian pizza or pasta are readily available but can get a bit monotonous. **Vegans** can always ask for a simple stir-fry if all else fails but in terms of snacks, you'll develop an unhealthy reliance on nachos and the ubiquitous veggieburger, though these days many new "organic" outlets offer home-made vegan and vegetarian pies.

If you are taking a multi-day expedition on which food is provided, give them plenty of notice of your dietary needs.

Eating out

The quality of **restaurants** in New Zealand is typically superb, portions are respectable, and many are good value for money – especially **BYO** establishments, where cost shrinks if you "bring your own" wine (corkage fees are typically $5 or under). In most restaurants you can expect to pay upwards of $20 for a main course, perhaps $45 for three courses without wine. **Service** tends to be helpful without being forced and there is no expectation of a tip, though a reward for exceptional service is always welcomed. However, legislation means that on public holidays you'll be expected to pay a surcharge (15–20 percent) to ensure staff wages compensate for their giving up their statutory holiday.

New Zealand's range of **ethnic restaurants** is constantly improving, with the major influx of East Asian immigrants enlivening the scene and lending a strong Thai, Chinese, Malaysian, Singaporian and Japanese flavour to the larger cities, alongside Indian and Mexican places. **Maori and Polynesian food** isn't widely represented in restaurants, but you shouldn't miss the opportunity to sample it when it's on offer, particularly in Wellington (see p.485) and Rotorua (p.311), or try a *hangi* (see box, p.52) – an earth oven producing delectable, fall-off-the-bone meat and delicately steamed vegetables.

Often there is little between restaurants and the better **café/bars**, which offer food that's just as good and a few dollars cheaper. Dining is less formal and you may well find yourself elbow to elbow with folk just out for a beer or coffee. Other **cafés** might only offer breakfasts and all-day snacks but nearly all serve good coffee.

Cosmopolitan cafés have all but replaced the traditional **tearooms**, self-service cafeteria-style establishments with no atmosphere but cheap food. Most were unlicensed and dished out machine coffee or tea, pre-packaged sandwiches, unsavoury savouries, sticky cakes and other crimes against the tastebud. On tourist routes, long-distance buses usually made their comfort stops at such tearooms but nowadays tend to opt for more modern cafés, though a few "trad" tearooms still hang on.

Most bars now serve **pub meals**, often the best budget eating around, with straightforward steak and chips, lasagne, pizza or burritos all served with salad for under $20.

The country's ever-burgeoning wine industry has also spawned a number of **vineyard restaurants**, particularly in the growing areas of Hawke's Bay and Marlborough. They're almost all geared to shifting their own vino but provide good, though often expensive, food to soak up the tastings. Most have outdoor seating close to or under the vines, and may well be an area for a post-prandial game of pétanque.

Breakfast, snacks and takeaways

New Zealanders generally take a light "continental" **breakfast** of juice, cereals, toast and tea or coffee. Visitors staying at a homestay or B&B may well be offered an additional "cooked breakfast", probably along the lines of bacon and eggs; if you're staying in motels, hostels or campsites, you'll usually have to fend for yourself. In bigger towns, you'll often find a **bakery** selling fresh croissants, bagels and focaccia, but at weekends New Zealanders tend to go out for breakfast or brunch, at cafés serving anything from a bowl of fruit and muesli to platefuls of Eggs Florentine or Benedict with smoked salmon or bacon.

In the cities you'll also come across **food courts**, usually in shopping malls with a dozen or so stalls selling bargain plates of all manner of ethnic dishes. Traditional **burger bars** continue to serve constructions far removed from the limp international-franchise offerings: weighty buns with juicy patties, thick ketchup, a stack of lettuce and tomato and the ever-present Kiwi favourite, beetroot. **Meat pies** are another stalwart of Kiwi snacking: sold in bakeries and from warming cabinets in pubs everywhere, the traditional steak and mince varieties are now supplemented by bacon and egg, venison, steak and cheese, steak and oyster, smoked fish and *kumara* and, increasingly, vegetarian versions.

Fish and chips (or "greasies") are also rightly popular – the fish is often shark (euphemistically called lemon fish or flake), though tastier species are always available for slightly more, and the chips (fries) are invariably thick and crisp. Look out too for paua fritters, battered slabs of minced abalone that are something of an acquired taste.

Self-catering

If you're **self-catering**, your best bet for supplies is the local supermarket: the warehouse-style Pak 'n' Save, slightly more expensive but reliable New World,

The hangi

In New Zealand restaurants you'll find few examples of **Maori** or Polynesian cuisine, though the cooking style does now have a foothold in forward-looking eateries. But you can always sample traditional cooking methods at a *hangi* (pronounced nasally as "hungi"), where meat and vegetables are steamed for hours in an earth oven then served to the assembled masses. The ideal way to experience a *hangi* is as a guest at a private gathering of extended families, but most people have to settle for one of the commercial affairs in Rotorua or Christchurch. There you'll be a paying customer rather than a guest but the *hangi* flavours will be authentic, though sometimes the operators may have been creative in the more modern methods they've used to achieve them.

At a traditional *hangi*, first the men light a fire and place river stones in the embers. While these are heating, they dig a suitably large pit, then place the hot stones in the bottom and cover them with wet sacking. Meanwhile the women prepare lamb, pork, chicken, fish, shellfish and vegetables (particularly *kumara*), wrapping the morsels in leaves then arranging them in baskets (originally of flax, but now most often of steel mesh). The baskets are lowered into the cooking pit and covered with earth so that the steam and the flavours are sealed in. A couple of hours later, the baskets are disinterred, revealing fabulously tender steam-smoked meat and vegetables with a faintly earthy flavour. A suitably reverential silence, broken only by munching and appreciative murmurs, usually descends.

Countdown or Woolworths. Failing that, you'll notice a marked drop in scope and hike in prices at smaller local supermarkets – IGA and Four Square are the most common. Recently opened and much vaunted small outlets, offering predominantly organic supplies, present a good alternative to the plethora of convenience corner shops (or dairies) stocking bog-standard essentials. Sadly, both types of store, along with shops at campsites and those in isolated areas with a captive market, tend to have inflated prices. Supermarkets sell **beer** and **wine**, but for anything else you'll need a **bottle store**, often attached to the local pub.

Drinking

New Zealand boasts many fine wines and beers, which can be sampled in cafés and restaurants all over the land. But for the lowest prices and a genuine Kiwi atmosphere you can't beat the **pub.** It's a place where folk stop off on their way home from work, its emphasis on consumption and back-slapping camaraderie rather than ambience and decor. In the cities, where competition from cafés is strong, pubs tend to be more comfortable and relaxing, but in the sticks little has changed. Rural pubs can initially be daunting for strangers, but once you get chatting, barriers soon drop. A few pubs are still divided into the **public bar**, a joyless Formica and linoleum place where overalls and work boots are the sartorial order of the day, and the **lounge bar**, where you are expected to dress up a bit more. Drinking hours are barely limited at all; you can drink in most bars until at least midnight on weeknights and until 3am or often later at weekends. The **drinking age** is 18, though anyone who looks under 25 can expect to be asked for identification and smokers are banished to open air, often in small purposely constructed shelters.

Beer

Beer is drunk everywhere and often. Nearly all of it is produced by two huge conglomerates – New Zealand Breweries and DB – who market countless variations on the lager and Pilsener theme, as well as insipid, deep-brown fizzy liquid dispensed from taps and in bottles as "draught" – a distant and altogether feebler relation of British-style bitter.

Increasingly, Kiwi beer drinkers are turning to lager, especially their beloved Steinlager and its newer "no-additive" version Pure. There really isn't a lot to choose between the beers except for alcohol content, normally around four percent, though five percent is common for premium beers usually described as "export".

To find something different and better tasting, seek out **boutique beers** such as those brewed near Nelson by Mac's. Try their dark and delicious stout-like Black Mac, the bitter-like Sassy Red or wait around for the Oktober Mac, a light and fresh concoction brewed in September and only available until it runs out. Small, regional brewers and in-house micro-breweries are increasingly establishing themselves on the scene – look out for the *Loaded Hog* and *One Red Dog* restaurant/bars, while in other pubs and bars, check for Emersons, from Dunedin, or Founders, from Nelson (to name but a couple of widespread superior ale producers). Recently, in the central North Island, the Waituna Brewing Company have started producing "Maori" beer, available in and around Palmerston North, but they've some catching up to do if they want to compete with other micro-breweries.

Most bottle shops stock a fair range of foreign brews and the flashier bars are always well stocked with international bottled beers – at a price. On tap, you will only find New Zealand beer, except for the odd ersatz Irish bar pouring Guinness and the like. A good source of information about all things beery in New Zealand is Ⓦwww.brewing.co.nz.

Measures are standard throughout the country: traditionalists buy a one-litre **jug**, which is then decanted into the required number of glasses, usually a **seven** (originally seven fluid ounces, or 200ml), a **ten**, or even an elegantly fluted **twelve**. Despite thirty years under the metric system, handled **pints** (just over half a litre) have now become widespread. Keep in mind that a half-pint will always be served as a ten fluid ounce glass and therefore will be a little over half the price of a pint. Prices vary enormously, but you can expect to pay around $5–8 for a pint. It is much cheaper to buy in bulk from a bottle shop where beer is either sold in six-packs or cartons of a dozen or twenty-four ($16–25). Serious drinkers go for refillable half-gallon **flagons** (2.25 litres) or their metric variant, the two-litre **rigger**; these can be bought for around a dollar and filled for $10–15 at taps in bottle shops.

Wines and spirits

Kiwis are justifiably loyal to New Zealand winemakers, who now produce **wines** that are among the best in the world. New Zealand is rapidly encroaching on the Loire's standing as the world benchmark for Sauvignon Blanc, while the bold fruitiness of its Chardonnay and apricot and citrus palate of its Rieslings attracts many fans. Wine menus feature few non-Kiwi **whites**, but reds are often of the broad-shouldered Aussie variety. Nevertheless, there are good New Zealand **reds,** particularly young-drinking varietals using Cabernet Sauvignon, Merlot and, perhaps best of all, Pinot Noir. A liking for **champagne** no longer implies "champagne tastes" in New Zealand: you can still buy the wildly overpriced French stuff, but good Kiwi Méthode Traditionelle (fermented in the bottle in the time-honoured way) starts at around $18 a bottle: Montana's Lindauer Brut is widely available, and justly popular. Another drinking trend is for **dessert wines** (or "stickies") typically made from grapes withered on the vine by the *botrytis* fungus, the so-called "noble rot".

Most bars and licensed restaurants have a tempting range of wines, many sold by the glass ($6–9, $8 and up for dessert wine), while in shops the racks groan under bottles starting from $10 ($14–20 for reasonable quality). "Chateau cardboard" wine bladders are considered passé nowadays, so buy a decent bottle if invited out.

If you want to try before you buy, visit a few wineries, where you are usually free to sample half a dozen different wines. There is sometimes a small fee, especially to try the reserve wines, but it is always redeemable if you buy a bottle. Among the established wine-growing areas, **Henderson and the Kumeu Valley**, 15km west of Auckland, is one of the more accessible, though its urban nature makes it the least appealing to tour. On the east coast of the North Island, the area around **Gisborne** is good for a tasting afternoon but wine connoisseurs are better off in **Hawke's Bay**, where Napier and Hastings are surrounded by almost thirty vineyards open to the public. Further south, **Martinborough** has the most accessible cluster of vineyards, many within walking distance. The colder climate of the South Island effectively limits wine production to the northern part, though there are increasing number of vineyards in **Central Otago** near Queenstown and Alexandra. The best are in **Marlborough**, close to Blenheim, which competes with Hawke's Bay for the title of New Zealand's top wine region. A good starting point for information on the Kiwi wine scene is ⓦwww.nzwine.com.

New Zealand also produces fruit **liqueurs**; some are delicious, though few visitors develop an enduring taste for the sickly sweet kiwifruit or feijoa varieties, which are mostly sold through souvenir shops. International spirits are widely available and their dominance is challenged only by one New Zealand-made **vodka** called 42 Below, and two single malt **whiskies**: Milford, made by the New Zealand Malt Whisky Co. (ⓦwww.milfordwhisky.co.nz); and Lammerlaw, made by Dunedin-based Wilson Distillers.

Soft drinks

New Zealand coolers are stocked with just about every international brand of carbonated soft drink, but one home-grown (though not Kiwi-owned) brand to look out for is L&P – originally **Lemon and Paeroa** after the Hauraki Plains town where it was first made – a naturally lemon-flavoured pop. **Milkshakes**, **thickshakes** (usually with a dollop of ice cream) and **smoothies** made with blended fruit are popular thirst quenchers, and almost any café worth its salt serves glasses of **spirulina**, a thick, green goo made from powdered seaweed and often mixed with the likes of apple juice and avocado. Enthusiasts claim restorative properties when drunk the morning after a bender.

Tea and coffee

Tea is usually a down-to-earth Indian blend (sometimes jocularly known as "gumboot"), though you may also have a choice of a dozen or so flavoured, scented and herbal varieties. **Coffee** drinking has been elevated to an art form with a specialized terminology: an Italian-style espresso is known as a **short black** (sometimes served with a jug of hot water so you can dilute it to taste); a weaker and larger version is a **long black**, which, with the addition of milk becomes a **flat white**; **cappuccinos** come regular or chocolate-laced as a mochaccino; while a milky café **latte** is usually sold in a glass but sometimes in a gargantuan bowl. Better places will serve all these decaffeinated, skinny or even made with soya milk. Flavoured syrups are occasionally available but are not common, and plunger and drip-style coffee is increasingly rare.

The media

For a country of only four million inhabitants, New Zealand has a vibrant media scene. Auckland apparently has more radio stations per capita than any city in the world, and the magazine racks groan with Kiwi-produced weeklies and monthlies. The standard of media coverage sometimes leaves a little to be desired, but for the most part this is a well-informed country with sophisticated tastes. On the web a good starting point is ⓦwww.publicaddress.net, the leading Kiwi blog site, which always features something interesting.

TV

New Zealanders receive five main free-to-air **broadcast channels**, a handful of local channels and Sky TV, a subscriber service offering fifty-plus channels plus assorted pay-per-view offerings. Travellers are always griping about low standards, but while much prime-time viewing is unashamedly populist there is high-quality stuff out there – you just have to look for it.

The biggest broadcaster is the state-owned **TVNZ**, which operates two channels (TV ONE and TV2) and has the unenviable task of being both a commercial broadcaster (with plenty of adverts) and delivering high-quality programmes according to its "charter". TV ONE has slightly older and more information-based programming while TV2 is younger and more entertainment-oriented. In practice there is a lot of crossover, and both channels present a diet of locally produced news, current affairs, sport, drama and entertainment, plus a slew of US, British and Australian programmes: you'll find most of your favourites, often 3–6 months behind. British readers may be surprised to hear that *Coronation Street* is huge in New Zealand.

The main opposition comes from **TV3**, which pitches itself roughly between TV ONE and TV2, and newcomer **Prime**, backed by Sky TV, which often has quirkier programming.

Lastly there's **Maori TV**, which was launched in 2004 with substantial government support (though it also has ads). Broadcasting in Maori and English, it is charged with promoting the language and culture but is far from a stuffy educational channel. Along with good movies you might catch Maori cooking shows, lifestyle makeovers, sitcoms, a gay show and Maori angles on news, current affairs and sport. You might not become a regular viewer, but it is well worth dipping into.

TV reception is virtually nationwide for TVONE, TV2 and TV3; the other channels have slightly narrower coverage. To compensate, many motels and some other accommodation come with Sky TV, featuring half a dozen channels including Discovery, BBC World, CNN, the Weather Channel, National Geographic, Animal Planet, E!, ESPN, plus cartoons, music channels, and some sport and movies.

Radio

New Zealand has few countrywide radio stations, but syndication means that some commercial stations can be heard in various parts of the country (principally the bigger cities) but with local commercials. All websites listed stream the channel over the **Internet**.

For news, current affairs and a thoughtful look at the arts and music, tune into the government-funded **Radio New Zealand National** (101.0–101.6 FM; ⓦwww.radionz.co.nz) which is the nearest New Zealand gets to, say, NPR or BBC Radio 4. You'll pick it up most places, though there are blank spots. Its sister station **Radio New Zealand Concert** (89–100 FM) concentrates on classical music, but reception is patchy.

Though sometimes pretty rough around the edges, **student radio stations** often provide excellent and varied "alternative" listening, though only in their home city. In Auckland tune to bFM (95.0; ⓦwww.95bfm.co.nz); in Wellington to Active (89.0; ⓦwww.radioactive.co.nz); in Christchurch to RDU (98.3; ⓦwww.rdu.org.nz); and in Dunedin to Radio One (91.0; ⓦwww.r1.co.nz).

A host of **other commercial stations** clog up the rest of the airwaves. Stations syndicated to various cities (on assorted frequencies) include the Top 40-oriented The Edge (ⓦwww.theedge.co.nz), the rock-oriented The Rock (ⓦwww.therock.net.nz), the classic rock of Hauraki, the self-explanatory NewstalkZB, and the middle-of-the-road music station ZM. In Auckland, listen out for the urban, hip-hop and Rn'B of Flava (96.1FM).

Print

New Zealand has no national **daily newspaper**, making do with four major regional papers (all published Mon–Sat mornings) and a plethora of minor rags of mostly local interest. Despite its title, the big-circulation *New Zealand Herald* (ⓦwww.nzherald.co.nz) is primarily an Auckland paper, with reach over the northern half of the North Island. The southern half of the North Island is covered by the Wellington-based *Dominion Post* (ⓦwww.dompost.co.nz) while *The Press* (ⓦwww.stuff.co.nz) covers Christchurch and its environs, and the *Otago Daily Times* (ⓦwww.odt.co.nz) is widely distributed over the far south of the country. All offer a pretty decent selection of national and international news, sport and reviews, often relying heavily on wire services and syndication deals with major British and American newspapers. All the main papers are politically fairly neutral.

There are two **Sunday papers** with national distribution, the tabloid-style *Sunday News* and the broadsheet *Sunday Star-Times*, which is probably the better of the two. The Auckland-based *Herald on Sunday* is distributed over much of the North Island.

Kiwi newspaper journalists get little scope for imaginative or investigative journalism, though the broad-ranging and slightly left-leaning **weekly magazine**, the *Listener* (ⓦwww.listener.co.nz), does its best. With coverage of politics, art, music, TV, radio, books, science, travel, architecture and much more, it is perhaps the best overall insight into what makes New Zealand tick, and it costs under $4.

Topics are covered in greater depth in the nationwide **monthly** *North and South*, though for an insight into the aspirations of Aucklanders you might be better off with the snappier glossy, *Metro*.

Specialist magazines cover the range: *Wilderness* (ⓦwww.wildernessmag.com) has a good spread of tramping, kayaking, climbing and mountain biking, and *Real Groove* is the best of the general music mags.

The bi-monthly *Mana* (ⓦwww.manaonline.co.nz) pitches itself as "the Maori news magazine for all New Zealanders", and gives an insight into what sometimes seems like a parallel world barely acknowledged by the mainstream media. It is in English, but comes peppered with Maori words and concepts which can make reading a little baffling at first, though it conveniently comes with a back-page glossary.

Festivals and public holidays

Holidays

In the southern hemisphere, **Christmas** falls in the middle of summer, during the school **summer holidays**, which run from mid-December until early February. From Boxing Day through to the middle of January Kiwis hit the beaches en masse and during this time you'll find a lot more people about. Motels and campgrounds can be difficult to book and often raise their prices, though B&Bs and hostels rarely up their rates. To help you chart a path through the chaos, visitor centres are open for longer hours, as are some museums and many other tourist attractions. Other school **holidays** last for two weeks in mid- to late April, a fortnight in early to mid-July and the first two weeks of October, though these have a less pronounced effect. **Public holidays** (marked **PH** in the listing in below) are big news in New Zealand and it can feel like the entire country has taken to the roads, so it's worth considering staying put rather than trying to travel on these days. Each region also takes one day a year to celebrate its Anniversary Day, remembering the founding of the original provinces that made up New Zealand. We've listed official dates below, but days are usually observed on the nearest Monday (or occasionally Friday) to make a long weekend. Although this isn't a good time to actually arrive in town, if you're there already you can join in the shenanigans, usually consisting of an agricultural show, horse-jumping, sheep-shearing, cake baking and best-vegetable contests, plus a novelty event like gumboot throwing.

Public holidays and festivals

Many of the festivals listed below are covered in more detail in the relevant section of the Guide. **PH** indicates a public holiday.

JANUARY

1 New Year's Day (PH) Whaleboat Racing Regatta, Kawhia; Highland Games, Waipu (Ⓦwww.highlandgames.co.nz).

2 (PH)

First Sat Glenorchy Races (Ⓦwww.glenorchy.com).

17 Anniversary Day (**PH** in Southland).

Third Fri Big Day Out, NZ's biggest one-day music festival, Auckland (Ⓦwww.bigdayout.com).

22 Anniversary Day (**PH** in Wellington).

29 Anniversary Day (**PH** in Auckland, Northland, Waikato, Coromandel, Taupo and the Bay of Plenty). Massive regatta on Auckland's Waitemata Harbour.

FEBRUARY

1 Anniversary Day (**PH** in Nelson).

6 Waitangi Day (**PH**) formal events at Waitangi.

First Sat Rippon music festival, Wanaka (Ⓦwww.ripponfestival.co.nz);

First weekend Waitangi weekend, Harvest Hawke's Bay (Ⓦwww.harvesthawkesbay.co.nz).

Second Weekend Coast-to-Coast multisport race (see p.742).

Second weekend Wine Marlborough Festival, Blenheim (Ⓦwww.wine-marlborough-festival.co.nz).

Third Sat Mission Bay Jazz and Blues Streetfest, Mission Bay, Auckland (Ⓦwww.jazzandbluesstreetfest.com).

Third weekend Art Deco Weekend, Napier (Ⓦwww.artdeconapier.com).

Devonport Food & Wine Festival (Ⓦwww.devonportwinefestival.co.nz).

Last week Flowers & Romance Festival, Christchurch (Ⓦwww.festivalofflowers.co.nz).

Mid-Feb to early March Wellington Fringe Festival (Ⓦwww.fringe.org.nz).

MARCH

Late Feb to late March NZ International Arts Festival, Wellington (even-numbered years only; Ⓦwww.nzfestival.telecom.co.nz);

Taranaki International Festival of the Arts (odd-numbered years only; Ⓦwww.aertsfest.co.nz).

First week Golden Shears sheep-shearing competition in Masterton (Ⓦwww.goldenshears.co.nz).

Early March Pasifika Festival, Auckland (Ⓦwww.aucklandcity.govt.nz/pasifika).

Second Sat Wildfoods Festival, Hokitika (see p.744); Te Houtaewa Challenge and Te Houtaewa Surf Challenge, Ahipara (Ⓦwww.newzealand-marathon.co.nz)

Mid-March WOMAD festival, New Plymouth (www.womad.co.nz).
Sun in mid-March Round-the-Bays fun run, Auckland (www.roundthebays.co.nz).
Closest Sat to March 17 Ngaruawahia Maori Regatta, near Hamilton.
23 Anniversary Day (**PH** in Otago).
31 Anniversary Day (**PH** in Taranaki).

APRIL
Late March to late April Good Friday (**PH**) and Easter Sunday (**PH**).
Easter week Waiheke Island Jazz Festival (www.waihekejazz.co.nz); Royal Easter Show, Auckland (www.royaleastershow.co.nz); Warbirds Over Wanaka International Airshow (even-numbered years only; see p.815); National Jazz Festival, Tauranga (www.jazz.org.nz).
25 ANZAC Day (**PH**).
Late April Five-day Festival of Colour (odd-numbered years only; www.festivalofcolour.co.nz) in Wanaka. Music, dance, theatre and arts.
Last week Arrowtown Autumn Festival (www.arrowtownautumnfestival.org.nz).

JUNE
First Mon Queen's Birthday (**PH**).
Middle weekend Fieldays. The southern hemisphere's largest agricultural show, Hamilton (www.fieldays.co.nz).
Mid- to late Matariki, Maori New Year festivities (www.taitokerau.co.nz/matariki.htm).
Late June to early July Two-week Queenstown Winter Festival (www.winterfestival.co.nz).

JULY
Mid- to late July Auckland International Film Festival (www.enzedff.co.nz); Wellington Film Festival (www.enzedff.co.nz).

SEPTEMBER
First full week Gay Ski Week, Queenstown (www.gayskiweeknz.com).
Fourth weekend Alexandra Blossom Festival (www.blossom.co.nz).
Last week and into Oct World of Wearable Art Awards Show, Wellington (www.worldofwearableart.com).

OCTOBER
Fourth Mon Labour Day (**PH**).
31 Halloween. General trick or treating.

NOVEMBER
1 Anniversary Day (**PH** in Hawke's Bay and Marlborough).
5 Guy Fawkes' Night fireworks.
Second week Canterbury Show week (www.nzcupandshow.co.nz).
Third Fri Anniversary Day (**PH** in Canterbury).
Third Sun Toast Martinborough Wine, Food & Music Festival (www.toastmartinborough.co.nz).

DECEMBER
1 Anniversary Day (**PH** in Westland).
25 Christmas Day (**PH**).
26 Boxing Day (**PH**).
31 Rhythm and Vines, New Year's Eve music festival, Gisborne (www.rhythmandvines.co.nz).

Outdoor activities

Life in New Zealand is tied to the Great Outdoors, and no visit to the country would be complete without spending a fair chunk of your time in intimate contact with nature.

Kiwis have long taken it for granted that within a few minutes' drive of their home they can find a deserted beach or piece of "bush" and wander freely through it, an attitude enshrined in a fabulous collection of national, forest and maritime parks. They are all administered by the **Department of Conservation** (DOC; www.doc.govt.nz), which seeks to balance the maintenance of a fragile environment with the demands of tourism. For the most part it manages remarkably well, providing a superb network of signposted paths studded with trampers' huts and operating visitor centres that present highly informative material about the local history, flora and fauna. They also publish excellent leaflets for major walking tracks.

The lofty peaks of the Southern Alps offer challenging **mountaineering** and great **skiing**, while the lower slopes are ideal for multi-day **tramps** which cross low passes between valleys choked with subtropical and temperate rainforests. Along the coasts there are sheltered lagoons and calm harbours for gentle **swimming** and **boating**, but also sweeping strands battered by some top-class **surf**.

The country also promotes itself as the **adventure tourism** capital of the world. All over New Zealand you will find places to go bungy jumping, whitewater or cave rafting, jetboating, tandem skydiving, mountain biking, stunt flying or scuba diving – in fact if you name it someone somewhere organizes it. While thousands of people participate in these activities every day without incident, standards of instructor training do vary. It seems to be a point of honour for all male (and they are almost all male) river guides, bungy operators and tandem parachute instructors to play the macho card and put the wind up you as much as possible. Such bravado shouldn't be interpreted as a genuine disregard for safety, but the fact remains that there have been quite a few well-publicized injuries and deaths – a tragic situation that's addressed by industry-regulated codes of practice, an independent system of accreditation and home-grown organizations that insist upon high levels of professionalism and safety instruction.

Before engaging in any adventure activities, check your insurance cover (see p.79).

Tramping

Tramping, trekking, bushwalking, hiking – call it what you will, it is one of the most compelling reasons to visit New Zealand, and for many the sole objective. Even if the idea sounds appalling, try it once, as the bug frequently bites reluctant trampers.

Hikes typically last three to five days, following well-worn trails through relatively untouched wilderness, often in one of the country's national parks. Along the way you'll be either camping out or staying in trampers' huts, and will consequently be lugging a pack over some rugged terrain, so a moderate level of fitness is required. If this sounds daunting, you can sign up with one of the guided tramping companies that maintain more salubrious huts or luxury lodges, provide meals and carry much of your gear. Details of these are given throughout the Guide.

The main tramping season is in summer, from October to May, although the most popular tramps – the Milford, Routeburn and Kepler – are in the cooler southern half of the South Island, where the season is shorter by a few weeks at either end.

The tramps

Rugged terrain and a history of track-bashing by explorers and deer hunters has left New Zealand with a web of tramps following river valleys and linking up over passes, high above the bushline. As far as possible, we've indicated the degree of difficulty of all tramps covered in the Guide,

Te Araroa – The Long Pathway

Since the mid-1970s it has been a Kiwi dream to have a continuous path from one end of the country to the other. In recent years, **Te Araroa – The Long Pathway** (Ⓦ www.teararoa.org.nz), has been championed by the Te Araroa Trust, a private group that intends to have the whole 2900km route, from Cape Reinga to Bluff, open by the end of 2010. Short trails, built with the trust's involvement, aim to link the fragmented network of existing tracks into a continuous whole. A provisional, impressively varied, route exists, much of it running through fairly remote country, although it intentionally visits small communities so that trampers can re-supply.

A handful of hardy souls have already tramped the whole route but it is envisaged that most people will tackle shorter sections.

broadly following DOC's classification system: a **path** is level, well graded and often wheelchair-accessible; **walking tracks** and **tramping tracks** (usually marked with red and white or orange flashes on trees) are respectively more arduous affairs requiring some fitness and proper walking equipment; and a **route** requires considerable tramping experience to cope with an ill-defined trail, frequently above the bushline. DOC's estimated **walking times** can trip you up: along paths likely to be used by families, for example, you can easily find yourself finishing in under half the time specified, but on serious routes aimed at fit trampers you might struggle to keep pace. We've given estimates for moderately fit individuals and, where possible, included the distance and amount of climbing involved, aiding route planning.

Invaluable information on walking directions, details of access, huts and an adequate map are contained in the excellent DOC tramp **leaflets** (usually $1 apiece). The title of each leaflet relating to an area is included in the appropriate places throughout this book, though we only include the price if it is $2 or over.

The maps in each DOC leaflet should be sufficient for trampers as long as they stick to the designated route, but experienced walkers planning independent routes and folk after a more detailed vision of the terrain should fork out for specialized **maps** that identify all the features along the way. Most trampers' huts have a copy of the local area map pinned to the wall or laminated into the table. In describing tramps we have used "**true directions**" in relation to rivers and streams, whereby the left bank (the "true left") is the left-hand side of the river looking downstream.

Eight of New Zealand's finest, most popular tramps, plus one river journey, have been classified by DOC as **Great Walks** and are covered in detail in the Guide and in the *Adrenalin heaven* colour section. Great Walks get the lion's share of DOC track spending, resulting in relatively smooth, broad walkways, with boardwalks over muddy sections and bridges over almost every stream. In short, they represent the slightly sanitized side of New Zealand tramping.

Access to tracks is seldom a problem in the most popular tramping regions, though it does require planning. Most finish some distance from their start, so taking your own vehicle is not much use; besides, cars parked at trailheads are an open invitation to thieves. Great Walks always have transport from the nearest town, but there are often equally stunning and barely used tramps close by which require a little more patience and tenacity to get to – we've included some of the best of the rest in the Guide, listed under "Tramps" in the index.

Backcountry accommodation: huts and camping

New Zealand's backcountry is strung with a network of almost nine hundred **trampers' huts**, sited less than a day's walk apart, frequently in beautiful surroundings. All are simple, communal affairs that fall into five distinct categories as defined by DOC.

Basic Huts (free) are often crude and rarely encountered on the major tramps. Next up is the **Standard Hut** ($5 per person per night): basic, weatherproof, usually equipped with individual bunks or sleeping platforms accommodating a dozen or so, an external long-drop toilet and a water supply. There is seldom any heating and there are no cooking facilities. **Serviced Huts** ($10) tend to be larger, sleeping twenty or more on bunks with mattresses. Water is piped indoors to a sink, and flush toilets are occasionally encountered. Again, you'll need to bring your own stove and cooking gear, but heating is provided; if the fire is a wood-burning one, you should replace any firewood you use. More sophisticated still are the **Great Walk Huts** – unsurprisingly found along the Great Walks. They tend to have separate bunkrooms, gas rings for cooking (but no utensils), stoves for heating, a drying room and occasionally solar-powered lighting. Children of school age generally pay half the adult fee and, thanks to a DOC initiative, under-18s can now use Great Walk huts and campsites for free – though you should still book in advance.

Hut fees are best paid in advance at the local DOC office, visitor centre or other outlet close to the start of the track. For most tramps you buy a quantity of $5 tickets and give the warden the appropriate number (one for a Standard hut, two for a Serviced hut) or post them in the hut's honesty box. You can sometimes buy tickets direct from wardens, but there is often a 25 percent premium on the price. If you are planning to tramp any of the Great Walks you **must** buy a **Great Walks Hut Pass**, covering the cost of your accommodation for the walk you intend to complete, and carry the confirmation with you, otherwise the wardens will charge you for each hut again. The pass and reservation, made simultaneously, guarantee trekkers a bed on the Kepler, Milford, Routeburn, Abel Tasman and Heaphy. No similar reservation is made with a hut pass bought for the remaining Great Walks, primarily because it's considered very unlikely that each hut will fill up.

The easiest way to make reservations and get Great Walk hut passes is online (@www.doc.govt.nz), or through the relevant/local DOC office (see accounts in the Guide) or, at a push, by using a booking agent, stating which hut you intend to use each night. To get more information about the Great Walks and other NZ tramps you can also log on to @www.tramper.co.nz. In winter (May–Sept) the huts on Great Walks are often stripped of heating and cooking facilities and downgraded to Standard status, so if you have an Annual Hut Pass (see below) you can use them, though possessing the pass or a ticket doesn't guarantee you a bunk. Beds go on a first-come-first-served basis, so if the trail is very busy you may find yourself in an undignified gallop to the next hut.

Should you wish to do a lot of tramping outside the Great Walks system, or on the Great Walks out of season, it's worth buying an **Annual Hut Pass** ($90), which allows you to stay in all Standard and Serviced huts.

Camping is allowed on all tracks except the Milford. Rules vary, but in most cases you're required to minimize environmental impact by camping close to the huts, whose facilities (toilets, water and gas rings where available, but obviously not bunks) you can use.

Equipment

Tramping in New Zealand can be a dangerous and/or dispiriting experience if you're not equipped for both hot, sunny days and wet, cold and windy weather. The best tramps pass through some of the world's wettest regions, with parts of the Milford Track receiving over six metres of rain a year. It is essential to carry a good waterproof jacket, preferably made from breathable fabric and fitted with a decent hood. Keeping your lower half dry is less crucial and most Kiwis tramp in shorts. Early starts often involve wading through long, sodden grass, so a pair of knee-length gaiters can come in handy. Comfortable boots with good ankle support are a must; take suitably broken-in leather boots or lightweight walking boots, and some comfortable footwear for the day's end. You'll also need a warm jacket or jumper, plus a good sleeping bag; even the heated huts are cold at night and a warm hat never goes amiss. All this, along with lighter clothing for sunny days, should be kept inside a robust backpack, preferably lined with a strong waterproof liner such as those sold at DOC offices.

Once on the tramp, you need to be totally self-sufficient. On Great Walks, you should carry **cooking** gear; on other tramps you also need a cooking stove and fuel. **Food** can be your heaviest burden; freeze-dried meals are light and reasonably tasty, but they are expensive, and many cost-conscious trampers prefer pasta or rice, dried soups for sauces, a handful of fresh vegetables, muesli (granola), milk powder and bread or crackers for lunch. Consider taking biscuits, trail mix (known in New Zealand as "scroggin"), tea, coffee and powdered fruit drinks (the Raro brand is good), and energy-giving spreads. All huts have drinking **water** but DOC advise treating water taken from lakes and rivers to protect yourself from giardia; see p.79 for more on this and water-purification methods.

You should also carry basic supplies: a first aid kit, blister kit, sunscreen, insect repellent; a torch (flashlight) with spare battery and bulb, candles, matches or a lighter; and a compass (though few bother on the better-marked tracks).

In the most popular tramping areas you will be able to **rent equipment**. Most important of all, remember that you'll have to carry all this stuff for hours each day. Hotels and hostels in nearby towns will generally let you leave your surplus gear either free or for a small fee.

Safety

Most people spend days or weeks tramping in New Zealand with nothing worse than stiff legs and a few sandfly bites, but **safety** is nonetheless a serious issue and there are deaths every year. The culprit is usually New Zealand's fickle **weather**. It cannot be stressed too strongly that within an hour (even in high summer) a warm, cloudless day can turn bitterly cold, with high winds driving in thick banks of track-obscuring cloud. Heeding the weather forecast (posted in DOC offices) is some help, but there is no substitute for carrying warm, windproof and waterproof clothing.

Failed **river crossings** are another common cause of tramping fatalities. If you are confronted with something that looks too dangerous to cross, then it is, and you should wait until the level falls or backtrack. If the worst happens and you get swept away while crossing, don't try to stand up in fast-flowing water; you may trap your leg between rocks and drown. Instead, lie on your back and float feet first until you reach a place where swimming to the bank seems feasible.

If you do get lost or injured, your chances of being found are better if you left word of your intentions with a **friend** or with a **trusted person** at your next port of call, who will realize you are overdue. DOC offices do stock **intention forms** for you to declare your planned route and estimated finishing time but by the time they are checked you could have been missing too long for it to matter. While on the tramp, fill in the hut logs as you go, so that your movements can be traced, and when you return check in with the folk you told about the trip.

Animals are not a problem in the New Zealand bush. Kiwis never tire of reminding you there are no snakes, and only two poisonous spiders, extremely rarely encountered. You might stumble upon the odd irate wild pig but the biggest irritants are likely to be sandflies whose bites itch or kea, boisterous green parrots that delight in pinching anything they can get their beaks into and, in the spirit of Rutherford, tearing it apart to fulfil their curiosity.

Swimming, surfing and windsurfing

Kiwi life is inextricably linked with the beach, and from Christmas to the end of March (longer in warmer northern climes), a weekend isn't complete without a dip or a waterside barbecue – though you should never underestimate the ferocity of the southern **sun** (see p.79 for precautions). Some of the most picturesque beaches stretch away into salt spray from the pounding Tasman surf or Pacific rollers. **Swimming** here can be very hazardous, so only venture into the water at beaches patrolled by surf lifesaving clubs and always swim between the flags. Spotter planes patrol the most popular beaches and warn of the occasional **shark**, so if you notice everyone heading for the safety of the beach, get out of the water.

New Zealand's tempestuous coastline offers near-perfect conditions for **surfing** and windsurfing. At major beach resorts there is often an outlet renting dinghies, catamarans, canoes and windsurfers; in regions where there is reliably good surf you might also come across boogie boards and surfboards, and seaside hostels often have a couple for guests' use. If you want to get deeper under the skin of the surf community in New Zealand, or just benefit from their local knowledge, take a squiz at Ⓦwww.surf.co.nz and Ⓦwww.surf2surf.co.nz.

Sailing

New Zealand's numerous harbours, studded with small islands and ringed with deserted bays, make **sailing** one of Kiwis' favourite pursuits, which explains why New Zealand and Kiwi sailors have been so influential in the fate of the America's Cup (see *Adrenalin heaven* colour section). People sail year-round, but the summer months from December to March are busiest. Unless you manage to befriend a yachtie you'll probably be limited to commercial yacht **charters** (expensive and usually with a skipper), more reasonably priced and often excellent **day-sailing trips**, or renting a dinghy for some inshore antics.

Grading of rivers

Both rivers and rapids are **graded** according to the scale below, the river grade dictated by the grade of its most demanding rapid. This lends itself to some creative marketing, and you need to take promotional material with a pinch of salt – a river hyped as Grade V might be almost entirely Grade III with one Grade V rapid. For maximum thrills and spills, the expression to look out for is "Continuous Grade …".

I Very easy; a few small waves.

II A flicker of interest, with choppier wave patterns. Dunking potential for inexperienced kayakers but no sweat in a raft.

III Bigger but still easily ridden waves make this bouncy and fun. Good proving ground for novice rafters.

IV Huge, less predictable waves churned up by rocks midstream make this excellent fun but dramatically increase the chance of a swim.

V Serious stuff with chaotic standing waves, churning narrow channels and huge holes ready to swallow you up. Best avoided by first-time rafters but thrilling nonetheless.

VI Dicing with death; commercially unraftable and only shot by the most experienced of paddlers.

Scuba diving and snorkelling

The waters around New Zealand offer wonderful opportunities to scuba **dive** and **snorkel**. What they lack in long-distance visibility, tropical warmth and colourful fish they make up for with the range of diving environments. Pretty much anywhere along the more sheltered eastern side of both islands you'll find somewhere with rewarding snorkelling, but much the best and most accessible spot is the **Goat Island Marine Reserve**, in Northland, where there's a superb range of habitats close to the shore. Northland also has world-class scuba diving at the **Poor Knights Islands Marine Reserve**, reached by boat from Tutukaka, and wreck diving on the *Rainbow Warrior*, from Matauri Bay. Other good spots include the **Hauraki Gulf Maritime Park**, off Great Barrier Island near Auckland, and the deliberately sunk wreck near Wellington. On the South Island, there are wrecks worth exploring off **Picton** and fabulous growths of **black and red corals** relatively close to the surface, in the southwestern fiords near Milford.

For the inexperienced, the easiest way to get a taste of what's under the surface is to take a **resort dive** with an instructor. If you want to dive independently, you need to be PADI qualified. For more information, pick up the free, comprehensive, bi-monthly *Dive New Zealand* brochure from dive shops and the bigger visitor centres, or consult their website at Ⓦwww.divenewzealand.com.

Rafting

The combination of challenging rapids and gorgeous scenery makes **whitewater rafting** one of the most thrilling of New Zealand's adventure activities. Visitor numbers and weather restrict the main **rafting season** to October to May, and most companies set an **age limit** at twelve or thirteen. You'll usually be supplied with everything except a swimming costume and an old pair of trainers. After safety instruction, you'll be placed in eight-seater rafts along with a guide and directed through narrow, rock-strewn riverbeds, spending an average of a couple of hours on the water, before being ferried back for refreshments.

Thrilling though it is, rafting is also one of the most **dangerous** of the adventure activities, claiming a number of lives in recent years. Operators have cleaned up their act with a self-imposed code of practice, but there are still cowboys out there. It might be stating the obvious but fatalities happen when people fall out of rafts: heed the guide's instructions about how best to stay on board and how to protect yourself if you do get a dunking.

For details of the best rafting see the *Adrenalin heaven* colour section.

Canoeing and kayaking

New Zealand is a paddler's paradise, and pretty much anywhere with water nearby has somewhere you can rent either canoes or kayaks. Sometimes this is simply an opportunity to muck around in boats but often there are guided trips available, with the emphasis being on soaking up the scenery. Grade II water is pretty much the limit for novices, making the scenic **Whanganui River** a perennial favourite. See the *Adrenalin heaven* colour section for details.

Jetboating

The shallow, braided rivers of the high Canterbury sheep country posed access difficulties for run-owner Bill Hamilton, who got around the problem by inventing the **Hamilton Jetboat** in the early 1960s. His inspired invention could plane in as little as 100mm of water, reach prodigious speeds (up to 80km per hour) and negotiate rapids while maintaining astonishing, turn-on-a-sixpence manoeuvrability.

The jetboat carried its first fare-paying passengers on a deep and glassy section of the Shotover River, which is still used by the pioneering Shotover Jet. **Rides** last around thirty eye-streaming minutes, time enough for hot dogging and as many 360-degree spins as anyone needs. **Wilderness trips** can last two hours or longer.

Bungy jumping and bridge swinging

For maximum adrenalin, minimum risk and greatest expense, bungy jumping is difficult to beat. For a bit of variety you could try a close relative of the bungy, **bridge swinging**, which provides a similar gut-wrenching fall accompanied by a super-fast swing along a gorge while harnessed to a cable. See the *Adrenalin heaven* colour section for locations.

Canyoning

The easiest way to get your hands on New Zealand rock is to go **canyoning** (or its near relative by the sea, **coasteering**), which involves following steep and confined river gorges or streambeds down chutes and over waterfalls for a few hours, sliding, jumping and abseiling all the way. Guided trips are available in a handful of places, the most accessible being in Auckland, Queenstown, Turangi and Wanaka.

Mountaineering

In the main, New Zealand is better suited to **mountaineering** than rock climbing, though most of what is available is fairly serious stuff, suitable only for well-equipped parties with a good deal of experience. For most people the only way to get above the snowline is to tackle the easy summit of Mount Ruapehu, the North Island's highest point, the summit of Mount Taranaki, near New Plymouth, or pay for a guided ascent of one of New Zealand's classic peaks. Prime candidates are the country's highest mountain, Aoraki Mount Cook (3754m), accessed from the climbers' heartland of Aoraki Mount Cook Village, and New Zealand's most beautiful peak, the pyramidal Mount Aspiring (3030m), approached from Wanaka. In both cases networks of climbers' huts are used as bases for what are typically twenty-hour attempts on the summit.

Multi-day tours

Tours that are included in this section involve taking part in one or other or, in extreme cases, all of the above activities. Although New Zealand is an easy place to explore independently, tours offer specialist insight, logistical help or just some company along the way.

Hiking and wildlife

Active Earth ⓣ025/360 268 & 0800/201 040, Australia ⓣ1800/141 242, ⓦwww.activeearthnewzealand.com. Suitable for anyone who is reasonably fit and wants to see things few other tourists will. Good-humoured and informative guides take small groups tramping, climbing and wilderness camping in virtually untouched country throughout the North Island – from $595 for five nights to $1120 for nine nights – excluding a daily food and camp-fee kitty (around $20 a day) and any extra adventure activities.

Fiordland Ecology Holidays ⓣ03/249 6600, ⓦwww.fiordland.gen.nz. These wonderful trips book up months in advance and take in Doubtful, Dusky and Breaksea sounds and Preservation Inlet, where you can snorkel and scuba dive and visit dolphins and seals (6 days; $1780). All profits go into ecological projects.

Hiking New Zealand ⓣ027/436 0268 & 0800/697 232, Australia ⓣ1800/141 242, ⓦwww.hikingnewzealand.com. Conservation-minded company, running outdoor trips and acting as agent for a number of like-minded operators that give them countrywide coverage. There's everything from hiking trips around the far north of Northland (5 days; $595) and trekking down the West Coast of the South Island (10 days; $1120) to boat trips to New Zealand's sub-Antarctic islands (8 days; $2467, plus $120 landing fees) – a camping and daily food fee of $20 a day applies.

Kiwi Wildlife Tours ⓣ09/422 6868, ⓦwww.kiwi-wildlife.co.nz. Upmarket small-group birding tours including day excursions from Auckland ($175 per person, $300 single supplement) and a comprehensive twenty-day all-inclusive NZ tour ($175 per day).

Kiwi Wildlife Walks ⓣ03/226 6739, ⓦwww.nzwalk.com. Expertly run guided walks in and around around Fiordland National Park and Stewart Island, where they go kiwi spotting (4 days; $995).

Real Journeys ⓣ03/249 6602, ⓦwww.realjourneys.co.nz. Trips include a cruise on the Milford Wanderer, taking in Milford, Doubtful, Dusky and Breaksea sounds (6 days; $1700), with onboard kayaks and a chance of seeing humpback whales.

Flying, skydiving and paragliding

Almost every town in New Zealand seems to harbour an airstrip or a helipad, and there is inevitably someone happy to get you airborne for half an hour's **flightseeing**. The best of these cross the truly spectacular mountain scenery of the Southern Alps or the ice-sculpted terrain of Fiordland, either from Fox Glacier, Franz Josef Glacier, Mount Cook, Wanaka or Queenstown. Helicopters cost around fifty percent more than planes and can't cover the same distances but score on manoeuvrability and the chance to land. If money is tight take a regular flight somewhere you want to go anyway. First choice here would have to be the journey from either Wanaka or Queenstown to Milford Sound, which overflies the very best of Fiordland.

In **tandem skydiving**, a double harness links you to an instructor, who has control of the parachute. After suitable tuition, the plane circles up to around 2500m and you leap out together, experiencing around 45 seconds of eerie freefall before the instructor pulls the ripcord. Again, the Southern Alps and Fiordland are popular jumping grounds,

Ruggedy Range ⓣ03/219 1066, ⓦwww.ruggedyrange.com. Stewart Island-based company offering enthusiastic and entertaining trips to Ulva Island and Masons Bay visiting the unique wildlife (3 days; $1950).

Cycling, horse-riding and kayaking

Adventure South ⓣ03/941 1222, ⓦwww.advsouth.co.nz. This environmentally conscious company runs guided cycling and multi-activity tours around the South Island, with accommodation in characterful lodges or track huts. Consider six days cycling along the West Coast of the South Island ($2390), seven days hiking in the South Island ($2990), and "Remarkable Tours", fourteen days throughout the country ($5890). All tours carry a single supplement.

Alpine Horse Safaris, Waitohi Downs ⓣ03/314 4293, ⓦwww.alpinehorse.co.nz. Treks intended for serious riders, including food and accommodation, that follow old mining tracks well away from civilization, or at least roads, for short (4 days; $930) or longer (12 days; $3275) trips.

Cycle Touring Company ⓣ09/436 0033, ⓦwww.cycletours.co.nz. Tailored self-led or guided tours of Northland, with several routes of two to twenty-one days, and the option to have your gear carried for you. Accommodation is in lodges and homestays (or a cheaper backpacker option) and prices are around $2073 for seven nights if their bus carries your gear, $1702 if you carry it.

New Zealand Sea Kayak Adventures ⓣ09/402 8596, ⓦwww.nzkayaktours.com. Fully catered Northland- and Bay of Islands-based guided sea kayak camping tours for three ($525), six ($1050) or ten days ($1500). Trips are quite adventurous but they cater to a full range of abilities and offer occasional women-only trips.

Pacific Cycle Tours ⓣ03/982 9913, UK freephone 0800/234 6780, US freephone 1-800/732 0921, ⓦwww.bike-nz.com. Christchurch-based mountain-bike, road-bike and hiking tours round both islands with varying degrees of adventurousness, including a Southern Jewel bike tour (14 days; $4825) and Hiking Highlights (19 days; $4865).

Pakiri Beach Horse Riding ⓣ09/422 6275, ⓦwww.horseride-nz.co.nz. Highly professional multi-day tours through native bush and along clifftops including an epic Coast to Coast trip (7 days; $2995).

Pedaltours ⓣ09/585 1338, US freephone ⓣ1-888/222-9187, ⓦwww.pedaltours.co.nz. Guided road- and mountain-biking tours of both islands, from a week-long ride around the Nelson Lakes ($2695) to a full sixteen-day Grand Tour of the South Island (around $5995). High-standard accommodation and hearty meals are included, and bikes can be rented if needed (cost depends on tour).

but Taupo has established itself as the low-cost, reliable venue with the most choice.

A hill, a gentle breeze and substantial tourist presence and you've all the ingredients for **tandem paragliding**, where you and an instructor jointly launch off a hilltop, slung below a manoeuvrable parachute, for perhaps ten to twenty minutes of graceful gliding and stomach-churning banked turns. Alternatively **tandem hang-gliding** or **parasailing** are usually available.

Skiing and snowboarding

New Zealand's **ski season** (roughly June–Nov) starts as snows on northern hemisphere slopes melt away, which, combined with the South Island's backbone of 3000-metre peaks, the North Island's equally lofty volcanoes and the relative cheapness of the skiing means New Zealand is an increasingly popular international ski destination. Most fields are geared to the domestic downhill market, and the eastern side of the Southern Alps is littered with **club fields** sporting a handful of rope tows, simple lifts and a motley collection of private ski lodges. They're open to all-comers, but some are only accessible by 4WD vehicles, others have a long walk in, and ski schools are almost unheard of. Throughout the country there are, however, a dozen exceptions to this norm: **commercial resorts**, with high-speed chairs, ski schools, gear rental and groomed wide-open slopes. What you won't find are massive on-site resorts of the scale found in North America and Europe; skiers commute daily to the slopes from nearby après-ski towns and **gear rental** is either from shops in these or on the field.

The best up-to-date source of skiing information is the annual **Ski & Snowboard Guide** published by Brown Bear Publications, PO Box 13717, 39 Carlisle St, Sydenham, Christchurch (ⓣ03/358 0935, ⓦwww.brownbear.co.nz). It is freely downloadable from their website, and the printed guide can be picked up from visitor centres and ski area hotels for a couple of bucks. For each field it gives a detailed rundown of facilities, season length, lift ticket prices and an indication of suitability for beginners, intermediates and advanced skiers. Heli-skiing is also dealt with and there's coverage of the main ski towns. Another **website** for all things skiing in New Zealand is ⓦwww.snow.co.nz. For the best skiing locations, see the *Adrenalin heaven* colour section.

Fishing

Kiwis grow up fishing: virtually everyone seems to have fond memories of long days out on a small boat trailing a line for snapper, if only to stock the beachside barbecue. All around the New Zealand coast there are low-key canoe, yacht and launch trips on which there is always time for a little **casual fishing**, but you'll also find plenty of trips aimed at more dedicated anglers. Most sea excursions look to land something of modest size with good flavour: snapper, *kahawai*, *moki* or flounder. Bigger boats might hope for *hapuku*, then there's a step up to the **big-game fishing** boats. From December to May these scout the seas off the northern half of the North Island for marlin, shark and tuna. Regulations and bag limits are covered on the Ministry of Fisheries website, ⓦwww.fish.govt.nz.

Inland, the **rivers** and **lakes** are choked with rainbow and brown trout, quinnat and Atlantic salmon, all introduced for sport at the end of the nineteenth century. Certain areas have gained enviable reputations: Lake Taupo is world-renowned for the abundance and fighting quality of its rainbow trout; South Island rivers, particularly around Gore, boast the finest brown trout in the land; and the braided gravel-bed rivers draining the eastern slopes of the Southern Alps bear superb salmon.

A national **fishing licence** ($96 for the year from Oct 1–Sept 30 and $19 for 24 hours) covers all New Zealand's lakes and rivers except for those in the Taupo catchment area, where a local licensing arrangement applies. They're available from sports shops everywhere and directly from Fish and Game NZ (ⓦwww.fishandgame.org.nz), the agency responsible for managing freshwater sports fisheries. The website also lists bag limits and local regulations.

Wherever you fish, **regulations** are taken seriously and are rigidly enforced. If you're found with an undersize catch or an over-full bag, heavy fines may be imposed and equipment confiscated. Be sure to find out the local regulations before you set out.

Other fishy websites include Ⓦwww.fishinginnewzealand.com and Ⓦwww.fishing.net.nz.

Horse trekking

New Zealand's highly urbanized population leaves a huge amount of countryside available for **horse trekking**, occasionally along beaches, often through patches of native bush and tracts of farmland; there may even be an opportunity to swim the horses. There are schools everywhere and all levels of experience are catered for, but more experienced riders might prefer the greater scope of full-day or even week-long wilderness treks (see p.67). We've highlighted some noteworthy places and operators throughout the Guide, and there's a smattering of others listed at Ⓦwww.truenz.co.nz/horsetrekking. As there are no nationwide safety standards, it's worth establishing your own and only using operators who offer riding helmets.

Mountain biking

If you prefer a smaller saddle, you'll find a stack of places renting out **mountain bikes**. The main trail-biking areas around Rotorua, Queenstown, Mount Cook and Hanmer Springs will often have a couple of companies willing to take you out on **guided rides**, usually dropping you at the top of the hill and picking you up at the bottom. For information about Kiwi **off-road biking** consult Ⓦwww.mountainbike.co.nz.

Mountain bikes aren't allowed off-road in national parks and reserves, and elsewhere you must respect the enjoyment of others by letting walkers know of your presence, avoiding skid damage to tracks and keeping your speed down. For more information, consult the specific biking guides available in New Zealand, including the "Kennett brothers" book (see p.921).

Spectator sports

If God were a rugby coach almost every New Zealander would be a religious fundamentalist. News coverage often gives headline prominence to sport, particularly the All Blacks, and entire radio stations are devoted to sports talkback, usually dwelling on occasions when Kiwi underdogs overcome better-funded teams from more populous nations. Kiwis are by and large an active bunch, most preferring to fish, play some form of sport or tramp.

As elsewhere, most major sports events are televised. Increasingly these are on subscription channels such as Sky TV, which encourages a devoted following in pubs with large-screen TVs.

Anyone with a keen interest in sport or just a desire to see the less reserved side of the Kiwi character should attend a rugby game. Local papers advertise games along with ticket booking details. **Bookings** for many of the bigger events can be made through Ticketek (Ⓦwww.ticketek.co.nz), although, except for the over-subscribed internationals and season finals, you can usually just buy a ticket at the gate.

Rugby

Opponents quake in their boots at the sight of fifteen strapping **All Blacks**, the national **rugby** team, performing their pre-match *haka*, and few spectators remain unmoved. Kiwi hearts swell at the sight, secure in the knowledge that their national team is always amongst the world's best, and anything less than a resounding victory is considered a case for national mourning in the leader columns of the newspapers. However, the All Blacks' relative failure in the four-yearly **Rugby World Cup** – in 2007 they were knocked out by the French – means the team doesn't quite carry the respect it once merited, particularly after the protracted national witch hunt of 2007 which curiously resulted in the re-appointment of the failed coach, Graham Henry.

Rugby (or Rugby Union, though it is seldom called this in New Zealand) is played through the winter, the season kicking off with the **Super 14 series** (mid-Feb to May) in which regional southern hemisphere teams (five from NZ, five from South Africa and four from Australia, though controversially none from the Pacific Islands) play each other with the top four teams going on to contest the finals series. Super 14 players make up the All Black team which, through the middle of winter, hosts an international test series or two, including the annual **tri-nations series** (mid-July to August) against South Africa and Australia. Games between the All Blacks and Australia also contest the **Bledisloe Cup**, which creates much desired bragging rights for one or other nation for a year.

The international season often runs over into the **National Provincial Championship** (NPC), played from the middle of August until the end of October. Each province has a team, the bigger competing in the first division with the minor provinces generally filling up the second division. At the time of writing, Auckland held the **Ranfurly Shield** (Ⓦwww.ranfurlyshield.com), affectionately known as the "log of wood". Throughout the season, the holders accept challenges at their home ground, and the winner takes all. Occasionally minor teams will wrest the shield, and in the smaller provinces this is a huge source of pride, subsequent defences prompting a huge swelling of community spirit.

Tickets for Super 14 games cost around $45, with international games costing a little more and NPC matches much less. For more information visit the NZ Rugby Union's official **website** Ⓦwww.nzrugby.co.nz, or the more newsy Ⓦwww.TheSilverFern.co.nz.

Rugby league (Ⓦwww.rugbyleague.co.nz and Ⓦwww.nzrl.co.nz) has always been regarded as rugby's poor cousin, though success at international level has raised its profile. Rugby League's World Cup was last held in 2000 with the NZ Kiwis only losing out in the final to their perennial nemesis, Australia. New Zealand's only significant provincial team are the Auckland-based **Warriors**, who play in Australia's NRL during the March to early September season. The top eight teams in the league go through to the finals series in September, and though the Warriors haven't done especially well in recent years, they did make it into the final eight in 2007. Home games are usually played at Ericsson Stadium, where you can buy tickets at the gate.

Cricket

Attending a rugby match is something you shouldn't miss if you have the chance, but most visitors spend their time in New Zealand from October to March, when the stadiums are turned over to the country's traditional summer sport, **cricket** (Ⓦwww.nzcricket.co.nz). The national team – the **Black Caps** – hover around mid-table in international test and one-day rankings but periodic flashes of brilliance – and the odd unexpected victory over Australia – keep fans interested. Unless you are an aficionado, cricket is an arcane game and much of the pleasure of attending is sitting in the sun with a beer in your hand soaking up the ambience. You can usually just turn up at a ground and buy a **ticket** (around $30), though games held around Christmas and New Year fill up fast and internationals sell out in advance.

Other sports

Other team sports lag far behind rugby and cricket, though women's **netball** (Ⓦwww.netballnz.co.nz) has an enthusiastic following and live TV coverage of international fixtures involving the Silver Ferns get good audiences.

Soccer in New Zealand has always been thought of as slightly effete (especially in macho rugby-playing circles) though there are now more youngsters playing soccer than rugby. The nation's only representative in the

Australian National Soccer League (NSL; Ⓦwww.footballaustralia.com.au), are the Wellington Phoenix (Ⓦwww.wellingtonphoenix.com). The season runs from October to early April and home games are played (usually on Fri or Sat evenings) at Westpac Stadium in Wellington; **tickets** (around $37) can be bought at the gate or on the team's website.

Beyond these major team sports there is a reasonable following for women's **softball** and men's and women's **basketball**. In recent years **yachting** has attracted heightened interest: Auckland is a frequent midway point for round-the-world yacht races and has twice hosted the **America's Cup**.

New Zealand's **Olympic** heritage is patchy, with occasional clutches of medals from rowing and yachting and a long pedigree of **middle-distance runners**, particularly in the 1960s with Murray Halberg and Peter Snell, and in the 1970s with John Walker, Dick Quax and Rod Dixon. These days, however, multi-event championships and endurance events like triathlons and Iron Man races seem to dominate.

Culture and etiquette

Ever since Maori settled in the land they named Aotearoa, New Zealand has been a nation of immigrants. The majority trace their roots back to Britain and Ireland, and northern European culture prevails with a strong Maori and Polynesian influence. Decades of attempted assimilation have now been replaced by a policy of bi-culturalism with Maori and Pakeha (white European) values at least nominally given equal status. In practice, British influences remain strong: the operation of Parliament and the legal system rooted in the old country, and the Queen continues as head of state and beams out from all coins and the $20 note.

Still, **Maori** are very much part of contemporary New Zealand society (see *Maori in the modern world* colour section). On the surface many seem integrated with the mainstream, but there's also a parallel Maori world you'll rarely see as a tourist, though some idea can be gleaned from commercial cultural tours. Occasionally Maori get fed up with perceived (and often real) injustices, and protests are fairly common. The racial tension that does exists mostly stays below the surface, and as a visitor you'll experience little and probably come away from New Zealand with the impression of a relatively tolerant society.

In the last couple of decades **Asian immigration** (principally from China and Korea, but also from the Indian subcontinent) has skyrocketed. Asians currently make up around seven percent of the population (around half that of Maori) but in the Auckland region Asians comprise over eighteen percent of the total. Currently Asians mostly live outside the mainstream of society but as they and their children gradually integrate some form of tri-culturalism will become a possibility.

Notwithstanding this mix, the archetypal **Kiwi personality** is rooted in the desire to make a better life in a unique and sometimes unaccommodating land. New Zealanders are inordinately fond of stories of plucky little Kiwis overcoming great odds and succeeding, perceiving the New Zealand persona to be rooted in self-reliance, inventiveness and bravery, tempered by a certain self-deprecating humour. Over-achieving "tall poppies" are routinely cut down.

Sport is a huge passion; the country has consistently punched above its weight in international competition, especially on the rugby field where the All Blacks are frequently at the top of the world rankings. Indeed, repeated losses in the Rugby World Cup (which Kiwis believe should be theirs by right) are cause for national mourning.

Despite a reputation for having a rugby-playing, beer-swilling, male-dominated culture, Kiwis like to point out that they run an open-minded and egalitarian society. In 1893, New Zealand became the first country with **women's suffrage**, generous pensions and free public health followed in the first half of the twentieth century, and in 1985 New Zealand declared its waters **nuclear-free**, angering its US and Australian defence partners. Broadly liberal social attitudes prevail with Japanese whaling and genetic modification hot topics.

New Zealand's relationship with its larger neighbour is a cause for endless entertainment on both sides of the Tasman. Kiwis and **Aussies** are like siblings: there are lots of scraps (mostly verbal), especially when it comes to sport, but they're the first to jump to each other's defence in everything from military conflict to pub brawls. Mostly it is just good-natured ribbing but you won't be in New Zealand long before you hear something disparaging about Australians. Of course, accusations of sheep-shagging go both ways.

Etiquette

"Gidday!" is as Kiwi as it is Australian, though you're also likely to be greeted with "Kia ora!" (Hi) or, more likely, "Kia ora, bro!" (Hi, mate). **Dress standards** are as informal as the greetings and unless you're on business or have a diplomatic function to attend you can leave your suit and tie at home; even the finest restaurants only require smart attire. The more pretentious nightclubs operate **dress policies**, mostly nothing more than a ban on work clothes and trainers. **Nudity** on beaches is pretty rare, but as long as you are reasonably discreet no one is likely to be too bothered.

Smoking is increasingly outlawed. It is banned on all public transport, in public buildings and is only permitted in outdoor areas of restaurants, cafés and bars. Cigarettes are expensive and best bought duty-free on arrival.

The Kiwi attitude to **tipping** is pleasingly uncomplicated. No tip is expected, though reward for excellent service in eating places is appreciated.

Living in New Zealand

New Zealand is the sort of place people come for a short visit and end up wanting to stay (at least for a few months). Unless you have substantial financial backing that will probably mean finding some work. And while your earning potential in New Zealand isn't necessarily going to be that great, you can at least supplement your budget for multiple bungy jumps, skydiving lessons and the like. Paid casual work is typically in tourism-linked service industries, or in orchard work.

For the last few years unemployment has been impressively low and finding casual work shouldn't be that difficult. Even better-paid, short-term **professional jobs** are quite possible if you have the skills. Employment agencies are a good bet for this sort of work, or simply look at general job-search websites such as Ⓦsearch4jobs.co.nz and the jobs section of Ⓦwww.trademe.co.nz. The minimum wage for all legally employed folk over the age of 18 is $12 an hour but if you'd rather not tackle the red tape you can simply reduce your travelling costs by **working for your board**. The Immigration Department still consider this to be work but are unlikely to track you down.

Working for board and lodging

A popular way of getting around the country cheaply is to work for your keep, typically toiling for 4–6 hours a day in return for board and lodging. **FHiNZ** (Farm Helpers in New Zealand; Ⓦwww.fhinz.co.nz), organize stays on farms, orchards and horticultural holdings for singles, couples and families, and no experience is needed. Almost 200 places are listed in their booklet ($25; apply online) and accommodation ranges from basic to quite luxurious. The international **WWOOF** (Ⓦwww.wwoof.co.nz) coordinates over a thousand properties (membership, for one or a couple, and booklet $40), mostly farms but also orchards, market gardens and self-sufficiency-orientated smallholdings, all using organic methods to a greater or lesser degree. They'll expect a stay of at least three nights, though much longer periods are common; armed with their booklet, you **book direct** (preferably a week or more in advance). Most hosts will work you three to four hours a day and vary the tasks to keep you interested, but there have been occasional reports of taskmasters; make sure you discuss what will be expected of you before you commit yourself.

Property managers are vetted but **lone women** may feel happier seeking placements with couples or families. Women taking up work through other organizations have fewer guarantees, though many are perfectly reputable operations.

A similar organization is the online **Help Exchange** (Ⓦwww.helpx.net), which supplies a regularly updated list of hosts on farms as well as at homestays, B&Bs, hostels and lodges, who need extra help for an average of four hours a day (sometimes less), in return for meals and accommodation; you register online for **free** and book direct.

Visas, permits and red tape

Australians can work legally work in New Zealand without any paperwork. Otherwise, if you're aged 18 to 30, the easiest way to work legally is through the **Working Holiday Scheme**, which gives you a temporary work permit valid for twelve months. An unlimited number of Brits and Dutch (plus 2800 Irish citizens, 2000 Canadians, and assorted Americans, Brazilians, French, Italians, Germans, Japanese, Koreans, Singaporeans and Malaysians) are eligible each year on a first-come-first-served basis; apply as far in advance as you can. You'll need a passport, NZ$120 for the application, evidence of a return ticket to New Zealand (or the funds to pay for it), and the equivalent of NZ$4200 to show you can support yourself. Brits can alternatively apply for a 23-month stay. Applications are made through the **New Zealand Immigration Service** (Ⓣ09/914 4100, Ⓦwww.immigration.govt.nz), which has all the details and downloadable forms on its website. Over-30s can't join the Working Holiday Scheme, and the only legal option is trying to get full immigrant status – not something to be tackled lightly.

Some visitors are tempted to **work illegally**, something for which you could be fined or deported. In practice, the authorities sometimes turn a blind eye to infringements, especially during the fruit-picking season, when there isn't enough local labour to fill demand.

Anyone working in New Zealand (including, oddly, those working illegally without permits) needs to obtain a **tax number** from the local Inland Revenue Department office (Ⓦwww.ird.govt.nz), a process that can take a week or more, though you can still work while the wheels of bureaucracy turn. If you don't have a number then you may find your employer has trouble paying you, and that the authorities will be more likely to take an interest in you. The tax department rakes in 24 per cent of your earnings and you probably won't be able to reclaim any of this. Many companies will also only pay wages into a **bank account**, so you may need to open one, which is easy (see p.81).

Casual work

One of the main sources of casual work is **picking fruit** or related **orchard work** such as packing or pruning and thinning. The main areas to consider are Kerikeri in the Bay of Islands for citrus and kiwifruit, Hastings in Hawke's Bay for apples, pears and peaches, Tauranga and Te Puke for kiwifruit, and Alexandra and Cromwell in

Central Otago for stonefruit. Most work is available during the autumn **picking season**, which runs roughly from January to May, but this is also when most people are looking for work so you can often find something just as easily in the off season. In popular working areas, some hostels cater to short-term workers, and these are usually the best places to find out what's happening.

Picking can be hard and heavy work and **payment** is usually by the quantity gathered, rather than by the hour. When you're starting off, the poor returns can be frustrating but with persistence and application you can soon find yourself pulling in a decent wage. Don't expect to earn a fortune, but in an eight-hour day you should gross $90–130. Rates do vary considerably so it's worth asking around, factoring in any meals and accommodation, which are sometimes included. Indoor packing work tends to be paid hourly.

Finding other types of casual work is more ad hoc, with no recognized channels other than newspapers and hostel notice-boards; just keep your ear to the ground, particularly in popular tourist areas – Rotorua, Nelson, Queenstown – where people running **cafés**, **bars** and **hostels** often need extra staff during peak periods. If you have no luck, try your chances in more out-of-the-way locales, where there'll be fewer travellers clamouring for work. Bar and restaurant work usually pays around $12–18 an hour and tips are negligible. Generally you'll need to commit to at least three months. **Ski resorts** occasionally employ people during the June to October season, usually in catering roles. The traditional $12–16 an hour may be supplemented by a lift pass and subsidized food and drink, though finding affordable accommodation can be difficult and may offset a lot of what you gain. Hiring clinics for ski and snowboard instructors are usually held at the beginning of the season at a small cost, though if you are experienced it is better to apply directly to the resort beforehand.

Local hostels and backpackers are always good places to hear about likely work opportunities, and there are a number of handy **resources** and **websites**. Perhaps the best is NZ Job Search, base ACB, 229 Queen St, Auckland (Ⓣ09/357 3996, Ⓦwww.nzjs.co.nz), which details the legalities, helps place people in jobs, and guides its clients through setting up bank accounts and dealing with the IRD. A new Christchurch office is planned: check the website for details.

For fruit picking and the like it's also worth checking out sites such as Ⓦwww.seasonalwork.co.nz and Ⓦwww.job.co.nz.

Volunteering

A useful starting point is the online service from the UK-based The Gapyear Company (Ⓦwww.gapyear.com), who offer free membership plus heaps of information on volunteering, travel, contacts and living abroad. The Department of Conservation's **Conservation Volunteer Programme** (search at Ⓦwww.doc.govt.nz) provides an excellent way to spend time out in the New Zealand bush while putting something back into the environment. Often you will get into areas most visitors never see, and learn some skills while you're at it. Projects include bat surveys, kiwi monitoring and nest protection, as well as more rugged tasks like track maintenance, tree planting and hut repair – all detailed on the website. You can muck in for just a day or up to a couple of weeks, and sometimes there is a fee (perhaps $50–200) to cover food and transport. Programmes are often booked up well in advance so it pays to send in an application (forms available on the website) before you reach New Zealand.

Travel Essentials

Costs

The relatively high Kiwi dollar means that New Zealand is no longer the bargain it once was, but with high standards of quality and service the country is still good value for money.

Daily costs vary enormously, and the following estimates are per person for two people travelling together. If you are on a tight budget, using public transport, camping or staying in hostels, and cooking most of your own meals, you could scrape by on $50 a day. A couple renting a car, staying in budget motels, and eating out a fair bit are looking at more like $120–150 per person. Step up to comfortable B&Bs and nicer restaurants, then throw in a few trips, and you can easily find yourself spending over $300 a day. With the prevalence of good hostels, **single travellers** can live almost as cheaply as couples, though you'll pay around thirty percent more if you want a room to yourself.

Though you are unlikely to return from New Zealand laden with souvenirs, you can completely blow your budget on **adventure trips** such as a bungy jump (around $150) or tandem parachuting ($240 and up). If you've got the money, by all means spend it; if not, it pays to think carefully about how best to get the maximum bang for your bucks.

New Zealanders are a straightforward bunch and the price quoted is what you pay. In almost all cases, the 12.5 percent Goods and Service Tax (**GST**) is included in the listed price, except for some business hotels, where rates will be clearly marked GST-exclusive. GST exemption is available on more expensive items bought at shops bearing the "Duty-Free Shopping" sticker that are to be sent or taken out of the country.

Student **discounts** are few and far between, but you can make substantial savings on accommodation and travel by buying one of the backpacker or YHA cards (see p.47); **kids** (see p.85) enjoy reductions of around fifty percent on most trains, buses and entry to many sights.

Crime and personal safety

New Zealand's rates of violent crime are in line with those in other developed countries and you'll almost certainly hear some grizzly stories through the news media. Still, as long as you use your common sense and don't drop your guard just because you're on holiday, you're unlikely to run into any trouble. Some caution is needed in the **seedier quarters** of the larger cities where it is unwise for lone women to walk late at night. Obviously the more isolated a spot the less chance of getting help. One major safety issue is the increasing number of **"boy racers"** using city and town streets as racetracks for customized cars, leading to bystander fatalities. Although the police do take action they are relatively thin on the ground so it's worth being on your toes when out late in city suburbs.

Theft can also be a problem. There is rarely any stealing in hostels apart from the odd case of mistaken identity when it comes to food in the fridge, although it doesn't do any harm to lock away stuff if you can. Car and campervan **break-ins** are a more widespread problem. When staying in cities it's easy enough (and a good idea) to move valuables into your lodging, but thieves also prey on visitors' vehicles left at trailheads and while you go to take a picture of a waterfall. Campervans containing all your travelling possessions make obvious and easy pickings. When you leave your vehicle, take your valuables with you, and put packs and bags out of sight as much as possible. Beyond this, there isn't really a great deal you can do except get good insurance. When setting out on long walks use a secure car park if possible, where your vehicle will be kept safe for a small sum.

Police and the law

As everywhere, there are cases of corruption and brutality but on the whole the police are friendly and helpful. If you do get arrested, you will be allowed one phone call; a solicitor will be appointed if you cannot afford one and you may be able to claim legal aid. It is unlikely that your consulate will take more than a passing interest unless there is something strange or unusual about the case against you.

The laws regarding **alcohol consumption** have traditionally been pretty lenient, though persistent rowdy behaviour has encouraged some towns to ban drinking in public spaces. Still, most of the time nobody's going to bother you if you fancy a beer on the beach or glass of wine at some wayside picnic area. Unless you are actively causing trouble, the police are tolerant. The same does not apply to drink driving (see p.38), which is taken very seriously.

Marijuana has a reputation for being very potent and relatively easily available. It is, however, illegal and although a certain amount of tolerance is sometimes shown towards personal use, the police and courts take a dim view of larger quantities and hard drugs, handing out long custodial sentences. New Zealand is, surprisingly, sixth in the world for methamphetamine usage, according to a recent survey. "Party Pills" – available, until recently, from high street shops and popular with some clubbers – are now illegal.

Most large-scale drug trafficking seems to be gang controlled, with around 2000 street gang members in Auckland alone. Gangs originated in the 1960s, with the Mongrel Mob and Black Power (who still exist), but have evolved to resemble their American counterparts. These days there are more gangs engaging in a broader range of activity, though tourists are about as likely to experience this first hand as they are a poisonous spider.

Emergency phone calls

Ⓣ111 is the free emergency telephone number to summon the police, ambulance or fire service.

Prejudice

New Zealanders like to think of themselves as a tolerant and open-minded people, and foreign visitors are generally welcomed with open arms. Racism is far from unknown, but you're unlikely to experience overt **discrimination** or be refused service because of your race, colour or gender. In out-of-the-way rural pubs, women, foreigners, and just about anyone who doesn't live within a 10km radius, may get a frosty reception, though this breaks down once you get talking.

Despite constant efforts to maintain good relations between Maori and Pakeha (white New Zealanders), tensions do exist. Ever since colonization, **Maori** have achieved lower educational standards, earned less and maintained disproportionately high rates of unemployment and imprisonment. Slowly Maori are getting some restitution for the wrongs perpetrated on their race, which of course plays into the hands of those who feel that such positive discrimination is unfair. "After all, we're all New Zealanders" is a refrain often heard, particularly of late, with the arrest of Maori activists in October 2007 on terrorism charges, later dropped.

Recent high levels of immigration from East Asia – Hong Kong, China and Taiwan in particular – have rapidly changed the demographics in Auckland, where most have settled. Central Auckland also has several English-language schools that are mostly full of Asian students. The combined effect means that in parts of Auckland, especially downtown, longer-established New Zealanders are in the minority. It is a sensation that some Maori and Pakeha find faintly disturbing. There's little overt racism, but neither is there much mixing.

Electricity

New Zealand operates a 230/240volt, 50Hz AC **power supply**, and sockets take a three-prong, flat-pin type of plug. Suitable socket adaptors are widely available in New Zealand and at most international airports; and for phone chargers and laptops that's all you'll need. In most other cases, North American appliances require both a transformer and an adaptor, British and Irish equipment needs only an adaptor and Australian appliances need no alteration.

Entry requirements

All visitors to New Zealand need a passport, which must be valid for at least three months beyond the time you intend to stay. When flying to New Zealand you'll probably need to show you have an **onward or return ticket** before they'll let you board the plane.

On arrival, British citizens are automatically issued with a permit to stay for up to six months, and a three-month permit is granted to citizens of most other European countries, Southeast Asian nations, Japan, South Africa, the USA and Canada, and several other countries. Australian citizens and permanent residents can stay indefinitely.

Other nationalities need to obtain a visitor visa in advance from a New Zealand embassy, costing the local equivalent of NZ$130 and usually valid for three months. Visas are issued by the New Zealand Immigration Service (Ⓦwww.immigration.govt.nz).

For **foreign embassies** and consulates in New Zealand see the "Listings" sections of the Auckland and Wellington chapters, on p.135 and p.489 respectively.

Embassies and consulates abroad

Websites and contact details for all New Zealand embassies and consulates abroad can be found at Ⓦwww.nzembassy.com.

Australia Canberra Ⓣ02/6270 4211, Ⓔnzhccba@bigpond.net.au; and consulates in Sydney and Melbourne.
Canada Ottawa Ⓣ613/238-5991, Ⓔinfo@nzhcottawa.org; and consulates in Toronto and Vancouver.
South Africa Pretoria Ⓣ012/342 8656, Ⓔenquiries@nzhc.co.za; and an honorary consul in Cape Town.
UK and Ireland London Ⓣ020/7930 8422, Ⓔaboutnz@newzealandhc.org.uk; and honorary consuls in Belfast, Dublin and Edinburgh.
USA Washington Ⓣ202/328-4800, Ⓔinfo@nzemb.org; and consulates in New York and Los Angeles.

Quarantine and customs

In a country all too familiar with the damage that can be caused by introduced plants and animals, New Zealand's Ministry of Agriculture and Forestry (MAF; Ⓦwww.maf.govt.nz/quarantine) takes a hard line. On arrival you'll be asked to **declare any food**, plants or parts of plants, animals (dead or alive), equipment used with animals, camping gear, golf clubs, bicycles, biological specimens and hiking boots. Outdoor equipment and walking boots will be taken away, inspected and perhaps cleaned then returned a few minutes later. After a long flight it can all seem a bit of a pain, but such precautions are important and there are huge fines for non-compliance. Be sure to dispose of any fresh fruit, vegetables and meat in the bins provided or you are liable for an instant $200 fine (even for that orange you forgot about in the bottom of your bag). Processed foods are usually allowed through, but must be declared.

Visitors aged 18 and over are entitled to a **duty-free allowance** (Ⓦwww.customs.govt.nz) of 200 cigarettes (or 250 grams of tobacco, or 50 cigars), 4.5 litres of wine or beer, three 1125ml bottles of spirits, and up to $700 worth of goods. There are **export restrictions** on wildlife, plants, antiquities and works of art.

Gay and lesbian travellers

New Zealand is a broadly gay-friendly place, defying the odds in what has always been perceived as a fairly macho country. There remains an undercurrent of redneck intolerance, particularly in rural areas, but it generally stays well below the surface.

Homosexuality was decriminalized in 1986 and the **age of consent** was set at sixteen (the same as for heterosexuals). The human rights section of the **legislation** was passed in 1993, with none of the usual exceptions made for the military or the police. This also makes it illegal to discriminate against gays and people with HIV or AIDS, and makes no limitation on people with HIV or AIDS entering the country.

The mainstream acceptance is such that the New Zealand Symphony Orchestra is quite upfront about one of its most prominent composers, Gareth Farr, doubling as a drag queen. This tolerant attitude has conspired to de-ghettoize the gay community; even in **Auckland** and **Wellington**, the only cities with genuinely vibrant gay scenes, there aren't any predominantly gay areas and most venues have a mixed clientele. Auckland's scene is generally the largest and most lively, but the intimate nature of Wellington makes it more accessible and welcoming. Christchurch has a few predominantly gay venues in the inner city, and Nelson has a moderately active gay community centred on Thursday nights at the Spectrum drop-in centre, 42 Franklyn St (7.30–10.30pm; ⓣ03/545 0814). Elsewhere it's hard to find a gay network to plug into; even Queenstown is fairly quiet, though it has a gay information service at ⓦwww.gayqueenstown.com.

Major **events** on the gay calendar include Auckland's Hero Festival (see box, p.132) each February and the annual **Vinegar Hill Summer Camp**, held just outside the small town of Hunterville, in the middle of the North Island, from Boxing Day to just after New Year. It's a very laid-back affair, with a couple of hundred gay men and women camping out, mixing and partying. There's no charge (except a few dollars for camping), no tickets and no hot water, but a large river runs through the grounds and everyone has a great time.

The best source of on-the-ground information is the gay newspaper **Express** (fortnightly, free; ⓦwww.gayexpress.co.nz), which is available free in almost any decent bookstore and graces the magazine racks of gay-friendly cafés and venues. Also keep your eyes peeled for the national bi-monthly *OUT!* (ⓦwww.out.co.nz).

Health

New Zealand is relatively free of serious health hazards and the most common pitfalls are not taking precautions or simply underestimating the power of nature. **No vaccinations** are required to enter the country, but you should make sure you have adequate health cover in your travel insurance, especially if you plan to take on the great outdoors (see p.63 for advice on tramping health and safety).

New Zealand has a good health service that's reasonably cheap by world standards. All visitors are covered by the accident compensation scheme, under which you can claim some medical and hospital expenses

Gay travel websites

ⓦ**www.gaynewzealand.com** A virtual tour of the country with a gay and lesbian slant.
ⓦ**www.gaytravel.net.nz** A gay online accommodation and travel reservation service.
ⓦ**www.adventureout.co.nz** Small-group outdoor adventure holidays for gay men.
ⓦ**www.gay.co.nz** Provides travel information aimed at gay, lesbian and bisexual visitors, and vets businesses for standards of service and hospitality.
ⓦ**www.gaynz.net.nz** A useful website that gives direct access to all manner of gay, lesbian, bisexual and transgender information including the *Pink Pages*, essentially a collection of linked pages including what's on in the gay community and a calendar of events all over the country.
ⓦ**www.rainbowtourism.com** An excellent resource for gay and lesbian travellers in both NZ and Oz, listing accommodation, events, clubs and tours.

in the event of an accident, but without full cover in your travel insurance you could still face a hefty bill. For more minor ailments, you can visit a doctor for a consultation (around $60) and, armed with a prescription, buy any required medication at a pharmacy at a reasonable price.

Sun, surf and earthquakes

Visitors to New Zealand frequently get caught out by the intensity of the **sun**, its damaging ultra violet rays easily penetrating the thin ozone layer and reducing burn times to as little as ten minutes in spring and summer. Stay out of the sun (or keep covered up) as much as possible between 11am and 3pm, and always slap on plenty of sunblock. Re-apply every few hours as well as after swimming, and keep a check on any moles on your body: if you notice any changes, during or after your trip, see a doctor right away.

The sea is a more immediate killer and even strong swimmers should read our **surf** warning (see box, p.139).

New Zealand is regularly shaken by **earthquakes**, but most are minor and it is not something to worry about. If the worst happens, the best advice is to stand in a doorway or crouch under a table. If caught in the open, try to get inside; failing that, keep your distance from trees and rocky outcrops to reduce the chances of being injured by falling branches or debris.

Wildlife hazards

New Zealand's wildlife is amazingly benign. There are no snakes, scorpions or other nasties, and only a few poisonous **spiders**, all rarely seen. No one has died from an encounter with a spider for many years but if you get a serious reaction from a bite be sure to see a doctor or head to the nearest hospital, where antivenin will be available.

Shark attacks are also rare; you are more likely to be carried away by a strong tide than a great white, though it still pays to be sensible and obey any local warnings when swimming.

A far bigger problem are **mosquitoes** and **sandflies** which are a great irritant, but generally free of life-threatening diseases. The West Coast of the South Island in the summer is the worst place for these beasts, though they appear to a lesser degree in many other places across the country: a liberal application of repellent keeps them at bay.

At the microscopic level, **giardia** inhabits many rivers and lakes, and infection results from drinking contaminated water, with symptoms appearing several weeks later: a bloated stomach, cramps, explosive diarrhoea and wind. The Department of Conservation advises you purify drinking water by using iodine-based solutions or tablets (regular chlorine-based tablets aren't effective against giardia), by fast-boiling water for at least seven minutes or by using a giardia-rated filter (obtainable from any outdoors or camping shop).

The relatively rare **amoebic meningitis** is another water borne hazard, this time contracted from hot pools. Commercial pools are almost always safe, but in natural pools surrounded by earth you should avoid contamination by keeping your head above water. The amoeba enters the body via the nose or ears, lodges in the brain, and weeks later causes severe headaches, stiffness of the neck, hypersensitivity to light, and eventually coma. If you experience any of these symptoms, seek medical attention immediately.

Insurance

New Zealand's Accident Compensation Commission (ⓦwww.acc.co.nz) provides limited medical treatment for visitors injured while in New Zealand, but is no substitute for having comprehensive **travel insurance** to cover against theft, loss and illness or injury.

Before paying for a new policy, it's worth checking whether you are already covered: some all-risks home insurance policies may cover your possessions when overseas, and many private medical schemes include cover when abroad. In Canada, provincial health plans usually provide partial cover for medical mishaps overseas, while holders of official student/teacher/youth cards in Canada and the US are entitled to meagre accident coverage and hospital in-patient benefits. Students will often find that their student health coverage extends during the vacations and for one term beyond the date of last enrolment.

Rough Guides travel insurance

Rough Guides has teamed up with Columbus Direct to offer you travel insurance that can be tailored to suit your needs. Products include a low-cost **backpacker option** for long stays; a **short break option** for city getaways; a typical **holiday package** option; and others. There are also annual **multi-trip policies** for those who travel regularly. Different sports and activities (trekking, skiing, etc) can be usually be covered if required.

See our website (Ⓦwww.roughguides.com/website/shop) for eligibility and purchasing options. Alternatively, UK residents should call Ⓣ08700 339988; US citizens should call Ⓣ1-800/749-4922; Australians should call Ⓣ1300 669999. All other nationalities should call Ⓣ+44 8708 902843.

After exhausting the possibilities above, you might want to contact a specialist travel insurance company, or consider the travel insurance deal we offer (see above).

A typical travel insurance **policy** usually provides cover for the loss of baggage, tickets and – up to a certain limit – cash or cheques, as well as cancellation or curtailment of your journey. Most of them exclude so-called **dangerous activities** unless an extra premium is paid. In New Zealand this can mean scuba diving, bungy jumping, whitewater rafting, windsurfing, skiing and snowboarding, and even tramping under some policies.

Many policies can be chopped and changed to exclude coverage you don't need – sickness and accident benefits, for example, can often be excluded or included. If you do take medical coverage, ascertain whether benefits will be paid as treatment proceeds or only after return home, and whether there is a 24-hour medical emergency number. When securing **baggage cover**, make sure that the per-article limit – typically under £500 – will cover your most valuable possession. If you need to make a claim, you should keep receipts for medicines and medical treatment, and in the event you have anything stolen, you must obtain an official statement from the police.

Internet

Internet access is abundant and fairly cheap though seldom blindingly fast. You'll find coin-operated machines at most **visitor centres,** backpacker hostels, motels and campsites, generally charging $6–10 an hour. At more expensive accommodation there'll often be a free-use computer, and laptop connections may be available.

Many machines (especially the coin-op ones) have limited functionality and can be frustrating if you want to do anything even slightly unusual. Many won't accept USB cables or flash memory sticks, so you may find yourself in need of one of the abundant **Internet cafés** lining city streets, which typically charge $6 an hour.

Wi-Fi access is rapidly becoming more widespread. Some hostels and many motels and hotels will have a hotspot which you can sign up to using your credit card. Rates vary considerably: an hour might cost $10 but you can often get a full 24hr day for under $25. The swankier B&Bs and lodges will usually have free Wi-Fi in all rooms. For more flexibility, consider Telecom's prepaid card, offering access to a **nationwide network** of several hundred wireless hotspots (various café chains, airports, Telecom stores, some libraries) charged at $10 an hour. You just pay for the minutes you use.

Mail

NZ Post (Ⓣ0800/501 501, Ⓦwww.nzpost.com) runs New Zealand's reliable mail service. Stamps, postcards, envelopes, packing materials and a lot more can be bought at **post shops** (aka post offices), which are open Monday to Friday 8.30am to 5pm, plus Saturday 9am or 10am to noon or 1pm in some large towns and cities. Red and silver **post boxes** are found outside post shops and on street corners, and mail is collected daily.

There are two forms of **domestic delivery**: Standard (50¢, or $1 for larger envelopes), delivered to any destination within 2–3 days; and FastPost ($1/$1.50), delivered in 1–2 days. **International air mail** takes 3–6 days to reach Australia ($1.50), and 6–12 days to Europe, Asia and the United States ($2). Postcards cost $1.50 to anywhere in the world. **Parcels** are quite expensive to send overseas as there is no longer any surface mail and the economy service only saves fifteen percent for a considerably delayed delivery. Your choice is either Airmail (1kg to Australia $13, USA $27, Europe $30), which takes about a week, or Economy (1kg to Australia $11, USA $23, Europe $25), which takes 2–5 weeks.

One post shop in each major town operates a **Poste Restante** (or **General Delivery**) service where you can receive mail; we've listed the major ones in the "Listings" section of each town account. Most hostels and hotels will keep mail for you, preferably marked with your expected date of arrival.

There is also an independent postal system called **Universal Mail** (ⓦwww.universalmail.co.nz) which only handles international mail and uses blue boxes. It is a little cheaper but there have been reports of very slow delivery.

Maps

Specialist outlets should have a reasonable stock of **maps** of New Zealand, including Rough Guides' own two-sided, 1:1,000,000 scale, waterproof fold-out sheet. The best of the rest is the map produced by International Travel Maps (ⓦwww.itmb.com), which displays important roads and has an attractive and instructive colour scheme giving a good sense of the country's terrain. **Road atlases** are widely available in New Zealand bookshops and service stations; the most detailed are those produced by Kiwi Pathfinder, which indicate numerous points of interest and the type of road surface.

With a road atlas and our city plans you can't go far wrong on the roads, but more detailed maps may be required for tramping. All the major walks are covered by the **Parkmap** series, complete with photos (around $15 from DOC offices and bookshops in New Zealand), while the larger scale 1:50,000 Topomaps ($13) cover the whole country.

Money

The Kiwi **dollar**, or "buck", is divided into 100 cents. There are $100, $50, $20, $10 and $5 notes made of a sturdy plastic material, and coins in denominations of $2 and $1, and 50¢, 20¢ and 10¢. Grocery prices are given to the nearest cent, but the final bill is rounded up or down to the nearest ten cents. All prices quoted in the Guide are in New Zealand dollars.

Exchange rates fluctuate substantially, but the New Zealand dollar currently trades at NZ$2.56 for £1, NZ$1.30 for US$1, NZ$2 for e1 and NZ$1.23 for A$1. Check current rates at ⓦwww.xe.com.

Cards, cheques and ATMs

For purchases, visitors generally rely on **credit cards**, particularly Visa and Mastercard/Bankcard, which are widely accepted, though many hostels, campsites and homestays will only accept cash. American Express and Diners Club are far less useful. You'll also find credit cards handy for advance booking of accommodation and trips, and with the appropriate PIN you can obtain **cash advances** through 24-hour ATMs found almost everywhere. Such withdrawals usually accrue interest immediately or are subject to a two percent premium – check with your bank before you go too wild. **Debit cards** are also useful for purchases and ATM cash withdrawals, though a fee of around 2 percent will be charged.

The safest way to carry your money is still in the form of **traveller's cheques** – they can be exchanged efficiently at banks and bureaux de change all over New Zealand and replaced if lost or stolen. Recognized brands – American Express, Thomas Cook, Mastercard and Visa – are accepted in all major currencies but traveller's cheques (even in New Zealand dollars) aren't accepted as cash.

Banks

The major **banks** – ASB, ANZ, BNZ, National Bank and Westpac – have branches in towns of any size and are open Monday to

Friday from 9.30am to 4.30pm, with some city branches opening on Saturday mornings (until around 12.30pm). The big cities and tourist centres also have **bureaux de change**, which are typically open from 8am to 8pm daily. The larger hotels will often change traveller's cheques at any time, but rates tend to be poor.

If you are spending over three months in New Zealand (and especially if you are working), you may want to open a **bank account**. A New Zealand EFTPOS (debit) card can be used just about anywhere for purchases or obtaining cash, so you can go for weeks without ever visiting a bank.

In Auckland, the branch of Westpac at 229 Queen St and the ASB at the corner of Wyndham and Hobson streets are well set up for dealing with working backpackers' needs. In Christchurch visit the ASB Migrant Banking Unit, 129 Riccarton Rd, Christchurch. An account can usually be set up within a day; remember to take your passport.

Opening hours

New Zealand's larger cities and tourist centres are increasingly open all hours, with cafés and bars open till very late, 24hr supermarkets abundant and shops open long hours every day. Once you get into rural areas, things change rapidly, and core **shopping hours** (Mon–Fri 9am–5.30pm, Sat 9am–noon) apply, though tourist-orientated shops stay open daily until 8pm.

An ever-increasing number of **supermarkets** (at least one in or near each major city) now open seven days a week, 24 hours a day and small "dairies" (corner shops or convenience stores) also keep long hours and open on Sundays. **Museums** and sights usually open around 9am, although small-town museums often open only in the afternoons and/or only on specific days.

Public holidays and festivals are listed on p.57.

Phones

Given the near-ubiquity of mobile phones, most people don't have much need for **public telephones**, though they are still fairly widespread across New Zealand. Coin-operated public phones are now rare, but all payphones accept major credit cards, account-based phonecards and slot-in disposable phonecards ($5, $10, $20 and $50). These can be bought at post shops, newsagents, dairies, garages, visitor centres and supermarkets.

A local call on a public payphone using coins or a slot-in phonecard costs $1 for the first fifteen minutes, then 20¢ a minute. NZ landline calls outside the local calling area cost $1 a minute, and calls to a cell phone are $1.20 a minute.

If you are staying with friends you may get to use a **private phone**, on which local calls are generally free and national calls typically cost around $0.20 a minute depending on what pricing plan your host is on.

Phone numbers

New Zealand **landline numbers** have only five area codes. The North Island is divided into four codes, while the South Island makes do with just one (☎03); all numbers in the Guide are given with their code. Even within the same area, you may have to dial the code if you're calling another town some distance away. **Mobile numbers** start with either ☎021, ☎027 or ☎029, and you'll come across **freephone** numbers which are all ☎0800 or ☎0508. Numbers prefixed ☎0900 are **premium-rated** and cannot be called from payphones.

National directory assistance ☎018 ($0.50 for up to two numbers, plus $0.50 to directly connect the call)

International operator ☎0170 (connecting a call costs $4)

International directory assistance ☎0172 ($1.50 for up to two numbers)

Emergency services Police, ambulance and fire brigade ☎111 (no charge)

International dialling codes

To call New Zealand from overseas, dial the international access code (☎00 from the UK, ☎011 from the USA and Canada, ☎0011 from Australia, ☎09 from South Africa), followed by ☎64, the area code minus its initial zero, and then the number.

To dial out of New Zealand, it's ☎00, followed by the country code (see p.83), then the area code (without the initial zero if there is one) and the number. Remember that there'll be a time difference between your country and New Zealand (see "Time" on p.84 to avoid rude awakenings).

Phonecards and calling cards

For **long-distance and international calling** you are best off with pre-paid account-based **phonecards** (denominations from $5 to $50) that can be used on any phone. To make a call, dial the access number followed by the number you are calling; the cost of the call is then deducted from your account, which can be topped up using your credit card. There are numerous such cards around offering highly competitive rates, but be wary of the very cheap ones: they are often Internet-based and the voice quality can be poor and delayed. One reliable card is Telecom's Yabba (Ⓦwww.yabba.co.nz) which charges just 10¢ to Australia, Ireland, the UK and most of Western Europe, 29¢ to Canada and the USA, and 25¢ to South Africa. Be warned, though, that public payphones now charge an additional 24¢ per minute for use of Yabba and all other account-based phonecards, so try to use them from private phones whenever possible.

There are also **discount phone centres** springing up in major cities and popular tourist destinations, which often undercut phonecards.

Mobile phones

For sheer convenience you can't do better than a **mobile phone**, and it needn't cost the earth. NZ has two mobile providers: Telecom (Ⓦwww.telecom.co.nz) run a CDMA network, while Vodafone (Ⓦwww.vodafone.co.nz) operate a GSM system. Both have excellent reception in populated areas but Telecom has broader coverage in remoter spots.

If you're thinking of bringing your phone from home check with your service to see if your phone will work in NZ. GSM users may want to use their own phone, buying a New Zealand SIM card ($35 from Vodafone) and going pre-pay; you'll have to tell friends and colleagues your new NZ number but it can save a fair bit of money.

Alternatively, you can rent an NZ phone (around $2 a day from airports and bigger cybercafés) or buy an NZ phone and use it during your stay: both companies sell basic models for under NZ$100.

Calling home

Note that the initial zero is omitted from the area code when dialling the UK, Ireland and Australia.

Australia 00 + 61 + city code.

Republic of Ireland 00 + 353 + city code.

South Africa 00 + 27 + city code.

UK 00 + 44 + city code.

US and Canada 00 + 1 + area code.

Photography

Camera shops everywhere will process your **digital images** onto CDs (for $5–8, less if you provide your own CD), and increasingly hostels have some way of allowing you to review your day's snaps. Uploading to websites or a home server is possible at some cybercafés, though many don't want you clogging up their lines. Standard colour print film is still fairly widely available, but professional and slide film is harder to come by outside the main cities.

Shopping

NZ is hardly a shoppers' paradise: you're more likely to take home fond memories than a bag full of goodies. But there is stuff worth seeking out. One of the most popular souvenirs is a curvaceous **greenstone** (jade) pendant, probably based on a Maori design. They're available all over the country, though it makes sense to buy close to the main source of raw material around Greymouth and Hokitika on the West Coast of the South Island. Most of the cheaper goods are manufactured from Chinese jade, which is regarded as inferior: for the genuine article insist on New Zealand *pounamu* carved locally (see box, p.746).

A variation on this theme is the **bone pendant**. Several places around the country give you a chance to work a piece of cattle bone into your own design or something based on classic Maori iconography. With a little talent and application you should be able to whip up something to be proud of in a few hours. Something similar can be made of irridescent paua shell, or you can simply buy ready-made pieces fashioned into anything from buttons to detailed picture frames.

As everywhere, gift shops come laden with tacky trinkets you wouldn't look twice at, but you will find **photo books** full of superb shots of magnificent scenery. Look out in particular for books by Craig Potton and Andris Apse, but there are many other worthy examples.

Sheepskin and **wool** products are also big, as are garments – socks, sweaters etc – at least partly made from **possum fur**. New Zealanders hate these Australian pests and will thank you for supporting any industry which hastens their demise. A quality possum-fur throw will set you back over $1000 but cushion covers come much cheaper. Sheepskins go for around $100.

On a more practical level, you may need to supplement your wardrobe of **outdoor clothing**. There's plenty of stuff around, but look out for the Icebreaker (ⓦwww.icebreaker.com) and Untouched World (ⓦwww.untouchedworld.co.nz) brands of stylish Merino-wool garments, which are fairly pricey but feel great, keep you warm and don't harbour nasty odours as much as some synthetics.

New Zealand doesn't do budget or mid-range **fashion clothing** all that well, but some of its top designers are world-class. Garments by Karen Walker, Kate Sylvester, Trelise Cooper, Zambesi and World are expensive for most Kiwis, but may seem quite affordable if you're travelling with a strong currency.

If you want to dress up in a more permanent fashion, you might even consider a **tattoo**. Curvilinear designs derived from ferns or based on Maori iconography are popular and you'll have little trouble tracking down skilled *moko* artists.

Time and seasons

New Zealand Standard Time (NZST) is 12 hours ahead of Greenwich Mean Time, but, from the last Sunday in September to the first Sunday in April, Daylight Saving puts the clocks one hour further forward. Throughout the summer, when it is noon in New Zealand, it's 10am in Sydney, 11pm the day before in London, 6pm the day before in New York, and 3pm the day before in Los Angeles.

New Zealand follows Britain's lead with **dates**, and 1/4/2009 means April 1 not January 4.

Don't forget that the southern hemisphere **seasons** are reversed: summer lasts roughly from November to March, and winter from June to September.

Tourist information

New Zealand promotes itself enthusiastically abroad through **Tourism New Zealand**, and its extensive website ⓦwww.newzealand.com.

Metric conversion table

Length
1 centimetre (cm) = 0.394in
1 metre = 39.37in
1 metre = 3.28ft
1 kilometre = 0.621 miles
1 foot (ft) = 30.48cm
1 yard (yd) = 0.91m
1 mile = 1.610km

Area
1 hectare = 2.471 acres
1 square km = 0.39 square miles
1 acre = 0.40 hectares
1 square mile = 2.59 square km

Weight
1 ounce (oz) = 28.57g
1 pound (lb) = 454g
1 gram (g) = 0.035oz
1 kilogram = 2.2lb

Volume
1 US gallon (gal) = 3.85 litres
1 litre = 0.22 UK gallons
1 litre = 0.26 US gallons

Temperature
To convert Celsius to Fahrenheit: multiply by 1.8 and add 32
To convert Fahrenheit to Celsius: subtract 32 and divide by 1.8

Many of the information centres listed below, as well as some cafés, bars and hostels, keep a supply of **free newspapers** and **magazines** oriented towards backpackers – they're usually filled with promotional copy, but are informative nonetheless. *NZ Backpackers News* (Ⓦwww.backpackersnews.co.nz) and *TNT* (Ⓦwww.tntdownunder.com) are two of the best.

Visitor centres

Every town of any size has an official **i-SITE visitor centre**, staffed by helpful and knowledgeable personnel and sometimes offering some form of video presentation on the area. Apart from dishing out local maps and leaflets, they offer a **free booking service** for accommodation, trips and activities, and onward travel, but only with businesses registered with them. Some (usually small) businesses choose not to register and may still be worth seeking out; we've mentioned them where relevant. In the more popular tourist areas, you'll also come across all manner of places representing themselves as **independent information centres** that usually follow a hidden agenda, typically promoting a number of allied adventure companies. While these can be useful, it's worth remembering that their advice may not be completely impartial.

Other useful resources are **Department of Conservation** (DOC; Ⓦwww.doc.govt.nz) offices and field centres, usually sited close to wilderness areas and popular tramping tracks, and often serving as the local visitor centre as well. These are highly informative and well geared to trampers' needs, with local weather forecasts, intentions forms and maps as well as historic and environmental displays and audio visual exhibitions. Their website contains loads of detail on the environment and the latest conservation issues plus details on national parks and Great Walks.

Tourism New Zealand offices

Australia Suite 3, Level 24, 1 Alfred St, Sydney, NSW 2000 ⓣ02/8220 9000.
Canada Information line only ⓣ1-866/639 9325.
New Zealand PO Box 95, Wellington ⓣ04/ 917 5400.
United Kingdom New Zealand House, Haymarket, London, SW1Y 4TQ ⓣ020/7930 1662, premium-rate information line ⓣ09069/101 010; also handles enquiries from Ireland.
USA Suite 300, 501 Santa Monica Blvd, Santa Monica, CA 90401 ⓣ310/395 7480 or 1-800/388 5494; Suite 2510, 222 East 41 St, New York, NY 10017 ⓣ212/661 7088.

Travelling with children

New Zealand is a child-friendly place, and while other people's kids aren't revered in the way they are in Mediterranean Europe, if you're **travelling with kids** you'll find broad acceptance. In fact getting you and your children to and from New Zealand might be the most difficult part. Unless you are coming from Australia, **flights** are inevitably long so it will probably pay to break your journey, or at least make sure your airline offers plenty of distractions to keep the little ones entertained.

Once in New Zealand, **accommodation** is easy. Family rooms are almost always available at motels and hostels, and holiday parks (campsites) typically offer self-contained units where the whole family can be together. The better holiday parks also have kids' play areas and often a swimming pool. To be more self-sufficient, consider renting a medium-sized **campervan**, possibly with its own shower and toilet, though the downside is that you'll have no escape.

Travelling around you'll find **public toilets** in most towns and anywhere tourists congregate – cleanliness standards are usually good.

Older kids can often join in adult **adventure activities**, though restrictions do apply. Bungy operators usually require a **minimum age** of ten, though this might rise to 12 or 13 for the bigger jumps. Whitewater rafting is typically limited to those 13 and over, though there are a few easier family-oriented trips. Similar restrictions apply to other activities, so ask when you book. **Family tickets** usually cost about the same as two adults and one child, so come into their own if you've got two or more children.

Children are welcomed in most cafés and **restaurants**, and most will make a reasonable effort to accommodate you.

Travellers with disabilities

New Zealand is disabled-traveller friendly, but that doesn't mean everything is rosy. While many public buildings, galleries and museums are **accessible** to the disabled, restaurants and local public transport make few concessions.

On the plus side, many tour operators are prepared to make a special effort to enable travellers with mobility problems or disabilities to participate in all manner of activities, such as swimming with dolphins or whales

Planning a trip

There are organized **tours** and **holidays** specifically for people with disabilities – the contacts listed below will be able to put you in touch with specialists for trips to New Zealand. If you want to be more independent, it's important to research where you must be self-reliant and where you may expect help, especially regarding transport and accommodation. It is also vital to be upfront with travel agencies, insurance companies and travel companions about your limitations. If your walking capabilities are limited, remember that you are likely to need to cover lengthy distances while travelling (often over rough terrain and in hot temperatures).

Reading your travel **insurance** small print carefully to make sure that people with a pre-existing medical condition are not excluded could save you a fortune. Your travel agent can help make your journey simpler: airline or bus companies can better cater to your needs if they are expecting you. A **medical certificate** of your fitness to travel, provided by your doctor, is also extremely useful; some airlines or insurance companies may insist on it. Make sure that you have extra supplies of medications – carried with you if you fly – and a prescription including the generic name in case of emergency. Carry spares of any clothing or equipment that might be hard to find; if there's an association representing people with your disability, contact them. Once you're in New Zealand, several organizations provide information for travellers with disabilities and give practical advice on where to go and how to get there.

Accommodation

Current New Zealand law stipulates that any newly built hotel, hostel or motel must have at least one room designed or modified for disabled access and use. Many pre-existing accommodation establishments have converted rooms to meet these requirements, including most YHA hostels, some motels, campsites and larger hotels. Older buildings, homestays and B&Bs are the least likely to lend themselves to such conversions.

For listings, go straight to ⓦwww.carers.org.nz which has a searchable database of lodging.

Travelling

Few airlines, trains, ferries and buses allow complete independence. Air New Zealand provides a special wheelchair narrow enough to move around in the plane, and the rear toilet cubicles are wider than the others to facilitate access; for more details search for "Special Assistance" on their website. Other **domestic airlines** will provide help, if not always facilities. Cook Strait **ferries** have reasonable access for disabled travellers, including physical help while boarding, if needed, and adapted toilets. If given advance warning, trains will provide attendants to get passengers in wheelchairs or sight-impaired travellers on board, but moving around the train in a standard wheelchair is impossible and there are no specially adapted toilets; the problems with **long-distance buses** are much the same.

In cities there are some **taxis** specifically adapted for wheelchairs, but these must be pre-booked; otherwise taxi drivers obligingly hoist wheelchairs into the boot and their occupant onto a seat. The **New Zealand Total Mobility Scheme** allows anyone unable to use public transport to use taxis at half-price; a list of participating areas and companies is available from the Disabled Persons Assembly (see "Contacts in New Zealand", on p.87), who can arrange for the necessary vouchers to be issued; they also provide advice about **parking** concessions for people with mobility problems. Alternatively, organizations in your home country, including those listed below, are good points of contact for advice. Staff on public buses will endeavour to lend a hand, but buses are difficult to board. Some small minibus conversions are available and shuttle buses will help you board and stow your chair, but it pays to let the operator know beforehand of your particular needs.

Contacts in New Zealand

Disability Resource Centre 14 Erson Ave, Royal Oak, Auckland ⓣ09/625 8069 & 0800/693 342, ⓦwww.disabilityresource.org.nz. General resource centre.
Disabled Persons Assembly Level 4/173–175 Victoria St, Wellington, New Zealand ⓣ04/801 9100 ⓦwww.dpa.org.nz. Resource centre with lists of travel agencies and tour operators for people with disabilities.
Enable New Zealand ⓣ0800/171 981, ⓦwww.enable.co.nz. Organization assisting people with disabilities, though not specifically focused on travellers.
Galaxy Motors ⓣ07/826 4020 & 0800/8642 5299, ⓦwww.galaxyautos.co.nz. Auckland company with rental vehicle for those with special mobility needs, plus personalized tours with a guide, companion, carer or translator.
Ucan Tours 8 Campbell St, Sumner, Christchurch ⓣ03/326 7881, ⓦwww.ucantours.com. Accessible group travel, customized independent tours and vehicle rental.

Contacts in Australia

NDS (National Disability Services) PO Box 60, Curtin ACT 2605 ⓣ02/6282 4333, ⓦwww.nds.org.au. Provides lists of travel agencies and tour operators for people with disabilities.

Contacts in the UK and Ireland

Holiday Care 2nd floor, Imperial Building, Victoria Rd, Horley, Surrey RH6 7PZ ⓣ0845/124 9971, Minicom ⓣ0845/124 9976, ⓦwww.holidaycare.org.uk. Provides a free list of accessible accommodation in New Zealand for older travellers, as well as those with disabilities.
Irish Wheelchair Association Blackheath Drive, Clontarf, Dublin 3 ⓣ01/818 6400, ⓦwww.iwa.ie. Useful information about travelling abroad with a wheelchair.
RADAR (Royal Association for Disability and Rehabilitation) 12 City Forum, 250 City Rd, London EC1V 8AF ⓣ020/7250 3222, Minicom ⓣ020/7250 4119, ⓦwww.radar.org.uk. Campaigning organization and general resource for the disabled.

Contacts in the USA

Access-Able ⓦwww.access-able.com. Online resource for travellers with disabilities.
Mobility International USA Suite 202, 451 Broadway, Eugene, OR 97401 ⓣ541/343-1284, ⓦwww.miusa.org. Information and referral services, access guides, tours and exchange programmes. Annual membership $35 (includes quarterly newsletter).
Society for the Advancement of Travelers with Handicaps (SATH) 347 5th Ave, New York, NY 10016 ⓣ212/447-7284, ⓦwww.sath.org. Non-profit educational organization that has actively represented travellers with disabilities since 1976.

Women travellers

Despite being burdened with a somewhat out-of-date macho reputation, most Kiwi men have fairly progressive attitudes towards women, and travelling in New Zealand doesn't present any particular problems. Of course, there are some unevolved specimens who will assume a lone female (any female) is fair game for their attentions, but this is rare and **harassment** may well be less of a problem than it is at home.

Nonetheless, New Zealand isn't all sweetness and light, and dangers do exist. Just because you're on holiday and the country seems benign you shouldn't let your guard down. Always follow the usual advice about not walking down empty city streets at night and avoiding hitch-hiking: a modicum of common sense and a short taxi ride can avert a disaster.

In the unlikely event of trouble, contact ⓦwww.rapecrisis.org.nz. For support, Women's Centres around the country are listed on the Ministry of Women's Affairs website at ⓦwww.mwa.govt.nz/directory. You might also consider partly organizing your holiday through Women Travel New Zealand (ⓦwww.womentravel.co.nz), which offers essential information for the woman traveller in New Zealand with links to retreats, women-oriented tour operators and their newsletter.

Guide

Guide

1

Auckland and around

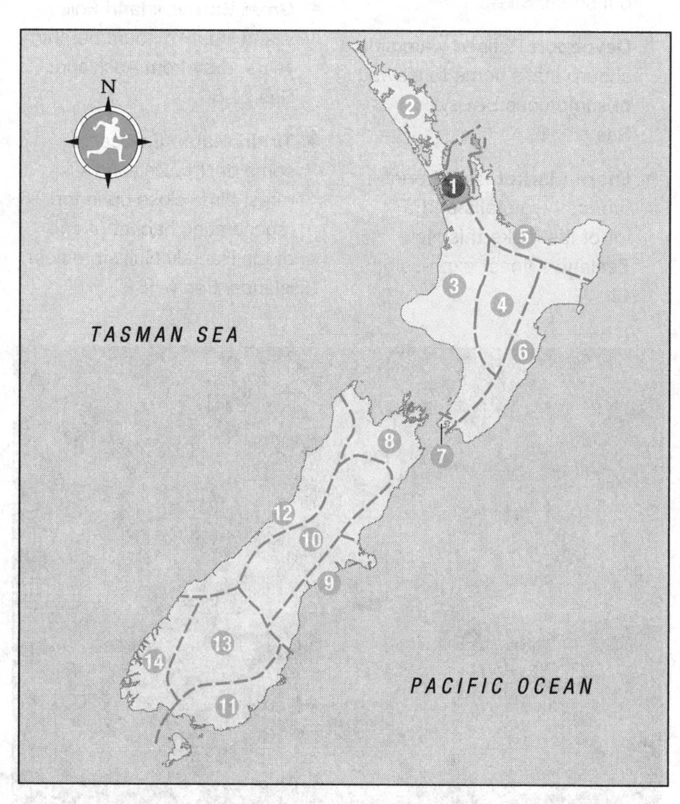

CHAPTER 1 Highlights

* **Auckland Museum** The exemplary Maori and Pacific Island collection is the highlight of this popular museum. See p.110
* **Ponsonby Road** Auckland's premier eating and hanging-out street. See p.116
* **Devonport** Refined waterside suburb that's home to a swag of sumptuous B&Bs. See p.119
* **Otara Market** Island print fabrics, veg stalls and a lot of life make this New Zealand's finest expression of Polynesian culture. See p.121
* **Rangitoto Island** Make a day-trip to this gnarled lava landscape draped in forest with great views back to the city. See p.146
* **Great Barrier Island** Enjoy island life, two hours but thirty years away from Auckland. See p.155
* **Tiritiri Matangi** Observe some of New Zealand's rarest birds close up in the regenerating habitat of one of the Hauraki Gulf's prettiest islands. See p.161

▲ Auckland skyline from Westhaven Marina

Auckland and around

Auckland is New Zealand's largest city and, as the site of the major international airport, most visitors' first view of the country. Planes bank over the island-studded Hauraki Gulf and brightly spinnakered yachts tack through the glistening waters towards the "City of Sails", but don't be fooled. Auckland looks best from air or sea, its skyscrapered downtown dominated by a Skytower that attracts the eye. Truth is the downtown area is relatively small, surrounded by the grassy humps of some fifty-odd extinct volcanoes that ring the Waitemata Harbour, and low-rise suburban sprawl that extends as far as the eye can see. Beyond the central business district little rises above two storeys and prim wooden villas surrounded by substantial gardens set the tone. This is one of the least densely populated cities in the world, occupying twice the area of London and yet home to just over a million inhabitants. With its attractive harbour and warm climate, Auckland's fans rank it alongside Sydney, though it fails to live up to the claim on most counts. Look beyond the glitzy shopfronts and Auckland has a modest small-town feel and measured pace, though this can seem frenetic in comparison with the rest of the country.

If Auckland stakes a claim to fame, it is as the **world's largest Polynesian city**. Around twelve percent of the population claim Maori descent while thirteen percent are families of migrants who arrived from Tonga, Samoa, the Cook Islands and other South Pacific islands during the 1960s and 1970s. Nevertheless, the Polynesian profile has traditionally been confined to small pockets, and it is only now, as the second generations reach maturity, that Polynesia is making its presence felt in mainstream Auckland life, especially in the arts.

Many visitors only stay long enough for a quick zip around the smattering of key sights before moving on to less metropolitan locales. You could be forgiven for doing the same, but don't miss the **Auckland Museum**, with its matchless collection of Maori and Pacific Island carving and artefacts. With more time it's worth grabbing a ferry from the centre of the city, to the **Hauraki Gulf islands**: Rangitoto, Waiheke Island, Tiritiri Matangi or Great Barrier.

Beyond these, you can get a taste of the city by ambling around the fashionable **inner-city suburbs** of Ponsonby, Parnell and Devonport, and using the city as a base for exploring the wild and desolate West Coast **surf beaches** and the **wineries** nearby.

Auckland's **climate** is often described as muggy; it's never scorching hot, and the heat is always tempered by a sea breeze. Winters are generally mild but rainy.

Auckland

AUCKLAND's urban sprawl smothers the North Island's wasp waist, a narrow isthmus where the island is all but severed by river estuaries probing inland from the city's two harbours. To the west, the shallow and silted **Manukau Harbour** opens out onto the Tasman Sea at a rare break in the long string of black-sand beaches continually pounded by heavy surf. Maori named the eastern anchorage the **Waitemata Harbour** for its "sparkling waters", which constitute Auckland's deep-water port and a focus for the heart of the city. Every summer weekend the harbour and adjoining Hauraki Gulf explode into a riot of brightly coloured sails.

In recent years, Auckland's downtown Viaduct Harbour has blossomed with hundreds of modern apartments and a welter of stylish cafés and restaurants. Yet despite Auckland's bustle and harbourside setting, few fall in love with the city

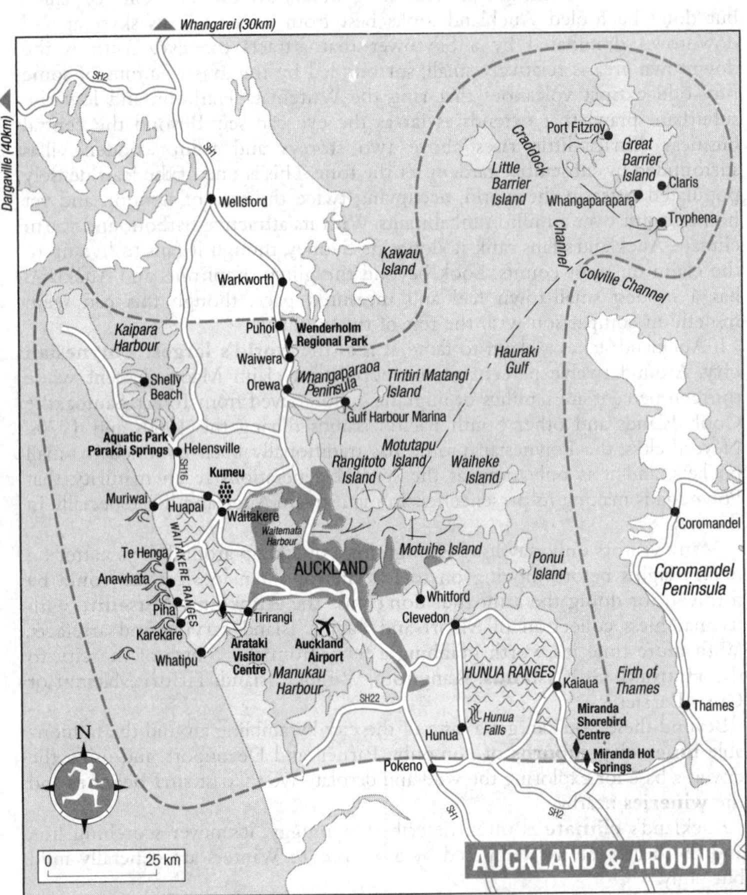

or stick around long enough to scratch below the surface. Those who persist might find themselves more enthusiastic about the place.

Some history

The earth's crust between the Waitemata and Manukau harbours is so thin that, every few thousand years, magma finds a fissure and bursts onto the surface, producing yet another volcano. The most recent eruption, some six hundred years ago, formed Rangitoto Island, to the horror of some of the region's earliest Maori inhabitants, settled on adjacent Motutapu Island. Legend records their ancestors' arrival on the Tamaki Isthmus, the narrowest neck of land between the Waitemata and Manukau harbours. With plentiful catches from two harbours and rich volcanic soils on a wealth of highly defensible volcano-top sites, the land, which they came to know as Tamaki-makau-rau ("the spouse sought by a hundred lovers"), became the prize of numerous battles over the years. By the middle of the eighteenth century it had fallen to **Kiwi Tamaki**, who established a three-thousand-strong *pa* (fortified village) on Maungakiekie ("One Tree Hill"), and a satellite *pa* on just about every volcano in the district, but was eventually overwhelmed by rival *hapu* (sub-tribes) from Kaipara Harbour to the north.

With the arrival of musket-trading **Europeans** in the Bay of Islands around the beginning of the nineteenth century, Northland Ngapuhi were able to launch successful raids on the Tamaki Maori which, combined with smallpox epidemics, left the region almost uninhabited, a significant factor in its choice as the new capital after the signing of the Treaty of Waitangi in 1840. Scottish medic **John Logan Campbell** was one of few European residents when this fertile land, with easy access to major river and seaborne trading routes, was purchased for £55 and some blankets. The capital was roughly laid out and Campbell took advantage of his early start, wheeling and dealing to achieve control of half the city, eventually becoming mayor and "the father of Auckland". After 1840, immigrants boosted the population to the extent that more land was needed, a demand which partly precipitated the **New Zealand Wars** of the 1860s (see p.881).

During the depression that followed, many sought their fortunes in the Otago goldfields and, as the balance of European population shifted south, so did the centre of government. Auckland lost its **capital status** to Wellington in 1865 and the city slumped further, only seeing the glimpse of a recovery when prospectors flooded through on their way to the gold mines around Thames in the late 1860s. Since then Auckland has never looked back, repeatedly ranking as New Zealand's fastest growing city and absorbing waves of migrants, initially from Britain then, in the 1960s and 1970s, from the Polynesian Islands of the South Pacific. A steady stream of rural Maori have been arriving on Auckland's doorstep for the best part of half a century, now joined by an influx of East Asians whose tastes have radically altered the city centre – high-rise apartments now pepper the CBD and Korean, Thai, Malaysian, Chinese and Japanese restaurants are everywhere.

Arrival and information

As New Zealand's major gateway city, Auckland receives the bulk of **international arrivals**, a few disembarking from cruise ships at the dock by the Ferry Building downtown, but the vast majority arriving by air.

Auckland International Airport (arrival and departure info at Ⓦwww.auckland-airport.co.nz) is located 20km south of the city centre in the suburb of Mangere. The international terminal is connected to the two domestic terminals – operated by Air New Zealand, Qantas and various regional airlines – by a shuttle bus (6am–10.30pm), but if you've a light load it's only a ten-minute walk. Before leaving the international terminal you can grab a free shower at The Collection Point, who also store baggage (towels $10, storage $3/day per item), though most travellers just head straight for the city. The well-stocked and helpful **i-SITE visitor centre** (Ⓣ09/275 6467) stays open for all international arrivals and will book you into a city hotel free of charge, or you can make use of the bank of courtesy phones nearby. There's also a branch of the BNZ **bank** that changes money at tolerable rates, and some **duty-free shops**.

A **taxi** into the city will set you back around $65, while the **AirBus** (every 20min 6.20am–10pm; $15 one way, $22 return; backpacker cardholder discount, $13 one way, $20 return) follows a fixed route into the city (roughly 1hr). Most travellers, however, end up catching one of the door-to-door **minibuses** that wait outside the terminals. Ask at the first in line and if they're not going to the part of town where you're staying they'll point you to one that is: you'll seldom have to wait more than fifteen minutes. Fares are around $23 to downtown and $40 to Devonport; most offer small discounts to those with a backpacker card, and groups travelling to the same location get a significant reduction, adding only $5 per additional person. For pick-up on departure call Super Shuttle (Ⓣ0800/748 885) or phone a taxi company (see p.137).

Long-distance bus services into Auckland mostly arrive at the InterCity Bus Terminal under the Sky City Casino complex at 102 Hobson St. This is used by InterCity, Newmans and Northliner Express. Smaller operators – Guthrey's, Mainline, Delroys, Go Kiwi and Supa Travel, as well as the AirBus – stop outside the Scenic Tours & Travel office at 172 Quay St, opposite the Downtown Ferry Terminal.

Overlander **trains** from Wellington and Hamilton arrive at the Britomart Transport Centre, at the harbour end of Queen Street.

Information

Auckland's two main **i-SITE visitor centres** share contact details (Ⓣ0800/2825 5263, Ⓦwww.aucklandnz.com). One is in The Atrium inside the Sky City, corner of Victoria and Federal streets (daily 8am–8pm;), and the other at 137 Quay St at the corner with Hobson St, close to Viaduct Harbour (daily: Oct–April Mon–Fri 8.30am–6pm, Sat & Sun 9am–5pm; May–Sept daily 9am–5pm). The former is a little cramped, but both are stocked with leaflets from around the country including a number of advertisement-heavy **free publications**, the best of which are the annual *Auckland A–Z Visitors Guide* and the monthly *Auckland What's On*. Both have sketch **maps** that are adequate for most purposes, or you could splash out on the *KiwiMap Auckland Pathfinder Directory* ($29.95), which includes 22 regional town maps. **Backpacker information** is best gleaned from notice-boards in hostels, where adverts cover rides, vehicle sales and job opportunities, and the hostels offer an extensive booking service for onward travel; try the *Auckland Central, base*, both YHAs and the *Fat Camel*.

The compact **Department of Conservation (DOC) office**, in the Ferry Building at 99 Quay St (Mon–Fri 9.30am–5pm, Oct–April only Sat 10am–3pm, closed every day for an hour for lunch; Ⓣ09/379 6476, Ⓔaucklandvc@doc.govt.nz), stocks DOC material and does track bookings for the whole country, although it specializes in the Auckland and Hauraki Gulf region.

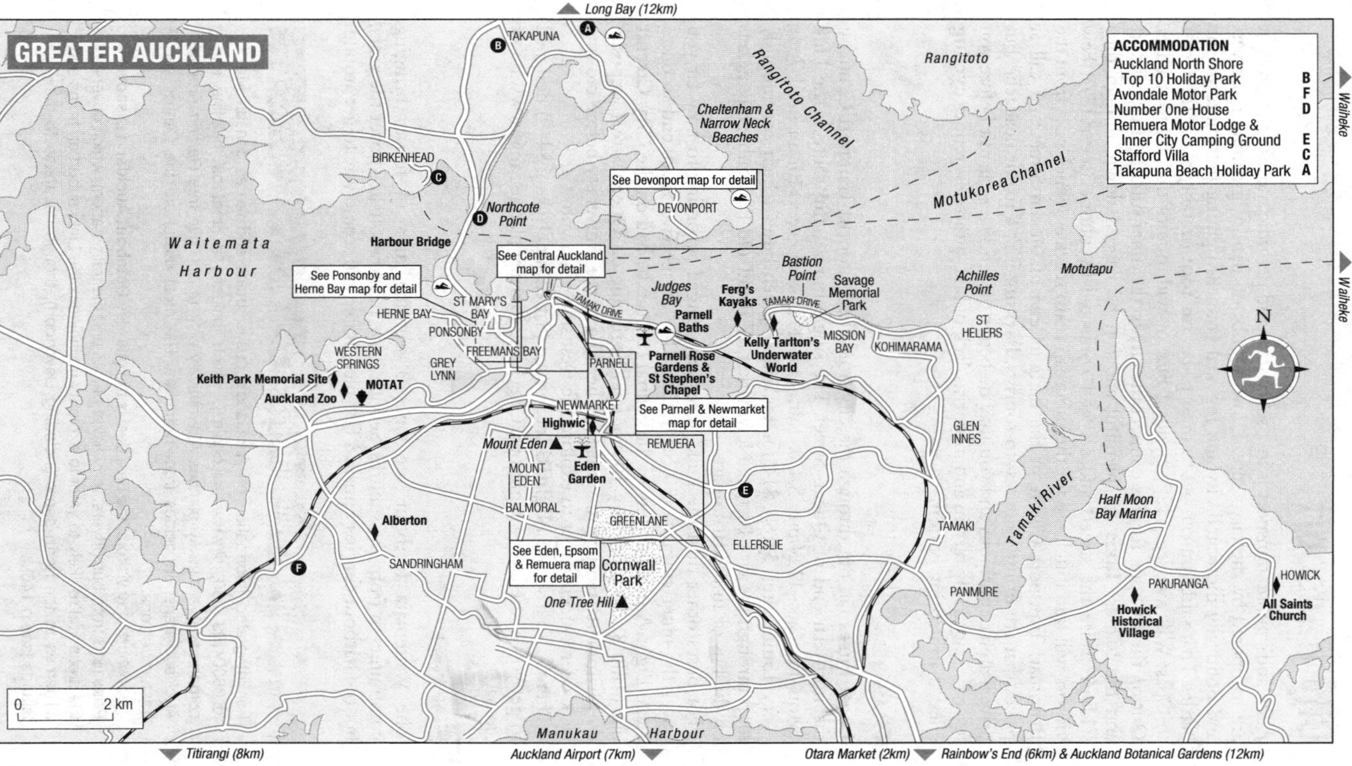
GREATER AUCKLAND
ACCOMMODATION
Auckland North Shore Top 10 Holiday Park B
Avondale Motor Park F
Number One House D
Remuera Motor Lodge & Inner City Camping Ground E
Stafford Villa C
Takapuna Beach Holiday Park A
Long Bay (12km)
Waiheke
Waiheke
Henderson (10km)
Titirangi (8km)
Auckland Airport (7km)
Otara Market (2km)
Rainbow's End (6km) & Auckland Botanical Gardens (12km)
TAKAPUNA
Rangitoto
Rangitoto Channel
Cheltenham & Narrow Neck Beaches
Motukorea Channel
BIRKENHEAD
Northcote Point
See Devonport map for detail
DEVONPORT
Waitemata Harbour
Harbour Bridge
See Central Auckland map for detail
See Ponsonby and Herne Bay map for detail
ST MARY'S BAY
HERNE BAY
PONSONBY
FREEMANS BAY
WESTERN SPRINGS
GREY LYNN
Keith Park Memorial Site
MOTAT
Auckland Zoo
TAMAKI DRIVE
Judges Bay
Parnell Baths
Bastion Point
Ferg's Kayaks
Savage Memorial Park
Kelly Tarlton's Underwater World
MISSION BAY
KOHIMARAMA
Achilles Point
ST HELIERS
Motutapu
N
PARNELL
Parnell Rose Gardens & St Stephen's Chapel
NEWMARKET
See Parnell & Newmarket map for detail
Highwic
Mount Eden
REMUERA
MOUNT EDEN
Eden Garden
GLEN INNES
BALMORAL
GREENLANE
Alberton
See Eden, Epsom & Remuera map for detail
ELLERSLIE
TAMAKI
Tamaki River
Half Moon Bay Marina
SANDRINGHAM
Cornwall Park
One Tree Hill
PANMURE
PAKURANGA
HOWICK
Howick Historical Village
All Saints Church
0 2 km
Manukau Harbour

City transport

Auckland's public transport is in a sorry state and periodic moves to improve it are hampered by the city's spread, low population density, groaning ratepayers and politically motivated city and regional councils fighting petty internecine battles. That said, you can get to most places **on foot** (notably along the Coast to Coast Walkway, see p.122), by local **bus**, or with one of the city tour buses. Out on the harbour, **ferries** connect the city to the inner suburb of Devonport and the islands. **Taxis** are plentiful and can be flagged down, though they seldom cruise the streets and are best contacted by phone (see p.137). Few visitors will find much use for the suburban **train** services, which start from the Britomart Transport Centre at the harbour end of Queen Street and call at places that are of little interest to tourists. **Parking** isn't a major headache, but drivers aren't courteous and you may be better off renting a car just before you leave the city. Hilly terrain and motorists' lack of bike-awareness render **cycling** a less than inviting option.

Buses

Local buses fan out through the city from the Britomart Transport Centre at the northern end of Queen Street. The single most useful route is the Link (Mon–Fri 6am–11.30pm, Sat & Sun 7am–11.30pm; every 10min until 7pm, every 15min after; $1.60, $14 for ten rides), green buses which continuously loop through the city, Parnell, Newmarket, K' Road and Ponsonby; buy tickets on the bus or in the Britomart.

For buses other than the Link, **fares** are charged according to how far you travel: the inner city is $0 50, Stage One $1.60, Stage Two $3.20 and so on to Stage Eight. A limited view of the central city can be had on the **City Circuit** bus (daily 8am–6pm; every 10min; free) beginning on Queen Street, opposite the Britomart Transport Centre, then heading to the University before crossing back over Queen Street to explore the west side of downtown.

There's also a secure **NightRider** service (Sat & Sun 1–3am; $4–9) designed to get you home after a night out. Check the journey planner at ⓦwww.maxx.co.nz.

Ferries

The Waitemata Harbour was once a seething mass of ferries bringing commuters in from the suburbs. Services have been rationalized over the years, but the harbour **ferries** remain a fast, pleasurable and scenic way to get around.

Information and transport passes

For integrated information on Auckland's buses, trains and ferries consult **Maxx** (ⓣ0800/103 080, ⓦwww.maxx.co.nz), which includes a timetable helpline and comprehensive journey planner. Alternatively pick up the five free *Getting Around Auckland* transport guides from Britomart. The most useful are the Central and Eastern regions.

For short-stay visitors, the best deal is the one-day **Getabout Auckland Discovery Pass** ($13 from bus drivers, ferry ticket offices and the train station), which covers all the areas you're likely to want to explore and includes the Link, suburban trains and all ferries to the north shore (including Devonport), though not those to the Gulf Islands (see p.146).

The main destinations are the Hauraki Gulf islands, but there are also services calling at Devonport, run by Fullers, the principal ferry company (T09/367 9111, Wwww.fullers.co.nz). The **Devonport Ferry** (see box, p.120) is the cheapest of the ferries and is included in the Getabout Auckland Discovery Pass (see p.98).

Driving

With many of the Auckland region's sights conveniently accessible on foot or by public transport, there isn't an advantage in having a car while in the city, though you'll need one to explore the Kumeu wineries and surf beaches of the West Coast. As the main point of entry, Auckland is awash with places to **rent a car** (see p.135 for details of outfits in the city); and if you're planning on some serious touring, you may be interested in **buying** one – see p.41 for some advice on the pros and cons, and p.135 for Auckland car markets.

Driving around Auckland isn't especially taxing, though it is worth avoiding the rush hours from 7 to 9am and 4 to 6.30pm. On first acquaintance, Auckland's urban freeways are unnerving, with frequent junctions, poor signage, a high density of private and commercial traffic, lane changing at whim and vehicles overtaking aggressively on all sides. Driving is on the left, though if you've just arrived after a long flight you should consider waiting a day or so before taking the plunge. Inner-city streets are metered, which means that parking is best done in the multistorey **car parks** dotted round the city; some are not open 24 hours, so check the latest exit time.

Cycling

Cycling around Auckland's hills can be a tiring and dispiriting exercise. However, a few areas lend themselves to pedal-powered exploration, most notably the harbourside Tamaki Drive east of the city centre, which forms part of a 50km **cycle route** around the city and its isthmus – detailed in a free leaflet available from visitor centres. **Rental bikes** cost around $25 per day ($140/week), depending on the sophistication of the model; see p.135 for details of outlets. In addition, some companies offer monthly rental and **buy-back schemes** for long-stayers (see p.43).

City tours

If you're keen to keep it simple, you can get around the main sights on the hop-on-hop-off **Explorer Bus** (T0800/439 756, Wwww.explorerbus.co.nz; 1-day pass $30, 2-day pass $45, pay the driver), which runs every half-hour (9am–4pm) and comes with a commentary. The circuit starts from the Ferry Building on Quay Street, goes along Tamaki Drive to Kelly Tarlton's Underwater World, up to Parnell and the Auckland Museum, and back via Victoria Park Market and Viaduct Harbour. Between October and April, a second loop takes in Mount Eden, MOTAT and the Auckland Art Gallery.

A different approach is taken by Tamaki Hikoi Tours (3hr, $80; T0800/282 5526), who offer **Maori-led walks** showcasing Mount Eden and the city including a *marae* visit. A similar Maori perspective is provided by Potiki Adventures (daily 10am–6pm; $145, on demand; T0800/692 3836, Wwww.potikiadventures.com) – see "Adventure Activities", p.124.

Accommodation

With a broad range of accommodation, Auckland meets the needs of most budgets but that doesn't stop everywhere filling up through December, January and February, when you should **book ahead**. At other times it's less critical and through the quiet winter months, from June to September, you'll be spoiled for choice and significant discounts on room rates can be had; it's worth asking.

Auckland is a place where you might choose to stay outside the **city centre**, as most sightseeing can be done as easily from **suburbs** such as **Ponsonby**, less than 2km west of the centre, **Mount Eden**, 2km south of the centre, **Devonport**, a short ferry journey across the harbour, and **Parnell**, 2km east of the centre. All are well supplied with places to eat and drink.

The city centre remains the place to find international four- and five-star **hotels**, mostly geared towards business travellers and tour groups; walk-in rates

First night accommodation

With several efficient door-to-door shuttle services into central Auckland there is little reason to stay near the airport unless you arrive at midnight or have a hideously early flight to catch. Most **airport accommodation** lines Kirkbride Road in Mangere, some 5km away, close to many of the car-rental pick-ups.

New arrivals picking up a car or campervan near the airport may baulk at tangling with central city traffic after a long flight. There are numerous tempting **beachside spots** only an hour or two from the airport, including **Miranda** (1hr southeast of airport, see p.145); **Muriwai** (1hr northwest of airport, see p.141); **Orewa** (1hr north of airport, see p.143); **Piha** (1hr northwest of airport, see p.140); and **Tawharanui Regional Park** (1hr 30min north of airport, see p.172), though this is reached by twisty, narrow roads and poor signage that might put off anyone driving a campervan for the first time.

Airport accommodation

All the places listed below provide their own free shuttle service to the airport (either on a fixed schedule or to order), and have a freephone at the airport: just give them a call and they'll pick you up. There isn't much of interest around the airport hotels, but some have bars and restaurants, and there are a couple of eateries and takeaways nearby.

Airport Bed & Breakfast 1 Westney Rd (at Kirkbride Rd) ⓣ09/275 0533, ⓦwww.airportbnb.co.nz. Ten rooms (four en suite) in a converted suburban house that's well placed for the airport, with a friendly owner, Wi-Fi and buffet breakfast thrown in. ❹

Airport Skyway Lodge 30 Kirkbride Rd ⓣ09/275 4443, ⓦwww.skywaylodge.co.nz. Several grades of basic budget accommodation in friendly and relaxed surroundings with guests' kitchen and free luggage storage. Accommodation is in four-bunk dorms, double and twin rooms and self-catering motel units. There's even free bikebox storage for cyclists. Doubles & twins ❷, en-suite rooms & units ❸

Jet Park Airport Hotel and Conference Centre 63 Westney Rd ⓣ0800/538 466, ⓦwww.jetinn.co.nz. The subject of a major re-brand, with tastefully decorated rooms and all the expected facilities – Sky TV, minibars, lovely outdoor pool, restaurant/bar – plus a deluxe wing. ❻, deluxe ❼, exec suite ❽

Ventura Inn and Suites 14 Airpark Drive ⓣ09/275 4540, ⓦwww.venturainns.co.nz. The nearest thing to the airport without camping by the runway just happens to be a swanky set of seventy air-conditioned rooms with all the usual business facilities at a surprisingly reasonable price. Housed in typical airport architecture, but if you're inside it won't matter. Standard Studio ❹, deluxe suite ❺

are usually prohibitively high, though there are sometimes weekend deals. Backpacker **hostels** congregate around the city centre and inner suburbs; **B&Bs** and **guesthouses** are strongest in Ponsonby, Devonport and the southern suburbs of Epsom and Remuera; and the widest selection of **motels** is just south of Newmarket in Epsom. Predictably, **campsites** are further out and not really worth the hassle.

Hotels and motels

An increasing number of **hotels** pepper the city centre and inner suburbs, ranging from budget to swanky five-star affairs. High city rents force **motels** further out and you'll see them mostly on the Great South Road in Epsom, immediately south of Newmarket, where at least a dozen nestle in one kilometre.

Central Auckland

See map on p.106.

Airdale Hotel 380 Queen St ⓣ09/374 1741, ⓦwww.scenic-circle.co.nz. Recently refurbished to its original 1950s Art Deco style, there are 100 rooms, all with kitchenette, some with city and harbour views from some rooms. Summer deals (6) make it good value for money. 7

Aspen House 62 Emily Place ⓣ09/379 6633, ⓦwww.aspenhouse.co.nz. Compact hotel right in the heart of the city but surprisingly quiet and with a small garden. Rooms aren't big (and some have little natural light) but it's great value and a help-yourself continental breakfast is included. Secure parking is available for $12.50 a day. Rooms 2 en suite 4

Elliott St Apartments Corner of Wellesley & Elliott sts ⓣ0800/565 665, ⓦwww.esapts.co.nz. Attractive, modern studio, one- and two-bedroom apartments (serviced daily) in a heritage building right in the heart of the city. Rooms at the back can be a little dark (but are quieter), and all have full kitchen, laundry, dataports and Sky TV. No on-site parking. Studios 5, 2-bedroom 6

Heritage 35 Hobson St ⓣ0800/368 888, ⓦwww.heritagehotels.co.nz. Top-class hotel partly fashioned from the original Farmers department store – once the city's grandest. Occasional bits of aged planking and wooden supports crop up in public areas, but it is fitted out to a very high standard and many rooms have views across the harbour or into the glassed-in atrium. There is also an outside pool with views over the city rooftops. 7

Hilton Princes Wharf, 147 Quay St, Auckland ⓣ09/978 2000, ⓦwww.1.hilton.com. Fabulously sited on a wharf jutting into the harbour. Beautifully decorated rooms, all with terrace or balcony, start from around $390 in summer but it is worth paying the extra $80 for a good view. Fabulous waterside suites are around a grand. If you decide this is out of your budget a visit to the Bellini cocktail bar on the ground floor will give you a taste of the high life and prices. 9

Parnell

See map on p.113.

Parnell Inn 320 Parnell Rd ⓣ0800/472 763, ⓦwww.parnellinn.co.nz. Compact and simple hotel tucked in behind the *Kosmic Café* right in the heart of Parnell. Rooms are fairly small, some with kitchenette, and off-street parking is available. Large rooms with view 4, basic rooms 3

Ponsonby

See map on p.117.

Abaco on Jervois 59 Jervois Rd ⓣ0800/220 066, ⓦwww.abaco.co.nz. Attractive motel close to the Ponsonby cafés, with a range of rooms and plenty of off-street parking. Budget options lack kitchens; standard rooms are much more spacious but nothing compared to the deluxe rooms, many with spa baths and distant harbour views. Budget 3, standard 4, deluxe 6

Epsom

See map on p.122.

Greenpark 66 Great South Rd ⓣ0800/888 819, ⓦwww.green-park.co.nz. Renovated motel with standard and executive suites, all with separate bedrooms and full facilities. 3

Hansen's & The Ascot Star 96 Great South Rd ⓣ09/520 2804 and 92 Great South Rd ⓣ0800/922 002, ⓦwww.ascotsyar.co.nz. One of the cheapest motels in town, with small s/c studios, has joined forces with its more illustrious next-door neighbour. 3

Off Broadway Motel Newmarket 11 Alpers Ave ⓣ0800/427 623, ⓦwww.offbroadway.co.nz. Business-oriented hotel with a/c, soundproofed en-suite rooms and a gym. Plump for the much larger suites if you can. Studios 4, suites 6

Siesta 70 Great South Rd ⓣ0800/743 782, ⓦwww.siestamotel.co.nz. Good modern family-run motel with kitchenless studios and self-catering units. Studios ③, units ④

Tudor Court 108 Great South Rd ⓣ0800/826 878, ⓔstay@tudor.co.nz. Compact motel with small hotel-style rooms and slightly larger ones with kitchenettes. ③

B&Bs and guesthouses

Auckland's stock of B&Bs and guesthouses is expanding. New places continually open, many pitching for the upper end of the market, with just a few rooms and an almost obsessive attention to detail. Places are scattered widely around the **inner suburbs** on the south side of the harbour and in the North Shore suburb of **Devonport**. Note that airport shuttle buses will drop you in Devonport for only a few dollars extra.

Parnell

See map on p.113.

Ascot Parnell St Stephens Ave ⓣ09/309 9012, ⓦwww.ascotparnell.com. Very swish and comfy accommodation with a large lounge opening onto a balcony overlooking the harbour, luxurious private bathrooms, Internet access and a filling breakfast. ⑧

Ponsonby and Herne Bay

See map on p.117.

Amitee's 237 Ponsonby Rd, Ponsonby ⓣ09/378 6325 ⓦwww.amitees.com. Petite urban hotel with smallish en-suite rooms sporting chic modern decor, all with access to the lounge (with honesty bar) where a help-yourself continental breakfast is served. If the rooms seem too small, step up to the penthouse with its own TV den and city views. Rooms ⑥, penthouse ⑨

The Great Ponsonby B&B 30 Ponsonby Terrace, Ponsonby ⓣ09/376 5989, ⓦwww.greatpons.co.nz. This welcoming boutique hotel, in a restored 1898 villa 3min walk from Ponsonby Rd, is the pick of the crop. Boldly decorated in ocean tones using native timbers and Pacific artworks; everyone has use of the sunny lounge and shaded garden and the breakfasts are a delight. The luxurious, en-suite rooms come with Sky TV; there are also self-catering studio units (⑧). Rooms ⑦

Herne Bay B&B 4 Shelly Beach Rd, Herne Bay ⓣ09/360 0309, ⓦwww.herne-bay.co.nz. Low-key B&B in a large, refurbished Edwardian house converted to accommodate several styles of room, some with their own kitchen. Basic rooms share facilities, the larger en suites have a separate living area and there's a two-bedroom apartment. Continental breakfast is included and there's also access to a partly restored rooftop turret. Basic ③, en suites ⑤, apartment ⑥

Devonport

See map on p.119.

108 Victoria Rd 108 Victoria Rd, Devonport ⓣ09/445 7565, ⓔsmj@ihug.co.nz. A B&B with two rooms overlooking a saltwater swimming pool and a cottage in lush gardens. Breakfast costs extra, there's a late checkout and both rooms can be rented as one. Rooms ④ cottage ⑦

The Garden Room 23 Cheltenham Rd, Devonport ⓣ09/445 2472, ⓦwww.devonportgardenroom.co.nz. Choose between the lovely private cottage in the leafy garden or the room inside the main house, both of which are done to a very high standard; sumptuous breakfasts can be served under an arbour or in your room. ⑤

Mahoe B&B 15b King Edward Parade, Devonport ⓣ09/445 1515, ⓦwww.mahoe.co.nz. Lovely property set back from the waterfront, in the heart of Devonport, tastefully furnished and offering either B&B in the house or a separate fully s/c apartment. ⑥

Parituhu Beachstay 3 King Edward Parade, Devonport ⓣ09/445 6559, ⓦwww.parituhu.co.nz. A gay-friendly budget B&B homestay in the heart of Devonport that overlooks the harbour, with just the one room, a private bath, access to a secluded garden and self-service breakfast. ⑤

Peace & Plenty Inn 6 Flagstaff Terrace, Devonport ⓣ09/445 2925, ⓦwww.peaceandplenty.co.nz. One of New Zealand's finest B&Bs, yet relaxed and well priced. Elegantly restored kauri floorboards lead through to a lovely veranda, past exquisite rooms filled with fresh flowers and equipped with sherry and port. Venture outside the bounds of the inn and you're right in the heart of Devonport. ⑨

Birkenhead and Northcote

See map on p.97.

Number One House 1 Princes St, Northcote Point ⓣ09/480 7659, ⓦwww.nz-homestay.co.nz. Hospitable B&B with views across the Waitemata Harbour to the city and Rangitoto Island. It has a small beach, easy city access by ferry, two rooms, a s/c apartment and a quirky garden with a little hobbit house. Great breakfast, plus the opportunity to go out on the owner's yacht (around $225 per person per day). Rooms & apartment ❻

Stafford Villa 2 Awanui St, Birkenhead ⓣ09/418 3022, ⓦwww.staffordvilla.co.nz. Located on a quiet street in one of the North Shore's more venerable waterside suburbs, where there are several good restaurants and an excellent cinema, this top-notch place offers just two period-furnished en-suite rooms in an elegant century-old villa. Guests have access to a drawing room and a comfy library (with complimentary port), and are treated to a sumptuous breakfast. Rates are $395–445. ❾

Mount Eden and Remuera

See map on p.122. Buses #274, #275 and #277 run from stand D16 on Customs St East in the CBD to Mount Eden shops, passing close to both these B&Bs.

Aachen House 39 Market Rd, Remuera ⓣ0800/222 436, ⓦwww.aachenhouse.co.nz. Elegant, if somewhat snooty boutique B&B in an Edwardian house decorated with antiques. Rooms are spacious, beds huge and breakfasts delicious. ❽

Bavaria 83 Valley Rd, Mount Eden ⓣ09/638 9641, ⓦwww.bavariabandbhotel.co.nz. Eleven-room B&B in a spacious, comfortable suburban villa that boasts a pleasant deck and garden. It's popular with German-speakers who appreciate the Teutonic touches to the buffet continental breakfast. Buses from downtown pass close by. ❺

Hostels

Auckland has stacks of **backpacker hostels** competing for your custom. Most are set up to assist new arrivals to plan onward travel, to the extent of having fully staffed on-site travel services – sometimes pushing favoured trips and activities, but generally offering impartial advice.

There's a definite trade-off between the convenice offered by **downtown** hostels and the relative quiet of places outside the centre. Most central hostels, with the exception of the YHAs, cram in the beds and, with bars and clubs only a short stagger away, cater to party animals. Hostels in the **inner suburbs** – Parnell, Ponsonby and Mount Eden – tend to be less boisterous affairs, often in old, converted houses, sometimes with gardens and usually with parking.

As you'd expect, **prices** are higher than in the rest of the country, though you can still get dorm bunks for around $22. Small dorms and four-shares hover around $25 and most doubles and twins are $55–80. If you're arriving during the peak summer season, try to book in advance.

Central Auckland

See map on p.106.

base Auckland 16–22 Fort St ⓣ09/300 9999, ⓦwww.stayatbase.com. Classy conversion of a city office building into a good hostel on seven floors complete with rooftop kitchen and outdoor barbecue area. There's also a spa pool, sauna, good travel desk, a bargain café and a lively bar that goes off most nights. Accommodation is in a range of dorms (4–12 beds), doubles and twins, and there's a separate women-only "sanctuary" floor with extra pampering. Dorms $26–28, sanctuary $30, en-suite double ❸

base Auckland Central 229 Queen St ⓣ0800/462 396, ⓦwww.stayatbase.com. Enormous, well-run hostel in a ten-storey converted office building. Despite the inevitable impersonality of housing several hundred, everything runs smoothly and it seldom feels too crowded. They've thought of everything, including a downstairs bar, separate terrace bar with nightly sausage sizzle, Internet centre, helpful travel office, laundry, gear storage and electronic key access to each floor and public areas. Mixed dorms sleep up to eight but it's worth the extra for a mixed four-bed dorm supplied with sheets. There's all sorts of evening activities, and parking nearby ($7 overnight, $20 for 24hr). Big dorms $25, small dorms $28, rooms ❸, en suites with TV ❸

BK Hostel 3 Mercury Lane ⓣ09/307 0052, ⓦwww.bkhostel.co.nz. Well-kept hostel in the heart of the lively K' Road district. No dorms as such, just three-bed shares, doubles and twins with cheaper rates for those without windows. Common areas are spacious and security is good. Shares $25–27, rooms ❷

City Groove 6 Constitution Hill ⓣ09/303 4768, ⓦwww.citygroove.co.nz. Small, slightly cramped accommodation, an easy walk from both the CBD and Parnell, that fills the gap between city and suburban hostels. Relaxed atmosphere, small garden and limited parking. Dorms $20, shares $22, rooms ❷, en suite ❷

The Fat Camel 38 Fort St ⓣ09/307 0181, ⓦwww.nomadsworld.com. Solid downtown hostel with a bar, café and travel desk. The emphasis is on twins and doubles, though small dorms are available, arranged in small flats with their own kitchens. Dorms $23, shares $26, windowless rooms ❷, with windows ❷

YHA Auckland City Corner of City Rd & Liverpool St ⓣ09/309 2802, ⓔyha.aucklandcity@yha.co.nz. Large and central YHA with seven floors of mostly twin and double rooms – the upper ones with fine city views – plus well-equipped common areas, a large travel centre and a bistro on site. Single-sex and mixed dorms $22, four-shares $24, rooms ❷

YHA Auckland International 5 Turner St ⓣ09/302 8200, ⓔyha.aucklandint@yha.co.nz. Just down the hill and even larger than its brother, this purpose-built YHA is thoroughly modern, with excellent cooking facilities, spacious rooms, separate TV and quiet lounges, Internet access and a travel centre. They even have a few free parking spaces; book early. Single-sex dorms $22, single-sex and mixed four-shares $26, rooms ❸, en-suite rooms ❹

Parnell

See map on p.113.

City Garden Lodge 25 St George's Bay Rd ⓣ09/302 0880, ⓦwww.citygardenlodge.co.nz. Friendly backpackers in a large, well-organized villa originally built for the Queen of Tonga, and surrounded by expansive lawns. Along with Internet access there are spacious dorms, some lovely doubles/twins and even a yoga/meditation room (classes available). Dorms $24, shares $25, rooms ❷

International Backpackers 2 Churton St ⓣ09/358 4584, ⓔinternational.bp@extra.co.nz. One-time home for wayward girls but now a friendly, spacious hostel on a quiet street 3min from Parnell with street parking and rejuvenated rooms. Large dorm $17, smaller dorms $22, rooms ❷, en suite ❷

Lantana Lodge 60 St George's Bay Rd ⓣ09/373 4546 ⓦwww.lantanalodge.co.nz. Small, clean and friendly hostel with wireless and a homely feel. Linen included. Dorms $23, rooms ❷

Ponsonby

See map on p.117.

Brown Kiwi 7 Prosford St ⓣ09/378 0191, ⓦwww.brownkiwi.co.nz. Compact, cosy little hostel in a restored Victorian villa on a quiet street close to the Ponsonby cafés. A patio and tiny garden at the back helps the relaxing atmosphere. Daytime parking is poor but it's easily accessible by the Link bus. Dorms $22, share $24, doubles and twins ❷

Uenuku Lodge 217 Ponsonby Rd ⓣ09/378 8990, ⓦwww.uenukulodge.co.nz. Comfortable, good-value hostel worked into a warren of an old boarding house just steps from the action on Ponsonby Rd and on the Link bus route. It's bright, clean, good value and there's parking. Dorms $25, shares $29, twins ❷, doubles ❷

Verandahs 6 Hopetoun St ⓣ09/360 4180, ⓦwww.verandahs.co.nz. Lovely, well-appointed, welcoming backpackers in a 1905 villa, overlooking a leafy park with city views that intentionally lacks TV. Offers off-street parking and a selection of spacious accommodation, as well as rooms in the recently renovated house next door. Dorms $25, shares $27–29, rooms ❷

Mount Eden

See map on p.122. Buses #274, #275 and #277 run from stand D16 on Customs St East in the CBD to Mount Eden shops, passing close to all these hostels.

Bamber House 22 View Rd ⓣ09/623 4267, ⓦwww.hostelbackpacker.com. Spacious, well-managed hostel partly in a lovely old colonial house and partly in a swish modern house. There's a large lawn out front and a host of other facilities including wireless Internet. Dorms $25, shares $28, rooms and en suites ❷

Oaklands Lodge 5a Oaklands Rd ⓣ09/638 6545, ⓦwww.oaklands.co.nz. Run by the folk above, this large two-storey Victorian house right by Mount Eden shops has mostly dorms with beds rather than bunks, and an abundance of separate lounge areas. Dorms $23, shares $25, rooms ❷

Pentlands 22 Pentlands Ave ⓣ09/638 7031, ⓦwww.pentlands.co.nz. Slightly ageing, laid-back hostel in a quiet suburban street 10min walk from Mount Eden shops and cafés. Big lounge, plenty of videos and loads of parking. Dorms $23, shares $25, rooms ❷

Campsites and motor parks

You'd have to travel a long way to find a genuinely attractive spot to pitch a **tent**. There are numerous, well-equipped motor camps within the city limits that are fine for **campervans** and offer bargain **cabins**, though without your own vehicle, you'll end up spending a lot of money on buses.

Auckland North Shore Top 10 Holiday Park 52 Northcote Rd, Takapuna ⓣ0508/909 090 & 09/418 2578, ⓦwww.nsmotels.co.nz. Well-appointed site on the North Shore just off the northern motorway, with an indoor swimming pool and extensive BBQ areas. Stagecoach buses stop nearby. Tents and vans $35 per site, cabins ❷, tourist flats ❸, motel units ❹

Avondale Motor Park 46 Bollard Ave, Avondale ⓣ0800/100 542, ⓦwww.aucklandmotorpark.co.nz. Restful, fairly central site 6km southwest of the city and accessible by bus #211 or #212 from Symonds St. Camping $14, on-site vans ❶, cabins ❷, tourist flats ❸

Remuera Motor Lodge and Inner City Camping Ground 16 Minto Rd ⓣ09/524 5126, ⓔremlodge@ihug.co.nz. About the most central and convenient site, 6km east of the city in a quiet residential area. There's even a swimming pool, and buses stop close by. Camping $14–15, dorms $24, tourist flats ❸, motel units ❹

Takapuna Beach Holiday Park 22 The Promenade, Takapuna ⓣ09/489 7909, ⓦwww.takapunabeach.kiwiholidaypark.com. Beachside caravan park on the North Shore overlooking Rangitoto and 5min walk from Takapuna shops and restaurants. There are regular buses to central Auckland. Camping $14, cabins & on-site vans ❷, en-suite caravans ❷, tourist flats ❸

Central Auckland

The central city street names represent a roll call of prime movers in New Zealand's early European history. The city's backbone, Queen Street, along with its attendant royal acolytes, Victoria and Albert streets, forms a central grid bedded with thoroughfares commemorating the country's first Governor-General, William Hobson, Willoughby Shortland, New Zealand's first colonial secretary, and William Symonds, who chivvied along local Maori chiefs reluctant to sign the Treaty of Waitangi.

Downtown clings to the southern shores of the **Waitemata Harbour**, the latter connected to the city through the developments round the **Maritime Museum** and the adjacent waterside rejuvenation of **Viaduct Harbour** and Princes Wharf; essentially flashy restaurants and swanky apartments dotted round a marina.

Downbeat **Queen Street**, the main drag, strikes south through the **city centre**, largely sustained by banks and insurance companies. There's little of abiding interest unless you're designer label shopping on the more exclusive side streets, or fancy something more cultural in the form of the **Auckland Art Gallery**, currently undergoing a transformation (see p.108). **Albert Park**, wedged between the Gallery and the **University**, makes a nice break from the concrete jungle.

At the top of Queen Street lies **Karangahape Road** (colloquially K' Road), an altogether groovier strip of cheaper shops, ethnic restaurants and more down and dirty clubs.

The Domain, an extensive swathe of parkland with trees and lawns, sweeps towards the harbour. It is Auckland's premier green space, laid out around the city's most-visited attraction, the **Auckland Museum**, exhibiting stunning Maori and Pacific Island artefacts.

Downtown and Viaduct Harbour

Auckland's waterfront was on **Fort Street** (originally Fore Street), but progressive reclamation shifted the shoreline 300m to the north, creating space for **Downtown Auckland**, which centres on the striking **Britomart Transport**

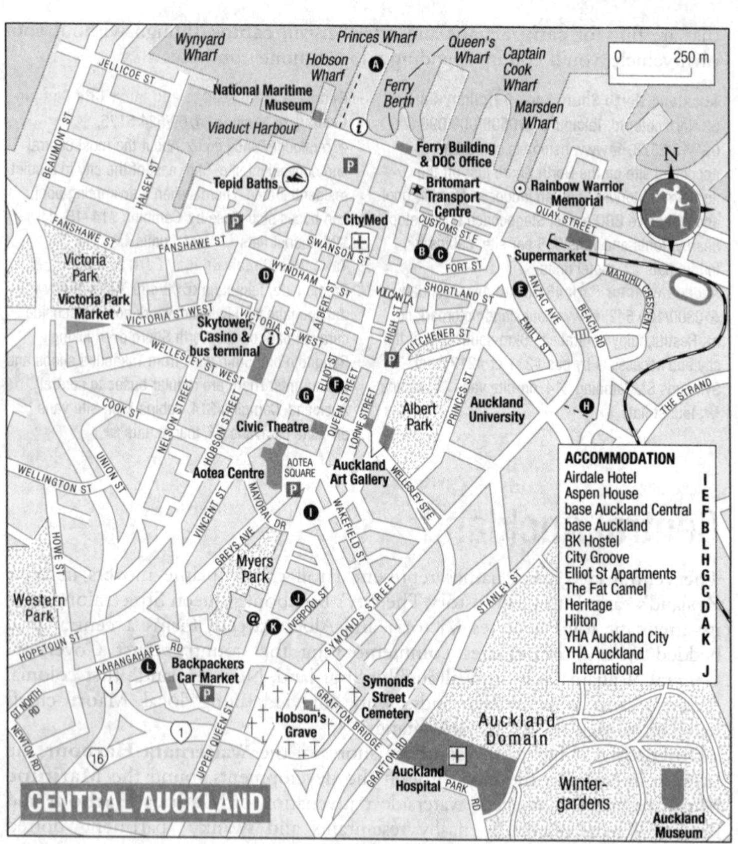

Centre, located inside the neoclassical 1910 former post office at the northern end of **Queen Street**. The street ends at the dockside **Ferry Building**, a neoclassical 1912 brick structure that is still the hub of the Waitemata Harbour ferry services and home to the local DOC office. The chaotic bustle of the days before the harbour bridge is now a distant memory, but the ebb and flow remains, as commuters and sightseers board speedy catamarans to Devonport and Rangitoto, Waiheke and Great Barrier islands.

Since the mid-1990s, the majority of the waterfront activity has shifted a couple of hundred metres west to **Viaduct Harbour**, smartened up in preparation for New Zealand's successful defence of the **America's Cup**, in 2000. Unfortunately the second defence, in 2003, suffered ignominious defeat at the hands of that famous ocean-sailing nation, the Swiss – primarily because of defections by crucial Kiwi personnel to the better-paying Swiss team. There's nothing left of the once-scruffy fishing port; instead, exclusive apartments, expensive yacht berths, flash restaurants and themed bars epitomize the new regime.

National Maritime Museum

The only sight downtown is the **National Maritime Museum**, Viaduct Harbour, on the corner of Quay and Hobson streets (daily: Nov–Easter

9am–6pm; Easter–Oct 9am–5pm; $16; ⓦwww.nzmaritime.org), which pays homage to the maritime history of an island nation reliant on the sea for colonization, trade and sport. The short *Te Waka* video shows an imagined Maori migration voyage, setting the scene for a display of outrigger and double-hulled canoes from all over the South Pacific. There's a huge variety of designs, employed for fishing, lagoon sailing and ocean voyaging – the last represented by the massive 23m-long *Taratai*, which carried New Zealand photographer and writer James Siers and a crew of thirteen over 2400km from Kiribati to Fiji in 1976. The creaking and rolling innards of a migrant ship and displays on New Zealand's coastal traders and whalers lead on to a collection of just about every class of yacht, culminating in the devotional exhibits on yacht racing. Other highlights include an early example of the Hamilton Jetboat, which was designed for shallow, braided Canterbury rivers; a replica of a classic 1950s holiday *bach* with great archival film footage adding to the nostalgic flavour; and the Edmiston and Fraser collections, containing maritime art.

There are interesting guided tours (usually Mon–Fri 11am, Sat 11am or 1pm; free), and rides on the little steam tug, SS *Puke* (two Sun each month, $5). There are also one-hour **cruises** on the *Ted Ashby* (Tues, Thurs, Sat & Sun noon & 2pm; $15, $24 including museum entry, twilight harbour cruises, two Thursdays each month, $30), a 1990s replica of one of the traditional flat-bottomed, ketch-rigged scows that once worked the North Island tidal waterways.

City centre

The liveliest section of the central city is **High Street**, south of downtown, energized by bookshops and trendy clothes stores. Most of the action happens around the junction with the former blacksmithing street of **Vulcan Lane**, now dominated by bars and restaurants.

The city centre is dominated by the concrete **Skytower**, on the corner of Victoria and Federal streets (Mon–Thurs & Sun 8.30am–10.30pm, Fri & Sat 8.30am–11.30pm; $25, upper viewing extra $3), built in the mid-1990s as a

▲ Skytower, New Zealand's tallest building

symbol for the city in the run-up to the new millennium. At 328m, it just pips the Eiffel Tower and Sydney's Centrepoint, and is New Zealand's tallest structure. The obligatory observation decks (192m and 220m) offer stupendous views over the city and Hauraki Gulf and there's also a revolving restaurant and a couple of **adventure activities** (see p.125). Normally floodlit white, it periodically gets a makeover – red and green for Christmas, red and gold for Chinese New Year and pink for breast cancer week. The tower sprouts from the **Sky City Casino**, whose gaming floor, awash in deep blue and green decor, contains all the usual distractions.

One of Queen Street's few buildings of distinction is the Art Nouveau **Civic Theatre**, on the corner of Wellesley Street. The talk of the town when it opened in 1929, the management went as far as to import a small Indian boy from Fiji to complement the ornate Moghul-style decor. After renovation in 2000 it reopened in its full splendour, complete with a star-strewn artificial sky and an ornate proscenium arch with flanking lions, their eyes blazing red. It's well worth a look, but unless you happen to strike one of the infrequent open days, the only way to get inside is to see a performance (see p.134).

Bang next door, but architecturally miles away, is a chunky postmodern multiplex cinema. It flanks **Aotea Square**, which is overlooked on its other sides by the Town Hall and the city's foremost concert hall, the **Aotea Centre**, which opened in a blaze of glory in 1990, with Kiri Te Kanawa performing on the inaugural night. On Friday and Saturday (10am–6pm), the arts, crafts, fashion, vintage clothing, local comestibles, jewellery and Pacifica stalls of the **Aotea Square Markets** bring the square to life and attempt to relieve visitors of a few dollars.

Albert Park and the Auckland Art Gallery

Moving east of Queen Street, Wellesley Street runs up to **Albert Park**, formal Victorian-style gardens which spread uphill from the Auckland Art Gallery to the university. Originally the site of a Maori *pa*, the land was successively conscripted into service as Albert Barracks in the 1840s and 50s, and then as a labyrinthine network of air-raid shelters during World War II, before relaxing into its current incarnation as parkland thronged with sunbathing students and office workers. It comes filled with a century's worth of memorials, a floral clock, some beautiful oaks, Morton Bay fig trees and the 1882 former gatekeeper's cottage. On the eastern edge of Albert Park, the **Auckland Art Gallery** (daily 10am–5pm; free but with fees for special exhibitions; infoline ⓣ09/307 7700, ⓦwww.aucklandartgallery.govt.nz) comes in two parts – one predominantly traditional, the other resolutely contemporary – that jointly make up the world's most important collection of Kiwi art. The Heritage Gallery was closed for a massive and highly impressive upgrade in 2008, due for completion in 2010.

The galleries

The elaborate mock-French **Heritage Gallery**, on the corner of Wellesley and Kitchener streets, is out of bounds while it's being enhanced, and all exhibitions are at the **New Gallery**, across the street on the corner of Wellesley and Lorne streets. It has two light and spacious floors and contains elements of the Heritage Gallery collection as well as site-specific installations by predominantly New Zealand, and particularly Maori, artists. One name to look out for is **Colin McCahon**, whose fascination with the power and beauty of New Zealand landscape informs much recent Kiwi art. Others, such as **Gordon Walters**, draw their inspiration from Maori iconography, in Walters' case controversially employing vibrant, graphic representations of traditional Maori symbols (for more on Maori design, see "Maoritanga", p.893). The Heritage Gallery collection includes a small, respectable representation of world art and an extensive collection of homegrown. At any one time you may see original drawings by artists on Cook's expeditions or overwrought oils depicting Maori migrations. These romantic images, seen through European eyes, frequently show composite scenes that could never have happened, contributing to a mythical view that persisted for decades.

Much of the rest of the early collection is devoted to works by two of the country's most loved artists – both highly respected by Maori as among the few to accurately portray their ancestors. Bohemian immigrant **Gottfried Lindauer** emigrated to New Zealand in 1873 and spent his later years painting lifelike, almost documentary, portraits of *rangatira* (chiefs) and high-born Maori men and women, in the mistaken belief that the Maori people were about to become extinct. In the early part of the twentieth century, **Charles F. Goldie** became New Zealand's resident "old master" and earned international recognition for his more emotional portraits of elderly Maori regally showing off their traditional tattoos, or *moko*, though they were in fact often painted from photographs (sometimes after the subject's death).

Contemporary landscape painters largely projected European visions of beauty onto New Zealand landscapes, reducing vibrant visions to subdued scenes reminiscent of English parkland, north European seas and Swiss Alps. It took half a century for more representative images to become the norm – an evolutionary process that continued into the 1960s and 70s, when many works betray an almost cartoon-like quality, with heavily delineated spaces daubed in shocking colours. Look out for works by **Rita Angus**, renowned for her images of Central Otago in the 1940s, and **Tony Fomison** (1939–1990), painter of one of the gallery's most expensive works, *Study of Holbein's "Dead Christ"*. Completed in 1973, it's typical of his later, more obsessive period, combining the artist's passion for art history and his preoccupation with mortality. Also worth a look are the works of **Russell Clark** (1905–1966), who painted scenes from everyday working life.

Karangahape Road

At its southern end, Queen Street climbs to the ridge-top **Karangahape Road**, universally known as **K' Road**. Formerly an uptown residential area for prosperous nineteenth-century merchants, it later became associated with Auckland's Polynesian community, but now only a couple of consulates and a Samoan church remain. For twenty years planners have hailed a mainstream shopping renaissance but K' Road remains determinedly niche. Groovy cafés, music shops specializing in vinyl and clothes shops selling budget designer garb rub shoulders with colourful stores run by East and South Asians. There are no specific sights, but you can easily pass an afternoon browsing the shops and eating in ethnic restaurants.

K' Road is much loved by those who know it and much maligned by those who don't – chiefly on account of the notoriety associated with its western end, a two-hundred-metre-long corridor of massage parlours, strip joints and gay cruising clubs. It is certainly one of the seedier parts of town but the raunchy places are interspersed with mainstream nightclubs and there is always a vibrant feel that is seldom intimidating, though the usual precautions should be exercised at night.

Further east, K' Road crosses Symonds Street by the little-known and somewhat neglected **Symonds Street Cemetery**, one of Auckland's earliest burial grounds, with allocations for Jewish, Presbyterian, Wesleyan, Roman Catholic and Anglican faiths – the last two areas largely destroyed by the motorway cut through Grafton Gully in the 1960s. A patch of deciduous woodland shades the grave of New Zealand's first Governor, William Hobson, tucked away on the eastern side of Symonds Street almost under the vast concrete span of Grafton Bridge.

The Domain

Grafton Gully separates the city centre from **The Domain**, a swathe of semi-formal gardens draped over the low, irregular profile of an extinct volcano known to Maori as Pukekawa or "hill of bitter memories", a reference to the bloodshed of ancient inter-tribal fighting. In the 1840s, when Auckland was the national capital, Governor Grey set aside the core of The Domain as the city's first park and it remains its finest, furnished with mid-nineteenth-century accoutrements: a band rotunda, phoenix palms, formal flowerbeds and spacious lawns. In summer, the rugby pitches metamorphose into cricket ovals and softball diamonds and marquees and stages are erected in the crater's shallow amphitheatre for outdoor musical extravaganzas.

The Domain's volcanic spring was one of Auckland's original water sources. It was used to farm the country's first rainbow trout in 1884 and by the Auckland Acclimatization Society to grow European plants, thereby promoting the rapid Europeanization of the New Zealand countryside. The spirit of this enterprise lingers on in the **Wintergardens** (Nov–March Mon–Sat 9am–5.30pm, Sun 9am–7.30pm; April–Oct daily 9am–4.30pm; free), a shallow fishpond in a formal sunken courtyard flanked by two elaborate barrel-roofed glasshouses – one temperate, the other heated to mimic tropical climes – filled with neatly tended botanical specimens. Next door, a former scoria quarry has been transformed into the **Fernz Fernery** (same hours; free), a green dell with over a hundred types of fern in dry, intermediate and wet habitats.

Auckland Museum

The highest point on The Domain is crowned by the imposing Greco-Roman-style **Auckland Museum** (daily 10am–5pm; $5, valid for repeated entry on one day; ⓦwww.akmuseum.org.nz). Built as a World War I memorial in 1929, the names of World War II battles were duly added around the outer walls. The contents of Auckland's original city museum were moved here and the holdings expanded to form one of the world's finest collections of Maori and Pacific art and craft. The museum has retained a traditional approach but is thoroughly contemporary in its execution, with each of the three floors taking on an individual identity – Pacific people (ground), natural history (middle) and New Zealand at War (top).

A 2006 revamp introduced a new atrium, containing a bowl-shaped building covered in Fijian kauri, hanging above the ground, the whole shebang housed beneath an undulating glass and copper dome. You can enter from this end of the building but the museum makes more sense from the foyer entrance, the new space providing an intriguing space in which to sit and have coffee or a snack (daily 10am–5pm).

Kids are catered for with the **Children's Discovery Centre** on the middle floor and if you're interested in buying Maori crafts, check out the high-quality traditional and contemporary work in the museum **shop**. To round off the experience, head along to the thirty-minute **Manaia cultural performance** (daily 11am, noon & 1.30pm, also Jan–March 2.30pm; $20) of song and dance, heralded by a conch-blast.

Auckland Museum is on the route of the Coast to Coast Walkway and the city tour **buses**. Both the Link bus and regular #283 bus stop on Park Road, five minutes' walk away.

Ground Floor

Entering from the foyer entrance, turn left as you enter to reach the **Pacific Lifeways** room, which mainly concentrates on daily life and is dominated by a simple yet majestic breadfruit-wood statue from the Caroline Islands depicting **Kave**, Polynesia's malevolent and highest-ranked female deity, whose menace is barely hinted at in this serene form. This leads on to the **Maori Court**, an extensive collection marking the transition from purely Polynesian motifs to an identifiably Maori style. It's exemplified in the **Kaitaia Carving**, a two-and-a-half-metre-wide totara carving (in the first case as you enter) thought to have been designed for a ceremonial gateway, guarded by the central goblin-like figure with sweeping arms that stretch out to become lizard forms at their extremities: Polynesian in style but Maori in concept. It was found in 1920 near Kaitaia and is estimated to date from the fourteenth or fifteenth century, predating most Maori art so far discovered.

As traditional Maori villages started to disappear towards the end of the nineteenth century, some of the best examples of carved panels, meeting houses and food stores were rescued. Many are currently displayed here, though some of the exhibits are claimed by Maori groups throughout the country and may ultimately be returned to their traditional owners. The main gallery is dominated by **Hotunui**, a large and wonderfully restored carved *whare whakairo* (meeting house), built near Thames in 1878, late enough to have a corrugated iron rather than rush roof, and re-erected here in 1929. Once again the craftsmanship is superb; the house's exterior bristles with grotesque faces, lolling tongues and glistening paua-shell eyes, while the interior is lined with wonderful geometric *tukutuku* panels. Outside is the intricately carved prow and stern-piece of **Te Toki a Tapiri**, a 25m-long *waka taua* (war canoe) designed to seat a hundred warriors, the only surviving specimen from the pre-European era.

Beyond the canoe you're into the main Pacific Island collection, known as **Pacific Masterpieces**, filled with exquisite Polynesian, Melanesian and Micronesian works. Look out for the shell-inlaid ceremonial food bowl from the Solomon Islands, ceremonial clubs and a wonderfully resonant slit-drum from Vanuatu. The textiles are fabulous too, with designs far more varied than you'd expect considering the limited raw materials: the Hawaiian red feather cloak is especially fine.

Middle Floor

The middle floor of the museum comprises the **natural history galleries**, an unusual combination of modern thematic displays and stuffed birds in cases. It charts the progress from the "Big Bang" through an exploration of plate tectonics and the break up of Gondwanaland, the geology and seismology of New Zealand and its flora and fauna. Dinosaur skeletons allude to their presence here until 65 million years ago, something scientists had discounted until the 1970s when fossils started turning up. Displays like the three-metre Giant Moa (an ostrich-like bird) and an 800kg ammonite can't be missed, but there's a lot of stuff virtually hidden so be prepared to take your time. Armed with the knowledge of how New Zealand came to be, you proceed to a series of ecosystems including a reconstruction of a cave in Waitomo and a three-storey-high model of a kauri tree. Also worth a look is the **Maori Natural History** display, which attempts to explain the unique Maori perspective unencumbered by Western scientific thinking, and the lively **volcanoes** display which relies heavily on said science.

Top Floor

A multi-levelled approach is used on the top floor in the **Scars on the Heart** exhibition, an emotional exploration of how New Zealanders' involvement in war has helped shape national identity. At any time you are able to divert from the main timeline and explore specific topics in more detail via interactive displays with personal accounts of the troops' experiences and the responses of those back home.

You enter Scars on the Heart through a slightly incongruous mock-up of an 1860s Auckland street that sets the scene for the New Zealand Wars, interpreted from both Maori and Pakeha perspectives. World War I gets extensive coverage, particularly the Gallipoli campaign in Turkey, when botched leadership led to a massacre of ANZAC – Australian and New Zealand Army Corps – troops in the trenches. Powerful visuals and rousing martial music accompany newsreel footage of the Pacific campaigns of World War II and finally New Zealand's foray into Vietnam is briefly documented.

The suburbs

You're likely to spend more time in the suburbs than you are in the centre of the city, as the bulk of the specific sights lie outside the CBD. **Parnell** forms the ecclesiastical heart of the city, with one of Auckland's oldest churches and a couple of historical houses. Beyond lies the waterfront Tamaki Drive, running past the watery attractions of Kelly Tarlton's to the city beaches of Mission Bay and St Heliers. West of the centre, the suburbs spread out beyond Freeman's Bay to Auckland's most concentrated cluster of restaurants and cafés along **Ponsonby Road**, and out to Western Springs, home of the **MOTAT** transport museum.

Across the Waitemata Harbour the seemingly endless suburbs of the **North Shore** stretch into the distance, though you're only likely to want to spend much time in the old waterside suburb of **Devonport** and perhaps the long golden beach at **Takapuna**.

Immediately south of the centre, two of Auckland's highest points, **Mount Eden** and **One Tree Hill** with its encircling **Cornwall Park**, provide wonderful vantage points for views of the city. The main reason for heading further south is to visit Saturday's **Otara Market**.

East of the city centre

The Auckland Domain separates the city from the fashionable inner suburbs of **Parnell** and **Newmarket**, the former an established, moneyed district of restaurants, boutiques and galleries with a modest line in churches and historical houses. To the east lies Auckland's prime waterfront, traced by **Tamaki Drive**, a twisting thoroughfare that skirts eight kilometres of Auckland's most popular city beaches – **Mission Bay**, **Kohimarama** and **St Heliers**. During the summer, the waterfront is the favoured hangout of rollerbladers and recreational cyclists. **Kelly Tarlton's Underwater World** is the only specific sight, but the harbour views out to Rangitoto and the Hauraki Gulf are excellent both from shore level and from a couple of headland viewpoints. The gentle hills behind are dotted with the secluded mansions of leafy Remuera, Auckland's old-money suburb. Further east is the suburban heartland of Panmure, Pakuranga and the former "fencible" settlement of **Howick**.

Parnell

Forty years ago **Parnell**, 2km east of the city centre, was not one of Auckland's most sought-after addresses but the restored kauri villas, fashionable shops and wealth of eating houses on the main thoroughfare, Parnell Road, now make it the place to be.

The district narrowly escaped a high-rise-concrete fate in the mid-1960s. Just as the bulldozers were closing in on its quaint but dilapidated shops and houses, eccentric dreamer **Les Harvey** raised enough money to buy the properties, whisking them from under the developers' noses. The area blossomed, with rent from the shops and restaurants funding much-needed restoration. Meanwhile, Harvey successfully campaigned against New Zealand's strict trading laws, with the result that during the 1970s and much of the 1980s Parnell was the only place in Auckland where you could shop on a Saturday. Parnell Road soon established an enviable reputation for chic clothes shops, swanky restaurants and, most evident of all, dealer art galleries.

Even if you're not buying, Parnell makes an appealing place to spend half a day, sipping lattes at pavement cafés and exploring some of the marks left by the area's long history. At the southern end of Parnell Road stands one of the world's largest wooden churches, the **Cathedral Church of St Mary** (Mon–Sat 10am–4pm, Sun 12.30–4pm; free), built from native timbers in 1886. Inside, the most interesting feature is a series of photos taken on the dramatic day in 1984 when the church was rolled in one piece from its original site across Parnell Road to join its more modern kin, the **Auckland Cathedral of the Holy Trinity** (Mon–Sat 10am–4pm, Sun 11am–5pm; free). The original Gothic chancel was started in 1959 then left half-finished until the late 1980s, when an airy nave with a Swiss chalet-style roof was grafted on, supposedly in imitation of the older church alongside. The result is shambolic. It is, however, worth

PARNELL & NEWMARKET

E (100m) & Parnell Rose Gardens (1km)

Highwic (200m) & Eden Garden (500m)

ACCOMMODATION		RESTAURANTS, CAFÉS & BARS			
Ascot Parnell	E	Asian Food Hall	13	Mustang Saloon	10
City Garden Lodge	C	Bodrum	12	Non Solo Pizza	5
International Backpackers	A	Chocolate Boutique	6	Pandoro	8
Lantana Lodge	B	Cibo	1	Portofino	3
Parnell Inn	D	Di Mare	4	Strawberry Alarm Clock	2
		Java Room	7	Sun World	11
		Mecca	9	Zarbo	14

admiring the modern stained-glass windows at the back; the bold and bright side panels symbolize Maori and Pakeha contributions to society. The most recent additions are the eighteen glass panels lining the nave. The more colourful set are by artist Robert Ellis but the most striking are by Maori artist Shane Cotton, who uses a unifying palette of muted reds, browns and greens.

The Gothic flourishes of the nineteenth-century church show the influence of New Zealand's prominent missionary bishop, George Selwyn. With his favoured architect, Frederick Thatcher, Selwyn left behind a trail of trademark wooden **Selwyn churches**, distinguished by vertical timber battens – examples include St Stephen's Chapel, down the hill at Judges Bay (see below) and All Saints' at Howick (see p.116). In 1857, Selwyn commissioned Thatcher to build the nearby **Kinder House**, at 2 Ayr St (Tues–Sun 11am–3pm; $4), for the headmaster of the new grammar school – a post filled by John Kinder, an accomplished watercolourist and documentary photographer. Built of rough-hewn Mount Eden volcanic rock, the house contains some interesting photos and reproductions of Kinder's paintings of nineteenth-century New Zealand. Just down the road is **Ewelme Cottage**, 14 Ayr St (Fri–Sun 10.30am–noon & 1–4.30pm; $7.50, $15 joint ticket with Highwic in Newmarket, see below and Alberton, see p.118; Ⓣ09/379 0202), a pioneer kauri house built as a family home in 1864 for the wonderfully named Howick clergyman Vicesimus Lush. The appeal of the place lies not so much in the house but in its furniture and possessions, left just as they were when Lush's descendants finally moved out in 1968, the family heirlooms betraying a desire to replicate the home comforts of their native Oxfordshire.

Judges Bay and Newmarket

From the cathedral you can continue south to Newmarket (see below) or northeast down Gladstone Road to Dove-Myer Robinson Park and the **Parnell Rose Gardens** (unrestricted entry; free), where five thousand bushes are at their glorious best from October to April. The park sweeps down to **Judges Bay**, named for three officers of the colony's Supreme Court who lived here from 1841, commuting to the courts on Symonds Street by rowboat. Bishop Selwyn used to stay with his friend, the Chief Justice William Martin, and had **St Stephen's Chapel** (usually closed) built nearby on a prominent knoll overlooking the harbour; the waterside Judges Bay Road leads to the open-air saltwater **Parnell Baths**.

The southern continuation of Parnell Road runs into Broadway, the main drag through fashion-conscious **NEWMARKET**, on the eastern flanks of Mount Eden. In the last decade it has transformed itself into one of the city's top shopping districts, complete with good places to eat. Just south of the shops, Great South Road is lined with motels (see p.101).

Specific sights are few in these parts, though you may be tempted by **Lionzone**, 380 Khyber Pass Rd (tours daily 9.30am, 12.15pm & 3pm; $15 bookings Ⓣ09/358 8366, Ⓦwww.lionzone.co.nz), a self-promoting introduction to New Zealand's largest brewery involving a historical perspective, a look at the packing lines and a chance to sample the product. It's better than your average brewery tour but at almost two hours a long-winded way to get a drink.

If you are staying over this way, consider visiting the Gothic timber mansion of **Highwic**, 40 Gillies Ave (Wed–Sun 10.30am–noon & 1–4.30pm; $7.50, $15 joint ticket with Ewelme Cottage in Parnell, see above, and Alberton, see p.118; Ⓣ09/524 5729), built as a "city" property by a wealthy rural auctioneer and landowner in 1862. The estate, complete with outbuildings and servants' quarters, gives a fair indication of the contrasting lives of the time. From here it's a short walk to **Eden Garden**, 24 Omana Ave (daily 9am–4.30pm; $5; Ⓦwww.edengarden.co.nz), an enclave created in a former quarry and tended by volunteers. There's year-round interest with a little of everything from water-gardens, cacti and proteas to Australasia's largest and most varied collection of camellias, in bloom from April to October.

Along the Tamaki Drive waterfront

Quay Street runs east from the foot of Queen Street, soon becoming **Tamaki Drive**, which separates Waitemata Harbour from Judges Bay. Crossing the causeway to Okahu Bay brings you to **Kelly Tarlton's Antarctic Encounter and Underwater World**, 23 Tamaki Drive (daily 9am–6pm; $29.50 valid all day; Ⓦwww.kellytarltons.co.nz). City tour **buses** and Stagecoach buses numbered #745 and #769 stop outside and Tarlton's shuttle runs from the Sky City atrium for $2 (one way). Opened in 1985, **Underwater World** was the brainchild of Kiwi diver, treasure hunter and salvage expert Kelly Tarlton, who converted some huge sewage tanks that, from 1910 until 1961, flushed the city's effluent into Waitemata Harbour on the outgoing tides. The aquarium pioneered the walk-through acrylic tunnels that have now become commonplace, and it is still a pleasure to stand on the moving walkway and glide through two tanks, both sculpted into the gnarled rock walls: one is dominated by flowing kelp beds, colourful reef fish and twisting eels; the other with smallish sharks, all appearing alarmingly close in the crystal-clear water. Newer tanks in the **Stingray Bay** section feature these graceful beasts, some with a two-metre wingspan. You can scuba dive with the sharks ($149) or stingrays ($69), or just snorkel with some less dangerous fish ($69).

The remaining sewage tanks form a couple of other diversions. **Antarctic Encounter** kicks off with some Antarctic history and an accomplished replica of the prefabricated hut used by Robert Falcon Scott and his team on their ill-starred 1911–12 attempt to be the first to reach the South Pole; the original hut still stands at Scott Base, New Zealand's Antarctic foothold. The capacious shelter has some unusual contents, including a pianola, a fully functional laboratory and a printing press – from which the *South Polar Times* rolled every few months throughout the three long years of the expedition. Contemporary footage and tales of their exploits add to the haunting atmosphere. Next up is a kind of penguin-atrium visited on a naff Disneyesque **Snow Cat** ride made bearable by the close-up views of king and gentoo penguins shooting through the water and hopping around on fake icebergs.

A little further along Tamaki Drive, Hapimana Street leads up onto the grassy range of Bastion Point and the **M.J. Savage Memorial Park**, the nation's austere Art Deco homage to its first Labour prime minister, who ushered in the welfare state in the late 1930s. More recently, **Bastion Point** was the site of a seventeen-month standoff between police and its traditional owners, the Ngati Whatua, over the subdivision of land for housing. The occupiers were removed in May 1977, but the stand galvanized the land-rights movement, and paved the way for a significant change in government attitude. Within a decade, the Waitangi Tribunal recommended that the land be returned.

Bastion Point looks down on **Mission Bay**, the closest of the truly worthwhile city **beaches**, where a grassy waterside reserve is backed by an enticing row of cafés and restaurants. Swimming is best here close to high tide; at other times the water remains shallow a long way out. Similar conditions prevail at the sheltered beaches of **Kohimarama** and **St Heliers Bay**, both a short way further along Tamaki Drive, which finishes on a high note with excellent harbour views from **Achilles Point**.

Howick

With your own transport it's easy enough to wind your way from St Heliers towards Howick, 15km east of central Auckland. Howick was one of four **fencible settlements** – along with Panmure and in the east, and Onehunga and Otahuhu in the south – set up around the young capital as a defence against disgruntled Maori and ambitious French. So-called "fencibles" (pensioned British soldiers) were re-enlisted to defend these sites for seven years, in return for free passage and a block of land. Skirmishes were few and the original shipments of men and their families formed the basis of small towns, all of which were subsequently engulfed by the Auckland conurbation. The best place to get a sense of fencible life is at the **Howick Historical Village**, Bells Road, Lloyd Elsmore Park (daily 10am–5pm, last admission 4pm; $13; ⓣ09/576 9506, ⓦwww.fencible.org.nz), 10km east of downtown between Pakuranga and Howick. Over thirty buildings dating from the 1840s and 1870s have been restored and re-sited from the four fencible settlements, and arranged in a believable village setting complete with a pond, a working blacksmith's and market gardens. Volunteers role-play the diligently researched lives of real 1850s characters as they amble between the tents and makeshift Maori-style *raupo* huts used on arrival, the officers' cottages, hostelry, school hall and village shop. The colonial village is 1km off Pakuranga Road, plied by all Howick & Eastern **buses**, which take about fifty minutes to get here from Britomart.

The suburb of **Howick**, a further 5km east, is a popular dwelling for East Asians, who have constructed huge, florid mansions on former farmland to the south of town which have become an attraction in their own right, mounting a challenge to Howick's more traditional sight, the distinctive, square-turreted **All Saints' Church**, the country's oldest active "Selwyn" church (see p.114), built in 1847.

West of the city centre

The suburbs of West Auckland developed later than their eastern counterparts, mainly because of their distance from the sea in the days when almost all travel was by ferry. The exceptions were the inner suburbs of Freeman's Bay, **Ponsonby** and Herne Bay, now enjoying renewed desirability for their proximity to the city and an unsurpassed array of restaurants, cafés and bars. Except for the flagging **Victoria Park Market**, sights are scarce until you get out to **Western Springs**, infant Auckland's major water source. The site is now part of **MOTAT**, a patchy transport and technology museum. To the south stands **Alberton**, once one of the city's grandest residences, but now just a brief distraction before you hit the wineries and West Coast beaches (see p.138 & pp.138–142).

Freeman's Bay, Ponsonby and Herne Bay

Victoria Street climbs the ridge west of Queen Street and descends into **Freeman's Bay**, a flat basin long since reclaimed from the Waitemata Harbour to accommodate early sawmilling operations. The land is now given over to the popular rugby and cricket fields of Victoria Park, all overshadowed by the 38m-high chimney of Auckland's defunct incinerator, occupied since 1984 by **Victoria Park Market** (daily 9am–6pm; ⓦwww.victoria-park-market.co.nz), a knot of stalls and restaurants. Check out the Awhina stall, full of handwoven *kete* (baskets) and carved *pounamu* (greenstone). The **Link bus** passes on its way to Ponsonby, and city tour buses also stop here.

Early in Auckland's European history, the areas around **Ponsonby** became fashionable neighbourhoods, only moving downmarket with the arrival of

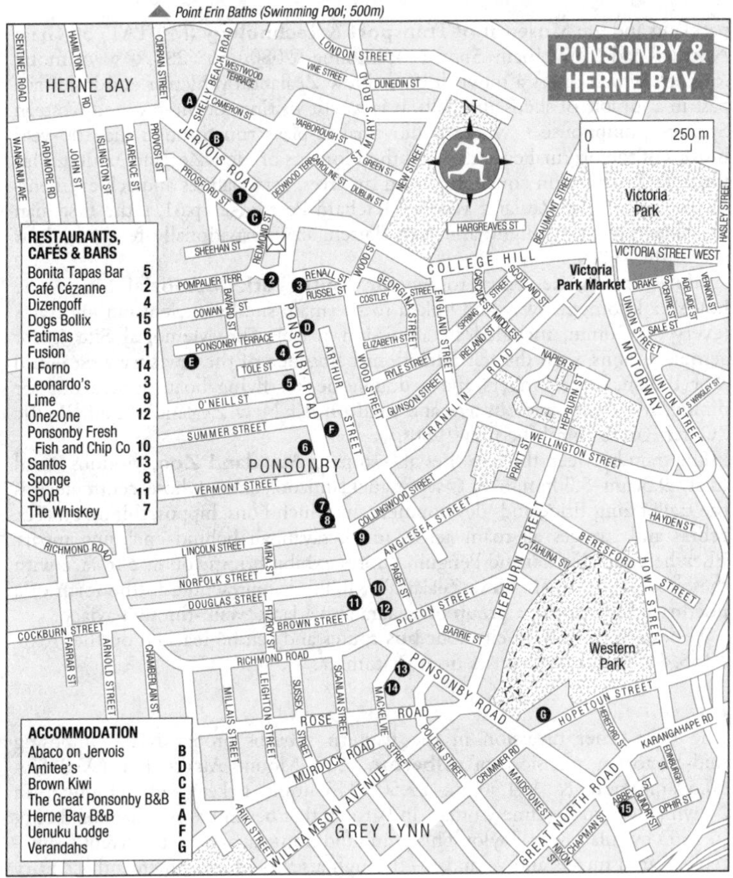

trams at the turn of the century. Inner-city living conditions deteriorated dramatically in the Depression of the 1930s, and the resulting low rents attracted large numbers of Pacific Islanders during the 1960s. Ponsonby took a bohemian turn in the Seventies and before long young professionals were moving in, restoring old houses and spending fistfuls of dollars in the cafés, restaurants and boutiques along Ponsonby Road. The street itself may not be beautiful, but the people sure are; musicians, actors and media folk congregate to lunch, schmooze and be seen in the latest fashionable haunt here. There's good reason to brave the poseurs, though, for some of New Zealand's classiest clothes shopping and eating.

Beyond Ponsonby lies **Herne Bay**, which followed its neighbours' economic ebb and flow and now ranks as Auckland's most expensive suburb, the merchants' water-view villas fetching astronomical prices.

Western Springs and MOTAT

In the late nineteenth century the burgeoning city of Auckland, with its meagre supply of unreliable streams, was heavily reliant on the waters of **Western Springs**, 4km west of the city. The area is now devoted to attractive parkland and the **Museum of Transport & Technology** (MOTAT) on Great North Road (daily 10am–5pm; $14; infoline ⓣ0800 668 286, ⓦwww.motat.org.nz), which offers a trawl through New Zealand's vehicular and industrial past in a jumble of sheds and halls. It is worth visiting for the restored Western Springs' pumphouse – where audiovisual displays run through the 100-year history of the original engine – and the Pioneers of New Zealand exhibit. This intriguing exhibition concentrates on the lives, personalities and achievements of two early New Zealand aviators: Richard Pearse (see p.611), the first man to achieve powered flight; and Jean Batten, an internationally recognized air ace of the 1930s.

Admission includes entry to the **Sir Keith Park Memorial Site** (same hours), a kilometre away and linked to the main site by ancient rattling trams (every 10–20min; included in admission price). The Memorial Site is for aeroplane buffs, with the star attractions being one of the few surviving World War II Lancaster bombers and a double-decker flying boat, decked out for dining in a more gracious age and used on Air New Zealand's South Pacific "Coral Route" until the mid-1960s.

The tram between the two sites also stops at **Auckland Zoo**, Motions Road (daily 9.30am–5.30pm; $18; ⓦwww.aucklandzoo.co.nz), whose centrepiece is the trailblazing Pridelands development, in which lions, hippos, rhinos, giraffes, zebras and gazelles all roam across mock savannah behind enclosing moats. Elsewhere, the Sealion and Penguin Shores exhibit brings you face to face with these loveable animals. New Zealand's wildlife is represented in the form of a nocturnal kiwi house, a group of tuatara and a large, walk-through aviary.

Western Springs is on city tour **bus** routes and can be reached on the #048, #163, #179 and #193 buses from Britomart.

Alberton

The only other diversion in the western suburbs proper is the imposing mid-Victorian mansion of **Alberton**, 100 Mount Albert Rd (Wed–Sun 10.30am–noon & 1–4.30pm; $7.50, $15 joint ticket with Highwic in Newmarket and Ewelme Cottage in Parnell) that began life as a farmstead built in 1863 by Allan Kerr-Taylor. This grand old house achieved its current form – replete with turrets and verandas – through a series of late-nineteenth-century additions befitting the centrepiece for an estate that once stretched over much of western Auckland.

The North Shore

The completion of the harbour bridge in 1959 provided the catalyst for the development of the **North Shore**, previously a handful of scattered communities linked by a web of ferries crisscrossing the harbour. By the early 1970s, the volume of traffic to the suburbs log-jammed the bridge – until a Japanese company attached a two-lane extension (affectionately dubbed "the Nippon Clip-ons") to each side. The bridge and its additional lanes can now be seen at close quarters on the Auckland Bridge Climb (see p.124).

The vast urban sprawl marches inexorably towards the Hibiscus Coast (see p.143), with most interest to be found in the maritime village of **Devonport** and the adjacent cove of **Cheltenham**, at the southern end of a long string of calm swimming **beaches**. Further north, try the more open and busier **Takapuna**, a short stroll from dozens of good cafés and reached by a host of buses mostly in the #800s and #900s, and **Long Bay** (buses #839, #858, #886 and others), with a grassy reserve and BBQ areas. All, to some degree, suffer

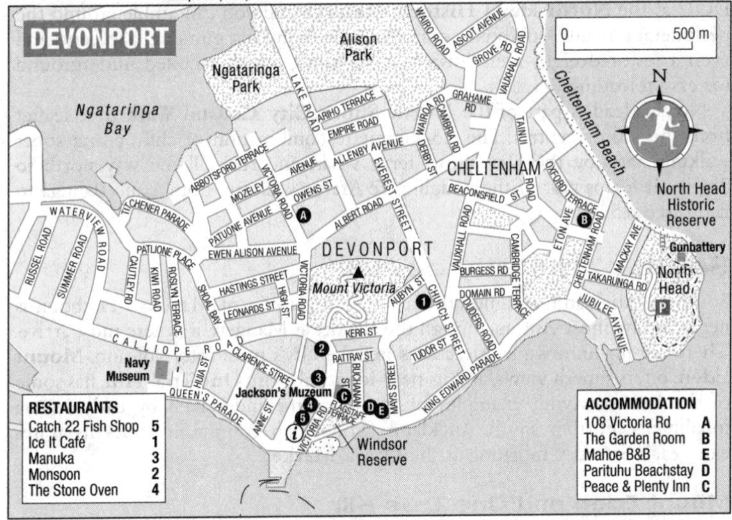

from the Auckland curse of being shallow at low tide, but beaches tend to be well attended throughout the summer.

Devonport

Devonport is one of Auckland's oldest suburbs, founded in 1840 and still linked to the city by a ten-minute ferry journey. The naval station was an early tenant, soon followed by wealthy merchants, who built fine kauri villas. Some of these are graced with little turrets ("widows' watches") that served as lookouts where the traders could scan the seas for their precious cargoes and wives watch hopefully for their returning husbands. Wandering along the peaceful streets and the tree-fringed waterfront past grand houses is the essence of Devonport's appeal and there's no shortage of tempting bookshops, small galleries, cafés and restaurants along the main street to punctuate your amblings.

Call at the **i-SITE visitor centre**, 3 Victoria Rd (daily 8.30am–5pm; ⓣ09/446 0677, ⓦwww.tourismnorthshore.org.nz), to pick up the *Old Devonport Walk* leaflet, or a map (both free).

Unless you have a soft spot for lifeless collections of uniforms and guns, you can blithely skip the **Navy Museum**, Spring Street (daily 10am–4.30pm; donation), in favour of a stiff walk up one of the two ancient volcanoes that back Devonport. The closest, about fifteen minutes' walk away, is **Mount Victoria** (Taka-a-ranga; unrestricted access for pedestrians; closed to vehicles from dusk on Thurs, Fri & Sat), from where you get fabulous gulf views. The hill was once the site of a Maori *pa* and fortified village and the remains of terraces and *kumara* pits can still be detected on the northern and eastern slopes. A kilometre east, the grass- and flax-covered volcanic plug of **North Head** (Maungauika; daily 6am–10pm, vehicles 6am–8pm; free) guards the entrance to the inner harbour, a strategic site for Maori before it was co-opted to form part of the young nation's coastal defences. In the wake of the "Russian Scares" of 1884–86, which were precipitated by the opening of the port of Vladivostok, North Head became Fort Cautley. It is now operated by

DOC as the **North Head Historic Reserve** and you can amble around the peripheral remains – pillboxes, concrete tunnels linking gun emplacements and even a restored eight-inch "disappearing gun", which recoiled underground for easy reloading.

North Head is part of the **North Shore City Coastal Walk** (free leaflet from the visitor centre). This 23-kilometre combination of clifftop and street walking starts by the Devonport ferry wharf and runs all the way north to Torbay. It forms part of the fledgling Te Araroa walkway from Cape Reinga to Bluff (see p.59).

South of the city centre

Southern Auckland, arching around the eastern end of Manukau Harbour, is neglected by most visitors, though the airport at Mangere is where most arrive. There are no unmissable attractions but the city's most lofty volcano, **Mount Eden**, offers superb views, and its near-identical twin, **One Tree Hill**, has some of the best surviving examples of the terracing undertaken by early Maori inhabitants. Further south, Auckland's Polynesian community plies its wares early each Saturday morning at the **Otara Market**.

Mount Eden and One Tree Hill

At 196m, **Mount Eden** (Maungawhau) is Auckland city's highest volcano and is named for George Eden, the first Earl of Auckland. The extensive views from the summit car park, just 2km south of the city, make it extraordinarily popular with tour buses, which grind up the steep slope through the day and well into the evening.

There's a more rewarding area 5km to the southeast around **One Tree Hill** (Maungakiekie; 183m), one of the city's most distinctive landmarks, topped by a 33m-tall granite obelisk. For a century, until just before the arrival of Europeans, Maungakiekie ("mountain of the kiekie plant") was one of the largest *pa* sites in the country; an estimated 4000 people were drawn here by the proximity to abundant seafood from both harbours and the rich soils of the volcanic cone, which still bears the scars of extensive earthworks including the remains of dwellings and *kumara* pits. The site was abandoned and then bought by the Scottish medic and "father of Auckland", Sir John Logan Campbell, one of only two European residents when the city was granted capital status in 1840. Through widespread land purchases and the founding of numerous shipping, banking and insurance companies, Campbell prospered, eventually becoming mayor in time for the visit of Britain's Duke and Duchess of Cornwall, in 1901. To commemorate the event, he donated his One Tree Hill estate to the people of New Zealand and named it **Cornwall Park** (daily 7am–dusk; free). The park puts on its best display around Christmas time, when avenues of pohutukawa trees erupt in a riot of red blossom. Campbell is buried at the summit, next to the obelisk, which bears inscriptions in Maori and English lauding Maori–Pakeha friendship. The summit is known in Maori as Te Totara-i-ahua, a reference to the single totara that originally gave One Tree Hill its name. Early

Devonport ferry

Devonport is best reached on the **Devonport ferry** (Mon–Thurs 6.10am–11.30pm, Fri & Sat 6.15am–1am, Sun 7.15am–10pm; every 30min; $10 return, bikes free), which forms part of the Getabout Auckland Discovery Pass (see p.98).

▲ Kumara-pit terracing on One Tree Hill

settlers cut it down in 1852, and Campbell planted several pines as a windbreak, a single specimen surviving until the millennium. Already ailing from a 1994 chainsaw attack by a Maori activist avenging the loss of the totara, the pine's fate was sealed by a similar attack in 1999 and the tree was removed the next year.

Free leaflets outlining a trail around the archeological and volcanic sites of the hill are available from the **visitor centre** (daily 10am–4pm), which is housed in **Huia Lodge**, originally built on the northern slopes by Campbell as a gatekeeper's house and now containing displays on the park and the man. Immediately opposite is **Acacia Cottage** (daily dawn–dusk; free), Campbell's original home and the city's oldest surviving building, built in 1841 and re-sited from central Auckland in the 1920s. Campbell devotees can round off their homage with a visit to the magisterial statue of him in mayoral garb at the northern end of the park by Manukau Road.

Fans of astronomy are better served on the southern side of One Tree Hill at the **Stardome Observatory**, just off Manukau Road, where a frequently changing schedule of 45-minute multimedia programmes are played out on the ceiling of the **planetarium** (Wed–Sun 8pm & 9pm, earlier in winter; $14; Ⓣ09/624 1246, Ⓦwww.stardome.org.nz). Weather and darkness permitting, the shows are followed by thirty minutes of telescope viewing.

Most of Cornwall Park is closed after dark but the observatory and the summit are accessible from the southern entrance off Manukau Road, which can be reached on **buses** #52, #68, #328, #347 and #472 from Britomart.

South Auckland

Beyond Cornwall Park is **South Auckland**, the city's poorest sector and the less-than-flatteringly-depicted gangland setting of Lee Tamahori's film *Once Were Warriors*. There isn't a great deal to see here, but neither is it a no-go zone, and **Otara Market** is certainly worth a look. Each Saturday morning, stalls sprawl across the car park of the Otara Town Centre. Plausibly billed as the largest Maori and Polynesian market in the world, its authenticity has been diluted by an influx of market traders flogging cheap clothes and shoddy trinkets. The tat is alleviated by displays of island-style floral print fabrics,

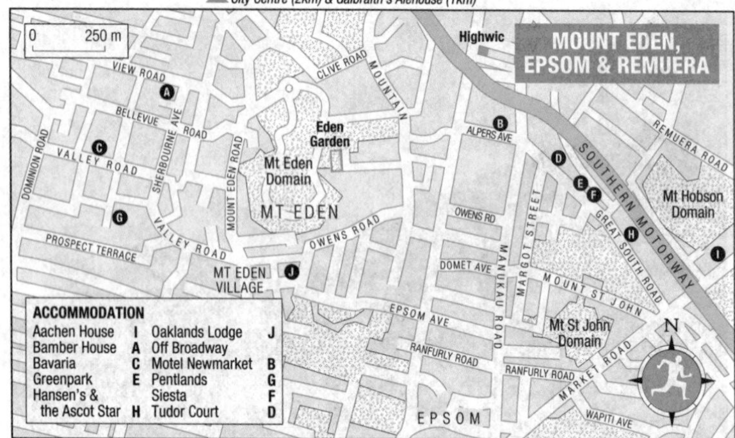

reasonably priced Maori carvings and truckloads of cheap fruit and veg. Your best bet is the food: there are stalls where you can buy home-made cakes and Maori bread, and a van has been ingeniously kitted out to produce an ersatz *hangi*. The market gets going around 6am and runs through to noon, so get there early. Take the Otara exit off the southern motorway or catch bus #487 or #497 for the fifty-minute journey from Britomart.

Walks, cruises and adventure activities

Few visitors linger long in Auckland, most being content to make travel arrangements then head out to the "real" New Zealand, but the city does boast a few adventure activities. There are diverting ways to get out in the harbour, including **sailing** an America's Cup yacht or **dolphin and whale safaris**, and two of Auckland's largest structures provide the framework for adrenalin thrills like the Auckland Bridge **bungy jump** and the Skyjump.

In addition, there are sightseeing tours to the city's West Coast beaches and gannet colony (see p.137) and **wine tours** to the wineries of Kumeu and Huapai (see p.138).

Walks

The most ambitious walking normally attempted by visitors to Auckland is a stroll through The Domain or a short hike up to one of the volcano-top viewpoints. The best of these have been threaded together as the well-marked **Coast to Coast Walkway**, a four-hour, thirteen-kilometre route straddling the isthmus from the Ferry Building on the Waitemata Harbour to Onehunga on the Manukau Harbour. By devoting a full day to the enterprise you can take in much of the best Auckland has to offer, including excellent harbour views from The Domain and the summits of Mount Eden and One Tree Hill, the Auckland Museum, Albert Park and numerous sites pivotal to the development of the city. All is revealed in the free "Coast to Coast Walkway" leaflet available from the tourist offices. At its northern end, the walkway links (by means of the Devonport Ferry) with the 23km North Shore City Coastal Walk (see p.120).

More ambitious hikers can head to Rangitoto Island (see p.146) or out into the hills, west to the Waitakere Ranges (see p.138).

Cruises, kayaking and dolphin safaris

Auckland is so water-focused that it would be a shame not to get out on the harbour at some point. The easiest and cheapest way is to hop on one of the **ferries** to Devonport (see p.120) or one of the outlying islands (see "Islands of the Hauraki Gulf" from p.146), but for prolonged forays, consider one of the many **cruises** available, while a **dolphin and whale safari** or **sea-kayaking** trip offers a more intimate experience.

Cruises and sailing

As well as their ferry services, Fullers offer a two-hour **Harbour Cruise** (daily 10.30am & 1.30pm; $30) that tours Viaduct Harbour and coasts past Devonport and the Harbour Bridge. Similar ground is covered when you crew on America's Cup **racing yachts** *NZL 40* or *NZL 41* (Ⓣ0800/724 569, Ⓦwww.sailnewzealand.co.nz; $140 for a two-hour sail or $195 as part of a team in a race between the two boats). Built for New Zealand's 1995 challenge in San Diego they are now based quayside at the Viaduct Harbour, and give a real sense of power and speed. The same company also offers an alternative way to get to the Bay of Islands: cruises on Peter Blake's old Whitbread Cup round-the-world yacht, *Lion*, run from Auckland to the Bay of Islands (Nov–May; 2 days & 2 nights one way; $595) with two departures weekly.

Romantics might prefer a gentler trip under sail with *Pride of Auckland* (Ⓣ09/373 4557, Ⓦwww.prideofauckland.com), based at the Maritime Museum and running a variety of cruises with coffee or a meal served on board: try the Coffee Cruise

Auckland's volcanic cones

Auckland is built on around **fifty small volcanoes**, yet the city hasn't been very respectful of its geological heritage. Even the exact number seems in doubt, not least because several cones have disappeared over the last 150 years, mostly chewed away by scoria and basalt quarrying.

That might sound a Herculean feat, but Auckland's largest volcano, Rangitoto Island out in the Hauraki Gulf (see p.146), is only 260m tall, and in the city itself none are taller than Mount Eden, just under 200 metres. Many are pimples barely 100m high that only just poke above the surrounding housing. Early on, **Maori** recognized the fertility of the volcanic soils, and set up *kumara* gardens on the lower slopes, usually protected by fortified *pa* sites around the summit. Europeans valued the elevated positions for water storage – most of the main volcanoes have **reservoirs** in the craters.

It is only in the last few decades that volcanic features have been protected from development, often by turning their environs into parks. City ordnances dictate that some summits can't be obscured from certain angles, and yet protection is limited. Debate raged for months recently when the edge of one volcano was marked for removal to make way for a motorway extension. Some see UNESCO World Heritage status as the best means of protection, but it is unlikely anything will happen soon.

In the meantime, the volcanoes make wonderful **viewpoints** dotted all over the city, notably from Mount Eden and One Tree Hill (see p.120) and from the top of Rangitoto Island (see p.146) where you can also explore lava caves.

Though it is over 600 years since the last eruption, the volcanic field remains active. No one knows when the next eruption will be, but it is unlikely to be through one of the existing volcanoes – meaning one day a new peak will emerge.

(3.45pm; 1hr 30min; $58), the Lunch Cruise (1pm; 1hr 30min; $68) or the Dinner Cruise (7pm; 2hr 30min; $95). All trips include entry to the Maritime Museum.

On most **summer weekends** you can help sail the *Søren Larsen* (Dec–Feb Sun 10am–3pm; $97 including lunch; ⓣ0800/707 265, ⓦwww.sorenlarsen.co.nz), a Danish Baltic trader built of oak in 1949 and later fitted with a nineteenth-century sailing rig. This majestic vessel starred in the 1970s TV series *The Onedin Line* and led the First Fleet re-enactment that formed a part of the Australian bicentennial celebrations in 1987. Passengers are free to participate – steering, hauling sheets and climbing the rigging – though maritime instruction tends to be a larger component of the midweek trips to Hauraki Gulf and Bay of Islands (5 nights; $1400).

Dolphin swimming and kayaking

The Hauraki Gulf is excellent territory for spotting marine mammals, best seen on five-hour dolphin-and whale-watching trips run by **Dolphin & Whale Safari** ($140; ⓣ0800/383 940, ⓦwww.dolphinsafari.co.nz) from Viaduct Harbour. Educational and entertaining trips head out daily (11am & 4pm, weather permitting) on a 20m catamaran and dolphins are spotted ninety percent of the time (you get a fifty percent discount on a second trip if none are seen), although strict controls restrict contact and passengers only occasionally get to swim with them. Bryde's whales and orcas are also frequently seen. For the same price you can do much the same trip with **DolphinPlanet** on *Dreamweaver* (ⓣ0800/220 111, ⓦwww.dolphinplanet.co.nz), an 18m catamaran.

For **kayaking** head to Fergs Kayaks, 12 Tamaki Drive, Okahu Bay (ⓣ09/529 2230, ⓦwww.fergskayaks.co.nz), who run guided trips 7km across the Waitemata Harbour to Rangitoto Island (9.30am & 5.30pm; 6hr; $120) hiking to the summit, then paddling back. They also do trips 3km to Devonport with a hike up North Head (9.30am & 5.30pm; 4hr; $95). In both cases, the later departure gives you a chance to paddle by moon or torchlight.

If you'd rather go it alone, Fergs offer **kayak rental** in either single sea kayaks ($20 1hr, $35 a half-day) or doubles ($40 1hr, $70 a half-day).

Adventure activities

Auckland has long tried to catch up with the rest of New Zealand by offering adventurous pursuits but walking to the top of the Harbour Bridge or jumping off the Skytower don't really match up, thankfully canyoning in the Waitakere Ranges does. However, if gentler activities call to you, try **rollerblading** along Tamaki Drive (shared with bikes and pedestrians) with good harbour views; in-line skates can be rented from Fergs Kayaks (see above) for $15 an hour.

For something a little out of the ordinary, consider a trip with **Potiki Adventures** (ⓣ0800/692 3836, ⓦwww.potikiadventures.com), run by a couple of Maori women who are passionate about the great outdoors and bring a Maori worldview to their Auckland-based full-day trips ($145 each). Snorkelling and kayaking at Goat Island (see p.172) are the objectives for their Marine Reserve Adventure (Mon, Wed & Fri, $185); the Urban Maori Experience (Tues & Sat, includes morning and afternoon tea) visits One Tree Hill, the Waitakere Ranges and Whatipu beach and gives you a change to learn flax weaving; and there's also the option of abseiling a waterfall (Thurs & Sun) on a trip that visits the gannets at Muriwai and a Maori tattoo studio.

Auckland Bridge Climb and Bungy

Based on the Sydney Harbour bridge climb, the **Auckland Bridge Climb** ($100, $80 for the abbreviated climb; ⓣ09/625 0445, ⓦwww.ajhackett.com), gives you the opportunity to sample excellent city views from the highest point on the city's harbour, crossing some 65 metres above the Waitemata Harbour. The ninety-minute trip doesn't actually involve climbing, just strolling along steel walkways under the roadway then emerging onto the upper girders by means of ordinary stairs, while clipped by safety harness to a cable. Guides relate detail on the bridge's fulcrums, pivots and cantilevers. Reservations are essential and anyone over seven can go. Cameras are not allowed but there'll be someone on hand to take a snap and sell it to you later.

If you crave an adrenalin rush, the **Auckland Bridge Bungy** (same contact details) should do the trick, with a 40m leap out over the water that will set you back $100 and includes a T-shirt.

Skyjump and Vertigo Climb

Auckland's 328-metre Skytower is the venue for two adventure activities, both exploiting its position as New Zealand's tallest building. On the **Skyjump** (daily 10am–6pm, and as late as 10pm on busy summer evenings; $195; booking recommended on ⓣ0800/759 586, ⓦwww.skyjump.co.nz) – claimed as the world's highest tower-based jump – you plummet 192m towards the ground in a kind of arrested freefall at 75kph, with a cable attached to your back. Alternatively, go for the more drawn-out sense of dread engendered by the **Skywalk** ($115, weather dependent ⓦwww.skywalk.co.nz), a nervous stroll round a 1.2m- wide walkway, 192m above the pavement. Although you are attached by safety line to a rail several feet above your head, there are no handrails and so confidence in your sense of balance suddenly becomes very important, for 75 minutes (total time including harness fitting and safety briefing). Two groups of six people can be on the walkway at any one time enjoying, the stupendous views.

Canyoning

About the most fun you can have in a wetsuit, particularly around Auckland, is **canyoning**, a combination of swimming, abseiling, jumping into deep pools and sliding down rock chutes. Two companies operate in the Waitakere Ranges, both making pick-ups in Auckland. Canyonz (ⓣ0800/422 696, ⓦwww.canyonz.co.nz) operates in Blue Canyon and offers a great variety of activities including an 8m waterfall-jump or abseil (standard full-day trip $175, 7hr). Awol Adventures (ⓣ0800/462 965, ⓦwww.awoladventures.co.nz) runs a similar trip near Piha, with more emphasis on abseiling. Join the day-trip ($155), half-day trip ($125) or go **night canyoning** ($145) with just a headtorch and glowworms for illumination. Both companies' trips often end up with a visit to one of the West Coast surf beaches.

Canyonz also offers day-trips down the magnificent **Sleeping God** canyon near Thames (Oct–May only; $235). In this wonderfully scenic spot you descend 300m in a series of twelve drops using slides, and abseils as long as 70m (some through the waterfall), with the opportunity to leap 13m from a rock ledge into a deep pool. It's tough enough to require previous abseiling experience.

Eating

Aucklanders take their eating seriously and there is no shortage of **restaurants**. For a more casual experience, **cafés** or **pubs** (see p.131), offer decent meals for under $20. On a fine summer evening it is tempting to flock to the waterside restaurants and bars of **Viaduct Harbour**, though it can be pricey and those on a budget will do better up on **Karangahape Road**. Dedicated foodies will find the best areas for grazing in the inner-city suburbs, chiefly along **Ponsonby Road**, Auckland's culinary crucible, or **Parnell Road**, the other main eat street.

City centre and Viaduct Harbour

The centre of Auckland is the best place to grab something quick during the day, with dozens of places geared to **lunching** city workers. Among the most popular are the **food halls**, seating plazas surrounded by inexpensive vendors, often in the basements of shopping arcades that spur off Queen Street. Downtown's eating scene is spiced with an increasing number of **Asian restaurants**, although in the evening parts of the city feel dead. **High Street** and **Lorne Street** are both good hunting grounds, but nowhere are the restaurants so densely packed as around the **Viaduct Harbour** – where good quality food is readily available but the venues lack soul and zealously embrace ostentation for its own sake, charging above the city average.

Food halls and takeaways

Atrium Food Gallery Elliot St. Slightly more salubrious than the competition, with a wide range of counters – Vietnamese, sushi, bagels, pizza, kebabs, roasts, Chinese – plus a bakery and decent coffee. Mon–Thurs 7am–6pm, Fri 7am–8pm, Sat–Sun 9am–5pm.

Food Alley 9 Albert St. Spartan, inexpensive two-level food hall with 13 kitchens exhibiting a strong East Asian bias. Open daily 10.30am–10pm.

Force Entertainment Food Hall In the basement of the 12-screen multiplex cinema, Queen St. This large food hall provides everything from pizza to Japanese for the hungry impatient cheapskate. Open daily 10am–10pm.

Cafés and restaurants

Euro Princes Wharf ⓣ09/309 9866. This popular, trendy place offers very high-quality food and service. Their signature dish of rotisserie chicken on a bed of mashed potato and peanut slaw ($32) is excellent.

French Café 210 Symonds St ⓣ09/302 2770. Consistently one of the finest restaurants in the city. The ever-changing seasonal menu leans towards contemporary European cuisine and the service is faultless. Six courses $90, add another $60 for matching wines. Dinner Tues–Sat plus Fri lunch.

Grand Harbour 18–28 Customs St West ⓣ09/357 6889. More opulent than most of the city's Chinese places and heavily patronized by the Chinese community, this bustling modern restaurant is popular for business lunches and serves great *yum cha*.

The Grove St Patrick's Square, Wyndham St ⓣ09/368 4129, ⓦwww.thegroverestaurant.co.nz. Tucked away off a quiet square in the city centre, this sophisticated place turns out some of the best modern New Zealand cuisine in Auckland. Mains cost $35 upwards and there are both omnivore ($100) and vegetarian ($80) tasting menus. Wine pairings are $80 extra. Closed Sat lunch and Sun.

Harbourside Seafood Bar & Grill Upstairs in the Ferry Building, 99 Quay St ⓣ09/307 0556. Classy but relaxed seafood restaurant. If it's warm, reserve a table on the harbour-view terrace and feast on beautifully prepared and presented fish and crustaceans. Expect to part with at least $75 for a full meal, not including drinks.

Merlot 23 O'Connell St ⓣ09/309 5456. Intimate, unpretentious candlelit restaurant with something of the feel of a French bistro. Mains from $26 and a selection of over a hundred wines.

Mezze Bar 1a Little High St ⓣ09/307 2029. Airy café offering respite from the buzz of Queen St. Great for tapas and meze ($9–20), with broadly Mediterranean and Middle Eastern leanings. Open for lunch and dinner with dishes such as Spanish tortilla and grilled mushroom on polenta or Moroccan meat bake ($25–30), washed down with a broad selection of beers and wines.

Middle East Café 23a Wellesley St, west. Tiny, simple, camel-themed eat-in or take-out unlicensed café that's an Auckland institution, deservedly celebrated for its *chawarma* and falafel ($7–10), both cloaked in creamy garlic, spicy tomato sauce or hot chilli sauce. Closed Sat lunch, & Sun.

New Gallery Café 18–26 Wellesley St, inside the New Gallery ⓣ09/302 0226. Excellent daytime

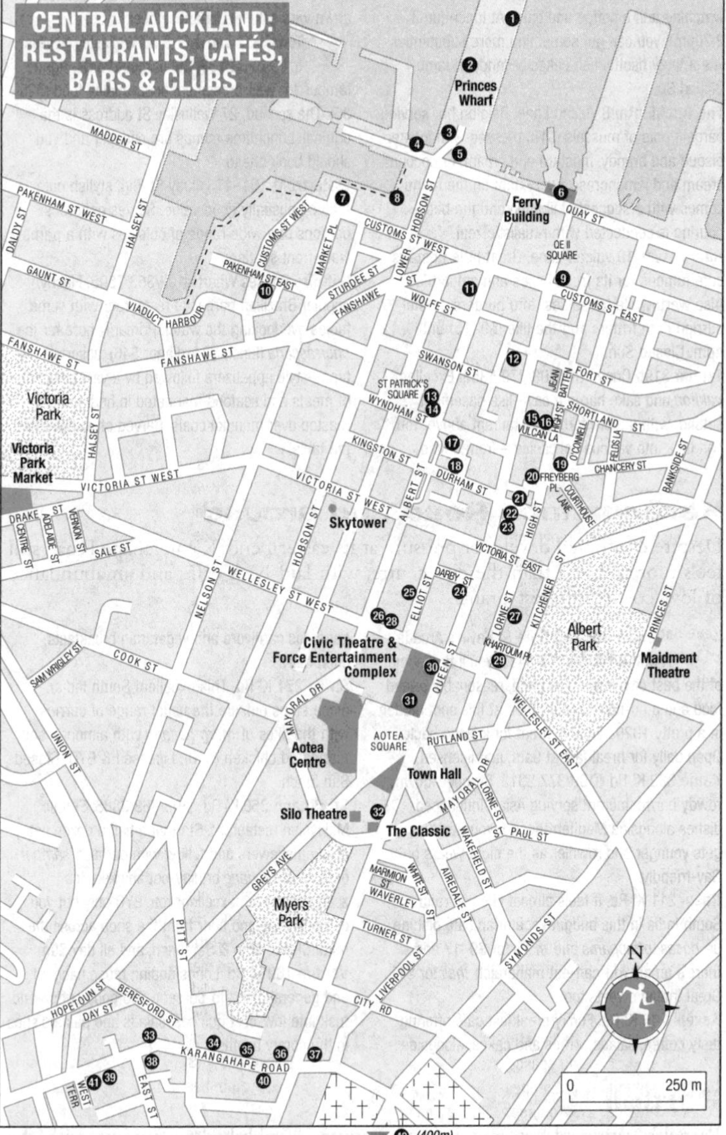

RESTAURANTS & CAFÉS

- Alleluya Bar and Café 35
- Atrium Food Gallery 25
- Bellini 1
- Euro 2
- Food Alley 11
- Force Entertainment Food Hall 31
- French Café 42
- Grand Harbour 10
- The Grove 13
- Harbourside Seafood Bar & Grill 6
- Kamo 41
- Merlot 19
- Mezze Bar 22
- Middle East Café 28
- New Gallery Café 29
- The Occidental 15
- Rasoi 34
- Raw Power 16
- Revels 40
- Satya 33
- Sri Pinang 39
- Tanuki 32
- Tony's 26 & 27
- Verona 36
- Waterfront 4
- Wildfire 3

BARS & CLUBS

- The Blue Stone Room 18
- Boogie Wonderland 9
- Crow Bar 17
- Degree 4
- Elbow Room 21
- Family 38
- Fu Bar 23
- Globe 24
- Khuja Lounge 37
- The Loaded hog 8
- Minus5 5
- O'Hagan's 7
- Rakino's 20
- Shakespeare Tavern 14
- Starks 30
- Tabac 12

oasis, with a comfortable terrace for people-watching and a coffee and cake. At lunch (until 2.30pm), you can get something more substantial like a tasty risotto, fish cakes or tandoori lamb. Closed Sun.

The Occidental 8 Vulcan Lane. Belgian bar serving bargain pots of mussels ($18) dressed with lobster bisque and brandy, mustard and cream, or coconut cream and lemongrass. Every item on the menu comes with a suggested libation and the beer-pouring is conducted with ritualistic zeal.

Raw Power 10 Vulcan Lane. Great little upstairs café famous for its fresh juices and smoothies. Also worthwhile for salads, tofu burgers, falafel, curried corn fritters and the like ($9–15) until 4pm. Closed Sun.

Tanuki 319b Queen St ⓣ09/379 5353. Excellent *yakitori* and sake bar in a cave-like basement setting, with a more formal restaurant above. You can tuck into various delicacies – from grilled cloves of garlic to teriyaki chicken, all washed down with sake or Japanese beer.

Tony's 32 Lorne St & 27 Wellesley St West ⓣ09/373 2138. Steak restaurants, rightly famous for well-presented, good-quality food ($25–35). The second, 27 Wellesley St address is the original. Lunchtime menus are cheaper and you should book ahead.

Waterfront 161–173 Quay St. Big, stylish café that is unusually good value. Serves generous portions of a wide range of cuisines with a prime waterfront seating.

Wildfire Princes Wharf ⓣ09/353 7595. Flashy, popular Brazilian barbecue restaurant with some tables overlooking the water. Primarily here for the *churrascaria* (lunch $34, dinner $46), assorted tapas-style appetizers followed by a vast selection of meats and seafood marinated in herbs and roasted over manuka coals. Carved off skewers at the table.

Karangahape Road and around

Despite continued developer pressure at its eastern end, Karangahape Road still feels more relaxed than the city centre, with laid-back cafés and an abundance of low-cost ethnic restaurants.

Alleluya Bar and Café St Kevin's Arcade, 179 K' Rd ⓣ09/377 8482. You'll find some of the best city views plus good, reasonably priced food and a no-nonsense attitude at this spot hidden in a pretty 1920s arcade, great for kicking back. Open daily for breakfast at 9am, and licensed.

Kamo 382 K' Rd ⓣ09/377 2313. Stripped-down, rowdy bar/restaurant serving Asian-influenced dishes alongside Mediterranean favourites that gets younger and rowdier as the night wears on. Gay-friendly.

Rasoi 211 K' Rd. It feels almost like you're in South India in this budget vegetarian café dishing up *dosas*, *uttappams* and *thalis* for $9–17 and there's an all-you-can-eat maharajah *thali* for $17. Great Indian sweets too.

Revels 146 K' Rd. Funky breakfast café offering tasty coffee, salads, wraps and cakes, alongside generous carnivore and vegetarian breakfasts, open daily.

Satya 271 K' Rd. This excellent South Indian place steps outside the usual range of curries with the likes of *murg badami* with almonds and marinated chicken ($18). Licensed & BYO. Closed Sun lunch.

Sri Pinang 356 K' Rd ⓣ09/358 3886. Simple Malaysian restaurant. Start with half a dozen satay chicken skewers and follow with perhaps *sambal* okra, beef *rendang* or clay-pot chicken rice scooped up with excellent roti. BYO only but you can buy wine and beer from the shop across the road. Closed Mon & Sat lunch, and all day Sun.

Verona 169 K' Rd. Longstanding muso hangout and general place-to-be-seen. Sip good coffee and tuck into low-cost quiches, salads and pasta dishes in the comfy booths.

Parnell

Parnell's eating places split into two camps: established restaurants with the accent on fine dining, and trendier, cheaper cafés catering to younger devotees and backpackers. See map on p.113.

Chocolate Boutique 323 Parnell Rd. Compact chocolate emporium selling handmade choccies and a range of chocolate (and coffee) drinks. Tables inside and out. Stays open until 10pm for that post-dinner dessert.

Cibo 91 St George's Bay Rd ⓣ09/303 9660. Fine dining a little off the main drag, and worth seeking out. Reliable favourites such as steak and duck leg are available but there's always something unexpected on the menu. Popular for business lunches so probably best left for evening visits. Mains $35–38.

Di Mare Shop 9, 251 Parnell Rd ⓣ09/300 3260. One of the best surf and turf restaurants in the city, serving delicious traditional and innovative dishes to an appreciative crowd, in an intimate, back alley courtyard restaurant off the main road. Well worth making the effort to find, particularly for the modern take on paella ($30 on request).

Java Room 317 Parnell Rd ⓣ09/366 1606. Intimate dinner-only restaurant serving loosely Indonesian-influenced dishes but also dim sum, spicy fish cakes, hot ruby prawns ($23) and Siamese snapper ($23).

Non Solo Pizza 259 Parnell Rd ⓣ09/379 5358. Choose the big airy room or more intimate patio for classy, but not too expensive Italian cuisine. The name means "Not just Pizza", but that is the specialty, done in crispy style with imaginative but classic Italian toppings.

Portofino 156 Parnell Rd ⓣ09/373 3740. Basic but reliable trattoria without the pretensions of much of this street, serving pasta and pizza around $20.

Strawberry Alarm Clock 119 Parnell Rd. Low-key café popular for inexpensive breakfasts, a snack or just hanging out over good coffee either inside or out in the rear courtyard.

Newmarket

There's plenty of good eating in Newmarket but unless you are staying nearby or have come here to shop it's a bit of a stretch from the centre.

Asian Food Hall Newmarket Plaza, Teed St, next to the fish market. Malaysian, Thai, Japanese, Korean and a couple of Chinese dishes all served up at bargain prices.

Bodrum 2 Osborne St. Boisterous Turkish restaurant, evenings only, serving chicken moussaka ($24), kebab plates ($26.50) and the obligatory baklava and *locum* for dessert. Low tables and cushions available for those who can sit cross-legged for an hour. Closed Mon.

Mecca 61 Davis Crescent. Relaxed café with speedy service dishing up excellent blueberry pancakes with fresh fruit ($11) and well-presented breakfast and lunch dishes including Thai chicken curry ($15).

Sun World 2 York St. Bustling, budget Chinese place popular with Asian English-language students. There's little attempt to appease delicate Western palates but everything is fresh and promptly served.

Zarbo 24 Morrow St. Auckland's finest deli/café with a fabulous range of products from around the world put to good use in a delicious range of breakfast and lunch dishes ($9–20). Lunch finishes at 3pm but they stay open until 5pm for salads, cakes and coffee.

Tamaki Drive: Okahu Bay and Mission Bay

If you find yourself peckish while visiting Kelly Tarlton's, rollerblading along Tamaki Drive, kayaking or out for a swim at Mission Bay, try one of this selection from a long line round the bay.

Bar Comida 81 Tamaki Drive. Quality version of the typical Kiwi cover-all-the-bases café/restaurant/bar with wood-fired gourmet pizza, great coffee and desserts and a strong line in tapas and Persian flatbreads, applied to anything from BLT to grilled vegetables with hummus.

Hammerheads 19 Tamaki Drive, Okahu Bay, by Kelly Tarlton's ⓣ09/521 4400. The perfect spot for a upmarket lunch on a sunny day, preceded by a cocktail while you admire the tremendous views over the water to the city skyline. Mains mostly under $37.

Tonino's Pizzeria 35 Tamaki Drive ⓣ09/528 8935, ⓦwww.toninos.co.nz. Small good-value Italian restaurant with tasty pasta dishes ($15–20) and pizza ($18–32) to dine in and take away. Licensed & BYO.

Ponsonby and Herne Bay

At the cutting edge of Auckland's foodie scene, **Ponsonby Road** is a street where devotion to style is as important as culinary prowess. But don't be intimidated; the food is mostly excellent and competition keeps prices reasonable. Popular daytime cafés frequently ease into more rambunctious drinking later on. See map on p.117.

Bonita Tapas Bar 242 Ponsonby Rd. Atmospheric little bar serving delicious tapas plates from $10–15 – try the tiny flavour-packed meatballs. Closed Sun & Mon.

Café Cézanne 296 Ponsonby Rd. This casual, ramshackle place is a welcome retreat from the glitz of the rest of Ponsonby Rd; great for reading the papers over hearty breakfasts, excellent quiches or huge wedges of cake.

Dizengoff 256 Ponsonby Rd ⓣ09/360 0108. Unlicensed breakfast and lunch café specializing in wonderful bagels, some Jewish deli favourites and luscious chargrilled vegetables, all at reasonable prices.

Fatimas 240 Ponsonby Rd ⓣ09/376 9303. If you fancy home-made, Middle Eastern food then look no further than this friendly wee café/bar where nothing costs more than $15.

Fusion 32 Jervois Rd. Friendly, relaxed daytime café with tables inside and in the small garden out the back. A good range of breakfasts all day, plus light lunches, great coffee and tasty fruit lassi drinks.

Il Forno 55 MacKelvie St. Great daytime bakery and café, especially notable for its delectable made-on-the-premises cakes, pastries and coffee, but also doing fine sandwiches and rolls.

Leonardo's 263 Ponsonby Rd ⓣ09/361 1556. About as authentic an Italian restaurant as you'll find in Auckland. No pizza, but a great antipasto plate ($31), pasta and gnocchi dishes (around $25–30), and *segundi piatti* ($30–35) such as fish in a paper parcel with garlic. Weekend lunches & dinner nightly except Mon, and Wed is live opera night.

One2One 121 Ponsonby Rd. Relaxed longstanding café where the fluffies (cappuccino foam), and a sandpit in the grapevine-shaded courtyard make it a great place for those with kids. Good coffee, plus excellent muffins and a blackboard full of macrobiotic and organic food.

Ponsonby Fresh Fish and Chip Co 127 Ponsonby Rd ⓣ09/378 7885. One of the best fish, chips and burger takeaways around, frequently lauded in *Metro* magazine's annual readers' poll and always busy, so call ahead or trot across the road to the *SPQR* bar and wait. The vegetarian burgers are sensational. Unlicensed.

Santos 114 Ponsonby Rd. Hip little café serving some of the best coffee on Ponsonby Rd and tasty panini.

SPQR 150 Ponsonby Rd ⓣ09/360 1710. Dimly lit and eternally groovy restaurant/bar that's always popular for its quality Italian-influenced food (especially the pizzas). Many treat it more as a bar and venue for spotting actors and rock stars. Excellent cocktails and a wide range of wines (sold by the glass).

▲ Dining alfresco at SPQR, Ponsonby Road

Devonport

Devonport has variety but few venues that live up to Auckland's better foodie hangouts. See map on p.119.

Catch 22 Fish Shop 19 Victoria Rd. On a nice evening it's hard to beat fish and chips or a straightforward burger on the beach. Pick some up at *Catch 22* and wander over. Closed Mon.

Ice It Café 29 Church St ⓣ09/446 3333. On a suburban street away from the bustle of Victoria Rd, this delightful daytime café has outside tables shaded by a nice tree. Delicate lemon syrup cakes go down well with coffee, and they apply equal attention to their lunches.

Manuka 49 Victoria Rd ⓣ09/445 7732. Quality restaurant specializing in pasta, wood-fired pizza ($21–28) and a few steak and chicken dishes, but good at any time of the day for light snacks and salads or just for coffee and cake.

Monsoon 71 Victoria Rd ⓣ09/445 4263. Value-for-money Thai/Malaysian place with tasty dishes such as fish and tiger prawns in a red curry sauce for around $18–23. Evenings only, from 5pm. BYO & licensed.

The Stone Oven 5 Clarence St. Large, bustling bakery and café with a solid reputation for organic sourdough, cakes and pastries to take away or eat in; also popular for all-day breakfasts (starting at 6.30am), light lunches, quiches, pies and stuffed panini.

Drinking, nightlife and entertainment

With a million plus people to entertain, there's always something going on in Auckland. The best way to find out **what's on** is to pick up the *New Zealand Herald, the Vulture*, an Auckland guide to music, art, theatre and film or the free *Groove Guide*, a music and clubbers listing and review. For more specialist gig information, buy the monthly *Real Groove* ($7.90), available from most record store and magazine shops or go to the entertainment guide section of the bFM radio station website ⓦwww.95bfm.co.nz.

At any time you should be able to find some quality local **bands** bashing away in a club or dedicated venue but due to New Zealand's remoteness, acts from North America or Europe are less frequent visitors. Auckland's **arts scene** is thriving, and on any night of the week there should be a choice of a couple of plays, comedy and dance or opera.

Pubs and bars

In Auckland, as in much of the rest of the country, the distinction between eating and drinking places is frequently blurred. The factor uniting those listed is their dedication to **drinking**: some are bars that may serve food; others are old-time hotels in the Kiwi tradition, though even these have been dramatically smartened up and do a sideline in inexpensive counter meals.

Drinking hours are relaxed, with most places staying open until 1–2am at weekends.

Viaduct Harbour, city centre and K' Road

See map on p.127.

The Blue Stone Room 9 Durham Lane ⓣ09/302 0930. Wood-floored, stone-walled former store from the 1850s right in the heart of the city. Monteith's real-ale-style beers predominate, there are pub-style meals and covers bands play at weekends.

Crow Bar 26 Wyndham St. Stylish cocktail bar whose upstairs Trophy Room provides a variation on the general theme of funky piped music and sophisticated chatter.

Degree 204 Quay St. Typical harbour-basin venue with a long bar and high chairs that serves good seafood and rewards the late-stayers with after-dinner DJing guaranteed to bring on crushed toes or indigestion.

Gay and lesbian Auckland

New Zealand has a fairly small but progressive and proactive **gay culture**, and Auckland and Wellington vie to be at its centre. Auckland hosts the annual **Hero Festival** (Ⓦwww.hero.org.nz), held over three weeks in the middle of February, which includes a tour around gay gardens, a tennis tournament, a lesbian tea party and a "big gay out" afternoon festival. It culminates in the **Hero Party** , a major dance event (and after-party) usually held around K' Road.

The best way to link into the scene is to pick up the free, fortnightly *Express* magazine (Ⓦwww.gayexpress.co.nz), found in racks in gay-friendly shops, cafés and bars, at branches of Maggazzino and at the Out! Bookshop, 37 Anzac Ave (Ⓣ09/377 7770). Alternatively get a copy of the free *GayNZ* leaflet and New Zealand venue guide. For counselling and support, contact the **Gay and lesbian helpline** (Ⓣ09/303 3584; Mon–Fri 10am–10pm, Sat & Sun 5–10pm; Ⓦwww.gayline.org.nz).

The gay scene is fairly low-key, woven into the café/bar mainstream of Ponsonby, Parnell and Newmarket, and the western end of K' Road, where strip clubs mingle freely with gay bars and cruise clubs. Among the **restaurants** and **bars**, *SPQR* on Ponsonby Road is always a good starting point, as is *Kamo* on K' Road.

For specifically gay **bars and clubs** try:

Dorothy's Sister 265 Ponsonby Rd. Great café and focal point for the scene at the far end of Ponsonby Rd.

Family Bar 270 K' Road. The focal point of K' Road's gay scene, operating as a café and bar during the day and getting more raucous into the evening. Expect karaoke on Wednesday and drag shows at weekends when basement club *GAY* comes alive.

Elbow Room 12 Durham St East. Fashionable little bar that is often quiet midweek but bouncy at the weekends, with live music.

Globe 229 Queen St, under *base Auckland Central* (see p.103). Long, thin, noisy backpackers-get-drunk bar that's full most nights of the week.

The Loaded Hog Viaduct Harbour. Vast, bustling, glass-walled bar with America's Cup paraphernalia around the walls. There's seating on the quay, bar food, an impressive range of wines and four micro-brewed beers. Turns clubby late on Fri & Sat nights.

Minus5 Princes Wharf Ⓣ09/377 6702, Ⓦwww.minus5experience.com. Stand in a room entirely sculpted from ice supping cocktails from a chunky ice "glass". The $30 cover charge gets you half an hour, a cocktail and coat.

O'Hagan's 101–103 Customs St West. Irish-themed pub spilling out onto the Market Square at the Viaduct Harbour. Guinness, Kilkenny and English ales on tap, a good range of meals for around $25 and occasional live bands.

Rakino's 1st floor, 35 High St. Daytime café with tables shaped like Hauraki Gulf islands. On Thurs, Fri & Sat evenings it transforms into a compact venue serving up anything from live jazz to DJs.

Shakespeare Tavern 61 Albert St. Unreconstructed Kiwi pub raised above the pack by brewing a handful of commendable ales and lagers. Best on the first-floor terrace.

Starks Corner of Queen & Wellesley sts. Cool, relaxing and stylish little cocktail bar offering the best gin and tonics in town, people-watching and highly polished professional service.

Tabac 6 Mills Lane. Cosy establishment co-owned by former Crowded House singer/songwriter Neil Finn; good for a drink in the bar (where there's often a DJ), or take it through to the sofas of the intimate Velvet Room out back. Closed Sun & Mon.

The suburbs

Dogs Bollix Corner of Karangahape & Newton rds. See map, p.117. Lively ersatz Irish bar with a soft spot for visitors, plus cheap bar food and live music every night (originals and cover bands).

Galbraith's Alehouse 2 Mount Eden Rd. See map, p.122. Micro-brew pub with some of New Zealand's finest English-style ales plus a handful of other local brews and fifty-odd bottled varieties. Back-to-basics bar meals include liver and onions and fish and chips – all at very reasonable prices.

Lime 167 Ponsonby Rd, Ponsonby. See map, p.117. Longstanding locals' favourite with a reputation as a singles bar – get more than thirty people and you're so close you can't help striking up a conversation. Good cocktails and singalong music make this a fun late-night hangout.

The Mustang Saloon 444–448 Kyhber Pass Rd, Newmarket. A Wild West theme sets the scene for this popular bar with saddles for stools and live music (Wed–Fri), thankfully not often country and western. They also serve generous portions of Tex-Mex and pizza.

Sponge 198 Ponsonby Rd, Ponsonby. See map, p.117. A flashy oval bar adorns the centre of this modern cocktail bar-cum-designer club where DJs spin house and hip-hop and well-dressed, slightly older partygoers canoodle on the leather booth seating. Always heaving at weekends when *Chicane*, the club upstairs, comes alive.

The Whiskey 210 Ponsonby Rd, Ponsonby. See map, p.117. Stylish modern bar with something of the feel of a groovy gentleman's club, all chocolate leather sofas and white brick walls hung with superb photos of Little Richard, the New York Dolls, Jimi Hendrix and more.

Clubs and gigs

Auckland by sheer weight of venues gets to see more bands than anywhere else; indeed, the bigger international acts often make it no further. The **clubbing** torch currently burns brightest along Karangahape Road, where you can join the nightly flow of young things meandering between the bars and clubs. Unless someone special is on the decks or a band is playing, few clubs charge more than $5 admission, and many are free, encouraging sporadic and unpredictable exits – just follow the crowds. Most of the venues mentioned in "Pubs and Bars" (see p.131) double as venues for live acts, employ DJs or put on some form of entertainment.

Many of the clubs have one area set up as a stage and on any night of the week you might find top Kiwi acts and even overseas **bands** blazing away in the corner; a few pubs may also put on a band from time to time. Bigger acts understandably opt for the larger venues; tickets can be booked through Ticketek (ⓣ09/307 5000, ⓦwww.ticketek.co.nz). One of the best ways to see local acts is to attend one of the **free summer concerts** held in The Domain and elsewhere under the *Music in Parks* banner (Jan–March; ⓣ09/379 2020, ⓦwww.aucklandcity.govt.nz;), mostly on Friday, Saturday and Sunday afternoons.

All venues listed are in the **city centre** unless otherwise specified; see map on p.127.

Boogie Wonderland Queen St, near the corner with Customs St ⓣ09/361 6093. Club that pays homage to seventies disco (plus a little funk and eighties pop), and even has a flashing, coloured-square dancefloor. The clientele is mostly over 25, though few can remember *Saturday Night Fever* from the first time around. $10 entry.

Fu Bar 166 Queen St. A cool basement club with a good dancefloor that kicks off about 10pm with occasional alternative and progressive sounds. Big-name spinners hit the spot regularly, when cover charges can rise to $25 plus.

Khuja Lounge 3rd floor, 536 Queen St ⓣ09/377 3711. *Khuja* means "melting pot" in Arabic and that sums up the feel in this lounge bar which calls itself the "Home of Aotearoa Soul". The funky jazz, soul and hip-hip (often with live bands) certainly attracts a slightly older, musically inclined crowd. $5–10 in. Closed Sun–Tues.

Kings Arms 59 France St, Newton ⓣ09/373 3240. Popular pub and second-string venue hosting local and touring acts who can't quite fill the bigger venues. Typically $5–25 in.

Safari Lounge 116 Ponsonby Rd. Swanky venue for cocktails, DJ-led dancing and occasionally live bands.

Classical music, dance, theatre and comedy

The **theatre** scene lacks a professional company with a permanent venue but the Auckland Theatre Company (ⓣ09/309 0390, ⓦwww.atc.co.nz) is firmly established at both the Aotea Centre and the Maidment, with occasional performances elsewhere. The Aotea Centre doubles as the major venue for **classical music**, **opera** and **ballet** but events are sporadic: the New Zealand

Festivals

As befits a city of its size, Auckland has numerous festivals and annual events. These are some of the best.

Anniversary Day (Jan, last Mon). Massive sailing regatta on Auckland's Waitemata Harbour.

Big Day Out (Jan, 3rd Fri). One day rock/pop/dance festival, with acts from all over the world at Mt Smart Stadium in the otherwise unvisited suburb of Penrose. Ⓦwww.bigdayout.com, tickets about $125.

International Buskers Festival (beginning of Feb). Ⓦwww.crackerjackpromotions.co.nz.

Mission Bay Jazz and Blues Streetfest (Feb, 2nd Sat). Ⓦwww.jazzandbluesstreetfest.com.

Devonport Food, Wine and Music Festival (Feb, 3rd weekend). Local retailers and vintners get together to charge extra (tickets $40) for their wares while mostly local acts play a little light music.

Pasifika (March, 1st or 2nd weekend). A celebration of Polynesian and Pacific Island culture (music, culture, food and crafts) held at Western Springs Park and stadium Friday night and all day Saturday.

Round the Bays Fun Run (March, 2nd or 3rd Sun). Up to 70,000 people jog 9km along the Tamaki Drive waterfront. Ⓦwww.roundthebays.co.nz.

Royal New Zealand Easter Show (Easter weekend). Family entertainment Kiwi style, with equestrian events, wine tasting and arts and crafts, all held at the ASB showgrounds along Greenlane.

International Comedy Festival (mid-May to early June). Ⓦwww.comedyfestival.co.nz.

Auckland International Film Festival (mid- to late July). The Auckland leg of this nationwide film tour. Ⓦwww.enzedff.co.nz.

Symphony Orchestra strikes up every month or so, the Wellington-based New Zealand Ballet calls in during its tours of the provinces and the Auckland Opera puts on several shows a year. The **Auckland Philharmonia** (Ⓣ09/638 7073, Ⓦwww.aucklandphil.co.nz) also present a number of shows, primarily at the Auckland Town Hall.

The **comedy** scene is relatively lively, with a dedicated venue hosting regular stand-up, while from mid-May to early June theatres and pubs are jumping with local stand-up comics and top-flight international acts for the three-week **International Comedy Festival**.

Aotea Centre Aotea Square, Queen St Ⓣ09/309 2677. New Zealand's first purpose-built opera house and the home stage for the New Zealand Symphony Orchestra and the New Zealand Ballet. The Auckland Theatre Company performs in its Herald Theatre.

Civic Theatre Corner of Queen and Wellesley sts Ⓣ09/307 2677. Lovely theatre worth visiting if there's anything at all on – could be dance, theatre or classic movies.

The Classic 321 Queen St Ⓣ09/373 4321, Ⓦwww.comedy.co.nz. Bar and comedy venue hosting top local names and touring acts. Shows Mon–Sat but the best line-ups are at weekends. $20–25 for the main acts, $15 for the nightly 10.30pm improv.

Maidment Theatre Corner of Princess & Alfred sts Ⓣ09/373 7599, Ⓦwww.maidment.auckland.ac.nz. Two university theatres, with mainstream works in the larger venue and more daring stuff in the studio.

Silo Theatre 1/108 Quay St Ⓣ0800/8425 3835, Ⓦwww.silotheatre.co.nz. Small venue specializing in less mainstream plays and events. Success varies, but there's usually something interesting on.

Cinema

Suburban multiplexes have virtually killed off smaller cinemas, leaving central Auckland with one twelve-screen monstrosity and two arthouse screens. We've listed the best of the smaller cinemas around the city, mostly in the inner suburbs. **Admission** is often reduced before 5pm (especially Mon–Wed); the *New Zealand Herald* has listings. The annual **Auckland International Film Festival**, usually held in mid-July, presses many of these cinemas into service for arthouse and foreign screenings.

Academy 44 Lorne St ⓣ09/373 2761, ⓦwww.academycinemas.com. Predominantly arthouse cinema with two screens tucked underneath the main library.
Bridgeway 122 Queen St, Birkenhead ⓣ09/418 3308, ⓦwww.bridgeway.co.nz. Renovated movie theatre on the North Shore that makes cinema-going even more of a pleasure with its intimate feel, good foyer food and coffee, luxurious seating and a wall-to-wall curved screen. Screens the smarter end of mainstream movies.
Lido 427 Manukau Rd, Epsom ⓣ09/630 1500, ⓦwww.lidocinema.co.nz. Grab a beer or wine, sink into wide seats, and enjoy mainstream and classic movies with digital sound.
Rialto 167 Broadway, Newmarket ⓦwww.rialto.co.nz. One of the most accessible of the fringe cinemas and resplendent after restorative work.

Listings

Automobile Association 99 Albert St ⓣ09/966 8800, ⓦwww.aa.co.nz.
Bike rental Adventure Cycles, 1 Laurie Ave, Parnell (ⓣ0800/335 566, ⓦwww.adventure-auckland.co.nz), has city bikes for $20 a day, mountain bikes from $25 a day and offers touring bikes at around $230 a month. Adventure Cycles also offer a service whereby you buy the equipment and they'll buy it back from you at the end of your trip for half the purchase price. Hedgehog Bikes, 72 Barrys Point Rd, Takapuna (ⓣ09/489 6559, ⓦwww.hedgehog.co.nz), also rent bikes (around $230/month plus fees for panniers etc) and will generally pick up from the airport and drop off a little out of Auckland.
Bookshops The biggest bookshops are on Queen St: Borders is at no. 291 (ⓣ09/309 3377), and Whitcoulls at no. 210 (ⓣ09/356 5400). Unity Books, 19 High St (ⓣ09/307 0731), is more highbrow; for a massive selection of second-hand books visit Hard to Find (But Worth The Effort), either at 238 K' Rd (ⓣ09/303 0555), or 81a Victoria St, Devonport (ⓣ09/446 0300).
Buying a car For general advice, consult Basics (see p.41), then peruse the noticeboards in hostels and at the main visitor centre. One of the best bets is the Backpackers Car Market, 20 East St (daily 9.30am–5pm; ⓣ09/377 7761, ⓦwww.backpackerscarmarket.co.nz), just off K' Rd, where backpackers buy and sell directly to each other. Alternatively head to the Auckland Car Fair, Ellerslie Racecourse, Greenlane (every Sun 9am–noon; ⓣ09/529 2233, ⓦwww.carfair.co.nz), which is well organized, with qualified folk on hand to check roadworthiness. Alternatively, glance through the page of cars for sale in the weekly *Auto Trader* or *Trade & Exchange* magazines, or pick up Wednesday's or Saturday's *New Zealand Herald*.
Camping and outdoor equipment For top-quality gear visit Bivouac, 210 Queen St ⓣ09/366 1966), and 300 Broadway, Newmarket (ⓣ09/529 2298). Kathmandu, 151 Queen St, (ⓣ09/309 4615), and 255 Broadway, Newmarket (ⓣ09/520 6041), are best for low-cost clothing and gear, especially during their frequent half-price sales. It's also worth checking hostel noticeboards for offers.
Car rental The international and major national companies all have depots close to the airport and free shuttle buses to pick you up; smaller companies are mostly based in the city or inner suburbs. In the central city, you'll find several close together along Beach Rd. The main international and local operators are listed in Basics (see p.40).
Consulates Australia (ⓣ09/921 8820; ⓦwww.australia.org.nz); Canada (ⓣ09/309 8516; ⓦwww.international.gc.ca/newzealand); Ireland (ⓣ09/977 2252); UK (ⓣ09/303 2973; ⓦwww.britishhighcommission.gov.uk); USA (ⓣ09/303 2724; ⓦwww.wellington.usembassy.gov.com).
Currency exchange Most places are clustered around the harbour end of Queen St. Travelex, 34 Queen St ⓣ09/377 2666; Money World, 155 Queen St ⓣ09/366 3280.
Emergencies Police, fire and ambulance, ⓣ111; Auckland Central police station ⓣ09/302 6400.

Laundry Clean Green Laundromat, 18 Fort St, ⓣ09/358 4370 (Mon–Fri 8am–6.30pm, Sat 8am–5pm).
Left luggage Lockers at the Sky City Bus Terminal, 102 Hobson St (accessible daily 7am–8.30pm), and most of the larger hostels also have long-term storage for one-time guests at minimal or no charge.
Library Auckland Public Library, 44–46 Lorne St, ⓣ09/377 0209 (Mon–Fri 9.30am–8pm, Sat 10am–4pm, Sun noon–4pm).
Maps Auckland Map Centre, National Bank Centre, Shop 3, 209 Queen St, ⓣ09/309 7725, ⓦwww.aucklandmapcentre.co.nz, or Speciality Maps, 46 Albert St, ⓣ09/307 2217.
Medical treatment Auckland City Hospital, Park Rd, Grafton, ⓣ09/367 0000; Travelcare, Level 1, 125 Queen St, ⓣ09/373 4621 (Mon–Fri 9am–5.30pm, Sat 10am–5pm, Sun noon–4pm), offers diving medicals, physiotherapy, X-rays and dental treatment; CityMed Medical Centre, corner Albert St and Mills Lane, has doctors and a pharmacy (Mon–Fri 8am–6pm, Sat 9.30am–2pm). Registered medical practitioners are listed separately at the beginning of the White Pages phone directory.
Newspapers and magazines Auckland's morning paper is the *New Zealand Herald* (ⓦwww.nzherald.co.nz), the closest New Zealand gets to a national daily. The best selection of international newspapers – mostly from Australia, UK and the US – is at Borders, 291 Queen St. This is also your best bet for specialist magazines, which are also sold at branches of Magazzino (123 Ponsonby Rd, Ponsonby; and 3 Mortimer Passage, Newmarket).
Pharmacy The most convenient late-opening pharmacy is the Auckland City Urgent Pharmacy, 60 Broadway, Newmarket (Mon–Fri 8.30am–1am, Sat & Sun 9am–1am); emergency departments of

Moving on from Auckland

Moving on from Auckland is a straightforward business. There's just one daily inter-city **train** service (ⓣ0800/872 467, ⓦwww.tranzscenic.co.nz) each way between Auckland and Wellington. Frequent **bus** services (see below) fan out from central Auckland: InterCity, Newmans and Northliner Express all leave from the Sky City terminal on Hobson Street; the rest depart from opposite the Ferry Building on Customs Street.

InterCity/Newmans ⓣ09/623 1503, ⓦwww.intercitycoach.co.nz: The widest selection of destinations.

Northliner Express ⓣ09/623 1503, ⓦwww.northliner.co.nz. Routes to Northland shared with Intercity.

Guthreys Express ⓣ0800/732 528, ⓦwww.guthreys.co.nz: Auckland–Hamilton–Rotorua.

Dalroy Express ⓣ06/759 0197, ⓦwww.dalroytours.co.nz: Auckland–Hamilton–New Plymouth–Hawera.

Go Kiwi ⓣ0800/446 549, ⓦwww.go-kiwi.co.nz: Auckland–Thames–Whangamata–Whitianga and Auckland–Hamilton.

Northbound **drivers** can take either SH1 directly over the harbour bridge, or go west around the head of the Waitemata Harbour past the wineries, West Coast beaches and Waitakere Ranges to meet SH1 at Wellsford. **Cyclists** must use the Devonport Ferry rather than the harbour bridge if heading north but will do well to take the western route, possibly riding a suburban train to Waitakere ($1 for the bike; travel outside peak hours). Southbound cyclists are better off following the Seabird Coast, avoiding the Southern Motorway, the main route south out of the city.

The network of **ferries** and **flights** linking the islands in the Hauraki Gulf presents more interesting ways to get out of the city. You might, for example, spend a few days on Great Barrier Island then continue to the Coromandel Peninsula without returning to Auckland (for details see our Great Barrier Island account from p.157).

Another option is the 360 Discovery ferry service (ⓣ0800/888 006, ⓦwww.360discovery.co.nz) to Coromandel Town. It runs four times a week and at just $49 one way is a viable alternative to taking the bus via Thames.

Finally, if you're on your way out of New Zealand, remember to keep $25 aside for your **airport tax**, payable on site.

hospitals (see "Medical treatment" above) have 24hr pharmacies.

Post office Auckland's main post office is just off Queen St in the Bledisloe Building, 24 Wellesley St, ⓣ09/379 6710 (Mon–Fri 7.30am–5.30pm), and has poste restante facilities.

Swimming Central pools include the indoor Edwardian-style Tepid Baths, 102 Customs St West (Mon–Fri 6am–9pm, Sat & Sun 7am–7pm; ⓣ09/379 4745), and the open-air saltwater Parnell Baths, Judges Bay Rd (Nov–Easter Mon–Fri 6am–8pm, Sat & Sun 8am–8pm; ⓣ09/373 3561). Otherwise, simply head for one of the beaches (see "The North Shore", p.118).

Taxis Alert ⓣ09/309 2000; Co-op ⓣ09/300 3000; Discount ⓣ09/529 1000.

Travel agencies Numerous in the city centre including Flight Centre with branches at 2 Fort St (ⓣ09/377 4655) and 350 Queen St (ⓣ09/358 4310), and STA Travel, 187 Queen St (ⓣ09/309 0458) and 267 High St (ⓣ09/356 1550).

Women's centres Auckland Women's Centre, 4 Warnock St, Grey Lynn (Mon–Fri 9am–4pm; ⓣ09/376 3227, ⓦwww.womenz.org.nz), offers counselling and health advice and has a library. The Women's Bookshop, 105 Ponsonby Rd (ⓣ09/376 4399), specializes in feminist literature and women's interest books.

Around Auckland

Real New Zealand begins, for many, in the immediate vicinity of Auckland, where verdant hills and magnificent beaches replace towerblocks, suburbs and sanitized wharfs. The **Waitakere Ranges**, to the **west** of the city offer a viable break from urban bustle. The hills also serve to deflect the prevailing westerly winds, providing shelter for the **vineyards** around Kumeu.

Spectacular expanses of sand are found along New Zealand's western seaboard, but it is only at Auckland's **West Coast beaches** that you will find surf-lifesaving patrols in reassuring numbers. Heading north, Auckland infringes on southern Northland, making the **Hibiscus Coast** a virtual suburb. South of Auckland, the **Hunua Ranges** offer a few modest walks and provide a windbreak for the **Seabird Coast**, where low shingle banks and extensive mudflats form an excellent breeding ground for dozens of migratory species.

West of Auckland

Auckland's suburban sprawl peters out some 20km west of the centre among the enveloping folds of the **Waitakere Ranges**. Despite being the most accessible expanse of greenery for over a million people, the hills remain largely unspoilt, with plenty of trails through native bush. On hot summer days, thousands head over the hills to one of half a dozen thundering **surf beaches**, largely undeveloped but for a few holiday homes (known to most Kiwis as *baches*) and the odd shop. The soils around the eastern fringes of the Waitakeres nurture long-established **vineyards**, mainly around Kumeu, just short of the Kaipara Harbour town of **Helensville** and the **hot pools** at Parakai.

You'll need your own transport to do justice to the beaches and most of the ranges, unless you join one of the West Coast **tours**: Bush & Beach (ⓣ0800/423 224, ⓦwww.bushandbeach.co.nz) offer afternoon trips ($125) or the more satisfying full-day tour ($185) taking in Piha Beach. You can also see the area on canyoning trips (see p.125).

As far as public transport goes, Auckland's suburban **trains** make it as far as Henderson and Waitakere – a boon for cyclists keen to get out of the city quickly – and Richies **buses** #066 & #067 run through Henderson to Kumeu and Helensville.

The Kumeu and Huapai wineries

Once a viticultural powerhouse, West Auckland has been eclipsed by bigger enterprises in Marlborough, Gisborne and Hawke's Bay. There is still some production, however, centred around the contiguous and characterless villages of **KUMEU** and **HUAPAI**.

As early as 1819 the Reverend Samuel Marsden planted grapes, ostensibly to produce sacramental wine, in Kerikeri in the Bay of Islands, but commercial winemaking didn't get under way until Dalmatians turned their hand to growing grapes after the kauri gum they came to dig ceased to be profitable (see p.226). Many of today's businesses owe their existence to immigrant families, a legacy evident in winery names such as Babich, Delegat, Nobilo and Selak. Today, the region produces quality wines, usually Cabernet Sauvignon, Pinot Noir and Chardonnay.

The free and widely available *Kumeu: Classic Wine Country* booklet details the half-dozen **wineries** that can be visited. One of the most pleasurable is Matua Valley, Waikoukou Valley Road, Waimauku (daily 10am–5pm; ⓣ09/411 8301, ⓦwww.matua.co.nz). Here you can taste, picnic or repair to the *Hunting Lodge* **restaurant** (ⓣ09/411 8259; closed Mon; $25–40 for main dishes) set beside the vines. Alternatively *Soljans*, 366 SH16 (ⓣ0508/765 526, ⓦwww.soljans.co.nz), right on the main road, has worthwhile cellar-door sales and a pleasing café.

If you plan some serious tasting, designate a non-drinking driver or leave the car behind and join one of the West Coast **tours** (see p.137), who visit wineries as part of wider explorations. Better still, spend the day with Fine Wine Tours (ⓣ0800/023 111, ⓦwww.insidertouring.co.nz), who offer a Kumeu half-day tour ($139), visiting three wineries and allowing time for lunch.

The Waitakere Ranges and the West Coast beaches

Auckland's western limit is defined by the bush-clad **Waitakere Ranges**, rising up to five hundred metres. The hills are a perennially popular weekend destination for Aucklanders intent on a picnic or a stroll and the western slopes roll down to the wild, black-sand **West Coast beaches**. Pounded by heavy surf and punctuated by precipitous headlands, these tempestuous shores provide a counterpoint to the calm, gently shelved beaches of the Hauraki Gulf.

The Kawarau a Maki people knew the region as Te Wao Nui a Tiriwa or "the Great Forest of Tiriwa", aptly describing the kauri groves that swathed the hills before the arrival of Europeans. By the turn of the century, diggers had pretty much cleaned out the kauri gum, but logging continued until the 1940s, leaving the land spent. The Auckland Regional Council bought the land, built reservoirs and designated a vast tract as the Centennial Memorial Park, with two hundred kilometres of walking tracks leading to fine vistas and numerous waterfalls that cascade off the escarpment.

The easiest access to the majority of the walks and beaches is via the **Waitakere Scenic Drive** (Route 24), which winds through the ranges from the dormitory suburb of **Titirangi**, in the foothills, to the informative **Arataki visitor centre** (Sept–April daily 9am–5pm; May–Aug Mon–Fri 10am–4pm,

Sat & Sun 9am–5pm), which shows an excellent twelve-minute DVD about the area on demand (free). A felled kauri has been transformed by Kawarau a Maki carvers into a striking *pou*, or guardian post, which marks the entrance and sets the tone for several smaller carvings within. Outside, walkways forge into the second-growth forest: the ten-minute plant identification loop trail identifies a dozen or so significant forest trees and ferns; a longer trail (1hr 15min) visits one of the few mature kauri stands to survive the loggers.

Arataki is also the place to pick up **camping** permits (call the Parksline in advance on ⓣ09/366 2000) for the seven sites ($5 per person) in the ranges, marked on the *Waitakere Ranges Recreation and Track Guide* map ($8, available from the visitor centre).

Beyond the visitor centre, the scenic drive swings north along the range, passing side roads to the **beaches**, noted for their foot-scorching gold-and-black sands and demanding swimming conditions. Before entering the water, read the box below, and heed all warning signs.

No **buses** run out this way, but Piha Surf Shuttle (ⓣ09/627 2644; reserve at least 24hr in advance) picks up in Auckland around 8.30am and leaves Piha for the city at 4pm (Dec–Feb daily; $50 return).

Whatipu

Whatipu is the southernmost of the West Coast surf beaches, 45km from central Auckland and located by the sand-bar entrance to Manukau Harbour, the watery grave of many a ship. The wharf at Whatipu was briefly the terminus of the precarious coastal **Parahara Railway**, which hauled kauri from the mill at Karekare across the beach and headlands during the 1870s. The tracks were

Always swim between the flags

The New Zealand coast is frequently pounded by ferocious surf and even strong swimmers can find themselves in difficulty in what may seem benign conditions. Every day throughout the peak holiday weeks (Christmas–Jan), and at weekends through the rest of the summer (Nov–Easter), the most popular surf beaches are monitored daily from around 10am to 5pm. Lifeguards stake out a section of beach between two red and yellow flags and continually monitor that area: **always swim between the flags**.

Before entering the water, watch other swimmers to see if they are being dragged along the beach by a strong along-shore **current** or **rip**. Often the rip will turn out to sea, leaving a "river" of disturbed but relatively calm water through the pattern of curling breakers. On entering the water, feel the strength of the waves and current before committing yourself too deeply, then keep glancing back to where you left your towel to judge your drift along the shore. Look out too for **sand bars**, a common feature of surf beaches at certain tides: wading out to sea, you may well be neck deep and then suddenly be only up to your knees. The corollary is moments after being comfortably within your depth you'll be floundering around in a **hole**, reaching for the bottom. Note that **boogie boards**, while providing flotation, can make you vulnerable to rips, and riders should always wear fins (flippers).

If you do find yourself in **trouble**, try not to panic, raise one hand in the air and yell to attract the attention of other swimmers and surf rescue folk. Most of all, don't struggle against the current; either swim across the rip or let it drag you out. Around 100–200m offshore the current will often subside and you can swim away from the rip and bodysurf the breakers back to shore. If you have to be rescued (or are just feeling generous), a large donation is in order. Surf lifeguards are dedicated volunteers, always strapped for cash and in need of new rescue equipment.

continually pounded by surf, but a second tramway from Piha covered the same treacherous expanse in the early twentieth century. Scant remains are visible, including an old tunnel that proved too tight a squeeze for a large steam engine whose boiler still litters the shore.

Over the last few decades, the sea has receded more than half a kilometre, leaving a broad beach backed by wetlands colonized by cabbage trees, tall toe toe grasses and waterfowl. It's a great place to explore, particularly along the base of the cliffs to the north where, in half an hour, you can walk to the **Ballroom Cave**, fitted with a sprung dancefloor in the 1920s that apparently still survives, buried by five metres of sand that drifted into the cave in the intervening years.

The only sign of civilization now is *Whatipu Lodge* (booking essential; ⓣ09/811 8860, ⓔwhatipulodge@xtra.co.nz; tents $15 per site, rooms ❸). Occupying an 1870 former mill manager's house, the lodge has no mains electricity (it generates its own for limited hours), but has communal cooking facilities and hot showers. Bring a sleeping bag.

Karekare, Piha and Te Henga

You can walk 5km north along the beach from Whatipu to **KAREKARE**, otherwise reached by a seventeen-kilometre road from Arataki visitor centre. Perhaps the most intimate and immediately appealing of the West Coast settlements, Karekare has regenerating manuka, pohutukawa and cabbage trees running down to a deep, smooth beach hemmed in by high promontories, and only a smattering of houses. In one hectic year, this dramatic spot was jolted out of its relative obscurity, providing the setting for beach scenes in Jane Campion's 1993 film *The Piano* and the inspiration for Crowded House's *Together Alone* album. The Karekare Surf Club patrols a safe swimming area on summer weekends, or there is a pool below **Karekare Falls**, a five-minute walk on a track just inland from the road. There is nowhere to stay here, and no facilities.

For decades **PIHA**, 20km west of the Arataki visitor centre, has been an icon for Aucklanders. A quintessential West Coast beach with a string of low-key weekend cottages and crashing surf, it lures a wide spectrum of day-trippers and the party set, whose New Year's Eve antics hastened in a dusk-till-dawn alcohol ban on holiday weekends.

Piha is on the brink of change, its quaint old-time *baches* displaced by upmarket beach houses, a gentrification that will be hastened by a proposed café, owned by TV celeb and former-All Black Marc Ellis. The 3km sweep of gold-and-black sand is hemmed in by bush-clad hills and split by Piha's defining feature, 101m **Lion Rock**. This former *pa* site, with some imagination, resembles a seated lion staring out to sea; the energetic climb to a shoulder two-thirds of the way up (20–30min return) is best done as the day cools. The **Tasman Lookout Track** (30–40min return) leaves the south end of the beach, climbing up to a lookout over the tiny cove of The Gap, where a spectacular blowhole performs in heavy surf.

Most **swimmers** flock to South Piha, where the more prestigious of the two surf-lifesaving clubs hogs the best **surf**. North Piha Road follows the beach for 2km to the second surf club; if battling raging surf isn't your thing, head for the cool **pool** below Kitekite Falls, a three-stage plunge reached on a loop track (1hr 30min) that starts 1km up Glen Esk Road, running inland opposite Piha's central Domain.

Day-trippers are catered for by a general store and surf shop, a traditional burger bar at South Piha (summer only) and the Piha Memorial RSA, 3 Beach Rd, which welcomes visitors. There's also a surf shop with a great view, Piha Surf (Ⓣ09/812 8723, Ⓦwww.pihasurf.co.nz), a couple of kilometres before the beach on the road in.

The self-contained caravans ($25) and cabins ($35) at the Piha Surf Shop provide good **places to stay.** For something upmarket, *Black Sands Lodge*, 54 Beach Rd (Ⓣ021/969 924, Ⓦwww.pihabeach.co.nz), offers jazzed-up Kiwi *baches* from the 1940s (❻). Their larger suites (❽) exude beach chic with big decks, French doors and quality furnishings and bedding. The lively hosts will also prepare romantic four-course dinners, served in your suite (around $125 a head, excluding wine). Three kilometres back from the beach, with great ocean views, *Piha Lodge*, 117 Piha Rd (Ⓣ09/812 8595, Ⓦwww.pihalodge.co.nz; ❺), has comfortable rooms and an outdoor pool.

The smaller and much less popular **TE HENGA** (also known as Bethell's Beach) lies at the end of a long road from Waitakere, 8km north along the coast. Less dramatic than Karekare, Piha or Muriwai, Te Henga is correspondingly less visited, making it good for escaping the crowds in the summer. There are no shops, but there is a surf club and luxurious **accommodation** at *Bethells Beach Cottages* (Ⓣ09/810 9581, Ⓦwww.bethellsbeach.com) – at either the elegant pohutukawa-shaded *Te Koinga Cottage* (❾), housing up to seven but comfortably sleeping two couples, or *Turehu Cottage* (❽), a smaller studio sleeping two; both with kitchens.

Muriwai

MURIWAI, the most populous of the West Coast beach settlements, lies 15km north of Piha and 10km coastwards from Huapai. Again, there's wonderful surf, and a long beach stretching 45km north to the heads of Kaipara Harbour. The main attraction is at the southern end of the beach where a **gannet colony** (late Oct to mid-Feb) occupies Motutara Island and Otakamiro Point, the headland between the main beach and the surfers' cove of Maori Bay. The

▲ Australasian gannet, Muriwai

gannets breed here before migrating to sunnier climes, a few staying behind with the fur seals that inhabit the rocks below. Gannets normally prefer the protection of islands, this is one of the few places where they nest on the mainland, just below viewing platforms from where you get a bird's-eye view. Short paths lead up here from near the surf club and off the road to Maori Bay.

To explore the beach, dunes and pine forests to the north, join a **horse trek** run by the Muriwai Beach Riding Centre, 290 Oaia Rd (2hr; $70; ⓣ09/411 8480, ⓦwww.aucklandhorsehire.org.nz). To try **surfing**, visit the Muriwai Surf School (ⓣ021/478 734, ⓦwww.muriwaisurfschool.co.nz), where you can rent gear (board and wetsuit $40/3hr), take a lesson (introductory $55, advanced $90) or muck around on blow carts ($45, 1hr) and mountain bikes ($10, 1hr). Its shed is located behind *Sand Dunz Beach Café*, at the road junction close to the beach, a modern café and takeaway that stays open well into the evening in summer.

If you want to **stay**, try the B&B at *Muriwai Beach Lodge*, 380 Motutara Rd (ⓣ0800/687 499, ⓦwww.muriwainz.co.nz; ⑤), half a kilometre back from the beach, or the shaded *Muriwai Beach Motor Camp*, (ⓣ09/411 9262; camping $12). For those without transport, Bush & Beach Ltd (see p.137) run half-day and day-trips out here.

The southern Kaipara: Helensville and Parakai

Venture beyond the vineyards of Kumeu and you'll soon find yourself in uninspiring **HELENSVILLE**, 45km from Auckland but more closely associated with the Kaipara Harbour (see p.223). Like many Kaipara towns, Helensville was founded on timber that, following the completion of the rail link to Auckland in 1881, was floated here in huge rafts then loaded onto freight wagons. Dairying has replaced the kauri trade and though the spread of the Auckland conurbation is threatening, Helensville still potters along. Photos and displays of the busier days can be seen at the new **Helensville Pioneer Museum** (Wed, Sat & Sun 1–3.30pm; $5; ⓦwww.helensvillemuseum.org.nz), at 98 Mill Rd as you enter town from Muriwai.

You'll get a better idea of what the kauri logging days were like with **Kaipara Cruises** (ⓣ09/420 8466, ⓦwww.helensville.co.nz/kewpie.htm), who run a series of trips from December to March on an old wooden ferryboat. Trip times are tide dependent (call or check the website) and leave either from the wharf at Springs Road in Parakai, north of the Aquatic Park (see below), or from Shelly Beach wharf, 20km north of Helensville. The three-hour Historical and Nature Cruise ($15) visits kauri mill sights and logging camps around the harbour, and the seven-hour Great West Coast Sand Safari ($55) includes a cruise to Poutu Point, south of Dargaville, where you link up with a 4WD sand bus to visit a historic lighthouse before returning by boat to Helensville.

To get to Kaipara Harbour you have to drive through **PARAKAI**, 3km north of Helensville, chiefly noted for its Aquatic Park (daily 10am–10pm; $15, private spa $6 extra per hour; ⓣ09/420 8998, ⓦwww.aquaticpark.co.nz), where pools are filled by natural hot springs; entry includes free use of a couple of buffeting water chutes. Richies **buses** #066 and #067 (ⓣ0800/103 080; not Sun) operate from Britomart to Parakai and Helensville. There's a **visitor centre**, 87 Commercial Rd (daily 10am–4pm; ⓣ09/420 8060, ⓦwww.helensville.co.nz), in the heart of town.

North of Auckland

The straggling suburbs of north Auckland merge into the **Hibiscus Coast**, which starts 40km north of the city and is increasingly favoured by retirees and long-distance commuters. The region centres on the suburban Whangaparaoa Peninsula – a launching point for trips to Tiritiri Matangi Island (see p.161) – and the anodyne beachside community of **Orewa**, now mostly bypassed by an extension of the northern motorway. Immediately to the north, the hot springs at **Waiwera** herald the beach-and-BBQ scene of **Wenderholm Regional Park** and the classic old **Puhoi** pub. Travelling north, the account continues on p.169 with Warkworth.

Orewa and the Whangaparaoa Peninsula

The most striking of the Hibiscus Coast beaches is the three-kilometre strand backed by **OREWA**, the region's main town and home to most of the area's accommodation and restaurants. Apart from swimming – and kitesurfing for those with their own gear – there isn't a great deal to do except a few bushwalks and minor diversions such as the town's stern-looking statue of Edmund Hillary.

South of Orewa, the **Whangaparaoa Peninsula** juts out 12km into the Hauraki Gulf, its central ridge traced by Whangaparaoa Road. This passes the small-time, narrow-gauge **Whangaparaoa Steam Railway**, 400 Whangaparaoa Rd (Sept–June, Sat & Sun 10am–5pm, plus school holidays Mon–Fri 10am–4pm; $6; Ⓦwww.rail.co.nz) on the way to **Shakespear Regional Park** (8am–dusk; free), a pleasant place to swim and wander through regenerating bush spotting pukeko, red-crowned parakeets and tui. The peninsula's most enticing diversion, though, is a trip to the bird sanctuary of Tiritiri Matangi (see p.161), with boats leaving from the vast Gulf Harbour Marina just before Shakespear Park.

Practicalities

A complex web of Auckland **buses** (call Maxx, Ⓣ0800/103 080) fan out from Auckland's Britomart Transport Centre to the Hibiscus Coast. The best routes are #893 and #896, which take an hour. These, and Northland-bound InterCity and Northliner buses, stop in central Orewa after passing the well-stocked **i-SITE visitor centre**, 214a Hibiscus Coast Hwy (daily 10am–4pm; Ⓣ09/426 0076, Ⓦwww.orewa-beach.co.nz). The buses continue along Whangaparaoa Road to Shakespear Park several times a day, passing within 2km of the Tiritiri Matangi wharf.

Campsites and backpackers offering budget **accommodation** are supplemented by dozens of motels and a few B&Bs. Motel prices peak from Christmas to the end of January.

Accommodation

Edgewater Motel 387 Hibiscus Coast Hwy Ⓣ09/426 5260, Ⓔedgewater.motel@xtra.co.nz. Comfortable budget motel with spa and a range of units, some beachside. Units ③, beachside ④

Orewa Beach Holiday Park 265 Hibiscus Coast Hwy Ⓣ09/426 5832, Ⓔobhpark@rodney.govt.nz. Orewa's only campsite, located at the south end of town and with a host of amenities. Camping $16, waterfront camping $18, cabins ②

Pillows Travellers Lodge 412 Hibiscus Coast Hwy Ⓣ09/426 6338, Ⓦwww.pillows.co.nz. Fairly central hostel with modern dorms, four-shares and rooms, some en suite. Dorms $20, rooms ①, en suites ②

The Ridge Greenhollows Rd, 10km north of Orewa Ⓣ0508/843 743, Ⓦwww.theridge.co.nz. Luxurious, eco-friendly lodge with panoramic views of the sea, farmland and bush, and a host of bushwalks fanning out from the house. Three-course dinners available ($65). ⑧

Eating and drinking

Asahi 6 Bakehouse Lane ⓣ09/426 0065. Simply furnished Japanese restaurant where the sushi is tasty and the teriyaki chicken ($18.50) to die for.

Hola! Moana Court ⓣ09/427 4652. A casual, good-value Mexican with all the favourites including $15 fajitas.

Muldoon's Westpac Plaza, Moana Ave. Convivial Irish Bar with moderately priced meals and a courtyard that catches the afternoon sun.

Waiwera and Wenderholm

The main highway north of Orewa (buses #893 and #896) runs through the cluster of holiday and retirement homes that make up Hatfields Beach to **WAIWERA**, 6km north of Orewa, where Maori once dug holes in the sands to take advantage of the natural hot springs. Bathing is now in the **Waiwera Infinity Thermal Spa Resort**, Waiwera Road (daily 9am–10pm; $22; ⓦwww.waiwera.co.nz), where a network of suicidal waterslides and indoor and outdoor pools are naturally heated to between 28 and 43°C. The Superpass ($40) gives you resort entry, half an hour private spa and a sunbed session.

Occupying a high headland between the estuaries of the Puhoi and Waiwera rivers, **Wenderholm Regional Park** was the first of Auckland's regional parks. Its sweeping golden beach is backed by pohutukawa-shaded swathes of grass and is often packed with barbecuing families on summer weekends. Walking tracks range from twenty minutes to two hours winding up to a headland viewpoint through nikau palm groves that have been turned into a "mainland island". By trapping and poisoning, the headland is kept free of introduced predators, allowing native birds to return, some reintroduced from Tiritiri Matangi (see p.161). You can also take a peek at **Coudrey House Museum** (Jan daily 1–4pm, Feb–Dec Sat & Sun 1–4pm; $2), an 1860 colonial homestead.

Buses terminate here on summer Sundays; if you need to stay there's a nicely sited water-and-toilets **campsite** ($10) with grassy plots and a BBQ beside the mangroves.

Puhoi

The village of **PUHOI**, 6km north of Waiwera, remains a bucolic place, settled by staunchly Catholic Bohemian migrants who arrived in 1863 from Egerland, in what was then the Austro-Hungarian Empire (now the Czech Republic). The land was poor, and settlers were forced to eke out a living by cutting the bush for timber: the horns of famed bullock teams are still ranged round the walls of the historic **Puhoi Tavern**, a colonial hotel containing a single-roomed bar festooned with pioneering paraphernalia and photos.

Few visit anywhere other than the pub, but **Puhoi Bohemian Museum** (Christmas–Easter daily 1–4pm; Easter–Christmas Sat, Sun & school holidays 1–3.30pm; $2) in the former Convent School, is interesting if only for the historic model of the village. Gentle activity beckons in the form of **kayaking**, or canoeing, along a tidal section of the river (1hr; double kayak or canoe $40) or downstream to Wenderholm (2hr; double kayak or canoe $80, including pick-up) with Puhoi River Canoe Hire (ⓣ09/422 0891, ⓦwww.puhoirivercanoes.co.nz; bookings essential). For refreshments, hit the pub or drive 3km north to *The Art of Cheese* **café** (9am–5pm) where they make tasty cheeses.

Southeast of Auckland

Most southbound travellers hurry along Auckland's southern motorway to Hamilton or turn off to Thames at Pokeno – either way missing out on the modest attractions of the **Hunua Ranges** and the **Seabird Coast** on its eastern shore. For **cyclists** in particular the coast road is an excellent way into and out of Auckland, following Tamaki Drive from the centre through Panmure and Howick to Clevedon and the coast.

Even for Auckland day-trippers the older and more rounded Hunuas play second fiddle to the more ecologically rich Waitakeres, but there are some decent walks – notably around the **Hunua Falls**. There are greater rewards further south with excellent seabird viewing and hot pools at **Miranda**.

The Hunua Ranges

A considerable amount of rain is dumped on the 700m-high **Hunua Ranges**, 50km southeast of Auckland, flowing down into a series of four dams that jointly supply over half the city's water. The bush surrounding the reservoirs was once logged for kauri but has largely regenerated, providing a habitat for birds, rarely seen in the city.

Access to the region is easiest through the village of **CLEVEDON**, whose cafés and craft shops shouldn't detain you from visiting, 9km east along SH25, Clevedon Coast Oysters (Mon–Fri 7am–4.30pm, Sat 9am–2pm, Sun 10–4pm; Ⓦwww.clevedonoysters.com), for a bargain bag or dozen pack of delicious local oysters. Pressing on south to Hunua, you'll come across the **Hunua Ranges Park visitor centre** (Mon–Fri 8am–4.30pm; Ⓣ09/292 4823), selling the *Hunua & Waitakere Recreation Areas* map ($12) – invaluable for extended walks in the ranges. The best of the walks are around the thirty-metre Hunua Falls, about 5km east, where the Wairoa River carves its way through the crater of an ancient volcano. There's good swimming here, or you could take the half-day loop hike crossing the Wairoa River at the falls and following the Massey Track to Cosseys Dam and back down the Cosseys Gorge Track to the falls.

The Seabird Coast and Miranda

The Firth of Thames, a sheltered arm of the Hauraki Gulf separating South Auckland from the Coromandel Peninsula, borders the Hunua Ranges to the east. Its frequently windswept western littoral has become known as the **Seabird Coast**, in recognition of its international importance for migrating shorebirds; almost a quarter of all known species visit the region. During winter, the vast inter-tidal flats support 30,000-strong flocks, with over fifty percent of the entire world population of the wrybill plover over-wintering here. During the southern summer (Sept–March), the arctic migrants, who fly 15,000 kilometres from Alaska, Siberia and Mongolia, are more significant – notably bar-tailed godwits and lesser knots, as well as turnstones, curlews, sandpipers and red-necked stints.

The tidal flats butt up against the geologically significant "chenier plain" around Miranda, where the land has been built up from successive deposits of shell banks; much has been converted to farmland but newer shell banks in the making can be seen along the coast.

From Clevedon the coast road winds 35km past the small beach settlements of Kawakawa Bay and Orere Point, and the **Tapapakanga Regional Park** (primitive camping $10) to **KAIAUA**. Here you'll find a couple of places to eat in the form of the *Bay View Hotel*, and the adjacent *Kaiaua Fisheries*, which operates a licensed seafood restaurant in the evening and serves good fish and chips.

The coast's birdlife is thoroughly interpreted at the excellent **Miranda Shorebird Centre**, 7km south of Kaiaua (daily 9am–5pm, and often later in the summer, when it's awash with twitchers reluctant to leave; ⓣ09/232 2781, ⓦwww.miranda-shorebird.org.nz); they'll fill you in on the current hot sightings and point you in the direction of the best viewing spots. With a sunny veranda for viewing, the centre also has good-value self-catering accommodation (bunks $17.50, flat ❷). A further 7km south are the slightly alkaline **Miranda Hot Springs** (daily 8am–9.30pm; $15, private spa $10 extra per 30min; ⓦwww.mirandahotsprings.co.nz), with a large, warm open pool and private kauri spa tubs. Guests at the adjacent *Miranda Holiday Park* (ⓣ0800/833 144, ⓦwww.mirandaholidaypark.co.nz; tent sites $19, rooms ❷, s/c units ❺) have access to their own landscaped mineral pool as well as a tennis court. From here it's a twenty-minute drive to Thames (see p.362).

Islands of the Hauraki Gulf

Auckland's greatest asset is the island-studded **Hauraki Gulf**, a seventy-kilometre-square patch of ocean to the northeast of the city. In Maori, Hauraki means "wind from the north" – though the gulf is somewhat sheltered from the prevailing winds and ocean swells by the islands of Great Barrier and Little Barrier, creating benign conditions for Auckland's legions of yachties. Most just sail but those who wish to strike land can visit some of the 47 islands, administered by the Department of Conservation, designated either for recreational use with full access, or as sanctuaries for endangered wildlife, requiring permits.

Auckland's nearest island neighbour is **Rangitoto**, a flat cone of gnarled and twisted lava that dominates the harbourscape. The most populous of the gulf islands is **Waiheke**, increasingly a commuter suburb of Auckland, with sandy beaches and some quality wineries. Such sophistication is a far cry from the largest island hereabouts, **Great Barrier**, but the advent of seasonal fast ferries has put its sandy surf beaches, hilly tramping tracks and exceptional fishing within reach of holidaying locals and international visitors. The Department of Conservation's policy of allowing access to wildlife sanctuaries is wonderfully demonstrated at **Tiritiri Matangi**, where a day-trip gives visitors an unsurpassed opportunity to see some of the world's rarest birds.

Frequent **ferries** run to the more popular islands from the Downtown Ferry Terminal by Auckland's Ferry Building, at the foot of Queen Street; the DOC **information centre** is conveniently located in the same complex. Assorted Fullers offices sell tickets for most island-bound boats, as do 360 Discovery. For more on cruising and kayaking the Gulf, see "Adventure activities", on p.123.

Rangitoto and Motutapu islands

The low, conical shape of **Rangitoto**, 10km northeast of the city centre, is a familiar sight to every Aucklander. Yet few set foot on the island, missing out on a freakish land of fractured black lava, the world's largest pohutukawa

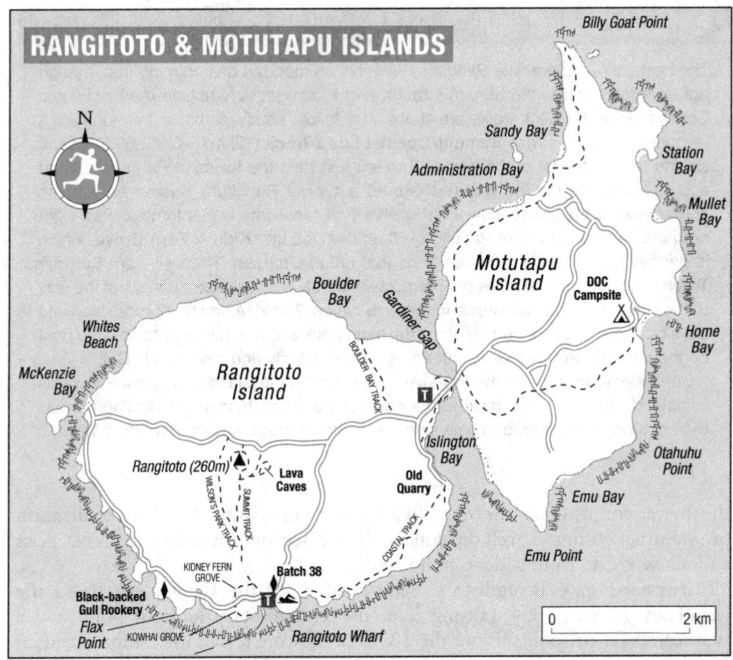

forest clinging precariously to its crevices. Alongside lies the older, and geologically quite distinct, island of **Motutapu** or "sacred island", linked to Rangitoto by a narrow causeway. A **day-trip** is enough to get a feel for Rangitoto, make the obligatory hike to the summit and tackle a few trails, but **longer stays** are possible if you pitch your tent at the primitive campsite at Home Bay on Motutapu.

Rangitoto is Auckland's youngest and largest **volcano**. Molten magma probably pushed its way through the bed of the Hauraki Gulf around six hundred years ago – watched by Motutapu Maori, who apparently called the island "blood red sky" after the spectacle that accompanied its creation. Others attribute the name to a contraction of Te Rangi i totongia a Tamatekapua ("the day the blood of Tamatekapua was shed"), recalling an incident when chiefs of the Arawa and Tainui clashed at Islington Bay.

Rangitoto's youth, lack of soil and porous rock have created unusual conditions for **plant life**, though the meagre supply of insects attracts few birds, making it eerily quiet. Pohutukawa trees seeded first, given a head start by their roots, which are able to tap underground reservoirs of fresh water up to 20m below the surface. Smaller and fleshier plants then established themselves under the protective canopy. Harsh conditions have led to some strange botanical anomalies: both epiphytes and mud-loving mangroves are found growing directly on the lava, an alpine moss is found at sea level, and the pohutukawa has hybridized with its close relative, the northern rata, to produce a spectrum of blossoms ranging from pink to crimson. The succulent pohutukawa leaves were a big hit with **possums** and wallabies, introduced in the 1880s, who ravaged the forests until the eradication programme of the early 1990s, which allowed the pohutukawa to rebound with vigour. Already Rangitoto is looking

Rangitoto summit walk

The best way to appreciate Rangitoto Island is on foot, but bear in mind that, though not especially steep, the terrain is rough and it can get very hot on the black lava. Consequently the best walks are those that follow shady paths to the summit. A favourite is the clockwise **Summit/Coastal Loop Track** (12km; 5–6hr; 260m ascent) around the southeast of the island. Turn left just past the toilets at Rangitoto Wharf and follow signs for the **Kowhai Grove**, a typical Rangitoto bush area with an abundance of the yellow-flowering kowhai that blossoms in September. Turn right onto the coastal road from Rangitoto Wharf then left into **Kidney Fern Grove**, which is packed with unusual miniature ferns that unfurl after rain. The well-worn **Summit Track** winds through patches of pohutukawa forest. Around three-quarters of the way to the summit, a side track leads to the **lava caves** (20min return) that probe deep into the side of the volcano. Further along the main track a former military observation post on the **summit** provides views out across Auckland city and the Hauraki Gulf.

Continue northwards to the east–west road across the island and follow it towards Islington Bay; from there, pick up the **coastal track** south, initially following the bay then cutting inland through some little-frequented forests back to Rangitoto Wharf.

the better for it. Over the next five years a concentrated rodent eradication programme, costing 5 million dollars, should see off any other mammal pests and allow DOC to introduce more birds.

Europeans gave Rangitoto a wide berth until the Crown purchased the island for £15 in 1854, putting it to use as a military lookout point and a workcamp for prisoners. From the 1890s, areas were leased for camping and, in keeping with the defiantly anti-authoritarian streak that thrived in early New Zealand, unauthorized *baches* were cobbled together on the sites. By 1937 over 100 *baches* had sprouted, but subsequent legislation decreed that they could be neither sold nor handed down and must be removed upon the expiry of the lease. In recent years the rules have been relaxed as the cultural value of this unique set of 1920s and 1930s houses has been appreciated. Only 34 remain and the people who still use them defend their right to do so. Some of the finest examples are being preserved for posterity, their corrugated iron chimneys and cast-off veranda-railing fenceposts capturing the Kiwi make-do spirit.

Bach 38, near Rangitoto Wharf, has been restored to its 1930s condition and you're free to look around the outside. If you're lucky you might strike one of the days when the Rangitoto Island Historic Conservation Trust (Ⓦwww.rangitoto.org) open it up for inspection.

The moment you step across the **causeway** onto **Motutapu**, the landscape changes dramatically; suddenly, you are back in rural New Zealand, with its characteristic grassy paddocks, ridge-top fencelines, corrugated iron barns and macrocarpa windbreaks. DOC's plan is to gradually restore its cultural and natural landscape, replanting the valleys with native trees – you can join their volunteer programme (see p.74) – restoring wetlands and interpreting the numerous Maori sites. Until the trees grow, Motutapu will continue to have a much more open, pastoral feel than Rangitoto, but the views of the Hauraki Gulf make time spent here worthwhile, particularly tramping the Motutapu Walkway to the campsite and beach at Home Bay (6km; 1hr 30min one way), then back again.

Practicalities

Fullers **ferries** (Mon–Sun 3 daily; $20 return) take forty minutes to reach Rangitoto Wharf, where there is a toilet block, the island's only **drinking**

water, and a sun-warmed saltwater swimming pool (filled naturally by the high tide) that's great for kids. Apart from the Home Bay campsite and a couple of toilets there's nothing else on the island, so bring everything you need – including strong shoes to protect you from the sharp rocks, a sun hat and a raincoat. If you're planning a walk, bring plenty of water. The first and last boats are met by the only transport on the island, a kind of tractor-drawn buggy that operates the two-hour **Volcanic Explorer Tour** ($50 including cost of ferry), a dusty summit trip with a full and informative commentary; the final 900m is on foot along a boardwalk.

The DOC has intentionally done all they can to ensure that the twin islands are the preserve of day-trippers. As a concession to the hardy and determined, there is a primitive but pleasant beachside DOC **campsite** ($5; booking essential Christmas–Jan on ⓣ09/379 6476), with toilets and water, at Home Bay on the eastern side of Motutapu, over an hour's walk from Islington Bay and almost three hours' walk from Rangitoto Wharf.

Waiheke Island

Pastoral **WAIHEKE**, 20km east of Auckland, is the second-largest of the gulf islands and easily most populous, particularly on summer weekends when day-trippers and weekenders quadruple its population. The traffic isn't all one way, though, as the fast and frequent ferry service makes it feasible for a growing proportion of the islanders to commute daily for work in the city – a trend that is turning Waiheke into a suburb. For the moment, with its chain of sandy beaches along the north coast and a climate that's slightly warmer and a lot less humid than Auckland, Waiheke retains its luxuriant character – and is popular with international visitors in search of a peaceful spot to recover from jet lag or to idle away a few days before flying home.

The **earliest settlers** on Waiheke trace their lineage back to the Tainui canoe that landed at Onetangi and gave the island its first name, Te Motu-arai-Roa, "the long sheltering island". Waiheke, or "cascading waters", originally referred to a particular creek but was assumed by **Europeans** to refer to the island. Among the first **settlers** to set foot on Waiheke was Samuel Marsden, who preached here in 1818 and established a mission near Matiatia. The island then went through the familiar cycle of kauri logging, gum digging and clearance for farming. Gradually, the magnificent coastal scenery gained popularity as a setting for grand picnics, and hamper-encumbered Victorians, attired in formal dress, arrived in boatloads.

Development was initially sluggish, but the availability of cheap land amid dramatic landscapes drew painters and **craftspeople**; others followed as access from Auckland became easier and faster.

Arrival, information and transport

Avoid Waiheke **at the weekend**, when it's flooded by Aucklanders shopping, tasting at vineyards and occupying the eateries and bars, where there's often live music. Lots of accommodation will demand a two-night minimum for Friday and Saturday, or will charge an additional fee. Better to visit midweek, the downside being a few wineries may not open, artists occasionally close their studios and trips requiring minimum numbers are harder to organize (outside the summer season).

Fullers operate fast **ferries** (ⓣ09/367 9111; roughly hourly; 35min; $28.50 return, bikes free) from the Ferry Building in Auckland to Matiatia Wharf ferry

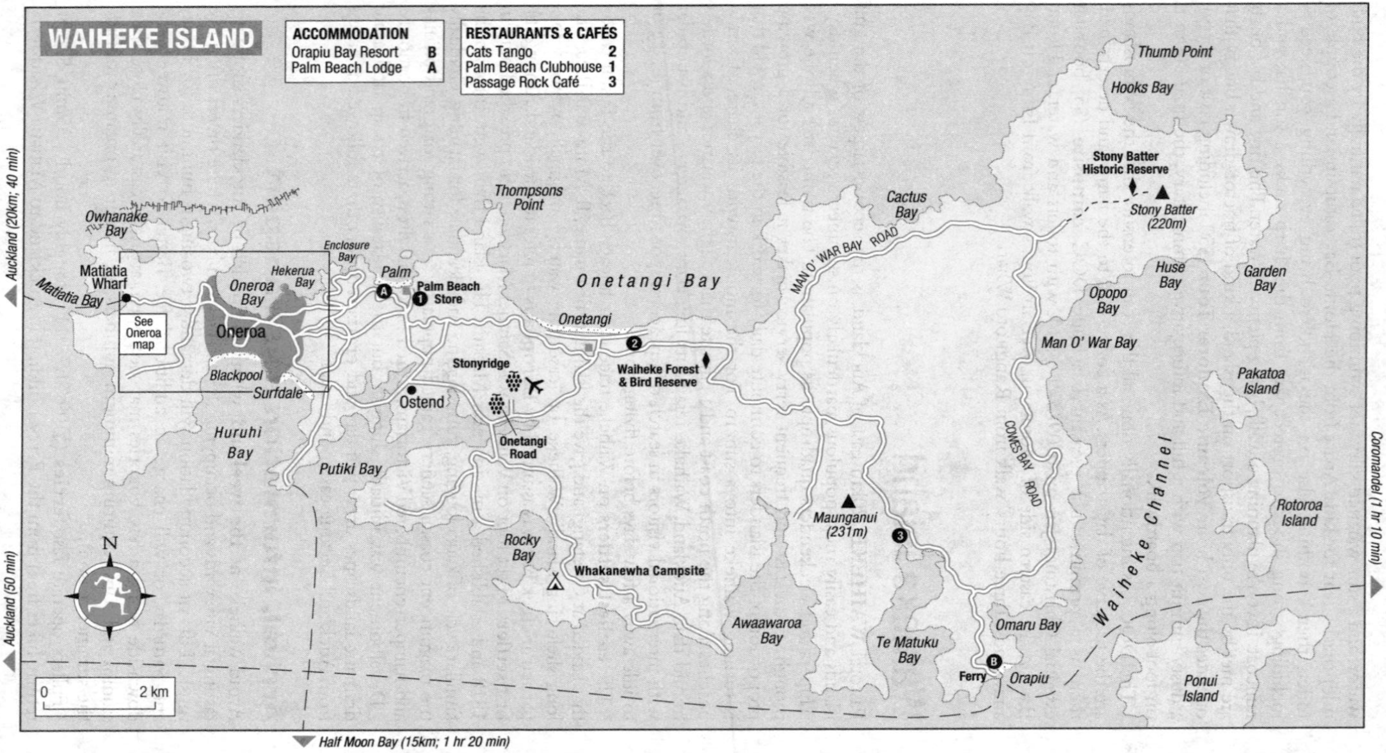

WAIHEKE ISLAND

ACCOMMODATION
Orapiu Bay Resort B
Palm Beach Lodge A

RESTAURANTS & CAFÉS
Cats Tango 2
Palm Beach Clubhouse 1
Passage Rock Café 3

Thumb Point
Hooks Bay
Stony Batter Historic Reserve
Stony Batter (220m)
Thompsons Point
Cactus Bay
Owhanake Bay
Enclosure Bay
Matiatia Wharf
Matiatia Bay
Hekerua Bay
Oneroa Bay
Palm
Palm Beach Store
Onetangi Bay
MAN O' WAR BAY ROAD
Huse Bay
Garden Bay
Opopo Bay
Oneroa
See Oneroa map
Onetangi
Man O' War Bay
Stonyridge
Waiheke Forest & Bird Reserve
Pakatoa Island
Blackpool
Surfdale
Ostend
Huruhi Bay
Onetangi Road
COWES BAY ROAD
Putiki Bay
Waiheke Channel
Rotoroa Island
Maunganui (231m)
Rocky Bay
Whakanewha Campsite
Awaawaroa Bay
Te Matuku Bay
Omaru Bay
Ferry
Orapiu
Ponui Island
N
0 2 km
Auckland (20km; 40 min)
Auckland (50 min)
Coromandel (1 hr 10 min)
Half Moon Bay (15km; 1 hr 20 min)

terminal, at the western end of Waiheke. The wharf is just over a kilometre from the main settlement of Oneroa. If you're staying for a couple of days or longer, you may find it cost-effective to bring your vehicle over using the daily **car ferry**, a flat-deck barge run by Sealink (Ⓣ0800/732 546, Ⓦwww.sealink.co.nz; $120–160 return for a car plus up to four people) from Half Moon Bay near Pakuranga in Auckland's eastern suburbs to Kennedy Point, between Huruhi and Putiki bays about 4km from Oneroa.

360 Discovery (Ⓣ0800/888 006, Ⓦwww.360discovery.co.nz) run a service from Auckland to **Coromandel** (Tues, Thurs, Fri & Sun; Auckland–Orapiu $32, Orapiu–Coromandel $65) via the small wharf at Orapiu on the southeast corner of Waiheke. There's no bus service down there, so it's of limited use unless you fancy staying at *Orapiu Bay Resort*, who can arrange a pick-up, or bring a bicycle.

Information

Waiheke's main source of information is the efficient **i-SITE visitor centre**, 2 Korora Rd, Oneroa (daily 9am–5pm; Ⓣ09/372 1234, Ⓦwww.waihekenz.com), where bags can be stored for $2 apiece. A further i-SITE exists in the ferry terminal but is rarely occupied. **Shops**, a couple of **banks** and a post office are also clustered in Oneroa. The weekly *Gulf News* ($1.50) comes out on Thursday afternoons and details of **what's on**, as well as a rundown of arts and crafts outlets. The free *Waiheke Week* is also informative.

Getting around

Ferry arrivals and departures connect with Fullers buses (Ⓣ09/3697 9111), which run to Onetangi via Oneroa, Surfdale and Ostend, and to Rocky Bay via Oneroa, Little Oneroa and Palm Beach. Tickets and a 10-day pass (only worthwhile for three or more long journeys) are available on the bus. For more flexibility, **rent a vehicle**. Waiheke Auto Rentals (Ⓣ09/372 8635, Ⓦwww.waihekerentalcars.co.nz), at Matiatia Wharf, are the most convenient and rent cars ($55 a day plus $0.60/km), 4WD ($80 plus $0.60/km), **scooters** ($55) and **motorbikes** ($75). Each car comes with an island pack, including an excellent map and a package of the more interesting brochures. Owned by the same company, Offshore Rentals, 2 Belgium St, Ostend (Ⓣ09/372 1018, Ⓦwww.offshorerentals.co.nz), market older budget models for as little as $40 a day with unlimited mileage.

Bikes from Waiheke Bike Hire (Ⓣ09/372 7937) at the Matiatia wharf cost $30 a day but remember Waiheke is undulating and you'll need to be pretty fit. For **taxis**, contact the companies on p.155, which all run tours and drop-offs at accommodation around the island, prices depend on numbers and destination.

Day-trippers are well catered for by a number of **island tours**. Fullers (Ⓣ09/3697 9111) run two. Their Explorer Tour (daily year-round departing Auckland 10am & noon; $44) includes an open-dated return ferry trip from Auckland, an hour-and-a-half island tour, plus an all-day bus pass so you can explore further on your own. The Vineyard Tour (Dec–Feb daily, March & Nov Wed–Sun, April–Oct Sat & Sun, departing Auckland 11am; $90) has the same benefits but spends four hours visiting three top vineyards including a light lunch at Stonyridge. On balance, this is the best way to tour the wineries, some of which are otherwise only open by appointment. Island-based operators include Ananda Tours (Ⓣ09/372 7530, Ⓦwww.ananda.co.nz), who run personalized wine, eco, art and scenic tours around the island from around $90 per person (minimum numbers apply).

Accommodation

If your visit coincides with the peak Christmas and January season or summer weekends, be sure to **reserve** a room as far in advance as possible – though this is less critical at the backpacker hostels. At other times, accommodation is plentiful, especially if you follow Aucklanders' lead and go for **B&Bs**; most are registered with the i-SITE.

Camping is restricted to the grounds of the various hostels and a simple but attractive site at *Whakanewha Regional Park* (reservations ⓣ09/366 2000; $5) on the tidal Rocky Bay, though it's a couple of kilometres' walk from the nearest bus stop.

There's a lot to be said for basing yourself at one of the quieter and more relaxing **beaches** like Palm Beach and Onetangi, but many people prefer to stay close to Oneroa, for the convenience of being near the buses, restaurants and shops.

Hotels, motels and B&Bs

Giverny Inn 44 Queens Drive, Oneroa ⓣ09/372 2200, ⓦwww.giverny.co.nz. Comfortable rooms in the main house and a separate independent cottage with fantastic views over the bay make this modern, friendly outfit one of the best places on the island. Rates (which start at $370) include welcome drinks and a sumptuous four-course breakfast. ⑨

Kiwi House 23 Kiwi St, Oneroa ⓣ09/372 9123, ⓔkiwihouse@clear.net.nz. A sociable place with several rooms (continental breakfast included), all with access to communal self-catering facilities, a TV lounge and BBQ. ④

Palm Beach Lodge 23 Tiri View Rd, Palm Beach ⓣ09/372 7763, ⓦwww.waiheke.co.nz/palmbeach.htm. Luxurious salmon-pink guesthouse with lovely each with a balcony overlooking the sea. ⑦

Punga Lodge 223 Ocean View Rd, Little Oneroa ⓣ09/372 6675, ⓦwww.pungalodge.co.nz. Delightful and hospitable B&B, well located in the bush close to Oneroa beach, with tea and muffins available from the helpful hosts. Accommodation consists of a range of comfortable and spacious en-suite doubles with verandas, and four self-catering apartments of different sizes. There's a spa pool, and good-value off-season deals. They also run the nearby *Tawa Lodge*, which has a well-priced B&B and a very comfortable apartment with wonderful sea views. Ferry transfers available. Rooms ④, garden rooms ⑤, apartments ⑥

Hostels

Fossil Bay Lodge 58 Korora Rd, Oneroa ⓣ09/372 8371. A relaxed, haphazard collection of huts located 5min walk from an all-but-private beach 1km from town on an organic farm. Single $30, rooms ①

Hekerua Lodge 11 Hekerua Rd, Little Oneroa ⓣ09/372 8990, ⓦwww.gotowaiheke.co.nz/hekerualodge.htm. Peaceful, pool-equipped backpackers set in the bush 10min walk from Oneroa. Some private rooms and a s/c unit. Tent sites $16, dorms $26, shares $30, rooms ③, unit ④

Orapiu Bay Resort 15 Anzac Rd, Orapiu ⓣ09/372 4443, ⓦwww.orapiubay.co.nz. Comfortable waterside backpacker resort on the southeast corner of the island, accessible by shuttle ($20, depending on numbers) from Matiatia and the 360 Discovery ferry between Auckland and Coromandel. It's a relaxing place, with great swimming and an in-house bar and restaurant (Sat & Sun), and is handy for *Passage Rock* winery and pizzeria. Bunks $25, rooms ②

Around the island

The bulk of Waiheke's population inhabits the western quarter of the island, chiefly around **Oneroa**, a kilometre east of the Matiatia Wharf. Waiheke's finest beaches lie east of Oneroa: the almost circular Enclosure Bay for snorkelling, Palm Beach for swimming, and the more surf-oriented Onetangi.

Waiheke has no shortage of diversions if you tire of the beaches. The bays and headlands lend themselves to short, often steep **walks**, detailed in the free *Waiheke Island's Walkways* leaflet, available from the i-SITE. One of the best and most accessible coastal tracks leads from Oneroa past Little Oneroa around to Enclosure Bay, while inland there's a shady stroll through regenerating bush of

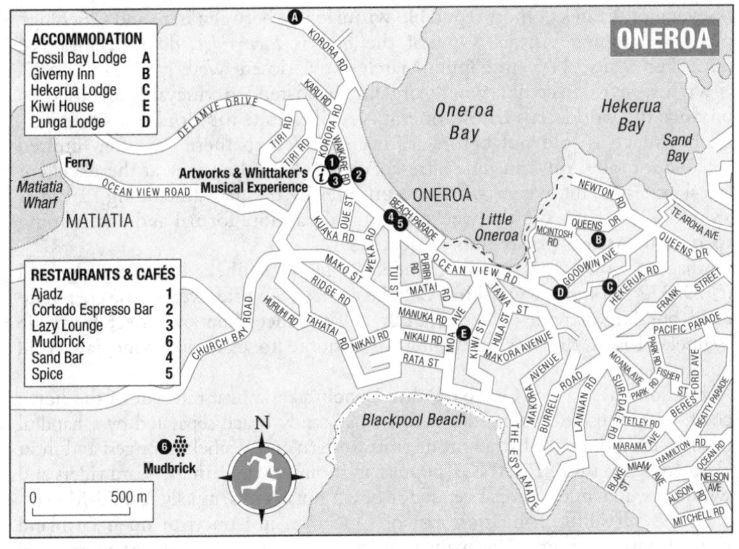

the **Waiheke Forest and Bird Reserve**, up behind Onetangi. If you're still restless, try kayaking or sailing (see p.155).

Oneroa and around

The settlement of **ONEROA** is draped across a narrow isthmus between the sandy sweep of Oneroa Bay and shallow, silty Blackpool Beach. The ridge-top main street runs up to the island's visitor centre (see p.151), where you can pick up the free *Waiheke Island of Wine Map* and *Waiheke Island Art Map*, a guide to the scattered **studios** of Waiheke's numerous artists and craftspeople. Artists' studio opening times tend to be erratic, so call ahead. For a primer on what the island has to offer, call in at the Community Gallery (daily 10am–4pm; free), by the visitor centre and adjacent to the library and cinema.

Next door is the eccentric **Whittaker's Musical Experience** (daily 10am–4pm, Sun noon–4pm; $3; Ⓦwww.musical-museum.org), a room full of flageolets, piano accordions, player pianos, xylophones and more, some dating back two hundred years and all ably demonstrated during the occasional musical performances (30min; $12.50).

The most accessible **vineyard** from Oneroa is Mudbrick, 2km west on Church Bay Road (Ⓣ09/372 9050, Ⓦwww.mudbrick.co.nz; tasting daily in summer), which has an excellent restaurant (see p.155).

The rest of the island

What passes for a main road on Waiheke winds east from Oneroa through the contiguous settlements of Little Oneroa, Blackpool and Surfdale, and across the lagoon at Putaki Bay to **Ostend**. The island's light-industrial heart, far from any appealing beaches, Ostend is best ignored except on Saturday mornings (7am–1pm) when the Ostend Hall, corner of Ostend Road and Belgium Street, is given over to the **Ostend Market**, with organic produce, arts and crafts, food stalls, massage, iridology readings and local entertainers.

Several of Waiheke's most reputable **wineries** lie between here and Onetangi, many welcoming visitors. One of the best is *Stonyridge*, 80 Onetangi Rd (Dec–Feb daily 11.50am–5pm; March–Nov closed Wed; ⓣ09/372 8822, ⓦwww.stonyridge.co.nz), where organic, hand-tended vineyards are used to produce the world-class Larose, one of New Zealand's top Bordeaux-style reds. Each vintage is sold out before it's even bottled so there are often limited cellar-door sales. You can dine alfresco, overlooking the vines, at the excellent low-key restaurant, where wines are on offer by the glass (including Larose at around $25 a pop). On the weekends they do a more formal and entertaining **tour and tasting** (Sat & Sun 11.30am; $10).

Adjacent, you'll find newly branded *Wild* on Waiheke, 82 Onetangi Rd (ⓣ09/372 1014, ⓦwww.wildonwaiheke.co.nz), who offer wearisome corporate team-building activities but thankfully still produce their own beer from the Waiheke Island Brewery, providing an antidote to excessive wine talk. Call before visiting.

Six kilometres east of Oneroa, **Palm Beach** takes a neat bite out of the north coast, with houses tumbling down to a small sandy beach separated by a handful of rocks from the nude bathing zone at its western end. Waiheke's longest and most exposed beach is **ONETANGI**, popular in summer with surfers, board riders and swimmers, and an occasional venue for beach horse races, usually in mid-March.

There's very little habitation east of Onetangi, just tracts of open farmland riddled with vineyards. The main goal in these parts is the mass of abandoned World War II defences at **Stony Batter Historic Reserve** (daily: Christmas–Jan 9am–7.30pm; Feb–Christmas 10am–3.30pm; $5, plus $5 extra for a torch; ⓣ09/372 5622) at the northeastern tip of the island 23km from Matiatia wharf. This labyrinth of dank concrete tunnels and gun emplacements was built to protect Auckland from a feared Japanese attack during World War II. The attack never came and after the war the guns and equipment were removed. The tunnels hold little allure but the views from the top are good. Stony Batter is a kilometre walk from the car park and visited by all the island tour buses.

▲ The Hauraki Gulf from Oneroa, Waiheke Island

Eating and entertainment

Oneroa is unchallenged on Waiheke for its **range** of places to eat, with restaurants catering to the demands of city day-trippers. Elsewhere, the scene is more ad hoc, with **beachside cafés** serving snacks and fast food. Entertainment is limited, though it is worth checking listings for the Waiheke Island Community **Cinema**, 2 Koroka Rd, near the visitor centre. **Live music** mostly happens at weekends, with *Sand Bar* and *Cats Tango* worthy bets.

Ajadz 2 Korora Rd. Surprisingly good Indian with authentic food at bargain prices. Dinner daily, lunch weekends only.

Cats Tango 21 The Strand, Onetangi. Lovely semi-formal licensed café with music on Fri & Sat, tasty food and a fantastic deck with sea views out to Little Barrier Island.

Cortado Espresso Bar 29 Waikare Rd, Oneroa. Wonderful cakes and coffee are served up in this stylish little café with great views and an excellent seafood menu, plus exceptional fish and chips dished up daily from the building next door, run by the same folk.

Lazy Lounge 139 Oceanview Rd. A good place to hang out and watch an endless parade of local characters call in for coffee, wine, beer or food options like Thai green curry, pizza, Mexican burritos or a hearty slice of cake.

Mudbrick Church Bay Rd, 2km west of Oneroa ⓣ09/372 9050. Expensive but highly regarded vineyard restaurant serving delicious meals. A red onion tarte tatin ($18) might be followed by seafood bisque medley ($35) perhaps washed down with wines produced on site.

Palm Beach Clubhouse Palm Beach. Sophisticated restaurant and bar open for brunch at weekends but otherwise only delicious dinners (mains approaching $35, closed Mon).

Passage Rock Café 438 Orapiu Rd, Orapiu ⓣ09/372 7257. A little inconveniently sited on a vineyard far from Waiheke's towns, but if you've got wheels it is *the* place to go for toothsome wood-fired pizza.

Sand Bar 153 Ocean View Rd ⓣ09/372 9458. Chic little bar, great for a cocktail as the sun goes down and frequently hosting DJs at the weekend. Opens 4pm.

Spice 153 Ocean View Rd, Oneroa. A licensed café open from breakfast through lunch, serving great coffee, snacks, sandwiches and cakes.

Listings

Internet access The library on Oceanview Rd (daily 9am–5pm) and i-SITE have Internet access.

Kayaking Ross Adventures (ⓣ09/372 5550, ⓦwww.kayakwaiheke.co.nz) run guided trips from Matiatia: half-day trips (4hr; $70), evening trips (3hr; $70), full-day trips including a shuttle back to your starting point ($135) and round-the-island camping trips (2–4 days; around $135 per day). They also rent sea kayaks (from $35/half-day). The Kayak Company (ⓣ09/372 2112, ⓦwww.thekayakcompany.co.nz) offers an almost identical range at similar prices, plus a 2hr jaunt ($45) and a full day around Cactus Bay ($120).

Medical emergencies Waiheke Island Community Health Services, 5 Belgium St, Ostend (ⓣ09/372 5005) and the Oneroa Accident and Medical Centre, Oceanview Rd (ⓣ09/372 3111).

Sailing Flying Carpet, 104 Wharf Rd, Ostend (ⓣ09/372 5621, ⓦwww.flyingcarpet.co.nz), offer day-trips on an ocean-going catamaran ($110), evening cruises ($50) and a range of others.

Taxis Waiheke Dial-a-Cab ⓣ09/372 3000; Waiheke Quality Cabs ⓣ09/372 7000.

Great Barrier Island (Aotea)

Rugged and sparsely populated **Great Barrier Island** (Aotea) lies 90km northeast of Auckland on the outer fringes of the Hauraki Gulf and, though only 30km long and 15km wide, packs in a mountainous heart which drops away to deep indented harbours in the west and eases gently to golden surf beaches in the east. It's a two-hour ferry or half-hour plane ride from the city but seems a world apart. There is no mains electricity or water, no industry, no towns to speak of, and no regular public transport. This lends Great Barrier a sense of peace and detachment, enhanced by **beaches**, **hot springs** and tightly packed **mountains** clad in bush and spared the ravages of deer and possums.

Ferries arrive in **Tryphena**, the southern harbour and major settlement, some continuing up the west coast to the minuscule hamlet of **Port Fitzroy**, an ideal jumping-off point for tramps in the Great Barrier Forest. **Claris**, in the east, is the site of the airport and is convenient for the best beaches at **Medlands** and **Awana Bay**.

Some history

Great Barrier is formed from the same line of extinct **volcanoes** as the Coromandel Peninsula and shares a common geological and human past. Aotea was one of the places first populated by **Maori**, and the Ngatiwai and Ngatimaru people occupied numerous *pa* sites when Cook sailed by in 1769. Recognizing the calming influence of Aotea and neighbouring Hauturu on the waters of the Hauraki Gulf, Cook renamed them Great Barrier Island and Little Barrier Island. The vast stands of kauri all over the island were soon seized upon for ships' timbers, the first load being taken in 1791. Kauri **logging** didn't really get under way until the late nineteenth century but continued until 1942, outliving some early copper mining at Miners Head and sporadic attempts to extract gold and silver from a large quartz intrusion in the centre of the island. Kauri logging and gum digging were replaced by a short-lived whale-oil extraction industry at Whangaparapara in the 1950s, but the Barrier soon fell back on tilling the poor clay soils and its peak population of over 5000 dropped to around 1000.

The space and tranquillity of the island appealed to budding alternative lifestylers, who trickled across from the mainland in the 1960s and 1970s. Much of the Seventies idealism has been supplanted by modern pragmatism, but **self-sufficiency** remains, more out of necessity than lifestyle choice. People grow their own vegetables, everyone has their own water supply and the strain on diesel generators is reduced by wind-driven turbines and solar panels. **Agriculture** takes a back seat to **tourism**, however, and wealthy second-home-owners are moving in. Islanders have resisted this trend but as land prices rocket, some on low incomes are forced to leave, while others head out when their kids reach high school age. Indeed, a dropping population and the need to cater for visitors means there's often **casual work** available in the summer.

Arrival, information and transport

Points of entry are the **airport** at Claris, the grass airstrip at Okiwi in the north and the two main **harbours** of Port Fitzroy and Tryphena. Around the first there's a couple of lodges and shops, leaving the bulk of the activity to the four main bays of Tryphena Harbour: Shoal Bay (where ferries arrive), Mulberry Grove, Stonewall Village (the largest settlement), and Puriri Bay (a short walk along the coast from Stonewall Village).

The vast majority of visitors arrive from Auckland over the summer months aboard Fullers **ferries** to Tyrphena (days of departure vary enormously and depend on the time of year; 2hr; $70 one way, bikes $10; ⓣ09/367 9111)

The slower Sealink **car ferry** (ⓣ0800/732 546, ⓦwww.sealink.co.nz), carries passengers, cars and just about all the island's freight, leaving Wynyard Wharf in Auckland (Christmas–Jan daily; Feb–Christmas 5 weekly; 4hr 30min) for Tryphena, with one service a week (Tues) to Port Fitzroy (foot passengers $68 one way, $110 return; cars $330/$205).

Ferries are met by **shuttle buses**, that generally run to the bays around Tryphena Harbour and on to Claris – if you want to go beyond Stonewall

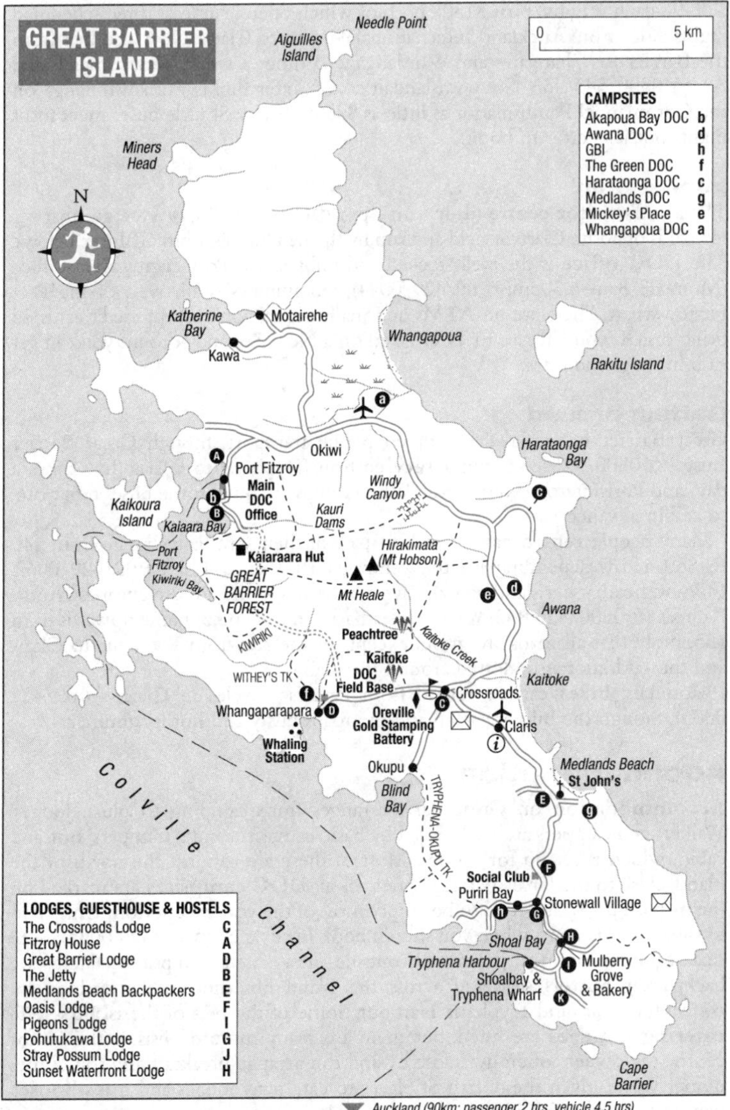

Village book in advance. Fares are around \$10 to Medlands, \$20 to Whangaparapara and \$12 to Claris, ask when you arrive.

Bad weather occasionally causes ferries to be cancelled, but you can pre-empt any inconvenience by buying a boat/fly deal with Great Barrier Express (see below), flying back or out and taking the ferry the other way.

Alternatively, **fly** both ways. The two main players are Great Barrier Airlines (GBA; ⓣ0800/900 600, ⓦwww.greatbarrierairlines.co.nz; \$75–96 each way) and Great Barrier Xpress (ⓣ0800/222 123, ⓦwww.mountainair.co.nz; generally

$79–98 each way, fly/boat $150), both of which operate at least three scheduled flights a day from Auckland International Airport to Claris. GBA also flies from the Barrier to Whangarei and Whitianga 2–3 times a week. Newcomer Island Air (Ⓣ0800/545 455, Ⓦwww.islandair.co.nz), offer flights from Whitianga on the Coromandel Peninsula for as little as $95 each way. Shuttle buses meet most flights but it's better to book.

Information

The island's **visitor centre** (daily 9am–4pm; Ⓣ09/429 0033, Ⓦwww.greatbarrier.co.nz) is opposite Claris airfield and run by the helpful folk from GBI (see below). The **DOC office** is the well-stocked and informative Port Fitzroy Area Office (Mon–Fri 8am–4.30pm; Ⓣ09/429 0044), ten minutes' walk west of the Port Fitzroy wharf. There are no **ATMs** and many places don't accept credit cards, so bring cash. If you have an EFTPOS card on a New Zealand account you can get cash in shops and cafés.

Getting around

Great Barrier has no real scheduled public transport, though Great Barrier Buses (Ⓣ0800/426 832) run a **service** from Tryphena to Claris (five times a day) and Port Fitzroy (Wed & Sat). When things are quiet some buses don't run, so call in advance.

Many people **rent a car** for at least part of their stay. Rates range from $40 to $80 a day, depending on the vehicle; GBI Rent-a-Car (Ⓣ09/429 0062, Ⓦwww.greatbarrierisland.co.nz), have a wide range and are the cheapest. Aotea Rentals (Ⓣ0800/426 832, Ⓦwww.greatbarriertravel.co.nz) range upwards from $55. Note that all roads are gravel except for the run from Tryphena to Claris and the odd kilometre dotted around the island.

Mountain **bikes** can be rented from Paradise Cycles in Claris (Ⓣ09/429 0303), though the hills are steep and the roads dusty and hot in summer.

Accommodation

Accommodation on Great Barrier ranges from camping to plush lodges. Walkers and campers are well served by basic campsites and a trampers' **hut** and cabin, which is set up for groups. Most of these are towards the north of the island, close to the Great Barrier Forest: all six **DOC campsites** are marked on the map on p.157 and tend to be empty most of the year except from Christmas to the end of January, when you should book in advance (Ⓣ09/429 0044); note that camping is not permitted outside designated campsites. There are backpacker **hostels** scattered across the island but most other options are concentrated around Tryphena Harbour. Some of the best of the island's **self-catering cottages** are listed, but there are many more on lists at the visitor centre; the owners often live close by and can arrange breakfast and sometimes dinner while, given the dearth of places to eat, many lodges and **guesthouses** have self-catering facilities.

Some places **pick up** from the harbours and airport, though those in Tryphena and Medlands will expect you to catch the shuttles that meet each boat or plane. The island's remoteness means that accommodation is generally more **expensive** than the mainland, particularly through the summer; some places further boost their rates from Christmas to the end of January when visitor numbers are at their peak – and you'll need to book well ahead to stand any chance of finding a place.

Lodges, guesthouses and cottages

Fitzroy House Glenfern Rd, Port Fitzroy ⓣ09/429 0091, ⓦwww.fitzroyhouse.co.nz and *Glenfern Sanctuary* (ⓦwww.glenfern.org.nz). The emphasis at *Glenfern* is on nature tourism and there is free use of canoes and a dinghy (sea kayaks are extra). Lodge guests can join a day-trip ($45–85 depending on numbers) that involves a Unimog 4WD journey, a hike and a botanical walkway to a suspension bridge into the top of a six-hundred-year-old kauri. Accommodation is in one comfortable s/c cottage sleeping six, with views over the northern shore of the inner harbour. 9

Great Barrier Lodge Whangaparapara Harbour ⓣ09/429 0488, ⓦwww.greatbarrierlodge.com. This harbourside lodge is pretty much all there is at Whangaparapara, and also serves as the local shop. Accommodation is in cottages and studio units and the main building houses a bar/restaurant. Bunkroom $40, cabin 3, studios & cottages 6

The Jetty Kaiaraara Bay, Port Fitzroy ⓣ09/429 0050, ⓔinfo@thejetty.co.nz. Sited around 2km from Port Fitzroy Wharf. B&B accommodation is in nicely decorated s/c chalets. 5

Oasis Lodge 50 Medlands Rd, Tryphena ⓣ09/429 0021, ⓦwww.barrieroasis.co.nz. Lovely en-suite rooms, great valley views and a separate s/c cottage for the reclusive. Rooms are let on a B&B basis, though you are encouraged to stay for delicious dinners (see p.161). 8

Pigeons Lodge 179 Shoal Bay Rd, Tryphena ⓣ09/429 0437, ⓦwww.pigeonslodge.co.nz. Small, comfortable and classy B&B (with delicious breakfasts) nestled in the bush near the sea, with en-suite accommodation and two self-catering chalets. Self-catering 5, B&B 6

Pohutukawa Lodge Stonewall, Tryphena ⓣ09/429 0211, ⓦwww.currachirishpub.com. The pick of the places around Tryphena, homely, small and welcoming, with a great pub and restaurant spilling out onto the veranda, all conveniently close to the shop. There are attractive en suites and backpacker rooms (linen supplied). Backpacker rooms $25, rooms 4

Sunset Waterfront Lodge Mulberry Grove, Tryphena ⓣ09/429 0051, ⓦwww.sunsetlodge.co.nz. Upmarket motel-style accommodation. 6

Hostels

The Crossroads Lodge 1 Blind Bay Rd, Crossroads ⓣ09/429 0889, ⓦwww.xroadslodge.com. Comfortable hostel well sited in the middle of the island, within walking distance of the hot springs and island tramps. Accommodation is in cabins or double rooms. Beds $30, rooms 3

Medlands Beach Backpackers 9 Mason Rd ⓣ09/429 0320, ⓦwww.medlandsbeach.com. Basic, low-key backpackers with two- and four-bed dorms, a secluded chalet and a couple of villas on a small farm 10min walk from Medlands Beach – making it popular with surfers. There are body boards for guests' use, but there are no meals and no shops nearby, so bring your own food. Dorms $30, chalet 3, villa 5

Stray Possum Lodge Shoal Bay ⓣ0800/767 786, ⓦwww.straypossum.co.nz. This hostel has a bar and on-site licensed pizza restaurant (which also serves breakfast) set in a spacious clearing in attractive bush. Beds are in six- to eight-bed dorms or in s/c chalets ideal for groups of up to six. Camping $12, dorms $25, rooms 3, chalets 5

Campsites

Akapoua DOC Campsite Orama. Harbour-edge site right by the DOC office and an easy walk to the harbour and shop at Port Fitzroy. It comes equipped with cold showers and toilets. Camping $8–9.

Awana DOC Campsite Awana. Exposed site with separate tent and vehicle sites, all 400m from a good surf beach. Cold showers and toilets. Camping $8–9.

GBI Campground Puriri Bay, Tryphena ⓣ09/429 0184. A quiet sheltered campsite nestled in bush by a freshwater stream near a safe swimming beach, 20min walk to shops. Camping $9.

The Green DOC Campsite Whangaparapara. Basic campsite with barbecues, water and toilets but no vehicle access. No showers but it's close to the sea and there's a stream to wash in. Camping $8–9.

Harataonga DOC Campsite Harataonga. Shady site 300m back from the beach, equipped with toilets and cold showers. Camping $8–9.

Medlands DOC Campsite Medlands Beach. Attractive beach-back site that gets very crowded in the peak season. Cold showers, stream water and toilets. Camping $8–9.

Mickey's Place Awana ⓣ09/429 0140. Hospitable commercial campsite 25km north of Tryphena that's less well located than the nearby DOC site but has hot showers, toilets and a cookhouse, all for $7.

Orama Karaka Bay, Port Fitzroy ⓣ09/429 0063. A Christian centre also operating as a waterfront holiday park with swimming pool, shop, small boats and kayaks and access to magnificent bushwalks, fishing and diving. Camping $10, cabins 3, s/c houses and cottages 4

Around the island

Much of the pleasure here is in lazing on the beaches and striking out on foot into the **Great Barrier Forest**, a rugged chunk of bush and kauri-logging relics between Port Fitzroy and Whangaparapara that takes up about a third of the island. If you're looking for more structure to your day, there are a few small-time operators keen to keep you entertained by means of various activities and tours (see p.161). **TRYPHENA** has a particular dearth of things to do, though there is the appealing **Tryphena to Okupu Walking Track** (4hr), which runs from Puriri Bay around coastal headlands to Okupu on Blind Bay.

Most people head straight for **Medlands Beach**, a long sweep of golden sand broken by a sheltering island and often endowed with some of the Barrier's best surf – though, be warned, there is no patrolled area. The pretty blue and white **St John's Church** looks suitably out of place, having only been moved here from the mainland in 1986 by barge before being dragged over the dunes.

North of Medlands, the road leaves the coast for the airport at **Claris**, where the post office claims to be the world's first place to have run an airmail service. The story goes that when the SS *Wairarapa* was wrecked on the northwest coast of Great Barrier in 1898, the news took a sobering three days to get to Auckland. In response the island set up a **pigeon-mail** service that was used until 1908, when a telephone was installed. Not far from the airport, the **Milk, Honey and Grain Museum**, 47 Hector Sanderson Rd (open most days, donation), boasts a collection of memorabilia neatly organized into three categories which reveals a lot more about the island than its name suggests – a worthwhile stop if the weather's bad.

Crossroads, 2km north of Claris, is just that – the junction of roads to Okupu, Port Fitzroy and the north of the island, and Whangaparapara. The Whangaparapara road runs past the scant roadside remains of the **Oreville gold stamping battery** (unrestricted entry) and the start of a path to **Kaitoke Hot Springs** (4km return; 1hr; also on the Great Barrier Forest Tramp – see p.162), sulphurous dammed pools that aren't especially pretty but are perfect for an hour's wallowing. At **Whangaparapara** itself, a short stroll around the bay brings you to the foundations of a whaling station built here in the 1950s.

North from Crossroads, the Port Fitzroy road passes two excellent camping spots by the surf beach at Awana Bay, then the start of a track to **Windy Canyon** (1km; 20–30min return), a narrow defile that gets its name from the eerie sounds produced by certain wind conditions. The narrow path winds through nikau palms and tree ferns to a viewpoint that gives a sense of the island's interior, as well as coastal views.

The island's highest point, Hirakimata, can be reached in three hours walking from Awana Bay or a similar time from **PORT FITZROY**, whose harbour remains remarkably calm under most wind conditions, a quality not lost on yachties who flock here in summer. Apart from the shop, burger bar and a few places to stay there's not a lot here, but Port Fitzroy makes the best base for **tramping** or shorter day-walks to some fine **kauri dams**. For three years from 1926, the Kauri Timber Company hacked trees out of the relatively inaccessible Kaiaraara Valley, shunning the tramways and trestle bridges employed in more manageable terrain in favour of six kauri dams – wooden structures up to twenty metres high and spanning the valley floor. Logs were cut and rolled into the reservoirs as the stream built up the water level behind the dams. The upper dams were then tripped, followed seconds later by the lower dams; the combined releases sent a torrent of water and logs sluicing down to Kaiaraara Bay, where they were lashed together in rafts and floated to Auckland.

Eating and drinking

The relative lack of stand-alone **restaurants** encourages lots of accommodation places to offer meals, and those that don't will almost certainly have self-catering facilities. Still, there are a few restaurants springing up, for which you should book in advance.

There are also a shops in Tryphena, Claris, Whangaparapara and Port Fitzroy, where you can get snacks and pick up picnic provisions. **Drinking** tends to happen in bars attached to accommodation establishments or in the social clubs at Tryphena and Claris.

Angasana Thai Restaurant just north of Crossroads, on Gray's Rd. Completely unexpected, brilliant Thai and Kiwi licensed restaurant, open for lunch and dinner with a wide-ranging menu and friendly service.

Claris Texas Café Claris ⓣ09/429 0811. Easily the best café on the island, with a sunny deck and a grassy patch for the kids. It's open daily 8am–4pm for light meals, good chowder, panini, great desserts and excellent coffee.

Currach Irish Pub Stonewall, Tryphena. An Irish Pub that's about as traditional as you can get on a South Pacific island – a lot of the paraphernalia came from the owner's grandmother's pub, in County Kerry, which closed in 1950. They have Guinness and Kilkenny on tap, and there's often live acoustic music, especially on Thurs when anyone is welcome to jam. Full breakfasts until 9.30am, and in the evening, great hot meals are served.

Mulberry Grove Store Mulberry Grove, Tryphena. Bar/eatery that's well worth a visit for excellent coffee and good grub alongside a range of shop goods.

Oasis Lodge 50 Medlands Rd, Tryphena ⓣ09/429 0021, ⓦwww.barrieroasis.co.nz. Delicious meals using local and homegrown produce (including their own Cabernet Sauvignon and olive oil), frequently with Thai, Indian or seafood themes. Evening meals are table d'hôte and will set you back $65 for three courses.

Tipi & Bob's Waterfront Lodge Puriri Bay, Tryphena ⓣ09/429 0550. A soulless public bar, leafy garden bar and spartan seafood and steak restaurant serving $15–35 mains.

Whale Boat Bistro *Great Barrier Lodge*, Whangaparapara Harbour. Bar and restaurant serving meals indoors or on the spacious deck with harbour views.

Listings

Fishing To test Great Barrier's enviable reputation, head out for a day's fishing in the Colville Channel aboard any of the Tryphena-based boats, who charge $380 a half-day ($640 a day) for four people including rod, tackle and bait. Try Tryphena Charters (ⓣ09/429 0596).

Golf Pioneer Park, Whangaparapara Rd, Claris (ⓣ09/429 0420; green fee and club rental are ridiculously cheap), is a nine-hole par-three course surrounded by bush with pukeko strutting across the fairways; every Thurs and Sun the lively bar serves cheap drinks and decent meals.

Internet *The Crossroads Lodge* (see p.159) has Internet facilities open to all, as does *Claris Texas café* (see above).

Kayaking Tryphena-based Great Barrier Kayaks (ⓣ027/660 022) run short paddling trips ($40 harbour cruise), joint 4–5hr kayak and snorkelling trips ($80) and sunset paddles ($50).

Package Tours If organizing your own Barrier Island itinerary is too much trouble, go for an all-in package (book through *Pohutukawa Lodge*, see p.159) including flights, two nights accommodation and car hire, all for $320 per person.

Shuttle bus companies Choose from The Barrier Tour Co (ⓣ09/429 0222), Great Barrier Buses/Great Barrier Travel (ⓣ09/429 0474), Kaka Tours (ⓣ09/429 0640), GBI Buses (ⓣ09/429 0062) and Sanderson Transport (ⓣ09/429 0640).

Tiritiri Matangi

A visit to **Tiritiri Matangi** is the highpoint of many a stay in Auckland. About 4km off the tip of the Whangaparaoa Peninsula and 30km north of Auckland, Tiritiri Matangi is an "open sanctuary", and visitors are free to roam through

The Great Barrier Forest tramp

The **Great Barrier Forest**, New Zealand's largest stand of possum-free bush, offers a unique **tramping environment**. Because the area is so compact, in no time at all you can find yourself climbing in and out of little subtropical gullies luxuriant with nikau palms, tree ferns, regenerating rimu and kauri, and onto scrubby manuka ridges with stunning coastal and mountain views. Many of the tracks follow the routes of mining tramways past old kauri dams.

The only decent walking **maps** are the four Topomaps that cover the island, though DOC also print a Track Information **leaflet** (from the Auckland DOC office) which will do for most purposes. Book huts in Auckland or use the local field office (see p.158).

Access and huts

The tramp can be done equally well from Port Fitzroy or Whangaparapara, both of which can offer accommodation and a reasonably well-stocked shop. Port Fitzroy also has the 28-bunk **Kaiaraara Hut** nearby ($10), and the main DOC office (Mon–Fri 8am–4.30pm; ⑦09/429 0044), which sells hut **tickets** and **maps**. In addition, Port Fitzroy's *Akapoua Bay* **campsite** is superior to Whangaparapara's simple *The Green*.

If you have come specifically to tramp it is best to catch one of the infrequent ferries direct to Port Fitzroy. Alternatively, call one of the shuttle operators in advance to organize transport from the airport or Tryphena.

The tramp

From the wharf at **Port Fitzroy**, follow the coast road fifteen minutes south to the DOC office. From there the road climbs for half an hour over a headland with views over Kaiaraara and Rarohara bays to a gate. The Kaiaraara Hut is roughly fifteen minutes on, along a 4WD track and across a couple of river fords. From **Kaiaraara Hut to Whangaparapara** (13km; 7–9hr; 800m ascent), the route leaves the 4WD track and crosses the Kaiaraara Stream several times as it climbs steeply to the first and most impressive **kauri dam** (see p.160), reached in under an hour. The well-defined path continues for another fifty minutes to one of the upper dams then begins a long and arduous series of boardwalks and wooden steps designed to keep

the predator-free bush where, within a couple of hours, it's possible to see rarities like takahe, saddlebacks, whiteheads, red-crowned parakeets, North Island robins, kokako and brown teals. To stand a chance of seeing the little-spotted kiwi and tuatara, you'll have to stay overnight.

Evidence from *pa* sites on the island indicate that Tiritiri Matangi was first populated by the Kawerau-A-Maki **Maori** and later by Ngati Paoa, both of whom are now recognized as the land's traditional owners. They partly **cleared the island** of bush, a process continued by Europeans who arrived in the mid-nineteenth century to graze sheep and cattle. Fortunately, **predators** such as possums, stoats, weasels, deer, cats, wallabies and the like failed to get a foothold, so after farming became uneconomic in the early 1970s Tiritiri was singled out as a prime site for helping to restore bird populations. The cacophony of birdsong in the bush is stark evidence of just how catastrophic the impact of these predators has been elsewhere.

Since 1984, a **reforestation** programme has seen the planting of over 300,000 saplings and though the rapidly regenerating bush is far from mature, the **birds** seem to like it. Most are thriving with the aid of feeding stations to supplement diets in the leaner months, with nesting boxes standing in for decaying trees.

Four of the species released here are among the rarest in the world, with total populations of around a couple of hundred. The most visible are the flightless **takahe**, lumbering blue-green turkey-sized birds long thought to be extinct (see

trampers on the path and prevent the disturbance of nesting black petrels. It'll take a good thirty to forty minutes to reach the summit of the 621-metre **Hirakimata** (Mount Hobson), where you'll be rewarded by panoramic views.

Less extensive boardwalks extend south around the dramatic spire of Mount Heale towards the junction of **two paths**. To the right a path follows the south branch of the Kaiaraara Stream **back to the Kaiaraara Hut** in around an hour and a half, making a four- to- five-hour circuit from the hut. The leftmost path follows an undulating but gradually descending route into Kaitoke Creek No.1, eventually reaching the edge of Kaitoke Swamp right by the hard-to-locate **Peach Tree Hot Spring** just beyond the northernmost tip of the swamp. Originally dug by kauri loggers, the pools here are hotter than the more widely used **Kaitoke Hot Springs** – the latter reached along a ten-minute track which spurs off south twenty minutes ahead; the more attractive hollows are to be found upstream. Back on the main track, you soon reach the 4WD forest road: follow it south for a hundred metres or so, then join the signposted track to the former site of Whangaparapara Hut, fifteen minutes on. From here it's ten minutes' walk to the DOC residence and half an hour to the Whangaparapara Wharf.

There are two main routes from **Whangaparapara to Kaiaraara Hut**, the direct and dull route following the Pack Track due north of the former site of Whangaparapara Hut and the 4WD forest road (11km; 5hr; 200m ascent), and the more appealing semi-coastal Kiwiriki Track (12km; 6hr; 300m ascent) which branches off the 4WD forest road just north of its junction with the Pack Track. The track cuts west from the forest road by the rocky knob of Maungapiko, leading to the picnic area at Kiwiriki Bay then climbing steeply over a ridge to Coffins Creek before a relatively gentle walk to a second picnic area at **Kaiaraara Bay**. From here it is half an hour to Kaiaraara Hut and another hour or so to the Port Fitzroy Wharf.

An alternative start to either route eschews the Pack Track and follows the far more interesting **Withey's Track**, which starts between the Whangaparapara DOC field base and the former hut site; it takes half an hour longer, but goes through some lovely bush with delightful streamside nikau groves.

p.845); birds moved here from Fiordland have bred well and are easily spotted as they are unafraid of humans and very inquisitive. **Saddlebacks**, **kokako** and **stitchbirds** stick to the bush and its margins, but often pop out if you sit quietly for a few moments on some of the bush boardwalks and paths near feeding stations. **Northern blue penguins** also frequent Tiritiri, and can be seen all year round – but are most in evidence in March, when they come ashore to moult, and from September to December, when they nest in specially constructed viewing boxes located along the seashore path west of the main wharf.

Practicalities

Tiritiri Matangi is typically visited as a **day-trip**, giving five hours on the island; you'll need to take your own **lunch**, as there is no food available. 360 Discovery **ferries** (ⓣ0800/888 006, ⓦwww.360discovery.co.nz) depart from Auckland's Downtown Ferry Terminal (Christmas to mid-Jan daily 9am, rest of year Wed–Sun and public holidays 9am; $59 return) then call at Gulf Harbour (see p.143: 9.50am; $26.80 return) before arriving at Tiritiri around 10.10am. Boats arrive back in Auckland around 5pm.

Visitors arriving on scheduled ferries can join **guided walks** (1–2hr; $5), leaving from the wharf and led by volunteers steeped in bird-lore. They typically finish near the lighthouse at the modern **interpretation centre**. Otherwise, you're free to wander the island or indulge in a little **swimming** from Hobbs Beach, a ten-minute walk west of the wharf and the only sandy strand around.

It's also possible to **stay overnight** in a self-contained bunkhouse – bring a sleeping bag and food in sealed rodent-proof containers – near the lighthouse (Ⓣ09/476 0010; $20); weekends are booked months ahead and for week nights you'll need to book two weeks in advance.

For more detail on the island go to the Supporters of Tiritiri Matangi website (Ⓦwww.tiritirimatangi.org.nz).

Little Barrier Island

Very few visitors make it out to **Little Barrier Island** (Hauturu), 80km north of Auckland, a nature reserve barred to those without the necessary DOC permit. Although around a third of its trees were felled for timber before the government acquired the island and set it aside as a wildlife sanctuary in 1884, mountainous Little Barrier remains largely unspoilt. Home to fascinating creatures – including giant earthworms up to a metre long, the prehistoric tuatara and a mouse-sized version of the grasshopper-like weta – the island became completely pest-free in 2007 and now DOC plans to create a refuge for native birds.

Travel details

For more on moving on from Auckland, see box, p.136

Trains

Auckland to: Hamilton (1 daily; 2hr 30min); National Park (1 daily; 5hr 30min); Ohakune (1 daily; 6hr 30min); Otorohanga (1 daily; 3hr); Palmerston North (1 daily; 9hr 30min); Wellington (1 daily; 12hr).

Buses

Auckland to: Dargaville (1 daily, not Sat; 3hr); Gisborne (1 daily; 9hr 30min); Hamilton (14–16 daily; 2hr); Hastings (3 daily; 7hr 50min); Helensville (Mon–Fri 8 daily; 1hr 10min); Huntly (14–16 daily; 1hr 20min); Kaitaia (1 daily; 7hr); Kerikeri (3–5 daily; 5hr); Kumeu (4–8 daily; 35min); Mangonui (1 daily; 6hr 30min); Napier (3 daily; 7hr 20min); National Park (1 daily; 5hr 30min); New Plymouth (3 daily; 5hr 30min–6hr 15min); Ngaruawahia (14–16 daily; 1hr 30min); Ohakune (1 daily; 6hr); Orewa (5–7 daily; 30min); Paihia (4–6 daily; 4hr 20min); Palmerston North (4 daily; 9hr); Rotorua (6 daily; 4hr); Taihape (3 daily; 6hr 45min); Taupo (4 daily; 4–5hr); Tauranga (3 daily; 3hr 40min); Thames (4 daily; 1hr 45min); Waipu (4–6 daily; 2hr 30min); Waitomo Caves (1 daily; 4hr 20min); Warkworth (6–8 daily; 1hr); Wellington (4 daily; 11hr); Whangarei (5–8 daily; 3hr).

Ferries

Auckland to: Coromandel (3 weekly; 2hr); Devonport (every 30min; 10min); Great Barrier (2–5 weekly; 2–5hr); Gulf Harbour Marina (3 daily; 50min); Rangitoto (2–4 daily; 40min); Tiritiri Matangi Island (4 weekly; 1hr 30min); Waiheke (7–10 daily; 35min).

Gulf Harbour Marina to: Tiritiri Matangi Island (4 weekly; 20min).

Half Moon Bay to: Waiheke (11 daily; 45min).

Flights

Auckland to: Bay of Islands (5 daily; 40min); Blenheim (4 daily; 1hr 20min); Christchurch (20–25 daily; 1hr 20min); Dunedin (1 daily; 1hr 50min); Gisborne (5–8 daily; 1hr); Great Barrier Island (5–10 daily; 30min), Hamilton (3 daily; 30min); Kaitaia (1–2 daily; 50min); Napier (5–8 daily; 1hr); Nelson (12–14 daily; 1hr 20min); New Plymouth (5–8 daily; 45min); Palmerston North (5–8 daily; 1hr); Queenstown (4 daily; 1hr 50min); Rotorua (3–5 daily; 40min); Taupo (2–3 daily; 45min); Tauranga (6–9 daily; 35min); Wanganui (3–4 daily; 1hr); Wellington (20–30 daily; 1hr); Whakatane (3–5 daily; 45min); Whangarei (7–10 daily; 35min).

Great Barrier Island: to Auckland (5–10 daily); Whitianga (2 weekly; 20min).

2

Northland

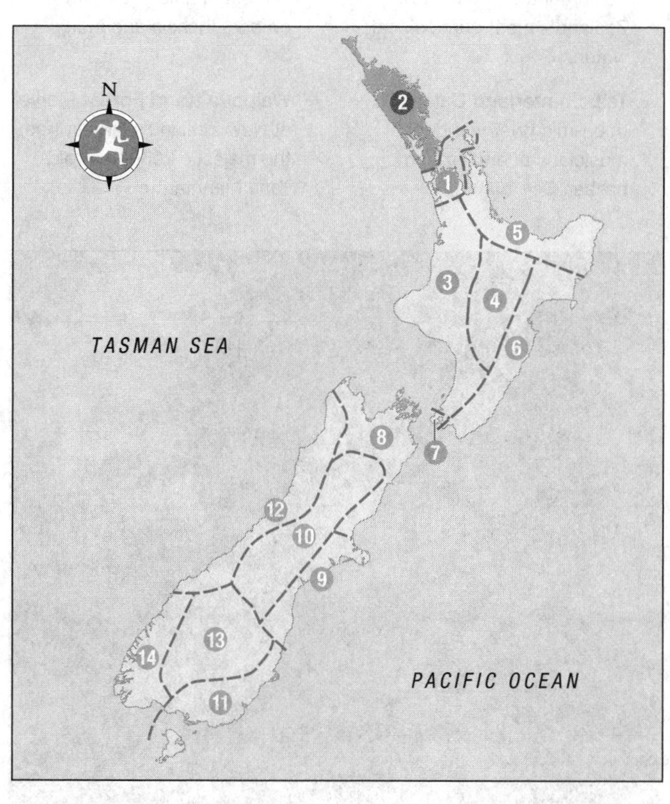

CHAPTER 2

Highlights

* **Poor Knights Islands** Scuba dive amid caves, fabulous rock arches, abundant fish, and wrecks including the *Rainbow Warrior*. See p.180
* **Whangaroa Harbour** Sail around some of New Zealand's most paradisiacal waters. See p.207
* **Taipa hinterland** Catch open-mic poetry and local musicians at a full moon bazaar. See p.209
* **Cape Reinga** Sandboard giant dunes and see the Pacific Ocean and Tasman Sea meeting in a maelstrom. See p.218
* **Hokianga Harbour** Watch the sun set in a fiery rainbow of orange, fuchsia and indigo. See p.219
* **Waipoua Kauri Forest** Marvel at New Zealand's largest tree, the majestic 2000-year-old Tane Mahuta. See p.223

▲ Red pigfish, Poor Knights Islands

2

Northland

Thrusting 350km from Auckland into the subtropical north, **Northland** separates the Pacific Ocean from the Tasman Sea. The two oceans crash together off Cape Reinga, New Zealand's most northerly road-accessible point. Kiwis often describe this staunchly Maori province as the "Winterless North", a phrase that rightly evokes the palms and citrus trees, warm aquamarine waters and beaches of white silica and golden sand that make the upper reaches of the region such a magnet.

Scenically, Northland splits down the middle. The **east coast** is a labyrinth of coves hidden between plunging headlands. Beaches tend to be calm and safe, with the force of occasional Pacific storms broken by clusters of protective barrier islands. There could hardly be a greater contrast than the long, virtually straight, **west coastline** pounded by powerful Tasman breakers and broken only by occasional harbours. Tidal rips and holes make swimming dangerous, and there are no lifeguard patrols. Some beaches are even designated as roads but are full of hazards for the unwary – and rental cars aren't insured for beach driving. Exploration of the undulating **interior** involves long forays down twisting side roads.

Beyond the Hibiscus Coast, on the east shore, is the rural **Kowhai Coast**, which is popular with yachties circumnavigating Kawau Island, and snorkellers exploring the underwater world of the **Goat Island Marine Reserve**. The broad sweep of **Bream Bay** runs to the dramatic crags of Whangarei Heads at the entrance to Northland's major port and town, **Whangarei**. Off the coast here lie the **Poor Knights Islands**, New Zealand's premier dive spot. Tourists in a hurry tend to make straight for the **Bay of Islands**, a jagged bite out of the coastline, dotted with islands perfect for cruising, diving and swimming with dolphins, and steeped in New Zealand history. Everything north of here is loosely referred to as **The Far North**, a region characterized by the quiet remoteness of the **Whangaroa Harbour**, **Doubtless Bay**, and the **Aupori Peninsula**, which backs **Ninety Mile Beach** all the way up to **Cape Reinga**.

The west coast is very different from the east, marked by economic neglect over the last fifty years as kauri logging ended and dairying never successfully replaced it. First stop on the way back south from Ninety Mile Beach is the fragmented **Hokianga Harbour**, one of New Zealand's largest, with spectacular sand dunes gracing the north head. South of here you're into the **Waipoua Forest**, all that remains after the depredations of the kauri loggers, a story best told at the excellent Kauri Museum at Matakohe.

Northland has no passenger train services so **getting around** by public transport means travelling by **bus**. If you're **driving** the choices are limited to

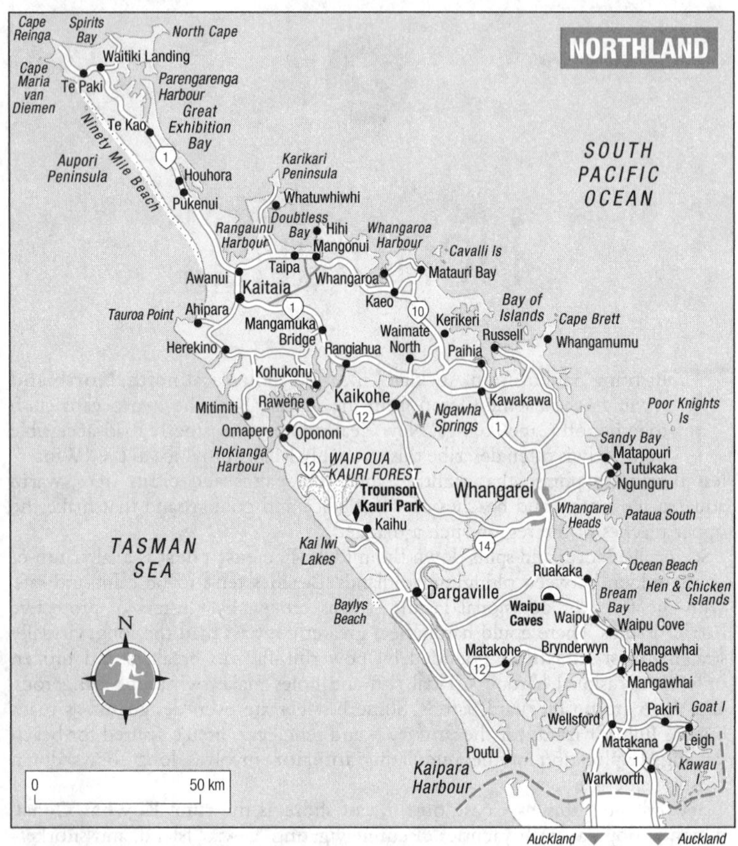

a major road up each side of the peninsula. This forms a logical loop formalized as the **Twin Coast Discovery Highway**: there's no need to follow it slavishly, but the brown signs emblazoned with a dolphin and curling wave make a good starting framework.

Some history

Northland was the site of most of the early contact between Maori and European settlers, and the birthplace of New Zealand's most important document, the **Treaty of Waitangi**. Maori legend tells of how the great Polynesian explorer Kupe discovered the Hokianga Harbour and, finding the climate and abundance of food to his liking, encouraged his people to return and settle there. It was their descendants in the Bay of Islands who had the dubious honour of making the first contact with white men, as European whalers plundered the seas and missionaries sought converts. Eventually, the northern chiefs signed away their sovereignty in return for assurances on land and traditional rights, which were seldom respected. There is still a perception among some Maori in the rest of the country that the five northern *iwi* gave Aotearoa away to the Pakeha.

As more fertile farmlands were found in newly settled regions further south, rapacious **kauri loggers** and **gum diggers** cleared the bush and later, as extractive industries died away, pioneers moved in, turning much of the land to **dairy country**. Local dairy factories closed as larger semi-industrial complexes centralized processing, leaving small towns all but destitute, though the planting of fast-growing exotic trees and sporadic horticulture keep local economies ticking over.

The Kowhai Coast to Bream Bay

Around 50km north of central Auckland the city's influence begins to wane, heralding the **Kowhai Coast**, a thirty-kilometre stretch of shallow harbours, beach-strung peninsulas and small islands. Its individual character becomes apparent, once you pass pretty **Warkworth** and head out either to **Kawau Island**, or up the coast to Leigh and the snorkelling and diving nirvana of **Goat Island**.

There's little to detain you on SH1 between Warkworth and Waipu as it passes the road junction at **Brynderwyn**, where SH12 loops off to Dargaville, the Waipoua kauri forest and the Hokianga Harbour. If you're heading north and want a scenic route, it's better to stay on the coast and follow **Bream Bay**, named by Cook when he visited in 1770 and his crew hauled in tarakihi, which they mistook for bream. The bay curves gently for 20km from the modest, rocky headland of Bream Tail in the south, past the entrance of Whangarei Harbour to the dramatic and craggy Bream Head. There are no sizeable towns here, only the small beach communities of **Mangawhai Heads** and **Waipu Cove**, looking out to the **Hen and Chicken Islands**, refuges for rare birds such as the wattled saddleback.

Warkworth and around

The Kowhai Coast's main township, **WARKWORTH**, sits at the head of Mahurangi Harbour, sheltered from the sea by its peninsula. A peaceful and slow-paced rural town, it only really comes to life in high summer when thousands of yachties moor their boats in the numerous estuaries and coves nearby. From the late 1820s for about a century, the languid stretch of river behind the town seethed with boats shipping out kauri, initially as spars for the Royal Navy and later as sawn planks; a boardwalk now traces its shores.

To learn more about the town's past, head 3km south to the **Warkworth and Districts Museum**, on Tudor Collins Drive, signposted off the main road (daily: 9am until at least 3.30pm, but hours vary according to season, $6), which offers a fairly prosaic exploration of the region's history through re-created rooms, and a five-metre-long, 130-link chain carved from a single piece of kauri. The two ancient kauri outside mark the start of two well-presented twenty-minute boardwalk nature trails through the preserved bush of the **Parry Kauri Park** (9am–dusk; donation). A free leaflet at the museum's entrance explains the trees in detail.

Just 4km south of Warkworth on SH1, stop in at the **Honey Centre** (daily 8.30am–5pm; ⓣ09/425 0132, ⓦwww.honeycentre.co.nz; free) for free honey tastings, a peek at bees, and the chance to buy everything from mead to honey ice cream and honey smoothies, along with café fare like *kumara* chips with honey mustard.

The Northland website is ⓦwww.northland.org.nz.

Following SH1 north of Warkworth, it's 4km to **Sheep World** (daily 9am–5pm; entry $9, entry & show $17.50; ⓣ09/425 7444, ⓦwww.sheepworld.co.nz/farm.htm), where there's an entertaining, indoor sheep-shearing show (daily 11am & 2pm) and the chance to have a go at shearing a sheep yourself. The complex also contains a mini-farm and a short nature trail, along with a campsite, a backpackers (see below) and a café. The **Dome Forest Walkway** begins 2km further north on SH1, leading through native forest to a lookout point (40min return), before climbing steeply to the summit (90min return) for superb views. The path then descends gently to the twenty magnificent trees of the Waiwhiu Kauri Grove (3hr return).

Practicalities

Warkworth's **i-SITE visitor centre**, 1 Baxter St (Nov–Easter Mon–Fri 8.30am–5.30pm, Sat & Sun 9am–4pm; Easter–Oct Mon–Fri 8.30am–5pm, Sat & Sun 9am–3pm, ⓣ09/425 9081, ⓦwww.warkworth-information.co.nz), is in the centre of town at the junction of Queen and Neville streets, where InterCity and Northliner buses stop. You can **eat** well in town, or the nearby vineyards (see p.171).

Accommodation

Rosemount Homestead 25 Rosemount Rd, 4km northeast of Warkworth on the way to Matakana ⓣ09/422 2580, ⓦwww.rosemount.co.nz. A lovingly restored kauri homestead dating from 1900, with wraparound verandas, extensive gardens and a pool; each of the three rooms is en suite. ❼

Saltings Guest House 1210 Sandspit Rd, Sandspit ⓣ09/425 9670, ⓦwww.saltings.co.nz. Gorgeous boutique B&B on a hill overlooking the estuary. All rooms are en suite with their own patio and views of the estuary, and fine breakfasts; independent self-catering in the Vintners Apartments at the edge of the vineyard. Rooms ❼, apartments ❼–❾

Sandspit Motor Camp 1334 Sandspit Rd ⓣ09/425 8610, ⓔsandspit@xtra.co.nz. Old-fashioned, well-kept estuaryside campsite offering free use of canoes, dinghies and a small golf course. Camping $15, cabins ❷

Sheep World Caravan Park, Camping Ground & Backpackers 4km north of town, ⓣ09/425 9962, ⓦwww.sheepworldcaravanpark.co.nz. Camping ground overlooking sheep-filled paddocks where campervans each get a private bathroom. Camping $15, dorms $25, on-site caravans & cabins ❷, s/c chalet ❺

Eating

Ducks Crossing Café Riverview Plaza. Good café with outdoor seating overlooking the river.

Flavour 7 Neville St. Friendly hole-in-the-wall where you can read the paper over excellent breakfasts and good strong coffee or tuck into lunches (around $15) such as warm beef salad or tofu burgers.

The Pizza Co 18 Neville St. Cosy little restaurant perfect for a great chowder or a fine pizza.

The Verandah Café & Restaurant 3 Neville St ⓣ09/422 2111. The first-floor timber veranda is a charming spot to enjoy coffee and pastries, lunches, and dinner mains ($26–29) such as mustard-seared salmon steak with fluffy mashed potatoes, with suggested wine pairings, and sinful desserts ($11–12) like Baileys double cream chocolate mousse. Closed Mon & Tues.

Kawau Island

With a resident population of around seventy (plus lots of weekenders), **KAWAU ISLAND** is chiefly given over to holiday homes each with its own wharf. Unless you have your own boat, however, you'll most likely only visit the Kawau Island Historic Reserve, a bayside enclave in the southwestern corner of the island. It's centred on the grand, kauri-panelled **Mansion House** (daily: Christmas–Feb & Easter 10am–4pm; rest of the year noon–3.30pm; $4), the former private home of George Grey – then doing his second stint as New Zealand's governor – and furnished much as it would have been in Grey's time, including his writing desk, books and some silverware.

Grey's pursuit of the Victorian fashion for all things exotic resulted in magnificent **grounds** stocked with flora and fauna from all over the world, such as Chilean wine palms and coral trees. He also brought in four species of **wallaby**, which have overtaken the island and have to be regularly culled. You might even see Australian kookaburras and a white peacock.

A path runs through the gardens to the tiny beach at **Lady's Bay** (5min) and on to a network of short tracks that weave through pine forest and kanuka scrub. The most popular destination is the ruins of the island's old **copper mine** (40min each way).

Practicalities

Boats to Kawau Island leave from the wharf (council-run parking available) at **Sandspit**, a small road-end community on the Matakana Estuary, 8km east of Warkworth. Throughout the year, Reubens (ⓣ0800/111 616, ⓦwww.reubens.co.nz) operate the **Royal Mail Run** (daily 10.30am; 4hr; $52 return; $70 with BBQ lunch), delivering mail, papers and groceries to all the wharves on the island and giving you around an hour and a half ashore at Mansion House Bay. Reubens also runs one to two Mansion House Bay trips daily that give you roughly twice the time ashore ($38).

The same company also operates **water taxi** services daily all year round to various bays on the island. Bring whatever you need to Kawau: there are no shops, though the **café** at Mansion House Bay is open daily from 10am till late (mains $14–26).

Matakana and around

MATAKANA, 9km northeast of Warkworth, is little more than a road junction at the heart of a fledgling **winemaking** region, though the surrounding area is dotted with crafts workshops.

The catalyst for the region's development was the **Morris & James Pottery & Tileworks**, 2km from Matakana at Tongue Farm Road (Mon–Fri 8.30am–4.30pm, Sat & Sun 10am–5pm; free), which in the late 1970s exploited New Zealand's fortress economy by producing handmade terracotta tiles and large garden pots from local clay. You can catch a free thirty-minute tour of the pottery (Mon–Fri 11.30am) before a visit to the café/bar.

Despite received wisdom about high humidity and proximity to the sea, newly planted **vineyards** have proliferated in the last decade or so. The free and widely available *Matakana Coast Wine Country* booklet currently details half a dozen wineries offering tastings (most for a small charge). First stop should be *Heron's Flight*, 49 Sharp Rd (daily from 10am; ⓣ09/422 7915, ⓦwww.heronsflight.co.nz), where Italian Sangiovese, Pinotage and Chardonnay have been planted with considerable success. You can dine at the lovely **restaurant** overlooking the vines, or wander through the gardens of heritage plants and Maori medicinal herbs.

Other good bets are *Ascension Vineyard & Café*, 480 Matakana Rd, 4km east of Warkworth (daily 10am–5pm; ⓣ09/422 9601, ⓦwww.ascensionvineyard.co.nz), where the pleasant café/restaurant serves Mediterranean-style dishes for lunch as well as dinner Fri and Sat (bookings advised); and Matakana's original winery, *Hyperion Wines* (Christmas–Jan daily plus rest of year Sat & Sun; ⓣ09/422 9375, ⓦwww.hyperion-wines.co.nz), on Tongue Farm Road 1km from Morris & James. For a high-quality **snack** head for the tiny *Pop-in Patisserie* on Matakana Valley Road in Matakana itself, and if you are around on a Saturday, you won't be able to (and shouldn't) miss the town's bustling Farmers' Market.

Tawharanui Regional Park

Just past Matakana, a side road runs about 10km southeast to **Tawharanui Regional Park**, with great beaches and swathes of regenerating bush. Predators have been eradicated and native birds are returning to this designated **open sanctuary**: come to swim, snorkel, picnic and walk or bike the easy trails, but you'll have to bring everything with you. The only facilities are the **campsite** ($10; book ahead on ⓣ09/366 2000).

Leigh and Goat Island

East of Matakana, the road runs 13km to the village of **LEIGH**, and a picturesque harbour with bobbing wooden fishing boats. Heading a further 4km northeast brings you to the **Cape Rodney–Okakari Marine Reserve**, usually known simply as **Goat Island** for the bush-clad islet 300m offshore. Established in 1975, this was New Zealand's first marine reserve, stretching 5km along the shoreline and 800m off the coast. More than three angling- and shellfishing-free decades later, the undersea life is thriving, with large rock lobster and huge snapper. Feeding has been discouraged since blue maomaos developed a taste for frozen peas and began to mob swimmers and divers. Easy beach access (from the road-end parking area), clear water, rock pools on wave-cut platforms, a variety of undersea terrains and relatively benign currents combine to make this an enormously popular year-round diving spot, as well as a favourite summer destination for families: aim to come midweek if you value tranquillity.

In fine weather, join forty-five-minute **glass-bottomed boat tours** around the island on the *Aquador* (Sept–April; $20; ⓣ09/422 6334, ⓦwww.glassbottomboat.co.nz), which depart from the beach.

Snorkellers can enjoy a lush world of kelp forest with numerous multi-coloured fish; those who venture deeper find more exposed seascapes with an abundance of sponges. The highly professional Goat Island Dive, 142a Pakiri Rd, Leigh (Mon–Fri 9am–5pm, Sat & Sun 8am–5pm; ⓣ0800/348 369, ⓦwww.goatislanddive.co.nz) rents snorkelling equipment plus full **dive** gear and also run trips to Goat Island Marine Reserve. Alternatively visit **Seafriends** (ⓣ09/422 6212, ⓦwww.seafriends.org.nz), a marine education centre, with an array of **aquarium** tanks recreating different Goat Island ecosystems about a kilometre along Goat Island Road; they also rent snorkelling gear and have a small café.

Practicalities

Without your own wheels, your only transport option is a taxi from Matakana (Matakabs, ⓣ09/422 2244), or Warkworth (Warkworth Taxi & Minibus Charters, ⓣ09/425 0000). Facilities are limited once you get here. You can stay at the welcoming *Goat Island Camping & Accommodation* (ⓣ09/422 6185, ⓦwww.goatislandcamping.co.nz; camping $16, cabins & on-site caravans ❷), about 500m back from the reserve on the way to Goat Island, which has great bay views, plus snorkel gear rental. *The Leigh Sawmill Café*, 142 Pakiri Rd (ⓣ09/422 6019, ⓦwww.sawmillcafe.co.nz; March–Christmas Thurs–Sun), has five spacious en-suite doubles (❺), two dorms ($25) and a communal kitchen. Its vast sawmill has been sensitively converted into a smart café/bar (summer daily; winter closed Thurs–Sun) serving fine gourmet pizzas and beers brewed on site; weekends typically draw touring bands. The best chippy around is *Leigh Fish and Chips*, Cumberland Street (closed Mon–Wed except during school holidays).

Pakiri

North of Leigh, a sealed road continues 10km to the tiny community of **Pakiri**, with a long, dune-backed white surf beach. The main land-based attraction here is horse-riding with the highly professional Pakiri Beach Horse Riding, Rahuikiri Road, Pakiri Beach (ⓣ09/422 6275, ⓦwww.horseride-nz.co.nz), who operate year-round and run a pleasant café. Rides range from a brief jaunt along the beach and through a pohutukawa glade, to multiday safaris through stands of native bush and along the tops of sea cliffs. Most people go for short rides (2hr for $85, half-day for $120), but it's worth considering the excellent overnight trips ($575) or even an epic seven-day Coast-to-Coast ride (see p.67). There's good reason to stay over in the farm's range of attractive on-site accommodation: riverside backpacker cabins ($25), self-contained beachside cabins for two (❻), and a luxurious four-bedroom beach house from $500 a day for up to eight. Campers can stay nearby at the well-sited, if rather haphazardly run, *Pakiri Beach Holiday Park*, Pakiri River Road (ⓣ09/422 6199, ⓦwww.pakiriholidaypark.co.nz; camping $15, dorms $25, cabins ❷, en-suite cabins ❸, flats ❹, cottages ❺) which also has a luxury beachfront lodge sleeping four (❽ plus $50 per extra adult).

Mangawhai Heads and around

Back on SH1 and heading north, your next chance to turn off towards the coast is at the small roadside settlement of **TE HANA**, 4km north of Wellsford. Here you'll find **The Arts Factory** (ⓣ09/423 8069, ⓦwww.artprimitiveandmodern.com; 9am–5pm Sat–Sun & by appointment), an innovative gallery specializing in work by Maori artists.

From here it is 20km along winding country roads to tiny **Mangawhai**, where you should stop at the *Smashed Pipi*, 40 Moir St (ⓣ09/431 4847; gallery daily 9am–5.30pm), a gallery crammed with colourful glass, jewellery, woven flax, ceramics and funky clothing, with an attached café and bar (closed evenings Mon–Wed April–late Dec; mains $5–29). An organic fruit-and-veg market is held on Saturday mornings in the village hall on the corner of Moir and Insley streets.

The road continues 3km north to meet the coast at **Mangawhai Heads** at the mouth of the Mangawhai Harbour, marked by holiday homes straggling over the hillsides behind a fine surf beach. Long a Kiwi summer-holiday favourite, Mangawhai Heads tends to be bypassed by outsiders due to its lack of specific attractions, but that's part of the charm. There's also the scenic **Mangawhai Cliffs Walkway** (2–3hr; closed Aug to mid-Oct for lambing). Walk north along the beach for fifteen minutes then follow the orange markers up through bush-backed farmland along the top of the sea cliffs until the path winds back down to the beach. Provided the tide is below half, you can return along the beach through a small rock arch.

Practicalities

For hostel **accommodation** head straight for *Coastal Cow Backpackers*, 299 Molesworth Drive (ⓣ09/431 5444; dorms $23, rooms ❷), in a pleasant modern house. There's far more luxury at *Milestone Cottages by the Sea*, 27 Moir Point Rd (ⓣ09/431 4018, ⓦwww.milestonecottages.co.nz; studio ❺, cottages ❻–❽), a cluster of beautiful cottages amid sumptuous organic gardens and coastal bush within sight of the sea; it's just a short walk to a secluded estuary beach. All are self-catering including a BBQ deck, and there's free use of a lap pool and kayaks.

At Mangawhai Heads most of the town's shops and **cafés** are in the Wood Street shopping complex, off Molesworth Drive, though it is also worth seeking out the licensed *Naja Garden Café*, 5 Molesworth Drive (ⓣ09/431 4111) at a garden centre, which makes a fine stop for a coffee and breakfast, or gourmet sandwiches; phone ahead to ask if they'll be open for dinner as hours vary.

Lang's Beach and Waipu Cove

Surfing is superb at both **Lang's Beach**, 12km north of Mangawhai Heads, and, a further 4km north, at **WAIPU COVE** – a cluster of houses and the excellent **Cove Café** (ⓣ09/432 0323; kitchen closes 8.30pm) by a sweeping stretch of Bream Bay. Accommodation is limited but right by the beach. There's camping at *Camp Waipu Cove*, 897 Cove Rd (ⓣ09/432 0410, ⓦwww.campwaipucove.com; $25 per tent, cabins ❷), and a dozen stylish, state-of-the-art poolside apartments at the *Waipu Cove Resort*, 891 Cove Rd (ⓣ09/432 0348, ⓦwww.waipucoveresort.co.nz; ❺). Or go for the modern cottages at the secluded *Waipu Cove Cottages and Camping*, 685 Cove Rd (ⓣ09/432 0851, ⓔcovecottages@xtra.co.nz; $30 per tent; rooms ❷, cottages ❹–❺), with free use of dinghies.

Half a kilometre further on, the *Stone House* (ⓣ09/432 0432 ⓔstonehousewaipu@xtra.co.nz; dorms $20, cabins & cottages ❹) occupies a couple of lovely buildings with grounds running down to the estuary, which you can explore with the free dinghy and kayaks.

Waipu and around

The increasingly chic yet delightfully quirky village of **WAIPU** is dominated by an Aberdeen granite monument surmounted by a Scottish lion. It's a historic nod to the settlers who followed charismatic preacher, the Reverend Norman McLeod, here in the mid-1800s by way of Nova Scotia, until famine and a series of harsh winters drove them here, where they formed a strict, self-contained Calvinist community built on farming and forestry. The settlers' Scottish history and genealogy is recounted in the Waipu Museum on the main street (daily 9.30am–4.30pm; $5) through a well-laid-out exhibition of settlers' photos and personal effects; and during the **Highland Games** (ⓦwww.highlandgames.co.nz; New Year's Day), in which competitors heft large stones and toss cabers and sheaves in the Caledonian Park. Nearby, the **Waipu Caves** make a popular excursion to view one of the longest stalagmites in New Zealand in a two-hundred-metre glow-worm-filled passage, in the limestone country 16km to the northwest. Obtain a free map from the visitor centre in the Waipu Museum, wear old clothes and good footwear, and take a couple of good torches per person. The cave is signposted from Waipu Caves Road and is impenetrable after heavy rain; you'll get muddy even in dry weather.

North from Waipu, the road runs parallel to Bream Bay, with occasional turnings accessing the long white **beach** to the east. The best place to head to the sands is at **Uretiti**, 6km north of Waipu, where there's a primitive DOC camping area ($7), with water and cold showers, and an adjacent unofficial naturist beach.

Practicalities

InterCity and Northliner **buses** drop off and pick up on request outside the liquor store on the main street, which also acts as a ticket agent (ⓣ09/432 0225). A block away, the Waipu Museum contains the town's **visitor centre** (daily 9.30am–4.30pm; ⓣ09/432 0746) and has **Internet access**. There are no banks or ATMs, but you can **exchange traveller's cheques** and currency (Mon, Wed & Fri 9.30am–3pm only) at the kiosk next door to the liquor store on the main road.

There's a better range of places to stay down the road at Waipu Cove, but you'll find welcoming budget **accommodation** here at *Waipu Wanderers*, 25 St Mary's Rd (Ⓣ09/432 0532, Ⓔwaipu.wanderers@xtra.co.nz; four-bed dorms 23, rooms ❶), which has beds in a separate house with its own kitchen and bathroom, within easy walking distance of the town centre.

For tasty **meals**, try the longstanding *Pizza Barn*, 2 Cove Rd (Ⓣ09/432 1011; closed Mon & Tues April–Nov) in Waipu's former post office, serving well-priced lunches and dinners (mains $13.50–18), including pizzas topped with gourmet ingredients such as brie, smoked salmon and fresh asparagus. Eat in the cosy corrugated iron and timber cabin dining room-bar, or in the garden room filled with surfboards and hibiscus flower candles; and peek inside the toilets, which are a veritable art installation of '70s kitsch. Alternatively, the contemporary *Artform Restaurant*, at the corner of South and Cove roads (Ⓣ09/432 0280), has cutting-edge artworks and inventive cuisine (mains $23–28).

Whangarei and around

Despite its prime gateway location to Whangarei Heads' sweeping beaches and world-class diving around the Poor Knights Islands, Northland's capital, **WHANGAREI** (pronounced Fahn-ga-RAY), remains refreshingly down to earth, with a laid-back local vibe and a complete absence of tourism overkill.

The main focal point for visitors is the riverside Town Basin, where sleek yachts moor outside a small redeveloped settler-style shopping and restaurant complex. Elsewhere there's a smattering of museums and rewarding walks, particularly the scenic track to Whangarei Falls.

Arrival and information

No passenger trains make it this far. InterCity and Northliner **buses** pull up on Bank Street, the hub of the skeletal local town service that runs frequently on weekdays, slightly less so on Saturday, and not at all on Sunday. Daily **flights** from Auckland, and five flights weekly from Great Barrier Island arrive at Onerahi Airport, 5km east of town and linked to Whangarei by local bus and two shuttle taxi firms – Kiwi Carlton Cabs (Ⓣ0800/438 4444) and A1 Shuttle (Ⓣ0800/483 3377). The main **i-SITE visitor centre** lies 2km south of town on the main route from Auckland at 92 Otaika Rd (Christmas–Jan daily 8.30am–6.30pm; Feb–Christmas Mon–Fri 8.30am–5pm, Sat & Sun 9.30am–4.30pm; Ⓣ09/438 1079, Ⓦwww.whangareinz.com), and there's a more central satellite office in the foyer of Chapham's Clocks, Town Basin (daily 9am–5pm; Ⓣ09/438 3993); both have **Internet access**. The **DOC office** (Mon–Fri 8am–4.30pm; Ⓣ09/430 2470) is at 149 Bank St.

Accommodation

Accommodation in Whangarei is seldom hard to find and prices are reasonable.

Hotels, motels and B&Bs

Central Court Motel 54 Otaika Rd Ⓣ0800/990 000, Ⓦwww.centralcourtmotel.co.nz. Ageing but decent budget motel close to the visitor centre with a free spa and cheap sauna. Basic units ❸, kitchen units ❹

Graelyn Villa 166 Kiripaka Rd, Tikipunga Ⓣ09/437 7532, Ⓦwww.graelynvilla.co.nz. Three pretty en-suite rooms in a hundred-year-old villa with a latticed veranda amid lush rose gardens in a tranquil setting close to Whangarei Falls. ❺

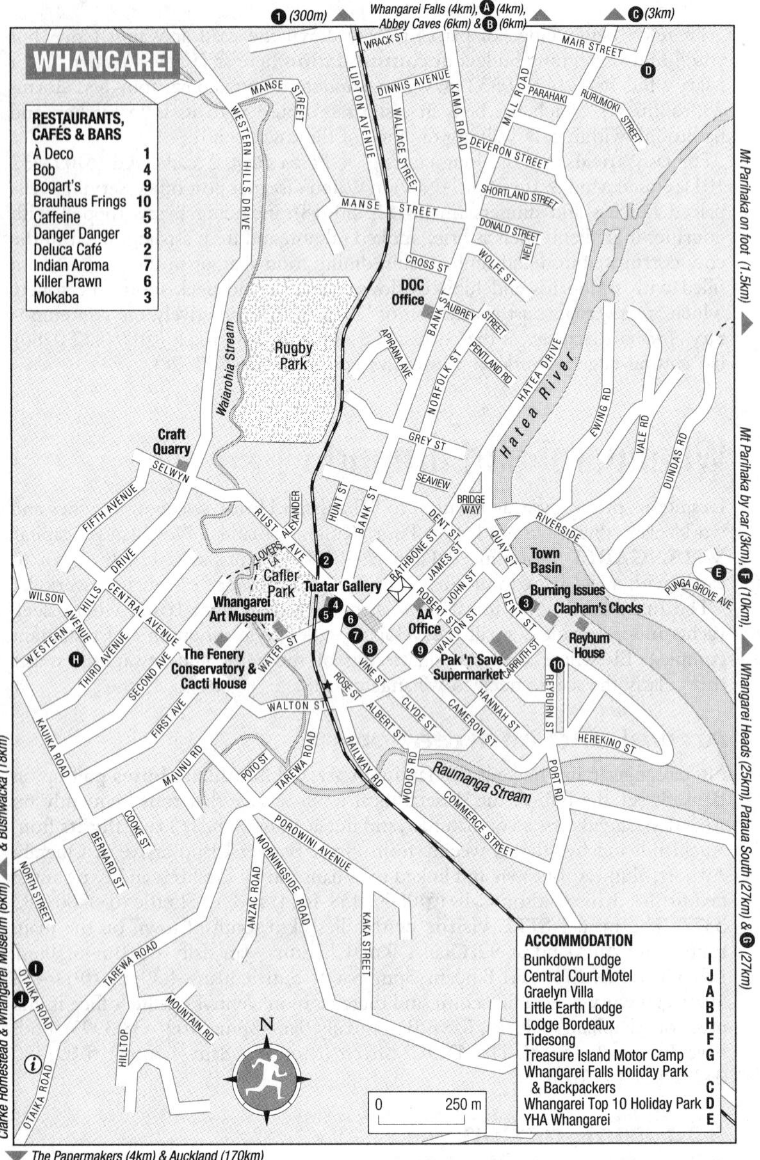

Lodge Bordeaux 361 Western Hills Drive ⓣ09/438 0404, ⓦwww.lodgebordeaux.co.nz. Elegant modern motel with a heated outdoor pool. All rooms come with a/c, heated tile floors, spa bath and DVD players, and some have dishwashers. Studios ⑥, suites ⑦

Tidesong Beasley Rd, Onerahi ⓣ09/436 1959, ⓦwww.tidesong.co.nz. Wonderfully relaxed B&B around 25min drive east of Whangarei surrounded by bush and overlooking the harbour. You get a spacious s/c apartment and meals can be provided. ④

Hostels and campsites

Bunkdown Lodge 23 Otaika Rd ⓣ09/438 8886, ⓦwww.bunkdownlodge.co.nz. A spacious, low-key hostel in a pretty 1903 villa, with cheap bike rental. There are two kitchens, dorm beds, four-shares, twins and doubles, with free tea and coffee and access to a heap of videos. Staff go out of their way to help, and also offer lessons in portraiture. Dorms $20, linen hire $2, rooms ❶–❷

Little Earth Lodge 85 Abbey Caves Rd ⓣ09/430 6562, ⓦwww.littleearthlodge.co.nz. Tucked into a pastoral valley 7km northeast of Whangarei, close to Abbey Caves. Free bikes, a DVD lounge, and camping by arrangement. Call ahead to check on winter closures. Dorms $26, rooms ❷

Treasure Island Motor Camp Pataua South ⓣ09/436 2390, ⓦwww.treasureislandnz.co.nz. Situated just 75m from one of New Zealand's best surf beaches about 30min drive east of Whangarei. Incredibly cheap powered sites cost the same as unpowered, and there's a general store, takeaway and bakery serving coffee and croissants. It's treasured by in-the-know Kiwis; book well ahead for high summer. Camping $12.

Whangarei Falls Holiday Park & Backpackers Ngunguru Rd at Tikipunga, 6km from town near Whangarei Falls ⓣ0800/227 222, ⓦwww.whangareifalls.co.nz. On the edge of the countryside, and with a pool and spa. Camping $13, dorms $18, cabins ❶

Whangarei Top 10 Holiday Park 24 Mair St ⓣ0800/455 488, ⓦwww.whangareitop10.co.nz. Small and tranquil site in a pretty setting 2km north of town with a wide range of accommodation. Camping $15, cabins ❷, en-suite cabins & s/c units ❹

YHA Whangarei 52 Punga Grove Ave ⓣ09/438 8954, ⓔyha.whangarei@yha.co.nz. Intimate, sociable hostel a steep 15min walk from the centre of Whangarei, with expansive views over town from several rooms, and glow-worms a short walk away in the bush (torches available). Accommodation is in glass-fronted cabins and four- and six-bed dorms and there's Wi-Fi. Reception closed noon–5pm. Dorms $25, rooms ❷

The Town

Whangarei's most appealing features are its peaceful parks and easy walks within a few minutes of the town, the best of which are outlined in the free *Whangarei Walks* leaflet, from the visitor centre. Extensive views over the harbour and town are the reward for climbing to the sheet-metal war memorial atop **Mount Parihaka** (240m), which can be approached by car along Memorial Drive or on foot along the steep Ross Track (40min ascent) from the end of Dundas Road.

Central Whangarei

Based around an 1880s villa, the redeveloped **Town Basin** is a small, prettified zone of upmarket galleries, shops and restaurants. Call in at the kauri and fudge shops, or play with the giant chessboard pieces outside the **Burning Issues Gallery** (daily 10am–5pm; free), a glass and ceramics studio where you can watch glass-blowing. The main sight is **Clapham's Clocks** (daily 9am–5pm; $8), a museum packed with 1500 clocks ranging from mechanisms taken out of church towers to cuckoo clocks. Outside is New Zealand's largest sundial. Nearby, Whangarei's oldest kauri villa, **Reyburn House** (Tues–Fri 10am–4pm, Sat & Sun 1–4pm; free), hosts the Northland Society of Arts' exhibition **gallery**, with monthly rotating exhibits.

In the centre of town, don't miss **Tuatara Gallery**, 29 Bank St (Mon–Fri 9.30am–5pm, Sat 9am–2.30pm, plus Nov–March Sun 10am–3pm; free), a small gallery space focusing on works by emerging Maori artists, fronted by an inventive shop stocking Maori-designed and -influenced goods from contemporary clothing to fine jewellery and greenstone carving. Immediately west, the well-kept **Cafler Park** is pleasant for a stroll – head for the Rose Gardens and the adjacent **Whangarei Art Museum** (daily 9am–5pm; gold coin donation), which houses a small permanent collection of heritage and contemporary New Zealand art. A footbridge crosses the stream running through Cafler Park to the cool, restful **Fernery Conservatory & Cacti House**, First Avenue (daily 10am–4pm; free), sheltering the country's largest public collection of native ferns. From here, it's ten minutes' walk but a step back in time to the **Craft Quarry** artists' co-operative, Selwyn Avenue (daily 10am–4pm; free), a focus for the local vibrant crafts community. You're free to wander among shacks built from adobe, timber and corrugated iron and watch the artisans at work.

Clarke Homestead, Whangarei Museum and the Native Bird Recovery Centre

There is a collection of museums at the **Whangarei Heritage Park**, 6km southwest of Whangarei on SH14 in Maunu (daily 10am–4pm; $10 combined ticket only). **Clarke Homestead,** a rare example of an unrestored original homestead, was built in 1886 for a Scottish doctor, Alexander Clarke. The house was at its most vibrant in the 1930s, when Alexander's son hosted high-society parties here, and much of what you see dates from that era. The **Whangarei Museum**, housed in a modern building in the homestead grounds, has an intriguing selection of objects relating to local history, flora and fauna and a small Maori collection. The prize exhibit is the *waka tupapuka*, a sixteenth-century wooden funerary chest decorated with bird-form carvings. The museum's Kiwi House is one of the best of its kind, well laid out and with clear views of the birds.

The adjacent **Whangarei Native Bird Recovery Centre** (Mon–Fri 10.30am–4.30pm; gold coin donation) attempts to rehabilitate birds that have been damaged in some way and can't fend for themselves. The star attraction is Woof-Woof the tui, who mimics his keeper perfectly and whistles *Pop Goes the Weasel*.

Whangarei Falls, the Kauri Park and Abbey Caves

A broad curtain of water cascades over a twenty-six-metre basalt ridge into a popular swimming hole at **Whangarei Falls**, 5km northeast of the town centre. Kamo-bound buses pass close by, but the nicest way to get here is to walk along a bushland walking trail following the Hatea River (90min one way) from the Parihaka Scenic Reserve on the opposite shore from the Town Basin – the visitor centre has a route map.

A couple of kilometres before Whangarei Falls, Whareora Road branches off 1.5km to the **A. H. Reed Memorial Kauri Park**, where shady paths through native bush pass 500-year-old kauri trees – look out for the ten-minute Alexander Walk, which links with a short, sinuous **canopy boardwalk** high across a creek before reaching some fine kauri. From the Elizabeth track it is possible to link up with the trail along the Hatea River to Whangarei Falls (30min one way).

Accessed from Whareora Road, the fluted and weather-worn limestone formations of **Abbey Caves** (unrestricted access) have stalactites and stalagmites in abundance, as well as glow-worms. Armed with a torch plus a moderate level of fitness you can explore them at leisure. A little scrambling is required to get into the first, Organ Cave, where you can walk a couple of hundred metres along an underground stream. Middle Cave and Ivy Cave are badly signposted but, once found, are also worth exploring. The owners of *Bunkdown Lodge* can provide guidance to guests, as can *Little Earth Lodge*, next to the caves (see p.177).

Eating and drinking

Cafés and **restaurants** cluster around the Town Basin, with some emerging hotspots in the city centre. Pak 'n' Save, on the corner of Robert and Carruth streets, has the cheapest groceries.

For details of **live music** gigs, check out Tuesday's *The Leader* newspaper.

À Deco 70 Kamo Rd ⓣ09/459 4957. Classy linen and crystal-ware service in a lovely Art Deco home 2km north of the centre. Easily worth the journey for exquisite meals that might start with mushroom risotto with aged parmesan and white truffle foam ($13), followed by steamed Northland flounder with aniseed bisque (mains $23–34). There's also a five-course tasting menu ($75) with matched wines ($115). Closed Sun & Mon.

Bob 29 Bank St. Airy terrazzo and polished concrete deli-café that does proper espresso, scrumptious warm berry-filled pinwheels, imaginative lunch mains ($14–17) and, though it's open daytimes only, a lush choice of cocktails.

Bogart's 84 Cameron St. Easy-going, licensed dinner restaurant that's lively at weekends and best value for its gourmet pizzas (from $17).

Brauhaus Frings 104 Lower Dent St ⓦwww.frings.co.nz. Welcoming micro-brewery and small bar. Also good bar food, plus regular live music at weekends.

Caffeine 4 Water St. Contemporary café with the best coffee in town, tasty muffins and wraps plus seasonal lunch mains (around $14–16.50).

Danger Danger 37 Vine St. Kickin' bar that boasts the biggest sports screen in Northland, which is switched to DJ use on dance nights. The bistro menu offers more than just basic bar food and there's a $6 Meal Steal (Tues–Sat; lunch & dinner).

Deluca Café 6 Rust Ave. Whangarei's best bet for breakfast – from home-made muesli or buttermilk pancake stacks to full-blown fry-ups ($9–17), in sleek white surrounds with moulded plastic seats and '70s-inspired wallpaper. Closed Sun.

Indian Aroma 23 Vine St ⓣ09/438 5005. Outstanding curries, including plenty of vegetarian options like a creamy butter Paneer (mains $11.90–16.50), to eat in or take away. Lunch Mon–Fri, dinner daily.

Killer Prawn 28 Bank St ⓦwww.killerprawn.co.nz. Conservatory-style bar and seafood restaurant; prawns served every which way (such as in tomato and rosemary broth, with dipping bread) are the speciality. Light snacks start at $7, enormous mains at $31. Closed Sun.

Mokaba Town Basin. The pick of Town Basin's cafés, with outside seating overlooking the yachts, decent coffee, cool music and fresh, healthy fare (mains $12–16.50).

Around Whangarei

It's worth hanging around Whangarei to explore the surrounding area, particularly to the east and north of the town where craggy, weathered remains of ancient volcanoes abut the sea. Southeast of the town, **Whangarei Heads** is the district's volcanic heartland where dramatic walks follow the coast to calm harbour beaches and windswept coastal strands. To the northeast, **Tutukaka** acts as the base for dive trips to the undersea wonderland around the **Poor Knights Islands**.

The only public transport is from Whangarei to Tutukaka with MVS Shuttles (ⓣ09/438 9912; $15 each way), which are coordinated with dive trip departure and return times.

Whangarei Heads

The winding road around the northern side of Whangarei Harbour runs 35km southeast to **Whangarei Heads**, a catch-all name for a series of small, residential beach communities scattered around jagged volcanic outcrops that terminate at Bream Head, the northern limit of Bream Bay. Numerous attractive bays provide safe swimming – **McLeod Bay** in particular – but otherwise there's no reason to stop until the road leaves the harbour and climbs to a saddle at the start of an excellent, signposted **walk** (3km return; 2hr–2hr 30min; 200m ascent) up the 430-metre **Mount Manaia**, crowned with five eroded pinnacles shrouded in legend. One story tells of a jealous dispute between Chief Manaia (whose *pa* stood atop Mount Manaia), and the lesser chief, Hautatu (from across the water at Marsden Point) who was married to the beautiful Pito. Hautatu was sent away on a raid, leaving the coast clear for Manaia to steal Pito. Hautatu returned and gave chase to Manaia, his two children and Pito across the hilltop when all five were struck by lightning, leaving the figures petrified on the summit. These pinnacles remain *tapu*, but you can climb to their base through native bush, passing fine viewpoints.

Beyond Mount Manaia, the road runs for 5km to **Urquharts Bay**, where a short walk (20min each way) leads to the white-sand **Smugglers Cove**. A longer trail (3hr return) continues to the small and pebbly beach of **Peach Cove**, which has a hut ($10; book through Whangarei DOC ⓣ09/430 2133). Very keen walkers could press on to **Ocean Beach** (5hr one way), a wild white-sand surf beach that's also accessible by road. Bring provisions, as there are no shops, and little shade. These walks are described in DOC's *Whangarei District Walks* leaflet, available from the visitor centres and the DOC office. There are also sweeping surf beaches at **Pataua South**, further north along the heads and also reachable by car, with a footbridge over the estuary and dunes to the ocean. You'll also find a smattering of shops here. Check with the visitor centre for updates on the limited **summertime bus service** to the beaches.

Panoramic views of Whangarei Heads are best seen by **skydiving**. Tandem jumps with Ballistic Blondes (ⓣ021 519 577, ⓦwww.skydiveballisticblondes.co.nz) start from $200 including pick-up from accommodation around Whangarei.

Tutukaka and the Poor Knights

Boats ply the waters from the tiny but growing village of **TUTUKAKA** – set on a beautiful, deeply incised harbour 30km northeast of Whangarei – for one of the world's premier dive locations, the **Poor Knights Islands Marine Reserve**, 25km offshore. The warm East Auckland current swirling around Cape Reinga and the lack of run-off from the land combine to create visibility approaching 30m most of the year, though in spring (roughly Oct–Dec) plankton can reduce it to 15–20m. The clear waters are home to New Zealand's most diverse range of sea life, including a few subtropical species found nowhere else, as well as a striking underwater landscape of near-vertical **rock faces** that drop almost 100m through a labyrinth of caves, fissures and rock arches teeming with rainbow-coloured fish, crabs, soft corals, kelp forests and shellfish. The Poor Knights lie along the migratory routes of a number of **whale** species, so blue, humpback, sei and minke whales, as well as dolphins, are not uncommon. The waters north and south of the reserve are home to two navy **wrecks**. The survey ship HMNZS *Tui* was sunk in 1999 to form an artificial reef, and it was so popular with divers and marine life that the obsolete frigate *Waikato* followed two years later.

Practicalities

The only amenities around the harbour at Tutukaka are **restaurants**, most notably the *Schnappa Rock Café*, Marina Road (ⓣ09/434 3774; daily 8am–late), a groovy bar/restaurant turning out a tempting range of dishes (mains $22–32.50), including vegetarian, as well as bar snacks; it's buzzing with divers, and it always pays to book ahead for dinner in summer.

Local **accommodation** is mostly on the headland just south of Tutukaka and accessed along Tutukaka Block Road, or 5km back towards Whangarei in **NGUNGURU**, which is strung along an attractive, sandy estuary that's fine for swimming if you dodge the jet skis.

Accommodation

Malibu Mal's Tutukaka Block Rd, Kowharewa Bay ⓣ09/434 3450 ⓦwww.malibumals.co.nz. Diving groups are welcome at the two spacious self-catering units (one sleeping four, the other six) in a secluded garden 5min drive from Tutukaka Marina. ❸

Pacific Rendezvous Motel Rd, off the Tutukaka Block Rd ⓣ0800/999 800, ⓦwww.oceanresort.co.nz. Fabulously sited on the peninsula that forms the southern arm of Tutukaka's harbour, offering tranquil s/c suites and apartments, as well as chalets with decks overlooking the ocean. ❻

Sands Motel Tutukaka Block Rd, 4km off the highway ⓣ09/434 3747, ⓦwww.sandsmotel.co.nz. Right beside the sands of Whangaumu Bay, this breezy motel offers one-and two-bedroom units. ④

Tutukaka Holiday Park Matapouri Rd, just around the corner from the harbour ⓣ09/434 3938, ⓦwww.tutukaka-holidaypark.co.nz. In a pretty valley that's a 2min walk from the harbour, this convenient site offers camping ($12–14), dorms ($20) and a variety of cabins (②) and flats sleeping up to six people. ④

Angling

Free-ranging species such as marlin, shark and tuna that stray outside the protected Poor Knights Reserve are picked off by **big-game anglers** from December to May. Anglers wanting to rent a quarter-share of a charter game-fishing boat for the day should expect to pay $250 or more: for a list of operators contact the Whangarei Deep Sea Anglers Club (daily 8am–6pm during season; ⓣ09/434 3818, ⓦwww.sportfishing.co.nz).

▲ Dive boat off the Poor Knights Islands

Diving and snorkelling

You'll need prior diving experience to sample the best the **Poor Knights** have to offer, but there's still plenty for novices and snorkellers. Several companies operate daily trips in the main season (Nov–April), and usually, at least one goes out most days the rest of the year. **Boats** leave from Tutukaka with most outfits picking up from backpackers in Whangarei at no extra charge. They offer broadly the same deal, with a full day out including two dives and a quick look around the Poor Knights coast.

The largest operator is the reliable Dive Tutukaka, Marina Road, Tutukaka (Ⓣ0800/288 882, Ⓦwww.diving.co.nz), who offer Poor Knights trips ($125; including gear $209) on one of several boats, so you are typically with similarly skilled divers. Snorkellers and sightseers ($119) are welcome, and everyone can use the on-board kayaks. Full-day dive trips onto the two wrecks cost the same. First-time divers can try a **resort dive** ($275) with full gear and one-to-one instruction; while a five-day PADI open-water dive qualification will cost $595.

Boat trips

Dive Tutukaka run a **fast boat** on the Perfect Day trip (5hr, $119), which zips you out for a look around the Poor Knights Islands then deep into Rikoriko Cave which penetrates 130m into the island. This is claimed to be the world's largest sea cave, and was formed 10 million years ago when a massive gas bubble got trapped during the volcanic formation of the islands. There's also time for snorkelling and kayaking.

For a more leisurely **cruise**, Ocean Blue Adventures (Ⓣ09/434 3678, Ⓦwww.oceanblue.co.nz) do overnight **sailing** trips out to the Poor Knights ($580 including at least 5 dives), and five-day trips ($1160 including at least 11 dives).

Surfing

Tutukaka Surf Experience (Ⓦwww.tutukakasurf.co.nz) run two-hour **surfing lessons** (group $60, private $90 including board and wetsuit hire) most mornings in summer, and on Saturdays and Sundays the rest of the year.

North of Tutukaka

It's a pleasant day-trip from Whangarei to the beachside holiday settlements north of Tutukaka for safe swimming in gorgeous sheltered bays. Favourites include the village of **MATAPOURI**, 6km north of Tutukaka, which backs onto a curving white-sand bay bounded by bushy headlands, and the pristine **Whale Bay**, signposted off Matapouri Road 1km further north and reached by a twenty-minute bushwalk. There are virtually no facilities along this stretch apart from a shop and takeaway at Matapouri.

From Tutukaka to the Bay of Islands

The roads that access the coast around Tutukaka and Matapouri rejoin SH1 at **Hikurangi** 16km north of Whangarei. About 6km further north you have a choice of roads: both go to the Bay of Islands but approach from different directions. Carry straight on and you go direct to Paihia with opportunities for side trips to the Maori redoubt of Ruapekapeka Pa, and the **Hundertwasser toilets** at Kawakawa. Turn right along Old Russell Road and you twist towards the coast on the tar-sealed but windy back road to Russell.

The direct route: along SH1

Sticking with SH1, a sign 17km north of Hikurangi directs you 5km northeast to **Ruapekapeka Pa** (unrestricted access; free), the site of the final battle in the

War of the North in 1846. Hone Heke's repeated flagpole felling in Russell (see p.196) precipitated nine months of fighting during which Maori learnt to adapt their *pa* defences to cope with British firepower. The apotheosis of this development is Ruapekapeka, the "Bat's Nest". Its hilltop setting, double row of totara palisades and labyrinth of trenches and interconnecting tunnels helped Hone Heke and his warriors defend the site, despite being heavily outgunned and outnumbered three to one. After ten days of bombardment the British attacked the *pa* but their victory was a hollow one; when Heke's uncle, Kawiti, offered New Zealand's new governor, George Grey, a truce saying "Mehe mea kua mutukoe" ("If you have had enough, I have had enough"), Grey replied "Kuamutu ahau" ("I have had enough"). The War of the North was over.

A modern carved **gateway** marks the entrance to the *pa* site where trench lines are clearly visible and large holes indicate at bunkers linking underground passages. There's even a small cannon pointing back at the British position.

Kawakawa

The direct route follows SH1 15km north of the Ruapekapeka junction to the small town of **KAWAKAWA**, where the only reason to stop is to visit its celebrated toilets on the main road and signposted from SH1. These works of art were created in 1997 by the reclusive Austrian émigré **Friedrich Hundertwasser**. Painter, architect, ecologist and philosopher, Hundertwasser made Kawakawa his home from 1975 until his death in 2000, aged 71. The ceramic columns supporting the entrance hint at the interior's complex use of broken tiles, coloured bottles and found objects such as the old hinges on the wrought-iron doors. A steady trickle of visitors take a peek in both the Gents and the Ladies after suitable warning. The columns are echoed across the road at the Grass Hut, 37 Gillies St, a quality gift shop selling Hundertwasser prints and cards.

For **eating**, try the central *Trainspotters Café*, 39 Gilles St; or the *Historic Fallowfield Café*, SH1 3km north toward Paihia (closed Mon & July–Sept), in a lovely 1894 kauri villa surrounded by mature gardens, where you can sit on the veranda to tuck into light meals and delicious cakes (some gluten-free) washed down with fresh lemonade and leaf teas made with filtered rainwater. From here it's another 14km to Paihia.

The back road to Russell: Whangaruru Harbour and the Cape Brett Track

With time on your hands, the most scenic way to approach the Bay of Islands is along **Old Russell Road**, which spurs off SH1 towards the coast. The narrow and winding seventy-five kilometre run to Russell takes around two hours, but you can spin it out over a lot longer, admiring the wonderful coastline around the **Whangaruru Harbour**, stopping for swims at numerous gorgeous bays, and perhaps a short walk in the mixed kauri forest of the **Ngaiotonga Scenic Reserve**.

Leaving SH1 you travel through 14km of farmland before reaching The Gallery Helena Bay Hill (Ⓣ09/433 9616, Ⓦwww.galleryhelenabay.co.nz), an imaginative **gallery** coupled with a great daytime **café** (closed June–Aug) with views across bush-clad hills down to Helena Bay. Stop if you're the slightest bit peckish as there's nowhere much to eat between here and Russell, sixty slow kilometres away. The first settlement is 11km on at **OAKURA**, where an island-studded bay is backed by a gently curving beach and a cluster of holiday homes. Not a great deal happens here, but that is its appeal, and there's no shortage of places to swim and walk.

The Cape Brett Track

Northland's best overnight tramp is the challenging but rewarding **Cape Brett Track** (20km each way; 6–8hr) which follows the hilly ridge along the centre of the peninsula with sea occasionally visible on both sides – a route outlined in DOC's *Cape Brett* leaflet. The track starts in Rawhiti (see below) and crosses private land, so all walkers must pay a **track fee** ($30, payable in advance). The Cape Brett lighthouse at the tip of the peninsula is now automatic but was once tended by keepers who lived in a house that now operates as a DOC **hut** ($23 beds; $12, annual hut pass not valid; booking required through DOC in Russell), with gas cooking stove but no cooking utensils. The hut is in a fabulous location surrounded by sea and views out to the Hole in the Rock, so you might want to stay more than one night.

You don't need to walk the track in both directions: Cape Brett Walkways/Kiwi Eco Tours (Ⓣ09/403 8823, Ⓦwww.capebrettwalks.co.nz) runs a **water taxi** service between Rawhiti and Cape Brett ($80 per person each way, minimum 4 people). Occasionally it is too rough for boats to drop off or pick up near the Cape Brett hut, but you can get dropped off at Deep Water Cove ($40 per person) two hours' walk away from the hut.

Cape Brett Walkways also give you the opportunity to tackle part of the Cape Brett Track as a one-day walk (6hr; $110) which entails a cruise from Russell or Paihia to the Cape Brett hut, an unguided walk to Deep Water Cove, then a cruise back with time for lunch and a swim. You can learn more about the bush and Maori stories of the area on a guided single group charter ($325 per person) with longer to appreciate the area and a crayfish lunch.

Along the next stretch of road, at *Coast Road Farm*, 12km north of Oakura (Ⓣ09/433 6894, Ⓦwww.thefarm.co.nz; camping $15, dorms $21, rooms and en suites ❷) you can get involved with dairy farm life, ride horses or motorbikes, go kayaking and much more. Breakfast is available for $6, lunch for $7, and dinner by arrangement for $12.

At Ngaiotonga, a further 2km north, a sealed side road runs 8km through hilly farmland to the broad sweep of **Bland Bay** with great beaches on both sides of an isthmus. Continue 2km beyond Bland Bay to reach **Whangaruru North Head Scenic Reserve**, with yet more lovely beaches, fine walks around the end of the peninsula and a DOC campsite ($7; only July–Nov) with water and toilets. Tent sites are around a hundred metres from the parking area.

Back on the coast road it is 7km north to a road junction where you turn left for Russell (25km further) and continue straight on for the scattered and predominantly Maori village of **Rawhiti**, the start of the Cape Brett Track (see box above). Just 1km along the Rawhiti road there's shorter, easier walking in the form of the **Whangamumu Track** (4km each way; 1hr; 150m ascent), a forest path which crosses the base of the Cape Brett Peninsula to a lovely beach. Here you can see the remains of a whaling station which closed in 1940.

Following the road towards Russell for 11km you'll come across a signposted side road to some fine stands of kauri. These can be visited on the **Twin Bole Kauri Walk** (around 200m; 5min), **Ngaiotonga Kauri Grove Walk** (1km; 20min), and the **Ngaiotonga–Russell Forest Walkway** (21km; 9hr); the last is best tackled over two days armed with a tent (more information is available from DOC in Russell, see p.196).

The Bay of Islands

THE BAY OF ISLANDS, 240km north of Auckland, lures visitors to its beautiful coastal scenery, scattered islands and clear blue waters. There are other equally stunning spots along the Northland coast, such as the Whangaroa and Hokianga harbours, but what sets the bay apart is the ease with which you can get out among the islands, and its pivotal history. This was the cradle of European settlement in New Zealand, a fact abundantly testified to by the bay's churches, mission stations and orchards. It's also a focal point for Maori because of the **Treaty of Waitangi** (see box, p.194) still, despite its limitations, New Zealand's most important legal document.

Perhaps surprisingly, much of your time in the Bay of Islands will be spent on the mainland, as there are no settlements on the islands. Most visitors base themselves in beachside **Paihia**, which is well set up to deal with the hordes who come here for the various cruises and excursions, as well as being the closest town to the Treaty House at **Waitangi**. The compact town of **Russell**, a couple of kilometres across the bay by passenger ferry is prettier and almost equally as convenient for cruises. To the northwest, away from the bay itself, **Kerikeri** is intimately entwined with the area's early missionary history, while **Waimate North**, inland to the west, was another important mission site and still has its Mission House.

As the main tourist centre in Northland, the Bay of Islands acts as a staging post for forays further north, in particular for day-long **bus tours** to Cape Reinga and Ninety Mile Beach (see box, p.214) – arduous affairs lasting eleven hours, most of them spent stuck inside the vehicle. You're better off making your way up to Mangonui, Kaitaia or Ahipara and taking a trip from there, though if time is short you can take your pick from a wide range of Paihia-based excursions, including scenic flights over Northland.

Some history

A warm climate, abundant seafood and deep, sheltered harbours all contributed to dense pre-European **Maori settlement** in the Bay of Islands, with many a headland supporting a *pa*. The bay also appealed to **Captain Cook**, who anchored here in 1769. Cook landed on Motuarohia Island at what became known as Cook's Cove, where he forged generally good relations with the inhabitants. Three years later the French sailor **Marion du Fresne**, en route from Mauritius to Tahiti, became the first European to have sustained contact with Maori, though he fared less well when a misunderstanding, probably over *tapu*, led to his death, along with twenty-six of his crew. The French retaliated, destroying a *pa* and killing hundreds of Maori.

Despite amicable relations between the local Ngapuhi Maori and Pakeha whalers in the early years of the nineteenth century, the situation gradually deteriorated. With increased contact, firearms, grog and Old World diseases spread and the fabric of Maori life began to break down, a process accelerated by the arrival in 1814 of Samuel Marsden, the first of many **missionaries** intent on turning Maori into Christians. In 1833, James Busby was sent as the "British Resident" to secure British interests and prevent the brutal treatment meted out to the Maori by whaling captains. Lacking armed back-up or judicial authority, he had little effect. The signing of the **Treaty of Waitangi** in 1840 brought effective policing yet heralded a decline in the importance of the Bay of Islands, as the capital moved from its original site of Kororareka (now Russell), first to Auckland and later to Wellington.

In 1927 American writer **Zane Grey** came here to fish for striped and black marlin, making the area famous with his book *The Angler's El Dorado*. Every

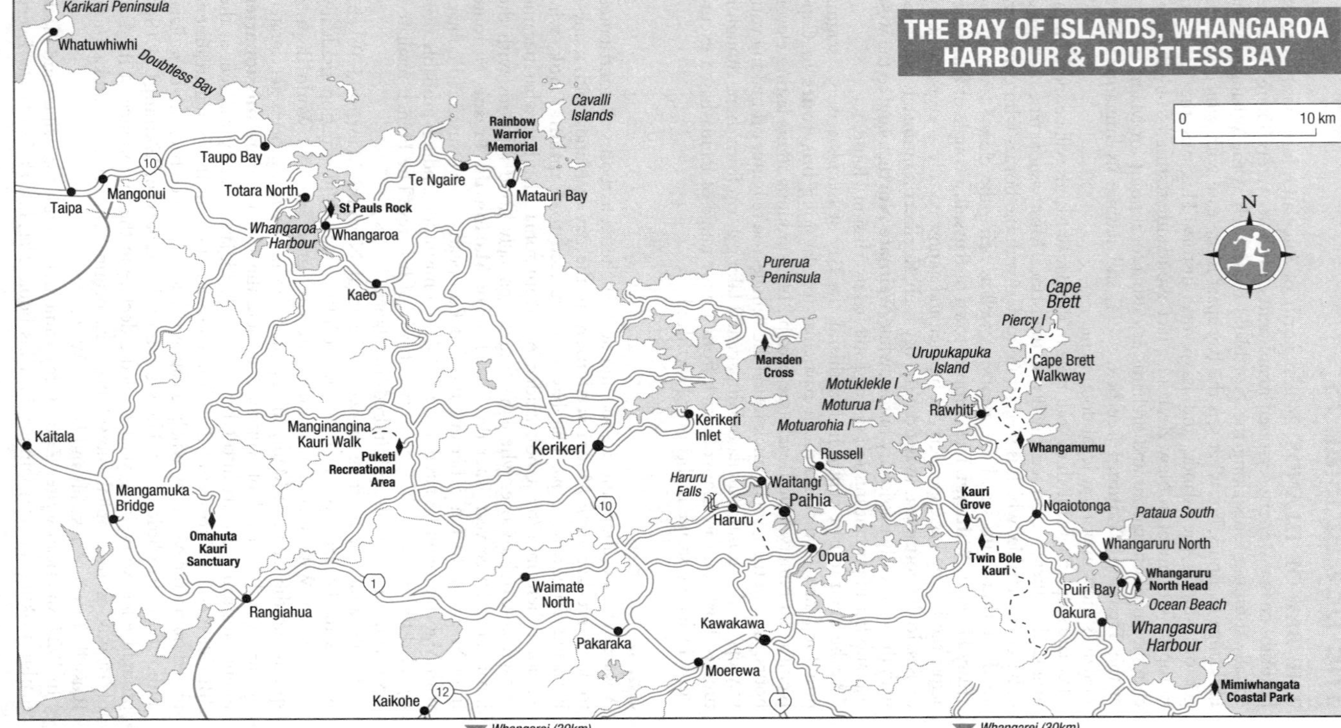
THE BAY OF ISLANDS, WHANGAROA HARBOUR & DOUBTLESS BAY
0
10 km
N
Karikari Peninsula
Whatuwhiwhi
Doubtless Bay
Cavalli Islands
Rainbow Warrior Memorial
Taupo Bay
Te Ngaire
Matauri Bay
Taipa
Mangonui
10
Totara North
St Pauls Rock
Whangaroa Harbour
Whangaroa
Kaeo
Purerua Peninsula
Cape Brett
Piercy I
Marsden Cross
Urupukapuka Island
Cape Brett Walkway
Motuklekle I
Moturua I
Rawhiti
Motuarohia I
Kerikeri Inlet
Whangamumu
Kaitala
Manginangina Kauri Walk
Puketi Recreational Area
Kerikeri
Russell
Haruru Falls
Waitangi
Paihia
Mangamuka Bridge
Kauri Grove
Ngaiotonga
Pataua South
Haruru
Omahuta Kauri Sanctuary
Opua
Twin Bole Kauri
Whangaruru North
Whangaruru North Head
Puiri Bay
Ocean Beach
1
Waimate North
Oakura
Rangiahua
Whangasura Harbour
Kawakawa
Pakaraka
Moerewa
Mimiwhangata Coastal Park
Kaikohe
12
Whangarei (30km)
Whangarei (30km)

summer since, the bay has seen game-fishing tournaments and glistening catches strung up on the jetties.

The islands

The only island that accommodates overnight guests to date is **Urupukapuka Island**, where Zane Grey, author of best-selling westerns and avid hooker of marlin, set up a fishing resort at Otehei Bay. The resort largely burned down in 1973, but you can still stay in the **accommodation** units, which now operate as the *Zane Grey Lodge* (☎09/403 7009, Ⓦwww.zanegrey.co.nz) with spartan dorms ($30), doubles (❶), en suites (❸), and a self-contained four-berth cottage (❺) all sharing a fully equipped kitchen. Adjacent to the lodge, the *Zane Grey* **restaurant** is a stopping point for Fullers cruises (see below), which provide regular access to the island ($39). There are also basic DOC **campsites** (☎09/403 9005, booked through DOC at Russell, $8) in all except the western bays of the island and there are several Maori *pa* and terrace sites all over the island, which can be explored in a few hours by following signs on the island and DOC's free *Urupukapuka Island Archeological Walk* leaflet.

Of the other six large islands, by far the most popular is **Motuarohia**, more commonly known as **Roberton Island** after John Roberton, who moved here in 1839. The Department of Conservation manages the most dramatic central section, an isthmus almost severed by a pair of perfectly circular blue lagoons, where it has installed an undersea nature trail for snorkellers, waymarked by inscribed stainless-steel plaques. At the time of writing, DOC was planning to open a **campsite** on the wildlife sanctuary of **Moturua**, which has a network of walks through bush alive with spotted kiwi, saddlebacks and North Island robins – check with the DOC office in Russell for updates.

Other sights that often feature on cruise itineraries include the **Black Rocks**, bare islets formed from columnar-jointed basalt – these rise only 10m out of the water but plummet a sheer 30m beneath. At the outer limit of the bay is the craggy peninsula of **Cape Brett**, named by Cook in 1769 after the then Lord of the Admiralty, Lord Piercy Brett. Cruises also regularly pass through the **Hole in the Rock**, a natural tunnel through Piercy Island, which is even more exciting when there's a swell running.

Exploring the bay

Unless you get out onto the water you're missing the essence of the Bay of Islands. The vast majority of yachting, scuba diving, dolphin watching, kayaking and fishing trips start in Paihia, but all the major **cruises** and bay **excursions** also pick up from Russell wharf around fifteen minutes later. Occasionally there are no pick-ups available, but you can catch the frequent, inexpensive passenger **ferry** between Paihia and Russell (p.190). From December to March, when demand outstrips supply, everything should be booked a couple of days in advance. Most hotels and motels book these trips for you and hostels can usually arrange some sort of "backpacker" discount of around ten percent.

Cruises

Dolphin Discoveries ☎0800/365 744, Ⓦwww.dolphinz.co.nz. The Discover the Bay trip on a fast catamaran (2 trips daily; 3hr 30min, $79) takes you to the Hole in the Rock and other sights on a flexible route, allowing for wildlife spotting throughout the year.

Fullers ☎0800/653 339, Ⓦwww.fboi.co.nz. Longstanding operator of large and stable craft. The leisurely Cream Trip is part of the Supercruise (daily Sept–May; June–Aug Mon, Wed, Thurs & Sat; 6hr 15min; $82) and delivers groceries and mail to wharves all around the bay. It includes a visit to the

For coverage of bus trips to Ninety Mile Beach and Cape Reinga see p.214.

Hole in the Rock and 90min at Otehei Bay. Their Hole in the Rock cruise (1–2 trips daily; 4hr; $77) speeds through the islands to Cape Brett and, when conditions permit, edges through the hole itself.

Kings ⓣ0800/222 979, ⓦwww.dolphincruises.co.nz. Family-run firm, running a Hole in the Rock Scenic Cruise (2 trips daily; 3hr; $77) which makes no island stops but includes dolphin and whale watching and an on-board Maori legend commentary. The Day in the Bay trip (Oct–May 1 daily; 6hr; $115) takes in the Hole in the Rock and an island stop of the captain's choice plus the possibility of swimming with dolphins.

The Rock ⓣ0800/762 2527, ⓦwww.rocktheboat.co.nz. Backpacker accommodation and activities aboard a former car ferry converted to sleep up to thirty. Board in the late afternoon and chug out to some gorgeous bays for fishing, swimming, snorkelling, kayaking, feasting on a big BBQ and then relaxing while someone plunks away on a guitar or the piano; arriving back around noon. Choose from six-berth dorms ($148) and private cabins ($168), all with sea views and all with dinner and breakfast included, but not drinks. Take a sleeping bag.

Fast boats

Mack Attack ⓣ0800/622 528, ⓦwww.mackattack.co.nz (4 trips daily in summer 2 trips daily in winter; 1hr 30min; $70). Open catamaran driven by 1320hp engines gives an adrenalin-pumping blast out to the Hole in the Rock and back at up to 50 knots; it's also the only boat that can take you right inside Cathedral Cave.

The Excitor ⓣ09/402 7020, ⓦwww.excitor.co.nz (5 trips daily in summer, 2 trips daily in winter; 90min; $77). Another catamaran that basically does the same thing.

Sailing and snorkelling

To combine sailing with **snorkelling**, join one of the smaller yachts which usually take less than a dozen passengers: competition is tight and the standards high, with all bringing snorkelling and fishing gear and typically going out for six hours and including lunch. See p.189 for trips focusing on dolphin watching and swimming.

Carino ⓣ09/402 8040, ⓦwww.sailingdolphins.co.nz. A large, fast, red catamaran based in Paihia, licensed to allow swimming with dolphins; $85, plus $5 for BBQ lunch.

Ecocruz ⓣ0800/432 6278, ⓦwww.ecocruz.co.nz. A three-day sail on the twenty-two-metre twin-masted *Manawanui*, which takes up to twelve people around the Bay with the emphasis on appreciation of the natural environment. Excellent meals are included, along with use of kayaks, snorkel gear, fishing tackle and a good deal of local knowledge and enthusiasm. Dorm bunk $495, double cabin $1150.

Gungha II ⓣ0800/478 900, ⓦwww.bayofislandssailing.com. A twenty-metre yacht on which you can also benefit from optional sailing tuition. $85, lunch included.

R. Tucker Thompson ⓣ0800/882537, ⓦwww.tucker.co.nz. A beautiful Northland-built schooner sails out on day-trips into the islands and anchors for a swim and BBQ lunch, taking up to twenty at a time. Daily late Oct–April; 6hr; $120 including morning tea with freshly baked scones and cream.

Scuba diving

Dive HQ, Williams Road (ⓣ0800/107 551, ⓦwww.divenz.com) is the main **scuba-diving** outfit and will take you out in the Bay of Islands, or the wrecks of the *Rainbow Warrior* (see p.206) and the *Canterbury*; all cost $205 for a two-tank dive including gear.

Kayaking and waka paddling

Lack of experience is no impediment to **kayaking** in and around Paihia, as plenty of operators offer guided trips. If you want to go it alone, there are a couple of rental outfits to choose from.

Bay Beach Hire South end of Paihia Beach ⓣ09/402 6078. Rents sit-on kayaks (single $10 per hr, $40/day; doubles $15/60), sea kayaks (singles $15/50; doubles $25/75), windsurfers ($25 per hr) and catamarans ($50 per hr). Also rents overnight allowing you to stay on Urupukapuka Island either camping or at *Zane Grey Lodge* (see p.187).

Coastal Kayakers Waitangi Bridge ⓣ09/402 8105, ⓦwww.coastalkayakers.co.nz. Open all year, running a variety of trips from half-day paddles upstream to Haruru Falls ($55) and full-day trips ($90), to two-day guided camping excursions (Nov–June; $130). They also rent out kayaks for two or more people at a time ($10 per hr, $40/day).

Island Kayaks at Bay Beach Hire ⓣ0800/611 440, ⓦwww.islandkayaking.co.nz. Operate all year, offering half-day ($55) and full-day ($90) trips exploring the inner islands and bays.

Taiamai Tours 09/405 9990, ⓦwww.taiamaitours.co.nz. Paddle your own canoe Maori-style. You and up to a dozen others will get the full works – *karakia* (prayers), *whaikorero* (speechmaking), and learn how to handle a *hoe* (paddle) – before propelling the *waka* (canoe) around the bay, getting a real feel for the Maori sense of spirituality and affinity with the land and sea. Daily at 10am & 1pm; 90min; $75.

Dolphin watching and swimming

Relatively warm water all year round and an abundance of marine mammals make the Bay of Islands a wonderful place for **dolphin watching**. You've around a 90 percent chance of seeing bottlenose and common dolphins in pretty much any season, orca from May to October and minke and Bryde's **whales** from August to January.

Be aware that swimming with dolphins is never a certainty, and swimming is forbidden when they have juveniles in tow (which can be any time of year). Generally your chances swimming with them are about 50 percent, but some (though not all) companies offer money back or a second trip if you miss out. These "raincheck" policies can vary according to the season; check with the visitor centre or direct with the operators when you book.

Your best chance to see dolphins is on a cruise with one of the companies licensed to actively search for and swim with dolphins, but only eighteen people are allowed in the water at a time and since most trips carry around forty people in the peak season, you can expect to be in the water about a third of the time that the dolphins are about.

Carino (see Sailing, p.188). A big catamaran that takes you on a day-trip around the islands, with a chance to swim with the dolphins if found in the right conditions.

Dolphin Adventures ⓣ09/402 7421, ⓦwww.fboi.co.nz. Run by Fullers (see p.187) this 4hr trip includes the option of a stopover on Urupukapuka Island for an extra few hours if you take the early boat at 8am; $105.

Dolphin Discoveries Marsden Rd, opposite the visitor centre ⓣ0800/365 744, ⓦwww.dolphinz.co.nz. The pioneers of dolphin swimming in this area and sensitive to the needs of the dolphins; 4hr, $99.

Dolphin Rendezvous (see p.208). Mangonui-based boat skippered by a local fisherman, who welcomes all travellers including those with disabilities. Enquire about pick-ups from Paihia. November to mid-June only.

Kings ⓣ0800/222 979, ⓦwww.dolphincruises.co.nz. Dolphin watching is a feature of all their trips or you can swim with dolphins as part of their Day in the Bay cruise (see p.188).

Fishing

Fishing trips range from a line fishing for snapper through to big-game boats in search of marlin, shark, tuna and kingfish. Ask around and speak to the skippers to find a trip that suits; daily charter rates range around $90 for light tackle and $280 upwards for the big-game boats.

Flights and parasailing

Salt Air Marsden Rd, near the Maritime Building, Paihia ☎0800/472 582, www.saltair.co.nz. Small plane trips ($115 for 30min, $195 for 1hr to the Hole in the Rock) and 20min helicopter flight (from $190, min 4 people).

Flying Kiwi Parasail based at Bay Beach Hire on Paihia waterfront ☎09/402 6078. 10–15min tandem or solo flights from the back of a speedboat to around 250m ($75) or 350m ($85).

Horse-riding and quad biking

The Adventure Company Tirohanga Rd, near Kawakawa ☎09/404 1142, www.adventurecompany.co.nz. Professionally run horse rides in small groups (90min; $55) and quad-biking tours (90min; $75) that climb rugged hill tracks to breathtaking views.

Paihia and Waitangi

PAIHIA is where it all happens. Until the mid-1990s it consisted of little more than a fish and chip shop but it's now a two-kilometre-long string of waterside motels, restaurants and holiday homes teeming with trip operators, backpacker hostels, party-oriented bars and hotels. Fortunately, Pahia's low-rise development is sympathetic to its three beautiful, flat beachside bays looking towards Russell and the Bay of Islands, encircled by forested hills. A plaque outside the current St Paul's Anglican Church on Marsden Road marks the spot where, in 1831, the northern chiefs petitioned the British Crown for a representative to establish law and order. In 1833 King William IV finally addressed their concerns by sending the first British resident, James Busby. Busby built a house on a promontory 2km north across the Waitangi River in **WAITANGI** – the scene some seven years later of the signing of the **Treaty of Waitangi**, which ceded the nation's sovereignty to Britain in return for protection.

Arrival, information and getting around

Northliner and InterCity buses arrive on the waterfront Marsden Road outside the Bay of Islands' main **i-SITE visitor centre** (daily 8am–5pm, extended hours Oct–April; ☎09/402 7345, paihia@visitnorthland.co.nz), which has **Internet** access and books tours. The Bay of Islands **airport** is twenty-two kilometres northwest, near Kerikeri, receiving planes from Auckland, which are met by a shuttle bus ($50 one way).

Paihia isn't big, and everywhere is within walking distance. If you've got bags to carry, engage the services of the **Paihia Tuk Tuk Shuttle Service**, based outside the visitor centre (☎0274/866 071), who will pick up and drop off one

Paihia–Russell ferries

Sticking to the highways Russell is almost 100km from Paihia, but drivers can shorten that to 15km by using the small **vehicle ferry** (7am–10pm; daily every 20min; car & driver $10 each way, pedestrians $1; buy your ticket on board) across the narrow Veronica Channel at **OPUA**, 6km south of Paihia.

Foot passengers can take one of several **passenger ferries** (Oct–May 7am–10.30pm; June–Sept 7.30am–7pm; $6 each way) between the main wharves in Paihia and Russell, a ten to fifteen minute journey.

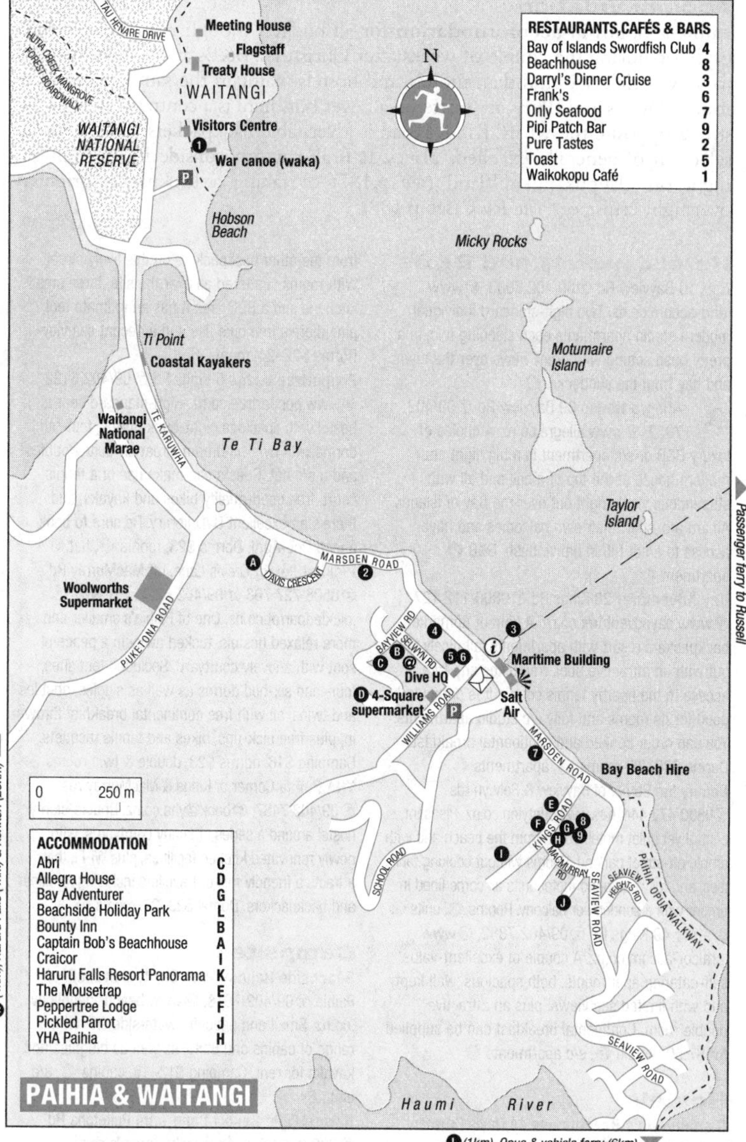

to six people pretty much anywhere in town for around $5 each and run up to Haruru Falls for around $10 each. Alternatively, you can rent good-quality **mountain bikes** from Bay Beach Hire, at the south end of Paihia Beach (☎09/402 6078; $15 a half-day, $20 per day, $25 overnight). **Parking** is difficult in high season; your best bet is the car park opposite the 4-square supermarket on Williams Road.

Accommodation

Paihia abounds in **accommodation** for all budgets though rates can be stratospheric during the couple of weeks after Christmas. B&Bs and homestays tend to vary their prices less than motels, and hostels maintain the same prices year-round. Motels and B&Bs are scattered all over but there is a central cluster in the streets opposite the wharf. Kings Road is a veritable backpackers' village with a selection of generally excellent places. It is also worth considering spending a night on Urupukapuka Island (see p.187) or taking a backpacker-oriented overnight cruise on *The Rock* (see p.188).

Hotels, motels and B&Bs

Abri 10 Bayview Rd ⓣ09/402 8003, ⓦwww.abri-accom.co.nz. Two high-standard individual modern studio apartments each sleeping two, in a pretty bush setting with great views over the town and bay from the sundecks. ❽

Allegra House 39 Bayview Rd ⓣ09/402 7932, ⓦwww.allegra.co.nz. A choice of luxury B&B or s/c apartment in a big, light and modern house at the top of a hill, and all with stupendous views right out over the Bay of Islands. All are a/c, sport their own balconies and have access to a hot tub in native bush. B&B ❺, apartment ❻

Bay Adventurer 28 Kings Rd ⓣ0800/112 127, ⓦwww.bayadventurer.co.nz. A kind of upmarket backpackers resort with apartments, all nicely laid out with an attractive pool, free bikes and free access to the nearby tennis courts. It is particularly good for its rooms and fully s/c studio apartments. You can order cooked and continental breakfasts. Dorms $20–25, rooms ❷, apartments ❹

Bounty Inn Corner of Bayview & Selwyn rds ⓣ0800/472 444, ⓦwww.bountyinn.co.nz. Pleasant, central yet quiet motel, 100m from the beach and with ample off-street parking. Rooms without cooking facilities, and fully equipped motel units all come lined in timber with a sundeck or balcony. Rooms ❺, units ❻

Craicor 49 Kings Rd ⓣ09/402 7882, ⓦwww.craicor-accom.co.nz. A couple of excellent-value self-catering apartments, both spacious, well kept and with limited sea views; plus an attractive double room. Continental breakfast can be supplied for $7.50.Double ❺, s/c apartments ❻

Hostels

Captain Bob's Beachhouse 44 Davis Crescent ⓣ09/402 8668, ⓔcapnbobs@xtra.co.nz. In Captain Bob's absence, Marie runs a tight ship in this attractive, well-maintained and homely hostel away from the hubbub of Kings Rd. There are good sea views and a separate women's dorm. Dorms $25, rooms ❷–❸, apartment ❸

The Mousetrap 11 Kings Rd ⓣ09/402 8182, ⓦwww.mousetrap.co.nz. Welcoming, nautically themed, wood-panelled hostel that sets itself apart from the other backpackers on this lively street. With rooms scattered all over the site, three small kitchens and a BBQ area it has an intimate feel, plus there's free bike use and a decent sea view. Dorms $22–24, rooms ❷

Peppertree Lodge 5 Kings Rd ⓣ09/402 6122, ⓦwww.peppertree.co.nz. High-standard central hostel with spacious eight-bunk dorms, four-bunk dorms with own bathroom, great en-suite doubles and a s/c flat. Guests can make use of a tennis court, free good-quality bikes and kayaks, and there's an excellent DVD library. Be sure to book ahead Oct–April. Dorms $23, rooms ❸, flat ❹

Pickled Parrot Grey's Lane, off MacMurray Rd ⓣ0508 727 768 or 09/402 6222, ⓦwww.pickledparrot.co.nz. One of Paihia's smaller and more relaxed hostels, tucked away in a peaceful spot with a lovely courtyard. Secluded tent sites; four- and six-bed dorms as well as singles, doubles and twins, all with free continental breakfast thrown in, plus free pick-ups, bikes and tennis racquets. Camping $16, dorms $23, double & twin rooms ❷

YHA Paihia Corner of Kings & MacMurray rds ⓣ09/402 7487, ⓔbook@yha.co.nz. Double-storey hostel around a series of sunny courtyards, with newly renovated kitchen facilities, plus Wi-Fi, that attracts a friendly mix of travellers including families and backpackers. Dorms $23–27, rooms ❷

Campsites

Beachside Holiday Park SH11, 3km south of Paihia ⓣ09/402 7678, ⓦwww.beachsideholiday.co.nz. Small and peaceful waterside site with a range of cabins and units, as well as dinghies and kayaks for rent. Camping $12–16, cabins ❷, s/c units ❸

Haruru Falls Resort Panorama Puketona Rd ⓣ0800/757 525, ⓦwww.harurufalls.co.nz. Fabulous location by the river with commanding views of Haruru Falls, 4km north of Paihia, offering riverside tent sites and motel units around a pool. The resort has outdoor games such as pétanque and volleyball, a BBQ, and its own restaurant bar, plus kayaks and pedalboats for rent; there's a courtesy shuttle to Paihia. Camping $12–19, motel units ❸

The Town

Paihia is primarily a base for exploring the bay, and there are no sights in town itself. If you'd like to study some fine bone and *pounamu* (greenstone) **carvings** check out the Cabbage Tree counter in the Maritime Building. Fans of mangroves and estuarine scenery can tackle the gentle **Paihia–Opua Coastal Walkway** (6km; 90min–2hr one way), which wanders along the wave-cut platforms and the small bays in between.

Waitangi Treaty Grounds

Crossing the bridge over the Waitangi River you enter the Waitangi Treaty Grounds, where in 1840 Queen Victoria's representative William Hobson and nearly fifty Maori chiefs signed the Treaty of Waitangi (see box, p.194). It's now home to the Waitangi Visitor Centre and Treaty House (daily: Oct–March 9am–6pm; April–Sept 9am–5pm; $12; free for New Zealand citizens), the single most symbolic place in New Zealand for Maori and Pakeha alike, and a focal point for the modern nation's struggle for identity. You can easily spend half a day here, taking in an audiovisual presentation that sets the historical framework, bolstered by a small exhibition of Maori artefacts, and perhaps a short daytime cultural performance or a guided tour (all $10), as well as daytime shows ($12), though most people give it around two hours then perhaps return in the evening for the Culture North Sound and Light Show (Ⓣ09/402 5990, Ⓦwww.culturenorth.co.nz), a highly recommended contemporary approach to presenting Maori culture (Oct–March Mon, Wed, Thurs & Sat 8pm; $45; book ahead), conducted inside the traditional meeting house. Over an hour and a quarter you're introduced to an extended family as the stories of Maori life from the arrival of Kupe to the present day are enacted with verve mixing drama, song and dance with storytelling. Free pick-ups are available from Paihia.

The **Treaty House** was built in Georgian colonial style in 1833–34. Its front windows look towards Russell over sweeping lawns, where marquees were erected on three significant occasions: in 1834, when Maori chiefs chose the Confederation of Tribes flag, which now flies on one yardarm of the central flagpole; the meeting a year later at which northern Maori leaders signed the Declaration of Independence of New Zealand; and, in 1840, the signing of the Treaty of Waitangi itself.

The northern side of the lawn is flanked by the *whare runanga*, or **Maori meeting house**, built between 1934 and 1940. Though proposed by Bledisloe and northern Maori chiefs, the construction of the house was a co-operative effort between all Maori, and the interior carvings represent all *iwi* rather than the usual single tribe. A short audiovisual presentation explains key elements on the richly carved panels.

Housed in a specially built shelter in the Treaty House grounds is the world's largest **war canoe** (*waka*), the *Ngatoki Matawhaorua*, named after the vessel navigated by Kupe when he discovered Aotearoa. It's an impressive boat, built over two years from two huge kauri by members of the five northern tribes and measuring over 35m in length. It has traditionally been launched each year on Waitangi Day, propelled by eighty warriors. Near the visitor centre is the excellent *Waikokopu Café* in a relaxing setting (see p.196).

Westwards, the Waitangi Treaty Grounds extend beyond the Waitangi Golf Course to the scenic viewpoint atop **Mount Bledisloe**, reached by car 3km away. Two kilometres beyond that and accessed from the main road, are the **Haruru (Big Noise) Falls**, formed where the Waitangi River drops over a basalt lava flow. Though not that impressive by New Zealand standards, there's

The Treaty of Waitangi

The Treaty of Waitangi is the **founding document** of modern New Zealand, a touchstone for both Pakeha and Maori, and its implications permeate New Zealand society. Signed in 1840 between what were ostensibly two sovereign states – the United Kingdom and the United Tribes of New Zealand, plus other Maori leaders – the treaty remains central to New Zealand's **race relations**. The Maori rights guaranteed by it have seldom been upheld, however, and the constant struggle for recognition continues.

The treaty at Waitangi

Motivated by a desire to staunch French expansion in the Pacific, and a moral obligation on the Crown to protect Maori from rapacious land-grabbing by settlers, the British instructed naval captain William Hobson to negotiate the transfer of sovereignty with "the free and intelligent consent of the natives", and to deal fairly with the Maori. Hobson, with the help of James Busby and others, drew up both the English Treaty and a Maori "translation". On the face of it, the treaty is a straightforward document, but the complications of having two versions (see Contexts, p.879) and the implications of striking a deal between two peoples with widely differing views on land and resource ownership and usage have reverberated down the years.

The treaty was unveiled on February 5, 1840, to a gathering of some 400 representatives of the five northern tribes in front of Busby's residence in Waitangi. Presented as a contract between the chiefs and Queen Victoria – someone whose role was comprehensible in chiefly terms – the benefits were amplified and the costs downplayed. As most chiefs didn't understand English, they signed the Maori version of the treaty, which still has *mana* (goodwill) among Maori today.

The treaty after Waitangi

The pattern set at Waitangi was repeated up and down the country, as seven copies of the treaty were dispatched to garner signatures and extend Crown authority over parts of the North Island that had not yet been covered, and the South Island. On May 21, before signed treaty copies had been returned, Hobson claimed New Zealand for Britain: the North Island on the grounds of cession by Maori, and the South Island by right of Cook's "discovery", as it was considered to be *in terrorium nullis* (without owners), despite a significant Maori population.

Maori fears were alerted from the start, and as the settler population grew and demand for land increased, successive governments passed laws that gradually stripped Maori of control over their affairs – actions which led to the New Zealand Wars of the 1860s (see Contexts, p.881). Over the decades, small concessions were made, but nothing significant changed until 1973, when **Waitangi Day** (February 6) became an official national holiday. Around the same time, Maori groups, supported by a small band of Pakeha, began a campaign of direct action, increasingly disrupting commemorations, thereby alienating many Pakeha and splitting Maori allegiances between angry young urban Maori and the *kaumatua* (elders), who saw the actions as disrespectful to the ancestors and an affront to tradition. Many strands of Maori society were unified by the *hikoi* (march) to Waitangi to protest against the celebrations in 1985, a watershed year in which Paul Reeves was appointed New Zealand's first Maori Governor General and the **Waitangi Tribunal** for land reform was given some teeth.

Protests have continued since as successive governments have vacillated over whether to attend the commemorations at Waitangi.

good swimming at their base. Haruru Falls are also reached from the Treaty House grounds via the very gentle **Hutia Creek Mangrove Forest Boardwalk** (2hr return) or on a guided **kayak** trip up the estuary and among the mangroves (see p.189).

Eating, drinking and entertainment

Paihia's range of **places to eat** is unmatched anywhere in the Bay of Islands and competition keeps prices reasonable – wander around town and you'll find any number of appealing restaurants and cafés, typically specializing in seafood. The restaurants are also good places to stick around for post prandial drinking, and there are several more raucous **bars** along Kings Road.

Paihia's winters are enlivened by two three-day **festivals** – **country rock** during the second weekend in May (Ⓦwww.country-rock.co.nz), and **jazz and blues**, usually held during the second weekend in August (Ⓦwww.jazz-blues.co.nz).

Cafés, restaurants, bars and dinner cruises

Bay of Islands Swordfish Club Marsden Rd. Private club, overlooking the bay and welcoming visitors outside the peak summer season: just sign yourself in. Simple but good-value food is served from 6pm, and "Swordy's" has some of the cheapest drinks in town.

Beachhouse 16 Kings Rd. Lively all-day café and juice bar with seating out under the shade sail and a menu of varied breakfasts, panini, and gourmet burgers ($7–15). There's the *Sand Pit* pool hall round the back, and live music most nights.

Frank's Marsden Rd. Chilled café, pizzeria and bar with good breakfasts, decent coffee and a wicked cocktail list.

Only Seafood 40 Marsden Rd Ⓣ09/402 7444. Stylish restaurant located in an atmospheric villa and open nightly for seafood extravaganzas such as rare yellowfin tuna with roasted langoustine (mains around $30).

Darryl's Dinner Cruise Ⓣ0800/334 6637, Ⓦwww.ddinner.co.nz. Convivial and leisurely cruise (2hr 30min, $78) from Paihia Wharf up the Waitangi River to Haruru Falls, where you tuck into prawns and mussels followed by T-bone steak, lamb and fish. Catch it for a good sunset and it is a great way to spend the evening. There's a cash bar on board or BYO wine.

Pipi Patch Bar 18 Kings Rd. Situated at Paihia's branch of the Base backpacker chain and the liveliest bar at this end of town, always full of backpackers and locals out on the deck, often tucking into the nightly $10 BBQ and competing for trip giveaways.

Pure Tastes 116 Marsden Rd Ⓣ09/402 0003. Acclaimed chef Paul Jobin is at the helm of this ultra-fine dining restaurant at the

▲The world's largest war canoe, Waitangi

2 NORTHLAND | The Bay of Islands

oasis-like *Paihia Beach Resort*. Breakfasts such as French sourdough toast with caramelized apples ($16) will see you through to intricately prepared lunches (poolside in summer; mains around $20), but it comes into its own with dinner choices like black lacquer duck with green banana, chilli and lime ($33). Also tasting menus (four-course $65, five-course $75).

Toast Selwyn Mall ☎09/402 8684. Chic and somewhat hidden restaurant and bar that draws the cognoscenti for a cocktail on the banquettes, one of their fine gourmet pizzas (around $20), or simply to curl up in the corner with a liqueur coffee and a book.

Waikokopu Café Treaty House Grounds, Waitangi ☎09/402 6275. Outstanding daytime café accessed by a track through the rainforest and surrounded by picnic table-strewn lawns. Perfect for tucking into unusual and beautifully prepared breakfasts and lunches ($13.50–18.50), plus an excellent range of cakes and great coffee. Licensed.

Russell

The isolated location of **RUSSELL** – on a narrow peninsula with poor road but good sea access – gives this small hillside settlement an island ambience. In summer, however, day-trippers pile off passenger ferries from Paihia and vehicle ferries from nearby Opua to explore the village's historic buildings and stroll along its quaint waterfront.

Evenings are more peaceful and romantic – a far cry from the 1830s when **Kororareka**, as Russell was then known, was a swashbuckling town full of whalers and sealers with a reputation as the "Hell Hole of the Pacific". Savage and drunken behaviour served as an open invitation to **missionaries**, who gradually won over a sizeable congregation and left behind Russell's two oldest buildings, the church and a printing works that produced religious tracts. By 1840, Kororareka was the largest settlement in the country, but after the signing of the Treaty of Waitangi, Governor William Hobson fell out with both Maori and local settlers and moved his capital progressively further south.

Meanwhile, initial Maori enthusiasm for the Treaty of Waitangi had faded: financial benefits had failed to materialize and the Confederation of Tribes flag that flew from Flagstaff Hill between 1834 and 1840 had been replaced by the Union Jack. This came to be seen as a symbol of British betrayal, and as resentment crystallized it found a leader in **Hone Heke Pokai**, Ngapuhi chief and son-in-law of Kerikeri's Hongi Hika. Between July 1844 and March 1845, Heke and his followers cut down the flagstaff no less than four times, the last occasion sparking the first **New Zealand War**, which raged for nearly a year, during which Kororareka was destroyed. The settlement rose from the ashes under a new name, Russell, and grew slowly around its beachfront into the tranquil village of today.

The main **cruises** (see p.187) all call here some fifteen minutes after leaving Paihia, though it's important to reserve in advance so that they know to pick you up. If you're only passing through, everything at Russell can be seen comfortably in a day.

Arrival and information

Most visitors reach Russell by **ferry** (see box, p.190), but it's also accessible along the back road described on p.183. Tourist information is available from **Russell Information**, at the end of the wharf (daily: Christmas–March 7.30am–8pm April–Christmas 8.30am–5pm; ☎09/403 8020, Ⓦwww.visitrussell.co.nz), who also make bookings for local trips and accommodation. For specific walking and environmental information make for DOC's **Bay of Islands Visitor Centre**, The Strand (daily: Nov–May 9am–5pm; June–Oct 9am–4.30pm; ☎09/403 9005) which is full of interesting displays and stocks the useful *Russell Heritage Trail* and *Bay of Islands Walks* leaflets.

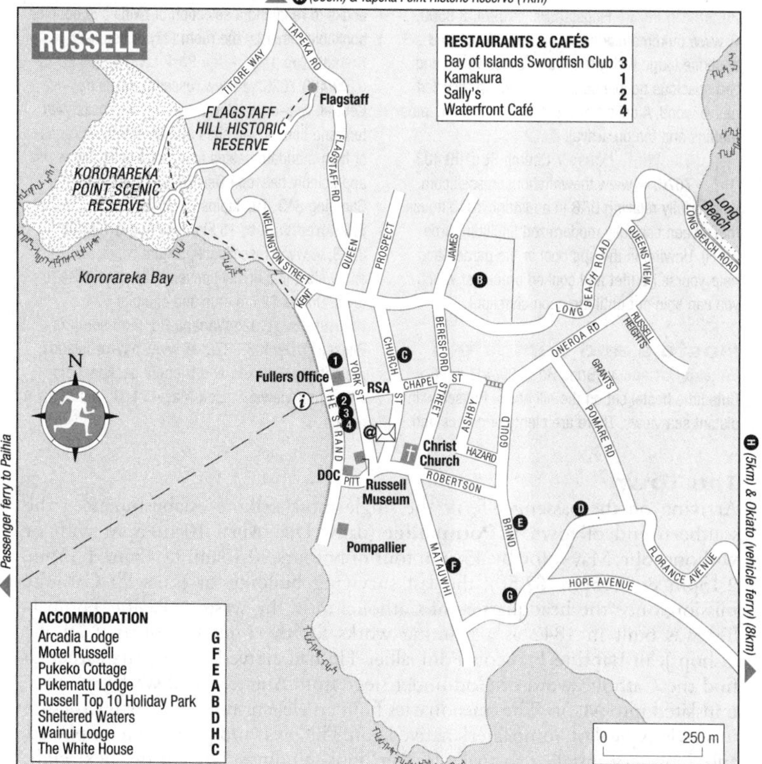

Few places are more than half a kilometre away from the wharf, though if time is limited you may fancy the **Russell Mini Tour** (3–5 tours daily; 1hr; $20; ⓣ09/403 7866), which leaves from outside the Fullers office on The Strand and visits the major sights. There's daytime **Internet access** at Enterprise Russell on York Street.

Accommodation

Accommodation in Russell is much more limited than in Paihia and tends to be more upmarket. Apart from a handful of motels, hotels and backpacker lodges, most accommodation is in B&Bs and homestays. Don't expect to find many vacancies in the three weeks after Christmas, when you'll have to book well ahead and pay inflated rates, which continue to the end of February.

Lodges, motels and B&Bs

Arcadia Lodge 10 Florance Ave ⓣ09/403 7756, ⓦwww.arcadialodge.co.nz. One of Russell's gems: B&B in an historic, rambling wooden house encircled by decks on a quiet hill overlooking English cottage gardens and the bay. It's a 5min stroll from the village and some of the half-dozen wooden-floored suites and rooms (one not en suite) enjoy sea views. Rooms ⑥, suites ⑧

Motel Russell Matauwhi Bay Rd ⓣ0800/240 011, ⓦwww.motelrussell.co.nz. Despite the lack of sea views, this is the pick of Russell's motels, with pleasant s/c units and units (some with kitchens), plus an attractive pool and spa. Studios ④, units ⑤

Pukematu Lodge Flagstaff Hill ☎09/403 8500, ⓦwww.pukematulodge.co.nz. Beautifully sited boutique lodge with great 360-degree views and two spacious double suites furnished in recycled native wood. A delicious breakfast is included, plus muffins and tea on arrival. ⑨

The White House 7 Church St ☎09/403 7676, ⓦwww.thewhitehouserussell.com. Wonderfully relaxing B&B in a historic 1840 house that's been carefully modernized (including free Wi-Fi). Unwind in the spa pool in the garden and help-yourself buffet and cooked breakfast which you can spin out until the noon checkout. ⑧

Hostels and campsites

Pukeko Cottage 14 Brind Rd ☎09/403 8498. Cute little hostel set on the hill above Russell with distant sea views. There are plenty of games and books to read and a selection of twins and doubles, bookable either by the room (②) or bed ($25).

Russell Top 10 Holiday Park Long Beach Rd ☎09/403 7826, ⓦwww.russelltop10.co.nz. Central, well-ordered and spotless campsite with tent and campervan sites and an extensive range of high-standard cabins and motel units. Rates rise appreciably between Dec 20 and end of Jan. Camping $13–19, cabins ②, units ④

Sheltered Waters 18 Florance Ave ☎09/403 8818, ⓦwww.russellbackpackers.co.nz. Modest and welcoming hostel conveniently sited close to town. Dorms $25, rooms and en suite ③

Wainui Lodge 92d Wahapu Rd, 5km south of Russell ☎09/403 8278, ⓦwww.bay-of-islands.pelnet.org. Relaxed and friendly backpackers with great views. Closed May–Oct. Dorms $23, rooms ②

The Town

Arriving on the passenger ferry, the single most striking establishment at the southern end of town is **Pompallier** (daily: Dec–April 10am–5pm with or without tour; May–Nov by 45-min tour only, tours 10.15am, 11.15am, 1.15pm, 2.15pm & 3.15pm; $7.50), the last surviving building of Russell's Catholic mission, once the headquarters of Catholicism in the western Pacific. Pompallier was built in 1842 as a printing works for the French Roman Catholic bishop Jean Baptiste François Pompallier. He had arrived three years earlier to find the Catholic word of God under siege from Anglican and Wesleyan tracts, translated into Maori. The missionaries built an elegant rammed-earth structure in a style typical of Pompallier's native Lyon. The press and paper were imported, and a tannery installed to make leather book-bindings. During the next eight years over a dozen titles were printed, comprising more than thirty thousand volumes, which were some of the first books printed in Maori.

The property became a private house in 1850, but restoration work has largely recreated its 1842 state. Today, artisans again produce handmade books – the production processes are explained in each room, and on the tour you can even get your hands dirty in what is New Zealand's only surviving colonial tannery. Outside, the grounds make a perfect place for a picnic.

Russell's only other building surviving from the same era is the prim, white, weatherboard **Christ Church** on Robertson Road, built in 1836 and New Zealand's oldest surviving church. Unlike most churches of similar vintage, it was not a mission church but built by local settlers: an appeal for public donations loosened the purse strings of Charles Darwin, who passed through the Bay of Islands at the time, long before he fell out with the church over his theory of evolution. In the mid-nineteenth century the church was besieged during skirmishes between Hone Heke's warriors and the British, leaving several still-visible bullet holes.

The small **Russell Museum**, York Street (daily: Christmas–Jan 10am–5pm; Feb–Christmas 10am–4pm; $5), shows a video telling the town's history and contains well-laid-out exhibits, including an impressive one-fifth scale model of Cook's *Endeavour*, which called in here in 1769. From the museum, a stroll along The Strand passes the prestigious Bay of Islands Swordfish Club, which was founded in 1924, and the *Duke of Marlborough Hotel* – the original building on this site held New Zealand's first liquor licence.

At the end of The Strand, a short track (30–40min return) climbs steeply to **Flagstaff Hill** (Maiki). The current flagpole was erected in 1857, some twelve years after the destruction of the fourth flagpole by Hone Heke as a conciliatory gesture by a son of one of the chiefs who had ordered the original felling. The Confederation of Tribes flag, abandoned after the signing of the Treaty of Waitangi, is flown on twelve significant days of the year, including the anniversary of Hone Heke's death and the final day of the first New Zealand War. From Flagstaff Hill it's a further kilometre to the **Tapeka Point Historic Reserve**, a former *pa* site at the end of the peninsula – a wonderfully defensible position with great views and abundant evidence of terracing.

Another worthwhile stroll is to **Oneroa Bay** (Long Beach), 1km east of Russell on the far side of the peninsula, a gently shelving beach sheltered from the prevailing wind and safe for swimming.

Eating and drinking

Russell has a limited range of **restaurants** and prices are fairly high, but quality is good. Outside the peak summer season, things close down pretty early. For **drinking** the best bets are often the cheap private **clubs** – the *RSA* on Cass Street and the *Bay of Islands Swordfish Club* on The Strand, for example – which usually welcome visitors.

Bay of Islands Swordfish Club The Strand. Technically a private club but you just sign yourself in. Always a winner for cheap beer, great sunset views from the veranda and simple but good bar meals.

Kamakura The Strand ☎09/403 7771. Probably the finest eating in town. A modern, licensed waterfront restaurant with an understated Japanese ambience and a varied menu of exquisite and beautifully presented dishes, particularly fish (mains around $30). Closed Mon & Tues.

Omata Estate Aucks Rd, 8km from Russell and 2km from ferry wharf ☎09/403 8007, www.omata.co.nz. Classy restaurant and bar overlooking young vineyards with the inner bay as a backdrop. Lunch platters cost around $45–65 for two, dinner mains around $30. Advance booking essential for meals in summer.

Sally's 25 The Strand ☎09/403 7652. Convivial, unpretentious and always busy day/night restaurant, strong on seafood (and especially seafood chowder; $10). It's worth booking ahead in peak season. Most mains $27–30.

Waterfront Café The Strand. Simple café with great coffee, waterfront seating as well as all-day breakfasts and delicious lunches such as chicken and shrimp laksa. Closed Mon in winter.

Kerikeri

KERIKERI, 25km northwest of Paihia, is central to the history of the Bay of Islands and yet geographically removed from it, strung out along the main road and surrounded by the orchards that form Kerikeri's economic mainstay. Two kilometres to the east of town, the thin ribbon of the Kerikeri Inlet forces its way from the sea to its tidal limit at **Kerikeri Basin**, the site chosen by Samuel Marsden for the Church Missionary Society's second mission in New Zealand.

In the 1920s the area was planted with the subtropical crops that continue to thrive here – mainly citrus fruit, along with tamarillos, feijoas, melons, courgettes, peppers and kiwifruit. For most of the year it's possible to get **seasonal work** in the orchards, weeding, thinning or picking. Work is most abundant from January to July, but this is also when competition for jobs is greatest, and you may find that your chances are just as good any month except August and September. The best contacts are the managers of the hostels and campsites, many of which also offer good weekly rates. In recent years Kerikeri has earned itself a reputation for its high-quality **craft shops** dotted amongst the orchards.

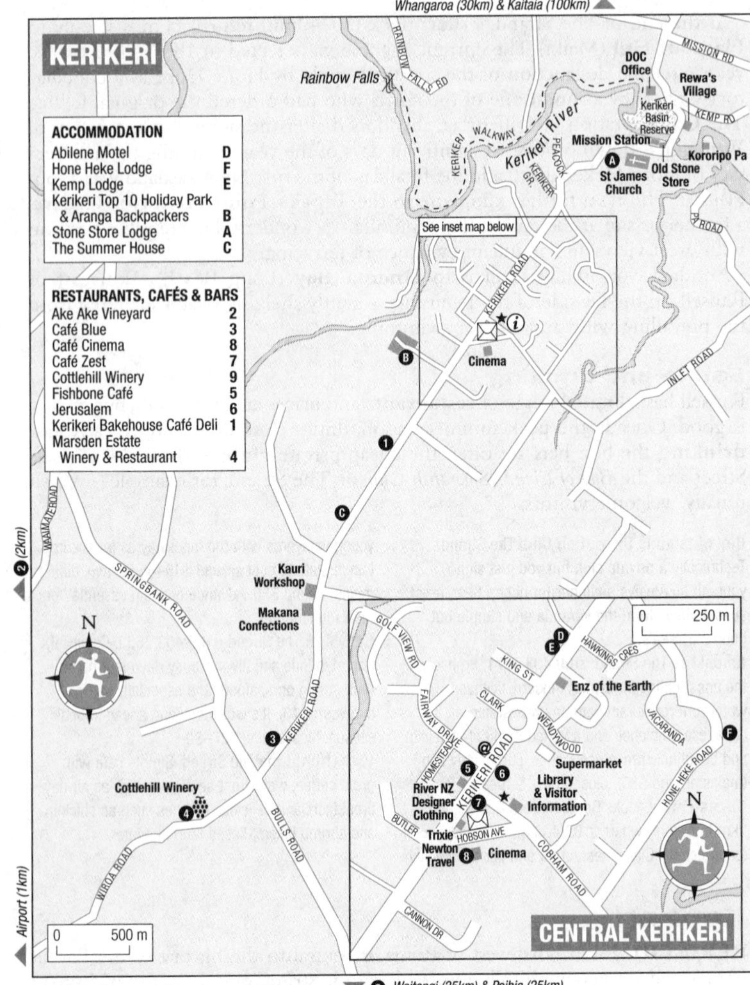

Arrival and information

Air New Zealand **flights** from Auckland land 5km out of town towards Paihia at Bay of Islands Airport, from where Paihia Taxis operate an airport shuttle ($10 per person to Kerikeri). Northliner and InterCity **buses** stop on Cobham Road, with several services to Paihia but just one bus heading north to Kaitaia daily (not Sun): book through Trixie Newton World Travel, 65 Kerikeri Rd (☎0800/108 001). There's no official visitor centre, but you can pick up **leaflets** inside the foyer of the library on Cobham Road (Mon–Fri 10am–5pm, Sat 9am–2pm; ☎09/407 9297); and there's a **DOC office** at 34 Landing Rd (Mon–Fri 8am–4.30pm; ☎09/407 8474), which can advise on local walks and more ambitious treks into the Puketi and Omahuta forests (see p.204) and has **Internet access**.

Accommodation

Kerikeri has a good selection of **accommodation** in all categories, particularly budget places – a consequence of the area's popularity with long-stay casual workers. The i-SITE office in Pahia keeps an updated list and can assist with bookings. Seasonal price fluctuations are nowhere near as marked as in Paihia, though it's still difficult to find accommodation in January.

Abilene Motel 136 Kerikeri Rd ⓣ09/407 9203, ⓦwww.abilenemotel.co.nz. Centrally located motel in a garden setting with a solar-heated pool, spa and Sky TV. ④

Hone Heke Lodge 65 Hone Heke Rd ⓣ09/407 8170, ⓦwww.honeheke.co.nz. Pleasant hostel that's recently undergone massive renovation and landscaping. Eight-bed dorms each come with a fridge and tea-making gear, plus there are doubles and twins, some en suite. There's also a games room and BBQ area. Dorms $23, rooms ②, en suites ③

Kemp Lodge 134 Kerikeri Rd ⓣ09/407 8295, ⓦwww.kemplodge.co.nz. Three pleasant s/c chalets close to town, complete with TV and video, and pool. ④

Kerikeri Top 10 Holiday Park and Aranga Backpackers Kerikeri Rd ⓣ0800/272 642, ⓦwww.aranga.co.nz. Large, beautiful streamside site on the edge of town with a spacious camping area, well-equipped standard cabins with good weekly rates, comfortable s/c units and a separate backpackers section (prices vary depending on length of stay). Other attractions are two spas and a big BBQ on Friday nights and the occasional sound of kiwi in the night. Camping $14–16, cabins ②, units ④

Stone Store Lodge 201 Kerikeri Rd ⓣ09/407 6693, ⓦwww.stonestorelodge.co.nz. Stylish B&B in a light and airy contemporary house with views down to Kerikeri Basin. Decor is tastefully minimal, the spacious rooms are all climate-controlled with private deck, and there's an option of dining on pizza cooked in (and eaten around) the outdoor oven. ⑥

The Summer House 424 Kerikeri Rd ⓣ09/407 4294, ⓦwww.thesummerhouse.co.nz. Classy boutique inn done out in French provincial style with three en-suite rooms. Sumptuous breakfasts are served in lovely gardens. Rooms ⑦, s/c suite ⑧

Kerikeri Basin

Kerikeri's past importance is evident at Kerikeri Basin, nearly 2km northeast of the current town. It was here, in 1821, that mission carpenters started work on what is now New Zealand's oldest European-style building, **Kerikeri Mission House** (daily: Nov–April 10am–5pm; May–Oct 10am–4pm; combined entry with Old Stone Store $7.50), a restrained two-storey Georgian colonial affair. The first occupants, missionary John Butler and family, soon moved on, and by 1832 the house was in the hands of lay missionary and blacksmith James Kemp, who extended the design. Since the last of the Kemps moved out in 1974 it has been restored, furnished in mid-nineteenth-century style, and surrounded by colonial-style gardens.

Next door is the only other extant building from the mission station and the country's oldest stone building, the **Old Stone Store**, constructed mostly of local stone, with keystones and quoins of Sydney sandstone. Completed in 1836 as a central provision store for the Church Missionary Society, it successively served as a munitions store for troops garrisoned here to fight Hone Heke, then a kauri trading store and a shop, before being opened to the public in 1975. The ground-floor **store** sells goods almost identical to those on offer almost 180 years ago, most sourced from the original manufacturers. You can still buy the once-prized Hudson Bay trading blankets, plus copper and cast-iron pots, jute sacks, gunpowder tea, old-fashioned sweets, and preserves made from fruit grown in the mission garden next door. The two **upper floors** house a museum stocked with old implements, including a hand-operated flour mill from around 1820, thought to be the oldest piece of machinery in the country.

From opposite the Old Stone Store, a path along the river leads to the site of local chief Hongi Hika's **Kororipo Pa**, passing the place where, in the 1820s, he had a European-style house built. The *pa* commands a hill on a prominent bend in the river, a relatively secure base from which attacks were launched on other tribes using newly acquired firearms. Signs help interpret the dips and humps in the ground, but you'll get a better appreciation of pre-European Maori life from **Rewa's Village**, 1 Landing Rd (daily: Dec & Jan 9am–5pm; late Oct–April 9.30am–4.30pm; May–late Oct 10am–4pm; $5), a reconstruction of a fishing village across the river from the *pa* site. It comes complete with *marae*, weapons and *kumara* stores, as well as an authentic *hangi* site with an adjacent shell midden. The entrance kiosk screens a short video on the history of the area and can supply you with a guide to the "Discoverers Garden" planted with over fifty species of plant Maori used for purposes as varied as eating, tattooing, healing and the lifting of *tapu*.

▲ Old Stone Store, Kerikeri

Opposite is the **Kerikeri Basin Reserve** and the start of a track past the site of Kerikeri's first hydroelectric station (15min each way) and the swimming holes at Fairy Pools (35min each way) to the impressively undercut **Rainbow Falls** (1hr each way). The latter are also accessible off Waipapa Road, 3km north of the Basin.

To explore the waters of Kerikeri Inlet, join the hour-long **steamboat cruise** (Mon–Sat 11am & 2pm; $25; ⓣ0800/944 785, ⓦwww.steamship.co.nz; booking essential) on one of two charming little boats: the replica nineteenth-century *Eliza Hobson* which carries fourteen, or the diminutive 1882 original *Firefly*, which only has space for half a dozen.

The rest of town

Elsewhere, Kerikeri is dominated by orchards and **craft outlets**. The free and widely available *Kerikeri Art & Craft Trail* leaflet advertises the major ones; they're mostly open daily from 10am–5pm, and you could easily spend a day pottering round them all. A few of the most highly regarded ones include The Enz of the Earth, right in town at 127 Kerikeri Rd (ⓣ09/407 8367), which combines Indian and Indonesian **handicrafts** with an exotic garden; The Kauri Workshop, 500 Kerikeri Rd (ⓣ09/407 9196), which stocks anything you could make from **kauri**; and next door, Makana Confections, Kerikeri Road (ⓣ0800/625 262) produce **handmade chocolates** and you can watch the process. Creations by New Zealand's top designers – including Kate Sylvester, Trelise Cooper and Doris De Pont – grace the racks of River NZ Designer Clothing, 86 Kerikeri Rd (Mon–Fri 9am–5.30pm, Sat 9am–2pm).

Further out, Kaleidoscopes, 265 Waipapa Rd (ⓣ09/407 4415, ⓦwww.scopesnz.com) make a fabulous range of devices out of mirrors made on site and a myriad coloured baubles. As well as classic swamp kauri tube **kaleidoscopes** they make wonderful jukebox kaleidoscopes and even a patented projecting kaleidoscope.

If the crafts trail does nothing for you, help may be at hand in the form of the **Steam Sawmill**, Inlet Road, 4km east of town (Mon–Fri 8am–4pm; $7.50; ⓣ09/407 9707), a working steam-driven mill powered by secondhand equipment garnered from all over the country. You can take a look anytime, but it is best to join one of the tours (Mon–Fri 10.30am & 1.30pm) when the steam whistle is blown. The mill is closed from Christmas to the middle of January.

Eating, drinking and entertainment

For its size, Kerikeri has an impressive selection of places to **eat**, particularly cafés. The town also boasts three **wineries**, all of which offer well-priced dining. **Entertainment** in Kerikeri is thinner on the ground, though there's always the lovingly restored, sixty-year-old Cathay Cinema, on Hobson Avenue (ⓣ09/407 4428), which shows mainstream first-run movies and has a good café attached (closed Sun).

Wineries

Ake Ake Vineyard 165 Waimate North Rd ⓣ09/407 8230, ⓦwww.akeakevineyard.co.nz. Newcomer whose cellar door is open Wed–Sun. Lunch Wed–Sun, dinner Fri & Sat plus Thurs & Sun Dec–April. *Ake Ake* also runs various tours ($3 to $9.50) and regular wine and food evenings.

Cottle Hill Winery Cottle Hill Drive, about 4km south of town off SH10 (ⓣ09/407 5203) Considerable range of table wines, as well as port and dessert wines; with a summertime café serving ploughman's lunches and antipasti platters.

Marsden Estate Wiroa Rd ⓣ09/407 9398, ⓦwww.marsdenestate.co.nz. Makes a broad variety of reds and whites sampled through free tastings, and runs a moderately priced restaurant (closed Mon in winter).

Restaurants & cafés

Café Blue Kerikeri Rd, 3km west of town ☎09/407 5150. Excellent licensed café for breakfast and lunch in a pretty garden setting. Dishes include a fine range of quiche, pizza and filo rolls stuffed with imaginative fillings, plus larger meals. Great coffee and cakes served outside or in the airy interior.

Café Zest 73 Kerikeri Rd. Vibrant new café with sweet and savoury muffins and scones and the best coffee in town, plus a huge range of wholesome hot lunches and salads under $15.

Fishbone Café 88 Kerikeri Rd ☎09/407 6065. Great licensed café for breakfast and lunch, perennially popular for its high-quality Kiwi fusion food.

Jerusalem Cobblestone Mall ☎09/407 1001. Small, friendly, licensed Israeli café beloved by Northlanders for its authentic, low-cost and wonderfully aromatic Middle Eastern dishes to eat in or take away. Closed Sun lunch.

Kerikeri Bakehouse Café Deli 334 Kerikeri Rd. Great, and reasonably priced, pastries, sandwiches, superlative vegetarian pies as well as soups and good coffee served in a large airy room or outside.

Around Kerikeri

Some 15km southwest from Kerikeri is **WAIMATE NORTH** and the colonial Regency-style **Te Waimate Mission House**, set in lush gardens (10pm–5pm; Nov–Dec 24 Mon–Wed, Sat & Sun; Dec 26–April daily; May–Oct Sat & Sun or by appointment ☎09/405 9734; $7.50), New Zealand's second-oldest European building. Now virtually in the middle of nowhere, in the 1830s this was the centre of a vigorous **Anglican mission**, the first to be established on an inland site, chosen for its fertile soils and large Maori population. Missionaries were keen to add European agricultural techniques to the literacy and religion they were teaching the Maori, and they made use of the grounds already cultivated by the missionaries' friend and Ngapuhi chief, Hongi Hika. By 1834 locally grown wheat was milled at the river, orchards were flourishing and crops were sprouting – all impressing Charles Darwin, who visited the following year. For two years from 1842 this was the home of Bishop Selwyn and headquarters of the Anglican church in New Zealand but, ultimately, shifting trade patterns made this first European-style farm uneconomic and the mission declined. The house itself was built by converts in 1831–32 and fashioned almost entirely of local kauri. Though slightly modified over the years, it has been restored as accurately as possible to its original design. Guided tours highlight prize possessions. The modest mission **Church of St John the Baptist** nearby is also open daily during daylight hours (free).

Ngawha Springs and the Puketi Forest

The nearest substantial town to Waimate North is **KAIKOHE**, almost equidistant from both coasts. There's little reason to stop, though you might like to soak your bones at **Ngawha Springs** (daily 9am–9.30pm; $5), pronounced "Naf-fa Springs" 7km southeast of Kaikohe, where eight individual pools (all with different mineral contents and at different temperatures) are enclosed by native timber but otherwise untouched by tourist trappings.

The stands of the **Puketi and Omahuta native forests**, 20km north of Kaikohe, jointly comprise one of the largest continuous tracts of kauri forest in the north. The easiest access is to the east of the forest: head north off SH1 at Okaihau, or west off SH10 just north of Kerikeri along Pungaere Road. Both routes bring you to the **Puketi Recreation Area**, where there's a basic DOC $7 campsite and a trampers' hut (from $7 in an 18-bunk main hut or two 3-bunk cabins; see Kerikeri DOC for keys) at the start of the twenty-kilometre **Waipapa River Track** – best done in one short (5hr) and one long (8hr) day, camping midway. This and several other decent tracks are detailed in DOC's free *Puketi and Omahuta Forests* leaflet which, along with camping and hut details, can be obtained from the DOC office in Kerikeri.

North to Doubtless Bay

North of the Bay of Islands everything gets a lot quieter. There are few towns of any consequence along the coast and it is the peace and slow pace that attract visitors to an array of glorious beaches and the lovely Whangaroa Harbour. The first stop north of Kerikeri is tiny **Matauri Bay**, where a hilltop memorial commemorates the Greenpeace flagship, *Rainbow Warrior*, which now lies off the coast. A sealed but windy back road continues north, offering fabulous sea views and passing gorgeous headlands and beaches before delivering you to **Whangaroa Harbour**, one of the most beautiful in Northland, and an excellent place to go sailing or kayaking. Further north is the idyllic surfing and fishing hideaway of **Taupo Bay**.

Continuing north brings you to the huge bite out of the coast called **Doubtless Bay**, which had two celebrated discoverers: Kupe, said to have first set foot on Aotearoa in **Taipa**; and Cook, who sailed past in 1769 and pronounced it "doubtless, a bay". A week later, French explorer Jean François Marie de Surville became the first European to enter the bay. Bounded on the west and north by the sheltering **Karikari Peninsula**, the bay offers safe boating and is popular with Kiwi vacationers. In January you can barely move here and you'll struggle to find accommodation, but the shoulder seasons can be surprisingly quiet, and outside December, January and February room prices drop to more affordable levels. Most of the bay's facilities cluster along the southern shore of the peninsula in a string of beachside settlements – **Coopers Beach**, **Cable Bay** and **Taipa Bay** – running west from picturesque Mangonui.

Matauri Bay

Some 20km north of Kerikeri, a high inland ridge provides a dramatic first glimpse of the long and sandy **MATAURI BAY** as it stretches north to a stand of Norfolk pines and the **Cavalli Islands** just offshore. The northern limit of

▲ Rainbow Warrior Memorial, Matauri Bay

the main bay is defined by Matauri Bay Hill, topped by a distinctive stone and steel **Rainbow Warrior Memorial** which remembers the Greenpeace flagship (see box below), now scuttled off Motutapere Island, one of the Cavalli Islands. Designed by sculptor Chris Booth, the memorial comprises a stone arch (symbolizing a rainbow) and the vessel's salvaged bronze propeller. It's reached by a well-worn path (20min return; 70m ascent) from near the holiday park at the foot of the hill.

Missionary Samuel Marsden first set foot in Aotearoa in 1814 at Matauri Bay, where he mediated between the Ngati Kura people – who still own the bay – and some Bay of Islands Maori, a process commemorated by the quaint wooden **Samuel Marsden Memorial Church** on the road into town, and a small memorial near the beach. The Ngati Kura tell of their ancestral *waka*, *Mataatua*, which lies in waters nearby. It was the resonance of this legendary canoe that partly led the Ngati Kura to offer a final resting place to the wreck of the *Rainbow Warrior*. Paihia-based dive operators (see p.188) run trips out to the wreck, 10 minutes offshore from Matauri Bay. The best visibility is in April; from September to November plankton sometimes obscure the view but it's still pretty good.

French nuclear testing in the Pacific

The French government has always claimed that nuclear testing is completely safe, and for decades persisted in conducting tests on the tiny Pacific atolls of **Mururoa** and **Fangataufa**, a comfortable 15,000km from Paris, but only 4000km northeast of New Zealand.

In 1966 France turned its back on the 1963 Partial Test Ban Treaty, which outlawed atmospheric testing, and relocated Pacific islanders away from their ancestral villages to make way for a barrage of tests over the next eight years. The French authorities claimed that "Not a single particle of radioactive fallout will ever reach an inhabited island" – and yet radiation was routinely detected as far away as Samoa, Fiji and even New Zealand. Increasingly antagonistic public opinion forced the French to conduct their tests underground in deep shafts, where another 200 detonations took place, threatening the geological stability of these fragile coral atolls. Surveys with very limited access to the test sites have since revealed severe fissuring; there is also evidence of radioactive isotopes in the Mururoa lagoon, as well as submarine slides and subsidence.

In 1985, Greenpeace co-ordinated a New Zealand-based protest flotilla, headed by its flagship, the **Rainbow Warrior**, but before the fleet could set sail from Auckland, the French secret service sabotaged the *Rainbow Warrior*, detonating two bombs below the waterline. As rescuers recovered the body of Greenpeace photographer Fernando Pereira, two French secret service agents posing as tourists were arrested. Flatly denying all knowledge at first, the French government was finally forced to admit to what David Lange (then Prime Minister of New Zealand) described as "a sordid act of international state-backed terrorism". The two captured agents were sentenced to ten years in jail, but France used all its international muscle to have them serve their sentences on a French Pacific island; they both served less than two years before being honoured and returning to France.

In 1995, to worldwide opprobrium, France announced a further series of tests. Greenpeace duly dispatched *Rainbow Warrior II*, which was impounded by the French navy on the tenth anniversary of the sinking of the original *Rainbow Warrior*. In early 1996 the French finally agreed to stop nuclear testing in the Pacific, paving the way for improved diplomatic relations between the French and New Zealand, and the following year the two foreign ministers met for the first time since the bombing of the *Rainbow Warrior*.

Accommodation in the bay is limited to the peaceful *Matauri Bay Holiday Park* (Ⓣ09/405 0525, Ⓦwww.matauribay.co.nz; camping from $12; on-site caravans ❷; chalets ❸), which has some lovely beachfront sites and a handy small shop. The only other place for a bite to **eat** is *Matauri Top Shop*, a combined store and good-value café at the top of Matauri Bay Road, just before you descend to the bay.

Whangaroa Harbour

Inland from Matauri Bay on SH10 the small town of **KAEO** heralds the virtually landlocked and sheltered **Whangaroa Harbour**. Time spent around here is the perfect antidote to Bay of Islands' commercialism. The scenery, albeit on a smaller scale, is easily a match for its southern cousin and, despite the limited facilities, you can still get out onto the water for a cruise or to join the big-game fishers. Narrow inlets forge between cliffs and steep hills, most notably the two bald volcanic plugs, **St Paul and St Peter**, which rise behind the harbour's two settlements, **WHANGAROA** and **TOTARA NORTH**.

The harbour wasn't always so quiet though, being among the first areas in New Zealand to be visited by European pioneers, most famously those aboard the *Boyd*, which called here in 1809 to load kauri spars for shipping to Britain. A couple of days after its arrival, all sixty-six crew were killed and the ship burned by local Maori in retribution for the crew's mistreatment of Tara, a high-born Maori sailor who had apparently transgressed the ship's rules. A British whaler avenged the incident by burning the entire Maori village, thereby sparking off a series of skirmishes that spread over the north for five years. Later the vast stands of kauri were hacked away; some were rafted to Auckland, while others were milled at Totara North. Even if you're just passing through, it's worth driving the 4km along the northern shore of the harbour to Totara North, passing a boatyard or two, the last commercial remnants of this historic community.

Activities

The single best thing to do around Whangaroa is to spend a day on the eleven-metre *Snow Cloud* **yacht** (Ⓣ09/405 0523, Ⓦwww.snowcloud.co.nz, Ⓔsnowcloud@xtra.co.nz; 10–11hr; $90, including meals) – trips typically involve sailing out to the rugged uninhabited Cavalli Islands, stopping to let the small group of passengers snorkel, sunbathe and walk; it's great value for money. Alternatively, sail on a similarly priced trip on the fifteen-metre steel cutter, *Sea Eagle* (Ⓣ09/405 1963, Ⓦwww.seaeaglecharters.com).

Summer **kayak** trips (half-day; $65; full-day $85, no credit cards) can be arranged with the knowledgeable Northland Sea Kayaking, on the northeastern flank of the harbour (Ⓣ09/405 0381, Ⓦwww.northlandseakayaking.co.nz); while the *Whangaroa Big Gamefish Club* are the people to see if you want to go out game fishing. One of the most immediately rewarding **walks** is the hike up the volcanic dome of **St Paul** (30min return; 140m ascent) from the top of Old Hospital Road in Whangaroa. The final few metres involve an easy scramble with fixed chains to assist. On the harbour's north side, DOC's Lane Cove Walk (90min–2hr each way) runs from Totara North, past freshwater pools, mangroves and viewpoints to DOC's *Lane Cove Cottage* ($12) on Pekapeka Bay, which sleeps sixteen people, but only opens for a minimum of four. It is accessible on foot and by boat, and has a solar-heated shower, water, toilets and plenty of sandflies. You'll need your own cooking gear and should book well in advance in summer through Kerikeri DOC.

Practicalities

Though a combined InterCity and Northliner **bus** plies SH10 at the head of the harbour, public transport reaches neither the small community of Whangaroa, 6km off SH10 on the southern side of the harbour, nor tiny Totara North, 4km off the highway on the northern side.

There's good accommodation around the harbour much of it clustered along the road to Whangaroa; try *Kahoe Farms Hostel* SH10 1.5km north of the Totara North turn-off (ⓣ09/405 1804, ⓦwww.kahoefarms.co.nz; dorms $25, rooms ❸), a small and extremely hospitable backpackers in a beautifully restored nineteenth-century property tucked into a corner of a working cattle farm, where you can enjoy excellent home-made pizza and pasta dinners and generous breakfasts, plus kayak rental and hiking trails to some superb swimming holes. Other **eating** options include the *Whangaroa Big Gamefish Club* overlooking the yacht harbour, and, across the road, the *Marlin Hotel*, which has surf 'n' turf fare and is a good spot for a beer and a game of pool.

Taupo Bay

A sealed 13km road from SH10 brings you to **TAUPO BAY**, a blissfully undeveloped holiday community with a smattering of beach shacks, and some of the best surfing and rock and beach fishing in Northland. Surfers of all levels, from beginners onwards, can take lessons with Isobar Surf, 43 Mako St (ⓣ09/406 0719, ⓦwww.isobarsurf.co.nz), with lessons starting from $65 for two hours; $180 for an "overnighter", staying at the school's surf lodge; and $690 for a five-day stay, including accommodation. Your only other accommodation option is the friendly *Taupo Bay Holiday Park*, on your right as you arrive into the township (ⓣ09/406 0315, ⓦwww.taupobayholidaypark.co.nz; camping & dorms $14–16; cabins ❷), which rents surf and boogie boards ($15 per hour), kayaks ($30 per hour), and sells bait and a few basic supplies at Taupo Bay's only shop. Easy and informative two-and-a-half-hour guided bushwalks (contact Murray Moses, ⓣ027 218 168; $20) depart from the holiday park.

Mangonui and around

There's an antiquated air to **MANGONUI**, strung along a sheltered half-kilometre-long harbour off Doubtless Bay. A handful of two-storey buildings with wooden verandas have been preserved, some operating as craft shops or cafés, but this is still very much a working village. With a lively fishing wharf and a traditional grocery perched on stilts over the water, it makes the most obvious stopping point on the way north, and has access to some excellent beaches nearby.

Don't miss the reasonably priced selection of handmade **woven flax items** and other locally made crafts at Flax Bush, The Waterfront: the deals on woven baskets (*kete*) are among the best you'll find. **Art** of a different kind is found along the Waterfront in the old courthouse at Exhibit A, which displays quality arts and crafts by artists from around the Far North.

Mangonui means "big shark", recalling the legendary chief Moehuri's *waka* which was supposedly led into the harbour by such a fish. But it was whales and the business of provisioning **whaling** ships that made the town: one story tells of a harbour so packed with ships that folk could leap between the boats to cross from Mangonui to the diminutive settlement of Hihi on the far shore. As whaling diminished, the kauri trade took its place, chiefly around Mill Bay, the cove five minutes' walk to the west of Mangonui.

Dolphin Rendezvous (ⓣ0800/732 432, ⓦwww.dolphinrendezvous.co.nz) is the only operator that can take you **swimming with dolphins** north of the

The Swamp Palace & Bush Fairy Dairy

If you're staying around Doubtless Bay and have your own transport, don't miss an evening at **The Swamp Palace** (℡09/408 7040), a quirky cinema in the Oruru Community Hall, 8km south of **Taipa** in the middle of nowhere. It caters to an eclectic mix of tastes – cult and classic movies, as well as the very latest releases. Call ahead to check programmes and opening hours, or ask at the **Bush Fairy Dairy**, at Peria (℡09/408 5508), signposted a further 4km down Oruru Road. Brimming with local art, craft, clothing and organic produce (plus standard dairy items), this authentic, hippie-style co-op also hosts full moon bazaars each month throughout the summer, complete with poetry readings and acoustic jam sessions around the bonfire along with craft and produce markets.

Bay of Islands, meaning that you're not sharing the water with boatloads of other tourists. Full-day trips cost $145, plus an extra $20 for an optional barbeque lunch (or BYO barbeque ingredients); ask about pick-ups from Paihia.

While ships were repaired and restocked at Mangonui, barrels were mended a couple of kilometres west beside a stream crossing the strand that became known as **COOPERS BEACH**. This glorious and well-shaded sweep of sand is now backed by a string of motels and construction sites for big new homes. The beach is popular in January and at weekends, but at other times you may find you have it pretty much to yourself.

Another couple of kilometres west is the smaller settlement of **CABLE BAY**, with an excellent swimming beach and good surf. The Taipa River separates Cable Bay from the beachside village of **TAIPA**, now the haunt of sunbathers and swimmers, but historically significant as the spot where Kupe, the discoverer of Aotearoa in Maori legend, first set foot on the land. There's a concrete memorial to him near the BP station by the Taipa River.

To get a feel for the layout of the bay, wander up to the views at **Rangikapiti Pa Historic Reserve**, off Rangikapiti Road, between Mangonui and Coopers Beach.

Mangonui also makes a good base for organized trips to **Cape Reinga and Ninety Mile Beach** (see box, p.214).

Practicalities

SH10 bypasses the Mangonui waterfront, which is reached on a two-kilometre loop road plied by the joint Northliner and InterCity **bus** service, which runs once a day in each direction between Paihia and Kaitaia. The volunteer-staffed **visitor centre** opposite the 4-Square grocery (daily: at least 10am–4pm; ℡09/406 2046, Ⓦwww.doubtlessbay.com) can point you to accommodation, both here and along the coast, and advise on bus bookings.

If you want to **dive**, contact Seabed Safaris (℡09/408 5885, Ⓦwww.divingseabedsafaris.com), who offer two-dive trips ($125) and *Rainbow Warrior* dives ($145), both including gear.

Accommodation

There are some nice places to **stay** around Mangonui, but not much budget accommodation and no camping.

Beach Lodge Coopers Beach ℡09/409 0068, Ⓦwww.beachlodge.co.nz. Five breezy yet elegant loft apartments, each with its own deck, full kitchen and Wi-Fi. Tranquillity is enhanced by the fact that it doesn't accept children under 8 years old. 7

Driftwood Lodge SH10, Cable Bay ℡09/406 0418, Ⓦwww.driftwoodlodge.co.nz. Great lodge right beside the beach with views of the Karikari Peninsula from the broad deck where everyone gathers for sundowners and perhaps a BBQ. Accommodation is in fully s/c units and there's free access to dinghies, kayaks and boogie boards. Always popular, so book well ahead. Studios ⑤, apartments ⑥

Mangonui Hotel Waterfront Rd, Mangonui ⓣ09/406 0003, ⓦwww.mangonuihotel.co.nz. Century-old, traditional hotel opposite the harbour opening to an upstairs veranda. Rooms (doubles are en suite) are cheerfully renovated in bright colours. Rooms with harbour views go quickly, so book ahead or arrive early. Dorms $25, single rooms ① double rooms ④

Eating and drinking

Doubtless Bay has the best range of **places to eat** north of Kerikeri, though admittedly it doesn't have much competition. Committed **drinking** mostly happens at the *Mangonui Hotel*, which often has bands at weekends. On Saturday mornings, a gourmet market sets up on the lawns outside *Coopers Café*.

Coopers Café 157 SH10, Coopers Beach ⓣ09/406 0860. Award-winning Maori chef Michael Venner cooked his way around the kitchens of the world, before opening his relaxed fine dining restaurant. Stop in for a Northland-roasted Ariki coffee, Belgian chocolate milkshake and impeccably prepared lunches (mains $12.50–22.50) and dinners (mains $22.50–35.50); you might also catch a wine-and-cheese night or classical quartet performance. Dinner bookings essential; closed Mon.

Fresh & Tasty Waterfront Rd, Mangonui. Rival chippy to neighbouring Mangonui, and much frequented by locals happy to trade location for lower prices, less waiting time and equally good tucker.

The Galley Waterfront Rd, Mangonui ⓣ09/406 1233. Eclectic restaurant in Mangonui's former post office serving a Mediterranean-leaning surf 'n' turf menu.

Mangonui Fish Shop Waterfront Rd, Mangonui. Ownership of this famed fish and chip restaurant, set on stilts over the water, has changed several times over the last few years, but its location remains idyllic. It's descended upon in mid-afternoons during summer by several of the Cape Reinga tour buses for the catch of the day – aim to arrive before or after they've left or you'll be in for a wait. Licensed and BYO.

Waterfront Café Waterfront Rd, Mangonui ⓣ09/406 0850. Respected café and bar opening out to pavement seating just over the street from the harbour. Good coffee, breakfasts, light lunches and a good range of dinner mains including fine pizzas.

The Karikari Peninsula

Doubtless Bay to the east and Rangaunu Harbour to the west are bounded by the crooked arm of the **Karikari Peninsula** which strikes north swathed in unspoiled golden- and white-sand beaches. Outside Christmas to mid-February, they have barely a soul on them. Once something of a backwater, the peninsula has been transformed since the millennium with the opening of **Karikari Estate**, a vast golf resort, vineyard and winery. That aside, facilities remain limited; there's no public transport, and without diving or fishing gear, you'll have to resign yourself to lazing on the beaches and swimming from them – and there can be few better places to do just that.

The initial approach across a low and scrubby isthmus is less than inspiring, though it's worth stopping briefly at **Lake Ohia**, 1km off SH10, which has gradually drained to reveal the stumps of a 40,000-year-old kauri forest thought to have been destroyed by some prehistoric cataclysm. A kilometre on, the **Gum Hole Reserve** has a short trail past holes left by kauri gum diggers (see box, p.226). Eight kilometres later, a side road leads to the peninsula's west coast and the **Puheke Scenic Reserve**, a gorgeous, dune-backed beach that's usually deserted. Another fine white strand spans the nearby hamlet of **RANGIPUTA**.

The peninsula's main road continues past the Rangiputa junction to the community of **TOKERAU BEACH**, a cluster of houses and a couple of shops at the northern end of the grand sweep of Doubtless Bay. There's accommodation nearby at the well-run *Whatuwhiwhi Top 10 Holiday Park*, Whatuwhiwhi Road (Ⓣ09/408 7202, Ⓦwww.whatuwhiwhitop10.co.nz; camping $17 cabins ❷, self-catering cabins ❸, units ❹, and deluxe units ❺) set back from a gorgeous beach; book ahead for summer, when prices jump considerably. Neighbouring A to Z Diving (Ⓣ09/408 7077, Ⓦwww.atozdiving.co.nz), offer **diving** off the Karikari Peninsula (two-tank dive $185), plus trips to the *Rainbow Warrior* wreck ($195), both including gear.

A kilometre north of Tokerau Beach you're into the Karikari Estate where an international-standard golf course surrounds *Carrington* (Ⓣ09/408 7222, Ⓦwww.carrington.co.nz; ❾) a sophisticated resort high on a hill with good sea views, and a fine **restaurant**. A few hundred metres further north a hillside swathed in grape vines is dominated by **Karikari Estate winery** (Ⓣ09/408 7222, Ⓦwww.karikariestate.co.nz) the northernmost in New Zealand, which produced its first vintage in 2003. It is a great spot with extensive views, perfect for leisurely sampling their wares, especially over lunch.

The Karikari Peninsula saves its best until last: **Maitai Bay,** 6km north of *Carrington*, is a matchless double arc of golden sand split by a rocky knoll, encompassed by the *Maitai Bay Campground* ($8), Northland's largest DOC campsite, with cold showers, toilets and drinking water. Much of the site is *tapu* to local Maori, and you are encouraged to respect the sacred areas.

Kaitaia and around

KAITAIA, 40km west of Mangonui, is the Far North's largest commercial centre, situated near the junction of the two main routes north. It makes a convenient base for some of the best trips to Cape Reinga and Ninety Mile Beach (see p.214), far preferable to the longer trips from the Bay of Islands. Kaitaia has suffered from a bad rap in some media, but the town is no more or less dangerous than elsewhere. That said, there's not a great deal to see in this working town and with your own transport, you might want to base yourself at the magnificent beach in **Ahipara** (see p.212), to sand toboggan the giant dunes or to pass through the old gumfields.

A Maori village already flourished here when the first missionary, Joseph Matthews, came looking for a mission site in 1832. The protection of the mission encouraged other European pastoralists to establish themselves here, but by the 1880s they found themselves swamped by the gum diggers who had come to plunder the underground deposits around Lake Ohia and Ahipara. Many early arrivals were young Dalmatians (mostly Croats) fleeing tough conditions in what was then part of the Austro-Hungarian Empire, though the only evidence of this is a Serbo-Croat welcome sign at the entrance to town, and a cultural society that holds a traditional dance each year.

The best place to gain a sense of the area is the Far North Regional Museum, 6 South Rd (daily 10am–4pm; $4), with arresting displays on local life and history. If you're here around the second weekend of March, you can also catch competitors from around the world take part in a series of running events on Ninety Mile Beach, including the Te Houtaewa Challenge (Ⓦwww.newzealand-marathon.co.nz), named after the tale of a great Maori athlete. The races are generally preceded by the combined five-day Kai Maori Food Festival and Te Houtaewa Arts & Crafts Festival, both held in Kaitaia. In the Te Houtaewa Waka Ama Surf Challenge, usually two or three weeks after the marathon, six-man outrigger *waka* race against each other, in 1000-, 3,000- and 5,000-metre sprints, finishing at Ahipara; again, anyone can enter. Locally made arts, crafts and clothing at Finders Gallery (Commerce Street) will fill up some suitcase space.

Practicalities

The daily InterCity–Northliner joint **bus** service pulls up outside Kaitaia's **visitor centre**, South Road (daily 8.30am–5pm; ⓣ09/408 0879, ⓔkaitaiainfo @xtra.co.nz), which sells bus tickets, rents sand toboggans ($10 per day) and has **Internet access**. They also stock DOC leaflets such as *Kaitaia Area Walks* and *Cape Reinga and Te Paki Walks*, but for detailed tramping info, you can also visit the **DOC office** on Matthews Avenue (Mon–Fri 8am–4.30pm, ⓣ09/408 6014).

The airport, 9km north of town near Awanui, is connected by direct **flights** to Auckland with Air New Zealand (ⓣ0800/737 000).

Accommodation and eating

Accommodation can be tight in peak season, but is otherwise plentiful, and prices are generally lower than at the coastal resorts to the east. Also consider places near Ninety Mile Beach, listed under Ahipara (see p.213). Self-caterers can stock up at the Pak 'n Save (West Lane).

Historic Wireless B&B 122 Wireless Rd, 4km north of Kaitaia ⓣ09/408 1929, ⓦwww.kaitaia-bnb.co.nz. Friendly kauri-floored homestay in a large 1912 house originally built as worker accommodation for the nearby wireless station. Shared-bath rooms are comfortable and breakfast is included. ❹

Main Street Lodge 235 Commerce St ⓣ09/408 1275, ⓦwww.mainstreetlodge.co.nz. Welcoming and well-equipped hostel that's always alive with folk headed for the Cape (tours pick up from the hostel); if you're hanging around town, you can also organize bone-carving lessons here. Dorms $26, rooms ❷

Beachcomber 222 Commerce St. Kaitaia's hippest new café/restaurant, with Asian-influenced dishes such as honey soy chicken, and bountiful fresh seafood. Lunch mains $15–16, dinner mains $26–28; closed Sun.

Birdie's 14 Commerce St. Old-school café, open from breakfast until lunch (and dinner in summer), and serving up huge portions of hearty Kiwi food at modest prices (mains $12–18). Closed Sun in winter.

Bridge Cottage 8 Redan Rd ⓣ09/408 2555. Kaitaia's finest dining in a converted house beside a stream. There's a hint of big city style mixed with a laid-back Kaitaia quality. Delicious lunch mains are around $16, with dinner mains under $30.

Kauri Arms Commerce St. The most popular of Kaitaia's workaday pubs, drumming up custom with local bands at weekends.

Ahipara and the gumfields

The southern end of Ninety Mile Beach finishes with a flourish at **AHIPARA**, a secluded scattered village 15km west of Kaitaia that grew up around the Ahipara gumfields. A hundred kilometres of sand recede into sea spray to the north, while to the south the high flatlands of the Ahipara Plateau tumble to the sea in a cascade of golden dunes. Beach and plateau meet at **Shipwreck Bay**, a surf and swimming beach with an underground following with surfers for its long tubes (sometimes 400m or more). The bay is named after the paddle-shaft of the *Favourite*, wrecked in 1870, whose funnel sticks out of the waves at low tide. At low tide you can pick mussels off the volcanic rocks and follow the wave-cut platform around a series of bays for about 5km to the dunes – about an hour's walk – although most do it by quad bike or mountain bike.

At their peak in the early twentieth century, the barren **gumfields**, on a sandy dune plateau to the south of town, supported three hotels and two thousand people. Unlike most gumfields, where experimental probing and digging was the norm, here the soil was methodically excavated, washed and sieved to extract the valuable kauri gum (see box, p.226). None of the dwellings remain on the plateau, and the gumfields are an eerie, desolately beautiful spot.

Practicalities

Ahipara is a broadly more appealing place to stay than Kaitaia, though there is no public transport, supermarket or bank. There is a small store, a takeaway and the decent *Gum Diggers Café*, 22 ReefView Rd, which benefits from sea views and serves a good choice of dishes under $15.

Virtually all the **accommodation** offers self-catering, and the village gets packed out for two weeks at Christmas.

Ahipara Bay Motel 22 Reef View Rd ⓣ0800/906 453, ⓦwww.ahipara.co.nz/baymotel. A choice of pleasant older motel units and six excellent luxury versions with tremendous sea views; and there's a decent on-site restaurant. Units ⑤, luxury ⑥

Beach Abode 11 Korora St ⓣ09/409 4070, ⓦwww.beachabode.co.nz. Three well-appointed beachfront units, each with Wi-Fi, a full kitchen, BBQ, deck and great views to the sea. Kids over 12 years only. Apartments ⑥

Endless Summer Lodge 245 Foreshore Rd ⓣ09/409 4181, ⓦwww.endlesssummer.co.nz. Well-managed hostel in an atmospheric 1880 timber homestead with kauri floors, right across the road from the beach. Relax in four comfortable doubles, two twins or two four-bed dorms; there's also a BBQ, free boogie boards, and surfboard hire; surfing instruction can be arranged. Bookings by phone only. Dorms $24, rooms ②

YHA Ahipara Motor Camp Takahe St ⓣ09/409 4864, ⓦwww.ahiparamotorcamp.co.nz. The best camping option in the Kaitai-Ahipara area, just 300m from the sea, has just joined the YHA network, offering accommodation-wide member discounts. Camping $14, basic cabins & on-site caravans ①, en-suite double rooms & s/c cabins ②

Activities

The best way to get into the dunes and gumfields is on a **quad bike** guided tour with Tua Tua Tours (ⓣ0800/494 288, ⓦwww.ahipara.co.nz/tuatuatours) whose excursions range from ninety minutes (single $100; double $110) to an excellent three-hour safari (single $175; double $185), which includes sandboarding. If you can manage without the local knowledge and riding instruction, head out on your own with quad bikes from the Ahipara Adventure Centre, Takahe Street, 100m past the store (ⓣ09/409 2055, ⓦwww.ahipara.co.nz/adventurecenter) who rent single-rider machines (1hr $60, $40 per hr thereafter; sand toboggan included). They also rent out surfboards, kayaks and mountain bikes (all $25 per half-day), and blo-karts ($30 for first 30min and $25 per 30min thereafter). Alternatively, you can saddle up with Ahipara Horse Treks (ⓣ027 333 8645 or ⓣ027 263 5269). Two-hour rides cost $60.

A short and worthwhile **walk** takes you from the western end of the beach to a **lookout** (500m, 10min return), giving spectacular views all the way to Cape Reinga. The track begins at the end of Foreshore Road. Keener hikers might fancy tackling the same area on a 6hr section of the tide-dependent **Gumfields Walk** (12km loop; free maps and tide times from the Ahipara Adventure Centre and Kaitaia visitor centre), which begins at the bridge at Shipwreck Bay and takes you into an eerie and desolate landscape of wind-sculpted dunes, then back along the beach. Let someone know where you're going, take plenty of water and look out for quad bikes.

Ninety Mile Beach and Cape Reinga

Northland's final gesture is the **Aupori Peninsula**, a narrow, 100km-long finger of consolidated and grassed-over dunes ending in a lumpy knot of 60-million-year-old marine volcanoes. To Maori it's known as Te Hika o te Ika ("The tail of the fish"), recalling the legend of Maui hauling up the North Island ("the fish") from the sea while in his canoe (the South Island).

The most northerly accessible point on the peninsula is **Cape Reinga**, believed by Maori to be the "Place of Leaping", where the spirits of the dead depart. Beginning their journey by sliding down the roots of an 800-year-old pohutukawa into the ocean, they climb out again on Ohaua, the highest of the Three Kings Islands, to bid a final farewell before returning to their ancestors

Getting to the Cape

The best way to experience the phenomenal length and wild beauty of Ninety Mile Beach is to take one of the **bus tours** based in Kaitaia, Ahipara, Mangonui and Paihia in the Bay of Islands. Those from Paihia are the most numerous but are also the longest (11hr), most leaving daily at around 7.30am. They go via Kerikeri, Mangonui and Awanui in one direction and passing Kaitaia and the kauri trees of the Puketi Forest in the other, with pick-ups along the way. Tours starting further north give you less time in the bus and more for exploring. The content varies but in essence the buses do the same trip, a loop up the Aupori Peninsula and back, travelling SH1 in one direction and Ninety Mile Beach in the other, the order being dictated by the tide. For many, the highlight is **sandboarding** on a boogie board or in a toboggan down the huge dunes that flank Te Paki Stream.

Smaller operators use more modest vehicles and take a less rigid approach, letting the group fine-tune the itinerary and not fussing overly if things run past the scheduled return time. Most companies give discounts to carriers of backpacker cards.

Going it alone on Ninety Mile Beach

Rental cars and private vehicles are not insured to drive on Ninety Mile Beach and for good reason. Vehicles frequently get bogged in the sand and abandoned by their occupants. As there are no rescue facilities near enough to get you out before the tide comes in, and mobile phone coverage is almost nil, you could end up with a long walk. Even in your own vehicle, **two-wheel-drives aren't recommended**, regardless of weather conditions, which can change rapidly.

If you are determined to take your own vehicle for a spin on the beach, seek local advice and prepare your car by spraying some form of water repellent on the ignition system – CRC is a common brand. Schedule your trip to coincide with a receding tide, starting two hours after high water and preferably going in the same direction as the bus traffic that day; drive on dry but firm sand, avoiding any soft patches, and slow down to cross streams running over the beach – they often have deceptively steep banks. If you do get stuck in soft sand, lowering the tyre pressure will improve traction. There are several access points along the beach, but the only ones realistically available to ordinary vehicles are the two used by the tour buses: the southern access point at **Waipapakauri Ramp**, 6km north of Awanui, and the more dangerous northern one along **Te Paki Stream**, which involves negotiating the quicksands of a river – start in low gear and don't stop, no matter how tempting it might be to ponder the dunes.

If you're intent on seeing Cape Reinga and not bothered about driving along Ninety Mile Beach, you can **drive to the Cape** via the main road and avoid the beach altogether.

in Hawaiiki. The spirits reach Cape Reinga along **Ninety Mile Beach** (actually around 64 miles long), a wide band of sand running straight along the western side of the peninsula. Most visitors follow the spirits, though they do so in modern buses specifically designed for belting along the hard-packed sand at the edge of the surf – officially part of the state highway system – then negotiating the quicksands of Te Paki Stream to return to the road. The main road runs more or less down the centre of the peninsula, while the western ocean is kept tantalizingly out of sight by the thin pine ribbon of the **Aupori Forest**. The forests, and the **cattle farms** that cover most of the rest of the peninsula, were once the preserve of gum diggers, who worked the area intensively early last century. The last twenty kilometres of the drive to Cape Reinga on the main road are the hardest, along an unsealed and twisty road shared with tour buses.

Tours from Kaitaia and Ahipara

Far North Outback Adventures Ahipara ⓣ09/408 0927, ⓦwww.farnorthtours.co.nz. Exclusive 4WD custom tours (8hr; $120 per person; $550 for personal tours) with a maximum of five people and including morning tea and lunch. They go off the beaten track, taking in the white sands of Great Exhibition Bay to explore flora, fauna and archeological sites.

Harrisons Cape Runner 123 North Rd, Kaitaia ⓣ0800/227 373, ⓦwww.ahipara.co.nz/caperunner. Their bargain basic tour ($45) includes the Cape, beach, pick-up and snacks.

Sand Safaris 221 Commerce St, Kaitaia ⓣ0800/869 090, ⓦwww.sandsafaris.co.nz. Good-value 8hr Cape Reinga tour in a small bus, also visiting the silica sands and the Gumdiggers Park Ancient Buried Kauri Forest. $65 including a picnic lunch.

Tours from Mangonui

Paradise Connexion Tours ⓣ0800/494 392, ⓦwww.paradisenz.co.nz. The standard bus tour (including pick-up from your accommodation) is $69, and there are 4WD customized tours for up to four people ($450 for one or two people; $600 for three, $700 for four).

Tours from Paihia

Awesome Adventures ⓣ09/402 6985, ⓦwww.awesomenz.com. Bus trip aimed at those with an adventurous spirit. $105; $125 including lunch.

Dune-Rider ⓣ09/402 8681, ⓦwww.dunerider.co.nz. Personalized cape trips in a comfortable high-clearance 4WD vehicle, though the route does not differ from the bus route. All the usual stops plus pick-ups in Kaeo, Mangonui, Taipa and Awanui. They will also drop you off along the route and pick you up another day at no extra cost. $105, backpackers $89.10.

Fullers ⓣ09/402 7421, ⓦfboi.co.nz. Major operator running swanky, custom-designed buses on the sight-seeing-orientated Cape Reinga Wanderer, with sand tobogganing, swimming and shellfish digging. Ten percent discount if you also sign up for one of their cruises. $105, $125 with lunch.

Kings ⓣ0800/222 979, ⓦwww.dolphincruises.co.nz. Fullers. Ten percent discount if you also sign up for one of their cruises. $105, plus $15 for picnic lunch.

Northern Exposure Tours ⓣ0800/573 875, ⓦwww.northernexposure.co.nz. The cheapest of the standard cape trips. $95, backpackers $85.

Salt Air ⓣ0800/475 582, ⓦwww.saltair.co.nz. Fly to the Cape, landing at Waitiki, then covering the last section to Cape Reinga by 4WD, and visiting an east-coast beach and a west-coast beach. $375 including morning or afternoon tea.Con vullan

Leave yourself plenty of time and remember not to park on a bend when you stop to take photos.

If you've made it this far north, you'll already be familiar with the paucity of facilities in rural Northland, so the Aupori Peninsula doesn't come as much of a surprise. There's sporadic **accommodation** along the way, ranging from some beautifully sited DOC campsites to motels, lodges and hostels. Most are reasonably priced, reflecting the fact that many visitors pass through without stopping; however, all are very busy immediately after Christmas. There are a few **places to eat**, though nothing stays open after around 8pm. You can refuel at Pukenui; petrol isn't always available in Waitiki.

Awanui

AWANUI, 8km north of Kaitaia on SH1, is a dilapidated rural backwater notable chiefly for being the meeting point of the eastern and western roads north. The name is Maori for "Big River", though all you'll find is a bend in a narrow tidal creek that makes a relaxing setting for the daytime *Big River Café*, corner of SH10 and SH1, serving a good range of light meals like fish tortillas to nachos plus proper espresso.

Almost all buses to Cape Reinga stop 1km north at the **Ancient Kauri Kingdom** (daily 8.30am–6pm; free; Ⓦwww.ancientkauri.co.nz), a defunct dairy factory now operating as a sawmill, cutting and shaping huge peat-preserved kauri logs hauled out of swamps where they have lain for between 30,000 and 50,000 years. You can wander around parts of the factory and watch slabs of wood being fashioned into all manner of things. Predictably, the emphasis is on the shop but be sure to climb up to the mezzanine on the spiral staircase hewn out of the centre of the largest piece of swamp kauri trunk ever unearthed, a monster three and a half metres in diameter.

Some 10km to the north of the Kauri Kingdom and 3km off SH1, the **Gumdiggers Park Ancient Buried Kauri Forest**, Heath Road (daily 9am–5.30pm summer, to 4pm winter; $8), features an easy thirty-minute nature trail through shady manuka forest. Holes have been excavated to show the methods used for gum digging, huts illustrate the living conditions and there's a small gecko house. The main southern entrance to Ninety Mile Beach, the **Waipapakauri Ramp**, is just south of the park's turn-off.

Houhora and Pukenui

Around 30km north of Awanui are the Aupori Peninsula's two largest settlements: scattered **HOUHORA**, and the working fishing village of **PUKENUI**, 2km to the north, where good catches are to be had off the wharf. At Houhora, a three-kilometre side road turns east to **Houhora Heads**.

The area around Houhora and Pukenui has the greatest concentration of places to stay on the Aupori Peninsula; the i-SITE visitor centre in Kaitaia can provide an updated list. Eating places are more limited; the best being the modern *Pukenui Pacific* on SH1 at Pukenui (Ⓣ09/409 8816), a good-value café/bar and takeaway with harbour views (kitchen closes around 8pm); and New Zealand's northernmost pub, the *Houhora Tavern*, 2km to the north.

The Parengarenga Harbour, Te Kao and Waitiki Landing

Beyond Houhora, the road runs out of sight of the sea, though side roads give opportunities to reach the east coast, particularly at **Rarawa Beach**, 10km north of Pukenui, where the pure white silica sand is backed by a shady streamside DOC **campsite** ($7), 4km off SH1. Its paradisiacal appeal is tempered by mosquitoes – bring plenty of insect repellent.

The beach stretches over thirty kilometres north of Rarawa to the straggling **Parengarenga Harbour**, a place largely forgotten by most New Zealanders until 1985, when it was identified as the drop-off point for the limpet mines (delivered by yacht from New Caledonia) that were used to sabotage the *Rainbow Warrior*. Bends in the road occasionally reveal glimpses of the harbour's southern headland. In late February and early March, hundreds of thousands of bar-tailed godwits turn the silica sands black as they gather for their 12,000km journey to Siberia. Insect repellent is also a must here.

This whole area is strongly Maori. The Ngati Kuri people own much of the land and comprise the bulk of the population, particularly in the settlement of **TE KAO**, just south of the harbour on SH1. The only reason to stop here is for the twin-towered Ratana Temple, on the main road – one of the few remaining houses of the Ratana religion, which combines Christian teachings with elements of Maori culture and spiritual belief.

The last place of any consequence before the land sinks into the ocean is **WAITIKI LANDING**, 21km from Cape Reinga. It is home to a shop, occasionally petrol, and the *Waitiki Landing Holiday Complex* (Ⓣ09/409 7508, Ⓔwaitiki.landing@xtra.co.nz; camping $7–18, dorms $20, en-suite cabins ❷; book ahead Dec–Feb), which has received complaints, but has a campsite, timber-lined cabins, smokehouse, and restaurant/bar open until around 8pm. The complex also rents boards for riding the dunes ($10; 4hr) and can arrange tramper transport (see box, p.215).

Alternatively you could join one of the very informative guided **adventure trips** run by Cape Reinga Adventures (Ⓣ09/409 8445, Ⓦwww.capereingaadventures.co.nz), based 2km south of Waitiki Landing beside SH1. They're a low-key outfit and extremely knowledgeable about the local area. All trips are customized, but might include a guided kayaking and fishing trip to the silica sands or a two-day combination of kayaking, fishing, horse trekking, snorkelling, dune surfing and a 4WD tour along Ninety Mile

▲ Cape Reinga Lighthouse

Beach with simple accommodation back at their base; prices vary but are consistently good value.

From Waitiki Landing, a dirt road twists 15km to the gorgeous and usually deserted seven-kilometre sweep of **Spirits Bay** (Kapowairua), where you'll find a DOC **campsite** ($7) with pitches in manuka woods and cold showers. It's also a favourite of large armies of mosquitoes – bring *plenty* of repellent.

The main road continues towards Cape Reinga, and is currently gravel for the last 20km, it should be fully sealed by mid-2010. While construction is underway, the road is prone to closure after heavy rain because of the risk of vehicles becoming bogged in the mud. After 6km along this final stretch, you pass a turn-off to the **Te Paki Stream entrance** to Ninety Mile Beach, where there's a small picnic area and parking, plus a twenty-minute **hike** to huge sand dunes ideal for **sandboarding** or **tobogganing**. Equipment can be rented at several places from Kaitaia northwards, as detailed; and also by calling ahead to Dave 'n' Rose (Ⓣ09/409 8228).

Cape Reinga

The last leg to **Cape Reinga** (Te Rerenga Wairua: the "leaping place of the spirits") runs high through the hills before revealing the Tasman Sea and the huge dunes that foreshadow it. Magnificent seascapes unfold until you reach the Cape Reinga car park. A well-trodden ten-minute path heads from here to the Cape Reinga **lighthouse**, dramatically perched on a headland 165m above Colombia Bank, where the waves of the Tasman Sea meet the swirling currents of the Pacific Ocean in a boiling cauldron of surf. On clear days the **view** from here is stunning: east to the Surville Cliffs of North Cape, west to Cape Maria van Diemen, and north to the rocky **Three Kings Islands**, 57km offshore, which were named by Abel Tasman, who first came upon them on the eve of Epiphany 1643.

The nearest shop and restaurant is back at Waitiki Landing, and the only place to stay is DOC's *Tapotupotu Bay* **campsite**, turn off 3km south of Cape Reinga, from where it's another 3km down an unsealed road ($7; toilets and

Cape Reinga Walks

A couple of worthwhile short **walks** radiate from the Cape Reinga car park: both form part of the much longer Cape Reinga Coastal Walkway. All these walks are described in the DOC leaflet **Cape Reinga and Te Paki Walks**, containing a useful map of the area, available at Kaitaia and elsewhere. Beware of **rip tides** on all the beaches hereabouts and bear in mind the wild and unpredictable nature of the region's weather.

Sandy Bay (3km return; 200m ascent on the way back; 50min–90min). Eastbound walk through scrub and young cabbage trees to a pretty cove. You can continue to the lovely **Tapotupotu Bay** (a further 3km one way; 1–2hr).

Te Werahi Beach (2.5km return; 200m ascent on the way back; 40min–1hr). Westbound walk gradually descending with Cape Maria van Diemen in your sights.

Cape Reinga Coastal Walkway (38km one way; 2–3 days; constantly undulating). This spectacular and increasingly popular coastal hike starts at Kapowairua (Spirits Bay), and heads west to Cape Reinga, continues to Cape Maria van Diemen, swings southeast to the northernmost stretch of Ninety Mile Beach, and then finally past the impressive dunes of Te Paki Stream. You need to be fit and self-sufficient: the only facilities are a couple of DOC campsites, and some ad hoc camping spots with no guaranteed water. Fresh water from streams is limited and you'll need mosquito repellent. You finish a good way from where you start, but fortunately *Waitiki Landing Holiday Complex* offers a $30 drop-off and pick-up combo.

cold showers); beautifully sited where beach meets estuary. It is a popular lunchtime picnic stop for tour buses. To properly enjoy its serenity, insect repellent is essential.

Hokianga Harbour

South of Kaitaia, the narrow, mangrove-flanked fissures of the **Hokianga Harbour** snake deep inland past tiny and almost moribund communities. For a few days' relaxation, the tranquillity and easy pace of this rural backwater are hard to beat. From the southern shores, the harbour's incredible, deep-blue waters beautifully set off the mountainous **sand dunes** of North Head. The dunes are best seen from the rocky promontory of South Head, high above the treacherous Hokianga Bar, or can be reached by boat for sand tobogganing. The high forest ranges immediately to the south make excellent hiking and horse-trekking territory, and the giant kauri of the Waipoua Forest are within easy striking distance.

According to legend, it was from here that the great Polynesian explorer **Kupe** left Aotearoa to go back to his homeland in Hawaiiki during the tenth century, and the harbour thus became known as Hokianganui-a-Kupe, "the place of Kupe's great return". Cook saw the Hokianga Heads from the *Endeavour* in 1770 but didn't realize what lay beyond, and it wasn't until a missionary crossed the hill from the Bay of Islands in 1819 that Europeans became aware of the harbour's existence. Catholics, Anglicans and Wesleyans soon followed, converting the local Ngapuhi, gaining their trust, intermarrying with them and establishing the well-integrated Maori and European communities that exist today. The Hokianga area soon rivalled the Bay of Islands in importance and notched up several firsts: European boat building began here in 1826; the first signal station opened two years later; and the first Catholic Mass was celebrated in the same year.

With the demise of kauri felling and milling (see p.226), Hokianga became an economic backwater, with little industry, high unemployment and limited facilities. Over the last couple of decades, city dwellers, artists and craftspeople have snapped up bargain properties and moved up here in a small and fairly inconspicuous way, settling in **Kohukohu** on the north shore, **Rawene**, a short ferry ride away to the south, and the two larger but still small-time resorts of **Opononi** and **Omapere**, opposite the dunes near the harbour entrance.

You'll need to stock up with cash before exploring the harbour and kauri forests: there are **no banks or ATMs** between Kaitaia and Dargaville, 170km away to the south.

Getting around is limited if you don't have your own wheels. Paihia-based tour operator, Kings (p.188) runs Hokianga excursions that can often work as a viable form of transport; contact them for schedules and options. Likewise, Crossings Hokianga, SH12, Opononi (ⓣ0800/687 836, ⓦwww.crossingshokianga.com) has a range of day-long cruises and tours ($69–119) that can double as handy transport for non-drivers, with various pick-up and drop-off possibilities.

Kohukohu and the northern Hokianga

Heading south from Kaitaia, the hilly SH1 twists its way through the forested Mangamuka Ranges for 40km to reach **Mangamuka Bridge**, the western entrance to the Omahuta Forest (see p.204), from where a narrower and equally tortuous road heads towards the north shore of the Hokianga Harbour. An alternative route from Kaitaia winds 23km south from the Ahipara road to tiny **HEREKINO**.

Both routes converge on **KOHUKOHU**, a waterside cluster of century-old wooden houses on the northernmost arm of Hokianga Harbour. Kohukohu was once the hub of Hokianga's kauri industry, but the subsequent years of decline have only partly been arrested by the recent influx of rat-race refugees. Four kilometres further east, Narrows Landing is the northern terminus of the **Hokianga Vehicle Ferry** (see below).

Practicalities

The beauty of **staying** on the north side of the harbour is that there's almost nothing to do except relax. There's no better place to do just that than *The Tree House*, 2km west of the ferry terminus (09/405 5855, www.treehouse.co.nz; camping $16, dorms $24, double ❷, cottage ❹). Accommodation is scattered among the trees in two spacious dorms, double and twin cabins with sundecks and a well-equipped house bus in a macadamia orchard.

Kohukohu's best **eating** is *The Waterline*, Kohukohu Road (kitchen closes 5pm Sun–Thurs, 8pm Fri & Sat), a licensed café fabulously sited on stilts over the water with panoramic harbour views from the deck. They serve tasty breakfasts, snacks and lunches, as well as pizza and great coffee, and often have live music such as blues sessions. There's also a traditional pub that serves meals, and a general **store** with a modest range of groceries.

For a personalized look at the work of **artisan woodturner** Neville Walker, who works with preserved swamp kauri up to 45,000 years old, and artist Emma Walker, who utilizes New Zealand ferns and other natural materials to decorate this beautiful timber, contact them on 09/401 9873 or through www.kaurigifts.co.nz to arrange a free, informal private tour.

Rawene and around

Delightful **RAWENE** occupies the tip of Herd's Point, a peninsula roughly halfway up the harbour. Though almost isolated by the mudflats at low tide, Rawene's strategic position made it an obvious choice for the location of a timber mill, which contributed material for the town's attractive wooden buildings, some perched on stilts out over the water.

The town's only significant distraction, **Clendon House**, Clendon Esplanade (Nov–April Sat–Mon 10am–4pm; $5), was the last residence of British-born US Consul James Clendon, a pivotal figure in the early life of the colony. The house itself is mostly pit-sawn kauri construction. Downstairs, one room beside the veranda has been retained as the post office it once was. Clendon Esplanade leads to the **Mangrove Walkway**, a pleasant fifteen-minute return boardwalk through the coastal shallows with boards telling of inter-tidal life and the sawmill which once operated here.

Hokianga Vehicle Ferry

Apart from a lengthy drive around the head of the harbour, the only way across the Hokianga is on the **Hokianga Vehicle Ferry** (car & driver $14 one way, $19 return, pedestrians $2 each way). This shuttles from Narrows Landing, 4km east of Kohukohu on the northern shores, to Rawene in the south, a journey of fifteen minutes. Departures (starting around 7.30am) are on the hour southbound (to 8pm) and on the half-hour northbound (to 7.30pm).

The main thoroughfare passes several places to stay, the best being The *Postmaster's Lodgings*, 1 Parnell St (Ⓣ09/405 7676, Ⓦwww.rawene.co.nz; ④), a B&B in a lovely century-old house with harbour views. Dinner is available, or you can BBQ on the sunny deck. The hilltop *Rawene Motor Camp*, Marmon Street, 1.5km from the ferry landing (Ⓣ09/405 7720, Ⓦwww.rawenemotorcamp.co.nz; camping $12, dorms $18, chalet cabins ①; no credit cards), has harbour views, a pool, tent sites and self-catering cabins in bush enclaves.

For **eating**, your first stop should be the daytime, licensed *Boatshed Café*, on Clendon Esplanade, a stone's throw from the ferry, which is built out over the water and offers magazines to read on the sunny deck as you tuck into gourmet pizza slices or home-made muffins, slices and soups and the best espresso for miles around; they also sell high-quality local arts and crafts.

Wairere Boulders

Detouring about 40km northeast of Rawene brings you to the **Wairere Boulders** (daily during daylight hours; Ⓣ09/401 9935, Ⓦwww.wairereboulders.co.nz; $10), a privately run park encompassing huge 2.8 million-year-old basalt rocks with natural fluting making them appear like carved corrugated iron. The main self-guided loop track takes 40 minutes; with several additional loops plus a spur trail leading through the rainforested valley. Approaching from SH12, the first 6km of road is sealed, but the next 8km is down a rough, narrow and twisting loose gravel road. From here, follow the signs right into McDonnell Road for a further 1km. Admission is paid into an honesty box in an information shed where you can pick up a trail map, and is good all day.

Opononi and Omapere

The two small resorts of **OPONONI** and **OMAPERE**, some 20km west of Rawene, comprise little more than a roadside string of houses running seamlessly for 4km along the southern shore of the Hokianga Harbour, with great views across to the massive sand dunes on the north side.

Kiwis of a certain age can tell you about Opononi and the summer of 1955–56 when a wild bottlenose dolphin, dubbed "Opo", started playing with the kids in the shallows and performing tricks with beach balls. At the time dolphin-watching trips were decades away. Christmas holidaymakers jammed the narrow dirt roads; film crews were dispatched; protective laws were drafted; and Auckland musicians wrote and recorded the novelty song *Opo The Crazy Dolphin* in a day. Their tape arrived at the radio station for its first airing just as news came in that Opo had been shot under mysterious circumstances. No one ever took responsibility, but amid the national mourning the song became a hit anyway.

Opononi has dined out on its fifteen minutes of fame ever since, though the only concrete reminders are a statue of Opo in the car park outside the *Opononi Resort Hotel* and her grave next door outside the War Memorial Hall. To get a sense of the frenzied enthusiasm for Opo, head to Omapere where the local museum inside the visitor centre shows a short video in classic 1950s-documentary style.

Practicalities

In Omapere, the Hokianga **i-SITE visitor centre** (daily: Oct–April 8.30am–5pm; May–Sept 9am–5pm; Ⓣ09/405 8869, Ⓦwww.hokianga.co.nz), stocks information on the immediate area and Waipoua Forest (see p.223), and can book **accommodation**, which is in good supply (book well ahead for high summer).

Eating options are improving: in Opononi look out for *Opo Takeaways* (daily 10am–7pm, later in summer), and the *Opononi Hotel*, which offers the district's best-value eating, both bar food and à la carte. In Omapere the small *Harbourside Café* (by the BP garage) dishes up simple, cheap fare, while the *Copthorne Hotel & Resort* serves good food in its elegant yet reasonably priced restaurant, and has a bar serving bistro meals. Both have great views over the lawns and harbour to the sand dunes.

Accommodation

Copthorne Hotel & Resort SH12, Omapere ⓣ0800/267 846, ⓦwww.millenniumhotels.com. The best of the hotels, set opposite the dunes, with a solar-heated pool, bar and licensed restaurant and a range of accommodation including some beautifully appointed waterside rooms. ❻

Globetrekkers Lodge SH12, Omapere ⓣ09/405 8183, ⓔglobetrekkers@hotmail.com. Relaxing and very well-kept hostel with some harbour views. The five- and six-bed dorms and doubles are all spacious and airy, and there's a couple of nice cabins in the grounds. TV is intentionally absent and the evening BBQ usually bring everyone together. Tent sites $10, dorms $20, rooms ❷

McKenzie's Accommodation 4 Pioneers Walk, Omapere ⓣ09/405 8068, ⓔdlmk@xtra.co.nz. Beachside options in either a spacious room rented as a double or a twin, with a separate bathroom and private entrance, or a s/c two-bedroom cottage. B&B ❺, cottage ❺

Opononi Beach Holiday Park SH12, Opononi ⓣ09/405 8791, ⓔharrybarlow@xtra.co.nz. Spacious if basic harbourside campsite. Camping $11–15, cabins ❷, self-catering cabins ❸

Around Opononi and Omapere

Boats ply the harbour to the sand dunes – though the vistas from the south side are so striking that it's enough just to visit the viewpoints. The most notable of these are immediately west of Omapere: **Arai te Uru Reserve**, along Signal Station Road, and the magical **Pakia Hill**, on SH12. Hokianga Express water taxi (ⓣ09/405 8872 or 021/405 872; $20) operate from 10am daily from Oponomi wharf and will drop you off with sandboards and pick you up a couple of hours later.

Tours run by Footprints Waipoua (p.224), through the Kauri forests 22km south, depart from the *Copthorne Hotel*; pick-ups from accommodation elsewhere in Opononi and Omapere are available.

Around 8km southeast of Opononi, **Labyrinth Woodworks**, Waiotemarama Gorge Road, (daily 9am–5pm, beep the horn if no one answers; ⓣ09/405 4581, ⓦwww.nzanity.co.nz), is one of the region's better craft shops, whose wares include carved kauri pieces and excellent woodblock prints. There are also mind-bending puzzles to play with and a maturing hedge maze.

Labyrinth marks the start of the **Waiotemarama Bush Walk** (2km loop), the best and most popular of the short walks in the district, running through a lovely fern-, palm- and kauri-filled valley. A ten-minute walk leads you to a waterfall with a small swimming hole, and after a further ten minutes you reach the first kauri. Another popular outing is along a section of the **Hokianga–Kai Iwi Coastal Track** (8km one way; 3hr), which heads from Hokianga South Head along Kaikai Beach and up the Waimamaku River back to SH12. More ambitious walkers could set two or three days aside for the entire Hokianga–Kai Iwi Coastal Track, a fifty-kilometre coastal trek that continues south from the Hokianga to Maunganui Bluff and on to Kai Iwi Lakes (see p.225). Details are available in DOC's *Waipoua & Trounson Kauri Forests* leaflet and from visitor centres. There are no facilities along the track – take all the drinking water and food you'll need. But sure to camp over the dunes and not the seaward side, to avoid being washed away by rapidly rising tides. There is currently **no bus service** through the Hokianga and Waipoua region, although Magic Bus (p.36) loops past Rawene, Omapere and Tane Mahuta en route from Paihia to Auckland.

The Kauri Forests and the northern Kaipara Harbour

Northland, Auckland and the Coromandel Peninsula were once covered in mixed forest dominated by the mighty kauri (see box, p.226), the world's second-largest tree. By the early twentieth century, rapacious Europeans had nearly felled the lot, the only extensive pockets remaining in the **Waipoua and Trounson kauri forests** south of the Hokianga Harbour. Though small stands of kauri can be found all over Northland, three-quarters of all the surviving mature trees grow in these two small forests, which between them cover barely 100 square kilometres. Walks provide access to the more celebrated examples, which dwarf the surrounding tataire, kohekohe and towai trees.

This area is home to the Te Roroa people who traditionally used the kauri sparingly. Simple tools made felling and working these huge trees a difficult task, and one reserved for major projects such as large war canoes. Once the Europeans arrived with metal tools, bullock trains, wheels and winches, clear felling became easier, and most of the trees had gone by the end of the nineteenth century. The efforts of several campaigning organizations eventually bore fruit in 1952, when much of the remaining forest was designated the Waipoua Sanctuary. It's now illegal to fell a kauri except in specified circumstances, such as culling a diseased or dying tree, or when constructing a new ceremonial canoe.

Driving through miles of farmland it's often hard to imagine the same landscape covered in dense forest. This is true of the lands to the south around the muddy shores of **Kaipara Harbour**, a labyrinth of mangrove-choked inlets, drowned valleys and small beaches that constitutes New Zealand's largest harbour. The harbour once unified this quarter of Northland, with sailboats plying its waters and linking the dairy farming and logging towns on its shores. Kauri was shipped out from the largest northern town, **Dargaville**, though the fragile boats all too often foundered on the unpredictable Kaipara Bar. Many eventually washed up on **Ripiro Beach**, which just pips Ninety Mile Beach to the title of New Zealand's longest, running for 108km.

Waipoua and Trounson kauri forests

South of the Hokianga Harbour, SH12 twists and turns through nearly 20km of mature kauri in the **Waipoua Kauri Forest**. Just after you enter the forest you reach a small car park, from where it's a three-minute walk to New Zealand's mightiest tree, the 2000-year-old **Tane Mahuta**, "Lord of the Forest". A vast wall of bark 6m wide rises nearly 18m to the lowest branches, covered in epiphytes. A kilometre or so further south on SH12, a ten-minute track leads to a clearing where three paths split off to notable trees: the shortest (5min return) runs to the **Four Sisters**, relatively slender kauri all growing close together; a second path (30min return) winds among numerous big trees to **Te Matua Ngahere**, the "Father of the Forest", the second-largest tree in New Zealand. The third path, the **Yakas Track** (3km return; 1hr), leads to Cathedral Grove, a dense conglomeration of trees, the

▲ Tane Mahuta kauri tree, Waipoua Kauri Forest

largest being the **Yakas Kauri**, named after veteran bushman Nicholas Yakas. Footprints Waipoua (Ⓣ09/405 8207, Ⓦwww.footprintswaipoua.co.nz) runs excellent **walks** to the kauri trees from Omapere (p.222). The pick of their trips is the Twilight Encounter ($75) through the forest to the two largest trees. You might see giant kauri snails, eels and *ruru* (native owl), but the emphasis is more on listening to and sensing the forest under the cover of darkness leavened with a strong Maori spiritual component – story, song and music.

Far and away the best **eating** in the area is the vaulted, barn-like *Morrell's Café*, 8km north of Tane Mahuta on SH12 (closed Mon mid-Oct–Easter), where you can enjoy all-day breakfasts under $14, light meals like gourmet burgers, wraps and salads (all under $10) and excellent coffee, or browse for handcrafted jewellery, silk scarves and local contemporary art.

Some 15km south of Tane Mahuta is the nearest formal **accommodation**, *Waipoua Lodge*, SH12 (T09/439 0422, Wwww.waipoualodge.co.nz; 9), with luxurious apartments converted from farm buildings – woolshed, stables, tack rooms and calf pen – in the tranquil grounds of a gracious and beautifully restored kauri villa. It's pricey but thoroughly relaxing, with a lounge, sunroom library and secluded hot tub in the grounds; you can dine on exquisite evening meals using mostly local produce. Immediately south of *Waipoua Lodge*, a side road leads 7km to the **Trounson Kauri Park**, a small but superb stand of kauri where the **Trounson Kauri Walk** (40min loop) weaves though lovely rainforest.

In 1997, Trounson was turned into a "mainland island" (see *Native Wildlife* colour section) in order to foster North Island brown kiwi survival. Numbers are up significantly, and you've a good chance of seeing them – along with weta and glow-worms – on two-hour guided **night walks** (every night, weather permitting, $20). These leave from the *Kauri Coast Top 10 Holiday Park*, 4km southeast of Trounson (T0800/807 200, Wwww.kauricoasttop10.co.nz; camping $20, standard cabins 2, self-contained cabins 4, motel units 4; book ahead Christmas–Feb). There's also a simple but popular DOC **campsite** ($10), right by the kauri forest, which is equipped with kitchen, toilets and hot showers.

A further 9km south of the Trounson turn-off, Aranga Coast Road branches west to **Maunganui Bluff** (460m), the northern limit of Ripiro Beach (see p.227). Budget accommodation is available at the appealingly rural *Kaihu Farm* hostel, SH12, 4km south of Aranga Coast Road (T09/439 4004, Wwww.kaihufarm.co.nz; tent site $15, dorm $21, rooms 2), with three- and five-bed dorms. From here it is a seven-kilometre walk to the Trounson kauris, and you might spot glow-worms in the bush.

Kai Iwi Lakes

The **Kai Iwi Lakes**, 11km west of SH12 and 20km south of Trounson, are a real change, with pine woods running down to fresh, crystal-blue waters fringed by silica-white sand. All three are dune lakes fed by rainwater and with no visible outlet. Though the largest, **Taharoa**, is less than a kilometre across, and **Waikere** and **Kai Iwi** are barely a hundred metres long, they constitute the deepest and some of the largest dune lakes in the country. People flock here in the summer to swim, fish and water-ski, but outside the first weeks in January you can usually find a quiet spot. Shallow and consequently warmer than the sea, they're good for an early-season dip.

There's no public transport to the lakes, but you'll find **accommodation** at the large and well-equipped *Kai Iwi Lakes Campground* (T09/439 8360; camping $10) which comprises the Pine Beach site on the gently shelving shores of Taharoa Lake, with water, toilets and cold showers; and the more intimate Promenade Point site with just long-drop toilets.

Dargaville and around

Sleepy **DARGAVILLE**, 30km south of Kai Iwi Lakes, is primarily a service town for the region's farming community, traditionally dairy-based but

The kauri and its uses

The **kauri** (*agathis australis*) ranks alongside the sequoias of California as one of the largest trees in existence. Unlike the sequoias, which are useless as furniture timber, kauri produce beautiful wood, a fact that hastened their demise and spawned the industries that dominated New Zealand's economy in the latter half of the nineteenth century.

The kauri is a type of pine which now grows only in New Zealand, though it once also grew in Australia and Southeast Asia, where it still has close relations. Identifiable remains of kauri forests are found all over New Zealand, but by the time humans arrived on the scene its range had contracted to Northland, Auckland, the Coromandel Peninsula and northern Waikato. Individual trees can live over 2000 years, reaching 50m in height and 20m in girth, finally toppling over as the rotting core becomes too weak to support its immense weight.

Kauri loggers

Maori have long used mature kauri for dugout canoes, but it was the "rickers" (young trees) that first drew the attention of **European loggers** since they formed perfect spars for sailing ships. The bigger trees soon earned an unmatched reputation for their durable, easy-to-work and blemish-free wood, with its straight, fine grain. Loggers' ingenuity was taxed to the limit by the difficulty of getting such huge logs out of the bush. On easier terrain, bullock wagons with up to twelve teams were lashed together to haul the logs onto primitive roads or tramways. Horse-turned winches were used on steeper ground and, where water could be deployed to transport the timber, dams were constructed from hewn logs. In narrow valleys and gullies all over Northland and the Coromandel, loggers constructed kauri dams up to 20m high and 60m across, with trap doors at the base. Trees along the sides of the valley were felled while the dam was filling, then the dam was opened to flush the floating trunks down the valley to inlets where the logs were rafted up and towed to the mills.

Gum diggers

Once an area had been logged, the **gum diggers** typically moved in. Like most pines, kauri exudes a thick resin to cover any scars inflicted on it, and huge accretions form on the sides of trunks and in globules around the base, further hardening off in time. In pre-European times, Maori chewed the gum, made torches from it to attract fish at night and burned the powdered resin to form a pigment used for *moko* (traditional tattoos). Once Pakeha got in on the act, it was exported as a raw material for furniture varnishes, linoleum, denture moulds and the "gilt" edging on books. When it could no longer be found on the ground, diggers – mostly Dalmatian, but also Maori, Chinese and Malaysian – thrust long poles into the earth and hooked out pieces with bent rods; elsewhere, the ground was dug up and sluiced to recover the gum. Almost all New Zealand gum was exported, but by the early twentieth century synthetic resins had captured the gum market. Kauri gum is still considered one of the finest varnishes for musical instruments, and occasional accidental finds supply such specialist needs.

burgeoning into the country's top *kumara*-growing district. The town was founded as a port in 1872, on the strongly tidal but navigable Northern Wairoa River, by Australian Joseph McMullen Dargaville. Ships came to load kauri logs and transport gum (see box above) extracted by Dalmatian settlers who, by the early part of the twentieth century, formed a sizeable portion of the community.

The Town

The only specific sight is the **Dargaville Museum** (daily 9am–4pm; $10), in the hilltop Harding Park, 2km west of town and marked by two masts rescued from the *Rainbow Warrior* (see box, p.206). It contains extensive displays of artefacts recovered from the shifting dunes, which occasionally reveal old shipwrecks. The only pre-European artefact is the Ngati Whatua *waka*, which lay buried under the sands of the North Head of the Kaipara Harbour from 1809 until 1972, and is a rare example of a canoe hewn entirely with stone tools. A fine collection of kauri gum gives pride of place to an 84kg piece, reputedly the largest ever found.

At the western end of town, at the **Woodturners Kauri Gallery & Working Studio**, 4 Murdoch St/SH12 (ⓣ09/439 4975, ⓦwww.thewoodturnersstudio.co.nz; daily 9am–dark), leading woodturner Rick Taylor demonstrates what can be done with the extraordinarily varied grains and colours of kauri, sells all manner of kauri products, and runs courses for those prepared to dedicate a day or more.

Baylys Beach and Ripiro Beach

West of Dargaville a minor road runs 14km to **Baylys Beach**, a conglomeration of mostly holiday homes on a central section of **Ripiro Beach**, the longest driveable beach in New Zealand. But beware: the sands of Ripiro Beach are renowned for their mobility, with several metres of beach often being shifted by a single tide, and huge areas being reclaimed over the centuries; the anchors or prows of long-lost wrecks periodically reappear through the sand. As elsewhere on the West Coast, tidal rips and holes make swimming dangerous and there are no beach patrols. Beach driving is no less fraught with danger and shouldn't be undertaken without prior local consultation; vehicles frequently get stranded. Nevertheless, it's a fine place for long walks, and spotting seals and penguins in winter. When easterlies are blowing the coastline is adorned with kites, flown out from the shore and drawing fishing lines for anything up to a kilometre. They're left for twenty minutes or so then hauled in, often heavy with fish.

Practicalities

Two **bus** services stop on Kapia Street in Dargaville: Westcoaster services run here to/from Whangarei twice daily; and Main Coachline (ⓣ09/278 8070) runs direct from Dargaville to Auckland six times a week, and from Auckland to Dargaville five times a week. Tickets for both are available from the **i-SITE visitor centre**, 69 Normanby St (mid-Dec–Feb Mon–Fri 8.30am–6pm, Sat &

Baylys Beach and Ripiro Beach Tours

A couple of operators run inexpensive beach tours in specially designed vehicles, and some offer quad biking on the dunes or cruising on the water. Call in advance as minimum numbers apply, and prices vary depending on customized itineraries; outside the peak summer season you may find little happening.

Pete's Safari Tours ⓣ09/439 0515, ⓦwww.petesafari.co.nz. Small personalized tours are taken along Baylys Beach in a Landrover, visiting the Kai Iwi Lakes and the kauri forests, and overnight trips to Pouto Point, surfcasting for trevally and kahwai.

Taylor Made Tours ⓣ09/439 1576. A specially designed six-wheeled truck carrying up to ten passengers operates along a wild and exposed section of Ripiro Beach to the disused Kaipara lighthouse, taking in shipwrecks on the way.

Sun 10am–4pm; March to mid-Dec Mon–Fri 8.30am–5pm, Sat & Sun 10am–4pm; ⓣ09/439 8360, ⓦwww.kauricoast.co.nz), which also has comprehensive accommodation listings for the region and **Internet access**.

Dargaville has a reasonable range of **places to stay**, though you might prefer the sands of Baylys Beach. **Eating** in Dargaville is somewhat limited, though you won't starve.

Accommodation and eating

Baylys Beach Holiday Park 24 Seaview Rd, Baylys Beach ⓣ09/439 6349, ⓦwww.baylysbeach.co.nz. Well-run place, a short walk from the beach. Some of the cabins are en suite and the cottage sleeps seven; there are also quad bikes for rent. Camping $12–13, caravans ❶, cabins ❶, units ❹, cottage ❺

Blah Blah Blah 101 Victoria St, Dargaville. Good licensed café specializing in Dargaville's famed *kumara*, incorporated in starters like *kumara* and mussel chowder ($10.50) followed by delicious mains (all $20–28) such as *kumara*, cashew and blue cheese cannelloni.

Dargaville Holiday Park 10 Onslow St, Dargaville ⓣ0800/114 441, ⓦwww.kauriparks.co.nz. Combined campsite and hostel only 10min walk from town, providing a good range of cabins and units set in secluded park-like grounds. Camping $14, cabins ❶, units ❸

The Funky Fish 34 Seaview Rd, Baylys Beach ⓣ09/439 8883. A groovy modern café and bar where you'll find great fish and chips, a speciality beer-battered dory with chargrilled lemon and salad, plus a range of burgers, baguettes and a varied à la carte evening menu, and a great garden bar. Closed Mon; reserve in advance for dinner in summer and for Sun lunch all year.

Greenhouse Hostel 13 Portland St, Dargaville ⓣ09/439 6342, ⓔgrahamdunnjack@hotmail.com. Somewhat old-fashioned hostel in a former 1920s schoolhouse in the town centre. Friendly and well managed. Dorms $21, cabins ❷

Kauri House Lodge Bowen St, Dargaville ⓣ09/439 8082, ⓔkaurihouse@xtra.co.nz. The town's grandest rooms in an engagingly low-key yet vast kauri villa with big en-suite rooms, a billiard room, library and swimming pool. ❼

Northern Wairoa Hotel Corner of of Victoria St and Hokianga Rd, Dargaville ⓣ09/439 8923. Simple, old-fashioned but well-kept pub rooms (some en suite) in a 1922 hotel, with bargain pub meals. ❸

Matakohe and the Kauri Museum

From Dargaville, SH12 runs 45km south to Matakohe, passing through countryside that is mostly flat except for the knobby **Tokatoka Peak**, 17km away. Panoramic views unfold from the 180-metre summit of this extinct volcanic plug, reached in ten breathless minutes from a trailhead 1km off SH12 near the *Tokatoka* pub.

If there's one museum you must see in the north it's the **Kauri Museum**, Church Road (daily: Nov–April 8.30am–5.30pm; May–Oct 9am–5pm; $12; ⓦwww.kauri-museum.com), on the outskirts of the village of **MATAKOHE**, 45km south of Dargaville. One of the best museums in the country, and deserving at least a couple of hours, it explains the way the kauri's timber and its valuable gum shaped the lives of pioneers in Northland. The displays focus on the makeshift settlements around logging camps, the gumfields, and the lives of merchants who were among the few who could afford to buy the fine kauri furniture or beautifully carved gum on show.

Practicalities

If you're travelling by public transport, visiting the museum will require **staying** overnight. Try *Matakohe House* (ⓣ09/431 7091, ⓔmathouse@xtra.co.nz; ❺), a big, inviting B&B right by the museum with simply furnished en-suite rooms opening out onto a veranda and a **café** with **Internet access** serving food throughout the day. Campers should head to the *Matakohe Top 10 Holiday Park* ⓣ0800/431 6431, ⓔmatakoheholidaypark@xtra.co.nz; camping $14, caravans ❶, cabins ❷, s/c units ❹, motels ❺), a small, hillside campsite 500m beyond the museum on a site offering great harbour views.

Travel details

Buses

The two major bus operators which serve Northland–InterCity (ⓦ www.intercitycoach.co.nz) and Northliner (ⓦ www.northliner.co.nz) – are owned by the same company. They still produce separate timetables, but in the far north one bus serves both companies. There is really only one route, from Auckland (SkyCity terminal) up the eastern side of the peninsula calling at Whangarei, Paihia and Kerikeri in the Bay of Islands, then finishing at Kaitaia; a jump-on-jump-off pass costs $50 one way.

Hokianga Harbour can be reached with Magic Bus (p.36), which does an anti clockwise loop around the North Island. There is also one short-range operator from Auckland: Main Coachlines (ⓣ 09/278 8070), who also serve Warkworth and continue on to Dargaville.

Auckland to: Dargaville (5 per week, not Wed or Sat; 3hr); Kaitaia (1 daily; 7hr); Kerikeri (3–5 daily; 5hr); Mangonui (1 daily; 6hr 30min); Orewa (5–7 daily; 30min); Paihia (4–6 daily; 4hr 20min); Waipu (4–6 daily; 2hr 30min); Warkworth (6–8 daily; 1hr); Whangarei (5–8; 3hr).

Dargaville to: Auckland (6 per week, not Wed or Sat; 3hr); Whangarei (2 Mon–Fri; 1hr).

Kaitaia to: Auckland (1 daily; 7hr).

Kerikeri to: Auckland (3–5 daily; 5hr); Paihia (3–5 daily; 20min).

Mangonui to: Auckland (1 daily; 6hr 30min).

Paihia to: Auckland (4–6 daily; 4hr 20min); Kaitaia (1 daily; 2hr); Kerikeri (3–5 daily; 20min); Mangonui (1 daily; 1hr 20min); Whangarei (4–6 daily; 1hr 15min).

Waipu to: Auckland (4–6 daily; 2hr 30min); Whangarei (4–6 daily; 30min).

Warkworth to: Auckland (6–8 daily; 1hr).

Whangarei to: Auckland (5–8 daily; 3hr); Dargaville (2 Mon–Fri; 1hr); Paihia (4–6 daily; 1hr 15min); Warkworth (4–6 daily; 1hr 45min).

Ferries

Kohukohu to: Rawene (hourly; 20min).

Opua to: Okiato (every 10–20min; 15min).

Paihia to: Russell by passenger ferry (every 20min; 15min).

Rawene to: Kohukohu (hourly; 20min).

Flights

Northland has a limited number of flights and since distances are relatively short you're unlikely to need them, except for flights from Whangarei to Great Barrier Island.

Bay of Islands (Paihia/Kerikeri) to: Auckland (5 daily; 40min); Wellington (1 weekdays; 1hr 30min).

Kaitaia to: Auckland (1–2 daily; 50min).

Whangarei to: Auckland (7–10 daily; 35min); Great Barrier Island (2 weekly; 30min); Wellington (1 Mon–Fri; 1hr 30min).

3

Western North Island

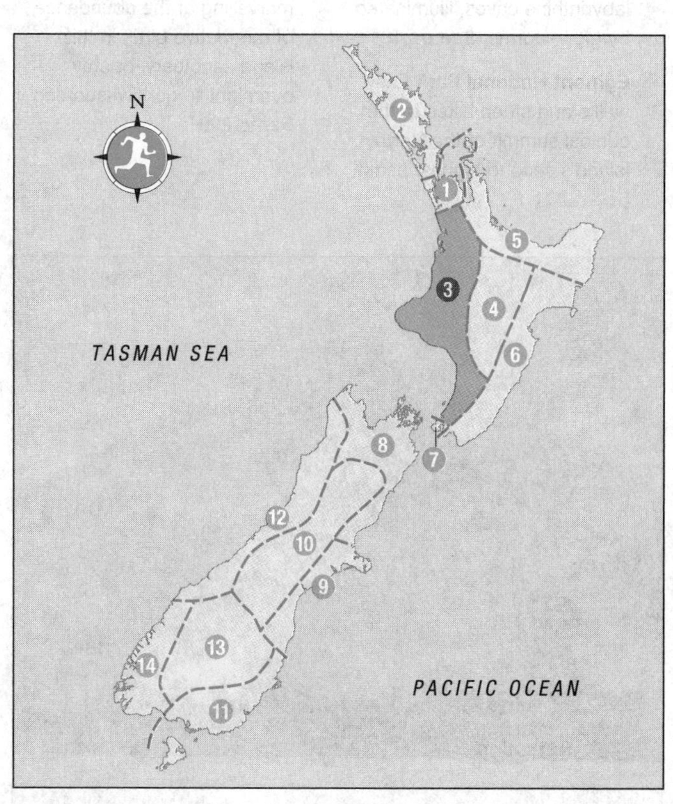

CHAPTER 3 Highlights

* **Raglan** Sociable harbourside town within easy reach of some of New Zealand's finest surf. See p.243
* **Waitomo** Abseil, squeeze or blackwater raft into labyrinthine caves, illuminated by glow-worms. See p.248
* **Egmont National Park** Easy walks and steep hikes to the conical summit of the North Island's second highest peak. See p.264
* **Whanganui River** Take a three-day canoe trip through the green canyons of New Zealand's longest navigable river. See p.271
* **Kapiti Island** Spend the day marvelling at the abundance of rare native birds in this island sanctuary, or stay overnight to go kiwi spotting. See p.290

▲ Mount Egmont (Taranaki)

3

Western North Island

Much of the **Western North Island** is ignored by visitors, who make a beeline for the wonders of Waitomo Caves and the graceful Mount Taranaki. In fact, there's much of interest in the area, which is best explored at a leisurely pace. Much of the region's appeal is tied to its extraordinary **history** of pre-European settlement and post-European conflict. The region is deeply rooted in Maori legend and history, for it was on the west coast, at **Kawhia**, that the Tainui people first landed in New Zealand; the *Tainui* canoe in which they arrived is buried there, and the waterside tree it was moored to lives on. Kawhia was also the birthplace of **Te Rauparaha**, the great Maori chief who led his people from here down the coast to Kapiti Island and on to the South Island, to escape the better-armed tribes of the Waikato.

Approaching the region from the north, you arrive in the **Waikato**, important farming country centred on the workaday provincial capital, **Hamilton**. There are few attractions here amid fields of cows and sheep, so head to the coast and **Raglan**, a laid-back town with world-class surf and a great selection of places to stay and eat.

South of the Waikato is the **King Country**, which took its name from the King Movement (see p.247), and was the last significant area in New Zealand to succumb to European colonization. Today it contains a number of stalwart communities coexisting with some extraordinary natural features – most famously the creamy limestone of **Waitomo Caves**, where unusual rock formations surmount a netherworld of glow-worm-filled caverns. Further down the coast, the giant thumbprint peninsula of **Taranaki** is dominated by the symmetrical cone of **Mount Taranaki**, within the **Egmont National Park**. At its foot, **New Plymouth** warrants a visit for its excellent contemporary art gallery and access to a multitude of **surf beaches**.

Inland from here, the farming town of **Taumarunui** isn't much in itself, but it is one of the main jumping-off points for spectacular multi-day canoe trips along the **Whanganui River**, through the heart of the verdant **Whanganui National Park**. The river runs down to the coastal city of **Wanganui**, a small, ordered place whose river-port past can be relived on a restored paddle steamer. Just 60km to the southeast, the university city of **Palmerston North** is at the centre of the rich farming region of **Manawatu**, and has some interesting Art Deco and modern architecture and a fine museum. A cluster of communities line the highway to the south, the former flax-weaving town of **Foxton** providing most interest until you reach the **Kapiti Coast**, where **Paraparaumu** is the launch point for boat trips to the bird sanctuary on **Kapiti Island**.

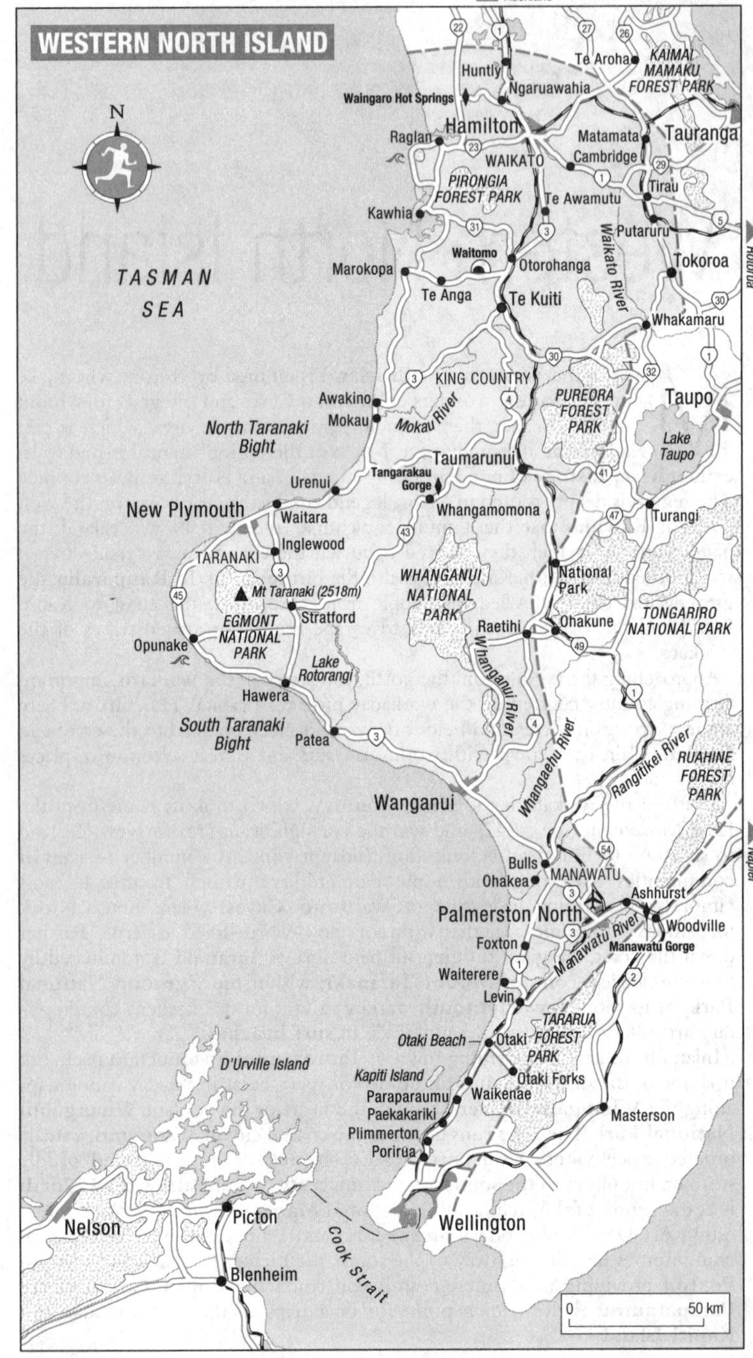
WESTERN NORTH ISLAND
N
Auckland
Rotorua
Napier
TASMAN SEA
Huntly
Ngaruawahia
Te Aroha
KAIMAI MAMAKU FOREST PARK
Waingaro Hot Springs
Hamilton
Raglan
Matamata
Tauranga
WAIKATO
Cambridge
PIRONGIA FOREST PARK
Tirau
Te Awamutu
Kawhia
Putaruru
Waikato River
Waitomo
Otorohanga
Marokopa
Tokoroa
Te Anga
Te Kuiti
Whakamaru
KING COUNTRY
PUREORA FOREST PARK
Taupo
Awakino
Mokau
Mokau River
North Taranaki Bight
Lake Taupo
Taumarunui
Urenui
Tangarakau Gorge
New Plymouth
Waitara
Whangamomona
Turangi
Inglewood
TARANAKI
WHANGANUI NATIONAL PARK
National Park
Mt Taranaki (2518m)
Stratford
EGMONT NATIONAL PARK
Raetihi
Ohakune
TONGARIRO NATIONAL PARK
Opunake
Whanganui River
Lake Rotorangi
Hawera
South Taranaki Bight
Patea
Whangaehu River
Rangitikei River
RUAHINE FOREST PARK
Wanganui
Bulls
Ohakea
MANAWATU
Ashhurst
Palmerston North
Woodville
Foxton
Manawatu River
Manawatu Gorge
Waiterere
Levin
TARARUA FOREST PARK
Otaki Beach
Otaki
D'Urville Island
Kapiti Island
Otaki Forks
Paraparaumu
Waikenae
Paekakariki
Masterson
Plimmerton
Porirua
Picton
Nelson
Wellington
Cook Strait
Blenheim
0
50 km
22
1
27
26
23
29
1
5
31
3
30
32
1
3
4
41
47
43
3
45
49
1
4
3
54
3
3
1
2

Western North Island transport

Most **bus** services are run by InterCity/Newmans, though there are a number of fairly short runs operated by competing companies, including Dalroy Express (ⓣ06/759 0197, ⓦwww.dalroytours.co.nz; Auckland–Hamilton–Otorohanga–Te Kuiti–New Plymouth–Hawera), Go Kiwi (ⓣ0800/446 549, ⓦwww.go-kiwi.co.nz; Hamilton–Auckland), Guthreys Express (ⓣ0800/732 528, ⓦwww.guthreys.co.nz; Auckland–Hamilton–Rotorua) and Waitomo Wanderer (ⓣ0508/926 337, ⓦwww.waitomotours.co.nz; Rotorua–Otorohanga–Waitomo Caves).

Transport through the Western North Island is piecemeal. The **rail line** runs partly through the region, with a single daytime service in both directions between Auckland and Wellington. There are also frequent commuter rail services from Wellington as far as Paraparaumu.

South from Auckland to Hamilton

Auckland's southern motorway turns to ordinary highway around **Huntly**, on the shores of the Waikato River. Having gazed across the river at the twin 150-metre-high chimneys of New Zealand's largest coal-fired power station, you may wish to pay a brief visit to the small but well-presented **Waikato Coalfields Museum**, 26 Harlock Place (daily 10am–4pm; $5), focusing on early life in the Waikato coalfield.

The most culturally significant spot in these parts is **NGARUAWAHIA**, 14km further south on SH1, a farming centre at the junction of the Waikato and Waipa rivers. Both rivers were important Maori canoe routes and the area has long held great significance for Maori: it is here that the **King Movement** (see p.247) has its roots. The town is home to the Maori king and was the scene of the signing of the Raupatu Land Settlement (1995), whereby the government agreed to compensate Tainui for land confiscated in the 1860s.

The Maori heritage is most evident on **Regatta Day** (the closest Saturday to March 17) when, watched by the Maori king, a parade of great war canoes takes place along the two rivers, and hurdle races and the like are run at the **Turangawaewae Marae** (open only on Regatta Day) on River Road, off SH1 just north of the river bridge. The rest of the year is significantly less satisfying for tourists as you can only view the *marae* through the perimeter fence, made of the dead trunks of tree ferns interspersed with robustly sculpted red posts and a couple of finely carved entranceways. From these you can glimpse the strikingly carved and decorated **Mahinarangi House**, housing the Maori throne; **Turongo House**, the official residence of the monarch; and the Kimi-ora Cultural Complex, with its conspicuous octagonal roof. On the opposite side of the river and road, on Eyre Street, is **Turangawaewae House**, also only viewable from the fence. Built in 1920 as the intended home of the Maori parliament it is an ordinary Edwardian-style stucco building, except for red-, black- and white-painted doors, carved barge boards and *pou* (guardian post).

Twenty-three kilometres west of Ngaruawahia, on Waingaro Road at the junction with SH22, is the **Waingaro Hot Springs** complex (daily 9am–10pm; $8). Though run-down, it still gets busy in the summer.

Hamilton

Most visitors pass straight through **HAMILTON**, 127km south of Auckland, but it's a pretty enough place, well sited on the banks of the languid green Waikato River and surrounded by parks. It's worth devoting a couple of hours to the **Museum of Art and History** and the tranquil **Hamilton Gardens**, and taking a **paddle-steamer cruise** on the river. And as befits New Zealand's fourth-largest city, there's a decent-sized student population, and lively term-time nightlife. In mid-June the town hosts the annual four-day **Fieldays festival** (ⓦwww.fieldays.co.nz), the largest agricultural field day in the southern hemisphere, at Mystery Creek Events Centre just outside the city.

Archeological evidence indicates that the **Tainui** settlement of Kirikirioa had existed on the current site of Hamilton for at least two hundred years before the Europeans arrived in the 1830s. The newcomers named their settlement after **John Fane Charles Hamilton**, an officer of the Royal Navy who died, bravely or foolishly (depending whose interpretation you believe), at the Battle of Gate Pa, near Tauranga, a few months earlier; a fictionalized account of the events leading up to his death appears in Maurice Shadbolt's excellent novel *The House of Strife*. The river remained the only supply route for the city until the railway came in 1878, effectively opening up the country to more European immigration, farming and commercial expansion.

Arrival, information and city transport

Super Shuttle (ⓣ0800/727 747), connects Hamilton's airport to the city for $20. The **train station** is on Fraser Street (ⓣ07/846 8353) in the suburb of Frankton, a twenty-minute walk west of the centre, or a #8 bus ride from the **Transport Centre**, on the corner of Anglesea and Bryce streets, which is the hub for local and long-distance **buses**. Bus and train tickets are sold at the **i-SITE visitor centre** (Mon–Thurs 7am–6pm, Fri 7am–7pm, Sat 9am–5pm, Sun 9am–7pm; ⓣ07/839 3580, ⓦwww.waikatonz.com), where there are **left luggage** lockers and a **taxi** rank. The **DOC office** is three minutes' walk north at Level 5, 73 Rostrevor St (Mon–Fri 8.30am–4.30pm; ⓣ07/858 1000).

Most of Hamilton's attractions are within walking distance of the centre; for those further afield (including Cambridge, Te Awamutu, Raglan and Paeroa), pick up the free Busit timetable or call the information line on ⓣ0800/800 401; one-way fares are $1.80, and there's a $4.60 all-day pass. Regional **bus** companies (see p.235) run scheduled services to neighbouring cities.

Accommodation

Hamilton specializes in business accommodation for farm company reps in **motels**, mostly lining Ulster Street. **B&Bs** are thin on the ground and there are limited **hostels**, so it may be worth basing yourself in Raglan (see p.243).

Bavaria Motel 203–207 Ulster St ⓣ0800/839 2520, ⓦwww.bavariamotel.co.nz. Large, comfortable units within 8min walk of the city. Units have DVD players, and access to a decent library of discs. ③

City Centre B&B 3 Anglesea St ⓣ07/838 1671, ⓦwww.citycentrebb.tk. Just one en-suite room with kitchenette and doors opening out to a garden and pool. Great value, free Internet access and an easy walk to town. ③

Eagles Nest 937 Victoria St ⓣ07/838 2704, ⓔeagles.nest.back@xtra.co.nz. Modern conversion of city-centre building to house six- and eight-bed dorms, plus rooms. There's a deck with BBQ overlooking the street. Dorms $24, rooms ②

Hamilton City Holiday Park Ruakura Rd ⓣ07/855 8255, ⓦwww.hamiltoncityholidaypark.co.nz. Smallish, well-tended campsite 1km east of the centre with camping ($14), basic and more

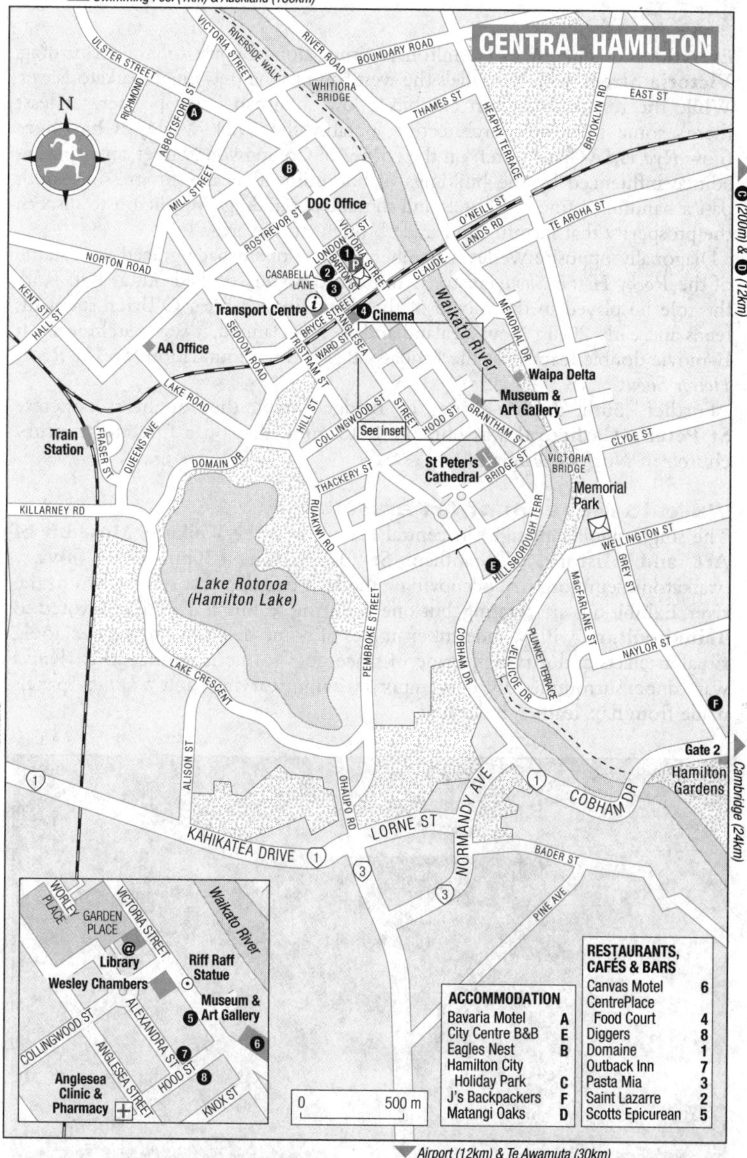

luxurious cabins, and slightly pricier s/c units. Cabins ②, units ②

J's Backpackers 8 Grey St ⓣ07/856 8934, ⓦwww.jsbackpackers.co.nz. Relaxed, low-key hostel 2km southeast of the centre, on the #10 bus route. Dorms $25, ②

Matangi Oaks 634 Marychurch Rd/SH1B, midway between Hamilton and Cambridge ⓣ07/829 5765, ⓦwww.matangioaks.co.nz. Upmarket B&B in an elegant house with extensive grounds, 12km from central Hamilton. Spacious rooms (one en suite, two sharing a bathroom). ⑥

The City

Everything of interest in Hamilton is either along or just off the main drag, **Victoria Street**, which parallels the west bank of the tree-lined Waikato River. While the rest of Hamilton exhibits a low, suburban cityscape, here at least there's some interesting architecture, notably the 1924 **Wesley Chambers** (now *Rydges Le Grand* hotel) on the corner of Collingwood Street, an imposing edifice influenced by the buildings of boomtime Chicago. Progressing south past a handful of fine old hotels and municipal buildings, you begin to discern the prosperity that farming and trade brought to the area.

Diagonally opposite Wesley Chambers a small open space graced by a statue of the *Rocky Horror Show* creator, **Richard O'Brien**, decked out as Riff Raff, the role he played in the movie of the show. English-born O'Brien spent his teens and early 20s in New Zealand and, so it is claimed, it was watching sci-fi B-movie double features at the Embassy that laid the foundation for *The Rocky Horror Show*.

Further south, at the corner of Bridge Street, the roughcast concrete **St Peter's Cathedral** was built in 1915, modelled on a fifteenth-century church in Norfolk, England.

Waikato Museum of Art and History

The single significant sight in central Hamilton is the **Waikato Museum of Art and History**, 1 Grantham St (daily 10am–4.30pm; free; Ⓦwww.waikatomuseum.org.nz), occupying a modern building that steps down to the river. Exhibitions are rotating, but one enduring feature is a section devoted to **Tainui culture**, with wonderful examples of domestic items, woven flax, tools, ritual artefacts and carvings. Pride of place goes to the magnificent *Te Winika* war canoe, surrounded by contemporary Tainui carvings and *tukutuku* panels made from flax, leather and wood.

▲ Waikato Museum of Art and History

Parks and gardens

Across the river in **Memorial Park** is the old **paddle steamer** *Waipa Delta* (☎0800/472 335, Ⓦwww.waipadelta.co.nz), still cruising daily along the Waikato River for sedate lunches (12.30pm), coffees (3pm) or dinners (7pm). Embark at the Memorial Park jetty and be prepared to part with $45, $20 or $59 respectively, more at weekends.

From Memorial Park, a riverside path heads 2km south to the huge, unfenced **Hamilton Gardens**, Cobham Drive/SH1 (free; Ⓦwww.hamiltongardens.co.nz; bus #10 from the Transport Centre), with extensive displays of roses, tropical plants, rhododendrons, magnolias and cacti. Pick up a free map from the gardens' visitor centre (daily 9am–5pm; café attached), then duck next door to the inner sanctum of the **Paradise Gardens Collection** (daily 7.30am–dusk; free), six beautiful enclosures each planted in a different style. Also watch or listen out for tui, a native New Zealand bird with a distinct call, recently returned thanks to a wildlife programme to attract native birds back to the city.

Eating, drinking and nightlife

The nucleus of Hamilton's food and drink scene lies on Hood Street and around the corner, along the southern end ofVictoria Street, where places start the day as **cafés** and progressively become **restaurant/bars** as the day wears on. Casabella Lane, between and parallel to London and Bryce streets, also has tempting cafés along a potted-plant alley. For information on happenings around town, check the *Waikato Times*; comprehensive entertainment **listings** appear on Friday and Saturday.

Canvas 1 Grantham St ☎07/839 2535. Stylish restaurant in the museum complex, popular for its considered menu of beautifully prepared modern Kiwi dishes. Lunches $10–20; dinners around $30. Closed Sat lunch & Sun.

CentrePlace Food Court Ward St. Mall-based, cheap Chinese, kebabs, Indian, sushi, etc.

Diggers 17 Hood St. Down-to-earth drinkers' den, with a long kauri bar, liveliest at weekends, with a great atmosphere and regular gigs on Sun.

Domaine 575 Victoria St ☎07/839 2100. Vibrant modern restaurant with streetside seating and booths at the back, that's good for café dining during the day and more formal evening meals. Closed Sun.

Outback Inn The Marketplace, off Hood St. Big boisterous student drinking hole, with pool tables and a selection of beers and snacks. Dancing Tues–Sat; DJ Wed–Sat; occasional live bands.

Pasta Mia Casabella Lane. Simple bistro serving a range of freshly made pasta dishes (for around $17), with tempting daily specials.

Saint Lazarre Casabella Lane. French-run café with the best Kiwi deli food in town, as well as French-style pastries.

Scotts Epicurean 181 Victoria St. Bustling daytime café/restaurant, good for coffee, snacks, and excellent cakes, plus a modern take on pea, pie and pud ($16).

Listings

Automobile Association 295 Barton St ☎07/839 1397.

Bookshops Dimensions Women's Bookshop, 67 Brookfield St; Browsers, 221 Victoria St; Crows Nest Books, Arcadia Building, Worley Place. Both buy and sell secondhand books.

Cinema Village Skycity, in the CentrePlace Mall on Ward St (☎07/834 1222), for mainstream releases.

Library The Central Library, Garden Place, off Victoria St (Mon–Fri 9am–8.30pm, Sat 9am–4pm, Sun noon–3.30pm); Internet access.

Medical treatment Anglesea Clinic and Pharmacy, corner of Anglesea & Thackeray sts (daily 7.30am–11pm; ☎07/858 0800).

Post office The main post office is in Bryce St.

Taxis Hamilton Taxis ☎0800/477 477.

Travel agents Air New Zealand Travel Centre, 25 Ward St ☎07/839 9835; Flight Centre, CentrePlace, Ward St ☎07/838 0888.

Southeast of Hamilton

Hamilton won't detain you long, but there's enough to soak up a couple of days' exploration in the immediate vicinity. The pick of the local towns is Raglan (see p.243), but Kawhia (see p.245) is worth a squiz for its cultural significance and remoteness, while southeast of Hamilton on SH1, there's a genteel English charm to **Cambridge** and further out, **Tirau** justifies a coffee stop. It also acts as a staging point for **Matamata**, where **Hobbiton tours** are an essential stop for *Lord of the Rings* nuts. If you're making for Taupo (see p.321), continue along SH1 through **Putaruru** and **Tokoroa**, neither of which warrants braking.

Cambridge

An undisturbed air – bordering on comatose – envelops **CAMBRIDGE**, 24km southeast of Hamilton. Founded as a militia settlement at the navigable limit of the Waikato River in 1864, Cambridge is today marooned in an agricultural belt dotted with stud farms. Attractive in a bucolic, Disneyesque way, it is of interest only to those fascinated by matters equine. A taste of the **horsey tradition** can be gleaned by following the town's **Equine Stars Walk of Fame**, with mosaics of Cambridge-bred winners embedded in the pavements. At Cambridge Thoroughbred Lodge, 6km southeast on SH1 (daily 10am–3pm; $8; ⓣ07/827 8118, ⓦwww.cambridgethoroughbredlodge.co.nz), you can watch contemporary **racehorses** getting a workout but it lacks conviction when there's no money riding on it.

Practicalities

Buses on the Auckland–Wellington run stop beside the town hall on Lake Street, while Cambridge Travel Lines (ⓣ07/827 7363) run a local service from Hamilton (Mon–Fri only) that stops by St Andrew's church. Both stops are two minutes' walk from the **visitor centre**, at the corner of Queen and Victoria streets (Mon–Fri 9am–5pm, Sat & Sun 10am–4pm; ⓣ07/823 3456, ⓦwww.cambridgeinfo.co.nz), a booking agent for buses. There's low-cost **Internet access** at the **library**, 23 Wilson St (Mon–Sat 10am–4pm, Sun 10am–2pm).

There's little reason to stay but *Park House*, 70 Queen St (ⓣ07/827 6368, ⓦwww.parkhouse.co.nz; ❻), offers temptation in an elegantly furnished 1920s house, the rooms in a separate wing. Cheaper B&B is available in *Pamade*, 229 Shakespeare St (ⓣ07/827 4916, ⓔpamades@hotmail.com; ❸), while 2km south of central Cambridge, over the river, is *Cambridge Motor Park*, 32 Scott St (ⓣ07/827 5649, ⓦcambridge.kiwiholidayparks.com; camping $13, cabins ❷, kitchen cabins ❷, self-contained units ❸).

Foodies could do worse than *The Deli*, 48 Victoria St (closed Sun after 2pm), a daytime venue for coffee, snacks, light meals and Devonshire teas; or *Fran's Café*, 62 Victoria St (closed Sun; BYO), a kitsch setting for home-baked snacks and light meals, under $15. *Rosso's*, Alpha Street (ⓣ07/827 6699; closed Mon), serves snacks and good Italian lunches and dinners while cheaper grub jumps the bar at the English-pub-style *Prince Albert*, Victoria Plaza, off Victoria Street.

Tirau

The farming settlement of **TIRAU**, 30km southeast of Cambridge, is a highwayside strip adorned with mild irony, in the form of a large corrugated-iron sheep and sheepdog. The sheep houses a wool shop, the sheepdog the **visitor centre** (daily 9am–5pm; ⓣ07/883 1202, ⓦtirauinfo.co.nz): where you can obtain a free leaflet highlighting the town's reinvention of itself as a centre for antiques and crafts. The corrugated iron constructions have attained iconic status and spawned a rash of sheet-metal structures and signs throughout Tirau, including a biblical shepherd in the grounds of a church. There's a handful of **places to eat** along SH1, notably the *Alley Cats Espresso Café* – opposite the dog – serving snacks; and the *Kinda Sheepish Koffee Bar* at the back of the sheep; and the *Loose Goose* (closed Tues) further east on SH1.

Matamata

The dairy-farming and racehorse-breeding town of **Matamata**, 20km north of Tirau, shot to prominence a few years back as the location of Hobbiton from the *Lord of the Rings* trilogy. All film sets were supposed to be destroyed after filming, but bad weather stopped the dismantling of seventeen hobbit-hole facades. The town has since built a minor industry round its association with celluloid Middle Earth but the only way to visit the Hobbiton location (on a working sheep farm 15km southwest of town) is with Rings Scenic Tours, who run two-hour trips (daily 9.30am, 10.45am, noon, 1.15pm, 2.30pm, 3.45pm, plus 5pm in the high season; $50; ⓣ07/888 6838, ⓦwww.hobbitontours.com). With unadorned frontages of the **hobbit holes** (all the interiors were filmed in Wellington studios) and grassed-over landscaping, the set retains little of the pastoral English feel created for the film. Still, you can see where it all happened, particularly the lake and the Party Tree (a big radiata pine). Die-hard fans will revel in the tour guides' unexpurgated tales of the filming.

Trips leave from the Matamata **i-SITE visitor centre**, 45 Broadway (daily 9am–5pm; ⓣ07/888 7260, ⓦwww.matamatanz.co.nz), where the InterCity/ Newmans **buses** drop off. Most people do the tour and press on, but it is worth staying to **eat** at the funky *Workman's Café*, 52 Broadway (ⓣ07/888 5498; daily except Mon from breakfast till 9pm or later, licensed), the best café in these parts.

Roads south

From Tirau, SH5 runs east to Rotorua, while SH1 continues southeast toward Taupo, passing through **PUTARURU**, 8km from Tirau. SH1 continues 25km southeast through rolling farmland to pungent **TOKOROA**, downwind of the nearby Kinleith pulp mill. Most likely you'll want to stick on SH1 to Taupo, but if the Tongariro National Park beckons, follow SH32 30km south from Tokoroa to **Whakamaru** and turn south for the **Western Bays Highway** (still SH32) direct to Turangi. The road flanks the eastern side of the Pureora Forest (p.253) accessible along Kakaho Road, 19km south of Whakamaru. Of additional interest 10km further south, a short side road leads to the **Waihora Lagoon Walk** (500m return; 15min), ending at a pretty lake surrounded by rimu and kahikatea trees.

Te Awamutu and around

TE AWAMUTU, 30km south of Hamilton, is a placid place, surrounded by rolling hills, dairy pasture and overlooked by Mount Pirongia. By the nineteenth century Maori had a heavy presence on the land, as evidenced by the many *pa* sites in the loops of rivers and on steep hilltops. During the 1863 **New Zealand Wars**, Te Awamutu was a garrison for government forces and site of one of the most famous battles of the conflict, fought at the hastily constructed

Orakau *pa,* where three hundred Maori stood off two thousand soldiers for three days.

Besides being the birthplace of fraternal Kiwi pop music icons Tim and Neil Finn, Te Awamatu is locally renowned for its extensive **rose gardens**, at the corner of Gorst and Arawata streets, at their best between November and May. Immediately across the road is the visitor centre (see below), where fans of **Split Enz** and **Crowded House** might want to get hold of the "Finn Tour" booklet ($5) for a self-guided jaunt round places of significance in the Finn brothers' unremarkable formative years. The visitor centre also holds the key to **St John's Church**, just across Arawata Street. Built as a garrison church in 1854, it was spared the fiery fate of most European buildings because the Maori chieftain, Te Paea Potatau, placed her *mana* upon it. Inside is a tribute from the British regiment, written in Maori, honouring Maori who crawled, under fire, onto the battlefield to give water to wounded British soldiers. The church also contains one of the oldest figurative stained-glass windows in New Zealand.

Te Awamutu Museum and library, 135 Roche St, ten minutes' walk west of the visitor centre (Mon–Fri 10am–4pm, Sat 10am–1pm, Sun 1–4pm; free; Ⓦwww.tamuseum.org.nz), contains an excellent collection of early Maori artefacts. The museum's pride and joy is *Uenuku*, a striking dark-wood carving representing a traditional god as a rainbow. This sacred relic of the Tainui people may date to around 1400. Along with displays about European settlers and the New Zealand Wars, there's the True Colours exhibit, devoted to the Finn brothers, but concentrating on Split Enz.

One of the largest remaining stands of kahikatea trees on the North Island, **Yarndley's Bush** (dawn–dusk; free), is just 4km north of Te Awamutu along SH3, then following the signposts 1500m along Ngaroto Road. A **loop walk** (30min) winds through huge root buttresses, with a raised platform midway along for a bird's-eye view of the constantly moving canopy. Kahikatea are one of New Zealand's most spectacular trees but the use of their odourless wood to make boxes to transport butter means this is one of the few places you will get the chance to appreciate them.

Practicalities

InterCity and Dalroy buses on the Auckland–New Plymouth run, stop at the **visitor centre**, 1 Gorst Ave (Mon–Fri 9am–4.30pm, Sat & Sun 10am–3.30pm, closing later in summer; Ⓣ07/871 3259, Ⓦwww.teawamutu.co.nz), from where just about everything in town is a short walk.

If you get hungry after a walk round the kahikatea stand **try** the small French-run patisserie at *Salvador's*, 50 Alexandra St (closed Sun), or the licensed *Olde Bank*, 201 Alexandra St, for good meals both day and evening.

Pirongia

Dominating the landscape to the west of Te Awamutu is **Mount Pirongia**, scarred by redoubt trenches from the New Zealand Wars. The peak lies within the **Pirongia Forest Park**, an area traversed by a series of interesting nature **walks** described in the DOC *Pirongia* leaflet (available from Te Awamutu visitor centre). The most popular is the Mangakara Nature Walk (3km; 1hr return), meandering through ancient forest. Longer **tramping routes** converge on the 959-metre summit, the most rewarding being the Mahaukura Track from the Grey Road car park (4km each way; 4–6hr up), taking you via the Wharauroa Lookout (2–3hr to the lookout; the last 30m are steep, with chains placed to help). On the summit ridge is DOC's **Pahautea Hut** (eight bunks; $5; book at Te Awamutu visitor centre or Hamilton DOC).

Raglan and around

Visitors often stay longer than they intend in **RAGLAN**, which hugs the south side of the large and picturesque Raglan Harbour, some 48km west of Hamilton. Once a day-tripper's paradise, Raglan now attracts an ever-growing number of permanent residents, drawn by the town's bohemian arts-and-crafts tenor and the laid-back spirit of the **surfing** community, here for some of the best left-handed breaks in the world. Aside from watersports there is **hiking** and **horse-riding** to the south of town, notably in the area around Mount Karioi, and further south at **Bridal Veil Falls**.

The horizon to the south of Raglan is dominated by **Mount Karioi**. According to Maori legend the mountain was the ultimate goal of the great migratory canoe *Tainui*, but on reaching the mouth of the harbour a bar blocked the way, hence the name Whaingaroa ("long pursuit"). The shortened epithet, Whangaroa, was the name used for the harbour until 1855, when it was renamed Raglan after the officer who led the Charge of the Light Brigade.

Arrival, information and accommodation

Almost everything of note in town is to be found along **Bow Street**, its central row of phoenix palms shading banks, restaurants and a selection of crafts shops. The street's western end butts against the harbour, where a slender footbridge provides access to the campsite and a safe swimming beach.

Hamilton City **buses** (ⓣ0800/800 401) stop outside the library on Bow Street. The **visitor centre** (Nov–March Mon–Fri 9.30am–5pm Sat 10am–5pm Sun 10am–4pm; April–Oct Mon–Fri 9am–3pm, Sat & Sun 10am–4pm; ⓣ07/825 0556, ⓦwww.raglan.org.nz) is at 4 Wallis St. Raglan Video, 6 Bow St, has **Internet access** (daily 10am–8.30pm).

One of the reasons you may overdo your expected stay here is the abundance of **accommodation** at all levels.

Accommodation

Belindsay's 28 Wallis St ⓣ07/825 6592, ⓔbelindsays@hotmail.com. Upmarket backpackers in a 1930s house with polished wood floors, stained-glass windows and a deep bath as well as shower. Three-bed shares, a single and doubles, plus a sunny lounge and kitchen. Dorms $20, ❷

Harbourview Hotel 14 Bow St ⓣ07/825 8010, ⓔharbourviewhotel@xtra.co.nz. Pleasant rooms, including singles in the town's archetypal hotel, some of them with a veranda overlooking the main street. ❸

Karioi Lodge, 5 Whaanga Rd, Whale Bay ⓣ07/825 7873, ⓦwww.karioi.co.nz. Pleasant hostel in native bush 8km southwest of Raglan, with four-bed dorms and doubles, a communal kitchen, sauna, bike hire, mountain tracks and a flying fox. At busy times evening meals may be available ($12), but it's best to bring supplies. Free pick-up from Raglan plus daily transport ($1 each way). Dorms $27, ❷

Raglan Backpackers & Waterfront Lodge 6 Nero St ⓣ07/825 0515, ⓦwww.raglanbackpackers.co.nz. Comfortable and friendly backpackers beautifully laid out round a courtyard that backs onto the estuary. Centrally located with cheap kayak, bike and surfboard ($20 per session) rental. Dorms $21, ❷

Raglan Kopua Holiday Park Marine Parade ⓣ07/825 8283, ⓦwww.raglanholidaypark.co.nz. Central campsite 1km by road from town but also accessible by footbridge. It is well sited next to Te Kopua, the harbour's safest swimming beach. Camping $12, backpacker bunks $20, cabins ❷, tourist flats ❸

Rohi Manu Rose St ⓣ07/825 6831, ⓦwww.rohimanu.co.nz. Three upmarket and centrally located houses, all with sea views and personalized dining as well as holistic therapies. ❼

Sleeping Lady Lodgings Raglan Surfing School, 5 Whaanga Rd, Whale Bay ⓣ07/825 7873, ⓦwww.sleepinglady.co.nz. Four delightful s/c holiday homes scattered through coastal bush 8km southwest of Raglan, sleeping from two to twelve ($120–220 a night for two, plus $30 for each additional person). ❻

Solscape Wainui Rd, Manu Bay, 6km south of Raglan ⓣ07/825 8268, ⓦwww.solscape.co.nz. Excellent if idiosyncratic accommodation in imaginatively converted train carriages, cottages and new eco cottages, on top of a hill with panoramic views. Other bonuses include a home-made solar water heating system, solar LED lights, tipi-style accommodation and individual earth-wood units (timber frames and roofs with mud walls) as well as free pick-ups from Raglan, and surf lessons (see p.245). Sheltered camping $15, dorms $20, ❷ shared cabooses and doubles ❸ eco units and s/c studios ❻

The town and its beaches

It's easy to pass a couple of hours wandering the foreshore, there is little specific to see in Raglan except for the **museum**, in an old police station on Wainui Road (Sat & Sun 1–3.30pm; donation), with a modest local history collection, mostly European. **Harbour cruises** are a better bet, taking in pancake rock formations, historic sites and birdlife; run by Raglan Harbour Adventures on the *Spruce Goose* (1hr 30min–2hr in the summer; $20; ⓣ07/825 8153, ⓔraglanmate@paradise.net.nz). Similar territory is covered on **guided kayak trips** with Raglan Kayaks (ⓣ825 8862, ⓦwww.raglaneco.co.nz), who run a variety of tours. The best is the Limestone Experience (3hr 30min; $65), involving paddling amid pancake-layered grey limestone formations.

The safest **swimming** beach is **Te Kopua**, in the heart of town, reached via the footbridge from lower Bow Street or by car along Wainui Road and Marine Parade. **Ocean Beach**, just outside the town off Wainui Road and on the way to Whale Bay, gives great views of the bar of rock and sand that stretches across the mouth of the harbour and is a fine picnic spot, but strong undertows make swimming unsafe.

Eating and drinking

With the steady flow of surfers and travellers, Raglan has some great relaxed café-style places to eat, most of them clustering around the intersection of Bow Street and Wainui Road.

Aqua Velvet Corner of Wainui Rd & Bow St. Spacious, licensed café with live music on Saturdays during the summer, otherwise daytime only, with good coffee and a knitting circle.

Harbour View Hotel Bow St. Reliable hotel/pub with good-value meals, plus draught beer and wine by the glass.

Raglan Club 22 Bow St. The atmosphere's nothing to shout about but there's good basic pub fare in the evenings, notably the $14 fish-and-chip meals, and the Thurs-night roast ($10). Closed Mon & Tues.

Salt Rock Café 2 Wallis St. Licensed breakfast and lunch hangout with great views over the bay, open evenings Dec–March, otherwise 9am–3pm daily.

Tongue and Groove Corner of Bow St & Wainui Rd. The laid-back vibe, steady flow of interesting locals, extensive range of imaginative café fare, and great cakes and coffee make this the pick of Raglan's eateries. Licensed & BYO.

Vinnie's World of Eats 7 Wainui Rd. One time trailblazer of the café scene hereabouts, *Vinnie's* remains excellent value (closed Mon–Wed except Dec–Mar) with everything from snacks to seafood mains via gourmet pizza. Licensed & BYO.

Around Raglan

Grand views of Raglan Harbour and up and down the coast can be had from the **summit** of Mount Karioi (755m), reached by the **Te Toto** track (8km

Surfing and kitesurfing

There are plenty of great surf breaks around the country but Raglan is New Zealand's main surfing destination, largely because of its international reputation for the best **left-handed break** in the world. The lines of perfect breakers appear like blue corduroy southwest of town. The best place for inexperienced surfers is **Ngarunui Beach**, 5km out of Raglan, which is rock-free; for the experienced, the main breaks are **Manu Bay** and **Whale Bay**, both around 8km from town.

The two main places for **surf lessons** are the Whale Bay-based Raglan Surfing School (ⓣ07/825 7873, ⓦwww.raglansurfingschool.co.nz), who offer a starter lesson (3hr; $89 including gear and transport) using a specially made soft board, plus a range of longer packages; and Manu Bay-based Solscape, who offer a range of deals, from $85 including a lesson, board and wetsuit. Both places also **rent gear**, as do GAg, 9a Bow St (ⓣ07/825 8702, ⓦwww.gagraglan.com; boards from $35 a day) and, in summer, a shack on Ngarunui Beach (boards $35 half-day; boogie boards $15 half-day; wetsuits $10 half-day; kite- or wind-surf gear $80 a day).

For those in need of the wind in their hair try kitesurfing with Ragaln Kitesurf School (ⓣ07/825 7453; 2hr $100).

return; 5–6hr; not to be attempted in bad weather). Starting 12km south of Raglan along Whaanga Road, the track heads up a gorge and, after a strenuous and difficult climb within a cliff-lined cut to a lookout, reaches the final, easier, section to the summit. A little further along this coast at Ruapuke, Extreme Horse Adventures (ⓣ07/825 0059, ⓦwww.wildcoast.co.nz) offer rides over their farm, through native bush and on to Ruakpuke Beach ($90 per person, $15 for transport from Raglan, minimum four).

Twenty-three kilometres southeast of Raglan, a short easy path (10min each way) leads to **Bridal Veil Falls**, hidden in dense native bush, and signposted from the Kawhia Road; at the falls themselves, water plummets 55m down a sheer rock face into a green pool where rainbows appear in the spray in sunny weather. The Te Toto track and the falls sights can be combined on a winding gravel-road loop around the Karioi Range, that passes Magic Mountain Horse Treks, 334 Houchen Rd (ⓣ07/825 6892, ⓦwww.magicmountain.co.nz), who charge $40 for an hour's riding, or $80 for a trek to Bridal Veil Falls. To get here, head 8km east of Raglan on SH23, then 6km up Te Mata Road, and 3km up Houchen Road; pick-ups can be arranged ($20, minimum two) from Raglan.

Kawhia

Sleepy **KAWHIA**, 55km south of Raglan, perches on the northern side of Kawhia Harbour and enjoys a massive population explosion in the summer. The six hundred souls who normally live there are joined by over four thousand holidaying Kiwis flocking to **Ocean Beach**, where **Te Puia Hot Springs** bubble from beneath the black sand. You can reach the springs along the unsealed four-kilometre Tainui–Kawhia Forest Road. At the car park a track leads over the dunes to the ocean. Go two hours either side of low tide (check times at the museum or in any of the local stores, and ask for detailed directions) – it's often hard to find the springs unless others have got there first, to dig the necessary shallow holes. Be warned, the black sand can scorch bare feet and dangerous rips make swimming unsafe.

The settlement of Kawhia is strung unattractively along Jervois Street. Lined with a couple of petrol stations and a handful of combined shop/cafés, the only site is **Kawhia Museum** (Oct–March Mon–Fri 11.30am–4.30pm, Sat & Sun 11am–4pm; April–Nov Wed–Sun 11am–3pm; donation; ⓣ07/871 0161), with interesting displays on local Maori culture, European settlers, and a kauri whaleboat built in the 1880s. As the spiritual home of the **Tainui**, the settlement does have other points of interest though. Legends tell of the arrival of the Tainui in 1350, in their ancestral **waka** (canoe), and of how they found Kawhia Harbour so bountiful that they lived on its shores for three hundred years. Tribal battles over the rich fishing grounds eventually forced them inland and in 1821, after constant attacks by the better-armed Waikato Maori, the Tainui chief, Te Rauparaha finally led his people to the relative safety of Kapiti Island.

When the original *waka* arrived in Kawhia, it was tied to a pohutukawa tree, Tangi te Korowhiti, still growing on the shore on Kaora Street, near the junction with Moke Street, 800m west of the museum – reached along the waterside footpath. The *Tainui* canoe is buried on a grassy knoll above the beautifully carved and painted **meeting house** of the **Maketu Marae**, further along Kaora Street at Karewa Beach, with Hani and Puna stones marking its stern and prow.

The arrival of **European** settlers and missionaries in the 1830s made Kawhia prosperous as a gateway to the fertile King Country, though its fortunes declined in the early years of the twentieth century, owing to its unsuitability for deep-draught ships. These days the settlement is known throughout New Zealand for annual **whaleboat races** (Jan 1), when eleven-metre, five-crew whaling boats dash across the bay. To sample something of this maritime spirit, join Kawhia Harbour Cruises (mid-Dec to Feb daily; $40, min 4; ⓣ027/350 3601) who visit the white-sand beaches and labyrinths of pancake rocks.

Practicalities

The museum acts as an unofficial **visitor centre**, dispensing free maps and details of local attractions. **Campers** can stay at the well-kept *Kawhia Camping Ground*, 73 Moke St (ⓣ07/871 0863, ⓦwww.kawhiacampingground.co.nz; camping $14, cabins ❶, caravans with awnings ❷), who also offer a ten-seater, 4WD shuttle to the hot springs. Alternatively try the waterfront *Kawhia Beachside S-cape*, 225 Pouewe St (SH31) (ⓣ07/871 0727, ⓦwww.kawhiabeachsidescape.co.nz; camping $15, dorms $25, cabins ❶, units ❹), for a range or accommodation, including some pleasant 'bottle and bonk' units.

Quintessential Kawhia **eating** is fish and chips from one of the town takeaways, eaten on the wharf overlooking the harbour. Follow this with a **beer** in the very traditional *Kawhia Hotel*, *Annie's* or the *Blue Chook Inn*.

The King Country

The rural landscape inland from Kawhia and south of Hamilton is known as the **King Country**, because it was the refuge of **King Tawhiao** and members of the **King Movement** (see p.247), after they were driven south during the New Zealand Wars. The area soon gained a reputation among *Pakeha* as a Maori stronghold renowned for difficult terrain and a welcome that meant few, if any, Europeans entered. However, the forest's respite was short-lived: when peace was declared in 1881, loggers descended in droves.

Tourist interest focuses on **Waitomo**, a tiny village at the heart of a unique and dramatic landscape, honeycombed by limestone caves eerily illuminated by

The King Movement

Before Europeans arrived, Maori loyalty was solely to their immediate family and tribe, but wrangles with acquisitive European settlers led many tribes to discard age-old feuds in favour of a common crusade against the Pakeha. **Maori nationalism** hardened in the face of blatantly unjust treatment and increasing pressure to "sell" land.

In 1856, the influential Otaki Maori sought a chief who might unite the disparate tribes against the Europeans, and in 1858 the Waikato, Taupo and other tribes (largely originating from the *Tainui* canoe; see p.246) chose **Te Wherowhero**. Taking the title of **Potatau I**, the newly elected king established himself at Ngaruawahia – to this day the seat of the **King Movement**. The principal tenet of the movement was to resist the appropriation of Maori land and provide a basis for a degree of self-government. Whether out of a genuine misunderstanding of these aims or for reasons of economic expediency, the settlers interpreted the formation of the movement as an act of rebellion – despite the fact that Queen Victoria was included in the movement's prayers – and tension heightened. The situation escalated into armed conflict later in 1858 when the Waitara Block near New Plymouth was confiscated from its Maori owners. The fighting spread throughout the central North Island: the King Movement won a notable victory at Gate Pa, in the Bay of Plenty, but was eventually overwhelmed at Te Ranga. Seeing the wars as an opportunity to settle old scores, some Maori tribes sided with the British and, in a series of battles along the Waikato, forced the kingites further south, until a crushing blow was struck at Orakau in 1864. The king and his followers fled south of the Puniu River into an area that, by virtue of their presence, became known as the **King Country**.

There they remained, with barely any European contact, until 1881, when **King Tawhiao**, who had succeeded to the throne in 1860, made peace. Gradually the followers of the King Movement drifted back to Ngaruawahia. Although by no means supported by all Maori, the loose coalition of the contemporary King Movement plays an important role in the current reassessment of Maori–Pakeha relations, and the reigning Maori King is the recipient of state and royal visits.

glow-worms, and overlaid by a geological wonderland of karst. North of Waitomo is the small dairy town of **Otorohanga**, with a kiwi house and aviary. To the south of Waitomo, **Te Kuiti** provided sanctuary in the 1860s for Maori rebel Te Kooti, who reciprocated with a beautifully carved meeting house. Further south is the **Pureora Forest Park**, an enclave of rich lowland podocarp forest that was the site of a conservation battle in the late 1970s, and now provides access to excellent walks and a home for the rare **kokako**, a bird that prefers walking to flight.

From Te Kuiti, SH4 runs south to the King Country's last community, the jaded town of **Taumarunui**, with access to the Whanganui River and the start of the **Forgotten World Highway** (see p.255).

Otorohanga

Surrounded by sheep and cattle country some 30km south of Te Awamutu, **OTOROHANGA** has one main attraction, the **Kiwi House Native Bird Park**, Alex Telfer Drive, off Kakamutu Road (daily: Sept–May 9.30am–4.30pm; June–Aug 9am–4pm; $15; Ⓦwww.kiwihouse.org.nz; kiwi get fed daily at 1.30pm and 4pm), five minutes' walk from the town centre. The grumpy little bird's lifestyle is explained in the well-laid-out nocturnal kiwi house. Outdoor enclosures contain most species of New Zealand native bird, many in a walk-through aviary.

Nearby on Kakamutu Road, the **Otorohanga Museum** (Sun 2–4pm; donation; Ⓣ07/873 8849) presents Maori flax weavings, dog-hair cloaks, and a glassed-in room where you can peer in at the remains of the half-built Maori *waka*, *Te Waonui O Tane*, carved from a totara. This rough-hewn canoe shape was found still on its construction cradle under layers of gravel and sand.

Otorohanga celebrates all things archetypally Kiwi with a series of light-hearted shop-window **Kiwiana displays** along Maniapoto Street. Take a glance in Hammer Hardware at no. 88 for Kiwi ingenuity, and Otorohanga Sheepskins at no. 52 for a celebration of Marmite. Perhaps more productively visit the Karam and John Haddad Menswear Store, 65–71 Maniapoto St (Ⓣ07/873 8377), 'world famous in New Zealand' for bargains on Swanndri bushwear and Kiwi-Stockman waxed coats and other vital rural gear, as well as their own specially designed, unique Kiwi hat, the Haddad 6045.

Practicalities

Trains pull in behind the **i-SITE visitor centre**, 21 Maniapoto St (Mon–Fri 9am–5pm, Sat & Sun 10am–3pm; Ⓣ07/873 8951, Ⓦwww.otorohanga.co.nz), buses stop out front. Waitomo has no bank, supermarket or petrol station, so make use of these amenities here.

There's a well-equipped central **campsite**, the *Otorohanga Holiday Park*, 12 Huiputea Drive (Ⓣ07/873 7253, Ⓦwww.kiwiholidaypark.co.nz; camping $15, cabin ❷, motel units ❸), if you wish to park your campervan, try the *Otorohanga & Waitomo Colonial Motels*, 59 Main North Rd/SH3 (Ⓣ0800/828 289, Ⓦwaitomomotels.co.nz; ❸).

The best bets for **eating** are the *Copper Tree*, 80 Maniapoto St (closed Sun), and *The Thirsty Weta*, 57 Maniapoto St.

Waitomo

Some 16km south of Otorohanga, **WAITOMO**, 8km west of SH3, is a diminutive village with an outsize reputation for wonderful **cave trips** and magnificent **karst features** – streams that disappear down funnel-shaped sinkholes, craggy limestone outcrops, fluted rocks, potholes and natural bridges caused by cave ceiling collapses. Below ground, seeping water has sculpted the rock into eerie and extraordinary shapes. The ongoing process of **cave creation** involves the interaction of rainwater and carbon dioxide from the air, that together form a weak acid. As more carbon dioxide is absorbed from the soil the acid grows stronger, dissolving the limestone and enlarging cracks and joints, eventually

Glow-worms

Glow-worms (*Arachnocampa luminosa*) are found all over New Zealand, mostly in caves but also on overhanging banks in the bush where in dark and damp conditions you'll often see the telltale bluey-green glow. A glow-worm isn't a worm at all, but the matchstick-sized larval stage of the fungus gnat (a relative of the mosquito), which attaches itself to the cave roof and produces around twenty or thirty mucus-and-silk threads or "fishing lines", which hang down a few centimetres. Drawn by the highly efficient chemical light, midges and flying insects get ensnared in the threads and the glow-worm draws in the line to eat them.

The six- to nine-month larval stage is the only time in the glow-worm **life cycle** that it can eat, so it needs to store energy for the two-week pupal stage when it transforms into the adult gnat that has no mouthparts. It only lives a couple of days, during which time the female has to frantically find a mate in the dark caves (the glow is a big help here) and lay her batch of a hundred or so eggs. After a two- to three-week incubation, they hatch into glow-worms and the process begins anew.

forming the varied caves you see today. Each year a further seventy cubic metres of limestone (about the size of a double-decker bus) is dissolved.

The caves can be visited on a number of tours, from a gentle underground float through grottoes illuminated by **glow-worms**, to full-on wetsuit-clad adventure trips involving squeezes and hundred-metre abseils into the void. Alternatively you can go glow-worm-searching independently on a night-time walk through a **natural tunnel**.

Appropriately enough, Waitomo means "water entering shaft" and, for over a hundred years, visitors have flocked here to explore the surrounding caves. Some passages were familiar to local Maori long before local chief **Tane Tinorau** introduced them to English surveyor **Fred Mace**, in 1887. The pair explored further, building a raft of flax stems and drifting along an underground stream, with candles their only source of light. So impressed were they that, within a year, the enterprising Tane was guiding tourists to see the spectacle. The government took over in 1906 and it was not until 1989 that the caves were returned to their Maori owners, who receive a percentage of all revenue generated and participate in the site's management.

Arrival and information

Trains and InterCity **buses** stop in Otorohanga, from where the Waitomo Shuttle (Ⓣ0800/808 279; $10 one way) ferries people to Waitomo, five times daily. Newmans buses run daily to Waitomo on their Auckland–Rotorua run, and there's also the Waitomo Wanderer (Ⓣ0508 926 337, Ⓦwww.waitomotours.co.nz) running daily from Rotorua.

Above ground there's not much to Waitomo Caves apart from the official **visitor centre** in the Museum of Caves building on the main road (daily: Jan & Feb 8.45am–7.30pm; April–Sept 8.30am–5pm, Oct–Dec & March 8.30am–5.30pm, Ⓣ07/878 7640, Ⓦwww.waitomoinfo.co.nz). The centre is a mine of information; booking agent for cave trips, trains and buses; a **post office**; and has **Internet access**. There is **no bank** or **petrol** at Waitomo and only a small store.

Accommodation

Backpackers are well provided for in Waitomo. Other **accommodation** is fairly limited so **book in advance**, particularly between November and January.

Abseil Breakfast Inn 709 Waitomo Caves Rd, 400m east of the museum Ⓣ07/878 7815, Ⓦwww.abseilinn.co.nz. Pick of the B&Bs, relaxing and stylish, on top of a hill with great views. Each of the four en-suite rooms is individually decorated. ❺

Hamilton Tomo Group Lodge 1700m west of Waitomo Ⓣ07/878 7422, Ⓦwww.htg.org.nz or book through visitor centre. Basic caving-club lodge plying visitors with local knowledge and offering dorms with access to a kitchen, wide sunny deck and BBQ. Bring your own sleeping bag. Dorm $12.

Juno Hall Waitomo Caves Rd, 1km east of Waitomo Ⓣ07/878 7649, Ⓦwww.junowaitomo.co.nz. Small, well-equipped hostel in a timber-lined building set on a low hill by a pool, BBQ deck and a tennis court. Free pick-ups from town, camping $15, dorms $25, ❷

KiwiPaka YHA Waitomo School Rd Ⓣ07/878 3395, Ⓦwww.kiwipaka-yha.co.nz. Excellent purpose-built YHA in the heart of Waitomo with beds and rooms in a lodge, separate chalets with private bathrooms, and a great café (see p.252). Three-shares $27, rooms ❸, chalets ❸

Te Tiro 9km west of Waitomo Ⓣ07/878 6328, Ⓦwww.waitomocavesnz.com. Cosy s/c cottages with fabulous views and a glow-worm grotto. Breakfast goodies are included, but if you're cooking, bring food or something for the BBQ. ❹

Waitomo Caves Guest Lodge 7 Waitomo Caves, 100m east of the museum Ⓣ07/878 7641, Ⓦwww.waitomocavesguestlodge.co.nz. Eight comfortable, good-value rooms on a hillside with a lovely garden. ❹

Waitomo Top 10 Holiday Park 12 Waitomo Caves Rd ⓣ0508/498 666, ⓦwww.waitomopark.co.nz. Well-equipped campsite in the heart of town, with a swimming pool and spa. Camping $18, cabins ❷, s/c units ❹

World Unique Waitomo Motels 900m up Waitomo Valley Rd, off Waitomo Caves Rd ⓣ07/878 6666, ⓦwww.woodlynpark.co.nz. Popular motel-style accommodation on the site of Billy Black's Kiwi Culture Show (see p.251). Sleep in a Bristol freighter aircraft imaginatively converted into two comfortable s/c units; a 1950s railway carriage containing a three-room unit; two hobbit holes with circular entrances sunk into a hillside and a converted World War II patrol boat. Book a month ahead for Dec–Feb. ❺

Visiting the caves

Only a fraction of the 45km of cave passages under Waitomo can be visited on guided tours, and the only caves you can safely explore **independently** are the Piripiri Caves, 28km west of the village (see p.252). To enhance your cave experience, stop at the **Museum of Caves**, beside the visitor centre (daily 8am–5pm, later Dec to early March; ⓦwww.waitomo-museum.co.nz); entry is $5, included in the price of most of the adventure-caving trips. The museum has informative exhibits on the geology and history of the caves, interactive displays on the life cycle of glow-worms and cave wetas and a free 18-minute multimedia show, screened on request, relating everything you'll ever need to know about glow-worms.

Waitomo's original cave experience is **Waitomo Glow-worm Caves**, 500m west of the visitor centre (daily 9am–5pm; $35; ⓦwww.waitomocaves.co.nz), geared to herding tour-bus passengers through forty-minute tours, beginning on the half-hour. Paved walkways and lighting pick out the best of the stalactites and stalagmites and there's a boat ride through the grotto, where glow-worms shed pinpricks of ghostly pale-green light. The best **tour** is the first of the day.

The Glow-worm Caves office also sells tickets for tours around the **Aranui Cave**, 3.5km west of the visitor centre (daily 10am, 11am, 1pm, 2pm & 3pm; 45min; $32). Although only 250m long it is geologically more spectacular, with high-ceilinged chambers and magnificent stalactites and stalagmites. A two-cave combo costs $50.

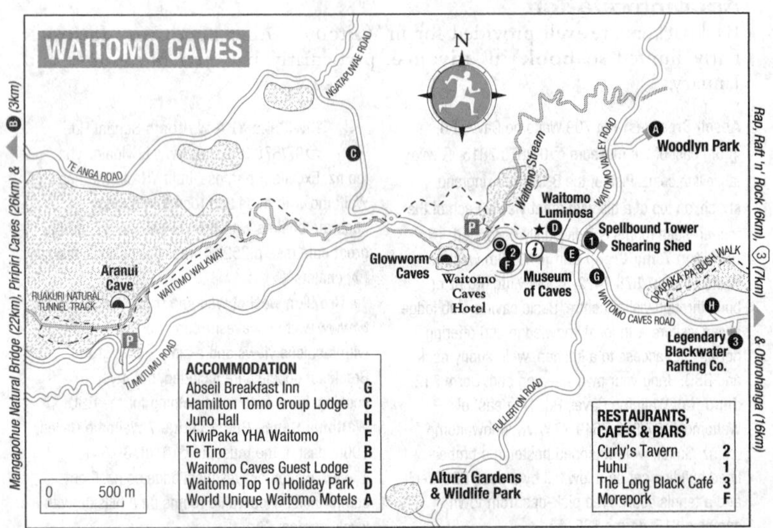

The pick of the other stay-dry caving trips are at **Ruakuri** (daily 9am, 11am, 1pm & 3pm; 2hr; $49, run by the Legendary Black Water Rafting Co, see below), whose tours draw on Maori stories of "The Den of the Dogs", as the cave's name translates.

Adventure caving

Waitomo excels at **adventure-caving trips**, which should be **booked in advance**, especially for the November to January period. The degree of commitment and level of fitness required varies considerably and the trick is to choose a trip that is exciting enough without scaring yourself witless (operators are adept at this). Most trips involve getting kitted out in a wetsuit, caver's helmet with lamp and rubber boots, and combine two or more adventure elements. In all cases, **heavy rain** can lead to cancellations if water levels rise too high, so it pays to have a day or two to spare. **Kids** under 12 are not usually allowed on adventure trips, and the wilder trips are for those of 15 and over.

Some trips feature **cave tubing** (also known as blackwater rafting), generally involving being wedged into the inner tube of a truck tyre for a gentle float through a pitch-black section of cave and gazing at pinpricks of glow-worm light overhead. Access to some caves is by **abseiling**; once underground you may do some genuine **caving**, working your way along passages, through squeezes, clambering over rocks and perhaps jumping into deep pools.

Adventure caving operators

Absolute Adventure ☎0800/787 323, Ⓦwww.absoluteadventure.co.nz. The closest thing to pure caving, physically demanding but rewarding, with gorgeous cave features. There's no tubing or glow-worms and only modest abseils, but the half-day Mission (2hr underground: $125) offers plenty to keep you occupied. Alternatively try Journey, a 24hr adventure ($380) involving hiking, a long abseil, overnight camp beneath a cliff overhang, and lots of caving. As the cave is near the top of the catchment, trips run when rainfall washes others out.

The Legendary Black Water Rafting Co ☎0800/228 464, Ⓦwww.blackwaterrafting.co.nz. The daddy of them all, who run two wetsuit-clad trips in Ruakuri Cave: Black Labyrinth (3hr, 1hr underground; $95), involving a short jump from an underground waterfall and an idyllic float through a glow-worm cave; and the more adventurous Black Abyss (5hr, 2–3hr underground; $185), which adds abseiling and an eerie flying-fox ride into darkness.

Rap, Raft 'n' Rock 95 Waitomo Caves Rd/SH37, 8km east of the Museum of Caves or 1km from the junction with SH3 ☎0800/228 372, Ⓦwww.caveraft.com. Small-group trips (4hr 30min; $125), starting with a 27m abseil into a glow-worm-filled cave explored partly on foot and partly floating on a tube, and ending with a rock climb out to the starting point.

Spellbound The Spellbound Tower, Waitomo Caves Road ☎0800/773 552, Ⓦwww.glowworm.co.nz. Housed in the silver, tapering beehive that is known as Spellbound Tower and offering low-impact glow-worm spotting on intimate trips four times daily, with gentle strolls and boat rides through two caves (3hrs 30min, $55).

Waitomo Adventures In the town centre ☎0800/924 866, Ⓦwww.waitomo.co.nz. Their signature trip is the Lost World Abseil (4hr; $245), a glorious, spine-tingling 100m rappel into the gaping fern-draped mouth of a spectacular pothole, followed by a relatively dry cave walk before climbing out on a seemingly endless ladder – the first trip of the day is best. Cave junkies should go for the Lost World Epic (7hr; $395), where an abseil is followed by several "wet" hours, working your way upstream through squeezes, behind a small waterfall and into a glittering glow-worm grotto.

Other attractions and activities

If the rain hits and caving is a wash-out head for **Woodlyn Park**, 900m up Waitomo Valley Road from the village (☎07/878 6666, Ⓦwww.woodlynpark.co.nz), where a rustic barn hosts the entertaining **Billy Black's Kiwi Culture Show** (daily 1.30pm; $22; 1hr), an offbeat look at the history of logging and farming with loads of audience participation. Otherwise try tackling the rugged karst countryside around Waitomo on 4WD **quad bikes** with Waitomo Big

Red (book through the visitor centre; 2hr; $105) or just get out and walk, pleasant enough even in the rain.

Waitomo Village and the Aranui Cave are linked by the **Waitomo Walkway** (10km; 3hr return) that starts opposite the museum, disappears into the bush then follows the Waitomo Stream to the Aranui Cave. The trail then links up with the **Ruakuri Natural Tunnel** track (2km return; 45min), one of the most impressive short walks in the country. Starting from the car park for the Aranui Cave on Tumutumu Road, the track follows the Waitomo Stream on boardwalks and walkways past cave entrances. Ducking and weaving through short tunnel sections, you eventually reach a huge cave where the stream temporarily threads underground. The walk is especially magical at night when lit by glow-worms in the bush. Both walks are shown on the free Waitomo Caves **map** from the visitor centre.

Eating and drinking

Waitomo has a limited range of **eating** options, particularly in winter, when opening times are restricted.

Curly's Tavern Immediately west of the museum. Almost everyone eventually ends up at this unreconstructed Kiwi pub, either for convivial boozing or good-value, meals in the steak, seafood and burger tradition. Occasional live music.

Huhu 10 Waitomo Caves Road, about 20m from the holiday park ⑦07/878 6676. Fine dining in a licensed café serving excellent evening meals ($21–28), and "small plates" (Kiwi tapas). Book in the evening.

The Long Black Café 2km east of the museum. Cooked breakfasts, Waitomo's best coffee, simple snacks and light meals, served from 8am in summer (8.30am in winter) until around 4pm in a spacious venue, busy with people setting off on caving trips or hanging out on the deck.

Morepork Inside the *KiwiPaka* YHA, School Rd. Good, all-day café open from breakfast, serving a limited menu of sandwiches, pasta and salads, plus good-quality dinners and pizza in the evenings. Licensed & BYO.

Towards the coast from Waitomo

For limestone scenery without all the commercialism, drive the Te Anga road for three free sights worth viewing in any weather. First is the **Mangapohue Natural Bridge**, 24km west of Waitomo, an easy fifteen-minute loop trail through forest to a riverside boardwalk which leads into a delightful, narrow limestone gorge topped by a remarkable double bridge formed by the remains of a collapsed cave roof. It's especially picturesque at night when the undersides glimmer with myriad glow-worms. In daylight, don't miss the rest of the walk, through farmland past fossilized examples of giant oysters, 35 million years old.

Four kilometres west is **Piripiri Caves**, a five-minute walk through a forested landscape full of weathered limestone outcrops. Inside the cavern you'll need a decent torch (and an emergency spare) to explore the Oyster Room, which contains more giant fossil oysters. A kilometre or so on, a track (15min return) accesses the dramatic multi-tiered **Marokopa Falls** through a forest of tawa, pukatea and kohekohe trees.

The road continues west past **TE ANGA** and its small tavern, past the turn-off for Kawhia (see p.245), and towards the wind-lashed communities and long black-sand beaches of the coast. At **MAROKOPA**, stop at the Albatross Anchor, at the end of the road overlooking the beach; the anchor was saved from the ship of the same name, which foundered crossing the harbour bar. Here you can take in the spot where the river meets the roaring white-capped waves – but be careful, the sea is dangerous and it's not unknown for fishermen to get dragged in.

Te Kuiti

The town of **TE KUITI**, 19km south of Waitomo, isn't much in itself but makes a reasonable base for visiting Waitomo. Promoting itself as the "Shearing Capital of the World", Te Kuiti has a seven-metre-high statue of a man shearing a sheep at the southern end of Rora Street; is home to five-time world shearing champion, David Fagan, who can shear a lamb in sixteen seconds; and, appropriately, hosts the annual New Zealand **Shearing and Wool Handling Championships** in late March or early April.

The town also has a proud Maori history, King Tawhiao and his followers fled here after the battle of Rangiriri in 1864. Eight years later, Maori rebel Te Kooti (see p.426) sought refuge and lived under the Maori king's protection until he was pardoned. In return for sanctuary, Te Kooti left a magnificently carved **meeting house**, Te Tokanganui-a-noho, opposite the south end of Rora Street, on Awakino Road.

Practicalities

The **visitor centre** (Oct–April daily 9am–5pm; May–Sept Mon–Fri 9am–5pm, Sat & Sun 10am–4pm; Ⓣ07/878 8077, Ⓔtkinfo@xtra.co.nz) is on Rora Street, by the **train station**. InterCity **buses** stop down the street outside *Tiffany's Restaurant*, others stop outside the visitor centre: Dalroy's (Ⓣ06/759 0197) between Auckland and New Plymouth; Perry's Bus (Ⓣ07/876 7596) running a regular shuttle to Waitomo. The **DOC office**, 78 Taupiri St (Mon–Fri 8am–4.30pm; Ⓣ07/878 1050), has details of the Pureora Forest Park. If you're heading on to Waitomo, Te Kuiti is the last stop for a bank, petrol or supermarket.

Accommodation is available 3km northeast at the rural hillside *Casara Mesa Backpackers*, Mangarino Road (Ⓣ07/878 6697, Ⓔcasara@xtra.co.nz; dorms $25, doubles ❷), with free pick-ups from the visitor centre. There are also units at the central *Motel Te Kuiti,* corner of Carroll and King streets (Ⓣ07/878 3448, Ⓔmoteltekuiti@xtra.co.nz; ❹) or camping $9, caravans & cabins ❶ at the *Te Kuiti Camping Ground*, 1 Hinerangi St (Ⓣ07/878 8966, Ⓔtewaka@hotmail.com).

The busiest place to **eat and drink** is *Tiffany's Restaurant*, at the corner of Rora and Lawrence streets, where cheap all-day meals and takeaways can be had until 9pm. Better, though pricier, food and coffee can be had at *Bosco*, 57 Te Kumi Rd (Ⓣ07/878 3633; daily 8am–3.30pm, Fri & Sat until 8pm), a couple of kilometres north. Back in town, *Riverside Lodge*, beside the river off King Street (turn off by the bridge; closed Mon), runs a restaurant bar that does good pizza.

Pureora Forest Park

Straddling the Hauhungaroa Range some 50km southeast of Te Kuiti, the **Pureora Forest Park** is accessible by SH30 from the west and SH32 from the east, though there is no public transport. The forest narrowly escaped clear-felling in 1978, and was saved, thanks to a treetop protest. Along with Little Barrier Island and a few pockets around Rotorua, this broad-leaf environment is now one of the few remaining habitats of the rare North Island **kokako**. A bluish-grey bird distinguished by the bright blue wattles on either cheek, it flies poorly, preferring to hop among the branches and nest close to the ground.

At the western entrance to the forest, 46km from Te Kuiti, is the **DOC Pureora Field Centre** (Mon–Fri 8am–4pm; Ⓣ07/878 1080). Here you can get leaflets describing various walks, and details of the simple *Ngaherenga* DOC **campsite** ($8), 1km north. Half a kilometre north of the field centre is the wheelchair-accessible **Totara Walk** (800m loop; 15–30min). Immediately south of the campsite, a signposted road runs 3km to the **Forest Tower**, giving a twelve-metre-high protestor's-eye view of the surrounding area, close to the site of the landmark anti-logging protest. A fifteen-minute drive northeast of the field centre, along SH30, leads to the **Pouakani Tree**, the largest totara ever recorded.

The SH3 from Te Kuiti to Taranaki

Southwest of Te Kuiti, **SH3** makes a beeline for the Tasman Sea and the small coastal town of **Mokau**, before twisting its way through tiny communities, sandwiched between spectacular black beaches and steep inland ranges. Opportunities for exploration focus on walks near the **Tongaporutu** rivermouth, and there's refreshment a little further on at an excellent micro-brewery. Eventually the scenery opens out onto the **Taranaki Plains** just north of New Plymouth (see p.258).

Mokau

The tiny community of **MOKAU**, 73km southwest of Te Kuiti, perches on a rise above the **Mokau Estuary** where the historic MV *Cygnet* (Ⓣ0800/665 2874) and *Glen Royal* (Ⓣ06/752 9036) operate **cruises** upriver (Oct–May; $40). Both concentrate on local history, passing a number of points of interest, old coal workings and abandoned farms. The river is noted for its run of whitebait, and in season (mid-Aug to end Nov), there are plenty of opportunities to sample the fish in local restaurants. The estuary also has good swimming, though the two local black-sand surf **beaches** – Mokau and Rapanui – have dangerous undertows and are best left to surfers and those after the region's abundant **shellfish**. The wild scenery hereabouts provided the backdrop for several scenes from Jane Campion's 1993 film *The Piano*, particularly in the bush scenes and the fence line, seen in silhouette, along which the daughter dances.

In town, the local **Tainui Museum** (daily 10am–4pm; donation), charts the history of the small Maori settlements on either side of the Mokau rivermouth and of the subsequent 1840 European settlement beside the coal-rich river. Just over 2km north along SH3, the **Maniaroa Marae** and *pa* is the resting place of the *Tainui* canoe's anchor stone (see p.246), a historic *waka* and some excellent woodcarvings; on entering the *marae* driveway, keep left to reach the cemetery, where the anchor stone must be observed from outside the gates.

Buses between Auckland and New Plymouth stop outside the *Whitebait Inn* (Ⓣ06/752 9713; camping $8.50, ❶), where you can get **accommodation** in cabins and excellent-value whitebait meals ($22) or whitebait burgers ($7.50). From there, it's 100m north to the cosy *Palm House Backpackers* (Ⓣ06/752 9081, Ⓦwww.mttaranaki.co.nz; dorms $25, plus $3 for linen, ❷) and a similar distance north to the museum, which acts as an unofficial **visitor centre**.

Tongaporutu and White Cliffs Brewery

Continuing south along the coast, after 18km you come to a fascinating **sea cave** just south of the **Tongaporutu rivermouth**. Signalled by two rock stacks on the beach opposite the entrance, the cave bears ancient footprints on its upper walls, about 4m up from the floor. For many years this coastal, tide-dependent route was the only access for Maori travelling between the Waikato and Taranaki districts, and the cave provided shelter. Local lore has it that the infamous chief Te Rauparaha, along with his most trusted female companion, rested in a sea cave to recover from a debilitating attack of boils. While the boils were lanced, the chief braced himself against the cave wall and, due to the combination of the sudden pain and his great strength, left impressions of his hands and feet in the rock. The chief was reputed to have six toes – as do eight of the foot imprints in the cave.

A little over 30km on, and just north of Urenui, keep your eyes skinned for the **White Cliffs Organic Brewery** (daily 10am–6pm; ⓣ06/752 3676, ⓦwww.organicbeer.co.nz), a tiny organic micro-brewery of international standing. It produces just two brews, Mike's Mild Ale and Mountain Lager; the friendly staff can give you a quick tour of the facilities.

Taumarunui

With its declining population and dwindling industries, five-thousand-strong **TAUMARUNUI**, 82km from Te Kuiti and 45km from National Park, feels run-down. For most travellers the only reason to stop is to use the town as a base for canoe or jetboat forays into the Whanganui National Park (see p.271) or follow the **Forgotten World Highway** towards Mount Taranaki.

Surrounded by national parks and forests at the confluence of the Ongarua and Whanganui rivers, Taumarunui was one of the last places to be settled by Europeans, who arrived in large numbers in 1908, when the railway came to town. Finding a suitable route for the track on its steep descent north towards Taumarunui from the area around the Tongariro National Park proved problematic, but surveyor R.W. Holmes' ingenious solution, the **Raurimu Spiral**, is a remarkable feat of engineering combining bridges and tunnels to loop the track over itself. The spiral, still in use, can be seen from a signposted viewpoint 37km south of Taumarunui on SH4. Rail fans will want to view the model of the spiral in the Taumarunui visitor centre.

Practicalities

Buses stop on Hakiaha Street (SH4) outside the **train station** and **visitor centre** (Mon–Fri 9am–4.30pm, Sat & Sun 10am–4pm; ⓣ07/895 7494, ⓦwww.visitruapehu.com), which has **Internet access**, Whanganui National Park Hut and Camp passes and other general information.

Motel **accommodation** is available at *Alexander Spa Motel*, 6 Marae St (ⓣ07/895 8501, ⓦwww.alexandermotel.co.nz; ❹), camping and decent cabins at *Taumarunui Holiday Park*, 4km south on SH4 (ⓣ07/895 9345, ⓦwww.taumarunuiholidaypark.co.nz; camping $11, cabins ❶, units ❷), wedged between a patch of native bush and the Whanganui River.

For **eating**, *Rivers II Café*, corner of Hakiaha and Marae streets, is good for snack lunches but for something a bit more classy head to the western end of town and *The Flax*, at the corner of Hakiaha Street and River Road (ⓣ07/895 6611; closed Mon, and Tues evening).

The Forgotten World Highway

For a taste of genuinely rural New Zealand, it's hard to beat the **Forgotten World Highway** between Taumarunui and Stratford (SH43), a rugged 155-kilometre road that twists through the hills west of Taumarunui. All but a ten-kilometre stretch through the Tangarakau Gorge is sealed, but reckon on three hours for the journey.

The first notable stop is the **Nukunuku Museum** (see p.274; entry by appointment ⓣ07/896 6365), 4km down Saddler Road. Back on SH43, the road snakes through the sedimentary limestone of the **Tangarakau Gorge**, possibly the highlight of the trip, with steep bush-draped cliffs rising up above the river. At the entrance to the gorge, a small sign directs you along a short trail to the picturesque site of **Joshua Morgan's grave**, the final resting place of an early surveyor. At the crest of a ridge you pass through the dark **Moki Tunnel**, then soon come across the delightful *Kaieto Café* (Ⓣ06/762 5858, Ⓦwww.kaietocafe.co.nz; camping and vans $10, cabins ❶), perched on a ridge with fabulous views.

Whangamomona

A steady descent brings you alongside a little-used rail line that runs parallel to the road as far as the village of **WHANGAMOMONA**, around 90km from Taumarunui. The thirty residents are boosted in January, every odd-numbered year, by hordes from Auckland and Hamilton who come to celebrate the town's independence, declared on October 28, 1989 after the government altered the provincial boundaries, removing it from Taranaki. The **republic** swears in a president and in full party mood hosts whip-cracking and gumboot-throwing competitions, amid much drinking and eating. Celebrations revolve around the 1911 *Whangamomona Hotel* on Ohura Road (Ⓣ06/762 5823, Ⓦwww.whangamomonahotel.co.nz), where you can get your passport stamped or buy a Whangamomonian version ($3), while wetting your whistle. The **hotel** serves **meals**, offers dinner, bed and breakfast for $100 a head and is open daily till the barman goes to bed. There's B&B accommodation across the road at *M&M's* (Ⓣ06/762 5596; $75 a head) and the simple *Whangamomona Village Motor Camp* (Ⓣ06/762 5822), a kilometre down the road: **camping** ($10 per tent) and bargain cabins ($20).

Leaving Whangamomona, SH43 climbs beside steep bluffs and passes a couple of saddles with views down the valley and across the **Taranaki Plains**. It then descends to flat dairy pasture, eventually rolling into **Stratford** (see p.268) as the permanently snowcapped Mount Taranaki looms into view, if the weather allows.

Taranaki

The province of **Taranaki** juts out west from the rest of the North Island forming a thumbprint peninsula centred on **Maunga Taranaki** (aka **Mount Egmont**), an elegant conical volcano rising 2500m from the subtropical coast to its icy summit. Taranaki means "peak clear of vegetation", an appropriate description of the upper half of "the mountain" as it is referred to locally.

The mountain remains a constant presence as you tour the region, though much of the time it is obscured by cloud. The summit is usually visible in the early morning and just before sunset, with cloud forming through the middle of the day – the bane of summit aspirants who slog for no view.

Much of your time in Taranaki is likely to be spent in **New Plymouth**, a vibrant provincial capital, with a couple of worthwhile sights and a decent selection of places to stay and eat. It's a good base for day-trips into the **Egmont National Park,** surrounding the mountain, or for short forays to the surfing and windsurfing hotspot of **Oakura**.

While New Plymouth and Egmont National Park are the undoubted highlights of the province, rural Taranaki has a few minor attractions, best sampled on a one- or two-day loop around the mountain. On the coastal SH45 **Surf Highway** west around the mountain, these are supplemented by ocean views from the multitude of surf beaches, while **Hawera**, has a couple of entertaining museums and the opportunity to go **dam dropping**.

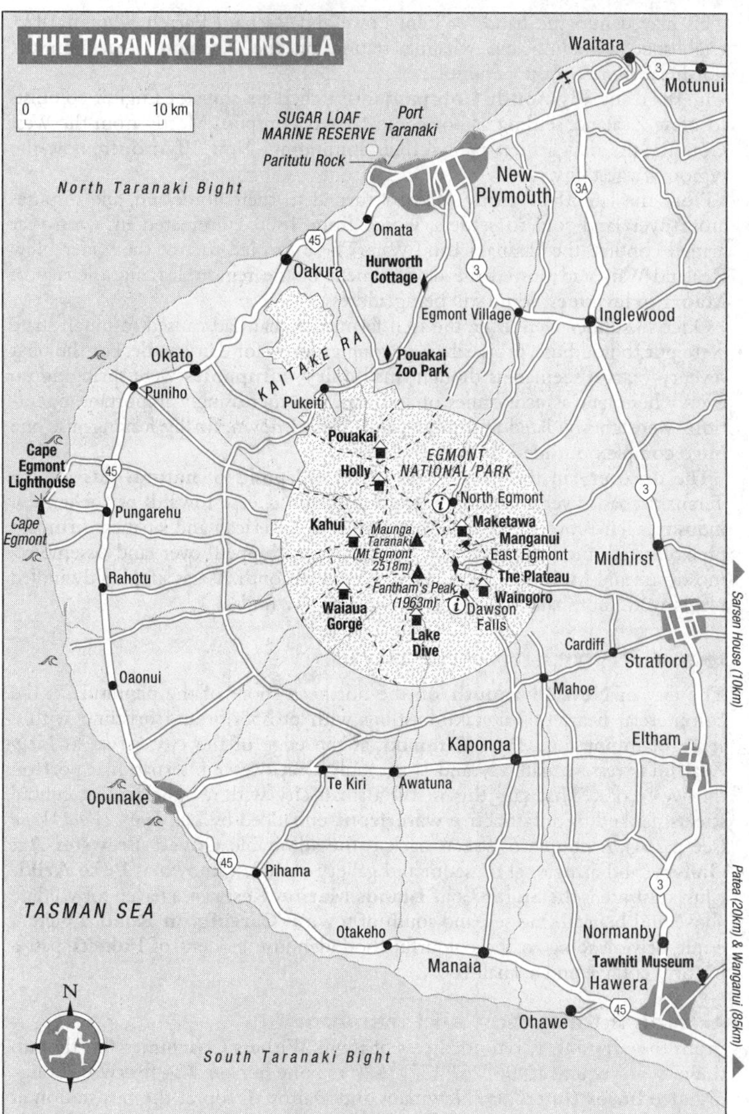

Some history

According to Maori (see box, p.334), the mountain-demigod Taranaki fled here from the company of the other mountains in the central North Island. He was firmly in place when spotted by the first European in the area, **Cook**, who named the peak Egmont after the first Lord of the Admiralty. In the early nineteenth century few **Maori** were living in the area as annual raids by northern tribes had forced many to migrate with Te Rauparaha to Kapiti Island.

This played into the hands of John Lowe and Richard Barrett who, in 1828, established a trading and whaling station on the Ngamotu Beach on the northern shores of the peninsula.

In 1841, the **Plymouth Company** dispatched six ships of English colonists to New Zealand, settling at Lowe and Barrett's outpost. Mostly from the West Country, the new settlers named their community **New Plymouth**, now the region's largest city.

From the late 1840s many Maori returned to their homeland, and disputes arose over land sold to settlers, which from 1860 culminated in a ten-year armed conflict, the Taranaki Land Wars. These formed part of the wider New Zealand Wars and slowed the development of the region, leaving a legacy of **Maori grievances**, some still being addressed.

Once hostilities were over, the rich farmlands that had caused so much strife were put to good use, primarily as grazing grounds for dairy cattle. For the next seventy years it seemed as though small **dairy companies** were springing up everywhere, but as economies of scale became increasingly important, operations were consolidated and most plants closed down, finally leaving just one huge complex outside Hawera.

The discovery in the early 1970s of large deposits of **natural gas** off the Taranaki coast diverted attention from milk and cheese towards petrochemical industries. The government paid huge sums to American and Japanese firms for prefabricated modular factories, which were shipped over and assembled, mostly around Motonui, 20km east of New Plymouth. As gas supplies dwindled plants were mothballed, awaiting hoped-for new finds.

New Plymouth and around

The city of **New Plymouth**, on the northern shore of the peninsula, is the commercial heart of Taranaki, bustling with prosperity and bristling with a sense of importance. **Port Taranaki**, at the edge of the city, serves as New Zealand's western gateway and is the only deep-water international port on the west coast. That said this is still a small city with a tight grid of central streets flanked by an attractive **waterfront** enhanced by Len Lye's *Wind Wand* (see p.261). A couple of streets back is the admirable **Govett-Brewster Art Gallery**, and a regional museum and gallery complex known as **Puke Ariki**.

Just offshore is the **Sugar Loaf Islands Marine Reserve**, a haven for wildlife above and beneath the sea, and south of town is **Carrington Road**, a picturesque drive leading to the colourful rhododendron gardens of **Pukeiti**, past a historic cottage and a small zoo.

Arrival, information and transport

From the **airport**, 12km northeast of town, Withers Coachlines shuttle into the city on request (ⓣ06/751 1777; $20 for one person, $24 for two). Long-distance **buses** (InterCity/Newmans and Dalroy's) stop at the bus station at 19 Ariki St, just along from the **i-SITE visitor centre**, 65 St Aubyn St (daily 9am–6pm except Wed till 9pm, Sat & Sun till 5pm; ⓣ06/759 6060, ⓦwww.newplymouthnz.com), in the foyer of the **Puke Ariki museum**. The visitor centre should be your first stop for Egmont National Park information, but there is also a **DOC office** at 220 Devon St West (Mon–Fri 8am–4.30pm). Both sell hut tickets.

Local bus services are run by Okato Bus Lines (ⓣ07/758 2799), but there are few useful routes and services are infrequent. A couple of companies, including Withers (see above), run shuttles to the mountain.

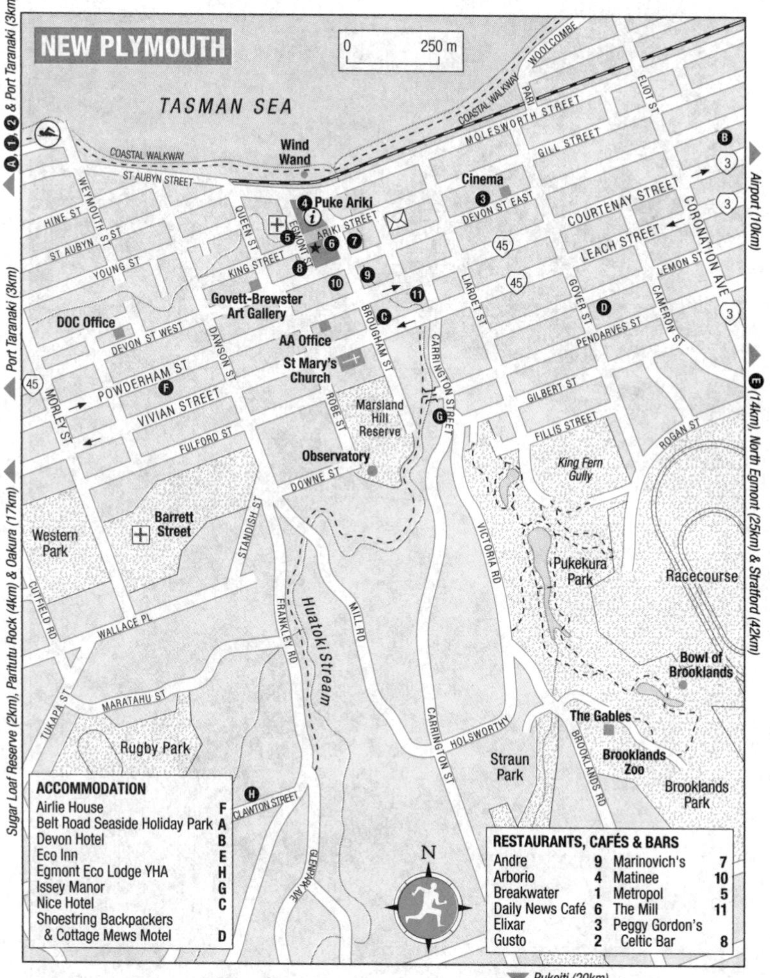

Accommodation

New Plymouth has a range of modestly priced **accommodation**, as well as options outside of town, either at the surf beach of Oakura (see p.269), or on the flanks of the mountain (see pp.266, 267).

Hotels, motels, farmstays and B&Bs

Airlie House 161 Powderham St ⓣ06/757 8866, ⓦwww.airliehouse.co.nz. Gracious, tastefully furnished B&B in a large villa dating from the turn of the last century, with crisp modern decor. There's a family suite and a studio apartment; one room is en suite, the other has a private bathroom with a claw-foot bath. ❺

Devon Hotel 390 Devon St East ⓣ0800/843 338, ⓦwww.devonhotel.co.nz. A smart business hotel with a heated pool and spa, buffet restaurant and range of rooms, including some pricey suites. ❹

Issey Manor 32 Carrington St ⓣ06/758 2375, ⓦwww.isseymanor.co.nz. Chic modern design characterizes these four rooms in a suburban house, with a good-sized deck overlooking a stream. ❺–❻

▲ Len Lye's Wind Wand

Nice Hotel 71 Brougham St ⓣ06/758 6423, ⓦwww.nicehotel.co.nz. Book in advance to ensure you get one of the seven unique rooms in this intimate, centrally located boutique hotel, with designer bathrooms, contemporary artworks and luxurious fittings. There's also a good on-site bistro (dinner only). ❼

Hostels and campsites

Belt Road Seaside Holiday Park 2 Belt Rd ⓣ0800 804 204, ⓦwww.beltroad.co.nz. A scenic, seaside clifftop site, 20min walk from the city centre, with camping and cabins (some en suite) in a tidy sheltered area. Camping $15, cabins ❶, kitchen cabins & units ❸

Eco Inn 671 Kent Rd, off SH3, between New Plymouth and Egmont Village ⓣ06/752 2765, ⓦwww.ecoinn.co.nz. 3km from the Egmont National Park boundary. Accommodation on an eco farm with wind turbines, a water wheel and the solar panels supplying energy. There's also a wood-fired hot tub, and good hiking. Pick-ups available. Camping $18, ❶

Egmont Eco Lodge YHA 12 Clawton St ⓣ06/753 5720, ⓦwww.mttaranaki.co.nz. A friendly hostel set in a peaceful garden, reached along a gentle streamside walking track (15min) from the city centre. Camping $16, dorms $25, rooms ❷, en-suite apartment ❸

Shoestring Backpackers & Cottage Mews Motel 48 Lemon St ⓣ06/758 0404, ⓦwww.shoestring.co.nz. A 5min walk from the visitor centre, this self-catering joint, with a roomy kitchen and dining room, is one of the best in town. Choose from four-shares, doubles, twins or singles in the charming old house, or stay in the bargain motel units next door. There's also a sauna ($8). Dorms $25, rooms ❷, units ❸

The waterfront

Arriving in the centre of New Plymouth, you can't miss the **Wind Wand**, a slender, bright-red, 45-metre carbon-fibre tube topped with a light globe that glows red in the dark and sways mesmerizingly in the wind. Designed by Len Lye (see box below) in 1962, it wasn't actually constructed until 2000, but has fast established itself as a regional icon. Though a smaller version was constructed in Greenwich Village in 1962, and a slightly larger one at the Toronto International Sculpture Symposium in 1966, Lye's true vision was restricted by the technology of the1960s; more recent advances in polymer engineering enabled the construction of the New Plymouth full-size model. That said, Lye's vision was greater still, but it seems unlikely

Len Lye

All of a sudden it hit me – if there was such a thing as composing music, there could be such a thing as composing motion. After all, there are melodic figures, why can't there be figures of motion?

Len Lye

New Zealand-born sculptor, film-maker and conceptual artist **Len Lye** (1901–80) was little known outside the art world but his work has now earned wider recognition. Born in Christchurch, Lye developed a fascination with movement, one that expressed itself in his late teens in early experiments in kinetic sculpture. His interest in Maori and other indigenous art encouraged him to travel widely, studying Australian Aboriginal and Samoan dance. Adapting indigenous art to the precepts of the Futurist and Surrealist movements coming out of Europe, he experimented with sculpture, batik, painting, photography and animated "cameraless" films (he painstakingly stencilled, scratched and drew on the actual film). Lye spent time working on his films in London, but towards the end of World War II joined the European artistic exodus and ended up in New York. Here he returned to sculpture, finding that he could exploit the flexibility of stainless-steel rods, loops and strips to create abstract "tangible motion sculptures" designed to "make movement real". The erratic movements of these motor-driven sculptures give them an air of anarchy, that is most evident in his best-known work, 1977's *Trilogy* (more commonly referred to as *Flip and Two Twisters*), three motorized metal sheets that wildly shake and contort until winding down to a final convulsion.

Lye envisaged his works as being monumental and set outdoors, but was always aware of the technical limitations of his era and considered his projects to be works of the twenty-first century. Just before his death in New York in 1980, friend, patron and New Plymouth resident, John Matthews, helped set up the Len Lye Foundation, which brought most of Lye's scattered work to New Plymouth's Govett-Brewster Art Gallery. The foundation has been instrumental in furthering Lye's work. The *Wind Wand* is the most visible and largest product of their efforts but the foundation has also been instrumental in creating Lye's *Water Whirler* on the Wellington waterfront (see p.470).

that his forest of 125 wind wands swaying together in the breeze will be built in the near future.

Landscaping and pathways stretch a couple of hundred metres either side of the *Wind Wand*, making a waterfront park that's pleasant for an evening stroll. More ambitious walkers can follow the **Coastal Walkway** that stretches some 3km in each direction.

Downtown New Plymouth

The **Govett-Brewster Art Gallery**, at the corner of Queen and King streets (daily 10.30am–5pm; free; Ⓦwww.govettbrewster.org.nz), is one of the country's finest contemporary art galleries. It is home to the **Len Lye Foundation**, owns a huge permanent collection of Lye's work, and as of 2010 will have a centre for exhibiting Lye's work adjacent to the gallery. Currently the gallery has only a small amount on display but some of Lye's films and a documentary on his life and work can usually be seen; if none are showing, ask. The gallery has no other permanent exhibits but puts on a series of temporary exhibitions with a contemporary bias. There's also a good art and design bookshop and an excellent café.

The other central highlight is **Puke Ariki**, St Aubyn Street (Mon–Fri 9am–6pm, Wed till 9pm, Sat & Sun 9am–5pm; free; Ⓦwww.pukeariki.com), a combined visitor centre, city **library**, interactive **regional museum and exhibition space**. The museum kicks off with the multimedia "Taranaki Experience" (12min; free), a rowdy promo for the province, but gets better upstairs, where the extensive Maori section includes the canoe that brought Taranaki Maori to New Zealand, and volcanic rock carvings and woodcarvings of a style unique to Taranaki. The museum site also encompasses **Richmond Cottage** on Ariki Street (Sat & Sun 11am–3.30pm; free), an 1854 stone dwelling built for local MP Christopher William Richmond, and moved to its current site in 1962.

Following Brougham Street south from Puke Ariki, you reach Vivian Street and the Frederick Thatcher-designed **St Mary's Church**, the oldest stone church in New Zealand. Built in 1845 along austere lines with an imposing gabled dark-wood interior, it contains a striking 1972 Maori memorial with carvings and *tukutuku* panels.

Immediately behind the church, Marsland Hill Reserve contains the **Observatory**, Robe Street (Tues: summer 8–10pm; winter 7.30–9.30pm; donation), where members of the Astronomical Society volunteer to point out highlights in the night sky for visitors.

Pukekura Park

One of New Zealand's finest city parks backs Downtown New Plymouth, **Pukekura Park and Brooklands** (daily dawn–dusk; free). The Pukekura section is mostly semi-formal, with glasshouses, a boating lake and a cricket pitch. The more freely laid out Brooklands section occupies the grounds of a long-gone homestead and includes the **Bowl of Brooklands** outdoor amphitheatre and numerous mature trees, among them a 2000-year-old puriri and a big ginkgo. Nearby, a former colonial hospital from 1847 is now the **Gables** (Jan daily 1–4pm; Feb–Dec Sat & Sun 1–4pm; free), containing an art gallery and medical museum. The area is best on summer evenings when the Pukekura section is given over to the annual **festival of lights** (mid-Dec to mid-Feb nightly dusk–10.45pm; free), a good time to walk gorgeously lit pathways between illuminated trees, and take out rowing boats festooned with lights while listening to live music, most nights.

Paritutu Rock and the Sugar Loaf Marine Reserve

New Plymouth's port and ugly power station lie 4km west of the town centre at the foot of the 200-metre-high **Paritutu Rock**, a feature of great cultural significance to Maori and a near-perfect natural fortress that still marks the boundary between Taranaki and Te Atiawa territories. Despite its cultural significance you are free to climb from a car park on Centennial Drive, signposted off Vivian Street. It's a steep scramble (20–50min return) with a steel rope providing support, but the reward is a great view of the coast and cluster of rocky islands that comprise the DOC-administered **Sugar Loaf Marine Reserve**. These eroded remnants of ancient volcanoes were occupied by Maori but were given their name by Captain Cook in 1770. The islands provide sanctuary for rare plants, little blue penguins, petrels and sooty shearwaters; the surrounding waters harbour abundant marine life, including 67 species of fish and a wealth of multicoloured anemones, sponges and seaweeds in undersea canyons. Humpback whales (Aug & Sept) and dolphins (Oct–Dec) migrate past the islands and the tidal rocks are populated by New Zealand's northernmost breeding colony of fur seals. The islands themselves are off-limits, but Chaddy's Charters run mildly eccentric **trips** around them (3 daily; 1hr; $30; ⓣ06/758 9133) in an old lifeboat, launched at high tide from its shed at Ocean View Parade marina, 3km west of downtown, otherwise boarded from the jetty.

Carrington Street

If you have your own wheels follow Carrington Street (which later becomes Carrington Road) south of the city towards the Taranaki foothills. First stop, 8km south, is the historic **Hurworth Cottage**, 906 Carrington Rd (Sat & Sun 11am–3pm and by appointment; $5; ⓣ06/753 3593). Built in 1856, the original occupier was Harry Atkinson, four times Prime Minister of New Zealand, famous for advocating women's suffrage and introducing welfare benefits.

Around 20km from New Plymouth lies **Pukeiti**, 2290 Carrington St (daily: Sept–March 9am–5pm; April–Aug 10am–3pm; $12; ⓦwww.pukeiti.org.nz), a rainforest garden with New Zealand's largest collection of rhododendrons and azaleas, best seen in October and November during the **rhododendron festival**.

Eating, drinking and entertainment

The majority of the cafés, restaurants, bars and clubs are on what is known as the **Devon Mile**, along Devon Street between Dawson and Eliot streets. Also along here is the Top Town Cinema 5, 119–125 Devon St East (ⓣ06/759 9077), showing mainstream **movies**. In recent times a second culinary hotspot has sprung up at Port Taranaki, where if you fancy harbourside dining you could do worse than *Bach on the Breakwater*, or *Gusto*.

For those of a more cultural persuasion, the biennial **Taranaki Festival of the Arts** (ⓦwww.taranakifest.org.nz) takes place every odd-numbered year at venues all over town in late July and early August. Lasting around three weeks, it's the biggest provincial arts festival in New Zealand. In mid-March the city hosts **WOMAD**, a three-day festival of world music (ⓦwww.womad.co.nz).

Andre 37–43 Brougham St (ⓣ06/758 4812). Stunning, legendary New Plymouth eatery where local ingredients are cooked to perfection with a guiding French influence, brought by the ruddy-faced Andre, something of a local character. Mains $35–45.

Arborio in Puke Ariki, overlooking the *Wind Wand* (ⓣ06/759 1241). A brilliant, licensed, modern café with imaginative breakfasts, including bubble and squeak, and delicious dinners ranging from steaks to clams, with DJ Fridays and Jazz Sundays.

Daily News Café Level 1 in the library, Ariki St. Small, tranquil daytime café, stocked with newspapers from across the country and around the world, serving coffee and snacks.
Elixar 117 Devon St East. Daytime café, with a small, well-made selection of panini, bagels and wraps. Closed Sun.
Marinovich's 19 Brougham St ☎06/758 4749. Fish and seafood restaurant that's been going in New Plymouth since 1927. Wonderfully fresh fish and good steaks (from $30).
Matinee 69 Devon St West. A cool all-day café, coffee shop and bar that gets lively on Friday and Saturday nights with DJs and bands.
Metropol Corner of King & Egmont sts ☎06/758 9788. A relaxed and airy restaurant with an imaginative European-influenced menu, and dishes around the $30 mark. They're well presented, tasty and accompanied by a select range of wines (many by the glass).
The Mill 2 Courtenay St. A massive converted flour mill with several bars for the late-night crowd, a wide range of beers and snacks, and live bands (or more likely a DJ playing Top 40 hits) at weekends.
Peggy Gordon's Celtic Bar Corner of Egmont & Devon sts With pictures of Irish and Scottish folk heroes on the walls, an extensive range of single malt whiskies, twelve beers on tap, meals under $20 and live Irish music on Fri & Sat nights, it's no surprise that this is a popular haunt for both locals and travellers. The *Basement Bar* showcases alternative bands.

Listings

Automobile Association 49–55 Powderham St ☎06/968 7840.
Banks and exchange Banks have branches along or just off Devon St. Holiday Shoppe, 120 Devon St East (☎06/968 3707) does foreign exchange and is the American Express agent.
Bike rental $20 a day at Cycle Inn, 133 Devon St East (☎06/758 7418).
Camping and outdoor equipment Kiwi Outdoors, 18 Ariki St (☎06/758 4152), rent and sell outdoor gear and camping equipment, including ice axes and crampons. They also have kayaks from $45 a day.
Car rental Major operators at the airport, local agencies include Russell Rentals (☎06/751 0772), who have vehicles from $40 a day.
Medical treatment There's medical and dental care and a pharmacy (daily 8.30am–9pm) at Medicross, Richmond Centre, 8 Egmont St (☎06/759 8915).
Post office The main post office, with a poste restante service, is at 21 Currie St (Mon–Fri 7.30am–5.30pm, Sat 9am–1pm).
Swimming The New Plymouth Aquatic Centre, Tisch Ave, Kawaroa Park (☎06/759 6060; daily till 7pm or later), is a massive complex with indoor and outdoor pools, water slides, wave machine, gym and fitness suite.

Egmont National Park

The whole western third of the North Island is dominated by **Taranaki** (Mount Egmont) a dormant volcano that last erupted in 1755. Its profile is a cone rising to 2518 metres, a purity of form favourably compared to Japan's Mount Fuji. In winter, snow blankets the mountain but as summer progresses only the crater remains white. The mountain is the focal point for **EGMONT NATIONAL PARK**, the boundary forming an arc with a ten-kilometre radius around the mountain, interrupted only on its north side where it encompasses the **Kaitake Range**, an older more weathered cousin of Taranaki.

Farmland lies all about, but within the national park the mountain's lower slopes are cloaked in native bush that gradually changes to stunted flag-form trees, lopsidedly shaped by the constant buffeting of the wind. Higher still, vegetation gives way to slopes of loose scoria (a kind of jagged volcanic gravel), hard work if you're hiking.

Three sealed roads climb the sides of the mountain, all on the eastern side, all ending a little under halfway up at car parks from where the park's 140km of walking tracks spread out. Of these **North Egmont** is the most easily accessible from New Plymouth but you can get higher up the mountain on the road through **East Egmont**; and there's particularly good walking (and the best

Maori in the modern world

Comprising roughly fifteen percent of the population, New Zealand's Maori are the country's largest minority. These days Maori culture is cool: it fascinates and inspires because of its voyaging history, its strong tribal customs and its contemporary take on traditional artistry. Interwoven with these appealing physical forms is a deep spirituality that connects the people with the natural world and their ancestors. The following is a glimpse of what it means to be Maori, and how visitors are likely to tap into it – there's more extensive coverage on issues and

Tino rangatiratanga flag ▲

The haka ▼

Maori identity

New Zealand's Maori have never been **marginalized** like Native Americans or Australian Aborigines. There are no reservations, and Maori take part in all walks of life – as lawyers, MPs, university lecturers, even as the Governor-General (the Queen's representative in New Zealand). But all is not rosy. Average incomes are lower than those of Pakeha, almost half of all prison inmates are Maori, only around a quarter of Maori achieve post-school qualifications and Maori health statistics make appalling reading.

There is considerable **intermarriage** between Maori and Pakeha, a fact that led one academic to speculate "race relations will be worked out in the bedrooms of New Zealand". Government policy calls for a **bicultural** approach, whereby everyone lives, works and plays together, but white and brown peoples can maintain a distinct identity. Among the more radical factions of Maoridom (see p.889), there are calls for Maori sovereignty under the banner of **Tino rangatiratanga**, meaning Maori control of all things Maori. Supporters might fly the flag at home or sport a T-shirt bearing the movement's symbol – a stylized white fern frond between fields of red and black.

Knowledge of **whakapapa** (tribal lineage) is central to a sense of place in the Maori world. At any formal event, elders will recite their *whakapapa*, stretching as far back as the canoes that their ancestors first came to New Zealand in, then honour the mountains, rivers, forests and seas that give meaning to their people. **Oratory**, and the ability to produce a song at a moment's notice are both highly valued. One Maori concept that has crossed over to general Kiwi culture is that of **mana**, a synthesis of prestige, charisma and influence, which increases through brave or compassionate actions and is reduced by foolish or lazy ones.

Kawa, hongi and hangi

The most direct and popular introduction to Maori culture is a **concert and hangi** (feast). Virtually all visitors to Rotorua attend one of these, generally authentic, gigs and it's also possible to visit one in Christchurch or Queenstown.

Both concert and *hangi* usually take place on a **marae**, a traditional compound that acts as meeting place, cultural hub, drop-in centre and spiritual home for a *hapu*, or group of extended families. **Kawa** (protocols) governing behaviour dictate that visitors must be challenged to determine friendly intent before being allowed onto the *marae*. As visitors, you elect a "chief" who represents you during this **wero**, where a fearsome warrior bears down on you with twirling **taiaha** (long club), flicking tongue and bulging eyes. Once a ritual gift has been accepted, the women make the **karanga** (welcoming call), followed by their **powhiri** (sung welcome). This acts as a prelude to ceremonial touching of noses, **hongi**, binding hosts and visitors.

And so begins the concert, performed in traditional costume. Highlights are the men's **haka**, familiar to all rugby fans, and the women's **poi dance**, in which tennis-ball-sized clumps of a kind of bulrush are swung rhythmically about the body and head. The concert is followed by the **hangi**, a feast traditionally steamed in an earth oven or, in Rotorua, over a geothermal vent.

▲ Hongi, the ceremonial touching of noses

▼ Wero – a challenge and a greetinga

▼ Poi dance

Hei tiki ▲

Traditional moko tatoo ▼

Exploring Northland with Taiamai Tours ▼

Carving and tattooing

Maori **woodcarving** is unmistakable, with a dense background of swirls, organic forms and fern fronds, overlaid with stylized figures and often inset with paua (abalone) shell. One, often repeated, element is the ancestor figure, the **hei tiki**, a human form distorted as to be almost unrecognizable, except for the challenge of a protruding tongue. Several places around the country offer the opportunity to try your hand at carving, usually on bone.

There's a more restrained style to carved **pounamu** (greenstone). Some of the best pieces follow ancient styles, featuring large areas of highly polished *pounamu* set off by small areas of intricately worked swirls. In recent years there's also been a return to the art of **moko** (tattooing), in which highly symbolic patterns are carved into a person's face from their teens onwards, reflecting birthright and key achievements. Today you'll usually see *moko* on arms, legs and back, but some Maori have gone for full-face *moko*.

Experiencing Maori culture

While the elements of concert and *hangi* nights are authentic enough, the ensemble can seem contrived. The following tours and lodgings offer opportunities to dig deeper.

Footprints Waipoua, Northland. See p.224.
Kapiti Island, near Wellington. See p.292.
Maori Tours, Kaikoura. See p.560.
Taiamai Tours, Northland. See p.189.
Waka Tours, Whanganui See p.275.

alpine accommodation) around **Dawson Falls**. Both the DOC office and visitor centre in New Plymouth have **information** on the park, and anyone interested in relatively easy hikes should obtain DOC's *Short Walks in Egmont National Park* brochure ($2.50). The main **visitor centre** is in North Egmont (see below).

Although the hike to the **summit** is exhausting and shouldn't be underestimated, it is possible in a day for anyone reasonably fit. The upper mountain is off limits to ordinary hikers in winter, but even during the **hiking season** (Jan to mid-April) bad weather, including occasional snow, sweeps in frighteningly quickly, and hikers starting off on a fine morning frequently find themselves groping through low cloud before the day is through. Deaths occur far too often: be sure to consult our **hiking advice** in Basics (see p.63) and get further advice and an up-to-date **weather forecast** from local visitor centres or DOC offices. You should always take **warm clothing**, at any time of year, climb with at least one companion or a mountain guide, and leave a **record of your intentions**. A free DOC information sheet supplied by the visitor centres outlines the routes, covered on pp.267–268. Ideally carry an **ice axe**, which can be rented from Kiwi Outdoors in New Plymouth (see p.264).

Transport and guides

With accommodation close to all three major trailheads, it makes sense for avid hikers to base themselves inside the park. Day visitors can easily visit from New Plymouth, Stratford (see p.268) or Hawera (see p.269) with all trailheads accessible in under an hour by **car**. **Shuttle buses** run from New Plymouth and Stratford, Cruise NZ Tours (ⓣ06/758 3222, ⓔkirkstall@xtra.co.nz; $38 return), dropping off at 7.30am in North Egmont, picking up at 4.30pm. Alternatively, try Taranaki Tours (ⓣ0800/886 877, ⓦwww.taranakitours.com; $40 return, on demand), who also run round the mountain trips (full-day $135).

If you'd rather go on **guided walks**, call either Adventure Dynamics (ⓣ06/751 3589, ⓦwww.adventuredynamics.co.nz) or Mac Alpine (ⓣ0800/866 484, ⓦwww.macalpineguides.com). Both offer bushwalking, guided summit treks and a range of more technical stuff. Guides will take up to ten clients for summer hiking and summit attempts but perhaps only two for winter expeditions, rock climbing or instruction. Guiding rates are around $350 a day, plus $50 for each extra person in the summer and start at $400 a day in the winter. If you're here in February try to join one of the local **alpine clubs**' inexpensive day-trips to the summit, enquire through DOC.

Egmont Village and North Egmont

The easiest access point to the park, and the closest to New Plymouth, is tiny **Egmont Village**, 13km southeast of New Plymouth on SH3. From here, the sixteen-kilometre sealed Egmont Road runs up the mountain to **North Egmont** (960m), the best base for summit ascents. Before heading up (or out on any of the numerous easier tracks), be sure to call at the park's main information source, the **North Egmont visitor centre** (daily: Oct–April 8am–4pm; May–Sept 8.30am–4pm; ⓣ06/756 0990, ⓔnevc@doc.govt.nz), that has displays about the mountain, maps of all the tracks, good viewing windows, weather updates and a decent café.

Short walks around North Egmont include an unusual and atmospheric **tramp** (1km loop; 45min–1hr; 100m ascent), through the hidden valley of the Goblin Forest, with its kaikawaka trees, alpine plants and gnarled trunks hung with ferns and mosses. There's also the **Veronica Loop Track** (2.5km loop;

2hr; 200m ascent) which climbs to a ridge through mountain forest and scrub, with fine views of the ancient lava flows known as Humphries Castle, and beyond to New Plymouth and the coast. Note that the supply of **water** at North Egmont is limited, so bring some with you.

Basic backpacker-style **accommodation** can be found at the *Camp House* (ⓣ0800/688 2727, ⓦwww.mttaranaki.co.nz; dorm $28, ❷), a large mountain hut built in 1891. It has bunks, a communal lounge with electric heating, a full kitchen and hot showers. Check-in is at the *Mountain Café* in the visitor centre (generally 8am–7pm). For non-guests, the *Camp House* offers services such as secure parking, use of a locker and a post-hike shower ($10). If you're heading up the mountain and expect to be back after the café closes, order in advance and they'll leave a ready-to-heat meal for you at the *Camp House*. A Nearby alternative is *Rahiri Cottage*, (ⓣ0800/688 2727, ⓦwww.mttaranaki.co.nz; ❺), a gatehouse by the park entrance.

East Egmont

The highest road on the mountain goes through **East Egmont**, a parking area and site of the *Mountain House* hotel, reached from Stratford, by the Pembroke Road from where it runs 14km west to East Egmont, then 3.5km to **The Plateau**. On the upper route of the Around the Mountain Circuit (see p.267), The Plateau is a rugged and windswept spot 1172m up on Taranaki's flanks, acting as the wintertime parking area for the tiny **Manganui Ski-field** (ⓦwww.snow.co.nz/manganui).

From East Egmont, the **Curtis Falls Track** (3.5km return; 2–3hr; 120m ascent) is part of the lower Around the Mountain Circuit and crosses several streams, via steps and ladders, to the Manganui River Gorge, where you can follow the riverbed (no track or signs) to the base of a waterfall. The **Enchanted Track** (3km one way; 3hr return; 300m ascent) also begins at the car park, heading through dense vegetation before climbing to The Plateau.

Accommodation is available at the beautifully sited, completely revamped *Mountain House* (ⓣ0800/668 682; ❹), 846m above sea level, with en-suite rooms and self-contained chalets, and a **restaurant** dishing up reliable mains from $30. The management also run *Anderson's Alpine Lodge* (same contact details; ❻), a chalet-style building with three B&B rooms, 5km downhill.

Dawson Falls

The most southerly access up Taranaki follows Manaia Road to **Dawson Falls**, roughly 23km west of Stratford and 900m above sea level. Here you'll find the **Dawson Falls visitor centre** (8.30am–4pm; ⓣ0274/430 248), outside of which stands an impressive eight-metre *pou whenua* (carved pole) depicting famous Maori associated with the area.

Only experienced hikers should tackle the summit from here (see p.267), but several easier tracks branch off from the visitor centre, notably a short one to the historic Dawson Falls Power Station, a small hydro plant providing power for the *Dawson Falls Mountain Lodge* since 1935.

An obvious goal is the seventeen-metre-high **Dawson Falls** (600m return; 40min; 30m ascent) that plummet over the end of an ancient lava flow. This hike begins down the road and can be extended along the **Kapuni Walk** (1km return; 1hr; 50m ascent). Another walk leads to **Wilkies Pool** (1km loop; 1hr; 100m ascent), where the waters of the Kapuni Gorge rush through a staircase of rock pools, and there's a tougher hike to **Hasties Hill** (2km; 1hr 30min–2hr; 100m ascent) involving a passage across the flank of the mountain to a lookout, returning the same way.

At Dawson Falls there's budget **accommodation** at *Konini Lodge* (☎06/756 0990; $20), an oversized hikers' hut, sleeping eight (bring a sleeping bag), with a communal lounge, hot showers and a kitchen equipped with stoves and fridges. You can go more upmarket at the nearby *Dawson Falls Maintain Lodge* (☎06/765 5457, ⓦwww.dawson-falls.co.nz), with views from most rooms and a bar and/or sauna for when the weather clags in. They offer a dinner, bed and breakfast deal (single $215, double $350), and non-guests can also dine (mains $20–30). TVs and radios are intentionally absent, and there's a simple daytime **café**.

Summit hikes and circuit hikes

There are two main **summit routes**, both requiring a full day, so set off early, around 7.30am. Ice axes and crampons are necessary up to January if you are visiting the crater. If you want to spend longer than a day on the mountain and are happy to forgo the summit climb, the **Pouakai Circuit** or the testing **Around the Mountain Circuit** (the latter for the most dedicated climbers only) might fit the bill. For those looking to explore the park further, note that a survey is being undertaken by DOC to introduce a new track, the Three Peaks. Loosely based around a three-day tramp taking in the summit of Taranaki, the Pouakai Range and the Kaitake Range, it's essentially a 40km line heading from North Egmont toward the sea. Check with DOC to see if it's in place.

Summit routes

The **Northern Route** (10km return; 6–8hr; 1560m ascent) is the most accessible, beginning at the top car park at North Egmont and initially following the gravel Translator Road (the appropriately named "Puffer") to Tahurangi Lodge, a private hut run by the Taranaki Alpine Club. A wooden stairway leads to North Ridge, after that you're onto slopes of scoria up the Lizard Ridge leading to the crater. After crossing the crater ice and a short scoria slope, you reach the summit.

The longer and poorly marked **Southern Route** (11km return; 8–10hr; 1620m ascent) is a more exacting proposition, suitable only for those with extensive mountain experience; you'll need crampons and ice axes year-round. The route starts at the Dawson Falls car park and climbs through bush before making a rapid ascent up a staircase to the Lake Dive Track. From there on, the ascent involves a steep and exhausting series of zigzags up scoria slopes.

The Around the Mountain Circuit

Dedicated hikers should consider tackling the **Around the Mountain Circuit** (44km; 3–5 days), an irregular loop around Taranaki varying in altitude from 500m to 1500m. The track is not fully maintained, so check conditions with DOC and in the absence of a printed leaflet, obtain the appropriate Topomap. From December through to February, the snow melts enough for hikers to occasionally loop off the main track onto the more strenuous **high-level route**, essentially making a few shortcuts by heading higher up the slopes. This way you can shave a day off the lower circuit. There are six well-spaced **huts** along the way ($10 except for the tiny Kahui hut, $5); use your DOC annual hut passes (see p.62) or buy tickets from the DOC visitor centres. **Camping** ($5) is only allowed outside the huts.

The Pouakai Circuit

Starting at North Egmont, the **Pouakai Circuit** (25km loop; 2 days) turns its back on the big mountain and heads north around the lower Pouakai

Range, from where views of Taranaki can be wonderful. The track varies in altitude from 700m to 1300m. Get advice from DOC before embarking. The route has two huts, the 36-bed Holly Hut, which can get very busy, and the less popular 16-bed Pouakai Hut ($10 each). Camping is only allowed outside the huts ($5).

Stratford

SH3 and SH3a meet at **Inglewood**, a nondescript service town worth a brief stop to sample fare from *MacFarlane's Café*, in an 1878 building at the corner of Kelly and Matai streets. Just over halfway between New Plymouth and Hawera, 23km south of Inglewood, is **STRATFORD**, providing direct access to the slopes of Mount Taranaki, particularly East Egmont and Dawson Falls. If you're bound for the centre of the North Island, Stratford marks the start of the **Forgotten World Highway** (see p.255). The town is not an attractive place, though it does have a kitsch mock-Elizabethan **clock tower** (built in 1996 to hide the 1920s version), from which a life-size Romeo and Juliet emerge to mark the hour (at 10am, 1pm and 3pm), accompanied by recordings of Shakespearean quotes. The logical extension of Stratford's Shakespearian theme is that every street name is a character from the bard's plays. From Stratford, 11km toward Mount Taranaki, however, one place of interest can be accessed, the Possum Fur and Leather Shop, 1103 Opunake Rd (ⓣ06/764 6133, ⓦwww.envirofur.co.nz), who are protecting New Zealand's native bush by offering truly lovely products made from possum, including some of the softest leather on the planet.

InterCity and Dalroy Express (ⓣ0508/465 622) **buses** stop outside the **i-SITE visitor centre** on Prospero Place (Mon–Fri 8.30am–5pm, Sat & Sun 10am–3pm; ⓣ06/765 6708, ⓦwww.stratford.govt.nz, ⓔinfo@stratford.govt.nz), up an alley opposite the clock tower.

Love of the bard may induce you to stay, in which case try the well-cared-for *Stratford Top 10 Holiday Park*, 10 Page St (ⓣ06/656 6440, ⓔstratfordtoppark@hotmail.com; camping $14, dorms in backpackers lodge $23, cabins ❶, units ❸), which is central and has bike rental for $25 a day. For something much more rural, visit *Sarsen House Country Lodge*, 636 Stanley Rd (ⓣ06/762 8775, ⓦwww.tepopo.co.nz; ❻), 15km northeast of Stratford amid the lovingly tended Te Popo gardens, offering en-suite rooms and an apartment ($170 per night for two, minimum stay three nights). You can self-cater or get dinner by arrangement ($45 including wine). In Stratford, next to the visitor centre is *Collage*, an airy, licensed **café** serving delicious meals into the evening.

Along SH45: the Surf Highway

You can either follow the eastern or western routes round Taranaki, but if you have time the best is the **Surf Highway** (SH45) from New Plymouth to Hawera, mostly running about 3km inland, with roads leading down to tiny uninhabited bays. It runs for about 100km, but its beachy charms can consume half a day, longer if you want to go surfing. Among surfers it is still something of a backwater but its glassy, even breaks offer consistent surfing. **Windsurfing** is good too, with near constant onshore winds. Surf beaches are everywhere, but the only surf-oriented communities are **Oakura**, increasingly populated by New Plymouth commuters, and **Opunake**, with more of a beach-resort feel. Between is **Cape Egmont**, with its picturesque lighthouse.

Oakura

Seventeen kilometres west of New Plymouth, **OAKURA** is a dormitory community retaining a hint of counter-cultural spirit thanks to board-riders, here to experience the best windsurfing beach in Taranaki. For **surfboard rental**, go to Vertigo, 605 Main St (ⓣ06/752 7363, ⓦthewavehaven.co.nz), who also have windsurfing gear, ($75 for a 2hr lesson).

If you want **to stay**, try the *Oakura Beach Holiday Park*, 2 Jan Terrace (ⓣ06/752 7861, ⓦwww.oakurabeach.com; camping $14, cabins ❷ unit ❹), with an on-site café; or head 4km southwest along SH45 to *Wave Haven* (who also run Vertigo, above), corner of SH45 and Ahu Ahu Road (ⓣ06/752 7800, ⓦwww.thewave.haven.co.nz; dorm $20, ❷), a low-key backpackers with good weekly rates. Ahu Ahu Road runs for 3km down to the coast and to *Ahu Ahu Beach Villas* at no. 321 (ⓣ06/752 7370, ⓦwww.ahu.co.nz; ❼), several gorgeous self-contained villas sleeping four, on a rise overlooking the ocean, built from an intriguing blend of salvaged materials with luxurious modern fittings. For food **try** the licensed *Café Wunderbar*, just before the BP station on SH45 and opposite the pharmacy (closed Mon).

Cape Egmont and Opunake

At Pungarehu, about 25km southwest of Oakura, Cape Road cuts 5km west to the cast-iron tower of **Cape Egmont Lighthouse**, moved here in 1877 from Mana Island, north of Wellington. It perches on a rise on the westernmost point of the cape overlooking Taranaki's windswept coast, a great spot around sunset with the mountain glowing behind.

The real surfing hub in these parts is 20km on at **Opunake**, a large village with a golden beach and little to do but swim, surf and cast a line. Try the Opunake Surf Co (Dreamtime), at the corner of Havelock and Tasman streets for board and gear rental.

Places to **stay** include the beachside *Opunake Beach Holiday Camp*, Beach Road (ⓣ0800/758 009, ⓔopunakebeach@xtra.co.nz; camping $13.50, on-site caravans ❶, cottages ❷), and *Opunake Motel and Backpackers*, 36 Heaphy Rd (ⓣ06/761 8330, ⓔopunakemotel@xtra.co.nz; ❷), which has motel units ❸ and a cottage ❹. The best place to **eat** is the upbeat *Sugar Juice Café*, 42–44 Tasman St (licensed; Tues–Sun daytime, plus Wed–Sat evening), which also does takeaways.

Hawera

A tidy town of eight thousand souls surrounded by gently undulating dairy country, Hawera, is the meeting point of the eastern and western routes around Taranaki. A service and administration centre for the district's farmers, Hawera's survival depends on the fortunes of the world's largest **dairy complex** south of town. Year-round it handles twenty percent of the country's milk production, mostly gathered from the rich volcanic soils of Taranaki but also brought by rail from other parts of the North Island. For entertainment try the **Tawhiti Museum** or possibly a bit of **dam dropping**.

The town and around

Hawera is dominated by its former **water tower** (daily 10am–2pm; $2), a 54-metre concrete structure offering views over South Taranaki. Completed in 1914 to help fight devastating fires, the tower casts its shadow over the birthplace and hometown of one of New Zealand's most celebrated authors, **Ronald Hugh Morrieson** (see p.918), who loved jazz, wrote well-observed and amusing Gothic novels about small-town life and liked a drink or two. The only memorial to his existence is *Morrieson's Café and Bar*, near the junction of Victoria and High streets, containing a few of his books, the old staircase from his house and tabletops made from timbers salvaged from the said building before it was demolished to make way for *KFC*.

Continuing the quirky theme is the **Elvis Presley Memorial Record Room**, 51 Argyle St (visits by appointment; ⓣ06/278 7624, ⓦwww.digitalus.co.nz/elvis; donation), a garage-shrine to the King. About ten minutes' walk from the visitor centre, it contains thousands of rare recordings, photographs and memorabilia.

The most interesting attraction hereabouts is the **Tawhiti Museum and Bush Railway**, 401 Ohangai Rd (Jan daily 10am–4pm; June–Aug Sun 10am–4pm; Sept–Dec & Feb–May Mon & Fri–Sun 10am–4pm; $10, with its own café; ⓦwww.tawhitimuseum.co.nz); just off Tawhiti Road, 4km east of Normanby, in turn 6km north of Hawera. The unique and ever expanding exhibits bring the past to life, using a multitude of life-size figurines modelled on local people by owner and creator, Nigel Ogle. The social and technological heritage of both Maori and Pakeha is explored through the extensive use of photographs, models and dioramas, some of the most impressive being representations of *pa* sites. Other highlights include a diorama of 800 miniatures depicting the 1820s musket wars; an extraordinary account of the 1860s Land Wars, seen through the eyes of a deserter from the British Army who lived out his days with the Ngati Ruanui tribe; and a small-scale **bush railway** (first Sun in the month; during school holidays also every public holiday & every Sun; $3) that trundles 1km through displays recounting Taranaki's logging history.

For something more adventerous try **dam dropping** ($100), a variation on whitewater sledging conducted by Kaitiaki Adventures (ⓣ06/752 8242, ⓦwww.damdrop.com). You'll be equipped with a buoyant plastic sledge, wetsuit, helmet and fins, ready to slide six to nine metres down the face of a dam. This is more fun (and less scary) than it sounds and you can do it as many times as you like before the gentle, guided, scenic float down the Wainongoro River.

Practicalities

Long-distance **buses** stop at the **i-SITE visitor centre**, 55 High St (Mon–Fri 8.30am–5.15pm, Sat & Sun 10am–3pm; ⓣ06/278 8599, ⓔvisitorinfo@stdc.govt.nz), found near the base of the water tower. There's no local transport other than taxis (ⓣ06/278 7171).

It's not really worth staying but if you need to, the cheapest **accommodation** is in the *King Edward Park Motorcamp*, 70 Waihi Rd (ⓣ & ⓕ06/278 8544; camping $8, cabins ❶). More expensive is boutique B&B in a grand 1875 kauri mansion called *Tairoa Lodge*, at the corner of Puawai Street and SH3 (ⓣ06/278 8603, ⓦwww.tairoa-lodge.co.nz; ❻), with a pool, mature grounds, en-suite rooms, a two-bedroom cottage and dinners on request (from $45). Out of town you'll find the peaceful and charming *Wheatly Downs Farmstay*, 484 Ararata St (ⓣ06/278 6523, ⓦwww.mttaranaki.co.nz; tent sites $16, dorms $28, ❷–❸), 5km past the Tawhiti Museum, with views of Mount Taranaki.

For eating, there's not much choice: *Mr Badger's* at the Tawhiti Museum, *Morrieson's Cafe and Bar*, or *II Chefs*, 47 High St (closed Mon & Sun).

Patea and Bushy Park

Cutting through heavily cultivated farmland, SH3 splits **PATEA**, the only major community between Hawera and Wanganui. The township has a model of the *Aotea* canoe at the western end of the main street, commemorating the settlement of the area by Turi and his *hapu*; a good surfing beach at the mouth of the Patea River; and a safe freshwater swimming hole, overlooked by the Manawapou Redoubt and *pa* site.

Some 47km southeast of Patea, 16km northwest of Wanganui, a well-signposted side road runs 8km east to **Bushy Park Homestead & Forest**, 791 Rangitatau East Rd (daily 10am–5pm; $6, children free; Ⓦwww.bushypark.co.nz). The park is the prime attraction in this area not for the charming historic homestead, B&B, backpackers or café but the native bush threaded by tracks. Encircled by a five-kilometre fence, the bush has witnessed the reintroduction of several native birds (North Island robins, moreporks and flocks of kereru) and allows Bushy Park to participate in the Operation Nest Egg programme (see *Protecting New Zealand's native wildlife* colour section). North Island brown kiwi run wild in the Park and it will soon be possible to participate in evening tours ($20, or accommodation and meal packages) whereby visitors can see them in the wild. An extension of this is the exciting prospect of joining rangers on monitoring trips, as part of the breeding programme: tracking tagged infant kiwi through bush at night to weighing and checking their progress (around $100, though this is still to be confirmed).

You'd need a couple of days to fully explore the bush tracks, but many are content to simply stroll the Ratanui Track (20min loop) past New Zealand's largest **rata tree**, 43m tall and 12m in circumference. The daytime entry fee gives access to the 1906 homestead (free guided tours on request), containing some attractive stained-glass windows at the entrance and a carved over-mantel and fireplace in the dining room. A Devonshire tea or light meal taken on the veranda or in the former billiard room seems entirely appropriate and you can **stay** overnight (Ⓣ06/342 9879, Ⓦwww.bushypark-homestead.co.nz), in the homestead (B&B ⑤; shared bathrooms) or the simple bunkhouse ($25; self-catering; bring a sleeping bag). Dinner is available by arrangement.

Whanganui National Park

The emerald-green Whanganui River tumbles from the northern slopes of Mount Tongariro to the Tasman Sea at Wanganui, passing through the **WHANGANUI NATIONAL PARK**, a vast swathe of barely inhabited and virtually trackless bush country east of Taranaki. The park contains one of the largest remaining tracts of lowland forest in the North Island, growing on a bed of soft sandstone and mudstone (*papa*) that has been eroded to form deep gorges, sharp ridges, sheer cliffs and waterfalls. Beneath the canopy of broad-leaved podocarps and mountain beech, an understorey of tree ferns and clinging plants extends down to the riverbanks, while abundant and vociferous **birdlife** includes the kereru (native pigeon), fantail, tui, robin, grey warbler, tomtit and brown kiwi.

The best way to explore the Whanganui National Park is on a multi-day **canoe trip**, providing a safe and reliable route to the wilderness well furnished with riverside campsites, as well as *marae* and lodge accommodation. You can also hike on two major tracks, relatively easy going despite the rugged country. The most popular exit point for canoe trips is **Pipiriki**, there's little to the place except for a few houses and offices for a couple of jetboat operators, running trips upstream, and a welcome café caravan.

Most, who aren't taking a river trip, drive the **roads** that nibble at the fringes. SH43 provides limited access to the northwest but only the slow and winding

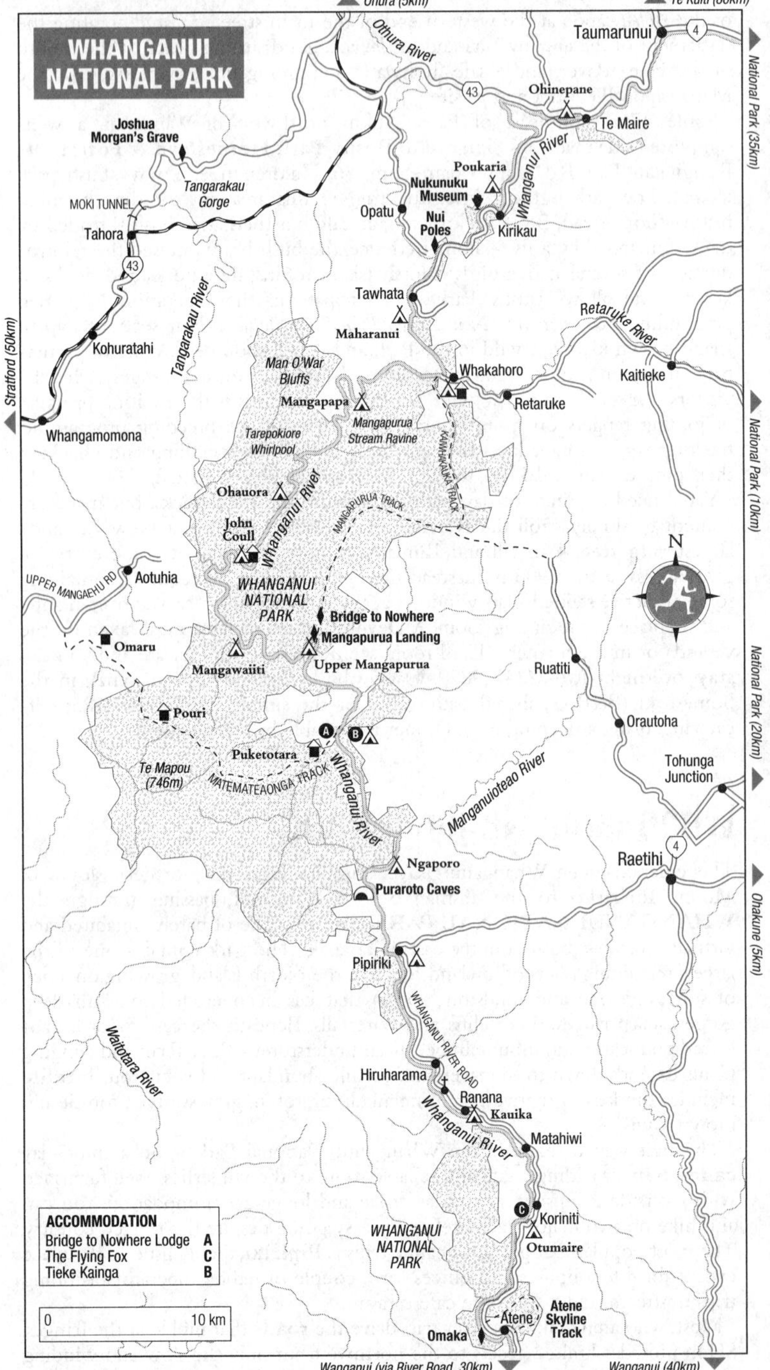
WHANGANUI NATIONAL PARK
Ohura (5km)
Te Kuiti (80km)
Taumarunui
National Park (35km)
Othura River
Ohinepane
Te Maire
Joshua Morgan's Grave
Tangarakau Gorge
MOKI TUNNEL
Tahora
Poukaria
Nukunuku Museum
Whanganui River
Opatu
Nui Poles
Kirikau
Tangarakau River
Tawhata
Maharanui
Retaruke River
Kohuratahi
Man O'War Bluffs
Whakahoro
Kaitieke
Stratford (50km)
Mangapapa
Retaruke
Whangamomona
Mangapurua Stream Ravine
Tarepokiore Whirlpool
KAIWHAKAUKA TRACK
National Park (10km)
Ohauora
MANGAPURUA TRACK
John Coull
Aotuhia
UPPER MANGAEHU RD
WHANGANUI NATIONAL PARK
Bridge to Nowhere
Mangapurua Landing
Omaru
Upper Mangapurua
Ruatiti
Mangawaiiti
National Park (20km)
Pouri
Orautoha
Puketotara
Te Mapou (746m)
MATEMATEAONGA TRACK
Tohunga Junction
Manganuioteao River
Raetihi
Ngaporo
Puraroto Caves
Ohakune (5km)
Pipiriki
WHANGANUI RIVER ROAD
Waitotara River
Hiruharama
Ranana
Kauika
Matahiwi
ACCOMMODATION
Bridge to Nowhere Lodge A
The Flying Fox C
Tieke Kainga B
Koriniti
Otumaire
WHANGANUI NATIONAL PARK
0 10 km
Atene
Atene Skyline Track
Omaka
Wanganui (via River Road, 30km)
Wanganui (40km)

Whanganui River Road stays near the river for any length of time. This runs off towards Wanganui from near Ohakune on the SH4, a seventy-kilometre drive south of Taumarunui.

Information on the national park and the river is most readily available from the DOC office in Wanganui (see p.280), from visitor centres in Wanganui and Taumarunui (see p.255), and from the widely available *In and Around the Whanganui National Park* booklet ($2.50).

Some history

At 329km, the Whanganui is New Zealand's longest navigable river, and one that plays an intrinsic part in the lives of local **Maori**, who hold that each river bend had a *kaitiaki* (guardian) who controlled the *mauri* (life force). The *mana* of the old riverside settlements depended upon the way in which the food supplies and living areas were maintained: sheltered terraces on the river-banks were cultivated and elaborate weirs constructed to trap eels and lamprey.

European missionaries arrived in the 1840s, and soon traders began to exploit the relatively easy route into the interior of the North Island, and by 1891 a regular boat service carried passengers and cargo to settlers establishing towns at Pipiriki and higher up at Taumarunui. In the early twentieth century **tourists** came too, making the Whanganui New Zealand's equivalent of the Rhine, with paddle steamers plying the waters to reach elegant hotels en route to Mount Ruapehu and central North Island.

European attempts to stamp their mark on this wild landscape have been ill-fated, in 1917 the **Mangapurua Valley**, in the middle of the park, was opened up for settlement by servicemen returning from World War I. Little did they realize they were trading one battlefield for another. Plagued by economic hardship, remoteness and difficulty of access, many had abandoned their farms by the 1930s. A concrete bridge over the Mangapurua Valley was opened in 1936, but after a major flood in 1942 the bridge was cut off, the three remaining families were ordered out, and the valley officially closed. Today, the only signs of habitation in the valley are the disappearing road, old fence lines, stands of exotic trees planted by the farmers, occasional brick chimneys and the poignant **Bridge to Nowhere**, a concrete span over a deep gorge that can be reached from the river or on the three-day Mangapurua Track.

With the coming of the railway and better roads, the riverboat tourist trade ceased in the 1920s but farms along the Whanganui continued to support a cargo and passenger service until the 1950s, thereafter the wilderness reclaimed land. This attracted recluses and visionaries fleeing the excesses of the civilized world, the most celebrated being poet **James K. Baxter**, who set up a commune in the 1970s and was held in great affection by local Maori. More recently the river was used extensively in the Vincent Ward movie *River Queen*.

Whanganui River trips

Canoes, kayaks and jetboats work the river, tailoring trips to your needs. The rapids are mostly Grade I with the occasional Grade II, making this an excellent paddling river for those with little or no experience. That said, the river shouldn't be underestimated: talk to operators about variations in river flows before embarking.

The navigable section of river starts at Cherry Grove in **Taumarunui**, site of a sporadically staffed DOC office. From here it is about two days' paddle to

Whakahoro, essentially just a DOC hut and a boat ramp at the end of a 45-kilometre road, mostly gravel, running west from SH4. Between these two points the river runs partly through farmland with roads nearby, and throws up a few rapids appreciably larger than those downstream (but still only Grade II). The journey also takes you past several spectacular water cascades and the **Nukunuku Museum** (entry by appointment; ⓣ07/896 6365). The collection was assembled by Jock Erceg (d. 2001), who spent the latter part of his life trawling the region's abandoned farmsteads, until eventually half the district started collecting ephemera for him.

Further on, a former stronghold of the Hau Hau (see p.400) is the site of a couple of **nui poles**. Here in 1862 the Hau Hau erected a war pole, **Rongo-nui**, with four arms indicating the cardinal points of the compass, intended to call warriors to their cause from all over the country. At the end of hostilities, a peace pole, **Rerekore**, was erected close by.

Downstream from Whakahoro, the rapids are generally Grade I and the paddling easier. You'll see the Mangapapa Stream Ravine, the **Man-o-war Bluff** (named for its supposed resemblance to an old iron-clad battleship) and the **Tarepokiore Whirlpool**, that once completely spun a river steamer. At Mangapurua Landing everyone stops for the easy walk to the **Bridge to Nowhere** (1hr 15min return), a trail that becomes the Mangapurua Track (see p.273) to Whakahoro. Further downstream you come to **Tieke Kainga** (aka Tieke Marae), a former DOC hut built on the site of an ancient *pa* that has been re-occupied by local Maori; you can stay or camp here or across the river at *Bridge to Nowhere Lodge*, an excellent base for river activities. The last stretch runs past the **Puraroto Caves** and into Pipiriki, where most paddlers finish.

River practicalities

The best source of practical **information** for river trips is the *Whanganui Journey* leaflet available from visitor centres and DOC offices in the region. The river is accessible all year, but the paddling **season** is generally from October to April, when all overnight river users must buy a **Hut and Camp Pass**. There are three options: "Taumarunui to Whakahoro only" ($10), valid for two days on the river plus a night in one of the three campsites along the upper section of river; "Full Journey" ($45), allowing five days on the river, with the intervening nights spent in any combination of huts and campsites, plus the *Tieke Kainga*; and the self-explanatory "Journey excluding Tieka Kainga" ($35), aimed mostly at those planning to stay at the *Bridge to Nowhere Lodge* (see p.275). As all passes carry a $15 surcharge if bought on the river itself, it's best to buy them at DOC offices or visitor centres in Taumarunui and Wanganui. One of these passes is generally included in the price of organized canoe trips, but it pays to check. From May to September, backcountry $10 hut tickets and annual passes are valid for the huts, and the campsites are free.

There are no shops along the river, so you need to take all your **supplies** with you: Taumarunui and Wanganui have the closest big supermarkets.

Accommodation

Apart from the huts and campsites, there's **accommodation** at the *Bridge to Nowhere Lodge* (ⓣ0800/480 308, ⓦwww.rivercitytours.co.nz), accessible by the river, which it overlooks. The lodge offers home cooking, a bar, simple bunkrooms, doubles and a twin, all sharing bathrooms; you can self-cater (from $45 per person) or go for a dinner, bed and breakfast deal (from $125). There is also a cabin that sleeps six (❶). Non-canoeists pay extra for a half-hour jetboat transfer from Pipiriki. Across the river is the relaxing *Tieke Kainga*, where you can stay in big sleeping huts for a small donation, or camp on terraces by the river (no alcohol allowed); if any of the residents are about, you'll be treated to an informal cultural experience. You can just turn up, or book ahead through the *Bridge to Nowhere Lodge*.

Jetboat trips and canoe rental

The quickest way to get about on the river is on **jetboat trips** (see below): they all run to the start of tramping tracks, drop off for a few days' hiking and take you pretty much anywhere else you fancy going, but the main destination is the Bridge to Nowhere, which is appreciably closer to Pipiriki. With each jetboat company competing for tourist dollars, the peace and isolation for which the river is famous is sometimes elusive.

The beauty, tranquillity and remoteness of the river are best appreciated on **canoeing** and **kayaking trips**. These range from one to five days, with most operators offering both **guided trips** as well as canoe or kayak **rentals**. The operators also supply most everything you need (except sleeping bags) and trips include transport to and from the river.

Taumarunui, National Park and Ohakune are the most common **bases**. Two-day canoe and kayak trips are normally on the upper section from Taumarunui to Whakahoro, but most people prefer the more scenic three-day run between Whakahoro and Pipiriki. Five-day marathons cover the whole stretch from Taumarunui to Pipiriki; few continue downstream from there.

Canoe tours and rentals

Blazing Paddles 1033 SH4, 10km south of central Taumarunui ☎0800/252 946, ⓦwww.blazingpaddles.co.nz. Gear rental for self-guided trips, with prices including drop-off, pick-up and the DOC Hut and Camp Pass; they can get you onto the water from Taumarunui, Whakahoro or Ohinepane.

Bridge to Nowhere ☎0800/480 308, ⓦwww.bridgetonowheretours.co.nz. Pipiriki-based operator offering combination trips – jetboating upstream and canoeing back down.

Canoe Safaris 6 Tay St, Ohakune ☎0800/272 335, ⓦwww.canoesafaris.co.nz. Top-end guided canoe trips, costing from $595 for three days. They also do canoe and kayak rentals, at a premium including transport to and from the river from Ohakune.

Wades Landing Outdoors ☎0800/226 631, ⓦwww.whanganui.co.nz. Whakahoro-based operator offering self-guided canoe and kayak trips, three days from Whakahoro to Pipiriki for $190. You can also kayak for a day downstream and catch a jetboat back ($120).

Waka Tours 19 George St, Raetihi ☎06/385 4811, ⓦwww.wakatours.net. Excellent three-day guided canoe tours ($610) from Whakahoro on the scenic middle reaches, during which you learn about the river environment from a Maori perspective in an effort to engender a true cultural exchange, take bushwalks and stay in *marae*.

Yeti Tours ☎0800/322 388, ⓦwww.yetitours.co.nz. Run in conjunction with *Matai Lodge* (see p.346) and offering guided and self-guided trips on the river from two to five days (three-day, guided, $575), including transport to launch points or for the tracks, a plethora of gear for hire and lots of help and advice.

Jetboat operators

Bridge to Nowhere see above. Popular and frequent jetboat tours from Pipiriki, principally to the Bridge to Nowhere (4hr; $105 return). They also work with Waka Tours to and from Tieke *marae*, for five to seven people.

Wades Landing Outdoors see above. Whakahoro-based jetboating trips from scenic joyrides and museum visits to visiting the Bridge to Nowhere (5–6hr; $140).

Whanganui River Adventures ☎0800/862 743, ⓦwww.whanganuiriveradventures.co.nz. Small jetboat operator running day-trips from Pipiriki to the Bridge to Nowhere ($105), a variety of other tours and tramper transport.

Whanganui Scenic Experience (☎0800/945 335, ⓦwww.whanganuiscenicjet.com, see p.278). Run tours on the lower reaches of the river and Bridge to Nowhere trips ($175).

Whanganui Jet ☎0800/538 8687 ⓦwww.whanganuijet.co.nz. From the Pungarehu Marae up-river a variety of trips are on offer, including the Bridge to Nowhere (6hr, $125).

Whanganui Park hikes

With the undoubted lure of canoe trips down the Whanganui River, few people tackle serious **hikes** in the area. In fact the country is so rugged that few tracks investigate the deep valleys and bush-clad slopes.

One that does, is wonderful the Mangapurua Track. Conditions are best from October to April. **Huts and campsites** in the park are managed by DOC. The best **map** is the new 1:80,000 *Whanganui National Park Parkmap* ($18.99).

The Mangapurua Track

The park's most manageable and appealing multi-day tramp follows the **Mangapurua Track** (40km one way; 3 days; 660m ascent), mostly on disused roadways through the Mangapurua and Kaiwhakauka valleys, passing through semi-open country that was once farmed. With the exception of the road-end DOC hut at Whakahoro there are no huts on the track but numerous campsites; most people pitch a tent within walking distance of the four toilets along the track.

The tramp is best tackled from Whakahoro, from where you can **jetboat** downriver to Mangapurua Landing (see p.274). From there it's a forty-minute walk to the Bridge to Nowhere, and a further ninety minutes to the camping area at Battleship Bluff. On the next section the track passes the remains of houses and rounds some sheer *papa* bluffs before climbing up to the highest point in the area, Mangapurua Trig (663m). Once you're into the Kaiwhakauka Valley, it's mostly easy riverside walking along abandoned roads back to Whakahoro. The tramp can be done in reverse, contact the jetboat and canoe operators to arrange transport.

The Whanganui River Road

The outlying sections of the park to the south can be accessed along the partly sealed **Whanganui River Road**, from either **Raetihi**, a small town on the SH4 near Ohakune, or Wanganui (see p.278). The River Road hugs the river's left bank from the riverside hamlet of **Pipiriki** 79km downstream to **Upokongaro**, just outside Wanganui. It's a rough twisting road, prone to floods and landslips, and even in the best conditions will take a minimum of two hours.

Day-trips along the Whanganui River Road

Ideally you'll want to spend a few days canoeing in the Whanganui National Park, but if time is short, consider one of the Wanganui-based **minibus trips** along the Whanganui River Road to Pipiriki and back. You may be able to extend the trip by staying overnight, see p.278.

The traditional choice is the **Rural Mail Coach Tour** (Mon–Fri at 7.30am; $40; ⓣ06/347 7534, ⓦwww.whanganuitours.co.nz), a genuine mail-delivery service stopping frequently at houses along the way as well as points of interest. Depending on numbers, you may be able to take a jetboat trip up to the Bridge to Nowhere and meet the minibus for the return journey. The trip is likely to take most of the day, so the $10 home-made lunch is a good bet.

By not delivering mail, Whanganui River Road Tours (daily 9am; $60; ⓣ06/345 8488, ⓦwww.whanganuiriverroad.com) run a quicker trip concentrating on the sights with full commentary, including the stories and legends of the river and a *marae* visit. Take or order a packed lunch.

Opened in 1934, the road is wedged between river, farmland and heavily forested outlying patches of the Whanganui National Park, and forms the supply route for the four hundred people or so who live along it. **Facilities** along the way are almost non-existent: there are no shops, pubs or petrol stations, and only a handful of places to stay. If you don't fancy the drive, consider joining one of the Wanganui-based bus tours (see box, p.276).

The road is detailed in the free and widely available *Whanganui River Road* leaflet. The leaflet highlights points of interest and lists their **distance from Wanganui**, a convention adopted in the parentheses in the following accounts, which take the road from north to south.

The southern reaches of the Whanganui National Park are accessed from Raetihi along the winding 27-kilometre Pipiriki–Raetihi Road, meeting the river at **PIPIRIKI** (79km), where you might make use of the unofficial **camping area** next to the toilets, with water.

Hiruharama

HIRUHARAMA (Maori for Jerusalem; 66km), 13km south of Pipiriki, was originally a Maori village and Catholic mission but is now best known as the site of the **James K. Baxter commune**, that briefly flourished in the early 1970s. Baxter, one of New Zealand's most (in)famous poets, attracted upwards of two hundred followers to the area. A devout Roman Catholic convert, but also firm believer in free love in his search for a "New Jerusalem", he became father to a flock of his own, the *nga moki* (fatherless ones), who soon dispersed after his death in 1972. The main commune house is situated high on a hill to the northeast of the church, and Baxter is buried just below. To pay homage at his grave, ask for directions from the three remaining Sisters of Compassion, who still live beside the 1892 **church** (from the north head up the first driveway, with a mailbox marked "The Sisters"), which features a Maori-designed and carved altar. Also in the church is a photo of Mother Mary Joseph Aubert (1835–1926), who established the first community of sisters. The small portrait of Baxter, looking suitably messianic, was removed at the time of writing but hopefully will by now have been retinstated. The original recently renovated wooden **convent** offers basic self-catering **accommodation** (ⓣ06/342 8190, ⓦwww.compassion.org.nz; $20, bed linen extra) for up to twenty people, in dorms with single beds.

From Moutoa Island to Koriniti

Moutoa Island (60km) was the scene of a vicious battle in 1864 when the lower-river Maori defeated the rebellious Hau Hau warriors, thus protecting the *mana* of the river and saving the lives of European settlers downstream at Wanganui. A cluster of houses 1km on marks **RANANA** (London; 60km) where there's a Roman Catholic mission church that's still in use today, and the *Kauika* **campsite** (ⓣ06/342 8762; tent sites $10, powered sites $20), adjacent to the river, with toilets, showers, fresh water and a small kitchen.

The two-storey 1854 **Kawana Flour Mill** (56km) is one of a number of water-powered flour mills that once operated along the river. It's also the only one that's been restored to its original condition (though it's not operational), along with the adjacent miller's cottage.

The only real settlement of note in these parts is **KORINITI** (Corinth; 47km), home to a lovely small church and a trio of traditional Maori buildings, the best being a 1920s **meeting house**, all down a side road. It is a private community, and while you can enter the church, the rest you should view from the road, unless you are invited into the compound.

Immediately south of Koriniti, *The Flying Fox* (46km; ⓣ06/342 8160, ⓦwww.theflyingfox.co.nz) is a wonderfully relaxing romantic hideaway accessible by boat or aerial cableway: prior booking essential, preferably a minimum of two nights. An eclectic range of found objects and scavenged pieces of old buildings have been imaginatively combined to create three separate self-contained buildings which encourage outdoor living amid the organic gardens and bush. Wood-fired bush baths, solar-heated showers, odourless composting toilets and a few spiders keeping the mosquitoes at bay add to the appeal. Choose from the James K (self-catering, sleeping five; ⑤), the Brewhouse (self-catering, sleeping three; ④), the Glory Cart (modelled on a gypsy caravan; ④), or camping ($15). Predominantly organic slow-food meals can be provided (breakfast $10, dinner $30–40), or you can bring your own food. There's a fascinating range of books, old vinyl and CDs to hire, and canoes for rent.

From Atene to SH4

Almost 10km south of Koriniti, a sign (35.5km) marks the start of the **Atene Viewpoint Walk** (5km return; 2hr; 100m ascent), giving great views of Puketapu, a hill that was once on a peninsula almost entirely encircled by the river. The river eventually cut through the isthmus to leave the hill surrounded by a dried-out ox-bow. The Viewpoint Walk comprises the first few kilometres of the **Atene Skyline Track** (18km loop; 6–8hr), making a wide loop following a gently ascending ridge line that ends with a two-kilometre walk along the road back to the start. There's camping midway around. Between the two track ends, a few occupied houses mark what's left of the settlement of **ATENE** (Athens; 35km).

A good base for the tracks is the **accommodation** at *Omaka* (32km; ⓣ06/342 5595, ⓦwww.omakaholiday.co.nz ④), a riverside farm with a modern self-catering lodge containing an en-suite double and two twins (B&B ⑤). They offer canoe rental and morning transport to Koriniti, so you can canoe back along the prettiest stretch of the lower reaches.

Further downriver are the **Oyster Shell Cliffs** (28km), roadside bluffs with oyster-shell deposits embedded in them. This is the base for Whanganui Scenic Experience (23km, see p.275), who run jetboat tours.

Soon the winding climb begins to the summit lookout of **Aramoana** (17km), giving a last look at the river below. On a clear day you can enjoy views of the northeast horizon, dominated by Mount Ruapehu. From the junction of the River Road and SH4, it's 14km to Wanganui.

Wanganui

There's an old-fashioned charm to the centre of **Wanganui**, the slow pace mirroring the speed of the river that bisects it, and museums and well-tended streetscape exuding civic pride. Founded on the banks of the **Whanganui River**, New Zealand's longest navigable watercourse, Wanganui is one of New Zealand's oldest cities and was the hub of early European commerce because of its access to the interior, and coastal links with the ports of Wellington and New Plymouth. The river traffic has long gone and the port is a shadow of what it was, but the city has given itself a facelift with an eye to its colonial past: the late Victorian and early Edwardian facades have been refurbished, and mock gas lamps installed along re-cobbled streets. All in all, Wanganui is a pleasant little place from which to take a ride on a restored

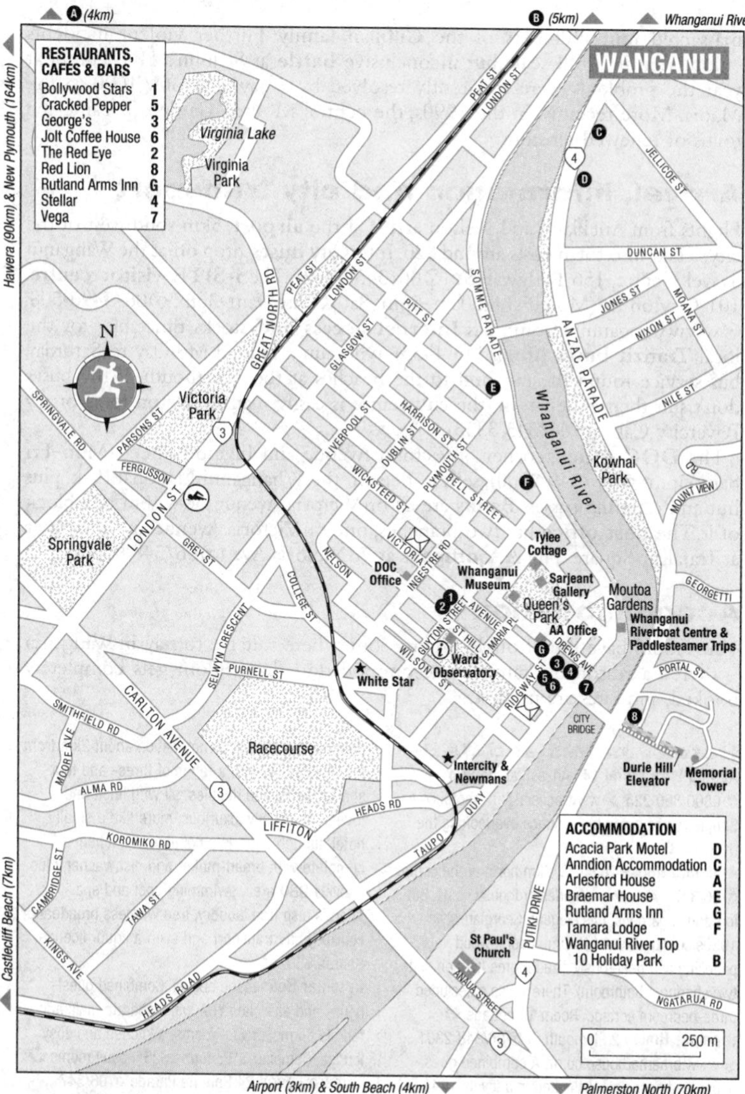

river steamer, visit the excellent museum, idle away an hour in the renowned **art gallery**, or enjoy the road to the tiny settlements along the Whanganui River (see p.276).

When **Europeans** arrived in the 1830s, land rights quickly became a bone of contention with the local Maori population. Transactions that Maori perceived as a ritual exchange of gifts were taken by the New Zealand Company to be a successful negotiation for the purchase of Wanganui and a large amount of surrounding land. Settlement went ahead regardless of the misunderstanding, and it was not until the **Gilfillan Massacre** of 1847 that trouble erupted – when a Maori was accidentally injured, his tribesmen massacred four members of the Gilfillan family. Further violent incidents culminated in a full-scale but inconclusive **battle** at St John's Hill. The next year the problems were apparently resolved by a payment of £1000 to the Maori. More recently, in the 1990s, the central Moutoa Gardens became the focus of renewed tensions.

Arrival, information and city transport

Flights from Auckland and Nelson arrive at the **airport**, 5km southwest of the city; a taxi into town costs around $20. InterCity **buses** drop off at the Wanganui Travel Centre, 156 Ridgway St (ⓣ06/345 4433). The **i-SITE visitor centre**, 101 Guyton St (Mon–Fri 8.30am–5pm, Sat & Sun 9am–3pm; ⓣ06/349 0508, ⓦwww.wanganuinz.com), has **Internet access and** stocks timetables for the local **Tranzit buses** (ⓣ06/345 4433), who run a limited Monday to Saturday bus service round the city and to the beaches at the rivermouth. If the buses don't suit then either walk (the city centre is easily manageable on foot) or try Rivercity Cabs (ⓣ06/345 3333).

The **DOC office**, corner of Victoria Avenue and Ingestre Street (Mon–Fri 8am–5pm; ⓣ06/349 2100), sells leaflets on the Whanganui National Park, plus hut and camping passes. **Banks** are all on Victoria Avenue or within one block of it. The **post office** has two branches, one on Victoria Avenue and the other at Trafalgar Square. The **AA office** is at 78 Victoria Ave (ⓣ06/348 9160).

Accommodation

You should have little trouble finding somewhere suitable to stay in Wanganui – there's a reasonable range of accommodation that seldom gets completely booked, and rates are modest.

Hotels, motels and B&Bs

Acacia Park Motel 140 Anzac Parade/SH4 ⓣ0800/800 225, ⓦwww.acacia-park-motel.co.nz. Simple rooms set in big grounds overlooking the river. ❸–❹

Arlesford House 202 SH3, 7km north of the centre ⓣ06/347 7751, ⓦwww.arlesfordhouse.co.nz. Set in tranquil gardens, this elegant, Georgian-style 1930s country home has rimu floors, wood panelling and generously sized rooms (two en suite, two sharing a bathroom). There's also a secluded three-bedroom cottage. Room ❺ cottage ❻

Braemar House 2 Plymouth St ⓣ06/348 2301, ⓦwww.braemarhouse.co.nz. A combined guest-house and associate YHA sited in a lovely 1895 homestead surrounded by lawns. The airy and quiet, shared-bath rooms front onto a veranda that catches the sun nicely. B&B ❸

Rutland Arms Inn Corner of Victoria Ave & Ridgway St ⓣ06/347 7677, ⓦwww.rutland-arms.co.nz. Upscale if somewhat soulless rooms in a, historic building, with a good bar and restaurant on site. ❺

Hostels and campsites

Anndion Accommodation 143 Anzac Parade ⓣ0800/343 056, ⓦwww.anndionlodge.co.nz. Backpacker-style accommodation about 2km from the city centre, with a range of three- and four-shares, twins and doubles, all with linen and towels. Unusually luxurious, more like a small hotel, though there is a communal kitchen complete with bread-maker and dishwasher, plus a lovely BBQ area, swimming pool and spa. There's also free laundry, free wireless broadband, courtesy city transport and even a liquor licence. Shares $30, ❸

Braemar House (see above). Combined guest-house and associate YHA with separate male and female dorms, private rooms, a kitchen and cosy lounge. Camping $12, dorms $25, hostel rooms ❷

Tamara Lodge 24 Somme Parade ⓣ06/347 6300, ⓦwww.tamaralodge.com. A large and well-kept historic building with pretty gardens and a friendly atmosphere. Offers free bikes, neat comfortable four-bed dorms, doubles and twins (some en suite), plus a balcony with a river view. Dorms $21, ❷

Wanganui River Top 10 Holiday Park 460 Somme Parade ⓣ0800/272 664, ⓦwww.wrivertop10.co.nz. Well-tended site 6km northeast of the city centre, beside the river in the shade of giant trees. Camping $16, cabins ❷, motel units ❹

The City

The cultural heart of Wanganui beats around Pukenamu, a grassy hill that marks the site of Wanganui's last tribal war in 1832. Now known as **Queens Park**, it contains three of the city's most significant buildings. Architecturally, the most impressive is the gleaming hilltop **Sarjeant Gallery** (daily 10.30am–4.30pm; donation; Ⓦwww.sarjeant.org.nz), best reached along Drews Avenue if you're driving. An engaging 1919 building of Oamaru stone, boasting a magnificent dome that filters natural light, and a highly regarded permanent collection concentrating on contemporary New Zealand art and photography, augmented by various touring exhibitions. Check to see if any of the Partington Collection are on display, black-and-white portraits of local Maori dating back one hundred years. Immediately to the north at the corner of Cameron and Bell streets, providing accommodation for artists in residence at the gallery, sits one of Wanganui's oldest buildings, the weatherboarded **Tylee Cottage**, built in 1853.

Southwest of the gallery, the Veteran Steps lead towards the centre of the city past the **Whanganui Museum** (daily 10am–4.30pm; $5). Founded in 1892, it contains an outstanding collection of Maori artefacts and three impressive canoes, all displayed in the central court, shaped like a traditional meeting house. In smaller galleries hang portraits of Maori in full ceremonial dress and *moko* (traditional tattoos) by Gottfried Lindauer. His portraits are sometimes criticized for the sitters' apparent passivity, but look long enough and the strongest impression is of great *mana*. Look out too for the photos of Whanganui river life, and models of ancient Maori methods of trapping eels and lampreys.

Towards the river, on Somme Parade, lie the historic **Moutoa Gardens**, a small but historic patch of grass. Traditionally Maori had lived at Moutoa during the fishing season until it was co-opted by Pakeha settlers, who renamed the area Market Square. It was here that Maori signed the document agreeing to the "sale" of Wanganui, an issue revisited on Waitangi Day 1995, when simmering old grievances and one or two more recent ones reached boiling point. Maori occupied Moutoa Gardens, claiming it as Maori land, for 83 days. This ended peacefully in the High Court, but created much bitterness on both sides. By 2001 a more conciliatory atmosphere prevailed, and the government, city council and local *iwi* agreed to share management of the gardens.

Following Ridgway Street until it meets Victoria Avenue, you reach the pretty **Watt Fountain**, which is surrounded by a number of ornate classical buildings, including the old post office and the striking Rutland Building. The Embassy 3 Complex provides a welcome counterpoint in the form of a stylish Art Deco (built in the early 1950s) exterior, foyer and mezzanine lounge, not to mention luxurious ladies' powder rooms.

Continuing west you come to **Cook's Gardens**, known in New Zealand as the place where, in 1962, local hero **Peter Snell** set a new world mile record of 3min 54.4sec, on grass. There's still a running track here, along with a velodrome and the wonderful 1901 **Ward Observatory**, where every Friday evening you can look through the 24-centimetre refractor (from around 8.30pm in summer, 8pm in winter; otherwise by arrangement through the visitor centre; $2).

The river

Wanganui's history is inextricably tied with the Whanganui River, and though commercial river traffic has virtually stopped, you can still ride the *Waimarie* **paddle steamer**, hopping aboard at Taupo Quay (Nov–April daily 2pm; May–July, Sept & Oct weekends, public & school holidays 1pm; $33; Ⓣ0800/783

2637, Ⓦ www.riverboat.co.nz; booking advisable). New Zealand's last surviving paddle-steamer, it makes a two-hour run up a tidal stretch of the river. The huffing of the coal-fired steam engine and the slosh of the paddles make for a soothing background to an afternoon's sunning on deck, or you can retire to the wood-panelled saloon for cakes and tea.

The *Waimarie* was built by Yarrow and Company of London in 1899, to a shallow-draught design with a tough hull, making it suitable for river work. It was transported to New Zealand in kit form, then put to work on the Whanganui River, where it saw service during the pre-Great War boom in tourism, when thousands from all over the world came to travel up the Whanganui River and stay at the hotel at Pipiriki. In 1949 the *Waimarie* made her last voyage and three years later sank at her moorings.

It wasn't until 1993 that the boat was salvaged and, thanks to skills passed on from half a century ago, the ship returned to the river in 1999. The restoration took place at the admirable **Whanganui Riverboat Centre & Museum** (Mon–Sat 9am–4pm, Sun 10am–4pm; donation), flanked by old warehouses and stores at Taupo Quay. Housed in an 1881 two-storey timber-framed building, the museum concentrates on the river and its history in relation to the town. Their most recent project, the *Wairua*, sistership to the *Waimarie* is now on the river, after twenty years restoration, and operating cruises for small groups. The *Wairua* was a service vessel for the upper reaches of the river, from Pipiriki to the Bridge to Nowhere, crossing 108 rapids in the course of its duties.

▲ The Waimare paddle steamer, on the Whanganui River

The left bank

Crossing City Bridge to the east bank of the river leads straight towards the **Durie Hill Elevator** (Mon–Fri 7.30am–6pm, Sat 9am–5pm, Sun 10am–5pm; $1 each way). A Maori carved gateway here marks the entrance to a 213-metre tunnel, at the end of which a historic 1919 elevator carries passengers 66m up through the hill to the summit. At the top of the hill two excellent vantage points grant extensive views of the city, beaches and inland. The viewpoint atop the elevator's machinery room is the easy option, but the best views are 176 steps up at the top of the 33.5-metre **Memorial Tower** (daily 8am–dusk; free). Head back to town using the 191 steps to the river – it only takes about ten minutes, and provides more satisfying views.

It's about 2km south along Putiki Drive to **St Paul's Memorial Church**, Anaua Street (donation requested), which looks like any other small, white-washed church but contains magnificent Maori carvings adorned with paua, a painted rib ceiling (as in Maori meeting houses), two beautiful etched-glass windows and two stained-glass, and *tukutuku* panels. The church is often locked: contact the visitor centre for access details.

Eating, drinking and entertainment

There are few culinary stars in Wanganui's firmament but there's enough choice to keep you sated for a night or so. For entertainment there's the Embassy 3 cinema, 34 Victoria Ave (☎06/345 7958). If you happen to be here in late March in an even-numbered year, check out the one-week Wanganui Arts Festival which has events all over town; late September in odd-numbered years brings the Blooming Artz Festival, a celebration of gardens and art. For listings of gigs or events, check out the daily editions of the *Wanganui Chronicle*.

Bollywood Stars 88 Guyton St ☎06/345 9996. Good curry house with the usual range of dishes, plus a daily lunch buffet and a more extensive evening menu.

Cracked Pepper 21 Victoria Ave. Licensed, daytime café serving excellent value food, including lambs fry and bacon, calamari risotto, meatballs and spaghetti and good chicken caesar salad, all under $20, daily.

George's 40 Victoria Ave. A local institution, this old-fashioned fish-and-chip shop also sells good-value fresh fish, the best in town. Closed Sun.

Jolt Coffee House 19 Victoria Ave. Upbeat daytime coffee house with an American diner feel, thanks to gleaming chrome and red plastic sofas (newspapers supplied). The great coffee is accompanied by rolls, cakes and sandwiches.

The Red Eye 96 Guyton St. Bohemian daytime café, with eye-brightening coffee and tasty dishes for breakfast and lunch, including great muesli cookies. Also open Fri evening, when there's often live music.

Red Lion 45 Anzac Parade. Atmospheric pub with a wide selection of beers and bar meals, plus live music at weekends. Closed Mon

Rutland Arms Inn Corner of Victoria Ave & Ridgway St. An old-style English-style pub with over a dozen beers on tap and a range of mainstream meals, served in the restaurant.

Stellar 2 Victoria Ave. Big all-day bar/restaurant, boasting lounge areas and a sports bar, with a comprehensive menu (mains $25–30); a lively spot at weekends.

Vega Corner of Victoria Ave & Taupo Quay ☎06/349 0078. Best restaurant in town, in an airy converted warehouse with two relaxing bars, one outdoors that backs onto the river; good-value café-style food both daytime and evening plus a DJ in the rear bar at weekends.

South through Bulls

South of Wanganui, SH1 and SH3 meet at **Bulls**, 44km north of Palmerston North, worth a brief pause for its signage – the police station comes billed as Const-a-Bull, the town hall as Soci-a-Bull and so on.

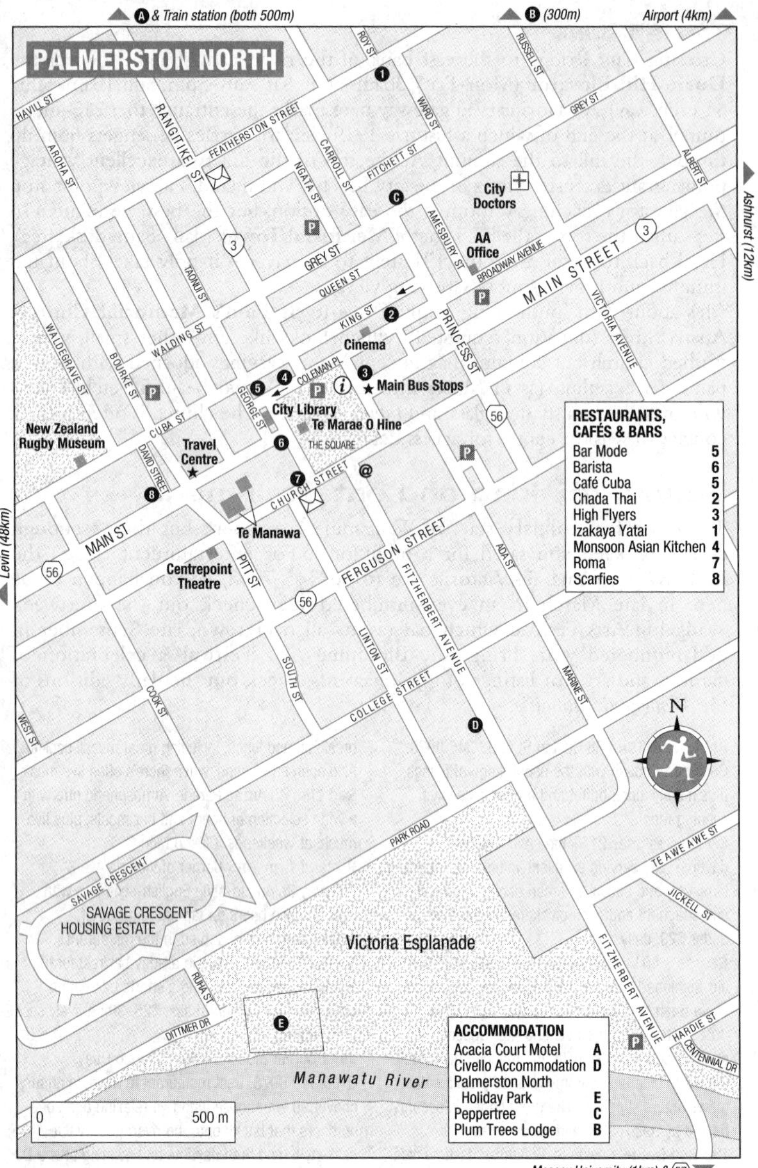

Palmerston North and around

PALMERSTON NORTH is the thriving capital of the province of Manawatu, and with around 75,000 people it's one of New Zealand's largest landlocked cities. After the arrival of the rail line in 1886, Palmerston North flourished, thanks to its pivotal position at the junction of road and rail routes.

Today its identity is reflected in some fine civic buildings, notably an excellent **museum** and **gallery** and a stunning **library**, though there's no single must-see attraction. The term-time presence of students from **Massey University** makes the city a livelier place, with plenty of buzzy restaurants and bars but it's a place now made infamous because of a comment by John Cleese, "If you want to kill yourself but lack the courage, I think a visit to Palmerston North will do the trick." The town's response was to name the local rubbish dump after him.

Arrival and information

Palmerston North centres on **The Square**, a simple grassy expanse marred by a central car park and by the ugly intrusion of the Civic Centre along part of the western side. The **train station** is on Matthews Avenue, about 1500m northwest of the city centre. **Long-distance buses** stop at the Palmerston North Travel Centre, at the corner of Pitt and Main streets. Frequent flights from Auckland, Wellington and Christchurch land at the **airport**, 3km northeast of the city, from where **taxis** (there are no buses) run into town: try Palmerston North Taxis (Ⓣ0800/355 5333; around $20).

Local bus services run from Main Street, near the visitor centre, in a series of loops ($2 single), with reduced services outside term time. Timetables can be obtained from the **i-SITE visitor centre**, The Square (Mon–Fri 9am–5pm, Sat & Sun 10am–4pm; Ⓣ06/350 1922, Ⓦwww.manawatunz.co.nz) that stocks a weekly events sheet.

Accommodation

Palmerston North has a decent range of **accommodation**, most geared toward the university, business or visiting parents.

Acacia Court Motel 374 Tremaine Ave Ⓣ0800/685 586, Ⓦwww.acaciacourtmotel.co.nz. Friendly, attractive spot with s/c units. ❸

Civello Accommodation 186 Fitzherbert Ave Ⓣ06/355 3653, Ⓔcontact.us@mail.com. Doubles with shared-bathrooms and a communal kitchen in a modern block 10min walk from The Square, offering excellent value for money. ❷–❸

Palmerston North Holiday Park 133 Dittmer Drive Ⓣ06/358 0349, Ⓦwww.holidayparks.co.nz. Spacious campsite close to the Manawatu River, with camping, cabins and tourist flats, and excellent facilities. Camping $18, cabins ❶, flats ❸

Peppertree 121 Grey St Ⓣ06/355 4054, Ⓔpeppertreehostel@clear.net.nz. Comfortable, well-appointed and welcoming associate YHA within easy walking distance of the central square. Dorms $23, ❷

Plum Trees Lodge 97 Russell St Ⓣ06/358 7813, Ⓦwww.plumtreeslodge.co.nz. Lovely self-catering loft in a quiet suburban street, tastefully decorated, with a leafy deck where you can pick your own plums if they're ripe. An extensive breakfast hamper is supplied. ❻

The city and around

In the heart of the town's square is **Te Marae o Hine**, or the Courtyard of the Daughter of Peace, an open area graced by a couple of five-metre-high Maori figures carved by renowned artist **John Bevan Ford**, who died in 2005. The Maori name is the one suggested for the settlement's central square by the chief of the Ngati Raukawa in 1878, in the hope that love and peace would become enduring features in the relationship between the Manawatu Maori and incoming Pakeha.

Around The Square, the mishmash of architectural styles – classical Victorian and Edwardian, Art Deco and so on – enhances the impact of the **City Library** (Mon, Tues & Thurs 10am–6pm, Wed & Fri 10am–8pm, Sat 10am–4pm & Sun

1–4pm), a postmodern conversion by Ian Athfield (see box, p.465). Sensitively poking its nose from behind the classical facade of the 1927 C.M. Ross building on the southeast side, the library presents a challenging environment of colour and contrast, light and texture in which all the reading materials are arranged according to "subject living rooms" furnished with armchairs and sofas.

Immediately west of the square lies **Te Manawa** (daily 10am–5pm; Ⓦwww.temanawa.co.nz), the city's main cultural focus. It's divided into three parts centred on the **Life Galleries** (free), a museum devoted to the history and culture of the Manawatu region. Much of the space is given over to high-quality touring exhibitions, but one room is devoted to a large impressive Maori exhibit. In the same building, **Mind Galleries** ($8) offers top-notch hands-on science displays and experiments predominantly for kids. Adjacent stands the **Art Gallery** (free), which displays Pakeha and Maori art from its permanent collection, alongside touring exhibitions.

A short stroll northwest of the square, the **New Zealand Rugby Museum**, 87 Cuba St (Mon–Sat 10am–noon & 1.30–4pm, Sun 1.30–4pm; $5), is chiefly a place for die-hard rugger fans to marvel at ephemera.

Ashhurst and the Manawatu Gorge

The town of **ASHHURST**, 13km northeast of Palmerston North, stands at the entrance to the **Manawatu Gorge** (Te Apiti in Maori), a narrow ten-kilometre-long defile through which a rail line, SH3 and the Manawatu River squeeze. The mouth of the gorge is framed by the hills of the Ruahine and Tararua ranges, where a couple of large **windfarms** enhance the landscape. The most impressive is **Te Apiti Windfarm**, with 55 70-metre-tall turbines, each fitted with 35-metre blades. They're a striking sight, typically seen from the Wind Farm Lookout on Cambridge Road (signposted off SH3), or by driving along Saddle Road: pick up a leaflet from the Palmerston North i-SITE.

The gorge itself can be explored on foot along the **Manawatu Gorge Track** (3–4hr one way), though with no public transport you'll have to either walk back or arrange transport with the i-SITE at Palmerston North.

Eating, drinking and entertainment

Palmerston North supports a lively **restaurant** scene, ranging from cafés to fancy eateries. In the late evening many places morph into vibrant **bars**, some of the best lining **George Street**, home of Palmerston North's café society.

For entertainment, there's an astonishing four theatres, The Regent on Broadway, Abbey Musical Theatre, and the two you should bother with, the **Centrepoint Theatre**, corner of Church and Pitt streets (Ⓣ06/354 5740, Ⓦwww.centrepoint.co.nz), an intimate performance space, with a pleasant bar open when there's a show on and the Globe, corner of Main and Pitt streets (Ⓣ06/358 8699) which has a range of good shows. **Movies** are less well represented at Downtown Cinemas, on Broadway Avenue between Princess Street and The Square (Ⓣ06/355 5655), a ubiquitous multiscreen.

Restaurants, cafés and bars

Barista George St Ⓦwww.barista.co.nz. Minimalist espresso bar where they grind their own coffee and serve great cakes, snacky meals, and a full range of breakfasts, including bagels. Mains around the $20 mark lunchtime, $30 upwards at dinner.

Bar Mode 1 Coleman Place Ⓣ06/357 4898. The only real venue sometimes packing in up to five hundred, for live bands or DJ twiddling, 4pm–very late, covers sometimes apply.

Café Cuba Corner of George & Cuba sts. Funky all-day café, a bit of a local institution for breakfast, all-day brunch, lunch and dinner. A good place for

late food Thurs–Sat, when the kitchen stays open until 11.30pm. Licensed & BYO.
Chada Thai 95 Broadway Ave ☎06/357 2555. Lively, brightly lit restaurant and takeaway serving tasty examples of Thai favourites, at bargain prices (mains $10).
High Flyers Corner of Main St & The Square. Central bar/club attracting a young crowd at night, especially to DJ dance nights Thurs–Sat, there's also bar food on offer.
Izakaya Yatai 316 Featherston St ☎06/356 1316. Excellent, Japanese-pub-style place serving tasty dishes at reasonable prices (mostly $15–20). Closed Mon & Sun, BYO.
Monsoon Asian Kitchen 200 The Square. Good-value Chinese, Malaysian and Singaporean cuisine. It isn't licensed, but they will order drinks for you from the bar across the street. Closed Mon & Sun.
Roma 51 The Square. Authentic Italian restaurant with a cosy atmosphere, easy-going service and many dishes available as a starter or main course. Dishes include an antipasto plate as well as thin-crust pizza.
Scarfies Corner of David & Main sts. A three-bar extravaganza in the old *Railway Hotel*, aimed at students, with DJ entertainment Thurs–Sat.

Listings

AA (Automobile Association) office 185 Broadway Ave ☎06/357 7039.
Banks and exchange Most banks are within a couple of blocks of The Square; there's also Thomas Cook, corner of Broadway Ave & Princess St ☎06/359 1655.
Internet access The library (see p.285).
Medical treatment City Doctors, 22 Victoria Ave ☎06/355 3300 (daily 8am–10pm). Full facilities and a pharmacy on site.
Post office The main post office is at 338 Church St.

South to the Kapiti Coast

South of Palmerston North and the Manawatu, the peaks of the rugged and inhospitable **Tararua Mountains** corral the **Horowhenua** region into a strip along the coast. Renowned for its gentle landscape and popularity with retirees, the area lacks substantial attractions, but has a few mildly diverting settlements. The pick of these is **Foxton**, with its plethora of museums and an extraordinary long flat beach facing its seaside offshoot community of **Foxton Beach**. The rugged bush country of the **Tararua Forest Park** to the east is most easily accessible from **Otaki Forks**, near the small town of **Otaki**.

It's better to press on to the Wellington commuter belt of the **Kapiti Coast**, a narrow coastal plain between the mountains and sweeping beaches that's peppered with dormitory suburbs and golf courses. The attraction is the wonderful bush-covered bird sanctuary and marine reserve of **Kapiti Island**, 5km offshore, though there's also interest in the birdlife of the Nga Manu Sanctuary at **Waikanae**.

Paekakariki marks the southern end of the Kapiti Coast, before the relaxing charms of **Plimmerton**, on the shores of Porirua Harbour. The minor attractions of **Porirua**, 20km from Wellington, won't detain you long. The north–south rail link between Auckland and Wellington and the main bus companies serve the coastal towns but away from the rail/road corridor your options are severely limited.

Foxton

It's not saying much but the most interesting town in these parts is **FOXTON**, 38km southwest of Palmerston North, where the old-style shop facades of the broad main street seem barely touched by the last fifty years or so. None of the town's several small museums is far from the **visitor centre**, housed in a crystal shop, so they know everything. **Buses** stop near the old rail and tram station that contains a horse-drawn tram that is hauled out every summer for tourist rides.

Archeological evidence suggests that there was a semi-nomadic **moa-hunter** culture in this area between 1400 and 1650, pre-dating larger tribal settlements. **Europeans** arrived in the early 1800s and settled at the mouth of the Manawatu River, but struck problems with land purchases and soon retreated to found Foxton. It quickly became the **flax-milling** capital of New Zealand, adapting techniques perfected by local Maori, who had long relied on handmade flax items for their everyday needs. Flax was exported from the small river port for use in woolpacks, as binder twine, fibrous plaster lashings and carpet. In an effort to streamline the stripping and weaving processes, mills were constructed by swamps and on riverbanks in Manawatu and Horowhenua.

In honour of those times a modern, full-scale replica of a seventeenth-century Dutch windmill known as **de Molen** (daily 10am–4pm; $5) now dominates the townscape, offering a fifteen-minute tour on which you're taken upstairs to watch the production of stoneground wholemeal flour. The broader history of the flax industry is recounted in the adjacent **Flax Stripper Museum** (daily 1–3pm; $3), behind which a hundred-metre-long strip of riverbanks contains a flaxwalk, an unkempt display of sixty-five types of flax. Pick up the free explanatory leaflet available from the museum.

The long, sandy **Foxton Beach** is 5km away on the coast, where there's good surfing, safe swimming areas and abundant birdlife around the Manawatu River estuary. The small community is full of *baches* for vacationing New Zealanders, as well as a campsite and a few motels. The beach stretches 20km north of here, making it a perfect spot for sand-yachting, a sport mostly conducted at **Himatangi Beach**, 10km north.

Otaki and around

The main southbound road routes converge 19km south of Foxton at **Levin**, the principal community in the Horowhenua region. There's little reason to stop except for a stroll through the **Papaitonga Scenic Reserve**, off SH1 some 4km south of town, where a boardwalk leads to the Papaitonga Lookout (20min return) and great **views** of Lake Papaitonga. The surrounding wetlands provide a refuge for many **rare birds**, including the spotless crake, Australasian bittern, and New Zealand dabchick.

OTAKI, 20km south of Levin, sits beside a broad, braided section of the Otaki River, in a market-garden area. For most of the year, this is a quiet place with a strong Maori heritage but, like other towns along this coast, swells to bursting point for the month or so after Christmas when Kiwi holidaymakers descend en masse.

Otaki comes in three parts: the train station and visitor centre on SH1; Otaki township 2km towards the sea along Mill Road; and the **beach**, a further 3km along Mill Road, safe to swim at in summer thanks to a surf patrol. In the township, Te Rauparaha Street leads 200m to **Rangiatea Church**, an exact replica of the 1849 original that was widely regarded as the finest Maori church in New Zealand (Mon–Fri, 9.30am–1.30pm, ⓣ06/364 6838, donation). The church was consecrated in 2003, eight years after the original was completely razed in an arson attack. Inside the building is simple, with *tukutuku* panels on the walls, the pattern representing both the stars and the departed. Notice, too, the rafters, painted in Maori designs representing hammerhead sharks (symbols of power and privilege), and the exquisite model of the Tainui *waka*, which escaped the blaze. Outside, the simple, grey-slate headstone of the Maori chief Te Rauparaha can be found in a row of three by a decapitated Norfolk pine, though his body is rumoured to have been exhumed and re-buried on Kapiti Island. Opposite the church is a memorial to the great chief, his likeness exuding an Alexandrian air.

Practicalities

Buses stop outside the **visitor centre**, corner of SH1 and Mill Road (Mon–Fri 9am–5pm, Sat & Sun 10am–3pm; ⓣ06/364 7620), which has free town maps and sells **hut passes** for tracks in the Tararua Forest. Two minutes' walk away is the unstaffed **train station**.

Daytime eating in Otaki is best done at *Brown Sugar*, on SH1 at the southern end of town (daily 9am–4pm), where veg frittata tops the menu, along with delicious cakes and good coffee.

Otaki Gorge and Otaki Forks

A kilometre south of the town, the scenic and partly unsealed **Otaki Gorge Road** branches off SH1 and threads 19km into the hills along the picturesque gorge of the Otaki River to **Otaki Forks**, the main western entrance to the **Tararua Forest Park**.

Most of the forest park is accessible only to serious trampers, though there are a few shorter and less intimidating **walks** from a series of three parking areas, all close to each other at the end of Otaki Gorge Road. First up is the **Boielle Flat** picnic area, immediately followed by **Gibbons Flat**, where a resident ranger provides assistance and information, and keeps an intentions book. Nearby, crossing a swingbridge over the river and walking 200m brings you to Parawai Lodge, a **trampers' hut** where those with a sleeping bag and cooking equipment can stay ($5). Two kilometres up the road from Gibbons Flat there's a basic **campsite** ($4) at the road end. Armed with the *Otaki Forks* leaflet (available from area visitor centres), you can explore the **Fenceline Loop** (3km; 2hr), offering excellent views of the river flowing down the valley to the coast.

Waikanae

WAIKANAE, 14km south of Otaki, is divided between the highwayside settlement and a beach community, 4km away along Te Moana Road, where the broad, dune-backed **beach** has safe swimming. Hikers heading for the Tararuas might want to call at the Kapiti Coast's main **DOC office**, 10 Parata St (Mon–Fri 8am–12.30pm & 1–4.30pm, but sometimes unmanned; ⓣ04/296 1112), one street west of the main highway (turn at the BP station). If you want to be outdoors, stop at the **Nga Manu Nature Reserve**, a large man-made bird sanctuary (daily 10am–5pm, later in Jan; $10; ⓦwww.ngamanu.co.nz), with easy walking tracks and some picnic spots. A circular track (1500m) cuts through a variety of habitats, from ponds and scrubland to swamp and coastal forest, which attract all manner of birds. There is also a nocturnal house containing kiwi, morepork and tuatara, plus eels, fed at 2pm daily and some walk-in aviaries where kea and kaka strut their funky stuff. To get here, follow Te Moana Road off SH1 for just over a kilometre and turn right at Ngarara Road; the sanctuary is a further 3km.

With over 250 vehicles in a specially built showroom, the **Southward Car Museum**, Otaihanga Road, 3km south of Waikanae (daily 9am–4.30pm; $12;

ⓦwww.southward.org.nz), contains one of the largest collections of cars, fire engines and motorbikes in Australasia, which is great if you like that sort of thing.

Paraparaumu and around

PARAPARAUMU, 7km south of Waikanae and 45km from Wellington, is the Kapiti Coast's largest settlement and the only jumping-off point to Kapiti Island. It's also a burgeoning dormitory community, with commuters lured here by the proximity of the long and sandy **Paraparaumu Beach**, 3km to the west along Kapiti Road, which is safe for swimming and looks out onto Kapiti Island.

There's precious little land-based interest here, though tour buses all flock to the **Lindale Centre**, 2km north on SH1 (daily 9am–5pm; free), where you can sample either ice cream or cheese at **Kapiti Cheeses**, both among New Zealand's finest. Its success has attracted a number of other food and craft shops, and the well-priced *Farm Kitchen* **café** (daily 7am–5pm), offering hearty snacks, light lunches and great cakes and coffee. Those with a sweet tooth might prefer the **Nyco Chocolate Factory**, at the corner of SH1 and Raumati Road, 1km south of Paraparaumu (Mon–Sat 9am–5pm, Sun 10am–4.30pm), which produces ninety thousand chocolates daily and sells them through a shop stuffed with goodies.

Practicalities

The **i-SITE visitor centre**, SH1, in the Coastlands shopping centre car park (Mon–Fri 9am–5pm, Sat & Sun 10am–3pm; ⓣ04/298 8195, ⓔparaparaumu@naturecoast.co.nz), has local and DOC information. InterCity **buses** drop off at the **train station** opposite, as do local services from Wellington. There are few genuinely tempting **places to stay**, though the revamped YHA *Barnacles Seaside Inn*, 3 Marine Parade, Paraparaumu Beach (ⓣ0800/555 856, ⓔstay@seasideyha.co.nz; dorms $25, ❷), in an attractive 1923 hotel, is comfortable and overlooks the beach. Just north of town, off SH1, is the *Lindale Motor Park* (ⓣ04/298 8046, ⓔlindalemotorpark@xtra.co.nz; camping $18, kitchen cabins ❷, self-contained unit ❸).

Apart from the *Farm Kitchen* at Kapiti Cheeses, and despite the plethora of new beachside restaurants, **eating** is still best done at the evening-only *Muang Thai*, 22 Maclean St (ⓣ04/902 9699; closed Sun), or the *Maclean Street Fish and Chip Shop*, 4 Maclean St, 11.30am–8pm daily.

Kapiti Island

One of the beast and most easily accessible island **nature reserves** in New Zealand, the ten-kilometre by two-kilometre **Kapiti Island** is a magical spot, its bush, once cleared for farmland, now home to birdlife that has become rare or extinct on the mainland. In 1822, infamous Maori chief **Te Rauparaha** captured the island from its first known Maori inhabitants and, with his people the Ngati Toa, used it as a base until his death in 1849: it's thought that he may be buried somewhere on the island, but the site of his grave is unknown. The island is considered extremely spiritual by Maori, and was designated a reserve in 1897.

Late January and February are the best months to visit, when the **birdlife** is at its most active, but at any time of the year you're likely to see kaka (bush parrots that may alight on your head or shoulder), weka, kakariki (parakeets), whiteheads (bush canaries), tui, bellbirds, fantails, wood pigeons, robins and a handful of the 250 takahe that exist in the world. The island can be explored on two fairly steep **walking tracks**, the Trig Track and the Wilkinson Track, which effectively form a loop by meeting near the island's highest point, Tuteremoana (521m). There are spectacular views from the summit, though the widest variety of birdlife is found along the lower parts of the tracks – take your time, keep quiet and stop frequently (allow about 3hr for the round-trip).

The **North End** of the island (about a tenth of its total area) is also part of the Kapiti Nature Reserve, though it is managed and accessed separately. Here the attractions are the **Okupe Lagoon** with its colony of royal spoonbills, though there are also plenty of rare forest birds about, a DOC walkway and kiwi spotting.

A wedge of sea between Kapiti Island and Paraparaumu has been designated a **marine reserve**, and its exceptionally clear waters make for great **snorkelling** around the rocks. You'll need your own gear to go **scuba diving**, which is particularly good to the west and north of the island, where there are some interesting formations, such as a rock archway known as the Hole-in-the-Wall. Three types of habitat – a boulder bottom, sheltered reef and sand bottom – are home to a rich variety of marine life, including orange and yellow sponges (some very rare), and luxuriant seaweed beds feeding kina and paua. Visiting ocean fish like moki and kingfish are common, and occasionally you'll see rare and subtropical fish as well as stingray and cruising orca.

▲ North Island robin, Kapiti Island

Practicalities

DOC manages the island and allows just fifty **visitors** a day to the main nature reserve, and a further 18 to the North End. Obligatory **landing permits** ($9 per person, valid for six months in case weather prevents a crossing) must be booked through DOC in Wellington (Ⓣ04/472 7356), though they'll fax them to the Paraparaumu visitor centre for pick-up. **Book** as far in advance as you can: a few days is generally OK, but on summer weekends the main reserve is often filled three months ahead. If you're visiting both ends of the island, get two permits.

The fifteen-minute crossing from Paraparaumu Beach to Kapiti Island ($55 return) can be done with either of two **launch operators**: Kapiti Marine Charter (Ⓣ0800/433 779, Ⓦwww.kapitimarinecharter.co.nz), or Kapiti Tours (Ⓣ0800/527 484, Ⓦwww.kapititours.co.nz). Boats leave at 9am and return around 3.30pm, with the option of a transfer to the North End (extra $5). DOC are sensitive about the reintroduction of pests so insist your bags are checked for any stray mammals before leaving for the island. At the main reserve, an excellent half-hour introduction by one of the island rangers, along with the free *Kapiti Island Nature Reserve* brochure, sets you up for a few hours' exploration, though there is an optional ninety-minute guided walk ($15). Facilities extend to toilets and a shelter at the landing point: take lunch and a drink, and bring back all the rubbish.

Adjacent to the northern reserve is a small plot of private land at Waiorua Bay, where one of the half-dozen houses offers the only **accommodation** on the island, at *Kapiti Nature Lodge* (Ⓣ06/362 6606, Ⓦwww.kapitiislandalive.co.nz). This sleeps a maximum of ten in simple bunkrooms, doubles or twins. Being Maori-run, it has a communal feel which runs through to the family-style meals, which might include fresh seafood. Rates (bunks $255, rooms from $265 a head) include breakfast, lunch and dinner and a chance to look for kiwi in the evening. There's also always the possibility of orca cruising by as you sit on the beach, after you've walked the track. If you can't stay overnight the day tour ($155) includes the ferry, DOC permit, lunch and hour-long guided walk.

Paekakariki

There'd be no reason to stop in **Paekakariki**, a tiny village 10km south of Paraparaumu, were it not for a safe swimming beach, and a place to park campervans within reach of transport into Wellington. The well-appointed *Paekakariki Holiday Park*, 180 Wellington Rd, almost 2km north (Ⓣ04/292 8292, Ⓔpaekakariki.holiday.park@xtra.co.nz; camping $14, cabins ❶, units ❷), fits the bill and is right by the beach. The village also contains a café and small store.

Porirua

There's more bustle at **PORIRUA**, which is booming on account of its proximity to Wellington. Consider stopping briefly in central Porirua at the **Pataka Museum of Arts and Cultures** (Mon–Sat 10am–4.30pm, Sun 11am–4.30pm; free; Ⓦwww.pataka.org.nz), at the corner of Norrie and Parumoana streets, that hosts local and travelling exhibitions, by leading contemporary New Zealand artists, plus regular Maori dance performances.

For a change of pace, tackle the **Colonial Knob Walkway** (7.5km loop; 3–4hr), a track across forested hills to the west of Porirua, reaching a 468-metre summit, the highest point within the Wellington urban area. It offers amazing

views of Mana and Kapiti islands, Mount Taranaki to the north, and south as far as the Kaikoura Ranges. This and other local walks are in the free *Walking and Cycling Tracks in Porirua City* leaflet.

Buses stop on the main road in Porirua, two minutes from the visitor centre. Trains and local buses between Wellington and the Kapiti Coast stop at the combined **bus and train station**, a few minutes' walk from the **visitor centre** at 8 Cobham Court (Mon–Sat 9am–5pm, Sat 9am–4pm, Sun 10am–2pm; ⓣ04/237 8088, ⓔvisinfo@pcc.govt.nz), which acts as a transport agent and has Internet access.

Travel details

Trains

Hamilton to: Auckland (1 daily; 2hr 30min); Ohakune (1 daily; 3hr 30min); Otorohanga (1 daily; 40min); Palmerston North (1 daily; 7hr); Te Awamutu (1 daily; 20min); Wellington (1 daily; 9hr 30min).
Otorohanga to: National Park (1 daily; 2hr 20min); Palmerston North (1 daily; 6hr 30min).
Palmerston North to: Auckland (1 daily; 9hr 30min); Hamilton (1 daily; 7hr); Wellington (1 daily; 2hr 30min).
Paraparaumu to: Paekakariki (half-hourly or more; 8min); Plimmerton (half-hourly or more; 25min); Porirua (half-hourly or more; 35min); Wellington (half-hourly or more; 50min–1hr).
Taumarunui to: Hamilton (1 daily; 2hr); Palmerston North (1 daily; 5hr); Wellington (1 daily; 7hr 30min).

Buses

Cambridge to: Hamilton (7 daily; 20min); Matamata (1–2 daily; 30min); Tauranga (1–2 daily; 1hr 30min).
Hamilton to: Auckland (14–16 daily; 2hr); Cambridge (7 daily; 20min); Matamata (2 daily; 50min); New Plymouth (3 daily; 3hr 40min–4hr 40min); Ngaruawahia (14–16 daily; 15min); Otorohanga (3–4 daily; 45min); Paeroa (1 daily; 1hr 30min); Raglan (2–3 daily; 45min); Rotorua (6 daily; 1hr 45min); Taupo (3 daily; 2hr 40min); Tauranga (2 daily; 1hr 45min); Te Aroha (1 daily; 1hr 10min); Te Awamutu (5 daily; 30min); Te Kuiti (3 daily; 1hr 30min); Thames (1–2 daily; 2hr 30min); Tirau (3 daily; 45min); Tokoroa (3 daily; 1hr 10min); Wanganui (2 daily; 6–8hr), Wellington (2 daily; 9hr).
Matamata to: Cambridge (1–2 daily; 30min); Hamilton (2 daily; 50min); Tauranga (2 daily; 1hr).
Otorohanga to: Hamilton (3–4 daily; 45min); Te Kuiti (3 daily; 15min); Waitomo Caves (6 daily; 30min).
New Plymouth to: Auckland (3 daily; 5hr 30min–6hr 15min); Hamilton (3 daily; 3hr 40min–4hr 40min); Te Kuiti (3 daily; 2hr 30min); Wanganui (2 daily; 2hr 40min); Wellington (3 daily; 7hr).
Palmerston North to: Auckland (4 daily; 9hr); Hastings (3 daily; 2hr 45min); Masterton (3 Mon–Fri; 2hr); Napier (3 daily; 3hr); Paraparaumu (6–7 daily; 1hr 30min); Rotorua (1 daily; 5hr 45min); Taupo (3 daily; 4hr); Wanganui (3–5 daily; 1hr–1hr 30min); Wellington (6–7 daily; 2hr).
Taumarunui to: Te Kuiti (1 daily; 1hr); Wanganui (1 daily; 3hr).
Te Awamutu to: Hamilton (5 daily; 30min); Otorohanga (5 daily; 20min).
Te Kuiti to: Hamilton (3 daily; 1hr 30min); New Plymouth (3 daily; 2hr 30min); Taumarunui (1 daily; 1hr).
Waitomo Caves to: Auckland (1 daily; 4hr 20min); Rotorua (2 daily; 2hr–2hr 30min).
Wanganui to: Hamilton (2 daily; 6–8hr); New Plymouth (2 daily; 2hr 40min); Palmerston North (3–5 daily; 1hr–1hr 30min); Taumarunui (1 daily; 3hr).

Flights

Hamilton to: Auckland (3 daily; 30min); Christchurch (1–2 daily; 1hr 45min); Nelson (1–2 daily; 1hr 15min); Palmerston North (3–4 weekdays; 45min); Wellington (5–10 daily; 1hr).
New Plymouth to: Auckland (5–8 daily; 45min); Nelson (1 daily; 1hr); Wellington (4–5 daily; 55min).
Palmerston North to: Auckland (5–8 daily; 1hr); Christchurch (4–6 daily; 1hr 15min); Hamilton (3–4 weekdays; 45min); Nelson (2 daily; 50min); Wellington (3 daily; 30min).
Wanganui to: Auckland (3–4 daily; 1hr).

4

Central North Island

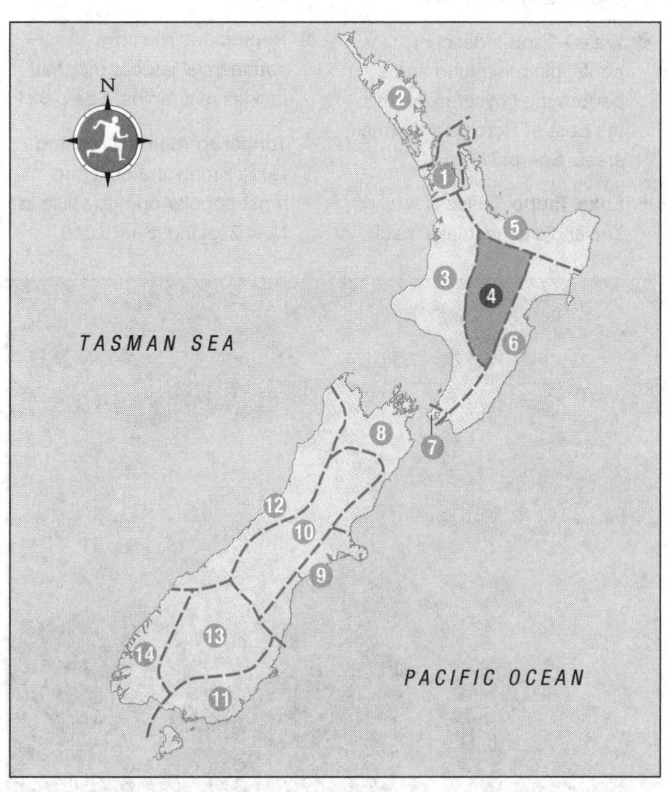

CHAPTER 4 Highlights

* **Kaituna River** Raft this excellent short river and shoot its seven-metre fall. See p.309
* **Maori cultural performance** Chants, dance, songs, stories and a *hangi* feast. See p.311
* **Wai-O-Tapu** Iridescent pools, glooping mud and a performing geyser make this the best of Rotorua's thermal areas. See p.317
* **Lake Taupo** Cruise New Zealand's largest lake, haul trout out of it, or approach at speed while skydiving. See p.320
* **Huka Falls** For volume and power alone this is the country's finest waterfall. See p.328
* **Rapids Jet** The only commercial jetboat trip that tackles real rapids. See p.331
* **Tongariro Alpine Crossing** Quite simply the best and most popular one-day hike in New Zealand. See p.340

▲ Tongariro National Park

4

Central North Island

The **Central North Island** contains more than its fair share of New Zealand's star attractions, many the result of its explosive geological past. It is dominated by three heavyweight features: **Lake Taupo**, the country's largest; **Tongariro National Park**, with its trio of active volcanoes; and the volcanic field that feeds colourful and fiercely active thermal areas, principally around **Rotorua**. If you are ticking off Kiwi icons, then time is well spent around Rotorua where boiling mud pools plop next to spouting geysers fuelled by super-heated water, drawn off to fill the hot pools around town. You'll also find the most accessible expression of Maori culture here, with highly regarded Arawa carvings and groups who'll perform traditional dances and *haka* before feeding you with fall-off-the-bone meat and juicy vegetables cooked in a *hangi* steam oven.

The dramatic volcanic scenery of Rotorua is striking for its contrast with the encroaching pines of the **Kaingaroa Forest**, one of the world's largest plantation forests, with serried ranks of fast-growing conifers marching to the horizon. When the country was carved up for farming, this region was all but abandoned as cattle grazed here soon contracted "bush sickness" and died. In the 1930s, scientists discovered that the disease was caused by an easily rectified deficiency of the mineral cobalt but by this stage the free-draining pumice soils had already been planted with millions of radiata (Monterrey) pine seedlings by gangs of convicts and Great Depression relief workers. Since then, sylviculture has consolidated its position as the area's chief earner through pulp and paper mills at Kinleith, near Tokoroa, and Kawerau.

The rest of the region is loosely referred to as the **Volcanic Plateau**, high country overlaid with a layer of rock and ash expelled two thousand years ago, when a huge volcano blew itself apart, the resultant crater and surrounds filled by **Lake Taupo**. This serene lake, and the streams and rivers feeding it, have since become a fishing mecca for anglers keen to snag brown and rainbow trout, while water-sports enthusiasts flock to the thundering rapids on the Waikato River, draining the lake. South of Lake Taupo rise three majestic volcanoes in **Tongariro National Park**, created in 1887 – a winter playground for North Island skiers and a summer destination for trampers drawn by spectacular walking trails.

If you're driving from Auckland you've a choice of **routes**: the direct SH1 through Hamilton; or the faster journey along SH2, which branches east at Pokeno, 50km south of Auckland, then along SH27 as it cuts south across the fringes of the Hauraki Plains. The two routes converge on Tirau, where SH1 heads south to Taupo and SH5 crosses the Mamaku Plateau to Rotorua, 52km to the east.

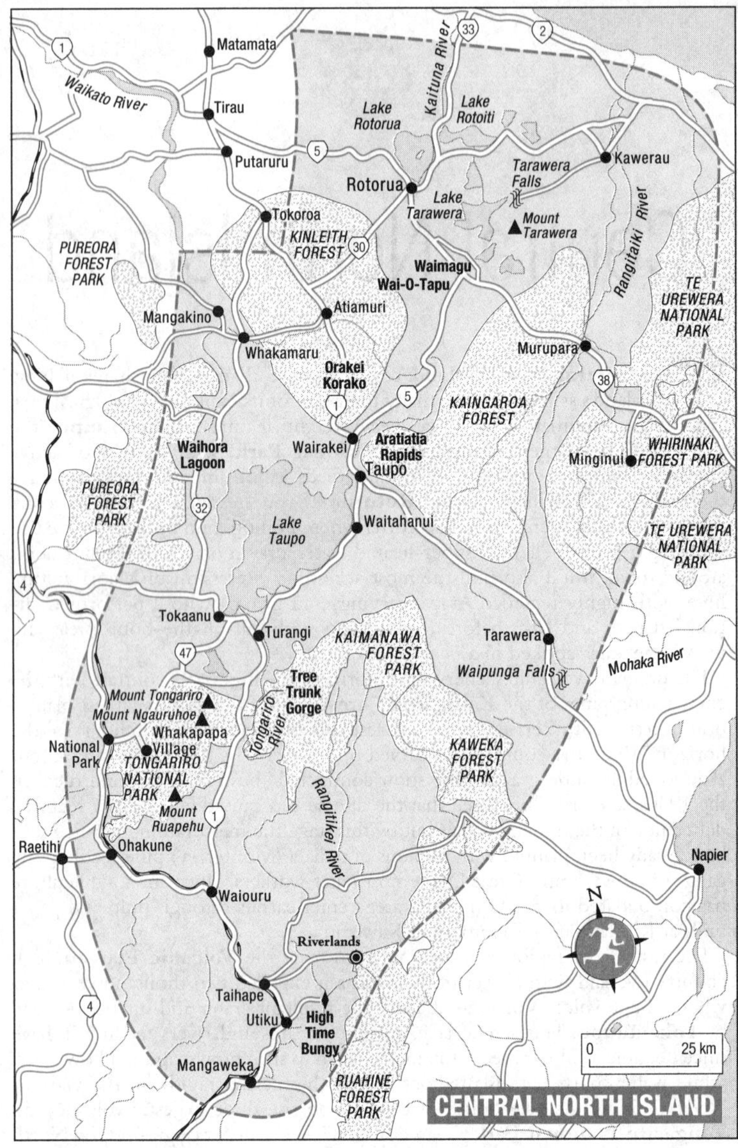

Climate wise, the altitude of the Volcanic Plateau lends Taupo, the Tongariro National Park and environs a crispness, even in high summer. Spring and autumn are tolerably warm and have the added advantage of freedom from the summer hordes, though the freezing winter months from May to October are best left to winter-sports enthusiasts. Rotorua is generally balmier but still cool in winter, making the thermal areas steamier and hot baths more appealing.

Rotorua and around

Rotorua is the North Island's tourist destination *par excellence*, one of the world's most concentrated and accessible geothermal areas, where twenty-metre geysers spout among kaleidoscopic mineral pools, steam wafts over cauldrons of boiling mud and terraces of encrusted silicates drip like stalactites. Everywhere you look there's evidence of vulcanism: birds on the lakeshore are relieved of the chore of nest-sitting by the warmth of the ground; in churchyards tombs are built topside as digging graves is likely to unearth a hot spring; and hotels are equipped with geothermally fed hot tubs, perfect for easing bones after a hard day's sightseeing. Throughout the region, sulphur and heat combine to form barren landscapes where only hardy plants brave the trickling hot streams, sputtering vents and seething fumaroles. There's no shortage of colour, however, from iridescent mineral deposits lining the pools: bright oranges juxtaposed with emerald greens and rust reds. The underworld looms large in Rotorua's lexicon: there's no end of "The Devil's" this and "Hell's" that, a state of affairs that prompted George Bernard Shaw to ruminate on his colourful past while visiting the Hell's Gate thermal area and famously quip, "It reminds me too vividly of the fate theologians have promised me".

But constant hydrothermal activity is only part of Rotorua's appeal. The naturally hot water lured **Maori** to settle around Lake Rotorua and Lake Tarawera, using the hottest pools for cooking and bathing, and building their *whare* (houses) on warm ground to drive away the winter chill. Despite the inevitably diluting effects of tourism there is no better place to get an introduction to Maori values, traditions, dance and song than at one of the concert and *hangi* evenings held all over Rotorua and in nearby *marae*.

Maori-owned and -operated tour companies often make insightful, not to mention entertaining, ways of exploring Rotorua's surrounding area. To the south and east, the forests are punctuated by sixteen **lakes** tucked into bush-girt hollows, overlooked by mountainous products of ancient volcanic activity and its more recent manifestation, the shattered five-kilometre-long chasm of **Mount Tarawera**. During one cataclysmic night of eruptions in 1886 this chain split in two, destroying the region's first tourist attraction (the reputedly beautiful Pink and White Terraces), entombing the nearest settlement, Te Wairoa, now known as the **Buried Village**, and creating the **Waimangu Volcanic Valley**. This is just one of many, often magnificent, thermal areas around Rotorua. As well as Waimangu, the superior paying attractions are the **Whakarewarewa Village** on the outskirts of town; the Lady Knox Geyser and the coloured pools at **Wai-O-Tapu**, to the south of Waimangu; and the fierce bubbling mud of **Hell's Gate**, in the northeast of Rotorua.

Some history

The Rotorua region is home to the Arawa people, who trace their ancestry back to the **Arawa canoe**, believed to have journeyed from the Polynesian homelands of Hawaiki in the fourteenth century, striking land at Maketu at the mouth of the Kaituna River on the Bay of Plenty. According to Maori history, one of the first parties to explore the interior was led by the *tohunga* (priest), **Ngatoroirangi**, who made it as far as the freezing summit of Mount Tongariro, where he feared he might die from cold. His prayers to the gods of Hawaiki were answered with fire that journeyed underground, surfacing at White Island in the Bay of Plenty, then at several more points in a line between there and the three central North Island volcanoes. Ngatoroirangi was saved, and he and his followers established themselves around Lake Rotorua, where they lived contentedly until another Arawa sailor, the wily **Ihenga**, duped Ngatoroirangi out of his land. The victor named the lakes as he reached them along the Kaituna River: Lake Rotoiti ("small lake") and Lake Rotorua ("second lake").

In revenge for an earlier raid on an island in nearby Green Lake, the Northland Ngapuhi chief, **Hongi Hika**, led a war party here in 1823. The Arawa got wind of the attack and retreated to Mokoia Island, in the middle of Lake Rotorua; undaunted, Hongi Hika and his warriors carried their canoes overland between lakes (the track between Lake Rotoiti and Lake Rotoehu still bears the name Hongi's Track). The Ngapuhi, equipped with muskets traded with Europeans in the Bay of Islands, defeated the traditionally armed Arawa then withdrew, leaving the Arawa to regroup in time for the New Zealand Wars of the 1860s, in which the Arawa supported the government. This worked in their favour when, in 1870, **Te Kooti** (see box, p.426) and his people attacked from the east coast, because colonial troops helped repulse them.

By this time a few **Europeans** – notably a Danish trader Philip Hans Tapsell and the missionary Thomas Chapman – had already lived for some years in the Maori villages of Ohinemutu and Whakarewarewa, but it wasn't until Te Kooti had been driven off that Rotorua came into existence. **Tourists** began to arrive in the district to view the Pink and White Terraces, using Ohinemutu, Whakarewarewa and Te Wairoa as staging posts. The Arawa, who up to this point had been relatively isolated from European influence, quickly grasped the possibilities of tourism, helping make Rotorua what it is today.

Rotorua

You smell **Rotorua** long before you see it. Hydrogen sulphide, drifting up from natural vents in the region's thin crust, means that a whiff of rotten eggs lingers in the air, but after a few hours you barely notice it. Certainly, the odour stops no one from visiting this small city on the southern shores of the near-circular **Lake Rotorua**, its northern and southern boundaries marked by two ancient villages of the Arawa sub-tribe, Ngati Whakaue: lakeshore **Ohinemutu** and inland **Whakarewarewa**, the only settlements before the 1880s, when Rotorua became New Zealand's only city with its origins firmly rooted in tourism. Specifically, Rotorua was set up as a **spa town** on land leased from the Ngati Whakaue, under the auspices of the 1881 Thermal Springs Districts Act. By 1885, the fledgling city boasted the Government Sanatorium Complex, a spa designed to administer the rigorous treatments deemed beneficial to the "invalids" who came to take the waters. The original **Bath House** is now part of **Rotorua Museum**, set in the grounds of the oh-so-English **Government Gardens**, which successfully and entertainingly puts these early enterprises into context.

Arrival and information

Long-distance **buses** pull up outside the information centre, as do Guthreys (Ⓣ0800/759 999) who run here from Auckland via Hamilton. Air New Zealand **flights** land 8km northeast of town at the lakeside airport (Ⓣ07/345 6175). The door-to-door Super Shuttle (Ⓣ07/349 3444) charges $17 for the run into town, while **taxis** are $25–30 (see p.312).

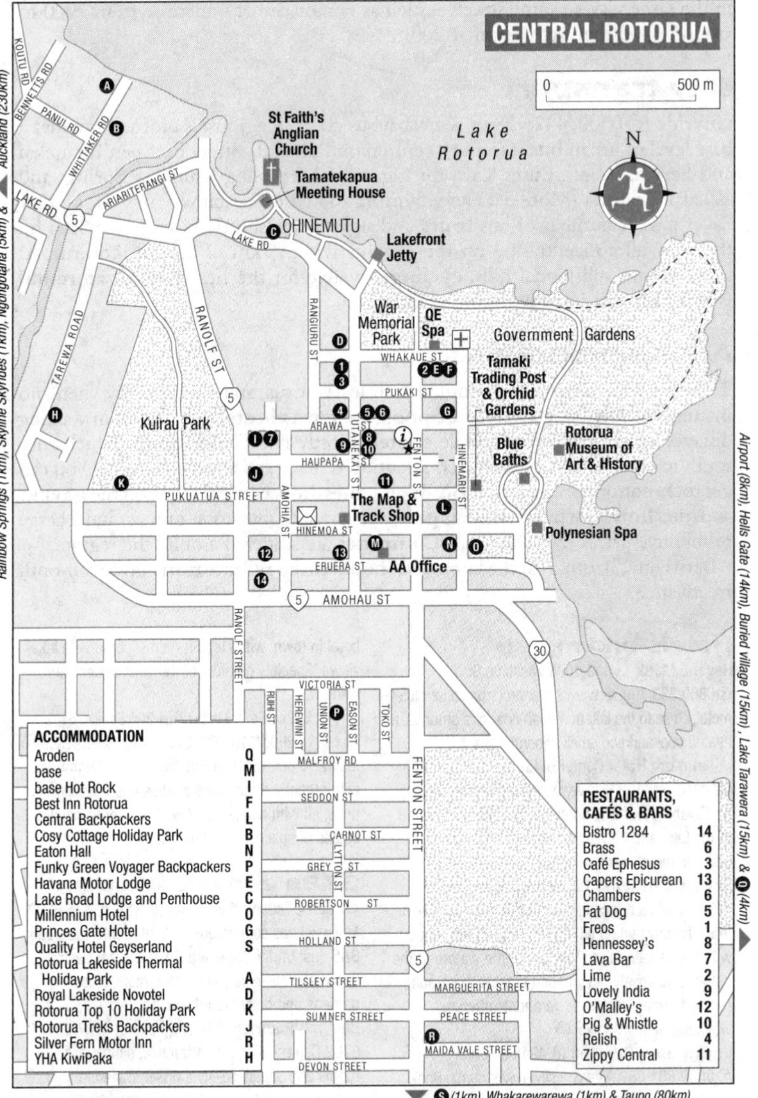

The **i-SITE visitor centre**, at 1167 Fenton St (daily: Nov–Easter 8am–6pm; Easter–Oct 8am–5.30pm; ⓣ07/348 5179, ⓦwww.rotoruanz.com), has two efficient, often busy, desks, one dealing with local tourism and DOC enquiries, the other with New Zealand-wide travel. For a general roundup of what's happening pick up the free weekly *Thermal Air Visitor's Guide*. Note that Central Rotorua **addresses** are subject to a block-based numbering system that increases south and west from the corner of Whakaue and Hinemaru streets near the lake, starting with the 1000 block. Confusingly, outlying areas haven't been numbered in the same way, so some streets – such as Fenton Street – increase from 1000 to around 1600 then start again at 200.

City transport

Cityride (ⓣ0800/442 928, ⓦwww.baybus.co.nz/Regions/Rotorua) provides a base level of urban **bus** transport, centred on Pukuatua Street between Tutanekai and Fenton streets. Buses leave for Ngongotaha, passing Rainbow Springs and Whakarewarewa (Mon–Sat every 30min), and cost $2 each way, or $6 for a Day Saver pass. A number of bus **tours** and sightseeing/shuttle buses (see p.313) fill the gaps, all concentrating on those sights within 7km of central Rotorua. As there are no substantial hills, **cycling** is viable for the fit, whereas **car rental** (see p.312) will suit the more sedentary.

Accommodation

There's a wide range of accommodation in Rotorua, and almost everywhere, no matter how low budget, has a **hot pool**. The town's **hostels** are all within walking distance of the city centre, while **motels** mostly line Fenton Street, which runs south towards Whakarewarewa; competition is fierce and at off-peak times you can get rock-bottom prices. Good **B&Bs** and **guesthouses** are thinner on the ground, and the **hotels**, while plentiful, generally cater to bus-tour groups and charge prohibitive prices for "walk-ins". **Campsites** are scattered around the region.

Between Christmas and March you should make **reservations** up to a month in advance.

Hotels and motels

Havana Motor Lodge 1078 Whakaue St ⓣ0800/333 799, ⓦwww.havanarotorua.co.nz. Quiet motel, close to the lakefront with spacious grounds, a heated pool and two small mineral pools. 3

Millennium Hotel Corner of Eruera & Hinemaru sts ⓣ07/3471234, ⓦwww.millenniumrotorua.co.nz. Swanky, tour-bus hotel within spitting distance of the lake and Polynesian Spa, facilities include a bar, restaurant, swimming pool and Sky TV. 6

Princes Gate Hotel 1057 Arawa St ⓣ07/348 1179, ⓦwww.princesgate.co.nz. The sole survivor from the days when all of Hinemaru St was lined with hotels catering to folk taking the waters at the bathhouse. Lovely old wooden hotel with en-suite rooms fronting onto wide verandas, offering weekend dinner shows. 5

Quality Hotel Geyserland 424 Fenton St ⓣ0800/881 882, ⓦwww.silverokas.co.nz. Book early to get a third- or fourth-floor room with unsurpassed views of the Whakarewarewa thermal area. Viewless rooms are cheaper, but that defeats the object of staying here. 5

Royal Lakeside Novotel Lake end Tutanekai St ⓣ0800/444 422, ⓦwww.novotel.co.nz. Swankiest hotel in town, with elegant rooms, some with lake views. Specials on most of the year, prices vary wildly. 6

Silver Fern Motor Inn 326 Fenton St ⓣ0800/118 808, ⓦwww.silverfernresort.co.nz. Knock-out, modern, top-of-the-line motel with recently refurbished studios and one-bedroom units, all with spa pools, Sky TV, sunny balconies, oodles of space and helpful staff. 5

B&Bs and guesthouses

Aroden 2 Hilton Rd (see map, p.313) ⓣ345 6303, ⓦwww.babs.co.nz/aroden. Comfortable suburban B&B, just off the Tarawera Rd 4km from central Rotorua, with -nicely appointed rooms, lush gardens and tasty breakfasts. 4

Best Inn Rotorua 1068 Whakaue St ⓣ07/347 9769.Central B&B with attractive, simple, clean rooms and Japanese-style onsen mineral baths. 4

Eaton Hall 39 Hinemaru St ⓣ0800/328 664, ⓦwww.eatonhallbnb.co.nz. Comfy B&B with three en suites and seven rooms with shared facilities, in the heart of town. 3

Lake Road Lodge and Penthouse 21 Lake Rd ⓣ0800/522 526, ⓦwww.jackanddis.co.nz. Two

> A continuing problem around Rotorua's centre is **theft from cars**, with thieves targeting those parked near hostels. Take any valuables into your room or ask to use a safe.

properties right by Ohinemutu with good lake views. A lodge with three doubles or luxury penthouse apartment, sleeping four, both non-hosted but including a continental breakfast. Rooms ④, apartment $249.

Hostels

Base 1140 Hinemoa St ⓣ0800/843 392, ⓦwww.basebacpackers.co.nz. Central and well-appointed hostel with separate music, TV and games rooms, a female-only floor and a 20-metre indoor climbing wall adjacent. Dorms $25, four-shares $28, doubles ②

Base Hot Rock 1286 Arawa St ⓣ0800/462 396, ⓦwww.basenz.co.nz. Large, lively hostel that's a perennial favourite of the backpacker tour buses, with two mineral pools, a heated outdoor swimming pool and the *Lava Bar* next door. Accommodation is mostly four-share dorms, each with private bathroom. There are backpacker doubles and en suites with kitchens, triple en suites and a female-only dorm. Dorms $25, twin & double rooms ②–③ triple rooms ③

Central Backpackers 1076 Pukuatua St ⓣ07/349 3285, ⓔrcbenquiry@slingshot.co.nz. Small, homely hostel, with beds rather than bunks in the four- and six-bed dorm rooms, plus a spa pool. Dorms $21–24, twins & doubles ①

Funky Green Voyager Backpackers 4 Union St ⓣ07/346 1754, ⓕ350 1100. Relaxed hostel in a suburban house, 10min walk from downtown, with an easy-going communal atmosphere fostered by the idiosyncratic owner of seventeen years. Cooking facilities in particular are excellent and there's a cosy, TV-less lounge and roaring log fire. Dorms $20, doubles and en suites ①

Rotorua Treks Backpackers 1278 Haupapa St ⓣ0508/487 357, ⓦwww.treks.co.nz. Large, well-managed hostel with clean rooms and spacious tasteful communal areas, plus a large kitchen and car park. The enthusiastic owner will create single-sex dorms on request and beds are separate rather than bunk. Triples as well as en-suite doubles and twins are offered. Dorms $27, rooms ②

YHA KiwiPaka 60 Tarewa Rd ⓣ07/347 0931, ⓦwww.kiwipaka-yha.co.nz. This well-organized complex is only a 5min walk from the town centre (on the far side of Kuirau Park), yet it's far enough away to avoid late-night party noise. Accommodation is great value and split between the "lodge", with four- or five-shares, singles, twins and doubles, and the en-suite chalets. There's also an excellent low-cost café and a travel desk. Camping $9, four- and five-shares $25, rooms ①, chalets ③

Campsites and motor parks

Blue Lake Top 10 Holiday Park Tarawera Rd, Blue Lake (see map, p.313) ⓣ0800/808 292, ⓦwww.bluelaketop10.co.nz. Well-organized site 9km from Rotorua, on the way to the Buried Village, just across the road from Blue Lake. Extensive facilities include a games room and a spa pool. Camping $15, cabins & kitchen cabins ②, s/c units ②

Cosy Cottage Holiday Park 67 Whittaker Rd ⓣ07/348 3793, ⓦwww.cosycottage.co.nz. Holiday park 2km from town with an extensive range of comfortable cabins, s/c cottages, powered and tent sites, some geothermally heated – great in winter. There's a swimming pool, a couple of pleasant mineral pools, naturally fed steam boxes for *hangi*-style cooking, and bikes ($20 a day). Camping $15, cabins ②, s/c cottages ③

Rotorua Lakeside Thermal Holiday Park 54 Whittaker Rd ⓣ07/348 1693, ⓔrelax@lakesidethermal.co.nz. Overlooking the lake, just 2km from town, with a mineral-water pool and mineral-water baths where you can adjust the temperature to suit. The accommodation, however, is rather run down. Camping $12.50, powered $30, cabins ②, kitchen cabins ②

Rotorua Top 10 Holiday Park 137 Pukuatua St ⓣ07/348 1886, ⓦwww.rotoruatop10.co.nz. The closest campsite to the city, with an outdoor pool and spa, a spacious camping area ($16), basic but serviceable cabins (②) and motel units (③).

The town, Lake Rotorua and Whakarewarewa

It's possible to spend half a day on foot visiting the fine collection of Maori artefacts and bathhouse relics in the **Rotorua Museum**, located in the old bathhouse in the formal **Government Gardens**, and strolling around the shores of **Lake Rotorua** to Ohinemutu, the city's original Maori village with its neatly carved church. Afterwards, you can ease your bones with a soak in the hot pools, set in a native bird sanctuary, by catching a boat out to **Mokoia Island**, the romantic setting for the tale of two lovers, Hinemoa and Tutanekai.

Otherwise, Rotorua's sights are so scattered you'll require some form of transport. Sightseeing/shuttle buses (see p.313) do the rounds to **Whakarewarewa**, a large thermal reserve now divided into two sections: the **Thermal Village**, where folk still go about their daily lives amid the steam and boiling pools; and the **Te Puia**, with its geyser, thermal park and a carving and weaving school. Where Rotorua's northwestern suburbs peter out, Mount Ngongotaha rises up, providing the necessary slope for a number of gravity-driven activities at the **Skyline Skyrides**. In its shadow, **Rainbow Springs Nature Park**, an aquatic farm, provides a window into the life cycle of trout, and an excellent **Kiwi Encounter**, while the nearby **Agrodome** fills the prescription for adrenalin junkies.

Government Gardens and around

In the early twentieth century, Rotorua was New Zealand's premier tourist town, a fact it celebrated in confident civic style by laying out the **Government Gardens,** east of the town centre. With their juxtaposition of the staid and the exotic, the gardens are a bizarre vision of an antipodean little England. White-clad croquet players totter round sulphurous steam vents, palm trees loom over rose gardens, and, commanding the centre, there's the neo-Tudor **bathhouse**, built in 1908. Heralded as the greatest spa in the South Seas, it was designed to treat patients suffering from just about any disorder – arthritis, alcoholism, nervousness – and offered ghoulish treatments involving electrical currents and colonic irrigation as well as the thermal baths. The bathhouse limped along until 1963, although the era of the grand spas had come to a close long before. For a modern sybaritic version of the experience head to the **Polynesian Spa** (see p.305), up the road, or the **QE Spa** near the lake.

Other than the attractions within the gardens themselves, on their southwestern edge you'll find the **Tamaki Trading Post & The Realm Of Tane**, a meeting point on the corner of Hinemaru and Pukuatua streets for tours of Tamaki Maori Village (see p.312).

The Rotorua Museum and the Blue Baths

The old bathhouse is now home to the wonderful **Rotorua Museum of Art and History** (daily: Oct to mid-March 9am–8pm; mid-March to Sept 9am–5pm; $12), which is currently being extended, in part to the original plans of 1908. Work on the north wing will be completed in 2008, while the south wing will be finished in 2011. For now, the recently opened viewing platform at the top of the building boasts great views over the town and lake and is well worth a visit, as is the basement which, because of the proximity of the thermal pools, gets hotter the further south you walk.

Above ground, the south wing houses *Taking the Waters*, an exhibition built around the old baths themselves, complete with gloomy green and white tiling and exposed pipes. Several rooms have been preserved in a state of arrested decay and filled with photos, some surprisingly frank, of the glory days, while an entertaining film recreates some of the history of both the area and baths. The north wing is devoted to three main exhibitions and will, when completed, contain an art gallery. Currently the small but exquisite and internationally significant **Te Arawa** display showcases the long-respected talents of Arawa carvers who made this area a bastion of pre-European carving traditions. Many pieces have been returned from European collections, and the magnificent carved figures, dog-skin cloaks, *pounamu* (greenstone) weapons and intricate bargeboards are all powerfully presented. Prized pieces include the flute played by the legendary lover Tutanekai (see p.306), an unusually fine pumice goddess, and rare eighteenth-century carvings executed with stone tools. The second exhibition covers the dramatic events surrounding the **Tarawera eruption**. The extensive displays include an informative relief map of the region, eyewitness accounts and reminiscences, an audiovisual presentation and photos of the ash-covered hotels at Te Wairoa and Rotomahana, both now demolished. Finally there's a small but moving section on the **Maori battalion**, with an evocative half-hour video.

While the main bathhouse promoted health, the adjacent **Blue Baths** promised only pleasure when it opened in 1933. Designed in the Californian Spanish Mission style, this was one of the first public swimming pools in the world to allow mixed bathing. It hit hard times and closed in 1982, not reopening until 1999. You can still swim in an ancillary outdoor pool ($9), or visit the museum, which concentrates on the Baths' early history (10am–5pm, $5), but the bulk of the building is given over to private functions, weddings and the like and so often closed at weekends.

The Polynesian Spa and QE Spa

Immediately south of the Blue Baths lies the **Polynesian Spa**, Hinemoa Street (daily 6.30am–11pm; Polynesian Pools $20, Lake Spa $40; ⓣ07/348 1328, ⓦwww.polynesianspa.co.nz), a mostly open-air complex landscaped for lake views and comprising three separate areas. The main Polynesian Pools have 35 hot mineral pools, claimed to treat all manner of ailments but principally arthritis and rheumatism. The vast majority of visitors bathe in either the slightly alkaline main pool or the small and turbid Radium and Priest pools, where the acidic waters bubbling up through the bottom of the tub vary from 36°C to 43°C. Private pools ($20 extra per person for 30min) are ranged around the Radium and Priest pools. But for real exclusivity opt for the adjacent **Lake Spa Retreat**, with four attractively landscaped shallow rock pools of differing temperatures along with private relaxation lounge and bar. Reserve in advance for massages, body scrubs, mud wraps and general pampering, from thirty minutes ($80, includes Lake Spa entry) onwards. Families are catered for in the new **Family Spa** ($32 for up to two adults and four kids), with one chlorinated 33°C pool, a couple of small mineral pools and a water slide.

If the Polynesian Spa is stuffed with visitors try the **QE Spa**, opposite the corner of Whakaue and Fenton streets (Mon–Fri 8am–10pm, Sat & Sun 9am–10pm, ⓣ07/348 0189, ⓦwww.qehealth.co.nz), which offers a variety of curative and therapeutic treatments, access to a public pool ($5), private pools ($10) and rheumatic consultation ($250).

Lake Rotorua and Mokoia Island

From the Government Gardens it's a short walk along the waterfront to the Lakefront Jetty, the starting point for trips on **Lake Rotorua** and to **Mokoia Island** (7km north of the jetty), New Zealand's only inland, predator-free bird sanctuary – the scene of a successful and longstanding breeding programme for saddlebacks and North Island robins (often spotted at the feeder stations) and the recently introduced kokako (see p.908). The island is better known, however, for the story of **Hinemoa and Tutanekai** (see box, p.306), the greatest Maori love story; the site of Tutanekai's *whare* and **Hinemoa's Pool** can still be seen on the island.

Mokoia Island Cruises offer **catamaran trips** ($70, or $95 with hot-pool, soak ⓣ0800/8627 8473, ⓦwww.mokoia-island.co.nz; 3 daily), with a guided tour of Mokoia Island, the emphasis on culture and conservation. If you fancy a more high-octane approach, roar out to the island on a **Kawarau Jet Boat**

The love story of Hinemoa and Tutanekai

The Maori love story of **Hinemoa and Tutanekai** has been told around the shores of Lake Rotorua for centuries. It tells of the illegitimate young chief Tutanekai of Mokoia Island and his high-born paramour, Hinemoa, whose family forbade her from marrying him. To prevent her from meeting him they beached their *waka* (canoe) but the strains of his lamenting flute wafted across the lake nightly and the smitten Hinemoa resolved to swim to him. One night, buoyed by gourds, she set off towards Mokoia but by the time she got there Tutanekai had retired to his *whare* (house) to sleep. Hinemoa arrived at the island but without clothes was unable to enter the village, so she immersed herself in a hot pool. Presently Tutanekai's slave came to collect water and Hinemoa lured him over, smashed his gourd and sent him back to his master. An enraged Tutanekai came to investigate, only to fall into Hinemoa's embrace.

90min; $89; (ⓣ07/3437 600; ⓦwww.nzjetboat.co.nz). If it's just a lake cruise you're after try the leisurely *Lakeland Queen* (ⓣ0800/572 784, ⓦwww.lakelandqueen.co.nz), a replica **paddle steamer** that runs a series of trips including meals – breakfast (7am & 8am; $37), lunch (12.30pm; $50) and dinner (6.45pm; $71).

Ohinemutu

Before Rotorua the principal Maori settlement in the area was at **Ohinemutu**, 500m north of the centre, on the lakeshore. Ohinemutu remains a Maori village centred on its hot springs and the small wooden **St Faith's Anglican Church**, built in 1914 to replace its 1885 predecessor. The church's simple half-timbered neo-Tudor exterior gives no hint of its rich interior, where there's barely a patch of wall that hasn't been carved or covered with *tukutuku* (ornamental latticework) panels. The main attraction is the window featuring the figure of Christ, swathed in a Maori cloak and feathers, positioned so that he appears to be walking on the lake. Outside is the grave of Gilbert Mair, a captain in the colonial army who twice saved Ohinemutu from attacks by rival Maori, becoming the only Pakeha to earn full Arawa chieftainship.

At the opposite end of the small square in front of the church stands the **Tamatekapua Meeting House**, again beautifully carved, though the best work, some dating back almost two hundred years, is inside. Unfortunately, it is inaccessible; although you may view the meeting house from outside you must not encroach on its perimeter.

Whakarewarewa Thermal Reserve

To New Zealanders, mention of Rotorua immediately conjures up images of the **Whakarewarewa Thermal Reserve** – or Whaka, as it is more commonly known – the closest thermal area to the city, with two distinct and separate attractions. Around two-thirds of the active thermal zone is leased to **Te Puia**, Hemo Road, 3km south of central Rotorua (daily: Nov–March 8am–6pm; April–Oct 8am–5pm; $50; ⓦwww.nzmaori.co.nz; free hour-long guided tours on the hour), the impressive start of a series of walkways past glooping pools of boiling mud, sulphurous springs and agglomerations of silica stalactites. The main attractions are New Zealand's most spectacular geysers, the ten-metre **Prince of Wales' Feathers** and the granddaddy of them all, the twenty-metre **Pohutu** ("big splash"), which performed several times a day until 2000, when it surprised everyone by spouting continuously for an unprecedented 329 days. It has since settled back to jetting water into the air around eighty percent of the time.

The complex also contains a **nocturnal house** with kiwi, a replica of a traditional **Maori village**, and an **Arts and Crafts Institute** (same hours; included with entry) where skilled artisans produce flax skirts and carvings which can be bought in the classy but expensive shop. The institute also hosts **Mia Ora** (daily: Nov–March 6.15pm; April–Oct 5.15pm; $90; ⓣ0800/837 842), comprising a Maori welcome, concert, steam-cooked feast and, weather permitting, floodlit tour of the geothermal valley. A Combo Package costs $130 and includes the cultural show, dinner and general admission.

▲ Maori carving, Rotorua

The rest of the thermal area falls under the auspices of **Whakarewarewa, The Thermal Village**, Tryon Street, 3km south of central Rotorua (daily 8.30am–5pm; guided tours 9.30am, 10.30am, 11.45am, 1.30pm & 3.30pm; $25; ⓦwww.whakarewarewa.com), a living village founded in pre-European times and undergoing continual, though sympathetic, modernization. The focus here is not on geysers but on how Maori interact with this unique environment. You can stroll at leisure around the village, attend the free **cultural performance** (11.15am & 2pm), and partake in a **hangi** (served at 12.30pm; $55; *hangi* taster $28.50).

The western fringe of the Whakarewarewa thermal area borders the **Whakarewarewa State Forest Park**, experimentally planted a century back to see which exotic species would grow well under New Zealand conditions. Redwoods were found to grow three times faster than in their native California, creating the impressive **Redwood Grove**, threaded by a number of short paths. The forest's **visitor centre**, Long Mile Road (Oct–March Mon–Fri 9am–5pm, Sat 9am–3pm; ⓣ07/350 0110), has details of these in its free *The Redwoods* recreation guide, and information on the excellent **mountain-biking trails**. The forest is also the venue for **horse rides** with Maori-run Peka Horse Trekking (ⓣ07/346 1755, ⓔpeka.info@xtra.co.nz), which offers one-hour ($50), two-hour ($80) and longer treks on request.

West of the Lake: Around Ngongotaha

Aside from visits to the thermal areas, much of Rotorua's daytime activity takes place around the flanks of **Mount Ngongotaha**, between five and ten kilometres northwest of the centre, which is increasingly being overtaken by the city's suburbs. Closest to downtown, there's all manner of gravity-driven activities at the **Skyline Skyrides** site, and gentler pursuits at either **Rainbow Springs** or around the mountain at **Paradise Valley Springs**. Sheep take centre stage (literally) a little further out at the **Agrodome**, an adventure park that wrestles for the adrenalin torch with the Skyline Skyrides.

Skyline Skyrides, Rainbow Springs and Paradise Valley

First stop, around 4km from town, is the **Skyline Skyrides**, where gondolas (daily 9am–late; $23; ⓣ07/347 0027, ⓦwww.skylineskyrides.co.nz) whisk you 200m up to the station on the mountain for superb views across the lake and town, scenic dining in the restaurant (the gondola runs return trips until the restaurant closes, 10–11pm most nights) and café, and a bevy of adventure activities including the **luge** ($7.50 per ride, $27.50 for 5) and the adjacent **Sky Swing** ride ($30), which drops semi-brave daredevils from 50m.

At the foot of the hill lies **Rainbow Springs Nature Park** (daily 8am–9pm, later in summer; $24.50, combo ticket with Kiwi Encounter $40, see below; ⓣ07/350 0440, ⓦwww.rainbowsprings.co.nz), a series of trout pools linked by nature trails where you can view massive rainbow, brown and North American brook trout. Also here is the excellent **Kiwi Encounter** (daily 10am–4pm; $27.50; ⓣ0800/724 626, ⓦwww.kiwiencounter.co.nz), an insightful celebration of the conservation work supporting the country's icon in the battle against extinction. A heart-warming 45-minute guided tour (on the hour, from 10am) of the "working nursery" demonstrates egg incubation and ends with a kiwi viewing.

For even more trout but in the company of lions, try **Paradise Valley Springs**, 13km west of Rotorua on Paradise Valley Road (daily 8am–late; $25; ⓣ07/348 9667, ⓦwww.paradisev.co.nz). A network of boardwalks guides you over pools of trout, native birds and an attractive wetland area, though the biggest draw is the breeding pride of lions, with the chance to touch a lion cub and, at 2.30pm, watch the adults feed. Trout superfans should continue along Paradise Valley Road to reach the **Ngongotaha Hatchery** (daily 9am–4pm; free; ⓣ07/357 5501), for an insight into the activities of Fish & Game New Zealand, the outfit that stocks most of the lakes. Paradise Valley Road continues to the Agrodome.

The Agrodome and Agrodome Adventure Park

Just about every bus touring the North Island stops 10km north of Rotorua at the **Agrodome**, Western Road, Ngongotaha (shows at 9.30am, 11am & 2.30pm; show $24, organic farm tour and show $46; ⓣ07/357 1050, ⓦwww.agrodome.co.nz), where the star attraction is a slick 45-minute **sheep show** involving lots of audience participation: rams representing the nineteen major breeds farmed in New Zealand are enticed onto the podium; a sheep is shorn; lambs are bottle-fed and there's a sheepdog display. Afterwards, the dogs are put through their paces outside – rounding up sheep and so on – and you can watch a 1906 industrial carding machine turn fleece into usable wool. There's also a 45-minute farm tour complete with honey tasting, a visit to an organic orchard, deer viewing and, between April and June, kiwifruit picking.

A different market is catered for at the adjacent **Agrodome Adventure Park** (daily 9am–5pm or later), where adrenalin junkies can get fixed. Attractions include a 43-metre **bungy jump** ($90), the **Swoop** swing ride ($45), and the **Agrojet** ($45) where tiny racing jetboats hurtle around a short course. The best attraction is the **Freefall Extreme** ($49 for 2min), which simulates freefalling, à la skydiving, using a powerful propeller and safety net above which you hover (or at least try to) five metres up. Less adrenalin glands get pumped but probably more laughter ensues at the **Zorb** ($49 a wet roll, $59 a dry) – another Kiwi-pioneered nutter ride. You dive into the centre of a huge clear plastic ball and roll down a two-hundred-metre hill or the slower but wilder zigzag course; you can choose from wet and dry rides, the former being the more fun. The Agrodome's latest attraction, the **Schweeb** ($45 for four laps), offers a chance to race bicycles inside clear plastic tubes attached to overhead rails forming an undulating circuit, either in teams or solo. Designed as a futuristic form of transport it's nowhere near as geeky as it sounds, particularly if you can get two teams together. Add to this the possibility of helicopter rides with HeliPro (see p.314) and you've got yourself quite a day out and an empty wallet.

Activities

As you'd expect in a place that attracts so many visitors, numerous companies have sprung up in Rotorua to offer all manner of adventure activities – rafting, kayaking, mountain biking and even fishing. **Adventure tourism** hasn't quite snowballed to the same degree as in Queenstown but there's plenty to keep you occupied. In addition to the activities detailed below you might want to try scenic **skydiving** with NZONE (15,000ft $399; ⓣ0800/3767 9663, ⓦwww.nzone.biz), although needlessly jumping out of a perfectly good aeroplane is cheaper down the road at Taupo.

Rafting, kayaking and sledging

Rotorua has a considerable reputation for its nearby whitewater rivers, which you can tackle aboard **rafts**, **kayaks** (usually tandems) or, more in-your-face, by "**sledging**" – floating down rapids wearing safety gear and clinging to a buoyant plastic sledge (really only for good swimmers). Much of the hype is reserved for the Grade V **Kaituna River**, or at least the two-kilometre section after it leaves Lake Rotoiti 20km north of Rotorua, which includes the spectacular seven-metre **Tutea's Falls**. The one to go for though, if you can get the timing right, is the Grade IV-plus **Wairoa River**, 80km by road from Rotorua, on the outskirts of Tauranga, which relies on dam-releases for raftable quantities of white water (Dec–March every Sun; Sept–Nov & April–May every second Sun). This is one of the finest short trips available in New Zealand, negotiating a hazardous but immensely satisfying stretch of water – essentially for those with experience and an appreciation of the dangers involved.

If your tastes lean more towards appreciation of the natural surroundings with a bit of a bumpy ride thrown in, opt for the Grade III **Rangitaiki River**, which also shoots Jeff's Joy, a Grade IV drop that's the highlight of the trip. With more time and money, it's worth considering a **multi-day wilderness rafting trip** on the East Cape's **Motu River** (see box, p.402). You could also **rent kayaks** or undertake **kayaking courses** and **guided trips** on several of the larger lakes in the region, with the emphasis on scenic appreciation, soaking in hot pools and a little fishing.

Adventure Kayaking ⓣ07/348 9451, ⓦwww.adventurekayaking.co.nz. Rents sea kayaks ($40 per seat per day) and undertakes guided trips including the Twilight Paddle ($80) on the Lake Tarawera Full Day Tour ($110), or individually tailored overnighters (from $210).

Kaitiaki Adventures ⓣ0800/338 736, ⓦwww.raft-it.com. Rafting and sledging trips down the Kaituna, Rangitaiki and Wairoa rivers with a cultural dimension - explaining the significance of the river to Maori. They also have modified rafts and sledges to better suit the conditions. Prices from $82–170, times from 3hr 30min to 8hr.

Kaituna Cascades ⓣ0800/524 886, ⓦwww.kaitunacascades.co.nz. Rafting on all the rivers mentioned above and the Motu, as well as extreme kayaking trips on the Kaituna and kayaking on Lake Rotoiti.

Kaituna Kayaks ⓣ0800/465 292, ⓦwww.kaitunakayaks.com. Offer tandem kayaking on the Kaituna River, including the seven-metre Tutea's Falls. Also specialize in kayak courses.

Raftabout ⓣ0800/7238 22688, ⓦwww.raftabout.co.nz. Rafting trips on the Kaituna, the Rangitaiki and the Wairoa, plus sledging from $99 (under the name Sledgeabout) on the Kaituna and a variety of combo deals including other adventure activities.

River Rats ⓣ0800/333 900, ⓦwww.riverrats.co.nz. Long-established company offering rafting on all the above rivers and adventure packages including various multi-adventure combo deals.

Sun Spots Kayak Shop SH33, Okawa Bay 14km north of Rotorua ☎07/362 4222, Ⓦwww.sunspots.co.nz. Kayak rental ($35 per seat per day) and courses including the half-day introduction and longer intermediate and advanced ones.

Wet'n'Wild ☎0800/462 7238, Ⓦwww.wetnwildrafting.co.nz. One-day trips on the Kaituna, Rangitaiki and Wairoa, and overnight to five-day rafting expeditions further afield on the Motu, and upper or lower Mohaka.

Mountain biking

Some fine and accessible **mountain biking** lies fifteen minutes' ride from central Rotorua, with large areas of the Whakarewarewa Forest's redwoods, firs and pines threaded by single-track trails especially constructed with banked turns and jumps under a sub-canopy of tree ferns. Altogether there's over 40km of track, divided into a dozen circuits in five grades of difficulty and all explained and colourfully illustrated on the waterproof **trail map** ($2) available from the forest visitor centre on Long Mile Road. Don't think that it's just for experts though; any level of pedaller can get great pleasure from half a day mucking about in this atmospheric forest. There is **no charge** to enter the forest or use the trails, most of which are accessed from the obvious car park on Waipa Mill Road, 5km south of town off SH38.

For **bike rental** try Planet Bike, 89 Vue Rd (☎07/346 1717, Ⓦwww.planetbike.co.nz), which rents bikes and gear for guided (from 2hr, $65), or self-guided mountain biking (full day, $55) through the forest, for all experience levels; it also offers women-only rides.

Fishing

The lakes adjacent to and around Rotorua have a reputation for trout fishing bettered only by the North Island rivers and streams flowing into Lake Taupo. The angling, in sixteen lakes, is both scenic and rewarding, with waters stocked with strong-fighting rainbow trout; a typical summer catch is around 1.5kg, while in winter it can creep up towards 3kg. The proximity of **Lake Rotorua** makes it a perennial favourite, reached by charter boats from the Lakefront Jetty (2hr minimum; $120 plus per hour, including tackle but not licences – see p.68).

If you are going it alone, obtain up-to-date information on lake and river conditions from O'Keefe's, 1113 Eruera St (☎07/346 0178), who stock the free *Lake Rotorua & Tributaries* leaflet published by Fish & Game New Zealand, explaining the rules of the fishery and will provide contacts for fly-fishing **guides**, generally around $500 for a half-day. **Licences** (24hr $19; year $96) are valid for the whole country except for the Taupo fishery region and can be bought with a credit card ($5 extra) from the licence helpline (☎0800/542 362).

Eating, drinking and entertainment

A few quality **restaurants**, most congregated along a short strip at the lake end of Tutanekai Street (known as "The Streat"), and lots of great cafés enliven eating in Rotorua. Unless you're part of a large group, there's little need to reserve a table. There are several good bars in Rotorua, but otherwise nightlife is limited: a few late-night venues have a bash at keeping you entertained but most visitors spend one evening of their stay at one of the **hangi** and/or **Maori concerts** in either a tourist hotel or, preferably, one of the outlying Maori villages.

Restaurants and cafés

Bistro 1284 1284 Eruera St. White linen tablecloths belie the relatively relaxed atmosphere in what is one of Rotorua's better restaurants. Dinner only (from 6pm); closed Sun & Mon.

Café Ephesus 1107 Tutanekai St. Unassuming and cheap, with generous portions of Turkish, Mediterranean and Middle Eastern fare dished up. Chomp on traditional delights like *dolmades* or *guveche* ($17–22).

Capers Epicurean 1181 Eruera St. Large airy café-cum-deli serving up wonderful breakfasts, from 7.30am daily, colourful salads, over-stuffed panini, Persian fish curry and pork spare ribs. Excellent-value lunches and dinners in a bustling cosmopolitan atmosphere.

Chambers 1151 Arawa St. Plenty of European fare but the Belgian grub's best. Mussel connoisseurs will salivate over the treats on offer from the Mosselen (from $17–18, other mains from $18–27). Occasional live music and a good selection of Belgian beers.

Fat Dog 1161 Arawa St. Friendly café/bar with a great atmosphere, engendered by mismatched furniture, daubed limericks on the walls and funky music. Drop in for lunch (from $10), or go for the wide-ranging selection of hearty breakfast or dinner mains ($19–31). For breakfast The Fat Dog Works ($14.90) should sort out hangovers and the coffee is some of the best in town. Takeaways available.

Freos 1103 Tutanekai St ⓣ07/346 0976. Modern Kiwi café offering dining at reasonable prices with alfresco option. Good for steaks, lamb and fish.

The Landing Tarawera Rd, 18km southeast of Rotorua (see map, p.313) ⓣ07/362 8595. European-influenced Kiwi grub at moderate prices in a waterside café, restaurant and bar – with great views across to Lake Tarawera towards Mount Tarawera.

Lime 1096 Whakaue St. Bustling all-day café serving stand-up coffee and tasty breakfasts as well as snacks and cakes.

Lovely India 1123 Tutanekai St ⓣ07/348 4088. Authentic, licensed Indian restaurant with a wide range of good-quality vegetarian dishes as well as the standard lamb kormas and tandoori chickens ($13–20). Takeaway available.

Relish 1149 Tutanekai St. Licensed café serving home-made toasted muesli, wood-fired pizzas and good cake. Daily 7am–4pm, dinners Wed–Fri.

Skyline Cableway Restaurant Skyline, Fairy Springs Rd ⓣ07/347 0027. Well worth a visit, if only for the beautiful view of the lights of Rotorua dancing by the lakeside at dusk. A surprisingly good NZ buffet combines the best available seafood, steaks, lamb, venison and vegetable selection in a value-for-money package. Plus excellent service.

Zippy Central 1153 Pukuatua St. Groovy licensed restaurant with haphazard retro 1950s and 1960s pop decor. Serves great coffee and imaginative and well-prepared food, from salads and bagels to smoothies. Mains from $15.

Bars and clubs

Brass1122 Tutanekai St ⓣ07/349 6306. Upscale downtown cocktail bar that does weekend brunches, good steak and fish dishes and hosts DJs (Fri), live acts and bands (Sat). Closed Sun & Mon.

Hennessey's 1206–1210 Tutanekai St. Dimly lit but pleasant enough Irish bar popular with backpackers, mainly because of the cheap "mad meal and pint" deals. Live music Thurs & Sat.

Lava Bar 1286 Arawa St. A house converted into a bar that's found favour with backpackers, rafting guides and local youth. Basic meals are available and there's an early-evening happy hour, pinball machines and a pool table if you can get to them, plus late-night music. Small cover charge on Sat.

O'Malley's 1287 Eruera St. Ersatz Irish bar with a strong line in draught Irish beers and bargain meals. Live Irish-style bands Fri plus regular happy hours.

Pig & Whistle Corner of Haupapa & Tutanekai sts. Lively bar in a former police station with some locally brewed beers on tap, a garden bar, and rock and pop covers bands or DJs and dancing at weekends when tidy dress is required and a $3 cover applies. There are also large and reasonably priced bar meals.

Hangi and Maori concerts

If you want to sample food steamed to perfection in the Maori earth oven or **hangi** and watch a **Maori concert**, typically an hour-long performance of traditional dance, song and chants, then Rotorua provides more opportunities than anywhere else. Although not an entirely satisfactory introduction to Maori culture, these are at least reliable and good value. Almost a dozen groups vie for your custom, the offerings falling into two distinct camps: extravaganzas laid on at the major hotels, invariably disappointing; or packages operated and organized by **Maori groups**. All run for three to four hours, most start around 6 or 7pm, with buses picking up and dropping off at hotels and hostels; some hotels offer *hangi*-only or concert-only deals. The **out-of-town packages** are more rewarding, though all follow largely the same format, giving instruction on *marae* customs and protocol (see "Maoritanga" in Contexts, p.893) as you are driven out to a Maori village, followed by a formal welcome.

Mitai ☎07/343 9132, ⓦwww.mitai.co.nz. You might end up with wood smoke in your eyes, but other than that this is a polished product with a solid initial show, the chance to see a fully manned *waka* and enjoy a decent *hangi* feed before looking at the natural springs, picked out by lights, bubbling up through the riverbed ($92).
Rotoiti Tours ☎0800/476 864, ⓦwww.worldofmaori.co.nz. In some ways more authentic than the others, or at least engaging because of its size, with almost the whole *whanau* (extended family group) contributing to the proceedings in the beautifully decorated meeting house on the Rakeiao Marae at Tapuaekura Bay on the shores of Lake Rotoiti, 20km north of Rotorua (around $80).
Tamaki Maori Village ☎07/346 2823, ⓦwww.maoriculture.co.nz. You, and several busloads, are driven out to a specially built "Maori village" south of town for a spine-chilling welcome. Everything is so professionally done that it is hard to quibble, though parts may feel a bit "Hollywood". Its popularity has become its biggest downfall and sightlines can be restricted, however, the *hangi* is probably the best on offer and the overall experience unforgettable ($90).
Te Puia ☎07/348 90 47, ⓦwww.tepuia.com. A "Mai Ora – Essence of Maori" evening performance is offered at Te Puia's extensive complex in part of the Whakarewarewa Thermal Reserve, which adds an extra layer to the generally professional show they put on during the day, plus some good food and a chance to look at boiling mud in the dark ($90).

Listings

Airlines Air New Zealand Travelcentre, corner of Hinemoa & Fenton sts ☎0800/737 000.
Automobile Association 1121 Eruera St ☎07/348 3069.
Bike rental Rotorua Cycle Centre, 1120 Hinemoa St ☎07/348 6588. See also "Mountain biking" p.310.
Bookshops Idle Hour Book Inn, 1112 Eruera St, for secondhand books; Whitcoulls, 1238 Tutanekai St, for new.
Car rental All the usual suspects including Budget, 1230 Fenton St (☎07/348 8127, ⓦwww.budget.co.nz), Handy Rentals, corner of Ranouf & Amohau sts (☎0800/479 849) and U-Drive, 153 Lake Rd (☎0800/837 483).
Cinema The local multiplex is Readings Cinema, 1263 Eruera St, but there's also the more intimate Basement Cinema, 1140 Hinemoa St (under *Base Backpackers*), an arthouse movie theatre of 33 seats and great character, plus a licensed café.
Left luggage At Travelex, in the visitor centre see p.301 ($2 for 3hr, $4 per day).
Library The public library is on Haupapa St (☎07/348 4177).
Medical treatment For emergencies and urgent healthcare go to Lakes Primecare, corner of Arawa & Tutanekai sts ☎07/348 1000 (daily 8am–11pm).
Pharmacy Lakes Care Pharmacy, corner of Arawa & Tutanekai sts ☎07/48 4385 (daily 9am–9.30pm).
Police 64–98 Fenton St ☎07/348 0099.
Post office The main post office, with poste restante facilities, is at 1195 Hinemoa St.
Taxis Fast Taxis ☎07/348 2444; Rotorua Taxis ☎07/348 1111.
Travelex Tourism Building, Rotorua Visitors Centre, 1167 Fenton St (☎07/348 0373), offers left luggage and foreign currency exchange.

Around Rotorua

Many of the best attractions in the area lie outside Rotorua, among the lakes to the north and east and around the most dramatic of the volcanic zones half an hour's drive south, toward Taupo. Shuttles and tours (see p.313) mean that just about every combination of sights can be packed into a day. Independent travellers can quickly dispatch minor sights along the eastern shore of Lake Rotorua, leaving time for the seldom-crowded **Hell's Gate** thermal area and the opportunity to watch terrified rafters plunging over **Tuteas Falls**. Hiring a boat opens up the best of lakes Rotoiti, Rotoehu and Rotama, though they're pleasing enough just to drive past on the way to Whakatane and the East Cape. Rewards are more plentiful to the east and south especially around Mount Tarawera which, in 1886, showered tonnes of ash on the settlement of Te Wairoa, now known as

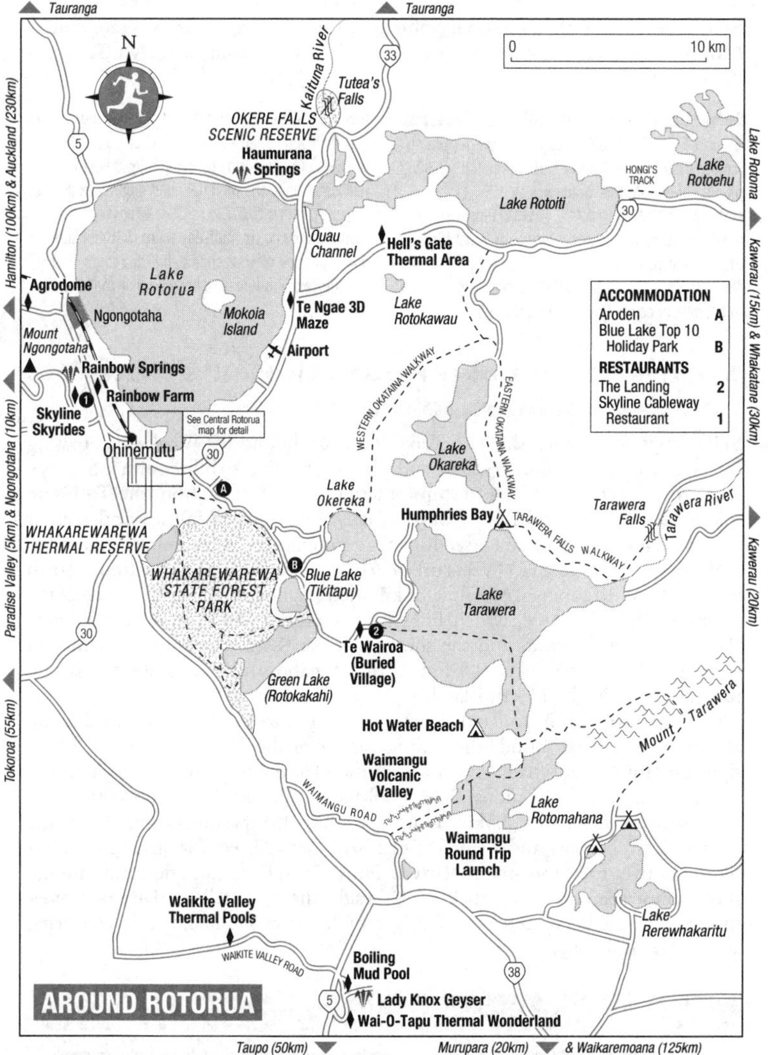

the **Buried Village**, where partly interred Maori dwellings graphically illustrate the volcano's power. As the village and the Pink and White Terraces were being destroyed the **Waimangu Volcanic Valley** was being created, and it now ranks as one of the finest collections of geothermal features in the region alongside kaleidoscopic **Wai-O-Tapu**, with its daily triggered **Lady Knox Geyser** and brilliantly coloured pools.

Getting around

Without your own transport, you need to choose between shuttles or a bewildering array of minibus tours, ranging from a couple of hours to a full day; to add confusion some shuttles also offer tours. One destination that isn't accessible with your own vehicle is the shattered line of craters atop Mount Tarawera, which can only be reached on a tour with Mt Tarawera NZ (see p.314).

Shuttle and minibus tours

Geyser Link ⓣ0800/004 321, ⓦwww.geyserlink.co.nz. Trips to Wai-O-Tapu and Waimangu for $25, plus a variety of other options.

Hotspotz ⓣ027/340 1744, ⓦwww.hotspotz.co.nz. Personalized shuttle service to most places at competitive rates.

Mt Tarawera NZ ⓣ07/349 3714, ⓦwww.mt-tarawera.co.nz. Have sole rights to the mountain, with a Rotorua-based half-day tour ($133). If you've got some spare dosh you can get the best of both worlds by doing a fly-drive tour, a helicopter up to the mountain and drive back ($435).

Superia Tours ⓣ07/357 2284, ⓦwww.superiatours.co.nz. Half-day tours ($85) include one attraction of your choice, full-day tours ($175) include two and lunch, or they'll tailor-make a tour for you.

Northeast of Lake Rotorua: Hell's Gate and the northern lakes

SH30 hugs the eastern shores of Lake Rotorua, bound for Whakatane, passing through a concentration of lakes and plenty of twisting hill country. Scenery aside, there isn't a great deal to stop for along the way apart from the **Te Ngae 3D Maze**, 10km northeast of Rotorua (daily 9am–5pm; $7.50), a wooden affair with bridges linking separate sections that complicate things immeasurably.

North of the maze, SH30 veers off to Whakatane while SH33 continues north to Te Puke and Tauranga. A couple of kilometres along the latter, you'll cross the riverine Ohau Channel, which links lakes Rotorua and Rotoiti. Haumurana Road then spurs left around the shores of Lake Rotorua passing **Hamurana Springs**, 773 Haumurana Rd (gold coin donation), which boast the largest natural spring in the North Island.

Sticking with SH33, you soon come upon signs to the **Okere Falls Scenic Reserve**, which surrounds the rafting mecca of the Kaituna River – follow signs up Trout Pool Road, 4km north of the Haumurana Road junction. From the first car park, 400m along Trout Pool Road, a broad track follows the river to a second car park (2.5km return; 40min–1hr) passing glimpses of the churning river below, and a viewing platform that's perfect for observing rafters plummet over the seven-metre **Tuteas Falls**. From here, steps descend through short tunnels in the steep rock walls beside the waterfall to **Tuteas Caves**, thought to have been used as a safe haven by Maori women and children during attacks by rival *iwi*.

Scenic flights

The scenery around Rotorua is breathtaking from the air. **Scenic flights** take in easily what you would find difficult to access from the ground, like the volcanic spine running through Rotorua. As a result there are various trips on offer, none cheap but many worthwhile if you're pushed for time.

Some say the majesty of Mount Tarawera is best appreciated from the air; **fixed-wing flights** with Volcanic Air Safaris (ⓣ0800/800 848, ⓦwww.volcanicair.co.nz) cost $185 for a Tarawera overview. **Helicopter** flights are usually more expensive but they do sometimes include a landing. Volcanic Safaris operate choppers on the same routes as their plane trips, with a couple of additional options. Similar deals are offered by HeliPro (ⓣ07/357 2512, ⓦwww.helipro.co.nz), with a short flight over Mount Tarawera and the local lakes at $175 (minimum numbers apply). HeliPro's other tours have vertically ascending prices.

Walks around Rotorua

Rotorua isn't especially well endowed with serious tramps though it does work well as a staging post for forays into the Whirinaki Forest and further afield to Waikaremoana. If you're keen to stretch your legs try there-and-back **day-walks**. Linking up multi-day hikes is all but impossible without a compliant driver to pick you up at the other end. The best **map** is Holidaymaker's 1:60,000 *Rotorua Lakes* ($15.95).

Day-walks

Blue Lake (Tikitapu; 5.5km loop; 2hr; 500m ascent). This none too arduous loop around the Blue Lake starts at the eastern end of the beach opposite the *Blue Lake Holiday Park*, 9km southeast of Rotorua, and heads through regenerating bush, Douglas firs and past some sandy beaches perfect for a dip. The single major climb takes you away from the lake to a viewpoint.

Okere Falls Scenic Reserve (2.5km return; 40min–1hr). An easy stroll starting 18km north of Rotorua, with river views and spectacular angles on rafters shooting Tuteas Falls.

Tarawera Falls Walk (1–8km return; 30min–4hr; 100m ascent). A gorgeous bushwalk to a great view of Tarawera Falls and on past swimming holes to the outlet of Lake Tarawera. The track starts 80km by road from Rotorua. Around 6km beyond Lake Rotoma a good side road leads to the timber-mill town of **Kawerau** – call at the **visitor centre** on Plunket Street (Mon–Fri 8.30am–4pm; ⓣ07/323 7550) for the compulsory **permit** for the walk ($3.50, or free from the forest's Visitor Centre in Rotorua – see p.307), which requires that you specify your car make, licence number and number of visitors). Note that **driving can be hazardous** on metalled forest roads – keep your headlights on at all times and keep clear of the billowing clouds of dust thrown up by huge logging trucks.

The falls are most impressive after rain when the underground section of the Tarawera River appears to **burst** in a solid stream from the cliff face. It's also worth the fifteen-minute walk (uphill) along the Tarawera Falls/Tarawera Outlet walkway to a point where you can see the Tarawera River dive underground and, by pressing on five minutes more, you'll come to a safe swimming hole, with natural diving spots and a rope swing.

Most traffic sticks to SH30, the route to **Hell's Gate** and **Wai Ora Spa** (daily 9am–5pm; $25; ⓦwww.hellsgate.co.nz), 14km northeast of Rotorua. The smallest of the major thermal areas, this is also one of the most active. Its fury camouflages a lack of notable features, however, and the only real highlights are the bubbling mud of the Devil's Cauldron and the hot **Kakahi Falls**, whose soothing 38°C waters once made this a popular bathing spot (now off-limits). Also worth a look on the way out are the interactive activities, including a quick carving lesson after which you can take home a design you've chipped away yourself. Substantial pleasure can also be taken from a wonderful soak in the sulphurous hot waters overlooking the park and a mud bath (an additional $55); massages are another $130, and other treatments rise in price from there.

Beyond Hell's Gate lies **Lake Rotoiti**, which translates as "small lake", though it is in fact the second largest in the region and is linked to Lake Rotorua by the narrow Ohau Channel. This passage, along with the neighbouring **Lake Rotoehu** and **Lake Rotoma**, traditionally formed part of the canoe route from the coast. A section of this route, apparently used on a raid by the Ngapuhi warrior chief Hongi Hika, is traced by **Hongi's Track** (3km; 1hr return), a beautiful bushwalk which runs through to Lake Rotoehu passing the Wishing Tree, which is often surrounded by plant offerings.

Southeast of Rotorua

Unsurprisingly, volcanic activity provides the main theme for attractions southeast of Rotorua, most having some association with **Lake Tarawera** and the jagged line of volcanic peaks and craters along the southeastern shore, collectively known as **Mount Tarawera**, which erupted in 1886. Before this, Tarawera was New Zealand's premier tourist destination, with thousands of visitors every year crossing lakes Tarawera and Rotomahana in whale boats and *waka*, frequently guided by the renowned Maori guide Sophia, to the **Pink and White Terraces**, two separate fans of silica that cascaded down the hillside to the edge of Lake Rotomahana. Boiling cauldrons bubbled at the top of each formation, spilling mineral-rich water down the hillside where, over several centuries, it formed a series of staggered cup-shaped pools, the outflow of one filling the one below. The White Terraces (Te Tarata or "Tattooed Rock") were the larger, but most visitors favoured the Pink Terraces (Otukapuarangi or "Cloudy Atmosphere"), which were prettier and better suited to sitting and soaking. All this came to an abrupt end on the night of June 10, 1886, when the long-dormant Mount Tarawera erupted, creating 22 craters along a 17km rift, and covering over 15,000 square kilometres in mud and scoria. The Pink and White Terraces were shattered by the buckling earth, covered by ash and lava, then submerged deep under the waters of Lake Rotomahana that, dammed by earth upheavals, grew to twenty times its previous size.

The cataclysm had been foreshadowed eleven days earlier, when two separate canoe loads of Pakeha tourists and their Maori guides saw an ancient *waka* glide out of the mist, with a dozen warriors paddling furiously, then vanish just as suddenly; this was interpreted by the ancient *tohunga* (priest) Tuhoto Ariki as a sign of imminent disaster. The fallout from the eruption buried five villages, including the staging post for the Pink and White Terrace trips, **Te Wairoa**, where the *tohunga* lived. In a classic case of blaming the messenger, the inhabitants refused to rescue the *tohunga* and it wasn't until four days later that they allowed a group of Pakeha to dig him out. Miraculously he lived, for a week.

The chain of eruptions that racked the fault line during that fateful night created an entirely new thermal valley, **Waimangu**, running southwest from the shores of the newly enlarged Lake Rotomahana. Still geothermally active, Waimangu competes to outdo the supremely colourful thermal area of **Wai-O-Tapu**, a few kilometres further south. Beyond the volcanic zone, the Kaingaroa Forest stretches east to the little-visited tramping territory of the **Whirinaki Forest Park**, and the Kinleith Forest straggles west to **Tirau**, **Putaruru** and **Tokoroa** (covered in Chapter Three).

The Blue and Green lakes, the Buried Village and Lake Tarawera

Passing a ridge-top viewpoint overlooking the iridescent waters of **Blue Lake** (Tikitapu) and **Green Lake** (Rotokakahi), the road reaches the shores of Lake Tarawera 15km southeast, just past the **Buried Village** (daily: Nov–March 8.30am–5pm; April–Oct 9am–4.30pm; $27; ⓣ07/362 8287, ⓦwww.buriedvillage.co.nz). By the entrance to the complex a **museum** provides a great introduction, capturing the spirit of the village in its heyday and the aftermath of its destruction, through photos, fine aquatints of the Pink and White Terraces and ash-encrusted knick-knacks. The Maori settlement here was larger than contemporary Rotorua until the Tarawera eruption when numerous houses collapsed under the weight of the ash; others were saved by virtue of their inhabitants hefting ash off the roof to lighten the load. You can either go for a free **guided tour** (11am, 1.30pm or 3pm), or make your own way through the grounds from here.

What you see today are the partly excavated and heavily reconstructed remains; much of the village was excavated in the 1930s and 1940s, though work continues slowly today. The village itself is less an archeological dig than a manicured orchard: half-buried *whare* and the foundations for the Rotomahana Hotel sit primly on mown lawns among European fruit trees gone to seed, marauding hawthorn and a perfect row of full-grown poplars fostered from a line of fenceposts. Many of the *whare* house collections of implements and ash-encrusted household goods, and contrast starkly with the simplicity of other dwellings such as **Tohunga's Whare**, where the ill-fated priest lay buried alive for four days (see p.316). Look out too for the extremely rare, carved-stone *pataka* (storehouse) and the bow section of a *waka* once used to ferry tourists on the lake and allegedly brought to the district by Hongi Hika, when he invaded in 1823. Beyond the formal grounds a steep staircase and slippery boardwalk dive into the hill alongside **Te Wairoa Falls**, then climb up through dripping, fern-draped bush on the far side.

Cruises on Lake Tarawera go from the Tarawera Landing, 2km east of the Buried Village, and are run by the owners of *The Landing* restaurant (see p.311; ⓣ07/362 8595; ⓦwww.purerotorua.com). Of the five cruise options, the Eruption Trail (Nov–April daily 10.30am; May–Oct by arrangement; 3hr; $38) is the most relevant, taking you to the approximate site of the Pink and White Terraces; it includes a picnic lunch and an hour's swim at a hot-water beach.

Waimangu

At the southern limit of the volcanic rift blown out by Mount Tarawera lies **Waimangu Volcanic Valley** (daily: Jan 8.30am–6pm; Feb–Dec 8.30am–5pm; $32.50; ⓣ07/366 6137, ⓦwww.waimangu.co.nz), 19km south of Rotorua on Waimangu Road, via SH5, and 5km off the highway. Among the world's youngest thermal areas, this is also New Zealand's largest and most lushly vegetated. The entrance fee includes a comprehensive leaflet for a self-guided walking tour; highlights include two recently cut trails that yield great views.

The visitor centre, by the entrance, hints at the sights lining the streamside path, which cuts through a valley choked with scrub and native bush that has re-established itself since 1886. The regeneration process is periodically interrupted by smaller eruptions, including one in 1917 that created the magnificent 100m-diameter **Frying Pan Lake**, the world's largest hot spring. Massive quantities of hot water well up from the depths of the **Inferno Crater**, an inverted cone where mesmerizing steam patterns partly obscure the powder-blue water and are stirred and swirled by breezes across the lake. The water level rises and falls according to a rigid 38-day cycle – filling to the rim for 21 days, overflowing for two then gradually falling to 8m below the rim over the next fifteen. More run-of-the-mill steaming pools and hissing vents line the stream, which also passes the muddy depression where, from 1900 to 1904, the **Waimangu Geyser** regularly spouted water to an astonishing height of 400m, carrying rocks and black mud with it.

The path through the valley ends at the wharf on the shores of Lake Rotomahana, where the rust-red sides of Mount Tarawera dominate the far horizon. From here, free shuttles run back up the road to the visitor centre and gentle, commentated, 45-minute **cruises** (6 daily; $37.50) chug around the lake past steaming cliffs, fumaroles and over the site of the Pink and White Terraces.

Wai-O-Tapu

The tussle for Rotorua's geothermal crown is principally fought between Waimangu and the **Wai-O-Tapu Thermal Wonderland** (daily 8.30am–5pm;

$27.50; ⓦwww.geyserland.co.nz), 10km south of Waimangu (and 30km from Rotorua), just off SH5. This combines a vast expanse of multi-hued rocks and pools, New Zealand's largest and most impressive lake of boiling mud and the **Lady Knox Geyser**, ignominiously induced to perform on schedule at 10.15am daily. Buy your ticket at the main entrance then double back 1km along the road to the geyser where, as the crowds fill the serried ranks of benches, a

▲ Lady Knox Geyser, Wai-O-Tapu

staff member pours a packet of soap flakes into the vent. Within a few minutes, the soap reduces the water's surface tension, and superheated steam and water are released in a jet initially reaching 10m before continuing at half that height for anything up to an hour. Everyone then bundles into their vehicles and drives back to the main site for the hour-long walking loop that wends its way through a series of small lakes which have taken on the tints of the minerals dissolved in them – yellow from sulphur, purple from manganese, green from arsenic and so on. The gurgling and growling black mud of the **Devil's Ink-Pots** and a series of hissing and rumbling craters pale beside the ever-changing rainbow colours of the **Artist's Palette** pools and the gorgeous, effervescent **Champagne Pool**, a circular bottle-green cauldron wreathed in swirling steam and fringed by a burnt-orange shelf. The waters of the Champagne Pool froth over **The Terraces**, a rippled accretion of lime silicate that glistens in the sunlight.

As you drive back to the main road, follow a short detour, along the same road you used to reach the geyser, to a huge and active **boiling mud pool** which plops away merrily, forming lovely concentric patterns.

Whirinaki Forest Park

Midway between Waimangu and Wai-O-Tapu, 25km south of Rotorua, SH38 spurs southeast, running through the regimented pines of the Kaingaroa Forest towards the jagged peaks of Te Urewera National Park, a vast tract of untouched wilderness separating the Rotorua lakes from Poverty Bay and the East Cape. The Kaingaroa Forest finally relents 40km on, as the road crosses the Rangitaiki River by the predominantly Maori timber town of **MURUPARA**. The only reason to pull over is DOC's **Rangitaiki Area Visitor Centre**, 1km southeast of town on SH38 (Mon–Fri 8am–5pm, Sat 9am–3pm; ⓣ07/366 1080), with diverting displays and stacks of information on Te Urewera National Park and Lake Waikaremoana (see p.422).

Particular emphasis is given to the easily accessible **Whirinaki Forest Park**, a wonderful slice of country that harbours some of the densest and most impressive stands of bush on the North Island: podocarps on the river flats, and native beech on the steep volcanic uplands between them, support a wonderfully rich birdlife with tui, bellbirds, parakeets and kaka. The forest is now protected, after one of the country's most celebrated environmental battles and is a wilderness paradise for hikers and mountain bikers alike (a dedicated mountain-bike track is detailed in the *Ride Whirinaki* leaflet from DOC visitor centres).

To get to the forest tracks from the visitor centre, head 25km south to **Minginui**, from where the River Road runs 8km south to the Whirinaki (or River Road) car park. In four hours or so, setting out from the car park, you can sample some of the best of the forest – the Whirinaki Falls, where the Whirinaki River cascades over an old lava flow, and the churning Te Whaiti-nui-a-tio Canyon – on the first stretch of the **Whirinaki Track** (27km; 2 days). If you're up for more than a day's hiking you can follow the rest of this gentle track, though you'll need to carry your own cooking stove, food and sleeping bag. By linking several tracks and staying in some of the nine standard **huts** (all $5, except central Whirinaki; $10) that pepper the park, robust walkers can tramp for four or five days – DOC's *Walks in Whirinaki Forest Park* leaflet covers the main routes.

It's also possible to explore the area with flexible Rotorua-based Whirinaki Trax (ⓣ07/366 4756, ⓦwww.getoutthere.co.nz), with pick-up and drop-off and one-day **guided treks**. Alternatively, you could try a day-long, guided tour with Whirinaki Rainforest Guided Eco-cultural Experiences ($155; ⓣ0800/869 9255, ⓦwww.indigenousbynature.co.nz), who offer a Maori perspective on the forest and its history in friendly, involving trips.

For other **transport** alternatives contact the Rangitaiki Area Visitor Centre, as it can be difficult to get to Whirinaki or through to Lake Waikaremoana without your own wheels. Even a car can be a liability as vehicles left at the Whirinaki car park aren't always safe.

Taupo and around

The unobtrusive resort town of **Taupo**, 80km south of Rotorua and slap in the centre of the North Island, is slung around the northern shores of Lake Taupo, the country's largest lake. It attracts Kiwi and foreign tourists alike, the latter increasingly due to its attraction as the **skydiving capital** of New Zealand. From Taupo, views stretch 30km southwest towards the three snow-capped volcanoes of the Tongariro National Park, the reflected light from the lake's glassy surface combining with the 360-metre altitude to create an almost alpine radiance. Here, the impossibly deep-blue waters of the Waikato River ("flowing water" in Maori) begin their long journey to the Tasman Sea and both lake and river frontages are lined with parks, lending Taupo a slow pace and appealing tenor.

For decades, Kiwi families have been descending en masse for a couple of weeks' holiday, bathing in the crisp cool waters of the lake, fishing its depths and lounging around holiday homes that fringe the lakeshore. Although you could easily follow their lead and just relax, there's no shortage of stuff to see and do, most notably around the spectacular rapids and geothermal badlands of **Wairakei Park**, immediately north of town. Thousands more come specifically for the **fishing**: the Taupo area is a most fecund trout fishery, extending south to Turangi and along the Tongariro River, with an enviable reputation for the quality of its fish. Year-round, you'll see boats drifting across the lake with lines trailing and, particularly in the evenings, rivermouths choked with fly casters in waist-high waders.

Lake Taupo (616 sq km, 185m deep) is itself a geological infant and, although no single eruption is responsible for its creation, a large part was played around 1800 years ago when the Taupo Volcano erupted, spewing out 24 cubic kilometres of rock, debris and ash – at least ten times more than was produced by the eruptions of Krakatoa and Mount St Helens combined – and covering much of the North Island in a thick layer of pumice. Ash was ejected so high into the atmosphere that it was carried around the world, enabling historians to pinpoint the date of the **eruption** as 186 AD – when the Chinese noted a blackening of the sky and Romans recorded that the heavens turned blood-red. As the underground magma chamber emptied, the roof slumped, leaving a huge steep-sided **crater**, since filled by, and forming part of, Lake Taupo. It is hard to reconcile this placid and beautiful lake with such colossal violence, though the evidence is all around: entire beaches are composed of feather-light pumice which, when caught by the wind, floats off across the lake. **Geologists** and **vulcanologists** continue to study the Taupo Volcano (currently considered dormant) and treat the lake as a kind of giant spirit-level, in which any tilting could indicate a build-up of magma below the surface that might trigger another eruption.

The local Tuwharetoa people ascribe the lake's formation to their ancestor, **Ngatoroirangi**, who cast a tree from the summit of Mount Tauhara, on the edge of Taupo, and where it struck the ground water welled up and formed the lake. The lake's full name is **Taupo-Nui-A-Tia**, "the great shoulder mat of Tia" or "great sleep of Tia", which refers to an explorer from the Arawa canoe said to have slept by the lake.

Taupo

Nowhere in **TAUPO**'s compact low-rise core is more than five minutes' walk from the waters of the Waikato River or Lake Taupo, which jointly hem in three sides. The fourth side rises up through the gentle slopes of Taupo's suburbs. Most of the commercial activity happens on, or just off, SH1, which passes through the middle of town as Tongariro Street and the aptly named Lake Terrace. Room for expansion is limited to the southeastern quarter, where ever more motels, second homes and timeshares are springing up along the lakeshore, often bizarre architectural creations which, depending upon your view, blight or enliven this otherwise unpretentious settlement.

Although Taupo bears little trace of the vigorous Tuwharetoa settlement that existed into the middle of the nineteenth century, there was scant European interest in the area until the New Zealand Wars of the 1860s, when the Armed Constabulary were trying to track down **Te Kooti** (see p.426). They set up camp one night in June 1869 at Opepe, 17km southeast of Taupo (beside what is now SH5), and were ambushed by Te Kooti's men, who killed nine soldiers. Garrisons were subsequently established at Opepe and Taupo, but only Taupo flourished, enjoying a more strategic situation and being blessed with hot springs for washing and bathing. By 1877, Te Kooti had been contained, but the Armed Constabulary wasn't disbanded until 1886, after which several soldiers and their families stayed on, forming the nucleus of European settlement.

Taupo didn't really take off as a domestic resort until the prosperous 1950s, when the North Island's roads had improved to the point where Kiwi families could easily drive here from Auckland, Wellington or Hawke's Bay. With the exception of a fantastic **museum** there are few attractions within the town but Taupo makes a great base for exploring the surrounding area and ticking off skydiving from your "must do" list.

Arrival, information and transport

Buses (direct connections from Rotorua, Tauranga, Hamilton, Auckland, Napier, Palmerston North and Wellington) stop at the Taupo Travel Centre bus station, 16 Gascoigne St (Ⓣ07/378 9032), around 200m from Taupo's **i-SITE visitor centre** on Tongariro Street (daily 8.30am–5pm; Ⓣ07/376 0027, Ⓦwww.laketauponz.com), in the heart of town. There's an alternative information centre across the road, Experience Taupo (daily: Oct–April 8.30am–7.30pm; May–Sept 8.30am–6.30pm; Ⓣ07/377 0704, Ⓦwww.experiencetaupo.com). The busy little **airport**, 10km south of the centre, is served by Air New Zealand flights; a taxi to town will set you back around $25.

Almost everything you'll want to visit in the centre can be reached either on foot or by **taxi** (see "Listings", p.328). For the surrounding sights, without your own vehicle, use the Hot Bus (daily: summer 9am–4pm; winter 10am–3pm; Ⓣ02/146 8287, Ⓦwww.hotbus.co.nz). This makes an hour-long **circuit** of all the main sights, such as Huka Falls, Craters of the Moon and Taupo Hot Springs,

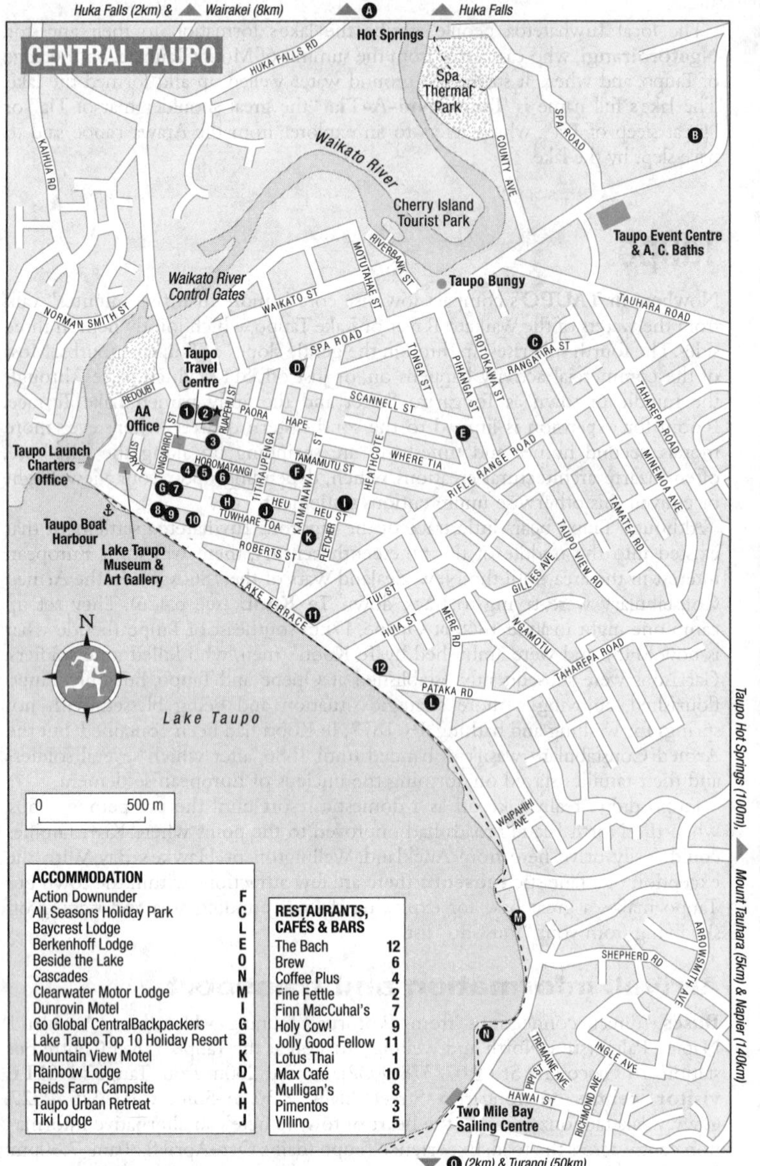

plus a few hostels, departing from the visitor centre on the hour; you pay $20 to visit two attractions, $25 for three and so on; buy a ticket from the i-SITE or on board. Alternatively, join a **guided tour** with Paradise Tours (start 10am; 4hr; $99; ⓣ07/378 9955, ⓦwww.paradisetours.co.nz) who visit most of the same places.

Renting a bike gives greater freedom: the most sophisticated machines will set you back roughly $30 a half-day. Another popular and fun way to get about town is on a **rented scooter** (see p.328).

Accommodation

Taupo maintains a high standard of accommodation for all budgets and the only time there's a problem finding somewhere is in the crush (Christmas to end Feb), when you must **book** well in advance. Much of the lakefront is taken up with **motels**, and grassy spots on the fringes of town given over to **campsites**, while **hostels** are abundant in the town itself, with a brand-new one (*Base*, 7 Tuwharetoa St ⓦwww.stayatbase.com) just about to open at the time of writing.

Hotels, motels and B&Bs

Baycrest Lodge 79 Mere Rd ⓣ0800/229 273, ⓦwww.baycrest.co.nz. Luxurious motel with spacious units, a heated pool, poolside bar and Sky TV. 6

Beside the Lake 8 Chad St, 5km south of Taupo ⓣ07/378 5847, ⓦwww.besidelaketaupo.co.nz. Two modern, tasteful, luxury rooms (one with private bath, one en suite) beside a small park fronting the lake. Rooms have lake views, a/c, and a terrace that catches the afternoon sun. A full breakfast is served. 8

Cascades SH1, Two Mile Bay ⓣ0800/996 997, ⓦwww.cascades.co.nz. Classy range of accommodation and access to an attractive pool. Studio and family units are spacious with deluxe fittings, a full kitchen, a mezzanine sleeping area, a patio and a spa bath. 4

Clearwater Motor Lodge 229 Lake Terrace ⓣ0800/639 639, ⓦwww.clearwatermotorlodge.co.nz. Beautiful lakeside accommodation with great views, in-room spas and some rooms with small balconies. 5

Dunrovin Motel 140 Heu Heu St ⓣ0800/386 768, ⓔinfo@dunrovintaupo.co.nz. Recently upgraded budget units, well kept and characterful, being built of wood rather than the ubiquitous concrete blocks. 3

Mountain View Motel 12 Fletcher St ⓣ0800/146 683, ⓦwww.mountainviewmotel.co.nz. Budget, central motel with spa pool, Sky TV, games room and kids' play area. The family units are huge, sleeping up to seven. Studios 3, family units 6

Hostels

Action Downunder 56 Kaimanawa St ⓣ07/378 3311, ⓦwww.yha.org.nz. Excellent and welcoming modern associate YHA hostel, close to town and with good lake and mountain views from the kitchen and BBQ balcony. There's a spa pool and a small gym, an outdoor cinema runs in the summer and bikes can be rented for $25 a day. Most dorm rooms hold four beds or less, families and disabilities are well catered for, plus en suites with private Internet access. Tents $15, dorms $25, rooms 2

Berkenhoff Lodge 75 Scannell St ⓣ07/378 4909, ⓦwww.berkenhofflodge.co.nz. Slightly cramped hostel 15min walk from the centre. The games room and on-site bar are perennially popular and they run a BBQ every evening by the pool and spa. Each dorm has a bathroom, and doubles and twins come with linen. Dorms $23, rooms 1

Go Global Central Backpackers Corner of Tongariro & Tuwharetoa sts ⓣ07/377 0044, ⓦwww.go-global.co.nz. With a recent makeover and yet another lot of new owners, this large, central hostel above a bar is still popular with the backpacker buses, though the new competition over the road may change things. Dorms and a multitude of rooms are all clean and there's Internet access. Dorms $25, rooms 2

Rainbow Lodge 99 Titiraupenga St ⓣ07/378 5754, ⓦwww.rainbowlodge.co.nz. Spacious, relaxed purpose-built backpackers with a comfortable lounge, sauna, bike rental at $20 a day and fishing gear for $11. A stack of local information and little touches create a homely atmosphere and the new themed rooms will put a smile on your face. Dorms have six to nine beds and there are triples and doubles, many of them en suite. Free pick-ups from the bus station. Dorms $22, rooms 2

Taupo Urban Retreat 65 Heu Heu St ⓣ0800/872 261, ⓦwww.taupourbanretreat.co.nz. Small hostel in central location with a small bar. Some doubles have lake views. Dorms $22, en-suite dorms $26, en-suite doubles 2

Tiki Lodge 104 Tuwharetoa St ⓣ0800/8454 56343, ⓦwww.tikilodge.co.nz. The best of the flashpacker-style hostels, with a spacious kitchen and lounge area plus a great balcony, a spa and an emphasis on cultural tourism; *hangi* can be ordered and Maori statues sit proudly in the small garden. Dorms $26, en-suite doubles 2

Campsites and motor parks

All Seasons Holiday Park 16 Rangatira St ⓣ0800/777 272, ⓦwww.taupoallseasons.co.nz. Compact site just 1km from town, with hedged tent sites scattered among cabins, some with kitchens, and a range of s/c units ($4 for linen) plus budget rooms in a lodge. Camping $20, cabins ❶, s/c units ❷

Lake Taupo Top 10 Holiday Resort 28 Centennial Drive ⓣ07/378 6860, ⓦwww.taupotop10.co.nz. Spacious site 2km from town with good communal facilities, kitchen cabins, park motels, fully s/c units, and easy access to the A.C. Baths. Camping $20, cabins ❸ motels & units ❻

Reids Farm Campsite 3km north of Taupo on Huka Falls Rd. Spacious free campsite right by the Waikato River just upstream of *Huka Lodge*, left to the world by a previous owner who liked backpackers. The makeshift slalom course makes it a popular spot with kayakers.

The Town

True to its family-resort status, Taupo specializes in entertainment for the kids and adventure activities for adults. However, a definite must-see is the intriguing **Lake Taupo Museum and Art Gallery**, Tongariro Park (daily 10.30am–4.30pm; $5), if only for the beautiful Reid Carvings, gifted to the museum in 1960 and then inexplicably kept under the floor of the old War Memorial Hall until a few years ago. Carved in 1927–28 by the famous master carver Tene Waitere, who produced "treasures" for *marae* throughout New Zealand, the pieces are exhibited in the form of a meeting house and are some of the finest Maori carving on display anywhere. Remarkably, Waitere was a survivor of the Buried Village of Te Wairoa, destroyed by the Tarawera eruption – reputedly he was responsible for much of the current Buried Village carving; the work on show here was intended as a gift for his niece, Mrs Lucy Reid. If this were not enough, the gallery section of the museum has regular exhibitions and contains a few Thomas Ryan watercolours of Ngati Tuwhareto chiefs which show the unmistakable influence of the artist's great friend Charles Goldie. Ryan, born in England was also famous for his rugby, playing for the first representative New Zealand Rugby (All Blacks) team. The remainder of the museum is given over to exhibits covering pioneering days and fishing in some depth, and a curious collection of scale models of every plane that took part in World War II. There's also a 150-year-old 14.5-metre *waka* (canoe), though its origins remain a mystery. One final point of interest is the stunning **Ora Garden**, a 2004 Chelsea Flower Show winner, recreated in all its thermal-New Zealand glory. From the museum, Tongariro Park sweeps down to the lakeshore and the **Taupo Boat Harbour**, the departure point for cruises, fishing trips and a multitude of aquatic pursuits.

Away from the town centre, 3km southeast on SH5, is the family-oriented **Taupo Hot Springs** (daily 7.30am–9.30pm; $14; ⓦwww.taupohotsprings.com), comprising a couple of large outdoor pools filled with natural mineral water and private mineral pools in a range of temperatures ($4 extra); an additional $5 buys as many descents as you like on the hot-water hydroslide. Without your own vehicle, you'll find it more convenient to head for the **Taupo Events Centre**, A.C. Baths Avenue (Mon–Fri 6am–9pm, Sat & Sun 7am–9pm), a sparkling new sports hall and twelve-metre climbing wall (harness, shoes and chalk $7, plus $8 entry), alongside the longstanding **A.C. Baths**, a complex of swimming and hot pools. The private hot pools ($5 per person, 45min) run off a thermal spring nearby while the swimming pool ($6.50) also gets you into the public hot pools.

From the junction opposite the baths, Spa Road forges north to the site of the first hot spring used by the Armed Constabulary. Just west, Spa Avenue runs down to the green swathe of **Spa Thermal Park**, where a path leads to the Waikato River past some naturally hot bathing pools (unrestricted entry) and, in an hour or so, downstream to Huka Falls (see p.328). A few hundred metres upstream, the river swirls through the narrows of Hell's Gate, the 47-metre white cliffs providing the launch pad for **Taupo Bungy**, 202 Spa Rd (daily 9am–5pm, until 7pm in high season; $109; ⓣ0800/888 408, ⓦwww.taupobungy.co.nz), one of New Zealand's finest bungy sites cantilevered 20m out from the bank, and with optional (so they say) dunking.

Activities

As you would expect, Taupo offers plenty of activities to relieve you of your holiday money, primarily **skydiving**: Taupo is now one of the busiest drop zones in the world and provides a spectacular setting toward which to plummet from a plane. Of the other activities the best are water-based, **cruising** or **kayaking** on Lake Taupo, **rafting** down the raging waters of the Tongariro or Rangitaiki rivers or **fishing** the lake and rivers.

Skydiving

Taupo is one of the cheapest places to go **tandem skydiving** – and one of the best, with magnificent scenery, if you dare to look. At times it can feel like a production line, with three very professional companies processing dozens of people a day, each offering an array of videos, DVDs, photos and T-shirts. From time to time price wars break out keeping the costs at reasonable levels, and you'll struggle to find cheaper skydiving in New Zealand. Many people go for 15,000ft for the longer freefall time (45 seconds at 12,000ft, around a minute at 15,000ft), and the only difference between the operators is the pre- and after-jump package. If you can afford to stay longer, each company also offers reasonably priced **solo skydiving** courses.

Great Lake Skydive ⓣ0800/373 335, ⓦwww.freefall.net.nz. A friendly and professional service. A 12,000-ft jump is $219, 15,000ft is $314. Ground videos and freefall videos and photos extra.

Skydive Taupo ⓣ0800/586 766, ⓦwww.skydivetaupo.co.nz The smallest company, offering a more personal experience: picking you up in a stretch limo and providing an individual, hand-held video – you choose the music. A jump from 12,000ft costs $220, 15,000ft is $315.

Taupo Tandem Skydiving ⓣ0800/275 934, ⓦwww.tts.net.nz The biggest operation in terms of publicity but primarily competes with Great Lake in terms of service and numbers. 12,000ft is $219, 15,000ft is $314. You pay extra for DVD and photos.

Scenic flights and helicopter trips

If you'd prefer to stay in the plane, a variety of **scenic flights** in a float plane, including a jaunt over the lake and its surrounds, are run by the imaginatively named Taupo's Float Plane (10min $70; Mount Ruapehu $270; ⓣ07/378 7500, ⓦwww.tauposfloatplane.co.nz). Similar trips are offered by Volcanic Aeroplane Adventures (ⓣ0800/2736 75263, ⓦwww.aeroplaneadventures.co.nz), Taupo Air Services (ⓣ07/378 5325, ⓔtaupoair@xtra.co.nz) and Air Charter Taupo (ⓣ07/378 5468, ⓦwww.airchartertaupo.co.nz). The best **helicopter trips** are run by Helistar Helicopters (ⓣ0800/435 478, ⓦwww.helistar.co.nz), on the Huka Falls Road, who offer a variety of flights, including ones over the Huka Falls (10min $99), while Clark & Jolly (ⓣ07/377 8805, ⓦwww.helinz.com) will also get you up and about, from $95.

Walking and horse-riding

There are a few easy **walks** near town. By far the most popular is the **Great Lake Walk**, which is more modest than it sounds: just follow the lakeshore east from town, covering as much of the seven-kilometre promenade as you like, passing hot springs right at the water's edge. On the northern edge of town, County Avenue leads to the **Spa Thermal Park**, where there's a pleasant thirty-minute bushwalk, which can be combined with a riverbank tramp to **Huka Falls** (4km;

1hr one way), and further extended to the Aratiatia Rapids (8km; 2hr one way), though you've then got to get back – if you set off early, you could conceivably walk back via the Wairakei visitor centre and the Craters of the Moon (12km; 3hr). Finally, if you have your own transport and a taste for magnificent lake and town views, try the track to the summit of **Mount Tauhara** (6km; 2–3hr return), the hill behind Taupo; it's approached on Mountain Road, which turns off SH5 to Napier after 6km.

If you fancy **horse-riding**, Taupo Horse Treks, Karapiti Road (Ⓣ07/378 0356, Ⓦwww.taupohorsetreks.co.nz), do one-hour ($45) and two-hour ($80) jaunts through the pine forests around the Craters of the Moon (see p.330), while Moehiwa Horse Ventures (Ⓣ07/378 3727, Ⓦmoehiwa.tripod.com) take a less traditional approach, preferring holistic methods of horsemanship; small groups trek through their 2500-acre farm for about an hour at similar rates.

Lake cruises

One way to relax in Taupo is on a **lake cruise**, from the Taupo Boat Harbour, setting out for the striking, modern, Maori rock carvings that can only be seen from the water at Mine Bay, 8km southwest of town. The ten-metre-high carvings date from the late 1970s and depict a stylized image of a man's face heavy with *moko*, together with tuatara (lizard-like reptiles) and female forms draped over nearby rocks.

The most characterful sailing trip – as much for the sea-dog skipper as the boat – is aboard *The Barbary* (daily, weather permitting, 10am & 2pm; 2hr 30min; $30; Ⓣ07/378 3444), a 1926 ketch once owned by Eroll Flynn (who, it is claimed, won it in a card game). For a touch of gin-palace style, opt for the *Cruise Cat* (daily 10.30am & 2pm; 1hr 30min; $35; Ⓣ0800/252 628), which motors up to and past the carvings while you recline. For an entirely different feel try the *Ernest Kemp* (daily Dec–Feb 10.30am, 2pm & 5pm; $30; Ⓣ07/378 3444;), a replica 1920s steamboat that chugs to the carvings and back in a couple of hours, though for sheer charm join up with the old sailors who restored and now run the *Alice*, a tiny vintage steam launch, built between 1861 and 1879, which pootles round the lake's edge for an hour or so at weekends ($20; Lakeside Bookings Office Ⓣ07/378 8659) – though at the time of writing it was up for sale.

Kayak tours and watersports

The most rewarding experiences on the lake come from being at wave level and putting in a little effort, so **kayak tours** fit the bill. Rapid Sensations, based behind Helistar Helicopters' office on the Huka Falls Road (Ⓣ0800/353 435, Ⓦwww.rapids.co.nz), run various such trips, including one to the carvings ($95, 4hr 30min) – and if the weather is against you they'll sort out a rewarding alternative.

There are no whitewater rivers right on Taupo's doorstep, but the town makes a viable base for **rafting**. The main trips running from Taupo paddle out onto the Tongariro (covered under Turangi – see p.334), the Rangitaiki and the Wairoa. Rapid Sensations (see above) run the Tongariro for $115, the Mohaka Gorge for $155, while Kiwi River Safaris (Ⓣ0800/723 857, Ⓦwww.krs.co.nz) organize rafting trips to the Wairoa ($109), the Rangitaiki ($99) and a one-day Mohaka trip ($175).

If this is all a bit energetic let the wind take the strain by heading for the Two Mile Bay Sailing Centre, Two Mile Bay (daily 9am–5pm in summer, otherwise sporadically; Ⓣ07/378 3299, Ⓦwww.sailingcentre.co.nz), who rent **catamarans** ($60 per hr), **windsurfers** ($30 per hr) and various other sail boats (from $50 per hr) to just about anybody with rudimentary knowledge.

Fishing

New Zealand's arcane fishing rules dictate that trout can't be sold, so if you've got a taste for them you'll need to catch them and the easiest way is to fish the lake from a charter boat. One of the best operators hereabouts is White Striker ($200 for 2hr on their smallest charter holding up to 6; ⓣ07/378 2736, ⓦwww.troutcatching.com) who have a good strike rate and a wealth of local knowledge. Alternatively look to one of the many charters offered by the Taupo Launch Charters Office (ⓣ07/378 3444). All **boats** go out for a minimum of two hours, more usually three or four, and although minimum numbers don't apply, the more on the boat the cheaper it is. **Book in advance** from mid-December to February – and at any other time of year if you want the booking office to help reduce your costs by matching you up with other interested parties. Boat operators have all the tackle you need and will organize the mandatory Taupo District Fishing Licence ($15.50) for you. Rivers flowing into Lake Taupo are the preserve of **fly-fishers**, particularly from March to September when mature rainbow trout enter the mouths of the streams and rivers and make their way upstream to shallow gravel hollows where they spawn. Brown trout are also in these waters but they tend to be more wily. You can **rent tackle** from Taupo Rod & Tackle, 34 Tongariro St (ⓣ07/378 5337), and pick your own spot, but average catches are much larger if you engage the services of a **fishing guide** (about $300 for half a day with gear and licence), two of the best are Chris Jolly and Will Kemp but the i-SITE has a complete list.

Eating, drinking and nightlife

Taupo's culinary stock has risen in recent years with new places opening all the time. The lakefront motor lodges have pricey **restaurants** but the best places to eat are in or around town, where there are plenty of modern **cafés**. Taupo's **nightlife** reflects its small-town status but is lively enough, with holidaymakers converging on several **pubs** and **clubs**.

Restaurants

The Bach 2 Pataka Rd ⓣ07/378 7856. Modern dining in a *bach*-style eatery with an easy-going atmosphere, slightly out of town. Choose from a select range of $30-plus mains and an extensive selection of cellared New Zealand wines by the bottle and glass.

Lotus Thai 137 Tongariro St. Highly regarded Thai, popular with locals. Though service can be abrupt there are very tasty and good-value curries and stir-frys. Mains from $14 (vegetarian). Takeaway option available.

Pimentos 17 Tamamutu St ⓣ07/377 4549. Stylish, dinner-only restaurant specializing in fusion European and Asian cookery, with jazzed-up European staples. Mains $25–30. Closed Tues. BYO.

Villino 45 Horomatangi St ⓣ07/377 4478. Classy downtown restaurant and café open daily for lunch and dinner and serving a typically eclectic range of dishes which lean towards Europe, though they also do wonderful Pacific oysters for $17. Mains ($30-ish) include duck confit, roast rack of spring lamb and fillet of beef. Open for cocktails till late Fri & Sat.

Cafés

Brew Marama Arcade (off Heu Heu St). Colourful, partly corrugated juice and espresso bar, offering a wide range of teas, fruit- and veg-based juices, all-day breakfasts and gourmet sandwiches. Try the cinnamon French toast (with banana, bacon and maple syrup) or a savoury muffin. Closed Tues.

Coffee Plus 11 Hiromatangi St. Relaxing coffee house, decorated predominantly yellow, with a juice bar on the street out front. The coffee is excellent, the energy-giving juices tasty and the food just about keeps apace.

Fine Fettle 39 Paora Hape St. Excellent daytime organic wholefood café that's good for breakfasts, including Eggs Benedict ($15.50) and the all-encompassing "FF classic" ($13). Lunches include an excellent mussel chowder ($9.50), panini and salads, many served with organic bread which is also available by the loaf. For brunch try the tasty buckwheat pancakes and slurp on one of their invigorating fruit drinks.

Max Café 38 Roberts St. Taupo's American-diner style fast-food mainstay (6am–10pm), serving a good standard of burgers ($10.50), big breakfasts, toasties and steak 'n' chips meals in an atmosphere-free zone with lake views.

Bars and clubs

Finn MacCuhal's Corner of Tongariro & Tuwharetoa sts. Large Irish bar very popular with the locals as well as the backpackers staying upstairs at *Go Global*. You come here for the Guinness, but they also do good-value steaks and fish and chips.

Holy Cow! 11 Tongariro St. Late, clubby bar run in conjuction with *Mulligan's*, spinning an eclectic selection of rock and dance tunes. Numerous drink specials through the week.

Jolly Good Fellow 76–80 Lake Terrace. The nearest Taupo gets to a British pub, nothing like one in style but with an excellent range of hand-pulled ales and a lively community feel. Most of the English and Irish beers on tap have travelled well. There are also pub meals in the English tradition, with toad-in-the-hole ($15.50) and all-day breakfast served all day including bacon butties. Lots of diners early on followed by revellers for the late shift.

Mulligan's 15 Tongariro St. Dimly lit, typical Irish-style bar with stout on tap, mischievous Kiwi bar staff, live music, quiz nights and massive plates of bar food. Popular with locals and tour buses alike. Pool tables, as well as table football.

Listings

Bike rental Most hostels have basic bikes for guests' use. *Rainbow Lodge* and YHA-associate hostel *Action Downunder* also rent to non-guests, while *Rainbow* also has motor scooters.

Car rental Backpackers Car Rentals, 2 Crown Rd (☎07/376 9209), and Pegasus Rental Cars (☎0800/258 394, ⓦwww.carrentalstaupo.co.nz) have reputations for good deals.

Left luggage Lockers are available at the Superloo, Tongariro St, opposite the visitor centre. Daily 7.30am–5.30pm, 8pm in the summer. $2 a day.

Medical treatment Taupo Health Centre, 115 Heu Heu St ☎07/378 7060 (Mon–Fri 8am–5pm).

Pharmacy Main Street Pharmacy, corner of Heu Heu & Tongariro sts (☎07/378 2636), is open daily until 8.30pm.

Police 21 Story Place, by the museum and art gallery ☎07/378 6060.

Post office Corner of Horomatangi & Ruapehu sts (☎07/378 9090), with poste restante facilities.

Scooter rental Scooter Rental (☎07/378 1551 & 021/158 4069) – driving licence and deposit needed.

Taxis Top Cabs (☎07/378 9250) and Taupo Taxis (☎07/378 5100).

Around Taupo

On the outskirts of Taupo is a concentration of natural wonders, all within a few minutes of one another. Here you'll find boiling mud, hissing steam harnessed by the **Wairakei power station**, and the clear blue Waikato River, which cuts a deep swirling course north over rapids and through deep-sided gorges. The highlights – **Huka Falls**, **Aratiatia Rapids**, **Wairakei Terraces** and the **Craters of the Moon** geothermal area – are all within 10km of Taupo, but you'll have to venture further to reach a second thermal park, **Orakei Korako**, 40km north. To get out this way, you'll need your own vehicle, or the services of one of Taupo's tour companies (see p.321).

Moving **south** from Taupo, SH1 follows the lakeshore to Turangi while SH5 heads east to Napier; both have worthwhile stops along the way.

Along Huka Falls Road

The bulk of the sights and activities flank the Waikato River as it wends its way north, and are lumped together under the collective title of **Wairakei Park**. The park is reached via Huka Falls Road, which loops off SH1 a couple of kilometres north of Taupo and passes the *Reids Farm* free campsite and the exclusive *Huka Lodge* en route to the first point-of-call, the impressive and justly popular **Huka Falls** (*hukanui*, or "great body of spray"). Here the full flow of the Waikato River, one of New Zealand's most voluminous rivers, funnels into a narrow chasm before plunging over a ten-metre shelf into a seething maelstrom of eddies and whirlpools; the sheer power of some four hundred tonnes of water per second make it a far more awesome sight than the short drop would suggest. A footbridge spans the channel, providing a perfect vantage point for watching the occasional mad kayaker making the descent, usually on weekend evenings. The car park, toilets and snack stand are only open until 6pm but you can park outside and walk in at any time.

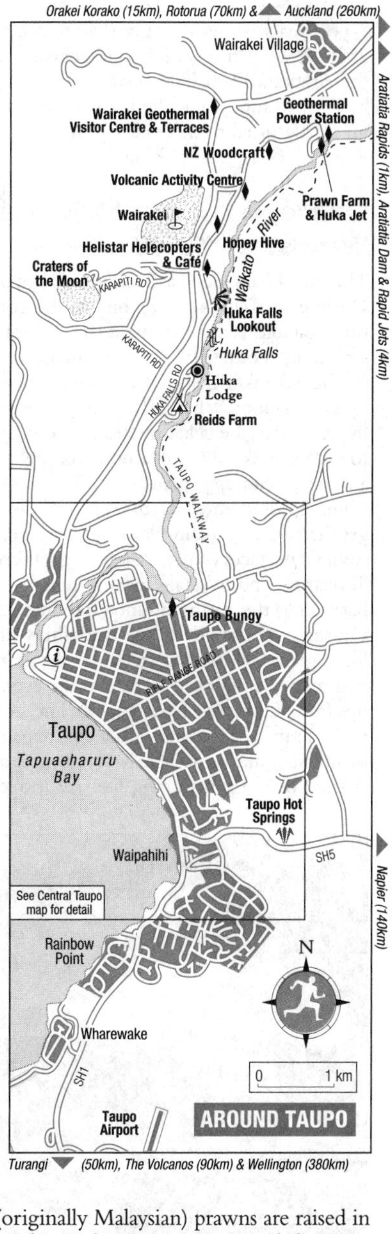

Continuing along Huka Falls Road, a large Russian helicopter marks the launch pad for Helistar flights (see p.325) en route to the cutaway hives and educational video at the **Honey Hive** (daily 9am–5pm; free; ⓣ07/374 8553), 1km further north. Press on to the **Volcanic Activity Centre** (Mon–Fri 9am–5pm, Sat & Sun 10am–4pm; $9.50), a highly instructional museum where the dense text is alleviated by striking photos and interactive computer displays on all things tectonic. Watch one of several films run continuously then check out the seismograph linked to sensors on Mount Ruapehu, an earthquake simulator and a large relief map of Taupo Volcanic Zone, which extends from Mount Ruapehu to White Island.

Moving on, you'll come to the Wairakei geothermal power station which discharges most of the excess heat it generates into the river, though a portion is channelled into large open ponds, where tropical (originally Malaysian) prawns are raised in a highly successful enterprise known as the **Huka Prawn Farm** (daily 9am–4pm, later in midsummer; tours every 30min 10am–4pm; $8; ⓦwww.prawnpark.co.nz). If learning about a day in the life of "Shawn the Prawn" doesn't fire your imagination, look forward to eating as many of Shawn's delicious little friends as you can (platter for two $60) in the adjacent *Prawn River Restaurant.*

The peace is periodically shattered by a **Huka Jet** (30min $95; ⓣ0800/485 2538, ⓦwww.hukfallsjet.com) roaring along the river between Huka Falls and the Aratiatia Dam. The boats leave from a jetty by the Prawn Farm (courtesy bus from Taupo), and the trips present great views of the falls as well as getting up to the usual tricks – close encounters with rock faces and 360-degree spins – but if you're just looking for thrills opt for Rapids Jet (see p.331).

Craters of the Moon and the Wairakei Terraces

The Huka Falls loop road rejoins SH1 opposite the **Wairakei International Golf Course** (ⓣ07/374 8152), one of the country's finest. Just south of the intersection, Karapiti Road runs west to **Craters of the Moon** (daily 8am–5.30pm; $5), a striking geothermal area that sprang to life in the 1950s, after the construction of the Wairakei geothermal power station drastically altered the underground hydrodynamics. What it lacks in geysers and colourful lakes it makes up for in hyperactivity: the belching steam is so vigorous that you must wear closed footwear to walk the 2km of trails among roaring fumaroles and rumbling pits belching out a pungent bad-egg smell.

Three kilometres north on SH1 is **Wairakei Terraces**, Taupo's original geothermal area (daily 9am–5pm; free entry, tour $18; ⓣ07/378 0913, ⓦwww.wairakeiterraces.co.nz), where a geothermal centre displays a relief map of the Tongariro and Waikato power schemes, plenty of stuff on the intricacies of harnessing the earth's bounty and an explanatory video shown on demand ($3). On the opposite side of the road, shiny high-pressure steam pipes twist and bend, like a giant ball-bearing racetrack, the 2km to the power station. Undoubtedly the best reason to visit the Terraces is the evening **Maori cultural experience** (pick-ups from Taupo can be arranged). The small-scale tour (every Wed or by appointment; 6pm; $79) begins with a challenge and welcome, followed by a guided tour of the site, during which Maori beliefs and history are interwoven with a look at the pools, a functioning life-size model village and carvings. Potentially more

▲ Craters of the Moon

impressive are the beginnings of some man-made terraces in the mould of the original Pink and White Terraces (see p.316). To round the evening off there's a *hangi* and concert.

Aratiatia Rapids and around

Around 2km downstream from the Wairakei power station lies the first of the Waikato River's eight hydroelectric dams, the Aratiatia Dam, which holds back the Waikato immediately above the **Aratiatia Rapids**, a long series of cataracts that were one of Taupo's earliest attractions. In the 1950s, plans to divert the waters around the rapids were amended by public pressure, thus preserving the rapids, though it's something of a hollow victory since they are dry most of the time, only seen in their full glory during three or four thirty-minute periods each day (Oct–March 10am, noon, 2pm & 4pm; April–Sept 10am, noon & 2pm). Stand on the dam itself or at one of two downstream viewpoints reached by an easy trail, and wait for the siren that heralds the spectacle of a parched watercourse being transformed into a foaming torrent of waterfalls and surging pressure waves, before returning to a trickle.

The most exhilirating way to experience the rapids is with **Rapids Jet** ($75; ⓣ0800/727 437, ⓦwww.rapidsjet.com), located on Rapids Road 3km beyond the Aratiatia Dam. This is no slick bus-them-in operation, but New Zealand's only true whitewater jetboating run, taking you down and up Fuljames rapid and throwing in a good deal of local lore and entertaining patter to boot. The entire boat gets airborne and the company makes no secret of having sunk three vessels, yet no one has been injured – just listen closely to the safety spiel, hang on and prepare to get very wet.

Diverting from either SH1 (14km) or SH5 (23km), about 40km north of Taupo is the atmospheric and, in places, spectacular thermal area of **Orakei Korako** (daily 8am–4pm; $28; ⓣ07/378 3131, ⓦwww.orakeikorako.co.nz;). Enjoyable boat trips ferry visitors to walkways threading through pools and belching fumaroles, and the whole experience can easily enthral you for a couple of hours.

The Taupo–Napier Road

Travelling beyond the immediate vicinity of Taupo, SH1 hugs the lake as it heads southwest to Turangi (see p.334), while SH5 veers southeast along the **Taupo–Napier Road**, a twisting ninety-minute run through some of the North Island's remotest country. Much of the early part of the journey crosses the Kaingaroa Plains, impoverished land cloaked in pumice and ash from the Taupo Volcanic eruption and of little use save for the pine plantations which stretch 100km to the north. The history of this route is traced by the **Taupo–Napier Heritage Trail**; pick up a free booklet from either town's i-SITE. Many of the 35 stops are of limited interest but be sure to call in at **Opepe Historic Reserve**, 17km from Taupo, where, on the north side of the road, a cemetery contains white wooden slabs marking the graves of nine soldiers of the Bay of Plenty cavalry, killed by followers of maverick Maori leader Te Kooti in 1869.

After another 11km, Clements Mill Road leads 30km south into the northern reaches of the **Kaimanawa Forest Park**, an untouched rugged mountain wilderness little visited by recreational trampers. If you are experienced and determined, get hold of the *Guide to Kaimanawa State Forest Park* map and set off on the remote **Te Iringa–Oamaru Circuit** (60km; 4–5 days), staying in Category 3 huts ($5 per night). Some 25km southeast of the Clements Mill Road turn-off, the Waipunga River, a tributary of the Mohaka, plummets 30m over the **Waipunga Falls**, and continues beside SH5 through the lovely Waipunga

Gorge, packed with tall native trees and dotted with picnic sites which double as overnight **campsites** with no facilities but river water. The highway descends to the Mohaka River and *Mountain Valley*, 5km south of SH5 (T06/834 9756, W www.mountainvalley.co.nz; camping $12, dorms $35 lodge rooms ❶, doubles, twins, chalets ❹, self-contained cottages ❻), a residential adventure lodge with a riverside bar and restaurant. Various excursions on offer include scenic **rafting** on Grade I–II stretches of the Mohaka (1hr $65, 2hr $95), or the more exciting and wonderfully scenic Grade III section (full day $150), which runs through a narrow gorge that's great for jumping off the cliffs either side. You can also **kayak** on similar stretches (2hr $65), or go on a wilderness **horse trek** (1hr $65), go mountain biking or try your hand on a guided fishing expedition. Beyond the Mohaka River, the highway climbs the Titiokura Saddle before the final descent through the grape country of the **Esk Valley** into Napier.

Tongariro National Park and around

New Zealand's highly developed network of national parks owes much to Te Heu Heu Tukino IV, the Tuwharetoa chief who, in the Pakeha land-grabbing climate of the late nineteenth century, recognized that the only chance his people had of keeping their sacred lands intact was to donate them to the nation – on condition that they could not be settled nor spoiled. His 1887 gift formed the core of the country's first major public reserve, **Tongariro National Park**, which became a **World Heritage Site** in 1991 owing to its unique landscape and cultural significance (see box, p.334). In the north a small, outlying section of the park centres on **Mount Pihanga** and the tiny **Lake Rotopounamu** but most visitors head straight for the main body of the park, dominated by the three great volcanoes which rise starkly from the desolate plateau: the broad-shouldered ski mountain, **Ruapehu** (2797m), its squatter sibling, **Tongariro** (1968m), and, wedged between them, the conical **Ngauruhoe** (2287m).

Within the boundaries of the park is some of the North Island's most striking scenery. The more forbidding volcanic areas were used as locations for Mordor and Mount Doom in the *Lord of the Rings*, though, in reality, it's a beautiful mixture of semi-arid plains, steaming fumaroles, crystal-clear lakes and streams, virgin rainforest and an abundance of ice and snow. All of this forms the backdrop to two supremely rewarding tramps, the one-day **Tongariro Alpine Crossing** and the three to four-day **Tongariro Northern Circuit**, one of New Zealand's Great Walks. The undulating plateau to the west of the volcanoes is vegetated by bushland and golden tussock, while on the eastern side the rain shadow of the mountains produces the **Rangipo Desert**. Although this is not a true desert, it is still an impressively bleak and barren landscape, smothered by a thick layer of volcanic ash from the 186 AD Taupo eruption. The park is part of the Taupo volcanic zone and captured world headlines in 1995, 1996 and 2007 when **Mount Ruapehu**, the highest and most massive of the three volcanoes, burst into life, emptying the crater lake down the side of the mountain in muddy deluges known as lahars. Although such **eruptions** drastically curtail the ski season there has (so far) been minimal lasting damage.

The northern approach to the region is through **Turangi**, not much in itself but a reasonable base both for the Tongariro tramps and for rafting and fishing the Tongariro River. What it lacks is a sense of proximity to the mountains – something much more tangible in the service town of **National Park** and more so again in **Whakapapa Village**, 1200m up on the flanks of Ruapehu. The southern gateway is **Ohakune**, a more appealing place than National Park but distinctly comatose outside the ski season. Heading south, the Army Museum at Waiouru marks the southern limit of the Volcanic Plateau, which tails off into the pastoral lower half of the region set around the agricultural town of **Taihape**, home to the North Island's highest bungy jump.

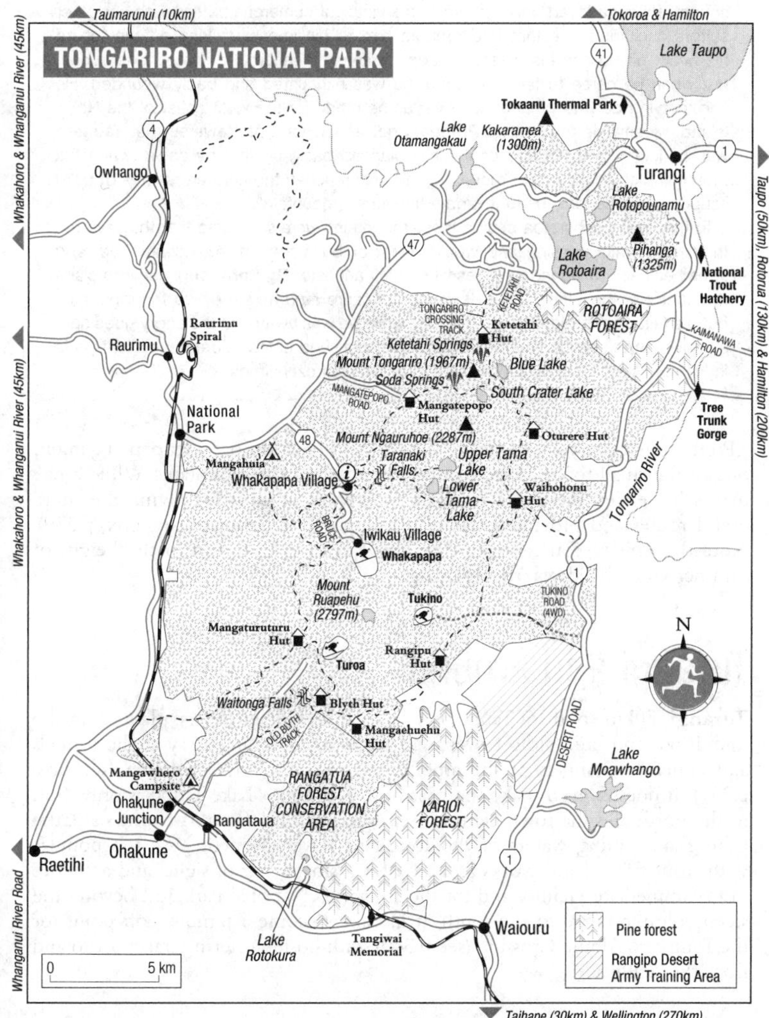

The Maori mountain legends

When Te Heu Heu Tukino donated Tongariro's central volcanoes to the Crown (see p.332), he was motivated by a deep spiritual need for their protection. According to Maori, the mountains at the heart of the park have distinct personalities and a genealogy and symbolize the links between the community and its environment. This significance was recognized in 1991 when the park became the first World Heritage Site included as a **cultural landscape**. The **Maori mountain legends** which follow explain some of the relationships between the peaks and their formation but vary from one *iwi* to another, so don't be surprised if the Taranaki Maori version is at odds with this one.

In the past, there were said to be a lot of smaller mountains clustered around the dominating **Ruapehu**, **Tongariro**, **Ngauruhoe** and **Taranaki**. Among these was the beautiful **Pihanga** in the northern section of the park, whose favours were widely sought. Pihanga loved only Tongariro, the victor of numerous battles with her other suitors, including one that had brought him to his knees, striking off the top of his head, giving him his present shape. Taranaki, meantime, defeated Ngauruhoe, but when he came to face Ruapehu, he was exhausted and badly wounded. He fled, carving out the Whanganui River as he made for the west coast of the North Island. Meanwhile the smaller **Putauaki** got as far north as Kawerau; but **Tauhara** was reluctant to leave and continually glanced back, so that by dawn, when the mountains could no longer move, he had only reached the northern shores of Lake Taupo, where he remains to this day, "the lonely mountain".

To the local Tuwharetoa people these mountains were so sacred that they averted their eyes while passing and wouldn't eat or build fires in the vicinity. The *tapu* stretches back to legendary times when their ancestor **Ngatoroirangi** came to claim the centre of the island. After declaring Tongariro *tapu* he set off up the mountain, but his followers broke their vow to fast while he was away and the angry gods sent a snowstorm in which Ngatoroirangi almost perished before more benevolent gods in Hawaiki saved him by sending fire to revive his frozen limbs.

Pretty much everyone comes to the park either to **ski** or to **tramp**, staying in one of the small towns dotted around the base of the mountains. While a **car** makes life easier, there is a reasonable network of **shuttles** plying the more useful routes and providing trailhead transport for trampers (see box, p.339). Note that this region is over 600m above sea level, so even in the height of summer you'll need **warm clothing**.

Turangi and around

Turangi, 50km south of Taupo, is small, flat and characterless, planned in the mid-1960s and built almost overnight for workers toiling away at the tunnels and concrete channels of the ambitious Tongariro Power Scheme (see box, p.337). It doesn't even make the best of its location – Lake Taupo is only 4km to the north and the town centre is separated by SH1 from its trump card, the fishing and rafting waters of the Tongariro River. Nonetheless, it is popular with trout fishers, and works as a base for a smattering of sights and activities in the immediate vicinity and for the Tongariro National Park, just beyond the steep volcanic range to the south. It has also become a jumping-off point for the Tongariro Alpine Crossing (see p.340) with hostels offering transport to and from the trailheads.

Practicalities

Alpine Scenic Tours and Tongariro Expeditions both run low-cost daily **bus** services from Taupo, dropping off pretty much where you want. InterCity drop near the **i-SITE visitor centre**, Ngawaka Place (daily 8.30am–5pm; ⓣ0800/288 726, ⓦwww.laketauponz.com), which sells bus tickets, has Internet access and is packed with local **information**, including stuff on fishing. It also sells Taupo fishing licences (it's the only place with the necessary paperwork for Rotaria), maps, DOC tramping brochures and hut tickets, though if you have detailed tramping enquiries you could trot down the street to the small **DOC office** on Turanga Place (Mon–Fri 8am–4.30pm; ⓣ07/386 8607).

Accommodation

Turangi's need to cater to anglers, skiers and trampers bound for the Tongariro National Park has left it with a range of **accommodation**; the budget places congregate in the town centre, while plusher lodges and B&Bs line the Tongariro River to the east.

Club Habitat 25 Ohuanga Rd ⓣ07/386 7492, ⓦwww.clubhabitat.co.nz. Refurbished accommodation with spacious games bar, dining complex, spa, sauna and luxurious "executive" units with TVs and a/c. Dorms $22, cabins ❸ units ❺

Creel Lodge 183 Taupahi Rd ⓣ07/386 8081. A simple, low-cost, fishing-oriented motel comprising a cluster of s/c one- and two-bedroom units in grounds running down to the river edge with communal fish smoker and BBQ. ❹

Extreme Backpackers 26 Ngawaka Place ⓣ07/386 8949, ⓦwww.extremebackpackers.co.nz. Simply decorated rooms in this purpose-built backpackers set around a central courtyard. The amenable hosts sometimes run guests to the Tokaanu hot pools in the evening; there's also a climbing wall ($15) and an amiable café. Dorms $23, rooms and en suites ❷

Founders Guest Lodge 253 Taupahi Rd ⓣ07/386 8539, ⓦwww.founders.co.nz. Four extremely comfortable double rooms in a quiet and relaxing homestay with cooked and continental breakfasts and friendly hosts. ❻

Ika Lodge 155 Taupahi Rd ⓣ07/386 5538, ⓦwww.ika.co.nz. This superior homestay-cum-fishing lodge by the Tongariro River has a two-bedroom and a double. Prices include breakfast. Double ❺, apartment ❼

Parklands Corner of SH1 & Arahori St ⓣ0800/456 284 & 07/386 7515, ⓦwww.parklandsmotorlodge.co.nz. Extensive motor lodge with an outdoor pool, private hot tubs, games room and a small restaurant serving home-style dinners. Camping $14, studios ❸, units ❹

Activities

To access activities around Turangi you'll either need your own transport or to arrange pick-up by the operators or the Tongariro shuttles (see p.339). Four companies offer **rafting** year-round on the lower reaches of the Tongariro River, which runs through one of the most scenic and accessible river gorges in the country. The Tongariro Power Scheme has modulated the Tongariro's natural flow patterns, limiting the possibility of a really wild time on the Grade II and Grade III rapids but there's a broad range of trips you can do on the water – traditional rafting, sit-on kayaks or a combination of fishing and rafting.

The handiest operators are Tokaanu-based Wai Maori (ⓣ0800/865 226, ⓦwww.raftingkayaking.co.nz; see p.336) and Turangi-based Tongariro River Rafting on Atirau Road, near Firestone Tyres (ⓣ0800/101 024, ⓦwww.trr.co.nz). Taupo's Rapid Sensations (ⓣ0800/227 238, ⓦwww.rapids.co.nz) and Kiwi River Safaris (ⓣ0800/7238 577, ⓦwww.krs.co.nz) are also competitive. All offer straightforward whitewater-rafting trips for about $99, with varying fringe benefits. Big rafts can make the modest scale of the lower Tongariro seem a little tame, so if you're after thrills **kayaking** ($99 for 4hr) in Grade II white water is the viable alternative offered by all the above operators.

If you're keen to haul a trout from Lake Taupo or one of the local rivers, the visitor centre will help pair you with a **fishing** guide to match your experience and aspirations as well as a licence ($15.50 a day); expect to pay anything from $180–300 for a half-day with gear and guiding. You can rent a boat and tackle at moderate prices from Hire Boats Motuoapa (around $40 an hour; ⓣ07/386 7000), 8km north of Turangi and just off SH1. River fishing takes place pretty much year-round, but the spawning season is from April to October.

To combine the last two activities, Wai Maori and Tongariro River Rafting will take you **raft fishing** (Dec–May only), which involves rafting the Tongariro and stopping off at otherwise inaccessible pools along the way to cast a fly. Rates are $650 a day for two people – roughly the same as you'd pay for a fishing guide alone.

Finally, the pleasant **Tongariro River Loop Track** (4km) is well worth the hour it takes to complete. The trail starts from the Major Jones footbridge at the end of Koura Street on the edge of town; it follows the right bank of the river north past a couple of viewpoints and over a bluff then crosses the river and returns along the opposite side. Ten kilometres south of Turangi, off SH47, the **Lake Rotopounamu Circuit** (5km; 90min) encircles a pristine lake surrounded by bush alive with native birds.

Eating and drinking

Eating in Turangi is limited but you can feed tolerably well for a couple of nights.

Brew Haus Bar & Restaurant At *Club Habitat* on Ohuanga Rd ⓣ07/386 7492. Moderately priced hearty meals at breakfast (7–9.30am) and dinner (6–10pm). The bar is probably the most hospitable in town.

Grand Central Fry Corner of Ohuanga Rd & Ngawaka Place ⓣ07/386 5344. Easily the best of the town's takeaways doing great fish and chips and, of course, run by an Englishman.

Kaimanawa Bistro 258 Taupahi Rd ⓣ07/386 8709. Traditional, dinner-only restaurant towards the Tongariro River, with mains $20–30. Closed Sun & Mon.

Mustard Seed Café 91 Ohuanga Rd. Casual, modern villa café with the usual range of breakfasts, panini, salads and cakes, plus decent espresso.

Red Crater Café At *Extreme Backpackers*, see p.335. Excellent little café serving great coffee, good-value snacks, burgers and more substantial fare.

Tokaanu

Turangi's smaller neighbour, **Tokaanu**, 5km west, was the main settlement in the area in pre-European times. Maori were drawn by the geothermal benefits of what is now the **Tokaanu Thermal Park** (unrestricted entry; free), a compact patch of low scrub, beautifully clear hot pools and plopping mud threaded by a fifteen-minute trail. The adjacent **Tokaanu Thermal Pools**, Mangaroa Road (daily 10am–9pm; $6), are great for soaking bones after a day's tramping in the national park, with an open-air public pool and hotter, partly enclosed and chlorine-free private pools ($8 for 20 min, including public pool access, closed at 9pm). Nearby you can spend a very pleasurable hour or two gently paddling along a narrow, lush, bush-fringed channel, past the hot tubs and back gardens of the locals in **kayaks** rented from Wai Maori (daily 10am–5pm; $40 per person per half-day; ⓣ0800/865 226, ⓦwww.raftingkayaking.co.nz); to find them, take the Tokaanu road out of Turangi and look for the sign on the left, just over the bridge. Alternatively stop by the *Dragonfly Café*, 426 SH41, at the Oasis General Store (9am–4pm, closed Wed), for a coffee and a cake and to browse the new and secondhand books.

The Tongariro Power Scheme

The **Tongariro Power Scheme** provides an object lesson in harnessing the power of water with minimal impact on the environment. Its two powerhouses produce around seven percent of the country's electricity, while the outflows that feed into Lake Taupo add flexibility to the much older chain of eight hydroelectric dams along the Waikato River. Some argue it is unacceptable to tamper with such a fine piece of wilderness and while it has caused fluctuations in the levels of nutrients in the Tongariro River and erosion along some of the service tracks, it's better than a nuclear power station.

In fact, if it weren't for the scale models in visitor centres and the ugly bulk of the Tokaanu power station, only astute observers would be aware of the complex system of tunnels, aqueducts, canals and weirs unobtrusively going about their business of diverting the waters of the Tongariro River and myriad streams running off the mountain slopes, back and forth around the perimeter of the national park, using modified natural lakes for storage. Mount Ruapehu poses its own unique problems: the threat of **lahars** (see p.333) is ever-present and, after the 1995 eruption, **tephra** (a highly abrasive volcanic ash) found its way into the turbines of the Rangipo underground powerhouse, causing an unscheduled seven-month shutdown.

Whakapapa and around

Tiny **Whakapapa**, the only settlement set firmly within the boundaries of the Tongariro National Park, hugs the lower slopes of Mount Ruapehu some 45km south of Turangi on SH48, which spurs off SH47. Approaching from the north, an open expanse of tussock gives distant views of the imposing *Grand Chateau* hotel which rises into view like an absurd mirage, framed by the snowy slopes of the volcano behind and overlooked by the arterial network of tows on the Whakapapa ski-field.

From Whakapapa, SH48 continues as Bruce Road 6km to **Iwikau Village** (known locally as the "Top o' the Bruce"), an ugly jumble of ski-club chalets which from late June through to mid-November, and in exceptional circumstances as late as Christmas, becomes a seething mass of wraparound shades and baggy snowboarders' pants. Outside the ski season, the village dies, leaving only a couple of **chair lifts** (Jan to mid-March; $20 return) to trundle up to the garish *Knoll Ridge Café*, New Zealand's highest at 2020m, from where you can take **guided walks** on the mountain.

Practicalities

The only **bus services** to Whakapapa are the once-daily shuttle buses from Turangi and National Park (see box, p.339), which drop off close to DOC's helpful **visitor centre** (daily: Dec–Feb 8am–6pm; March–Nov 8am–5pm; Ⓣ07/892 3729, Ⓔwhakapapavc@doc.govt.nz). The centre contains all the maps and leaflets you'll need and extensive displays on the park, including the tiny Ski History museum and a couple of videos that are shown on demand – *Volcanoes of the South Wind* (15min) is a fairly simplistic discussion of vulcanism in general and its manifestations here, while *The Sacred Gift of Tongariro* (25min) combines Maori legends surrounding Tongariro with impressive footage of the landscape through the seasons and the activities that take place in it. Each costs $3, or you can see both for $5.

Accommodation

There's not much to Whakapapa besides cafés, a pub and **places to stay**, all within a couple of minutes' walk of each other and often booked in advance. Reserve as far ahead as possible through the ski season and over the Christmas and January school holidays. The most prominent hotel is the *Grand Chateau* (Ⓣ0800/242 832, Ⓦwww.chateau.co.nz; ❸), a vast 1929 brick edifice with gracious public areas including a huge lounge with full-size snooker table and great mountain views; it's worth a visit for a cup of tea even if you're not a resident. Guests have use of the highest nine-hole golf course in New Zealand, tennis courts, gym and a small indoor pool, and stay in rooms modernized to international hotel standard; you'll need a premium room (❼) if you're after space and good views, but you can save money in spring and autumn when there are often discounts of around thirty percent. The *Chateau* also has self-contained chalets (❻), some sleeping up to six; and helps guests organize Tongariro treks (see p.340). The only other hotel is the *Skotel*, about 50m up the hill beside the *Grand Chateau* (Ⓣ0800/756 835, Ⓦwww.skotel.com; backpacker beds $30, standard rooms ❷, hotel rooms & cabins ❺), an "alpine retreat" with a sauna. Note that rates are hiked considerably in the ski season. The best budget option is the *Whakapapa Holiday Park*, its entrance diagonally opposite the visitor centre (Ⓣ07/892 3897, Ⓔwhakapapaholpark@xtra.co.nz; camping $17, dorms $25, cabins ❸, unit ❹), set in a patch of bushland with spacious tent and powered sites. There is also DOC's toilets-and-water self-registration *Mangahuia Campsite* ($4), on SH47 close to the foot of the Whakapapa access road.

Iwikau Village has no accommodation, only daytime cafés open throughout the year.

Eating and drinking

Snacks are cheap at *Fergussons Café*, opposite the visitor centre, though you might prefer the better quality across the road at the *Chateau*'s *Pihanga Café and T Bar*, which serve more substantial fare (from 11.30am to 9pm). Alternatives are the *Skotel*, which serves breakfast and good-value bistro meals and has a bar. The cheapest booze and food, and some might say the most atmospheric place to **drink**, is the *Tussock Pub* (open at 3pm with big-screen TV) where the few locals tend to congregate. If you want to reward yourself for the successful completion of a major tramp, the *Chateau*'s *Ruapehu Room* has good à la carte meals at à la carte prices. Five kilometres up the hill is the basic *Lorenz's Café*, in the ski resort by the base of the chair lift, while a chair-lift ride away is *Knoll Ridge*, the highest café in New Zealand – not much to write home about but with good views nonetheless.

Around Whakapapa

Outside the skiing season (see box, p.342) Whakapapa is much less frenetic, though swarms of trampers use it as a base for short walks or long tramps. The Tongariro Northern Circuit and the Round the Mountain track (see p.341) can both be tackled from here, but there are also easier strolls covered by DOC's *Whakapapa Walks* leaflet. Three of the best of these are the **Whakapapa Nature Walk** (1km; 20–30min), highlighting the unique flora of the park; the **Taranaki Falls Walk** (6km; 2hr), which heads through open tussock and bushland to where the Wairere Stream plunges 20m over the end of an old lava flow; and the **Silica Rapids Walk** (7km; 2hr 30min), which follows a stream through beech forests to some creamy-coloured geothermal terraces.

If you've a good few dollars to spare and want to take some of the strain out of hiking, head up to the ski village and on to the chair lift. From the top **guided crater walks** (6hr, $90 including the lift, Jan–March 9.30am; ⓣ07/892 3738, ⓦwww.mtruapehu.com) give a taste of the majesty of Ruapehu.

Tramping in Tongariro National Park

Tongariro National Park contains some of the North Island's finest walks. The **Tongariro Alpine Crossing** alone is rated as the best one-day tramp in the country, but there are many longer possibilities, notably the three- to four-day **Tongariro Northern Circuit**; both pass through spectacular and varied volcanic terrain. Mount Ruapehu has the arduous but rewarding **Crater Rim Walk** and a circuit, the **Round the Mountain Track**, which offers a narrower variety of terrain and sights than the Tongariro tramps, but is consequently less used.

Getting to the Tongariro National Park treks

The major bus companies don't run through the Tongariro National Park, leaving several smaller companies, many associated with backpacker hostels, to fill the void. Some offer an Early Bird service getting you to the trailhead before the masses, others only run at peak times; most charge extra for early starts. The best places to visit the park from are Ohakune, National Park, Whakapapa and Turangi; Taupo is simply too far away to make it an enjoyable or sensible option.

From National Park: Shuttle buses serve the trailheads in summer and ski-fields in winter. All the hostels will arrange transport, but the biggest operator is *Howard's Lodge* (ⓣ07/892 2827), which runs all-comer buses, charging $25 for drop-off and pick-up at either end of the Tongariro Alpine Crossing. Tongariro Track Transport picks up in National Park at 7.45am then continues to Whakapapa and Mangatepopo. Matai Shuttles call in too (see below).

From Ohakune: Matai Shuttles, operated by *Matai Lodge*, (ⓣ06/385 9169, ⓦwww.matailodge.co.nz), run reliable buses every morning, the first departing Ohakune at 6am, calling in at National Park 30min later and getting to the start of the walk for a crowd-dodging 7.15am, or 8.15am and 9.15am, if you pressed the snooze button. They charge $30 and will pick up at 3, 4 and 5pm – bookings are essential.

From Taupo: Alpine Scenic Tours (ⓣ07/378 7412, ⓦwww.alpinescenictours.co.nz) and Tongariro Expeditions (ⓣ0800/828 763, ⓦwww.tongariroexpeditions.com) compete, but to attempt the crossing from Taupo involves a ridiculously early start and puts you on the crossing when it is at its busiest.

From Turangi: Alpine Scenic Tours (ⓣ07/386 8918, ⓦwww.alpinescenictours.co.nz) do a particularly useful run three times a day, calling at Whakapapa and the start and end of the Tongariro Alpine Crossing including one run (11am from Turangi) going right through to National Park. *Bellbird Lodge* (ⓣ07/386 8281), *Club Habitat* (see p.335), *Extreme Backpackers* (see p.335) and new operator Mountain Shuttle (ⓣ0800/117 686, ⓦwww.tongarirocrossing.com) all offer similar services, with most running an early bus giving you a head start on the pack. Fares are competitive – each charges around $30 for the Tongariro Alpine Crossing drop-off and pick-up and $25 one way to either Whakapapa or National Park. Alpine becomes a ski-field shuttle in winter.

From Whakapapa: Tongariro Track Transport (ⓣ07/892 3716) runs a daily shuttle leaving the visitor centre at 8am for the start of the Tongariro Alpine Crossing (around $25 return), and meeting you at Ketetahi at either 4.30 or 6pm.

Practicalities

The *Tongariro Park* **maps** ($13.50 or $19) are ideal for these tramps, but **DOC leaflets** covering the tramps are informative and adequate. The main **points of access** to the walks are Mangatepopo Road and Ketetahi Road for the Tongariro Alpine Crossing and Tongariro Northern Circuit; and Whakapapa for the Tongariro Northern Circuit, the Ruapehu Crater Rim and the Round the Mountain Track. Shuttle **buses** serve the trailheads (see p.339). With the exception of the unmarked Crater Rim walk, the tracks are all well maintained and sporadically signposted, so you can judge your progress if you've a bus to catch.

Other than accommodation in Whakapapa Village, the only places to stay are **trampers huts**, all of which have adjacent **campsites**. In summer (roughly late Oct–May), huts on the Tongariro Northern Circuit – Mangatepopo, Ketetahi, Waihohonu and Oturere – are classed as Great Walk huts ($20); in winter they lose their cooking facilities and revert to Category 2 ($10, camping $5). Hut tickets do not guarantee a bunk, so at busy times you could end up on the floor. Campers (summer $15, winter $5) stay close to the huts and use the same facilities. Huts on the Round the Mountain Track – Whakapapaiti, Mangaturuturu, Blyth, Mangaehuehu and Rangipo – are Category 2 huts all year ($10, camping $5). Hut tickets can be bought in advance from DOC in Whakapapa and Ohakune, or DOC and the visitor centre in Turangi; if bought from a hut warden you pay an extra $5.

There are several **organized treks**: the *Grand Chateau* hotel in Whakapapa Village (mid-Dec to mid-April; ⓣ0800/242 832, ⓦwww.trek.co.nz) offers a variety of Tongariro tramping options, though at the time of writing no guided trips were allowed on the Tongariro Alpine Crossing, a situation currently under review by DOC. Guided Walk (see p.339) ascend to the Ruapehu Crater Rim, providing a commentary on geology and flora and some magnificent view over the range.

The **weather** in the mountains is extremely changeable, and the usual provisos apply. Even on scorching summer days, the increased altitude and exposed windy ridges produce a wind-chill factor to be reckoned with, and storms roll in with frightening rapidity. Any time from the end of March through to late November there can be snow on the tracks, so if you are planning a tramp during this period, enquire locally about current conditions. Always take warm **clothing** and rain gear – and if you plan to scramble up and down the steep volcanic cone of Mount Ngauruhoe, take gloves and long trousers for protection from the sharp scoria rock.

Tongariro Alpine Crossing

The **Tongariro Alpine Crossing** (16km; 6–8hr; 750m ascent) is by far the most popular of the major tramps in the region and for good reason. Within a few hours you climb over lava flows, cross a crater floor, skirt active geothermal areas, pass beautiful and serene emerald and blue lakes and have the opportunity to ascend the cinder cone of Mount Ngauruhoe. Even without this wealth of highlights it would still be a fine tramp, traversing a mountain massif through scrub and tussock before descending into virgin bush. Note that this isn't a wilderness experience – on weekends and through the height of summer well over a thousand people complete the Crossing, so it pays to aim for spring or autumn, or stick to weekdays. It is a long and arduous day if you're not particularly fit, so consider the pleasing alternative of turning the walk from a one-day into a two-day experience by doing it in reverse (see box opposite).

Car parks at both ends of the track have a reputation for break-ins so it's a good idea to leave your vehicle in Ohakune, Turangi, National Park or Whakapapa and

Easing the pain, avoiding the crowds

To avoid the worst of the crush on the Tongariro Alpire Crossing, steal a march on other walkers by choosing a shuttle operator prepared to drop off at Mangatepopo Road a little earlier; or dawdle behind the mob and plan to stay the night at Mangatepopo Hut. Much more practical and enjoyable, allowing you more mountain time, is to do the trek in reverse, get dropped off at Ketetahi Road in the afternoon, walk leisurely to the Ketetahi Hut, spend the night and be ready for a crack-of-dawn start next day, allowing you to be the first to leave footprints in the snow and enjoy views unsullied by armies of other trampers.

make use instead of the shuttle buses (see p.339). The track can be walked in either direction but by going from west to east you save roughly 300m of ascent, unimportant if you're doing it in two days, noteworthy if you're taking one; all shuttle buses are scheduled around a west to east traverse, usually depositing their charges at Mangatepopo Road End car park, six gravel kilometres east of SH47, at about 8.30am and picking up at Ketetahi Road around 4.30pm. Some shuttle operators do a 6pm pick-up allowing you to tack on an ascent of Ngauruhoe.

From Mangatepopo Road End the first hour is gentle, following the Mangatepopo Stream through a barren landscape and passing the Mangatepopo Hut. The track steepens as you scale the fractured black lava flows towards the **Mangatepopo Saddle**, passing a short side track to the **Soda Springs**, a small wildflower oasis in this blasted landscape. The Saddle marks the start of the high ground between the bulky and ancient Mount Tongariro and its youthful acolyte, **Mount Ngauruhoe**, which fit walkers can climb (2km return; 2hr return; 600m ascent) from here and still make the shuttle bus at the end of the day. The two-steps-forward-one-step-back ascent of this thirty-five-degree cone of red and black scoria is most exhausting and dispiriting but the views from the toothy crater rim and the thrilling headlong descent among a cascade of tumbling rocks and volcanic dust make it a popular excursion. If you're attempting it in **winter**, bear in mind that the ascent becomes an "alpine" climb and the use of mountaineering gear, like ice axes, is advisable.

From the Mangatepopo Saddle, the main track crosses the flat pan of the South Crater and climbs to the rim of **Red Crater**, with fumaroles belching out steam, which obscures the banded crimson and black of the crater walls. Colours get more vibrant still as you begin the descent to the Emerald Lakes, opaque pools shading from jade to palest duck-egg, and beyond to the crystal-clear Blue Lake. Sidling around Tongariro's **North Crater**, you begin to descend steeply on golden tussock slopes to **Ketetahi Hut**, a major rest stop with views of Lake Rotoaira and Lake Taupo. From here you pass close to the steaming Ketetahi Springs, then begin the final descent through cool streamside bush to the car park on Ketetahi Road.

Tongariro Northern Circuit and the Round the Mountain track

If the Tongariro Alpine Crossing appeals, but you are looking for something more challenging, the answer is the **Tongariro Northern Circuit** (42km; 3–4 days at a gentle pace), one of New Zealand's Great Walks. The section from **Whakapapa to Mangatepopo Hut** (9km; 2–3hr; 50m ascent) is boggy after heavy rain but usually passable, though you could always get a shuttle to Mangatepopo. If you decide to walk, you'll find the track undulating through tussock and crossing numerous streams before meeting the Tongariro Alpine Crossing track close to Mangatepopo Hut. From **Mangatepopo Hut to Emerald Lakes** (6km; 3–4hr; 660m ascent), you follow the Tongariro Alpine Crossing (described above), then have the choice of continuing on the Crossing to **Ketetahi Hut** (4km;

Mount Ruapehu ski-fields

Mount Ruapehu, recently the subject of a major revamp, is home to the North Island's only substantial **ski-fields**, which attract around two-thirds of the nation's skiers. Every weekend from **late June to early November**, cars pile out of Auckland and Wellington (and everywhere in between) for the four-hour drive to either Whakapapa, the more extensive ski-field on the northwestern slopes of Mount Ruapehu, or Turoa, on the south side. Both have excellent reputations for pretty much all levels of skier and the orientation of volcanic ridges lends itself to an abundance of dreamy, natural half-pipes for snowboarding.

With over thirty groomed runs (fifteen beginner, eight intermediate, seven advanced), a dozen major chair lifts and T-bars and the dedicated learners' area of Happy Valley, **Whakapapa** is New Zealand's largest and busiest ski area. It offers the longest North Island season (usually late June to early Nov and sometimes through to Christmas), 675 vertical metres of piste, plus snow-making equipment, ski schools, a huge gear-rental operation and some café/bars. **Access** is along the toll-free, sealed Bruce Road. Tyre chains are sometimes required, in which case a fitting service miraculously appears at a parking area beside the road. Car parking is free and there is a free courtesy bus from the lower car parks. Shuttle buses run from Whakapapa Village, National Park, Turangi and Taupo.

Turoa (typically mid- to late June through to late Oct) has developed in a much more controlled fashion than Whakapapa, and offers the country's greatest vertical range of piste (720m) and a skiable area almost as extensive as Whakapapa's with wide, groomed trails (four beginner, eleven intermediate, five advanced) particularly aimed at intermediate skiers; it also offers the region's best après-ski at Ohakune. It is usually possible to drive straight up the sealed, toll-free, 17km access road from Ohakune without chains, and park for nothing. Again, the ski-field operators will fit chains ($25) when needed, or you can rent from shops in Ohakune for a little less and fit them yourself. Several shuttle buses run up from Ohakune, charging around $25 return. The lesser-known **Tukino** Ski Field on the east of Mount Ruapehu is owned and operated by club members, who provide a back-to-basics option. The lack of crowds, cheaper passes and more stable weather conditions are countered by comparative inaccessibility and a lack of ski rental, though this can be arranged in outlets close to Tukino. Their season usually lasts from July to late September.

Practicalities

Mt Ruapehu (☎07/892 3738, Ⓦwww.mtruapehu.com) look after the two major ski areas and $80 a day will get you a pass for either; $360 for five days; or a Discover Ski pack ($80) and a Discover Snowboard pack ($85) including gear rental, 1-hour-50-minute lesson and a learners' area lift pass. On-site ski rental for one day costs $35, $45 for snowboard and boots. Several places in National Park and Ohakune also offer competitive rates and a wide selection of equipment. A day pass on Tukino is just $40, though you either need a 4WD to reach it or pick-ups can be arranged from Turangi and Waiouru as part of ski and accommodation packages, which also offer on-mountain accommodation options (☎0800/885 466, Ⓦwww.tukino.co.nz). Ski and snowboard lessons are available.

No field has public accommodation on site. Ski clubs maintain dozens of chalets at the foot of the main lifts in Whakapapa's Iwikau Village, but casual visitors (unless invited as a guest) have to stay 6km downhill at Whakapapa Village or 22km away at National Park (see p.343). Almost everyone skiing Turoa stays in Ohakune.

2–3hr; 400m descent) and returning to this point the next day, or branching right to **Oturere Hut** (5km; 1–2hr; 500m descent), descending steeply through fabulously contorted lava formations towards the Rangipo Desert. The initial section from **Otuere Hut to Waihohonu Hut** (8km; 2–3hr; 250m descent) crosses open, rolling country, then descends into the beech forests before a final climb over a ridge brings you to the hut, where you can drop your pack and press on for twenty minutes to the cool and clear Ohinepango Springs. The final day's walk, from **Waihohonu Hut to Whakapapa** (14km; 5–6hr; 200m ascent), cuts between Ngauruhoe and Ruapehu, passing the Old Waihohonu Hut (no accommodation) that was built for stagecoaches on the old road in 1901. The path then continues alongside Waihohonu Stream to the exposed **Tama Saddle** and, just over a kilometre beyond, a junction where side tracks lead to Lower Tama Lake (20min return) and Upper Tama Lake (1hr return), both water-filled explosion craters, where you can swim, if you don't need your water warmed. It is only around two hours' walk from the saddle back to Whakapapa, so you should have time to explore the **Taranaki Falls** before ambling back through tussock to the village.

If you'd prefer to steer clear of the popular Northern Circuit but still want to circle the mountain, try the aptly named **Round the Mountain Track** (71km; 4–5 days), most easily tackled from Whakapapa. Combined with the Northern Circuit it makes a mighty five- or six-day **circumnavigation** of all three mountains. For these two you need backcountry hut tickets or an annual hut pass; huts are Category 2 ($10), camping is $5. A Great Walks pass is necessary for Waihohonu hut, also part of the Northern Circuit Great Walk.

Ruapehu Crater Rim

The ascent to the **Ruapehu Crater Rim** takes around eight hours return from the Top o' the Bruce (15km), and a much more appealing five hours from the top of the **Waterfall Express chair lift** (9km), avoiding a long slog through a barren, rocky landscape. Even from the top of the chair lift this is a tough short hike but the destination makes it worthwhile. Volcanic instability renders this a high-risk area; it is dangerous to go beyond **The Dome** (no accommodation), at 2672m typically surrounded by snow. It perches on the rim of the crater, with great views across the upper reaches of a small glacier to the dramatic silhouettes of Cathedral Rocks, west to Mount Taranaki and down into the crater lake, currently refilling after the September 2007 eruption. The route is not well marked but from Christmas until the first snows arrive, the ascent can usually be made in ordinary walking boots without crampons. If you are in any doubt or would appreciate some company, join an organized trek (see p.339).

National Park

The evocative moniker attached to **National Park**, 15km west of Whakapapa Village, belies the overwhelming drabness of this tiny settlement – a dispiriting collection of A-frame chalets sprouting from a scrubby plain of pines, eucalyptuses and flax, with only the views of Ruapehu and Ngauruhoe to lend it grace. The place owes its continued existence to skiers and trampers bound for the adjacent Tongariro National Park, and paddlers heading for **Whanganui River trips**. With limited accommodation at Whakapapa Village, visitors are often forced to stay here, using shuttle buses (see box, p.339) to get to the tramps.

Practicalities

National Park comprises a grid of half a dozen streets wedged between SH4 and the parallel rail line. **Trains** stop at the deserted platform on Station Road, while **buses** pull up outside what used to be the National Park Store, now just a telephone box 100m north on Carroll Street. Bus tickets can be bought a further 100m up the road at *Howard's Lodge* (see below). There are no banks or cash machines in National Park so unless you have an EFTPOS card, bring cash.

Accommodation

Accommodation is in great demand during the **ski season** – when prices will be at least one price code higher than those given here – and can fill up from Christmas to the end of January, but otherwise it's plentiful. *Pukenui Lodge*, SH4 (Ⓣ0800/785 368, Ⓦwww.tongariro.cc; four-shares no linen $25, doubles/twins ❹, chalet ❼), offers a lounge and kitchen with great mountain views, a spa pool, plenty of assistance arranging activities, and a range of accommodation from dorms and doubles to a three-bedroom chalet (sleeps 7; 2 nights minimum). It also runs transport to the Tongariro Alpine Crossing and 42 Traverse (a 44-kilometre mountain-biking track. Similar standards apply at *Howard's Lodge*, two- thirds of the way down Carroll Street (Ⓣ07/892 2827, Ⓦwww.howardslodge.co.nz; dorms $22, rooms ❷, deluxe rooms ❹), which has two accommodation sections – one catering to backpackers, the other offering a plusher kitchen and lounge for better-heeled guests. There's also a spa bath, track transport, mountain bikes ($60 a day), and tramping and climbing gear. Alternatively try the excellent *National Park Backpackers*, Finlay Street (Ⓣ07/892 2870, Ⓦwww.npbp.co.nz; camping $14, dorms $22, rooms ❷, doubles ❷), with outdoor hot tub, good facilities and Internet access, and notable for being built around an excellent indoor climbing wall ($10, plus $3 for boots and harness). It also runs track transport (under the name Tongariro Volcanic Adventures), as well as local tours. Last but not least is *The Park*, on the corner of SH4 and Millar Street (Ⓣ07/892 2748, Ⓦwww.the-park.co.nz; dorms $30, rooms ❸), an 82-room hotel complex with a bar and restaurant, where the accommodation, for no very good reason, ignores the views of the mountains, preferring to look in on its own courtyard.

Eating and drinking

The lodges serve breakfasts for guests, while for main **meals** try steaks and bar-style meals at the rowdy *Schnapps Bar*, on SH4, next to *Pukenui Lodge*, or fish and chips and a jug of **beer** at the *National Park Hotel* on Carroll Street. *The Station* at the railway station is the high-class option, serving café-style dishes and lovely cakes before morphing into a formal restaurant in the evening, while *Eivin's*, at the corner of Carol Street and SH4, offers large portions of Kiwi favourites from 4pm (mains $18–30).

Ohakune and around

Ohakune, 35km south of National Park, welcomes you with a huge (artificial) carrot, celebrating its position at the heart of one of the nation's prime market-gardening regions. This is easily forgotten once you are in town among the chalet-style lodges and ski-rental shops geared to cope with the massive influx of winter-sports enthusiasts who descend from mid-June to early November for the **skiing** at Turoa (see box, p.342). During these months, the bars and restaurants swing into action, everyone makes their money for the year and

Trails around Ohakune

Some of the best **walks** include the Round the Mountain track (see p.341), while the pick of the shorter trails are: the **Mangawhero Forest Walk** (3km return; 1hr), a short and well-marked loop track from opposite the DOC field centre; the **Waitonga Falls Walk** (4km return; 1hr 10min) to a spectacular waterfall, starting 11km up the Mountain Road; and the hike to **Lake Surprise** (12km return; 5hr), an undulating route along the Round the Mountain track to a shallow lake which starts from the 15km mark on Ohakune Mountain Road and passes evidence of volcanic debris which swept down the mountain during the 1975 and 1995 eruptions. All the walking tracks, and any inside the bounds of the national park, are off-limits for **mountain biking**, but you can coast 17km down Ohakune Mountain Road, a 1000-metre descent, or head 12km east to the forest roads around Rangataua – consult Scenic Cycles, 6 Tay St (Nov–June; $45–50; ⓣ02/1607 294, ⓦwww.sceniccycles.co.nz) who have everything two-wheeled sewn up. They will even drive you to the top of the road, adding a spot of local history and botany, before letting you cruise the 17km down. A less arduous approach is to let **horses** take the strain on a tour at *Ruapehu Homestead*, 4km east on SH49 (ⓣ06/385 8799, ⓦwww.ruapehuhomestead.co.nz), starting at $40 for an hour in the saddle.

then most shut until next season. Consequently it is pretty quiet in summer, but once the snows have melted, the trails are open for tramping, mountain biking and horse trekking.

Practicalities

Ohakune is strung between two centres. The Auckland–Wellington rail line passes through **Ohakune Junction** where there's the **train station** and a cluster of hotels and restaurants mostly serving the skiing fraternity. **Central Ohakune**, the commercial heart of the town, lies 2km to the southwest, where **buses** on the Hamilton–Taumarunui–Wanganui run (daily except Sat) stop close to the **i-SITE visitor centre**, 54 Clyde St (daily 9am–5pm; ⓣ06/385 8427, ⓦwww.visitruapehu.com), which contains all the information you'll need and sells transport tickets. For specific tramping information, the mountain weather forecast and a detailed low-down on local flora and fauna, make for the DOC **field centre** at the foot of Ohakune Mountain Road (Mon–Fri 9am–3pm; ⓣ06/385 0010, ⓔohakunevc@doc.govt.nz); the foyer stays open 24hr and contains tramping information. **Internet access** is available in The Video Shop, on the corner of Goldfinch and Ayr streets.

Accommodation

Ohakune has stacks of **places to stay**, though several of them close outside the ski season and are packed once the snows arrive when prices get hiked up by around thirty percent more than those quoted here. Enough places are open in summer to satisfy almost all budgets, including two campsites. Those arriving by bus will find it more convenient to stay in the main town rather than Ohakune Junction. For a quieter and cheaper option, it can be worth resting up 10km down the road in **Raetihi**.

Alpine Motel Lodge 7 Miro St, Ohakune Central ⓣ06/385 8758, ⓦwww.alpinemotel.co.nz. Budget beds with basic four-share dorms and rooms, some studio units and fully s/c chalets, all with access to Sky TV, a spa and drying room. Dorms $20, units & chalets ❸

Mangawhero Campsite 1.5km up Ohakune Mountain Rd from the field centre. A basic DOC toilets-and-water site. $4

Matai Lodge 15–17 Clyde St, Ohakune Central ⓣ06/385 9169, ⓦwww.matailodge.co.nz. Excellent, YHA-affiliated budget accommodation in two buildings, offering various extras including tours and regular transport to and from the Tongariro Alpine Crossing, and anywhere else in the national park, including the Waihohonu Traverse – a good alternative when rough weather means the crossing is off-limits. It also runs a variety of guided and self-guided trips on the Whanganui River, all with knowledgeable leaders. Dorms $26, rooms ❷

Ohakune Top 10 Holiday Park 5 Moore St ⓣ06/385 8561, ⓦwww.ohakune.net.nz. Campsite on the edge of bush but still central. Camping $18, cabins ❷ kitchen cabins ❸, motel units ❺

Powderhorn Chateau 194 Mangawhero Terrace, at base of Ohakune Mountain Rd, Ohakune Junction ⓣ06/385 8888, ⓦwww.powderhorn.co.nz. Immense, log-cabin style edifice with tiny indoor swimming pool ($8 for non-guests), sunbeds and en-suite rooms, the best with balconies and forest views. ❻

Rimu Park Lodge 27 Rimu St, Ohakune Junction ⓣ06/385 9023, ⓦwww.rimupark.co.nz. One of the most comprehensive choices, this 1914 villa contains six-bunk dorms and doubles. The grounds are dotted with simple cabins, en-suite units with TV and fridge but no kitchen, fully s/c chalets sleeping between four and ten, and several railway carriages fitted out as s/c units with separate lounge and sleeping quarters. Dorms $20, rooms & cabins ❷, units & carriages ❸, chalets ❹

Eating, drinking and nightlife

During the ski season, Ohakune Junction is *the* happening place to spend your evenings, while in summer the focus switches to **central Ohakune**. The tastiest meals are served at the daytime *Utopia*, 47 Clyde St, the ideal spot for coffee and all-day brunches. Also good are the succulent gourmet kebabs at *Mountain Kebabs*, 29 Clyde St (winter only), and *O Bar and Restaurant*, 72 Clyde St, inside the *Ohakune Country Hotel*, a kind of upscale bar serving a range of dishes including pizza and steaks. Alternatively, try the *Mountain Rocks*, 53 Clyde St, an appealing café/bar offering good beer and value-for-money grub or the *Cyprus Tree*, Goldfinch Street, for a range of Kiwi restaurant classics and some fine wine.

At the **Ohakune Junction**, the regal *Powderhorn Chateau*, 194 Mangawhero Terrace, harbours two restaurants: the fine-dining *Matterhorn* (ⓣ06/385 8888) and the more modest *Powderkeg* brasserie/bar, known as "the Keg". In winter, the *Turoa Lodge* bar, 10 Thames St, is a popular spot to eat or drink and has live music and DJs at least once a week. Also worth a look is the *Projection Room*, 4 Thames St, open from 4pm daily and serving excellent café fare. For a good rowdy bar you could do worse than *Kings* on Miro Street, a massively renovated accommodation and nightspot with a good atmosphere in the evenings.

The Desert Road and Waiouru

South of Turangi, past the trout hatchery, SH1 sticks to the east of the Tongariro National Park running roughly parallel to the Tongariro River. This is the eerily scenic **Desert Road** (SH1), which climbs up over an exposed and barren plateau. This isn't a true desert (the rainfall is too high), but it'll do until something better comes along. Road cuttings reveal the cause as they slice through several metres of volcanic ash – a timeline of past eruptions – that's so free-draining vegetation struggles to take hold.

Initially you're deep in pine forest with side roads periodically ducking off to the east and the assortment of hydroelectric tunnels, intakes and tailraces of the Tongariro River. Some 9km south of Turangi, Kaimanawa Road runs 2km down to the river and beyond to a good free camping area by a stream (best found in daylight). After crossing the river, keep left on a tarmac road following signs to

▲ Desert Road and Mount Ruapehu

Waihaha Valley. The site is 500m back from the substation at the end of the road. A further 5km south along SH1, Tree Trunk Gorge Road leads again to the Tongariro River at a spot where it squeezes through a narrow fissure known as **Tree Trunk Gorge**.

Back on the highway you soon climb out of the forest for great views of the three volcanoes off to the west and the blasted territory ahead. It is a dramatic scene, somehow made even more elemental by the three lines of electricity pylons striding off across the bleak tussock towards Waiouru.

Waiouru and the Army Museum

The Desert Road and the roads flanking the western side of Ruapehu, Ngauruhoe and Tongariro meet at **WAIOURU**, an uninspiring row of service stations and tearooms perched 800m above sea level on the bleak tussock plain beside New Zealand's major **army base**. The serene view of the mountains from here can be fabulous but troop movements and target practice often disturb the peace.

The place to take cover is in the three concrete bunkers of the **QEII Army Memorial Museum** (daily 9am–4.30pm; $10), a showcase of national military heritage from the New Zealand Wars through the Anglo-Boer and two World Wars to New Zealand's involvement in Vietnam. In 2007 the museum hit the national headlines when thieves stole, probably to order, some of the rare medals on display, including Victoria Crosses awarded to various famous Kiwi war heroes. Little can prepare you for the impact of the *Roimata Pounamu* ("Tears on Greenstone") **wall of remembrance**, where a veil of tears symbolizes mourning and cleansing as it streams down a curving bank of heavily veined greenstone tiles while the name, rank and place of death of each of the 33,000 New Zealanders who have died in the various wars is recited. A twenty-minute audiovisual presentation sets the scene for the rest of the chronologically arranged exhibits, which are brought to life by oral histories, including some heart-rending ones that recount the bungled Gallipoli campaign of World War I. The emphasis is small-scale and personal: one particularly affecting case contains artefacts made by soldiers in the trenches – cribbage boards, chess sets and a cigarette holder that completely encased the cigarette so it could be smoked at night without risk of the enemy seeing the telltale glow. Plans are afoot for an extension to the building, to showcase military vehicles.

The *Rations* **café**, inside the Army Museum, shows a surprising lack of taste, labelling French toast "Somme Toast". You might prefer to head over the road to the *Angkor Wat Bakery and Coffee Shop*, 65 Ruataniwha, SH1, where they dish up cheap breakfasts and some of the best pies for miles around.

Taihape and around

Continuing south along SH1, you descend from the volcanic plateau into the **Rangitikei District**, with the Rangitikei River never far away though seldom seen as its waters have carved through the soft rock to leave off-white cliffs as the only evidence of the river's course. This is farming country, the pastoral nature of the region reflected in the character of its largest town **Taihape** (30km south of Waiouru), an agricultural service centre of only passing interest. Taihape promotes itself as "New Zealand's one and only Gumboot City", something it marks by a corrugated iron boot and, each year on Labour Day in late October with **Gumboot Day**, a tongue-in-cheek celebration of this archetypal Kiwi footwear that culminates in a gumboot-throwing competition.

Practicalities

Most people hurry on by but if you fancy a bite to eat the main contenders here are the cottagey but expensive *Brown Sugar Café*, Huia Street (Ⓣ06/388 1880), a small café serving light lunches daily as well as dinners on Friday and Sunday evenings (until 7pm; booking advisable); and the more modern *Café Exchange*, Huia Street (Ⓣ06/388 0599), which has a good deli selection. A newcomer to the scene is the *Soul Food Café*, on Huia Street, good for coffee, snacks or pizza. The best **places to stay** are the well-run and friendly *Stockman's Lodge Backpackers* (Ⓣ06/388 1584, Ⓦwww.thestockmanslodge.co.nz; dorms $20, double ❷), 1km out of town, and the welcoming hilltop homestay at *Korirata*, 25 Pukeko St (Ⓣ06/388 0315, Ⓔkorirata@xtra.co.nz; ❸), which does dinners on request ($25). There's a basic **information centre**, 90–92 Hautapu St (daily 9am–5pm; Ⓣ06/388 0604, Ⓦwww.rangittikei.com).

Activities

Driving through Taihape, there is little to suggest that the hilly country to the east hides one of New Zealand's most thrilling whitewater-rafting trips and the North Island's highest bungy jump.

The Grade V gorge section of the **Rangitikei River** is one of the toughest regularly used sections of **whitewater-rafting** river in the country. Ten major rapids are packed into the two- to three-hour run. Operators will take first-timers, but novices can make it safer for everyone if they choose to raft elsewhere first. Trips on the Rangitikei are run from Mangaweka (see below), or more directly from *River Valley Venture*, Pukoekahu (T 06/388 1444, W www.rivervalley.co.nz), a mostly backpacker-oriented complex sited right by the river, at the pull-out point for rafting trips, some 30km east of Taihape. Morning, and occasionally afternoon, trips ($145) are run throughout the year, though if water levels are low, rafts are replaced by one-person inflatable **kayaks** (also $145) launched in convoy with guides helping out tentative paddlers. *River Valley* also offer scenic rafting ($145; 5hr) down the quieter Grade II section immediately downstream of the lodge, and **horse trekking** ($85 for 2hr). Customers, many of them from the Kiwi Experience buses that call nightly, stay in sixteen-bunk ($22, no linen) or slightly pricier six-berth dorms ($27), pleasant double or twin rooms (2), camping ($11), or appealing en-suite cabins (5). Straightforward low-cost meals are served, including a celebrated roast, and there's a bar on site.

If you are an adventure seeker get a detailed map and follow the back roads from *River Valley Venture* to Gravity Canyon, or alternatively turn off SH1 at Uhutu, 7km south of Taihape, and follow the signs 15km east. Here you'll find an eighty-metre **bungy jump** ($125; booking advisable; T 0800/802 864, W www.gravitycanyon.co.nz) and the longest and fastest **Flying Fox** in New Zealand (160m high, 1km long; $99, combo deals available), both of which have a unique and rather pleasant water-powered lift to get you back to jumping-off height.

Mangaweka

A DC3 airplane beside SH1, 24km south of Taihape, is about the only indication that there might be a reason to stop in the dilapidated hamlet of **MANGAWEKA**, scattered across a plain high above the Rangitikei River. About 50m north of the plane is the Up the Creek River Centre, HQ of the Manaweka Adventure Company (T 0800/655 747, W www.mangaweka.co.nz), which offers a number of **whitewater-rafting** and **kayaking** trips: a Rangitekei River and Grand Canyons tour (3–4hr; $180), the Grade V Mokai Gorge trip ($145), or family-oriented rafting (1hr; $55). From here it's 60km to Bulls (see p.283).

Travel details

Trains

National Park to: Auckland (1 daily; 5hr 30min); Ohakune (1 daily; 30min); Palmerston North (1 daily; 3hr 30min); Waiouru (1 daily; 1hr); Wellington (1 daily; 5hr 30min).
Ohakune to: Auckland (1 daily; 6hr); Wellington (1 daily; 5hr).

Buses

Kawerau to: Rotorua (1 daily; 45min).
National Park to: Auckland (1 daily; 5hr 30min); Ohakune (1 daily; 30min).
Ohakune to: Auckland (1 daily; 6hr).
Rotorua to: Auckland (6 daily; 4hr); Gisborne (1 daily; 4hr 30min); Hamilton (5 daily; 1hr 45min); Kawerau (1 daily; 45min); Opotiki (1 daily; 2hr 10min); Palmerston North (2 daily; 5hr 30min); Taupo (4 daily; 1hr); Tauranga (3 daily; 1hr 30min); Waitomo (1 daily; 2hr–2hr 30min); Whakatane (1 daily; 1hr 30min).
Taihape to: Auckland (3 daily; 6hr 30min); Taupo (3 daily; 2hr); Turangi (4 daily; 1hr 10min); Wellington (4 daily; 4hr).

Taupo to: Auckland (4 daily; 4–5hr); Hamilton (4 daily; 2hr 30min); Hastings (3 daily; 2hr 30min); Napier (3 daily; 2hr); Palmerston North (4 daily; 3hr 30min); Rotorua (5 daily; 1hr); Taihape (3 daily; 2hr); Tauranga (4 daily; 2hr 30min); Turangi (4 daily; 45min); Wellington (4 daily; 6hr).
Tokoroa to: Hamilton (3 daily; 1hr 45min); Taupo (2 daily; 45min).
Turangi to: *The Chateau* (1 daily; 1hr).

Flights

Rotorua to: Auckland (5 daily; 45min); Christchurch (9 daily; 1hr 15min); Queenstown (3 daily; 3hr 15min); Wellington (6 daily; 1hr 10min).
Taupo to: Auckland (2 daily; 50min); Wellington (2 daily; 1hr).

5

The Coromandel, Bay of Plenty and the East Cape

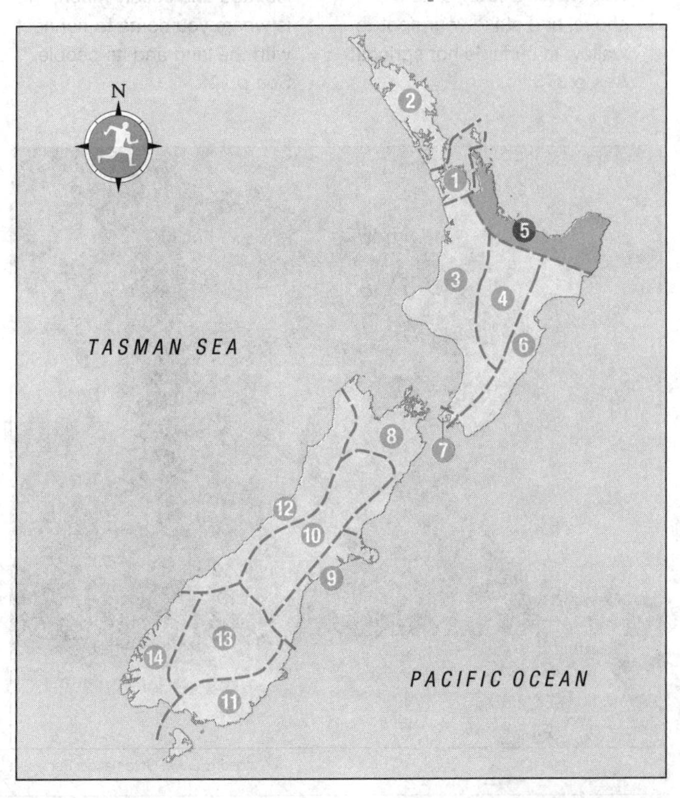

CHAPTER 5 Highlights

* **Coromandel Peninsula** Untouched beaches, rich bush and a slow pace lull you into peninsula time. See p.359

* **Driving Creek Railway** This modern narrow-gauge line climbs high through the bush for long coastal views. See p.367

* **Hot Water Beach** Grab a shovel and stake your spot to wallow in surfside hot springs. See p.376

* **White Island** Visit the otherworldly moonscape and sulphur deposits of New Zealand's most active volcano. See p.397

* **Dolphin swimming** There's always a high success rate in the abundant waters off Whakatane. See p.398

* **The East Cape** Rugged, isolated and solidly Maori, this is where you come to connect with the land and its people. See p.402

▲ Cathedral Cove, Coromandel Peninsula

5

The Coromandel, Bay of Plenty and the East Cape

The long coastal sweep east of Auckland is split into three distinct areas, the Coromandel, Bay of Plenty and the East Cape. The first two are among the most popular summer-holiday destinations on the North Island; the latter one of the least-visited parts of the country. Heading from Auckland by road, you'll cut across the **Hauraki Plains**, a wedge of dairy country at the foot of the Coromandel Peninsula with a few pleasant surprises for anyone willing to dawdle. In the spa town of **Te Aroha** you can luxuriate in a private soda bath, while at nearby **Paeroa** there are walks in the lush **Karangahake Gorge**, once the scene of intensive gold mining.

Directly across the Hauraki Gulf from Auckland, the long and jagged **Coromandel Peninsula** is blessed with some of the country's best sandy beaches and a gorgeous climate. It is an area of great coastal scenery, offering solitude, walks to pristine beaches and tramps in luxuriant mountainous rainforest. The two coasts are markedly different, the east supplying idyllic tourist beaches and short coastal walks and the west a more rugged and atmospheric coastline, plus easier access to the volcanic hills and ancient kauri trees of the **Coromandel Forest Park**. The countryside is best explored from bases such as **Coromandel**, set in rolling hills beside a harbour, and **Thames**, while **Whangamata** and **Whitianga**, the principal towns in the east, are blessed with long sandy beaches. The latter is handy for **Hot Water Beach**, where natural thermal springs bubble through the sand, and **Cathedral Cove Marine Reserve**, ideal for dolphin spotting and snorkelling.

From the open-cast gold-mining town of **Waihi** at the base of the Coromandel Peninsula, the **Bay of Plenty** sweeps south and east to Opotiki, punctuated by golden beaches and thundering surf, and traced along its length by the Pacific Coast Highway (SH2), which links Auckland with Gisborne. The bay earned its name in 1769 from **Captain Cook**, who was impressed by the number of Maori settlements living off the abundant resources and the generous supplies they gave him. This era of peace was shattered by the **New Zealand Wars** of the 1860s, when fierce fighting led to the establishment of garrisons at both Tauranga and Whakatane, while Opotiki gained notoriety because of the death of a European missionary – murdered by a Maori prophet.

The Bay of Plenty has the best climate on the North Island, making it a fertile fruit-growing region (particularly citrus and kiwi). The coast, though popular with Kiwi holidaymakers, has remained relatively unspoiled, offering great surf beaches and other offshore activities. The western part of the region is home to one of the country's fastest-growing urban areas, centred on **Tauranga** and the contiguous beach town of **Mount Maunganui**. The eastern Bay of Plenty revolves around **Whakatane**, primarily of interest for boat excursions to the fuming, volcanic **White Island**, opportunities to swim with dolphins, and as a base for wilderness rafting on the **Motu River**.

Contrasting with these two regions is the rugged and isolated **East Cape**, once a wealthy part of New Zealand but today run-down and sparsely populated. With a dramatic coastline, a rich and varied Maori history and great hospitality, the region provides a taste of a more old-fashioned way of life. At its easternmost point – the **East Cape** – is a lighthouse overlooking East Island, the first place in the country to see the sunrise. The region's communities are dotted along the coastline, against the backdrop of the **Waiapu Mountains**.

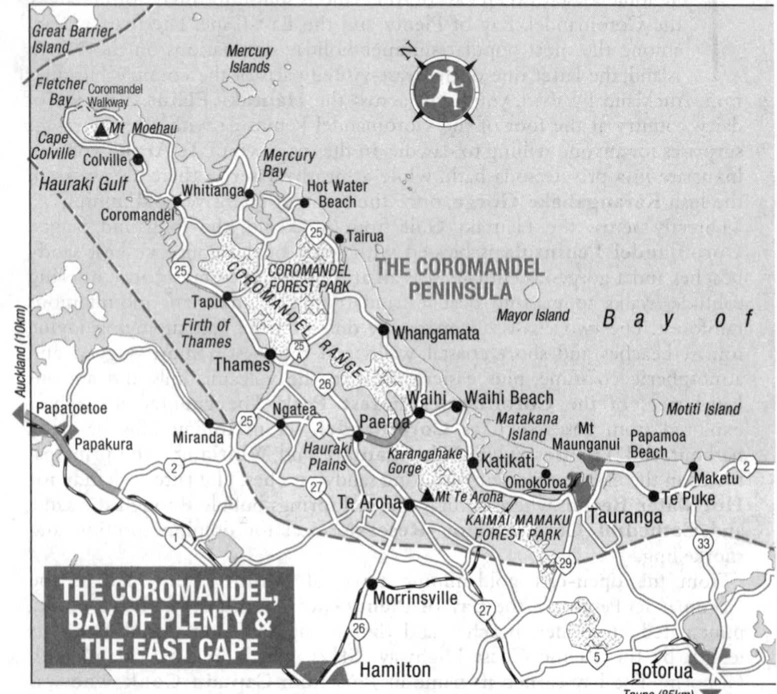

The Hauraki Plains

Approaching the Coromandel Peninsula from the west you'll pass through at least part of the fertile **Hauraki Plains**, a block of former swamp at the peninsula's southern end. The Firth of Thames, the final destination for a number of meandering rivers, borders it to the north. Attractions are limited and most people rush through on their way to the scenic splendours of the north or further east, although there is enough of interest here to warrant a short detour.

The hub of the plains is **Paeroa**, not much in itself, but handy for walks in scenic **Karangahake Gorge**, running from Paeroa to Waihi (see p.380). The real interest hereabouts is **Te Aroha**, an Edwardian town tucked away at the southern extremity of the plains, where you can hike Mount Te Aroha and soak your bones in natural hot soda springs.

Paeroa

Not worth a special detour, the small, dreary town of **PAEROA** briefly became a significant port during the early gold-mining days when boats from Auckland could go no further up the Ohinemuri River. To Kiwis, it is the birthplace of

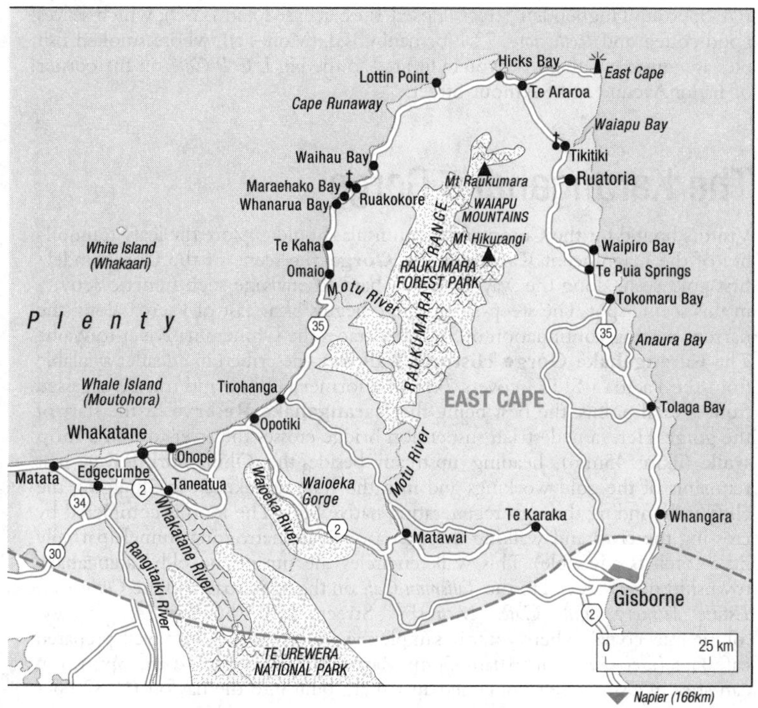

> **Getting around** the Plains by public transport isn't too difficult, with InterCity running daily services from Auckland through Paeroa and the Karangahake Gorge to Waihi and Tauranga, and Supa Travel (Ⓣ07/571 0583, Ⓦwww.supatravelexpress.co.nz) operating between Auckland and Paeroa. Te Aroha is a bit more out on a limb, but Turley-Murphy (Ⓣ07/884 8208) run a service once daily (except public holidays) between Hamilton and Thames via Te Aroha and Paeroa.

Lemon and Paeroa (L & P), a homegrown, though not home-owned, soft-drink. A giant brown L & P bottle stands at the junction of SH2 and SH26, greeting those arriving from the south, and Paeroa gets as much mileage as it can from the drink's catchphrase "World Famous in New Zealand".

On Paeroa's main thoroughfare, Belmont Road, the **Paeroa and District Museum**, at no. 37 (Mon–Fri 10.30am–3pm; $2), neatly covers the town's history, shipping and gold mining in the Karangahake Gorge.

Practicalities

Belmont Road (SH2) runs south through Paeroa's centre before morphing into Normanby Road, but the guts of the town are concentrated on a small area wedged between the Domain and the junction with SH26. Supa Travel **buses** stop at the *L & P Café* on the corner of Taylor Avenue and Seymour Street. InterCity and Turley-Murphy buses stop at the shelter outside the **i-SITE visitor centre**, 1 Belmont Rd (Mon–Fri 9am–4.30pm, Sat & Sun 10am–2pm; Ⓣ07/862 8636).

Café culture has come to Paeroa in the form of the *Lazy Fish*, 56 Belmont Rd, opposite Hughenden Street (closed Tues; licensed and BYO), which serves good coffee, and *Reflexions*, 72 Normanby Rd, (Mon–Fri), whose smoked fish pies are yummy. Otherwise, you're limited to the big *L & P Café*, on the corner of Taylor Avenue and Seymour Street.

The Karangahake Gorge

Visitors bound for the Coromandel Peninsula should explore the leafy tranquillity of the magnificent **Karangahake Gorge**, the scene of the Coromandel's first gold rush, along the way. Today it's hard to envisage such frenetic activity in this scenic spot. The steep-sided gorge begins 8km east of Paeroa along the narrow, snaking continuation of SH2 as it traces the Ohinemuri River to Waihi. The **Karangahake Gorge Historic Walkway** (described in a leaflet available from the Paeroa i-SITE) covers 7km of a former rail line and can be accessed from several points, the best being the **Karangahake Reserve**, at the start of the gorge. Here, a pedestrian suspension bridge crosses the river to join a **loop walk** (3km; 45min), heading upstream beside the Ohinemuri River, past remnants of the gold workings and into the Karangahake Gorge, hugging the cliffs and winding through regenerating native bush. The loop is completed by crossing the river and walking through a one-kilometre-long tunnel (partially lit; a torch is advisable). This walk encircles the site of the old Karangahake township, now reduced to the *Talisman Café* on the main road and the *Ohinemuri Estate Winery and Café*, Moresby Street (Ⓣ07/862 8874, Ⓦwww.ohinemuri.co.nz), where you can sample the wines and tuck into well-prepared café fare (Dec–Feb daily 10am–5pm; March–Nov Wed–Sun 10am–5pm). You can **stay** in a smart, self-contained apartment built into the hayloft (❹, $20 per extra person), and on fine Sunday afternoons in summer there's music.

At the eastern end of the gorge, the tiny village of **WAIKINO** is little more than a train station, the western terminus for the Goldfields Railway (see p.381), running three trains daily to Waihi and back. Inside are displays on local history and walks in the area, as well as the daytime *Waikino Station Café*, with outdoor seating on the platform.

Te Aroha

On the fringes of the Hauraki Plains, 21km south of Paeroa on SH26, the town of **TE AROHA** is famed for New Zealand's only intact **Edwardian spa**. Those prepared to make the journey for a peaceful day-trip are rewarded with a neat little town hunkered beneath the imposing bush-clad slopes of the **Kaimai-Mamaku Forest Park**. The 954-metre **Mount Te Aroha** rears up immediately behind the town centre, providing a reasonably challenging goal for hikers, while gentler pleasures await in the hot **soda baths and spas**, the latter fed by the **Mokena Geyser**.

The town itself was founded in 1880 at the furthest navigable extent of the Waihou River. A year later, rich deposits of gold were discovered on Mount Te Aroha, sparking a full-scale **gold rush**, the gold-bearing quartz producing handsome yields until 1921. Within a few months of settlement, the new townsfolk set out the attractive Hot Springs Domain around a cluster of soda springs which, by the 1890s, had become New Zealand's most popular mineral spa complex. Enclosures were erected for privacy, most rebuilt in grand style during the Edwardian years. The fine suite of original buildings have been restored and integrated with more modern pools fed by the hot soda springs and nearby geyser. Aucklanders frequently make the trip to soak in the tubs, often compared with those of Vichy or Baden.

The Town

Te Aroha's centrepiece is the **Hot Springs Domain** at the southern end of town on Whitaker Street, a 44-acre **thermal reserve** of gardens and rose beds. The **Spa Baths** complex is well signposted (daily 10am–10pm; 30min; $15,

Walks in and around Te Aroha

The most rewarding of Te Aroha's **walks** is the ascent of **Mount Te Aroha**, which tops out on the crest of the Kaimai Range to give sweeping views to the Bay of Plenty and, on exceptionally clear days, across to mounts Ruapehu and Taranaki. The **Te Aroha Mountain Track** (8km return; 4hr; 950m ascent) starts from just behind the Mokena Geyser in the Domain and climbs steeply through native bush, zigzagging up a well-defined path to a viewing platform at **Whakapipi** (or Bald Spur), before dipping to a small saddle. From here, the final climb (which can be muddy and slippery after rain) becomes increasingly arduous, and you'll need to use your hands to pull yourself up in places. To return, follow the **Tui Mine Track**, dropping through a stark, heavily mined landscape to link with the Tui Road back to town in one direction and the **Tui–Domain Track**, a pleasant bushwalk past a waterfall back to the Domain, in the other. If the thought of an uphill slog right to the top is too much, the section as far as the **Whakapipi Lookout** (2km; 50min) gives good views over the town and its surroundings. These walks and others are listed in the *Te Aroha and Waiorongomai Walks* leaflet from the Te Aroha i-SITE.

$25 for two; book ahead at weekends ⓣ07/884 8717, ⓦwww.tearohapools.co.nz), comprising eight private, enclosed pools, each with hydrotherapeutic water jets. Choose a stainless-steel one if you fancy adding aromatherapy oils; otherwise the wooden tubs are bigger. A half-hour soak is plenty, said to extract polluting heavy metals from your system; after a bath don't shower as the mineral water leaves the skin incredibly soft. If you'd prefer more space, book the private three-metre-long **No. 2 Bathhouse** (Mon–Fri 10am–6pm, Sat & Sun 10am–7pm; same prices as Spa Baths), opened in 1900 as one of the original communal bathhouses. This is contained in the nearby outdoor **Leisure Pool** complex ($5 entry if you want to swim too). The bathhouse is usually heated to 40°C and can be booked by one person or a couple, although it takes up to sixteen people.

Just uphill from the baths is the erratic **Mokena Geyser**, which goes off roughly every forty minutes. It can spurt to an impressive height on good days, but often disappoints. From here, a **trail** (see p.357) leads to the top of **Mount Te Aroha** which, legend has it, was named by a young Arawa chief, Kahumatamomoe, who climbed it after losing his way in the region's vast swamp while making for Maketu in the Bay of Plenty. Delighted to see the familiar shoreline of his homeland, he called the mountain Te Aroha, "love", in honour of his father and kinsmen. If a soak in the spa has left you too blissfully lethargic to contemplate the climb up Mount Te Aroha, Mountain High River Wide Tours will run you up there for $45 (min 3 people; ⓣ027/445 2090).

An old sanatorium, just below the spa baths and in front of the croquet lawn, houses the town **museum** (daily: Dec–March 11am–4pm; April–Nov 1–4pm; donation), three exhibit-packed rooms and two finely decorated Royal Doulton Victorian lavatories. Highlights are a chemical analysis of the local soda water, and memorabilia from a silent movie called *Tilly of Te Aroha*, something of a racy picture.

By the Boundary Street exit from the Domain you'll find the 1926 **St Mark's Anglican Church**, on the corner of Church and Kenrick streets, insignificant but for the incongruous 1712 organ, said to be the oldest in the southern hemisphere.

Practicalities

The town's main thoroughfare is Whitaker Street and everything of interest – banks, post office, library – is either along it or close by. The **i-SITE** (Mon–Fri 9.30am–5pm, Sat & Sun 9.30am–4pm; ⓣ07/884 8052, ⓦwww.tearohanz.co.nz) is at 102 Whitaker St by the entrance to the Domain, and has DOC information for the area.

For a small place, Te Aroha has a reasonable choice of **accommodation**. The small *YHA* on Miro Street, off Brick Street (ⓣ07/884 8739, ⓦwww.stayyha.com; dorms $18, rooms ❶), is one of the oldest and simplest in New Zealand, about ten minutes' walk from the visitor centre in a cosy wooden cottage on the lower slopes of Mount Te Aroha, with lovely views and free bike use. Campers should head 4km out on the road to Hamilton (SH26) to the *Te Aroha Holiday Park*, 217 Stanley Rd South (ⓣ07/884 9567, ⓦwww.tearoha-info.co.nz/holidaypark; tent sites $9, dorms $15, on-site vans and cabins ❶, flats and cottages ❶–❸), set among oak trees.

Eating in Te Aroha is limited to *Pearls Café Bar*, 174 Whitaker St, a former bank serving breakfast, lunch and dinner (closed Tues eve); café/bar *Ironique*, 159 Whitaker St for snacks and evening meals; *Pulse*, 140 Whitaker St, which offers fine coffee and cake (until 5pm); *The Crossing*, 183 Whitaker St, with good-value breakfasts and pizza (Tues–Sun until 8pm); while the unfortunately titled

Berlusconi on Whitaker (149), serves fine wine and a weird array of Spanish-style tapas with a Tuscan/Asian leaning, including tiger prawns with chilli and black olives (Wed–Sun).

The Coromandel Peninsula

The Hauraki Gulf is separated from the Pacific Ocean by the long, broad thumb of the **Coromandel Peninsula**, a mountainous, bush-cloaked interior fringed with beautiful surf and swimming beaches, basking in a balmy climate. Although genuine sights are few, there's no denying the allure of a relaxing few days spent scouting aound.

In the **west**, cliffs and steep hills drop sharply to the sea, leaving only a narrow coastal strip shaded by **pohutukawa** trees that erupt in a blaze of red from mid-November to January. The beaches are sheltered, safe and ripe for exploration, but most are only good for **swimming** when high tide obscures the mudflats. The majority of tourists prefer the **east coast**, a land of sweeping white-sand beaches pounded by impressive but often perilous **surf**. This is where Kiwis flock for long weekends and holidays, and the more fashionable beaches are lined with million-dollar holiday homes.

Low property prices in declining former gold towns, combined with the wonderful juxtaposition of bush, hills and beaches, exerted a powerful attraction on hippies, **artists** and New Agers in the 1960s and 70s. Most eked out a living from organic market gardens, or holistic healing centres and retreats, while painters, potters and **craftspeople**, some very good, hawked their work (the free *Coromandel Craft Trail* leaflet details rural craft outlets all over the peninsula). These days the peninsula is a more commercial animal, and the old spirit is fading fast. Increasingly Aucklanders are finding ways to live here permanently or commute, and are converting one-time *baches* into expensive designer properties, raising both the area's profile and the cost of living.

The **Coromandel Range** – sculpted millions of years ago by volcanic activity, its contorted skyline clothed in dense rainforest – runs through the interior and is interpreted by local Maori as a canoe, with **Mount Moehau** (the peninsula's northern tip) as its prow, and Mount Te Aroha in the south as its sternpost. The summit area of Mount Moehau is sacred, Maori-owned land, the legendary burial place of Tama Te Kapua, the commander of one of the Great Migration canoes, *Te Arawa*.

At the base of the peninsula, the former gold town of **Thames** exhibits its heritage and makes a good base for exploring the forested **Kauaeranga Valley**'s walking tracks. Further north, the town of **Coromandel** offers the opportunity to ride the narrow-gauge **Driving Creek Railway** and is close to the trans-peninsular 309 Road, where the **Waiau Waterworks** and an impressive stand of **kauri** are the main attractions. For really remote country, head to **Colville** and the peninsula's northern tip. The sealed Highway 25 continues east to **Mercury Bay**, centred on more populous **Whitianga**, near which you can dig a hole to wallow in the surfside hot springs that lure hundreds to **Hot Water Beach**, or snorkel in a gorgeous bay at **Cathedral**

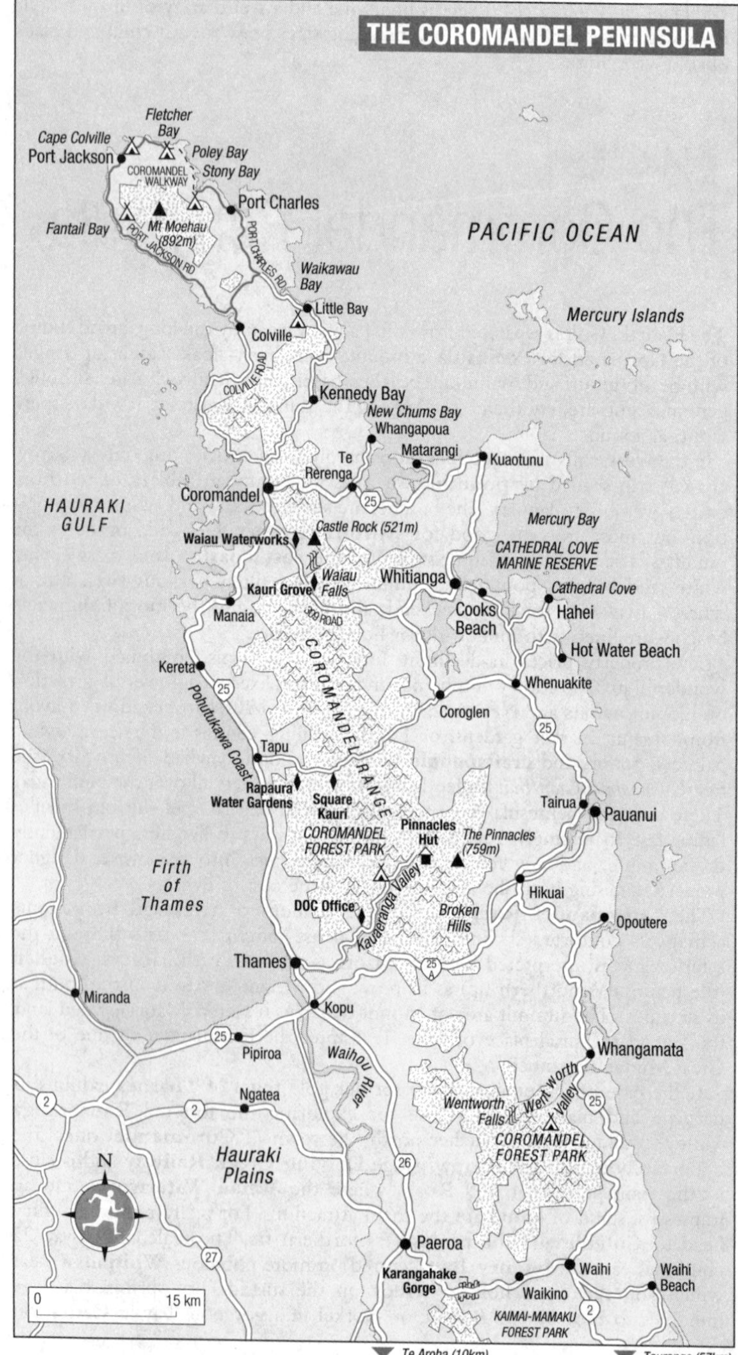
THE COROMANDEL PENINSULA
Fletcher Bay
Cape Colville
Port Jackson
Poley Bay
COROMANDEL WALKWAY
Stony Bay
Port Charles
Fantail Bay
Mt Moehau (892m)
PORT JACKSON RD
PORT CHARLES RD
PACIFIC OCEAN
Waikawau Bay
Little Bay
Mercury Islands
Colville
COLVILLE ROAD
Kennedy Bay
New Chums Bay
Whangapoua
Matarangi
Kuaotunu
Te Rerenga
Coromandel
HAURAKI GULF
Mercury Bay
Castle Rock (521m)
Waiau Waterworks
CATHEDRAL COVE MARINE RESERVE
Waiau Falls
Whitianga
Kauri Grove
Cathedral Cove
Cooks Beach
Hahei
Manaia
309 ROAD
Hot Water Beach
COROMANDEL RANGE
Kereta
Whenuakite
Pohutukawa Coast
Coroglen
Tapu
Rapaura Water Gardens
Square Kauri
Tairua
Pauanui
Pinnacles Hut
COROMANDEL FOREST PARK
The Pinnacles (759m)
Firth of Thames
Hikuai
Kauaeranga Valley
DOC Office
Broken Hills
Opoutere
Thames
Miranda
Kopu
Pipiroa
Waihou River
Whangamata
Ngatea
Wentworth Falls
Went worth Valley
COROMANDEL FOREST PARK
Hauraki Plains
N
Paeroa
Karangahake Gorge
Waihi
Waihi Beach
Waikino
KAIMAI-MAMAKU FOREST PARK
0
15 km
Te Aroha (10km)
Tauranga (57km)

Cove Marine Reserve. Yet more beaches string the coast further south, some of the best (and busiest) around **Whangamata** and **Waihi Beach**, the coastal acolyte of **Waihi**.

Peninsula practicalities

As one of the North Island's principal holiday spots, the Coromandel Peninsula becomes the scene of frenetic activity from **Christmas** until the end of January, when finding accommodation can become impossible – book well ahead. Numbers are more manageable for the rest of the summer, while in **winter** much of the peninsula is deserted, though the **climate** remains mild.

Negotiating the peninsula is easiest by **car**: main roads are mostly sealed, and though many of the more remote stretches are gravel, very few pose any real danger if you take it steadily – even the infamous roads beyond Colville to the northern tip are a lot better than of old. **Bus** travel is more problematic, timetables dictating that you cover the peninsula in a clockwise direction, with InterCity providing a regular loop service from Thames north to Coromandel, across to Whitianga and back south and across to Thames: a **Top Half** pass costs $145 and incorporates the fare from Auckland to Rotorua. Go Kiwi (Ⓣ0800/446 549, Ⓦwww.go-kiwi.co.nz) offers a competitive door-to-door service between Auckland and numerous Coromandel Peninsula stops, running to Auckland in the morning and back in the afternoon.

You can **fly** to the peninsula with Great Barrier Airlines (Ⓣ0800/900 600, Ⓦwww.greatbarrierairlines.co.nz; $99 one way), from Auckland to Whitianga via Great Barrier Island two to three times a week. **Sailing** is on the 360Discovery ferry ($49 one way; 2hr; Ⓣ09/424 5510, Ⓦwww.360discovery.co.nz), which leaves pier 4 in Auckland (Tues, Thurs, Fri & Sun at 9am, Fri 6pm) and docks in Coromandel Harbour. They also time trips to coincide with their full-day Coromandel Discovery Tours ($129; Thurs, Fri, Sat & Sun).

▲ Pohutukawa trees, Coromandel Peninsula

Thames and around

The small and rather dull former gold town of **THAMES** is packed into a coastal strip between the Firth of Thames and the Coromandel Range. As the peninsula's main service town, it has functional value, with a range of accommodation, a few places to eat, and transport connections for both the immediate surroundings and the rest of the peninsula.

The first big discovery of gold-bearing quartz was made in a Thames creek-bed in 1867, but mining activity tailed off during the 1880s and had mostly finished by 1913. Nonetheless, the legacy of **mining** forms the basis of the town's attractions, and you can easily spend half a day visiting them. The

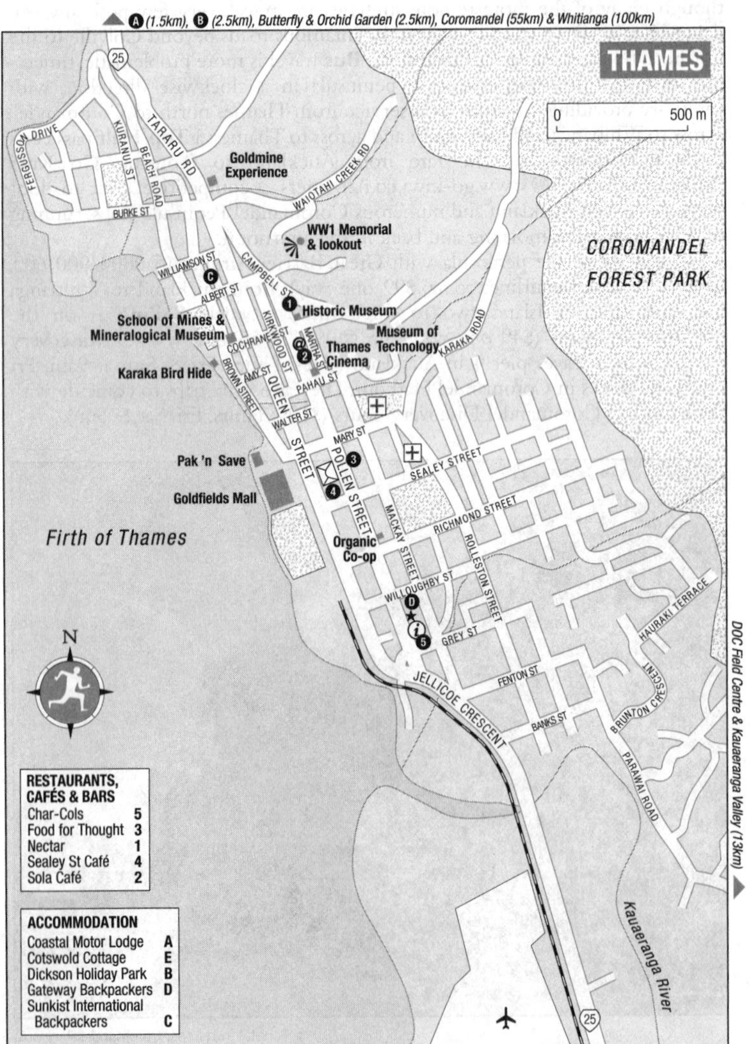

Kauaeranga Valley, a popular centre for hikers visiting the Coromandel Forest Park, is within easy reach, and is often busy at weekends.

Arrival, information and transport

Buses drop off outside the **i-SITE visitor centre**, 206 Pollen St (Mon–Fri 8.30am–5pm, Sat & Sun 9am–4pm; ⓣ07/868 7284, ⓦwww.thamesinfo.co.nz), which has **Internet** access, while Pollen Street, the main shopping thoroughfare, is home to banks and the post office. Nowhere is far from here but you can get **taxis** from Thames Gold Cabs (ⓣ07/868 6037), or rent **touring bikes** from Paki Paki Bike Shop, in the Goldfields Mall off Mary Street ($25 a day; ⓣ07/867 9026, ⓦwww.pakipakibikeshop.co.nz) or **mountain bikes** from Price & Richards, 430 Pollen St ($25 a day; ⓣ07/868 6157). Michael Saunders Motors (ⓣ07/868 8398), John Davy Rentals (ⓣ07/868 6868) and *Sunkist International Backpackers* (see below) all rent budget cars and allow them onto the peninsula's roughest roads.

Accommodation

Accommodation in Thames is dominated by B&Bs and backpackers, scattered away from the town centre, but the standard is generally good.

Coastal Motor Lodge 608 Tararu Rd (SH25), 2.5km north of town ⓣ07/868 6843, ⓦwww.staycoastal.co.nz. Well-equipped "cottage" units and modern, spacious A-frame chalets (all s/c and designed for two), overlooking the Firth. The best views are from the pricier chalets. Cottages ❺, chalets ❻

Cotswold Cottage 46 Maramarahi Rd, 3km south of town off SH25 ⓣ07/868 6306, ⓦwww.cotswoldcottage.co.nz. Grand old villa set in mature grounds on the outskirts of Thames with lovely views of the adjacent river and peninsula hills, offering B&B. ❺

Dickson Holiday Park Victoria St, off SH25 ⓣ07/868 7308, ⓦwww.dicksonpark.co.nz. Large, well-run campsite in a pretty valley 3.5km north of the centre. The excellent facilities include a pool, and there's bus pick-up from Thames. Dorms $20, cabins & on-site caravans ❷, flats ❸, units ❹

Gateway Backpackers 209 Mackay St ⓣ07/868 6339, ⓦwww.gatewaybackpackers.co.nz. Intimate hostel just a few paces from the visitor centre and bus stop. Has free bikes, a large video collection, luggage storage and transfer to Kauaeranga Valley. Dorms $23, rooms ❷

Sunkist International Backpackers 506 Brown St ⓣ07/868 8808, ⓦwww.sunkistbackpackers.com. An atmospheric hostel in a historic building, with hammocks set up in the appealing garden and a large balcony. Services include baggage and bike storage, free bikes, daily shuttles to the Pinnacles and Kauaeranga Valley and on-site car rental, plus free pick-ups from the bus station. Tent sites $14, dorms $21, rooms ❶

The Town

The best introduction to Thames's gold-mining past is at the **Goldmine Experience**, Tararu Road (10am–4pm: summer daily; winter Sat, Sun & public holidays; $10; ⓣ07/868 8514, ⓦwww.goldmine-experience.co.nz), where you join an atmospheric and informative 45-minute tour underground along a narrow horizontal shaft originally cut by hand by Cornish miners, and then take a look at the stamper battery, which is briefly kicked into deafening gear. The **Historic Museum** (daily 1–4pm), **Technological Museum** (10am–4pm, key in the glass shop attached) and the **School of Mines & Mineralogical Museum** (Wed–Sun, 11am–3pm) are also worth a look ($5 each) in Bella, Cochrane and Brown streets, respectively, no more than 100m from each other.

Near the junction of Brown and Amy streets, a one-minute boardwalk across the mangroves leads to the **Karaka Bird Hide**: a couple of hours either side of high tide is the best time to spot migratory birds such as knots, godwits, shags and terns, especially between October and February. Winged creatures of the tropical variety can be seen at the magical **Butterfly and Orchid Garden**, 3.5km north of Thames, at the *Dickson Holiday Park*, Victoria Street, just off SH25 (daily: Nov–March 10am–4pm; April–Oct 10am–3pm; $9.50; Ⓦwww.butterfly.co.nz), where you can happily spend half an hour inside a hothouse delighting in the acrobatics of hundreds of butterflies.

Kauaeranga Valley

The steep-sided **Kauaeranga Valley**, east of town, stretches towards the spine of the Coromandel Peninsula, a jagged landscape of bluffs and gorges topped by **the Pinnacles** (759m), with stupendous views to both coasts across native forest studded with rata, rimu and kauri. All this is reached along a scenic and mostly sealed road snaking beside the river, providing access to some of the

Kauaeranga walks

The Kauaeranga Valley is blessed with a variety of easily accessible tramps ranging from a thirty-minute stroll to a satisfying two-day circuit with a night spent at the large and relatively plush **Pinnacles Hut** (80 bunks; $15; advance booking essential through Kauaeranga DOC Ⓣ07/867 9080). There are also a couple of remote and very basic DOC **campsites**: one near the Pinnacles Hut and another at Moss Creek (both $9). The *Kauaeranga Kauri Trail* DOC leaflet covers the basics, though you might prefer the detail provided by the 1:50,000 Thames Topomap ($14.95). Both are available from the refurbished DOC office at the road-end, where you can also **store luggage** or tents for $2 per person. The ease of access to these tracks can lead trampers not to take them as seriously as other tramps but in bad weather the conditions can be treacherous, so go properly prepared (see p.63).

Nature Walk to Hoffman's Pool (1.5km loop; 30min). A short, easy loop beginning 1km beyond the DOC office. Information panels make it a classic introduction to the valley's native forest. The track leads to a tranquil sand-edged pool in a river bend, an ideal picnic and swimming spot (toilets and changing sheds nearby). You return the same way or in a loop along the road.

Pinnacles Moss Creek Circuit (14km loop; 2 days). This upgraded track (with new ladders and steps) is a great way to get a taste of the region, following the Kauaeranga Kauri Trail and overnighting in the Pinnacles Hut (see above) about a third of the way along. It is really just a day and a half, starting at the road-end and spending the first 2–3hr following Webb Creek up to Pinnacles Hut and the well-restored Dancing Camp kauri dam. From the hut a steep 50-minute climb reaches the Pinnacles. The second day is longer (7–8hr) and can be muddy and difficult, involving a few unbridged stream crossings (either being bridged at the time of writing or due to be). It passes the remnants of a couple of kauri dams, an old logging camp and some fine viewpoints, with Moss Creek campsite along the way. The more popular option however, is a there-and-back trip to the Pinnacles, possible in 7hr.

Webb Creek–Billygoat Circuit (9km loop; 4–5hr). The most interesting walk if you like your history, with information panels telling the story of the loggers. From the road-end the track crosses the river on a swingbridge and follows Webb Creek along an old packhorse route (steep in places) used by kauri bushmen in the 1920s. Linking with the Billygoat Track leads to a saddle with views down the valley to the Hauraki Plains.

Wainora Track (6km return; 2–3hr). Moderate, well-formed track to a couple of large kauri – pretty much the only accessible ones left standing hereabouts – that starts from the Wainora campsite, 6km beyond the DOC office, heading northeast.

finest walks in the Coromandel Range, and the only backcountry DOC hut on the peninsula. *Sunkist International Backpackers* and *Gateway Backpackers* (see p.363) both run shuttle buses along the road ($25 return; min 2 people), or you can **drive** by heading out of the southern end of Thames, along Parawai Road, which becomes Kauaeranga Road.

Thirteen kilometres along you reach the recently refurbished **DOC office** (daily 8am–4pm; ☎07/867 9080), where you can stock up on maps, buy hut tickets and examine displays on early kauri logging in the valley. From here a loop track (500m; 10min) leads to a scale model of a kauri driving dam, a type once used extensively in this forest. Along the eight unsealed kilometres beyond the DOC office to the road-end, an assortment of tracks (see box, p.364) lead off into the bush containing scattered "pole stands" of young kauri that have grown since the area was logged a century ago: only a handful in each stand will reach maturity. Most of the hikes head into the bush near one of the half-dozen simple roadside **campsites** ($9; toilets and stream water) dotting the length of the stretch.

To really get off the beaten track consider **canyoning** down the Sleeping God canyon with Canyonz (see p.125), whose trips begin in Auckland but pick up in Thames.

Eating and entertainment

The traditional, sometimes larrikin **bars** of Thames are not worth the hassle, so head instead either for *Nectar* or the Multiplex **cinema** at 708 Pollen St. For **stocking up**, consider the small and friendly Organic Co-op, 736 Pollen St (Mon–Fri 9am–5pm, Sat 9am–noon), and the Saturday morning **market** (9am–noon; food, clothing and more) held at the northern end of Pollen Street.

Char-Cols 206 Pollen St. Right next to the bus stop and popular with backpackers, all items here are home-made. Try the full-flavoured mussel fritters. Licensed; closes at 5pm.

Food for Thought 574 Pollen St. Central daytime café, specializing in pastries, good home-made pies, cakes and vegetarian dishes – and great coffee. Closed Sun.

Nectar 748 Pollen St. Cool, intimate front-room bar with an eclectic mix of entertainment including live bands, big-city DJs, poetry readings and a Thurs night jam session. Listings are usually posted on the door. Open from 5pm Tues–Sun.

Sealey Street Café 109 Sealey St, ☎07/868 8641. High-quality food, including Coromandel sirloin, served in a stylish, turn-of-the-century wooden villa, fully licensed and BYO. Mains around $30.

Sola Café 720b Pollen St. Popular modern vegetarian café and restaurant for excellent coffee and snacks during the day with a short vegan menu (plus some wheat-free).

North to Coromandel

From Thames, SH25 snakes 58km north to Coromandel town, tracing the grey rocky shoreline of the "**Pohutukawa Coast**" past a series of tiny, sandy bays, most with little more than a few houses and maybe a campsite. Hills and sand-coloured cliffs rise dramatically from the roadside for the first 19km to **Tapu**, where the **Tapu–Coroglen Road** peels off to the Coromandel's east coast. It is a wonderfully scenic 28km run of narrow, unsealed yet manageable driving, leaving behind the marginal farmland on the coast and climbing over the peninsula's mountainous spine. Even if you aren't tackling the traverse, it is worth making a detour 6.5km along the road (and just beyond the end of the asphalt), to **Rapaura Water Gardens** (daily 9am–5pm, winter hours may vary;

$12; ⓣ07/868 4821, ⓦwww.rapaurawatergardens.com), a cleverly landscaped "wilderness" of bush and blooms, punctuated by lily ponds and a trickling stream. Against a backdrop of bush and threaded by paths, the gardens tap into the Coromandel ethos with philosophical messages urging you to stop and think. There are a few picnic areas and an excellent **café**. You can enjoy the gardens at night in luxury accommodation: an enchanting cottage for two (❻) or a serene two-bedroom house lined with rimu (❽).

The road continues for 3km on to the (easily missed) "**square kauri**" signpost near the road's summit, opposite a rough lay-by and just before a small bridge. Steep steps through bush (175m; 10min) lead to this giant of a tree (1200 years old, just over 41m high and 9m wide), whose unusual, angular shape saved it from loggers. From here it's another rough and twisty 19km across the peninsula to Coroglen, linking with the main road between Whitianga and Whangamata, or 9.5km back to Tapu and the continuation of SH25 north.

Back on **SH25**, the road lurches inland soon after Kereta (about 12km north of Tapu), snaking over hills to the roadside **Manaia-Kereta Lookout** (206m), which has great views of the northern peninsula, the majestic Moehau Range and Coromandel Harbour. Beyond, Great Barrier Island, a giant block of rock with vertical cliffs, may be visible on a clear day. Ducking and diving along the rocky shoreline and the blue-green vistas of the Firth of Thames, SH25 continues for 23km before reaching Coromandel.

Coromandel

The northernmost town of any substance is charming little **COROMANDEL**, 58km north of Thames, huddling beneath high, craggy hills at the head of Coromandel Harbour. It's the jumping-off point for the **Coromandel Walkway** (see p.370), 57km away amid the jagged landscape of the northern peninsula, but it's also worth taking time to ride the **scenic railway** into the hills.

The town and peninsula took their name from an 1820 visit by the British Admiralty supply ship *Coromandel*, which called into the harbour to obtain kauri spars and masts. A more mercenary European invasion was precipitated by the 1852 discovery of **gold**, near Driving Creek, in the northern part of town. The subsequent boom left a string of fine wooden buildings along the main street. There are a couple of supermarkets and petrol stations, a BNZ bank, a cluster of cafés and a broad range of accommodation.

Moving on, you've a choice of striking **east to Whitianga**, via the continuation of SH25 (see p.371) past the deserted beaches of Whangapoua and Kuaotunu, or taking the more rugged 309 Road (see p.371).

Arrival, information and transport

The combined **i-SITE visitor centre** and **DOC office**, 355 Kapanga Rd (Nov–Easter daily 9am–5pm, Easter–Oct Mon–Sat 9am–5pm, Sun 10am–2pm; ⓣ07/866 8598, ⓦwww.coromandeltown.co.nz), at the northern end of town, just over the bridge, supplies **tide times** for Hot Water Beach and **Internet access**. Daily **buses** pull into the car park opposite the visitor centre. The only **car rental** firm in town is the G.A.S. BP service station, 226 Wharf Rd (ⓣ07/866 8059), which allows its cars onto the unsealed roads north of Colville.

Accommodation

For a small place, Coromandel offers a fair range of **places to stay**.

Buffalo Lodge Buffalo Rd, signposted north of town and past the Gold Stamper Battery ⓣ07/866 8960, ⓦwww.buffalolodge.co.nz. Comfortable accommodation in a specially designed house, high up in the bush with superb views across the Hauraki Gulf. Give two days' notice for superb three-course dinners ($95 a head). Reserve well in advance; closed May–Sept. Not suitable for children. ⑧

Celadon Cottages Motel & B&B Alfred St, about 1km north of town ⓣ07/866 8058, ⓦwww.celadonmotel.com. Four attractive places tucked away on a bush-clad hillside, with town and harbour views. Choose between a self-catering cabin for two, a large chalet for up to eight, a two-bedroom studio and a lodge that fits up to five. ④

Coromandel Colonial Cottages 1737 Rings Rd, 1.5km north of town ⓣ07/866 8857, ⓦwww.corocottagesmotel.co.nz. Eight good-value luxury cottages (some sleeping up to six) in tranquil gardens. The excellent facilities include a big solar-heated swimming pool, a playground including a trampoline and a BBQ area. ⑥

Coromandel Town Backpackers 732 Rings Rd ⓣ07/866 8327, ⓔcoromandeltownbackpackers@orkon.net.nz. Modern, spick-and-span hostel 3min walk north of town with budget bunks and several attractive rooms. Luggage and bike storage. Dorms $20, rooms ①

Jacaranda Lodge 3km south on Tiki Rd (SH25) ⓣ07/866 8002, ⓦwww.jacarandalodge.co.nz. A modern house in farmland offering B&B in extremely comfortable and spacious rooms (two en-suite doubles). ⑤

Long Bay Motor Camp 3200 Long Bay Rd, 3km west of town ⓣ07/866 8720, ⓔlbmccoromandel@xtra.co.nz. Attractive beachfront campsite with great views, safe swimming and good facilities such as kayak rental ($10 per hour). There are bunkhouse units, and additional tent sites at the secluded Tucks Bay, less than 1km away through the bush or a 5min walk around the headland. Tent sites $13, powered sites $15, units ①, caravans and cabins ②

Tidewater Tourist Park 270 Tiki Rd ⓣ07/866 8888, ⓦwww.tidewater.co.nz. A very comfortable motel with an associate YHA tagged on, 200m from town and near the harbour, with BBQ area and low-cost bike rental. Tents $15, dorms $25, rooms ②, motel units ④

Tui Lodge 60 Whangapoua Rd, just off SH25 ⓣ07/866 8237, ⓔtuilodge@paradise.net.nz. Good-value hostel 10min walk south of town (and on the InterCity bus route), set in a big rambling house surrounded by an orchard and tranquil garden. Perks include free linen, laundry, tea and coffee, fruit (in season), BBQ, use of bikes, a trampoline and friendly hosts. Tent sites $12, dorms $22, rooms ②

The town and around

The town centre spreads along the main road, distinguished by a few old buildings left from gold-mining days. From the south, SH25 becomes Tiki Road and then splits into two: Wharf Road skirts the harbour and Kapanga Road immediately enters the heart of the town, lined with shops and cafés. A couple of blocks further on, it becomes Rings Road, before heading northwards out of town as Colville Road.

About 300m north of the i-SITE is the small **Coromandel Historical Museum**, at 841 Rings Rd (Sat & Sun 10am–2pm; $2). Based in the old School of Mines (1898), it contains a mishmash of items including evocative black-and-white photographs of the old miners.

The main attraction in the immediate vicinity is the very popular **Driving Creek Railway and Potteries**, Driving Creek Road, 3.5km north of town (daily; check times with visitor centre or phone ⓣ07/866 8703; ⓦwww.drivingcreekrailway.co.nz). Built mostly by hand over 27 years and completed in 2003, though they still keep maintaining and adding to it, this is the country's only narrow-gauge hill railway, the brainchild of Barry Brickell, an eccentric local potter and rail enthusiast who wanted to access the clay-bearing hills. Today it mainly carries visitors on a well-organized **train trip** with an informative commentary (daily 10.15am & 2pm plus 12.45pm during the summer; 1hr return; $20; book ahead). The track is only 381mm wide and climbs 120m over a distance of about 3km, rewarding with spectacular views, extraordinary feats of engineering and quirky design; at the end of the line are panoramic views from a specially constructed wooden lodge, the Eyefull Tower. The journey starts and ends at the **workshops**, where you can see various types of **pottery**: stoneware, bricks and earthenware items, and sculptures made from terracotta. There's also a video about Brickell and a sculpture garden in a newly created wildlife sanctuary, designed to protect the local and visiting birdlife.

Around 1.5km north of town is the turn-off to the **Coromandel Goldfields Centre & Stamper Battery**, another 300m or so along Buffalo Road (Mon–Thurs 2.30pm & 3.30pm, Sat & Sun 1.30pm, 2.30pm & 3.30pm; 1hr guided tour; $10), where the peninsula's gold-mining history is explained. The fully functional 1899 stamper battery is also briefly operated to demonstrate the processing of gold.

Three kilometres west of town, along Wharf Road, lies the beach of **Long Bay** and a pleasing **walk** through a scenic reserve (40min loop). A hundred metres inside the *Long Bay Motor Camp*, a signpost marks the track, which

▲ Driving Creek Railway, Coromandel

climbs through bush to an ancient kauri tree and on to a small grove of younger ones. Beyond that, at the junction with a gravel road you can turn right to Tucks Bay and follow the coastal track back to the motor camp.

Eating and entertainment

For a small town, Coromandel has a disproportionate number of places to eat, of widely varying quality. As far as evening **entertainment** goes, there's a fair bit of live music going on, particularly in summer. Also worth a look is the **Coromandel Oyster Company**, who specialize in roadside sales of mussels, oysters, crayfish and scallops, about 5km before you hit town, or in the township at 70 Tiki Rd, **The Coromandel Smoking Company** (daily 8.30am–5.30pm) who smoke shellfish and fish delightfully.

Admirals Restaurant 46 Wharf St ⓣ07/866 8020. Boasting that it's "the only restaurant in town with sea views", this overly expensive but popular establishment specializes in seafood and steaks.

Driving Creek Café 180 Driving Creek Rd, 3.5km north of town ⓣ07/866 7066. Classic Coromandel, a laid-back and welcoming hideaway for great coffee, snacks and meals, with beautiful hill views from the veranda and garden. Acoustic music on summer afternoons.

Peppertree 31 Kapanga Rd ⓣ07/866 8211. A popular bar and restaurant open from breakfast to dinner, with main courses for $20–30 and an all-day snack menu. Eat indoors – there's an open fire in winter – or in the garden. Licensed and BYO; book ahead on summer weekends.

The Success Café & Restaurant 102 Kapanga Rd ⓣ07/866 7100. Good café that turns into a so-so bistro/bar in the evenings; licensed & BYO.

Star and Garter 5 Kapanga Rd. Newish bar in the centre of town, great for the full range of Monteith's brews and some palatable vino with a more urbane atmosphere than the competition.

Top Pub *Coromandel Hotel*, 611 Rings Rd ⓣ07/866 8760. A pleasant evening dinner bar, good for its seafood, but also serving pizzas, steaks and other meat dishes; open for lunch in summer too. Beer garden.

North to Fletcher Bay and Port Charles

The landscape **north of Coromandel** is even more rugged than the rest of the peninsula, its green hills dropping to apparently endless beaches, clean blue sea and white surf. The tourist authorities have dubbed the area the **Pohutukawa Cape**, and indeed the dirt roads are lined with ancient pohutukawa trees, blazing red from early November until January. With its dairy farms long deserted, it is a virtually uninhabited land and there are **few facilities**: replenish your supplies in Coromandel. As elsewhere on the peninsula, signs have sprung up to deter freelance **camping** and the Department of Conservation has responded by opening five waterside campsites around the northern peninsula. For the two weeks after Christmas the campsites are full, but for most of the rest of the year you can have this unspoilt area to yourself.

From Coromandel, the road snakes 20km along the coast, then cuts inland to the tiny settlement of **COLVILLE**, little more than a post office, petrol pump and the Colville General Store, set in a quiet green valley that appealed to counter-culture aspirants in the 1970s. The store is a good place to stock up on dry goods for the Coromandel Walkway (see p.370) and check on the state of the road north of Port Jackson; there's also a café, open for coffee and snacks during the daytime and dinner (BYO) in the summer. If you fancy **staying** up this way, try *Colville Farm*, Colville Road, 1.5km south of Colville (ⓣ07/866 6820), a soothing spot on a sheep and cattle farm offering **horse trekking** (1hr $30; 5hr $100). Accommodation includes a campsite ($12) backpacker

The Coromandel Walkway and cycle route

Other than a bit of swimming, fishing or lolling about on the beaches, the only activity in the far north of the peninsula is to hike from Fletcher Bay to Stony Bay along the **Coromandel Walkway** (11km; 3hr one way), a gentle and clearly marked path with lovely views. The walk starts at the far end of the beach in Fletcher Bay and heads off into a no-man's-land, first following gentle coastal hills that alternate between pasture and bush, before giving way to wilder terrain as you head further south past a series of tiny bays. Several hilltop **vantage points** yield spectacular vistas of the coast and Pacific Ocean beyond. **Stony Bay** is a sweep of pebbles with a bridge across an estuary that's safe for swimming. The DOC leaflet *Coromandel Recreation Information* briefly describes the walk and shows a map, but you're unlikely to need it.

The Strongman Coachlines **shuttle bus** run a taxi service between Coromandel town and Fletcher Bay (Ⓣ0800/668 175, Ⓦwww.coromandeldiscoverytours.co.nz; $90 return; complimentary tea, coffee and biscuits), dropping off walkers and collecting them at Stony Bay before returning to Coromandel, as well as stopping off for photos. It also picks up from *Fletcher Bay Backpackers*.

dorms in a cottage ($22), a couple of bush lodges (❷) and two self-contained houses (❸–❹) with fabulous views.

Beyond Colville the road is unsealed. It becomes narrower, rougher and dustier the further north you go, though it's not that difficult to drive if taken at a steady pace (allow an hour to reach Fletcher Bay from Colville in fine weather). Three kilometres north of Colville the road splits, the right fork heading east over the hills to Stony Bay and the southern end of the Coromandel Walkway. The left fork runs 35km north to Port Jackson and Fletcher Bay at the very tip of the peninsula, following the coast all the way. An abandoned **granite wharf** marks the halfway spot. A couple of kilometres beyond, you'll find the diminutive and lovely *Fantail Bay Recreation Reserve* ($9), the first of the DOC **campsites**, which comes equipped with basic toilets and a water supply. The road then cuts inland, over hills rising straight from the shore, to reach **PORT JACKSON**, just two houses and a one-kilometre sandy crescent of beach. It's safe for swimming and is backed by a grassy DOC reserve, where you can **camp** ($9) with views across to Great Barrier and Little Barrier islands. From here the road deteriorates on the final 6km to **FLETCHER BAY**, probably the best beach of all, safe for swimming, its eastern end marking the start of the **Coromandel Walkway**. The beach is backed by another DOC **campsite** ($9), with flush toilets and cold showers; the cosy *Fletcher Bay Backpackers* (Ⓣ07/866 6712, Ⓔjs.lourie@xtra.co.nz; dorm beds from $20), is set on a hill 400m away from the beach, with four-bed dorms.

Stony Bay, at the southern end of the Coromandel Walkway, is reached by two perilous and twisty gravel roads – one, via Little Bay, across the Coromandel Range from just beyond Coromandel, the other traversing the Moehau Range from just beyond Colville. The latter runs 14km from Colville to the small holiday settlement of **Port Charles**, and a further 6km to Stony Bay, where there's another DOC campsite ($9).

East to Whitianga

The drive east from Coromandel to Whitianga can be done in under an hour, but you could easily spend a day on either of two highly **scenic roads** that cross the mountains: the more direct, snaking **309 Road** (33km, of which 14km are gravel; no public transport) spends much of its time in the bush, while the main (and mostly sealed) **SH25** climbs through forested hills before zigzagging down to the coast, 46km away.

Coromandel to Whitianga: the 309 Road

From the junction with SH25, 4km south of Coromandel, the 309 Road twists 5km east to **Waiau Waterworks** (daily: Oct–March 9am till dusk; April–Sept 9am–5pm; $12), a rambling garden carved from the bush and dotted with whimsical water-powered contraptions and contrivances.

One hundred metres past the waterworks, a rough access road on the left crosses a ford and climbs steeply for 3km to the trailhead for the track to **Castle Rock** (2km return; 40min–1hr 30min), the most easily accessible peak on the Coromandel Peninsula. It's a climb that gets steeper towards the final tree-root claw onto the 521-metre summit of this old volcanic plug, but your efforts are rewarded by fantastic views to both coasts: the Whangapoua peninsula and the Mercury Islands on the east, and Coromandel and the Firth of Thames on the west.

A further 2.5km along the 309 Road, the **Waiau Falls** crash over a rockface into a pool below. They're not that impressive, but they are right next to the road and offer a gorgeous spot to cool off. Half a kilometre further on, a car park heralds the easy bush track to the magnificent **Kauri Grove** (1km return; 30min) and "**Siamese**" **Kauri** a little further on. Fortuitous gaps in the bush make this one of the best places in the country to really get a sense of the size of the kauri, and appreciate just how they stand head and shoulders above the rest of the forest: a boardwalk allows you to get face-to-bark with these giants.

The road tops out at the 306-metre saddle and descends towards Whitianga, passing some relaxing **accommodation** (see p.374).

Coromandel to Whitianga: SH25

From Coromandel, **SH25** follows an attractive route through lush native forest, passing a couple of isolated but pretty beachside settlements with campsites. About 14km from Coromandel is the 5km turn-off to the secluded village and beach of **WHANGAPOUA**, whose long stretch of white sand is lined by *baches*, expensive beach houses and a single general store/petrol station. At the end of the road (along the right fork into town) is a pleasing walk to the sandy beach of **New Chums Bay** (4km return; 1hr): from the beach, cross the estuary and follow the bushline around the headland to a saddle, on the other side of which is New Chums Bay (accessible at low tide only). Continuing along SH25, about 30km from Coromandel, you descend to diminutive **KUAOTUNU**, beside a lovely white-sand beach. There's **accommodation** here: the shady *Kuaotunu Motor Camp*, Bluff Road (Ⓣ07/866 5628, Ⓦwww.kuaotunumotorcamp.co.nz; tent sites $18, cabins ❷, units ❹), with kayak rental; the *Black Jack Lodge*, SH25 (Ⓣ07/866 2988, Ⓦwww.black-jack.co.nz; dorms $25, twins and doubles ❷); and the ultra-friendly *Kuaotunu Bay Lodge*, SH25 (Ⓣ07/866 4396, Ⓦwww.kuaotunubay.co.nz), set on a rise with sea views, a self-contained unit (❼), B&B en-suite doubles (❽), and dinner ($45) by arrangement.

From here, if you have your own transport and an afternoon to spare, it's worth taking the first left turn off SH25 to **Otama Beach**, though the road is a little rough in places. Head for the far end of the beach, where pohutokawa lean over a white quartz sand beach. The road continues over to the even more deserted **Opito Bay**, rougher still but well worth the effort before returning, the way you came.

Nine kilometres north of Whitianga on SH25, Twin Oaks Riding Ranch is the base for scenic two-hour **horse treks** (book ahead ⓣ07/866 5388, ⓦwww.twinoaksridingraunch.co.nz; daily 9.30am & 1.30pm, plus twilight trek at 6pm Dec–March; $50), with breathtaking views of Mercury Bay and the northern Coromandel; transport from Whitianga can be arranged. From here, SH25 continues through farmland to Whitianga and Mercury Bay.

Whitianga and around

The attractive town of **WHITIANGA** clusters where Whitianga Harbour meets the broad sweep of **Mercury Bay**, a huge bite out of the Coromandel Peninsula coastline named by Captain Cook, who stopped here in 1769 so that his party of scientists could observe the planet passing across the face of the sun. Today it's a popular Kiwi summer-holiday destination, the population of 4000 swelling dramatically during January as vacationers flock to the town's **Buffalo Beach**, a long sweep of surf-pounded white sand.

Whitianga makes a good base from which to make a series of half-day and **day-trips** to wonderfully secluded spots. Just across the narrow harbour mouth and strung along Mercury Bay's eastern shore are several lovely beaches, reached by passenger ferry to **Ferry Landing**, from where you can catch a **bus** or strike out along scenic coastal tracks; an area also served by roads branching off the southbound SH25, which loops around the deeply indented harbour. Two gems are **Cathedral Cove**, a stunning geological formation, and **Hot Water Beach**, renowned for the natural hot-water springs that bubble from beneath its sand. Bordering part of the eastern shore is **Cathedral Cove Marine Reserve**, whose protected waters are great for snorkelling and scuba diving. In addition, **boat trips** to the outer reaches of Mercury Bay and the volcanically formed **Mercury Islands**, 25km offshore, explore pristine waters and shoreline – and search for bottlenose **dolphins** and **whales**.

Arrival, information and transport

SH25 runs through town, becoming Albert Street along the main shopping thoroughfare, then Buffalo Beach Road along the shore. Virtually everything happens on these streets or The Esplanade, which branches off to the wharf and ferry.

Buses drop off at accommodation around town and outside the **i-SITE visitor centre** at the corner of Albert Street and Blacksmith Lane (Boxing Day–Jan daily 8am–6pm; Feb–Christmas Eve Mon–Fri 9am–5pm Sat–Sun 9am–4pm; ⓣ07/866 5555, ⓦwww.whitianga.co.nz), where **Internet access** is available. Great Barrier Airlines' (ⓣ0800/900 600) flights from Auckland (twice a day on Mon, Fri & Sun) and Great Barrier Island (2–3 weekly) land at the **airport**, 4km south of the town centre, reached for roughly $15 with Mercury Bay **Taxis** (ⓣ07/866 4141) or Paradise Cabs (ⓣ07/869 5555).

The surrounding **beaches** are served by ferry and buses; the **passenger ferry** to Ferry Landing (daily: 7.30am–6.30pm, 7.30–8.30pm & 9.30–10.30pm or until midnight in summer; $2 each way) takes three minutes and leaves from The Esplanade. Go Kiwi (ⓣ0800/446 549, ⓦwww.go-kiwi.co.nz) and Purangi Shuttles and Tours (ⓣ07/866 3724) run **shuttle tours** from Ferry Landing to

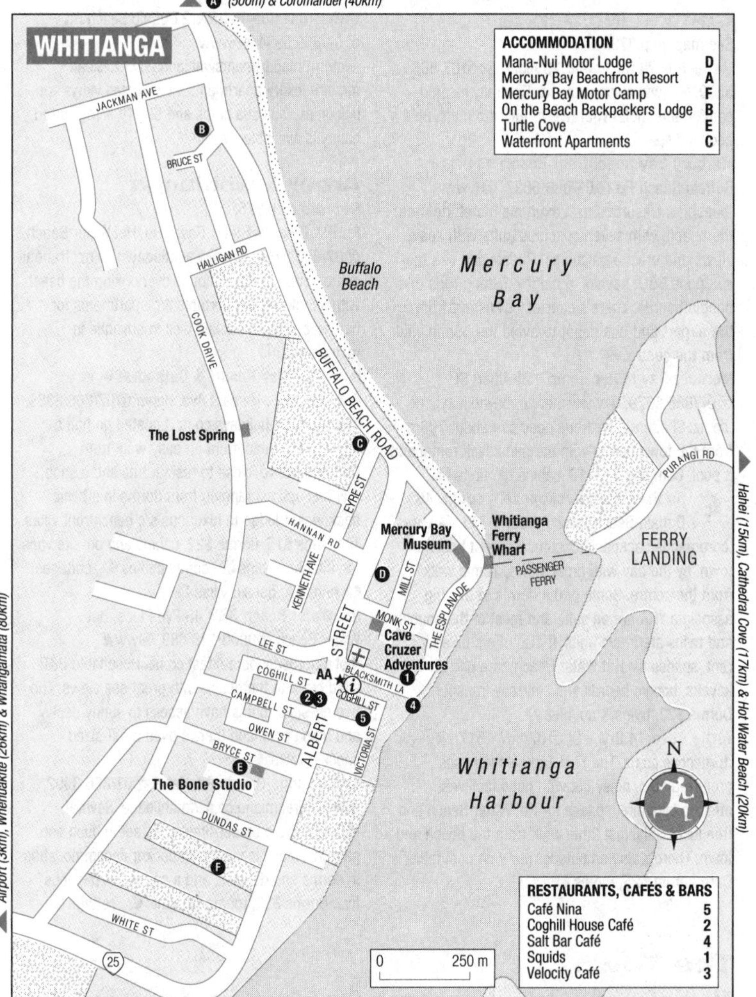

Cooks Beach, Hahei and Hot Water Beach (4–5hr, $40), with services connecting with buses to Auckland and Whitianga.

Accommodation

As one of the Coromandel's main tourist centres, Whitianga has plenty of **accommodation**. Further out, beside the secluded **beaches** of Mercury Bay there's less choice, mostly at Hot Water Beach and Hahei; it's also worth staying at Kuaotunu, 16km north (see p.371). Throughout summer you'll need to **book** two months ahead. Also, be prepared for **higher prices** than on the rest of the peninsula, especially anywhere with a sea view.

Central Whitianga

See map on p.373.

Mana-Nui Motor Lodge 20 Albert St ⓣ07/866 5599, ⓦwww.mananui.co.nz. Centrally located, comfortable motel with twelve fully s/c units, plus a pool and spa. ⑤

Mercury Bay Beachfront Resort 111–113 Buffalo Beach Rd ⓣ07/866 5637, ⓦwww.beachfrontresort.co.nz. Luxurious motel, right on the beach, with seven spacious units with sea views and private balconies. Guests can use the spa pool, BBQ, kayaks, a dinghy, fishing rods and boogie boards. There's courtesy transport from the airport and bus depot to avoid the 35min walk from the centre. ⑦

Mercury Bay Motor Camp 121 Albert St ⓣ07/866 5579, ⓦwww.mercurybayholidaypark.co.nz. Sheltered, well-equipped site about 700m from the town centre with bargain kayak rental and a pool. Camping $13–18, cabins ②, units ③

On the Beach Backpackers Lodge 46 Buffalo Beach Rd ⓣ07/866 5380, ⓦwww.coromandelbackpackers.com. The best hostel in town, by the bay with great views, 10min walk from the centre. Some of the dorms at this big associate YHA are en suite and most of the doubles and twins are in s/c units. It also offers bikes for rent, spades for Hot Water Beach, free use of kayaks, boogie boards and courtesy transport. Dorms $23, twins & doubles ②

Turtle Cove 14 Bryce St ⓣ07/867 1517, ⓦwww.turtlecove.co.nz. The Kiwi Experience buses' preferred stop, noisy but with good facilities, offering bike hire, spades for Hot Water Beach and free local calls, just 2min walk from the beach and town. There's also an outdoor bar with pool table. Dorms from $25, rooms ②

Waterfront Apartments 2 Buffalo Beach Rd ⓣ07/869 5994, ⓦwww.waterfrontapartmentswhitianga.co.nz. Clean modern luxury apartments, all with sea views and balconies. Plus spa baths and Sky TV. A registered nanny is available. ⑤

Around Whitianga

See map on p.375.

Auntie Dawn's Place Radar Rd, Hot Water Beach ⓣ07/866 3707, ⓦwww.auntiedawn.co.nz. Tranquil contemporary hillside house overlooking the beach with simple yet comfortable s/c apartments for two. Needs to be booked well in advance in midsummer. ④

Hahei Holiday Resort & Cathedral Cove Backpackers Harsant Ave, Hahei ⓣ07/866 3889, ⓦwww.haheiholidays.co.nz. Located on half a kilometre of beachfront an easy walk from Cathedral Cove, close to restaurants and a shop, this has options ranging from dorms in a basic backpacker lodge to luxurious s/c beachfront villas. Tent sites $15, dorms $22, cabins and on-site vans ②, kitchen cabins ②, comfy cabins ③, cottages ④ units ⑤, deluxe villas ⑥

Hot Water Beach B&B 48 Pye Place, Hot Water Beach ⓣ0800/146 889, ⓦwww.hotwaterbedandbreakfast.co.nz. Hospitable B&B sited close to the beach with great sea views. The two en-suite rooms have access to sunny decks and a spa pool, and there's even a full-sized snooker table. ⑧

Tatahi Lodge Grange Rd, Hahei ⓣ07/866 3992, ⓦwww.dreamland.co.nz/tatahilodge. Several welcoming s/c timber-lined units set in bush and gardens, plus pleasant backpacker accommodation in dorms and doubles, and a cottage that sleeps five. Dorms $22, rooms ②, units ⑥, cottage ⑦

The Town

Much of the pleasure in this area is got from getting out of town, easily done at Cathedral Cove or Hot Water Beach, or by taking boat trips on Mercury Bay (see p.376). Alternatively, consider a **bone-carving course**, where a skilled carver helps you produce a high-quality pendant within a day ($100). Ian Thorne at The Bone Studio, 6b Bryce St (book ahead on ⓣ07/866 2158, ⓦwww.carving.co.nz), takes only a few prospective carvers at a time, gives just the right amount of guidance and encourages self-expression. If you lack the patience, check out the ready-carved pieces at Bay Carving, The Esplanade (ⓣ07/866 4021, ⓦwww.bonecarving.com), who also offer shorter (2–3hr) carve-your-own courses ($40), based on set patterns.

In an old butter factory on The Esplanade is the **Mercury Bay Museum** (daily 10am–4pm; $5), with displays on Kupe, the first Maori explorer to visit the area, Captain Cook and the subsequent families that settled. An attractive alternative is a soak in the new **hot water spring**, located at The Lost Spring, 121a Cook Drive (ⓣ07/866 0456, ⓦwww.thelostspring.co.nz), the brainchild

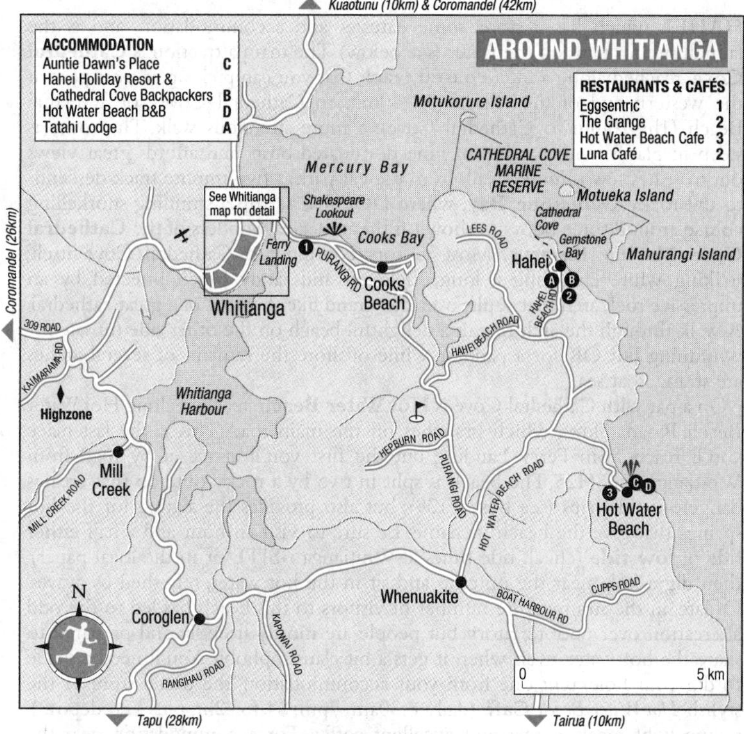

of Alan Hopping; the epic tale of how he has brought this venture to fruition, tapping a local hot spring, is pure Disney meets number-eight-wire. The pools themselves, camouflaged behind a town-centre street, are a extraordinary mix, spa kitsch standing alongside a recreation of natural bush spendour (entry prices were still to be determined at the time of writing).

Ferry Landing and the beaches

The beaches across the estuary are accessible by car, by boat, or by passenger ferry (see p.372) to **Ferry Landing**, where buses continue on. The longer **road route** travels south along SH25, skirting the harbour and cutting inland at the signposted turn-off at Whenuakite, 26km from Whitianga. **Facilities** at Ferry Landing are limited to a store; there are no banks or liquor stores on this side, so stock up if you're planning to stay more than a day.

From Ferry Landing, the first point of interest is **Shakespeare Lookout**, signposted 1.5km along the road and reached after another kilometre uphill to a car park. From the lookout – viewed from the sea it once supposedly resembled the Bard's profile – panoramic views stretch east to Cooks Beach and across Mercury Bay, west to Buffalo Beach, and north towards Mount Maungatawhiri. Signposted tracks lead from the car park to the secluded Lonely Bay and onto the popular family holiday spot of **Cooks Beach** (2km one way; 20min), also accessible from the main road 2km further east.

About 4km southeast of Cooks Beach along the main road lies the junction with Hahei Beach Road, leading 6km to the tiny beachside community of

HAHEI, which has a store, some eateries and accommodation, and is the launch site for trips on the water (see below). The main attraction is **Cathedral Cove**, reached along a hilly **coastal track** that you can pick up at a car park at the western end of the village (30–40min to Cathedral Cove), or at Hahei Beach (1hr 20min to Cathedral Cove), a more strenuous walk. The route is steep in places, with patches of pine-dominated bush, and affords great views out to sea. A few minutes' walk from the car park, a five-minute track descends to the rocky **Gemstone Bay**, where DOC has set up a stunning snorkelling course around three buoys to show off the undersea wonders of the **Cathedral Cove Marine Reserve**. Most visitors continue to Cathedral Cove itself; striking white cliffs hug a long, sheltered and sandy beach bisected by an impressive rock arch that vaults over the strand like the nave of a great cathedral. A walk through the arch reveals a delightful beach on the other side (unsafe for swimming but OK for a paddle), while offshore the remains of several arches are stranded at sea.

On a par with Cathedral Cove is **Hot Water Beach**, reached along Hot Water Beach Road (5km), which branches off the main road. This is the last place you'll reach from Ferry Landing but the first you'll arrive at by road from Whitianga via SH25. The beach is split in two by a rocky outcrop that creates dangerous tidal rips (see box, p.139), but also provides the setting for the hot springs that give the beach its name. Be sure to visit an hour and a half either side of **low tide** (check tide times at Whitianga i-SITE or in the local paper), then dig a hole near the outcrop and sit in the hot water, refreshed by waves. Of late, in the summer, the number of visitors to this beach has led to the odd altercation over pool territory but people are mostly friendly and prepared to share the hot water, even when it gets a bit claustrophobic. You'll need a spade to dig your hole: rent one from your accommodation, the beach store or the stylish *Hot Water Beach* **Café** (daily 8.30am–7pm; $4 for 2hr, plus $20 deposit), selling light meals, snacks and excellent coffee. For accommodation near the beach, see p.374.

Activities around Mercury Bay

The abundant waters of Mercury Bay make **dolphin and seal sightings** a common event on **scenic trips** from Whitianga, along the coast to Cathedral Cove and Hot Water Beach, or out to the various island groups dotted off the coast, all of which take in the extraordinary array of volcanic features on the coastline and within the many sea caves. A variety of companies vie for your trade, with Cave Cruzer Adventures (Ⓣ0800/427 893, Ⓦwww.cavecruzer.co.nz) and Sea Cave and Island Adventures (Ⓣ0800/806 060, Ⓦwww.ocenwave.co.nz) among the best of the bunch. Tours range from 90min ($60) to three hours ($100), depending on the distance travelled, features visited and wildlife spotted, and leave from the Whitianga Ferry Wharf.

Great boat trips also run **from Hahei**, the best being Hahei Explorer (book previous evening or before 9am on the day on Ⓣ07/866 3910, Ⓦwww.haheiexplorer.co.nz; $60), a rigid-hull inflatable that takes small groups on exhilarating hour-long sea-cave trips, visiting Cathedral Cove and an amazing blowhole, with an entertaining commentary. They also rent out snorkel gear and wetsuits for use at Gemstone Bay ($40 a day). Alternatively, join one of the **guided sea kayak trips** run from Hahei by Cathedral Cove Sea Kayaking (Ⓣ07/866 3877, Ⓦwww.seakayaktours.co.nz), who take up to twenty people; their half-day trip ($75) visits Cathedral Cove and selected islands and caves, sometimes in conjunction with Sea Cave and Island Adventures.

Scuba diving and snorkelling in Cathedral Cove Marine Reserve can be arranged through Hahei-based Cathedral Cove Dive (☎07/866 3955, Ⓦwww.hahei.co.nz/diving), 48 Hahei Beach Rd, who pick up from Ferry Landing, or Whitianga-based Dive HQ, 7 Blacksmith Lane (☎07/867 1580, Ⓦwww.divecoromandel.co.nz). Snorkel-gear rental costs around $20 a day and a one-dive scuba trip $95 with full gear. **Non-divers** can learn basic scuba skills ($145), and both companies run PADI courses.

Eating and entertainment

Whitianga and its environs are well supplied with places to **eat**, with many clustered along The Esplanade near the marina. Entertainment options are limited: live **bands** occasionally play the *Whitianga Marina Hotel* (see *Salt Bar Café*, below) in summer and there is music at *Eggcentric*, a ferry ride away.

Whitianga

See map on p.373.

Café Nina 20 Victoria St. Great coffee at this friendly daytime café. The food is made to order, with vegetarian and vegan options. Try the signature seafood chowder ($9.50) or a delicious home-made carrot cake.

Coghill House Café 10 Coghill St. Relaxing spot for high-quality snacks (including great pies) or generous meals during the day. Ease yourself into the lounging area or outdoor seating.

Salt Bar Café *Whitianga Marina Hotel*, The Esplanade. Airy lunch and dinner café/bar with decking onto the marina. Known for à la carte mains such as pan-seared tuna steaks and veal sirloin with herb risotto ($20–35).

Squids 1 Blacksmith Lane. Popular cocktail/wine bar, good for a few drinks and well-priced food, including lambs fry and bacon, salmon with roast *kumara* and steak with garlic mash.

Velocity Café 69 Albert St. A stylish licensed café, friendly with outdoor seating and a selection of salads, veggie tarts, cookies and fritters (closed Sun & Mon).

Around Whitianga

See map on p.375.

Eggcentric 1047 Purangi Rd, Ferry Landing ☎07/866 0307. Quirky place that comes alive in the evenings when live music vies for prominence with poetry readings, all alongside some well-presented grub (closed Mon).

The Grange 7 Grange Rd, Hahei. Highly regarded licensed spot, currently undergoing a revamp, but still retaining more of a party atmosphere than the competition, open from brunch until dinner. Closed Mon and all of May.

Luna Café 1 Grange Rd, Hahei. Cool little number where you can pick from a range of seafood and pizzas for lunch and dinner. Licensed and BYO (closed Tues & Wed).

South to Whangamata

The run along SH25 from Whitianga **south to Whangamata** is a pleasant journey, though the brief glimpses of the coast often show over-development. If **Tairua**, the midway point is a little spoilt, its neighbour across the harbour, the luxury retirement and holiday resort of **Pauanui**, is reminiscent of the worst excesses of Florida. All is not lost though – unspoilt beaches can be found, particularly the delightful **Opoutere**, a tiny harbourside retreat at the foot of a mountain with a wild sweep of beach and a beautifully located hostel.

Tairua

Small but with a residential density that would put some cities to shame, **TAIRUA** lies on SH25, 16km south of the turn-off to Hot Water Beach and 42km from Whitianga. Huddled between pine-forested hills and the estuary of the Tairua River, it is separated from the crashing Pacific breakers by two opposing and almost touching peninsulas. One is crowned by the impressive volcanic Mount Paku, the other covered by the suburban sprawl of exclusive **Pauanui**, accessible by a five-minute passenger **ferry** ride from Tairua (around 9am–5pm; Sept–Nov roughly hourly; Dec–end Jan continuous; rest of the year twice daily; $5 return), or a 25km drive.

You could stop briefly for a dip or to climb **Mount Paku** (15min ascent) for spectacular views over the town, its estuary and beaches; the track starts at the end of Paku Drive, reached by following the estuary around to the north. InterCity buses from Thames, Auckland and Whitianga drop off outside the information centre, 223 Main St (daily 9am–5pm; ⓣ07/864 7575). Go Kiwi buses (see p.372) pass through once a day in each direction as part of their tours.

Opoutere

Around twenty kilometres south of Tairua is a 5km side road to **Opoutere**, a gorgeous and usually deserted 4km-long surf beach backed by pines – behind them a campsite, YHA and a few houses. The pohutukawa-fringed road hugs the shores of the Wharekawa Harbour where wetlands make good bird-watching spots, mudflats yield shellfish and the calm waters are good for kayaking.

From a signposted parking area at the end of the sealed road a footbridge leads to two paths, both reaching the beach in ten minutes or so: the **left-hand fork** runs straight through the forest to the beach; the **right-hand track** follows the estuary to the edge of a protected sandspit where endangered New Zealand dotterels breed from November to March. The white-sand Opoutere Beach can have a strong undertow and there are no lifeguards, so don't swim. For a wider view over the estuary and the coastline, tackle the track up **Mount Maungaru-awahine** (2km return; 40–50min), climbing through gnarled pohutukawa and other native trees to the summit.

The summit track begins by the gate to the relaxing, old-fashioned and wonderfully sited ★ **YHA** (ⓣ07/865 9072, ⓦwww.yha.org.nz, dorms $23, rooms ❷), beside the estuary in a 1908 schoolhouse and surrounding buildings, in mature bush surrounded by the calls of native birds, with free kayaks and the chance for nocturnal glow-worm spotting. The attractive **campsite**, *Opoutere Coastal Camping* (Dec 1 to April 30 only; ⓣ07/865 9152, ⓦwww.opouterebeach.co.nz; tent sites $15, powered sites $17.50, cabins ❹, chalets ❺ plus $15 per extra person), is about 700m towards the beach from the hostel.

There's no regular **bus** service, but drop-offs can be arranged – call the YHA in advance – and bring all your food as both places have only basic **provisions** for sale.

Whangamata

The long, straggling resort of **WHANGAMATA**, on SH25 towards the southern end of the Coromandel Peninsula, is bounded on three sides by estuaries and the ocean, and on the fourth by bush-clad hills. This single-storey town of 4500 grows tenfold in January, when holidaymakers flock to four-kilometre **Ocean Beach**, a crescent of white sand that curves from the harbour to the mouth of the **Otahu River**. The bar at the harbour end has an excellent break, making this a **surf** mecca.

Practicalities

Whangamata is an umbrella of land, its canopy facing the sea, estuaries on either side and its streets sprouting out from long roads running north to south. Port Road runs straight through the small town centre, linking it with the highway. **Buses** drop off next door to the centrally located **i-SITE visitor centre**, 616 Port Rd (Mon–Sat 9am–5pm, Sun 10am–2pm; Sun until 4pm in summer; ⓣ07/865 8340, ⓦwww.whangamatainfo.co.nz), and most places are within easy walking distance. **Internet access** is available at Bartley Internet & Graphics, 706 Port Rd (ⓣ07/865 8832).

Accommodation

From Christmas until the middle of January **accommodation** is scarce and high prices are jacked skywards. For the rest of the year Whangamata is fairly quiet.

Brenton Lodge 2 Brenton Place ⓣ07/865 8400, ⓦwww.brentonlodge.co.nz. Beautiful retreat in pretty gardens on the edge of Whangamata with sea views from two cottages (each sleeping four) and one suite. Understated decor, pool, spa and delicious breakfasts. ❽

Southpacific Tourist Lodge Corner of Port Rd & Mayfair Ave ⓣ07/865 9580, ⓦwww.thesouthpacific.co.nz. Immaculate motel and budget lodge. The well-equipped budget lodge has four-shares, double rooms, surf lessons ($20), board hire ($40), kayaks ($15) and mountain bikes ($25). The modern and comfortable motel offers smart and spacious units, some with full kitchen. Four-shares $20, rooms ❷, units ❹–❻

Palm Pacific Resort 413 Port Rd ⓣ07/865 9211, ⓦwww.palmpacificresort.com. A big motel complex, equipped with fairly modern, spacious units sleeping up to eight. Facilities include a BBQ, several bars, a bistro, tennis courts, a large pool, spas and a sauna. ❺

Wentworth Valley Campground End of Wentworth Valley Rd, 7km southwest of Whangamata. Lovely DOC campsite with streamside pitches, BBQs and coin-operated hot showers right by the start of the track to Wentworth Falls. $9.

Eating, drinking and entertainment

Considering its size and tourist credentials, there are surprisingly few places to **eat** of any merit in town and only one **cinema**, at 708 Port Rd (ⓣ07/865 6566).

Caffe Rossini 646 Port Rd. Modern café serving a range of breakfasts, cakes and good coffee.

Minato Sushi 715 Port Rd. Wonderful daytime sushi café, the fish prepared with care and exactness. Rich seafood chowder is also available.

Nero's Port Rd, near northern junction with SH25. Evening venue with the best pizzas in town (around $19), offering combinations such as salmon and shrimp or chicken and mango.

Whangamata Ocean Sports Club Harbour-end of Port Rd. Private club and home of the Whangamata Boat & Gamefishing Club, open to non-members when they're not busy; ask at the bar. It's worth the effort for great harbour and sea views, cheap drink and hearty good-value fare, including roasts for $12.

Whanga Bar Port Rd, set back behind *Vibes Coffee Bar* (638 Port Rd). Intimate, licensed, spot for breakfast, lunch or dinner, serving burgers, Thai fish cakes and steaks. Closed Sun–Wed.

The town and around

Surfies should make for the Whangamata Surf Shop, 634 Port Rd (ⓣ07/865 8252; Mon–Fri 9am–5pm, daily in the summer) to **rent a surfboard** ($40/day), **boogie boards** ($20/day) and wetsuits ($20/day). The shop also offers one-on-one surfing tuition ($50 per hr).

There are a couple of other diversions in the foothills of the Coromandel Range, on the edge of town, including a pleasant **walk** to Wentworth Falls (10km return; 2hr) in the nearby Wentworth Valley. Take SH25 2km south to the signposted turn-off to Wentworth Valley Road and follow it 4km to its end. Here you'll find a campsite (see p.379) and the start of the track through regenerating bush past numerous small swimming holes. The route continues into the heart of the mountains, but most turn around at the two-leap Wentworth Falls, best viewed from a small deck.

The other reason to come here is to join either of two popular **eco-tours**. Choose from Kiwi Dundee Adventures (Ⓣ07/865 8809, Ⓦwww.kiwidundee.co.nz; book well in advance) or Wildman Milne (Ⓣ07/865 6575, Ⓦwww.wildman.co.nz); both cover similar areas but differ considerably in scale. Kiwi Dundee have grown from small beginnings to deal with bus tours and bigger groups and are run by dedicated conservationist Doug Johansen (popularly known as "Kiwi Dundee"). Wildman Milne is a one-man operation offering intimate tours with his own well-considered perspective on the brain-load of history he has at his disposal, both Pakeha and Maori. The year-round operations offer a variety of trips (some tailored to individual needs), with wildlife experiences and paths off the beaten track. A full-day trip with Kiwi Dundee, including lunch is around $210, a 4hr trip with Wildman Milne is $75, both offer departures from Tairua, Pauanui and Whangamata, Milne also picks up at Opoutere YHA.

Waihi and Waihi Beach

SH25 continues 30km south from Whangamata to **WAIHI**, where it meets SH2 at the entrance to the Karangahake Gorge. Gold was first discovered at Waihi in a reef of quartz in 1878, but it was not until 1894 that a boom began with the first successful trials in extracting gold using cyanide solution at Karangahake. By 1908 Waihi was the fastest-growing town in the Auckland Province, and it remains a mining district some five-thousand strong. Although underground mining stopped in 1952, extraction was cranked up again in 1987 in the opencast but well-hidden Martha Mine. You can visit the mine, learn about its past in a good **museum**, or hop on a 1930s train for a scenic ride into the nearby **Karangahake Gorge**.

For light relief, the popular surf beach of **WAIHI BEACH** lies 12km east of town, off SH2: its long, thin strip of golden sand, stretching for 8km, is one of the safest ocean beaches in the country.

The Town

At the eastern end of town stands the **Martha Mine**, whose influence has dominated Waihi, while in the centre of town the old pumphouse dominates the town physically, looming like a warty sentinel against the skyline. Though the mine was due to close in 2006, further exploration, the prospect of discovering more accessible deposits and the long-winded rehabilitation of the land mean it will continue to operate until at least 2012. **Guided tours** (book ahead through the i-SITE, see p.381, Ⓦwww.marthamine.co.nz; Mon–Fri according to demand; 75–90min; donation) take visitors from the i-SITE around the opencast gold mine and processing areas, providing history and details of the environmental work the company is doing. Even if you decide against the gold-mine tour it's worth heading to the viewing platform next to the old pumphouse, based on a Cornish design, which allows you to peer into the vast pit, where the laden trucks are dwarfed by the sheer scale of the earthworks. Opposite the viewing platform on Upper Seddon Street is the **i-SITE** and in its basement is an interactive **museum** (same hours) that details Waihi's golden history. Little mention is made of the violent Waihi Strike of 1912, which helped galvanize the labour movement and led to the creation of the Labour Party. The strike is conjured up evocatively in a display in the **Gold-mining Museum & Art Gallery**, 54 Kenny St, currently closed for refurbishment. At the western end of town, the wooden station at the end of Wrigley Street is home to the **Goldfields Railway**, operating scenic 6km rail trips year-round to Waikino in the **Karangahake Gorge** (trains daily 11am, 12.30pm & 2pm, returning from Waikino 45min later; 20min each way; $15 return; ⓣ07/863 8640). The 1930s diesel engines follow a route alongside SH2 giving spectacular views of the Ohinemuri River.

Practicalities

Buses pull up near the **i-SITE visitor centre,** Upper Seddon Street (daily 9am–5pm; ⓣ07/863 6715) in the centre of town. **Internet access** is available in the i-SITE and at the library on Seddon Street, 100m away (Mon–Thurs 10.30am–4.30pm, Fri 10am–5pm, Sat 10am–noon). The best accommodation is at Waihi Beach, as are the better places to eat.

Accommodation

Beaches Motel 40 Seaforth Rd, Waihi Beach ⓣ07/863 5439, ⓦwww.beachesmotel.co.nz. Small and reliable waterfront motel near the shops. ④

Bowentown Beach Holiday Park Seaforth Rd, Bowentown Beach ⓣ07/863 5381, ⓦwww.bowentown.co.nz. Lovely, secluded site right at the southern end of the beach with a range of accommodation. Wireless Internet is available, and kayaks ($13), boogie boards ($4) and bikes ($7) can be rented from the cheery hosts. Tents and powered sites from $17, cabins ①, s/c units ③, new units ⑥

Athenree Hot Springs and Holiday Park Athenree Rd, Athenree (off SH2 in Tauranga Harbour, on the opposite arm from Waihi Beach) ⓣ07/863 5600, ⓦwww.athenehotsprings.co.nz. Between Waihi and Katikati, this motorcamp is almost on a par with Bowentown, lacking the stunning beach but gaining by having its own hot springs. Powered and tent sites ($18), chalets ⑥, motels and studios ⑤, cabins ①

Eating

Cactus Jack's 31 Wilson Rd, Waihi Beach. An evening sit-in and takeout burger bar perfect for a chilli burger and shake (closed Tues–Thurs).

Ti-Tree Café 14 Haszard St, Waihi. Small, cheerful licensed daytime eatery (till 3pm) with a pretty garden. Dinners served Fri–Sun.

Porch 23 Wilson Rd, Waihi Beach, ⓣ07/863 1330. Fine dining at a beach in an award-winning spot with a broad, imaginative menu and solicitous service. Dinner mains $18–26. Live music on Sun afternoons.

Waitete Orchard 31 Orchard Rd, Waihi. All food at this café and ice-creamery is home-made; their famous ice creams and fat-free sorbets are comprised of natural products made in a small on-site factory. By night they become a restaurant (mains $24–35) with a good wine list. Restaurant open Thurs–Sat from 6pm, café open Tues–Sun 10am–5pm.

Katikati and around

Waihi and the Karangahake Gorge mark the southern limit of the Coromandel Peninsula. From here on the coast begins to curl eastwards into the Bay of Plenty, leaving the bush-clad mountains behind to take on a gentler, more open aspect, with rolling hills divided by tall evergreen shelter belts that protect valuable hectares of kiwifruit vines. In summer, numerous roadside stalls spring up selling ripe fruit straight from the orchards, often at knockdown prices. It takes less then an hour to drive from Waihi to Tauranga, but you might pause a while over the murals of **Katikati**, 20km south of Waihi.

This ordinary little town was dealt a devastating economic blow when the price of kiwifruit collapsed in the late 1980s. It reacted by fashioning itself as "**Mural Town**", to catch passing tourist traffic. Colourful and well-painted murals have sprung up on buildings, many reflecting the heritage of the original settlers from Ulster: a couple of the best are "Waitekohe No. 3", on a block wall on the right as you enter the main street from the north, and the photo-realist "Central Motors", a little further along on the left. More information on the town is available in the **i-SITE visitor centre**, 36 Main Rd/SH2, in the council building (Mon–Fri 9am–4.30pm, Sat 9am–2pm, Sun 9.30am–2.30pm; ⓣ07/549 1658, ⓦwww.katikati.co.nz), where **buses** from Auckland stop.

For something to **eat**, head 8km south of Katikati on SH2 to *The Vineyard* in the Morton Estate winery (sales and tastings daily 9.30am–5pm; ⓣ0800/667 866, ⓦwww.mortonestateswines.co.nz). The restaurant offers well-presented lunches (summer Thurs–Sun) or dinner (year-round Thurs–Sat, reservations advised, ⓣ07/552 0620) and a chance to enjoy this charming spot, ringed by mountains and standing at the foot of a sloping **vineyard** with roses planted at the end of each row in classic French fashion. All the grape juice is tankered here from more extensive plantings in Hawke's Bay and Marlborough, allowing the production of a range of quality wines, and free tastings are offered.

The western Bay of Plenty

The western end of the **Bay of Plenty** centres on the prosperous port city of **Tauranga** ("safe anchorage") and its beachside acolyte, **Mount Maunganui**. This amorphous settlement, sprawled around the glittering tentacles of Tauranga Harbour, is one of the fastest-growing cities in the land. A combination of warm dry summers and mild winters initially attracted retirees, followed by telecommuters and folk running small businesses from home.

Visit outside the peak weeks of summer madness, when thousands of holidaying Kiwi children and their families clog the beaches, and the region's charms become more apparent – though you'll do best if you have access to the surrounding area. Mount Maunganui's appeal is limited to the beach and a couple of walks around its extinct volcano, although it shares a decent **restaurant** and **bar** scene with its larger neighbour. Tauranga is best used to get out on the water: trips primarily head to **Tuhua (Mayor) Island**, while boats also take clients to **swim with dolphins**, cruise the harbour, or on full-day **sailing trips**. If the weather prohibits such activity head for the new **art gallery**, a fine achievement for a city with practically no cultural ambitions.

Beyond the city limits are opportunities to go **kayaking**, ride horses or engage in more peaceful pursuits like **wine tasting**, or picnicking beside the swimming holes at **McLaren Falls**. Tauranga is in a major **kiwifruit-picking region**, but be warned, it's tough and prickly work and you must commit yourself to a minimum of three weeks (if this doesn't put you off, check out "Listings" on p.390).

Tauranga and Mount Maunganui

Once through the protecting ring of suburbs, it's apparent that rampant development hasn't spoilt central **TAURANGA**, which occupies a narrow peninsula with several city parks and gardens backing a lively waterfront area. Progress has been less kind to the over-commercialized beach resort of **MOUNT MAUNGANUI**, huddling under the extinct volcanic cone of the same name – a landmark visible throughout the western Bay of Plenty. "The Mount", as hill and town are often known, was once an island but is connected to the mainland by a narrow neck of dune sand (a tombolo), covered with apartment blocks, shops, restaurants and houses. The Mount's saving grace is the 20km-long golden strand of Ocean Beach, wonderful for swimming and surfing. No surprise, then, that the area's a big draw for Kiwi **holidaymakers** from mid-December to Easter (March or April) and on summer weekends, when Tauranga and Mount Maunganui can be overwhelming and accommodation hard to come by.

Arrival, information and transport

The **airport** receives daily Air New Zealand flights from Auckland and Wellington, and lies midway between Tauranga and Mount Maunganui, roughly 3km from each: a taxi to either costs around $20. **Buses** stop at the visitor centres in both towns, the Tauranga **i-SITE**, corner of Willow and Wharf stret (Mon–Fri 8.30am–5.30pm, Sat & Sun 9am–5pm; ⓣ07/578 8103, ⓦwww.tauranga.govt.nz), handles transport and accommodation bookings and sells maps. The Mount Maunganui **i-SITE** is on Salisbury Avenue, just off Maunganui Road (daily 9am–5pm; ⓣ07/575 5099, ⓦwww.bayplentynz.com). There is a **DOC office**, 253 Chadwick Rd, Greerton (Mon–Fri 8am–4.30pm; ⓣ07/578 7677), 6km south of central Tauranga. For topographic **maps**, try Absolute Adventure, 94 Willow St, by the visitor centre. You can avoid Tauranga's **metered parking** by choosing streets just outside the city centre.

Local transport

Timetables for the local **Bay Hopper Bus** (ⓣ0800/422 9287, ⓦwww.hopper.citynews.co.nz), running Monday to Saturday services covering most places in the immediate vicinity, including a half-hourly Tauranga–Mount Maunganui run ($6 all-day ticket from driver), are available in the i-SITEs. These dry up at around 6pm; after that you'll have to shell out for a taxi (up to $30), either from the **taxi** stand in Hamilton Street (between The Strand and Willow St) in Tauranga or by calling one of the radio-cab companies (see p.390). Spirit of Tauranga (ⓣ07/579 1325, ⓦwww.kiwicoastcruises.co.nz) run a ferry service from 9am (two hourly until 5.20pm; $8), to the Mount and back.

Accommodation

Tauranga offers a broader choice of accommodation at lower prices than **Mount Maunganui**. Alternatively, you might like to stay further afield at the

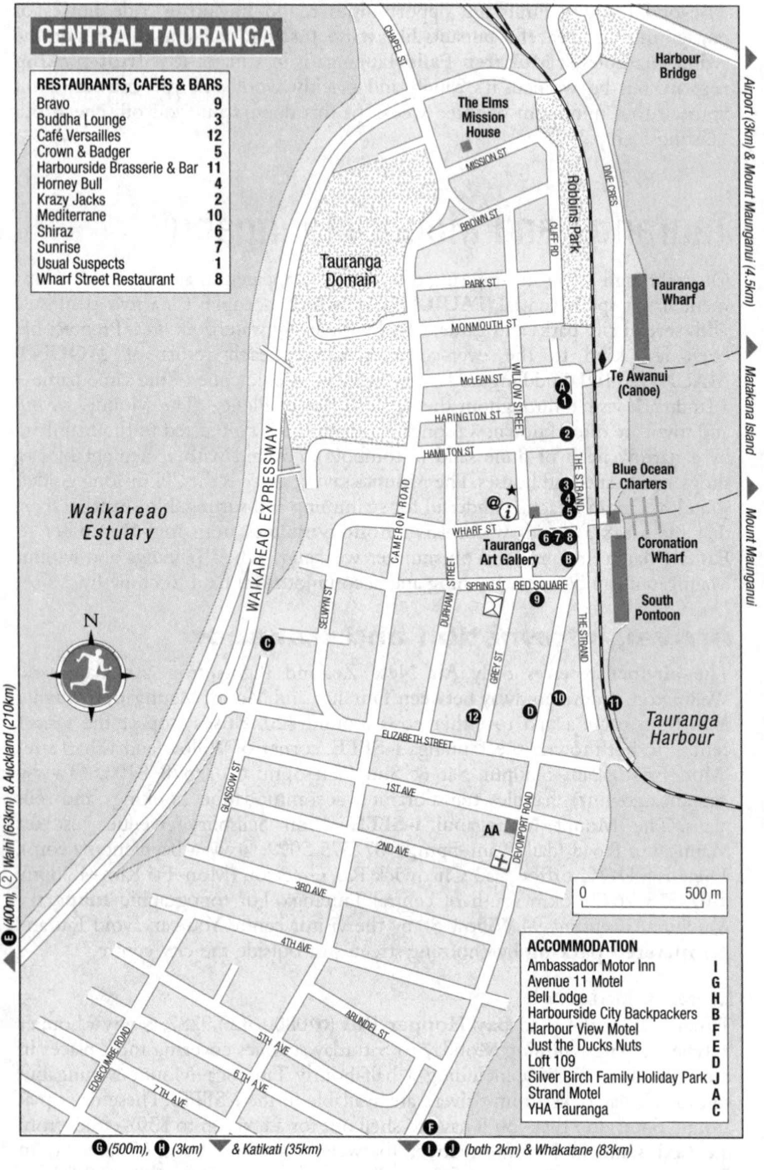

beachside campsites out of town – including Omokoroa to the west and Papamoa Beach to the east.

Tauranga

Tauranga has numerous **hostels** and **motels** within walking distance of the centre, and plenty more out in the suburbs. A plethora of motels line 15th Avenue, some offering good deals at slack times of year.

Motels & B&B

Ambassador Motor Inn 9 15th Ave ⓣ0800/735 294, ⓦwww.ambassador-motorinn.co.nz. See map, p.392. A 5min drive from the city centre, near the estuary, this has popular, well-equipped budget units and more luxurious options. There's a heated pool, some rooms have a spa bath, and some river views. ❹

Avenue 11 Motel 26 11th Ave ⓣ07/577 1881, ⓦwww.avenue11.co.nz. See map, p.392. Great-value boutique motel in a central but quiet location overlooking a small park and part of the harbour, with four spacious, sumptuously decorated units (with good views). Extra touches include personalized service, bathrobes and a spa. ❸

Harbour View Motel 7 5th Ave East ⓣ07/578 8621, ⓦwww.harbourviewmotel.co.nz. Quiet and homely, just 10min walk from town and a stone's throw from the bay, with spa and free kayaks. Ideal for families. ❹

Strand Motel Corner of The Strand & McLean St ⓣ07/578 5807, ⓦwww.strandmotel.co.nz. Budget, central and near the waterfront, but on a fairly noisy corner. You get sea views from the decks of most of the fully equipped units. ❸

Hostels & campsites

Bell Lodge 39 Bell St, off Waihi Rd (take Otumoetai exit off SH2) ⓣ07/578 6344, ⓦwww.bell-lodge.co.nz. See map, p.392. A clean, modern and comfortable hostel in a peaceful spot 4km from the centre, with spacious dorms, comfortable en-suite rooms and some motel units. Excellent facilities include BBQ, free pick-up and a free daily shuttle to Mount Maunganui on request, departing at 10am. Tent sites $18, dorms $25, rooms ❷, units ❸

Harbourside City Backpackers 105 The Strand ⓣ07/579 4066, ⓦwww.backpacktauranga.co.nz. Large hostel in the middle of it all. The waterfront views and tranquil atmosphere of the rooftop garden make up for the basic rooms and noise on Fri & Sat nights. A popular hostel for fruit-pickers, with job-seeking assistance given. Dorms $23, rooms ❷

Just the Ducks Nuts 6 Vale St ⓣ07/576 1366, ⓦwww.justtheducksnuts.co.nz. See map, p.392. A small, friendly hostel 1.5km from the city centre, with great views of the harbour and the Mount, free bikes, free pick-ups and harbour views. Dorms $21, rooms ❷

Loft 109 109 Devonport Rd ⓣ07/579 5638, ⓦwww.loft109.co.nz. Little yet central, friendly hostel with a roof deck and nautical decor. Dorms $23, rooms ❷

Silver Birch Family Holiday Park 101 Turret Rd ⓣ07/578 4603, ⓦwww.silverbirch.co.nz. See map, p.392. Fairly central campsite right on the river's edge with a family atmosphere, playground and thermal pools. Tent sites $14, cabins ❷, units ❸, park motels ❸

YHA Tauranga 171 Elizabeth St ⓣ07/578 5064, ⓦwww.yha.org.nz. Well-equipped, modern and welcoming hostel in secluded grounds 5min walk from the centre, with BBQ, volleyball and mini-golf. Tent sites $18, dorms $25, rooms ❷

Mount Maunganui

Much of the accommodation here is geared towards long-staying Kiwi holiday-makers, but you'll also find several **motels** and a couple of **hostels**. The following places are marked on the map on p.387.

Belle Mer 53 Marine Parade ⓣ0800/100 235, ⓦwww.bellemer.co.nz. Plush apartments for 4–6 with modern decor, just across the road from the beach. All have spa baths, luxurious kitchens, stereo and access to a heated lap pool. ❽

Mount Backpackers 87 Maunganui Rd ⓣ07/575 0860, ⓦwww.mountbackpackers.co.nz. Small hostel right in the thick of things – close to restaurants, bars and the beach. Low-cost bike and boogie-board rental and job-seeking help. Dorms $25, rooms ❷

Mount Maunganui Beachside Holiday Park 1 Adams Ave ⓣ07/575 4471, ⓦwww.mountainbeachside.co.nz. A sizeable, terraced, well-equipped campsite very close to the beach in a pleasant spot beside the hot saltwater pools, right at the foot of the Mount. Camping $40 per site.

Pacific Coast Lodge 432 Maunganui Rd ⓣ0800/666 622, ⓦwww.pacificcoastlodge.co.nz. Vast hostel with good facilities (spacious dorms, large kitchen, games room, BBQ area) and a strong recycling ethic, although it is a fair way from the restaurants and the fashionable end of the beach. Dorms $24, rooms ❸

The city centre

Tauranga's flat **city centre** is concentrated between Tauranga Harbour and Waikareao Estuary. It's a dense kernel of shops, restaurants and bars where you'll

The Battle of Gate Pa

In 1864 the tiny community of Tauranga became the scene of the **Battle of Gate Pa**, one of the most decisive engagements of the **New Zealand Wars**. In January the government sent troops to build two redoubts, hoping to prevent supplies and reinforcements from reaching the followers of the Maori King (see p.247), who were fighting in the Waikato. Most of the local Ngaiterangi hurried back from the Waikato and challenged the soldiers from a *pa* they quickly built near an entrance to the mission land, which became known as Gate Pa. In April, government troops surrounded the *pa* in what was New Zealand's only naval blockade, and pounded it with artillery. Despite this, the British lost about a third of their assault force and at nightfall the Ngaiterangi slipped through the British lines to fight again in the Waikato.

find just about everything you need, but little of abiding interest other than boat trips onto the bay and its islands (see p.387) and the art gallery. You can easily spend half a day checking out exhibitions, strolling along the waterfront or mooching about minor sights.

First stop should be the new **Tauranga Art Gallery**, opened after a determined fifteen-year campaign to give the city a contemporary cultural attraction; sadly the accompanying museum was lost to council cuts. Sited in an old bank on the corner of Wharf and Willow streets, 108 Willow St (daily 10am–4.30pm, donation; ⓣ07/578 7933, ⓦwww.artgallery.org.nz), the building has been described by local wags as a nuclear bunker or the armadillo. Inside it's a clean-lined, fit for purpose, modern series of display spaces over two floors, intended to house travelling exhibitions, both national and international, depending what is on the circuit.

Next stop is the ornately carved traditional **war canoe**, *Te Awanui*, in a shelter on the corner of Dive Crescent and McLean Street; still used on ceremonial occasions on the harbour. About one block up and entered from Cliff Street **Robbins Park** (dawn–dusk; free), is a swathe of green decorated by a rose garden and begonia house, and yielding fine views of Mount Maunganui. At the northern end of town, on Mission Street, **The Elms Mission House** (Wed, Sat & Sun 2–4pm, and by appointment on ⓣ07/577 9772; $5) is one of the country's oldest homes, built from kauri between 1835 and 1847 by an early missionary, Archdeacon A.N. Brown, who tended the wounded of both sides during the **Battle of Gate Pa** (see above). The house has maintained its original form complete with dark-wood interior and a dining table at which Brown entertained several British officers on the eve of the Battle of Gate Pa, little suspecting that over the next few days he would bury all of them.

Mount Maunganui

The eastern end of the 3.5km-long Tauranga Harbour Bridge is 3km from the heart of **Mount Maunganui**, reached through an industrial estate. Things improve at the northern tip where the 232-metre Mount (Mauao in Maori) rises above the golden **beach**, an unbroken sweep stretching more than 20km east to Papamoa (see p.391) and beyond. It's habitually sun-kissed in summer, and condos and apartments have colonized the beach's fashionable northern kilometre. The Mount also has a reputation as a party town, especially at New Year, while the beach is still great, perfect for a day or two of volleyball and swimming, but within easy reach of good restaurants and bars where everyone gravitates for sundowners.

If you fancy trying your hand at **surfing**, wander along to 24 Pacific Avenue, where teachers at Assault (ⓣ07/575 7831, ⓦwww.assault.co.nz)

conduct one-hour **lessons** ($25) and provide equipment rental (boards $10 per hr, wet suit $5 per hr). They also offer bodyboards, windsurfing and kite-boarding instruction and equipment, and can advise on surf conditions. **Sea kayakers** should contact Oceanix (ⓣ07/572 2236, ⓦwww.oceanix.co.nz; $85–$95), who head out from the i-SITE for both daytime and evening trips: the latter are more spectacular as the town lights illuminate the water.

Apart from the beach, the big draw is the mountain itself, which has a fine **walking track** around the base (3km loop; 45min), mostly level and offering a sea and harbour outlook from under the shade of ancient pohutukawas. The base track links with a **hike to the summit** (2km one way; 1hr), tough going towards the top but well worth the effort for views of Matakana Island and along the coast. Both tracks start at the northern end of the beach, right by the outdoor, chlorinated **Hot Saltwater Pools**, Adams Avenue (Mon–Sat 6am–9.45pm, Sun 8am–9.45pm; public pool $9, private spa $13 per half-hour; use of towel $3; ⓣ07/575 0868), Mount Maunganui's other main attraction, best visited out of season when it is at its most relaxing.

Cruises and day-trips

The main reason to come to the western Bay of Plenty is to get **on the water**. A full range of boats is ready to take you cruising, fishing, sailing, parasailing and swimming with dolphins.

The island retreat Tuhua (Mayor) is a prime Bay of Plenty boat-trip destination, a cone-shaped dormant volcano, protruding from the Bay of Plenty 40km off the coast of Tauranga, increasingly geared towards eco-tourism.

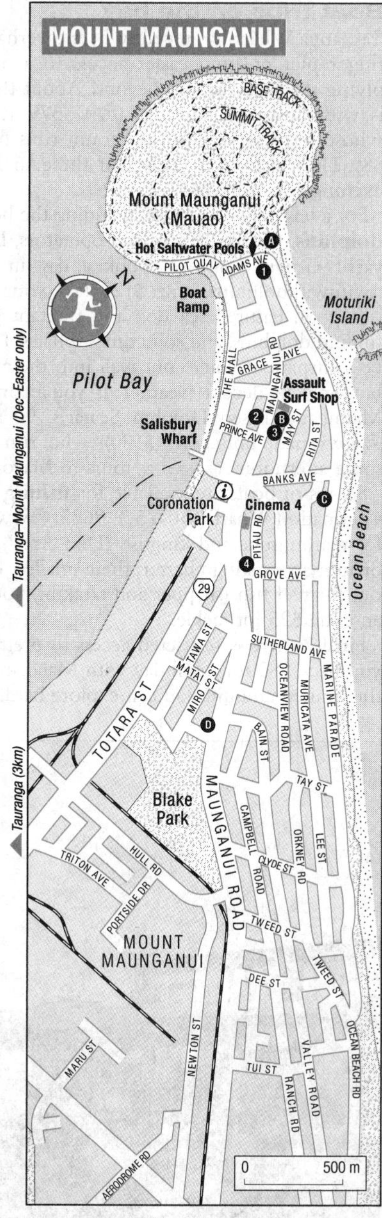

ACCOMMODATION		RESTAURANTS & BARS	
Belle Mer	C	Astrolabe	2
Mount Backpackers	B	Mount Mellick	4
Mount Manganui Beachside Holiday Park	A	Sidetrack Café Pacifica	1
Pacific Coast Lodge	D	Volantis	3

Boat trips on the bay

Tauranga Wharf has recently been overhauled, with a barge converted into a finger pier creating easier access to a number of trips and a ferry service plying the harbour and beyond. About the cheapest way to get on the water is with Spirit of Tauranga (ⓣ07/579 1325, ⓦwww.kiwicoastcruises.co.nz), whose ferry service to the mount runs from 9am (two hourly until 5.20pm; $8). They also offer cruises of three to four hours ($400 for the boat) and evening trips for $60.

For a leisurely day at sea, including the bonus of seeing and **swimming with dolphins**, try the best of the operators, Butler's Swim with Dolphins on the yacht *Gemini Galaxsea* (book a day in advance ⓣ0508/288 537, ⓦwww.swimwithdolphins.co.nz; $125, take your own lunch). Skipper Graham Butler is a good-natured sea dog and militant greenie with a high success rate of finding dolphins, and sometimes whales. He allows plenty of time and it won't be a surprise if you're out well into the afternoon. Trips run most of the year, but only in decent weather. If you're on a really tight schedule, try Mount Maunganui-based Dolphin Seafaris, 90 Maunganui Rd (ⓣ0800/326 8747, ⓦwww.nzdolphin.com; $120), who run half-day trips in the morning and some afternoons, as well as tours to Mayor Island (see p.389).

Scores of boats are available for **fishing charters**; try Blue Ocean Charters, Coronation Wharf (ⓣ07/578 9685, ⓦwww.blueocean.co.nz) for game fishing for marlin, tuna and kingfish (Dec–April), which involves chartering the boat, or join an existing charter; their smallest boat costs $1200 a day, but if you go out for reef fish (snapper and tarakihi) you'll pay around $80 per person, with an extra $25 for tackle.

Finally, there is restricted access to pretty **Matakana Island**. A tour will set you back $83 for a full day with Matakana Island Tours (ⓣ0800/276 391) but the limited amount you can explore hardly makes it worthwhile.

▲ Eating out in Tauranga

Tuhua (Mayor) Island

TUHUA (Mayor) ISLAND is a dormant volcano, its crater virtually overgrown and a third of its coast designated a **marine reserve**. There are some great **walking tracks** around the island's base and through its centre, and boats coming out here will rent out snorkelling gear (around $20 per day) so you can explore the aquatic world. **Wasps** are abundant, however, and anyone allergic to stings should pack medication or stay away.

Tuhua Island is privately owned by the Tuhua Trust Board, and day visitors are charged a **landing fee** ($5 plus $6 if you are camping). Both Dolphin Safaris (see p.389) and Blue Ocean Charters (see p.389) run trips, though you'll need to contact them to establish what days they are going. Marine-reserve **diving** trips are run by Dolphin Seafaris (above, $120), while Blue Ocean run day-trips to the island for $105, or $132 including an overnight stay.

Eating

Tauranga and Mount Maunganui have fully embraced modern café/bar culture, Tauranga in particular rating as something of a regional culinary hotspot. The distinctions between eating and drinking places are blurring and you may well find yourself enjoying a drink at one of the places listed below. There's also a Saturday morning farmers' **market** from 8am, at the Compass Community Village, 17th Avenue West in Tauranga.

Most of **Tauranga**'s cafés and restaurants are in the centre – notably along Devonport Road and The Strand and the streets running back from it. A little further afield, the western suburb of Bethlehem is home to a popular winery restaurant. **Mount Maunganui** doesn't have Tauranga's selection, but you can find something appealing on the half-dozen blocks of Maunganui Road that make up the centre, or on the waterfront strip by the mount in the lee of apartment buildings.

Tauranga and Bethlehem

Bravo Red Square ⓣ07/578 4700. Cool urban café and restaurant that spills onto the pedestrianized Red Square. An energizing spot for breakfast, gourmet snacks and pizzas, or dinner (mains for around $30). Book for a lunchtime table outdoors in summer.

Café Versailles 107 Grey St ⓣ07/571 1480. Award-winning traditional French restaurant serving a wonderful range of Gallic fare from snails to bouillabaisse, taking in several inspired standards along the way, all fabulously presented with a glass of home-grown cabernet.

Harbourside Brasserie & Bar Under the railway bridge at the southern end of The Strand ⓣ07/571 0520. A big, airy restaurant and bar right on the harbour, with great views and a covered deck over the water. Lively, cosmopolitan ambience and food, with lunch and dinner (mains averaging $40), as well as cheaper light meals and weekend breakfast. Book ahead for a table on the deck or just drop in for a beer.

Mediterrane Café and Restaurant (aka The Med) 60 Devonport Rd. Popular daytime café with moderately priced salads, sandwiches and paninis (from $12) and some outdoor seating. Try the gorgeous, home-made honey-crunch muesli with fruit and yoghurt.

Mills Reef Restaurant 143 Moffat Rd, Bethlehem ⓣ07/576 8800. See map, p.392. Highly regarded winery restaurant in an elevated position that's Tauranga's favourite brunch and lunch spot – or just pop in for coffee and a cake. There's live music outdoors every summer Sun lunchtime. Open till 3pm.

Shiraz 12 Wharf St ⓣ07/577 0059. Tasty Middle Eastern and Mediterranean food, excellent service and reasonable prices for lunch and dinner mean reservations are recommended. The small café and covered courtyard and helpful staff make this a great spot for a leisurely meal. Closed Sun.

Sunrise 10 Wharf St. Intimate, friendly, funky and very popular licensed café where good breakfast standards vie with tasty chowder, salads and home-made cakes and slices. Open 7am–4pm with occasional summer Sat evening events that include live music. Closed Sun.

Wharf Street Restaurant Corner of Wharf St & The Strand ⓣ07/578 8322. Upper-floor brasserie and bar, with great views over the harbour, open for lunch (Mon–Fri only) and dinner (mains $29 upwards).

Mount Maunganui

Astrolabe 82 Maunganui Rd. Large, popular diner-cum-drinking hole, with a beachy vibe and lively evening crowds at the weekend. Open for brunch, lunch and dinner, with salads and pasta, chargrilled steak and fish, and a large range of beers.

Sidetrack Café Pacifica Marine Parade, under the Twin Towers. A great place to go for breakfast or morning coffee, when you can gaze across the beach to the ocean in the warming early sun. Also open for lunch.

Volantis 105 Maunganui Rd. One of the best spots on the strip for a casual coffee, or snacks along the lines of gourmet burgers and paninis, with several vegetarian options. Liqueur shots accompany some of the highly extravagant sundaes. Dinner mains $19–30. Licensed & BYO.

Drinking, nightlife and entertainment

Neither town pumps in the off season but Tauranga currently holds the clubbing baton with summer revelry continuing into the small hours along The Strand and at a few venues nearby at weekends. In both Tauranga and Maunganui most restaurants double as **bars**.

Films are shown at Cinema 8 on Elizabeth Street in Tauranga (infoline ⓣ07/577 0800) and the new Rialto Cinema, Goddard Centre, 21 Devonport St (infoline ⓣ07/577 0445). Screening times are listed in *Bay of Plenty Times*, the best source of entertainment **listings**.

For something different, consider a visit to **Paparoa Marae**, Paparoa Road, 15km west ofTauranga (ⓣ07/552 5904, ⓔpaparoamarae@ihug.co.nz) Performances are for groups only (or when there's a cruise ship in town), but you might be able to tag along, and evening events may include a *hangi*.

Clubs and bars

Buddha Lounge 61b The Strand. This small but cool venue with a balcony reverberates to soul, house and drum 'n' bass till 3am, with alluring sofas upstairs. Can be a bit of a squeeze on a Fri or Sat night.

Crown & Badger Corner of The Strand & Wharf St. Lively (sometimes frenetic) English pub with a good range of beers and pub-style meals, mostly for around $15.

Horney Bull 67 The Strand. Texan-style food keeps energy levels up at this jolly and often-packed bar.

Krazy Jacks 47 The Strand. Popular restaurant and bar with regular music events: acoustic evenings (Wed), electric jam nights (Thurs), live local talent (most Fridays) and a covers band (Sat). Open 4pm–3am.

Mount Mellick 317 Maunganui Rd. Popular and friendly Irish bar with well-priced food and an exciting calendar of events including courtyard cricket, jam nights, live music, quiz nights and big-screen sports.

Usual Suspects Corner of Hamilton St & The Strand. Bouncy bar with live music Wed–Sat, the music kicking off about 10pm, plus the *Sugar Bar* upstairs, open the same nights with DJ-inspired poppy bopping.

Listings

Buses InterCity and Newmans (both at the i-SITE) run several daily services to Auckland, Hamilton, Rotorua and Thames (via Katikati, Waihi and Paeroa). Go Kiwi (ⓣ07/866 0336) run daily services in summer to Auckland, Hamilton and Rotorua, with limited services in winter.

Internet access Tauranga Library, in the Civic Shopping Centre behind the visitor centre (Mon–Fri 9.30am–5.30pm, Sat 9.30am–4pm, Sun 12.30–4pm).

Kiwifruit picking The best time for picking is late April to mid-June, but pruning is also necessary from mid-June to early Sept and again from end of Oct to Jan. For picking, you're paid by the bin or by the kilo, so speed is of the essence. The best sources of up-to-date information are the backpacker hostels, which will often help you to find work.

Medical treatment After-hours medical care and an emergency pharmacy is available at the Baycare Medical Service Centre, corner of Edgecumbe Rd & Tenth Ave ⓣ07/578 8111; Mon–Fri 5pm–8am, Sat & Sun 24hr.

Taxis Citicabs ⓣ07/577 0999; Tauranga Taxis and Mount Taxis are the same company ⓣ07/578 6086.

Tours The Touring Company (ⓣ07/577 0057, ⓦwww.newzealandadventure.co.nz), offer a variety of North Island tours, including one that leaves from the i-SITE covering Tauranga and its Gate Pa heritage, heading as far as the murals of Katitkati ($79).

Around Tauranga

Unless you're happy spending days on the beach you'll soon exhaust the temptations of Tauranga and Mount Maunganui. Help is at hand in the hinterland, where **Mills Reef winery** drapes across fertile countryside, backed by the angular peaks of the Kaimai-Mamaku Forest Park. Rivers, cascading down the slopes and across the coastal plain, supply water for assorted activities at **Waimarino Adventure Park**, and periodically fire up **McLaren Falls**, where shallow rock pools make excellent swimming holes. At the coast, the long sweep of Mount Maunganui's Ocean Beach extends to **Papamoa Beach**, great for surfing and swimming away from the glitz of the Mount.

Bethlehem: Mills Reef winery and Waimarino Adventure Park

The suburb of **Bethlehem** is home to the Art Deco-style **tasting rooms** at Mills Reef, 143 Moffat Rd (daily 10am–5pm; Ⓦwww.millsreef.co.nz), where you can sample (free), and purchase some of the excellent Reserve Chardonnay or the Rieslings, Sauvignons and Merlots. There's a classy on-site restaurant open for brunch and lunch (see p.389).

Wine tasting could work as a perfect finale to a half-day spent at the riverside **Waimarino Adventure Park**, 36 Taniwha Place (daily 10am–6pm; ⓣ07/576 4233, Ⓦwww.waimarino.com), where water-based courses and activities are the order of the day. The most accessible are the **kayaking** trips, the Wairoa River Trip (3hr; $75), a tide-assisted and unguided flat-water paddle down a lower stretch of the Wairoa River to the adventure park; or a three-hour glow-worm version. Booking is essential.

McLaren Falls

Most summer Sundays, **McLaren Falls**, signposted 11km south of Tauranga off SH29, becomes the scene of frenetic activity as hundreds of rafters and kayakers congregate to run the Grade IV–V rapids of the Wairoa River. Pretty much every day of the summer, meanwhile, locals flock here to wallow in a lovely series of shallow pools hewn out of the bedrock. It can get crowded, but a few minutes' rock-hopping should secure you a pool to yourself: bring a picnic and sunscreen.

Papamoa Beach

Mount Maunganui's stunning Ocean Beach stretches 20km east to **Papamoa Beach**, a burgeoning community accessed off SH2. Backed by the dramatic Papamoa Hills, it makes a pleasant spot for a beach break away from the city, facilitated by *Papamoa Beach Top 10 Holiday Park* in the domain at the eastern end of Papamoa Beach Road (ⓣ07/572 0816, Ⓦwww.papamoabeach.co.nz; camping $20, cabins ❸, units ❹, four-bed villas ❻ and park motel units ❻). Accommodation ranges from beachfront campsites to waterside villas, all near the shops. The licensed, nautically themed *Bluebiyou* café/restaurant next door has a covered deck overlooking the sea just metres away, and serves light meals, lunch, dinner and weekend brunch.

Papamoa is also home to the world's only purpose-built **blokart speedway track** at Blokart Heaven, 176 Parton Rd (15min $15, 30min $30, 60min $50; ⓣ07/572 4256, Ⓦwww.blokartheaven.co.nz): think go-kart with a sail. Tuition is offered, and with a fair wind you can get up to 60km; naturally it's weather-dependent, so no wind equals no fun.

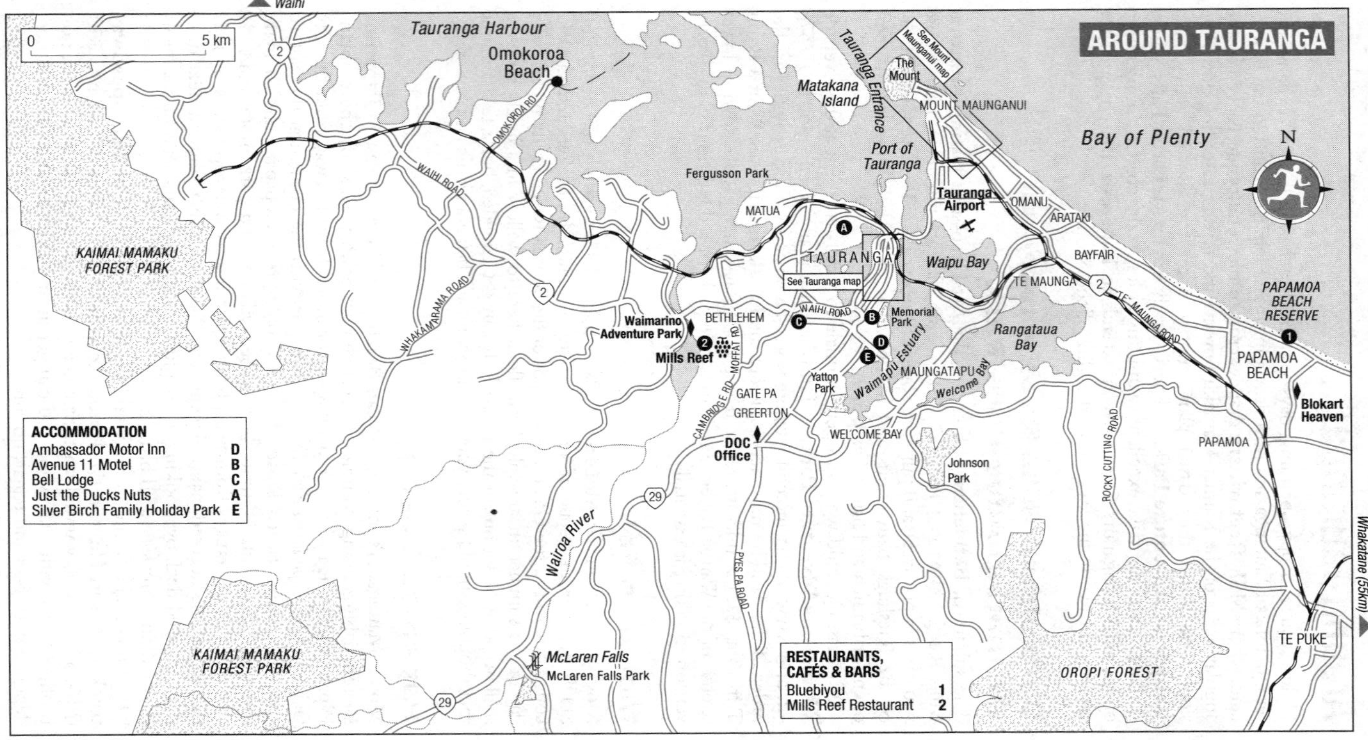
AROUND TAURANGA
Waihi
0 5 km
Tauranga Harbour
Omokoroa Beach
OMOKOROA RD
Matakana Island
Tauranga Entrance
The Mount
See Mount Maunganui map
MOUNT MAUNGANUI
Bay of Plenty
N
Port of Tauranga
Fergusson Park
Tauranga Airport
OMANU
ARATAKI
MATUA
TAURANGA
See Tauranga map
Waipu Bay
BAYFAIR
TE MAUNGA
TE MAUNGA ROAD
PAPAMOA BEACH RESERVE
WAIHI ROAD
KAIMAI MAMAKU FOREST PARK
WHAKAMARAMA ROAD
Waimarino Adventure Park
BETHLEHEM
Mills Reef
MOFFAT RD
Memorial Park
Rangataua Bay
Waimapu Estuary
MAUNGATAPU
Welcome Bay
Yatton Park
GATE PA
GREERTON
CAMBRIDGE RD
DOC Office
WELCOME BAY
Johnson Park
ROCKY CUTTING ROAD
PAPAMOA BEACH
Blokart Heaven
PAPAMOA
Wairoa River
PYES PA ROAD
Whakatane (55km)
TE PUKE
McLaren Falls
McLaren Falls Park
OROPI FOREST
ACCOMMODATION
Ambassador Motor Inn D
Avenue 11 Motel B
Bell Lodge C
Just the Ducks Nuts A
Silver Birch Family Holiday Park E
RESTAURANTS, CAFÉS & BARS
Bluebiyou 1
Mills Reef Restaurant 2

The eastern Bay of Plenty

Moving away from Tauranga toward the **eastern Bay of Plenty**, along the Pacific Coast Highway, the urban influence wanes, the pace slows and everything seems more rural, with orchards and kiwifruit vines gradually giving way to sheep country. You'll also find a gradual change in the racial mix, for the eastern Bay of Plenty is mostly Maori country; appropriate since some of the first **Maori** to reach New Zealand arrived here in their great *waka* (war canoes). In fact Whakatane is sometimes known as the birthplace of Aotearoa, for it was here that the Polynesian navigator **Toi te Huatahi** first landed.

The westernmost town, **Te Puke**, is very much New Zealand's kiwifruit capital, and is well inland, but the sea is still the focus of the region. The heyday of its port has long passed, but **Whakatane** remains the largest town, prettily set between cliffs and a river estuary. It makes a great base for forays to volcanic **White Island** or the bird reserve of **Whale Island**. Further east, **Opotiki** is the gateway to the East Cape in one direction, and Gisborne in the other, as well as providing access to interesting walks in the hills to the south and to trips on the remote and scenic **Motu River**.

Te Puke

Te Puke, 31km southeast of Tauranga on SH2, is justifiably billed as the "kiwifruit capital of the world", a claim driven home at **Kiwi360**, 6km east of Te Puke (daily 9am–5pm; 45min guided tours $20; ⓣ0800/549 4360, ⓦwww.kiwi360.com), a massive orchard and processing plant that also operates as a horticultural theme park. A giant, surreal slice of kiwifruit stands near the gateway. The complex is as tacky and commercialized as you would expect, but it's the only place to be if you're curious about how these little green, furry fruits (and their gold counterparts) grow and are harvested.

From Te Puke it's 66km along SH2 to Whakatane, the road hugging the coast for some of the way.

Whakatane and around

The main settlement of the eastern Bay of Plenty is **WHAKATANE**, a 14,000-strong town sprawled across flat farmland around the last convulsions of the Whakatane River. The dull suburbs surround a vaguely attractive centre wedged between the river and bush-clad hills that rise steeply from the town. The town itself has little to recommend it but that is about to change, with the re-erection of the **Great Carved House** and its interpretation centre. The remainder of Whakatane's real appeal lies off the coast, either swimming with **dolphins**, or on trips to the bird sanctuary of **Whale Island** and volcanic **White Island**, which billows plumes of steam into the sky. Back on land, there are walks along the spine of hills above the town and to the viewpoint at **Kohi Point**, and you can body-surf and sunbathe at **Ohope Beach**.

The Whakatane area has had more than its fair share of dramatic events. The **Maori** word *Whakatane* means "to act as a man" and comes from a legendary incident when the women of the *Mataatua* canoe were left aboard while the men went ashore; the canoe began to drift out to sea, but touching the paddles was *tapu* for women. Undeterred, the high-spirited Wairaka paddled back to the safety of the shore, shouting *Ka Whakatane Au i Ah au* ("I will deport myself as a man"); a statue at Whakatane Heads commemorates her heroic act. The first **Europeans** to set foot in the area, apart from a brief sortie by Cook, were flax traders in the early 1800s and a trader called Philip Tapsell, who established a store in 1830. The next turning point in Whakatane's history came in March 1865, when missionary **Carl Völkner** was killed at Opotiki, and a government agent, **James Falloon**, arrived to investigate. At this unwelcome intrusion, supporters of a fanatical Maori sect, the Hau Hau, attacked Falloon's vessel, killing him and his crew. In response, the government declared **martial law**, and by the end of the year a large part of the Bay of Plenty had been confiscated and Whakatane was a military settlement. The memory of this led **Te Kooti** (see p.426) to choose Whakatane as his target for a full-scale attack by his Maori force in 1869, burning and looting buildings before being driven back into the hills of Urewera. In more **recent times**, Whakatane has led a relatively quiet life as a trading area and service town for the surrounding regions, and as a jumping-off point for many areas of natural beauty.

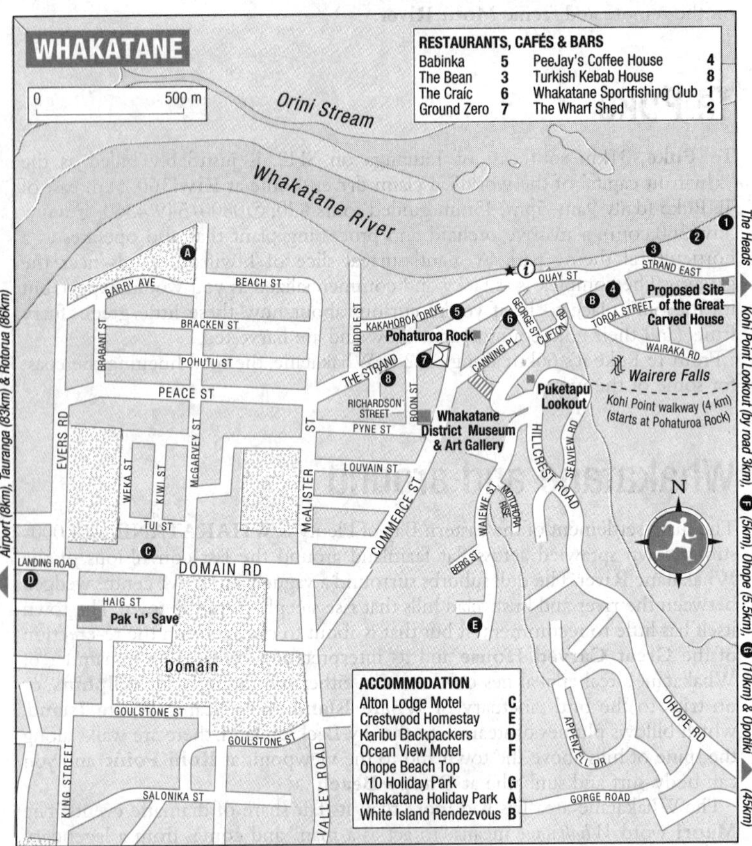

Arrival, information and transport

Long-distance **buses** running along SH2 between Rotorua and Gisborne stop once a day in each direction outside the **i-SITE visitor centre**, corner of Quay Street and Kakahoroa Drive (Christmas–March Mon–Fri 8am–6pm, Sat & Sun 9am–5pm; April–Christmas Mon–Fri 8am–5pm, Sat & Sun 10am–4pm; ⓣ07/308 6058, ⓦwww.whakatane.com), which is well stocked with DOC leaflets for the local area and offers free **Internet access**. The **post office**, corner of Commerce Street and The Strand (ⓣ07/307 1155), has poste restante facilities. Whakatane **airport** receives several flights daily from Auckland and is about 10km west of the centre, connected by the Dial-A-Cab shuttle (ⓣ0800/308 0222; around $25). A **local bus** service is run by Eastern Bay (ⓣ0800/422 9287, ⓦwww.baybus.co.nz) to Tauranga and Mount Maunganui (Mon–Sat), Ohope (Mon–Sat), Opotiki (Mon & Wed) and Kawerau (Mon & Wed).

Accommodation

There's a reasonable selection of **accommodation** in Whakatane, much firmly mid-range with a preference for motels, although you might prefer a campsite or B&B at Ohope Beach.

Alton Lodge Motel 76 Domain Rd ⓣ0800/425 866, ⓦwww.altonlodge.co.nz. Comfortable motel with eleven spacious kitchen units and a heated indoor pool. 4

Crestwood Homestay 2 Crestwood Rise ⓣ07/308 7554, ⓦwww.crestwood-homestay.co.nz. Attractive, friendly B&B in a quiet hilltop setting with scenic views, 20min walk from the town centre. Stay in the twin or double. 4

Karibu Backpackers 13 Landing Rd ⓣ07/307 8276, ⓦwww.karibubackpackers.co.nz. Suburban house converted into a big, well-maintained and welcoming hostel 1.5km from the town centre, with an attractive garden for camping and off-street parking, plus free bikes and free pick-up from the bus stop. Tent sites $14, dorms $24, rooms 2

Ocean View Motel West End, Ohope Beach ⓣ07/312 5665, ⓦwww.oceanviewmotel.co.nz. Relaxing motel at the western end of the beach, with safe swimming, bushwalks and s/c units. 3

Ohope Beach Top 10 Holiday Park Harbour Rd, Ohope, 10km east of Whakatane ⓣ07/312 4460, ⓦwww.ohopebeach.co.nz. Upmarket holiday park right behind Ohope Beach at the eastern end of Ohope, with a pool complex, camping ($18) and a range of cabins & kitchen cabins. Cabins 3, s/c units 3, motel units 4, luxury apartments 6

Whakatane Holiday Park McGarvey Rd ⓣ07/308 8694, ⓦwww.whakataneholiidaypark.co.nz. A reasonable, sheltered campsite 10min walk from The Strand. Tent sites $15, cabins 2 kitchen cabins 2 s/c units 3

White Island Rendezvous 15 Strand East ⓣ0800/242 299, ⓦwww.whiteisland.co.nz. Spotless, big modern motel in a quiet yet central location. Some rooms have spa baths, and all are equipped with Sky TV and microwave. There's also a peaceful cottage in a renovated villa, sleeping five (and at the lower end of the 7 price bracket). Disabled needs are well catered for. 4

The Town

Driving into Whakatane, Commerce Street hugs cliffs that were once lapped by the sea. The junction with The Strand is effectively the town centre, marked by Whakatane's defining feature, a large rock outcrop called **Pohaturoa** ("long rock"). The place is sacred to Maori and the small park surrounding the rock contains carved benches and a black marble monument to Te Hurinui Apanui, a great chief who propounded the virtues of peace and is mourned by Pakeha and Maori alike. The site was once a shrine where Maori rites were performed, and the seed that grew into the karaka trees at the rock's base is said to have arrived on the *Mataatua* canoe. From here, it is a three-minute walk along Canning Place, then Clifton Road and Toroa Street, to the base of **Wairere Falls** from where you can rejoin The Strand and stroll a 1km section of the

▲ Statue of Wairaka, Whakatane Heads

four-kilometre **river walk** to the heads, a lovely late-afternoon stroll that passes a replica of the *Mataatua waka* in a reserve (also reached by car along Muriwai Drive), and a sprightly bronze statue of Wairaka on a rock.

Back in town, the **Whakatane District Museum and Gallery** (Mon–Fri 10am–4.30pm, Sat & Sun 11am–3pm; donation; Ⓦwww.whakatanemuseum.org.nz) lies on Boon Street. One room is packed with well-conceived displays on geological, Maori and European history: the house collection is rich and varied with over 30,000 photographs and an important collection of Maori *taonga* (treasures) from the local *iwi*, tracing their descent from the *Mataatua* canoe. The others host travelling exhibitions.

The **Great Carved House**, Mataatua of Whakatane, will (from 2009) be a fascinating opportunity to visit the "lost marae", a meeting house beautifully carved to restore the pride of the local *iwi* after a disastrous campaign in the

Whakatane's islands

Whale Island

Whale Island (Motohora), 10km offshore from Whakatane, is a DOC-controlled haven where considerable efforts were made decades ago to eradicate goats and rats. Native bush is rapidly returning and the island has become a bird reserve and safe environment for saddlebacks, grey-faced petrels, sooty shearwaters, little blue penguins, dotterels and oystercatchers, as well as three species of lizard – geckos and speckled and copper skinks – and the reptilian tuatara; occasional visits are made by the North Island kaka and falcon, as well as fur seals.

Access to the island is on one of a variety of **guided tours** (between Dec and mid-Feb) that depart from Whakatane, run by a number of operators, the best of which are Dive Works Charters ($90, 4–5hr, see p.398) and White Island Tours ($60, 4hr, see p.398).

White Island

Many people ignore Whale Island in favour of the more obvious and spectacular attractions of **White Island** (Whaakari), named by Cook for its permanent shroud of mist and steam. Over twice the size of Whale Island, White Island lies 50km offshore, sometimes a rough ride. Neither this nor its seething vulcanism deters visitors, who flock to appreciate its desolate, other-worldly landscape, with billowing towers of gas, steam and ash spewing from a crater lake sixty metres below sea level. They marvel at the smaller fumaroles surrounded by bright yellow and white crystal deposits that re-form in new and bizarre shapes each day. The crystal-clear and abundant waters around the island make this one of the best **dive** spots in New Zealand.

Whaakari embodies the ongoing clash between the Indo-Australian Plate and the Pacific Plate that has been driven beneath it for the last two million years. This resulted in the upward thrust of super-heated rock through the ocean floor, creating a massive **volcanic** structure. **Sulphur**, for use in fertilizer manufacture, was sporadically mined on the island from the 1880s but catastrophic eruptions, landslides and economic misfortune plagued the enterprise. The island was abandoned in 1934, and these days it is home only to 60,000 grey-faced **petrels** and 10,000 **gannets**.

An excellent **guided boat trip** to White Island runs from Whakatane. White Island Tours, also known as Pee Jay, 15 The Strand East (Ⓣ0800/733 529, Ⓦwww.whiteisland.co.nz; daily; 6hr; $160, including lunch) operate big boats – book at least a couple of days in advance if you can and allow a week in midsummer. Their two-hour tour of the island takes in the site of a 1923 sulphur-processing factory, partially submerged by a landslide, the remains being gradually eaten away by the high sulphur content of the atmosphere, and the tour progresses to an open-sided crater. Here, amid pools of bubbling mud and pillars of smoke and steam, you get the chance to study sulphur deposits and stand in the wind-driven clouds (with a gas mask on).

With plenty of cash and clement weather, you can also visit White Island by **helicopter** with Vulcan Helicopters (Ⓣ0800/804 354, Ⓦwww.vulcanheli.co.nz; 2hr 30min; $435, min 3 people, including a walking tour of the island).

Undersea explorers should approach the excellent Dive White Island, at Sportsworld, 186 The Strand (Ⓣ0800/348 394, Ⓦwww.divewhite.co.nz) who offer **dive trips** (with two dives) in the waters off White Island, where visibility is commonly around 20m. Costs range from $225 with your own gear to $275 for full rental and $440 for a one-to-one beginner's dive with an instructor. They'll also take you on a sightseeing trip with a chance to **snorkel** (full-day $180 including lunch, minimum 5 people).

land wars. The meeting house (Mataatua means "the eye of God") was allegedly gifted to the Queen in 1875 and then lent to the Sydney Exhibition of 1880, before ending up in England as part of the British Empire Exhibition in 1924 (because of the quality of the timber and carving). It was recovered after a Kiwi soldier, visiting London to recover from his wounds, spotted it in a museum, and it is being restored to Whakatane as part of a Waitangi Settlement, where it will be the centre of a Maori visitor complex (The Wharf, Strand East).

Activities

You can get noisily out on the local **Rangitaiki River** with Kiwi Jetboat Tours (Ⓣ0800/800 538, Ⓦwww.kiwijetboattours.com), run by an ex-world champion jetboat racer who will take you from the Matahina Dam, 25km south of Whakatane, to the beautiful Aniwhenua Falls over a number of modest white-water sections ($70). There are also innumerable **fishing** guides, mostly working on a charter basis from the local marina; the visitor centre stocks a free leaflet listing charter boats.

The rich waters around Whakatane give abundant opportunities for **whale and dolphin watching** and **dolphin swimming** from December to March – anybody offering to take you outside those months is either wildly optimistic or less than scrupulous. The best trip from Whakatane is run by the Dive Works Charters, 86 The Strand (Ⓣ07/308 5896, Ⓦwww.whaleislandtours.co.nz; 3–4hr, $140), who run two trips a day. Pee Jay, White Island Tours (Ⓣ07/308 9588, Ⓦwww.whiteisland.co.nz, $80) are almost as good but run less frequently.

Ohope

Seven kilometres east of Whakatane, the tiny settlement of **OHOPE** extends along the beach in a thin ribbon to the entrance of **Ohiwa Harbour**. Ohiwa ("a place of watchfulness") is the site of a natural shellfishery for pipi and cockles, and a place of numerous *pa* sites, signifying the importance of a convenient and renewable food source to the Maori way of life.

Kohi Point Lookout walk

There are several interesting **walks** in the area, all detailed in a free map or the more detailed *Discover the Walks Around Whakatane* booklet ($2) from the I-SITE. Easily the best is to **Kohi Point Scenic Reserve** (5.5km one way, 4hr), combining part of the Whakatane Town Centre Walk with the Nga Tapuwae o Toi ("Sacred Footsteps of Toi") Walkway, which traverses the domain of the great chieftain Toi and continues to Kohi Point, giving panoramic views of Whakatane, Whale and White islands and Te Urewera National Park.

The walk starts either from the car park at the bottom of Mokorua Gorge on Commerce Street or from the car park on Seaview Road. From the Mokorua Gorge car park head north along Commerce Street and turn right just before Pohaturoa to climb the steps to Hillcrest Road. Turn left to Seaview Road, where the track leads to **Kapu-te-rangi**, passing the head of the **Wairere Falls**, a cool and peaceful spot. Head through regenerating bush to the **Toi pa**, the oldest in New Zealand, before continuing along the clifftop past a number of other *pa* sites and food pits through bushland, including honeysuckle and pohutukawa, and emerging onto flax and scrub towards the Kohi Point. Either return the same way for a shorter walk or continue along the headlands to **Otarawairere Bay**, an excellent swimming and picnic spot (unreachable one hour either side of high tide); the steep descent to the bay is quite beautiful.

Otherwise, this is very much a beach resort, and when you've had enough of the surf and sand you'll want to press on, though Ohope makes a pleasant enough base from which to explore Whakatane and its surroundings.

If you're after cheap supplies of fresh **seafood**, including mussels, oysters and smoked fish, stop off at the *Ohiwa Oyster Farm* (daily 9am–8pm, except Christmas Day), a shack beside Ohiwa Harbour, 1km south of the beach and on the road to Opotiki with a couple of picnic tables at the water's edge. For more formal **eating**, try the cosy, licensed *Café Surfside*, 22 Pohutukawa Ave (☎07/312 4675; book ahead for dinner, Thurs–Sun); or the harbourside *Pier 5*, Fisherman's Wharf, off Harbour Road and at the eastern end of the beach – a lovely relaxing spot with deck seating for drinks, lunch or moderately priced dinners (mains from $28, closed Mon). The popular attached fish-and-burger takeaway (daily 5pm–late) has a few outdoor tables for BYO dining.

Eating, drinking and nightlife

Whakatane has a few decent spots for espressos and a couple of appealing waterside **restaurants**, which double as good places for an evening tipple. There's virtually no entertainment, except for the **Cinema 5** multiplex, 99 The Strand (☎07/308 7623) and a couple of bars in the *Whakatane Hotel* (see *The Craic* below), one of them an occasional club venue.

Babinka Kakahoroa Drive ☎07/307 0009. Very popular, specially built restaurant and bar with big windows, a marine theme and a versatile menu for brunch, lunch and dinner, including a selection of curries (around $25). Book ahead for dinner.

The Bean 72 Strand East. Laid-back, groovy daytime café and coffee roastery, so you can be sure of a good hit, or opt for a juice or one of their speciality teas. Closed Sun.

The Craic Whakatane Hotel, corner of The Strand & George St. Atmospheric Irish bar furnished in mellow dark wood to include booths, serving tasty fare. Most of the town's nightlife happens here, with live bands on Fri night and some Sun afternoons, and dancing in the bar.

Ground Zero 163 The Strand. Large and stylish daytime café with outdoor seating, specializing in quiches, filled rolls, home-made pies and muffins. Free Wi-Fi.

PeeJay's Coffee House 15 Strand East. The best espresso in town helps wash down daytime snacks and light meals. Early opening hours (6.30am) make it a good spot for a tasty breakfast before a morning boat trip. Located in the *White Island Rendezvous Motel* building.

Turkish Kebab House 113 The Strand. Tiny takeaway with a just a couple of tables that dishes up great-value kebabs and rice dishes until late.

Whakatane Sportfishing Club Strand East. Spacious bar with huge windows overlooking the boats and river, great for cheap drinks, good-value bar meals at lunch and dinner, and live music in the summer on most Fri & Sat evenings. It is a private club but visitors can call in.

The Wharf Shed Strand East ☎07/308 5698. All-day café-cum-restaurant, with a mellow riverside setting in a converted wooden butter store. Good for a late breakfast, lunch or watching the sun set over the water while tucking into seafood, lamb or venison. Book ahead for dinner.

Opotiki

The small settlement of **OPOTIKI**, 58km east of Whakatane, is the easternmost town in the Bay of Plenty and makes a useful stopping-off point for exploring its beautiful surroundings. Despite some recent growth, it doesn't amount to much, but does act as an effective gateway to the East Cape and is your last place to stock up on supplies and petrol before heading on.

From Opotiki, SH2 strikes inland to **Gisborne**, while SH35 meanders along the more circumspect roads around the perimeter of **the East Cape**, never straying far from its rugged and windswept coastline.

Arrival and information

Buses from Whakatane and Gisborne drop off on Bridge Street near its junction with Opotiki's main drag, Church Street. From here it's five blocks to the combined **i-SITE visitor centre** and **DOC office**, on the corner of St John and Elliott streets (daily: mid-Dec to end Feb 8.30am–5pm; March to mid-Dec 9am–4.30pm; ⓣ07/315 3031, ⓦwww.opotikinz.com), a good place to pick up information and advice for Opotiki and the whole of the East Cape. The Eastern Bay **local bus** (Mon & Wed; ⓣ0800/422 9281) heads to Whakatane and Tauranga. **Internet** access is available at the library, 101 Church St.

Accommodation

Opotiki has accommodation options for all budgets, though the mid- to lower-price ranges are best catered for.

Central Oasis Backpackers 30 King St ⓣ07/315 5165, ⓦwww.centraloasisbackpackers.co.nz. Somewhat cramped but friendly hostel in a renovated kauri villa right in town. Camping $12, dorms $18, rooms ❶

Eastland Pacific Motor Lodge 44 St Johns St ⓣ0800/103 003, ⓦwww.eastlandpacific.co.nz. Probably the best of the motels, with comfortable modern units (six with spa baths) and some wheel-chair units. ❸

Glow Worm Cove Cottage (aka Fighting Trout Lodge) 15km south of Opotiki on SH2 heading for Gisborne ⓣ07/315 5553, ⓦwww.newzealandsbestspot.co.nz. A modern and spacious two-bedroom cottage on a pretty farm property by the Waioeka River. The hosts run kayak trips and are opening up a small backpackers (dorms $20). ❹

Ohiwa Holiday Park Ohiwa Harbour Rd, off SH2 ⓣ07/315 4741, ⓦwww.ohiwaholidays.co.nz. This little-known gem has a range of appealing cabins and units right on the beach, with safe swimming, kayaks for rent and a "jumping pillow" – massively popular with kids (and a few adults). Camping $17, cabins ❷, kitchen cabins ❸, units ❹ park motels ❺

Opotiki Backpackers Beach House 7 Appleton Rd, off SH2 and 5km west of Opotiki ⓣ07/315 5117, ⓔhangout@paradise.net.nz. Laid-back beachside backpackers with free use of kayaks, bodyboards and so forth. Closed July & Aug. Tents $18, dorms $22, rooms ❷

Opotiki Holiday Park Corner of Potts Ave & Grey St – follow King or Elliott St west to Potts Ave ⓣ07/315 6050. Small and sheltered, with a range of cabins plus some good child-orientated facilities, such as an adventure playground, a swimming pool and a basketball hoop. Tents $14, on-site caravans & cabins ❶, units ❸ motel ❹

The Hau Hau

Zealous missionaries encouraged many Maori to abandon their belief structure in favour of **Christianity** but, as land disputes with settlers escalated, the Maori increasingly perceived the missionaries as agents for land-hungry Europeans.

When **war** broke out and the recently converted Maori suffered defeats, they felt betrayed not only by the Crown but also by their newly acquired god, and some formed the revivalist **Hau Hau** movement, based on the Old Testament. Dedicated to routing the interlopers, disciples danced around *nui* **poles**, chanting for Pakeha to leave the country. The name is derived from the **battle cry** of the warriors, who flung themselves at their enemies with their right arms raised to protect them from bullets, believing that true faith prevented them from being shot. The movement began in 1862 and by 1865, having capitalized on widespread Maori unrest, there was a *nui* pole in most villages of any size from Wellington to the Waikato. The Hau Hau were some of the most feared **warriors** and involved in the bloodiest and bitterest battles, but the movement began to fade after their **leader** and founder, Te Ua Haumene, was captured in 1866. Some of the sect's ideas were **revitalized** when the infamous rebel **Te Kooti** (see p.426) based parts of his **Ringatu** movement on Hau Hau doctrine.

The Town

Opotiki has few sights of interest to delay your departure for the wilds of the East Cape or the bright lights of Gisborne, but it does have some lush countryside and beaches around it. All the significant historic buildings cluster around the junction of Church and Elliot streets, including the **Opotiki Museum**, 123 Church St (Mon–Fri 10am–4pm, Sat 10am–2pm; $5), which occupies the whole block between Elliot and Kelly streets. The museum is undergoing a major and protracted renovation and is currently stuffed to the gunnels with a mishmash of exhibits, some quite interesting. Opposite, the innocent-looking white clapboard **St Stephen's Church** was once the scene of a notorious murder, for it was here, in March 1865, that local missionary **Carl Völkner** was allegedly killed by prophet Kereopa Te Rau from the Hau Hau sect (see box, p.400). The case is far from clear-cut: at the time, many Maori believed that missionaries doubled as spies, reporting their findings to the settlers and military, and it appears that Völkner had indeed written many letters to Governor Grey espousing the land-grabbing ambitions of settlers, and local Maori claim Völkner was justly executed. Whatever the truth, settlers used the story as propaganda, fuelling intermittent skirmishes over the next three years. The Op Shop next to the church (Mon–Sat 9am–3pm) will let you have a key so that you can nip in and see the gorgeous *tukutuku* panels around the altar. Völkner's gravestone is to one side of the entrance.

A welcome retreat into the bush is given by the small and unspoiled **Opotiki (Hukutaia) Domain** (daily dawn–dusk; free), full of native flora, including a puriri tree thought to date from 500BC and once used as a burial tree by local Maori. The bush also contains a good lookout over the Waioeka Valley and a series of short yet interesting rainforest tracks. To get here, head south from the centre of town on Church Street as far as the Waioweka River Bridge, cross it and bear left along Woodlands Road for 7km.

Activities

If all the running water is tickling your adventure glands, consider water-based activities either on the **Waioeka River** south of town, or on the **Motu River**, which surges through the hills to the east of Opotiki and meets the sea 45km to the northeast. On the former, Waioeka River Kayak Trips (Ⓣ07/315 5553, Ⓦwww.newzealandsbestspot.co.nz) run gentle paddles down a beautiful stretch (1hr; $40). There are superb backcountry **rafting trips** (see p.402) on the Motu River, and scenic flat-water **jetboating** on the lower 50km with Motu River Jet Boat Tours (Ⓣ07/325 2735, Ⓦwww.motujet.co.nz; 1hr $85; 3 times daily during summer, minimum of two people, other times by request, booking essential).

Eating

The pick of the daytime **cafés** are the *Flying Pig* at 95 Church St (closed Sat & Sun, but open Sat in Jan), and the *Hot Bread Shop Café*, on the corner of Bridge and St John streets, which does the town's best coffee, yummy cakes and pastries, brunch and snacks. Another good bet is the excellent *Two Fish*, 102 Church St (8am–4pm, later in the summer, closed Sun), with a wide range of gourmet home-made food. Traditional, if slightly pricey, **meals** are served day and evening at *Honey's* in the *Opotiki Hotel*, on the corner of Church and Kelly streets, but in fine weather go for the wonderful **fish and chips** from *Ocean Seafoods Fish and Chips* at 88 Church St, to eat in or take away (9am–8.30pm).

Wilderness rafting on the Motu River

Some of the best **wilderness rafting** trips in New Zealand are on the Grade III–IV **Motu River**, hidden deep in the mountain terrain of the remote Raukumara Ranges, with long stretches of white water plunging through gorges and valleys to the Bay of Plenty coast. In 1981, after a protracted campaign against hydro-dam builders, the Motu became New Zealand's first designated "wild and scenic" river. Access by 4WD, helicopter and jetboat makes one- and two-day trips possible, but to capture the essence of this remote region you should consider one of the longer trips in which you'll see no sign of civilization for three days – a magical and eerie experience.

Rotorua-based Wet 'n' Wild Rafting (Ⓣ0800/462 723, Ⓦwww.wetnwildrafting.co.nz) starts trips from Opotiki, generally using 4WD vehicles to get you in there. On all but the dedicated wilderness trips, the final flat drift to the coast is skipped in favour of a jetboat ride. Trips (minimum 6 people) range from two days (with helicopter access, $875), to the full five-day adventure (without helicopter access, $875) from the headwaters to the sea. In all cases transport, camping equipment and food are provided, though you may need to supply your own sleeping bag.

The inland route to Gisborne

From Opotiki, **SH2** strikes out south to **Gisborne**, 137km away. It is one of New Zealand's great scenic drives, dotted with tiny settlements, weaving up and down steep hills cloaked in bush and winding gingerly along the lower echelons of the plunging **Waioeka Gorge**. Following the river for 30km, the route becomes increasingly narrow and steep before emerging onto rolling pastureland on the Gisborne side and dropping to plains. From there it runs straight as an arrow through orchards, vineyards and sheep farms to Gisborne (see p.414).

The only part of the route worth breaking your journey for, or exploring from Opotiki, is the first 72-kilometre stretch to Matawai, along which a number of interesting **walks** branch off either side of the road. Ten scenic tracks through forest, ranging from fifteen minutes to ten hours one way, are described in the DOC leaflet *Walks in Waioeka and Urutawa*, available at Opotiki i-SITE.

The East Cape

The East Cape (also known as the East Coast or Eastland), the nub of land jutting into the South Pacific northeast of Opotiki and Gisborne, is one of the most sparsely populated areas in New Zealand, rarely visited, an unspoilt backwater that feels lost in time. Between Opotiki and Gisborne, the Pacific Coast Highway (SH35) runs 330 scenic kilometres around the peninsula, hugging the rugged coastline much of the way and providing spectacular sea views on a fine day. The **climate** here tends towards extremes – hot in summer, wet in winter, and extremely changeable at any time of year.

As soon as you enter the region you'll notice a change of pace, epitomized by the occasional sight of a lone horseback rider clopping along the road. Contemporary **Maori**, who make up a significant percentage of the population, draw on their strong culture to cope with the hardships of this untamed landscape and uncertain economic prospects. Over eighty percent of land tenure here is in Maori hands, something that sits well with the people: most feel in greater control of their destiny than Maori do elsewhere.

The East Cape is a reminder of how New Zealand once was, and the response to strangers splits into two camps: generally people are warm, friendly and welcoming, but sometimes it can feel as if they're standoffish, a slightly intimidating experience. However, this feeling usually evaporates after you have adjusted to the cape's slower pace.

The **coast** is very much the focus here, and if you're not gazing out of the car or bus window you're likely to be on the beach or in the water. That said, there are some hiking opportunities, and just about everywhere you go there will be someone happy to take you **horse trekking**, either along the beach or into the bush. In general, the **towns**, such as they are, don't have much to recommend them and you're better off planning to stay between towns, though at weekends you might like to find a pub if you fancy a country-music jukebox singalong.

Inland, the inhospitable **Waiapu Mountains** run through the area, encompassing the northeastern Raukumara Range and the typical native flora of the Raukumara Forest Park. The isolated and rugged peaks of Hikurangi, Whanokao, Aroangi, Wharekia and Tatai provide a spectacular backdrop to the coastal scenery, but are only accessible through **Maori land** and **permission** must be sought (further information is available at the DOC offices in Gisborne and Opotiki).

Legends of the East Cape Maori

According to legend, a great *ariki* (leader) from the East Cape was drowned by rival tribesmen, and his youngest daughter swore vengeance: when she gave birth to a son called **Tuwhakairiora**, she hoped he would make good her promise. As a young man, Tuwhakairiora travelled and encountered a young woman named **Ruataupare**; she took him to her father, who happened to be the local chief. A thunderstorm broke, signalling to the people that they had an important visitor among them, and Tuwhakairiora was allowed to marry Ruataupare and live in Te Araroa. When he called upon all the *hapu* of the area to gather and avenge the death of his grandfather, many warriors travelled to Whareponga and sacked the *pa* there. Tuwhakairiora became renowned as a warrior, dominating the area from **Tolaga Bay** to Cape Runaway, and all Maori families in the region today trace their descent from him.

Ruataupare, meanwhile, grew jealous of her husband's influence. While their children were growing up, she constantly heard them referred to as the offspring of the great Tuwhakairiora, yet her name was barely mentioned. She returned to her own *iwi* in **Tokomaru Bay**, where she summoned all the warriors and started a war against rival *iwi*; victorious, Ruataupare became chieftainess of Tokomaru Bay.

Another legend that has shaped this wild land is one of rivalry between two students – **Paoa**, who excelled at navigation, and **Rongokaka**, who was renowned for travelling at great speed by means of giant strides. At the time, a beautiful maiden, Muriwhenua, lived in Hauraki and many set off to claim her for their bride. Paoa set off early but his rival took only one step and was ahead of him; this continued up the coast, with Rongokaka leaving huge footprints as he went – his imprint in the rock at Matakaoa Point, at the northern end of Hicks Bay, is the most clearly distinguishable. En route, they created the **Waiapu Mountains**: Paoa, flummoxed by Rongokaka's pace, set a snare for his rival at Tokomaru Bay, lashing the crown of a giant totara tree to a hill; recognizing the trap, Rongokaka cut it loose. The force with which the tree sprang upright caused such vibration that Mount Hikurangi partly disintegrated, forming the other mountain peaks. Finally, Rongokaka stepped across the Bay of Plenty and up to Hauraki, where he claimed his maiden.

East Cape practicalities

The road is sealed all the way round the coast, but twists in and out of small bays so much that driving right around takes a full six hours – so around three days might be better to gain an appreciation of the area and allow for stop-offs. The further around you go, the fewer the **services**, including food stores, which are small and close at around 5 or 6pm, and petrol pumps, some of which run out from time to time.

Public transport on the East Cape is limited to **shuttle buses**. Polly's Passenger Courier (☎06/864 4728) and Cooks Couriers (☎06/864 4711) run from Gisborne to Hicks Bay for $40 one way, while Matakoa Transport (☎06/864 4654) run from Hicks Bay to Whakatane, $40 one way, $60 round trip. Note that none of the companies work at weekends and timetables change frequently, so call to check or contact the Gisborne or Opotiki i-SITEs. Shuttles will pick up and drop off anywhere en route, so you can manage half a dozen stops in three or four days.

Campsites are the staple accommodation, though free beachside camping, once the norm, is now prohibited. **Hostels** are scattered along the route, with the occasional motel and B&B, but upmarket accommodation is almost non-existent. Apart from a couple of steak-and-chips places attached to pubs and motels, there isn't anywhere on the East Cape that you'd describe as a real **restaurant**. Unless you've arranged to stay in B&Bs that serve meals you need to be prepared for self-catering or accept a diet of toasted sandwiches and fish and chips.

Opotiki to Waihau Bay

The road from Opotiki to **Waihau Bay** covers 103km, generally sticking close to the sea, but frequently twisting up over steep bluffs only to drop back down to desolate beaches heavy with driftwood. The logs have been washed down from the Raukumara Range by the numerous rivers that reach the sea here, often forming delightful freshwater swimming holes. This is probably the section of the East Cape where you'll want to spend most of your time. You'll find family campsites every few kilometres, none of them far from the beach but never right beside it either. Nonetheless, most make the best of their proximity to the sea with a wealth of aquatic activities offered to guests – from boogie boards and canoes to half-day fishing and dive trips – along with horse riding and bikes to search out your own secluded cove.

Omaio and Te Kaha

Leaving Opotiki you soon hit a section of the coast that sets the scene for the next couple of hours' driving. Swimming beaches are scarce initially and, once past Tirohanga, the only place you are likely to want to **stay** is the hillside *Oariki Coastal Cottage*, Maraenui, almost 40km east of Opotiki (☎07/325 2678, Ⓦwww.oarikicoastalcottages.co.nz; ❺), a self-catering cottage for four surrounded by native bush overlooking the sea. Call ahead for directions and if the option of a three-course meal made largely from organic produce ($45) doesn't appeal, be prepared to self-cater. There are opportunities to go jetboating, fishing and diving, dependent upon numbers.

Continuing, you soon cross the Motu River and after 11km reach **OMAIO**, where there is a store with a petrol pump, and one of the few places in these parts where you can **camp** for free: turn sharp left onto Omaio Marae Road by the store. A further 13km on, **TE KAHA** spreads 7km along the highway in a beautiful crescent shape, with spectacular headlands and a deserted beach strewn with driftwood, where you can swim safely. Its beginning is marked by the super-relaxing *Te Kaha Homestead Lodge* (Ⓣ07/325 2194, Ⓔpaora@hotmail.com; dorm $28, room ❸), a hostel at the water's edge with an outdoor spa, access to the beach, and opportunities for kayaking and fishing. You can self-cater or pay for breakfast and dinner ($30 for both meals). A little further along the main road is the brand spanking new beachside *Te Kaha Hotel* (Ⓣ07/325 2830, Ⓔtekahahotel@xtra.co.nz; ❼), providing conference facility-style accommodation and a decent restaurant and bar with great views. Striking inland just after the hotel, along Loop Road to Copenhagen Road, you'll come to *Tui Lodge* (Ⓣ07/325 2922 Ⓦwww.tuilodge.co.nz; ❺), a secluded and spacious B&B with en-suite rooms and dinner for $35. Back on the main road, 2km past the hotel, lies the well-run *Te Kaha Holiday Park & Motels* (Ⓣ07/325 2894, Ⓦwww.tekahaholidaypark.co.nz; tent sites $12, powered sites $14, dorms $20, kitchen cabins ❸, units ❹), a **campsite** with a store, post office and café as well as kayak rental and access to the beach.

Whanarua Bay and Maraehako Bay

Te Kaha is about the closest land to White Island, 50km offshore, which remains in view as you continue 6km to the tranquil *Waikawa B&B* (Ⓣ07/325 2070, Ⓦwww.waikawa.net; B&B ❺, *bach* ❻, *bach* $35 extra per person), a pretty spot above a rocky cove with a couple of en-suite **rooms** with their own access and an attractive *bach* with two bedrooms. The adjacent communities of **WHANARUA BAY** and **MARAEHAKO BAY**, 10km further on, make another ideal opportunity to stop and enjoy the beaches and rugged countryside. At Whanarua Bay, foodies will want to stop at the peaceful *Pacific Coast Macadamias* (daily 9am–5pm) set back from the main road, which has a small shop amid the nut orchards, selling delicious home-made macadamia products, and a simple café (closed May–Sept).

There's **budget accommodation** at Maraehako Bay: the idyllic *Maraehako Bay Retreat* (Ⓣ07/325 2648, Ⓔmaraehako@xtra.co.nz; tents $20 (for a two-person), dorms $28, rooms ❷), signposted off the main road, a beautiful waterside hostel in a rocky cove with a safe, private swimming beach and opportunities to go kayaking, fishing, diving and on trips to White Island or whale and dolphin watching. The beachside *Maraehako Camping Ground* (Ⓣ07/325 2047; camping $10), discreetly signposted off the main road at the far end of Maraehako Bay, has toilets and solar-heated showers, and organizes **horse treks**.

Waihau Bay

Still hugging the coast, SH35 winds 13km to **Ruakokere**, where a picture-perfect, white clapboard Anglican church stands on a promontory framed by the blue ocean. From here it's five minutes' drive to **WAIHAU BAY**, another sweeping crescent of sand and grass that's ideal for swimming, surfing and kayaking. The abundance of shellfish and flat fish here might encourage you to sling a line for a tasty supper from the wharf beside the *Waihau Bay Lodge*, a pretty basic pub adjacent to a store, post office and petrol station, and 3km further on, the *Waihau Bay Holiday Park* (Ⓣ07/325 3844; camping $18, dorm & on-site vans $25, cabins ❸, units ❹), which has another store and the closest thing to a daytime **café** between Opotiki and Gisborne. The best places to **stay** are the hospitable and friendly *Waihau Bay Homestay* (☎07/325 3674; ❸), 2km on at the far end of the bay, with two self-contained units and an en-suite room in a house overlooking the beach (book in advance for a superb $30 seafood dinner) and *Oceanside Apartments* (☎07/325 3699, Ⓦwww.waihaubay.co.nz; ❹, plus $20 per extra person), whose suites sleep four to seven; there's dinner for $30, as well as diving and fishing trips and kayaks for hire.

Cape Runaway to Te Puia Springs

Beyond Waihau Bay the highway continues close to the water for a few more kilometres before veering inland at **Cape Runaway**, the East Cape's northernmost point. For the next 125km you hardly see the coast again, with the significant exceptions of **Hicks Bay**, **Te Araroa** and **East Cape**. Further on, the church at **Tikitiki**, **Ruatoria** – the East Cape's largest community – and the hot springs at **Te Puia** are points of interest.

In the Cape Runaway area a range of worthwhile **guided walks** are led by vibrant Maori elder June McDonald (☎07/325 3697; 90min; $30; minimum 2 people), whose tours explore the area's history, culture (including a *marae* visit), landscape and medicinal uses of native plants. If you have your own transport, a worthwhile side trip is the mercurial road to Lottin Point, where a beautiful little bay encourages paddling and loafing. If you really fall in love with the place you can stay at the motel, the only building for some distance with a restaurant and bar (☎06/864 4455 ❸).

Hicks Bay and Onepoto Bay

The small coastal township of **HICKS BAY** (Wharekahika), 44km from Waihau Bay, shelters between headlands and coastal rock bluffs almost halfway along SH35 and makes a good base from which to visit the East Cape Lighthouse and enjoy water-based activities. Nearby are the secluded sands of **Onepoto Bay**, a safe swimming beach also popular for kayaking and surfing. Hicks Bay was named after Lieutenant Zachariah Hicks, who sighted it on Cook's *Endeavour* expedition. There are numerous *pa* sites in the area, in varying states of repair, some of which were modified for musket fighting during the 1860 Hau Hau uprising.

Entering the community along Wharf Road, off SH35, you'll find a general store and a takeaway. Small self-catering beachside **accommodation** is provided by *Mel's Place*, Onepoto Beach Road (☎06/864 4694, Ⓦwww.eastcapefishing.co.nz; tents $18, dorms $25, caravans ❷), in a simple bunkroom and caravan by a rocky bay. The Maori hosts run eco-sightseeing boat trips, which often include dolphin spotting, fishing trips (3hr; $60) and tours out to the cape lighthouse ($30; minimum 3 people). Alternatively, continue 2km east of Hicks Bay along SH35 to *Hicks Bay Motel Lodge* (☎06/864 4880; ❹), set high above both bays with great views, a licensed **restaurant**, a **bar** and access to a glow-worm grotto.

Horse Trekking In Hicks Bay (☎06/864 4859) offer exactly what their name suggests (from 2hr, $40; Oct–May).

Te Araroa

From Hicks Bay SH35 climbs over a hill and drops back to the coast, 6km on, at *Te Araroa Holiday Park* (☎06/864 4873, Ⓔbill.martin@xtra.co.nz; tent sites

$11, powered sites $13, dorms $18, cabins ❷, flats ❹), which has a handy shop and a takeaway van in summer, plus sea kayaks and mountain bikes for hire.

From here it's 4km to **East Cape Manuka Oil** on SH35 (daily 9am–5pm; ⓦwww.manukaproducts.com), a producer of essential oils extracted by steam distillation from the twigs of manuka trees grown in the surrounding hills. Highly valued for its healing abilities, the oil is exported all over the world. Manuka-oil products such as soaps and medicinal creams are on sale in the small shop and café, where they will explain the process over a flat white coffee.

A further 2km on, the broad surf-washed shore of Kawakawa Bay is graced by the drab village of **TE ARAROA** ("long pathway"), which marks the midway point between Opotiki and Gisborne. Te Araroa was once the domain of the famous Maori warrior Tuwhakairiora and the legendary Paikea, who is said to have arrived here on the back of a whale. Ironically, the first Europeans in the area occupied a **whaling station** not far from the present township. These days the settlement contains little more than a petrol station, two stores and a takeaway selling fresh **fish and chips**. In the grounds of the local school on Moana Parade stands a giant pohutukawa tree, reputedly the largest in New Zealand.

East Cape Lighthouse

The New Zealand mainland's easternmost point is marked by the **East Cape Lighthouse**, reached by a cliff-clinging partly sealed 21km road from Te Araroa: follow the sign east along the foreshore. This dramatic coastal run ends in a car park, from which you climb 755 steps to the lighthouse perched atop a 140m hill – an atmospheric spot with views inland to the Raukumara Range and seaward towards East Island (a bird sanctuary), just offshore. To find the path, head 50m back down the road and go through a gate near the derelict huts.

If you're relying on public transport along SH35, you can still get there at sunrise with East Cape 4WD **trips** (ⓣ06/864 4775; 2–3hr $60), who pick up at accommodation in Te Araroa and Hicks Bay before dawn – you could also contact *Mel's Place* (see p.406).

Tikitiki, Ruatoria and Te Puia Springs

From Te Araroa SH35 cuts inland through 24km of sheep-farming country before reaching **TIKITIKI**, a village that will only delay you long enough to peek inside the modest restored Anglican **church**, on a rise as you enter the town. The plain wooden exterior hides a treasure-trove of elaborate Maori design, *tukutuku* and carving; unusually, the stained glass is also in Maori designs, and the rafters are painted in the colours of a Maori meeting house. You can **stay** at *Eastender Backpackers*, Rangitukia Road, off SH35 (ⓣ06/864 3820), with beds in dorms ($23) and cabins (❶). They also offer **bone carving** (2–3hr $35) and some of the best **horse treks** in the area (2hr; $60) including a gallop on the beach.

Inland **RUATORIA**, 19km south of Tikitiki, is the largest town since Opotiki, though that's not saying much. The main highway skirts the town, but it's worth stopping if only for the petrol station, pub, grocery shop, the biggest supermarket on the Cape and two serviceable cafés, *Just Rob's* and the *Sunburst*. There's also an office for Ngati Porou Tourism (ⓣ06/864 8660) who, among other things, arrange guided trips to Mount Hikurangi (see p.408).

The hill country to the west of Ruatoria comes under the jurisdiction of the Raukumara Conservation Area, which includes the upper catchments of several rivers that drain into the Bay of Plenty. The desolate terrain and limited access discourage most visitors from exploring the park, but it is possible to tackle the four-hour trek up the 1754m **Mount Hikurangi** (the highest peak in the range), offering the early riser the chance to be among the first in New Zealand to see the sunrise. The local Ngati Porou control the land and you should consult them for the access details (see p.407).

At Kopuaroa, around 15km south of Ruatoria, a loop road heads 6km to the broad sweep of **Waipiro Bay**, a busy port in its heyday, but now a beautiful and secluded inlet. The loop road to Waipiro Bay rejoins SH35 at the small settlement of **TE PUIA SPRINGS**, where a small lake is picturesquely surrounded by deciduous trees. The mineral-rich **hot springs** (daily 10am–8pm; 30min; $5; book ahead from Christmas to end of Jan) have seen better days, today comprising just one pool that accommodates around six people, but you can book it for a private soak. The pool continuously fills with fresh water and lies behind the *Te Puia Hot Springs Hotel* (ⓣ06/864 6755; ❸), which has a decent bar and café.

Tokomaru Bay to Gisborne

At **Tokomaru Bay** the road emerges from inland bush and pastoral country to reveal the North Island's east coast in all its glory. For the remaining 80km to Gisborne you stay mostly inland but catch frequent glimpses of yawning bays and crashing surf, accessed either on SH35 itself, or by taking short side roads to little-visited coves.

Tokomaru Bay

TOKOMARU BAY (or just "Toko"), 11km south of Te Puia Springs, is a gorgeous spot to idle for a day, exploring the steep green hills, rocky headlands and the broad expanse of **beach**, which is dotted with driftwood, pounded by surf, and provides a good spot to swim. The Maori who settled here trace their descent to Toi te Huatahi, the great navigator and the first to arrive from the ancestral home of Hawaiki. In 1865 the Mawhai Pa was the scene of several attacks by a party of Hau Hau, but they were repulsed by a small garrison of old men and women.

At the far northern end of town, a long wooden wharf and the ruined buildings of a freezing works (abattoir) testify to the former prosperity of this once-busy port, which thrived until improved road transport forced the factory's closure in 1953. The town now gets by on the merest hint of a craft industry; call in at the **craft shop** on Waitangi Street (usually Mon–Fri 10am–3pm), near the general store to see flax goods, possum-fur hats, pottery and more.

Backpackers can chose either *Footprints In The Sand*, 13 Potae St (ⓣ06/864 5858 ⓦwww.footprintsinthesand.co.nz; tents $17, dorms $22, private room ❷); or head up the hill to the enthusiastically run *Brian's Place*, Potae Street (ⓣ06/864 5870; tents $18, dorms $25, rooms & cabins ❷), a small and welcoming hostel.

Te Puka Tavern on Beach Road serves inexpensive pub **meals** in hefty portions and is the only place in town for a drink; it can get boisterous at the weekends. The only other alternative is the supermarket on Waitangi Street, where you can stock up for a picnic.

Anaura Bay

Some 22km south from Tokomaru, a 6km long sealed side road runs to rugged **ANAURA BAY**, a prized surf spot with a broad sweep of sand and jagged headlands. At the north end of the bay, the **Anaura Scenic Reserve** harbours a large area of mixed broadleaf bush noted for its large puriri trees and abundance of native birds. Starting near the end of the road, and signposted to the west by the reserve, the **Anaura Bay Walkway** (3.5km loop; 2hr) follows the course of the Waipare Stream into thick green bush, up a gently climbing valley and out into scrubland before turning back towards the bay and a lookout point with magnificent views.

Beside the beach immediately beyond the start of this walk there's a very basic DOC **campsite** (free, with water but no shower), and at the opposite end of the bay, superbly sited just back from the beach, the *Anaura Bay Motor Camp* (Ⓣ06/862 6380; tents $12, powered sites $14). Facilities are in the former schoolhouse and there's a store selling essentials.

Tolaga Bay and beyond

TOLAGA BAY (Uawa), 36km from Tokomaru, is the first place since Opotiki that feels like a viable town, its population of six hundred one of the better-serviced communities on the East Cape. Once again, rugged headlands enclose the bay, the scene of a 1769 visit by Captain Cook and his crew. They are commemorated in the town's street names: Banks, Solander, Forester and, of course, Cook.

Cook, anchoring to replenish his stocks of food and water, named the bay "Tolaga", a misinterpretation of the Maori name for the prevailing wind (*teraki*). One individual who stayed a little longer – and may well have provided the historical basis for the character played by Harvey Keitel in the film *The Piano* – was an early flax trader called Barnet Burns. He wore full *moko*, and stayed in the bay for three years, marrying a Maori woman and fathering three sons, before decamping; his wife, Amotawa, went on to marry the great Maori chief Te Kani-a-Takirau.

Just over 1km south of town, Wharf Road cuts seaward past the start of **Cooks Cove Walkway** (2.6km; 45min), which involves a steep and often muddy climb through bush and birdlife, rewarding the effort with good views across the bay. Another 300m along Wharf Road you'll find the 660m-long concrete **wharf** itself, the longest concrete jetty in the southern hemisphere, jutting out past

▲ Wharf at Tolaga Bay

steep sandstone cliffs. Built in the late 1920s to service coastal shipping, it soon became redundant and is in a near-ruinous state, with no safety rails. It's not strong enough for vehicles, but you can wander to the end for a picturesque picnic spot.

Having seen the sights, there's little reason to linger, unless you fancy a **coffee** and some cake in *Maria's* at the incongruous mock-Tudor *Tolaga Bay Inn*, on the corner of Solander and Cook streets. If you decide to stay, go for the beachfront **accommodation** at *Tolaga Bay Holiday Park*, Wharf Road (ⓣ06/862 6716; tent sites $11, caravans & cabins ❶–❸), which has a store and great views.

The 47km stretch from Tolaga Bay to Gisborne becomes both tamer and bleaker the further south you travel, the land despoiled by clearance for farming. The road climbs in and out of more small bays, occasionally providing panoramic vistas of sea and close-ups of the slate-grey rock shelves that characterize this coast. It passes through the modest settlement of **Whangara**, where the film *Whale Rider* was shot, but there's not much to see here apart from a sweep of sand and an offshore island said to be the fossilized remains of the whale that the legendary Paikea rode all the way from Hawaiki. For a guided introduction to the area contact Tipuna Tours (ⓣ06/867 6558, ⓦwww.tipunatours.com; full day $160; minimum two people), who offer enlightening trips and visit one of the three *marae* at Tolaga Bay.

After Whangara there's little to stop you heading straight for Gisborne except a dip in the water at the surf mecca of **WAINUI BEACH**, 9km from the city.

Travel details

Buses

Coromandel to: Thames (1 daily; 1hr 15min); Whitianga (1 daily; 1hr).
Opotiki to: Gisborne, via SH2 (1 daily; 2hr); Hicks Bay via SH35 (2 daily; 3hr); Rotorua (1 daily; 2hr 10min); Whakatane (1 daily; 40min).
Paeroa to: Auckland (2 daily; 2hr 30min); Hamilton (2 daily; 1hr 30min).
Tauranga to: Auckland (2 daily; 3hr 40min); Hamilton (1 daily; 2hr); Rotorua (3 daily; 1hr 30min); Taupo (2 daily; 2hr 30min).
Te Aroha to: Hamilton (2 daily; 1hr 5min).
Thames to: Auckland (3 daily; 2hr); Coromandel (2 daily; 1hr 15min); Hamilton (1 daily; 1hr 30min); Mount Maunganui (1 daily, 2hr); Tauranga (1 daily; 1hr 45min); Whitianga (2 daily; 1hr 40min).
Whakatane to: Gisborne (2 daily; 3hr); Kawerau (1 daily; 45min); Opotiki (3 daily; 40min); Rotorua (1 daily; 1hr 30min).
Whitianga to: Rotorua (1 daily; 4hr 30min); Thames (2 daily; 1hr 45min).

Flights

Tauranga to: Auckland (6–8 daily; 35min); Wellington (9–14 daily; 1hr 15min).
Whakatane to: Auckland (3–4 daily; 45min).
Whitianga to: Auckland (5 weekly; 30min), Great Barrier Island (2 weekly; 30min).

6

Poverty Bay, Hawke's Bay and the Wairarapa

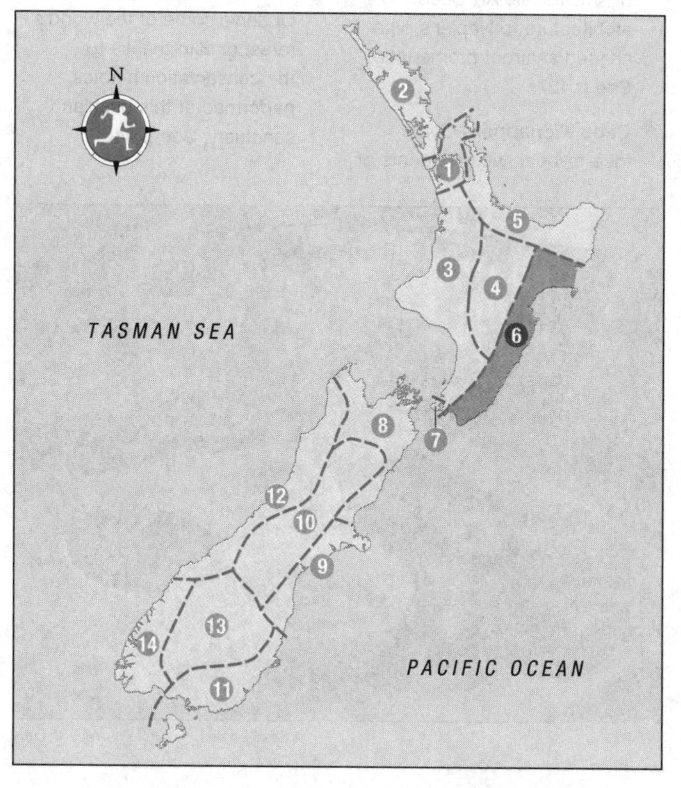

CHAPTER 6

Highlights

* **Gisborne** Swim with the sharks off the coast of New Zealand's easternmost city. See p.414
* **Lake Waikaremoana** Take in this picturesque lake on short hikes or the North Island's most prized multi-day tramp. See p.422
* **Napier** Wander through the world's finest collection of small-scale Art Deco architecture to Napier's pine-shaded seafront promenade. See p.427
* **Cape Kidnappers** Come face-to-beak with residents of the world's largest mainland gannet colony after a tractor ride along the beach. See p.436
* **Vineyards** Sip to your heart's content in Hawke's Bay Wine Country, or stroll to almost a dozen fine wineries from appealing Martinborough. See p.438
* **Pukaha Mount Bruce National Wildlife Centre** Observe some of the world's rarest birdlife thanks to the conservation heroics performed at this bushland sanctuary. See p.445

▲ Sileni Estates, Hawke's Bay Wine Country

6

Poverty Bay, Hawke's Bay and the Wairarapa

From the eastern tip of the North Island, a mountainous backbone runs 650km southwest to the outskirts of Wellington, defining and isolating the **east coast**. The Raukumara, Kaweka, Ruahine, Tararua and Rimutaka mountain ranges protect much of the region from the prevailing westerlies and cast a long rain shadow, the bane of the area's sheep farmers, who watch their land become a parched dusty brown each summer. Increasingly, these pastures are being given over to viticulture, and the regions of Poverty Bay, Hawke's Bay and the Wairarapa are now renowned around the world for their **wine**. Any tour of the wineries has to take in **Poverty Bay**, a major grape-growing region, where the main centre of Gisborne was the first part of New Zealand sighted by Cook's expedition in 1769. Finding little, other than the wary local Maori, he named it Poverty Bay and sailed south to the bay he later named **Hawke Bay** after his boyhood hero Admiral Sir Edward Hawke (the name of the surrounding province has since evolved into **Hawke's Bay**). Here Cook had a clash with Maori at **Cape Kidnappers**, now the site of an impressive gannet colony.

Hawke's Bay has long been dubbed "the fruit bowl of New Zealand", and its orchard boughs still sag under the weight of apples, pears and peaches. The district, now one of New Zealand's foremost wine regions, is best visited from the waterfront city of **Napier**, famed for its Art Deco buildings, constructed after the city was flattened by a massive earthquake in 1931. Nearby Hastings suffered much the same fate and wove Spanish Mission-style buildings into the resulting Art Deco fabric, though this won't delay you long from continuing south into the sheep lands of the Wairarapa and its wonderfully accessible vineyards of Martinborough.

Access to the mountainous **interior** of this region is limited, with only six roads winding over or cutting through the full length of the ranges. The tortuous, scenic SH38 forges northwest from the small town of **Wairoa**, the gateway to the remote wooded mountains of Te Urewera National Park and

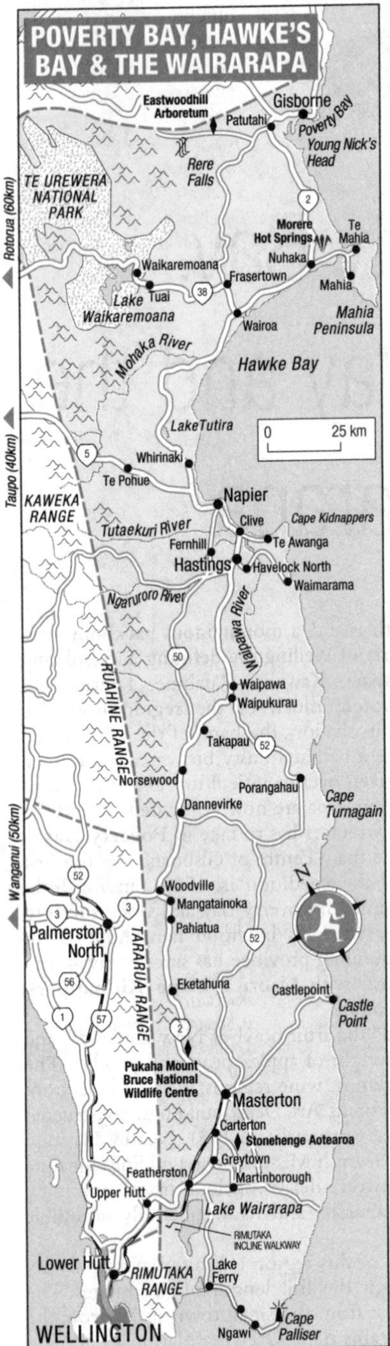

beautiful **Lake Waikaremoana**, which is encircled by the four-day Lake Waikaremoana Track tramping route, as well as shorter lakeside strolls.

The east coast is blessed with the North Island's most favourable summertime **climate** – the grape-ripening heatwaves come with just enough sea breeze to make vigorous activity tolerable – though winters can be cold and damp. As elsewhere, it's best to book ahead when the **Christmas and January** madness packs out accommodation, and during the area's many **festivals**.

Gisborne and around

New Zealand's easternmost city, **GISBORNE**, is the first to catch the sun each new day, and, thanks to the surrounding mountain ranges, its relatively isolated location has spared it from overdevelopment. Broad streets lined with squat weatherboard houses warmed by long hours of sunshine are interspersed with expansive parkland hugging the Pacific, the harbour and three rivers – the Taruheru, Turanganui and Waimata.

It was here in October 1769 that **James Cook** first set foot on the soil of Aotearoa, an event commemorated by a shoreside statue. He immediately ran into conflict with local Maori, killing several of them before sailing away empty-handed. He named the landing site **Poverty Bay**, since "it did not afford a single item we wanted, except a little firewood". Despite the fertility of the surrounding lands, the name stuck and looks set to prevail, against the wishes of some **Maori**, who would rename it Turanganui a Kiwa – honouring a Polynesian navigator.

Early-nineteenth-century Poverty Bay remained staunchly Maori and few Pakeha moved here, discouraged by both the Hau Hau rebellion and Te Kooti's uprising (see p.426). It wasn't until the 1870s that **Europeans** headed here in numbers to farm the rich alluvial river flats. After a decent port was constructed in the 1920s, sheep farming and market gardening took off, followed more recently by the grape harvest and the rise of plantation forestry. Today Gisborne's Maori and Pakeha population is almost exactly 50:50; and the city's relaxed pace and easy-going beach culture makes it one of New Zealand's more gently appealing places. The land itself rumbles occasionally, though: in December 2007, the city was rocked by an earthquake measuring 6.8 on the Richter scale. Thankfully, although some buildings tumbled, there were no fatalities.

Arrival and information

Gisborne sits near the junction of the region's two main highways, SH35, which skirts the rugged East Cape, and the inland SH2, which straddles the Raukumara Range and continues south to Napier. InterCity **buses** along these routes converge on the **i-SITE visitor centre**, 209 Grey St (daily: Nov–Easter 8.30am–5.30pm; Easter–Oct 8.30am–5pm; ⓣ06/868 6139, ⓦwww.gisbornenz.com), which has **Internet access** and helpful displays on walks in Te Urewera National Park. For specialist outdoor information, visit the **DOC office** at 63 Carnarvon St (Mon–Fri 8am–4.30pm; ⓣ06/867 8531).

Flights arrive at Gisborne **airport**, on the edge of town about 2km west of the town centre, which can be reached by **taxi** (around $15) – try Gisborne Taxis (ⓣ06/867 2222) or Eastland Taxis (ⓣ06/868 1133). **Getting around** most of the city is easily done on foot, though **rental bikes** from Maintrax Cycles, corner of Gladstone and Roebuck roads ($15–20 per day; ⓣ06/867 4571), are good for a spin around the wineries.

Accommodation

Despite the huge number of motels – chiefly along the main strip, palm-shaded Gladstone Road, and the waterfront Salisbury Road – **accommodation** can be hard to come by during the month or so after Christmas, when booking is advisable and prices rise a little from their normally modest levels.

Motels and B&Bs

Beachcomber Motel 73 Salisbury Rd ⓣ06/868 9349. Welcoming, well-cared-for motel with broadband Internet and a range of comfortable units 50m from the beach. ④

Knapdale Eco Lodge 114 Snowsill Rd, Waihirere, 13km northwest of Gisborne ⓣ06/862 5444, ⓦwww.knapdale.co.nz. Luxurious accommodation in a tranquil farm setting on the forest edge. Wake up to the dawn chorus in attractive and modern rooms, then tuck into a sumptuous breakfast. Animal lovers will appreciate the chickens, deer and horses, and gourmands might want to book one of the exquisite dinners ($75 a head). ⑧

Pacific Harbour Motor Inn Corner of Reads Quay and Pitt St ⓣ06/867 8847, ⓦwww.pacific-harbour.co.nz. Glass bricks and panoramic windows overlooking the harbour flood this contemporary motel with natural light. Large, fully equipped rooms, some with balconies and spa baths. Units ⑤, apartments ⑥

Te Kura 14 Cheeseman Rd ⓣ06/863 3497, ⓦwww.tekura.co.nz. There's just one guest suite in this grand, beautifully timbered Arts & Crafts homestead overlooking the Waimata River in central Gisborne. Guests can relax in their own lounge or make use of the deep clawfoot bath. Other facilities include a pool and free Wi-Fi, and the generous hosts serve full breakfasts. ④

Whispering Sands 22 Salisbury Rd ⓣ0800/405 030, ⓦwww.whisperingsands.co.nz. Well-appointed beachfront motel with fourteen large modern units, all with great sea views. ④

Hostels and campsites

Flying Nun 147 Roebuck Rd ⓣ06/868 0461, ⓦwww.flynun.co.nz. This hippie-style former

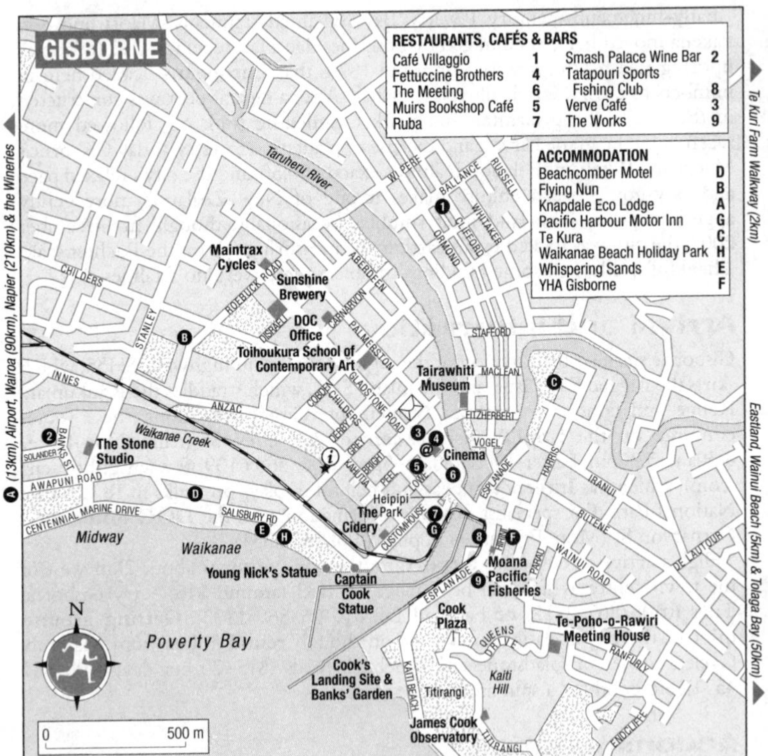

convent, a 15min walk from town, is where Dame Kiri Te Kanawa first trained her voice. Some of the spacious dorms front onto broad verandas, and although doubles can be a little cramped, singles ($33) are good value. Spacious grounds include a BBQ area and games room. No credit cards. Tent sites $13, dorms $21, doubles and twins ❷

Waikanae Beach Holiday Park Grey St ⓣ06/867 5634, ⓦwww.gisborneholidaypark.co.nz. Idyllically sited motor park right by Gisborne's main beach and 5min walk from town, with tennis courts, comfortable cabins and s/c units. Camping $11–14, cabins ❶, en-suite cabins ❷, units ❸

YHA Gisborne Corner of Harris St & Wainui Rd ⓣ06/867 3269, ⓔyha.gisborne@clear.net.nz. Spacious and central hostel in a weatherboard homestead with a sunny deck, a cheery paint job and a manager switched onto the local surf hotspots. Dorms $20, twins and doubles ❷, en suites ❷

The Town

Almost everywhere in this compact city is an easy stroll from Midway Beach. Swimming, surfing and sunbathing aside, most of Gisborne's sights are connected in some way to the historical accident of James Cook's landing - and the dynamic between Maori and Pakeha cultures it engendered. The first of Cook's crew to spy the mountains of Aotearoa, a couple of days before the first landing, was twelve-year-old surgeon's boy Nick Young, who Cook rewarded by recording this white-cliffed promontory, 10km south of Gisborne across Poverty Bay, on his chart as Young Nick's Head. Young's keen eyes are commemorated with a pained-looking statue on the western side of the rivermouth in Gisborne. Nearby is a modern **statue of Cook** atop a stone hemisphere.

Early Maori explorers are likewise honoured with **Te Tauihu Turanga Whakamana** – a striking wooden sculpture depicting a Maori *tauihu* (canoe prow) carved with images of Tangaroa (god of the sea), the demi-god Maui, and Toi Kai Rakau (one of the earliest Maori to settle in New Zealand).

Across the river at the **Tairawhiti Museum**, 18 Stout St (Mon–Fri 10am–4pm, Sat & Sun 1.30–4pm; $5, free entry Mon), temporary exhibitions augment extensive displays on East Coast Maori and a strong line in contemporary Maori arts including beautiful *kete* (flax baskets) and greenstone finely carved into *tiki* (pendants). A maritime wing incorporates the original wheelhouse and captain's quarters of the 12,000-tonne *Star of Canada*, which ran aground on the reef off Gisborne's Kaiti Beach in 1912, along with exhibits on Cook's arrival, the role of shipping, and a shrine to the local surfing. Several disused buildings from around the region are clustered outside the museum, notably the six-room 1872 **Wyllie Cottage**, the oldest extant house in town, and the **Sled House**, built on runners at the time of the Hau Hau uprising so that it could be hauled away by a team of bullocks at the first sign of unrest.

A striking modern whale-tail sculpture near the corner of Gladstone Road and Cobden Street heralds the **Toihoukura School of Contemporary Art** (generally Mon–Fri 9am–5pm during school term times, and by appointment ☎06/868 0347; free), where existing Maori carvings are restored and students are instructed in the oral history and traditions of Maori design. Modern interpretations using contemporary materials and techniques are encouraged, and many vibrant and stunning pieces find their way onto the public gallery.

If you've worked up a thirst, repair to the boutique **Sunshine Brewery**, 109 Disraeli St (Mon–Sat 9am–6pm; free) for a brief tour of the tiny brewhouse before sampling their Pilsener-style Gisborne Gold, delectable English-style ale and the Black Magic stout. The beers are available in bars around town, but the shop prices are the best around. Alternatively, you can watch an industrial cider production plant, **The Cidery**, 91 Customhouse St (Mon–Fri 9am–5pm, Sat 10am–3pm; also Nov–March Sun 10am–3pm; free), in action, and try fresh-tasting ciders, local mead and ginger beer.

Kaiti Hill and around

An obelisk on the eastern side of the rivermouth marks **Cook's landing site**, now a couple of hundred metres inland following reclamation for the harbour. Beside the obelisk, Cook's botanist gets recognition in **Banks' Garden**, a small collection of low-growing species – including ngaio, tutu, karo and puriri – that he and his accomplice Solander collected along this coast. Behind, Titirangi Domain climbs the side of **Kaiti Hill** to Cook Plaza, designed around a sculpture intended to represent Cook. The hill's highest point is occupied by the **James Cook Observatory**, which runs public stargazing nights on Tuesdays (Nov–March 8.30pm; April–Oct 7.30pm; $2).

On the eastern side of the hill lies **Te Poho-o-Rawiri Meeting House**, one of the largest in the country. The interior is superb, full of fine ancestor carvings, interspersed with wonderfully varied geometric *tukutuku* (woven panels). At the foot of the two support poles, ancient and intricately carved warrior statues provide a fine counterpoint to the bolder work on the walls. This is one of the most easily accessible working *marae*, but you'll need to arrange permission to enter the site (☎06/868 5364), preferably a day or two in advance. You're pretty much left to your own devices, so remember to remove your shoes before entering the meeting house and take photographs only if you've asked permission; a *koha* (donation) is appreciated.

If all the protocol seems a bit daunting, one alternative is a half-day, guided tour of the *marae* with Tipuna Tours ($80, minimum two people, ⓣ06/867 6558, ⓦwww.tipunatours.com). They will meet you, run through the introductory etiquette, take you to the *marae*, explain the history and cultural context of the meeting house and get you weaving, playing stick games or singing an action song. They also run wide-ranging, full-day tours in Tolaga Bay (see p.409). *Whale Rider* tours ($60), covering the locations in the film, in and around Whangara (see p.410), are occasionally available either from Tipuna or the Taumanu family (book well in advance through the Gisborne i-SITE).

Outdoor activities

Gisborne offers one of New Zealand's few opportunities for heart-pounding **shark encounters**. Surfit (Nov–March; $250; bookings essential on ⓣ06/867 2970, ⓦwww.surfit.co.nz) take small groups about 15km offshore from where, two at a time, you climb into a tough metal cage, which is partly lowered into the water where **mako sharks** lurk. Standing chest deep, you get around half an hour in the water – quite long enough – ducking down with a mask and snorkel or regulator to observe these curious three-metre-long, eighty-kilo killing machines. There's a fifty-percent refund in the unlikely event of not seeing any sharks. Dive Tatapouri (ⓣ06/868 6138, ⓦwww.divetatapouri) also offers shark encounters for $250 as well as **stingray feeding** ($40), where you don a wetsuit and wade onto the reef, and **eco-tour boat trips** ($115).

To take advantage of Gisborne's renowned surf, go **Surfing With Frank** (ⓣ06/867 0823, ⓦwww.surfingwithfrank.com; private lesson $65, group lesson $45 including board and wetsuit hire; maximum of four people per group). Those who'd rather stay on dry land can head off through the pine forest on a horse trek with **Stoney Horse Treks** (ⓣ027/292 4496, ⓦwww.stoneyhorse.co.nz) – beginners are welcome and prices depend on the length of trek you'd like to take.

Eating, drinking and nightlife

For its size, Gisborne is surprisingly well supplied with decent **cafés** and **restaurants** for all budgets. Many are beside the city's rivers or harbour making them ideal for an evening drink, though there are several traditional **pubs** too.

For **self-caterers**, affordable, straight-off-the-boat fish can be found at **Real Fisheries** shop (Mon–Fri 8.30am–5.30pm & Sat 8.30am–12.30pm), on The Esplanade, and fruit and vegetables are best at the bustling **farmers' markets**, held each Saturday morning in the park next to the visitor centre (6.30am to around 8.30am), and at the Army Hall car park (9.30am–1pm). Movies are shown at the Odeon **cinema**, 79 Gladstone Rd (ⓣ06/867 3339).

Cafés and restaurants

Café Villaggio 57 Ballance St ⓣ06/868 1611. Award-winning casual restaurant that spills out of a suburban Art Deco house. Offers simple, delicious meals (mains $26.50–32). Breakfast and lunch daily, dinner Thurs–Sat.

Fettuccine Brothers 12 Peel St ⓣ06/868 5700. Relaxing, longstanding Italian restaurant (with adjacent bar), lit by candelabras, serving a full range of dishes from pasta ($22) to substantial meat and fish dishes ($26–36). Closed Sun.

Muirs Bookshop Café 62 Gladstone Rd. Airy café tucked above Gisborne's best bookshop, adjacent to the second-hand section. A sundrenched balcony overlooks the main street, where you can enjoy panini, salads and delicious "bookshop brownies".

Ruba 14 Childers Rd. Chic, modern café, perfect for coffee and warm lemon curd and cream cheese muffins, or something delectable like tempura-fried feta from their all-day "grazing menu" ($4–14.50). Also full lunches and dinner daily (mains $25–32).

Verve Café 121 Gladstone Rd. With rotating art exhibitions by up-and-coming local artists, this groovy but low-key daytime café and restaurant serves gorgeous, moderately priced food from savoury muffins to falafel, steak sandwiches and cakes.

The Works Corner of The Esplanade & Crawford Rd ⓣ06/863 1285. This former freezing works, with bare-brick walls and wood floors, is abuzz with folk in for a coffee and a snack and serious diners here for impeccably cooked dishes such as Moroccan-spiced roast veg and excellent wines by the glass or bottle. Lunch mains $16.50–27.50, dinner mains $28–36.

Pubs and bars

The Meeting Corner of Gladstone Rd & Reads Quay. Convivial and convincing Irish bar with good Guinness and a range of toothsome meals at good prices.

Smash Palace Wine Bar 24 Banks St. Wonderfully oddball bar where overalls from the surrounding industrial area rub shoulders with suits in a corrugated iron barn. Food basically comprises snacks – favourites include flaming pizzas and nachos that have been flame-toasted with a blow torch.

Tatapouri Sports Fishing Club The Esplanade. Sociable club right on the wharf with veranda seating for seafood, steaks or gourmet burgers (all under $22), while watching the sun set behind the hills beyond the dock. Visitors can usually be signed in: ask at the bar.

Around Gisborne

Winery visits, gentle walks and a smattering of specific attractions make a day or so spent in Gisborne's surrounds an agreeable prospect. If you don't have a car, your best bet is to **bike** out on the flat roads to the wineries before perhaps embarking on one of the **short walks** just north of the city; ask the visitor centre for a leaflet outlining trails. Alternatively, join Unique Bay Tours (ⓣ06/863 0907, ⓦwww.uniquebaytours.co.nz), for a spin around the wineries ($65, minimum two people), or out to Eastwoodhill Arboretum ($65, minimum two people).

The wineries

Occupying a free-draining alluvial plain in the lee of the Raukumara Range and blessed with long hours of strong sun and warm summer nights, Poverty Bay's wineries (ⓦwww.gisbornewine.co.nz) have made Gisborne a viticultural workhorse, churning out vast quantities of Chardonnay, Riesling, Müller-Thurgau and Gewürztraminer grapes to be blended into cheerful wines for everyday glugging. National giants Corbans and Montana account for over eighty percent of the regional production, but tours are generally only available to groups by appointment. The exception is Montana's **Lindauer Cellars**, 11 Solander St, around 1km west of downtown ($5; ⓣ06/868 2757), where a historic tour is followed by tasting (there's also good-quality food available). For more interesting boutique wineries, follow the road towards Napier some 6km out of town to **Bushmere Estate**, 166 Main Road South (ⓣ06/868 9317) for tastings (including a refreshing rosé) plus a good café in a pretty vineyard setting.

Millton, Papatu Road, Manutuke, 4km west (tastings free; ⓣ06/862 8680) is one of New Zealand's few organic wineries to apply bio-dynamic principles. The timing of planting, harvesting and bottling are dictated by the moon's phases to produce some delicious, surprisingly inexpensive wines (especially Riesling, Chenin Blanc and late-harvest dessert wines) that, they claim, can be enjoyed even by those who experience allergic reactions to other wines. You can also indulge in a picnic among the vines and a leisurely game of pétanque on the winery's pitch.

Eastwoodhill Arboretum

A bottle of wine tucked under your arm and a groaning picnic hamper is the most conducive way to enjoy New Zealand's largest collection of northern hemisphere vegetation at **Eastwoodhill Arboretum**, Ngatapa-Rere Road, 35km northwest of Gisborne (daily 9am–5pm; $10; Ⓦ www.eastwoodhill.org.nz). The parched hills surrounding the Poverty Bay plains stand in stark contrast to the arboretum's lush glens and formal lawns. Planting began in 1918 and the arboretum became the life's work of William Douglas Cook, who spent time recuperating in England during World War I and grew to love British gardens and parks. Concerned that war would break up the great estates of Europe and destroy their genetic stock of trees, he made it his business to import the best he could. Cook died in 1967 leaving numerous trails threading through a unique mixture of over 3500 species – magnolias, oaks, spruce, maples, cherries – brought together in an unusual micro-climate in which both hot- and cold-climate trees flourish.

Mahia, Wairoa and the road to Napier

Routes **south** from Gisborne involve lengthy travel through vast swathes of farmland with tiny villages and little incentive to linger. There are two roads: the inland SH36, which sees very little traffic – and no public transport – and the faster SH2, which sticks closer to the coast before veering around Hawke Bay. From Wairoa south to Napier, the road becomes considerably narrower, steeper and twistier, so allow plenty of time to take it slowly.

Morere

Following **SH2** from Gisborne, the Poverty Bay vineyards soon give way to the hill country of the Wharerata State Forest, where the first real diversion is the **Morere Hot Springs** (daily 10am–5pm, late summer opening if busy; $5, private pools an extra $3 for 30min), 60km south of Gisborne. The highly saline and pleasantly non-sulphurous waters that well up along a small stream here result from ancient sea water, warmed and concentrated along a fault line. This is also one of the east coast's last remaining tracts of native coastal forest, and

▲ Morere Hot Springs

grassy BBQ areas surround the pools and form the nucleus of numerous trails that radiate out through stands of tawa, rimu, totara and matai; a short streamside walk (10min) takes you to the Nikau Plunge Pools, where soaking tanks are surrounded by nikau palm groves.

It's a wonderfully relaxing spot, so you might want to hang around the adjacent settlement of **MORERE**, which has a couple of **places to stay**, both on SH2 as it passes through the village. A spacious, broad-verandaed house tucked away amid trees forms the heart of the welcoming *Moonlight Lodge* (ⓣ06/837 8824, ⓔmoonlightlodge@xtra.co.nz; shares $25, rooms ❶, cabins ❸); there's also accommodation at *Morere Tearooms & Camping Ground* (ⓣ06/837 8792, ⓔmorere@xtra.co.nz; camping $13, cabins ❷), which in addition to its tearooms stocks a limited range of staples in its shop.

Mahia Peninsula

At Nuhaka, 8km south of Morere, the highway flirts briefly with the sea before turning sharp right for Wairoa. Mahia Road spurs east to the pendulous **Mahia Peninsula**, a distinctive high promontory that separates Hawke's Bay from Poverty Bay, linked to the mainland by a narrow sandy isthmus. Surfers make good use of the rougher windward side, while the calmer beaches on the leeward side offer safe bathing and boating. Outside the mad month after Christmas it makes a relaxing place to break your journey, or to stretch your legs on the 4km looped track through the **Mahia Peninsula Scenic Reserve**.

Almost 1km along Mahia Road you can learn how paua (abalone) are farmed in a large shed at **Paua Farm Aquaculture Tours** (tours daily 1.30pm, 2.30pm and 3.30pm; 20min; $7.50; ⓦwww.pauanzabalone.co.nz). They also sell live paua along with the minced meat (around $60 a kilo), and glittering paua-shell jewellery.

The peninsula's main settlement, **MAHIA BEACH**, lies 15km on, at the southern end of the five-kilometre strand. The *Mahia Beach Motels & Holiday Park* (ⓣ06/837 5830, ⓔmahiabeach.motels@xtra.co.nz; camping $13–15, cabins ❷, units ❹) has spacious camping, simple tourist cabins and flashier motel units. Eating is limited to takeaways and the lively *Sunset Sports Bar and Bistro*, which does hearty meals (steaks, crayfish etc) and comes alive at weekends when there is often a DJ.

Just over the hill, closer to the surf beaches at tiny **TE MAHIA**, you can stay at the self-contained, log-built *Cappamore Lodge*, 435 East Coast Rd (ⓣ06/837 5523, ⓦwww.cottagestays.co.nz/cappamore/cottage.htm; ❺), and eat at the classy, licensed *Café Mahia*, 476 East Coast Rd.

Wairoa and south towards Napier

The launch pad for trips to Lake Waikaremoana, peaceful **WAIROA**, some 40km west of the Nuhaka junction, hugs the banks of the willow-lined Wairoa River a couple of kilometres from its mouth, where ships once entered to load the produce of the dairy-and sheep-farming country all around. Today the riverside wharves have all but disappeared, but if you have time, stroll along the waterfront past the 1877 kauri-wood **lighthouse** beside the bridge at the town centre.

Nearby, the **Wairoa Museum**, on Marine Parade (Mon–Fri 10am–4pm, Sat 10am–1pm; gold coin donation), deserves thirty minutes for its small but well-presented displays on local history (including the devastating cyclone Bola, which swept through the region in 1988) and its beautifully carved Maori figure dating back to the eighteenth century, and also presents rotating exhibitions.

Buses to Waikaremoana and InterCity buses to Gisborne and Napier pick up daily at the **i-SITE visitor centre**, corner of SH2 and Queen Street (Nov–March Mon–Fri 9am–5pm, Sat & Sun 10am–4pm; April–Sept Mon–Fri 9am–5pm, Sat & Sun 10am–11pm & 3–4pm; ⓣ06/838 7440, ⓦwww.wairoadc.govt.nz).

Accommodation options include the *Riverside Motor Camp* at 19 Marine Parade (ⓣ06/838 6301, ⓔriversidemotorcamp@quicksilver.net.nz; camping $28, cabins ❶), or the *Vista Motor Lodge*, on SH2 north of the Wairoa bridge (ⓣ0800/284 782; ❹), which has a heated pool. Backpackers can get a great insight into Maori culture at *Haere Mai Cottage*, 49 Mitchell Rd, 2km west of the centre (ⓣ06/838 6817; dorms $23, doubles ❷), partly through visits to the local school's *kapa haka* group.

The best place to **eat** is precisely 2.87km south of town at *Café 287*, SH2, a white-painted timber house opening daily for breakfast, lunch and dinner (mains $12–27), with retro fare like shrimp cocktail and beef stroganoff – it also has some attractive cabins (❸). In town, choose from 23 varieties of home-made pies at the award-winning *Osler's Bakery & Café*, 116 Marine Parade (Mon–Fri 4.30am–4.30pm, Sat & Sun 5am–3pm), first established in the early 1900s and something of a local institution.

En route from Wairoa to Napier at little lakes **Tutira** and **Waikopiro**, 75km south of Wairoa, you could tackle one of three farmland loop walks (1km, 20min; 3.5km, 2hr; and 9km, 5hr; all closed Aug & Sept for lambing season). Some 12km further south **White Pine Bush Scenic Reserve** is a dense clump of kahikatea, rimu and other podocarps, where loop tracks (650m, 30min; and 3km, 1hr) thread through the bush alongside the Kareaara Stream. Wairoa's visitor centre stocks a brochure ($1) on these and other walks.

Te Urewera National Park

Te Urewera National Park (ⓦwww.teurewera.co.nz), 65km northwest of Wairoa, straddles the North Island's mountainous backbone and at 212,000 hectares encompasses the largest untouched expanse of native bush outside Fiordland. Unusually for New Zealand, it is almost completely covered in vegetation; even the highest peaks – some approaching 1500m – barely poke through this dense cloak of primeval forest, whose undergrowth is trampled by deer and wild pigs and whose rivers are filled with trout. One road, SH38, penetrates the interior, but the way to get a true sense of the place is to hike, particularly the celebrated Lake Waikaremoana Track encircling **Lake Waikaremoana**, the "Sea of Rippling Waters" and the undoubted jewel of the park. The lake's deep clear waters, fringed by white sandy beaches and rocky bluffs, are ideal for swimming, fishing and kayaking.

Habitation is very sparse. The Tuhoe people, the "Children of the Mist", still live in the interior of the park (the largest concentration around the tramping base of **Ruatahuna**), but most visitors make straight for **Waikaremoana**, a visitor centre and motor camp right on the lakeshore. Immediately to the south, the *Big Bush Holiday Park* and the quiet former hydroelectrical development town of **Tuai** provide some additional basic services, but otherwise you're on your own.

Lake Waikaremoana

Shrouded by bushland, **Lake Waikaremoana** fills a huge scalloped bowl at an altitude of over 585m, precariously held back by the Panekiri and Ngamoko ranges. The lake came into being around 2200 years ago when a huge bank of

sandstone boulders was dislodged from the Ngamoko range, blocking the river that once drained the valleys. The Maori have a more poetic explanation of the lake's creation, involving Hau-Mapuhia, the recalcitrant daughter of Mahu, who was drowned by her father and turned into a *taniwha*, or "water spirit". In a frenzied effort to get to the sea, she charged in every direction, thereby creating the various arms of the lake. As she frantically ran south towards Onepoto, the dawn caught her, turning her to stone at a spot where the lake is said to ripple from time to time, in memory of her struggle.

One of the beauties of the lake is that there is no town nearby, just the DOC-operated Aniwaniwa visitor centre and a motor camp, both well set up for helping hikers tackle the Lake Waikaremoana Track. Short visits are still worthwhile, repaid by the opportunity to see the **Papakorito Falls**, a twenty-metre-wide curtain of water 2km east of the visitor centre. But to really see and get a feel for the place you'll need to walk a little further afield, preferably armed with DOC's *Lake Waikaremoana Walks* leaflet ($2.50), which details the region's rewarding shorter hikes such as the stroll to the double-drop **Aniwaniwa Falls** (1km; 20min return; 50m ascent), starting from beside the visitor centre, or the **Black Beech Track** (2km; 30min one way; 50m descent), which follows the old highway from the visitor centre to the motor camp. If you've the best part of a day to spare, take on the **Waipai–Ruapani–Waikareiti Round Trip** (15km; 6hr; 300m ascent), which starts 200m north of the visitor centre and winds up through dense beech forest past the grass-fringed Lake Ruapani to the beautiful and serene **Lake Waikareiti**, where you can rent rowboats (around $15 per half-day, $40 bond), though you'll need to plan ahead as the key is held at Aniwaniwa visitor centre. Return down the Waikareiti Track or head on around to the northern side of the lake (3hr one way) and stay at **Sandy Bay Hut** (18 bunks; $25). You can also explore Lake Waikaremoana on single **kayaks** ($40 a day) and open **canoes** ($50 a day) – call ⓣ0800/469 879.

Waikaremoana practicalities

Along with the Wairoa visitor centre (see p.422), the **Aniwaniwa visitor centre** (daily 8am–4.30pm; ⓣ06/837 3803, ⓔurewerainfo@doc.govt.nz) is a fount of information on Lake Waikaremoana and Te Urewera National Park. Renovations were underway at the time of writing: the centre should still be open but the extensive displays on the geology and ecology of the region, and Colin McCahon's epic *Urewera Mural* (1976), are unlikely to be accessible until their completion.

The only **accommodation** inside the park itself is at the well-equipped *Waikaremoana Motor Camp*, on SH38, 2km south of the visitor centre (ⓣ06/837 3826, ⓦwww.lake.co.nz; cabins & units ❸), which has a compact but grassy camping area ($10); showers are available for non-guests at $2 a time. Just outside the park on SH38, 15km south of the Aniwaniwa visitor centre, the best bet is the ever-expanding *Big Bush Holiday Park* (ⓣ0800/525 392, ⓦwww.lakewaikaremoana.co.nz), which is fully set up for track trampers and offers camping ($10), dorms ($25) and some comfortable self-contained units (❸) with television and a small sunny deck. A further kilometre south in Tuai is the *Kaitaua Outdoor Education Centre* (ⓣ06/837 3806), which charges $15 for dorms during school holidays only, while construction workers' quarters have been converted into *Lake Whakamarino Lodge* (ⓣ06/837 3876, ⓦwww.lakelodge.co.nz; rooms ❷, self-contained units ❹), which is wonderfully sited right on the shores of the trout-filled Lake Whakamarino. There are also a couple of DOC **campsites** along SH38: *Mokau Landing* ($5), 11km northwest of the visitor centre, and *Taita a Makora* (free), 11km further on. You'll largely have to fend for yourself when it comes to **eating**, with the only food in the park being the good range of groceries at the *Waikaremoana Motor Camp*. Outside the park, Tuai's *Big Bush Holiday Park* has reasonably priced meals and decent coffee in its *Rangers Café*, a authentic cowboy-style bar and restaurant, and meals are available on request at the *Lake Whakamarino Lodge* with mains around $25.

See p.425 for trailhead transport.

The Lake Waikaremoana Track

The **Lake Waikaremoana Track** (46km; 3–4 days; 900m ascent) is one of New Zealand's "Great Walks". It is also the most popular multi-day tramp in the North Island and often compared with the South Island's renowned Routeburn and Milford tracks though, with the exception of an exhausting climb on the first day, this is a much gentler affair, with plenty of opportunities to fish, swim and listen to the melodious birdlife.

Comprehensive walking **information** is covered in DOC's *Lake Waikaremoana Track* leaflet, though **map** enthusiasts might like the detailed 1:100,000 *Urewera Parkmap*, both available from the Aniwaniwa and Wairoa visitor centres. Three days is enough for fit walkers, but it's normally done in four, spending nights in the five "Great Walk" **huts** ($25) and five designated **campsites** ($10) scattered around the lakeshore. Throughout the year, huts and campsites must be **booked in advance** through the Aniwaniwa visitor centre or DOC offices nationwide; your chances of getting a place are much better outside the busy month or so after Christmas and the week of Easter. The winter months (June–Sept) can be cold and wet, making spring and autumn the best times to undertake the walk. Each hut is supplied with drinking water, toilets and a heating stove, but a cooking stove, fuel and all your food must be carried. Campsites just have water and toilets.

About sixty percent of walkers prefer to travel clockwise around the lake, getting the challenging but panoramic ascent of Panekiri Bluff over with on the first day, though if the weather looks bad there's no reason why you shouldn't go anticlockwise in the hope that it will improve.

If you don't fancy going it alone, consider a four-day **guided walk** ($950) with Walking Legends (ⓣ07/345 7363, ⓦwww.walkinglegends.com), whose

▲ Lake Waikaremoana

accommodation is in the same DOC huts used by independent walkers. Transport from Rotorua, enthusiastic and knowledgeable guiding, excellent meals and wine are provided. All you have to do is carry a daypack. The longest day is around seven hours, and there's usually enough time for a bit of trout fishing.

Trailhead transport

You can **drive** to the trailheads at either end of the tramp, but there are occasional thefts and most people instead park free of charge either at *Big Bush Holiday Park*, or in the car park beside the *Waikaremoana Motor Camp* store. Three companies then provide **access** to the start and finish of the Waikaremoana Circuit either by **shuttle bus** or **ferry service**: Waikaremoana Guided Tours (Ⓣ0800/469 879), Homebay Water Taxi & Cruises (Ⓣ06/837 3826) and Big Bush Water Taxi (Ⓣ0800/525 392). They each run several times a day to the ends of the track, charging $30 to $35 for a joint drop-off and pick-up package: all will get you started by 9am. They will also run a **water taxi** service to anywhere else you might want to start or finish, enabling you to walk shorter sections of the circuit by means of prearranged pick-ups from specified beaches – prices are dependent on numbers but are broadly comparable with the regular services.

The route

When tackled clockwise, as outlined below, the first leg is the toughest; carry plenty of drinking water.

Onepoto to Panekiri Hut (9km; 4–5hr; 750m ascent, 150m descent) The track starts at a shelter by the lakeshore close to SH38 and climbs steeply past the site of a redoubt set up by soldiers of the Armed Constabulary in pursuit of Te Kooti (see box, p.426). It then undulates along the ridge top, occasionally revealing fabulous lake views. Wonderfully airy steps up a rocky bluff bring you to the Panekiri Hut (36 bunks), magnificently set on the brink of the cliffs that fall away to the lake far below. Camping in this fragile environment is prohibited; committed campers must press on to Waiopaoa, an exhausting 8hr walk from the start at Onepoto.

Te Kooti Rikirangi

Te Kooti Rikirangi was one of the most celebrated of Maori "rebels", a thorn in the side of the colonial government throughout the New Zealand Wars of the late 1860s and early 1870s. An excellent fighter and brilliant strategist, Te Kooti kept the mountainous spine of the North Island on edge for half a decade eluding the biggest manhunt in New Zealand's history.

Born near Gisborne around 1830, Te Kooti was not of chiefly rank but could trace his ancestry back to the captains of several *waka* (canoes) that brought the Maori to New Zealand. By the middle of the 1860s, he was fighting for the government against the fanatical, pseudo-Christian Hau Hau cult that started in Taranaki in 1862. The cult spread to the east coast where, in 1866, Te Kooti was unjustly accused of being in league with its devotees. Denied the trial he demanded, he was imprisoned on the Chatham Islands, along with 300 of his supposed allies. In 1867, he was brought close to death by a fever, but rose again, claiming a divine revelation and establishing a new religion, **Ringatu** ("the uplifted hand"), which still has some ten thousand believers today. Ringatu took its cues from the Hau Hau, but developed into a uniquely Maori version of Catholicism, drawing heavily on the Old Testament. Some say Te Kooti saw himself as a Moses figure – apparently given to dousing his uplifted hand in phosphorus so that it glowed in the dim meeting houses.

After two years on the Chathams, Te Kooti and his fellow prisoners commandeered a ship and engineered a dramatic escape, returning to Poverty Bay. He sought safety in the **Urewera Range**, with the Armed Constabulary in hot pursuit. Te Kooti still managed to conduct successful campaigns, exacting revenge against government troops at Whakatane on the Bay of Plenty, Mohaka in Hawke's Bay and at Rotorua. With the end of the New Zealand Wars in 1872, Te Kooti took refuge in the Maori safe haven of the King Country. He was eventually pardoned in 1883, and in 1891 was granted a plot of land near Whakatane, where he lived out the last two years of his life.

Panekiri Hut to Waiopaoa Hut (7.5km; 3–4hr; 600m descent) Descends the ridge, then rapidly loses height through an often muddy area where protruding tree roots provide welcome hand-holds. Occasional lake views and the transition from beech forests to rich podocarp woodlands make this an appealing, if tricky, section of track down to the hut (30 bunks) and campsite.

Waiopaoa Hut to Marauiti Hut (11km; 4–5hr; 100m ascent) Largely follows the lakeshore, crossing grassland and then kanuka scrub before reaching the Korokoro campsite (1hr 30min from Waiopaoa Hut). A side track leads to the impressive twenty-metre Korokoro Falls (45–60min return). Meanwhile, the main track climbs slightly above the lake past barely accessible bays, eventually reaching the Maraunui campsite and, after ascending the low Whakaneke Spur, descends to the waterside Marauiti Hut (25 bunks).

Marauiti Hut to Waiharuru Hut (6km; 2hr; 150m ascent) Passes the lovely white-sand Te Kopua Bay and climbs an easy saddle, before dropping down to Te Totara Bay and following the lake to the large and modern Waiharuru Hut (40 bunks) and campsite.

Waiharuru Hut to Whanganui Hut (5.3km; 2–3hr; 100m ascent) A short hike across a broad neck of land to the Tapuaenui campsite and beyond, following the shore to the characterful old hut, fitted with built-in three-tier bunks (18 bunks).

Whanganui Hut to Hopuruahine (5km; 2–3hr; 50m ascent) This easy final section skirts the lake to the point where water taxis pick up (45min). The track then follows grassy flats beside the Hopuruahine River and crosses a suspension bridge to the access road to a camping area (free).

Central Te Urewera National Park

Beyond Lake Waikaremoana, SH38 twists and turns for over two hours before regaining its tar seal just before Murupara, almost 100km northwest of the lake and just an hour (62km) short of Rotorua. The road, which took 45 years to build and wasn't completed until 1930, makes a tortuous journey through the heart of Te Urewera National Park, the ancestral home of the Tuhoe people.

Historically, the Tuhoe had limited contact with Europeans; even today, they live in relative isolation in ramshackle roadside villages such as **RUATAHUNA**, 48km from Waikaremoana, which has the road's only store and takeaway. Ruatahuna also serves as a base for a couple of little-used tracks into beautiful and remote country north of SH38. These are most often used by anglers and hunters, but are excellent for tramping (and covered by DOC leaflets), with backcountry huts ($5) at regular intervals; seek local advice on the likelihood of flooding.

Napier and around

Seaside **NAPIER** is an easy place to warm to, thanks to its Mediterranean climate, affordable prices and the world's best-preserved collection of Art Deco architecture. With its laid-back population of 54,000, Napier is Hawke's Bay's largest city, and the jumping-off point for trips out to the gannet colony at Cape Kidnappers as well as the barrel-load of world-class **wineries** on the surrounding plains.

Some history

In 1769, James Cook sailed past **Ahuriri**, the current site of Napier, noting the sea-girt Bluff Hill linked to the mainland by two slender shingle banks and backed by a superb saltwater lagoon – the only substantial sheltered mooring between Gisborne and Wellington. Nonetheless, after a less-than-cordial encounter with the native Ngati Kahungunu people he anchored just to the south, off what came to be known as Cape Kidnappers. Some thirty years later,

Hawke's Bay festivals

During January and February, Napier and nearby Hastings flip into festive mode. Small-scale events take place in January, but the first of the major events is the **Harvest Hawke's Bay** (first weekend in Feb; ⓦwww.harvesthawkesbay.co.nz), when food- and wine-lovers from around the country flock here for two days of drinking and entertainment. A constant stream of buses connect over two dozen wineries, each offering something different: vertical tastings (sampling a particular wine from a series of vintages), food matching, special tours or music. Either buy the special weekend glass ($15) and make your own way, or get the Saturday bus pass ($40), which is good for entry and unlimited bus rides. Saturday's jazz concert ($55) at Church Road Winery in Taradale is the acclaimed highlight, but many other wineries offer free concerts.

The **Mission Vineyard Concert** usually takes place in early February (the precise dates are dependent on artists' bookings), when an internationally famous vocalist – Kiri Te Kanawa, Ray Charles and Rod Stewart have starred in recent years – performs outdoors at the Mission Estate Winery to an audience of around 25,000.

No sooner has the Hawke's Bay summer festival wound up than Napier gears up for the **Art Deco Weekend** (ⓣ06/835 0022, ⓦwww.artdeconapier.com), featuring guided walks, open-house tours of domestic Art Deco architecture, vintage cars, 1930s dress picnics, champagne breakfasts, dress balls, silent movies and the like; and the associated **Wine & Food Festival**, both held on the third weekend in February and continuing for five light-hearted days. Heading into winter, the **Deco Decanted & Jazz Festival** takes place on the third weekend in July.

when early whalers followed in Cook's tracks, Ahuriri was all but deserted, the Ngati Kahungunu having been driven out by rivals equipped with guns – the dubious contribution of European settlers in the Bay of Islands. During the uneasy peace of the early colonial years, Maori returned to the Napier area, which weathered the **New Zealand Wars** of the 1860s relatively unscathed. The port boomed, but by the early years of the twentieth century all the available land was used up.

Everything changed in two and a half minutes on the morning of February 3, 1931, when the city was rocked by the biggest **earthquake** in New Zealand's recorded history, measuring a massive 7.9 on the Richter scale. More than six hundred aftershocks followed over the next two weeks, hampering efforts to rescue the 258 people who perished in the Bay area, 162 of them in Napier alone. The centre of the city was completely devastated, crumbling into smouldering rubble and consumed by the ensuing fire. The land twisted and buckled, finding a new equilibrium more than two metres higher, with three hundred square kilometres of new land wrested from the grip of the ocean – enough room to site the Hawke's Bay airport, establish new farms and expand the city; cast your eye inland and you can still pick out a stranded line of sea cliffs a couple of kilometres away.

Napier embraced the opportunity to start afresh: out went the trams, telephone wires were laid underground, the streets were widened and, in the spirit of the times, almost everything was designed according to the precepts of the **Art Deco** movement. The simultaneous reconstruction gave Napier a stylistic uniformity rarely seen – ranking it alongside Miami Beach as one of the world's largest collections of Art Deco buildings.

Arrival, information and transport

Regular direct **flights** from Auckland, Wellington and Christchurch touch down at Hawke's Bay Airport, 5km north of town on SH2, where they are met by the Super Shuttle (Ⓣ06/844 7333, Ⓦwww.supershuttle.co.nz), which charges around $15 to get into town depending on the number of passengers and the drop-off point. Long-distance **buses** pull in at the Napier Travel Centre, Munroe Street (Ⓣ06/834 2720), some ten minutes' walk from the busy **i-SITE visitor centre**, 100 Marine Parade (Mon–Fri 8.30am–5pm, Sat & Sun 9am–5pm, often until 6 or 7pm in summer; Ⓣ06/834 1911, Ⓦwww.hawkesbaynz.com), which has Internet access. The nearby **DOC office**, 59 Marine Parade (Mon–Fri 9am–4.15pm; Ⓣ06/834 3111) has tide tables for Cape Kidnappers and information about walks into the remote Kaweka and Ruahine ranges to the west. Napier's **post office** is on the corner of Hastings and Dickens streets. Entertainment **listings** are covered in the weekday-only *Hawke's Bay Today* newspaper, especially on Thursday.

Getting around Napier's central sights is easily done on foot. For trips around the region, the Nimons **local bus** services (not Sun; check with the visitor centre for pick-up points) are of use for visits to Hastings, or the Mission Estate Winery (where they drop off within walking distance). To venture further afield, either join a **winery tour** (see p.440), **rent a car** (try Hertz Ⓣ06/835 6169; Rent-a-Dent Ⓣ06/834 0688, or Pegasus Ⓣ0806/354 526), **rent a bike** from Marineland on Marine Parade ($25 a day), or hop in a **taxi** with Napier Taxis (Ⓣ06/835 7777).

Accommodation

Apart from the usual shortage of rooms during the month or so after Christmas and during February's festivals (see p.427), you should have little trouble finding

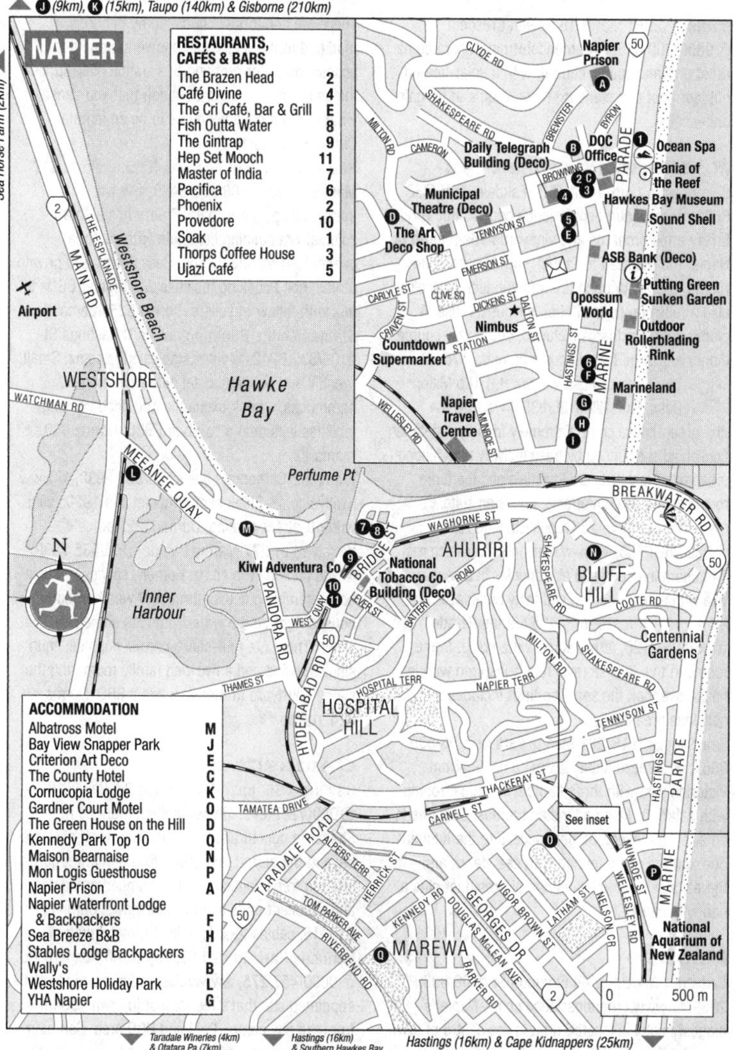

accommodation in Napier. There are dozens of **motels** around town, many concentrated in Westshore, a beachfront suburb a couple of kilometres from the centre, beside the northbound SH2. Right in the thick of things, Marine Parade has low-cost backpacker **hostels** and classy **B&Bs**.

Hotels and motels

Albatross Motel 56 Meeanee Quay, Westshore ⓣ0800/252 287, ⓦwww.albatrossmotel.co.nz. Large, good-value motel close to Westshore Beach and Ahuriri's restaurants, with a pool, spa, studio units and self-catering family rooms. ❸

The County Hotel 12 Browning St ⓣ0800/843 468, ⓦwww.countyhotel.co.nz. Elegant, beautifully decorated business and tourist hotel in the Edwardian former council offices building, one of the few to survive the earthquake. Rooms all come with en-suite facilities and Sky TV. ❽

Gardner Court Motel 16 Nelson Crescent ☎0800/000 830, Ⓔ gardencourtmotel@xtra.co.nz. Quiet and reasonably central, with a solar-heated outdoor pool and standard motel rooms at bargain prices. ❸

B&Bs and homestays

Cornucopia Lodge 361 SH5, Eskdale ☎06/836 6508, Ⓦ www.cornucopia-lodge.com. A little rural luxury amid orchards and vineyards 15km north of Napier (on the road to Taupo), with two en-suite rooms, each with open fire and sundeck. There's also a fully equipped kitchen for guests' use. A wonderful breakfast is included, and a two-course dinner and wine for two costs an extra $75. ❻

The Green House on the Hill 18b Milton Oaks, Bluff Hill ☎06/835 4475 Ⓦ www.the-green-house.co.nz. Extremely friendly vegetarian household surrounded by trees halfway up a hidden urban hill. Breakfasts are inventive and the three rooms quiet and comfortable; one is en suite. ❹

Maison Bearnaise 25 France Rd, Bluff Hill ☎0800/624 766, Ⓦ www.maisonbearnaise.co.nz. Two charming open and airy doubles in a century-old villa with a lovely garden and tasty breakfasts. ❺

Mon Logis Guesthouse 415 Marine Parade ☎06/835 2125, Ⓔ monlogis@xtra.co.nz. Some rooms in this two-storey, French-inspired wooden house overlook the sea. The tariff includes a delicious breakfast. ❹

Sea Breeze B&B 281 Marine Parade ☎06/835 8067, Ⓔ sbreeze.napier@xtra.co.nz. Seafront Victorian villa with three flamboyant guest rooms with Asian, Turkish and Indian themes. Only one is en suite, but everyone gets access to the kitchenette and the guest lounge with sea views, and there's a self-service continental breakfast plus a handy laundry. ❹

Hostels

Criterion Art Deco 48 Emerson St ☎06/835 2059, Ⓦ www.criterionartdeco.co.nz. Napier's biggest hostel is located right in the centre of town, in an Art Deco former hotel with large communal areas. There are good-value dorms as well as doubles, some en suite. Guests get discounts in *The Cri* café/bar downstairs. Rates spike sharply during festivals. Dorms $24, rooms ❷

Napier Prison 55 Coote Rd ☎06/835 9933, Ⓦ www.napierprison.com. Stay in what was Napier's fifty-bed prison from the 1860s to 1993. There are comfortable beds (some in barely modified former cells), hot showers, free Internet access, bikes for rent and bus station pick-up, but things are kept primitive enough that you sense what it might have been like to be an inmate. Dorms $23, rooms ❷

Napier Waterfront Lodge & Backpackers 217 Marine Parade ☎06/835 3429, Ⓦ www.napierbackpackers.co.nz. Breezy hostel in a colonial-era building complete with veranda overlooking Marine Parade. Cosy dorms and private rooms, good cooking facilities and regular BBQs to mix with fellow travellers. Dorms $25, rooms ❷

Stables Lodge Backpackers 370 Hastings St ☎06/835 6242, Ⓦ www.stableslodge.co.nz. Small, friendly and relaxed hostel with free Internet, hammocks, a book exchange and good cooking facilities including a courtyard BBQ. Dorms $20, rooms ❷

Wally's 7 Cathedral Lane ☎06/833 7930, Ⓦ www.wallys.co.nz. Sleek central hostel in a 1920s villa with off-street parking. Dorms $22, rooms ❷

YHA Napier 277 Marine Parade ☎06/835 7039, Ⓔ yha.napier@yha.co.nz. Homely, spotlessly clean hostel rambling across three airy weatherboard houses right on the waterfront with some sea views. There are four-share dorms, doubles, snug singles, twins and a five-bed family room, and the sunny courtyard at the back has a BBQ. Dorms $24, rooms ❷

Campsites

Bay View Snapper Park 10 Gill Rd, Bay View ☎0800/287 275, Ⓦ www.snapperpark.co.nz. Sheltered beachfront campsite 9km north of Napier, beyond the airport and 200m from a market garden offering fresh vegetables. The campervan spots and excellent units all have sea views. Camping $15–16, cabins ❷, s/c units ❹, motel units ❺

Kennedy Park Top 10 Storkey St, off Kennedy Rd ☎0800/457 275, Ⓦ www.kennedypark.co.nz. Well-appointed site that's the closest to town at 3km from the city centre. Pool and BBQ area. Camping $16–17, cabins & kitchen cabins ❷, s/c units ❹

Westshore Holiday Park 88 Meeanee Quay, Westshore ☎06/835 9456, Ⓔ westshoreholiday@xtra.co.nz. Located midway along Westshore Beach, 3km north of town, this site is a little less formal than *Kennedy Park* but still has all the facilities you're likely to need. Camping $12–14, cabins & kitchen cabins ❶, s/c units ❷

The Town

Steep roads and even steeper steps switchback down the southern flank of **Bluff Hill** (Mataruahou) to the grid pattern of Napier's Art Deco **commercial**

centre where, at the whim of mid-nineteenth-century Land Commissioner Alfred Domett, streets were given the names of literary luminaries – Tennyson, Thackeray, Byron, Dickens, Shakespeare, Milton and more. Bisecting it all is the partly pedestrianized main thoroughfare of Emerson Street, whose terracotta paving and palm trees run from Clive Square – one-time site of a makeshift "Tin Town" while the city was being rebuilt after the earthquake – to the Norfolk pine-fringed **Marine Parade**. The long strip of grey shingle flanking Marine Parade is Napier's main **beach**, but treacherous undertows and surf breaking close to the shoreline make it unsafe for swimming – you'll find golden-sand swimming beaches out of town north from Whirinaki, and south from Cape Kidnappers.

Around the northeastern side of Bluff Hill, about 5km from the city centre, lies the original settlement site of **Ahuriri**, currently experiencing a renaissance, its waterside warehouses now smartened up and occupied by trendy restaurants and cavernous bars.

The commercial centre: Art Deco Napier

The 1931 earthquake saw Napier rebuild in line with the times. Although **Art Deco** embraced modernity, glorifying progress, the machine age and the Gatsby-style high life, the onset of the Great Depression pared down these excesses, and Napier's version was informed by the privations of an austere era. At the same time, the architects looked for inspiration to California's Santa Barbara – which, just six years earlier, had suffered the same fate as Napier and risen from the ashes. They adopted fountains (a symbol of renewal), sunbursts, chevrons, lightning flashes and fluting to embellish the highly formalized but asymmetric designs. In Napier, what emerged was a palimpsest of early-twentieth-century design, combining elements of the Arts and Crafts movement, the Californian Spanish Mission style, Egyptian and Mayan motifs, stylized floral designs and even Maori imagery. For the best part of half a century, the city's residents merely daubed the buildings in grey or muted blue paint. Fortunately, this meant that when a few visionaries recognized the city's potential in the mid-1980s and formed the **Art Deco Trust**, everything was still intact. The trust continues to promote the preservation of buildings and provides funding for shopkeepers to pick out distinctive architectural detail in pastel colours similar to those originally used.

Art Deco Napier tours and trails

Keen observers will find classic Art Deco everywhere, but for a systematic exploration of Napier's Art Deco revival, begin at **The Art Deco Shop**, 163 Tennyson St (daily 9am–5pm), where you can watch a free twenty-minute introductory video and buy a leaflet for the **self-guided Art Deco Walk** ($5), outlining a stroll (1.5km; 1hr 30min–2hr) through the downtown area. Dedicated Deco buffs meet here for the **Art Deco Afternoon Walking Tour** (daily 2pm; 2hr; $20), which brings 1930s Napier to life through anecdote-laden patter and gives you the chance to gaze around the interiors of shops and banks without feeling quite so self-conscious. The shorter **Art Deco Morning Walking Tour** (daily 10am; 1hr; $14) and **Art Deco Evening Walk** (daily end Dec to March; 1.5hr; $16) both start at the i-SITE visitor centre. The Art Deco Trust (☎06/835 0022), based in the same building as The Art Deco Shop, operates **Vintage Deco Car Tours** (subject to availability; 1hr; $130 per tour for a maximum of 3 people), and the **Deco Tour**, a minibus tour of Napier's Art Deco attractions outside the central city (daily 11.30am; 75min; $38 per person for a maximimum of 8 people).

You can get a sense of Art Deco Napier by wandering along the half-dozen streets of the city centre, notably **Emerson Street**. Worth special attention here is the **ASB Bank**, on the corner of Hastings Street. Its exterior is adorned with fern shoots and a mask from the head of a *taiaha* (a long fighting club), while its interior has a fine Maori rafter design. On Tennyson Street, look for the flamboyant **Daily Telegraph** building, with stylized fountains, and the **Municipal Theatre**, built in the late 1930s in a strikingly geometric form.

▲Pania of the Reef, Marine Parade

Pania of the Reef

Local Maori tell the tale of **Pania**, a beautiful sea-maiden who would swim from the watery realm of Tangaroa, the god of the ocean, each evening to quench her thirst at a freshwater spring in a clump of flax close to the base of Bluff Hill, then return to her people each morning. One evening, she was discovered by a young chief who wooed her and wanted her to remain on land. Eventually they married, but when Pania went to pay a final visit to her kin they forcibly restrained her in the briny depths, and she turned to stone as what is now known as **Pania Reef**. Fishers and divers still claim they can see her with her arms outstretched towards the shore.

Marine Parade

Napier's defining feature is **Marine Parade**, a two-kilometre-long boulevard lined with stately Norfolk pines and fashioned in the British seaside tradition (pebbly beach and all). A popular walking and cycling path links its string of attractions. Marine Parade starts by Napier's port at the northern end of town and passes the foot of Bluff Hill before arriving at the **Ocean Spa**, 42 Marine Parade (Mon–Sat 6am–10pm, Sun 8am–10pm; $6.50; ⓣ06/835 8553), a lavish salt-chlorinated hot-pool complex overlooking the beach with bubbles, jets, spouts, massages ($35 for 30min), beauty treatments and a lap pool. The long hours and warm waters make it a great place for a relaxed summer evening.

A little further south you'll pass a floral clock and the ornamental Tom Parker Fountain before reaching the bronze cast of the curvaceous **Pania of the Reef**, a siren of Maori legend (see box above). Opposite, the **Hawke's Bay Museum & Art Gallery**, 65 Marine Parade (daily 10am–6pm; $7.50), has a newly overhauled collection of exhibits that give you a deeper insight into the local area; check with the visitor centre for updates.

Up ahead, the curving colonnade of the Veronica Sun Bay and the **Sound Shell** stage give way to a **putting course** (daily 9.30am–4.30pm; $7.50 per 18-hole round) and some attractive **sunken gardens**. Opposite, at 157 Marine Parade, **Opossum World** (daily 9am–5pm; free) presents all you ever need to know and more about New Zealand's greatest pest and sells all sorts of possum products – including fur hats and garments knitted from possum fur blended with merino wool – with the motto that every item bought saves a tree.

Continuing beyond the sunken gardens and popular outdoor **rollerblading/skateboarding** rink you reach **Marineland** (daily 10am–4.30pm; dolphin & seal shows 10.30am & 2pm; $11, $18 for a "Behind the Scenes" tour; ⓦwww.marineland.co.nz), a small marine zoo that houses a leopard seal, sea lions and penguins – many of them recovering from injuries sustained in the wild. During the outdated shows, performing seals and one ageing dolphin are put through their paces. In the summer months you should try to book a couple of days in advance (a couple of weeks immediately after Christmas) if you fancy **feeding** one of the creatures (just which one depends on who's hungry on the day), or an half-hour-long **swim with the dolphin** in the pool (ⓣ06/834 4027; $50, plus $10 for the recommended wetsuit); she can usually be persuaded to play ball.

Further along the seafront, past the boating lake, lies the **National Aquarium of New Zealand** (daily 9am–5pm; $14.60; ⓦwww.nationalaquarium.co.nz.) Constantly revamped, it is consolidating its position as the finest such establishment in the country, with distinct marine environments from Africa, Asia and Australia, plus a substantial New Zealand section. The most spectacular section is the **ocean tank** (hand-feeding at 2pm), its Perspex walk-through tunnel giving intimate views of rays and the odd shark. There's more hand-feeding at the **reef tank** at 10am, plus "Behind the Scenes" tours (daily by reservation; $28) and the chance for qualified scuba-divers to swim with the sharks in the ocean tank ($62.50, plus $31 for gear). There are also non-aquatic sections on New Zealand's reptilian tuatara, and a nocturnal **kiwi house**.

Bluff Hill and Napier Prison Tour

The city centre's northern flank butts up against the steep slopes of **Bluff Hill**, a three-kilometre-long hummock of winding streets that houses some of Napier's more desirable suburbs. There's little to see, but at its eastern summit is **Bluff Hill Domain Lookout** (daily 7am–dusk) offering views of Cape Kidnappers to the west, and right across to the distant Mahia Peninsula in the east. Wind back down to Coote Road where, near the foot of the hill, native and exotic trees have been cultivated in **Centennial Gardens** (unrestricted entry), a former quarry with an artificial waterfall.

The quarry was originally worked by convicts who hacked out rock for the imposing sandstone wall of the nearby prison. Decommissioned in 1993, this is now a backpacker hostel (see p.430), and can be visited on entertaining, hour-long **Napier Prison Tours** (daily 9.30am & 3pm; $15; prison backpacker guests $5). This is no Alcatraz but a very Kiwi jail, all weatherboard and corrugated iron. Founded in 1863, it had a chequered career, housing women, children and lunatics as well as hardened male inmates. Several cells have been left as they were, complete with gang graffiti and, reputedly, the ghosts of former inmates.

Ahuriri

Napier's European beginnings are all around the harbourside suburb of **Ahuriri**, 5km northwest of downtown. James Cook found shelter for the *Endeavour* in the Ahuriri Estuary, and the fledgling town grew up around the harbour. When the industrial port and the commercial heart moved around the headland Ahuriri languished, but in the last few years the old wool stores and warehouses around the inner harbour (also known as the Iron Pot) have been reborn as cavernous bars and restaurants, all typically buzzing from Thursday evening through the weekend.

During the day it's a pleasant place to stroll, though the only real sight is the **National Tobacco Company Building**, on the corner of Bridge and Ossian streets. Its exterior is the most frequently used image of Deco Napier and exhibits a decorative richness seldom seen on industrial buildings, including Art Nouveau motifs of roses and raupo (a kind of Kiwi bulrush).

In one of the former wool stores, the Kiwi Adventure Co, 58 West Quay (ⓣ06/834 3500, ⓦwww.kiwi-adventure.co.nz), has an indoor **climbing wall** ($15 all day), and offers **gorging** and **kayaking** trips (each $149 for 5hr return).

Unique behind-the-scenes tours of a **sheepskin tannery** are offered by Classic Sheepskins, 22 Thames St (daily 11am & 2pm; free; ⓣ06/835 9662, ⓦwww.classicsheepskins.co.nz). You also have the opportunity to buy discounted products including ugg boots; they'll even pick you up for free from the city centre.

Eating, drinking and entertainment

Napier has plenty of places to keep you fed and watered, with assorted **cafés** and **restaurants** scattered around the centre and harbourside Ahuriri, although the very best chefs ply their trade at the region's premier **wineries** – Mission, Sileni and Craggy Range. Self-caterers have plenty of **supermarkets** to choose from, including a large Countdown Supermarket, Station Street, open daily from 6am to midnight.

It's rare to find any really exciting entertainment, unless you hit town at **festival time** (see box, p.427), but a couple of the **bars** host live music at weekends and when touring bands pass through. Straightforward drinking happens along Hastings Street, mostly the short stretch between Browning and Emerson streets, while a trendier crowd converges on Ahuriri's converted warehouse bars.

There are mainstream **movies** at Downtown Cinema 4, corner of Station and Munroe streets (☎06/831 0600), and more arthouse films at Century Cinema, 65 Marine Parade (☎06/835 9248), in the Hawke's Bay Museum building.

City Centre

The Brazen Head 21 Hastings St. Napier's best Irish-style bar with good-value grub, outdoor seating and a lively, boozy atmosphere at weekends.

Café Divine 53 Hastings St. Lives up to its name with enormous slices of healthy home-made veggie slices and filos and wraps, a delicious seafood chowder ($9.50), and other inexpensive breakfasts and lunches.

The Cri Café, Bar & Grill Market St. Standard Kiwi café fare at some of the best prices in town including nightly backpackers specials under $12. The lively bar has pool tables, big-screen TVs and occasional live music.

Pacifica 208 Marine Parade ☎06/833 6335. Sophisticated, marine-blue modern restaurant concentrating on fish and seafood with mains around the $32–40 mark. The hapuka fillets and teriyaki gurnard are particularly good. In fine weather, head for the bamboo-screened garden. Closed Mon.

Phoenix 43 Hastings St. A real nightclub (Wed–Sat), with live bands and DJs playing breaks, hip-hop and more. Very popular with both locals and visitors.

Soak 42 Marine Parade. Excellent café/restaurant that's part of the Ocean Spa complex, overlooking the pools. Drop in for well-prepared Kiwi café lunches and dinners, or just a coffee.

Thorps Coffee House 40 Hastings St. Wonderfully old-school eat-in or takeaway build-your-own sandwich place also serving good breakfasts, cakes, shakes and great coffee. The interior features bevelled Art Deco detailing and aqua lino floors. Closed Sun.

Ujazi Café 28 Tennyson St. Chilled daytime café spinning reggae and serving largely vegetarian snacks for breakfast and lunch: quiches, sandwiches and salads, plus scrumptious juices and good strong coffee.

Ahuriri

Fish Outta Water 81 Bridge St. Napier's best chipper, churning out tasty fish and chips (including *kumara* chips and at least a couple of choices of fish) as well as gourmet oyster, paua or mussel fritters. Closed Mon lunch.

The Gintrap 66 West Quay. This cobalt-blue corrugated iron shed serves mains like pan-roasted peppered eye fillet ($32), with few-to-no veggie options. You can do better food-wise along this strip, but its timber deck and huge interior are packed with drinkers at weekends; midweek usually sees some action, too.

Hep Set Mooch 58 West Quay. Art-filled daytime café in another vast warehouse, with fun, friendly staff, serving a wide range of breakfasts (such as steaming porridge with stewed apple), great muffins (sweet and savoury) and a healthy selection of salads, frittatas and filo pies.

Master of India 79 Ahuriri Shopping Centre ☎06/834 3440. Atmospheric curry house with ornate gilded decor and a broad menu of vegetarian delights and goat specialities, mostly under $20. Dinner nightly; BYO & licensed. Takeaways too.

Provedore 60 West Quay ☎06/834 0189. Ahuriri's classiest dining with an intimate but spirited atmosphere and delicious food that might include lemon-infused chicken breast on sweetcorn and polenta cakes ($27.50) followed by white chocolate, drambuie and macadamia tart ($12).

Cape Kidnappers and the wineries

No visit to Napier or Hastings is complete without spending some time exploring the surrounding fifty or so **wineries** and the gannet colony at **Cape Kidnappers**. Heading from Napier towards Cape Kidnappers, Marine Parade

(SH2) trawls south through an industrial sprawl on the outskirts of Napier, passing the windswept Waitangi Mission site after about 9km, where a plaque records the establishment of Hawke's Bay's first mission station by William Colenso in 1844. From here it's a couple of kilometres to the village of **Clive**, where a signed turn leads to the beachside settlements of Te Awanga and Clifton, starting point for trips to Cape Kidnappers.

Cape Kidnappers

After James Cook's ill-starred initial encounter with Maori at Gisborne, he sailed to the southern limit of Hawke Bay and anchored off the jagged peninsula known to the Ngati Kahungunu as Te Matua-a-maui, "the fishhook of Maui" – a reference to the origin of the North Island, which was, as legend has it, dragged from the oceans by Maui. Here, Cook experienced a second unfortunate meeting. This time Maori traders noticed two young Tahitian interpreters aboard the *Endeavour*; believing them to be held against their will, the traders captured one of them and paddled away. The boy escaped back to the ship, but Cook subsequently marked the point on his chart as **Cape Kidnappers**.

Neither Cook nor Joseph Banks, both meticulous in recording flora and fauna, mentioned any gannets on the peninsula's final shark-tooth flourish of pinnacles. However, a hundred years later, twenty or so pairs were recorded, and now there are over five thousand pairs – making this the world's largest mainland **gannet colony**.

Gannets are big birds, members of the booby family distinguished by their gold-and-black head markings and their lack of fear of humans. The birds start nesting here in June, laying their eggs from early July through to October, with the chicks hatching some six weeks later. Once fledged, at around fifteen weeks, the young gannets embark on their inaugural flight, a marathon, as-yet-unexplained three-thousand-kilometre journey to Australia, where they spend a couple of years before flying back to spend the rest of their life in New Zealand, returning to their place of birth to breed each year.

During the **breeding season** (June to late Oct), the cape is closed to the public, and one colony, the Saddle, is always reserved for scientific study. At other times you can get within a metre or so of the remaining two sites: the Plateau, a few hundred metres back from the Saddle, where two thousand chattering pairs nest beak-by-jowl; and the beachside Black Reef, the largest colony, a couple of kilometres back from the tip of the peninsula, where there are a further 3500 pairs.

Practicalities

There are several ways to visit the gannets, all starting from well-signposted points in the adjacent settlements of **Clifton** and **Te Awanga**, 20km southeast of Napier, both reached from the Napier or Hastings visitor centres with Kiwi Shuttle (booking essential; $25 return, tour $50; ⓣ0800/147 488). Most tours are tide-dependent, travelling to the colony along the beach below rock fall-prone, hundred-metre-high cliffs. The least expensive way to get to the gannets is simply to walk the 11km along the beach from Clifton (roughly 5hr return). No permits are needed, but you'll need to check **tide tables** with DOC or the Hastings or Napier visitor centres, set off from Clifton between three and four hours after high tide, and head back no more than ninety minutes after low tide. The useful DOC *Guide to Cape Kidnappers* contains a **map** and handy tips.

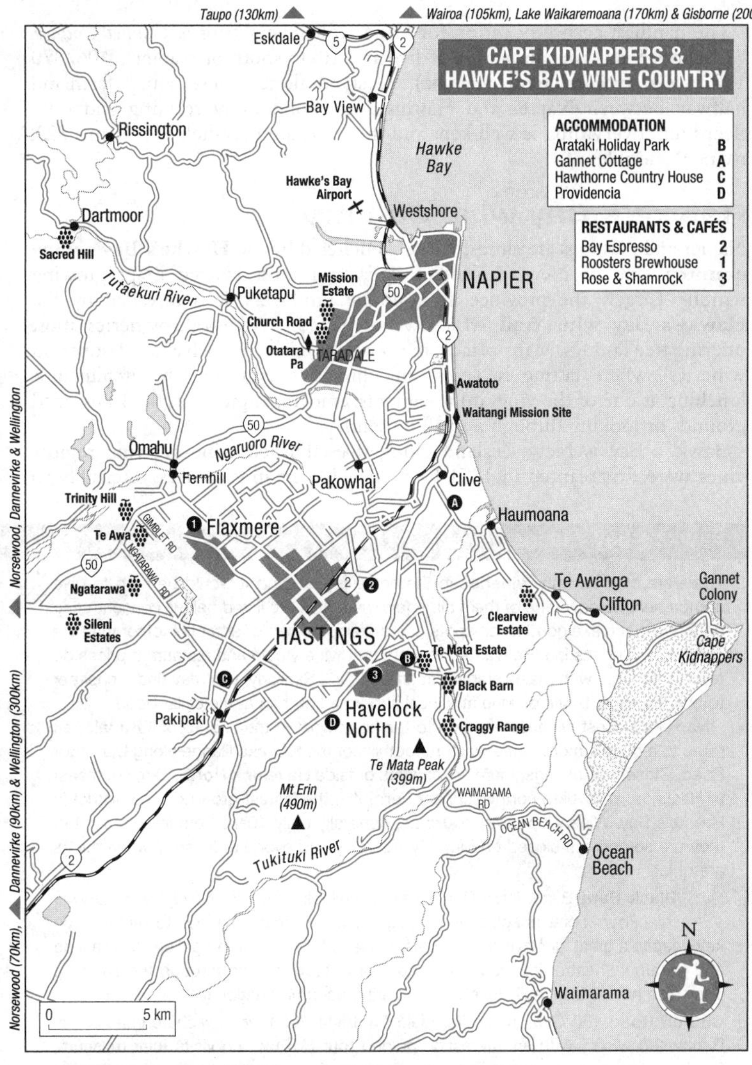

The traditional and best gannet **trip** is aboard tractor-drawn trailers along the beach with Gannet Beach Adventures (daily mid-Oct to early May; 4hr; $33; ⓣ0800/426 638, ⓦwww.gannets.com), whose pace and approach give plenty of opportunities to appreciate the geology along the way and observe the birds at close quarters. These end at a DOC shelter, from where you face a twenty-minute uphill slog to the Plateau, where you'll have half an hour to admire the birds. A worthwhile alternative, which takes you right to the gannets with almost no walking, is with eco-friendly Gannet Safaris (ⓣ0800/427 232, ⓦwww.gannetsafaris.com), which gains access **overland** through Summerlee Station on three-hour trips in air-conditioned 4WD minibuses; prices vary so check with the company directly.

The handiest accommodation for Cape Kidnappers' trips is *Gannet Cottage*, 77 School Rd, 1km southeast of Clive and 10km south of Napier (Ⓣ06/870 1222, Ⓦwww.gannetcottage.co.nz). A stand-alone house amid farmland halfway between Napier and Hastings, it's wonderfully relaxing and only sleeps ten. Everything is well kept and the hosts are ever-helpful. Dorms $23, twins ❶, doubles ❷.

Hawke's Bay wine country

Napier and Hastings are almost entirely encircled by the **Hawke's Bay's wine country**, one of New Zealand's largest and most exalted grape-growing regions. Largely the province of boutique producers, it is threaded by the **Hawke's Bay wine trail**, which wends past thirty-five-odd wineries, most offering free tastings. Many places are now fashioning themselves as "destination wineries" where tasting is almost an adjunct to admiring the architecture, lunching at one of the vineyard restaurants, enjoying a picnic in the landscaped grounds or looking through a small museum.

Hawke's Bay is New Zealand's longest-established wine-growing region: vines were first planted in 1851 by French Marist missionaries, ostensibly to

Hawke's Bay wineries

There are over seventy **wineries** in the entire region, and it would be hard to give comprehensive coverage of them all. A few favourites are listed below, concentrating on those that make good lunch spots or feature some sort of attraction other than the obligatory wine tasting. Be warned though, that winery café and restaurant prices do tend to be high, with mains starting at around $28. Similarly, you may find it cheaper to buy the same bottle of wine at a local supermarket than at the cellar door.

Napier's closest wineries are 8km to the southwest in the suburb of **Taradale**, en route to a couple more in the western foothills of the Kaweka Range along Dartmoor Road. Closer to Hastings, there are clusters outside **Havelock North**, 5km southeast of Hastings, and 10km northwest near **Fernhill** – the fastest-growing wine district in Hawke's Bay. Winery **opening hours** are generally daily 10am–5pm in summer, but they are sometimes closed on Monday, Tuesday and even Wednesday when things are quiet.

Black Barn Black Barn Road, near Havelock North Ⓣ06/877 7985, Ⓦwww.blackbarn.com. Imaginatively designed winery that manages to remain low-key despite a great lunch bistro and café (closed Mon), a small art gallery, free tasting and an amphitheatre that hosts a number of outdoor events through the summer. They also have some really lovely self-catering accommodation (❼).

Church Road 150 Church Rd, Taradale Ⓣ06/844 2053, Ⓦwww.churchroad.co.nz. Renowned winery with an interesting guided tour ($10) which visits their museum, fashioned from old underground vats. Tastings (free; reserve tastings extra) often include their famed Church Road Chardonnay. There's also a restaurant that uses fresh local produce and spills out into the gardens, serving Mediterranean-style dishes at reasonable prices.

Clearview Estate 194 Clifton Rd, Te Awanga Ⓣ06/875 0150, Ⓦwww.clearviewestate.co.nz. Some of New Zealand's most highly rated wines are produced here in tiny quantities and sold only from the family-run vineyard. You pay a premium for the attention to detail but the wines are superb, especially when enjoyed with the restaurant's classy Mediterranean lunches.

Mission Estate 198 Church Rd, Taradale Ⓣ06/845 9350, Ⓦwww.missionestate.co.nz. Worth a visit for its pivotal position in the development of the Hawke's Bay's

produce sacramental wine. The excess was sold, and the commercial aspect of the operation continues today as the Mission Estate Winery. Some fifty years later, other wineries began to spring up, favouring open-textured gravel terraces alongside the Tutaekuri, Ngaruroro and Tukituki rivers, which retain the day's heat and are free from moist sea breezes. In this arena the vineyards of the **Gimblett Road** area produce increasingly sought-after wines With a climatic pattern similar to that of the great Bordeaux vineyards, Hawke's Bay produces fine **Chardonnay** and **Cabernet Sauvignon**. **Merlot** has gained a foothold north of Napier along the Esk Valley, while some experts predict that Hawke's Bay may one day topple the Marlborough region's **Sauvignon Blanc** primacy.

Practicalities

If you have your own transport, head out with a copy of the *Winery Guide* leaflet (free from visitor centres), which lists wineries open to the public – see the box below for the pick of the bunch. Much of the country covered by the wine trail is also part of the region's **art and food trails**. The free *Hawke's Bay Art Guide* booklet directs you to the workshops and galleries of some of the best painters,

wine industry alone, yet New Zealand's oldest winery hasn't rested on its laurels, offering well-organized, free guided tours (daily 10.30am & 2pm). There's an à la carte restaurant on site.

Ngatarawa 305 Ngatarawa Rd, Bridge Pa ⓣ06/879 7603, ⓦwww.ngatarawa.co.nz. An excellent first stop, a small winery with free tastings of quality tipples (notably Chardonnay, Sauvignon Blanc and Merlot as well as highly acclaimed dessert wines from Riesling) in a century-old stable complex with attractive picnic areas and a pétanque pitch.

Sacred Hill 1033 Dartmoor Rd, 20km west of Taradale ⓣ06/844 0138, ⓦwww.sacredhill.com. A lengthy excursion rewarded by a few sips of their superb wine (Dec–Feb only; 11am–4.30pm).

Sileni Estates 2016 Maraekakaho Rd, Bridge Pa ⓣ06/879 8768, ⓦwww.sileni.co.nz. This relative newcomer has brought a new level of professionalism to the area, with landscaped grounds and striking buildings that incorporate a classy café/restaurant, a gourmet food store and a culinary school, plus a vineyard and winery with tastings ($12).

Te Awa 2375 SH50, Fernhill ⓣ06/879 7602, ⓦwww.teawa.com. Sited near the famed Gimblett Road, this winery produces exceptional reds (Merlot, Cabernet Merlot and Pinotage) that are more aromatic and livelier than many of their Hawke's Bay rivals; their Chardonnays are pretty good too. The indoor and outdoor lunchtime restaurant is highly regarded.

Te Mata Estate 349 Te Mata Rd, Havelock North ⓣ06/877 4399, ⓦwww.temata.co.nz. New Zealand's oldest winery on its existing site, now making a fairly small volume of premium handmade wines, notably a Coleraine blend of Cabernet Sauvignon, Merlot and Cabernet Franc. Free tastings with the added bonus of the architecturally controversial house among the grapes designed by Ian Athfield.

Trinity Hill 2396 SH50, Fernhill ⓣ06/879 7778 ⓦwww.trinityhill.com. Strikingly modern winery in the Gimblett Road area, producing excellent reds and Chardonnay. They're increasingly experimenting with varietals rare in New Zealand such as Montepulciano, Tempranillo, Arneis and even make a port blended from Tempranillo and Touriga Nacional. Antipasto platters are on offer for outdoor picnicking.

sculptors, potters and craftspeople hereabouts, while the *Hawke's Bay Wine Country Food Trail* leaflet (also free) includes a map showing the whereabouts of all manner of places producing and selling quality produce – everything from chocolate makers to olive oil producers and cheese manufacturers – along with gourmet cafés and restaurants.

If you can't find an abstemious driver, you could hop on the Nimons local bus services (not Sun), which run from Napier and drop within walking distance of Mission Estate Winery, or, better yet, take a **wine tour**. At least half a dozen are on offer, most visiting four or five wineries over the course of a morning or afternoon. They're mainly Napier-based but will pick up in Hastings and Havelock North, either free or for a small fee. Vince's Vineyard Tours ($55; ⓣ06/836 6705, ⓦwww.vincestours.co.nz) are great fun, with an entertaining and knowledgeable guide and a flexible schedule. Another good bet is Grape Escape (ⓣ0800/100 489, ⓦwww.grapeescapenz.co.nz), who run half-day trips ($55).

A great alternative is to **cycle** around the vineyards with On Yer Bike, 129 Rosser Rd, Hastings (ⓣ076/879 8735,ⓦwww.onyerbikehb.co.nz), who have put together a series of easy routes from two wineries in 14km to six in 23km. All-day bike rental (tandems available), route map, emergency mobile phone and a packed lunch are included in the $50 fee.

Hastings and around

Inland **HASTINGS**, 20km south of Napier, was once a rival to its northern neighbour as Hawke's Bay's premier city, buoyed by the wealth generated by the surrounding farmland and orchards. In recent years, shifting economic patterns and Napier's ascendancy as a tourist destination have put Hastings firmly in second place. Nonetheless, it has an attractive core of buildings, erected after the same 1931 earthquake that rocked Napier. It was saved from the worst effects of the ensuing fires, which were quenched using the artesian water beneath the city before they could take hold. As in Napier, **Art Deco** predominates and, though Hastings lacks the flamboyance and exuberance of its neighbour, there are some harmonious townscapes along Russell, Eastbourne and Heretaunga streets. Hastings also enthusiastically embraced the **Spanish Mission** style, and two exemplary buildings warrant a brief visit.

The area is at the heart of the wonderful Hawke's Bay wine country, and most of its vineyards are within easy reach. Apples, pears and peaches also continue to be grown in huge quantities, and the harvest, which begins in February and lasts three or four months, provides casual, hard-going, low-paying **orchard work** for those willing to thin, pick or pack fruit. The hostels are the best sources of work and up-to-the-minute information and will soon have you organized. Often there is so much work that you can be picky about what you accept. For more information about working in the region see Basics, p.73.

Hastings' neighbour is the upmarket **Havelock North**, 3km southeast and at the foot of the striking ridgeline of **Te Mata Peak**. There isn't a great deal to it, and the only diversion is a drive up the peak, but the cobbled central streets lined with pavement cafés give it a village atmosphere.

Arrival and information

Long-distance **buses** pull up on Russell Street North, a few steps from the **i-SITE visitor centre**, corner of Russell and Heretaunga streets (Mon–Fri

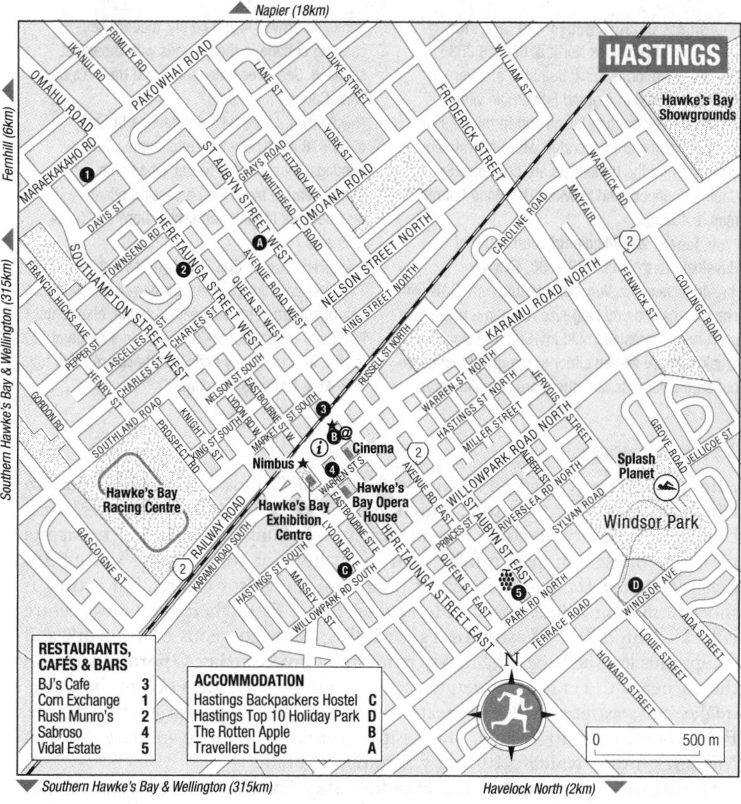

8.30am–5pm, Sat & Sun 9am–4pm; ⓣ06/873 0080, ⓦwww.hastings.co.nz), where you can buy tickets. There's **Internet** access opposite at Hectic Netway, 102 Heretaunga St East. Local bus operator Nimbus (ⓣ06/877 8133) runs to Napier and Havelock North (Mon–Fri; limited services Sat) from the corner of Eastbourne Street East and Russell Street.

Accommodation

The availability of Hastings' budget-oriented **accommodation** is greatly affected by the **fruit-picking season**: from mid-February to May you'll struggle to find cheap accommodation, especially if you're looking for self-catering or a long-stay, unless you've booked well ahead, but nearby Napier makes a good alternative base if you're able to commute. For more luxurious accommodation, head for Havelock North, where **B&Bs** and swanky self-catering houses predominate. The *Black Barn* winery (p.438) has some superb self-catering accommodation.

Hastings Backpackers Hostel 505 Lyndon Rd East ⓣ06/876 5888, ⓦwww.medcasa.co.nz. Comfortable house near the centre, with good facilities and Internet access, packed with pickers in the season. Closed from around May to mid-Oct. Dorms $20, rooms ❷

Hastings Top 10 Holiday Park 610 Windsor Ave ⓣ06/878 6692 & 0508/427 846, ⓦwww.hastingsholidaypark.co.nz. Appealing campsite on the edge of Windsor Park, with tent sites, a range of modern units and good facilities, though it does get busy over the fruit-picking season. Camping $28–32, cabins ❶, kitchen cabins ❸, units and chalets ❹

Hawthorne Country House 420 SH2, 7km southwest of Havelock North ⓣ06/878 0035, ⓦwww.hawthorne.co.nz. Beautiful and very welcoming B&B in a grand Edwardian villa surrounded by croquet lawns and farmland. Five en-suite rooms are decorated with understated elegance and the breakfasts are delicious. See Cape Kidnappers and Hawke's Bay Wine Country map, p.437. ⑧

Providencia 225 Middle Rd, 3km south of Havelock North ⓣ06/877 2300, ⓦwww.providencia.co.nz. Very comfortable rural B&B with one queen- and one king-size room in a beautifully preserved homestead built in 1903. Delicious breakfasts are served either in the guest lounge or out on the veranda, and there are complimentary drinks on arrival. Also a comfy, modern self-catering cottage in the grounds with breakfast supplied. See Cape Kidnappers and Hawke's Bay Wine Country map, p.437. ⑦

The Rotten Apple 114 Heretaunga St East ⓣ06/878 4363, ⓦwww.rottenapple.co.nz. Hastings' most central hostel, albeit with lived-in dorms bearing more than a passing olfactory resemblance to their namesake. Dorms $20–24, rooms ②

Travellers Lodge 606 St Aubyn St West ⓣ06/878 7108, ⓦwww.tlodge.co.nz. Garden-set hostel in a pair of suburban houses, with a sauna, bike rental, Wi-Fi and off-street parking. There is a range of rooms, all with comfy beds, but these are often full Nov–May. Dorms $21, rooms ②

The Town

After the 1931 earthquake, Hastings looked to the Californian-inspired **Spanish Mission** style of architecture: roughcast stucco walls, arched windows, small balconies, barley-twist columns and heavily overhung roofs clad in terracotta tiles. The finest examples can be seen in an hour or so, using the self-guided *Spanish Mission Hastings* walk leaflet (free from the visitor centre), but if time is short, limit your wanderings to Heretaunga Street East, where the visitor centre is located inside the **Westerman's Building**, with gorgeous bronzework and sumptuous lead lighting. The newly renovated **Hawke's Bay Opera House**, on the corner with Hastings Street, was actually built fifteen years before the earthquake, but was remodelled to create the region's finest Spanish Mission facade. From November to March, the visitor centre runs ninety-minute Spanish Mission **guided walks** ($10) every Saturday at 11am.

Also worth a quick look is the **Hawke's Bay Exhibition Centre**, opposite the junction of Eastbourne Street and Karamu Road (daily 10am–4.30pm; free except for special exhibitions), which hosts all manner of art shows and has a relaxing café with good coffee.

Families may well find themselves at **Splash Planet**, Grove Road (daily late Sept to Easter 10am–6pm; adults $25, kids $20; ⓣ06/876 9856, ⓦwww.splashplanet.co.nz), which offers waterpark amusements and slides along with mini race cars, a narrow-gauge train and crazy golf. If you're planning to spend the day there, it's worth taking a picnic.

Te Mata Peak

Driving from Hastings to Havelock North, the long ridge of limestone bluffs which make up the 399m **Te Mata Peak** loom into view. The ridge is held to be the supine form of a Maori chief, Rongokako, who choked on a rock as he tried to eat through the hill – just one of many Herculean feats he attempted while wooing the beautiful daughter of a Heretaunga chief. The long and winding Te Mata Peak Road climbs the hill to a wonderful vantage point that's great towards sunset. Views stretch over the fertile plains, north across Hawke's Bay and Cape Kidnappers, and east to surf-pounded Ocean Beach and Waimarama, the main swimming **beaches** for Hastings and Havelock North.

The peak is encompassed by the Te Mata Peak Trust Park, entered 3.5km up Te Mata Peak Road, where there is a parking area and a number of **walking**

tracks through the hill's patches of parkland. These are outlined in the free brochure on the park available at Napier and Hastings visitor centres and can be combined to create a route through groves of native trees and redwoods and a wetland area before reaching the summit (2–3hr return).

According to legend, overcome with grief at her father's death, Rongokako's daughter threw herself off the peak – something you can emulate by **tandem paragliding** with Airplay Paragliding (Ⓣ06/845 1977, Ⓦwww.airplay.co.nz), who ride the thermals and Pacific winds for 15min ($140). You can also head cross-country for an hour ($250), or even longer.

Eating and drinking

For a town of its size, Hastings is relatively poorly supplied with good places to **eat**, though an ever-expanding selection of places in neighbouring Havelock North bumps up the quota, and lunches at the region's **wineries** are a good (if often pricey) option. Foodies in town at the weekend should make for the **Hawke's Bay Farmers' Market** (Sun 8.30am–12.30pm), at the Hawke's Bay Showgrounds on Kenilworth Road to enjoy fresh local produce. Drinkers will find a smattering of welcoming places in both towns. All establishments are shown on the Hastings map on p.441, unless otherwise stated.

Bay Espresso 141 Karamu Rd. North of the Hawke's Bay Showgrounds, this rustic coffee roastery is the locals' weekend home-from-home. Offers superb coffee, light and healthy lunch specials under $15 and "survival kits" of plunger coffee, locally made biscotti and Fair Trade chocolate ($12) as well as beans by the kilo ($35). See map, p.437.

BJ's Cafe 127 Heretaunga St West. Decent daytime café chiefly notable as outlet for Hastings' award-winning pie maker. Choose from sumptuous, bargain pies such as seafood and veg or the ever-popular steak and cheese. Vegetarians should get in early as non-meat pies quickly sell out.

Corn Exchange 118 Maraekakaho Rd. Stylish restaurant and bar converted from an attractive 1930s grain store on the western fringes of the city, serving moderately priced lunches and dinners.

Roosters Brewhouse 1470 Omahu Rd, 7km west of central Hastings. Welcoming micro-brewery offering traditional natural brews, best supped in their pleasant café or outdoors at garden tables while tucking into straightforward hearty dishes at reasonable prices. There's also free tasting of their English ale, lager and dark beers, and you can buy a flagon to take away, which is a wise move considering the prices elsewhere. Closed Sun. See map, p.437.

Rose & Shamrock 15 Napier Rd, Havelock North. A fair attempt at an Irish pub, with Guinness and a broad range of Irish beers, draught ales and guest beers from Kiwi micro-breweries, plus well-priced bar meals and occasional Irish folk bands. See map, p.437.

Rush Munro's 704 Heretaunga St West. A small ice-cream garden that's been packing in the locals for years. For the retro experience go for the feijoa peaked cone.

Sabroso 219 Heretaunga St East. All-organic and GM-free Slow Food café creating authentic, nourishing Mexican and world fare from local produce, and serving specially roasted coffee (also organic). Kids' menu and play area, too. Closed Sun & Mon.

Vidal Estate 913 Aubyn St East; book at weekends Ⓣ06/872 7440. Popular formal restaurant attached to a winery with linen and polished glassware set amid huge wine barrels. Lunch dishes (each matched with a Vidal wine) might be sundried tomato-crusted lamb rump or seared scallops with *kumara* fritters ($19.50–24.50); dinner mains run from $25–34.

Southern Hawke's Bay

South of Hastings, the main road (SH2) gives the coast a wide berth, taking you through the relentless sheep stations of **Southern Hawke's Bay**, a region uncluttered by places of genuine interest. Small farming towns stand

as fitting memorials to the pioneers who tamed the region, spending the latter half of the nineteenth century clearing the huge totara trees of Seventy Mile Bush, pushing through communication links and establishing sheep runs on the rich plains.

If time is short you'd do as well to push straight on through, but with a little more leisure, you can make a brief pit stop at the "**Scandinavian**" **settlements** of Norsewood and Dannevirke. The New Zealand Wars of the 1860s discouraged British immigrants and, as new areas were opened up for colonization, the authorities took their search for settlers elsewhere. In 1872, Danes, Norwegians and a few Swedes answered the call for rugged folk with strong ties to the land, arriving in Napier ill-prepared for the hardship ahead – many promptly upped sticks for North America, leaving little trace of their sojourn.

The more northern of the two settlements, the hilltop village of **NORSEWOOD**, has a more Scandinavian tenor. Invisible from the highway and easily missed, Upper Norsewood is basically just one short, quaint and deathly quiet main street, Coronation Street, which runs past a glassed-in boathouse containing the fishing boat *Bindalsfaering*, a gift from the Norwegian government commemorating Norsewood's centenary. Kiwis are more familiar with Lower Norsewood, 1km to the south, which is mainly strung along Høvding Street and home to Norsewear, an outdoor clothing company with an excellent reputation among Kiwis for producing hard-wearing woollen garments, originally in rustic Scandinavian designs. The socks in particular last for years – check for bargains in the **factory shop**.

Some 20km south of Norsewood, the Danish heritage of the larger farming town of **DANNEVIRKE** is borne out by a modern windmill in Copenhagen Square on the main street, along with cut-out signs of smiling Vikings greeting and farewelling visitors. If you're after sustenance for the onward journey, try *Black Stump Dannevirke*, 21 High St, a reputable **café** and espresso bar.

South of Dannevirke, SH2 runs 25km to Woodville, the junction of SH3, which strikes west through the Manawatu Gorge to Palmerston North, and SH2. Just 10km south of Woodville on SH2 in **Mangatainoka**, you can watch beer being made at the original headquarters of **Tui Brewery** (open Mon–Thurs 10am–4pm, Fri–Sun 10am–5pm, tours 11am & 2pm Thurs–Sun, plus 2pm Mon–Wed Oct to late March; tours or tastings $12.50; ⓣ06/376 0815, ⓦwww.tui.co.nz), established here in 1889. Book ahead for tours, which conclude with tastings, after which you get to keep your handle (beer glass); otherwise it costs the same to drop in for a tasting. From Mangatainoka, the S2 continues south into the Wairarapa.

Long names and famous flutes

Almost all traffic through Southern Hawke's Bay follows SH2, but visitors in search of the esoteric might want to stray along SH52, which makes a 120km tar-sealed loop east towards the rugged coastline from dull Waipukurau, 50km south of Hastings, re-emerging at Dannevirke. Almost 50km south of Waipukurau (and 6km south of Porangahau), a sign marks the hill known as Taumatawhakatangihanga-koauauotamateaturipukakapikimaungahoronukupokaiwhenuakitanatahu, which, unsurprisingly, rates as one of the world's longest place names; roughly, this mouthful translates as "the hill where Tamatea, circumnavigator of the lands, played the flute for his lover". Whichever way you head south, the coastline is almost entirely inaccessible, apart from Castlepoint, reached by a sixty-five-kilometre road from Masterton.

The Wairarapa

Most of the **Wairarapa** valley is archetypal Kiwi sheep country, with white-flecked green hills stretching into the distance. In recent years, however, the southern half of the region has increasingly benefited from free-spending day-trippers and weekenders coming over the hills from Wellington to visit the boutique hotels and innovative restaurants of Martinborough and Greytown.

The Wairarapa is separated from the capital by the Rimutaka Range, a persistent barrier to communication that kept the region relatively isolated for decades, until the establishment of New Zealand's earliest sheep station close to present-day Martinborough in the 1840s. Soon the rich alluvial lands were selected for development by the **Small Farm Association** (SFA), the brainchild of Joseph Masters, a Derbyshire cooper and longtime campaigner against the separation of landowner and labourer. Aided and abetted by liberal governor George Grey, Masters founded the progressive association, which had the express aim of giving disenfranchised settlers the opportunity to become smallholders. At Grey's suggestion, in 1853 SFA representatives persuaded Maori to sell land for the establishment of two towns – **Masterton** and **Greytown**.

Initially Greytown prospered, and it retains an air of antiquity rare among New Zealand towns, but the routing of the rail line favoured Masterton, which soon became the main commercial centre, famed chiefly today for the annual Golden Shears shearing competition. North of Masterton, the **Pukaha Mount Bruce National Wildlife Centre** provides a superb opportunity to witness ongoing bird conservation work; to the south, **Featherston** is a base for walks up the bed of the Rimutaka Incline Railway.

The goal of many Wellingtonians and visitors is **Martinborough**, the region's wine capital and far and away its most appealing town. Back on the coast, the laid-back holiday settlement of **Castlepoint** is the place for swimming and surfing, and **Cape Palliser** is a good destination for blustery mind-clearing walks and dramatic coastal scenery.

Cross the **Rimutaka Range** towards Wellington and you're into the Hutt Valley, full of commuter-belt communities, none of which really warrant a stop until you reach Petone, on the outskirts of the capital.

Pukaha Mount Bruce National Wildlife Centre and around

The northern half of the Wairarapa is very much a continuation of southern Hawke's Bay, but instead of speeding through this pastoral country, make a brief stop at the **Eketahuna Kiwi Country Information Centre**, 23 Main St (daily 10am–4pm; ⓣ06/375 8545; ⓦwww.eketahunakiwicountry.co.nz) to snap a photo of its Big Kiwi out front, and to buy unique kiwi postage stamps. The centre has reams of information about the **Pukaha Mount Bruce National Wildlife Centre**, in majestic forest a few kilometres to the south (daily 9am–4.30pm, 90min guided tours 10.30am & 2pm Sat & Sun; $8, guided tours $15 including entry; ⓦwww.mtbruce.org.nz). This is one of the best places in the country to view endangered native birds, and some of the world's rarest – kokako, kakariki, Campbell Island teal, hihi, kiwi and takahe – can be found in spacious aviaries set along a one-kilometre trail through lowland primeval forest. Beyond the trail several thousand hectares of forest are used for reintroducing birds to the wild. The generous size of the cages on the trail and the thick foliage often make the birds hard to spot, so you'll need to be patient – Jan & Feb are the best times. More immediate gratification comes in the form of a stand of Californian redwoods, a nocturnal **kiwi house**, reptilian tuatara, and a closed-circuit camera trained on the birds' nests in the breeding season (Oct–March). A twenty-minute audiovisual gives a moving account of the decline of birdlife in New Zealand, long-fin eels are fed at 1.30pm and at 3pm each day a flock of kaka come to feed. You can use the picnic area or relax in the café, which serves good coffee and snacks. There's no useful public transport out here, other than very limited bus services from Masterton.

High above the wildlife centre, you can **stay** at *The Hut* (Ⓣ06/375 8681, Ⓦwww.thehut.co.nz; ❷), a wonderfully rustic but comfy bush cottage with an outdoor tub for a romantic bath (warmed by a thermette) under the stars and a log burner to cook meals. It's a steep forty-minute walk, or you can arrange four-wheeler transport with the owners for a small additional charge.

Masterton and around

Though it is Wairarapa's largest town, workaday **MASTERTON**, crouched at the foot of the Tararua Mountains some 30km south of Pukaha Mount Bruce, is of only passing interest. Central Masterton is bounded on its eastern side by the large **Queen Elizabeth Park**, and strolling around the formal gardens is a pleasant way to pass an hour or so. Opposite, **Aratoi**, corner of Bruce and Dixon streets (daily 10am–4.30pm; gold coin donation; Ⓦwww.aratoi.co.nz), offers regularly changing insights into the history of the Wairarapa region along with some excellent art exhibitions.

The town's major event is the annual **Golden Shears** competition, effectively the Olympiad of all things woolly, held on the three days leading up to the first Saturday in March. Contestants flock from around the world to demonstrate their prowess with the broad-blade handpiece; a top shearer can remove a fleece in under a minute, though for maximum points it must be done with skill as well as speed and leave a smooth and unblemished, if shivering, beast. For a couple of bucks you can just walk in on the early rounds, but to attend the entertaining finals day on Saturday you'll need to book well in advance. For details see Ⓦwww.goldenshears.co.nz.

On a similar theme, **Shear Discovery**, 12 Dixon St (daily 10am–4pm; $5) is an excellent little museum on all things woolly. Housed in two century-old shearing sheds relocated from rural Wairarapa, it's filled with everything from sheep pens and shearing handpieces to pressed bales of wool stencilled with the marks of sheep stations.

Draped over the hills to the west of town, the **Tararua Forest Park**, while not among New Zealand's tramping hotspots, offers some excellent walking through beech and podocarp forests to the sub alpine tops, where the notoriously fickle weather can be dangerous. For details of tramps, pay a visit to the Masterton DOC field centre (see p.447), where you should also buy hut tickets. Serious walkers should consider the **Holdsworth–Jumbo Tramp**, a highly worthwhile twelve-hour circuit that can be broken down into two or more manageable days by staying at **huts** (two at $10 and one at $5) evenly spaced along the route. The track starts at the backcountry hut-style *Holdsworth Lodge* (tent sites $4, lodge $8), 25km west of Masterton at the end of Norfolk Road, off southbound SH2, where day-trippers can undertake easy riverside walks (1–2hr).

Practicalities

Masterton's commercial heart is strung along the parallel Chapel, Queen and Dixon streets. Tranzit **buses** (Ⓣ06/377 1227) pull up outside the **i-SITE visitor centre**, 316 Queen St (Mon–Fri 9am–5pm & Sat–Sun 10am–4pm;

(Ⓣ06/370 0900, Ⓦwww.wairarapanz.com). Tranz Metro (Ⓣ04/801 7000) run commuter services from Wellington to the **train station**, at the end of Perry Street, a fifteen-minute walk from the centre, or call Masterton Radio Taxis (Ⓣ06/378 2555). Trampers should visit the **DOC field centre** (Ⓣ06/377 0700; Mon–Fri 8am–5pm), 3km south at the southern end of South Road, the continuation of Queen Street.

Masterton's best budget **accommodation** is the spacious and attractive *Mawley Park Motor Camp*, 15 Oxford St (Ⓣ06/378 6454, Ⓦwww.mawleypark.co.nz; camping $10, cabins ❶). There's peaceful motel rooms at the well-appointed *Cornwall Park*, 119 Cornwall St (Ⓣ06/378 2939, Ⓦwww.nzmotels.co.nz/cornwall; ❸), in a quiet suburb 2km west of the town centre, with a pool and spa.

You can **eat** well enough for the short time you're likely to be in Masterton. Try *Entice*, the lively café at Aratoi, for a simple snack, or *Café Strada*, on the corner of Queen and Jackson streets next to the Regent cinema, serving good-value imaginative grub from breakfast through to dinner. In Queen Elizabeth Park, the chic *Café Cecille* (Ⓣ06/370 1166; closed dinner Sun & Tues and all day Mon) occupies the genteel former aquarium building and has wide verandas where you can dine while watching the miniature train chug by the boating lake. If you're here on a Saturday morning, stop by the local **farmers' market** at the Solway Showgrounds, off York Street.

Castlepoint

The 300km of coastline from Cape Kidnappers, near Napier, south to Cape Palliser is bleak, desolate and almost entirely inaccessible – except for **CASTLEPOINT**, 65km east of Masterton, where early explorers found a welcome break in the "perpendicular line of cliff". A lighthouse presides over the rocky knoll, which is linked to the mainland by a boardwalk set over a thin hourglass double **beach** that encloses a sheltered **lagoon** known as the Basin. Nearby is a small settlement where Wairarapa families retreat for summer fun and surfers ride the breakers. Castlepoint is at its most frenetic around the third or fourth Saturday in March, when there's an informal **horse race** along the beach most years.

In the absence of a visitor centre, ask for **information** at the Castlepoint Store (Ⓣ06/372 6823), which can let you know about *baches* that can be rented (some by the night). You can also **stay** at the *Castlepoint Holiday Park & Motels* (Ⓣ06/372 6705, Ⓦwww.castlepoint.co.nz; camping $15–20, cabins ❷, kitchen cabins ❸, units ❺) and a garden cottage (❺). The only places to eat are the daytime **café** at the store, and, on Friday and Saturday nights only, at the excellent little attached restaurant, *The Berley Pot*, with seafood and other bar-style fare costing between $15 and $26.

Carterton

South of Masterton, a string of small towns guide you towards the Rimutaka Range to **CARTERTON**, 15km south, home to **Paua World**, 54 Kent St (Mon–Fri 8am–5pm, Sat & Sun 9am–5pm; free; Ⓦwww.pauashell.co.nz). An Aladdin's Cave of objects fashioned from this beautiful rainbow-swirled seashell, you can pick up anything from wonderfully kitsch fridge magnets to elegant jewellery here. The factory supplies just about every tourist knick-knack shop in the country and you can even take a brief, free self-guided tour to see how the stuff is made. There's free tea and coffee, as well as picnic benches and a kids' playground on site, but if making sandwiches sounds like hard work, make for

▲ Stonehenge Aotearoa, near Carterton

Wild Oats, 127 High St, a good **bakery** and deli with decent coffee and plenty of outside seating.

For a magical view over the Wairarapa, drift up and away in a **hot air balloon**. Flights cost $290 including return transport to Carterton and a champagne breakfast.

Around Carterton: Stonehenge Aotearoa

Some 5km south of Carterton, a rough road runs 15km west into the foothills of the Tararua Range to **Waiohine Gorge**, a picturesque chasm that's also ideal for picnics.

Twelve kilometres southeast of Carterton, **Stonehenge Aotearoa** (Sat & Sun 1.30pm & 3pm; $12; bookings essential ⓣ027/246 6766, ⓦwww.stonehenge-aotearoa.com) appears like some vision of neolithic Britain on a low hill amid Wairarapa farmland. Though built on the same scale as its kin on Salisbury Plain, there the similarity ends. Opened in 2005, this is a modern wood and concrete edifice, technically classed as a garden ornament by the local council when planning permission was sought. The resulting "open-sky observatory" is primarily educational, with detailed ninety-minute tours covering a fascinating array of information ranging from pure astronomy through Maori star stories and navigation to astrology and myth-busting comparative religion.

Greytown

Laid out in 1853, the gracious settlement of **GREYTOWN**, 9km south of Carterton, still retains something of its original Victorian feel. Until the end of the nineteenth century, this was the Wairarapa's main settlement, but railway planners diverted the new line around its flood-prone environs, contributing to a decline that was only arrested by the development of profitable orchards and market gardens in the latter half of the twentieth century. The two-storey wooden buildings either side of the highway now house assorted art galleries, "collectibles" shops, excellent cafés and chi-chi B&Bs mostly geared to the Wellington weekender set.

There's no real reason to stay, but if you want a break, the reliable *Main Street Deli*, at no. 88 (Ⓣ06/304 9022), serves moderately priced **meals** and sells a good range of breads and cheeses. If you feel you need to earn your lunch, take a historical **walk** guided by the *Heritage Trails of Wairarapa* booklet ($2) from the volunteer-run **visitor centre** (hours vary) on Main Street, or the i-SITE visitor centre in Masterton.

Featherston and the Rimutaka Incline

The last of the Wairarapa towns before SH2 climbs west over the Rimutakas is **Featherston**, 13km south of Greytown. Steam buffs cross the country to visit the **Fell Locomotive Museum** on Lyon Street (daily 10am–4pm; $5), which contains the last surviving example of the locos that, for 77 years (until the boring of a new tunnel in 1955), climbed the 265-metre, one-in-fifteen slope of the Rimutaka Incline.

Although the rails have long been pulled up, you can follow the trackbed on the **Rimutaka Rail Trail** (17km; 4–5hr; 265m ascent), which starts 10km south of Featherston at Cross Creek, passes old shunting yards and shuffles through the 576-metre summit tunnel before descending to Kaitoke. A detailed

Martinborough wineries

For visitors, Martinborough has the edge over other wine regions in that ten of its wineries are accessible on foot, and a dozen more easily reached by car or a bike rented locally (see p.451). The best **guide** is the widely available and free *Wairarapa and Martinborough Wine Trail* brochure which details the hours and facilities of almost forty wineries, most of which conduct **tastings**, often charging a few dollars – especially if there are reserve wines on offer. During the summer places generally open 11am–4pm at weekends and shorter hours midweek, with some of the smaller places closing if they've sold their year's stock. Here's our pick of the wineries to kick-start your explorations.

Ata Rangi Puruatanga Road Ⓣ06/306 9570, Ⓦwww.atarangi.co.nz. A great place to start as it's central. Increasingly well known for its Pinot Noir and Chardonnay, as well as Pinot Gris and rosé.

Margrain Vineyard Ponatahi Road Ⓣ06/306 9202, Ⓦwww.margrainvineyard.co.nz. Good-quality wine, a great little café (see p.452) and some accommodation in a pleasing setting.

Martinborough Vineyard Princess Street Ⓣ06/306 9955 Ⓦwww.martinborough-vineyard.co.nz. A Martinborough original and still one of the largest, producing top-quality Pinot Noir and Chardonnay. Picnicking is encouraged. Open all year.

Muirlea Rise 50 Princess St Ⓣ06/306 9332. Top-quality Pinot Noir to go with a ploughman's lunch and lovely coffee. Open all year.

Palliser Kitchener Street Ⓣ06/306 9019, Ⓦwww.palliser.co.nz. This pioneering Martinborough winery limits its impact on the environment while producing premium wines – Pinot Noir, Chardonnay, Sauvignon Blanc and Riesling; picnics are encouraged in the pleasant formal garden. Open all year.

booklet ($3.50) from the Fell Museum lays out the route, provides background information and pinpoints three basic, grassy campsites along the way.

There's not much point in **staying** in Featherston but you may want to break for a **meal** of inexpensive pastas, meat and seafood dishes or a woodfired pizza at *Chapelli's Eatery & Wine Bar*, 29 Fitzherbert St (ⓣ06/308 6969; 11am until at least 8.30pm) on the main highway. You can eat in its contemporary interior or pleasant leafy courtyard, or pick up takeaway meals.

Martinborough

Over the last couple of decades, tiny **MARTINBOROUGH**, 18km southeast of Featherston, has been transformed from a small and obscure farming town into the centre of a compact wine region synonymous with some of New Zealand's finest reds. It's within easy striking distance of Wellington, and weekends see the arrival of the smart set to lunch at the contemporary cafés and restaurants and load up their shiny 4WDs at the two dozen wineries that are within a kilometre or so of town. On Mondays and Tuesdays much of the town simply shuts down to recover.

The town was initially laid out in the 1870s by landowner John Martin, who named the streets after cities he had visited on his travels and arranged the core, centred on a leafy square, in the form of a Union Jack. Martinborough languished as a minor agricultural centre for over a century until the first four

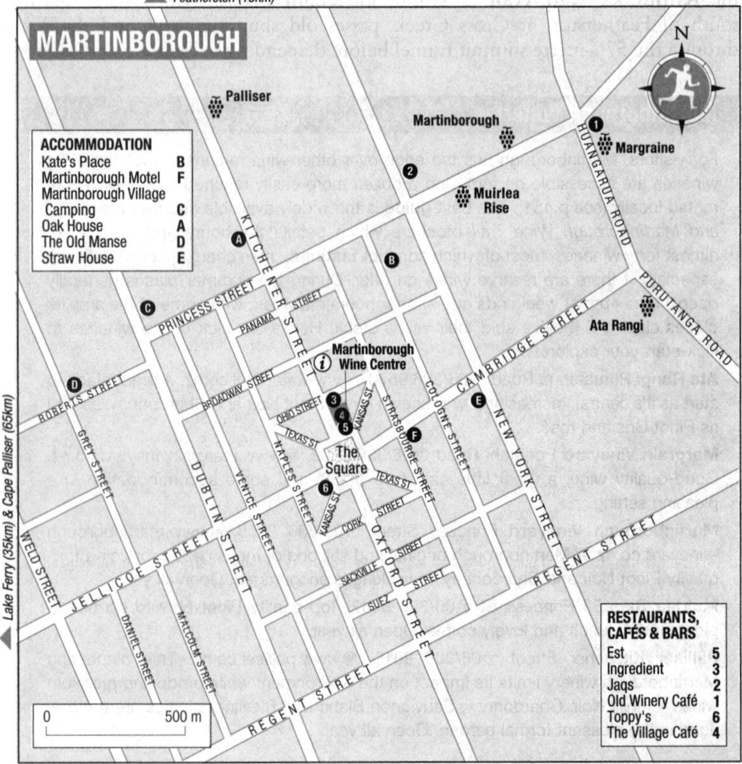

wineries – Ata Rangi, Dry River, Chifney and Martinborough (all of which produced their first vintages in 1984) – re-invented Martinborough as the coolest, driest and most wind-prone of the North Island's grape-growing regions. With the aid of shelter belts that slice the horizon, the wineries produce some outstanding Pinot Noir, very good Cabernet Sauvignon, crisp and fruity Sauvignon Blanc and wonderfully aromatic Riesling.

Martinborough is no slouch at promoting its viticultural prowess, and the best time to visit is during one of its **festivals**. The first of the summer is Toast Martinborough (third Sun in Nov), a wine-orientated affair with buses free and most of the vineyards open to ticket holders, and top Wellington and local restaurants selling their wares. It is an exclusive event and tickets (sold from early Oct through Ⓦwww.toastmartinborough.co.nz; $60) are hard to obtain. There's a considerably more egalitarian feel to the two Martinborough Fairs (first Sat in Feb & March) – huge country fetes during which the streets radiating from the central square are lined with art and craft stalls.

Outside these times, the best starting point is **Martinborough Wine Centre**, 6 Kitchener St (daily 11am–5pm; Ⓦwww.martinboroughwinecentre.co.nz), where you can taste a variety of local wines ($1.50–2.50 per taste) and **rent bikes** ($35 per day) for a spin through the vineyards.

Practicalities

Tranzit Coachlines **buses** (Ⓣ0800/471 227), shuttling between Featherston, Masterton and Martinborough, meet the TranzMetro commuter **trains** from Wellington (Ⓣ04/801 7000) and drop off diagonally opposite the **i-SITE visitor centre**, 18 Kitchener St (Mon–Fri 9am–5pm, Sat & Sun 10am–4pm; Ⓣ06/306 9043, Ⓔmartinborough@wairarapanz.co.nz), which also has **Internet access**.

The town's **accommodation** options lean heavily towards mid- and upper-price B&Bs and homestays, most of them in rural surroundings out of town, as well as self-contained cottages starting at around $120 midweek, $150 at weekends. Martinborough caters to discerning diners with around a dozen **restaurants** charging moderate to high prices, in return for high-quality dishes; pickings should be even finer when the new Cordon Bleu culinary school opens in Martinborough in early 2009. Self-caterers can stock up on gourmet local produce such as wine, olives, cheese and charcuterie at *Ingredient*, 8 Kitchener St, or try antipasti platters and wines by the glass on the premises.

Accommodation

Kate's Place 7 Cologne St Ⓣ06/306 9935, Ⓦwww.katesplace.co.nz. Cosy, laid-back homestay and backpacker combo in a weatherboard cottage on a quiet street. There's just one en-suite double plus a couple of top-quality four-share dorms with super-comfy timber bunks. Breakfast isn't served, but you can use Kate's kitchen, there are heaps of books to read and guests can borrow a bike and use the Internet for free. Dorm $25–30, room ④

Martinborough Motel 43 Strasbourge St Ⓣ06/306 9408. Very central budget motel with ageing but comfortable units. ③

Martinborough Village Camping Princess St Ⓣ06/306 8919, Ⓦwww.martinboroughcamping.com. Impeccably maintained campsite 10min walk from the centre, with tent sites separate from van hookups, and bike rental for $35 per day. Modern kitchen and showers. Camping $12.50, cabins ①

Oak House 45 Kitchener St Ⓣ06/306 9198, Ⓦwww.buringswines.co.nz. Welcoming homestay run by a local winemaker with attractive rooms in a Californian-style bungalow and substantial breakfasts included. ⑤

The Old Manse 19 Grey St Ⓣ06/306 8599, Ⓦwww.oldmanse.co.nz. Boutique B&B in a wonderful old villa amid the vines on the edge of town. ⑥

Straw House 24 Cambridge Rd Ⓣ06/306 8383, Ⓦwww.thestrawhouse.co.nz. Choose from a studio or s/c two-bedroom house, both built of straw bales and stylishly decorated. Breakfast goodies are provided and there's a small reduction for second and subsequent nights. Studio ⑤, house ⑧

Eating and drinking

Est The Square ☎06/306 9665. Classy restaurant and wine bar in Martinborough's nineteenth-century former post office serving contemporary cuisine (mains $26–32) matched to an outstanding wine list.

Jaqs New York St. Popular new local haunt where you can cook your own BBQ and sip boutique bottled New Zealand and imported beers. Open Wed–Sat noon–late, Sun 10am–7pm.

Old Winery Café Margrain Vineyard, Ponatahi Rd ☎06/306 8333. Great dining in relaxed surroundings overlooking the vines. Most of the well-priced dishes are matched to Margrain wines. Generally open noon–3pm.

Toppy's The Square. One of the best all-day cafés in town, offering great coffee, snacks, all-day brunches, light meals and takeaways in an attractive old building with a garden bar. Closed Mon–Wed in winter.

The Village Café 6 Kitchener St. Daytime café with seating in the rustic-chic, barn-like interior and the pergola-covered courtyard, serving a range of tasty brunches, pizzas and salads, and good espresso.

Cape Palliser

Low-key, cosmopolitan Martinborough stands in dramatic contrast to the bleak and windswept coast around **Cape Palliser**, 60km south. The southernmost point on the North Island, the cape was named in honour of James Cook's mentor, Rear Admiral Sir Hugh Palliser. Apart from a few gentle walks and the opportunity to observe fur seals at close quarters, there's not a lot to do out here but kick back, especially since swimming is unsafe and the weather changeable owing to the proximity of the Tararua Range.

From Martinborough, a sealed road leads 35km south to **Lake Ferry**, a tiny, laid-back surfcasting settlement on the sandy shores of Lake Onoke. Here, the *Lake Ferry Hotel* (☎06/307 7831, ⓦwww.lakeferryhotel.co.nz; dorms $25, rooms ❸) – the southernmost on the North Island – is renowned for its traditional Kiwi public **bar** and deck, overlooking the water, where you can tuck into good-value **meals**, notably the locally famed fish and chips. It is particularly good on a sunny evening, though packed at weekends, when you'll need to arrive early to get a table. Nearby, the *Lake Ferry Holiday Park* (☎06/307 7873; camping $10–12, cabins ❶, self-contained units ❸) is a little cramped but handy for the pub.

From a road junction just before Lake Ferry, the Cape Palliser road twists for 13km through the coastal hills until it meets the sea near the **Putangirua Pinnacles**, dozens of grey soft-rock spires and fluted cliffs up to 50m high, formed by wind and rain selectively eroding the surrounding silt and gravel. The pinnacles lie within the little-visited Aorangi (Haurangi) Forest Park, and can be explored along an easy streambed path (2hr return) from the roadside Putangirua Scenic Reserve, where there are BBQ areas and a primitive DOC **campsite** ($5); longer walks of up to 5hr are outlined on a map in the car park.

From here, the partly metalled road hugs the rugged, exposed coastline for 15km to **Ngawi**, a small fishing village where all manner of bulldozers grind out their last days, hauling fishing boats up the steep gravel beach. It is five rough kilometres on to the Cape proper, where a **fur seal colony**, right beside the road, is overlooked by the century-old Cape Palliser **lighthouse**, standing on a knoll 60m above the sea at the top of a long flight of some 250 steps, worth climbing at sunrise or sunset. It's easy enough to get within 20m of the seals, but they can become aggressive if they feel threatened, and move surprisingly quickly, given their bulk – keep your distance from pups or their parents, and don't get between any seal and the sea.

Travel details

Trains

The only rail services in the region are commuter services from Wellington to Masterton. Buses meet every train and run through the Wairarapa valley to Masterton.

Masterton to: Carterton (2–5 daily; 15min); Featherston (2–5 daily; 40min); Wellington (2–5 daily; 1hr 30min).

Buses

Gisborne to: Auckland (2 daily; 9hr 30min); Hastings (1 daily; 5hr); Napier (1 daily; 4hr); Opotiki, via SH2 (1 daily; 2hr); Rotorua (1 daily; 4hr 45min); Wairoa (1 daily; 1hr 30min); Wellington (1 daily; 10hr); Whakatane (1 daily; 3hr).

Hastings to: Auckland (3 daily; 7hr 50min); Dannevirke (4 daily; 1hr 30min); Gisborne (1 daily; 5hr); Napier (Mon–Fri hourly or better, Sat 5 daily; 1hr); Norsewood (4 daily; 1hr 10min); Taupo (3 daily; 2hr 30min); Wellington (4 daily; 4hr 45min).

Masterton to: Carterton (5–6 Mon–Fri, 3 Sat–Sun; 25min); Featherston (6 Mon–Fri; 1hr); Greytown (6 Mon–Fri; 30–40min); Palmerston North (1–2 Mon–Sat, 1 Sun; 2hr).

Napier to: Auckland (4 daily; 7hr 20min); Dannevirke (4 daily; 2hr); Gisborne (1 daily; 4hr); Hastings (Mon–Fri hourly or better, Sat 5 daily; 1hr); Norsewood (4 daily; 1hr 30min); Palmerston North (3 daily; 3hr); Taupo (3–4 daily; 2hr); Wellington (4 daily; 5hr 15min).

Wairoa to: Gisborne (1 daily; 1hr 30min); Napier (1 daily; 2hr 30min).

Flights

Gisborne to: Auckland (5–8 daily; 1hr); Wellington (1–4 daily; 1hr 10min).

Napier to: Auckland (7–12 daily; 1hr); Christchurch (1–2; 1hr 30min); Wellington (5–6 daily; 50min).

7

Wellington and around

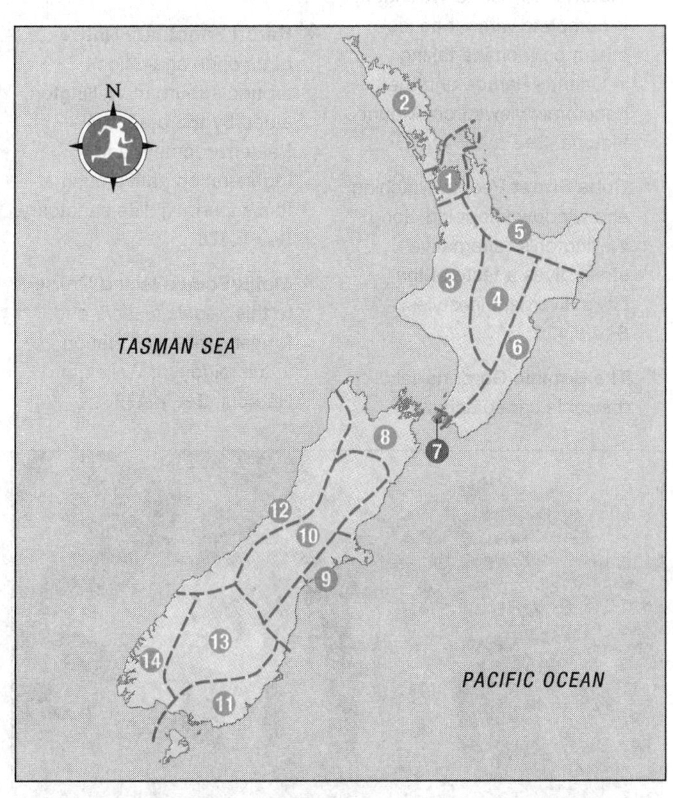

CHAPTER 7 Highlights

* **Te Papa** The national museum has become Wellington's premier attraction, with intriguing displays of pre-European Maori culture, and some of the country's finest art. See p.468

* **Oriental Parade and Mount Victoria** No visit to Wellington is complete without an ice-cream promenade taking in Oriental Parade and the panoramic views from Mount Victoria. See p.468

* **Cuba Street** People-watching and window shopping along Wellington's "alternative" street gives a taste of the city's divergent lifestyles. See p.470

* **The Botanic Gardens** Take the cable car up and stroll back down for great views, beautiful roses and the lovely Begonia House. See p.471

* **The Parliamentary District** Visit the country's seat of power and associated national institutions, including a chance to see the original Treaty of Waitangi. See p.472

* **Karori Sanctuary** Native birds once again flock around suburban Wellington, aided by the predator-free environment and regenerating native bush at this superb wildlife sanctuary. See p.475

* **Matiu/Somes Island** Cruise to this wildlife reserve and former quarantine station in the middle of Wellington Harbour. See p.479

▲ The Beehive and Parliament House

7

Wellington and around

The North Island finishes with a flourish at **Wellington**, New Zealand's capital and its most interesting and exciting city. Wedged between steep hills, the glistening waters of **Wellington Harbour** (technically **Port Nicholson**) and the turbulent seas of Cook Strait, Wellington is, with around 400,000 residents, New Zealand's second most populous city. As the principal departure point to the South Island it is sometimes only afforded a fleeting glimpse, but it certainly warrants a stay of a couple of nights, more if you can manage it.

Tight hills restrict Wellington to a compact core, mostly built on reclaimed land, whose stimulating blend of historical and modern architecture spills down to the bustling waterfront with its beaches, marinas and restored warehouses. All this is overlooked by Victorian and Edwardian weatherboard villas and bungalows, which climb the steep hillsides to an encircling belt of parks and woodland, a natural barrier to development. Houses are accessed by narrow winding roads, or sometimes just a precipitous stairway flanked by a small funicular railway to haul groceries and just about anything else up to the house. As if this weren't enough to contend with, Wellington is New Zealand's **windy city**, buffeted most days by air funnelled through Cook Strait, its force amplified by the wind-tunnelling effect of the city's high-rise buildings.

Perhaps to escape the inclement weather, Wellingtonians have cultivated the nation's most sophisticated **café society** and a buzzing arts scene. While Auckland grows more commercially important (and self-important in the eyes of much of the rest of the country) Wellington reaches for higher ground, promoting itself as the nation's **cultural capital**. It is certainly a cosmopolitan place, especially in late summer when the city hosts a series of arts and fringe **festivals** (see p.488). High levels of investment in recent years have buffed the city's biceps, making it worthy of its capital status. The beacon in this rejuvenation is **Te Papa**, New Zealand's modern and inventive national museum, dramatically sited on the waterfront.

Central Wellington is easily walkable and, if the weather behaves, it's a pleasant stroll from Te Papa along the waterfront past the Civic Square to Queens Wharf and the **Museum of Wellington**, which recounts the city's development and seafaring traditions. Politicians and civil servants populate the streets of the **Parliamentary District**, where a brief tour of the Parliament building sets you

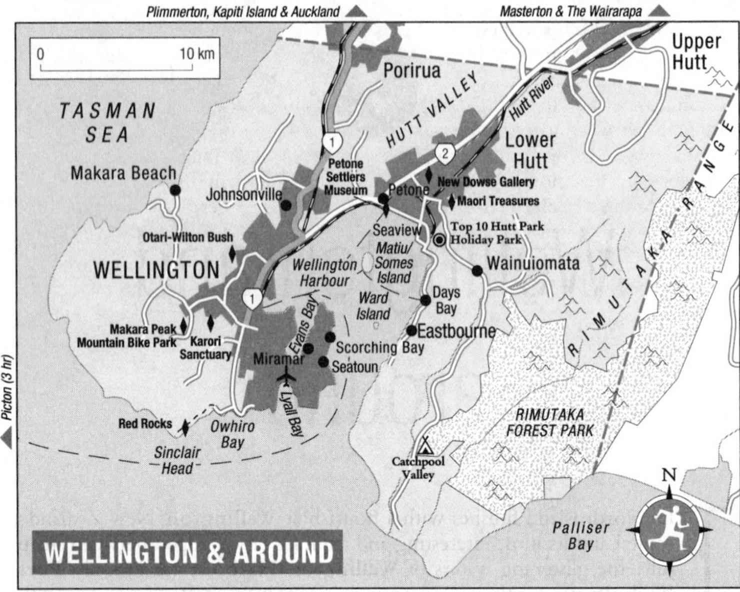

up for viewing the **original Treaty of Waitangi** in Archives New Zealand. Nearby, you can visit the childhood home of New Zealand's most famous short-story writer, **Katherine Mansfield's Birthplace**, now suitably furnished in period style.

Enticing though the indoor sights may be, it's certainly worth venturing beyond the central city. Given Wellington's unpredictable weather, you should make the best of the good days, riding the stately **Cable Car** to Kelburn and either wandering down through the **Botanical Gardens** or continuing further out to see the results of ambitious and important conservation work at the **Karori Sanctuary**. Take time, too, for the simple pleasures of strolling along **Oriental Parade** and up to one of the city's hilltop viewpoints, such as Mount Victoria.

Farther afield, you can **hike** to the seal colony at Red Rocks or wander one of the city's many trails, notably the **Southern Walkway**, and bikers are also spoilt for choice. At some point you should really get out on the water to the wildlife sanctuary of **Matiu/Somes Island** and beyond to **Lower Hutt** and the Ian Athfield-designed **New Dowse Gallery**.

Wellington can also be used as a base to explore **Kapiti Island** (p.290) and the **Wairarapa** (see p.445), with its windswept coastline and compact wine district around Martinborough.

Some history

Maori oral histories tell of the first Polynesian navigator, **Kupe**, discovering Wellington Harbour in 925 AD and naming the harbour's islands Matiu (Somes Island) and Makaro (Ward Island) after his daughters. Several *iwi* settled around the harbour, including the Ngati Tara people, who enjoyed the rich fishing areas and the protection that the bay offered. Both Abel Tasman (in 1642) and Captain Cook (in 1773) were prevented from entering Wellington Harbour by fierce winds and, apart from a few whalers, it was not until 1840 that the first wave of **European settlers** arrived. They carved out a niche on a large tract of harbourside land, purchased by the New Zealand Company, who set up their initial beachhead, named Britannia, on the northeastern beaches at Petone. Shortly afterwards, the Hutt River flooded, forcing the settlers to move around the harbour to a more sheltered site known as Lambton Harbour (where the central city has grown up) and the relatively level land at Thorndon, at that time just north of the shoreline. They renamed the settlement after the Iron Duke and began **land reclamations** into the harbour, a process that continued for more than a hundred years.

By the turn of the twentieth century the original shoreline of Lambton Harbour had been replaced by wharves and harbourside businesses, which formed the hub of the city's coastal trade. In 1865, the growing city succeeded Auckland as the **capital** of New Zealand; Wellington has prospered ever since.

Arrival, information and city transport

Wellington International Airport (Ⓦwww.wlg-airport.co.nz), about 10km southeast of the city centre, is an important domestic hub, linking around twenty airports across New Zealand and handling international flights from Australia. There's an unstaffed information station, a bureau de change (open for all arrivals and departures), and free Wi-Fi.

To get into town, grab a **taxi** (see p.489) for about $35, or hop on the Stagecoach Flyer city **bus** outside the terminal (daily 7am–8pm; $5.50), which runs about every half-hour and takes fifteen minutes to Courtenay Place. Alternatively, use one of the shuttle bus companies such as Super Shuttle (Ⓣ0800/748 885), who charge $20 for the first person to a particular destination, plus $5 for each extra person travelling to the same place.

The Overlander **train** from Auckland (see p.37) arrives at the main train station (see p.461), while Newmans and InterCity **buses** (see Basics, p.34) terminate nearby, alongside Platform 9.

Arriving by **car** is almost painless. State Highway 1 through Porirua and SH2 via Lower Hutt both turn into short urban motorways that merge, run scenically along the harbourside and deposit you downtown. Finding cheap parking close to the centre of the city can be a problem (for more see p.462), so if you are planning to relinquish your rental car here you might as well get rid of it as soon as you arrive.

Visitors from the northern tip of the **South Island** arrive via Cook Strait (see box, p.460).

Information

Wellington's **i-SITE visitor centre**, on the corner of Wakefield and Victoria streets (Dec to mid-March Mon–Fri 8.30am–5.30pm and Sat & Sun 9.30am–5pm, mid-March to Nov Mon–Fri 8.30am–5pm, Sat & Sun 9.30am–4.30pm; Ⓣ0800/933 536, Ⓦwww.wellington.nz.com), is stocked with leaflets, maps and brochures, and shares a glass-fronted section of the Civic Centre with a café and an Internet-access business. They give away a city map, sell a better one for $1 and also stock the handy free *Wellington: Official Visitor Guide* booklet.

DOC's Wellington Visitor Centre, 18 Manners St (Mon–Fri 9am–5pm Sat 10am–3.30pm; Ⓣ04/384 7770) has stacks of information on walks in the Wellington region. They also sell hut tickets and issue permits to visit Kapiti Island (both of which can also be obtained online).

Crossing Cook Strait

To travel between the bottom of the North Island and top of the South Island you need to cross **Cook Strait**, either using a vehicle ferry between Wellington and Picton or flying. The latter avoids a potentially choppy ferry crossing, is much quicker and gives the option of parachuting onto the South Island (see p.503) – but does mean missing the cruise through the beautiful Marlborough Sounds. Around half the journey is across open water, but the southern half is spent negotiating the narrow channels of the Sounds, where you cruise past barely inhabited bays and might catch sight of dolphins. The ferries even offer an audio tour about Cook Strait on most services.

By sea

Two companies run combined passenger and vehicle ferry services. **Interislander** (all year 3–5 daily; 3hr; ⓣ0800/802 802, ⓦwww.interislander.co.nz) operate three **ferries** which leave Wellington just over a kilometre north of the train station. A free shuttle bus leaves the train station (by Platform 9) 35 minutes before each sailing.

Interislander offers three fare categories: **Web Saver** is the cheapest but the least flexible and non-refundable; the mid-range **Saver Change** allows bookings to be amended up to the time of departure (depending on space) and offers a fifty percent refund if cancelled; **Easy Change** is the most expensive and most flexible, allowing changes right up until departure, and is fully refundable. In general, expect to pay around $52–72 one way for a single passenger, $165–235 for a car and driver, and $15 for bicycles. In addition, the Kaitaki ship offers Kaitaki Plus ($110/$245), which includes the use of a private lounge, the latest movies and complimentary food and drinks.

In summer it is often cheaper travelling with **Bluebridge** (all year 3–4 daily; 3hr 20min ⓣ0800/844 844, ⓦwww.bluebridge.co.nz), who operate on the same route from their terminal opposite Wellington's train station. All bookings are non-refundable but fully transferable, and they charge a flat fare all year: passengers $55 one way; driver and car up to 5.5 metres $130; bicycles $10.

By air

Soundsair (ⓣ0800/505 005, ⓦwww.soundsair.co.nz) fly between Wellington and Picton (6–8 daily; 25min; $84 each way, see p.503), and offer small backpacker discounts. Foot passengers keen to get directly to Nelson, Christchurch, Queenstown or Kaikoura will find it quicker and possibly cheaper if they fly direct from Wellington, though you'll miss a lot of the scenery.

City transport

Wellington's integrated bus, train and ferry systems all work well, although if you are staying centrally, you'll be able to see almost everything on foot. As well as the various discounts mentioned below, the very useful **Metlink Explorer** ($15) gives one day of unlimited bus and train travel throughout the Wellington region from 9am on weekdays and all day at weekends. For Wellington region **train and bus information**, pick up the free *Metlink Network Map* or any of the individual timetables at the visitor centre or train station, or call Metlink (ⓣ0800/801 700, ⓦwww.metlink.org.nz). You might even consider cycling (see p.482).

Buses

Wellington's extensive network of **buses and trolley buses** operates from Lambton Interchange, just west of the train station, and has an After Midnight service (Sat & Sun hourly 1–3am), centred on Courtenay Place, to get revellers home safely.

All tickets and day-passes can be bought direct from the bus driver. One-way **fares** are $1.50 within the inner city, beyond which a zone system comes into operation: for example Karori Sanctuary costs $3.50. After midnight services cost $3.50–7. If you intend to use the transport system extensively it's worth picking the **Daytripper** ($5) on the first bus you board, which covers all central city bus travel for the day, or a **Star Pass** ($10), which also includes the After Midnight buses. There's also the airport Flyer service, discussed on p.459.

Suburban trains

Wellington's train station, on Bunny Street, contains little more than a café, a small supermarket and a rail booking office but remains the hub of Wellington's public transport network, and commuter services all terminate here. The fast and efficient **suburban train service** is run by Tranz Metro (Ⓣ04/498 3000, Ⓦwww.tranzmetro.co.nz). Trains on both main lines – to the Hutt Valley (p.478) and the Kapiti Coast (p.287) – leave the train station roughly every half-hour for Waterloo (for Lower Hutt; 20min; $3); Porirua (20min; $3.50); Plimmerton (30min; $4.50); and Paraparaumu (1hr; $6.50). A further line runs to Johnsonville and provides handy access for hiking the Northern Walkway (see p.481). Add around 30 percent for peak-hour fares, which apply before 9am and from 4 to 7pm.

A one-day Rover ticket ($10) gives you the run of the train network after 9am weekdays and all weekend, plus there's a three-day weekend Rover ($15) valid all day Friday to Sunday. Bikes cost the same as the adult fare, up to a maximum of $4. Tickets can be bought at the Tranz Rail Travel Centre at the main train station or on the train.

Driving and parking

The compact centre of Wellington and its good public transport mean there is little value in having a car in the city. Still, a vehicle is useful for exploring the

City tours

A number of clued-up local outfits offer entertaining and informative tours of the city, the best of which are listed below.

4WD Seal Coast Safari Ⓣ0800/732 527, Ⓦwww.sealcoast.com. Three-hour tours to the Red Rocks seal colony (see p.481), charging $90 for a lift and some commentary.

Flat Earth Ⓣ0800/775 805, Ⓦwww.flatearth.co.nz. Upmarket outfit who take very good care of you on their full-day tours (around $300): Capital Arts, Wild Wellington, Inspiration and *Lord of the Rings*.

Hammond's Scenic Tours Ⓣ04/472 0869, Ⓦwww.wellingtonsightseeingtours.com. Slightly staid trips, ranging from a City Sights Tour (2 daily; 2hr 30min; $50) to extended visits to the Kapiti Coast (2 daily; 4hr; $85) and the Palliser Bay Seal Colony and *Lord of the Rings* Tour (daily; 8hr; $170).

Walk Wellington Ⓦwww.walk.wellington.net.nz. Entertaining ninety-minute walking tours of the downtown area (daily 10am plus Nov–March Mon, Wed & Fri 5.30pm; $20), leaving from the visitor centre (which is where you book).

Wellington Rover Ⓣ021/426 211, Ⓦwww.wellingtonrover.co.nz. Hop-on-hop-off minibus service making a loop around the city's outer sights – Mount Victoria, Red Rocks, the zoo and a couple of LOTR locations – three times a day ($40), with small discounts for entry to various sights along the way. There's also a Twilight Rover ($45) visiting the south coast, Otari-Wilton's Bush and Mount Victoria, and several other trips.

bays and outer suburbs, and **driving** around the inner city is simple enough once you get used to the extensive one-way system and remember to avoid the rush hour (roughly 7–9am & 4.30–6.30pm). There is no free **parking** downtown, but there are numerous car parks charging $4 an hour during the day, typically only $2 from 6pm to midnight and often with a one-day maximum of $8–10. The car park by the Te Papa museum is suitable for campervans ($12 all day; $6 after 5pm), and there are several others nearby. If you don't want to bother with moving the vehicle all the time, some places charge $15–20 to leave it for the full 24-hour day.

Most downtown streets have **parking meters** (usually Mon–Thurs 8am–6pm & Fri 8am–8pm $4 per hr; otherwise free) that limit you to a two-hour stay during the metered hours. A little further out you get **coupon parking** (Mon–Fri 8am–4pm) where the first two hours are free, but to stay longer you have to display a coupon ($5 all day), available from dairies and petrol stations. These areas are also free outside the set hours.

Accommodation

With so much of Wellington easily accessible on foot, most visitors plump for **accommodation** in the city centre close to the action. There's plenty of choice at all levels, including a selection of good **backpacker hostels**. **B&Bs** are also in abundant supply, many in beautifully preserved Victorian villas. Wellington is a great place to breakfast or brunch out, so you might not want a place where breakfast is included in the tariff. Centrally sited **motels** are in short supply, but there are plenty of downtown **hotels**, catering mostly to the business crowd but also offering good-value deals, especially at weekends.

For a little peace and quiet, you might want to stay outside the city centre, particularly if you have a vehicle. You could stay at the nearest **campsite**, inconveniently sited in the Hutt Valley, or the excellent hostel in **Plimmerton** (see p.292) with good train access into Wellington.

Prices are only a touch above the Kiwi average, but **availability** is limited during the busiest part of the summer (mid-Dec to Feb), so it pays to book as far ahead as possible: at least a week for the more popular places. All the following are shown on the map on p.466 unless otherwise stated.

Hotels and motels

Apollo Lodge Motel 49 Majoribanks St ⓣ0800/361 645, ⓦwww.apollo-lodge.co.nz. Central, medium-sized motel with modern decor 200m from Courtenay Place. There's off-street parking and many units have fully equipped kitchens. Studios ❹, deluxe with kitchen ❺

Duxton 170 Wakefield St ⓣ0800/655 555, ⓦwww.duxton.com. A gleaming modern corporate hotel close to Te Papa, with an à la carte restaurant, a brasserie and plenty of rooms with harbour views. Short notice and weekend deals for ❻, normally ❼

Halswell Lodge 21 Kent Terrace ⓣ04/385 0196, ⓦwww.halswell.co.nz. Comfortable, central and welcoming establishment with plain but good-value hotel rooms, relatively pricey motel units and some lovely deluxe rooms (some with spa) in a lodge set back from the street. Free off-street parking. Hotel ❸, motel ❺, lodge ❺

Just Hotel 166 Willis St ⓣ0800/458 784, ⓦwww.justhotel.co.nz. Budget modern hotel with 60 rooms, all with phone, Sky TV, tea and coffee and access to on-site restaurant, bar and parking ($15; book ahead). Deals (especially at weekends) as low as $90. ❺

Museum Hotel 90 Cable St ⓣ0800/994 335, ⓦwww.museumhotel.co.nz. Big, black business hotel locally famous for having been trundled across the street from the Te Papa construction site, hence its nickname, the Hotel de Wheels. Rates are reasonable for the high standards and some of the better rooms have harbour views. Contemporary NZ art is on show, and there are good weekend and last-minute reductions. Rooms ❻, harbour view ❼

Wellington Motel 14 Hobson St ⓣ04/472 0334, ⓔwellington.motels@clear.net.nz. Not really a motel at all, but ageing, self-catering rooms with Sky TV and phone in a large house in the diplomatic quarter, close to ferries and Parliament. ❹

B&Bs and guesthouses

Austinvilla B&B 11 Austin St, Mount Victoria ⓣ04/385 8334, ⓦwww.austinvilla.co.nz. Two lovely and very private s/c apartments (one studio, the other with a separate bedroom and a small garden), both with bathtubs, in an elegant villa with leafy surrounds 10min walk from Courtenay Place. Off-street parking, free Wi-Fi and a breakfast basket is delivered. Studio ❺, one-bedroom ❻

Booklovers B&B 123 Pirie St, Mount Victoria ⓣ04/384 2714, ⓦwww.booklovers.co.nz. For charm and comfort there are few better than this literary B&B in an unfussy Victorian villa 10min walk from Courtenay Place and Mount Victoria Park. There are books in every room and they even encourage you to take one away to read on your travels. A full, cooked breakfast is served any time. ❼

Koromiko Homestay 11 Koromiko Rd, Highbury (see map, p.476) ⓣ04/938 6539, ⓦwww.adventureout.co.nz. City homestay for "gay men and their friends" in a quiet street overlooking the Botanical Gardens. Great harbour views, free Internet and meals ($25) on request. ❹

The Mermaid 1 Epuni St, corner with Aro St ⓣ04/384 4511, ⓦwww.mermaid.co.nz. A luxurious guesthouse for women only, set in a restored century-old house on eclectic Aro St, 10min walk from downtown. The four opulently furnished rooms (one with private bathroom) all come with a view of the garden or hills. Everyone has full use of the kitchen. Room ❹, en suite ❺

Rawhiti 40 Rawhiti Terrace, Kelburn ⓣ04/934 4859, ⓦwww.rawhiti.co.nz. Gorgeous and peaceful B&B right by the upper cable-car terminus, set in a classic century-old home. The two casually but elegantly decorated rooms both get the morning sun. Breakfasts are delicious and there's a nice garden out the back. ❽

Tinakori Lodge 182 Tinakori Rd, Thorndon ⓣ04/939 3478, ⓦwww.tinakorilodge.co.nz. Modest but comfortable B&B in a big, well-appointed Victorian villa, a short walk from the Parliamentary District, with nine airy rooms and a conservatory that looks onto a bushland reserve. Rooms ❺, en suites ❻

Hostels

base Wellington 21–23 Cambridge Terrace ⓣ0800/227 369, ⓦwww.basebackpackers.com. Slick and well-organized 280-bed hostel converted from an office building. Facilities include cheap Internet, lockable cupboards, bike rental and a bar in the basement with theme nights, though the kitchens are small. There's a women-only "Sanctuary" floor ($3 a night extra) with towels and shampoo provided. Dorms $26, en suite ❸

Cambridge Hotel 28 Cambridge Terrace ⓣ0800/375 021, ⓦwww.cambridgehotel.co.nz. Nicely renovated 1930s hotel that partly operates as a backpackers. Spacious four- to eight-bed dorms come with made-up bunks, and there's a good restaurant and bar, but there's only one barely adequate common area used for cooking, eating and TV watching. The smallish hotel rooms are en suite, well appointed and good value. Dorms $23, rooms ❸, en suite ❹

Downtown Backpackers 1 Bunny St ⓣ04/473 8482, ⓦwww.downtownbackpackers.co.nz. Large and ageing hostel in the Art Deco *Waterloo Hotel* that's very convenient for train, bus and ferry arrivals. Dorms (one a 20-bedder) and rooms are adequate but unexciting, though there's a good bar with cheap beer and a café serving low-cost breakfasts and dinners. Dorms $21, rooms ❷, en-suite doubles ❸

Lodge in the City 152 Taranaki St ⓣ0800/257 225, ⓦwww.lodgeinthecity.co.nz. Rambling former student lodgings that offers a range of rooms, plus free off-street parking, an on-site bar and free shuttle to the ferry, bus and train. Dorms $23 , rooms ❷, s/c units for four ❹

Nomads Capital 118 Wakefield St ⓣ0508/666 237, ⓦwww.nomadscapital.com. New and comfortable 180-bed hostel (with vertigo-inducing top bunks) right in the centre of the city with cool bar-cum-eatery *Blend* attached. There are women-only dorms for no extra charge and, best of all, plush en-suite doubles. Dorms $23, en suite ❸

Worldwide 291 The Terrace ⓣ04/802 5590, ⓦwww.worldwidenz.co.nz. Bright and cheerful hostel in an attractive house with singles, doubles and twins, four-shares and six-bunk dorms, plus free local calls and free Internet. Breakfast included. Dorms $27, rooms ❷

YHA Wellington City 292 Wakefield St ⓣ04/801 7280, ⓔyha.wellington@yha.co.nz. This 320-bedder is one of the best urban hostels in the country, right in the heart of the city and with great harbour views from some of the upper floor rooms. It has spacious and comfortable common areas, a well-equipped kitchen, bike storage, an info and travel desk and a full day and evening activities programme. Many of the doubles, twin, four- and six-share dorms have en suites. Book at least a week in advance in summer. Dorms $29, rooms ❸, en suites ❹

Campsites

Catchpool Valley, Rimutaka Forest Park, 30km northeast of Wellington. See map, p.458. Pleasant drive-in DOC campsite with toilets, water supply and barbecues. $10

Matiu/Somes Island Twelve-person DOC campsite on this wildlife reserve in the middle of Wellington Harbour with great city views. There are flush toilets, and gas cooking stoves but you need to bring pots and all food. It is on a trial basis, so contact Ⓔ matiusomes@doc.govt.nz to see if it is still operating. $6

Top 10 Hutt Park Holiday Park 95 Hutt Park Rd, Lower Hutt Ⓣ 0800/488 872, Ⓦ www.huttpark.co.nz. See map, p.458. Located 12km north of Wellington on the harbour's northeastern shore, this is the capital's closest campsite. It's near beaches, shops and bushwalks and can be accessed on buses #81 and #83 from Courtenay Place and Lambton Interchange. Camping $17, cabins ❷, s/c units ❸, motel units ❹

The City

Wellington's **city centre** is compact and easy to cover on foot. The heart of the city stretches south from the train station to Courtenay Place through the central business and shopping district along Lambton Quay. The main areas for eating, drinking and entertainment are further south around Courtenay Place, Cuba Street, Willis Street, and down to the waterfront at Queens Wharf. **Cuba Street** is also the "alternative" shopping district with secondhand bookshops, record stores, retro clothes retailers and quirky cafés.

The **Civic Square** is the nearest thing to a real centre that Wellington has. From there, points of interest run both ways along the waterfront. The area south of Civic Square contains New Zealand's national museum, **Te Papa**, the city's number one attraction, its cerebral pleasures nicely balanced by shopping and entertainment districts around **Courtenay Place** and **Cuba Street** to the south. For further contrast, take a stroll along **Oriental Parade** and up to **Mount Victoria** beyond for some excellent views of the city.

North of the Civic Centre, Jervois Quay runs past the engaging **Museum of Wellington** and a couple of minor attractions on Queens Wharf. A couple of blocks inland, **Lambton Quay** forms the backbone of the central business district, its **cable car** running up to the leafy suburb of Kelburn. Lambton Quay runs to Thorndon and the **Parliamentary District**, seat of New Zealand's government and home to institutions like **Archives New Zealand**, the national library, the new and old **cathedrals** and **Katherine Mansfield's Birthplace.**

Heading out from the centre, the lovely **Botanic Gardens** lead west towards a couple of sylvan sites: **Karori Sanctuary**, with its growing population of native birds, and **Otari-Wilton's Bush**, one of the last remnants of virgin bush in the area. These form part of the **Town Belt**, a band of greenery across the hills that encircle the city centre. Originally set aside in 1840 by the New Zealand Company for aesthetic and recreational purposes, it contains several good walks and many of the city's best lookout points. Further south, the Town Belt runs past Wellington Zoo, and to the east it cuts the city off from the quiet suburbs and beaches of the **Miramar Peninsula**.

Civic Square

The city's main visitor centre backs onto **Civic Square**, a compact open space which was extensively revamped in the early 1990s by Wellington architect Ian

The architecture of Ian Athfield

The work of New Zealand's most influential and versatile living architect, **Ian Athfield**, generates the kind of love-hate reaction associated with the likes of the Pompidou Centre in Paris or Seattle's Experience Music Project. His principal motif is the juxtaposition of old and new, regular and irregular, as seen in the facade of the **Palmerston North City Library** (see p.285). Many of the finest examples of Athfield's work are in his home town of Wellington, where the facade of the **Moore Wilson Building** from 1984 (a food warehouse at the corner of College and Tory streets) explores fractures, while the **Oriental Parade Apartments**, built in 1988 near the start of the Southern Walkway on Oriental Parade (see p.468), have an almost Egyptian feel. Athfield also likes artwork to appear as part of his buildings, as demonstrated by the sculptural forms of the **Wellington Central Library** (see below). Perhaps the best recent example of his work is his revamp of the The New Dowse in Lower Hutt (see p.479), where he has cleverly combined an old structure with a new one, revitalizing a somewhat drab building. However, many people's favourite Athfield building is a house-cum-office on a hillside in the northern suburb of **Khandallah** (at 105 Amritsar St; closed to the public). Visible from the Wellington motorway and – at some distance – from the ferry to Days Bay, it seems to grow organically down the hill, showing a respect for the environment and a willingness to engage with it that's often lacking in New Zealand architecture. In contrast, the house adjoining the **Te Mata Estate Winery** in Havelock North (see p.439) is a sly backhanded tribute to the modernists of the 1930s and an expression of the architect's humour, though it still manages to look perfectly placed in its surroundings.

Athfield (see box above). Now a popular venue for outdoor events, it's full of interesting sculptures including Neil Dawson's *Ferns*, interlinking metal fern fronds formed into a ball that seems to float above the square.

The most immediately arresting building is Athfield's 1991 **Central Library** (Mon–Thurs 9.30am–8.30pm, Fri 9.30am–9pm, Sat 9.30am–5pm, Sun 1–4pm), a spacious high-tech statement in steel, stone and timber with its inner workings – air ducts, water pipes, etc – exposed. Athfield also created the supporting steel nikau palms which ring the building and provide a link to the rest of the Civic Square by continuing out beyond the building itself.

Adjacent to the library, the 1939 Art Deco **City Gallery** (daily 10am–5pm; free; ⓣ04/801 3021, ⓦwww.city-gallery.org.nz), is a contemporary art gallery that hosts touring shows of national and international works and is attached to the bijou **City Cinema**. This often shows works relating directly to exhibits elsewhere in the gallery and also screens films in conjunction with some of the city's many specialist film festivals (see p.488). To round it all off, the stylish *Nikau Gallery Café* (see "Eating", p.484), opens onto an external terrace.

Across the square, the **City-to-Sea Bridge** was intentionally made broad in an attempt to link downtown to the long-ignored waterfront as seamlessly as possible. It is decorated with Para Matchitt's timber sculptures of birds, whales and celestial motifs which symbolize the arrival of Maori and European settlers and, by extension, that of present-day visitors.

South of Civic Square

You're likely to spend much of your time south of the Civic Square either at **Te Papa** or eating and drinking around Courtenay Place and Cuba Street, but don't miss out on **Oriental Parade** – a lovely stroll with great harbour views, a small city beach and the chance to hike up to the summit of **Mount Victoria**.

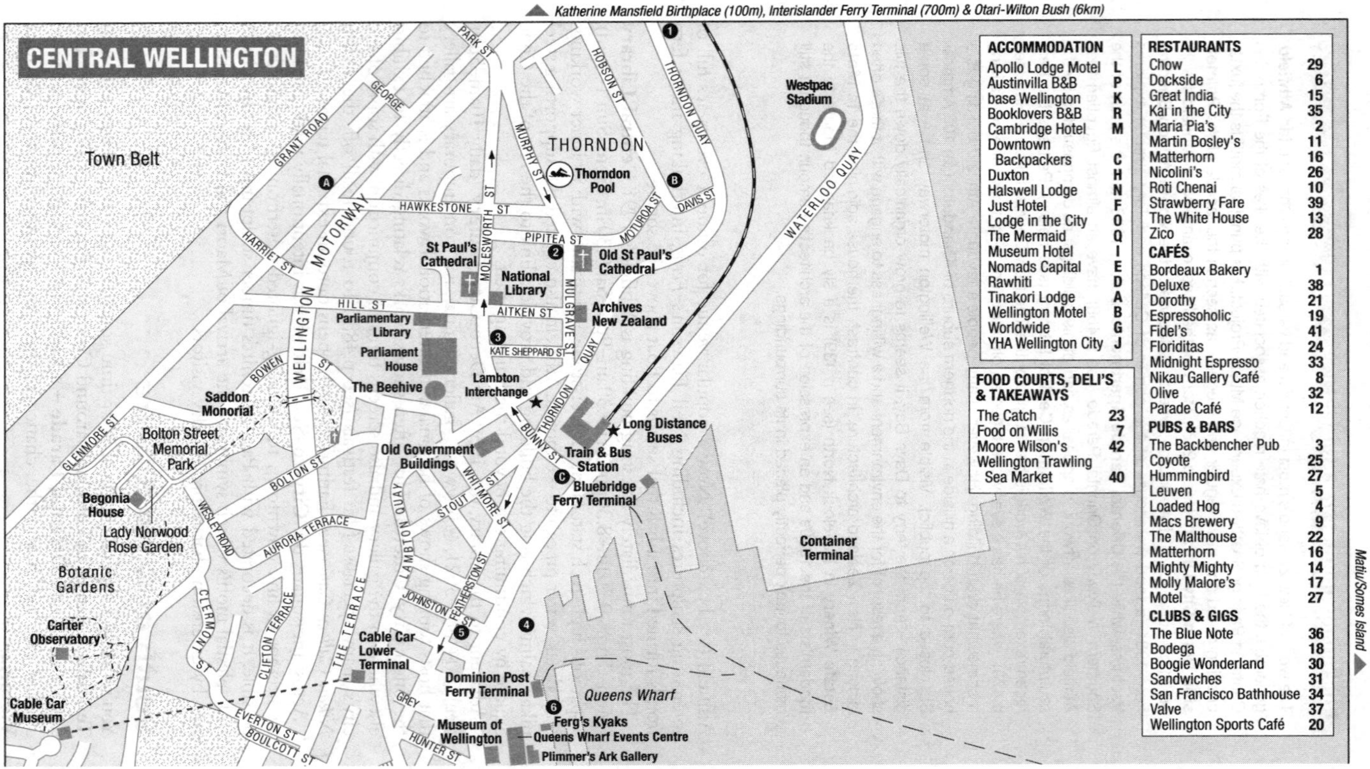

CENTRAL WELLINGTON

Katherine Mansfield Birthplace (100m), Interislander Ferry Terminal (700m) & Otari-Wilton Bush (6km)

Matiu/Somes Island

ACCOMMODATION	
Apollo Lodge Motel	L
Austinvilla B&B	P
base Wellington	K
Booklovers B&B	R
Cambridge Hotel	M
Downtown Backpackers	C
Duxton	H
Halswell Lodge	N
Just Hotel	F
Lodge in the City	O
The Mermaid	Q
Museum Hotel	I
Nomads Capital	E
Rawhiti	D
Tinakori Lodge	A
Wellington Motel	B
Worldwide	G
YHA Wellington City	J

FOOD COURTS, DELI'S & TAKEAWAYS	
The Catch	23
Food on Willis	7
Moore Wilson's	42
Wellington Trawling Sea Market	40

RESTAURANTS	
Chow	29
Dockside	6
Great India	15
Kai in the City	35
Maria Pia's	2
Martin Bosley's	11
Matterhorn	16
Nicolini's	26
Roti Chenai	10
Strawberry Fare	39
The White House	13
Zico	28
CAFÉS	
Bordeaux Bakery	1
Deluxe	38
Dorothy	21
Espressoholic	19
Fidel's	41
Floriditas	24
Midnight Espresso	33
Nikau Gallery Café	8
Olive	32
Parade Café	12
PUBS & BARS	
The Backbencher Pub	3
Coyote	25
Hummingbird	27
Leuven	5
Loaded Hog	4
Macs Brewery	9
The Malthouse	22
Matterhorn	16
Mighty Mighty	14
Molly Malore's	17
Motel	27
CLUBS & GIGS	
The Blue Note	36
Bodega	18
Boogie Wonderland	30
Sandwiches	31
San Francisco Bathhouse	34
Valve	37
Wellington Sports Café	20

Town Belt
THORNDON
Thorndon Pool
Westpac Stadium
St Paul's Cathedral
Old St Paul's Cathedral
National Library
Archives New Zealand
Parliamentary Library
Parliament House
The Beehive
Lambton Interchange
Long Distance Buses
Train & Bus Station
Bluebridge Ferry Terminal
Container Terminal
Old Government Buildings
Saddon Monorial
Bolton Street Memorial Park
Begonia House
Lady Norwood Rose Garden
Botanic Gardens
Carter Observatory
Cable Car Museum
Cable Car Lower Terminal
Dominion Post Ferry Terminal
Queens Wharf
Ferg's Kyaks
Queens Wharf Events Centre
Plimmer's Ark Gallery
Museum of Wellington
PARK ST
GEORGE
GRANT ROAD
HARRIET ST
MOTORWAY
WELLINGTON
HAWKESTONE ST
MOLESWORTH ST
MURPHY ST
HOBSON ST
THORNDON QUAY
MOTUROA ST
DAVIS ST
PIPITEA ST
MULGRAVE ST
AITKEN ST
KATE SHEPPARD ST
HILL ST
WATERLOO QUAY
THORNDON QUAY
BUNNY ST
BOWEN ST
GLENMORE ST
BOLTON ST
WESLEY ROAD
AURORA TERRACE
WHITMORE ST
STOUT ST
LAMBTON QUAY
FEATHERSTON ST
JOHNSTON ST
THE TERRACE
CLIFTON TERRACE
CLERMONT ST
GREY
EVERTON ST
BOULCOTT ST
HUNTER ST

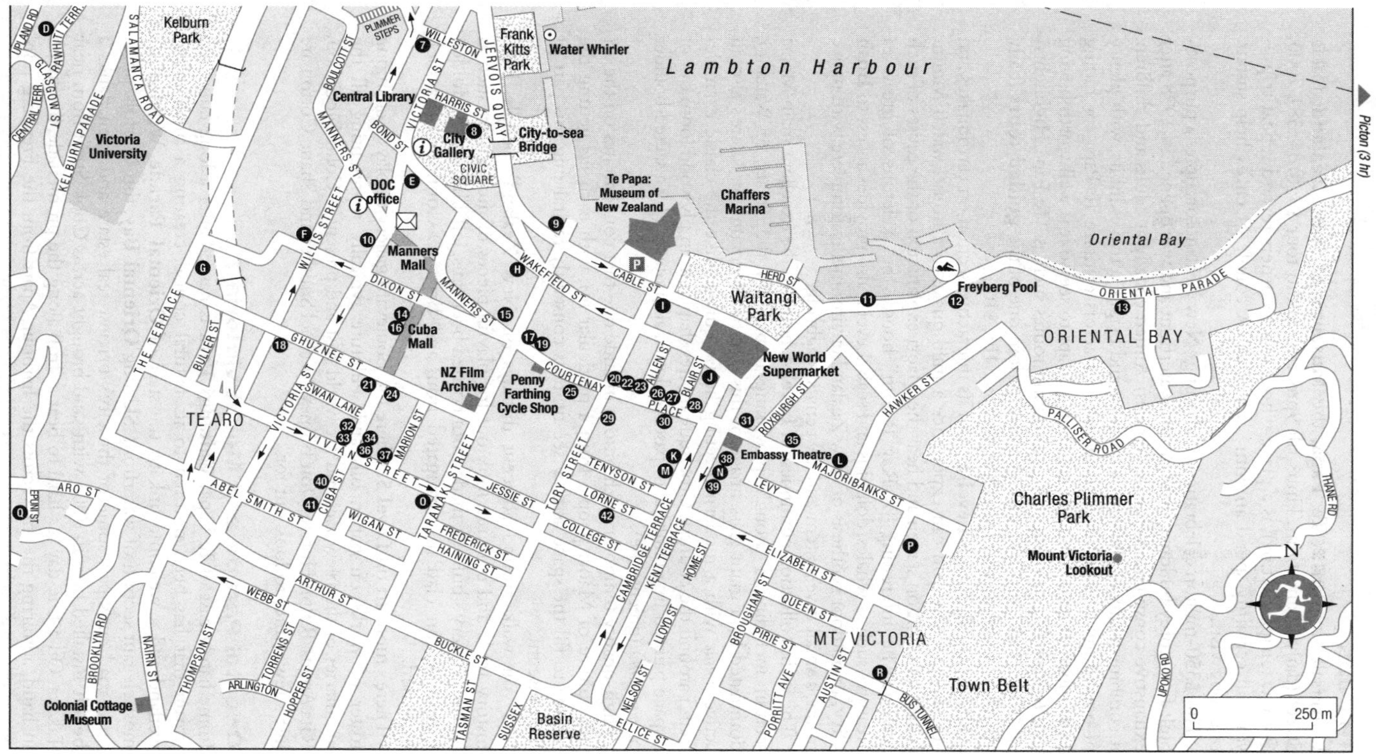
Lambton Harbour
Picton (3 hr)
Water Whirler
Frank Kitts Park
Kelburn Park
Central Library
City Gallery
City-to-sea Bridge
CIVIC SQUARE
DOC office
Te Papa: Museum of New Zealand
Chaffers Marina
Oriental Bay
Freyberg Pool
ORIENTAL PARADE
ORIENTAL BAY
Waitangi Park
New World Supermarket
Manners Mall
Cuba Mall
NZ Film Archive
Penny Farthing Cycle Shop
Embassy Theatre
Victoria University
TE ARO
Charles Plimmer Park
Mount Victoria Lookout
MT VICTORIA
Town Belt
Basin Reserve
Colonial Cottage Museum
UPLAND RD
RAWHITI TERR
GLASGOW ST
CENTRAL TERR
KELBURN PARADE
SALAMANCA ROAD
PLIMMER STEPS
WILLESTON
BOULCOTT ST
VICTORIA ST
HARRIS ST
JERVOIS QUAY
MANNERS ST
BOND ST
WILLIS STREET
WAKEFIELD ST
CABLE ST
HERD ST
DIXON ST
MANNERS ST
GHUZNEE ST
THE TERRACE
BULLER ST
COURTENAY PLACE
ALLEN ST
BLAIR ST
ROXBURGH ST
HAWKER ST
PALLISER ROAD
THANE RD
SWAN LANE
VICTORIA ST
VIVIAN STREET
MARION ST
TARANAKI STREET
TORY STREET
TENYSON ST
LORNE ST
MAJORIBANKS ST
LEVY
ARO ST
EPUNI ST
ABEL SMITH ST
CUBA ST
JESSIE ST
WIGAN ST
FREDERICK ST
HAINING ST
COLLEGE ST
CAMBRIDGE TERRACE
KENT TERRACE
HOME ST
ELIZABETH ST
ARTHUR ST
WEBB ST
LLOYD ST
BROUGHAM ST
QUEEN ST
PIRIE ST
BROOKLYN RD
NAIRN ST
THOMPSON ST
TORRENS ST
HOPPER ST
ARLINGTON
BUCKLE ST
TASMAN ST
SUSSEX
NELSON ST
ELLICE ST
PORRITT AVE
AUSTIN ST
BUS TUNNEL
UPOKO RD
N
0
250 m

Te Papa

Universally known as **Te Papa**, the **Museum of New Zealand**, Cable Street (daily 10am–6pm, Thurs till 9pm; free; audio tour $5; ⓣ04/381 7000, ⓦwww.tepapa.govt.nz), is a place whose many corners reward repeat trips – you can certainly spend an entire day there. A couple of **cafés** help sustain one long visit.

This $350-million celebration of all things New Zealand occupies a purpose-built five-storey building right on the waterfront and was opened in 1998 after exhaustive consultation with *iwi* (tribes). Aimed equally at adults and children, it combines state-of-the-art technology and bright active exhibits, with plenty of opportunity to dig deeper, though detractors criticize Te Papa for hiding away much of its collection. Still, there's heaps to see, so it is well worth buying the *Te Papa Explorer* guide ($3), outlining routes such as "Te Papa Highlights" or "Kids Highlights", or calling ahead to join one of the **guided tours** (daily 10.15am, 11am, noon, 1pm, 2pm & 3pm; 1hr; $10).

The hub of Te Papa is **Level 2**, with its interactive section on earthquakes and volcanoes, where you can experience a mild quake in a house, watch Mount Ruapehu erupt on screen and hear the Maori explanation of the causes of such activity. The interesting "X-Ray Room" houses the skeletons of great sea creatures such as whales, dolphins and seals. Level 2 also provides access to **Bush City**, an outdoor synthesis of New Zealand environments complete with native plants, a small cave system and a weeny swingbridge.

The main collection continues on **Level 4**, home to the excellent main Maori section including a thought-provoking display on the Treaty of Waitangi, dominated by a giant glass image of this significant document. There's also an active *marae* with a modern meeting house quite unlike the classic examples found around the country. Grotesque figures shaped from plywood loom out of a space painted in a rainbow of pastel colours, all protected by a sacred boulder of *pounamu* (greenstone).

High-quality temporary exhibitions include one that concentrates on the art and culture of Maori people from a particular *iwi*, with each *iwi* getting the chance to fill the space as they see fit, thus constantly revitalizing this part of the museum.

As you walk around adjacent displays on New Zealand's people, land, history, trade and cultures, look out for playful pieces of modern art such as Michel Tuffery's bullock made from corned beef cans, Jeff Thomson's Holden station wagon clad in corrugated iron, and Brian O'Connor's paua-shell surfboard.

There's more art on **Level 5**, where the Boulevard gallery displays a changing roster of works on paper, oils and sculpture typically representing all the luminaries of the New Zealand art world past and present – Colin McCahon, Rita Angus, Ralph Hotere, Don Binney, Michael Smither and Shane Cotton are just a few names to look out for.

Oriental Parade and Mount Victoria

Immediately east of Te Papa, **Waitangi Park** is named after a long culverted stream that has been restored to its natural course, creating a small urban wetland and a welcome link to the start of **Oriental Parade**, Wellington's most elegant section of waterfront. Skirting **Oriental Bay**, this Norfolk pine-lined road curls past some of the city's priciest real estate and even flanks a **beach** installed here in 2003 with sand brought across Cook Strait from near Takaka. On a fine day it's hard to beat a stroll along the promenade, ice cream in hand, admiring the city across the harbour. Apart from the Freyberg pool

▲ Chaffers Marina and the houses above Oriental Bay

(see "Swimming", p.489) and a couple of restaurants, there are no sights as such, but your stroll can be extended out into a full afternoon by continuing to Charles Plimmer Park and joining the Southern Walkway (see p.481) to the summit of **Mount Victoria**.

At 196m, **Mount Victoria Lookout** is one of the best of Wellington's viewpoints, offering sweeping views of the city, waterfront, docks and beyond to the Hutt Valley; all particularly dramatic around dusk. If you don't fancy the steep but rewarding walk, you can also reach the summit by bus (#20; Mon–Fri), using the Wellington Rover (see p.461), or by car following Hawker Street, off Majoribanks Street, then taking Palliser Road, which twists uphill to the lookout.

Courtenay Place and Cuba Street

If the weather isn't up to a stroll along the waterfront, repair to the excellent **New Zealand Film Archive**, 84 Taranaki St (Mon & Tues 9am–5pm, Wed–Fri 9am–10pm, Sat 4–10pm; free; ⓣ04/384 7647 ⓦwww.filmarchive.org.nz), a couple of blocks south of Te Papa. Small film-themed exhibits will interest movie buffs, but the main attraction is the ability to watch just about any New Zealand movie ever made, plus TV programmes, old commercials and assorted home movies. Much can be readily accessed from computer terminals, or search the archive and retrieve anything you fancy. Watch on a monitor or join friends in one of the small viewing rooms (all free). They also have evening screenings in their cinema (Wed–Sat usually 7pm; $8), which on Wednesday will be an NZ feature film.

Walk a block north and you're in the heart of Wellington's dining and entertainment district, centred on **Courtenay Place**. You'll continually find yourself here for a coffee, a few drinks, a meal or a movie. For mooching around during the day there's more interest along **Cuba Street**, traditionally Wellington's alternative quarter but becoming ever more chic with designer clothing stores and fancy restaurants moving in. Between Dixon and Ghuznee streets, Wellington's colourful and iconic **Bucket Fountain** was installed in 1969 and is still splashing unsuspecting passers-by.

There's little specific to see beyond here, though die-hard heritage fans could press on a couple of hundred metres south to the **Colonial Cottage Museum**, 68 Nairn St (Christmas–Easter daily 10am–4pm, Easter–Christmas Sat & Sun noon–4pm; $5; ⓦwww.colonialcottagemuseum.co.nz), central Wellington's oldest building. Though dating from 1858 (two decades into Victoria's reign), it is built in late Georgian style and has been decorated so that it feels as though the family has just left for Sunday church and will be back in an hour.

North of Civic Square

Over the last few years the northern waterfront has become livelier as the city progressively reconnects itself to the harbour. Much of the action goes on around **Queens Wharf**, where expensive harbour-view apartments, the Museum of Wellington and some bars and fine restaurants attract a lively throng.

The business heart of Wellington beats along Lambton Quay, which runs north to the **Parliamentary District**, the administrative and ecclesiastical heart of the city. Parliament marks the southern edge of **Thorndon**, Wellington's oldest suburb and the location of the **Katherine Mansfield Birthplace**, the former home of New Zealand's most famous writer.

Queens Wharf and the Museum of Wellington

North of the Civic Square lies **Frank Kitts Park**, where the mast of the *Wahine* (see p.471) stands proud on the waterfront. A few metres further along is the *Water Whirler*, a kinetic sculpture designed by Len Lye (see p.261) and opened in 2006, a quarter of a century after the artist's death. Roughly every hour (10am–10pm but not 2pm; 5–10min), it erupts into action, a sequence of complex and increasingly energetic gyrations with jets of water spewing everywhere. Nearby, **Queens Wharf** is a good place to come on a fine day to soak up the relaxed atmosphere, eat at one of the restaurants, shop and visit a couple of worthwhile sights.

A Victorian former bond store houses the **Museum of Wellington** (daily 10am–5pm: free; ⓦwww.museumofwellington.co.nz), which follows a more traditional approach than Te Papa, providing a nice counterpoint. Wellington's social and maritime history unfolds through well-executed displays on early Maori and European settlement and the city's strong seafaring heritage. For Kiwis of a certain age, the main focus is the coverage of the **Wahine disaster**, remembering the inter-island ferry which sank with the loss of 52 lives on 10 April 1968. The *Wahine* foundered in one of New Zealand's most violent storms ever, with 734 people on board. Rescue attempts were repeatedly thwarted until the weather calmed enough for passengers to start abandoning ship, only to find the ship had listed so much that the lifeboats on the upper side were unusable. Elsewhere in the museum, an impressive display tells the Maori legends of the creation of Wellington Harbour and a tall screen features a roster of short films. Free tours take place on Sundays at 2pm.

Lambton Quay and the Cable Car

Traditionally Wellington's main shopping and business street, **Lambton Quay** formed the original waterfront but was cut off by the docks formed by reclamation. Many of the more interesting shops have moved elsewhere, but the street remains the heart of the central business district, becoming more formal as you head north to the Parliamentary District.

At the southern end of Lambton Quay, glass floor panels in the basement of the Old Bank Arcade reveal some of the bow of **Plimmer's Ark**. This nineteenth-century wooden ship was scuttled then operated as a trading store by John Plimmer, a Shropshire carpenter who became known as the Father of Wellington for his devotion to the growing community. The boat was eventually abandoned, only to be rediscovered in 1997. The bulk of the remains are being preserved on Queens Wharf, but are not currently open to the public. From here, head straight along Lambton Quay to the Parliamentary District, or detour up the Cable Car (see box below) and back down through the Botanic Gardens.

The Botanic Gardens and observatories

At the top of the Cable Car (see box below) there's a lookout which gives spectacular views over the city. Here, you're also at the highest point of Wellington's **Botanic Gardens** (daily dawn–dusk; free), a huge swathe of green on peaceful rolling hills with numerous paths that wind down towards the city. You could easily while away a couple of hours here visiting the observatory, begonia house and rose garden, or simply strolling through stands of pohutukawa, remnants of dense native forest and ornamental flowerbeds. Pick up the useful free map from the Cable Car Museum.

Riding the Cable Car

Even if you never use the rest of Wellington's public transport system, be sure to take the short and scenic ride up to the leafy suburb of Kelburn and the upper section of the Botanic Gardens on the **Cable Car** (Mon–Fri 7am–10pm, Sat & Sun 9am–10pm; $2.50 one way, $4.50 return), originally built in 1902. Its shiny red railcars depart every ten minutes from the lower terminus on Cable Car Lane, just off Lambton Quay, and climb a steep, one-in-five incline, making three stops along the way and giving great views over the city and harbour. At the upper terminus on Upland Road, the **Cable Car Museum** (Mon–Fri 9.30am–5.30pm, Sat & Sun 9.30am–4.30pm; free) contains the historic winding room with the electric drive motor and a cat's cradle of cables. Three century-old cars are on display along with plenty of background on this and other cable cars around the world. Spend time watching the short movies, particularly the one about the 400-plus mini cable cars people use to access their properties around Wellington.

Two minutes' walk from the upper Cable Car terminus is the revamped 1941 **Carter Observatory** (Ⓦwww.carterobservatory.org) which by the time you read this should have reopened with all sorts of astronomical displays, and telescopes used to give a New Zealand angle on the exploration of the southern skies, from Maori astronavigation through to recent planet searches. Check the website of opening hours, prices and details of their planetarium shows.

The *tour de force* of the Botanic Gardens, and their most visited section, is the fragrant **Lady Norwood Rose Garden**, where a colonnade of climbing roses frames beds of over 300 varieties set out in a formal wheel shape. The adjacent **Begonia House** (daily: Oct–March 10am–5pm; April–Sept 10am–4pm; free) is divided into two areas: the tropical, with an attractive lily pond, and the temperate, which has seasonal displays of begonias and gloxinias in summer, changing to cyclamen, orchids and impatiens in winter. There's also a good café.

A couple of hundred metres northeast, the monolithic Seddon Memorial (to New Zealand's most lauded politician, Richard Seddon) marks the entrance to **Bolton Street Memorial Park**, an atmospheric Victorian cemetery where many of the city's early pioneers are buried. Established in 1840 as the city's only non-Catholic burial ground (with sections for Anglicans, Jews and others), the cemetery was closed in 1892. In the 1960s, amid public outcry, over 3700 bodies were exhumed and relocated to make way for the motorway that now bisects it. The main path crosses the motorway by a footbridge to an isolated remnant of the cemetery and a pretty weatherboard chapel (daily 10am–4pm) containing burial records. Here you're up against the high-rise buildings of The Terrace, only a short walk from the Parliamentary District. Old-fashioned roses clamber over the ageing headstones and twist through ironwork in the shade of mature trees.

Parliamentary District

The northern end of Lambton Quay marks the start of the **Parliamentary District**. It is dominated by the grandiose **Old Government Buildings**, which at first glance appears to be an opulent Italian Renaissance palace constructed from cream stone but is in fact wooden. Designed by Colonial Architect William Clayton (1823–77) to mark the country's transition from provincial to centralized government, it was supposed to be built in stone but cost-cutting forced a rethink. When completed in 1876 it was the largest building in New Zealand, and except for an ornamental palace in Japan remains the largest timber building in the world. It is now occupied by Victoria University's Law Faculty, but you can usually duck inside and nip up the fine rimu staircase to see a series of photos of the building as a backdrop to various demonstrations and protests.

The Parliament Buildings

Visible across Lambton Quay are the **Parliament Buildings**, the seat of New Zealand's government, a trio of highly individual structures that somehow manage to sit quite harmoniously together. The most distinctive is the modernist **Beehive**, a seven-stepped truncated cone that houses the Cabinet and the offices of its ministers. Designed by British (and Coventry Cathedral) architect Sir Basil Spence in 1964, it was finally completed in 1982, six years after Spence's death. The Beehive is connected directly to the Edwardian Neoclassical **Parliament House**, a suitably solid and reliable seat of government – which is more than can be said for the almost frivolous Victorian Gothic **Parliamentary Library** next door.

Hour-long guided tours (on the hour: Mon–Fri 10am–4pm, Sat 10am–3pm, Sun 11am–3pm; free; ⓣ04/471 9503, ⓦwww.parliament.nz) start from a visitor centre on the ground floor of the Beehive. Informative and anecdotal, the tour begins with a short video on the detailed restoration work that was carried out after a fire in 1992 and a look at the earthquake-isolating foundations retrofitted under Parliament House to protect it from the fault line just 400m away. An undoubted highlight is the highly decorative **Maori Affairs Select Committee Room** with its specially commissioned carvings and woven *tukutuku* panels from all the major tribal groups in the land. A brief look at the ornate and beautifully restored Victorian Gothic library gives a sense of its ecclesiastical feel; no accident as it was designed in 1899 by Thomas Turnbull, who was famous for his work on churches. Finally, if Parliament isn't sitting, you are led through the Debating Chamber; when the house is sitting you're able to watch proceedings from the public gallery, after the tour.

MPs occasionally venture across Molesworth Street to the **Backbencher Pub** (see p.486).

The National Library and Archives

Opposite Parliament on Molesworth Street, the **National Library of New Zealand** (Mon–Fri 9am–5pm, Sat 9am–1pm; free), is mostly off limits to all but researchers, but it is worth ducking into the large public **gallery**, which regularly hosts free and usually worthwhile exhibitions.

A stone's throw east along Aitken Street, **Archives New Zealand**, 10 Mulgrave St (Mon–Fri 9am–5pm, Sat 9am–1pm; free; ⓦwww.archives.govt.nz), is home to the nation's most important documents. Again, much of the building is devoted to research, but you can visit the **Constitution Room**, a dimly lit, climate-controlled vault where the prize exhibit is the original Maori-language **Treaty of Waitangi** (see p.194). This barely survived a long spell lost in the bowels of the Old Government Buildings, suffering water damage and the gnawings of rodents before it was rescued in 1908. Various copies of the Treaty did the rounds of the country collecting Maori chiefs' signatures, giving a sense of how haphazard the whole process was. Other archives highlight milestones on the country's road to nationhood, notably the 1835 Declaration of Independence of the Northern Chiefs and **Maori petitions** dating back to 1909, which complain of broken treaty promises. Look also for the facsimile of the 1893 **petition for women's suffrage**, put together by New Zealand's iconic suffragette, Kate Sheppard – who features on the $10 note. At this third attempt she managed to amass 32,000 signatures, a quarter of the adult female population, ushering in legislation which made New Zealand the first country to give women the vote. Outside the Constitution Room is a small bowl of water to help Maori neutralize the effect of being in the presence of such a sacred object.

The Cathedrals – old and new

Long before the houses of the Parliamentary District were taken over by government departments and foreign delegations, this area of Thorndon was a thriving suburb, its religious needs served by the modest **Old St Paul's**, at the corner of Mulgrave and Pipitea streets (daily 10am–5pm; free). Possibly the finest European timber church in the country, it operated as the parish church of Thorndon from 1866 to 1964 and was only saved from demolition in the 1960s by sustained public protest. It remains a consecrated building popular for weddings. You'll understand why when you see its beautiful interior, crafted in early English Gothic style (more commonly seen in stone) from native timbers that have since darkened with age to a rich mellow hue. Lovely stained-glass windows and the sheen of polished brass plaques on the walls highlight the ranks of dark pews, arches, pulpit and choral area. The church was the major work of an English ecclesiastical architect, Reverend Frederick Thatcher, who designed it for Bishop Selwyn and was vicar here for a few years.

Old St Paul's could hardly stand in greater contrast to **St Paul's Cathedral** (Mon–Fri 8.30am–5pm, Sat 10am–4pm, Sun 8am–6pm; free), its modern successor, a block away on Molesworth Street. A curious mix of Byzantine and Santa Fe styles, it was designed in the 1930s by Cecil Wood of Christchurch, a renowned ecclesiastical architect. Queen Elizabeth II laid the foundation stone in 1954 but the cathedral wasn't finally complete until 1998. The interior is cavernous, dwarfing the dark-wood choir stalls, which look completely out of place amongst all the powder-pink concrete. Note the distinctive pipe organ, which was built in London, and was originally installed in Old St Paul's.

Thorndon and the Katherine Mansfield Birthplace

Walk north from Parliament for about ten minutes to reach the **Katherine Mansfield Birthplace**, 25 Tinakori Rd (Tues–Sun 10am–4pm; $5.50; Ⓦwww.katherinemansfield.com; bus #14 stops on nearby Park Street). A modest wooden house with a small garden, this was the childhood home of Katherine Mansfield (see box below) and comes stuffed with antiques and ornaments. The house has a cluttered Victorian/Edwardian charm and unusual decor, avant-garde for its time, inspired by Japonisme and the Aesthetic Movement. This has been beautifully restored and the walls are bright with colour and reprints of original wallpapers. In the kitchen is a doll's house representing the one in the story of the same name, while an upstairs room is set aside to recount a history of the author's life and career, with some black-and-white photos of Wellington and the people that shaped her life – and an excellent 54-minute video, *A Woman and a Writer*. The connections between the suburb of Thorndon and Mansfield's life and works are explored through more photos in the lean-to at the back of the house.

The suburbs

Wellington's suburbs offer a few worthwhile distractions from the bustle of the city. The groundbreaking **Karori Sanctuary** is within easy striking distance of the centre and is nicely complemented by a couple of other sites: the fine stand of native bush a few kilometres north at **Otari-Wilson's Bush**, and the **Wellington Zoo**, just south of downtown. A number of good walks thread

Katherine Mansfield

Katherine Mansfield Beauchamp (1888–1923), is New Zealand's most famous short-story writer. During her brief life, she revolutionized the form, eschewing plot in favour of a poetic expansiveness. Virginia Woolf felt that her work was "the only writing I have ever been jealous of".

Mansfield lived here on Tinakori Road for five years with her parents, three sisters and beloved grandmother and the place is described in some of her works, notably "Prelude" and "A Birthday". The family later moved to a much grander house in what is now the western suburb of Karori until, at 19, Katherine left for Europe, where she lived until dying of tuberculosis in France, aged 32.

through the greenery of the Town Belt or head beyond to the quiet pleasures of **Scorching Bay** on the Miramar Peninsula.

Karori Sanctuary

The **Karori Sanctuary**, 31 Waiapu Rd (Dec–March daily 10am–5pm; April–Nov Mon–Fri 10am–4pm, Sat & Sun 10am–5pm; $12; ⓣ04/920 9200, infoline ⓣ04/920 2222, ⓦwww.sanctuary.org.nz), 3km west of downtown, is an ambitious project to restore a sliver of New Zealand native bush (and attendant wildlife) to 225 hectares of urban Wellington. Sited around two century-old reservoirs which formerly supplied Wellington's drinking water, the managing trust first designed an 8.6km-long **predator-proof fence** which is intended to keep out all introduced mammals. As well as restocking the area with native trees and eradicating weeds, the trust has introduced native birds – little spotted kiwi, weka, saddleback, kaka, morepork, tui, bellbird, whitehead and North Island robins – plus tuatara (back in a natural mainland environment for the first time in over 200 years) and the grass-hopper-like weta to the sanctuary from the overspill of the successful conservation and restocking programme on Kapiti Island (see p.290).

Started in the late 1990s, this far-reaching project won't be entirely complete until the forest has matured in around 500 years. You can already walk the 35km of paths (some almost flat, others quite rugged) listening to birdsong heard almost nowhere else on the mainland – making it easy to understand why early European arrivals to New Zealand were so impressed with the avian chorus.

It's worth spending half a day here wandering past viewing hides, areas noted for their fantails or saddleback, and even the first few metres of a gold-mine tunnel from the 1869 Karori gold rush. You should seriously consider joining one of the **guided tours**: the Introductory (daily at 11am; 1hr; $22); the Escape (Sept–April daily 3hr 30min before sunset; 2hr; $40); or the Night (daily 30min before sunset; 2hr; $45), which gives you a chance to watch kaka feeding, see banks of glow-worms and hear (and maybe see) kiwi.

The sanctuary's existence is already having a wider effect, with increasing numbers of tui, bellbirds and kaka spotted in neighbouring suburbs. A big new visitor centre and restaurant is due to open in late 2009.

To reach the sanctuary, either walk the 2km from the Cable Car upper terminus, catch the frequent #3 bus from Lambton Quay or Courtenay Place, or if you're booked on a tour use the bus service provided that picks up at the i-SITE (see p.459).

Otari-Wilton's Bush

The Karori Sanctuary may be predator-free and is undoubtedly an impressive achievement, but the flora is far from mature. For a glimpse of the New Zealand bush as it was, you're better off at **Otari-Wilton's Bush** (daily dawn–dusk; free), 6km northwest of the city centre. The remains of the area's original podocarp-northern rata forest was set aside in 1860 by one Job Wilton and forms the core of the luscious 80 hectares preserved here.

At the unstaffed visitor centre, 160 Wilton Rd (daily 9am–5pm), you'll find a map of the walks, which initially follow a hundred-metre **Canopy Walkway** of sturdy decking high in the trees across a gully. This leads to the **Native Botanic Garden**, laid out with plants from around the country, and the informative **Nature Trail** (30min), a good introduction to the New Zealand forest and its many plants. Assorted trails (all 30min–1hr) wander through the bush, one passing an 800-year-old rimu. To reach the reserve, either walk the 3km from the Karori Sanctuary or take bus #14 (every 30min from the Lambton Interchange).

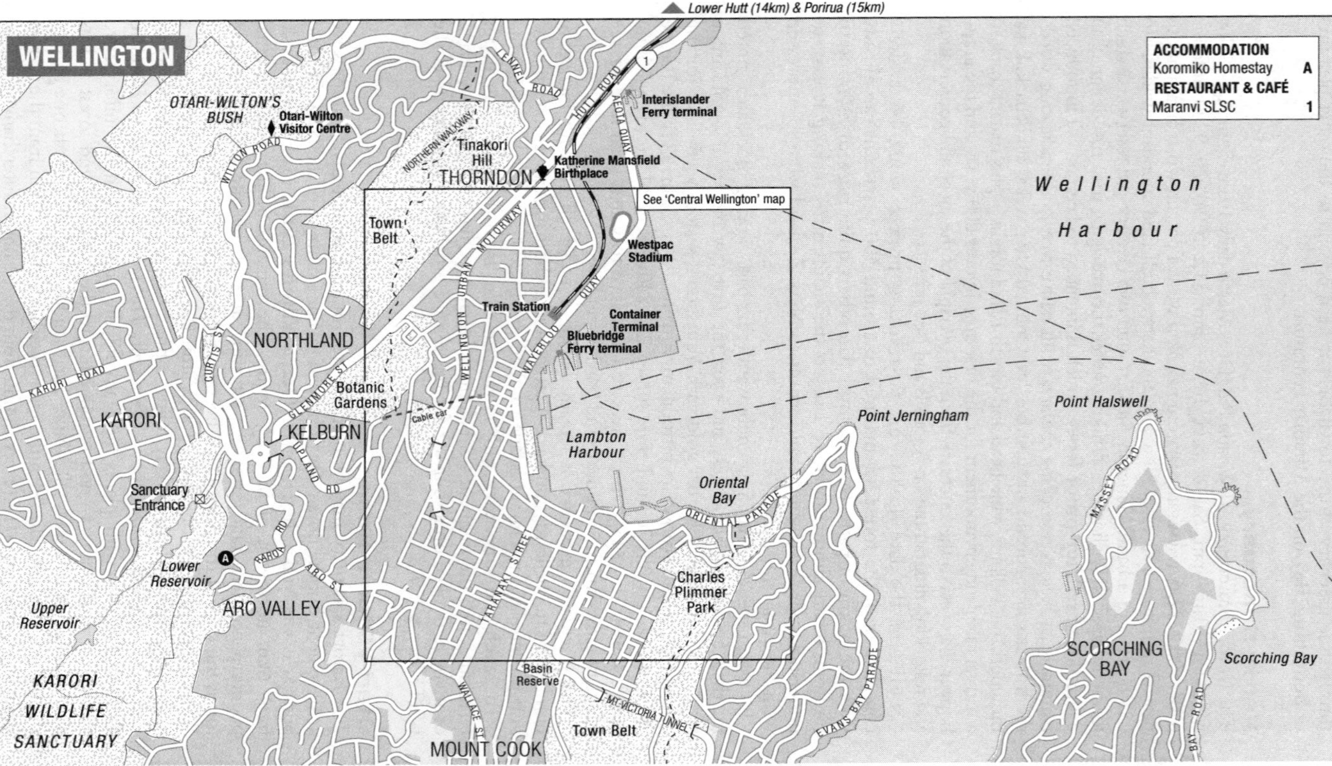
WELLINGTON
Lower Hutt (14km) & Porirua (15km)
Makara Peak (5km)
Matiu/Somes Island (20 min)
Picton (3 hr)
ACCOMMODATION
Koromiko Homestay A
RESTAURANT & CAFÉ
Maranvi SLSC 1
OTARI-WILTON'S BUSH
Otari-Wilton Visitor Centre
WILTON ROAD
NORTHERN WALKWAY
Tinakori Hill
TENNEL ROAD
HUTT ROAD
AEOTA QUAY
Interislander Ferry terminal
THORNDON
Katherine Mansfield Birthplace
See 'Central Wellington' map
Wellington Harbour
Town Belt
URBAN MOTORWAY
WELLINGTON
Westpac Stadium
QUAY
Train Station
Container Terminal
Bluebridge Ferry terminal
WATERLOO
NORTHLAND
CURTIS ST
KARORI ROAD
GLENMORE ST
Botanic Gardens
Cable car
KARORI
KELBURN
UPLAND RD
Point Jerningham
Point Halswell
Lambton Harbour
Oriental Bay
ORIENTAL PARADE
MASSEY ROAD
Sanctuary Entrance
ARO RD
A
Lower Reservoir
ARO ST
Upper Reservoir
ARO VALLEY
TARANAKI STREET
Charles Plimmer Park
SCORCHING BAY
Scorching Bay
Basin Reserve
MT VICTORIA TUNNEL
EVANS BAY PARADE
BAY ROAD
KARORI WILDLIFE SANCTUARY
WALLACE ST
Town Belt
MOUNT COOK

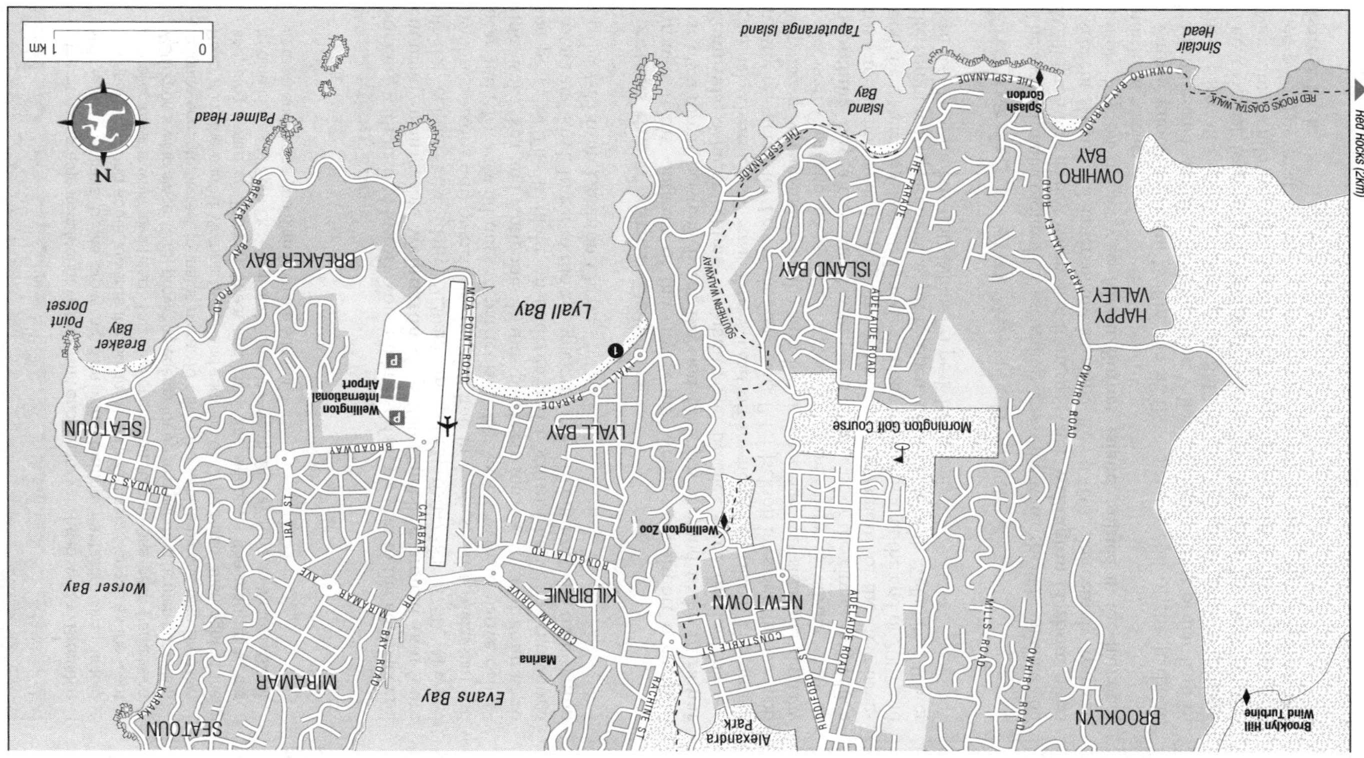
SEATOUN
KARAKA
Worser Bay
DUNDAS ST
SEATOUN
Point Dorset
Breaker Bay
BREAKER BAY ROAD
Palmer Head
BREAKER BAY
MIRAMAR
IRA ST
MIRAMAR AVE
BROADWAY
Wellington International Airport
BAY ROAD
DR
CALABAR
MOA POINT ROAD
Evans Bay
Marina
COBHAM DRIVE
KILBIRNIE
RONGOTAI RD
LYALL BAY
PARADE
LYALL
Lyall Bay
RACHINE ST
Wellington Zoo
Alexandra Park
CONSTABLE ST
NEWTOWN
SOUTHERN WALKWAY
THE ESPLANADE
Taputeranga Island
RIDDIFORD ST
ADELAIDE ROAD
Mornington Golf Course
ISLAND BAY
Island Bay
THE PARADE
MILLS ROAD
OWHIRO ROAD
THE ESPLANADE
Splash Gordon
HAPPY VALLEY ROAD
OWHIRO BAY
BROOKLYN
HAPPY VALLEY
OWHIRO BAY PARADE
Sinclair Head
RED ROCKS COASTAL WALK
Brooklyn Hill Wind Turbine
Red Rocks (2km)
N
0
1 km

The best view in Wellington

If the city panorama from Mount Victoria isn't enough for you, head west to **Brooklyn Hill**, easily identified by its crowning 32m **wind turbine**. Fantastic views unfold across the city and south towards the South Island's Kaikoura Ranges as the giant propeller blades whirr overhead. This demonstration turbine has been harnessing Wellington's wind since 1993, providing energy for up to a hundred homes but failing to ignite enough interest to install more. To reach the turbine by car, take Brooklyn Road from the end of Victoria Street and turn left at Ohiro Road, then right at the shopping centre up Todman Street and follow the signposts (the road up to the turbine closes at 8pm Oct–April and 5pm May–Sept). Bus #7 runs up Victoria Street in town and drops you 3km from the summit.

Wellington Zoo

Sticking with natural history, you might also fancy a visit to the compact and eminently manageable **Wellington Zoo**, 200 Daniell St, around 4km south of the central city (daily 9.30am–5pm; $15; ⓣ04/381 6750, ⓦwww.wellingtonzoo.com), which does a nice line in exotics – the Malaysian sun bear and African wild dogs in particular – but excels with its native collection. Kaka, kea and Antipodes Islands parakeets squawk, a great contrast to the peace of The Twilight, an underground nocturnal house for morepork, tuatara and kiwi. To get to the zoo, pick up the #10 bus from the train station or the #23 from Lambton Quay.

Around the Miramar Peninsula

Around 10km southeast of the city centre, Wellington's airport occupies a narrow isthmus between Evans Bay and Lyall Bay. Beyond is the **Miramar Peninsula**, a lumpy chunk of suburbs and beaches, some overlooking the channel where Cook Strait ferries head off to the South Island. The area is mostly of interest for *Lord of the Rings* fans: Peter Jackson lives out this way, and Miramar is where much of the non-location footage was shot and digitally processed. Cast and crew often stayed out here, many favouring visits to **Scorching Bay**, a crescent of white sand 13km east of the city centre, which has safe swimming and a play area. It was formerly famous for the crew hangout, the waterside *Chocolate Fish Café*, though this closed at the end of 2007 and the rumoured replacement is yet to open. Come here with Wellington Rover (see p.461) or on bus #30 (Mon–Fri peak hours only).

The harbour and the Hutt Valley

The sight of multicoloured sails scudding across the water should convince you Wellington is at its best when seen from the water. **Wellington Harbour** offers excellent sailing and entertaining kayaking (see p.480); alternatively you can simply hop on the ferry to **Matiu/Somes Island**, isolated in the harbour's northern reaches.

Fifteen kilometres from Wellington at the northern end of the harbour, commuterland spreads along the Hutt Valley, the largest tract of flat land in these parts, all easily accessible along SH2 and by suburban trains and buses. The original founding of Wellington is remembered in Petone's Settlers Museum, while nearby Lower Hutt has Wellington's closest campsite (see p.464), a great art gallery and is on the way to the rugged **Rimutaka Forest Park**.

Matiu/Somes Island

One of Wellington's best day-trips is to **Matiu/Somes Island**, isolated in the northern reaches of the harbour. Legendary navigator Kupe is said to have named it Matiu (meaning "peace"), in the tenth century, and his descendants lived on the island until deposed by European settlers in the late 1830s. They renamed the island after Joseph Somes, then deputy governor of the New Zealand Company that had "bought" it. For eighty years it was a quarantine station where travellers carrying diseases such as smallpox were held until they recovered or died. During both world wars anyone in New Zealand considered even vaguely suspect – Germans, Italians, Turks, Mexicans and Japanese – were interned until the end of the war, after which it became an animal quarantine station for a number of years.

In the early 1980s its conservation value was recognized and it's now managed by DOC, who oversee continued efforts to revitalize **native vegetation** and restore the historic buildings. Introduced mammalian predators have now all been eradicated and threatened native species are being introduced in an effort to save them from extinction. Already there are six types of lizard, kakariki (the red-crowned parakeet), North Island robins, little blue penguins, the cricket-like weta and the ancient reptilian tuatara. Over fifty of these ancient lizard-like beasts were captive-bred at Wellington's Victoria University and released in 1998. They seem to like it as numbers are increasing.

Access is on the **Dominion Post Ferry** (3–4 services daily; 20min each way; $18.50 return; timetable ⓣ04/499 3339, ⓦwww.eastbywest.co.nz) which stops at the island on its cross-harbour journey to Days Bay, enabling you to explore for up to five hours before catching a ferry back to Wellington. From the wharf at the island's northeastern end, a surfaced road runs uphill for 400m to the **DOC field centre** in an old hospital, which has maps of the island, or you can pick one up in advance from the city DOC office (see p.459). A popular option is to take a picnic lunch onto the island. Note that this is a protected reserve and smoking is not allowed.

Petone and Lower Hutt

The northern shore of Wellington Harbour is occupied by the suburb of **Petone**, the site of the first, short-lived European settlement in the Wellington region: the **Petone Settlers Museum**, The Esplanade, Petone (Tues–Fri noon–4pm, Sat & Sun 1–5pm; donation; ⓦwww.petonesettlers.org.nz), tells the tale of the early Maori life in the region and the subsequent colonial settlement. The museum is 2.5km east of the Petone train station, so access is easier on buses #81, #83 or the Flyer from Courtenay Place and Lambton Quay.

Some 6km north of Petone sprawls **Lower Hutt**, home to **The New Dowse**, 45 Laings Rd (Mon–Fri 10am–4.30pm, Sat & Sun 10am–5pm; free; ⓣ04/570 6500, ⓦwww.dowse.org.nz), a progressive art museum which recently underwent a major redevelopment by Athfield Architects (see box, p.465). It's a real stunner, a great modern space always filled with beautiful and frequently challenging works, regularly cycled from their permanent collection. Renowned for its collection of modern art and crafts, the Dowse might have shows on modern fashion, photography, jewellery or wider subjects, and is always keen to engage local artists, who bring a strong Kiwi flavour to the place. It is not a huge space, but it's still worth breaking your visit with time in the excellent café. The gallery is almost 2km west of the Waterloo train station, so access is easier on the same buses as the Petone Settlers Museum.

The Dowse is adjacent to the i-SITE visitor centre, 25 Laings Rd (Mon–Fri 9am–5pm, Sat & Sun 9am–3pm; ⓣ04/560 4715, ⓦwww.huttvalleynz.com), which is a good place to find out about casual visits 3km southeast at **Maori Treasures**, 58 Guthrie St (ⓣ04/939 9630). This classy private Maori art studios, gallery and shop is normally visited on three-hour tours from Wellington ($85) which include a chance to watch artists at work, learn something of Maori artistic traditions and customs, touch a kiwi-feather cloak and see fine carving in wood, greenstone and bone, plus painting, basketry, fibre arts, clay works and stone sculpture.

Rimutaka Forest Park

Due south of Lower Hutt is the main entrance to the **Rimutaka Forest Park**, popular among city-dwellers for its series of easy, short and **day-walks** in the attractive Catchpool Valley; there's also picnic and BBQ facilities, and a well-maintained **campsite** (see p.464), the nearest DOC site to Wellington. Some 20km from Wellington along the Coast Road, a signpost marks the park **entrance** (gates open 8am–dusk), from where Catchpool Road winds a further 2km up the valley to the car park, the starting point for most of the walks. Keen walkers and campers will want to get as far as the braided Orongorongo River, from where a startlingly grand landscape begins; camping is free along the riverbanks. There is no convenient bus service, so you'll probably want to drive.

Pick up the *Catchpool Valley/Rimutaka Forest Park* leaflet from DOC in Wellington.

Activities

As the capital city, Wellington isn't perhaps the sort of place you would expect to get into the outdoors much, but there are a number of worthwhile **activities**. Walking along the waterfront (particularly Oriental Parade) provides an atmospheric antidote to city pursuits, while tougher **hikes** are on offer out around the Town Belt (see box, p.481). **Bikers** can make use of much the same territory plus an excellent mountain-bike park, while folk after water-based adventures can explore the harbour. Oriental Bay has a small, handy beach, but if you're making an afternoon of it head out to Scorching Bay (see p.478). For watersports, try windsurfing, kayaking or diving on the wreck of the frigate *Wellington*.

Watersports

Apart from Dominion Post Ferry out to Matiu/Somes Island (see p.479) Wellington makes only limited use of its harbour, though reliable winds make it a great place for kiteboarding. Most action is centred on Kio Bay, to the east of Oriental Bay and around the point towards Evans Bay. For windsurfing lessons, try Wildwinds, Chaffers Marina, Overseas Terminal (ⓣ04/384 1010, ⓦwww.wildwinds.co.nz), just east of Te Papa, who offer a two-hour taster lesson ($95) or a series of four sessions ($395) to really get you going.

If the sun's out and it's not too windy, **kayaking** along the waterfront is a great way to spend a couple of hours. Nip down to Queens Wharf and Fergs Kayaks in Shed 6 (Oct–April daily 9am–8pm; May–Aug Mon–Fri 10am–8pm, Sat & Sun 9am–6pm; ⓣ04/499 8898, ⓦwww.fergskayaks.co.nz) for **rental kayaks** (sit-on-top kayaks $12 for 2hr; singles $18 for 2hr, $40 per day; doubles

Walks around Wellington

With its encircling wooded Town Belt, great city views from nearby hills and the temptation of watching seals along the southern coast, Wellington offers some excellent and easily accessible walking. Pick up relevant free leaflets from the i-SITE (see p.459).

Red Rocks Coastal Walk

The easy and popular **Red Rocks Coastal Walk** (4km each way; 2–3hr return) traces Wellington's southern shoreline to Sinclair Head, where a colony of bachelor New Zealand **fur seals** takes up residence from May to October each year. The walk follows a rough track along the coastline from Owhiro Bay to Sinclair Head, passing a quarry and the eponymous **Red Rocks** – well-preserved volcanic pillow lava, formed about 200 million years ago by underwater volcanic eruptions and coloured red by iron oxide. Maori variously attribute the colour to bloodstains from Maui's nose or blood dripping from a paua-shell cut on Kupe's hand, while another account tells how Kupe's daughters cut themselves in mourning, having given up their father for dead.

The track starts around 7km south of the city centre at the quarry gates at the western end of Owhiro Bay Parade, where there's a car park. To get there by **bus** either take the frequent #1 to Island Bay, get off at The Parade at the corner of Reef Street and walk 2.5km to the start of the walk or, at peak times, catch #4, which continues to Happy Valley, only 1km from the track. Both leave downtown on Courtenay Place heading east. Alternatively join the Wellington Rover hop-on-hop-off bus or come with Seal Coast Safari (see p.461 for both).

The Southern Walkway

The **Southern Walkway** (11km; 4–5hr) cuts through the Town Belt to the south of the city centre, between Oriental and Island bays. Despite a few steep stretches it is fairly easy going overall. The walk offers plenty of variety, yielding excellent views of the harbour and central city. Fantails, grey warblers and wax-eyes provide company, and Island Bay offers some of the city's best swimming.

The walk can be undertaken in either direction and is clearly marked by posts bearing orange arrows. To start at the city end, simply walk along Oriental Parade (or take **bus** #14 or #24) to the entrance to Charles Plimmer Park just past 350 Oriental Parade. To begin at the southern end, take the #1 bus to Island Bay and follow the signs from nearby Shorland Park.

The Northern Walkway

Extending through tranquil sections of the Town Belt to the north of the city centre, the **Northern Walkway** (16km; 4–5hr) offers spectacular views. Stretching from Kelburn to the suburb of Johnsonville, it covers five distinct areas – Botanic Garden, Tinakori Hill, Trelissick Park, Khandallah Park and Johnsonville Park – each accessible from suburban streets and served by public transport. Highlights are the **birdlife** on Tinakori Hill (tui, fantails, kingfishers, grey warblers, silver-eyes); the regenerating native forest of **Ngaio Gorge** in Trelissick Park; great views across the city and the harbour and over to the Rimutaka and Tararua ranges from a lookout on **Mount Kaukau** (430m); and, in **Johnsonville Park**, a disused road tunnel hewn through solid rock.

Start at the top of the Cable Car and head north through the Botanic Garden, or join the walk at Tinakori Hill by climbing St Mary Street, off Glenmore Street, and following the orange arrows through woodland. To begin at the northern end, take a **train** to Raroa station on the Johnsonville line.

$35/$80), or join one of their **guided trips** such as the Lights at Night trip (when calm), with romantic city-illuminated views and including a light supper (6–9pm; $85 each 4 or more; $105 each for 2; book a week in advance).

Sub-surface explorations are best conducted with Splash Gordon, 432 The Esplanade, Island Bay (Ⓣ04/939 3483, Ⓦwww.splashgordon.co.nz), who offer scuba diving on the frigate *Wellington*, scuttled just off the coast in 21m of water in 2005. Experienced divers can do two dives with all gear for $110.

Cycling

With little flat land, super-steep hills and a reputation for fierce winds, **cycling** around Wellington may not be your first choice, but on a fine day there is little to beat renting a bike for a spin around the coastal roads that follow the bays east of the city. Start by heading east from Te Papa along Oriental Parade and follow the coast as far as you want; even right past the airport and around the northern tip of the Miramar Peninsula to Scorching Bay (see p.478) and Seatoun (25–30km one way).

There's also a stack of **off-road riding**, much of it outlined in the *Mountain Biking in Wellington City* leaflet (available free from the visitor centre), which contains maps of key areas a short ride from the city. Ones to consider include the coastal track out to Red Rocks (see "Walks around Wellington" box, p.481) and the single-track trails around Mount Victoria. Committed mountain bikers flock to **Makara Peak Mountain Bike Park** (Ⓦwww.makarapeak.org.nz), an area of forest and farmland centred on the 412m Makara Peak, up behind Karori some 8km west of downtown Wellington. There's no entry fee and you'll have the run of 40km of tracks suitable for all abilities.

Bikes are best rented from Mud Cycles, 338 Karori Rd, Karori, 2km short of the bike park (Ⓣ04/476 4961 Ⓦwww.mudcycles.co.nz), who charge $30 a half-day and $45 a day for hardtails. In town, try Penny Farthing Cycle Shop, 89 Courtenay Place (Ⓣ04/385 2279, Ⓦwww.pennyfarthing.co.nz), who charge $50 a day for a hardtail.

Skating and rock climbing

In-line skates ($15 for 2hr) are available at Ferg's Kayaks (see p.480) and are perfect for use in nearby Frank Kitts Park or around Oriental Parade. Ferg's also offer an excellent and very popular indoor climbing wall ($12; harness and shoes $3 each).

Eating, drinking and entertainment

In central Wellington you're spoilt for choice by some of the finest eateries in the country. There's little need to venture much beyond the bounds of the central business district, though we've picked out a couple of reasons to stray. The scene is cosmopolitan, and as the country's self-professed **coffee** capital, you'll find the good stuff served up at numerous spots, from the cosy to the *très chic.*

In the streets around **Courtenay Place** and **Cuba Street** there's a plethora of ethnic restaurants – Malaysian and Indian places are particularly abundant – and a number of fancier places trying to lure the crowds. The area is also home to some of the best **nightlife** in the country, with a huge array of late-night cafés, bars and clubs within walking distance of each other. New places constantly spring up and tired ones quietly drop off their perch or, after a lick of paint, reinvent themselves under a different name. The partying goes on late into the next morning, and pumps hardest from Thursday to Saturday, when more secluded places nearby offer a less frenetic setting.

The **arts** are also strong, with several theatres and a healthy festival season.

Eating

During the day budget-minded visitors should make for one of the **food courts**, which offer bargain grazing from an array of international outlets, though there are also budget lunch specials at many ethnic restaurants. For **groceries** try New World Metro, 68 Willis St, or the larger New World, at the eastern end of Wakefield Street near Te Papa. The following are marked on the map on p.466, unless otherwise stated.

Food courts, delis and takeaways

The Catch 48 Courtenay Place. Inexpensive sushi bar with dishes revolving on the countertop conveyor belt (plates are colour-coded according to price), to take away or eat in; also does side orders and bigger meals ($10–22) from a set menu. Closed Sun lunch.

Food on Willis Basement at 1 Willis St. Daytime food court with counters selling sushi, Thai, Chinese, Mexican, Indian and Turkish plus a bakery and licensed café. Closed Sun.

Moore Wilson's Corner of of Tory & College sts. Tucked under a parking building this superb deli, charcuterie and bakery is the place to come for top-quality picnic supplies.

Wellington Trawling Sea Market 220 Cuba St. The best fish-and-chip shop in the city, eat in or take away, which also sells wet fish. Closed Sun evening.

Cafés

Bordeaux Bakery 127 Thorndon Quay. A treat for lovers of French baking, this casual daytime bakery and café serves wonderfully crusty loaves and baguettes, flaky croissants and pains au chocolat, all washed down with good coffee. Lunches extend to beef entrecote ($17) and vegetable risotto ($13). Licensed.

Deluxe 10 Kent Terrace. Great coffee and low-cost cakes and savouries, many of them vegetarian, vegan or gluten-free, served in a slightly offbeat café, with tiny and uncomfortable infant-school-sized chairs, that's popular with the post-cinema and theatre crowd.

Dorothy 136 Cuba St. Perch in little booths in this small patisserie and chocolaterie where hot chocolate drinks, handmade chocolates and French pastries add some glamour to the usual espresso coffee menu.

Espressoholic 128 Courtenay Place. Longstanding Wellington favourite famed for being cooler than a cucumber; sinful desserts and hot chocolates are served until at least 1am (more like 4am at weekends). Come for breakfast, panini, cakes, pasta dishes ($16), mains (under $20) and assorted beers and wine. There's backyard seating for the smokers.

Fidel's 234 Cuba St. Located at the offbeat southern end of Cuba St, this funky and fun café/restaurant comes plastered with revolution-era pics of Castro and includes a camouflage-netted open-air seating area for smokers. A very un-Cuban expansion policy has recently seen them take over the barber's next door and turn it into a cool bar, though in the spirit of Castro they've kept the old Super Cuts sign. Come for coffee, booze, smoothies or excellent-value, good-quality meals for under $20.

Floriditas 161 Cuba St ☎ 04/381 2212. This stylish, light and airy café is always busy with folk here for wonderful breakfasts, fresh-baked breads, oatcakes, tarts and cakes as well as a small but clever menu which might include clam fritters with salad ($18) or a nibbling platter ($13–16) followed by a delicious amaretto afogatto ($8). Evening mains cost $20–25.

Maranui SLSC 7 Lyall Parade, Lyall Bay. See map, p.476. Wonderful unlicensed Bohemian café in a still-operational surf lifesaving club (sign in for free membership on your first visit). Gaze out over Lyall Bay to Cook Strait and the airport as you tuck into green-lipped mussel pasta ($17), a fish burger ($14), green tea soba noodles with coriander, chilli and lime or quinoa tabbouleh. Great desserts too.

Midnight Espresso 178 Cuba St. Caffeine junkiey heaven, peddling beans for all palates, this mellow coffee house offers its own brand of java plus delicious veggie and vegan fare, counter food, breakfasts and a selection of reading material to pore over. Open until around 3am.

Nikau Gallery Café City Gallery, Civic Square. A stylish, contemporary daytime café/bar and Friday-evening dinner venue (until 8pm) with an airy setting and outdoor terrace. Excellent coffee and a reasonably priced menu: try the pan-fried haloumi with bread or one of the lip-smacking desserts.

Olive 170 Cuba St ⓣ04/802 5266. Relaxed and spacious bare-boards café that's great for coffee and cakes, but also does delicious breakfasts (organic porridge $7; French toast with bacon and banana $13) and full meals, such as their antipasti plate ($18) and lamb shanks in a red wine sauce ($23). Great sunny courtyard out back. Closed Sun & Mon evenings.

Parade Café 148 Oriental Parade. A great spot to break your Oriental Bay stroll, with fine coffee and cakes and a full range of breakfasts and lunches at moderate prices. Try the garlic calamari salad, roast pumpkin panini or gourmet bangers and mash (all $14–18).

▲ Café life on Wellington waterfront

Restaurants

Chow 45 Tory St ⓣ04/382 8585. Hip restaurant serving tasty and beautifully presented Southeast Asian dishes in a stylish setting. Lunch specials ($12) are great and there's a wide selection of "long plates" ($12–15), ideal as side dishes or in combination as a banquet – go for the mussel fritters with coriander and chilli soy mayo. Linked to *Motel* (see p.486).

Dockside Shed 3, Queens Wharf ⓣ04/499 9900. Flashy restaurant and bar in a vast converted wooden warehouse with a deck area overlooking the harbour; dress up unless you want to sit outside. The place is hot on seafood – try the Dockside fish and chips, $28 or whole baby snapper ($32), and book ahead if you want a window seat.

Great India 141 Manners Str, ⓣ04/384 5755, ⓦwww.greatindia.co.nz. Probably the best curry restaurant In Wellington. More expensive than some and the service isn't always top-notch but the food is hard to beat, with plenty of tandoori and vegetarian options. Lunch specials for $10.

Kai in the City 21 Marjoribanks St ⓣ04/801 5006. Come to this lively dinner-only restaurant for Maori-inspired eating with a modern twist. They dish up *Nga O Tangaroa* (gifts from the sea) and *Nga Uri O Tane* (gifts from the land) and wonderful Maori bread, as well as fine wine and a unifying singalong that creates a truly special atmosphere. Try the *hangi* ($30), seafood platter to share ($40) or the seasonal muttonbird. Closed Mon.

Maria Pia's Trattoria 55 Mulgrave St ⓣ04/499 5590. Maria Pia is passionate about her food, and it shows in this cosy southern Italian trattoria and wine bar. The menu varies seasonally and almost everything is cooked from scratch using mostly organic ingredients. Stop in for lunch while touring the Parliamentary District, or make a special effort and come for dinner – expect to pay $30 for a main course. Lunch Tues–Fri, dinner Mon–Sat.

Martin Bosley's 103 Oriental Parade ⓣ04/920 8302. Quite simply one of Wellington's finest restaurants. Innovative cuisine focuses on seafood to complement the views from the upper floor of the Port Nicholson Yacht Club. Every detail is attended to but there's nothing over fussy. Dinner mains start at $45 and the *dégustation* menu ($100) can come with matched wines ($70). Lunch Mon–Fri, dinner Tues–Sat.

Matterhorn 106 Cuba St ⓣ04/384 3359. It is rare to find a place that successfully merges a glam bar and a fancy restaurant, but *Matterhorn* does it admirably. This delicious haven of cream concrete, dark-wood panelling and red velvet is always popular with the beautiful people but very welcoming to anyone who pops in to eat or for a beer or a cocktail (try the basil and manuka honey martini) perhaps with a selection of tapas. Food is served all day and is beautifully done: try the breakfast avocado on toast with grilled lime ($11) or the juniper-spiced venison with celeriac and potato gratin ($32).

Nicolini's 26 Courtenay Place. Genuine no-fuss, inexpensive Neapolitan restaurant: small, bustling and full of divine smells and colourful food. Delicious pork scaloppini, fish marinara, reasonably priced wine and a friendly atmosphere. Mains under $24.

Roti Chenai 120 Victoria St ⓣ04/382 9807. Tiny simple South Indian and Malaysian café with an open kitchen where roti are prepared before your eyes, as well as *dosai*, *murtabak*, curries and *rendang*. Lunch specials ($7–10) and dinner mains $14–17, are great value. Licensed & BYO.

Strawberry Fare 25 Kent Terrace ⓣ04/385 2551. A sweet-lover's delight, this restaurant is principally known for its fabulous range of two dozen sumptuous calorific indulgences ($14–17). Licensed & BYO.

The White House 232 Oriental Parade ⓣ04/385 8555. Great harbour views and exquisite food makes *The White House* one of Wellington's best and most romantic dining picks. Expect the likes of grilled venison with an orgy of mushrooms and truffle oil ($40), chargrilled lambs loin ($40) and grilled salmon on wasabi mash followed by a palate-clearing blackberry sorbet ($19). Open every night & lunch Fri.

Zico 8 Courtenay Place ⓣ04/802 5585. Young, exuberant, authentic Italian that won't break the bank, with veal medallions, creamy risotto, calamari fritti, plus shrimp and salmon in pasta with pesto, mostly around $24–31 mark. Daily for lunch & dinner.

Drinking and nightlife

Most **pubs** and **bars** are open daily, from around eleven in the morning until midnight or later. Those closest to the business district, The Terrace and Lambton Quay tend to be the most expensive. The distinction between bars and **clubs** is often blurred, with many bars having free live music and dancing in the evenings, especially at weekends. Resident and guest DJs mix broad-ranging styles to create a party- or club-style atmosphere. Live **bands** (usually Kiwi but sometimes international) are a regular fixture, playing in bars, dedicated smaller venues or bigger halls like the Queens Wharf Events Centre (☎04/472 5021) and occasionally in **free concerts** in the waterfront Frank Kitts Park or at the Civic Square. The following are marked on the map on p.466.

Pubs and bars

The Backbencher Pub Corner of Molesworth & Kate Sheppard sts. A favourite with MPs and civil servants, partly for the satirical cartoons and outsized latex puppets of notable local politicians and sportsmen from the 1970s. There's also a convivial pub ambience, a dozen or more draught beers and unpretentious meals – risotto ($20), pork rib-eye ($25), etc – all named after current MPs.

Coyote 63 Courtenay Place. Urban Santa Fe-style bar that pulls in the dance crowds on Fri & Sat nights with its own brand of commercial dance music, reasonably priced drinks, Kiwi-Mex dishes and hedonistic crowd.

Hummingbird 22 Courtenay Place ☎04/801 6336. Popular bar/restaurant with large windows opening out onto Courtenay Place, allowing customers to watch – and be watched by – the passing crowds. There's an extensive wine list and great cocktails helped down with share platters for two ($15–35) or full meals ($25–35). Live jazz on Sunday afternoons. Open until 3am most nights.

Leuven 135 –137 Featherston St ☎04/499 2939. Belgian-style beer café in the heart of the business district, good for breakfasts of Belgian porridge ($10) and full meals such as 1kg of mussels in coconut cream, apple and coriander and lemon-grass with fries and mayo ($20) – but especially popular for lunch or early-evening tie-loosening sessions over a few Hoegaarden or a glass of wine.

Loaded Hog Backing onto Waterloo Quay. Big boozy bar overlooking the harbour with plenty of tap beers and quality food; lively at weekends.

Macs Brewery Corner of Cable & Taranaki sts. Big, popular, bare-wood bar with brewery attached. Spills out onto the waterfront and serves *Macs'* excellent home-brewed ales and some filling meals.

The Malthouse 50 Courtenay Place. A beer drinker's paradise with over two dozen on tap – including some of New Zealand's best micro-brews – plus scores more by the bottle. Also small dining plates and pizzas.

Matterhorn 106 Cuba St. Eternally cool, and the best spot for a beer or a cocktail anytime (see p.485).

Molly Malone's Corner of Taranaki St & Courtenay Place. An atmospheric, loud and in-your-face Irish-style pub, with foot-tapping live Irish-ish and rock music.

Mighty Mighty 104 Cuba St. Cool, off-beam late-night bar that regularly hosts bands of just about any stripe, but might also have a weird play, a pie-eating contest, country ping pong, or hip-hop bowls – you'll just have to go and find out. Food extends to toasted sandwiches and there's usually a $5–10 cover. Wed–Sat until 4am.

Motel Foresters Lane ☎04/384 9084. Brilliant retro-chic bar that was once so exclusive it reputedly turned away Liv Tyler when she was shooting *The Lord of the Rings*. It still cuts it, with semi-private booths and cool sounds (mostly jazz). Tucked in behind *Chow*, and closed Sun.

Clubs and gigs

The Blue Note 191 Cuba St ☎04/801 5007. Dark, untidy and rough-around-the-edges club open from 4pm (till 6am weeknights, 8am weekends). The only blues venue in the city, with live jazz and acoustic bands; usually free midweek with occasional cover charges of $5–15 at weekends, more if big-name acts.

Bodega 101 Ghuznee St. This ever-popular and fairly scruffy venue has recently reopened after some downtime. Expect cutting-edge Kiwi bands and the odd offbeat international act.

Boogie Wonderland 25 Courtenay Place. Wild and wonderfully cheesy, this retro joint is for you if you remember (or just love) flares and roller disco. Open Thurs–Sat 9pm until late. Cover typically $10.

San Francisco Bathhouse 171 Cuba St ☎04/801 6797 ⓦwww.sfbh.co.nz. The city's main indie, alternative rock and reggae venue with good Kiwi bands, occasional international touring acts and a balcony looking out on the assorted life passing along Cuba St.

Sandwiches 8 Kent Terrace. Posher clubby venue for dancing, with a restaurant attached, which attracts the weekend urbanites. Jazz (Wed), funk and soul (Thurs) and drum 'n' bass at the weekends. Sometimes free, but covers can be up to $45.

Valve 154 Vivian St ☎04/385 1630. A lively, well-respected venue with gigs and DJs most nights and everything from hardcore and garage punk to drum 'n' bass; occasional cover charges.

Wellington Sports Café Corner of Courtenay Place & Tory St. A late-night, post-pub, loud dancing venue and flash sports bar with live music, DJs playing middle-of-the-road dance and chart music and serving expensive drinks and food that is ideal for soaking them up.

Gay and lesbian Wellington

The scene in Wellington is focused in the inner city, particularly around **Courtenay Place**, and woven into the general café/bar mainstream; and though smaller than that of Auckland, it tends to be less cliquey and judgemental. In the centre, at least, gay people openly express affection in public, and gays, lesbians, transgender and bi-folk mix freely together. Currently, the only genuinely gay club is *Imerst*, 13 Dixon St, with three floors of dancing. There's also *Club Wakefield*, 15 Tory St (ⓣ04/385 4400), which is basically a sauna and cruise club.

Wellington's big gay event is the annual Pride Week (in early August), with dances, parties, films and art.

For **information** on venues and events, check out the national gay fortnightly **newspaper** *Express* (ⓦwww.gayexpress.co.nz), available free from the YHA and Unity Books (see "Bookshops", p.488); or the national *OUT!* magazine, available through OUT! Bookshop, 15 Tory St.

Performing arts and festivals

Performing arts are strong in Wellington, which is home to several professional theatres, the Royal New Zealand Ballet, the New Zealand Symphony Orchestra and assorted opera and dance companies. The best introduction is the *Wellington – What's On* booklet, free from the visitor centre and from accommodation around the city. There are also weekend **listings** in *The Dominion Post*, while bland reviews and more useful listings appear in the city's free, weekly *Capital Times*, which you can pick up from racks around town, and the monthly *Feeling Great*, a glossy arts and entertainment guide.

Look out too for flyers about the council-sponsored Summer City festival (Jan–March) with free music and performances in the Civic Square, Frank Kitts Park, the Botanic Garden and elsewhere.

Classical music, theatre and cinema

The city regularly hosts **orchestral** and other performances, while four professional **theatres** stage Kiwi and international shows. Tickets normally cost $40 upwards, but the visitor centre sells theatre tickets at a discount depending on availability. In addition to its quota of multiplexes, Wellington also has a smattering of arthouse **cinemas**: you can usually save a couple of dollars by going during the day or any time early in the week, though expect to pay around $15 on average.

Book **tickets** direct at venues or, for a small fee, through Ticketek (ⓣ04/384 3840, ⓦwww.ticketek.co.nz), who have outlets at the St James Theatre, 77–87 Courtenay Place.

Theatres and concert halls

Bats Theatre 1 Kent Terrace ⓣ04/802 4175, ⓦwww.bats.co.nz. Lively theatre concentrating on developmental works served up at affordable prices, often under $20.

Circa Corner of Taranaki & Cable sts ⓣ04/801 7992, ⓦwww.circa.co.nz. One of the country's liveliest and most innovative professional theatres, which has fostered the skills of some of the best-known Kiwi directors and actors. At either of the two spaces in this new complex (the main house and a 100-seater studio) you can count on intimate, imaginative productions.

Downstage 12 Cambridge Terrace ⓣ04/801 6946, ⓦwww.downstage.co.nz. Stages its own productions and the best touring shows: a mix of mainstream and new drama, dance and comedy, with the emphasis on quality Kiwi work. Cheaper gallery seats available.

Opera House 111–113 Manners St ⓣ04/384 4060, ⓦwww.stjames.co.nz. Hosts touring opera, ballet and musicals.

St James Theatre 77–87 Courtenay Place ⓣ04/802 4060, ⓦwww.stjames.co.nz. This refurbished theatre in a fine 1912 building is the major venue for the Royal New Zealand Ballet and hosts opera, dance, musicals and plays. It also has a licensed café for pre- and post-performance drinks.
Westpac Stadium Between Aotea Quay and Waterloo Quay. Dubbed "the cake tin" by its detractors for its iron-clad design, this modern purpose-built stadium near the ferry terminal is the venue for all things rugby and cricket (although cricket tests are still played at the Basin Reserve), and acts as an occasional rock concert venue.

Cinemas

Embassy 10 Kent Terrace ⓣ04/384 7657, ⓦwww.deluxe.co.nz. Revamped for the December 2003 world premiere of *The Return of the King*, the Embassy shows mainstream and independent movies on a single giant screen in the city centre.
The New Zealand Film Archive See p.470.
Paramount 25 Courtenay Place ⓣ04/384 4080, ⓦwww.paramount.co.nz. Central multi-screen showing art and mainstream movies with the added joy of being able to watch while sipping a beer or wine.
Reading Cinemas 100 Courtenay Place ⓣ04/801 4610, ⓦwww.readingcinemas.co.nz. Mostly mainstream movies ($15) with the option of going for their plush Gold Lounge seats ($32) which come with unlimited free pop and popcorn plus an in-seat food and drink service.
Regent on Manners 73 Manners St ⓣ04/472 5182, ⓦwww.hoyts.co.nz. Mainstream movies for $10 ($6 on Tues): the cheapest in town.

Festivals

Whenever you visit Wellington there's a good chance there'll be some sort of arts-related festival happening. The visitor centre has full details, but the following are the biggest occasions, listed chronologically.

New Zealand International Arts Festival ⓦwww.nzfestival.nzpost.co.nz. The country's biggest cultural event is a month-long festival held in March in even-numbered years, drawing top performers from around the world. Fashioned along the lines of the Edinburgh Festival, it celebrates the huge diversity of the arts, and performances include classical music, jazz and pop, opera, puppet shows and the Grotesque, cabaret, poetry readings, traditional Maori dance, modern ballet and experimental works – and most of the venues are downtown.
Wellington Fringe Festival ⓦwww.fringe.org.nz. Originally part of the Arts festival, this vibrant affair is now run as a separate and roughly concurrent event, filling the inner city with street and indoor theatre.
Wellington Film Festival ⓦwww.enzedff.co.nz. Typically held from mid-July to early Aug, with less mainstream offerings playing at cinemas around town.
Wellington International Jazz Festival ⓦwww.jazzfestival.co.nz. A two-week festival in Nov bringing some of the world's best performers primarily to the Ilott Theatre at the Town Hall, but also to Happy, corner of Vivian & Tory Sts.
World of WearableArt ⓦwww.worldofwearableart.com. This glorious spectacle of weird costumes runs like a bizarre fashion show over the last two weeks in Sept. Tickets go like hot cakes, and previous winners are displayed at WOW in Nelson (see p.516).

Listings

Airlines and flights For details of transport to the airport see p.459, and remember there is a $25 airport tax when leaving the country that is not included in your ticket price, though you'll end up paying it at Auckland or Christchurch if one of those airports is your final stop in the country.
Automobile Association 342–352 Lambton Quay ⓣ04/931 9999.
Banks and foreign exchange Banks are dotted all over the CBD, but to change money head along the southern end of Lambton Quay to ANZ at 215–229 Lambton Quay, BNZ at 1 Willis St and Travelex at 120 Lambton Quay.
Bike rental See "Cycling", p.482.
Bookshops The best selection of New Zealand and special-interest (especially gay and lesbian) books is Unity Books, 57 Willis St ⓣ04/499 4245. It is also good for more mainstream fare, as are the majors: Whitcoulls, 312 Lambton Quay ⓣ04/472 1921, at 91 Cuba St and 80 Courtenay Place; Dymocks, 360 Lambton Quay ⓣ04/472 2080; and Borders, 226 Lambton Quay ⓣ04/471 1900. For

good secondhand and book exchanges try Arty Bee's Books, 17 Courtenay Place ⓣ04/385 1819, ⓦwww.artybees.co.nz.

Camping and outdoor equipment Several good shops – Mountain Designs, Fairydown and Kathmandu – cluster around the junction of Willis & Mercer str. Bivouac, 39 Mercer St ⓣ04/473 2587, have the top brands and knowledgeable staff.

Car rental As well as the companies covered in Basics (see p.40) various local firms offer good deals: Nationwide, 37 Hutt Rd, Thorndon ⓣ0800/803 003, ⓦwww.nationwiderentals.co.nz; Rent-a-Dent, 24 Tacy St, Kilbirnie ⓣ0800/736 823, ⓦwww.rentadent.co.nz; and Ace Rental Cars, 126 Hutt Rd, ⓣ0800/535 500, ⓦwww.acerentalcars.co.nz.

Embassies and consulates Australia, 72 Hobson St, Thorndon ⓣ04/473 6411; Canada, 125 The Terrace ⓣ04/473 9577; Germany, 90 Hobson St, Thorndon ⓣ04/473 6063; Netherlands, Investment House, Featherston St ⓣ04/471 6390; Thailand, 2 Cook St ⓣ04/476 8618; South Africa ⓣ04/234 8006; UK, 44 Hill St ⓣ04/924 2888; USA, 29 Fitzherbert Terrace, Thorndon (ⓣ04/462 6000); for other countries, look in the Yellow Pages, under "Diplomatic and consular representatives".

Internet access Plenty of places, mostly along Courtenay Place, generally charging $4–5 per hr, including @Internet, 97 Courtenay Place. There's also access at the i-SITE visitor centre.

Library Wellington's Central Library (Mon–Thurs 9.30am–8.30pm, Fri 9.30am–9pm, Sat 9.30am–5pm, Sun 1–4pm; ⓣ04/801 4060) is on Victoria St, where it backs onto Civic Square.

Market James Smith's Market is a popular flea market on the corner of Cuba & Manners sts. Open to 6pm, and 9pm on Fri.

Medical emergencies For emergencies call ⓣ111. For 24hr emergency treatment, the After Hours Medical Centre is at 17 Adelaide Rd, Newtown, near Basin Reserve ⓣ04/384 4944. Wellington Hospital is on Riddiford St, Newtown ⓣ04/385 5999.

Newspapers *The Dominion Post* is the local morning paper, its influence spreading over much of the southern half of the North Island. Events and entertainment listings are best on Thurs and Sat. The free weekly *Capital Times* has a round-up of events and plenty of listings: pick it up in cafés and the like.

Pharmacy Radius Pharmacy, 204 Lambton Quay ⓣ04/472 0362 is handy, but for late service go to After Hours Pharmacy, 17 Adelaide Rd, Newtown ⓣ04/385 8801 (Mon–Fri 5–11pm, Sat, Sun & public holidays 8am–11pm).

Photographic supplies Wellington Photographic Supplies, 11–15 Vivian St ⓣ04/384 3713 is the place for digital and film needs.

Police Wellington Central Police Station, corner of of Victoria and Harris sts ⓣ04/381 2000.

Post office There are several throughout the downtown area. For poste restante go to the Post Shop, 43 Manners St (Mon–Fri 8am–5.30pm, Sat 10am–3pm).

Swimming Freyberg Pool and Fitness Centre, 139 Oriental Parade (daily 6am–9pm; ⓣ04/801 4530), has a 33-metre indoor pool ($5 to swim), plus gym, spas, saunas, steamroom, fitness classes and massage therapy. Also the Thorndon Pool, 26 Murphy St (Nov–March Mon–Fri 6.30am–7pm, Sat & Sun 8am–6.30pm; $5), a classy lido near Parliament.

Taxis Green Cabs ⓣ0508/447 336 use hybrids; otherwise try Wellington Combined Taxis ⓣ04/384 4444. Authorized stands are located at the train station, on Whitmore St (between Lambton Quay & Featherston St), outside the *James Smith Hotel* on Lambton Quay, off Willis St on the Bond St corner, at the corner of Courtenay Place & Taranaki St, and at the junction of Willis & Aro sts.

Travel details

Unsurprisingly, Wellington is a major transportation hub with trains and buses homing in on the ferries that cross Cook Strait to Picton and the South Island (see p.460). Here we've only listed direct buses and flights but there are numerous connections to further-flung places. Only direct, non-stop flights are listed.

Ferries

Wellington to: Matiu/Somes Island (3–4 daily; 20min); Picton (5–8 daily; 3hr).

Trains

The Auckland–Wellington Overlander runs once daily in summer (Dec–April) and Fri, Sat & Sun for the rest of the year.

Wellington to: Auckland (1 daily; 12hr); Hamilton (1 daily; 9hr 30min); Hutt Central/Waterloo (every 30min; 20 min); Masterton (2–5 daily; 1hr 30min); National Park (1 daily; 5hr 30min); Otaki (2 daily; 1hr 10min); Otorohanga (1 daily; 8hr 45min); Paekakariki (every 30min; 50min); Palmerston North (2 daily; 2hr–2hr 20min); Paraparaumu (every 30min; 1hr).

Buses

Wellington to: Auckland (3–4 daily; 11hr); Masterton via the Hutt Valley (1–2 daily; 2hr); Napier (3 daily; 5hr 15min); New Plymouth (3 daily; 6hr 30min); Palmerston North (5–7 daily; 2hr); Paraparaumu (10 daily; 50min); Rotorua (5 daily; 7hr); Taupo (5 daily; 6hr).

Flights

Wellington to: Auckland (20–25 daily; 1hr); Blenheim (8–13 daily; 25min); Christchurch (15 daily; 45min); Dunedin (2 daily; 1hr 15min); Gisborne (3–4 daily; 1hr); Greymouth (5 weekly; 1hr); Hamilton (7 daily; 1hr); Kaikoura (1–2 daily in summer; 1hr); Napier/Hastings (5 daily; 50min); Nelson (6–10 daily; 35min); New Plymouth (4 daily; 50min); Palmerston North (3 daily; 30min); Picton (6–8 daily; 25min); Rotorua (3 daily; 1hr); Takaka (1 daily; 30min); Taupo (3 daily; 1hr); Tauranga (4 daily; 1hr 10min); Timaru (4 daily; 1hr 10min); Westport (1 daily Mon–Fri; 55min); Whangarei (1 daily; 1hr 30min).

8

Marlborough, Nelson and Kaikoura

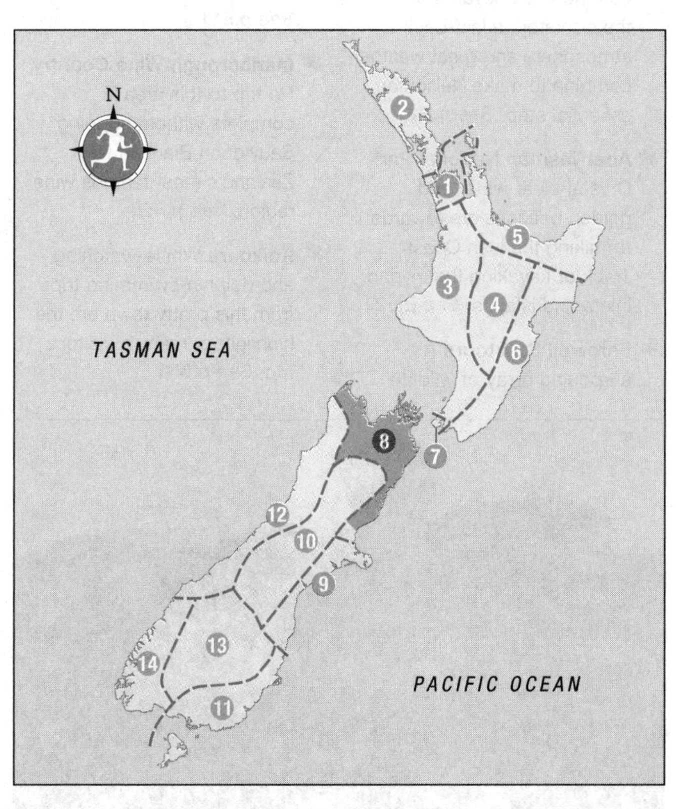

CHAPTER 8

Highlights

* **The Queen Charlotte Track** This beautiful multi-day hike is make all the more manageable by staying in great backpackers and B&Bs, and having your bags carried for you. See p.504
* **Nelson** A vibrant arts community, vineyards on the doorstep, a laid-back atmosphere and great weather combine to make Nelson an essential stop. See p.510
* **Abel Tasman National Park** Crystal-clear water and golden beaches are rewards for hiking the lush Coast Track or kayaking the myriad inlets and islands. See p.522
* **Farewell Spit tours** A surprising array of wildlife can be seen on four-wheel-drive tours along this thin strip of ocean-girt desert. See p.539
* **Heaphy Track** The huge range of dramatic scenery and final sense of achievement puts this Great Walk up with the best. See p.541
* **Marlborough Wine Country** No trip to this area is complete without supping Sauvignon Blanc in New Zealand's most famous wine region. See p.550
* **Kaikoura** Whale-watching and dolphin-swimming trips from this pretty town are the highlight of many a visitor's trip. See p.554

▲ Highfield Estate winery, near Blenheim

8

Marlborough, Nelson and Kaikoura

The South Island kicks off spectacularly. The whole northern section is supremely alluring, from the indented bays and secluded hideaways of the Marlborough Sounds and the sweep of golden beaches around Nelson, to an impressive array of national parks, sophisticated wineries around Marlborough and the natural wonders of Kaikoura. In fact, if you had to choose only one area of New Zealand to visit, this would be a strong contender.

Most visitors travel between the North Island and the South Island by ferry, striking land at the town of **Picton** – drab in the winter, lively in the summer and surrounded by the beautiful **Marlborough Sounds**. Here, bays full of unfathomably deep water lap at tiny beaches, each with its rickety boat jetty, and the land rises steeply to forest or stark pasture.

To the west, the lively yet relaxed city of **Nelson** is the starting point for forays to wilder spots further north. Some of the country's most gorgeous walking tracks and dazzling golden beaches populate the **Abel Tasman National Park**, while yet further north the relatively isolated **Golden Bay** offers peaceful times in relaxed settings. The curve of the Golden Bay culminates in a long sandy bar that juts into the ocean, **Farewell Spit**, an extraordinary and unique habitat. It borders the Kahurangi National Park, through which the rugged and spectacular **Heaphy Track** forges a route to the West Coast.

The least visited of the region's well-preserved areas of natural splendour is the sparsely populated **Nelson Lakes National Park**, principally a spot for tramping to alpine lakes or fishing, though the nearby **Buller River** also lures raft and kayak rats.

South of Picton, you can slurp your merry way through **Marlborough**, New Zealand's most renowned winemaking region centred on the modest towns of **Blenheim** and **Renwick**. A night or two in one of the rural B&Bs and some time spent around the wineries happily balances the more energetic activities of the national parks, and sets you up nicely for a few days of eco-tourism in **Kaikoura**. **Whale watching** and **swimming with dolphins** and **seals** are the main draws, but there's also pleasure in local walks or just relaxing outside one of the cafés.

The region's **weather** is some of the sunniest in the land, particularly around Blenheim and Nelson, who regularly compete for the honour of the greatest number of sunshine hours in New Zealand. The climate is mild throughout the year though the **peak season** is December to February when the Abel Tasman

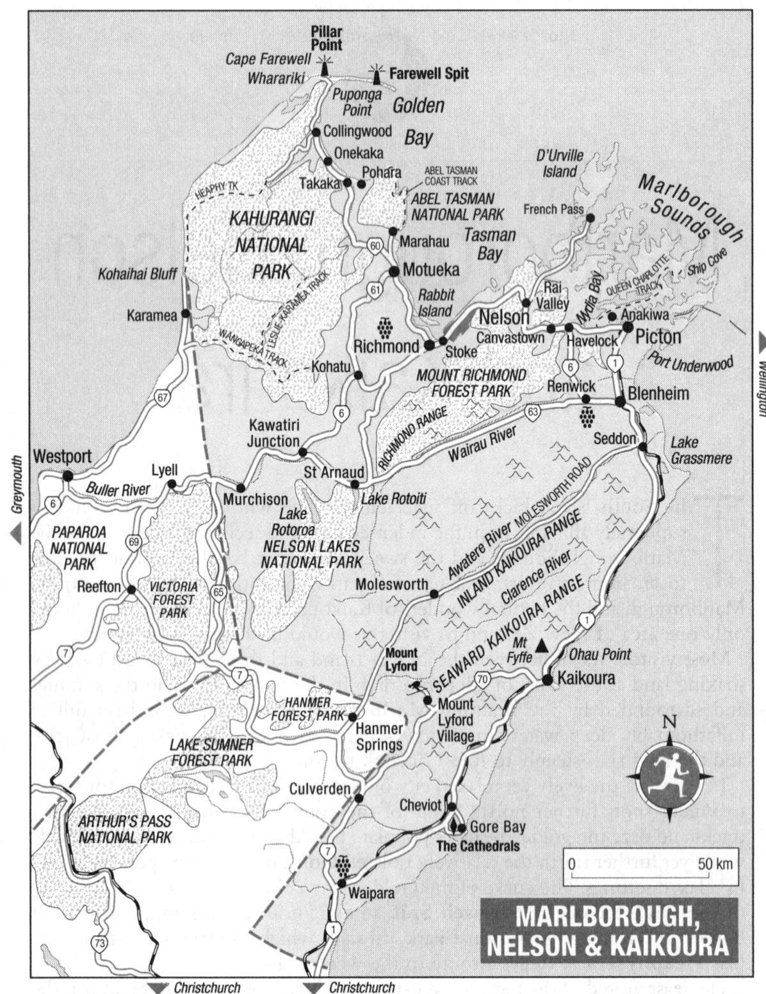

National Park and Queen Charlotte Track are enormously popular. For greater solitude and the chance to travel without booking everything in advance, try to visit either side of high season.

The Marlborough Sounds

The **Marlborough Sounds** are undeniably picturesque, a stimulating filigree of bays, inlets, islands and peninsulas rising abruptly from the water to rugged, lush green wilderness and open farmland. Large parts are only accessible by sea, which also provides the ideal vantage point for witnessing its splendour. The area is part working farms, including salmon or mussel farms, and part given over to

For details of **transport** between the **North and South islands**, see box, p.460.

some fifty-nine reserve areas – a mixture of islands, sections of coast and land-bound tracts. The Sounds' nexus, **Picton**, is the jumping-off point for **Queen Charlotte Sound** where cruises and water taxi provide access to the rewarding and very manageable **Queen Charlotte Track**. Heading west, Queen Charlotte Drive winds precipitously to the small community of **Havelock**, which is well worth a stop to indulge in green-lipped mussels before exploring the delightful **Pelorus Sound** and maybe tramping the **Nydia Track**. Most then carry on to Nelson and the Abel Tasman National Park, but if you've got time to spare consider exploring the road to the swirling waters of **French Pass**.

Picton and around

Cross-strait ferries arrive at **Picton**, a nicely set small town sandwiched between the hills and the deep, placid waters of Queen Charlotte Sound. Many people only stop for a coffee looking out over the water before pressing on, but Picton makes a great base for a few days' exploring Queen Charlotte Sound. In town, don't miss the historic *Edwin Fox* ship, or head out on excellent **cruises and kayak trips**. Water taxis buzz across the water taking trampers to various points on the **Queen Charlotte Track**. Picton also makes a decent base for exploring the **wine region** around Blenheim, half an hour's drive to the south.

There was a European settlement in the region as early as 1827 when John Guard established a whaling station, but Picton itself didn't come into being until the New Zealand Company purchased the town site for £300 in 1848. Picton flourished as a port and **service town** for the Wairau Plains to the south but predominantly as the most convenient port for travel between the islands.

Arrival and information

Interislander ferry foot passengers disembark close to the town centre, while Bluebridge foot passengers and all **vehicles** disembark on the western side of town about 1km from the centre: Bluebridge operates a free shuttle bus to the i-SITE. Interislander ferry schedules work in well with the daily TranzCoastal **train** to Christchurch: one-way fares range from $52–88. **Buses** stop outside the Interislander ferry terminal and again at the visitor centre. Picton **airport**, 9km south of town, is served by Soundsair (Ⓣ0800/505 005, Ⓦwww.soundsair.com), with flights from Wellington and deals with those brave enough to skydive into the South Island: a bus ($3 one-way) meets flights and runs into Picton.

The combined **i-SITE visitor centre** and **DOC office** (daily: Jan–Feb 8.30am–6pm; Oct–Dec & March–Sept 8.30am–5pm; Ⓣ03/520 3113, Ⓦwww.destinationmarlborough.com) is on the foreshore, five minutes' walk from the ferry terminal. It is packed with leaflets on the town and the rest of the South Island, including a free Picton map and DOC's *Queen Charlotte Track* map.

Accommodation

As a major **transit centre**, Picton is disproportionately well endowed with accommodation, ranging from backpacker hostels to upscale lodges. You should have no difficulty finding somewhere to suit your needs within walking distance of the gangplank throughout most of the year, although from mid-December to the end of February you should definitely **book** in advance.

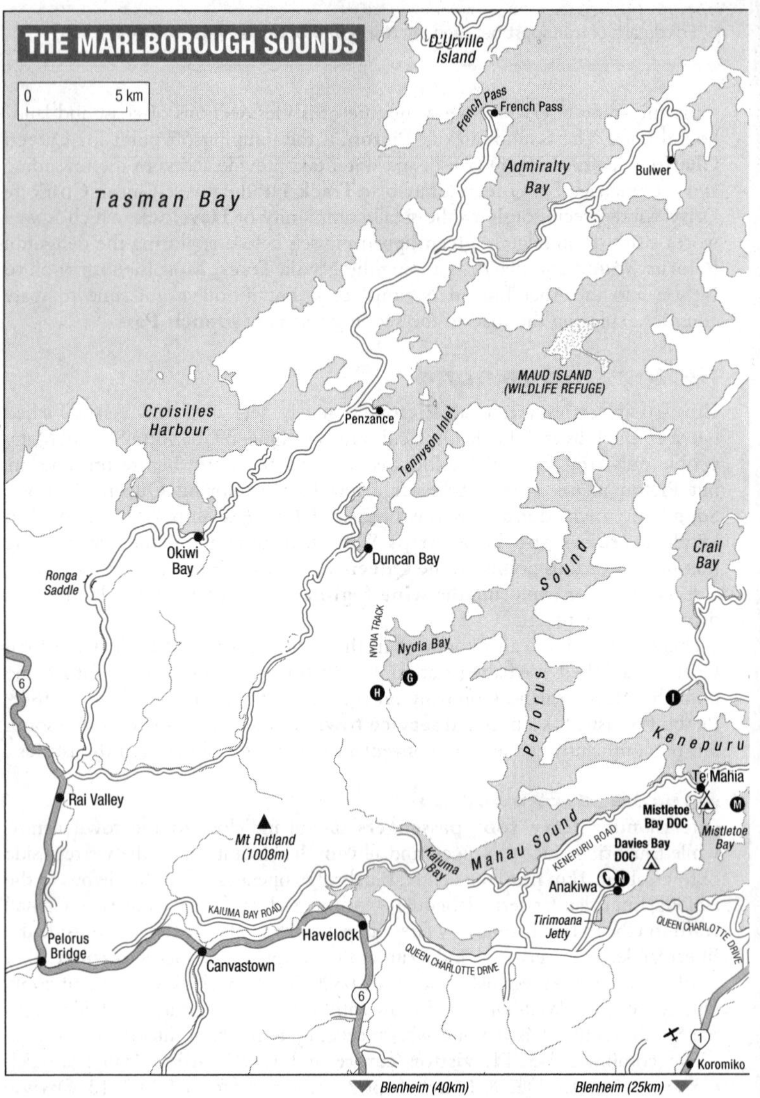

Motels

Broadway Motel 113 Picton High St ⓣ0800/101 919, ⓦwww.broadwaymotel.co.nz. Attractive modern motel units in the centre of town with good views from the first-floor balcony. ❺

Harbour View Motel 30 Waikawa Rd ⓣ0800/101 133, ⓦwww.harbourviewpicton.co.nz. Twelve spacious, tastefully appointed, s/c units, each with a balcony and with great views over the harbour. ❺

Jasmine Court 78 Wellington St ⓣ0800/421 999, ⓦwww.jasminecourt.co.nz. Top-of-the-line, modern motel with no-smoking, luxury units, including DVD & CD players and sunny verandas, plus a sauna room, free email and pay Wi-Fi. ❻

Tourist Court 45 High St ⓣ0800/366 555, ⓦwww.tourist-court.co.nz. Centrally located, small but tolerable en-suite doubles at low prices. ❸

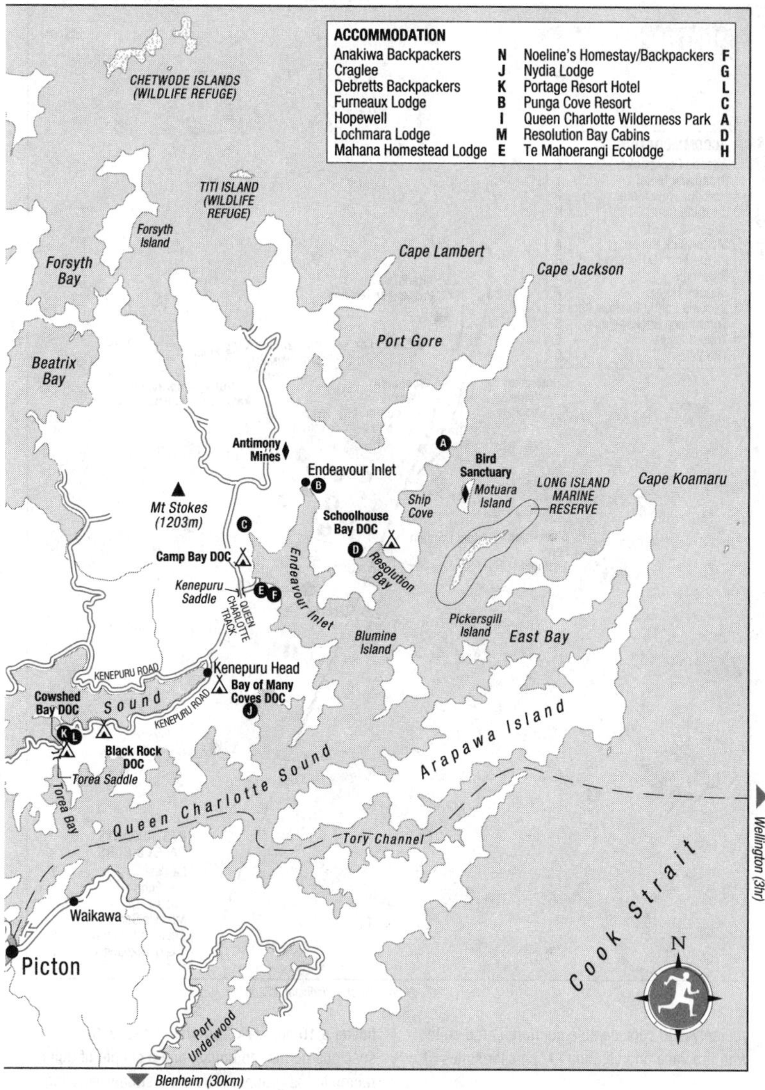

B&Bs and homestays

McCormick House 21 Leicester St ⓣ03/573 5253, ⓦwww.mccormickhouse.co.nz. Atmospheric Edwardian villa with an original rimu-panelled staircase, luxurious, individually decorated, rooms and indulgent breakfasts made from local produce. There's a good stock of Kiwi movies and music in the public lounge. ❽

Rivenhall 118 Wellington St ⓣ03/573 7692, ⓦwww.rivenhall.kol.co.nz. Recently rejuvenated, historic homestay with two big rooms, grand views and a warm welcome from the hosts. Both rooms come with private bathroom and robes. ❺

Sennen House 9 Oxford St ⓣ03/573 5216, ⓦwww.sennenhouse.co.nz. Gorgeous, 1886, grand villa 10min walk from town, which has been tastefully converted into a B&B with five suites, all with kitchen facilities; a breakfast hamper is also supplied. After a glass of wine with the owners on the rear deck you're left to

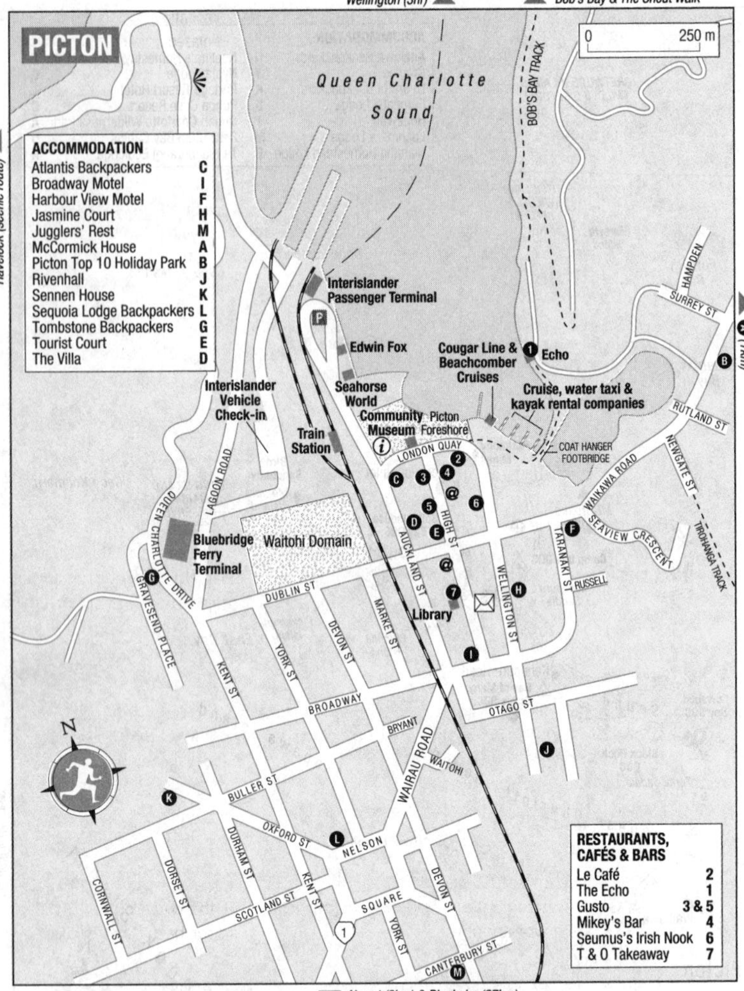

yourselves in considerable comfort. Large suite with fireplace and veranda ⑨, smaller suites ⑧

Hostels and campsites

Atlantis Backpackers London Quay ⓣ03/573 7390, ⓦwww.atlantishostel.co.nz. Central hostel close to ferry with the town's cheapest bunks, if you're prepared to share with 27 others, though there are also smaller dorms, twins and doubles plus free breakfast and the use of an indoor heated pool shared by the local dive school (see p.501). Dorms $18, rooms ②

Jugglers' Rest 8 Canterbury St ⓣ03/573 5570, ⓦwww.jugglersrest.com. Small and relaxed hostel a 10min walk from the ferries, with spacious dorms (no bunks) and a couple of quiet rooms in the grounds. There's a strong recycling ethic, the vegetable garden is open to all and there's home-made jam to spread on each morning's fresh bread. And should you fancy it, there are devil sticks, balls and even fire to juggle. Closed May–Oct. Tents $16, dorms $27, rooms ②

Picton Top 10 Holiday Park 70–78 Waikawa Rd ⓣ0800/277 444, ⓦwww.pictontop10.co.nz. Centrally located campsite with swimming pool, children's playground, cabins (bedding $5) and motel-style units, in a pleasant spot with sheltering trees. Camping $15, cabins ❷, kitchen cabins ❸, s/c units ❸

Sequoia Lodge Backpackers 3 Nelson Square ⓣ0800/222 257, ⓦwww.sequoialodge.co.nz. Well-organized hostel shoehorned onto a site 10min walk from the town centre (and with free pick-ups). Beds and bunks all come with bedlights and side tables, rooms have heated towel rails, and there's a separate, en-suite female dorm. Breakfast, hammocks, spa and home cinema are all free, making this a great deal. Dorms $24, rooms ❷, en suites ❸

Tombstone Backpackers 16 Gravesend Place ⓣ0800/573 7116, ⓦwww.tombstonebp.co.nz. Wonderful hostel right by the town cemetery with a tastefully decorated, purpose-built accommodation block that's all carpeted and double-glazed, making it super-quiet for a place that's an easy walk from the port. A barbecue area, piano, hot tub, bikes and a continental breakfast are all available for no extra charge. Dorms are single sex, and private rooms even have electric blankets and a sunny balcony. Dorms $25, rooms ❷, en suites ❸

The Villa 34 Auckland St ⓣ03/573 6598, ⓦwww.thevilla.co.nz. Youthful hostel based around a century-old house and a more modern one next door. When busy it can feel a little cramped, but it works well and there are all manner of inducements such as free bikes, apple crumble in winter and a hot tub. Dorms $24, rooms ❷, en suites ❸

The Town

Pretty much everything of interest in Picton is along the waterfront, close to **Picton Foreshore**, a strip of park that has been spruced up with brick paving and native plantings around the line of phoenix palms. At its western end, close to the ferry terminal, a large steel shed houses the hulk of the 1600-tonne **Edwin Fox** (daily 9am–5pm; $8), the sole survivor of the fleets that once brought migrants to New Zealand and the last of some four thousand

Staying out in the Sounds

The best way to soak up something of the spirit of the Marlborough Sounds is to stay in one of the swanky lodges, modest resorts or superb backpacker hostels inaccessible (or barely accessible) by road. Many of the best dot the Queen Charlotte Track but there's no need to go tramping as water taxis will get you there in a few minutes from Picton (and to a lesser extent Havelock; see p.507). As well as those listed below, consider staying at *Lochmara Lodge* and *Furneaux Lodge* (for both see p.506).

Craglee Queen Charlotte Sound ⓣ03/579 9223, ⓦwww.craglee.co.nz. A mermaid welcomes you to this romantic boutique lodge set in bush by the water. Rates ($450 per couple) include wonderful meals, pre-dinner drinks, outdoor baths and endless relaxation. ❾

Hopewell Kenepuru Sound ⓣ03/573 4341, ⓦwww.hopewell.co.nz. A gorgeous backpacker hostel in a dreamy setting where even a couple of nights isn't enough to fully appreciate the relaxing setting, wonderfully welcoming hosts, waterside hot tub, kayaks, fishing and opportunities to visit the local mussel farm or go water-skiing. Access is either on a tortuous 2–3hr drive along Kenepuru Road, or by a sequence of water taxis from Picton ($50 each way per person): call the hostel for details. Closed June–Sept. Dorms $30, rooms ❷, en suites ❸, self-contained cottage sleeping four ❹

Queen Charlotte Wilderness Park Port Jackson ⓣ03/579 9025, ⓦwww.truenz.co.nz/wilderness. Set amid regenerating bush northeast of Ship Cove and accessible from the northern end of the Queen Charlotte Track, this place describes itself as "a wildlife sanctuary with visitors". A minimum two-night stay ($298) gets you an en-suite room with dinner and breakfast provided, water taxi transfer from Picton and free use of canoe and dinghy. Self-catering is available and each extra night costs $84.

Hiking around Picton

The best of the local **trails** run through Victoria Domain, a mostly bush-clad peninsula immediately east of Picton. As most trails link up at some point it can be a little confusing, though several free and widely available maps of town show the way.

Bob's Bay Track (1km one way; 30min; gently undulating). Starting at Shelly Beach near the *Echo*, this extends along the shoreline to a safe swimming and picnicking beach at Bob's Bay providing great views across the water to the ferry terminal and up the Queen Charlotte Sound. From Bob's Bay a short steep path climbs away from the bay to the **Harbour View** parking area.

The Snout (5km one way; 1hr 15min; 200m ascent on return). From the Harbour View parking area (see above) follow the top of the ridge past the self-explanatory Queen Charlotte View to the tip of the promontory, The Snout, whose evocative Maori name, Te Ihumoeone-ihu, translates as "the nose of the sand worm".

Tirohanga Track (3km one way; 1hr 15min; 300m ascent). Fairly strenuous walk up the hills behind Picton passing the lovely Hilltop Viewpoint. The track starts on Newgate Street.

"Indiamen" built in India throughout the nineteenth century. This 1853 example operated as a troop carrier in the Crimean War and transported convicts to Australia, before bringing free settlers to New Zealand. After years working as a merchant vessel and helping to establish the frozen meat trade in New Zealand, it was towed into Shakespeare Bay (just west of Picton) in 1967. Vandalized and weather-beaten for twenty years, but still afloat, it was finally moved to Picton Harbour where in 1999 it was dry-docked and preserved. A small but well-designed museum explains the life and significance of the ship, preparing you for the age-blackened hull itself. Standing on the small part of the deck that remains gives a sense of what it must have been like to sail, but the best bit is below decks in the large open hold, all heavy planking partly rotted away to reveal the teak ribs.

Beside the *Edwin Fox*, **Seahorse World** (daily 9am–5pm; $16; Ⓦwww.seahorseworld.co.nz) offers an insight into the lives of seahorses, a collection of local marine life, a few small sharks and a preserved giant squid. Twenty-minute narrated tours include a little of the significance of sea creatures to Maori.

Heading further east around the bay onto London Quay, the **Picton Community Museum** (daily 10am–4pm; $4) continues the maritime theme with displays on the Perano Whaling Station, which operated in Queen Charlotte Sound until 1964. There are photographs of the station in its heyday, and a harpoon gun from one of the steamboat chasers as well as some excellent examples of carved whalebone. Smaller displays deal with local history.

Eating and entertainment

Picton offers enough decent **restaurants** to satisfy for a couple of days, and plenty of **cafés**, but little in the way of organized **entertainment**.

The Echo East Harbour. While this permanently moored top-sail schooner serves food, such as a seaman's snack ($16) and a cooked breakfast ($14), it's primarily a fine place for a beer on deck. Built in 1905, the *Echo* was the last ship to trade commercially under sail in New Zealand waters; spend some time looking at the maritime paraphernalia around the walls.

Gusto 33 High St. Cosy and popular daytime café dishing up delicious home-made cakes and salads. Dinner (Thurs–Sat only) might be steamed mussels, followed by wild pork sausages and roast garlic, herb-crusted lamb rack or fresh fish with creamy potato puree – all made from local produce (mains $26–30).

Le Café 14 London Quay. Bustling café and bar with pavement seating just across from the Sound, serving mouth-watering steaks with home-made chutney and all sorts of seafood at reasonable prices.

Mikey's Bar 18 High St. Modern bar with a pool table, and a barn-like nightclub out back where DJs are interspersed with bands trying to scrape together enough money to play somewhere bigger.

Seumus's Irish Nook Wellington St. Above-average Irish bar, authentically poky and with a great drinking atmosphere, straightforward bar meals ($15–20) and outdoor seating.

T & O Takeaway 85 High St ⓣ03/573 6115. Serves the freshest and best fish and chips in town plus a variety of other fruits of the sea.

Listings

Banks Several along High St.

Bike rental Marlborough Sounds Adventure Co rents bikes for use on the QCT for $50 a day and kayaks (see p.503), while Adventure Tours Down Under, 1 Auckland St (ⓣ03/573 8565, ⓦwww.toursdownunder.com), also rents bikes for the track at $50 a day, and does wine tours including drop-off and pick-up.

Buses You can book all the buses through the i-SITE or directly. Atomic Shuttles (ⓣ03/349 0697) run to Christchurch, St Arnaud, Nelson, Greymouth and Fox Glacier; Richies (ⓣ03/578 5467) go to Blenheim; InterCity (ⓣ03/379 9020) run to Nelson, Blenheim and Christchurch via Kaikoura, and Southern Link K Bus (ⓣ0508/458835) go to Takaka via Blenheim, Havelock, Nelson and Motueka. Most buses do the 40min run to Blenheim for $10.

Car rental Most of the major international and Kiwi companies have offices at the Ferry Terminal or scattered around town. The visitor centre has a free sheet listing them all, but local numbers for the most commonly used companies are: Ace ⓣ03/573 8939; Avis ⓣ03/573 6363; Avon ⓣ03/573 6009; Budget ⓣ03/573 6081; Hertz ⓣ03/573 7224; National ⓣ03/573 8800; NZ Rent A Car ⓣ03/573 7282; Pegasus ⓣ03/573 7733; Rent-a-Dent ⓣ03/573 7787; Thrifty ⓣ03/573 7387.

Diving Dive Picton, corner of London Quay & Auckland St (ⓣ0800/728 223, ⓦwww.scubadive.co.nz), offers gear rental ($77 for full kit and one tank), two-wreck dives ($165), and runs 4-day PADI courses ($495). Divers with some experience should dive the *Michael Lermontov* (3 days; $699), a Soviet cruise ship that became the southern hemisphere's largest diveable wreck when it hit rocks in 1986.

Internet access There are computers at the i-SITE plus cheaper machines at United Video, 60 High St (Mon–Sat to 9pm).

Library 67 High St (Mon–Fri 8am–5pm, Sat 10am–1pm).

Luggage storage Most lodgings store luggage while you walk the Queen Charlotte Track. Cars can be left unsecured on the streets around Picton, or safely with Sounds Storage, 7 Market St ($30 first 2 nights then $15 a night; ⓣ021/335136).

Medical treatment Picton Medical Centre, 71 High St ⓣ03/573 6092.

Movies Picton Cinema, by the aquarium, shows mainstream movies.

Pharmacy Picton Healthcare, 6 High St (Mon–Fri 9am–6pm, Sat 9am–1pm).

Post office Mariners Mall on High St (Mon–Fri 8.30am–5pm).

Rural Mail Bus Service You can ride the Rural Mail Bus Service (ⓣ027/255 8882), essentially a minivan serving remote spots linking the main post offices in Havelock and Picton, and the southern end of the Queen Charlotte Track at Anakiwa. There are several runs each day and fares start at $15.

Taxis Gateway Taxis ⓣ03/573 7662; see also "Water taxis" below.

Water taxis Arrow Water Taxis ⓣ03/573 8229; Beachcomber Cruises ⓣ0800/624 526, ⓦwww.mailboat.co.nz; Cougar Line ⓣ0800/504 090, ⓦwww.cougarlinecruises.co.nz; Endeavour Express ⓣ03/573 5456, ⓦwww.boatrides.co.nz; and West Bay Water Transport ⓣ03/573 5597, ⓦwww.westbay.co.nz.

Winery tours Tours of the Marlborough wine country are covered in detail in "Listings" on p.551, and most companies do Picton pick-ups for a small additional fee.

Exploring Queen Charlotte Sound

Picton is a pretty spot, but you've barely touched the region's beauty until you've explored **Queen Charlotte Sound**. This wildly indented series of drowned valleys encloses moody picturesque bays, small deserted sandy beaches, headlands with panoramic views and cloistered islands while grand lumpy

▲ Heading into Picton Harbour from Queen Charlotte Sound

peninsulas offer shelter from the winds and storms, and solitude for the contemplative fisherman or kayaker. For a taste of these labyrinthine waterways, take one of the many **day-cruises** from Picton, but to really appreciate the tranquil beauty you're far better off **kayaking** round the bays or **tramping** the Queen Charlotte Track. The relatively calm waters of the Sounds also give the opportunity for **scuba diving**, either checking out the wrecks and rich marine life or just taking an open-water qualification (see p.501).

The sights

The principal pleasure in exploring Queen Charlotte Sound is just being out on the water, but there are a couple of sights which crop up on most itineraries. The DOC-managed **Motuara Island** is a predator-free wildlife sanctuary that is home to the saddleback, South Island bush robin, bellbird and a few Okarito brown kiwi. All the birds are quite fearless and will rest and fly startlingly close to you. A steep trail climbs to the island's higher reaches where the best birdsong can be heard. Throughout the island little blue penguins choose to nest in boxes provided, rather than build their own, and in spring (Oct–Dec), you can gently lift the top of the box and see the baby penguins inside.

Just across a channel from Motuara Island, **Ship Cove** marks the bay where Captain Cook spent a total of 168 days during his three trips to New Zealand. A large white concrete monument commemorates his five separate visits.

Cruises and tours

Water taxis are always flitting about Queen Charlotte Sound taking hikers to the Queen Charlotte Track or delivering guests to swanky lodges. If you just want to get out on the water this may be all you need but several companies also run excellent **cruises**. The cheapest are Nellie Harbour Trips ($20; ⓣ03/573 7301), leaving from the Town Wharf several times a day for one-hour inshore jaunts.

Along with Rural Mail Runs (see p.503), Beachcomber Fun Cruises offer a cruise to Ship Cove (3hr; $65), and one to Motuara Island (3hr; $65). Some of the most sympathetic wildlife trips in the Sounds are run by Dolphin Watch Ecotours, Wellington Street (T0800/945 354, Wwww.naturetours.co.nz), who offer **dolphin swimming** and watching (2–4hr; $130 to swim, $80 to watch) with dusky, common, bottlenose or the endemic Hector's dolphins. To combine dolphin watching with the Sounds' other sights, join their trips to either Motuara Island ($65) or Ship Cove ($65), both of which can be used as a drop-off for QCT walkers. Finally, there's the Birdwatchers Expedition (Oct–April daily 1.30pm; $95) especially for birders.

One particularly fine way to get out on the water is with Myths and Legends **Eco Tours** (T03/573 6901, Wwww.eco-tours.co.nz), run by a sixth-generation local Pakeha and his Maori wife who tour the bays in their 1930 kauri launch, explaining the history and culture of the region (4hr $150 or 8hr $200 including lunch). They also run a Stargazer BBQ ($150) that rolls in late – it's weather dependent but well worth the extra time.

For something a little different, join Waterways Boating Safaris (T03/574 1372, Wwww.waterways.co.nz) who guide flotillas of small motorboats around Kenepuru Sound (7hr, $99). You get to drive your own boat, allowing access to bushwalks and beaches.

Kayaking

Visitors dashing across to Abel Tasman National Park often overlook the uncrowded waters and breathtaking views to be had kayaking in Queen Charlotte Sound. The friendly and professional Marlborough Sounds Adventure Company, Town Wharf (T0800/283 283, Wwww.marlboroughsounds.co.nz), offers a huge range of **guided kayaking trips** including a lovely twilight paddle around Picton (Dec–Feb daily, 3hr; $60), a gentle one-dayer (7hr; $95), a two-day trip ($150) on which you join the one-day trip then camp out by yourselves and paddle home the next day, and a fully guided three-day trip in the outer sounds ($465); rentals are $50 for one day, $80 for two.

Also consider the smaller Sea Kayaking Adventure Tours (T03/574 2765, Wwww.nzseakayaking.com), based at Anakiwa by the end of the Queen Charlotte Track. They have one-day guided trips ($85) as well as a three-day trip along the length of the track either camping ($300) or upgrading to fancier accommodation. Independent rentals are $50 per day, reducing to $40 a day for three days or more.

Skydiving

One of the most exhilarating ways to see the grandeur of the Sounds is to **skydive** into, or from the local airstrip, with Skydive The Sounds ($245 from

Delivering the mail with dolphins

Several companies run great cruises around Queen Charlotte and Pelorus sounds, but there is something special about the **Rural Mail Runs**, pulling up at a lonely wharf and having some farmer's wife (or the whole family) coming out to receive their only mail delivery of the week and perhaps a few perishable groceries. The journey includes golden beaches with bush-clad shorelines and dolphins sometimes escort the boat.

In **Queen Charlotte Sound**, Beachcomber Fun Cruises (T0800/624 526, Wwww.mailboat.co.nz) run the four-hour **Magic Mail Run** (Mon–Sat 1.30pm; $80) which leaves from Picton. Three routes are plied on different days of the week, but there's little to choose between them so hop on whichever is convenient. All call into Endeavour Inlet, pass a salmon farm and allow fifteen minutes ashore at Ship Cove.

Alternative postal routes explore **Pelorus Sound** from Havelock (see p.507).

9000ft, $295 from 12,000ft; ⓣ0800/373 2648, ⓦwww.skydivethesounds.com). Even better, instead of crossing Cook Straight by ferry, skydive into the South Island ($620) with a Wellington pick-up and a landing at Picton airport that makes you feel like some kind of secret agent. The plane brings your gear down in a more leisurely fashion.

The Queen Charlotte Track

The **Queen Charlotte Track** (QCT: 71km one way; 3–5 days; open all year; ⓦwww.qctrack.co.nz) is a spectacularly beautiful walk partly tracing skyline ridges with brilliant views across dense coastal forest to the waters of Queen Charlotte and Kenepuru sounds on either side. It is broad, relatively easy going and is distinguished from all other Kiwi multi-day tramps by the **abundant accommodation** along the way. There are no DOC huts and no fees to hike the track, but with the temptation of some lovely places to stay, it may cost you more than you bargained for. Access and egress is generally by boat from Picton, and your water taxi will **transport your bags** to your next destination each day, making hiking the Queen Charlotte Track a thoroughly pleasurable experience. Since boats call at numerous bays along the way, less ambitious walkers can tackle shorter sections, do day-hikes from Picton or tackle the track as part of a guided walk (see p.505). Though the track is less crowded than some, its popularity is rapidly increasing.

Queen Charlotte Sound was an important trade route and provided good shelter and bountiful food for **Maori**, who carried canoes over the low saddles of the walkway to avoid long and hazardous sea journeys around the full length of the Sounds. **Captain Cook** stopped at Ship Cove on five occasions and made it his New Zealand base, spending almost six months there between 1770 and 1777. The shelter and fresh water made it an ideal spot and its plentiful supplies of (what became known as) Cook's scurvy grass were particularly valued for the vitamin C content.

The changing seasons are reflected by splashes of colour: native clematis (*puawanga*) is festooned with creamy-white **flowers** in the spring; karaka groves are laden with bright yellow berries in the summer; and supplejacks produce red and orange fruits in the autumn. As a result, there is no shortage of **birds**, with tui and bellbirds in profusion, as well as the ever-friendly fantails and little piebald robins. Rocky shorelines boast an abundance of shags, gannets, terns and shearwaters, as well as the stooping oystercatchers patrolling in pairs. If you're lucky, you may spot a little blue penguin making its way to the fishing grounds in the morning.

Biking the QCT

Though the Queen Charlotte Track is primarily for hikers, **mountain bikers** can ride the whole thing in a couple of days. There are a couple of steep ascents but it is not overly technical, and with pack transfers and abundant accommodation you won't need to lug heavy panniers. Most of the track is open to bikers year-round, though the northern quarter (Ship Cove–Punga Cove) is off-limits from December to February.

Marlborough Sounds Adventure Company (see p.503) operates a three-day Freedom Bike Ride ($595–635) with bike rental, transfers and comfortable accommodation at *Punga Cove* and *Portage Resort*. Alternatively it can rent you a mountain bike ($50 a day) and you can organize your own trip, perhaps camping or staying in cheaper accommodation.

Adrenalin heaven

With an extraordinary range of climatic conditions and geographical phenomena spread over both islands, New Zealand is a true playground for adrenalin junkies and outdoor enthusiasts. Couple this with the often innovative Kiwi approach to adventure activities, and you can easily find yourself overwhelmed. The quick, big-buck thrills of bungy jumping and skydiving compete with stomach-churning days canyoning or whitewater rafting. For the cost of a day heli-skiing you could go scuba diving, swimming with dolphins and kayaking. Or shun the lot and spend your whole time tramping some of the world's most gorgeous scenery.

Swingbridge on the Routeburn Track ▲

The Kepler Track ▼

Kaiteriteri, near Abel Tasman National Park ▼

Tremendous tramps

New Zealand is crisscrossed by thousands of kilometres of walking tracks. Eight of New Zealand's finest tramps, and one river journey, have been classified as **Great Walks**; even the most well-trodden of these reveal magnificent natural wonders in the raw.

On the North Island

▸▸ The gentle **Lake Waikaremoana Track** (3–4 days; see p.424) circumnavigates one of the country's most beautiful lakes.

▸▸ The **Tongariro Northern Circuit** (3–4 days; see p.341) takes in magnificent volcanic and semi-desert scenery.

▸▸ The **Whanganui River Journey** (2–4 days; p.273) is best explored by canoe and a series of highly atmospheric short walks.

On the South Island

▸▸ The **Heaphy Track** (4–5 days; see p.541) passes through the Kahurangi National Park, balancing subalpine tops and surf-pounded beaches.

▸▸ The **Abel Tasman Coastal Track** (2–4 days; see p.531) skirts beaches and crystal-clear bays, ideally explored by sea kayak.

▸▸ The world-famous **Milford Track** (4 days; see p.857) accesses stunning glaciated alpine scenery and stupendous waterfalls.

▸▸ The **Routeburn Track** (3 days; see p.806), one of the country's finest walks, spends quality time above the bushline.

▸▸ The **Kepler Track** (4 days; see p.847) is renowned for ridge walks and virgin beech forest.

For more on outdoor activities in New Zealand see pp.58–69.

▸▸ The **Rakiura Track** (3 days; see p.713), on Stewart Island, follows the rainforest-bordered coast and provides opportunities to see kiwi in the wild.

Wet and wild

Torrents of water cascade from the high mountains of the North and South Islands, and there's enormous fun to be had by joining the gurgling whitewater mass.

Rafting is a perennial favourite, with both **Rotorua** and **Queenstown** offering an enviable selection of river runs. Less frequented but equally exciting rafting areas include Canterbury's **Rangitata River** and the **West Coast** of the South Island, which offers the best rafting in the land – often accessed by chopper.

Sea kayaking is at its best around the **Abel Tasman National Park**, **Marlborough Sounds**, **Fiordland** and **Kaikoura**, where there's always the chance of bumping into fur seals, penguins and rare seabirds. **River kayakers** can enjoy a relaxing paddle on the Whanganui River Journey or take on fast-flowing white water, best tackled at the kayak school in **Murchison**.

Jumping mad

Diving off tall towers with vines tied around the ankles has been a rite of passage for centuries in the South Pacific islands of Vanuatu, but commercial bungy jumping was pioneered by Kiwi speed skiers A.J. Hackett and Henry Van Asch. They began pushing the bungy boundaries, culminating in Hackett's jump from the Eiffel Tower in 1987. He was promptly arrested, but the publicity sparked worldwide interest that continues to draw bungy aspirants to

▲ Rafting the Kaituna River, Rotorua

▼ Ledge Urban Bungy, Queenstown

Exploring Franz Josef Glacier ▲

Going off-piste in the Southern Alps ▼

New Zealand's sites – some of the world's best, with bridges over deep canyons and platforms cantilevered out over rivers. The first commercial operation was set up just outside Queenstown on the 43m **Kawerau Suspension Bridge**. Its accessible location and the chance to be dunked in the river make this the most popular jump of many on both the South and North islands.

Winter wonderland

The main **North Island ski-fields** include the country's two largest and most popular skiing destinations, **Turoa** and **Whakapapa**, both on the volcanic Mount Ruapehu. Along with the chance to ski a dormant volcano, visitors can take advantage of some beautiful, virtually deserted **tramps**, including the Tongariro Alpine Crossing, where frozen lakes and vibrant colours are thrown into relief by steaming fumaroles.

On the **South Island**, the west coast of the Southern Alps offers a variety of glacier-climbing experiences on the **Franz Josef and Fox glaciers**. On the other side of the Alps you can shoot up to **Mount Cook** and take a boat or a kayak to the foot of a glacier and watch the ice crumble. Mix all this in with the party atmosphere and uncrowded runs on the commercial **ski-fields** – Coronet Peak and The Remarkables by **Queenstown**; Treble Cone, Cardrona and the Waiorau Snow Farm near **Wanaka**; and further north, Porter Heights and Mount Hutt, both within two hours' drive of **Christchurch** – and you're guaranteed a memorable time, as well as some of the most spectacular snow-dusted scenery you'll ever see.

Information and access

First stop should be Picton's i-SITE where you'll be given a free leaflet detailing all the latest transportation costs and frequencies, and outlining the accommodation options. Staff will also talk you through organizing your trip and sell you DOC's *Queen Charlotte Track* leaflet (which can also be downloaded free).

Trampers normally **travel north to south** from Ship Cove to Anakiwa, using **water taxis** to drop them off and pick them up. Sections of the track are also **accessible from Kenepuru Road** (see p.507), but there is no public transport and hitching or using your own vehicle seems counter to the spirit of the whole enterprise.

Water taxi companies (see p.501 for details) all offer a standard package with drop-off at Ship Cove, bag transfers and pick-up at Anakiwa or the nearby Tirimoana Jetty for $80–95. Endeavour Express is cheapest but other companies may have more convenient schedules. **Bikes** are charged at $5 per journey. Equally you can just walk a short section of the track and be picked up pretty much anywhere you want: one-way transfers are around $30.

Most water taxis run a late-afternoon service back to Picton from Anakiwa, which is also accessible using the Rural Mail Bus Run (see Picton listings, p.501).

Guided walks, combos and day-trips

All sorts of companies around Picton offer organized encounters with the QCT with varying degrees of assistance. Marlborough Sounds Adventure Company offers **freedom walks** (4-day $560; 5-day $650) with nights spent at *Furneaux Lodge*, *Punga Cove Resort* and *Portage Resort Hotel*, which costs about the same as organizing it yourself but avoids booking hassles and includes a packed lunch each day. Its **guided walks** (4-day $1270; 5-day $1540) add in a knowledgeable guide accompanying you the whole way and the five-dayer includes free guided kayaking. Better still, try its four-day Paddle and Walk ($1270) which includes a visit to Moturua Island with Dolphin Watch (see p.503), the first two days of the guided walk from Ship Cove to Punga Cove, a day kayaking on Kenepuru Sound, then a final day paddling back to Picton. To pack in a day each of hiking, biking and paddling, go for the excellent three-day Ultimate Sounds Adventure ($495–695 depending on accommodation).

Beachcomber Fun Cruises (see p.503) offer a series of one-day walks ($45–61), some with afternoon tea at *Furneaux Lodge*, and the Cougar Line offers walks from one to five hours (all $63).

Accommodation

A hot shower, a good meal and a comfy bed are three things seldom encountered on long tramps but the Queen Charlotte Track offers comfort in spades plus a good deal of backpacker-style accommodation for $25–40 a night: around twenty places in all. **Booking** is essential, not just to guarantee a bed for the night but also to ensure your water taxi company knows where to deliver your bags. Many of the cheaper places don't accept EFTPOS or credit cards, so **take plenty of cash**. The seven DOC **campsites** (all marked on the map on p.496) cost $6 and have water and toilets but only four have water taxi access.

The accommodation below is listed geographically from north to south, with hiking distances measured from Ship Cove.

Resolution Bay Cabins Resolution Bay Km5 ⓣ03/579 941, ⓔreso@xtra.co.nz. The closest accommodation to Ship Cove, a 1920s-style mini-resort in a pretty and atmospheric spot offering swimming, kayaks and fairly rustic accommodation. Camping $15, basic cabins $35 per person, s/c cabins ❸, cottages for four ❻

Furneaux Lodge Endeavour Inlet, Km14 ⓣ 03/579 8259, ⓦ www.furneaux.co.nz. One of the region's bigger lodges built in attractive grounds around a century-old homestead, with a convivial bar serving good meals and an excellent restaurant ($30 mains). Rooms range from basic backpackers (bring a sleeping bag) and made-up bunk rooms to s/c cottages, and swanky modern suites. Internet access and phone available. Dorms $30, bunk rooms $40, chalets ❻, suites ❽

Punga Cove Resort Endeavour Inlet, Km26 ⓣ 03/579 8561, ⓦ www.pungacove.co.nz. A large resort straggling from the boat-shed bar by the wharf, up the hillside to a classy restaurant with panoramic views; with pool, spa, sauna, fishing gear and kayaks. Dorms $35 (linen $12 extra), budget rooms ❹, chalets ❺, deluxe ❼

Mahana Homestead Lodge Endeavour Inlet, Km27 ⓣ 03/579 8373, ⓦ www.mahanahomestead.com. Modern and functional 12-bed hostel with four-shares and twin/family rooms all with sea views. A good kitchen supplemented by home-cooked dinners and it's only a 10min stroll to the restaurant and bar at Punga Cove. Free kayaks. Dorms $31, rooms ❸

Noeline's Homestay / Backpackers Near Punga Cove, Km27 ⓣ 03/ 579 8375. A friendly welcome from the redoubtable Noeline and comfortable accommodation in a relaxing atmosphere– you may not want to leave. Linen $5. Dorms $25.

Portage Resort Hotel Kenepuru Rd, Km51, ⓣ 03/573 4309, ⓦ www.portage.co.nz. A stylish hotel beside Kenepuru Sound, a 10min walk from the QCT at Torea Bay. Remodelled, bold-coloured rooms and designer bathrooms, along with a classy restaurant, café and bar, swimming pool and great views. Dorms have a full kitchen. Access is by car along Kenepuru Rd, or by water taxi from Picton ($30 each way). Dorms $40, with linen $50, backpacker en suite ❹, non-view hotel rooms ❻, view rooms ❽

Debretts Backpackers Kenepuru Rd, Km51, ⓣ 03/573 4522, ⓦ www.stayportage.co.nz. Tranquil and well-appointed hostel sleeping six with great views of Portage Bay and Kenepuru Sound. Pick-ups from the track at Torea Bay are included in the price. Dorms $35 (linen $5), rooms ❸

Lochmara Lodge Lochmara Bay, Km58 ⓣ 03/573 4554, ⓦ www.lochmaralodge.co.nz. Beautiful eco-lodge with its own excellent café, restaurant and bar overlooking the still waters of Lochmara Bay. A portion of your bill goes to fund predator control and a captive breeding programme for kakariki (native parakeets), geckos and tuatara (due in 2008). It is a great place to stroll along a couple of kilometres of bush tracks past sculptures and artworks (some for sale, others just to beautify), into the kakariki aviary, past the glow-worm grotto, then relax in a hammock: some are waterside, others swing in the shady bush and a few are set up for star-gazing. There are also free kayaks and snorkelling gear, a lovely hot tub ($3/30min), and massage available. All rooms are en suite with kettle and toaster but are not set up for cooking and don't have TV or phone. The lodge is almost an hour's walk off the QCT or a 15min water taxi ride from Picton. The lodge runs its own water taxi ($25 each way; Picton departures daily 9am, noon, 3.15pm & 5.30pm). Closed June–Aug. Viewless twin ❸, bay-view double ❹, deluxe ❻

Anakiwa Backpackers Anakiwa, Km71 ⓣ 03/574 1388, ⓦ www.anakiwabackpackers.co.nz. Clean, simple and relaxed homestay/hostel with made-up beds, some nice doubles and a s/c unit. Bed $33, rooms ❷, unit ❸

The route

The track passes through some grassy farmland and open gorse-covered hills, but both ends of the track are forest reserves with lush greenery right down to the shoreline. There are a number of **detours** off the main track to places of interest, including a short walk from Ship Cove to a pretty forest-shrouded waterfall where Cook frequently bathed, a scramble down to the Bay of Many Coves, or a foray to the Antimony Mines (where there are exposed shafts – stick to the marked tracks).

To do the whole track in three days, get an early start from Ship Cove and plan to hike to Punga Cove. From there you have a fairly long day to Portage, then a relatively easy finish.

Ship Cove to Resolution Bay (4.5km; 1–2hr; 200m ascent). The track climbs steeply away from the shore through largely untouched forest to a lookout with great views of Motuara Island, before dropping down to Resolution Bay, where there's a DOC campsite and *Resolution Bay Cabins*.

Resolution Bay to Endeavour Inlet (15km; 3–5hr; 200m ascent). Follows an old bridle path over the ridge to *Furneaux Lodge* and *Endeavour Resort*.

Endeavour Inlet to Punga Cove (11.5km; 3–4hr; 100m ascent). Coastal track through regenerating forest thick with birdlife. DOC campsite and several lodges.

Punga Cove to Portage (24.5km; 6–8hr; 650m ascent). The longest stretch without convenient roofed accommodation (just two DOC campsites) is also the most rewarding, mostly following a ridge with views down to the Sounds on both sides.

Portage to Mistletoe Bay (7.5km; 3–4hr; 450 ascent). A steep initial climb is followed by a pleasant ridge walk through manuka, gorse and shrubs with the chance to break the journey at the lovely *Lochmara Lodge*, some 2km off the track.

Mistletoe Bay to Anakiwa (12.5km; 3–4hr; 100m ascent). Follows an old bridle path well above the water with great views, then finishes off through some lovely beech forest.

Queen Charlotte Drive and Kenepuru Road

With water taxis providing convenient access to fabulous out-of-the-way spots, it seems a little perverse to try to see the Marlborough Sounds by car; doubly so when you start weaving your way around the mostly paved but narrow and twisting roads – don't expect to average more than 40km an hour. In compensation, the views through the ferns to turquoise bays are magical.

The 35-kilometre Queen Charlotte Drive between Picton and Havelock is a picturesque and spectacular back road sliding past the flat plain at the head of Queen Charlotte Sound and climbing up the hills overlooking Pelorus Sound before descending to SH6 and Havelock itself. It is a slow and winding drive, but you may want to take it even slower by stopping to wander down to a couple of sheltered coves.

Around 18km west of Picton, a narrow road heads north to **Anakiwa**, the southern end of the Queen Charlotte Track. Here you'll find a wharf used by water taxis taking hikers back to Picton, *Anakiwa Backpackers* (see p.506) and the *Blist'd Foot Garden Café*.

A couple of kilometres further along Queen Charlotte Drive, **Kenepuru Road** cuts right and begins its 75-kilometre journey out along the shores of Kenepuru Sound. There are no real sights along the way, though Kenepuru Road provides access to several points along the Queen Charlotte Track, and runs past a handful of DOC campsites and several places to stay – *Resort Hotel*, *Debretts Backpackers* and *Punga Cove* – all listed on pp.506. The road ends at the wonderful *Hopewell* **backpackers** (see p.499).

Havelock and Pelorus Sound

Nestled in the heart of the Sound, **Havelock**, 35km west of Picton, comprises little more than a thin ribbon along the main road linked to an expanded and gentrified marina. The town won't detain you long, but it is an excellent base for hiking, kayaking or cruising the stunning **Pelorus Sound**, an intricate maze of steep-sided bays, crescent beaches and sunken sea passages surrounded by forested peaks.

Once a gold and timber boom town, then a sleepy fishing village, Havelock's fortunes have begun to revive with an influx of travellers who discover the fun to be had in these quiet environs, and feast on **green-lipped mussels**. Havelock is the world capital for these choice bivalves and you simply can't leave without tucking into a plateful.

You'll only need a few minutes in the **Havelock Museum** on SH6 (sporadic but generally open daily 9am–5pm; donation requested), a miscellaneous collection of bric-a-brac plus a wood-milling display and the honour rolls from Havelock School which feature pioneering atom-nucleus discoverer, **Ernest**

Rutherford, who went to school here for two years from 1882 in what is now the YHA. There's a memorial in the centre of town detailing Rutherford's life story along with that of local boy **William Pickering**, a NASA scientist during the Cold War.

The town's other famous son is the itinerant author **Barry Crump,** who died in 1996. Crumpy, as he was affectionately known, began life as a hunter and bushman, culling deer and pigs in some of New Zealand's roughest country – a way of life he described in a series of humorous, nostalgic and emotively descriptive novels and short stories.

To see the best of Pelorus Sound, get aboard the **Pelorus Mail Run** ($110; ⓣ03/574 1088, ⓦwww.mail-boat.co.nz), which departs from the marina on Tuesdays, Thursdays and Fridays at 9.30am and follows a different route each day. All the trips are a scenic delight, though Friday's is the most comprehensive, delivering mail and essential supplies to the far-flung residents at a pace from a bygone age, and dropping in on a mussel farm. The trips return late in the afternoon so bring your own lunch.

Practicalities

Buses between Picton and Nelson all stop at Havelock, while local bus and **water taxi** operators offer services to Kenepuru and Pelorus sounds. For information and bookings call at the **Havelock Infocentre**, 70 Main Rd (daily 8.30am–5pm; ⓣ03/574 2114), which also acts as the local **DOC** agent. Just down the street, Soundz Interesting, 60 Main Rd (Dec–March Mon–Fri 8.30am–5.30pm, Sat & Sun 9am–4pm; April–Nov Mon–Fri 8.30am–5pm, Sat & Sun 9am–4pm; ⓣ0800/428 356, ⓦwww.havelock.co.nz), sells camping and fishing gear, has Internet access, books trips and organizes fishing charters (from $135, min 2 people).

Accommodation options include *Havelock Garden Motel*, 71 Main Rd (ⓣ03/574 2387, ⓦwww.gardenmotels.com; ❹), with fully self-contained units and helpful hosts; and *Havelock Motor Camp*, 24 Inglis St (ⓣ03/574 2339; camping $10, cabins and on-site vans ❶), just off Main Road in the heart of town. The traditional *YHA Rutherford Hostel*, 46 Main Rd (ⓣ03/574 2104, ⓔrutherford@meet.co.nz; camping $12, dorms $25, rooms ❷), occupies a characterful old schoolhouse, which has been much rejuvenated in recent years, and has a sunny garden out back. The small *Blue Moon Backpackers*, 48 Main Rd (ⓣ03/574 2212, ⓔcombatnelson@yahoo.co.nz; dorms $23, rooms ❷), is a welcoming spot with a nice deck with views of the marina.

Food in Havelock is surprisingly good, especially if you like mussels. The place to eat them is the *Mussel Pot,* 73 Main Rd ⓣ03/574 2824 (closes 6–7pm outside the summer season), where they dish up green-lipped mussels in myriad different sauces ($17) with various accompaniments, along with excellent chowder ($10) and a farmer's platter ($16). Around the restaurant are details about mussels and a step-by-step guide on the best way to eat them. Café fare is best at *The Wakamarinian*, 70 Main Rd, while the *Havelock Hotel*, 54 Main Rd, serves simple cuisine in massive portions for under $20. For a sundowner, make for the marina-side *Slip Inn* (ⓣ03/574 2345) which does excellent gurnard and chips ($17), pizzas and more sophisticated dishes.

Pelorus and the road to Nelson, French Pass

Twelve kilometres west of Havelock along SH6, a twisting mostly dirt road heads to the start of the Nydia Track. Continue a further 6km along SH6 to reach the **Pelorus Bridge Scenic Reserve**, a gorgeous forested spot run through by the crystal-clear trout-filled Pelorus River with sandy beaches,

The Nydia Track

If you are looking for excellent bushwalking with few fellow travellers, consider the **Nydia Track** (27km one way; 2–3 days), preferably tackled from Havelock and explained on DOC's *The Nydia Track* leaflet. It follows a series of bridle paths, making its way through pasture, shrubland and virgin forest, with great views from the Kaiuma Saddle (387m) and Nydia Saddle (347m), as well as along the head of Nydia Bay. The first day (5–6hr) is pleasant, but the second (4–5hr) is the real gem. **Mountain biking** is allowed on the track all year round, though it's a tough proposition in the dry and near impossible when wet.

Start at **Kaiuma Bay**, most easily accessed by water taxi from Havelock, but also driveable in around an hour and a half: turn off SH6 12km west of Havelock onto Daltons Road. The track finishes at Duncan Bay, in **Tennyson Inlet**, about an hour's drive from Havelock. The most convenient approach is to buy a package from Havelock Infocentre ($65) that includes a shuttle bus to the start and shuttle bus pick-up from the end back to Havelock. They'll also organize **accommodation** somewhere around Nydia Bay, roughly halfway along the track. Groups are best served by DOC's *Nydia Lodge* ($15 per person), which will only open if there are four or more people. Otherwise go for the small and relaxed *Te Mahoerangi Ecolodge* (Ⓣ03/579 8411, Ⓦwww.nydiatrack.org.nz; dorm $25, room ❸) where home-cooked meals are available. There is also a **campsite** ($6) at the north-western end of Nydia Bay, and a waterside one at the Duncan Bay end of the track (dusk to dawn only; $6).

abundant swimming holes and verdant bush enlivened by tui, grey warblers and bellbirds. This fertile area saw a succession of Maori settlements, which prospered until Te Rauparaha conquered the north of the South Island in the 1820s. The misery caused by the war and the encroachment of European settlers drove most of the Maori away – the few that remained produced flax that Te Rauparaha could trade for rifles.

The place is understandably popular in summer. Facilities include a basic DOC **camping** area (Ⓣ03/571 6019; tent sites $10, cabins ❶), and a **DOC office** adjoining a modest daytime **café** (daily: Nov–March 8.30am–7pm; April–Oct 8.30am–4.30pm).

The **walking tracks** in the reserve are fairly flat, well maintained and clearly marked and there's a swingbridge to add a little extra excitement: the **Totara** track (1.5km return; 30min) and **Circle** (1km return; 30min) route pass through the low-lying woodland for which the area is famous, while the **Trig K** (2.5km one way; 2hr), after a steady climb to 417m, offers stunning views of the whole area.

SH6 continues west past the turn off to French Pass (see below) at the small settlement of **Rai Valley** and climbs the hills past Happy Valley Adventures (see p.516) to Nelson.

Duncan Bay and French Pass

Narrow winding roads head north from Rai Valley towards French Pass, a two-hour, sixty-kilometre drive. **Duncan Bay**, 30km off the highway at the northern end of the Nydia Track (see box, above), is the easier of the two destinations, a gorgeous hamlet of a couple of dozen houses. Bring all you need for a picnic lunch and a swim, then walk along the Nydia Track, perhaps to Pipi Beach (15min one way).

The road to French Pass winds 22km to **Okiwi**, a small settlement set on a broad curving bay with no facilities except for a summer-only café and the

Okiwi Bay Holiday Park & Lodge (Ⓣ03/576 5006, Ⓦwww.okiwi.co.nz; camping $15–17, lodge $31 per person, on-site vans ❷). The next forty-kilometre drive is through pockets of bush locked in sheep country and pine plantations with occasional, tantalizing glimpses of inaccessible bays and coves. French Pass itself is a narrow channel between the mainland and D'Urville Island where nineteenth-century French explorer Dumont d'Urville was spun by tumultuous whirlpools. If you're here at mid-tide it is easy to understand why these seething waters were so feared. The maelstrom is best seen from a couple of short tracks in **French Pass Scenic Reserve**, 1km before the road end at **French Pass**. This tiny settlement is little more than a wharf, a shop, DOC's basic *French Pass* **campsite** ($7) and *Sea Safaris & Beachfront Villas* (Ⓣ03/576 5204, Ⓦwww.seasafaris.co.nz; B&B ❻) with meals available on request ($35). Sea Safaris also run all manner of dive trips, boat charters, rent sea kayaks ($55 a day) and take groups over to D'Urville Island for mountain biking and walking ($130), wildlife trips ($75), and dolphin and seal swimming ($110, watching $75).

Nelson and around

The thriving, small city of **Nelson**, set on the coast in a broad basin between the Arthur and Richmond ranges, is a beguiling place. Initially it is not much to look at, but on longer acquaintance it gets its hooks into you and the Nelson region has become one of the most popular visitor destinations in New Zealand. A warm, sunny climate, access to good beaches and a cluster of worthwhile wineries in the hinterland are powerful lures, but Nelson is also supremely placed for accessing Golden Bay and three national parks – Abel Tasman, Kahurangi and Nelson Lakes. Over the years it has become a bit of a haven for painters and potters drawn by the sunlight, the landscape and the unique raw materials for ceramic art that lie beneath the rich green grass.

You'll initially spend much of your time in central Nelson, where the **Suter Gallery** and the lively **Saturday Market** are good diversions. But you'll soon want to venture further, notably to **Tahunanui Beach** and the western suburb of **Stoke** for the fascinating **World of WearableArt** museum. Further west, the satellite town of **Richmond**, 14km out, is the starting point for the arts, crafts and wine district to the north. To get further away from Nelson, on a short day-trip, head for Mapua Wharf or the beaches of **Rabbit Island**, accessible at low tide.

Some history

Nelson is one of the oldest settlements in New Zealand. By the middle of the sixteenth century, it was occupied by the Ngati Tumatakokiri people, some of whom provided a reception committee for **Abel Tasman**'s longboats at Murderer's Bay (now Golden Bay), where they killed four of his sailors. Nonetheless, Nelson is where many early European immigrants got their first taste of the South Island.

By the time Europeans arrived in earnest, Maori numbers had been decimated by internecine fighting and the nearest *pa* site to Nelson was at Motueka, though this did little to prevent land squabbles, culminating in the **Wairau Affray** in 1843. Despite assurances from Maori chiefs Te Rauparaha and Te Rangihaeata that they would abide by the decision of a land commissioner, the

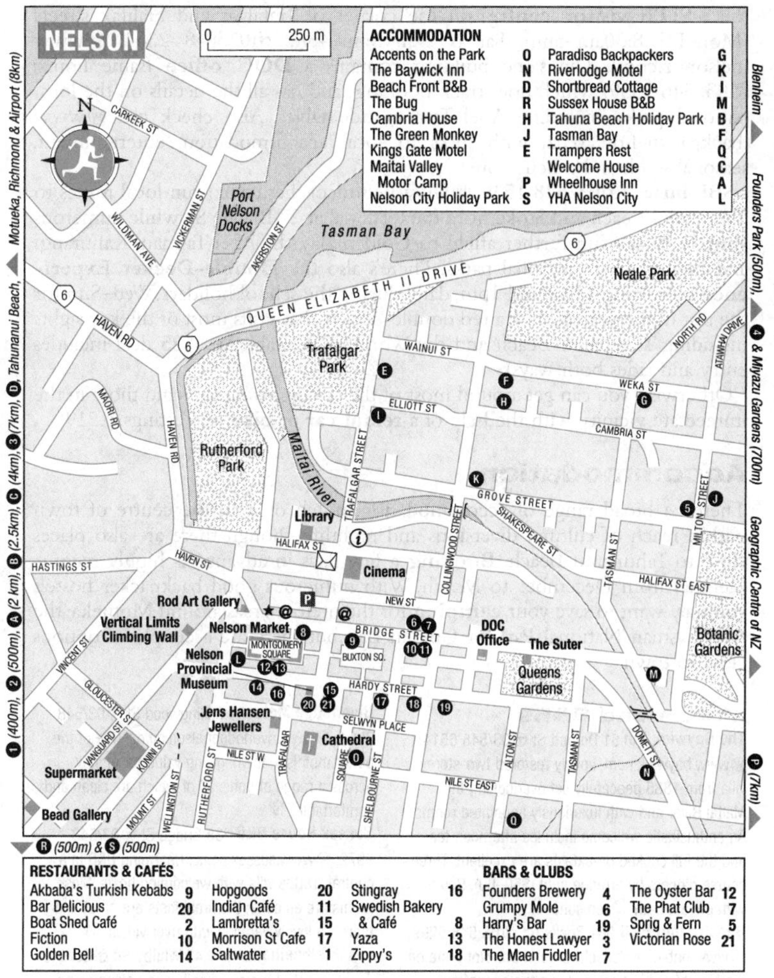

New Zealand Company pre-emptively sent surveyors south to the Wairau Plains, the catalyst for a skirmish during which Te Rangihaeata's wife was shot. The bereaved chief and his men slaughtered twenty-two people in retaliation but the settlers continued their land acquisition as numbers were boosted by a small wave of immigrants from Germany.

Arrival, information and transport

Flights arrive at Nelson **airport**, 8km west of the centre. The Airporter (ⓣ0800/400 110; $10 one person, $12 for two) meets most flights, or you can grab a taxi (ⓣ03/548 8225; $20–25). Long-distance **buses** drop you near the centre of the city, within easy walking distance of most accommodation. InterCity pulls in at 27 Bridge St, while the other companies all stop outside the **i-SITE visitor centre**, on the corner of Trafalgar and Halifax streets (Mon–Fri 8.30am–5pm, Sat & Sun 9am–4pm; ⓣ03/548 2304, ⓦwww.nelsonnz.com). The same building contains a **DOC office** (same hours; ⓣ03/546 9339) which does track bookings and has all the details on the local national parks, including Abel Tasman tide tables. Also check out ⓦwww.backpacknelson.co.nz, with links to local accommodation, entertainment, seasonal work and much more.

SBL **buses** (ⓣ03/548 1539, ⓦwww.nelsoncoaches.co.nz) run local routes to Tahunanui Beach and Stoke from the terminal at 27 Bridge St, while numerous **shuttle buses** run further afield to Golden Bay, the Abel Tasman, Kahurangi and Nelson Lakes national parks. There's also the **Double-Decker Experience** (departing 11am and 1pm, daily during the school holidays, Wed–Sun for the rest of the year; $7.50), a red double-decker that visits most of the key sights including Tahunanui Beach and the World of WearableArt ($25 deal includes entry and rides both ways).

Otherwise, you can get around most of the city sights on foot and those in the immediate vicinity with the help of a **rental car** or **bike** (see listings, p.519).

Accommodation

There's a broad range of accommodation, much of it in the centre of town within reach of cultural diversions and nightlife, though there are also places close to Tahunanui Beach. **Booking** a few days in advance is highly recommended from December to March. With numerous good backpacker hostels you may want to save your **camping** for the prettier areas around Motueka, the Abel Tasman National Park or Golden Bay, but there are a couple of options close to town.

Motels and B&Bs

The Baywick Inn 51 Domett St ⓣ03/545 6514, ⓦwww.baywick.com. Lovely restored two-storey villa from 1885 peacefully set overlooking the Maitai River and with luxuriously appointed rooms. An enthusiastic welcome includes afternoon tea, and the full cooked breakfasts are excellent. Three-course dinners by arrangement ($50–60). Room with private bath ⑤, en suite ⑥

Beach Front B&B 581 Rocks Rd ⓣ03/548 5299, ⓦwww.bnb.co.nz/beachfrontbb.html. Not quite on the beachfront but certainly on the beachfront road, with great views of sand and sea from the deck out front and from the spa bath. Two pleasant rooms (one en suite, the other with private bathroom), very helpful hosts and a hearty full breakfast. ⑤

Cambria House 7 Cambria St ⓣ0800/548 4681, ⓦwww.cambria.co.nz. This late-nineteenth-century weatherboard house boasts a lovely back deck and garden, beautiful fireplaces, and a wide choice of breakfasts – all just 10min walk from town on a quiet road. Suites ⑦, deluxe ⑧

Kings Gate Motel 21 Trafalgar St ⓣ0800/104 022, ⓦwww.kingsgatemotel.co.nz. Central motel with comfortable well-kept rooms including full kitchens and a pool. ⑤

Riverlodge Motel 31 Collingwood St ⓣ03/548 3094, ⓦwww.riverlodgenelson.co.nz. One of the better motels in town, giving value for money across a range of units, all of which are clean and comfortable. ⑤

Sussex House B&B 238 Bridge St ⓣ03/548 9972, ⓦwww.sussex.co.nz. Charming B&B in a central, 1880s villa with welcoming hosts. Most rooms are en suite, the breakfasts are great and there's a lovely veranda with river views. ⑤

Wheelhouse Inn 42 Whitby Rd ⓣ03/546 8391, ⓦwww.wheelhouse.nelson.co.nz. Magical bay views from the picture windows in these nautically themed, self-catering apartments high on the hill 2km west of central Nelson. All are very private and come with full kitchen, laundry, TV/DVD, Internet access and BBQ. The Captain's Quarters is the largest apartment, sleeping up to six. ⑥

Hostels

Accents on the Park 335 Trafalgar Square ⓣ03/548 4335, ⓦwww.accentsonthepark.com. An excellent, large backpackers, partly in a restored nineteenth-century house that balances the Victorian theme with a host of modern amenities, including spa pool, BBQ and luggage storage.

Cheaper dorms have three-tier bunks but there are pricier dorms, a range of rooms, and a bar/café downstairs that dishes up cheap fare to the residents. Dorms $23, rooms ❷, en suite ❸

The Bug 226 Vanguard St ⓣ03/539 4227, ⓦwww.thebug.co.nz. Excellent and welcoming small hostel about 1km from the centre of Nelson with VW Beetle paraphernalia everywhere. Free bikes, free Internet and local pick-ups make this a popular choice. Dorms $23, rooms and en suites ❷

The Green Monkey 129 Milton St ⓣ03/545 7421, ⓦwww.thegreenmonkey.co.nz. A quiet, boutique hostel in a converted villa that's well kept and has a relaxed atmosphere. Free Internet and bikes. Book well in advance. Dorms $24, doubles ❷

Paradiso Backpackers 42 Weka St ⓣ03/546 6703, ⓦwww.backpackernelson.co.nz. This large, converted villa with purpose-built outbuildings houses a lively hostel with a youthful feel that's packed in summer, though the pressure is eased somewhat by a small outdoor pool. Dorms $23, rooms and en suites ❷

Shortbread Cottage 33 Trafalgar St ⓣ03/546 6681, ⓔshortbread_cottages@xtra.co.nz. Boutique hostel with polished wood floors, a small number of beds and lots of home comforts. Book ahead. Dorms $23, rooms ❷

Tasman Bay 10 Weka St ⓣ0800/222 572 ⓦwww.tasmanbaybackpackers.co.nz. A sound choice, this comfortable purpose-built hostel, just minutes from the town centre, has clean, spacious rooms and enthusiastic, friendly management who ensure you always get more than you pay for. Free bikes. Dorms $24, rooms ❷

Trampers Rest 31 Alton St ⓣ03/545 7477. Cosy backpackers with just eight beds in homestyle accommodation with comparatively small rooms. TV watching is by consensus only, but there's free Internet and Wi-Fi, a tuned piano, and the wee garden boasts a hammock, avocado tree and bike storage. There are free bikes for exploring the Nelson surrounds, and Alan is a real tramping enthusiast, an absolute mine of information on Nelson and all things track. Dorms $25, doubles ❷

Welcome House 108a Parkers Rd ⓣ03/548 5462, ⓔwelcomehouse@xtra.co.nz. Welcoming hostel (though without dorms) in a suburban home close to Tahunanui Beach and with plenty of outdoor space for summer relaxing. It's 4km from the centre but there's a bus stop nearby. Rooms ❷

YHA Nelson City 59 Rutherford St ⓣ03/545 9988, ⓔyha.nelson@yha.co.nz. This purpose-built hostel in a central location is one of the best in town, with a wide range of accommodation, including connecting rooms for families and two disabled-access units. One big and one smaller kitchen and plenty of communal areas mean you never feel crowded and the staff are well informed and helpful. Dorms $28, rooms ❷

Campsites and holiday parks

Maitai Valley Motor Camp 472 Maitai Valley Rd ⓣ03/548 7729, ⓔmaitaivalleymc@xtra.co.nz. Bargain, friendly camping in a bush setting beside the Maitai River (with good swimming holes) 7km southeast of Nelson. Camping $16 per site, cabins ❶

Nelson City Holiday Park 230 Vanguard Rd ⓣ0800/778 898, ⓦwww.nelsonholidaypark.co.nz. Small, very well-maintained and sited van park with limited tent space but various grades of room plus bikes at $25 a day. Camping $16, cabins ❶, kitchen cabins ❷, s/c units ❸

Tahuna Beach Holiday Park 70 Beach Rd, Tahunanui ⓣ0800/500 501, ⓦwww.tahunabeach.co.nz. Enormous estuary-side campsite with many facilities, 5min walk from Tahunanui Beach with a wide range of accommodation – from tent and campervan sites through assorted cabins and units to full-blown motel units. There's also a mini-golf course, kids' playgrounds and TV room. Camping $15, cabins ❶, kitchen cabins ❷, s/c units ❹

The city and around

The grid pattern streets of Nelson are dominated by the glowering, grey-stone **Christ Church Cathedral**, perched on a small hill peering down Trafalgar Street towards the sea. English architect Frank Peck's original 1924 design was gradually modified over many years due to lack of money; World War II further intervened, and even now the cathedral tower looks as if it's still under construction. However, the cathedral's grim exterior contrasts with its interior, illuminated by dazzling stained-glass windows, ten noteworthy examples of which are tucked away in a small chapel to the right of the main altar.

About two minutes' walk north the **Nelson Provincial Museum**, on the corner of Hardy and Trafalgar streets (Mon–Fri 10am–5pm, Sat & Sun

10am–4.30pm; donation requested; ⓣ03/548 9588, ⓦwww.nelsonmuseum.co.nz), makes imaginative use of an existing building by Ian Athfield (see p.465). The ground-floor permanent collection takes a fresh, multimedia approach to local exhibits and then draws strands from them to the rest of New Zealand and the wider world. The Maori displays are each curated by the various local *iwi* with their choice of treasures from their own *marae*; witness the fine bone club, delicate flax and feather cloak, and interpretation of the designs in *tukutuku* panels. The death masks from the Mangatapu Murders highlight a grisly tale of robbery, murder and betrayal from 1866, and there's a collection of traditional Maori musical instruments whose sounds echo throughout the galleries.

Just east of the centre on Bridge Street, the pretty Victorian **Queens Gardens** (daily 8am–dusk; free), with its mature trees and well-populated duck pond, hosts **The Suter**, 208 Bridge St (daily 10.30am–4.30pm; $3; ⓦwww.TheSuter.org.nz). This small public art museum is one of the finest in the South Island, built in 1899 as a memorial to Andrew Burn Suter, Bishop of Nelson from 1866 to 1891. It hosts visiting exhibitions and shows relating to the local area, as well as changing displays from the gallery's own collection. During the summer try to catch something of its stock of **watercolours** – especially those of John Gully, a friend of the bishop whose works largely depict scenes from the surrounding area. Also look out for oils by "**Toss**" **Woollaston**, a founder of the modernist movement in New Zealand and one of a group of artists and writers who, during the 1930s and 1940s, began exploring notions of a New Zealand culture independent of colonial Britain. Another must is Gottfried Lindauer's painting of Huria Matenga, a Maori woman who helped save many lives from the wreck of the *Delaware* in 1863. Her status is indicated by feathers, bone, greenstone jewellery and the ceremonial club she holds; in the background is the foundering American ship.

Continue further east along Bridge Street, across the Maitai River to the lacklustre **Botanic Gardens** where New Zealand's first ever rugby game was played in 1870. The adjacent small hill commands a good view over the town and, it is claimed, marks the **geographical centre of New Zealand**.

About 1km north of the Botanical Gardens, **Founders Park**, 87 Atawhai Drive (daily 10am–4.30pm; $5), presents relocated and replica buildings and gives a somewhat sanitized version of early colonial history. It is good for the kids, though, and adults will appreciate the Founders Brewery (see p.518).

For a relaxing half-hour, continue 300m north along Atawhai Drive to the delightful Japanese-style **Miyazu Gardens** (daily 8am–dusk; free), a quiet oasis of reflective pools, ornamental cherry trees and restrained statuary; the gardens are at their best during December and January.

Arts and crafts

Many of the region's artists and craftspeople display at galleries outside Nelson (see account from p.519) but you can get an idea of what's in store by visiting galleries in town. A good starting point is Red Art Gallery, 1 Bridge St

> Saturday morning should involve a pilgrimage to the renowned **Nelson Market** (8am–1pm), which takes over Montgomery Square. Artists are flushed out of their rural bolt holes and stalls groan with hand-dipped candles, turned wooden bowls, bracelets made from forks and all manner of produce from the crafts community. Food stalls with mounds of fruit, endless varieties of fresh bread and fish, Thai and vegetarian dishes, preserves, coffee and cakes sustain you while you browse.

▲ The fruits of the sea, Nelson Market

(ⓣ03/548 2170), which specializes in contemporary New Zealand fine art, glass and jewellery.

Just southeast of the centre, the **Bead Gallery**, 18 Parere St (Mon–Sat 9am–5pm, Sun 10am–4pm; ⓦwww.beads.co.nz), packs a small 1920s cottage to the rafters with a heady collection of over 10,000 bead styles, all for sale. The idea is simple; you can either design your own bead-piece or have one custom-made for you using anything from 10¢ baubles to some of the most exotic anywhere in the world (up to $200 apiece). They have a particularly fine range of psychedelic century-old Venetian glass trade beads from West Africa at relatively modest prices and even some broken 2000-year-old Roman bracelets.

Another opportunity to put your creativity to work comes in the form of **bone carving**; one-day workshops with Stephan ($65 with pick-up from your accommodation; ⓣ03/546 4275, ⓦwww.carvingbone.co.nz) should see you complete a relatively attractive pendant by the end of the day.

If you're committed to exploring your artistic potential while getting closer to local practitioners then contact Creative Tourism New Zealand (ⓦwww.creativetourism.co.nz), who coordinate **creative workshops** with topics ranging from *harakeke* (flax) weaving to bone carving, via wood turning, organic brewing, Maori medicines, ecology and seafood cookery.

Lord of the Rings fans will, of course, want to visit the jeweller's Jens Hansen, at the corner of Church Street and Selwyn Place (Mon–Fri 9am–5pm, Sat 10am–1pm; ⓦwww.jenshansen.com), who Peter Jackson got to make "**The one ring to rule them all**", or a few dozen of them to suit various cast members. Replicas are available, but remember what happens to the owner of such a ring.

Tahunanui Beach and WOW

Haven Road (SH6) runs northwest out of central Nelson and, after a kilometre, becomes **Wakefield Quay**, a popular spot for strolling along the waterfront but primarily known for the *Boat Shed Café* jutting picturesquely out over the water, and one or two newer sea-view restaurants (see p.517). Continue 3km along SH6 to reach **Tahunanui Beach Reserve**, a long golden strand backed by grassland and drifting dunes. It is where Nelson comes to relax on sunny weekends, with safe swimming, a fun park, zoo and children's playgrounds: buses run here frequently along SH6 from the city.

A further 3km out along SH6 follow signs to the **World of WearableArt and Classic Cars**, 95 Quarantine Rd (WOW; daily 10am–5pm; $18; Ⓦwww.wowcars.co.nz), for a theatrical and memorable experience. It is primarily a purpose-built showcase for the best designs from the annual WearableArt show, a fashion show with a difference first put on by Suzie Moncrieff in Nelson in 1987 and now held in Wellington (see p.488). Participants from around the world submit sculptures or pieces of art that can be worn as clothes –many made from the most unusual materials such as household junk, food, metal, stone, wood and tyres. A thirty-minute video of past shows sets the scene for the best of the costumes themselves, displayed in a manner that owes more to colourful theatre productions than to static gallery or museum exhibitions. Adjacent galleries are devoted to highly desirable shiny automobiles, both old and relatively new, all displayed in inventive ways. To get there, take an SBL bus and ask for directions, or join Double-Decker Experience (see p.512) which drops off at the door. Both leave from 27 Bridge St in Nelson.

Activities

Nelson is the sort of place where sunbathing at Tahunanui might be as active as you want to get, though there is no shortage of energetic diversions. On a wet day retreat to Vertical Limits, 34 Vanguard St ($12–16; Ⓣ0508/837 842, Ⓦwww.verticallimits.co.nz) for some indoor **rock climbing** and when the weather improves join their full-day climbing trips ($130) to Payne's Ford in Takaka.

Another good destination, in the wet or dry, is Happy Valley Adventures, 194 Cable Bay Rd, 17km northeast of Nelson off SH6 (Ⓣ03/545 0304, Ⓦwww.HappyValleyAdventures.co.nz), a large forested farm explored on **quad bikes**. Assorted **safaris** explore their 40km of track, climbing hills, passing monstrous matai trees, stopping to learn a little about the forest and its stories and eventually reaching a high spot with expansive views of Cable Bay and the ocean. The most popular trips are the Bayview Circuit (2hr; rider $105, passenger $30), and the Blue Hill Special (3hr; $145, no passengers) designed for the more skilled and ambitious rider.

Some rides visit the site of the **Skywire** ($85), a four-seater cable-car chair that swoops almost a kilometre across a forested valley then back to their hilltop café with its panoramic deck.

Visiting Abel Tasman National Park from Nelson

Most people visiting the Abel Tasman National Park base themselves at Motueka, Kaiteriteri or Marahau (for all see p.524), but it is quite possible to visit the park directly from Nelson. Abel Tasman Coachlines (Ⓣ03/548 0285, Ⓦwww.abeltasmantravel.co.nz) run a couple of daily services to Marahau ($18 each way), giving you enough time for a water taxi ride and a few hours' walking along the Coast Track. An alternative is to go with Abel Tasman Cruises (Ⓣ0508/488 066, Ⓦwww.abeltasmancruises.co.nz), who run a small cruise boat from Nelson along the Abel Tasman Coast into Golden Bay with the option of getting off at several spots in the park and returning at a later date. Their Summer Cruise (Dec–March daily; $160) leaves Nelson at 9am, reaches Pohara in Golden Bay by noon and spends a couple of hours there before returning to Nelson by 5pm.

For **horse-riding** you'll have to head 17km southwest of Nelson through Richmond to Stonehurst Farm Horse Treks, Haycock Road (Ⓣ0800/487 357, Ⓦwww.stonehurstfarm.co.nz). The majority of the shorter treks (1hr $55, 2hr 30min $95, 3hr 30min $105 and a summer sundowner starting at 6pm; 2hr 30min; $95) take place in the foothills of the Richmond ranges and offer great views of the coast and beyond; there are horses to suit all abilities, the routes are challenging but not frightening and there's a full safety briefing.

To get airborne try **tandem paragliding** with Nelson Paragliding (Ⓣ03/544 1182, Ⓦwww.nelsonparagliding.co.nz): a hair-raising drive up the hill to the launch site reveals a spectacular landscape, before you run like hell then glide off into the quiet up draughts for 15 to 20 minutes of eerily silent flight. Tandem flights go for $150 and a one-day introductory lesson costs $200, or try Adventure Paragliding and Kiteboarding (Ⓣ0800/212 359, Ⓦwww.skyout.co.nz; $150 for a tandem). For a birdlike quality to your flight, go with Nelson Hang Gliding (Ⓣ03/548 9151, Ⓦwww.flynelson.co.nz; $150, tandem flight of roughly 15min).

Eating

Nelson's enviable lifestyle is reflected in the **broad choice** of eating options within easy reach of the town centre. And when you tire of these, there's always fine food on the waterfront, at Mapua Wharf or in the gorgeous settings of the **wineries**. Don't forget Nelson's pubs and bars (see p.518) for a quick snack either.

Akbaba's Turkish Kebabs 130 Bridge St. Plenty of tasty cheap kebabs and salads ($7–13) to take away, munch in the courtyard out back, or in booth seating on low floor cushions; Turkish decor and music create a lively and casual atmosphere for lunch and dinner.

Bar Delicious 276 Trafalgar St Ⓣ03/546 9400. This suave, pseudo-Belgian beer café serves delicious, inventive, mostly Italian-based, cuisine ($17–27) in a louche, loungy atmosphere that gets a little skittish on Fri & Sat nights when the in-house DJs kick off. Closed Sun.

Boat Shed Café 350 Wakefield Quay Ⓣ03/546 9783. You can certainly get good seafood meals here (mains $28–35), but the reason to come is the location, in a converted boat shed perched out over the water with matchless views over Tasman Bay – perfect for romantic sunset dinners. Make the effort to come on one of the quieter nights or at lunchtime and save room for the fab desserts.

Golden Bell 104 Hardy St. Top Thai, relaxed and with all your favourites dishes for under $20.

Hopgoods 284 Trafalgar St Ⓣ03/545 7191. Nelson's finest dining is found in this airy restaurant or at tables outside on Trafalgar. Its commitment to locally sourced, organic produce informs its range of seasonal dishes fashioned by a perfectionist chef into lovely European-influenced meals. Expect the likes of confit of lamb with sweetbreads ($32) and pineapple tarte tatin ($12). Impeccable service. Closed Sun.

Indian Café 94 Collingwood St Ⓣ03/548 4098. The town's best curry restaurant set in a historic villa and serving all your favourites for around $16. The malai prawns are particularly good. Closed Sat lunch and Sun.

Lambretta's 204 Hardy St Ⓣ03/545 8555. Lambretta scooters lord it over this cavernous and bustling restaurant specializing in exotic pizzas, with names like "Fender Bender Pork" and "Scootin tootin chicken", and slightly more prosaic pasta dishes (mains $20–25).

Morrison St Cafe 244 Hardy St. Semi-formal café with tasty brunches, lunches, snacks (many dishes dairy or gluten free) and a liberal sprinkling of local art adorning the walls. Favourites include poached pork dumplings ($15), and chorizo and mushroom pilaf ($17), and there's plenty of outdoor seating.

Saltwater 272 Wakefield Quay Ⓣ03/548 3361. Bar-cum-restaurant with seating on the quay and grand views across the harbour to the beautiful blue bay and beyond. Seafood is the *raison d'être* here so don't pass up dishes such as seafood chowder ($10) followed by pan-seared scallops with lemon risotto ($30).

Stingray 8 Church St Ⓣ03/545 8957. This eco-designed backstreet café uses local organic ingredients to ensure delicious, good-value breakfasts, lunches and dinners. Obligatory kick-arse coffee and a select bunch of wines and beers encourage lingering, as does berry crumble with vanilla-bean ice cream. Live music and jam sessions (Wed,

Thurs & Sun) liven up the evenings and local DJs turn up to change the mood on Fri & Sat until late.
Swedish Bakery & Café 54 Bridge St. Tiny coffee joint serving genuine Danishes, Swedish marzipan treats and sandwiches including classic Swedish meatball and beetroot combos.
Yaza Montgomery Square. Hip, licensed café selling excellent breakfasts, lunches, coffees and the cheesiest cheese scones around. Also worth seeking out for its occasional alternative gigs late in the week – poetry, music, DJs, talks, etc.
Zippy's 276 Hardy St. If you're looking for home-baked veggie or wheat-free food, wicked vegan curries, tofu burgers, marvellous muffins and smoothies, and you can bear the purple and yellow walls then this is it. Dinner served in summer. Closed Sun.

Drinking, nightlife and entertainment

While most of its suburban neighbours retire early to sip cocoa, Nelson stays up all night and parties – at least on Friday and Saturday. Most restaurants and bars around town lay on some form of entertainment but for raucous boozing and some dancing head for Trafalgar Street or the half-dozen bars on Bridge Street between Trafalgar and Collingwood streets. Pubs and **bars** of all stripes often have **live music**, karaoke and DJ **nights**; check out the Friday edition of the *Nelson Mail* to find out **what's on**.

Mainstream **movies** play at the State Cinema 6 (☎03/548 8123), while flicks of more minority interest turn up at the cinema in the Suter Art Gallery, 208 Bridge St (Thurs–Sun only).

Founders Brewery Founders Park. Four delicious and potent organic beers are brewed on site and can be sampled at the café/bar, best on a sunny afternoon out on the grass. No need to pay Founders Park entry – just say you are going for a beer and they'll let you through.
Grumpy Mole 141 Bridge St. Cavernous and always open late, with DJs playing top 40 and pop in all the bars including the garden and early-evening happy hours and big video screens as well as free pool (Sun–Thurs 7–9pm) to drag in the punters. There are half a dozen broadly similar places within a short stagger if this doesn't suit.
Harry's Bar 306 Hardy St ☎03/539 0905. Smooth-operator cocktail bar attached to a delightful Asian restaurant, serving everything from a sushi to an Indian curry and local Sauvignon Blanc to a Singapore Sling. Closed Sun & Mon.
The Honest Lawyer 1 Point Rd, Monaco, 7km west of town. A comfortable, English-style country pub, with a beer garden overlooking the beach serving a wide range of local and foreign beverages and wholesome grub – live music late in the week, often Irish-style folk or covers.
The Maen Fiddler 145 Bridge St ☎03/546 8516. Best live music venue in town (Tues–Sat from 9pm) otherwise no pool, no TV, no stupid promotions, so good beer and a good sense of humour rule. Closed July & Aug.
The Oyster Bar 115 Hardy St. Tiny, chic bar serving the best gin and tonic in town and Californian-style sushi, a good bet for a quiet drink, cool sounds and a discerning crowd. Thurs–Sat only.

Nelson's festivals

The summer festival season kicks off with the **Nelson Arts Festival** (10 days in mid-Oct; Ⓦwww.nelsonfestivals.co.nz), presenting all manner of arts, theatre, music, writers' readings and street entertainment, much of it either free or costing just a few dollars. Headline events such as rock gigs and major plays command $25–65 ticket prices.

Nelson also hosts the **Nelson Jazz Festival** (5–6 days finishing Jan 2; Ⓦwww.nelsonjazz.co.nz) with musicians from around the country, and a New Year's Eve hard rock and metal event call **The Cusp** in Trafalgar Park.

Later, the **Nelson Summer Festival** (early Feb; Ⓦwww.nelsonnz.com/events) presents a series of events including street performers, Shakespearean theatre, outdoor films, lantern parades, a home-made trolley race and the like, mostly to engage and occupy holidaying schoolchildren and families.

The Phat Club 137 Bridge St ⓣ03/548 3311, ⓦwww.phatclub.co.nz. The main venue for touring bands and name DJs. Check the website or the door for what's on.
Sprig & Fern 134 Milton St. A villa in a suburban street converted into a cosy bar with open fires and a wonderful selection of locally brewed, unpasteurized Tasman Brewing Co beers – crisp lagers and wheat beers to a ruby porter and a delicious pale ale – plus scrumpy, cider and a selection of local wines. Daily to 10pm.
Victorian Rose 281 Trafalgar St. Olde-English-style pub with good beer, homestyle meals (including a $13 Sun roast) and plenty of live music: jazz on Tues, rock and pop sounds Thurs–Sat.

Listings

Automobile Association 45 Halifax St ⓣ03/548 8339.
Bike rental Stewarts, 114 Hardy St ⓣ03/548 1666, from $30 for half a day, depending on what type of bike you need.
Buses and shuttles Abel Tasman Coachlines leaves Nelson at 6.45am daily for Marahau and Totaranui, via Motueka, connecting with launch services deeper into the park, and operates a service to the head of the Heaphy Track; Atomic does a daily run from Picton to Fox Glacier via Blenheim, Nelson and Greymouth; InterCity offers daily services to Picton, Blenheim and Fox Glacier; and Southern Link K Bus goes to Motueka, Golden Bay, Blenheim, Picton, St Arnaud, Christchurch, Westport and Greymouth.
Car rental Summer daily rates start at about $60–70; $50 a day for week-long rentals. Try Nelson Car Hire (ⓣ0800/283 545, ⓦwww.nelsoncarhire.co.nz). Also Apex ⓣ03/546 9028; Hardy Cars ⓣ03/548 5125; Rent-a-Dent ⓣ03/546 9890; and Thrifty ⓣ03/547 5563.
Internet access Best rates at KiwiNet, 95 Hardy St. Also Aurora, 161 Trafalgar St, and Boots Off Travellers Centre, 53 Bridge St.
Library 27 Halifax St (Mon–Thurs 10am–6pm, Fri 10am–7.30pm, Sat 10am–1pm, Sun 1–4pm).
Left luggage Limited lockers at Boots Off Travellers' Centre, 53 Bridge St.
Medical treatment Nelson Public Hospital, Waimea Rd ⓣ03/546 1800.
Pharmacy Prices Pharmacy, corner of Hardy & Collingwood sts, open daily till 8pm, 6pm on Sun.
Post office Corner of Trafalgar & Halifax sts (Mon–Fri 8am–5pm, Sat 9.30am–12.30pm).
Taxis Nelson City Taxis ⓣ03/548 8225.

West of Nelson and the road to Motueka

Much of the pleasure in hanging around Nelson is what lies on its doorstep, particularly to the west where what at first looks just like standard New Zealand farmland turns out to harbour some excellent **wineries**. Here the vines appreciate the combination of natural spring water, New Zealand's sunniest climate and either the free-draining alluvial gravels of the Waimea Plains or the clay gravels of the Moutere Hills. Wineries are interspersed with the studios of a number of contemporary artists working in the Nelson region, many of whom exhibit in their own small **galleries**, showcasing ceramics, glass-blowing, woodturning, textiles, sculpture, installations and painting.

Almost everywhere of interest is located on or just off SH60, which runs north from Richmond towards Motueka through some lovely scenery big on sea views. You can sample the best of the region on an extended drive from Nelson to Motueka but the region is appealing enough to warrant a couple of leisurely days.

What follows is an introduction to some of the best places; for more thorough investigations equip yourselves with the leaflets *Nelson Wine Guide*, *Nelson's Creative Pathways* and *Nelson Potters*: all free and available from visitor centres.

Driving or cycling is probably the best way to get around, though you may want to join a **guided tour**, some of which combine the wineries and art galleries. Bay Tours (ⓣ0800/229 868, ⓦwww.baytoursnelson.co.nz) offer afternoon trips (4 vineyards; $75) or full-day tours (6 wineries; $95), which include an excellent lunch, or combination wine and art tours (half-day; $75).

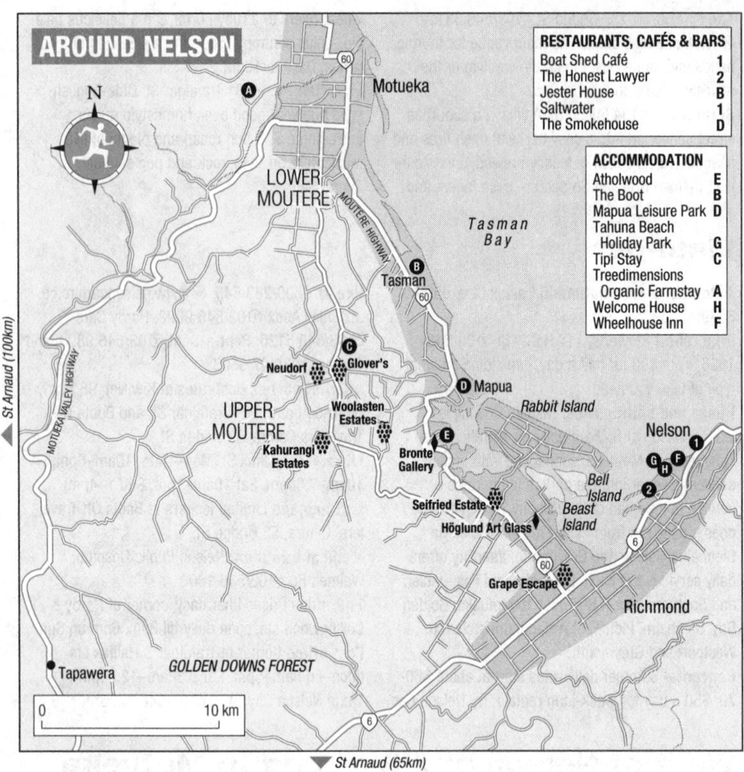

Around Waimea Inlet

Highway 6 runs 15km southwest of Nelson to Richmond where SH60 cuts north towards Motueka around the shores of **Waimea Inlet**. A couple of kilometres along SH60, the Grape Escape makes a good starting point for a wine tour of the region (see box opposite). Craft fans are better off 3km further along at **Höglund Art Glass**, Lansdowne Road (daily 10am–5pm; ⓣ03/544 6500, ⓦwww.nelson.hoglund.co.nz), a slick international-standard glass centre with a gallery (free) displaying an amazing array of its work, mostly tableware. The style is Scandinavian-influenced, which works best in the bigger, bolder pieces with clean lines and bright, unusual colours. Some pieces are valued at several thousand dollars but there are also seconds available, where minor blemishes get you large discounts. The glass museum introduces you to the history and techniques of handblown glass manufacture – partly through early works by Swedish owners Ola and Marie Höglund.

A couple of kilometres north along SH60, the Moutere Highway cuts left for **Upper Moutere** and a cluster of atmospheric wineries. Almost opposite the Moutere Highway junction, Redwood Road runs past the Nelson area's largest winery, *Seifried*, and on to picture-book-pretty **Rabbit Island**, one of Nelson's most popular beaches with golden sands backed by trees: note that the access road is barred at dusk each day.

Back on SH60 it is another 5km north to the **Bronte Gallery**, Bronte Road East (daily 9am–5pm), recommended for the highly individual work by internationally recognized ceramic artist, Darryl Robertson, all done on site. He also does notable abstract oils, a medium used by his partner, Lesley Jacka Robertson, whose work is on display. There's luxurious **accommodation** next door in the form of *Atholwood* (ⓣ03/540 2925, ⓦwww.atholwood.co.nz; ⑨), with swimming pool, spa, mature gardens and bush running down to Waimea Inlet. Self-contained and B&B rates are around $350 a night.

Mapua and the Motueka road

There's not much to **Mapua**, a couple of kilometres off SH60 and some 34km from Nelson, though there's much to be said for eating good fish on the ramshackle wharf looking across the picturesque Waimea Estuary to the north-western end of Rabbit Island. Head straight for *The Smokehouse* restaurant (book for dinner on ⓣ03/540 2280), a polished affair with plenty of waterside seating and mains costing $22–28. And for later, consider buying some of the excellent manuka-smoked fish (of several species) and a widely acclaimed fish pâté. For something cheaper, try the fish and chip shop (open for lunch and

Nelson region wineries

A pleasant day can be spent touring Nelson's wineries, perhaps stopping for lunch at one of several good restaurants, or picking up picnic requisites and heading for Mapua Wharf or Rabbit Island. They're located on the free *Nelson Wine Guide* which lists opening hours, typically daily 10am–4.30pm in summer.

Glover's Gardner Valley Road ⓣ03/543 2698, ⓦwww.glovers-vineyard.co.nz. A good small-output winery run by the slightly eccentric Dave Glover, once renowned for tucking a Wagner CD into every package destined for overseas. Wagner usually plays in the background while you taste (free) European-structured wines crafted to produce highly tannic reds (Pinot Noir and Cabernet Sauvignon) and acidic whites (Sauvignon Blanc and Riesling) that stand up for themselves.

Grape Escape Corner of SH60 and McShane Road ⓣ03/544 4054. Taste organic wines by Te Mania and Richmond Plains (50¢ each) at this complex which includes speciality food shops and schnapps tasting.

Kahurangi Estate Sunrise Road ⓣ03/543 2980, ⓦwww.kahurangiwine.com. Respected winery, offering tastings ($2, refunded with purchase) from some of the South Island's oldest commercial vines (though that's only 1973). Its stylish café is popular for alfresco dining which includes an antipasto platter for two ($36). Try the Rieslings, Chardonnay and also the estate's own brand of olive oil.

Neudorf Neudorf Road, Upper Moutere ⓣ03/543 2643, ⓦwww.neudorf.co.nz. Relaxed winery in a low-slung wooden building covered by vines with simple outdoor seating in the shade of tall ancient trees. It is a lovely spot for sampling the superb wines (free), some produced from the 30-year-old vines on site. Everything is available by the bottle and glass, so bring a picnic and relax in the garden with an elegant Pinot Gris or Riesling.

Seifried Estate Corner of SH60 and Redwood Road ⓣ03/544 5599, ⓦwww.seifried.co.nz. The area's largest winery, offering a wide range of wines to taste ($3, redeemable with purchase). Try the Austrian Würzer and Zweigelt varietals, unique within NZ. The large restaurant does platters, great desserts and meals for kids. Restaurant open for lunch daily and dinner on summer weekends.

Woollaston Estates School Road, Mahana ⓣ03/543 2817, ⓦwww.woollaston.co.nz. Swish modern winery landscaped into the Moutere Hills with tussock-roofed buildings where operations (primarily Pinot Noir production) are all gravity-fed. A huge steel sculpture welcomes visitors and the art collections includes works by relative "Toss" Woollaston (see p.514).

dinner, until 7.30pm) attached and search out one of the uncluttered bits of the wharf to sit and munch.

While here, stroll around the small galleries and the surprisingly interesting **aquarium** (daily Oct–April 9.30am–8pm; May–Sept 10am–4.30pm; $7.50), with its touch-tanks full of fish and some informative video and static exhibits. More exhilaration can be had with Mapua Adventures (Ⓣ03/540 3833, Ⓦwww.mapuadventures) whose **jetboat** at the wharf does a $59 zoom around the estuary (30min), stopping off along the way to identify some of the rare birds that inhabit the shores.

There's great beachside **camping** nearby at *Mapua Leisure Park*, 33 Toru St (Ⓣ03/540 2666, Ⓦwww.nelsonholiday.co.nz; camping $16, beachfront cabins ❷, motel units ❹) which includes the excellent, summer-only *Boat Shed Café* and bar. In February and March the place is **clothing-optional**, though plenty of non-nudists still visit at this time.

North of Mapua, SH60 runs 7km to the tiny settlement of **Tasman**, and the *Jester House* (Ⓣ03/526 6742, Ⓦwww.jesterhouse.co.nz; closed Mon–Thurs in winter), an eccentric and rewarding licensed daytime café popular with Motueka residents for its garden seating, rose arbours, maze, giant chess set and **tame eels** to keep the kids entertained.The food is all home-baked and reasonably priced, and the coffee is strong. It is all very tempting and there's even fairy-tale **accommodation** around the back in *The Boot* (B&B; ❽), an enormous red Mother Hubbard boot with a luxurious lounge area, a romantic bedroom upstairs and its own little garden patio.

Abel Tasman National Park and around

The **Abel Tasman National Park**, 60km north of Nelson, is a stunningly beautiful area of golden sandy beaches lapped by crystal-clear waters and lush green bushland, all interspersed with granite outcrops and inhabited by abundant wildlife. It comes with an international reputation that draws large crowds of trampers, kayakers and day-trippers from November to the end of March. Some contend it is better to come in early spring, mid-autumn, or even winter, but if you have to come in summer, don't be put off. Despite being New Zealand's smallest national park – just 20km by 25km – the Abel Tasman absorbs the crowds tolerably well and packs in some real beauty.

The goal of most visitors is the coastline. Some come to hike the **Abel Tasman Coast Track** with its picturesque mixture of dense coastal bushwalking, gentle climbs to lookouts and walks across idyllic beaches. Abundant water taxis allow you to pick the sections you want to hike and get a lift back when you've had enough. Others come for the wonderful **kayaking** around the mercurial coastline spending leisurely lunchtimes on golden sands before paddling off in the late afternoon sun to some campsite or hut. The two can be combined and you might even tack on **sailing** the limpid waters and **swimming with seals** to round off the experience.

The park isn't entirely devoid of habitation: a few dozen private residences are scattered around the more popular bays generally accessed only by foot or boat. That doesn't stop a handful of places operating as lodges, making overnighting in the park a comfortable experience. Of course, there are also DOC huts and campsites for hardier types looking for a more authentic taste of the locale.

With **advance trip booking** you'll be whisked from Nelson straight into the park obviating the need for nights in the surrounding gateway towns, though they're pleasant enough places to spend a little time.The service town of **Motueka**,

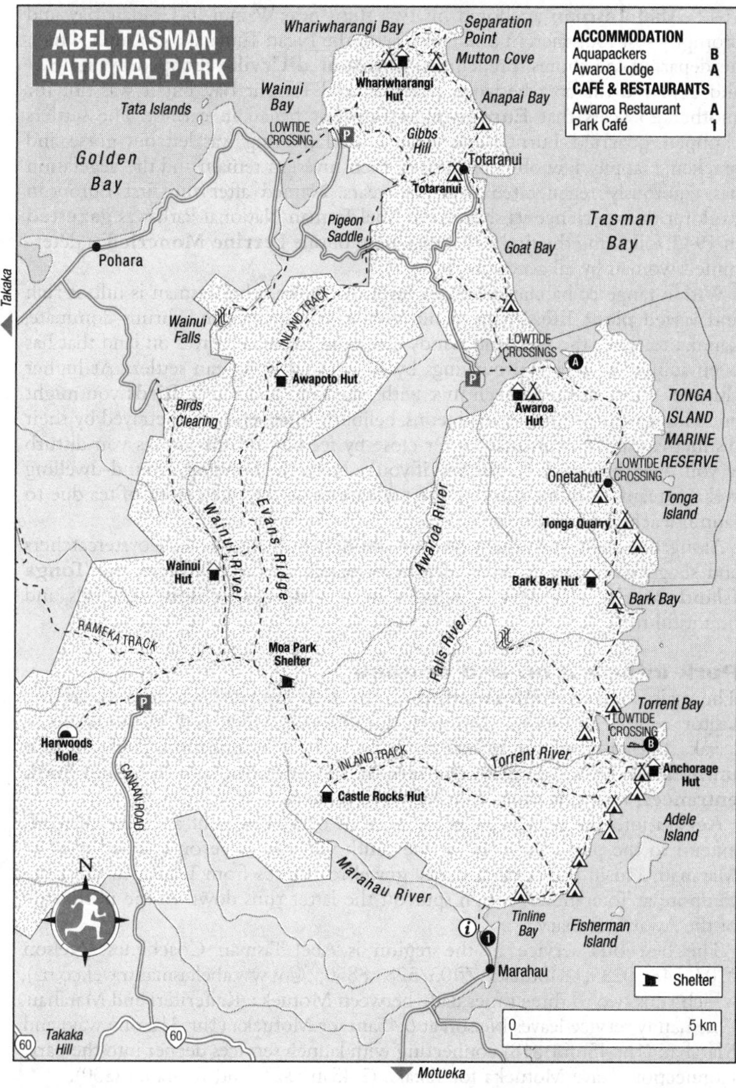

is good for general organizing, but trips mostly depart from tiny **Marahau**, at the park's southern entrance. A few trips depart from diminutive **Kaiteriteri**, which might lure you to stay awhile to relax on the gorgeous beach.

The northern reaches of the park are accessed from **Takaka** (see p.533) where Abel Tasman Drive leads to Wainui, Awaroa and **Totaranui**, all on the Coast Track.

Some history and natural history

Since around 1500, Maori made seasonal encampments along this coast and some permanent settlements flourished near the mouth of the Awaroa River. In

1642, **Abel Tasman** anchored his two ships near Wainui in Golden Bay and promptly lost four men in a skirmish with the Ngati Tumatakokiri, after which he departed the shores. Frenchman **Dumont d'Urville** dropped by in 1827 and explored the area between Marahau and Torrent Bay, but it was not for another 23 years that **European settlement** began in earnest. The settlers chopped, quarried, burned and cleared until nothing was left but gorse and bracken. Happily, few obvious signs of their invasion remain and the vegetation has vigorously regenerated over the years. Named after the first European explorer to experience its shores, the Abel Tasman National Park was **gazetted** in 1942, following the tireless campaigning of one **Perrine Moncrieff**, a determined woman by all accounts.

With a range of habitats from sea level to 1000m, Abel Tasman is full of rich and varied **plant life**. In the damp gullies, beech trees and shrubs dominate, kanuka tolerates the wild and windy areas and manuka thrives on land that has been subject to repeated burnings by Maori and European settlers. At higher altitudes, silver and red beech mix with rata, miro and totara. **Birds** you might encounter include tui, native pigeons, bellbirds (their presence betrayed by their distinctive call), fantails that flutter close by feeding off the insects you disturb as you walk through the bush, and if you're lucky the bobbing, ground-dwelling weka. Streams burbling through the park are invariably the colour of tea due to tannin leached from the soil.

Along the coast you might see the distinctive orange-beaked oystercatchers and shags, who dive to great depths in search of fish. Offshore, the **Tonga Island Marine Reserve** is famous for its **fur seal colony**, seabirds and bountiful fish.

Park information and access

The main sources of **information** on the Abel Tasman National Park are the visitor centres at Nelson, Motueka and Takaka, which will all book boats, kayaks, hut and camping tickets, transport and accommodation. There are also **unmanned** DOC **display shelters** at the Marahau and Totaranui **park entrances**, with tide times and safety precautions.

Access into the park is generally on foot or by boat, but a couple of roads extend to the park entrances: in the south you can drive on a sealed road to Marahau; and in the north a partly gravel road leads from Takaka to the large campsite at Totaranui. A rough spur off the latter runs down to the north side of the Awaroa Estuary.

The best **bus** service in the region is Abel Tasman Coachlines (Nelson ⓣ03/548 0285, Motueka ⓣ03/528 8850; ⓦwww.abeltasmantravel.co.nz), which runs two to three times daily between Motueka, Kaiteriteri and Marahau. One handy service leaves Nelson at 6.45am for Motueka (1hr; $12 one way) and Marahau (1hr 45min; $18) connecting with launch services deeper into the park. Connections leave Motueka for Takaka (7.45am; $21) and Totaranui ($30).

For details of onward travel see "Cruises, water taxis, sailing and seal swimming" on p.529.

Motueka

The modest town of **MOTUEKA**, 47km northwest of Nelson, is a great base for exploring the Abel Tasman National Park: there's a complete booking service, a range of accommodation and places you can rent hiking gear.

The name Motueka means "island of the weka", a reference to the abundance of these edible birds which provided sustenance for Maori. European settlers arrived in 1842 and established a horticulture industry based mainly around hops. Orchards and vineyards have since taken over, making this a good place for **seasonal work**, particularly from December to March: contact the work coordinator at Work and Income at 236 High St (Ⓣ03/528 4037).

The town and activities

Motueka is strung along SH60, with quieter streets spurring off from the main highway. Head a kilometre down Old Wharf Road to reach **Motueka Quay**, where the ghost of this once-busy port lingers among the scant remains of the old jetty and storehouses. Here lies the rusting hulk of the Scottish-built *Janie Seddon* – named after the daughter of Richard Seddon, premier of New Zealand from 1893 until his death in 1906. The tiny **Motueka District Museum** (Nov–May Mon–Sat 10am–4pm; June–Oct Tues–Fri 10am–3pm; $2) delves into the area's history through a few Maori and European artefacts, as well as the *Motueka Carvings*, a modern four-panel frieze in the foyer that skilfully depicts the livelihoods that have traditionally sustained Tasman Bay.

People are usually too desperate to get to the Abel Tasman National Park to bother with other activities around Motueka, but there's excellent **hiking** in the hills to the west (see box below) and the opportunity to go **tandem skydiving** with Skydive Abel Tasman (Ⓣ0800/422 899, Ⓦwww.skydive.co.nz). Based at Motueka airport, 3km southwest of town, it offers all the usual jumps ($219 from 9000ft; $269 from 12,000ft; $289 from 13,000ft) plus excellent scenery and helpful, friendly parachuting "buddies".

A less intense but no less rewarding experience is **adventure horse-riding** with Western Ranges Horse Treks (Oct–May only; Ⓣ03/522 4178, Ⓦwww.thehorsetrek.co.nz), located around 40km southwest of Motueka on SH61: call for directions. They take you to wild and challenging places often involving river crossings: half a day ($90; no credit cards) gives you a taster but for the full experience you really need a full day ($180), two days ($450) overnighting in a comfy hut with meals cooked outdoors over a wood fire, or, for those with loads of money ($2500), the intrepid ten-day trek.

Practicalities

Buses pick up and drop off on Wallace Street, close to the **i-SITE visitor centre** (daily: Christmas–Feb 8am–5pm; March–Christmas 9am–4.30pm; Ⓣ03/528 6543, Ⓦwww.motuekaisite.co.nz). Staff will help you organize your

Walks around Motueka

Some of the best subalpine hiking in the north of the South Island is around the 1795-metre **Mount Arthur** and the associated uplifted plateau, the **Mount Arthur Tablelands**, all detailed in DOC's *The Cobb valley, Mount Arthur and the Tablelands* leaflet available from the visitor centre in Motueka. Traditionally, few visitors have bothered coming up this way, so what company you find will mostly be Kiwis and wildlife.

The principal starting point is the Flora car park, on the Graham Valley Road that leads off SH61 south of Motueka. From the car park, commanding views of the lowlands spread before you with Mount Arthur dominating the southern skyline. It's only an hour from the car park to the Mount Arthur Hut ($10), from where you can continue on to the top of Mount Arthur in another 3 hours. Alternatively, head up, from the car park, to the 1448m summit of Mount Lodestone (2hr). Penetrating the moor-like **Tablelands** requires a little more effort, though you can stay at Salisbury Lodge Hut ($10), around 4hr from the Flora car park, and explore from there.

visit to the Abel Tasman National Park or the Heaphy Track so you'll have little need for the **DOC office**, on the corner of High and King Edward streets, 2km south of the visitor centre (Mon–Fri 8am–4.30pm; ⓣ03/528 1810).

You can rent gear for **camping** and tramping from most hostels or from SportsWorld, 201 High St (ⓣ03/528 9845), who offer packs, two-person tents, stove and pots and sleeping bags (all $10 a day each), and there are discounts for rentals over three days.

For a small town Motueka has a decent range of **accommodation** and there are enough **places to eat** for the couple of nights you might spend here. You might even want to catch a **movie** at the intimate Gecko Theatre, 78 High St (ⓣ03/528 4272).

Accommodation

Abel Tasman Motel and Lodge 45 High St ⓣ0800/845 678, ⓦwww.motuekamotel.co.nz. Old but clean and well-maintained budget motel 500m north of the centre, with fully self-catering units plus a range of lodge rooms with access to a large communal cooking area and lounge. En-suite lodge rooms ❸, units ❸

Equestrian Lodge Motel Tudor St ⓣ0800/668 782, ⓦwww.equestrianlodge.co.nz. Well-kept, renovated upscale motel with units backing onto a large grassy area with a pool. ❺

Hat Trick Lodge 25 Wallace St ⓣ03/528 5353, ⓦwww.hattricklodge.co.nz. Conveniently located opposite the i-SITE and bus stop, this modern hostel comes with high standards and a warm welcome. Along with a spacious and well-equipped kitchen and lounge, bike rental and free gear storage, there's a separate women's dorm and a family room with its own bathroom and kitchen. Dorms $23, rooms ❷, en suites ❸

The Laughing Kiwi 310 High St ⓣ03/ 528 9229, ⓔmarknwendy@xtra.co.nz. Attractive, friendly and central backpackers with a convivial atmosphere. spacious dorms and rooms, plenty of outdoor seating and a hot tub. Camping $15, dorms $25, rooms and en suite ❷

Motueka Top 10 Holiday Park 10 Fearon St ⓣ0800/668 835, ⓦwww.motuekatop10.co.nz. Verdant campsite with plenty of trees for shelter and clean, well-kept facilities (including spa pool) just 1km north of the town centre. Camping $34 per site, cabins ❶, kitchen cabins ❹, s/c units ❹, motel units ❹

Nautilus Lodge Motel 67 High St ⓣ0800/628 845, ⓦwww.nautiluslodge.co.nz. Modern motel, recently renovated, with tasteful decor, flat-screen TVs, DVD and nice courtyards on the lower units. One-bedroom units have full kitchen and spa baths. Studios ❺, units ❻

Rowan Cottage 27 Fearon St ⓣ03/528 6492, ⓦwww.rowancottage.net. Tastefully styled cottage with two polished-floor rooms set in an attractive garden where chickens lay eggs for the full breakfast (optional). One room comes with its own secluded deck with sunken bath. ❹

Tipi Stay Upper Moutere Hwy, 15km southwest of Motueka ⓣ03/543 2119, ⓦwww.tipistay.com. A great place to decompress, this alternative 15-bed backpackers offers accommodation in tipis and a yurt which operates as a double or family room. An outdoor bath ($4), indoor/outdoor shower and a communal fireplace give this place bags of character and there are organic eggs available. Closed June–Sept. Dorms $26, rooms ❷

Treedimensions Organic Farmstay Shaggery Rd, 10km west of Motueka ⓣ03/528 8718, ⓦwww.treedimensions.co.nz. Wake up to birdsong then breakfast on the deck of these attractive, modern s/c units with polished wood floors, comfy beds and stereo. They overlook an organic orchard with 45 types of fruit and 700 species and you can usually try whatever's ripe. ❹

Eating and drinking

Chokdee 109 High St ⓣ03/528 0318. Reliable Thai cuisine to eat in or take away. All the usual soups, curries and noodle dishes at modest prices.

Hot Mama's 105 High St. Motueka's pick for pizza or simply hanging out over a beer or a coffee either in the breezy, bright interior or in the patio garden. The music's always interesting and at weekends it is usually live with occasional appearances by touring New Zealand folk, jazz, acoustic and rock acts.

Muses Café Beside the Museum Building, High St. Small daytime café with good coffee, reasonably priced breakfasts, lunches and tasty snacks.

Swinging Sultan 172 High St ⓣ03/528 8909. Kebab takeaway with just a couple of tables out on the pavement where you can tuck into chicken and beef kebabs and falafel (all $7–9) plus good coffee.

T.O.A.D Hall 502 High St, 3km south of the town centre. Organic fruit-and-veg vendor with a flower-filled garden that's perfect for imbibing delicious home-made ice cream and good coffee.

Kaiteriteri

The tiny resort settlement of **KAITERITERI**, 15km north of Motueka and just south of the Abel Tasman National Park, ranks high in the pantheon of Kiwi summer-holiday destinations and is consequently packed to its limited gills from Christmas through to mid-January, and is busy well into March. There's an understandable appeal, with a golden arc of safe swimming beach looking out towards Tasman Bay where a couple of small islands add perspective. With Marahau (see p.528) becoming too congested for some tastes, Kaiteriteri has fashioned itself as an alternative embarkation point for Abel Tasman cruise, water taxi and kayaking trips.

Accommodation is very limited. Kiwi families flock to the beachside *Kaiteriteri Beach Motor Camp* (Ⓣ03/527 8010, Ⓦwww.kaiteriteribeach.co.nz; camping $12, cabins ❶, en-suite cabins ❷: bedding $5 per person) which is booked solid months in advance from Christmas to early February. *Kaiteri Lodge*, just back from the beach on Inlet Road (Ⓣ0508/524 8374, Ⓦwww.kaiterilodge.co.nz; dorms $35, rooms ❺), is something between a motel and an upscale backpackers with modern four-share rooms and tasteful en-suite doubles plus the usual hostel accoutrements.

Bellbird Lodge, Sandy Bay Road (Ⓣ03/527 8555, Ⓦwww.bellbirdlodge.com; ❼) offers two comfortable suites, welcoming hosts and great breakfasts, but for something astonishingly relaxing and unexpected, stay at *Kimi Ora Spa Resort* (Ⓣ0508/546 4672, Ⓦwww.kimiora.com; rooms ❻, suites ❼), a hillside complex set in pine forest on Martin Farm Road, signposted 1km back from the beach road, with heated indoor and outdoor pools. You can just stay, but the emphasis is on fitness, therapy and indulgent massage sessions ($90 for 1hr).

For beach views from the terrace and pretty decent **meals** ($19–26), go for the *Shoreline* on the main road; or go for the summer-only restaurant at *Kimi Ora* (Ⓣ03/527 8668) which is open to all and serves healthy, vegetarian **lunches** and à la carte **dinners** (mains around $25), with a small selection of wines and beers or range of juices.

▲Water taxi pick-up, Abel Tasman National Park

Marahau

About 8km north of Kaiteriteri, tiny **MARAHAU** is poised right at the southern entrance to the Abel Tasman National Park, something that affects almost everything that happens here. Most of the tours, water taxis and kayak operators working in the park are based here making this a very popular last or first night of civilization.

The beach road runs through the settlement to the **park entrance**, marked by an unstaffed DOC display shelter. From here, a long boardwalk across marshland leads into the national park.

Tramping and kayaking dominate, but Marahau is also a good place to go **mountain biking**. Abel Tasman Mountain Biking (ⓣ0800/808 018, ⓦwww.abeltasmanmountainbiking.co.nz) runs a fully guided half-day drip down the Rameka Track (see p.533; $145), offers logistics and bikes for a two-day trip into the mountains, and works with a kayaking company to offer a one-day bike and paddle combo ($110).

There are only a few **places to stay**, all geared towards the needs of park visitors and detailed below. The best place to **eat** is the licensed *Park Café*, by the start of the track (Sept–May daily 8am–late), which is legendary among appreciative walkers emerging from the park for its wholesome food, good coffee, restorative beers and range of delicious mains ($22–27) and desserts ($10).

Abel Tasman Stables Accommodation 100m along Marahau Valley Rd ⓣ03/527 8181, ⓦwww.abeltasmanstables.co.nz. Two in one: a two-room homestay (one en suite) plus three motel-style units. B&B ❹, motels ❺

The Barn Harvey Rd ⓣ03/527 8043, ⓦwww.barn.co.nz. A peaceful backpackers by the park entrance, with a rather public dorm plus several other dorms and doubles, some in a separate house beautifully sited with estuary views. Camping $13, dorms $25, rooms ❷

Marahau Beach Camp Beach Rd ⓣ0800/808 018, ⓦwww.abeltasmanmarahaucamp.co.nz. Unpretentious but well-kept campsite with tent sites ($15 for 1 / $25 for 2), backpackers $20, rooms ❶ and kitchen cabins ❷

Marahau Lodge Beach Rd ⓣ03/527 8250, ⓦwww.abeltasmanmarahaulodge.co.nz. Studio and larger chalets scattered about the lawns give a relaxed feel to this upscale lodge with outdoor spa, sauna and breakfast delivered to your room on request. ❺

Ocean View Chalets Beach Rd ⓣ03/527 8232, ⓦwww.AccommodationAbelTasman.co.nz. Wooden planking gives a kind of alpine-chalet feel to these ten spacious units, all with balconies and distant sea views from your bed. Studio ❹, s/c unit ❻

Old MacDonald's Farm Harvey Rd, by the park entrance ⓣ03/527 8288, ⓦwww.oldmacs.co.nz. A family-run farm with alpacas a host of other animals, a few cottages and a s/c studio. But it is primarily good for camping with a huge wooded area next to a couple of swimming holes. There's also secure parking ($5 a night), along with a well-stocked shop and gear storage. Camping $12, van sites $30, dorms $22, cabins ❸, motel unit ❺

Exploring the Park

There is an almost infinite variety of ways to explore the Abel Tasman National Park. It is beyond the scope of this guide to cover every permutation, but no matter what combination of activities you'd like to try, there's bound to be an operator who can oblige. Relatively few people tramp the **Inland Track**, most are keen to stick to the park's **coastline**, with its long golden beaches, clear water, spectacular outcrops and the constant temptation to snorkel in some of the idyllic bays. Also, near the coast is where you'll find a good array of **accommodation** ranging from beachside campsites to swanky lodges. **Water taxis** can take you virtually anywhere along the coast as far north as the lovely beach at Totaranui. They usually give a bit of a commentary along the way, though there are also dedicated **cruises**, some visiting the seal colony on the **Tonga**

Island Marine Reserve and **Split Apple Rock**, a large apple-like boulder that has split and fallen into two halves.

The intricate details of the coast are best explored by **kayak**, preferably on a guided trip or by getting a partially guided trip and then renting kayaks and setting your own itinerary. This is enormously popular, but even more people **tramp the Coast Track**, which can easily be combined with sections of kayaking, water taxi rides and even a little sailing.

Accommodation and food

Unlike many of New Zealand's national parks, the Abel Tasman offers a range of accommodation, some on private land, most of it on or close to the coast where it can be accessed either by boat or the Abel Tasman Coast Path. We've listed the best below.

There are also **multi-day all-inclusive** trips to consider. Wilson's Experiences (ⓣ0800/223 582, ⓦwww.AbelTasman.co.nz) run 2 to 5-day guided walking and kayaking holidays ($716–1545) with accommodation at their two trackside lodges at Torrent Bay and Awaroa.

Many people stay at the four **DOC huts** (Oct–April $30; May–Sept $12) that are spaced around four hours' walk apart along the coast. These come with potable water, heating, good toilets, basic but comfortable bunks and most have showers, but there are no cooking facilities: bring a sleeping bag, cooking stove, pans, utensils, food and a torch. Hardened trampers will want to camp at some of the twenty-one **DOC campsites** (Oct–April $12; May–Sept $8) strung along the coast, all either beside beaches or near the DOC huts (whose facilities you are not supposed to use); all sites have a water supply and toilets, but it means carrying more gear and you'll need an ocean of sandfly repellent. Huts and campsites both have a two-night maximum stay in summer.

Bookings are required all year for all huts and campsites and should be made at least a week in advance in summer. Book online (ⓦwww.doc.govt.nz) or at information centre's DOC offices.

The following places are listed from south to north through the park.

Aquapackers Anchorage ⓣ0800/430 744, ⓦwww.aquapackers.co.nz. Relaxed backpacker accommodation in made-up dorms and doubles aboard two converted boats moored for the summer just off the beach in Anchorage Bay: there's a free ferry from beach to boat. The package includes BBQ dinner, B&B, free use of sit-on kayaks and access to a pay bar. It can be a little cramped but the stillness of the park at night and sounds of lapping water make it worthwhile. Dorms $60, doubles ❻

Awaroa Lodge Awaroa ⓣ03/528 8758, ⓦwww.awaroalodge.co.nz. Nestled in the bush with great wetland views, this upscale lodge uses ingredients from its organic garden in its classy restaurant. Hikers and casual visitors can still drop in for a coffee or a drink by their enormous fireplace, but it is increasingly aimed at well-heeled guests arriving by water taxi or plane and staying in the delightful en-suite rooms and suites. Rooms ❽, suites ❾

Totaranui Campground Totaranui. The only car-accessible accommodation on the Abel Tasman coast, this huge campsite (room for 850; $12) is so busy in summer that places are obtained by lottery for Christmas to the end of Jan. A form can be downloaded from ⓦwww.doc.govt.nz. A separate section for track hikers usually has space, though you might want to press on.

Cruises, water taxis, sailing and seal swimming

Kayaking and hiking may be the bread and butter of the Abel Tasman National Park, but you don't have to be quite so energetic. Many are quite happy taking a cruise or perhaps hopping on a water taxi in Kaiteriteri, Marahau or Totaranui, riding to some gorgeous beach and getting another water taxi back. You might even include a little walking along the track or even stay overnight in the park.

Wilson's Experiences (ⓣ0800/223 582, ⓦwww.AbelTasman.co.nz) offer leisurely launch **cruises** from Kaiteriteri such as one to Totaranui and back (Oct to late April; 5hr 30min; $56). Their Seals, Bush & Beach trip (7hr; $53) adds in a visit to the seal colony and the chance to walk from Onetahuti to Torrent Bay. The launch calls 2 to 5 times daily at the beaches along the way on a regular schedule allowing you to plan your own escape.

If their timetable doesn't work for you, try a **water taxi**. Aqua Taxi (ⓣ0800/278 282, ⓦwww.aquataxis.co.nz) are fast, efficient and run their trips from Marahau to coincide with incoming buses and include a commentary along the way. They also have a fixed schedule and charge slightly less than Wilson's (Anchorage $25, Bark Bay $29 and Totaranui $36).

If you'd rather let the zephyrs of this coast propel you along, contact Abel Tasman Sailing (ⓣ0800/467245, ⓦwww.sailingadventures.co.nz) who offer small-group all-day **sailing** trips ($150) and sail-walk combos ($70) using the yacht to access a four-hour coast walk.

To spend a **night on a yacht**, join Nelson-based Catamaran Sailing (ⓣ03/547 6666, ⓦwww.sailingcharters.co.nz) who run an Abel Tasman Overnighter ($130) which includes a little sailing, a bunk on board, dinner and breakfast.

Abel Tasman **Seal Swim** (Nov–March only; ⓣ0800/252 925, ⓦwww .sealswim.com)offer an hour with these sleek amphibians (swimming $149, watching $70) accessed by an entertaining 45-minute water taxi trip. Swimming with seals can be a lot more fun than swimming with dolphins simply because seals are more manoeuvrable and curious. The water is usually crystal-clear and the impact on the seals is minimized by ensuring that you wait for the seals to come and swim with you rather than just leaping in and splashing about among them.

Kayaking

One of the best ways to explore the park's remoter shores is by **sea kayak**. It is hard to beat gently paddling along exploring little coves (and possibly being accompanied by seals or dolphins), stopping on a golden beach for a dip then continuing to a nearly deserted campsite where you cool your beer in a stream. Of course, you're not the first to discover such pleasures and in the height of summer over one hundred kayaks may form a brightly coloured armada at any one time.

Kayaking central is Marahau at the southern end of the park: the initial stretch north of here is known as the "Mad Mile", but congestion quickly eases further north. Only Golden Bay Kayaks (see p.531) work from the quieter north end of the park.

Half a dozen companies (four of them – Abel Tasman Kayaks, Kiwi Kayaks, Ocean River and Kaiteriteri Kayak – owned by a local Maori tribal corporation) offer a broadly similar range of one- to five-day guided trips, and "freedom rentals" where you are typically given some shore-based instruction then let loose (though you are not allowed to go solo nor to venture north of Abel Head at the north end of the Tonga Island Marine Reserve). Conditions are generally benign and suitable for complete beginners, though if you've any doubts about your ability you may prefer a guided trip.

Freedom-rental prices are quoted per person regardless of whether you paddle a single or double kayak. Some of the best deals are with Ocean River (ⓣ0800/732 529, ⓦwww.oceanriver.co.nz) and the independent Kahu Kayaks (ⓣ03/527 8300, ⓦwww.kahukayaks.co.nz), who might come in fractionally cheaper depending on your itinerary. Expect to pay $50–55 for each of the first two days, $35–40 for the third then $30–35 for each subsequent day. One-way rentals are available, with a fee ($35–50) for returning the kayak to base by water taxi. Most companies have a range of camping **gear rental**, will store your vehicle while you are away and operate year-round, though the range of trips is reduced in winter.

There is an enormous range of **guided trips** combining paddling with walking, water taxi rides, overnight stays visiting seals and more. A good all-round taster is Kahu Kayaks' full-day cruise (5hr; $127), which gives you three hours paddling the Mad Mile followed by a water taxi visit to the seal colony, a short coastal walk and a water taxi back to Marahau. The Sea Kayak Company (ⓣ0508/252 925, ⓦwww.seakayak.co.nz) offers a more leisurely variation with its Ab Fab Paddle and Walk (7.5hr; $165) where you paddle around the seal colony and spend longer walking. **Multi-day guided trips** let you ease into the pace of the park. Abel Tasman Kayaks (ⓣ0800/732 529, ⓦwww.abeltasmankayaks.co.nz) offer a two-day camping and kayaking trip to the Tonga Island seals ($370), and kayak and tramp trips, including a three-day gourmet-catered camping trip to the park's northern reaches ($540) and a lodge-based variation ($850). If you'd rather explore the much quieter northern section of the park around Golden Bay, join Pohara-based Golden Bay Kayaks (ⓣ03/525 9095, ⓦwww.goldenbaykayaks.co.nz), who offer rentals ($40 a day) and half-day guided tours ($70).

Hiking the Coast Track

The **Abel Tasman Coast Track** (51km; 2–5 days) is one of the **easiest** of New Zealand's Great Walks – one for people who wouldn't normally think of themselves as trampers. You should obtain DOC's *Abel Tasman Coast Track* leaflet, but the track is clear and easy to follow. Lack of fitness is no impediment as you can use water taxis to skip some sections or just pick the bits you fancy walking. Entry and exit to the beach sections are clearly marked and you are never more than four hours from a hut or campsite. In dry conditions you don't even need strong boots – trainers will do fine. All this combines to make the Coast Track extremely popular, especially from December to the end of February when some sections seem like a hikers' highway: heading for the section north of Totaranui can deliver a less frenetic experience.

The **route** traverses broad golden beaches lapped by emerald waters, punctuated by granite pillars silhouetted against the horizon and zigzagging gentle climbs through valleys. The main planning difficulty is coping with two **tide-dependent** sections at Onetahuti and across the Awaroa Estuary. Tide times will help you decide which way you're going to do the track – if there are low tides in the afternoon you'll probably want to head south, if they're in the morning, north. Before setting off you should also arrange your transport drop-offs and pick-ups (see "Park information and access" on p.524).

Marahau to Anchorage (11.5km; 4hr). The track follows a wooden causeway across the Marahau Estuary to the open country around Tinline Bay before rounding a point overlooking Fisherman and Adele islands just off the coast. As the track winds in and out of gullies, the surroundings are obscured by beech forest and tall kanuka trees until you emerge at Anchorage, with its hut, campsite and summertime offshore backpackers.

Anchorage to Bark Bay (9.5km; 3hr). Aim to cross Torrent Bay two hours either side of low tide or be prepared to skirt the bay (adding an hour) to reach the few dozen houses that constitute the settlement of Torrent Bay. Climb out of the bay through pine trees then meander through valleys to reach the gorgeous Falls River, crossed by a long swingbridge. The Bark Bay hut and campsites are 1hr ahead.

Bark Bay to Awaroa (11.5km; 4hr). After crossing (or skirting) Bark Bay Estuary you cut away from the coast only to return at Tonga Quarry where there's a campsite and views out to Tonga Island and its associated Marine Reserve. You soon reach the golden beach at Onetahuti. The stream at its northern end is tidal (cross 3hr either side of low tide). The track then climbs to the Tonga Saddle and descends to Awaroa Inlet and the settlement of two dozen houses and a DOC hut with a campsite alongside; *Awaroa Lodge* and its restaurant are also within easy walking distance.

Awaroa to Totaranui (5.5km; 1hr 30min). You must cross the Awaroa Estuary (2hr either side of low tide) to reach Goat Bay then up to a lookout above Skinner Point before reaching Totaranui with its great arc of beach and extensive campsite.

Totaranui to Whariwharangi (7.5km; 3hr). After rounding the Totaranui Estuary, press on over and around rocky headlands as far as Mutton Cove then wander through alternating shrubland and beaches to the hut at Whariwharangi. From here it's possible to take a short hike to Separation Point, where there is a fur seal colony and a good lookout, or to tackle the strenuous climb up Gibbs Hill for even better views.

Whariwharangi to Wainui (5.5km; 1hr 30min). It is an easy walk to the road on the eastern side of Wainui Bay where buses pick up, but it is also possible to cross Wainui Bay (2hr either side of low tide) or following the road around the bay. If you follow the road, you can also take in the short hike up to the Wainui Falls which heads off the road at the base of Wainui Bay.

Inland Track

The **Inland Track** (42km; 3–5 days) between Marahau and Totaranui is far less popular than the Coast Track and is strenuous enough to require moderate fitness and decent tramping gear. The route climbs from sea level to **Evans Ridge** past many granite outcrops and views of the coast: highlights include the **Pigeon Saddle**, the moorlands of Moa Park and the moon-like Canaan landscape. The track can be combined with the Coast Track to make a six- to seven-day loop.

Camping is not recommended on the Inland Track, but there are **three DOC huts** ($5; annual hut passes valid) mostly spaced less than five hours' walk apart. They are first-come-first-served but there is rarely competition for bunks. Water supplies and toilets are provided, but you'll need to take a cooking stove.

From Marahau to Castle Rocks Hut (11.5km; 5hr 30min) the Inland Track splits away from the Coastal Track at Tinline Bay and climbs steadily through regenerating forest to the **Castle Rocks Hut** (8 bunks) which is perched near rocky outcrops and has great views of the Marahau Valley and Tasman Bay. From **Castle Rocks to Awapoto Hut** (13km; 5–6hr) you climb steeply, followed by an undulating section over tussock to Moa Park shelter. The route then traverses **Evans Ridge** and descends to the Awapoto Hut (12 bunks). Accommodation is also available at **Wainui Hut** (4 bunks) an hour's walk off the main track.

From **Awapoto Hut to Wainui car park** (13km; 5hr 30min) the route involves topping **Pigeon Saddle** then dropping down before ascending to the summit of **Gibbs Hill**, from where you get some of the most expansive views across the park, and meet up with the select few Coast Track walkers who had the energy to make the arduous climb from Totaranui. Afterwards, it is an easy descent to the **Wainui car park**.

Golden Bay

Occupying the northwestern tip of the South Island, **GOLDEN BAY** curves gracefully from the northern fringes of the Abel Tasman National Park to the encircling arm of **Farewell Spit**, all backed by the magnificence of the Kahurangi National Park. With bush-clad mountains on three sides and waves lapping at its exposed fourth side, Golden Bay's inaccessibility has kept it outside the mainstream and it can seem a world apart. The coastline is washed by clear, sparkling water, creating excellent conditions for windsurfing, while its hinterland is home to the country's largest freshwater springs, **Te Waikoropupu Springs**, as well as a number of other curious geological phenomena.

Wainui Bay, just east of the main town of **Takaka**, is most likely the spot where Abel Tasman first anchored, guaranteeing his place in history as the first European to encounter Aotearoa and its fierce inhabitants. The isolating presence of **Takaka Hill** and lack of any road access from the West Coast keep today's bayside communities small and very manageable. This isolation goes some way to explaining the region's spirit of **independence** and self-reliance, and why the bay has lured such a cross section of alternative lifestylers, craftspeople and artists. Sunny, beautiful and full of fascinating sights, Golden Bay deserves a couple days of your time and has a knack of inducing you to stay longer.

For some insight into what makes the place tick, pick up the home-produced newspaper, *The G.B. Weekly*.

Takaka Hill

The only way to get to Golden Bay by road is on SH60 over the **Takaka Hill** that skirts the inland border of the Abel Tasman National Park. It twists and turns endlessly to get up to 791m and then down again, but it is paved all the way, and taken steadily is no problem. Along the way, viewpoints provide glorious mountain and seascapes from Nelson north to D'Urville Island.

After climbing Takaka Hill, some 20km out of Motueka, a short bumpy track leads to the **Ngarua Caves** (Oct–April daily 10am–4pm; 45min guided tours on the hour; $13, cash only), a celebration of tackiness with music to accompany viewing of illuminated stalactite formations such as the Wedding Cathedral. Tour guides also point out moa bones and regale you with an informative commentary on the caves' history and geology.

Half a kilometre further north, the twisting, unsealed Canaan Road runs 11km to a car park (long-drop and water supply) with access to **Harwoods Hole**, a huge vertical shaft 176m deep and over 50m in diameter, which links up to a vast cave system below. Its lip is reached by an enchanting trail (6km return, 1hr 30min; mostly level) through silver beech forest, then follows a dry rock-strewn riverbed to the hole itself dropping away in front. There is no viewing platform, so only the brave and foolhardy get much of a look down the hole. About 30min along the trail a side trail (20min return) leads to a **clifftop viewpoint** with views down towards the Takaka Valley and the coast. The marble under foot has been eroded into what looks like micro-mountain ranges. A spot beside Canaan Road 3km back from the car park is one of several sites in the area used by the **Lord of the Rings** crew, in this case a scene with Strider leading the hobbits from Bree through Chetwood Forest. From Harwoods Hole hikers can tackle the clearly signposted **Rameka Track** (5km; 3hr one way; 750m descent), which follows one of the earliest surveyed routes down into the Takaka Valley with superb views of the granite outcrops and the surrounding country. The Rameka Track is particularly popular with downhill **mountain bikers**, especially those with an amenable driver who can meet them at the bottom thus avoiding the slog back up SH60 and Canaan Road.

Takaka and around

The small town of **TAKAKA**, almost 60km north of Motueka, is set slightly inland turning its back on the crook of Golden Bay. It is Golden Bay's largest settlement, and one that's increasingly pitching itself to summer tourists while continuing to cater for the local farming community and barefoot crusties who emerge from their shacks and tipis to sell their crafts and healing services. Immediately north, **Te Waikoropupu Springs** emerge from their underground lair, while to the north yawns a considerable stretch of beautiful bay, running parallel to SH60 as it rolls into Collingwood and Farewell Spit. To the east, Abel Tasman Drive winds past the safe swimming beach at **Pohara** and a few minor sights before heading into the northern section of the Abel Tasman National Park (see p.522).

Arrival and information

Golden Bay Coachlines (Ⓣ03/525 8352, Ⓦwww.goldenbaycoachlines.co.nz) and Southern Link K Bus (Ⓣ0508/458 835, Ⓦwww.kahurangi.co.nz) both run from Nelson and continue north to Collingwood and the Heaphy Track, and east to Totaranui. Both **bus** companies drop off outside the **i-SITE** visitor centre (Nov–April daily 9am–5pm May–Oct Mon–Fri 9am–5pm Sat & Sun 9am–4pm; Ⓣ03/525 9136, Ⓦwww.nelsonnz.com), on SH60 as you enter town from the south. It carries all DOC information, handles bookings and hut tickets for the national parks and tracks, and organizes **rental cars**. Pick up the free *Golden Bay Visitors Guide* booklet and the *Guide to Artists in Golden Bay* (also free) pinpointing the artists and craftspeople who open their studios to the public.

Most of the hostels have free bikes for guests, and The Quiet Revolution, 11 Commercial St (closed Sat afternoon & Sun; Ⓣ03/525 9555, Ⓔquietrev@hotmail.com), **rents mountain bikes** for $30–45 a day (depending on where you're taking them) and can sell you *Fat Tyre Fun* ($2), containing over a dozen great mountain-bike rides in Golden Bay. **Internet access** is available at the library, 63 Commercial St (Mon–Thurs 9.30am–5pm, Fri 9.30am–6pm, Sat 9.30am–12.30pm), and at Unlimited Copies, 4 Commercial St (Mon–Fri 9am–5pm, Sat 10am–1pm).

Accommodation

Golden Bay is a popular holiday spot for both Kiwis and foreign visitors; as a result there is plenty of good-quality accommodation, from backpackers to fairly swanky lodges. Camping ranges from the enormous DOC campsite at Totaranui to wayside spots where you can park your campervan overnight.

Takaka

Annie's Nirvana Lodge 25 Motupipi St Ⓣ03/525 8766, Ⓦwww.nirvanalodge.co.nz. Comfortable and friendly associate YHA right in town with a homely atmosphere, a nice garden, a spa pool, rental bikes, and private rooms. Dorms $25, rooms ❷

Autumn Farm Lodge 3km south of Takaka off SH60 Ⓣ03/525 9013, Ⓦwww.autumnfarm.com. Charming gay-friendly lodge, on a six-hectare plot, with comfortable rooms, a big bathhouse and a laid-back (clothing optional) atmosphere. Also hosts a 10-day annual gay summer camp over New Year. Reservations essential. Camping $20, backpackers $30, B&B ❸

Golden Bay Motel 132 Commercial St Ⓣ0800/401 212, Ⓦwww.goldenbaymotel.co.nz. Well-kept little motel with off-street parking and spacious rooms. ❹

Kiwiana 73 Motupipi St Ⓣ0800/805 494. Beautifully kept and well-run hostel in a large villa where the Kiwiana theme runs to the labelling of the airy rooms – paua, jandals, tiki, etc – and collection of books in the games room where they have table football, pool and table tennis. Space for tents ($15) still leaves room for a free hot tub and BBQ area. Closed July & Aug. Dorms $24, rooms ❷

Mohua Motels SH60, Ⓣ03/525 7222, Ⓦwww.mohuamotels.com. Takaka's newest motel, on the southern entrance to town with attractive well-appointed units, Sky TV and in-room Internet. ❺

Rose Cottage Motel and B&B SH60, 5km south of Takaka Ⓣ03/525 9048. Three beautifully maintained motel units set in a large, lovingly tended garden (complete with indoor pool), plus a homestay option, all with friendly and helpful hosts. Very good value. ❹

Shady Rest 139 Commercial St ⓣ03/525 9669, ⓦwww.shadyrest.co.nz. Lovely new B&B in a historic house on the main street. Comfortable, wood-panelled rooms, a generous breakfast and an outdoor bath make this a treat. ❻

Takaka Caravan & Motel Park 56 Motupipi St ⓣ03/525 7300. Simple but good campsite close to the centre of Takaka. Camping $12, cabins ❶

Around Takaka

Adrift Tukurua Rd, ⓣ03/525 8353, ⓦwww.adrift.co.nz. Five gorgeous s/c cottages (and one studio) decorated in chic, modern style and all with direct access across lawns to the beach. All rooms have a sea view, making them perfect for a leisurely breakfast in bed. With double spa baths, free use of bikes and kayaks and a small penguin colony on site you may never want to leave. Studio ❻, cottages ❽

Golden Bay Lodge and Garden Tukurua, signposted off SH60 17km north of Takaka ⓣ03/525 9275, ⓦwww.goldenbaylodge.co.nz. Two fully s/c units overlooking a lovely garden and the sea, with easy beach access. Self-catering ❻

The Nook Abel Tasman Drive, Pohara, 9km east ⓣ03/525 8501, ⓔthenook@paradise.net.nz. A relaxed backpackers in a lovely wood-floored house where TV and the Internet are intentionally absent. Apart from the comfy dorms and doubles there's a fairly luxurious, straw-and-plaster cottage, rented as a s/c unit or two doubles. Free pick-up from Takaka by arrangement and free bikes once you're here. Dorms $25, doubles ❷, cottage for up to four ❺

Pohara Beach Top 10 Holiday Park Abel Tasman Drive ⓣ0800/764272, ⓦwww.poharabeach.com. A popular, well-equipped, beachfront holiday park with a broad range of accommodation. Camping $16, cabins ❷, en-suite cabins ❸ motels ❺

Sans Souci Inn Richmond Rd, Pohara Beach, 10km east ⓣ03/525 8663, ⓦwww.sanssouciinn.co.nz. Endearing B&B, offering a friendly welcome, in a mud-brick building with sod roof and handmade floor tiles. Most rooms share one large bathroom with shower stalls, bath and composting toilets, though there's also a s/c cottage sleeping four and an excellent restaurant (see p.538). Rooms ❹, cottage ❺

Shambhala SH60,16km north at Onekaka ⓣ03/525 8463, ⓦwww.shambhala.co.nz. Welcoming backpackers with a slightly spiritual bent, including yoga classes, located 2km down a track almost opposite the *Mussel Inn* (see p.537), from where free pick-up can be arranged. Dorms are in the main house, or there are spacious twins and doubles with good views in a separate block, with solar-heated showers and composting toilets. Closed June–Oct. Camping $15, dorms $26, rooms ❷

Totaranui Campground (see p.529). Large and popular beachside campsite within Abel Tasman NP, 26km east of Takaka. $12.

Waitapu Bridge Pleasant riverside freedom camping site with toilets and river water 4km north of Takaka on SH60. For s/c motor homes only. Maximum 2 nights. Free.

The town and around

Most of the action in Takaka takes place along Commercial Street (SH60 as it passes through town), where you'll find the **Golden Bay Gallery** at no. 67 (daily 10am–5pm; free), an art and gift store with wonderful silk paintings by Sage Cox. Walk through the gallery to access the **Golden Bay Museum** (Nov–March daily 10am–5.30pm; April–Oct Mon–Sat 10am–4pm; free), worth a peek even if it's only for the breathtakingly detailed diorama depicting Abel Tasman's ill-fated trip to Wainui Bay in 1642. The rest of the museum houses Maori artefacts, some fascinating geological and natural history material, as well as the usual mishmash of bits and bobs rooted out of attics.

Most of the rest of the diverting sights are east of town along Abel Tasman Drive (see p.536) but be sure to nip 4km north along SH60 to a turn-off for **Te Waikoropupu Springs** Scenic Reserve (aka Pupu Springs; unrestricted access). They're the largest in New Zealand, set amid old gold workings, regenerating forest and a vestige of mature forest. Here vast quantities of fresh water well up through at least sixteen crystal-clear vents. The two largest form the main pool and several more create Dancing Sands (where the sands, pushed by the surging water, appear to perform a jig). The colourful aquatic plant life can be seen by means of a large reverse periscope on one of the boardwalks.

Abel Tasman Drive

East of Takaka, **Abel Tasman Drive** threads its way past the small waterside settlement of Pohara then splits into three, each road ending at a trailhead for the Abel Tasman Coast Track: Awaroa, Totaranui and Wainui Bay. Many of the features are shown on the Abel Tasman National Park map on p.523.

The first point of some interest, just over 2km out of Takaka, is **Labyrinth Rocks Park** (daily noon to an hour before dark; $7), a family-oriented maze of naturally sculpted limestone formations in a garden setting. "The Keeper of the Rocks", Dave, encourages a light-hearted approach and bakes wonderful rock cakes.

Hikers interested in limestone formations should head for **Rawhiti Cave** (1hr 20min–2hr return; instruction sheet available from the Takaka i-SITE), its cavernous mouth hung with myriad pendulous stalactites, transparent stone straws and a discarded billy now encrusted in rock deposited from the dripping ceiling. To reach the trailhead, drive 5km along Abel Tasman Drive from Takaka, turn right into Glenview Road then left into Packard Road and follow it to the end. A poorly signed track leads to the cave: be sure to take a torch.

Two kilometres further along Abel Tasman Drive, follow signs to the wonderful **Grove Scenic Reserve** (unrestricted access), a mystical place that could have been transplanted straight from Arthurian legend. Massive rata trees sprout from odd and deformed limestone outcrops, and a ten-minute walk takes you to a narrow slot between two enormous vertical cliffs where a lookout reveals expansive views of the coast and beaches around Pohara. Self-caterers should drop in to the nearby Golden Salami (Ⓣ03/525 9385) on a local farm where a variety of delicious, totally natural **salami** are made from the aggressively healthy Sussex beasts with a handful of secret ingredients added.

Pohara, 10km east of Takaka, has a couple of places to stay (see p.535) and eat (see p.538) and a relaxing sandy beach but otherwise you'll want to press on past the former site of a cement factory, a jarring industrial ruin in such a wonderfully scenic spot. The ugly **Abel Tasman Memorial** at least offers great views of the coast ahead: Ligar Bay and **Tata Beach** with the Tata Islands picturesquely offshore.

Beyond Tata Beach signs guide you half a kilometre inland to a trailhead for **Wainui Falls** (40min return), reached by heading up through dense bush with the roar of the falls growing ever louder. Nikau palms shade the banks of the river, and a curtain of spray swathes the rather lovely falls.

The road now splits and deteriorates to winding gravel. The Wainui Bay road runs past the **Tui Community** (one of the last of several started in Golden Bay in the 1970s), and ends at the northernmost access point to the Coast Track. Other roads go to a car park at Awaroa Estuary, and the wonderful golden arc of **Totaranui Beach**. This is a common place to finish the Coast Track, right by the *Totaranui Campground* (see p.529).

Eating and entertainment

Takaka's Commercial Street has some good places to **eat**, and there are more a few kilometres out that just about justify the journey. **Drinking** and music tend to be confined to the big old hotels/pubs, the *Wholemeal Café* or *Mussel Inn* some way out of town. **Movies** are shown at the atmospheric **Village Theatre**, 34 Commercial St (Ⓣ03/525 8453), where the seating includes beanbags and there are cups of tea to sip during the films.

Takaka

The Brigand 90 Commercial St Ⓣ03/525 9636. Relaxed establishment, that caters for the rib-eaters and steak-lovers in town and has live music a couple of nights a week. Mains are around $25 and there's some outdoor seating.

▲ Grove Scenic Reserve

Dangerous Kitchen 46 Commercial St (☎03/525 8686 for takeaway orders). This peculiarly named café spilling out onto the pavement specializes in exotic pizzas, good coffee and muffins. Try the seafood pizza with mussels, squid and prawns.

Wholemeal Café 60 Commercial St. A Takaka institution that's endearingly sloppy at times, but it's always good value, and still way ahead of the competition. It also makes a decent spot to hang out over a coffee and cake. Return for pizza, colourful and healthy salads, assorted fish dishes and a good range of curries (all $17–23) in the cavernous interior or on the back deck. Summer evenings sometimes bring live music from local and touring bands. Daily until 7pm, and later in summer.

Around Takaka

Mussel Inn SH60, 18km north of Takaka. Do not miss this place – whether you want to eat, enjoy wine or ale (they brew their own), sit and read, play chess or soak up the lively atmosphere of a live band. The wooden building is adorned with local art and some clumpy but comfortable wooden furniture. You can always get a simple, fresh and wholesome meal; try a plate of the local mussels for around $16. Open daily, 11am until late.

Penguin Café Abel Tasman Drive, Pohara. Spacious modern, café/restaurant and bar that's worth the drive out from Takaka if only to sip a beer or coffee on the roadside deck which catches the sun most of the day. Well-presented dishes might include Anatoki salmon, seafood pizza and home-made ice cream. Mains $23–30.

Sans Souci Inn see p.535. This simple licensed restaurant has a daily set menu that can include hot smoked fish or beef fillet or a veggie option (all $27–30). There's also a choice of sumptuous freshly made desserts. Booking essential.

The road to Collingwood: arts and crafts

Many of the region's best **artists and craftspeople** live and work between Takaka and Collingwood, so the winding roads offer endless opportunities for mooching around country galleries armed with the free, widely available *Artists in Golden Bay* leaflet.

Following SH60 north out of Takaka look for roadside signs for Onekaka Arts, 13km north (ⓣ03/525 7366, ⓦwww.onekakaarts.co.nz), a gallery containing hand-crafted silver jewellery and scrimshaw created by Peter Meares, and jade carved by Geoff Williams. A little further along, Tim Jessep Pottery (ⓣ03/524 8663), specializes in large courtyard pieces, water features and very funky little dragons. Next up, Rosie Little and Bruce Hamlin run Estuary Arts (ⓣ03/524 8466), one of the best pottery and painting galleries in the bay. Their work features a mix of brightly coloured and more Pacific-influenced tableware and handmade low-relief art tiles, plus Rosie's evocative, almost organic, landscapes.

Collingwood and around

Golden Bay's northernmost settlement of any consequence is laid-back **COLLINGWOOD**, a useful base for tours to **Farewell Spit** (see p.539) or hikes along the **Heaphy Track** (see p.541). The town occupies a thread of land wedged between the sea and Ruataniwha Inlet and comprises little more than a store, a couple of cafés, a pub and a few places to stay. However, during the 1850s gold rush the site of Collingwood was briefly championed as the nation's new capital; street plans were drawn up but as the gold petered out, so did the enthusiasm. The details are spelled out in the diminutive **Collingwood Museum** (daily 9am–6pm; donation).

Some 7km southwest of Collingwood in the Aorere Valley, on the road to the Heaphy Track trailhead, is the turn-off for a striking natural sculpture: two plinths of limestone on either side of the road support bulbous overhangs, dubbed the **Devil's Boots** for their resemblance to two feet protruding from the ground, with tree and shrubs sprouting from their soles. Just before the Boots the road forks 1km to **Te Anaroa Caves** where there are guided tours (daily 2pm & 6pm; $25), bookable at the Takaka i-SITE and the *Collingwood Café*.

The last piece of living history from the Golden Bay gold rush is **Langford's Store** (open afternoons only) at Bainham, a further 10km inland. A combined general store and post office it was built in 1928 by the grandparents of the current owner, Lorna Langford. She has worked here since 1947 and has been postmistress for over fifty years during which time little looks to have changed. Wooden shelves are stacked with ageing goods, you can still get an assorted bag of sweets for 50¢ and the hand-cranked Burroughs adding machine is used to tally up your bill.

Practicalities

Buses from Takaka drop off in the centre of Collingwood, near the **general store** on Tasman Street. There are a few **places to stay** in town, all within

Farewell Spit tours

Two companies make an excellent job of running trips to the end of Farewell Spit (some 22km north of Collingwood). Operating since 1946, **Farewell Spit Eco Tours**, based on Tasman Street in Collingwood (Ⓣ0800/808 257, Ⓦwww.farewellspit.com), run the **Original Farewell Spit Safari** (4hr 30min; $80) which heads out along the sands of the spit to its historic lighthouse in a purpose-built 4x4. The trip comes with a bright commentary, peppered with local lore. During the day you'll see vast numbers of birds, seals and fossils, climb an enormous sand dune and maybe see the skeletons of wrecked ships if the sands reveal them.

To see the massive gannet colony towards the very end of the spit you'll need to take the company's more eco-oriented **Gannet Colony Tour** (6hr 30min; $110), which includes most of the above plus a 20-minute walk to the gannets. Trips operate year-round with departure times dependent on tides: check the website for expected departure times up to several months ahead. On both trips lunch ($10) is optional.

Equally professional and fun trips are run by **Farewell Spit Nature Experience** (Ⓣ0800/250 500, Ⓦwww.farewellspittours.com) who operate from the Old School at Pakawau, 15km north of Collingwood. They offer four-hour tours ($75) and a six-hour trip ($95) which includes a visit to Pillar Point lighthouse.

a couple of minutes' stroll of the centre, plus a couple of good spots on the road to Farewell Spit (see below). For cheap **accommodation** visit the *Collingwood Motor Camp* on William Street (Ⓣ03/524 8149; camping $16, cabins ❶, self-contained units ❸), or *Somerset House*, Gibbs Road (Ⓣ03/524 8624, Ⓔinfo@backpackerscollingwood.co.nz; dorms $25, rooms ❷), a low-key backpackers with estuary views, free breakfast and cheap bikes. Alternatively try *Beachcomber Motels*, Tasman Street (Ⓣ0800/270 520; ❹), which back onto the river estuary.

Collingwood has a decent cheap café, a pub selling bar **meals** and the *Courthouse Café* (closed Mon in winter; Ⓣ03/524 8025) where fine coffee, rich cakes and imaginative mains using mainly organic and local produce ($20–25) are served in the atmospheric 1901 courthouse.

North to Farewell Spit

Heading north out of Collingwood the road skirts Ruataniwha Inlet, and after 10km, passes *The Innlet* (Ⓣ03/524 8040, Ⓦwww.goldenbayindex.co.nz/theinnlet.html; camping $19, dorms $26, rooms ❷, self-contained cottages ❸, motel ❹), an excellent **hostel** offering spacious dorms and doubles in the main house and a collection of delightful cottages nearby, plus a BBQ area and several heated outdoor baths. Ride the rental bikes ($15 a day) to the base of Farewell Spit, go caving, rent kayaks ($35 a day), hike up through the on-site bush track or simply relax in the garden. Almost opposite, *Twin Waters Lodge*, 30 Totara Ave (Ⓣ03/524 8014, Ⓦwww.twinwaters.co.nz; ❼; closed May–Oct) offers comfortable B&B, a lounge with great estuary views, access to a sandy beach with cockle beds, and three-course dinner ($50) by arrangement.

The road now follows the coast 11km to **Puponga Farm Park**, a coastal sheep farm open to the public at the northern tip of the South Island. Here, the daytime *Paddle Crab Kitchen* café (Ⓣ03/524 8454; closed July & Aug) acts as the area **visitor centre**, complete with information on a mass whale-stranding in 1991 and a network of Maori middens. There are great views right along **Farewell Spit** – named by Captain Cook at the end of a visit in 1770 – which stretches 25km east, curling slightly south to follow the tidal flows which formed it. Debris sluiced out of flooding West Coast rivers is carried by coastal currents and deposited here to form an uninterrupted desert of sand which curls back towards Golden Bay, whose shores capture much of the windblown sand from the spit's exposed side. The whole vast sand bank is a **nature reserve** of international importance, with saltmarshes, open mudflats, freshwater brackish lakes and bare dunes providing habitats for over a hundred **bird species**: bartailed godwit, wrybill, long-billed curlew and Mongolian dotterel all come to escape the Arctic winter, and there are breeding colonies of Caspian terns and gannets, and large numbers of black swans. Sadly, the unusual shape of the coastline seems to fool whales' navigation systems and beachings are common.

To protect shipping, the original **Farewell Spit Lighthouse** was erected in 1870, from materials carried along the spit, and trees were transplanted to the area to provide shelter for the keepers' dwellings. Since rebuilt of steel and now automated, the lighthouse (and most of the rest of the spit) can only be accessed on guided tours from Collingwood (see p.539).

From the *Paddle Crab Kitchen*, short **walks** head to the outer beach (2.5km) and the inner beach (4km); both provide good views of the spit and its wading-bird population and offer an undiluted experience of this rather odd landscape. Away from the spit, walks head through the farm park to **Cape Farewell** (the northernmost point on the South Island), to the strikingly set **Pillar Point Lighthouse**, and to the wave-lashed **Wharariki Beach**. Here, rock bridges and towering arches are stranded just offshore, while deep dunes have blocked rivermouths, forming briny lakes and islands where fur seals and birds have made a home. Visit within a couple of hours of low tide when you can access some sea caves where the seals hang out.

Nearby, the well-signposted Cape Farewell Horse Treks (Ⓣ03/524 8031, Ⓦwww.horsetreksnz.com) offer some of the most visually spectacular **horse-riding** in the South Island – with Mount Beale on one side, views of Farewell Spit, and the Burnett Range forging away down the West Coast. Trips don't actually go onto Farewell Spit, but visit Pillar Point (90min; $45), Puponga Beach (90min; $50) and Wharariki Beach (3hr; $95).

Kahurangi National Park

The huge expanse of **Kahurangi National Park** was created in 1996, and encompasses 40,000 square kilometres of the northwestern South Island; appropriately enough, its name means "treasured possession". The park enfolds the exposed western side of the Wakamarama Range (among the wettest mountains in the country) and the peaks of Mount Owen and Mount Arthur. A remote and beautiful place with relatively few visitors, the only way to see much of the park is on foot. Some of the best of the extraordinary landscape lies along the **Heaphy Track**, though its lesser-tramped cousins offer equal rewards and more solitude. The best bases for visiting the northern section of the Kahurangi National Park are **Collingwood** and **Takaka**, from where buses run to the head of the Heaphy Track (summer only). **Motueka** provides access to the Tablelands, Mount Arthur and the Leslie–Karamea Track from the Flora Saddle car park; and the southern reaches of the park are best approached from Murchison (see p.546).

Some natural history and history

Geologically Kahurangi is an incredibly diverse area, comprising sedimentary rocks faulted and uplifted from an ancient sea leaving limestone and marble riddled with deep caves, natural bridges and arches, sink holes and strange outcrops. Over half of New Zealand's native **plant species** are represented in the park, as are most of its alpine species, while the remote interior is a haven for birds and **animals**, including rare carnivorous snails and giant cave spiders.

Around 800 years ago, the area was well travelled by **Maori**, as they made their way to central Westland in search of *pounamu* for weapons, ornaments and tools. From Aorere, they traversed the Gouland Downs, crossed the Heaphy rivermouth and headed down the coast, constantly at risk of being swept away. The first **Europeans** to arrive, via Australia, were sealing gangs in the 1820s that, within twenty years, almost wiped out the entire population. In 1856 the first **gold rush** ignited interest in the area and although it had petered out three years later, prospectors tarried on at the Aorere Gold Fields (now a reserve) and deeper into the interior. Ironically, now the area is protected it faces its greatest test as millions of **possums**, which invaded the area in the late 1960s, obliviously munch their way through the native plants and devastate the snail population.

The Heaphy Track

The **Heaphy Track** (82km; 4–5 days) is one of New Zealand's Great Walks. It can be walked year-round and links Golden Bay with Kohaihai Bluff on the West Coast by way of the northern reaches of the Kahurangi National Park. It is appreciably tougher than the nearby Abel Tasman Coast Track but compensates with its beauty and the diversity of the landscapes it covers: the confluence of the turbulent Brown and Aorere rivers, broad tussock downs and forests, and nikau palm groves at the western end. The track is named after Charles Heaphy who, with Thomas Brunner, became the first Europeans to walk the West Coast section of the route in 1846, accompanied by their Maori guide Kehu.

Information, accommodation and guided walks

DOC's *Heaphy Track* **brochure** is available from visitor centres and DOC offices, and includes a schematic map that is satisfactory for hiking, though it is helpful to carry the detailed 1:150,000 *Kahurangi Park* map ($19). Along the route, there are seven **huts** that **must be booked** and paid for all year round (Oct–April $20; May–Sept $10), with heating, water and toilets (mostly flush): all except Brown and Gouland Downs have cooking stoves, but you need to carry your own pots and pans. There are also seven designated **campsites**, which again must be booked (Oct–April $10, May–Sept $7), mostly close to huts (though you can't use hut facilities). Before setting off, you must book online (Ⓦwww.doc.govt.nz) and there is a two-night limit in each hut. There is nowhere along the track to pick up **supplies** so you must take all provisions with you, and go prepared for sudden changes of weather and a hail of sandflies.

Guided walks along the track (and elsewhere in the park) are handled admirably by the ecologically caring Bush and Beyond Guided Walks (Ⓣ03/528 9054, Ⓦwww.naturetreks.co.nz) who run five-day trips either driving back from Karamea ($1150), or flying back ($1325).

Trailhead transport

The Heaphy Track is particularly awkward in one respect: the western end is over 400km by road from the eastern end, so if you leave gear at one end, you'll have to re-walk the track, undertake a long bus journey, or fly back to your base at Nelson, Motueka or Takaka.

The Heaphy starts at **Brown Hut**, 28km southwest of Collingwood. Abel Tasman Coachlines (Ⓣ03/548 0285) run there from Nelson (departing

6.45am; $50), Motueka (7.45am; $41), Takaka (9.15am; $26) and Collingwood (9.45am; $22).

At the West Coast end of the track you'll arrive at Kohaihai shelter, 10km north of Karamea. Shuttle buses (see p.731 for details) run you into Karamea where you'll need to spend the night (unless you are flying back). Even catching an early-morning bus from Karamea and changing at Westport there is no guarantee you'll make your connection in Nelson and make it back to Takaka in one day. A better solution is to engage the services of Nelson-based Trek Express (Ⓣ0800/128 735, Ⓦwww.trekexpress.co.nz), who will run you direct from Nelson to Brown Hut then, several days later, pick up at Kohaihai Shelter and run you back to Nelson that evening, all for $160.

Flying also gives you the chance to return to your car the same day you finish the track: it is obviously more expensive but if you can get four or more people together the price can be very competitive. Remote Adventures (Ⓣ025/384 225, Ⓦwww.remoteadventures.co.nz) pick up in Karamea and fly to Takaka ($170, min 2).

Track transport only runs from late October to late April: in **winter** months *everything* becomes more difficult requiring taxis to reach trailheads.

The route

Ninety percent of hikers walk the Heaphy Track from east to west, thereby getting the tough initial climb over with and taking it relatively easy on subsequent days.

Brown Hut to Perry Saddle Hut (17km; 5hr; 800m ascent). A steady climb all the way along an old coach road passing the Aorere campsite and shelter, and Flanagans Corner viewpoint – at 915m, the highest point on the track.

Perry Saddle Hut to Gouland Downs Hut (8km; 2hr; 200m ascent). It's a very easy walk across Perry Saddle through tussock clearings and down into a valley before crossing limestone arches to the hut. This is a great little 8-bunk hut (no cooking facilities) where you might hear kiwi at night.

Gouland Downs Hut to Saxon Hut (5km; 1hr 30min, 200m descent). Crossing Gouland Downs, an undulating area of flax and tussock.

Saxon Hut to James Mackay Hut (14km; 3hr; 400m ascent). This involves crossing grassy flatlands, winding in and out of small tannin-stained streams as they tip over into the Heaphy River below.

James Mackay Hut to Lewis Hut (13.5km; 3–4hr; 700m descent). If you have the energy it is worth pressing on to a haven of nikau palms – and less welcome sandflies.

Lewis Hut to Heaphy Hut (8km; 2–3hr; 100m ascent). It is possible to get from Lewis Hut to the track end in a day but it is more enjoyable to take your time and stop at the Heaphy Hut, near where you can explore the exciting Heaphy river-mouth: its narrow outlet funnels river water into a torrid sea, resulting in a maelstrom of sea and fresh water.

Heaphy Hut to Kohaihai (16km; 5hr; 100m ascent). This final stretch is a gentle walk through forest down the coast until you reach Crayfish Point, where the route briefly follows the beach. Avoid this section within an hour of high tide, longer if it is stormy. Once you reach Scott's Beach, you have only to climb over Kohaihai Bluff to find the Kohaihai Shelter car park on the other side – and hopefully your prearranged pick-up from Karamea.

The rest of the park

The Heaphy Track is all that most people see of Kahurangi, but there are a number of other worthwhile **walking** tracks, all of which offer a taste of this unusual and still relatively unknown area. Visitor centres in Takaka, Motueka and Nelson have plenty of **information** on the area and can advise on the limited transport to trailheads.

Two quite arduous but rewarding tracks are the **Wangapeka Track** (60km; 4–5 days) to Little Wanganui, just south of Karamea on the West Coast, and the **Leslie–Karamea Track** (90km; 5–7 days), which links the Wangapeka Track with Mount Arthur and the Tablelands above Motueka. Trampers searching for something quieter than the Heaphy should pick up DOC's *Wangapeka Track* leaflet. The Leslie–Karamea Track starts at the Flora Saddle car park near Motueka (see p.524) and heads south along the Leslie and Karamea rivers and through beech forest before joining the Wangapeka Track near the Luna Hut. There are seven main huts (all $5–10) along the track, which is quite rough in places and should only be attempted by reasonably fit and well-equipped trampers.

Nelson Lakes National Park and around

Two glacial lakes characterize the **Nelson Lakes National Park**, around 120km southwest of Nelson, **Rotoiti** ("little lake") and **Rotoroa** ("long lake") nestled in the mountains at the northernmost limit of the Southern Alps. Both are surrounded by tranquil mountains and shrouded in dark beech forest, and jointly form the headwaters of the Buller River. Tramping is undoubtedly the main event and you could easily devote a week to some of the longer circuits, though short lakeside walks reward a briefer visit.

Anglers, kayakers and yachties mostly base themselves in tiny **St Arnaud**, draped around the northern shores of Lake Rotoiti 100km west of Blenheim. It is possible to stay in the mixed beech and podocarp forest beside the deep-blue waters of Lake Rotoroa in rather more seclusion hemmed in by mountains, but track access is poorer from here unless you take a water taxi across the lake.

The park's subalpine rivers, lakes, forests and hills are full of birdlife, but it has offered little solace to humans: Maori passed through the area and caught eels in the lakes, but the best efforts of European settlers and gold prospectors yielded meagre returns. Now, recreation is all.

St Arnaud

ST ARNAUD (pronounced Snt-AR-nard) is a speck of a place scattered around the north shore of Lake Rotoiti, with around a hundred residents but over four hundred houses, mostly used by holidaying Kiwis. It is where you'll come to stay and eat, though the choice is limited. Aside from beautiful lake and mountain vistas and a heap of walks (see box, p.545) there's little to detain you except the DOC **visitor centre**, on View Road (daily: Christmas–Feb 8am–6pm; March–Christmas 8.30am–4.30pm; ⓣ03/521 1806), which has all the hiking, biking, fishing and ecology information you could need as well as local accommodation and transport listings. The centre is guarded by a red statue depicting Rakaihautu, creator of the lakes. According to Maori legend, the area's topography and peppering of lakes is due to this famous chief who travelled the great mountains with his *ko* (digging stick), digging enormous holes that he filled with water and food for those that followed.

Rotoiti **Water Taxis** operate on Lake Rotoiti from St Arnaud to the head of the lake, ($60 for up to 3 people, then $20 per person; ⓣ03/521 1894), so if you fancy sections of hiking at the southern end of the lake there's no need to walk the whole way. Alternatively, you can pay them to take you on a scenic cruise around the lake, or they'll rent **kayaks** ($40 half-day, $60 per day), rowboats and canoes ($60 half-day, $80 full-day).

▲ Lake Rotoiti at dawn

Practicalities

The Southern Link K Bus visits St Arnaud on demand on its daily run between Nelson to Westport, though if there are two or more of you it may be more convenient to use Trek Express (Ⓣ0800/128 735, Ⓦwww.trekexpress.co.nz) which runs from Nelson to St Arnaud on demand for $30 a head. Once in St Arnaud, use Nelson Lakes Shuttles (Ⓣ03/521 1900, Ⓦwww.nelsonlakesshuttles.co.nz) for services to the Mount Robert car park ($10, min 2) and Lake Rotoroa $25 (min 3).

The hub of St Arnaud is the **St Arnaud Village Alpine Store** (generally daily 8.30am–5.30pm) a combined petrol station, post office, store and takeaway. Opposite, *Alpine Lodge and Alpine Chalet* (Ⓣ03/521 1869, Ⓦwww.alpinelodge.co.nz; dorms $23, budget rooms ❷, hotel rooms ❺) has **accommodation** in modern wooden buildings plus a licensed restaurant, bar and spa pool.

About 150m up the street is the pick of the local places to stay, the combined *Nelson Lakes Motels* and *Travers-Sabine Lodge* (ⓣ03/521 1887, ⓦwww.nelsonlakes.co.nz; dorms $26, rooms ❷, self-contained units ❹): the former is a mid-sized, neat hostel with some doubles, twins and shared rooms, kitchen, TV and a wealth of information; the latter a cluster of comfortable, fully self-contained log-built chalets next door. Both have access to a hot tub ($5).

Most of the year holiday homes are available for rent through St Arnaud Holiday Cottages (ⓦwww.starnaudholidaycottages.co.nz), and costing $90–120 a night for up to four people. There's a one-night surcharge of $10 and you'll

Nelson Lakes hikes

With 270km of track served by twenty huts there is no shortage of walking options. For **day-walks**, arm yourself with DOC's *Walks In Nelson Lakes National Park* booklet. The two **multi-day tramps** have their own leaflets supplemented by the 1:100,000 *Nelson Lakes National Park* map. These are alpine tracks so you must be equipped with good boots, and warm, waterproof clothing – it can snow in almost any month up here – and **crampons** are likely to be needed from April to November. Both tracks start from the upper Mount Robert car park, 5km from St Arnaud, which can be reached on foot, by car, or by bus with Nelson Lakes Shuttles ($10, min 2; ⓣ03/521 1900, ⓦwww.nelsonlakesshuttles.co.nz).

The following hikes are listed in approximate order of difficulty.

Bellbird Walk Kerr Bay, St Arnaud (10–15min loop; flat). Easy meander through beech forest alive with the sound of tui, bellbirds and fantails thanks to the Rotoiti Nature Recovery Project, an attempt to replicate the successful offshore island pest clearances by concerted trapping and poisoning. Several of these "mainland islands" have been set up across New Zealand since the late 1990s with apparent success. Visit in the early evening when the birds are particularly noisy and frisky.

Honeydew Walk Kerr Bay, St Arnaud (30–45min loop; flat). An extension of the Bellbird Walk, named for the sweet excretions of the scale insect that burrows into the bark of the beech trees, its produce attracting the nectar-loving tui and bellbirds.

Whisky Falls Mount Robert trailhead (3–5hr return, 10km; 100m ascent). From a parking area on the Mount Robert Road, follow the Lakeside Trail to these 40-metre falls. Often shrouded in mist and fringed by hanging ferns, the falls are particularly grand after heavy rain.

Mount Robert Circuit (4–5hr loop; 9km; 600m ascent). An excellent loop around the visible face of Mount Robert starting at the Mount Robert car park, ascending the steep Pinchgut Track to the edge of the bush then traversing across to Bushline Hut ($10) before zigzagging down Paddy Track to the start.

Angelus Hut Loop Mount Robert trailhead (2-day loop; 28km; 1000m ascent). One of the most popular overnighters, this loop follows the occasionally exposed **Robert Ridge** to the beautiful Angelus Basin with its welcoming hut ($10) and alpine tarn. Two common routes complete the loop: the exposed Cascade Track and the Speargrass Track, a bad-weather escape route.

Travers-Sabine Circuit (80km; 4–7 days; 1200m ascent). This major tramp is the scenic equal of several of the Great Walks, but without that status it is far less crowded. The track probes deep into remote areas of lakes, fields of tussock, 2000-metre mountains and the 1780-metre Travers Saddle. At the height of summer, the track verges are briefly emblazoned with yellow buttercups, white daisies, sundew and harebells. The circuit requires a good level of **fitness**, but is fairly easy to follow with bridges over most streams. There are six huts along the track ($10; tickets from DOC) and **camping** is allowed – but fires aren't, so carry a stove and fuel.

need your own bedding and towels. Comfy B&B accommodation is available amid beech forest and rhododendrons at *Avarest*, 1 Kerr Bay Rd (Ⓣ03/521 1864, Ⓦwww.avarestbnb.co.nz; ❼).

Finally, there are two DOC **campsites** (Ⓣ03/521 1806; $10–12), both close to town overlooking the lake with toilets and pay showers. *Kerr Bay* is open all year and has cooking facilities and a BBQ area; *West Bay* is only open from December to March.

Eating is limited to takeaways from the shop, meals at the *Alpine Chalet and Lodge*, and the excellent nosh at the welcoming, licensed *Elaine's Alpine Café* (Ⓣ03/521 1979), next door to the *Alpine Lodge*, which provides strong coffee, home-made cakes, all-day snacks and generous dinners ($20–24).

Lake Rotoroa

Lake Rotoroa feels a good deal more remote than the area around St Arnaud. Approached along the Gowan Valley Road which veers off SH6 some 20km northwest of St Arnaud, it ends near a self-registration DOC **campsite** (non-powered sites only $6; no showers), and the exclusive, 1920s *Lake Rotoroa Lodge* (Ⓣ03/523 9121, Ⓦwww.lakerotoroalodge.com; ❾), the preserve of dedicated anglers, stressed-out executives and jittery minor celebrities who can afford almost $590 plus each per night.

The lake itself is pretty and there are a few short walks but nothing like the range at St Arnaud. It is possible to follow the Lakeside Track all the way to Sabine hut and hook up with the Travers–Sabine Circuit, but the walk along the lake is dull and you're better engaging Lake Rotoroa Water Taxis ($40pp, min 3; Ⓣ03/523 9199) who ply the length of the lake. Nelson Lakes Shuttles (Ⓣ03/521 1900) run here on demand from St Arnaud to Lake Rotoroa ($25, min 3).

Murchison and around

MURCHISON, 125km southwest of Nelson and 60km west of St Arnaud is a small service town much favoured by hunting and fishing types as well as rafters and river kayakers. Numerous rivers feed the Buller nearby providing excellent white water and plenty of opportunities for bagging trout.

A couple of colonial hotels stand as testimony to Murchison's glory days, during a series of **gold rushes** in the district between 1862 and 1915 but the workings were in rugged hard-to-reach areas. However, prospectors flocked here, some paddling up the Buller River in Maori canoes in search of their fortune.

Tales of the gold days fill the **Murchison Museum**, 60 Fairfax St (daily 10am–4pm; donation requested), in the 1911 former post office with newspaper clippings, photographs and various oddities. There are also ancient telephone exchanges, gold-rush era Chinese pottery and opium bottles, and a bike belonging to Bob Bunn, local pioneer, longtime sawmiller and avid cyclist.

Murchison is one of the few places in the country with public **gold panning**: pick up a pan ($10) and the *Recreational Gold Panning* leaflet from the visitor centre which lists places to try your hand. The visitor centre also stocks DOC's *Murchison Day Walks* leaflet featuring the **Skyline Walk** (3km return; 1hr 30min) which climbs through the native forest to the skyline ridge above Murchison with views of the confluence of the Buller, Matakitaki, Maruia and Matiri rivers. The track starts from the car park 500m west of the bridge crossing the Matakitaki River, at the junction of SH6 and Matakitaki West Bank Road.

Once clear of Murchison, SH6 romps alongside the Buller River through the Buller Gorge to the **West Coast** town of Westport, a route covered in Chapter 12 (see p.525).

Rafting, river kayaking and jetboating

There's considerably more fun to be had getting wet on excellent **rafting** and inflatable **kayak** trips on the Buller, Mokihinui and Karamea. Wherever you go the scenery is breathtaking – and the water swift. **Ultimate Descents**, 51 Fairfax St (Ⓣ0800/748 377, Ⓦwww.rivers.co.nz), regularly run the Buller (Gd III–IV; 4hr 30min; $105), spending at least two hours on the water and including snacks and a post-trip hot tub. There are also gentler family rafting trips (Gd II; 4hr 30min; $95), and combo trips (Gd II–IV; 9hr; $195) rafting the tougher bits then kayaking down some easier sections. Check the website for helicopter-access and multi-day trips on fabulous West Coast rivers.

White Water Action Rafting Tours, behind the visitor centre on Main Road (Ⓣ0800/100 582, Ⓦwww.whitewateraction.co.nz), combine with Buller Adventure Tours (see p.728) for the "Earthquake Slip" run down the Buller ($110).

Those keen to learn **whitewater kayaking** or brush up some skills should visit the highly respected New Zealand Kayaking School, 111 Waller St (Ⓣ03/523 9611, Ⓦwww.nzkayakschool.com); four-day intensive courses go for $795 and include lodging at the school's hostel. Petrolheads will prefer Buller Experience Jet (Ⓣ0800/802 023, Ⓦwww.murchsion.co.nz) who do one-hour **jetboat rides** on two sections of the Buller (both $75).

Practicalities

Everything of note is on SH6 (Waller St in Murchison), or Fairfax Street that crosses it. **Buses** drop off at several places around town, none more than 100m from the **visitor centre**, 47 Waller St (Oct–April daily 10am–5pm; May–Sept Mon–Fri 10am–4pm; Ⓣ03/523 9350). Like many small towns Murchison has **no bank or ATM**.

Cycling is a good way to explore the area, perhaps using the free pamphlet from the visitor centre which details several trails fanning out from town. Bike rentals are available from *Riverview Holiday Park* ($15 for 3hr).

There's a reasonable selection of good **accommodation** and **places to eat** around town.

Accommodation

Kiwi Park 170 Fairfax St, 1km south of the town centre Ⓣ03/523 9248, Ⓦwww.kiwipark.co.nz. Family holiday park with all the amenities, an animal park and a full range of accommodation. Camping $11, cabins and motel ❶, kitchen cabins ❸, motel units ❹, luxury cottages ❻

Lazy Cow 37 Waller St Ⓣ03/523 9451, Ⓔlazycow@paradise.net.nz. Small, low-key hostel in the centre of town. Dorm $25, doubles & twins ❷

Mataki Motel 34 Hotham St, Ⓣ0800/279 088, Ⓦwww.matakimotel.co.nz. Clean and quiet motel clearly signposted about 1km from town. Some units have a full kitchen. ❸

Murchison Lodge 15 Grey St Ⓣ03/523 9196, Ⓦwww.murchisonlodge.co.nz. Very comfortable and convivial eco-conscious lodge with airy rooms, welcome drinks and a barbecue breakfast including eggs laid in the grounds where you'll also find a few cows and pigs. Free Internet and Wi-Fi. Private bathroom ❺, en suite ❻

Riverview Holiday Park SH6, 1km east Ⓣ03/523 9591. Simple campsite by the gurgling Buller River, much frequented by kayakers and rafters. Camping $16 for two, cabins ❶, tourist flat ❸, motel unit ❸

Eating

Commercial Hotel 37 Fairfax St. Fairly standard Kiwi pub with a straightforward drinkers' bar and a separate restaurant/café with reliable bar meals. Closed Mon in winter.

Rock Snot Café at the *Riverview Holiday Park*. Relaxed open-air café beside the Buller River with good coffee and a selection of pizzas,

Our account of the Buller Gorge and the road west continues on p.719.

enchiladas and toasted sandwiches. It takes its name from the slang term for the invasive alga didymo which spread through the river a few years back. Open Sept–April daily 8am–7pm, later in summer.

River Café 51 Fairfax St (in the Ultimate Descents Centre). This chilled-out spot does some imaginative and reasonably priced snacks and good coffee, as well as more substantial main meals ($18–30) on summer evenings.

Blenheim and the Marlborough wine country

In the early 1970s, **Blenheim**, 27km south of Picton, was a fairly sleepy service town set amid pastoral land: now it is a fairly sleepy service town completely surrounded by some of the most fecund and highly regarded vineyards in the land – the **Marlborough wine country**. In the intervening years Marlborough Sauvignon Blanc has helped put the New Zealand wine industry on the world map, and increased plantings have now edged the region ahead of

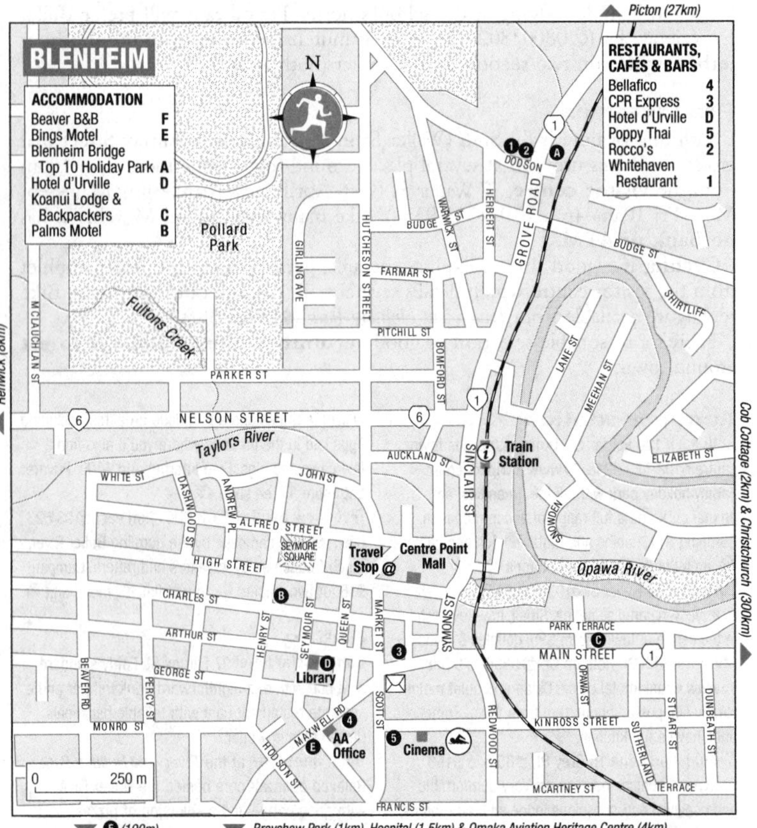

Hawke's Bay as the country's largest producing region with over fifty percent of the national grape crop.

Many wineries go all out to attract visitors using distinctive architecture, classy restaurants, art and gourmet foodstuffs. The profusion of weekend visitors from Nelson, Wellington and further afield has spawned a number of smart B&Bs throughout the district, trying to out-luxury one another. If this is what you're after there's little need to bother with Blenheim itself, particularly since most of the vineyards are closer to the small, unremarkable town of **Renwick**, 10km to the west.

Arrival, information and accommodation

Trains and long-distance **buses** all stop outside the **i-SITE** visitor centre, in the train station on Sinclair Street (Mon–Fri 8.30am–5pm, Sat & Sun 9am–3pm; ⓣ03/577 8080, ⓦwww.destinationmarlborough.com), which stocks an assortment of **leaflets** including the *Marlborough Wine Region* map, the *Art and Craft Trail* brochure (both free) and the detailed *Wines of Marlborough* Map ($2). The **airport** is 7km south of town, and flights are met by Airport Super Shuttle (ⓣ0800/748 885; about $20).

As befits a major wine region there's an abundance of high-priced luxury **accommodation** scattered around the district, plus more modest places in town. Budget places are thinner on the ground and most cater to seasonal workers, though there are a couple of good hostels, particularly *Watson's Way* in Renwick.

During the first full week of February nearly all accommodation is booked far in advance for the **festival season** (see box, p.553), so either plan well ahead or steer clear of the region.

Blenheim

Beaver B&B 60 Beaver Rd ⓣ03/578 8401, ⓦwww.beaverhomestay.co.nz. Attractive s/c unit 10min walk from central Blenheim, with a continental breakfast supplied. ❹

Bings Motel 29 Maxwell Rd ⓣ0800/666 999, ⓔemail@bingsmotel.co.nz. Classic older-style motel close to the centre of Blenheim with plenty of space and low rates. ❸

Blenheim Bridge Top 10 Holiday Park 78 Grove Rd ⓣ0800/268 666, ⓦwww.blenheimtop10.co.nz. Sited a little too close to the main road and railway line but central and with all the expected facilities. Camping $15, cabins ❷, kitchen cabins ❸, s/c units ❹

Hotel d'Urville 52 Queen St ⓣ03/577 9945, ⓦwww.durville.com. This former bank right in the centre of town has been turned into a chic and stylish small hotel with restaurant and cocktail bar. The best, and some say the only, place to stay in town and a good place to eat and party. Rates include continental breakfast. ❼

Koanui Lodge & Backpackers 33 Main St ⓣ03/578 7487, ⓦwww.koanui.co.nz. The pick of Blenheim's fairly poor crop of hostels; modern with a well-equipped kitchen and BBQ area, plus doubles, some en suite with TV. Dorms $23, rooms ❷

Palms Motel Corner of Henry & Charles sts ⓣ0800/256 725, ⓦwww.blenheimpalmsmotel.co.nz. Nicely decorated central motel, with Sky TV and a range of individually styled units, some with spa bath. Cooked breakfast available. ❹

The wine region

Cranbrook Cottage 145 Giffords Rd, about 9km northwest of town ⓣ03/572 8606, ⓦwww.cranbrook.co.nz. Romantic, picture-book 1860s cottage sleeping four, set in a tree-filled paddock amid the vines. The place is self contained and breakfast (delivered to your door in a basket) is to die for. ❻

Dry Olive Homestay 15 Dry Hills Rise ⓣ03/577 8648, ⓦwww.dryolivehomestay.com. Purpose-built B&B peacefully set among young olive trees, some 3km south of central Blenheim. The two bedrooms share a bathroom and living area with kitchenette and there's a separate three-bedroom family-friendly cottage. ❻

St Leonard's Vineyard Cottages 18 St Leonard's Rd ⓣ03/577 8328, ⓦwww.stleonards.co.nz. A broad range of former farm buildings beautifully converted into rustically luxurious s/c quarters, with access to a lovely solar-heated pool, free bikes, barbecue areas and gorgeous grounds amid the vines. Choose from The Dairy (4; max 2), Shearers Quarters (5; max 3), the Stables (6; max 2), the Cottage (7; max 3) and the Woolshed (8; max 5), which comes with an outdoor bath. Breakfast ingredients are supplied, often with home-laid eggs. 4–8

Uno Più 75 Murphys Rd ⓣ03/578 2235, ⓦwww.unopiu.co.nz. Run by friendly, former Italian-restaurant owner, Gino, who makes this homestay magical. It's hard to imagine being looked after any better, either in the 1917 homestead ($370) or out in the modern mud-brick self-catering cottage ($430). Breakfasts are great and excellent dinners ($80) are available by arrangement. Book in advance. 9

Watson's Way Backpackers 56 High St, Renwick ⓣ03/572 8228, ⓦwww.watsonswaybackpackers.co.nz. Easily Marlborough's best hostel: a very comfortable spot in the shade of large trees in a wonderful garden, with a public tennis court over the fence, snug rooms, made-up doubles, easy access to the wineries, low-cost bikes ($25 a day), an outdoor bath, BBQ and owners who can't do enough for you. Several buses pass the gate. Closed Sept. Tents $14, dorms $25, rooms 2, en suites 3

The Town

With the exception of the wineries, Blenheim is light on sights. Easily the most diverting is the **Omaka Aviation Heritage Centre**, 79 Aerodrome Rd (daily 10am–4pm; $18; ⓦwww.omaka.org.nz), located beside an airfield 4km southwest of Blenheim. Two large hangars contain twenty-one World War I planes, some original and still airworthy, others authentic replicas, and many set in amazingly realistic dioramas made by film-maker Peter Jackson's Weta Workshop. Indeed, Jackson, who is a huge World War I buff, owns much of the collection and chairs the trust which set the place up and will guide its growth over the next few years. The planes are fine examples of their kind and some, such as the German Halberstadt D.IV and the American Airco DHS, are unique. Check out the crash-landing scene depicting the death of Manfred von Richthofen complete with an original fabric cross from the plane, and a group of Australian soldiers souveniring his boots. A collection of the Red Baron's own memorabilia is displayed nearby. Elsewhere there's the flight suit of US ace Eddie Rickenbacker and a mass of models, badges and love letters – the collection of an obsessive. Everything is made more poignant when you chat to the guides and interpreters, who are themselves mostly former aviators.

Of the remaining sights there's just a lacklustre reconstruction of an early settlers' community and a collection of vintage farm machinery and vehicles out in **Brayshaw Park**, off New Renwick Road, 2.5km south of the town centre (daily 10am–4pm; museum $5), and the tiny 1860s **Cob Cottage**, on SH1, 3km southeast of town (Sat 10am–4pm, Sun 1–4pm; donations requested), which has been restored to house yet more displays on the lives of early settlers.

Wine country

The gravel plains that flank the Wairau River around the towns of Blenheim and Renwick make up some of New Zealand's most prized **wine country**. The region, sheltered by the protective hills of the Richmond Range, basks in around 2400 hours of sunshine a year making it perfect for ripening the grapes for its esteemed Sauvignon Blanc. Chardonnay and Pinot Noir grapes also grow well (almost guaranteeing tasty bubbly), and the region is gaining a reputation for its light and golden olive oil.

Over seventy wineries call this home, most of them accessible for cellar-door sales and **tasting** (either free or for a small charge, which is often deducted from any subsequent purchases). Some add a short tour, tack on a restaurant or even link up with outlets hawking olive oil, fruit preserves and the like. Most of the notable wineries are around Renwick or immediately north along Raupara

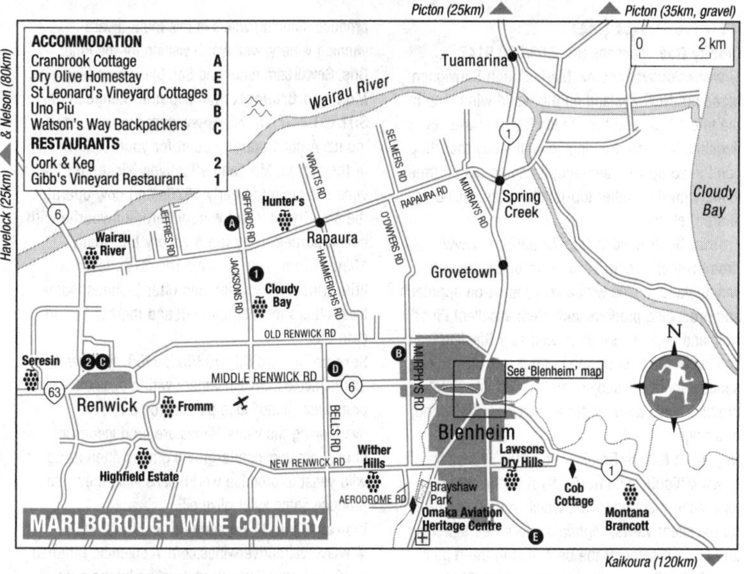

Road, all listed on the free *Marlborough Wine Region* sheet (along with their opening hours and facilities), and most also feature on the more detailed *Marlborough Wineries and Wines* fold-out map ($2). **Opening hours** are generally 10am–4pm daily, though often much reduced in winter.

Armed with these you're ready for a day among the vines, preferably with lunch at one of the winery restaurants. Few wines are available for much under $20 a bottle, and wineries like to show off with their restaurants, so although it will almost certainly be a pleasurable experience it won't be cheap. And don't be tempted to cram too many into a day; most vineyards are more suited to leisurely vineyard tastings than whistle-stop tours.

There's benefit (certainly for the driver) in taking an organized **wine tour**. Some of the cheapest are with Marlborough Wine Tours (ⓣ03/578 9515, ⓦwww.marlboroughwinetours.co.nz) who offer trips of three hours ($43), four hours ($54) and seven hours ($75) with time for lunch (not included) at one of the wineries. Sounds Connection (ⓣ0800/742 866, ⓦwww.soundsconnection.co.nz) specialize in half-day tours visiting four or five wineries ($59), a full-day circuit of six or seven wineries ($79, lunch at your own expense), and a full-day gourmet tour ($179) including lunch with matched wines and a visit to a chocolate factory. Tours pick up at accommodation around Blenheim.

Rental bikes are also a possibility, though the wineries are fairly spread out and you may find that after a couple of visits your desire to cycle diminishes rapidly. Spokeman Cycles, 61 Queen St (ⓣ0800/422 453), offer rental for $40 a day, while Wine Tours by Bike (ⓣ03/577 6954, ⓦwww.winetoursbybike.co.nz) charge $55 for the day's bike rental but include accommodation pick-ups and will come and rescue you if you have some mechanical breakdown.

Most of the wineries will **ship cases** of wine anywhere in the world, but shipping costs and high import duties mean that it seldom works out good value: expect $155 a case to the UK, $270 to the US. Buy what you can drink and carry, and when you know what you like, enquire as to who distributes those wines in your home country.

The wineries

Cloudy Bay Jacksons Rd ⓣ03/520 9147, ⓦwww.cloudybay.co.nz. Marlborough Sauvignon Blanc put New Zealand on the world wine map in the late 1980s and the Cloudy Bay Sav was its flagship. It is still drinking so well today that they can't keep up with demand; it can be tasted (free) along with their other top-notch wines, including limited releases.

Fromm Godfrey Rd ⓣ03/572 9355, ⓦwww.frommwineries.com. A vineyard that is turning winemakers' heads with a very hands-on approach and producing predominantly red: excellent Pinot Noir, and peppery Syrah as well as a Riesling with echoes of the best German efforts. Visit if you're serious about the subject and you'll taste (free) a product that's a match for anywhere in the world, at a price.

Highfield Estate Brookby Rd ⓣ03/572 9244, ⓦwww.highfield.co.nz. Easily recognizable by its Tuscan-inspired tower, which you can climb for excellent views, *Highfield* offers free tastings and lays on some of the best food in the region, with $19–26 mains, antipasto platters ($50) that will easily feed two and delectable desserts ($10), all served inside or on the terrace overlooking the vines.

Hunter's Rapaura Rd ⓣ03/572 8489, ⓦwww.hunters.co.nz. Jane Hunter is recognized as one of the world's top female winemakers. Drop by to taste, visit the art gallery or eat in the classy restaurant.

Lawsons Dry Hills Alabama Rd ⓣ03/578 7674, ⓦwww.lawsonsdryhills.co.nz. Established vines produce stunning wines in this multi-award-winning winery, well worth visiting for the Pinot Gris, Gewürtztraminer and Sav Blanc if nothing else.

Montana Brancott 5km south of Blenheim on SH1 ⓣ03/577 5775, ⓦwww.montanawines.co.nz. A good starting point for your exploration of the region. Montana effectively kicked off the wine region in the early 1970s and now operate the country's largest winery here, a favourite with coach parties. They run a winery tour (daily 10am, 11am, 1pm & 3pm; 1hr; $15), teach a little wine appreciation and offer tastings (some free, others for a small fee), and there's a good café too.

Seresin Bedford Rd ⓣ03/572 9408, ⓦwww.seresin.co.nz. Stylish winery with a distinctive primitivist "hand" logo perched on a rise overlooking the vines. Wines are produced from largely organic, estate-grown grapes often using wild yeast to produce world-class vino, they also produce some killer olive oil.

Wairau River 11 Rapaura Rd ⓣ03/572 9800, ⓦwww.wairauriverwines.com. A splendid rammed earth and rimu timber construction by the river, at the foot of the Richmond mountain range. Free tastings and fabulous lunches served under shady vines in summer and by the fire in winter.

Wither Hills 211 New Renwick Rd ⓣ03/578 4039, ⓦwww.witherhills.co.nz. A striking, modern roadside winery, all concrete and tussock. Nip in for free tastings of the popular Sauvignon Blanc, Chardonnay and Pinot Noir along with a sweet but clean dessert wine only available at the cellar door.

Eating, drinking and entertainment

A few hours spent visiting vineyards should be accompanied by **lunch** at one of the wineries – especially *Highfield Estate* and *Wairau River* (see p. 000). A few are also open in the evenings, but for dinner you may prefer to head into Blenheim where there's a reasonable choice of **restaurants**.

For entertainment, there's the Top Town Cinema 3, 4 Kinross St, Blenheim (ⓣ03/577 8273).

Bellafico 17 Maxwell Rd, Blenheim ⓣ03/577 6072. Relaxed and fairly upscale restaurant with relatively traditional à la carte dining (mains $23–30) made more affordable by the three-course signature menu ($49) which has a choice of just two mains. Closed Sun.

CPR Express 1c Main St, Blenheim. The region's top roaster delivers primo espresso alongside the panini, frittata slices and cakes in modern surroundings. Closed Sun.

Cork and Keg Inkerman St, Renwick. Friendly English-style local with a stone hearth, traditional games like dominoes and a cursory nod to modern sporting coverage, a big-screen TV. The beer is made to order, in Westport, and includes excellent natural brews, dark, draught, lager and old English Hurricane. All day pub meals around $15.

Gibb's Vineyard Restaurant 258 Jacksons Rd, 7km northwest of Blenheim ⓣ03/572 8048, ⓦwww.gibbs-restaurant.co.nz. Superb restaurant in a former winery building with vines all around and tables set with white linen and highly polished cutlery. You might start with celeriac and ricotta ravioli ($18) and follow with rack of lamb ($38) or

Marlborough festivals

Blenheim springs to life during the first full week of February. On the first Saturday, the **Blues, Brews and BBQ Festival** (Ⓦwww.bluesbrews.co.nz) kicks off proceedings at the Blenheim A&P Showground with a combination of musicians and brewers parading their wares from all over the country. This is mixed in a heady cocktail with some good old-fashioned Kiwi snags, kebabs and burgers, as well as some more adventurous fare. Well worth a look if you're in party mode.

Various arts and crafts demonstrations, exhibitions, markets and special events pad out the next week, but Blenheim's big event is the annual **Wine Marlborough Festival** ($40, includes a glass for slurping; noon–8pm; Ⓦwww.wine-marlborough-festival.co.nz) on the second Saturday. Around 10,000 people flock to the *Montana Brancott* winery, where a vast field of marquees, containing local wines and food for purchase and consumption, throb with the sound of live music and revelry.

Deluxe Travel Line run **buses** ($6) to the festival site from the town and the airport, as well as from Picton ($16).

veal with lemons and chorizo ($35). The wine list leans heavily on Marlborough with a few quality Central Otago Chardonnays and Pinot Noirs. Dinner only and closed Sun & Mon from May–Oct.

Hotel d'Urville 52 Queen St, Blenheim ⓣ03/577 9945. A classy restaurant with stylish modern decor and exemplary cuisine, making the best of seasonal produce, so expect something special. Be prepared to pay around $30 for mains and book in advance.

Poppy Thai 31 Scott St ⓣ03/579 4496. The service is sloppy and the decor is nothing to shout about but it is cheap and the meals are always tasty and delicately spiced. Lunch specials cost $8–10.

Rocco's 5 Dodson St, Blenheim ⓣ03/578 6940. Enjoyable authentic Italian restaurant that could unabashedly sit on a New York or Rome street. For a blowout, order the awesome chicken Kiev alla Rocco – chicken breast filled with ham, garlic butter and cheese, all wrapped in a veal schnitzel ($26) or the fillet alla Rocco. Fresh pasta is made daily. Dinner only, closed Sun.

Whitehaven Restaurant & Black Creek Bar and Café 1 Dodson St, Blenheim ⓣ03/577 6634. Upstairs, the à la carte restaurant specializes in fresh, high-quality produce with mains a little under $30, and some scrumptious desserts; downstairs, the relaxed pizzeria dishes up tasty pizzas and serves the Renaissance beers brewed on site – Scotch ale, porter and a superbly hoppy American-style pale ale.

Listings

Automobile Association 23 Maxwell Rd ⓣ03/578 3399.

Bike rental See p.551.

Internet access Computers and Wi-Fi at the i-SITE, and also at the Travel Stop Cyber Café, 17 Market St (Mon–Sat 10am–9pm).

Medical treatment Wairau Hospital, Hospital Rd (ⓣ03/520 9999), about 3km southwest of town.

Post office Central post office, corner of Scott & Main sts (Mon–Fri 8.30am–5.15pm, Sat 9.30am–12.30pm).

Swimming Pool Kinross St, ⓣ03/577 8300 (Mon–Thurs 6am–8pm, Thurs & Fri 6am–6pm, Sat & Sun 10am–5pm).

Taxis Marlborough Taxis ⓣ03/577 5511.

South from Blenheim: the Kaikoura Coast

From Blenheim it is a 130-kilometre run down between the coast and the brooding Seaward Kaikoura Range to the next place of any consequence, Kaikoura. It can be done in an hour and a half, but is best if allotted more time for frequent stops along some gorgeous stretches of coastline. Around 20km south of Blenheim a sign points inland along the Awatere Valley, mostly of interest for the few weeks each year when it provides access through **Molesworth Station** to **Hanmer Springs** (see box below).

Driving through Molesworth Station

Timing is everything if you want to drive the Acheron Road through **Molesworth Station**, at 180,000 hectares New Zealand's largest farm. The central 59-kilometre section of road is only open to traffic for a few weeks each summer (late Dec to March). It is an impressive run through New Zealand's most accessible high country passing historic cob houses with towering mountains all around. The drive from Blenheim to Hanmer Springs (190km) takes over five hours, a couple of them on gravel, and since there are no services make sure your rig is in good nick and the tank topped up. **Camping** is only permitted at *Molesworth Cob Cottage* and *Acheron Accommodation House* (both $6). For the latest information obtain DOC's *Molesworth* leaflet ($2) and check the DOC website, ⓦwww.doc.govt.nz.

Access is also possible from October to May with Molesworth Station Tours (ⓣ03/577 9897 or 0800/104 532, ⓦwww.backcountrysafaris.co.nz) who explore the region on one-day trips ($235), overnight ($590) and a three-day experience ($950).

The highway then continues 30km to Lake Grassmere, a vast shallow salt lake put to use producing much of New Zealand's table salt. Drivers will probably want to press on, but **cyclists** may want to overnight 20km south of the salt works at the small but beautifully formed *Pedallers Rest Cycle Stop* (ⓣ03/575 6708, ⓔpedallers@ callsouth.net.nz; bunks $16, camping $12) which even has a small shop: it is 1.5km off SH1; look for the water tank and sign beside the road.You're now following the coast with grey gravel beaches all the way, accessible at various points. Almost 90km out of Blenheim, the rocky Kekerengu Point juts out and makes a great place to watch the crashing waves while tucking into the delicious sandwiches, fish and chips, cakes and coffee at *The Store* (ⓣ03/575 8600).

Another 35km on and you hit the best stretch of coastline, signalled by **Ohau Point**, a roadside parking area right beside the South Island's largest seal colony with (usually) dozens of seals lolling on the rocks not more than twenty metres away. Along the final 30km into Kaikoura, the shoreline is dotted with craggy rocks making this a perfect habitat for **crayfish**, which are sought by the locals and sold at good prices from roadside shacks, notably at Rakautara, 3km south of Ohau Point.

Kaikoura and around

The small town of **Kaikoura**, 130km south of Blenheim and 180km north of Christchurch, enjoys a pretty setting in the lee of the Kaikoura Peninsula, wedged between the mountains and the ocean. Offshore, the sea bed drops away rapidly to the Kaikoura Canyon – 1000 metres deep a kilometre from land – a phenomenon that brings sea mammals in big and varied numbers. **Whale watching** and **swimming with dolphins** are big business here, and the presence of expectant tourists has spawned a number of eco-oriented businesses offering swimming with seals, sea kayaking and hiking.

The town's aquatic activities are very popular and visitors often book well in advance to be sure of getting a place. Unfortunately, because trips are in the open ocean the sea easily chops up in **bad weather** and trips quite often get cancelled. If you don't want to miss out, allow yourself a couple of days' flexibility here.

Kaikoura got its name when an ancient **Maori** explorer who stopped to eat crayfish and found it so good he called the place *kai* (food) *koura* (crayfish).

Maori legend also accounts for the extraordinary coastline around Kaikoura. During the creation of the land, a young deity, Marokura, was given the job of finishing the region: first he built the Kaikoura Peninsula and a second smaller peninsula (Haumuri Bluff), then he set about creating the huge troughs in the sea between the two peninsulas, where the cold waters of the south would mix with the warm waters of the north and east. Tuterakiwhanoa (a god), realizing the depth of Marokura's accomplishment, said that the place would be a gift

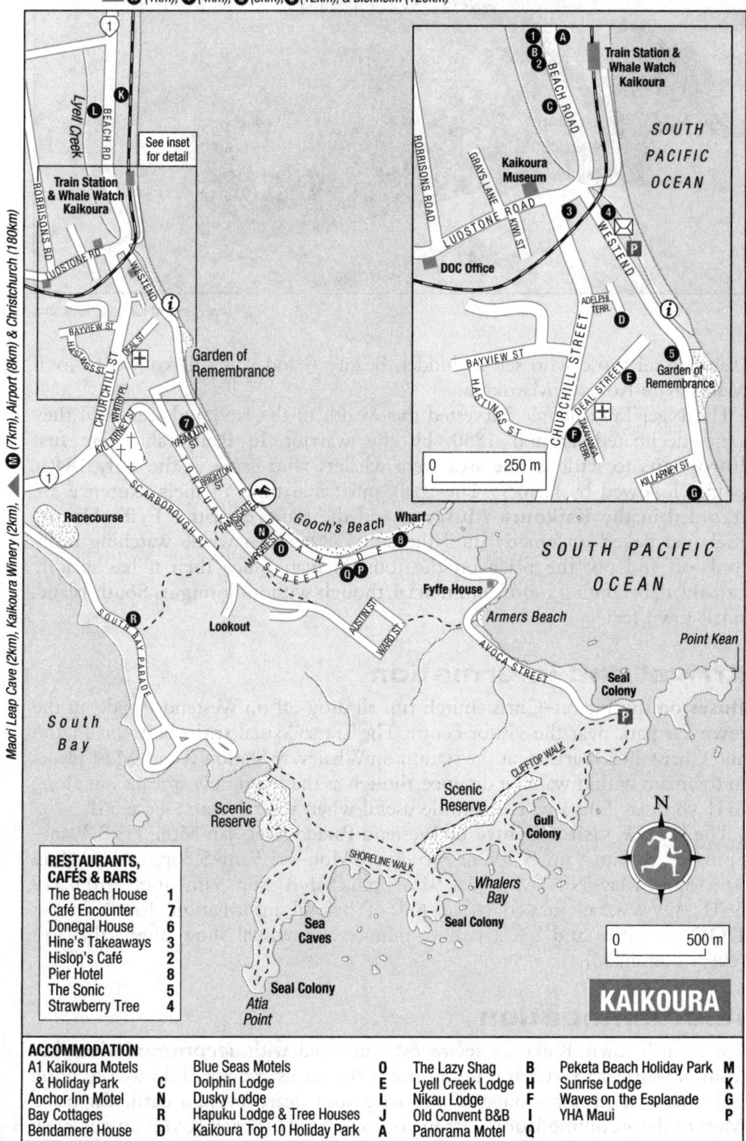

▲ New Zealand fur seal, Kaikoura

(*koha*) to all those who see its hidden beauty – and it is still known to local Maori as Te Koha O Marokura.

The Ngai Tahu people harvested the wealth of the land and seas until they were decimated, around 1830, by the warrior Te Rauparaha. The first **Europeans** to settle in the area were whalers who came in the early 1840s, swiftly followed by farmers. The trials and tribulations of their existence are recorded in the **Kaikoura Museum** and the more evocative **Fyffe House**. Kaikoura ticked on quietly until the late 1980s when whale watching really took off and put the place on the tourism map. Since then it has steadily expanded, becoming more commercial, though without losing its South Island, small-town feel.

Arrival and information

Buses on the Picton–Christchurch run all drop off on Westend Parade, in the town car park near the visitor centre. The TranzCoastal **train** between Picton and Christchurch arrives at the station on Whaleway Station Road. Most places in town are within walking distance, though as the town now spreads out along SH1 you may find a bike or shuttle useful when you're weary; see p.561.

The **i-SITE visitor centre** on Westend Parade (Dec–Jan Mon–Fri 8.30am–6pm, Sat & Sun 9am–5.30pm; Feb–April Mon–Fri 9am–5.30pm, Sat & Sun 9am–5pm; May–Nov Mon–Fri 9am–5pm, Sat & Sun 9am–4pm; ⓣ03/319 5641, ⓦwww.kaikoura.co.nz), is full of helpful information, handles most **DOC** enquiries and has a twenty-minute audiovisual show about the area (every 30min; $3).

Accommodation

For a small town, Kaikoura seems overburdened with **accommodation**, but from November to March it is splitting at the seams and you'll do well to book a few days in advance, longer if you have your heart set on a particular place. Most of the accommodation is strung out along SH1 (Beach Road) immediately north of the centre, or along The Esplanade which heads out onto the peninsula east of town.

Hotels, motels B&Bs and homestays

Anchor Inn Motel 208 The Esplanade ⓣ0800/720 033, ⓦwww.anchor-inn.co.nz. Luxurious motel with tastefully decorated, a/c units that come with every convenience (some with spa bath). Standard ❻, sea view ❼

Bay Cottages 29 South Parade, South Bay, 2km from the town centre ⓣ03/319 5506, ⓦwww.baycottages.co.nz. Excellent-value accommodation in purpose-built, well-equipped, s/c units, in a quiet spot at a silly price. The owner is exceptionally friendly and sometimes takes guests out crayfishing for breakfast in the morning. Free laundry service. ❸, deluxe ❹

Bendamere House 37 Adelphi Terrace ⓣ0800/107 770, ⓦwww.bendamerehouse.co.nz. Five high-standard rooms with kitchenette in the grounds of a large villa on the hill. Great sea views, and hearty breakfasts. ❻

Blue Seas Motels 222 The Esplanade ⓣ0800/507 077, ⓦwww.blueseasmotel.co.nz. Small, simple and good-value older motel units, close to the sea but only the newer ones have sea views. ❹, sea view ❺

Hapuku Lodge & Tree Houses SH1, 13km north of Kaikoura ⓣ0800/524 568, ⓦwww.hapukulodge.com. Set on a deer farm amid young olive trees, the rooms in the modern country lodge ($390) are gorgeous, but the five supremely luxurious treehouses ($490 and $650) are even better: nothing like a child's back-garden den, these have great sea and mountain views and you can even select the type of music you'd like supplied to them. There's also a great restaurant on site and breakfast is included. ❾

Nikau Lodge 53 Deal St ⓣ03/319 6973, ⓦwww.nikaulodge.com. Most of the six tastefully decorated en-suite rooms in this lovely, wooden, 1925 house have great mountain or sea views. There's also satellite TV with in-room movies, free Internet access, an outdoor spa pool and a good breakfast. Free Wi-Fi. ❼

Old Convent B&B Corner of Mount Fyffe & Mill rds, 4km northwest of town ⓣ03/319 6603, ⓦwww.theoldconvent.co.nz. Something of a curiosity, this French-styled 1911 ex-convent is set in spacious grounds and has a quiet rural atmosphere. Bright, en-suite rooms are atmospheric, if relatively modest, and there's a swimming pool, a bar and a gift shop where you can buy a chocolate nun. ❻

Panorama Motel 266 The Esplanade ⓣ0800/288 299 ⓦwww.panoramamotel.co.nz. There are superb views from the stripped-pine units with a chalet feel; you'll pay $10 extra for the better view from the upper floor. ❹

Waves on the Esplanade 78 The Esplanade ⓣ03/319 5890, ⓦwww.KaikouraApartments.co.nz. Luxurious two-bedroom, motel-style apartments with sea views. ❼

Hostels, campsites and motor parks

A1 Kaikoura Motels & Holiday Park 11 Beach Rd ⓣ0800/605 999, ⓦwww.a1kaikouramotel.co.nz. Basic and cheap this central complex offers a variety of ageing accommodation from motel units through four different types of cabin, to backpacker bunks and campsites, all on a site that backs onto the river. Tent sites $14, dorms $20, cabins ❶–❷, motels ❸

Dolphin Lodge 15 Deal St ⓣ03/319 5842, ⓦwww.dolphinlodge.co.nz. Secluded hostel with lovely gardens (complete with spa) overlooking the sea. It offers dorms and pleasant little doubles, plus free bikes. Dorms $23, rooms and en suite ❷

Dusky Lodge 67 Beach Rd, ⓣ03/319 5959, ⓦwww.duskylodge.com. Large and well-organized hostel with sauna, spa pool, swimming pool and a Thai restaurant along with log fires and a big sunny terrace. One level is devoted to deluxe en suites with their own upscale lounge and kitchen. Popular with the backpacker tour buses. Dorms $23, rooms and en suites ❷, deluxe en suites ❸

Kaikoura Top 10 Holiday Park 34 Beach Rd ⓣ03/319 5362, ⓦwww.kaikouratop10.co.nz. This central, shaded, award-winning park maintains high standards and offers a range of accommodation, including van sites, cabins and motels, and has an outdoor private spa. Camping $18, cabins ❸, s/c unit ❹, motel ❺

The Lazy Shag 37 Beach Rd ⓣ03/319 6662, ⓔlazy-shag@xtra.co.nz. Modern, purpose-built hostel where guests' comfort is the priority. Rooms are warm and quiet, common rooms are spacious and well equipped, and all dorms, twins and doubles are en suite. Dorms $22, rooms ❷

Lyell Creek Lodge 193 Beach Rd ⓣ03/319 6277, ⓦwww.lyellcreeklodge.co.nz. Small and quiet hostel 2km north of the town centre with no dorms, just comfy doubles and twins. Daily muffins or barbecue, and free winter roasts. Rooms and en suites ❷

Peketa Beach Holiday Park 665 SH1, 8km south of Kaikoura ⓣ03/319 6299, ⓔbeachfront@kaikourapeketabeach.co.nz. A peaceful

beachside campsite that's very popular with surfers who make use of the excellent waves on the doorstep. Camping $12, cabins ❶, beachfront cabins ❷

Sunrise Lodge 74 Beach Rd ⓣ03/319 7444, ⓔsunrisehostel@xtra.co.nz. Handy for the beach and with plenty of off-street parking, this friendly hostel is one of the best in town. No bunks, maximum 3 to a room, free bikes and a separate s/c studio out back. Dorms $25, rooms ❷

YHA Maui 270 The Esplanade ⓣ03/319 5931, ⓔyha.kaikoura@yha.co.nz. A comfortable, well-run hostel with tremendous sea and mountain views, particularly from the lounge and kitchen, and well-informed, knowledgeable staff. Dorms $28, rooms ❷, en suite ❸

The town and the peninsula

Most visitors are dead-set on seeing whales or swimming with dolphins, and the smattering of other sights and activities are often treated as ways of filling in the time until their turn comes, or a means of waiting out bad weather.

Some distraction is provided by the **Kaikoura Museum**, 14 Ludstone Rd (Mon–Fri 12.30–4.30pm, Sat & Sun 2–4pm; $3), with exhibits spanning the millennia. A large rock containing the fossilized ribcage of a Cretaceous-period plesiosaur sits beside the jawbone of an equally monstrous sea creature, the mosasaur. The Maori collection illustrates the stages needed to convert a mussel shell into effective fish hooks, while out back there's an early 1900s jailhouse (complete with padded cell) that was used in Kaikoura until 1980.

Out on the peninsula, don't miss the town's oldest building, **Fyffe House**, 62 Avoca St (daily 10am–5pm, excellent 30min guided tours; $7), an old whaler's cottage occupying a great site with views up and down the coast. Still on its original whalebone foundations, the house began life as part of the Waiopuka Whaling Station that was founded by Robert Fyffe in 1842. Originally an unprepossessing two-room cooper's cottage, it was extended by George Fyffe in 1860, and looks now much as it did then.

Avoca Street follows the edge of the peninsula round to a car park (the start of the Kaikoura Peninsula Walkway; see box below) where fur **seals** often lounge on flat, sea-worn rocks watching the plentiful birdlife, gulls, shags, and black oystercatchers, who in turn explore the rock pools full of rich tidal detritus.

South of town, SH1 runs 2km to the sea-formed **Maori Leap Cave** (35min tours daily on the half-hour 10.30am–3.30pm; $12; ⓣ03/319 5023), named

Walks around Kaikoura

Kaikoura isn't all about spending money watching marine mammals. There's plenty to be seen on foot, best accessed on these two walks.

Kaikoura Peninsula Walkway (11km loop; 3hr; undulating). A superb circuit of the peninsula covered on DOC's *The Peninsula Walkway* leaflet. Pick it up at the i-SITE and follow the route along The Esplanade past Fyffe House to the seal colony. From here it loops over the grassy cliffs to South Bay, with views down to the seals lolling on the rocks below. Several options follow paths back over the peninsula back to the i-SITE. Chances are you'll see red-billed and black-backed gulls, oystercatchers, herons and shags: be warned that gulls nesting during September and October are likely to attack if they feel that their nests are threatened: steer well clear.

Mount Fyffe (16km return; 6–8hr; 1400m ascent). Several walks close to town are outlined in DOC's *Mount Fyffe and the Seaward Kaikoura Range* leaflet. The most immediately appealing is this hike to the 1602-metre summit of Mount Fyffe. Starting at a poorly signposted car park 12km northwest of town, the route climbs steadily up a 4WD road to the summit with its glorious views over the Kaikoura Peninsula and coast.

after a Maori warrior who jumped to his death from the hills above the cave to escape capture by another tribe. Stalagmites and stalactites sprout from the floor and ceiling of the cave, and translucent stone straws seem to defy gravity by maintaining their internal water level. There are also examples of cave coral and algae that survive in the dank cave by turning darkness into energy.

Roughly 300m further south, **Kaikoura Winery** (daily 10am–5.30pm; tastings $3; Ⓦwww.kaikourawines.co.nz) perches on the steep hillside overlooking South Bay, a seaside location that flies in the face of conventional viticultural wisdom. Gauge how successful they've been on tours of their subterranean cellars (on the hour, last tour 4pm; $9.50) which conclude with a tasting.

Marine life and activities

Less than a kilometre off the Kaikoura Peninsula the coastal shallows plummet into the 1000-metre-deep Kaikoura Canyon, a network of undersea troughs that funnel warm subtropical waters and cold sub-Antarctic flows into a nutrient-rich upwelling. This provides an unusually rich habitat supporting an enormous amount and variety of marine life, including fourteen species of whale. Marine mammals come for an easy meal, and tourists come to watch. You can expect to see gigantic sperm **whales** (all year), **dolphins** (all year), migratory humpback whales (June–July) and **orca** (Dec–Feb), all at relatively close quarters.

Whale watching

Kaikoura's flagship activity is **whale watching**, conducted by the Maori-owned and operated Whale Watch Kaikoura (Ⓣ0800/655 121, Ⓦwww.whalewatch.co.nz), who run trips (2hr 30min; $130) on five boats, each with an excellent introductory video. You meet at their office at the train station and are bussed around to South Bay where a speedy catamaran whisks you a couple of kilometres offshore (much closer than similar trips elsewhere in the world). Hopefully there'll be several whale sightings along with dolphins and seabirds before you head back: if you see no whales there's a 70–80 percent refund. The office sells pills and bands to alleviate **sea sickness** – often a wise investment.

An alternative is **aerial whale watching** with Wings Over Whales (Ⓣ0800/226 629, Ⓦwww.whales.co.nz) who have thirty-minute flights for $145; and Kaikoura Helicopters (Ⓣ03/319 6609, Ⓦwww.worldofwhales.co.nz) who offer a thirty-minute flight for up to three people ($600). You won't get as close to whales as you would by sea, so bring a good pair of binoculars.

Swimming with dolphins and seals

The other main reason people visit Kaikoura is to go **swimming with dolphins**, an experience many find almost spiritual. Trips are run by the highly professional Dolphin Encounter, based at 96 The Esplanade (5.30am, 8.30am & 12.30pm; swimming Nov–March $150 April–Oct $130, watching $80/70; Ⓣ0800/733 365, Ⓦwww.dolphin.co.nz) where there is a good café (see p.560). There are only thirteen places on each boat, so book four weeks in advance for the December–February peak season (though standbys do become available at short notice). You'll get most out of it if you're a reasonably confident swimmer; the more you duck-dive the more eager the dolphins will be to investigate. They seem to find it attractive listening to you humming through your snorkel – any tune will do. Don't get too carried away though: dolphins have a penchant for swimming in ever decreasing circles until lesser beings are quite dizzy and disorientated.

Seals tend to be even more curious than dolphins, so you may fancy **seal swimming** with Seal Swim Kaikoura, 58 Westend (ⓣ0800/732 579, ⓦwww.sealswimkaikoura.co.nz; Oct–May only) who offer shore-based trips ($70) and more flexible trips by boat ($80). There's a fair bit of swimming involved so it helps if you've snorkelled before.

Still in the water, Dive Kaikoura, Yarmouth Street (ⓣ0800/728 223, ⓦwww.scubadive.co.nz), run resort **scuba-diving** trips for folk who've never done it before ($150) and other dive trips for those qualified ($120 per dive), with the chance to see a temperate reef with kelp forests, nudibranchs and sponges.

Birdwatching and sea kayaking

Fans of seabirds won't be able to resist birdwatching trips run by **Albatross Encounter**, 96 The Esplanade (2–3 trips daily; 2–3hr; $80; ⓣ0800/733 365, ⓦwww.oceanwings.co.nz), who take you a kilometre or two offshore in a small boat. Bait is laid to attract all manner of seabirds – shags, mollymawks, gannets, petrels and a couple of varieties of albatross. They come amazingly close and it is a rare opportunity to see endangered species, but you should try to stay upwind of the smelly bait used to attract the birds. Breakfasts have been lost.

Another way to see the wildlife is **sea kayaking** with the well-run Kaikoura Kayaks (ⓣ0800/452 456, ⓦwww.kaikourakayaks.co.nz) who offer half-day guided trips ($75) and a full-day unguided one ($75) which they've cleverly titled *Seal Kayaking*.

Other activities

If you'd rather stay on dry land, and learn something of the Maori culture hereabouts, join **Maori Tours** (ⓣ0800/866 267, ⓦwww.maoritours.co.nz) who offer a selection of emotionally engaging trips, organized and guided by an ex-whale-watch boat driver and his family, that give a real taste of *Maoritanga* and the genuine hospitality it demands. Three-hour tours ($99) take in various local sights, storytelling, explanations of Maori ways and medicines, cultural differences and involve learning a song, that you then surprise yourself by singing.

There's great **horse-riding** around 13km inland at Fyffe View Horse Treks (from $45; ⓣ03/319 5069), and aspiring fliers might like to **Pilot a Plane** ($120; ⓣ03/319 6579), a chance to take the controls for thirty minutes: an adrenaline buzz with great scenery to boot.

Once the sun goes down, crystal-clear nights offer a great chance to experience **Kaikoura Night Sky** (1–1hr 30min; $40; ⓣ03/319 6635, ⓦwww.kaikouranightsky.co.nz), with small groups clustered around a mobile eight-inch telescope in the fields away from the bright lights of Kaikoura. The chance planets, moon craters and distant galaxies come alive with tales of celestial navigation and what the southern sky means to Maori.

Eating and drinking

Kaikoura is a small town but the steady flow of tourists helps keep a decent selection of **cafés** and **restaurants** alive. Prices are a little on the high side, especially if you're keen to sample the local crayfish, though if that's your aim, you might want to buy them ready-boiled from one of the shacks and caravans alongside SH1 around 22km north of town.

The Beach House 39 Beach Rd. Kaikoura's cool set hang out here, imbibing good coffee over an extended breakfast ($8–18) or returning for lunches which include nachos, seafood chowder, quiches and panini from the cabinet. Casual atmosphere inside and out.

Café Encounter at Dolphin Encounter, 96 Esplanade. On a nice day it is hard to beat sitting outside across from the beach tucking into mussels in a tomato chilli sauce on focaccia ($18) or grilled haloumi with asparagus ($20). Good coffee and muffins too. Daytime only.

Donegal House School House Rd ⓣ03/319 5083, ⓦwww.donegalhouse.co.nz. A local legend, this purpose-built Irish bar and restaurant in the middle of a farm works surprisingly well with a short but decent menu (mains $26–30) and a buzzing atmosphere, occasionally enhanced by live music. It is 10min drive north of town (follow SH1 for 4km then 2km west) so you may want to go by cab or arrange to stay at the on-site, recently expanded B&B (5). Daily 11am–whenever.

Hine's Takeaways 18 Westend. Top fish and chips. Perfect for sunset on the waterfront.

Hislop's Café 33 Beach Rd ⓣ03/319 6971. The pick of the cafés in Kaikoura, this lovely wooden-floored eatery is a must for coffee and cakes, inside or out, as well as sumptuous breakfasts, organic meals (some vegetarian or gluten-free), tasty seafood and toothsome daily fresh-baked bread. Wine by the glass including vegan varieties. Open for breakfast ($10–19), lunch salads and sandwiches ($16–19) and dinner (mains $25–30).

Pier Hotel 1 Avoca St ⓣ03/319 5037. Old colonial hotel that has evolved into an excellent gastropub, with a friendly bar and restaurant serving hearty portions of tasty chowder ($16) and the likes of fish of the day ($28) and an indulgent half-crayfish in lemon dill sauce ($45).

The Sonic The Esplanade. Lively café/bar that becomes the town's main nightspot as the evening wears on, often with bands or a DJ. The menu runs from plates of nachos to gourmet pizza via lamb shanks and seafood mains, but that's not really why people come here.

Strawberry Tree 21 Westend. Loosely Irish-styled bar that's mostly busy with a mix of locals and travellers. Decent bar meals for $15–22.

Listings

Bike rental R&R Sport, 14 Westend (ⓣ03/319 5028) charge $20 for a half-day, $30 full. They also rent surfboards and act as agents for Board Silly Surf School (ⓣ03/319 6464).

Buses InterCity and Atomic run frequently to Christchurch and Picton via Blenheim and the Hanmer Connection (ⓣ0800/377 378) run three days a week to Hanmer Springs via Mount Lyford, while Southern Link (ⓣ0508/458 835) offer a number of services.

Car rental Good deals from Ace Rentals (ⓣ0800/226 629, ⓦwww.acerentals.co.nz).

Cinema Mayfair Cinema, 80 The Esplanade ⓣ03/319 5859.

Internet access Global Gossip, 19 Westend, have plenty of machines and Wi-Fi. Daily 9am–8pm.

Medical treatment Kaikoura Hospital and Doctor's Surgery, Deal St, 50m from corner of of Churchill St ⓣ03/319 5040.

Pharmacy Kaikoura Pharmacy, 37 Westend (Mon–Fri 9am–5pm, Sat 9am–1pm).

Post office 41 Westend (Mon–Fri 8.30am–5pm, Sat 9am–noon).

Taxis Kaikoura Shuttles (ⓣ03/319 6214) operate a taxi service and trailhead transport.

South from Kaikoura

South of Kaikoura you have a choice of routes. It is a two- to three-hour run down SH1 to Christchurch with only relatively minor points of interest along the way. The road initially follows a 20-kilometre stretch of delightful rocky coastline then ducks inland through farming country for most of the rest of the way to Christchurch. In winter, however, you may want to head inland on a scenic route past **Mount Lyford** (mid-June to mid-Oct; ⓦwww.mtlyford.co.nz) which offers some of the best **skiing** in the upper South Island. It's a small field and has limited lift facilities ($50 a day), but caters for a broad range of abilities (three beginner runs, eleven intermediate, six advanced) and is rarely crowded. Just down from **Mount Lyford Village**, on SH70, there's **accommodation** at the *Mount Lyford Lodge* (ⓣ03/315 6446, ⓦwww.mtlyfordlodge.co.nz; vans $25, dorms $30, rooms 3, motels 4), which also has a welcoming restaurant and bar.

There are various opportunities to see more of the coast, one of the best being the excellent, privately owned **Kaikoura Coast Track** (43km; 3 days; 600m ascent), a manageable way to explore the area. The trail climbs through farmland and native bush across the Hawkeswood Range and along beaches, with spectacular views of the seaward Kaikoura mountains and the Southern Alps, starting and ending at *The Staging Post*, 75 Hawkeswood Rd, Hawkeswood, 50km south of Kaikoura (camping $12, cabins $25, B&B rooms ⑤). Only a limited number are allowed to walk the track at any one time so you must **book in advance** (ⓣ03/319 2715, ⓦwww.kaikouratrack.co.nz) and pay the fee of $160. In return you get bag transport (so you only need carry a daypack), and three nights' **accommodation** in warm, clean cottages with fully equipped kitchens, baths and showers as well as fresh farm produce, milk, bread and home-cooked meals by arrangement. The track is now also open to **mountain bikers**, who pay $80 for a two-day ride, one night's accommodation and bag transport.

Cheviot and Gore Bay

The only significant town between Kaikoura and Christchurch is the sleepy farming town of **CHEVIOT**, 70km south of Kaikoura, which played a pivotal role in changes to colonial land distribution. In the early years of settlement most agricultural land was in vast estates, but in 1893 one Sir John McKenzie (see p.623) parcelled the land into small farms and holdings, so the same land could support 650 people, rather than just 80 – a process that was to be replicated across New Zealand, breaking up the enormous landholdings of a few rich and powerful men (as recounted in John Wilson's book, *Cheviot: Kingdom to Country*). The story is detailed in the **Cheviot Museum**, 6 Main St (open on request ⓣ03/319 8038; by donation). The village has a handful of cafés and the *Broadview Motel*, 6 Hall St (ⓣ03/319 8594, ⓔbroadview.motel@xtra.co.nz; ④).

To dispel driving fatigue or museum ennui, take a walk by the sea at **Gore Bay**, a small collection of homes, 8km east of Cheviot. There's a lovely beach with safe swimming, and one sight in the shape of **The Cathedrals**, 500m up the hill at the southern end of the beach. A viewpoint overlooks a dramatic example of badland erosion where siltstone cliffs have weathered into huge stalagmite-like fingers that resemble the pipes of a cathedral organ.

Waipara Valley

Some 50km south of Cheviot, paddocks full of newly planted vines announce one of New Zealand's fastest growing wine regions. Thanks to its long warm days, combination of alluvial gravels and limestone clays, and protection from cooling sea winds, the **Waipara Valley** produces quality wines, particularly its Pinot Noirs and Rieslings. As a wine destination it is very much in its infancy: a dozen places offer tastings and several have restaurants on site, but there isn't much else.

Everywhere is within a five-kilometre radius of the hamlet of **Waipara** at the junction of SH1 and SH7 to Hanmer Springs and the Lewis Pass. Around 4km north on SH1, *Waipara Springs* (daily 11am–5pm; ⓣ03/314 6777, ⓦwww.waiparasprings.co.nz) was first planted in 1982 and offers tastings of their latest vintages, though they are perhaps best appreciated in their modestly priced family-oriented **café** which always has wholesome fresh-baked bread to go with their daily specials. There's a considerably more upscale tenor to *Pegasus Bay*, Stockgrove Road, 4km south of the junction along SH1 then 3km east (daily

10.30am–5pm, ⓣ03/314 6869, ⓦwww.pegasusbay.com) with contemporary artworks surrounding diners in their classy **restaurant** (daily noon–4pm). Nip in to taste some of their delicious wines or stay for lunch when each course is matched with an appropriate wine.

Much more workaday needs are satisfied by *The Corner Cupboard*, at the corner of SH1 and SH7 which does light **meals** and sells ice creams, and there is simple backpacker **accommodation** just around the corner at *Waipara Sleepers*, 12 Glenmark Drive (ⓣ03/314 6003, ⓦwww.inet.net.nz/~waipara.sleepers; camping $10, dorms $20, rooms ①) where disused 1940s railway guards' vans have been converted into dorms and doubles, and an old station functions as a kitchen.

From Waipara it is only 50km down SH1 to Christchurch.

Travel details

Ferries cross Cook Strait and link up with the region's only train, from Picton to Christchurch. Buses fill in the gaps, many doing the same Picton–Christchurch run via Kaikoura with others running to Blenheim and Nelson where there are connections for the Abel Tasman National Park and Golden Bay. Flights listed are nonstop direct flights; there are many others that stop, or require changes in Wellington or Christchurch.

Ferries

Picton to: Wellington (5–8 daily; 3hr).

Trains

Picton to: Blenheim (1 daily; 30min); Christchurch (1 daily; 5hr 20min); Kaikoura (1 daily; 2hr 30min).

Buses

Blenheim to: Christchurch (11 daily; 4hr 45min–5hr 30min); Murchison (1 daily; 3hr 45min); Nelson (12 daily; 1hr 45min); Picton (13 daily; 30min).
Kaikoura to: Christchurch (11 daily 2hr 30min); Hanmer Springs (3 weekly; 2hr); Picton (8 daily; 2hr 15min).
Motueka to: Collingwood (3 daily; 1hr 30min); Heaphy Track (2 daily; 2hr 15min); Kaiteriteri (4–5 daily; 15min); Marahau (7 daily; 40–50min); Nelson (9–10 daily; 1hr); Takaka (5 daily; 1hr 10min); Totaranui (1 daily; 2hr 15min).
Murchison to: Blenheim (1 daily; 3hr 45min); Greymouth (1 daily; 2hr 15min); Nelson (4 daily; 2hr); St Arnaud (1 daily; 45min); Westport (3 daily; 1hr 15min–1hr 45min).
Nelson to: Blenheim (12 daily; 1hr 45min); Christchurch (4 daily; 7hr); Collingwood (3 daily; 2hr 45min); Greymouth (1 daily; 4hr 45min); Heaphy Track (2 daily; 3hr 30min); Motueka (9–10 daily; 1hr); Murchison (4 daily; 2hr); Picton (8 daily; 2hr); St Arnaud (1 daily; 1hr 15min); Takaka (5 daily; 2hr 15min); Totaranui (1 daily; 3hr 30min); Westport (3 daily; 3hr 30min–4hr).
Picton to: Blenheim (13 daily; 30min); Christchurch (8 daily; 5hr–5hr 30min); Greymouth (1 daily; 7hr); Kaikoura (8 daily; 2hr 15min); Nelson (8 daily; 2hr); St Arnaud (1 daily; 1hr 45min).
St Arnaud to: Murchison (1 daily; 45min); Nelson (1 daily; 1hr 15min); Picton (1 daily; 1hr 45min); Westport (1 daily; 1hr 45min).
Takaka to: Collingwood (3 daily; 30min); Heaphy Track (2 daily; 1hr); Motueka (5 daily; 1hr 10min); Nelson (5 daily; 2hr 15min); Totaranui (1 daily; 1hr).

Flights

Blenheim to: Auckland (4–5 daily; 1hr 20min); Christchurch (2 daily; 50min); Wellington (8–13 daily; 25min).
Kaikoura to: Wellington (1–2 daily in summer; 1hr).
Nelson to: Auckland (7–10 daily; 1hr 15min); Christchurch (5–8 daily; 50min); Palmerston North (1 daily; 50min); Wellington (6–10 daily; 35min).
Picton to: Wellington (6–8 daily; 25min).
Takaka to: Wellington (daily; 30min).

9

Christchurch and south to Otago

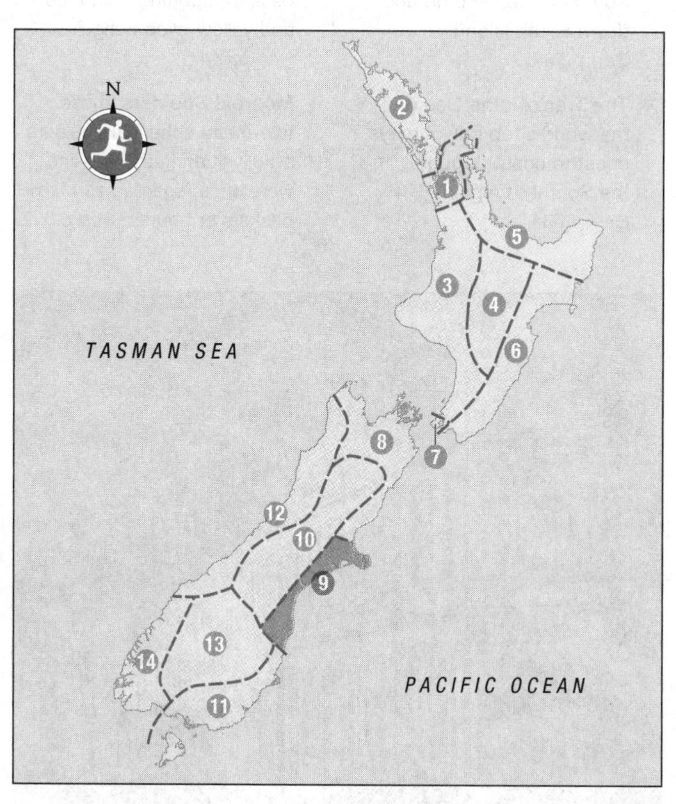

CHAPTER 9 **Highlights**

* **Christchurch Art Gallery** New Zealand's newest major gallery, with a fine collection of Kiwi art. See p.579

* **Ballooning** The Canterbury Plains are one of the best ballooning spots in the world, with views to the Southern Alps and up and down South Island. See p.584

* **The TranzAlpine** One of the world's top rail journeys, coast to coast through the Southern Alps. See p.585

* **Akaroa** Stay in a fine B&B in this relaxed French-influenced village and swim with Hector's dolphins. See p.602

* **Oamaru** The fine core of Neoclassical buildings in the slowly gentrifying Historic District make this a perfect base for spotting both blue and yellow-eyed penguins. See p.614

* **Moeraki Boulders** These two-metre spherical boulders artfully littering the tide line were once regarded as Maori baskets or gourds. See p.622

▲ Oamaru Historic Precinct

9

Christchurch and south to Otago

In many ways, the South Island's east coast comes closer to expectations of New Zealand than any other part of the country. Huge sweeps of pastoral land come wedged between snowy mountains and a rugged coast. The main hub of the region is New Zealand's third city, **Christchurch**, stretched out between the Pacific Ocean and the agriculturally rich flatlands of the Canterbury Plains. It is a relaxed city with a lively café and bar scene, where parks and gardens rub shoulders with some fine Victorian architecture. **The beach suburbs** of New Brighton and Sumner are within easy reach of the centre, and just over the bald **Port Hills** you'll find the appealing port town of **Lyttelton**. Lyttelton harbour is a drowned volcanic crater and geologically part of **Banks Peninsula**, a popular escape for city residents, its coastline indented with numerous bays and harbours. The largest settlement is the slightly twee "French village" of **Akaroa**, a great place to relax and a good base for exploring the peninsula.

South of Banks Peninsula, the main road (SH1) forges across the Canterbury Plains, a patchwork of fertile fields and vineyards bordered by long shingle beaches littered with driftwood. Further south the countryside again changes character, with undulating coastal hills and crumbling cliffs announcing the altogether more rugged terrain of North Otago. Historic settlements dotted along the coast testify to the wealth that farming has brought to the region. The first significant town is the workaday port of **Timaru**, close to a series of Maori rock paintings, evidence of a far longer history than the imposed European feel would have you believe. Further south, **Oamaru** is much more beguiling, with wonderfully accessible penguin colonies and an impressive core of nineteenth-century mercantile buildings in the process of being restored. Beyond, routes lead on towards Dunedin and the south, passing the unearthly Moeraki boulders, perfect spherical rocks formed by a combination of subterranean pressure and erosion.

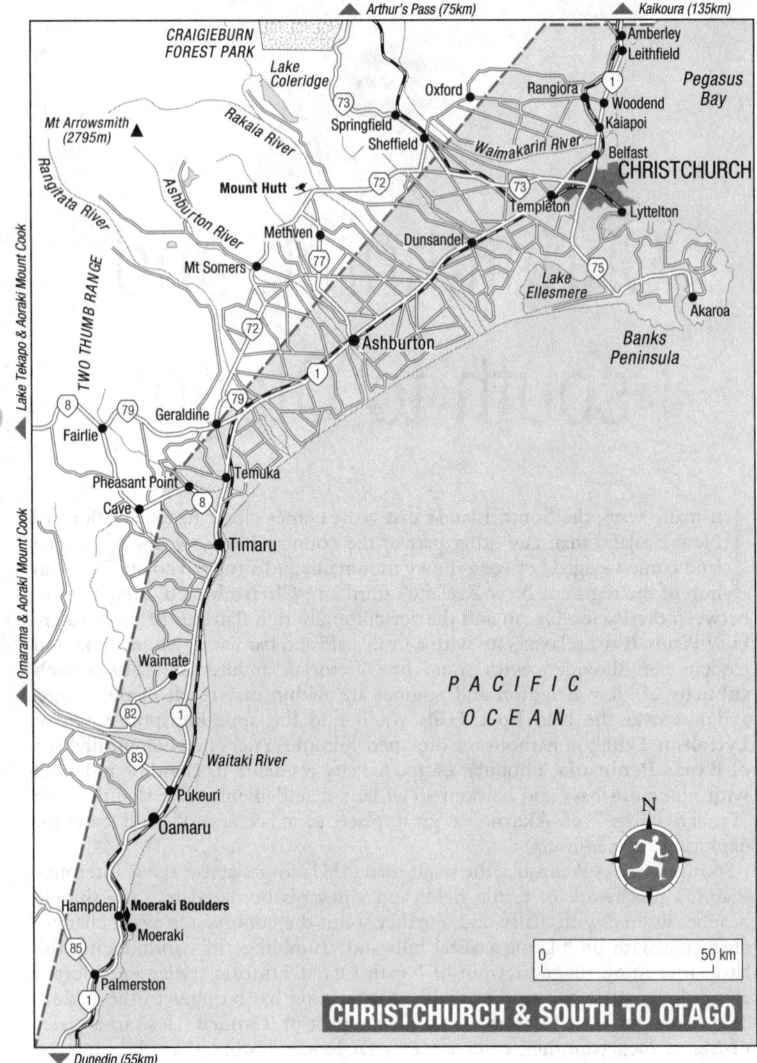

Christchurch

With a population of over 300,000, **CHRISTCHURCH** is the largest city on the South Island and capital of the Canterbury region. It exudes a palpable air of gentility and a strong connection with the mother country. After all, it was founded as an outpost of Anglicanism by its first settlers, was named after an Oxford college, and has some of the feel of a traditional English university town, with its neo-Gothic architecture and gently winding river. To some extent it pursues an archetype – the boys at Christ's College still wear striped blazers, and punts slide along the Avon – but the Englishness is largely skin-deep. In recent years the traditional conservatism of the settlement has developed a youthful, bohemian edge, with an explosion of lively bars and restaurants and a burgeoning visual arts, theatre, music and street entertainment scene. These urban and cultural pursuits are balanced by relaxed beach life at the Pacific Ocean suburbs of **New Brighton** and **Sumner**. On the southern skirts of the city, the **Port Hills** provide a playground for hikers and mountain bikers, or a great destination for an evening drive.

The city can be used as a base for exploring further afield, with a plethora of city-based companies offering **activities** such as rafting, paragliding, ballooning and mountain biking, all in the surrounding countryside (see box, p.584). Christchurch is also within a two-hour drive of several good **ski-fields** to the west, making it possible to combine a day on the pistes with an evening in the city's restaurants and bars.

Some history

Located in what was once a dry and windswept area only sparsely populated by Maori, Christchurch came into being as the result of a policy of colonization instigated by the **Canterbury Association**. Formed in 1849 by members of Oxford's Christ Church College, and with the Archbishop of Canterbury at its head, the association had the utopian aim of creating a new Jerusalem in New Zealand: a middle-class, Anglican community in which the moralizing culture of Victorian England could prosper. The association's surveyor, Captain Joseph Thomas, quickly recognized the agricultural potential of the surrounding plain and chose the site of the city. A few Europeans were already farming the area (notably the Scottish Deans brothers, who had arrived here in 1843; see p.583), although the main centre of white settlement at the time was the port of Lyttelton to the southeast, a base for whalers since the 1830s.

It was at Lyttelton that four ships containing nearly 800 **settlers** arrived in 1850, bound for the new city of Christchurch, by this stage little more than an agglomeration of wooden shacks. The earliest settlers weren't all Anglicans by any means, and the millenarian aspirations upon which the city was founded soon faded as people got on with the exhausting business of carving out a new life in unfamiliar terrain. Nevertheless, the association's ideals had a profound effect on the cultural identity of the city and descent from those who came on the "four ships" still carries social cachet among members of the Christchurch elite.

Arrival and information

Christchurch Airport, 10km northwest of the city centre, stays open 24/7 and you may find yourself arriving at some ungodly hour. Fortunately, there are ATMs, foreign exchange booths and a couple of **visitor centres** (ⓣ03/353 7774), at least one of which will be open. In addition, there's a freephone board for accommodation and car-rental bookings, and many Christchurch hotels provide a free pick-up service if you've already booked a room. A couple of places accept **left luggage**, notably the post shop in the domestic terminal, which charges $8 a day and allows you to retrieve bags after hours.

The Airport Flier bus runs into the city centre every 30–60 minutes (Mon–Fri 6am–midnight, Sat & Sun 8am–midnight; $7 one way), as does bus #10 (Mon–Fri 6am–midnight, Sat & Sun 8am–11pm; $7 one way). You may find it more convenient to look out for one of the airport–city **shuttle buses** which are usually parked outside the terminal and only charge $5 to the Square. Various other **shuttle** buses (see "Listings" for numbers) operate a frequent door-to-door service. There'll often be several waiting outside the terminal: hop in and once there is a viable load (this usually takes under 10min) they'll take you to your lodging for $17 per person. **Taxis** also wait outside and charge $35–40 into town.

The **train station** is on Clarence Street near the corner of Hagley Park, over 2km southwest of Cathedral Square. City buses don't serve the train station directly – you have to walk almost 1km up Clarence Street to Riccarton Road where there are numerous buses into town. Alternatively get a **shuttle bus** ($6) or **taxi** ($10–20) from the station into the centre. Long-distance **buses** all stop near the Square (see box, p.594).

Orientation and information

The low-rise, grid-plan city centre, together with many of its more compelling sights, is encased within the **Four Avenues** – Moorhouse, Fitzgerald, Bealey and Deans. They define a useful border round the downtown area, in the very centre of which is **Cathedral Square** (usually known as "the Square") with its landmark spire.

Christchurch's **i-SITE visitor centre** is in the former Post Office on the south side of Cathedral Square (daily Nov–mid-Jan 8.30am–6pm; mid-Jan–March 8.30am–7pm; April–Oct 8.30am–5pm; ⓣ03/379 9629, ⓦwww.christchurchnz.net). You can book all forms of transport here as well as trips and activities; be sure to pick up the free *Christchurch City Centre Walks* leaflet, which provides a good introduction to local history, as well as the *Tramway* map, which details the main stops on this popular sightseers' route (see "City transport" below). The visitor centre is also the place to find out which of the city's many excellent **festivals** (see "Listings" on p.594) is currently in progress.

The i-SITE is often busy and you may find it easier to nip into the **Adventure Centre**, 69 Cathedral Square (daily Dec & Jan 9am–9.30pm, Feb–Nov 9am–8pm; ⓣ0800/847 486), a convenient commercial enterprise which makes its money by booking trips.

For tramping and national parks information visit the **DOC office** (Mon–Fri 8.30am–5pm; ⓣ03/341 9102), which stocks a good selection of maps and brochures, and sells hut tickets and annual hut passes. The office is currently on the fourth floor of Torrens House, 195 Hereford St, but is likely to move some time in 2009.

City transport

You can easily see most of what Christchurch has to offer **on foot**, resorting to public transport for the odd trip out to the suburbs. The City Bus Exchange on the corner of Colombo and Lichfield streets is the hub for **bus** services run by several companies, but unified under Metro and Red Bus (info desk Mon–Sat 6.30am–10.30pm, Sun 9am–9pm; ⓣ03/366 8855, ⓦwww.metroinfo.org.nz, ⓦwww.redbus.co.nz). In the immediate vicinity along Colombo Street, between the Town Hall and Moorhouse Avenue, there's the free yellow environmentally friendly **Shuttle**, running every 10–15min (7.30am–10.30pm) but it is only marginally useful. With the exception of the yellow shuttle and the Airport Bus (see p.570), the **fare** anywhere in the city's zone one, including the beaches and Lyttelton, is $2.50, more for every zone thereafter ($5 to Diamond Harbour). If you are here for a few days, save money by buying a **Metrocard** from the Bus Exchange (minimum $10) which you swipe each time you board. Standard fares drop to $1.90 and once you've paid for two fares on a certain day subsequent journeys are free for the rest of the day. Most routes run from 6.30am until around midnight.

Familiarize yourself with the central city by hopping on the **Christchurch Tramway** (daily Nov–March 9am–9pm; April–Oct 9am–6pm; Ⓦwww.tram.co.nz), which weaves a 2.5km circuit past many of the central sights, including the Arts Centre and Cathedral Square, and comes with an individual commentary delivered by the driver. The tramway was only installed in 1995, but the rolling stock is largely made up of lovingly restored 1905 originals. Tickets ($14) are valid for two days and you can get on and off as often as you like.

Several key sights – the Antarctic Centre, Willowbank Wildlife Reserve and Christchurch Gondola – have joined forces and offer a **Best Attractions bus** ($6 return to one attraction, $12 for two, and $17 all four within 24 hours) the last only worthwhile if you're intent on bagging all these sights in one hectic day.

Driving in Christchurch is straightforward, and even the morning and evening rush hours are pretty tame. Most central parking spaces are metered from Monday to Saturday between 7am and 6pm (otherwise free). If you have

Staying by the beach: Sumner

The beachside suburb of Sumner (see p.586) has a selection of appealing places to stay, all accessible on fast and frequent city buses (#3). Places to eat and drink are listed on p.591.

Abbott House 104 Nayland St Ⓣ0800/020 654, Ⓦwww.abbotthouse.co.nz. Attractively restored 1870s villa set a block back from the beach with accommodation in either a studio with kitchenette, or in a suite with large lounge, kitchen and laundry. Both have TV/DVD, dataport, private entrances and continental breakfast ingredients (including freshly baked bread) are supplied. Studio ❹, suite ❺

Cave Rock 16 Esplanade Ⓣ03/326 5600, Ⓦwww.caverockguesthouse.co.nz. Appealing guesthouse just across the road from the beach and with sea views from some rooms and the sun lounge. Large en-suite rooms and breakfast ingredients delivered to your room. ❺

The Marine 26 Nayland St Ⓣ03/326 6609, Ⓦwww.themarine.co.nz. Former pub converted into a bright and cheerful backpackers hostel with spacious four-share rooms and several doubles, some with doors opening out onto a upstairs veranda. Toast is provided for a light breakfast, there's free use of a barbecue, and the lounge has a piano. Dorms $23, rooms and en suites ❷

Sumner Bay Motel 26 Marriner St Ⓣ0800/496 949, Ⓦwww.sumnermotel.co.nz. Stylish motel a block from the beach, with a range of studios and apartments all with a balcony or courtyard, Sky TV and DVD player. There's also bike and board rental. ❺

Villa Alexandra 1 Kinsey Terrace, Clifton Hill Ⓣ03/326 6291, Ⓦwww.villaalexandra.co.nz. An excellent-value homestay in a spacious villa overlooking Sumner Bay with a sunny veranda and turret, offering two bedrooms and one spacious loft apartment all with their own bathrooms. They also offer a full cooked breakfast. There is also a modern self-contained apartment overlooking the beach let with a 3-night minimum. Rooms ❹, loft ❺, apartment ❺

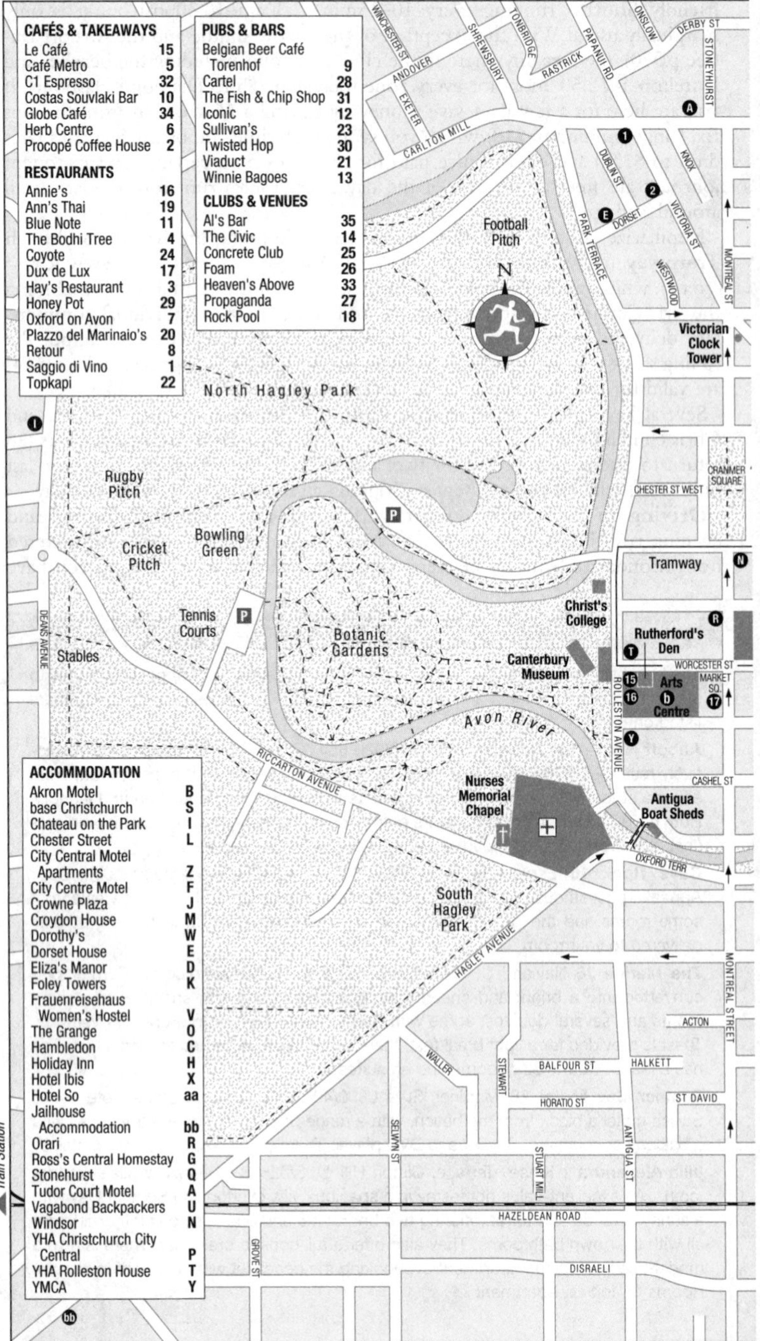
CAFÉS & TAKEAWAYS
Le Café 15
Café Metro 5
C1 Espresso 32
Costas Souvlaki Bar 10
Globe Café 34
Herb Centre 6
Procopé Coffee House 2
RESTAURANTS
Annie's 16
Ann's Thai 19
Blue Note 11
The Bodhi Tree 4
Coyote 24
Dux de Lux 17
Hay's Restaurant 3
Honey Pot 29
Oxford on Avon 7
Plazzo del Marinaio's 20
Retour 8
Saggio di Vino 1
Topkapi 22
PUBS & BARS
Belgian Beer Café Torenhof 9
Cartel 28
The Fish & Chip Shop 31
Iconic 12
Sullivan's 23
Twisted Hop 30
Viaduct 21
Winnie Bagoes 13
CLUBS & VENUES
Al's Bar 35
The Civic 14
Concrete Club 25
Foam 26
Heaven's Above 33
Propaganda 27
Rock Pool 18
ACCOMMODATION
Akron Motel B
base Christchurch S
Chateau on the Park I
Chester Street L
City Central Motel Apartments Z
City Centre Motel F
Crowne Plaza J
Croydon House M
Dorothy's W
Dorset House E
Eliza's Manor D
Foley Towers K
Frauenreisehaus Women's Hostel V
The Grange O
Hambledon C
Holiday Inn H
Hotel Ibis X
Hotel So aa
Jailhouse Accommodation bb
Orari R
Ross's Central Homestay G
Stonehurst Q
Tudor Court Motel A
Vagabond Backpackers U
Windsor N
YHA Christchurch City Central P
YHA Rolleston House T
YMCA Y
N
North Hagley Park
Football Pitch
Rugby Pitch
Cricket Pitch
Bowling Green
Tennis Courts
Botanic Gardens
Stables
South Hagley Park
Avon River
Christ's College
Canterbury Museum
Nurses Memorial Chapel
Antigua Boat Sheds
Arts Centre
Rutherford's Den
Tramway
Victorian Clock Tower
CRANMER SQUARE
Train Station
WINCHESTER ST
SHREWSBURY
TONBRIDGE
ONSLOW
DERBY ST
STONEYHURST
ANDOVER
EXETER
RASTRICK
PAPANUI RD
CARLTON MILL
DUBLIN ST
KNOX
DORSET
VICTORIA ST
PARK TERRACE
WESTWOOD
MONTREAL ST
CHESTER ST WEST
WORCESTER ST
MARKET SQ
ROLLESTON AVENUE
CASHEL ST
OXFORD TERR
DEANS AVENUE
RICCARTON AVENUE
HAGLEY AVENUE
MONTREAL STREET
ACTON
HALKETT
BALFOUR ST
WALLER
STEWART
HORATIO ST
ST DAVID
SELWYN ST
STUART MILL
ANTIGUA ST
HAZELDEAN ROAD
GROVE ST
DISRAELI

CENTRAL CHRISTCHRUCH: INSIDE THE 4 AVENUES
After Hours Surgery
Johnson's Grocers
Casino
Convention Centre
Town Hall
Victoria Square
Provincial Government Buildings
Library
Theatre Royal
Christchurch Art Gallery
Aquarium
Cathedral Sq.
Cathedral
Intercity Bus Stop
Centennial Pool
DOC Office
AA Office
The Strip
City Exchange Bus Station
St Michael's & All Angels
Sol Square
Cathedral of the Blessed Sacrament (RC)
CINEMAS
Academy b
Hoyts 8 d
Regent a
Rialto c
0 250 m

to drive into town, there's convenient **parking** in the centre of Hagley Park (Armagh Street entrance): free for the first hour and all day at weekends.

Given the city's relatively quiet roads and flat terrain, **cycling** is an ideal way of exploring some of the more out-of-the-way suburbs. Expect to pay $30–40 a day for **bike rental** (see "Listings", p.593, for details of outlets).

Accommodation

Christchurch has an impressive range of accommodation, and although prices are by no means extortionate, they're understandably higher than in the South Island's smaller towns and cities. Most of the **business hotels** and backpacker **hostels** are situated within the city centre, as are a number of the better **B&Bs**, though there are also several out in the leafier suburbs. Probably the best value for money are the hostels, none too far away from the action and most offering good deals on rooms and en suites. Convenient **motels** are mostly strung out along Papanui Road to the northwest of the city centre. Predictably, **campsites** are scattered outside the city centre, mostly within walking distance of a bus stop.

Christchurch is a walkable city and staying in the centre is pleasant, but if you want to wake up to the sound of the sea slapping the beach, go for **Sumner** (see box, p.571).

With Christchurch operating a 24-hour airport, most places are well used to accommodating **late arrivals** and early departures: when making a reservation it pays to double-check that your date of arrival has been understood, especially if you're arriving around midnight.

Hotels and motels

Central Christchurch has plenty of large, flashy, expensive **hotels** often with rooms overlooking Hagley Park, Cathedral Square or Victoria Square, but there are cheaper hotel and **motel** rooms not far away. The best hunting ground is around fifteen minutes' walk northwest of Cathedral Square: upwards of a dozen highly competitive places line **Papanui Road** which leads to the classy suburb of Merivale. Rates are competitive, and you shouldn't have any trouble finding a studio for around $110 a night. In addition, many establishments offer **special deals** for weekend and long-term stays.

City centre

Akron Motel 87 Bealey Ave ⓣ0800/778 787, ⓦwww.akronmotel.co.nz. Combined budget motel and hostel in a quiet area set back off the road with plain but functional units, all of which open out onto a small garden; about 10min walk from Cathedral Square. The hostel section is comfortable with a good kitchen and has no dorms, just doubles, twins and quads, all with shared bathroom. Hostel rooms ❸, units. ❹

Chateau on the Park 189 Deans Ave ⓣ0800/808 999, ⓦwww.chateau-park.co.nz. Two-hundred-room hotel, memorable for its lovely surroundings on the edge of Hagley Park, with an outdoor pool, restaurants and cocktail bar. 25min walk from the Square but they have a special shuttle. ❻

City Central Motel Apartments 252 Barbadoes St ⓣ0508/800 888, ⓦwww.citycentral.co.nz. Recently renovated motel with flatscreen TV-equipped, stylish rooms and parking just 5min walk from the city centre. It is on a busy intersection but rooms are double-glazed. ❹

City Centre Motel 876 Colombo St ⓣ03/372 9294, ⓦwww.citycentremotel.co.nz. Plush modern motel with flatscreen TVs and off-street parking. Surprisingly quiet for such a central location. ❺

Crowne Plaza Corner of Kilmore & Durham sts ⓣ0800/154 181, ⓦwww.crowneplaza.co.nz. Spectacular ziggurat-shaped business hotel overlooking Victoria Square with a magnificent lobby plus assorted bars and restaurants. ❼

Holiday Inn 356 Oxford Terrace ⓣ0800/801 111, ⓦwww.holidayinnchristchurch.nz-hotels.com.

Business hotel on the edge of the Central Business District, beside the Avon River with relaxing courtyard gardens and a high standard of rooms, plus all the expected facilities including indoor pool, restaurant and bar. ⑦

Hotel Ibis 107 Hereford St ⓣ0800/444 422, ⓦwww.ibishotels.co.nz. Brand-new, no-frills business hotel in the heart of the city. Rooms are small and without minibar though they're tastefully decorated and have phone, fridge, tea and coffee and LCD TV, and there's a restaurant and bar on site. Parking nearby for $15 a day. ⑤

Hotel So 165 Cashel St ⓣ0508/165 165, ⓦwww.hotelso.co.nz. Brand-new hotel where space is sacrificed for stylish lodging at budget prices. Chic rooms (all en suite) come with flat-screen TV, free Wi-Fi, MP3-player link to sound system, and controllable mood lighting, plus there's a small gym/sauna, a café/bar and a communal kitchenette. Doubles are tiny (and many lack windows), so you may want to step up to the slightly more spacious queen or king (both ④). Housekeeping and car parking (if required) both cost $15 a day extra. ③

Tudor Court Motel 57 Bealey Ave ⓣ0800/488 367, ⓦwww.tudorcourt.co.nz. Very small motel in a peaceful environment with simple, comfy units, about 10min walk from Cathedral Square. Cooked and continental breakfasts are available. ④

Papanui Road

Lodgings are marked on the map on p.582.

Colonial Inn Motel 43 Papanui Rd, Merivale ⓣ0800/111 232, ⓦwww.colonialinnmotel.co.nz. A modern motel about 15min walk from Cathedral Square with clean and comfortable units. ④

Diplomat Motel 127 Papanui Rd, Merivale ⓣ0800/109 699, ⓦwww.diplomatmotel.co.nz. Situated in the heart of Merivale, 2km north of Cathedral Square, this smart motel has large s/c units with separate kitchens, where the extra few dollars are justified by a nice outdoor pool and spa. ④

Randolph 79 Papanui Rd ⓣ0800/537366, ⓦwww.randolphmotel.co.nz. Excellent modern motel in grounds overshadowed by a huge copper beech tree. Rooms with bold decor are extremely well equipped with cooking facilities, TV/DVD, stereo and in-room laundry. Deluxe rooms come with double spa bath and there's even a small gym. ⑤

Strathern Motor Lodge 54 Papanui Rd, Merivale ⓣ0800/766 624, ⓦwww.strathern.co.nz. Spacious and well-presented modern units with kitchenette or full kitchen a 15min walk from Cathedral Square. One unit has its own spa bath. ④

B&Bs and guesthouses

Christchurch has an impressive range of **B&Bs**, in the centre, in the leafy inner suburbs, and at the seaside community of Sumner. Prices start around $120.

City centre

Croydon House 63 Armagh St ⓣ0800/276936, ⓦwww.croydon.co.nz. Pleasant and well-run B&B with smallish modernized rooms in the main house and a couple of lovely cottages in the compact but appealing garden. There's a guest lounge with TV and chess, 24hr tea and coffee, and a cooked breakfast. Shared bath ⑤, en suite ⑥

Dorothy's 2 Latimer Square ⓣ03/365 6034, ⓦwww.dorothys.co.nz. Boutique hotel with seven lovingly restored en-suite rooms with an appreciable gay following. There's an on-site restaurant and the *Rainbow Bar* (open to all) themed around the *Wizard of Oz*. Rooms ⑥, Queen suite ⑧

Eliza's Manor 82 Bealey Ave ⓣ03/366 8584, ⓦwww.elizas.co.nz. Luxury B&B in a grand 1861 house with eight rooms all period furnished and with heat pump temperature control. Go for the spacious Heritage rooms if you have the funds. Rooms ⑥, Heritage ⑧

The Grange 56 Armagh St ⓣ0800/932 850, ⓦwww.thegrange.co.nz. Good central, budget option, very popular and with eight small and modestly appointed en-suite rooms which are let either B&B or room-only. There are also eight more spacious self-catering apartments. Room ④, B&B ⑤, apartments ⑤

Hambledon 103 Bealey Ave ⓣ03/379 0723, ⓦwww.hambledon.co.nz. Luxurious, but homely family-run B&B with plush Victorian furniture in one of the city's oldest and grandest houses, built in 1856 for one of the early city fathers. The array of high-standard, spacious suites all come with complimentary port and sherry and delicious breakfasts. ⑧

Orari 42 Gloucester St ⓣ03/365 6569, ⓦwww.orari.net.nz. Informally run and art-adorned B&B in a large 1893 home just steps from the Arts Centre. Ten bright, sunny rooms all have TVs, phones, artworks and either en suites or private bathrooms (one with a tub). Tasty continental breakfasts. ⑥

Ross's Central Homestay 410 Oxford Terrace ⓣ03/366 0962 ⓔrossed@xtra.co.nz. Gay, lesbian and mixed homestay on the banks of the Avon. ❸

Windsor 52 Armagh St ⓣ0800/366150, ⓦwww.windsorhotel.co.nz. Traditional guesthouse with forty rooms in a 1907 former student hall of residence. Nothing flash and none of the rooms have en-suite bathrooms, but they are comfortable, clean and mostly quiet, the staff are friendly and the cooked breakfast keeps you going all day. ❹

Outside the Four Avenues

These lodgings are marked on the map on p.582.

The CharlotteJane 110 Papanui Rd ⓣ03/355 1028, ⓦwww.charlotte-jane.co.nz. Named for one of Canterbury's founding "Four Ships, this elegant boutique hotel has beautiful wood-panelled rooms, breakfast when you want it and an atmospheric restaurant (dinner only). Standard rooms ($375) are gorgeous but the next level up ($475) have spa baths and working fireplaces. ❾

Elm Tree House 236 Papanui Rd, Merivale ⓣ03/355 9731, ⓦwww.elmtreehouse.co.nz. A very welcoming B&B fashioned out of a listed 1920s building in Merivale, just 2km from Cathedral Square. Largely built from dark native timbers with clean lines and plain colours, all rooms are en suite, and there is a conservatory and courtyard. Breakfasts are hearty. Room ❽, suite ❾

Onuku 27 Harry Ell Drive, Cashmere, 7km south of central Christchurch ⓣ03/332 7296, ⓦwww.onukubedandbreakfast.co.nz. Welcoming B&B in a stylish modern house high in the Port Hills with fab views of the city and great access to walking and mountain biking. Rooms are simple but tasteful with very comfy beds, pick-ups can be arranged and there's a full breakfast to set you up for the day. Private bath ❹, en suite ❺

Hostels

Most **backpacker hostels** in Christchurch are within the Four Avenues, or just beyond, and almost all offer excellent value for money. We've picked a range of the best: quiet modern hostels; party-oriented downtown places; and those a few blocks out with gardens and a homely atmosphere (something Christchurch specializes in). Prices don't vary a great deal, generally around $23 for dorm beds and around $60 for doubles and twins, with sheets and towels. None of the hostels listed here have tent sites.

During the peak summer months try to **book** a couple of days in advance; most hostels are prepared for late plane arrivals, and many have long-term storage for bike boxes and gear you might not need in the South Island.

base Christchurch 56 Cathedral Square ⓣ03/982 2225, ⓦwww.basebackpackers.com. Modern 300-bed hostel in an 1880 building in the heart of the city with card-swipe entry, a café and bar and a separate women's section known as "Sanctuary". It is a fun place to stay with plenty of lounges, pool table and an Indian restaurant on the doorstep. Free light continental breakfast. Dorms $27, rooms ❷, en suites ❸

Chester Street 148 Chester St East ⓣ03/377 1897, ⓦwww.chesterst.co.nz. With just 14 beds (no bunks) this is the city's smallest hostel and feels more like a shared house with comfy doubles and a 3-bed dorm. Separate TV lounge, limited off-street parking and a pleasant garden. Dorm $25, rooms ❷

Dorset House 1 Dorset St ⓣ03/366 8268, ⓦwww.dorsethouse.co.nz. Renovated, small and spacious hostel in an 1871 house located in a quiet area, with firm beds (no bunks). There's Sky TV and pool in a huge lounge fitted with stained-glass windows, and free tea and coffee, Off-street parking. Dorms $28, rooms ❸

Foley Towers 208 Kilmore St ⓣ03/366 9720, ⓔfoley.towers@backpack.co.nz. Largish hostel built around a couple of old houses that manages to maintain an intimate feel thanks to attractive gardens and an abundance of doubles and twins. Dorms $22, rooms & en suites ❷

Frauenreisehaus Women's Hostel 272 Barbadoes St ⓣ03/366 2585, ⓔjesse-sandra@quicksilver.net.nz. Wonderfully relaxed and superbly well-equipped women-only hostel in an old and central house. Much loved by those looking for scented candles, mood music, spring water direct from the garden and heaps of DVDs. Dorms $26, twins ❷

Jailhouse Accommodation 338 Lincoln Rd ⓣ03/982 7777, ⓦwww.jail.co.nz. A jail as recently as 1999, this Victorian Gothic prison has been imaginatively turned into an atmospheric hostel with mostly double and twin-bunk rooms plus some bunk-free dorms, all kauri-floored. Whimsical touches include barbed-wire inlaid toilet seats and a couple of cells left as they were. Helpful owners, bike rental ($15 a day), wireless internet, a free Kiwi and prison-related DVD library and espresso round out the deal. Located almost 2km southwest of the Square: bus #7 drops off at the door. Dorms $25, rooms ❷

The Old Countryhouse 437 Gloucester St ⓣ03/381 5504, ⓦwww.oldcountryhousenz.com. One of Christchurch's most peaceful hostels, fashioned from a couple of wood-floored villas with bold decor and spacious dorms. 15min walk east of the Square (bus #21). Dorms $23, rooms ❷, en suites ❸

Stonehurst 241 Gloucester St ⓣ0508/786633, ⓦwww.stonehurst.co.nz. Central and very popular hostel with a wide range of accommodation, 24hr reception, a basic restaurant and outdoor pool and BBQ area. All beds are made up and private rooms have TV and phone. There's off-street parking and even campervan hookups. Dorms $26, backpacker rooms & en suites ❷, motels ❹, apartments ❺

Vagabond Backpackers 232 Worcester St ⓣ03/379 9677, ⓔvagabondbackpackers@hotmail.com. Very friendly place with only thirty beds, some in an annexe at the back of the house; all are well kept, quiet, clean and recently redecorated. There's off-street parking, BBQ and a lovely garden area. Dorms $23, rooms ❷

YHA Christchurch City Central 273 Manchester St ⓣ03/379 9535, ⓔyha.christchurchcity@yha.co.nz. Large, very central, purpose-built hostel with lots of high-quality rooms, two kitchens, two common rooms and well-informed staff that run the travel, events and booking office. If you're staying in the older wing go for one of the exterior doubles. Limited free parking. Dorms $29, rooms ❸, en suites with TV ❸

YHA Rolleston House 5 Worcester Blvd ⓣ03/366 6564, ⓔyha.rollestonhouse@yha.co.nz.The best-located hostel in Christchurch: opposite the Arts Centre and full of character. Plenty of dorms but a limited number of twins and doubles, so book ahead for a room. Limited parking. Dorms $25, rooms ❷, en suite ❸

YMCA 12 Hereford St ⓣ0508/962 224, ⓦwww.ymcachch.org.nz. Very central, state-of-the-art YMCA with dorms, singles, basic doubles and deluxe en-suite doubles with phone, tea and coffee, and TV. Guests get significant discounts at the fitness centre, gym, squash courts, climbing wall and sauna, and there's an on-site café. Dorms $25, rooms ❷, en suites ❸

Campsites

Christchurch's **campsites** are well set up for tents and campervans, and offer good deals on cabins, though given their distance from the centre you might find it more convenient to stay in one of the city's excellent hostels.

The campsites are marked on the map on p.582.

Amber Park 308 Blenheim Rd, Upper Riccarton ⓣ03/348 3327, ⓦwww.amberpark.co.nz. Spacious, grassy site with all the expected features just 4km south of the city (bus #5 stops right outside), and handy for the train station and Canterbury University. Camping $15, en-suite cabins ❷, kitchen cabins ❸, motels ❹

Christchurch Top 10 39 Meadow St, St Albans ⓣ0800/396 323, ⓦwww.meadowpark.co.nz. Situated 5km north of the Square on SH74 (reached by buses #11, 12 & 13) this large campsite, close to supermarkets and restaurants, has a full range of facilities including a heated indoor pool. Camping $22, cabins ❷, s/c chalets ❸, tourist flats ❹, motels ❺

South New Brighton Motor Camp Halsey St, South New Brighton ⓣ03/388 9844, ⓦwww.southbrightonmotorcamp.co.nz. Handily sited near the beach 7km east of the city centre, this medium-sized site has good facilities and a limited range of cabins and flats. Camping $15, cabins ❶, s/c cabins ❷

The City

Scattered in the streets around Cathedral Square are the city's most attractive buildings, predominantly nineteenth-century Gothic, though with some outstanding modern structures such as the new **art gallery**. Beyond the art gallery on the western edge of the city centre is **Hagley Park**, a focal point for leisure activities at weekends. It is threaded by the placid River Avon, and there's no more relaxing way to experience some of the prettier parts of the city than by **punt**.

Outside the Four Avenues you pass into well-tended suburban districts like Riccarton, Fendalton, Merivale and St Albans, each characterized by one- and

▲ Punting on the River Avon

two-storey residential housing and beautifully kept gardens. Further east, the coastal suburbs of New Brighton and Sumner provide access to the picturesque and atmospheric Pacific Ocean **beaches**.

Within the Four Avenues

Christchurch is centred on **Cathedral Square** a large, open, paved area typically abuzz with lunching office workers, skateboarders and tourists. Above it rises the Gothic Revival Anglican **Cathedral** (free guided tours Mon–Fri 11am & 2pm, Sat 11am, Sun 11.30am), designed by George Gilbert Scott, architect of London's St Pancras Station. It was begun in the 1860s and, when completed in 1904, revealed a cool and spacious interior and a 63-metre spire ($5 to ascend the claustrophobic 134-step staircase) with the best panoramic views of the city. On the left-hand side of the nave, look out for the Maori contribution of *tukutuku* panels made of leather and rimu wood, celebrating the Maori proverb: "What is the most important thing in life? It is people, people, people". To sample the marvellous acoustics of the building, drop by for choral evensong (Tues & Wed 5.15pm for the full choir, Fri 4.30pm for boys' choir only).

Outside stands the 1867 statue of Robert Godley, founding father of Christchurch and agent of the Canterbury Association. It is said to be the earliest public sculpture in New Zealand and is the work of Pre-Raphaelite Thomas Woolner, who was briefly in New Zealand after failing on the Australian goldfields. The vessels that brought the city's founding fathers are also remembered in the nearby Memorial of the Four Ships. Neither work matches the scale of Neil Dawson's *Chalice* sculpture, which looks like a monstrous ice-cream cone, silver on the outside and metallic blue on the inside, with leaf and fern patterns cut out of its higher reaches. It was unveiled just before September 11, 2001, after which it became a focal point for flowers, messages and public grief. Since then, it has taken a place of affection in most locals' hearts and is now climbed quite regularly by people with something to protest about.

The grandest of the buildings surrounding the Square are the Italianate 1879 **Old Post Office** and adjacent 1901 Palladian-style former **Government Building**. The former contains the i-SITE and the **Southern Encounter Aquarium** (daily 9am–5pm; $14; Ⓦwww.southernencounter.co.nz), a fishy extension of Orana Wildlife Park (see p.584) that replicates many of the damper habitats of the South Island. Although it is small, many native saltwater and freshwater species of fish are represented, with touch tanks fashioned after rock pools, plus artificial eel and salmon runs and a mock-up of a fly-fishing lodge. Come for **feeding time** (11am, 1pm & 3pm) and to be guided through a nocturnal house to view North Island **brown kiwi**.

North of Cathedral Square

A grid of shopping streets spreads north from the Square, the most interesting section being around **New Regent Street**. Built in 1932 in the Spanish Mission style, it was gussied up and painted in pastel shades a few years back, though it is looking a bit tired now.

One block west, manicured Victoria Square is bounded to the north by the languid River Avon and Christchurch's starkly modern **Town Hall**. Epicureans should nip around the corner to the venerable **Johnson's Grocers**, 787 Colombo St, a tiny treasure-trove stacked to the rafters with just about every packaged gourmet product imaginable, plus some British favourites.

Following the river a few steps to the southwest you find the **Provincial Council Buildings**, corner of Durham and Armagh streets (Mon–Sat 10.30am–3.30pm; free), built between 1858 and 1865. They're the only provincial government buildings left in New Zealand and are widely regarded as the masterpiece of Christchurch's most renowned early architect, **Benjamin W. Mountfort**. Built in neo-Gothic style, the older wooden portion of the chambers has a fine flagstone-paved corridor. The Gothic Revival Great Hall, built in 1869 as the council chamber, is magnificently decorated with an intricate ceiling and elaborate stonework. Head north from here past the **casino** and along Victoria Street to reach the Victorian **clock** tower, which houses a clock originally imported from England in 1860 to adorn the government buildings.

South of Cathedral Square

The area **south of Cathedral Square** has the city's greatest concentration of shops, restaurants and bars, and you'll continually find yourself back here in the evening. There are no sights to speak of, but one area to make for is a region dubbed **South of Lichfield** (or SOL) along High Street lined with the more offbeat music and clothes shops as well as the cooler end of the café scene.

Christchurch Art Gallery

With so much neo-Gothic architecture in Christchurch it is refreshing to come face to face with the **Christchurch Art Gallery**, corner of Worcester Boulevard and Montreal Street (daily 9am–5pm & until 9pm on Wed; free; iPod tour narrated by Sam Neill ($5) Ⓦwww.christchurchartgallery.org.nz), with its striking frontage of curving glass intersecting at odd angles. Natural light floods into the large atrium – all grey stone slabs and pale wood – from where a grand staircase leads up to an interconnected series of large rooms containing the historical, twentieth-century and contemporary collections. International works are displayed, but the Gallery is strongest on New Zealand creations, particularly those by Christchurch and Canterbury artists.

The European landscape tradition comes through forcefully in nineteenth-century paintings by Charles Goldie and Dutch émigré Petrus van der Velden, such as *Mountain stream Otira Gorge*. More recent works include Tony Fomison's compellingly dark *No!*, Rita Angus' *Cass*, depicting a lone customer on the platform of a desolate station, and Bill Hammond's primordial *The Fall of Icarus*, liberally scattered with iconic bird-headed humanoids.

Elsewhere, the ceramics and glass collection contains superb pieces by Ann Robinson and Shona Firman, especially the latter's blue canoe prow, *Te Waka Taniwha*. Lastly, check out what's on show from the "Works on Paper" collection which includes a Rembrandt etching, a Goya aquatint, a Blake engraving, a Warhol screenprint of Chairman Mao and Bill Frizell's *From Mickey to Tiki Tu Meke*, a seven-head transformation from Mickey Mouse to a Maori Tiki.

The Arts Centre

The **Arts Centre**, diagonally across from the Art Gallery, was built in 1874 as the University of Canterbury and Christchurch Girls' and Boys' High Schools. After the university decamped to suburban Ilam in 1975, the Arts Centre took over, with restaurants, food stalls, galleries, cinemas and the Court Theatre (see p.592). Benjamin Mountfort, the architect of the Christchurch Museum, Christ's College and the Provincial Chambers, was at his Gothic best here using volcanic "bluestone" and Oamaru limestone. Today the leafy courtyards and grassy quadrangles make a great place to watch the world go by, especially at weekends when the Market Square on the east side is turned over to a lively **craft market**, complete with buskers and musicians. Much of what's on sale is made in workshops dotted throughout the building. To the rear of the Arts Centre, via the *Dux de Lux* pub and courtyard, a collection of ethnic food stalls (Sat & Sun 10am–4pm) offer Czech, Lebanese, Thai, Korean, Chinese and a planet-load of other national dishes dirt-cheap. The **information centre** (daily 9.30am–5pm ⓣ03/366 0989, ⓦwww.artscentre.org.nz) runs free 20min **tours** of the buildings on demand, and provides access to **Rutherford's Den**, which honours Nobel Prize-winning atomic nucleus discoverer **Ernest Rutherford** – he on the $100 banknote. It is an appropriately reverential place with thoughtful displays, a look at the tiny basement laboratory where he did postgraduate research, and a fine old lecture theatre with copiously graffitied benches.

Canterbury Museum, Hagley Park and around

Across Rolleston Avenue from the Arts Centre stands the **Canterbury Museum** (daily Oct to mid-March 9am–5.30pm; mid-March to Sept 9am–5pm; $5 donation requested), occupying an 1870 neo-Gothic structure. Founding director and archeologist Julius Haast (who gave his name to the Haast Pass) supplied the museum with an Egyptian mummy bought for $24 in 1886. Christchurch's association with the Antarctic is explored with a flimsy unreliable motor tractor from Shackleton's 1914–17 expedition, a Ferguson tractor that became the first vehicle to reach the Pole as part of Edmund Hillary's push in 1958, and the far more robust Sno-Cat used by Brit Vivian Fuchs on the same expedition. Charmingly retro dioramas of penguins and Weddell seals set the tone for the Maori collection, full of great carvings but also featuring dioramas of bronzed natives going about their daily lives.

Next door stands **Christ's College**, the city's most elite private school. There are no tours, but you are free to wander round the grounds and admire the Victorian architecture. The Museum and Christ's College block the city off from **Hagley Park** which, it is whispered by the mischievous priest of St Michael's, was situated to protect the Anglican residents within the Four Avenues from the Presbyterians, who arrived on the same four ships but resided in the outer suburbs. The park contains the spectacular Botanic Gardens, a golf course and playing fields, and at weekends it seems like the entire population of Christchurch is there, strolling around or playing some form of sport.

One corner is devoted to the **Botanic Gardens** (Rolleston Avenue gate; daily 7am until 1hr before sunset; conservatories 10.15am–4pm; free), which does all it can to live up to Christchurch's Garden City moniker. It has a collection of indigenous and exotic plants and trees unrivalled on the South Island. From summer to autumn perennials give a constant and dazzling display of colour, the herb garden, containing a variety of culinary and medicinal plants, exuding lovely aromas. Beginning in December the rose garden proudly displays over 250 varieties while the Cockayne Memorial Garden, an area of native bush named after one of New Zealand's greatest botanists, provides a restful spot to meander. Best of all, though, it is just a great place to hang out on a sunny day with picnicking families, studying students and couples flattening the grass and listening to the distant hum of the city.

The gardens are enclosed by a loop of the River Avon which you can explore by heading along to the **Antigua Boat Sheds**, 2 Cambridge Terrace (daily 9.30am–5.30pm ⓣ03/366 5885, ⓦwww.boatsheds.co.nz) and renting a paddleboat ($16 per half-hour for two), canoe (single $8 per hour, double $16), or rowboat ($15 per half-hour). Adjacent, **Punting on the Avon** (ⓣ03/366 0337, ⓦwww.punting.co.nz) supply a guide nattily dressed in a striped blazer and straw boater, to **punt** you along the river ($20 per person for 30min).

On the southern borders of Hagley Park, Christchurch Hospital almost engulfs the tiny brick-and-slate 1928 **Nurses' Memorial Chapel**, Riccarton Avenue (daily 1–4pm; free), dedicated to nurses who served in World War I. It was constructed after the death of three Christchurch-trained nurses aboard a torpedoed troopship in 1915, and contains four stained-glass windows by the English glass artist Veronica Whall, with an uneven texture and a variety of colours set off by the otherwise dark, low-ceilinged interior.

Heading back into town along Oxford Terrace, the eye-catching stand-alone **belltower** houses a bell from one of the first four migrant ships that once served as a timepiece for the settlers and was rung on the hour. The belltower belongs to the adjacent 1872 **St Michael and All Angels Church** (Nov–April Mon–Fri 10am–5pm, Sat & Sun 2–5pm; guided tours on demand; April–Oct open for regular church services only), built in French and English medieval Gothic styles. The stained-glass windows covering both east and west wings are particularly beautiful, their bright colours contrasting with the dark hues of the surrounding timber. Look out also for the bi-culturally significant **Te Tapenakara o te Ariki** ("The Tabernacle of the Lord"), a small Maori war canoe carved with grapes and wheat and holding the reserve sacrament.

Beyond the Four Avenues

Inspired by a couple of hours spent in the Botanic Gardens, you might fancy a stroll across North Hagley Park to the beautiful precincts of **Mona Vale** at 63 Fendalton Rd (grounds open daily 8.30am to just before dusk; free). Originally part of the Deans' estate (see p.583), the site became the property of the city in 1969 and is now tended by the Canterbury Horticultural Society. The gardens have majestic displays of roses, dahlias, fuchsias and irises, as well as

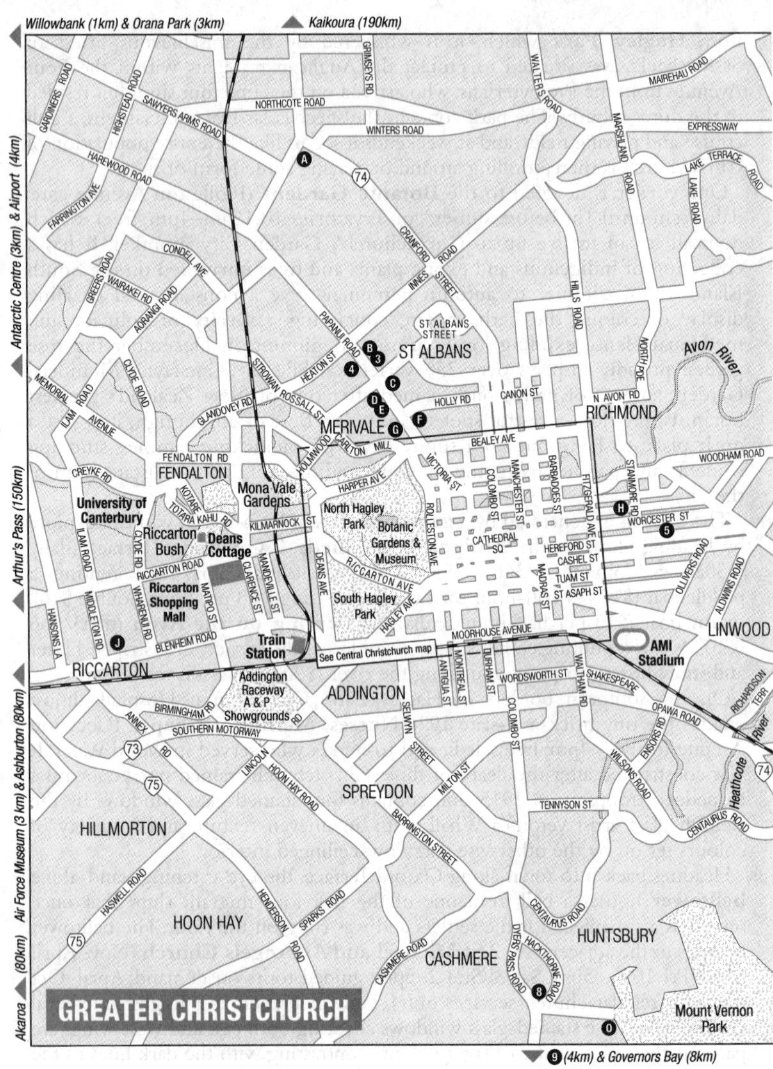

magnolias, rhododendrons and herbaceous perennials, while the Bath House has been converted for use as a greenhouse and the old homestead is open for lunch daily.

You could hardly make a greater botanical leap than to wander ten minutes to the southwest to the suburb of Riccarton and **Riccarton Bush** (aka **Deans** Bush; daily dawn–dusk; free), an area of native forest containing several 500-year-old kahikatea trees. Access is off Kahu Road (bus #24). The survival of this valuable area of forest is largely due to Scottish brothers William and John Deans, who came here to farm in 1843 and somehow resisted the temptation to put all their property to immediate agricultural use. Today a concrete path navigates the bush, with signs pointing out the various species. The tiny black-pine **Deans**

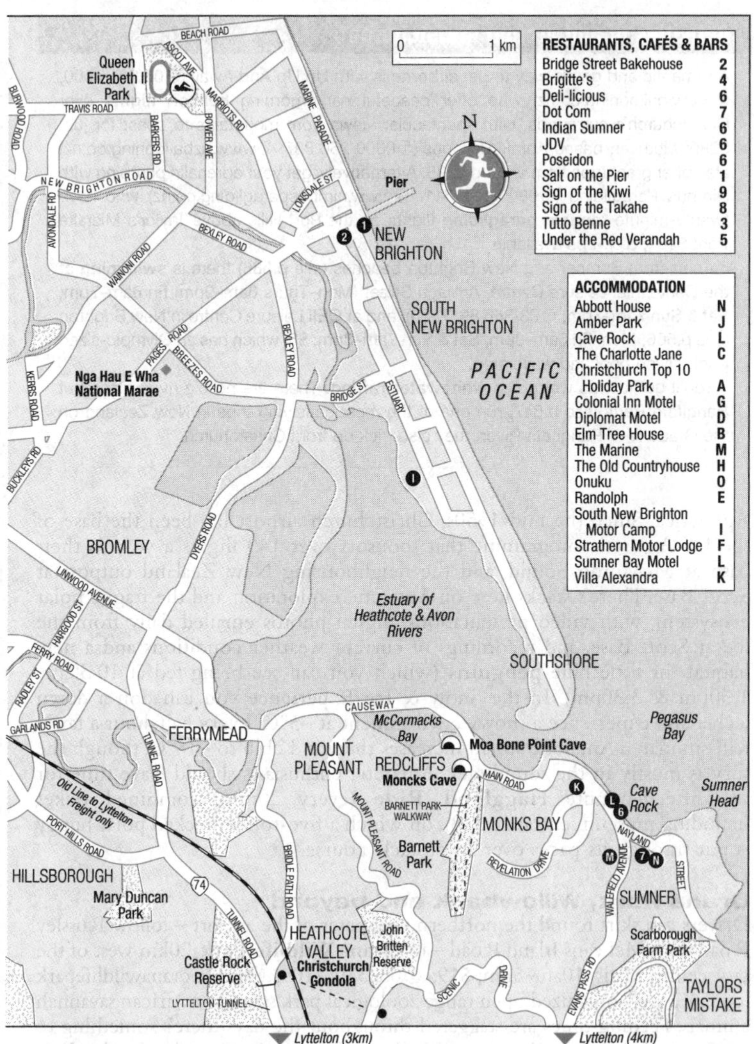

Cottage (daily 9am–dusk; free), was built by the Deans brothers on their arrival, and is furnished as it would have been when the Deans lived there. Their descendants built the adjacent, grand Victorian **Riccarton House** (guided tours daily except Sat, 2pm; $12; Ⓦ www.riccartonhouse.co.nz), all oak panelling and stag heads.

The International Antarctic Centre

Beyond Deans Bush, Memorial Avenue runs northwest to the airport and the **International Antarctic Centre**, 38 Orchard Rd (daily Oct–March 9am–7pm; April–Sept 9am–5.30pm; $30; Ⓦ www.iceberg.co.nz), a well-presented and dynamic exhibit concentrating on New Zealand's involvement in

Activities in and around Christchurch

A romantic and gentle way to get airborne is with Up Up And Away (☎03/381 4600, ⓦwww.ballooning.co.nz) who offer peaceful early-morning **balloon flights** over Christchurch's surrounds, with spectacular views from mountains to coast for just $280. Methven-based Aoraki Balloons (☎0800/256 837, ⓦwww.nzballooning.co.nz) also offer great trips from around $295. Alternatively, get your adrenalin pumping with Nimbus Paragliding (☎0800/111 611, ⓦwww.nimbusparagliding.co.nz) who have twenty-minute **tandem paragliding** flights on the Port Hills above Taylor's Mistake from $160; pick-ups available.

Apart from Sumner and New Brighton beaches (see p.586) there is **swimming** at the Centennial Leisure Centre, Armagh Street (Mon–Thurs 6am–9pm, Fri 6am–7pm, Sat & Sun 7am–7pm; ☎03/366 8917; $5), and at QEII Leisure Centre in New Brighton (see p.586; Mon–Fri 6am–9pm, Sat & Sun 7am–8pm; $5) which has an Olympic-sized pool, diving pool and wave area.

You'll get just as wet going **whitewater rafting**. There are no big rivers near, but Rangitata Rafts (see p.647) run one of the most satisfying trips in New Zealand on the Grade IV–V Rangitata River; they also pick up from Christchurch.

Antarctica. Since the mid-1950s, Christchurch airport has been the base of the US Antarctic programme that sponsors over 140 flights a year to their base at McMurdo Sound, and the neighbouring New Zealand outpost at Scott Base. There's stacks here on Antarctic exploration and the fragile polar ecosystem, with video presentations, digital photos emailed daily from the ice at Scott Base, and recordings of current weather conditions and a new habitat for little blue **penguins** (which you can see being fed at 10.30am, 1.30pm & 3.30pm). In the Snow & Ice Experience you can don a down jacket and experience a snowy environment at –5°C. Every half-hour a fairly naff simulated Antarctic storm increases the wind chill to –18°C, though the fury is mostly in the soundtrack. Antarctic enthusiasts should leave time for the fifteen-minute **Hägglund Ride** (every 20min; combined ticket including museum entrance $48), on which a five-tonne tracked polar buggy is put through its paces over an obstacle course.

Orana Park, Willowbank and beyond

Drivers can skirt round the northern perimeter of the airport – follow Russley Road then McLeans Island Road – to **Orana Wildlife Park**, 20km west of the city centre (daily 10am–5pm; $19; ☎03/359 7109, ⓦwww.oranawildlifepark.co.nz), a well-organized open range zoological park strong on African savannah animals. Feeding times are staggered throughout the day (there's something to see every half-hour). You can even hand-feed a giraffe and join the **lion encounter** (daily 2.15pm; $15) touring the lion enclosure on the caged back of a truck. New Zealand is represented by kiwi, tuatara, an active aviary and a gecko house where the little beasties are perfectly camouflaged in the foliage. The only public transport out here is the Sunshine Shuttle (☎03/379 1699; $20 return), which leaves from the visitor centre at 10am and 1pm.

Although nowhere near as exciting as Orana Park, the smaller and more intimate **Willowbank Wildlife Reserve**, 60 Hussey Rd (daily 10am to an hour before sunset; $21, ☎03/359 6226, ⓦwww.willowbank.co.nz), has some good displays of native birds including a kiwi house. This is also the site of the Ko Tane Maori Experience (see p.593). To get here use the Best Attractions bus ($6; see p.571).

Around twenty minutes' drive southwest of Hagley Park and accessible via Blenheim and Great South roads is the **Air Force Museum** (daily 10am–5pm; $15; ⓣ03/343 9532, ⓦwww.airforcemuseum.co.nz), located on the former RNZAF base at Wigram. Among the two dozen aircraft you'll see the Dakota converted for use on the British Queen's state visit in 1953, and several World War II veterans including a Spitfire. Three flight simulators will keep the (big) kids happy, particularly the one simulating the World War II Mosquito as it engages in combat in the Norwegian fjords. Enthusiastic volunteer guides conduct free tours of the restoration and storage hangars (daily 11am & 2pm).

The Christchurch Gondola

For quick access to great views and easy hiking on the Port Hills on the south-eastern flank of the city, ride the **Christchurch Gondola**, 10 Bridle Path Rd (daily 10am–10pm or later; $22 return; ⓦwww.gondola.co.nz), located by the entrance to the Lyttelton tunnel 15 minutes' drive from Cathedral Square, and is served by the Lyttelton bus (#28) and the Best Attractions bus (see p.571). The Gondola cable cars whisk you to the upper station on the 945-metre summit of **Mount Cavendish**. Here, time is best spent in the café admiring the 360-degree views of Christchurch, the Canterbury Plains, the volcanic outcrops of the Banks Peninsula and the Southern Alps. There's also an indifferent restaurant and the uninspiring Heritage Time Tunnel Experience (same hours; free), where the history and culture of the region are told as you creep through tableaux on a motorized buggy.

The TranzAlpine

When completed in 1923, the train line from Christchurch to Greymouth was a massive boon for travellers, covering in five hours what formerly took two days by horse-drawn coach – a passage tough enough to shorten the average life expectancy of the draught horses to just eighteen months. The journey is covered by the **TranzAlpine** (4hr 30min; prices vary according to demand so book well ahead for best prices; $97–118 one way, $140–215 day return, ⓦwww.tranzscenic.co.nz), leaving Christchurch train station at 8.15am every morning and returning by 6.05pm. It passes through sixteen tunnels and crosses numerous viaducts, all seen from the train's large viewing windows and open-sided observation car. The scenic, 224km coast-to-coast journey starts out across the Canterbury Plains as far as Springfield, after which you start gently up into the mountains. The halfway point is reached around Craigieburn, open tussock country dried throughout the summer by strong nor'wester winds that leave it crisp and golden. As you head up to Arthur's Pass the annual rainfall increases, encouraging transition-zone vegetation of mossy beech forests. There's a pause at Arthur's Pass to add an extra locomotive, after which the train dives through the 8.5km-long Otira Tunnel that burrows under the 920m pass itself. The train then descends to the high-rainfall West Coast, the predominant, lush podocarp forests appearing particularly around Lake Brunner just before you trundle down the Grey Valley into the town of Greymouth.

If you travel in December you will see red and white rata in bloom, but the trip is at its romantic, snow-cloaked best in the winter months (June–Aug). A good strategy for those with a vehicle is to catch the train at Darfield, 45km west of Christchurch, allowing a later start, slightly cheaper fares and fewer parking problems. You only miss Christchurch's suburbs and a few farms.

Wherever you board, consider alighting at Moana for a relaxed three-hour lakeside lunch before boarding for the return journey. It beats a hurried snack in Greymouth and should save you a few dollars.

From the summit, you can explore the paths that run along the ridge tops before descending back to the lower station. Alternatively try a combined gondola ride and **mountain bicycle descent** with the Mountain Bike Adventure Company ($50; reservations essential ⓣ0800/424 534, ⓦwww.cyclehire-tours.co.nz) who meet you with bikes near the top of the gondola and give you two hours to explore one of three possible descents with bird's-eye views of Sumner's beaches, Lyttelton and Banks Peninsula.

Christchurch's beaches

As the summer sun bakes the city streets it's tempting to head for the beach, and Christchurch has plenty on offer, all accessible by frequent buses. The area around **Redcliffs** and **Sumner** is particularly appealing.

Around eight kilometres east of the centre, a long swathe of sand runs from Waimari Beach south along a spit to the mouth of the Avon estuary – the whole area is a great place to swim or sunbathe. The centre of activity is **New Brighton** (bus #5 or #40 from the city), resplendent with its long concrete **pier**. Have a beer, coffee or decent light meal at the *Salt on the Pier* restaurant at the base of the pier, or head down the developing café strip along Bridge Street, opposite the pier. Here, the *Bridge Street Bakehouse*, at no.107, stocks an excellent range of pies – spinach, feta and mushroom, Akaroa cod in white wine and their award-winning Cointreau soaked plums & apricots with almond custard (all around $4).

Redcliffs and Sumner

On the whole, you are better off on the southern side of the river estuary where Redcliffs, and particularly Sumner (both accessed by bus #3 from the City Exchange bus station), have developed into tight beachside communities with plenty going on and a number of good places to stay and eat.

Redcliffs lies at the mouth of the estuary on and around the fractured dull red cliffs that give the community its name. The sea has eroded the base of the cliffs to leave a series of caves, the largest of which once contained moa bones and shellfish remnants indicating Maori habitation up to 700 years ago. As you drive along Main Road, look out for the large entrance to **Moa Bone Point Cave** a now sadly much graffitied recess once used by European settlers. Half a kilometre further along, the smaller **Moncks Cave** heralds Barnett Park, the starting point for the **Barnett Park Walkway** (5km loop; 1hr 45min), a well-formed track which climbs through grassland onto rock outcrops, with steps giving access to a large rock shelter and several caves. The walkway then bisects a copse of native bush and passes a seasonal waterfall, before crossing a creek and descending via bluffs past **Paradise Cave**, home of a Maori family in the 1890s.

As you follow the coast around from Redcliffs, estuary beaches become sea beaches, the best being at **Sumner**, a Norfolk pine-backed strip of craft shops, restaurants, cafés, wine bars, surf shacks and a cinema, all fronting a broad patch of golden sand. Named after Dr J.B. Sumner, Archbishop of Canterbury and president of the Canterbury Association in the 1850s, it's now one of Christchurch's more desirable suburbs. It is a popular destination on summer weekends and a great place just to hang out anytime (see box, p.571).

The highlight of the beach is **Cave Rock**, a geological anomaly of honeycombed rock – its underside is peppered with little caves like an enormous Swiss cheese – accessible at low tide. The lifeguard's lookout point on top can be reached by clambering up the rock. Elsewhere, you can stroll the clifftop paths around Sumner Head (see p.587) or visit Urban Surf, 25d Marriner St in the heart of the village (Ⓣ03/326 6023, Ⓔthegirls@urbansurf.co.nz) where you can rent boards ($20 for 2hr) and wetsuits ($10 for 2hr). They also deal with **surf coach** Doug Young (Ⓣ0800/478 734) who charges around $40 for a two-hour lesson complete with gear.

The best **surfing** is 2km south at **Taylor's Mistake** (reached along Nayland Street), a narrow beach and small community named, according to local lore, for a captain who ran aground here after mistaking the bay for the entrance to Lyttelton Harbour. The best way to get here from Sumner is to walk along the **Scarborough Head/Taylor's Mistake Walk** (1hr each way; 3km; constantly undulating), which makes its way over the headlands with great coastal views and passing a few *baches* tucked away in Hobson Bay. To get there, follow The Esplanade south onto Scarborough Road then hugging the coast onto Whitewash Head Road.

Drivers can continue beyond Sumner following the extension of Wakefield Street inland and over Evans Pass to Lyttelton, only 6km away (see p.596).

Exploring the Port Hills

On a fine evening there's no finer drive or bike ride in Christchurch than a traverse of the Port Hills along the **Summit Road** (see box below) perhaps dropping down to explore Lyttelton. Akaroa-bound drivers can even continue along a sequence of connecting backroads that forms a giant S-shaped circuit around the peninsula's two crater harbours. Designed with pedestrians and wagons in mind, it keeps as close as possible to the ridge tops marking an undulating course – with few sustained ascents – and offers stupendous views all around.

A variety of roads (see Banks Peninsula map on p.596) wind around the hills offering all sorts of variations, but this is the classic **Port Hills drive**: allow at least two hours. Start by following Colombo Street south from the city centre

Harry Ell and the Summit Road

The Summit Road was the consuming passion of the public-spirited liberal MP and conservationist **Harry Ell**. He dreamed of building a highway with **walking tracks** and fourteen rest stations along the summit of the Port Hills and right around the peninsula to Akaroa. The project got under way at the beginning of the twentieth century, but when Ell died in 1934 only four rest stations (all of local stone and mostly named after native birds) had been built.

The first was the **Sign of the Takahe**, Dyers Pass Road, a Gothic-style baronial house distinguished by enormous kauri beams, salvaged from a bridge that once spanned the Hurunui River. This building now houses a classy restaurant and a more casual café/bar (for both see p.591), and for the price of a coffee you can take a look at some unique friezes fashioned from old packing cases and stone quarried from the peninsula. Look out for the heraldic embellishments relating to early governors of New Zealand, coats of arms of local families and shields portraying significant events in British history.

From the *Sign of the Takahe*, Dyers Pass Road runs 4km uphill to the Summit Road and the second rest station, the **Sign of the Kiwi**, now a reasonable café (see p.591). This is perhaps the best place to start the exploration of the Summit Road.

From the *Sign of the Kiwi* the Summit Road follows the ridge tops 9km southwest to the single remaining room of the third of Ell's structures, the **Sign of the Bellbird**, a stone picnic shelter with exceptional views.

The last rest station, the **Sign of the Packhorse**, is now a trampers' hut between Mount Bradley and Remarkable Dykes near Diamond Harbour (see p.600).

and when you hit the foothills continue straight ahead up **Dyers Pass Road**. This takes you past the *Sign of the Takahe* and on up to the *Sign of the Kiwi* (for both see p.591) at Dyers Pass. At the latter, turn left. You're now on the Summit Road with alternate views north down to Christchurch and south to Lyttelton and its harbour. There are numerous rocky outcrops and wayside viewpoints along this twisting 14km route to Evans Pass: many make great spots for a picnic or to watch the sun drop behind the Southern Alps.

At Evans Pass either turn right to reach **Lyttelton** and return to Christchurch through the tunnel; or turn left for the **beaches** of Sumner and Taylor's Mistake. Straight ahead is Godley Head (see p.600).

Cyclists could easily spend a day following the same route. Traffic is sparse, but what there is tends to hare round blind corners, so keep your wits about you. Mountain bikers can often get off the road on parallel tracks, which make for some excellent riding.

Walkers are also well served with paths. The lack of useful buses makes one-way hikes inconvenient, but you can stop pretty much anywhere along the ridge and find appealing walks. The Port Hills brochure (available free from visitor centres) shows where all the footpaths go and includes details on the **Crater Rim Walkway** (18.5km one way; 5hr; continuously undulating), a magical path right along the crater rim.

Eating and drinking

Christchurch has more restaurants, cafés, bars and pubs than anywhere else on the South Island, the bulk of them in the city centre. There's everything from cheap little **ethnic** places to the **finest dining**, along with an abundance of **cool café/bars**. As ever, many places operate as restaurants during the day and bars at night, or as bars that morph into dance and club venues as night turns to morning. We've listed places where they seem to fit best, but it is worthwhile scanning other categories.

Central Christchurch

There is little reason to venture beyond the Four Avenues for food and drink; you'll find most of what you need in the grid of **downtown** streets close to Cathedral Square. Places are quite broadly scattered, but a few areas warrant special mention. The southeastern end of **High Street** (around Lichfield and Tuam streets) is particularly good for offbeat cafés and good lunch spots. **The Strip**, a section of Oxford Terrace between Cashel and Gloucester streets, overlooking the river Avon, is a great place for lunch in the sun, with a dozen or so almost indistinguishable restaurant/bars spilling out onto the pavement, attracting the after-work set for dinner, then settling down to serious drinking (and weekend DJs) later on. In the last year or so much of the cooler action has moved to **SOL Square**, just off Lichfield Street, where there are some great bars, many serving food. If you're **self-catering**, head for the New World **supermarket** at 555 Colombo St and the **City Seafood Market**, 277 Manchester St.

You can combine sightseeing with dining by clunking around Christchurch's streets on the **dinner tram** (daily 7.30pm; from $68 for 4 courses; ⓣ03/366 7511, ⓦwww.tram.co.nz), operating from 7.30pm and offering local delicacies as well as a broader selection of Kiwi cuisine.

Cafés and takeaways

Café Metro Corner of Colombo & Kilmore sts. One of the best cafés in this part of town, right by the Town Hall with great coffee, a good range of quiche, pies, muffins and cakes, and a varied stack of up-to-date mags.

C1 Espresso 150 High St. Tardis-like young and funky café where filling gourmet sandwiches ($10) fight for your attention with omelettes, pizza, flatbreads, breakfasts, smoothies, juices and dynamite coffee. There's a selection of mags and papers, a mishmash of 50s and 60s furniture and a DJ holding forth from a little booth most evenings and weekends.

Costas Souvlaki Bar 150 Armagh St. Unpretentious and cheap little kebab, falafel, Greek salad and, obviously, souvlaki café that has been around since time began. Closed Sun.

Globe Café 171 High St. Wonderful coffee spot and lunchtime hangout for students from the jazz school across the road, with a spacious interior and pavement seating. Great for teas, all manner of panini, salads, quiches and stunning cakes. Licensed.

Herb Centre 225 Kilmore St. Daytime café specializing in a range of caffeine-free drinks, smoothies, organic coffee, gluten-free nosh and quality food at lowish prices. Next door Piko Healthfoods sell organic bread and food. Closed Sun.

Le Café The Arts Centre, Worcester St ⓣ03/366 7722. Atmospheric, wood-beamed café that's open from 7am–midnight daily and is understandably popular for breakfast specials, focaccia sandwiches ($14), mains ($15), great tiramisu ($10) and scrumptious boysenberry smoothies.

Procopé Coffee House 165 Victoria St. Great little unlicensed café serving delicious salads, mushroom and chicken crepes and a fine lunch platter for two ($22).

Under the Red Verandah 502 Worcester St. Delightful suburban daytime café 20min walk east of the centre, but worth the effort for its breakfast/brunch menu, pumpkin and corn cakes, bacon and *kumara* frittata, organic breads and coffee served in the bare-boards interior or in the sunny courtyard. There's a resident cat as well. Closed Mon.

Restaurants

Annie's The Arts Centre, Worcester St ⓣ03/365 0566. Charming wine bar and restaurant within the polished-wood-floor confines of the Arts Centre, that spills into the sun-dappled courtyard outside. Lunches ($12–20) might include a field mushroom,

▲ Café culture, New Regent Street

feta and sweet-pepper gateau or a smoked chicken salad; mains ($24–35) a cut of herb-roasted ostrich. Licensed.

Ann's Thai 165 Hereford St ⓣ03/379 9843. Classic Thai cooking in a simple restaurant with a pleasant bar and broad wine list. Try the spicy salad, roast duck or whole fish. Good $8–10 weekday lunch specials.

Blue Note 22 New Regent St ⓣ03/379 9674. Restaurant and bar where diners spill out onto the pedestrianized street as they tuck into $26–30 mains, such as Canterbury lamb fillets or fish and garlic mash accompanied by zingy New-World wines. Live jazz Thurs–Sat with no cover. Closed Sun.

The Bodhi Tree 808 Colombo St ⓣ03/377 6808. Casual dinner-only Burmese place popular for dishes such as fish fillet with tamarind, coriander, chilli and tomato ($16), tempura whitebait on mango salad ($13) and yellow split-pea tofu salad ($10). Order several dishes and share. Booking almost essential. Closed Mon.

Coyote 126 Oxford Terrace. The heart of The Strip, this restaurant and bar serves everything from top-notch nachos to whitebait omelettes and rib-eye, and later becomes a regular watering hole for the city's bright young things. Shame about the imitation adobe walls and fake beams.

Dux de Lux Corner of Hereford & Montreal sts. Slightly dated but ever-popular restaurant with outdoor and indoor seating and a longstanding reputation for superb seafood and vegetarian meals at moderate prices: Thai green mussel curry or gourmet pizza for under $24. Wash it down with award-winning beers brewed on the premises (tasting tray $12). Live music Thurs–Sat and generally no cover charge.

Hay's Restaurant 63 Victoria St ⓣ03/379 7501. Classy restaurant that's a must for lamb aficionados: the animals are mostly reared on the owners' Banks Peninsula property. Imaginative and delicious food is accompanied by something from their wonderful wine list – mains go for $35. Closed Sun & Mon in winter.

Honey Pot 114 Lichfield St. Casual restaurant with rustic wooden tables, where you can enjoy all-day breakfasts and a wide range of rich and hearty food at reasonable prices. The service is a bit sloppy but it is worth waiting for the likes of delicious naan bread with dips ($9), vegetable and mushroom stuffed cannelloni ($22), venison burger ($16) and grilled porterhouse with lime mash ($28).

Oxford on Avon 794 Colombo St ⓣ03/379 7148. Pub on the banks of the Avon, famed for its large portions of straightforward, cheap nosh (including a $16 all-you-can-eat breakfast); $10 roast lunches; $10 mains Mon–Thurs). Always busy with the food-bargain hunters.

Palazzo del Marinaio 108 Hereford St ⓣ03/365 5911. If you've been saving up for a week then this is the place to treat yourself to seafood and steaks, plus the finest wine, port, brandy and malt whisky. Mains $30–35. Daily, lunch and dinner.

Retour Corner of Cambridge Terrace & Manchester St ⓣ03/365 2888. Some of the best fine-dining meals in town are served in this dinner-only restaurant beautifully located in a glass-sided bandstand on the banks of the Avon. A gem.

Saggio di Vino 185 Victoria St corner of Bealey Ave ⓣ03/379 4006. Classy Italian dinner-only restaurant where dishes such as roasted pumpkin and Bergamo cheese risotto ($32) can be accompanied by wine from an extensive award-winning cellar; all available by the glass.

Topkapi 185 Manchester St. Budget Turkish joint with quality kebabs ($11–14), iskandars ($18–22) and rich baklava. Licensed & BYO wine.

Pubs and bars

Belgian Beer Café Torenhof 88 Armagh St ⓣ03/377 1007. Central bar with a good range of beers, Belgian-style dishes like steamed mussels ($25) and a bustling atmosphere. Catch the afternoon sun on the deck overlooking the Avon.

Cartel His Lordship's Lane, 96 Lichfield St. Diminutive dark bar in the heart of the action, that spills out onto the lane where the connected get to lounge on the bean bag in front of the big fire.

Dux de Lux (see above). Award-winning beers and live music.

The Fish & Chip Shop His Lordship's Lane, 96 Lichfield St. Funky and bustling bar with a retro Kiwiana theme. The subtleties might be lost on foreign visitors but you'll still enjoy the vibe and they do sell expensive fish and chips, served wrapped in newspaper at formica tables.

Iconic 200 Manchester St, corner of Manchester and Gloucester sts. Big brash sports bar with large screens, pool tables, a loud PA system, drinks specials, events, filling pub grub and covered external smoking areas for an illicit ciggie.

Sullivan's 150 Manchester St. Fairly traditional Irish bar with pictures of the old country, gallons of beer, live Irish-style bands from Wed–Sat, and late-night dancing towards the end of the week.

Twisted Hop 6 Poplar St. Rough concrete floor and stylish lighting gives a modern Kiwi slant to this pub selling several cask-conditioned English-style beers brewed on site. Meals run from pizzas ($19) to steak frites ($28) and fish, chips and mushy peas ($20). Five-beer tasting tray for $15.

Viaduct 136 Oxford Terrace. One of almost a dozen near-identical restaurant/bars along "The Strip" and as good a starting point as any. Its Greek-column-and-Spanish-tile interior help create a cocktail atmosphere midweek, and weekends are always rowdy.

Winnie Bagoes 194 Gloucester St. Wood, metal and red-brick conversion, exuding urban chic. Tap and bottle beers, cocktails, a fair selection of wine, good pizzas and weekend DJs. On Thursdays you can hear mellower acoustic sounds.

Papanui Road and Merivale

There's little culinary reason to leave the city centre and head out to the suburbs, but villagey Merivale is well placed if you are staying along Papanui Road or in the northern reaches of the city.

The following places are marked on the map on p.582.

Brigitte's Hawkesbury Building, Aikmans Rd, Merivale. Very busy but relaxed restaurant and wine bar with open courtyard at the back, serving good-quality Mediterranean and Kiwi-style food, as well as some New Zealand–Thai combinations, at moderate prices.

Tutto Bene 192 Papanui Rd ⓣ03/355 3744. Hugely popular trad Italian restaurant where hearty portions are dished up on gingham tablecloths. Pizza, pasta and risotto go for around $23 while main courses are $30. Licensed and BYO ($7 corkage). Dinner only; booking highly recommended.

Sumner

You won't starve at **Sumner**, and there are new places opening all the time. If you are bored with the city it's worth coming out here for a beach stroll, beer and bite in the evening: the #3 bus back to the city runs until gone 11pm.

The following places are marked on the map on p.582.

Deli-licious 21 Marriner St. Straightforward, quality café with the best espresso on the beach.

Dot Com 42 Marriner St. Sleek, tiny modern café with good coffee, a range of light and tasty meals and Internet access.

Indian Sumner 11a Wakefield Ave ⓣ03/326 4777. Good name, great curries. Dine outside on the pavement, take away or hope to get into their cramped but atmospheric interior for something from their small but well-chosen selection of mains ($12–17). Dinner only; closed Mon.

JDV 22a The Esplanade ⓣ03/326 5358. Probably the best dining in Sumner, in a relaxed setting with pavement tables just across the road from the sea. Dinner mains (around $30) might include beef fillet with wild mushroom gratin, desserts an Italian ricotta cake with espresso anglaise ($12). Book on summer evenings.

Poseidon 25 The Esplanade ⓣ03/326 7090. Perfect spot for a sundowner right on the beach, though the food and service can be hit and miss.

The Port Hills

There are few places to eat when exploring the **Port Hills**, though these two should satisfy most needs. Both are in original rest stations for Harry Ell's Summit Road (see box, p.582).

Sign of the Kiwi corner of Dyers Pass and the Summit Rds. Fairly basic tearoom perfectly sited on a col with great views over Christchurch to the Alps. Daily 10am–4pm.

Sign of the Takahe Dyers Pass Rd, Cashmere ⓣ03/332 4052, ⓦwww.signofthetakahe.co.nz. This grand baronial building houses two restaurants. The *Signature Restaurant* offers evening fine dining in a classy setting with long views towards the Southern Alps. A Kiwi take on French cuisine produces a menu which might include mains ($32–38) of Akaroa salmon in chive *beurre blanc* or horopito-rubbed loin of lamb, followed by raspberry crème brûlée. The more modest *SOH* is a low-key café/bar in a stone-flagged former half-cellar (check out Harry Ell's signature on the wall) spilling out onto the lawns. Open all day for quality breakfasts, coffee, muffins and the likes of chicken caesar salad ($19), beef stroganoff pie ($22) and a charcuterie platter ($28).

Nightlife and entertainment

Most of Christchurch's nightlife takes place along or just off Manchester Street between Gloucester and Lichfield Streets. The lanes off Lichfield Street, particularly **His Lordship's Lane**, and **Poplar Street**, have recently become the city's dining and partying hub.

Serious **music and drama** are centred on venues like the Town Hall and the Arts Centre, and there's a clutch of city-centre cinemas. The Megaguide in Monday's *The Press* newspaper covers theatre and live music **listings** for the whole week.

Clubs and gigs

Things are pretty quiet early in the week, but begin to rev up from Thursday when a sprinkling of places within the Four Avenues open. Some of these are full-on **clubs**, though a growing number of bars transform into dancing venues at weekends by drafting in a DJ or two. There's a surfeit of bars offering **live music**, although most places content themselves with a meagre diet of cover or Irish-style bands and minor local rock acts. If you want to stroll around and see where the crowds are going, make for Lichfield Street around the intersection with High Street. For a general idea of who is playing or spinning platters check out the fortnightly *JAGG* clubguide (Ⓦwww.jagg.co.nz), available free in bars.

Al's Bar 31 Dundas St Ⓣ03/366 6877. The most rock 'n' roll venue in town. Live gigs from local Kiwi bands and occasionally small international acts, mostly Thurs–Sun.

The Civic 194 Manchester St Ⓣ03/374 9988. Popular and huge clubbing venue offering a range of themed nights (funk, hip-hop, rare groove, house and techno) and some headline live acts; check listings in *The Press* to see what's on. Also *Zinc* lounge bar on the same site. Open Wed–Sat.

Concrete Club 132 Manchester St, under the *Loaded Hog*. Take a mole's-eye view of the world in this cool atmospheric basement club, with music ranging from roots to drum'n'bass. Open Tues–Sat.

Foam 30 Bedford Row. Laid-back speakeasy type atmosphere, smooth grooves and good cocktails.

Heavens Above 170 Tuam St. Christchurch's only genuine gay bar. Open Thurs–Sun.

Propaganda 88–90 Lichfield St Ⓣ03/379 2910. One of the biggest and liveliest of the clubs, with two dancefloors. Deep, dark and with thumping drum'n'bass and hardcore till sunup. Also a lounge bar. Kicks off around midnight and there's sometimes a small cover charge.

Rock Pool 85 Hereford St. A broad spectrum of imported beers, cocktails and 22 pool tables, as well as a PA rarely turned below ear-splitting level. Daily 9am till late; attached to *Mickey Finn's Irish Bar* upstairs.

Concerts, theatre, cinema and spectator sports

Christchurch runs a busy cultural calendar with shows at the various theatres, a selection of movie theatres and cricket, rugby and big gig at AMI Stadium. Tourists are wooed with Maori cultural experiences at both Ko Tane and Tamaki Heritage Village, and the Arts Centre typically hosts a bunch of gigs and shows – and even a Ghost Walk. There is also a varied programme of music events in Hagley Park throughout the summer (Ⓦwww.summertimes.org.nz).

Concerts and theatre

Court Theatre 20 Worcester Blvd, Arts Centre Ⓣ0800/333 100, Ⓦwww.courttheatre.org.nz. The shining star in Christchurch's drama firmament. This longstanding and highly reputed theatre company puts on a professional roster of mainstream and more edgy works. Performances are well advertised around town and in *The Press*. Tickets $30–37.

Ghost Walk ⓣ03/963 0870. Actors from the Court Theatre lead entertaining evening strolls (Wed–Fri, Oct–March 9pm, April–Sept 8pm; $20) through the dark and creepy cloisters of the Arts Centre.

Ko Tane: The Maori Experience ⓣ03/359 6226, ⓦwww.kotane.co.nz. If you've missed your chance in Rotorua (see p.311), you can catch a Maori concert and *hangi* evening here at Willowbank Wildlife Reserve (see p.584). The basic package is the cultural performance and tour of Willowbank (several times nightly; $39, or $49 if you want to include a guided tour round the park) complete with *powhiri* greeting and Maori cultural performance. Or step up to the full Maori Experience (dining at 6.30pm & 7.30pm; $89) with added *hangi* dinner.

Tamaki Heritage Village Ferrymead Historic Park, 8km southeast of central Christchurch ⓣ03/366 &333, ⓦwww.christchurchinfo.co.nz. A diverting and instructional, though not wholly successful, attempt to illustrate the impact of colonization on Maori society and how the two societies forged a path together. Actors role-play in a mock-up Maori *pa* and village where you can see traditional crafts being practised as a colonial force attacks. As you ride a tram through the relocated Victorian buildings of the Ferrymead Historic Park you're given a sense of the tensions bubbling under as Pakeha ways gradually submerge Maori values. A *hangi*, and short steam train ride complete the evening's entertainment. Takes place most evenings; $120.

Theatre Royal 145 Gloucester St ⓣ03/377 8899. Concerts by touring mainstream jazz and rock acts often take place in this fine old Edwardian venue.

Town Hall Victoria Square. Touring shows frequently play in the main auditorium, which also has a programme of classical music and ballet. Tickets through Ticketek ⓣ03/377 8899.

Cinema

Academy Cinema Arts Centre ⓣ03/366 0167, ⓦwww.artfilms.co.nz. Arthouse cinema with a smaller sister cinema, Cloisters.

Hoyts 392 Moorhouse Ave ⓣ03/377 9941. Major multiplex at the southern end of Manchester St.

Regent 94 Worcester St ⓣ 03/366 0140. Four-screen multiplex right by Cathedral Square.

Rialto 250 Moorhouse Ave corner of Durham St ⓣ03/374 9404. Three-screen multiplex with arty leanings.

Sport

AMI Stadium Southeast of the centre near the junction of Moorhouse Ave & Ferry Rd. Generically known by its historic name of Lancaster Park, this is the main venue for the big spectator sports, hosting cricket in the summer and rugby on weekends throughout the autumn and winter. Visit ⓦwww.amistadium.co.nz for information and Ticketek (ⓣ03/377 8899, ⓦwww.ticketek.co.nz) for tickets.

Listings

Automobile Association 210 Hereford St ⓣ03/964 3650.

Banks and exchange Most banks have branches and ATMs on Colombo St a block north or south of the Square or near Colombo and Hereford sts.

Bike rental The most convenient bike rental is Wheels 'n' Deals Cycles, 159 Gloucester St between Manchester and Colombo (Mon–Fri 9am–5.30pm, Sat 10am–4pm. Sun 11am–3pm; ⓣ03/377 6655) who rent out mountain bikes and tourers for $18 a half-day and $25 a day.

Bookshops Whitcoulls in the Cashel St Mall. Otherwise try: Scorpio Books, 79 Hereford St; Liberty Books, 147 High St & 145 Manchester St, good for secondhand paperbacks; Map World, 173 Gloucester St has the best range of maps and guides; and Madras Cafe Bookshop, 165 Madras St, stocks quality books and has a good little café.

Car and campervan rental There are dozens of car and van rental places in Christchurch many of them clustered along Lichfield between Montreal and Barbados sts. From Jan to March you may have trouble landing anything if you don't book ahead; for more on car hire and contact details for international and nationwide companies, see Basics, p.41. The following are reputable local and national

Moving on from Christchurch

Christchurch is the hub of air, road and rail routes for the South Island: see Travel Agencies in "Listings" (p.585) for bookings. There are direct **flights** to Blenheim, Dunedin, Hokitika, Invercargill, Nelson, Queenstown, Wanaka and several North Island cities. Two very scenic passenger **trains** operate: the TranzCoastal to Picton (meeting ferries to the North Island) and the TranzAlpine to Greymouth (see box, p.585). Most inter city journeys are best done by **bus**. There are usually 2–4 services a day to most destinations, but bear in mind that journeys from, say, Christchurch to Nelson or Queenstown are likely to take up most of the day.

Independent companies run the following services:

Akaroa French Connection ⓣ0800/800 575, ⓦwww.akaroabus.co.nz. To Akaroa twice daily. Free central pick-ups.

Akaroa Shuttle ⓣ0800/500 929, ⓦwww.akaroashuttle.co.nz. To Akaroa 2–3 times daily. Departs Christchurch i-SITE.

Atomic Shuttles ⓣ03/439 0697, ⓦwww.atomictravel.co.nz. North to Kaikoura, Blenheim and Picton; south to Timaru, Oamaru and Dunedin; west to Greymouth; and inland through Geraldine and Twizel to Wanaka and Queenstown. Departs from 88 Worcester St, but free pick-ups inside the Four Avenues.

Coast to Coast ⓣ0800/800 847, ⓦwww.coast2coast.co.nz. To Greymouth and Hokitika via Arthur's Pass. Departs Cathedral Square with some local pick-ups.

Hanmer Connection ⓣ0800/242 663, ⓦwww.atsnz.com. Daily to Hanmer Springs. Departs Cathedral Square.

InterCity/Newmans ⓣ03/365 1113, ⓦwww.intercitycoach.co.nz. North to Kaikoura, Blenheim, Picton and Nelson; south to Timaru, Oamaru, Dunedin and Invercargill; and inland to Methven, Aoraki Mount Cook, Wanaka and Queenstown. Services depart from Richies Travel at 123 Worcester St behind the cathedral.

Knightrider ⓣ0800/317 057, ⓦwww.knightrider.co.nz. Evening/night trips to Dunedin and Invercargill. Departs from Victoria Square on Colombo Street.

Methven Travel ⓣ03/302 8106, ⓦwww.methventravel.co.nz. Daily to Methven.

South Island Connections ⓣ0508/742 669: daily runs to Dunedin and Picton.

Southern Link K Bus ⓣ0508/458 835, ⓦwww.southernlinkcoaches.co.nz. South to Timaru, Oamaru and Dunedin; inland via Geraldine, Tekapo, Twizel and Wanaka to Queenstown; north to Kaikoura, Blenheim & Picton; and to Nelson via Hanmer Springs and the Lewis Pass. Departs from 88 Worcester St near the Square.

West Coast Shuttle ⓣ03/768 0028, ⓦwww.westcoastshuttle.co.nz. Daily to Greymouth. Services depart from Richies Travel at 123 Worcester St behind the cathedral.

agencies: Ace ⓣ0800/202 029, ⓦwww.acerentalcars.co.nz; Apex ⓣ0800/939 597, ⓦwww.apexrenrentals.co.nz; Apple ⓣ03/366 4855, ⓦwww.applerentalcars.co.nz; Avon Percy ⓣ0800/736 828, ⓦwww.avonrentacar.co.nz; Explore ⓣ0800/447 363, ⓦwww.exploremore.co.nz; Jucy ⓣ0800/399 107, ⓦwww.jucy.co.nz; Nationwide ⓣ0800/803 003, ⓦwww.nationwiderentals.co.nz; Omega ⓣ0800/626 210, ⓦwww.omegarental.co.nz; Scotties ⓣ0800/736 825, ⓦwww.scotties.co.nz; U-Save ⓣ0508/112 233, ⓦwww.rental-car.co.nz.

Festivals The local city council enthusiastically backs a number of summer festivals. Look out particularly for the Jazz Festival (mid-Oct); the free World Buskers Festival (late Jan), which is lots of fun and mostly takes place around the Arts Centre, in front of the *Dux De Lux* and in the Square; and the Festival of Romance (early to mid-Feb) on the lead up to Valentine's Day. Check at the information centre for more details or consult ⓦwww.bethere.org.nz.

Internet access The City library (see p.595) has free Wi-Fi , and Internet access for $3 per hr. Numerous Internet places around the Square (mostly charging $3–4 per hr) including E Blah Blah, 77 Cathedral Square.

Left luggage (see p.569 for airport storage). Most hostels offer a left-luggage facility at usually no

more than $5 a day. Also E Blah Blah, 77 Cathedral Square (packs $3/calendar day; daily 8am–10pm).
Library Central Library, Gloucester St (Mon–Fri 9am–9pm, Sat & Sun 10am–4pm).
Medical treatment In emergencies call ☎111. For a doctor at any time call The 24 Hour Surgery, corner of Bealey Ave & Colombo St (☎03/365 7777, no appointment necessary). Biggest of the hospitals is Christchurch Hospital, corner of Oxford Terrace & Riccarton Ave (☎03/364 0640).
Outdoor gear Loads of places along Lichfield St between Colombo and Durham sts, notably Bivouac, corner of Colombo & Lichfield sts.
Pharmacies After-hours pharmacy at The 24 Hour Surgery (see "Medical Treatment" above; ☎03/366 4439), stays open daily until 11pm.
Police Central Police Station, corner of Hereford St & Cambridge Terrace ☎03/363 7400.
Post office The main post office is at 680 Colombo St at Gloucester St (☎03/374 4381) has poste restante facilities.
Shuttle buses For airport and train station transfers, shuttle buses offer a cheaper alternative to taxis. Try Super Shuttle (☎0800/748 885) which runs from Cathedral Square to the airport ($17 per person). They'll also pick you up from your accommodation. If you're catching a morning flight you should book your transfer the evening before. There are also $5 no-name shuttles from the tram stop in the Square leaving for the airport roughly every 20min: take your chance.
Taxis Blue Star (☎03/379 9799) and Gold Band (☎03/379 5795) all have heaps of cabs.
Tours Guided walking tours (daily Oct–April 10am & 1pm; May–Sept 1pm; 2hr; $10; ☎03/365 8480), led by local volunteers who really know their stuff, start from a kiosk in Cathedral Square near the cathedral entrance. Christchurch Sightseeing Tours (☎0508/669 660, www.christchurchtours.co.nz) offer a City, Beach and Harbour tour (3hr, $46); a summer-only Private Gardens tour (3hr; $40); and a Heritage Homes tour (3hr; $40).
Train information ☎0800/872 467.
Travel agencies Flight Centre, 116 Cashel St (☎03/366 6371) and STA, corner of Colombo & Cashel sts (☎03/379 9098).

Banks Peninsula

Flying into Christchurch you'll be struck by the dramatic contrast between the flat plains of Canterbury and the rugged, fissured topography of **Banks Peninsula**, a volcanic thumb sticking out into the Canterbury Bight. When James Cook sailed by in 1769 he mistakenly charted it as an island and named it after his botanist Joseph Banks. His error was only one of time, as this basalt lump initially formed an island, only joined to the land as silt sluiced down the rivers from the eastern flanks of the Southern Alps.

The fertile **volcanic** soil of the peninsula's valleys sprouted totara, matai and kahikatea trees that, along with the abundant shellfish in the bays, attracted early Maori around a thousand years ago. The trees soon succumbed to the fire stick, a process accelerated with the arrival of European timber-milling interests. The lumber yards ground to a halt when the trees ran out in the late 1880s, and the peninsula is now largely bald, with large areas of tussock grass on the rolling hills, and small pockets of regenerating native bush and trees.

Today, the two massive drowned craters that form Banks Peninsula are key to the commerce of the region. Lyttelton Harbour protects and nurtures the port town of **Lyttelton**, disembarkation point for countless European migrants and now the South Island's major port. It remains a workaday town but is rapidly gentrifying with several entertaining places to eat and drink plus its historic timeball station, harbour cruises and dolphin watching. There's an altogether more refined tone to the picturesque and visitor-oriented town of **Akaroa**; lent a gentle French influence by its founders. Elsewhere on the peninsula, a network of narrow, twisting roads wind along the crater rims and dive down to

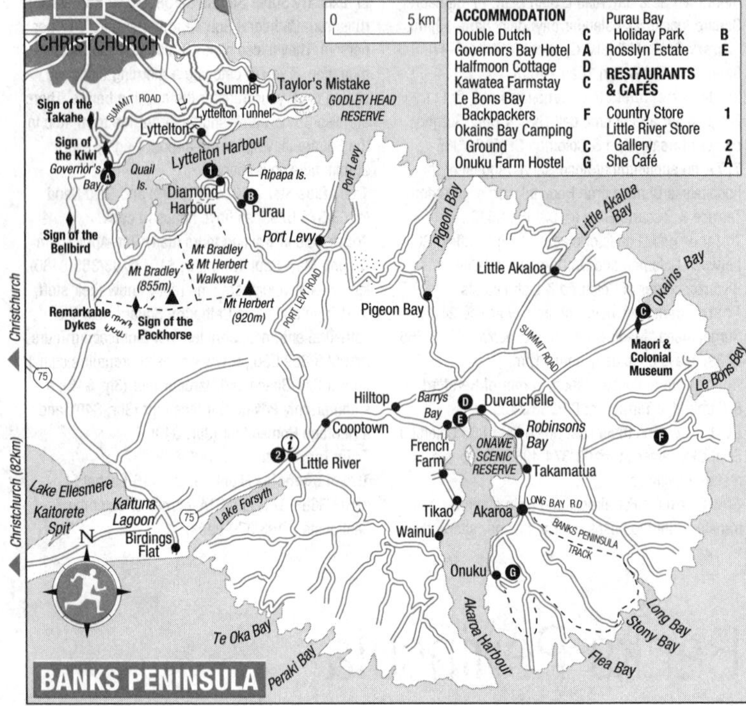

gorgeous, quiet bays once alive with whalers, sealers and shipbuilders, but now seldom visited except during the peak of summer.

Despite the denuded grassland of much of the landscape, Banks Peninsula is very popular for relatively easy scenic **walks**, with panoramic views, ancient lava flows, relics from the earliest Maori and European settlers and great beaches. As befits a city playground, the peninsula is also well endowed with country-style B&Bs and farmstays, while Akaroa and Lyttelton both have a host of decent restaurants.

From Christchurch, the main route to Akaroa is **SH75**, via Lake Ellesmere and Little River, though a more picturesque journey follows the **Summit Road** from Sumner via Lyttelton, along the Port Hills and ridges of the peninsula. **Buses** from Christchurch serve only the main towns of Lyttelton and Akaroa, and to reach the smaller communities tucked into the bays you'll need your own transport. If you're planning on cycling, bear in mind that the peninsula is extremely hilly, and the routes linking the summit road with the various bays below can be steep.

Lyttelton

Just 12km southeast of Christchurch city centre, **LYTTELTON** is a world apart, hemmed in by the rocky walls of the drowned volcanic crater that forms **Lyttelton Harbour**. It is an attractive setting that is rapidly drawing a coterie of city escapees to the smart cafés and restaurants, but Lyttelton is foremost a working port that retains a raffish air: rowdy clanking from the docks and rumbustiousness from the waterfront bars, with plenty of overheard snippets of Polish, Russian and Filipino. Boats servicing the New Zealand and the US bases in Antarctica leave from here, and cruise ships visit a few dozen times a year, though the passengers are mostly bussed off to Christchurch as soon as they arrive.

The town itself overlooks the docks and quays, climbing up the Port Hills behind and spreading southwest along the coast toward Governors Bay. The web of streets spreading up the hill are primarily residential but running parallel with the docks are the best bars, restaurants, shops and accommodation possibilities, mostly on London Street.

Arrival, information and accommodation

The quickest way from Christchurch to Lyttelton is through the 2km Lyttelton Tunnel, which brings you right to the heart of town, just twenty minutes after leaving Christchurch; the #28 **bus** from Cathedral Square leaves every 15–30min (a journey of 35min; $2.50). The small **visitor centre** resides in Anchor Fine Arts, 34 London St (daily 9am–5pm; ⓣ03/328 9093, ⓦwww.lytteltonharbour.co.nz) and has a leaflet describing a self-guided **walk** around Lyttelton's many historic sites.

Accommodation right in Lyttelton is somewhat limited, though there is a good backpackers and a couple of attractive B&Bs. Most of the best places are

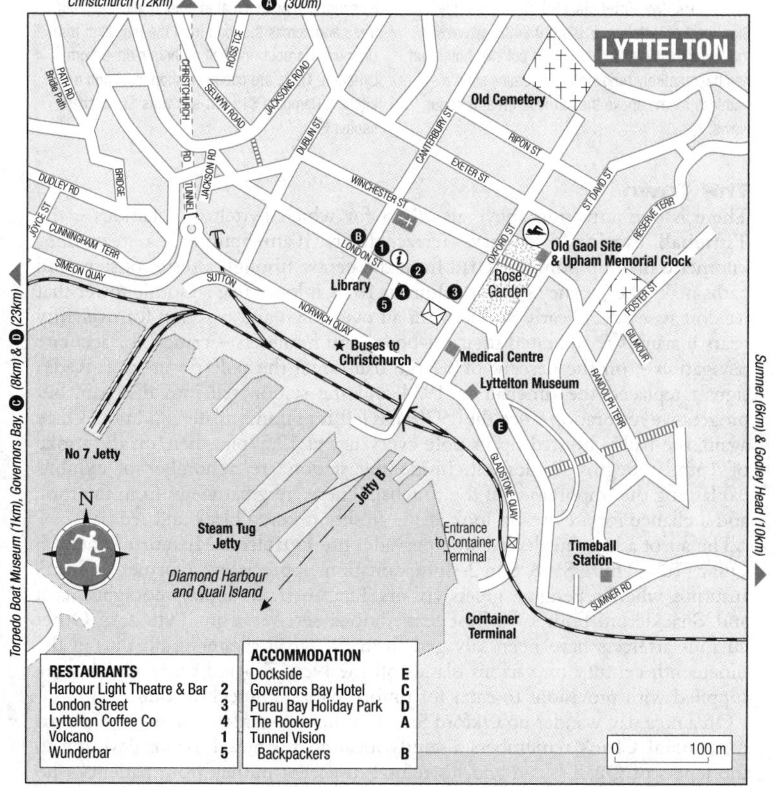

some way out of town around Lyttelton Harbour, along with the only campsite that is remotely close.

Lyttleton centre

These hotels are on the Lyttleton map p.597.

Dockside 22 Sumner Rd ⓣ027/448 8133. ⓦwww.dockside.co.nz. Well-run, self-catering B&B apartment with a sunny en-suite room and a deck with panoramic harbour views plus one very pleasant bedsit. Continental breakfast. Bedsit ❸, apartment ❹

The Rookery 9 Ross Terrace, Lyttelton ⓣ03/328 8038, ⓦwww.therookery.co.nz. Appealing B&B imaginatively designed with unconventional features that can make you feel like you're aboard ship. Both main bedrooms have private entrance and underfloor heating, and the en suite has great harbour views and a digital cinema. The cosy second room has Port Hills views, and there's also a single room let for $84. Great breakfast and convivial hosts. It is a steep 10min walk up from town: call for driving directions. Shared bathroom ❺, en suite ❺

Tunnel Vision Backpackers 44 London St ⓣ03/328 7576, ⓦwww.tunnelvision.co.nz. A brightly decorated, well-maintained, hostel occupying a renovated old hotel in a central location with a good selection of double and twin rooms, some with harbour views. Dorms $25, rooms ❷

Around Lyttleton

These hotels are on the Banks Peninsula map p.596.

Governors Bay Hotel Main Rd, Governors Bay 8km west of Lyttelton ⓣ03/329 9433, ⓦwww.governorsbayhotel.co.nz. A large colonial hotel that has been entirely renovated but retains simple bathless rooms above the bar with great harbour views. ❹

Purau Bay Holiday Park Diamond Harbour ⓣ0800/468 678, ⓦwww.holidayparks.co.nz. Pleasant campsite situated among tall sheltering trees and across the road from the bay, 2km from Diamond Harbour and half an hour's drive from Lyttelton. There are cabins, a shop, pool and a kitchen. Camping $15, On-site vans ❶, kitchen cabins ❷

The Town

There is one attraction above all others for which Lyttelton is famous – the **Timeball Station**, 2 Reserve Terrace (daily 10am–5pm; $7), a steep one-kilometre hike up Sumner Road from the centre (though a series of steps and paths make the journey shorter). Built in 1876, it looks like a Gothic tower that has lost its castle. Clearly visible from all over town and harbour, for over fifty years mariners recalibrated their on-board chronometers – critical for accurate navigation – on the descent of a large ball down the pole on its roof. Radio signals replaced the timeball in 1934 and the station fell into disrepair, but progressive restoration since the 1970s has left it in immaculate condition. Once again, the ball is hoisted up its pole every day at 12.57pm, then, on the stroke of 1pm, it begins its descent. Inside the station are a number of exhibits explaining the importance of the timeball. There are great views from the roof, and a chance for a close-up look at the freshly restored black and red ball.

The air of a long-neglected attic pervades the **Lyttelton Museum**, Norwich Quay (Tues, Thurs, Sat & Sun 2–4pm; donations appreciated) a former Seaman's Institute, where a penguin greets visitors. The Antarctic display spotlights Scott and Shackleton, both of whose expeditions set out from Lyttelton. Other curious artefacts have been salvaged from the small shelters built during the nineteenth century on various islands off the New Zealand shore, which were supplied with provisions to cater for unfortunate shipwrecked souls.

On a nice day, wander up Oxford Street to the rose garden where the **Upham Memorial Clock** remembers a saintly local doctor noted for his devotion to the lepers of Quail Island and his refusal to accept money from patients who could not afford to pay. This is also the site of the old jail – the remains of a couple of the cells can be seen on the northern side of the gardens. Built in 1851, the jail became the South Island's major penal institution, even accommodating sheep rustler James McKenzie (see p.649) for a time.

Further up Oxford Street you'll find the **Old Cemetery**, which featured in Peter Jackson's 1996 movie *The Frighteners*.

Boats and harbour cruises

To get a sense of Lyttelton's maritime importance, particularly in time of war, visit the **Torpedo Boat Museum** (Nov–March Tues, Thurs, Sat & Sun 1–3pm; April–Oct Sat & Sun 1–3pm; $2) reached by a five-minute shoreline walk from a car park on Charlotte Jane Quay about 1km west of town. After the Russian invasion of Afghanistan in 1885, the fear of further Russian expansion spread around the western Pacific. New Zealand responded by building a Torpedo Boat to protect Lyttelton Harbour, designed to charge up to an invading ship, detonate a charge below the waterline then scarper before it could be attacked itself. The boat was, in fact, never used and has only recently been restored after years of abandonment. Its remains (principally the bow, stern and a fully restored engine) are now displayed in a former powder magazine along with a good video.

For a piece of living history, visit the **Steam Tug Lyttelton**, the older of only two steam tugs still operating in the country. It is docked at the wharf opposite Norwich Quay, over the Overhead Bridge, and on most summer Sundays the tug fires up for round-trip **cruises** (booking required ⓣ03/322 8911; 2.30pm, 90min; $15), steaming all the way to the head of the harbour. Built in Glasgow by the Ferguson brothers in 1907, this beautiful antique boat is maintained in full working order by an impassioned bunch of volunteers. The boiler room is particularly impressive: all burnished brass and oily pistons, cutting edge in its heyday, with steam-power-assisted steering.

Apart from the regular ferry services to Diamond Harbour and Quail Island (see p.600) Black Cat Cruises (ⓣ0800/436 574, ⓦwww.blackcat.co.nz) run a **Wildlife Cruise** (daily at 1.30pm; $55), departing from jetty B, that includes the prospect of seeing Hector's dolphins up close. There's a free shuttle from the Square in Christchurch; book in advance.

Eating and drinking

Lyttelton has a well-founded reputation for good-quality **food**, and is way livelier than you'd expect for such a small town. In fact, a trip to Lyttelton is justified solely on the intention of dining and sampling the curious pleasures of the *Wunderbar*. If you're here on Saturday morning, call in to the small **Farmers' Market** in the school grounds on Oxford Street.

Governors Bay Hotel Main Rd, 8km west of Lyttelton ⓣ03/329 9433. A renovated colonial hotel with outdoor seating where you can enjoy straightforward but tasty fare such as crumbed hoki or prawn laksa ($17–19).

Harbour Light Theatre and Bar 22 London St. Old theatre that still hosts some pretty lively gigs, usually advertised on the door with a functional little bar that opens when someone's playing.

London Street 2 London St ⓣ03/328 7171. This lively brick-lined restaurant is Lyttelton's finest, and a place that consistently meets high expectations. Local ingredients are used in seasonal dishes (mains $25–35) which draw influences from around the world: perhaps spinach ricotta and pine nut tart or pork cutlet with mustard mash. Everything is well matched with something from their huge wine list. Open for dinner Wed–Sun plus Sat brunch.

Lyttelton Coffee Co 29 London St. Cool, rough-hewn café with beans roasted on site and a hearty range of meals. A perfect brunch spot, with cakes, deep sofas and a sunny deck overlooking the port.

She Café 79 Main Rd, 8km west of Lyttelton at Governors Bay ⓣ03/329 9825, ⓦwww.shecafe.co.nz. With tables inside and out all looking straight down Lyttelton Harbour to the sea, this makes a great place for a leisurely lunch or a cinnamon and chilli spiced Mayan hot chocolate. Prices are a little high (lunch mains $20), but ingredients are mostly local, free range and organic, and there's a selection of veggie and vegan options. Try the mushroom and eggplant gateau or Akaroa salmon. Closed Tues.

Volcano 42 London St ⓣ03/328 7077. A Lyttelton institution fashioned out of a former fish and chip shop with bright, eclectic decor and meals served on formica tables all with fresh flowers. The cuisine draws on Cajun, Mexican, Spanish and Italian influences, with all sorts of home-made treats in substantial portions (mains $25–32). Licensed and BYO.

Wunderbar London St ⓦwww.wunderbar.co.nz. An idiosyncratic late-night drinking-hole and club, with decor ranging from crushed velour to a gruesome doll's-head lightshade, and a deck overlooking the harbour that's great for a peaceful drink if you can't take the clamour within. Entertainment ranges from 1940s and 50s cabaret nights, through poetry, live bands, stand-up comics, club and disco music, to film-noir evenings. Entry is down steps beside the supermarket, and up an iron fire escape. Check the website for upcoming events. Mon–Fri 5pm–late, Sat & Sun 1pm–even later.

Around Lyttelton Harbour

Lyttelton would be nothing without its **harbour**. Boats reach Lyttelton through "the heads", best seen from Godley Head – a moody, grass- and rock-covered promontory with steep sea cliffs offering excellent views. Across the harbour, the main destinations are the small community of **Diamond Harbour**, and **Quail Island**, a haven for birds.

Godley Head

At the northernmost tip of the harbour, **Godley Head** stands guard – a spectacular piece of land with high cliffs and excellent views, administered by DOC. Follow the signs east out of Lyttelton to the Summit Road that takes you out onto Godley Head (about 10km) and the **Godley Head Reserve**, a delightful spot for walks and picnics. The walkway network is extensive, in places stumbling across installations left behind after World War II, including dark warren-like tunnels and searchlight emplacements perched like birds' nests on the cliffs – from here, walk down to the tiny coastal settlements of Boulder Bay and Taylor's Mistake (see box, p.587).

Diamond Harbour

In bright sunlight the water sparkles like a million gems at **Diamond Harbour**, directly across the water from Lyttelton. Passenger **ferries** (sailings every 30–60min; $5 each way; ⓦwww.metroinfo.co.nz) make the fifteen-minute run across the harbour arriving at the Diamond Harbour wharf. Here you can generate a thirst with a 500-metre walk uphill, then slake it at either the *Country Store*, which does coffee, muffins and toasted sandwiches, or at **Godley House** (ⓦwww.godleyhouse.co.nz) a popular vantage point with gardens and lawns overlooking Diamond Harbour that have attracted visitors from Christchurch and beyond for more than a century. The house has been taken over by the conference market in recent years but on summer weekends you can still buy a beer or lunch and sprawl out on the grass. Keen hikers should head for the Mount Herbert Walkway (see box, p.601), and if you want to stay over this way there's the *Purau Bay Holiday Park* (see p.598) at Purau 2km east.

Quail island

Set in mid-harbour, the 86 hectare **Quail Island** was known by the local Maori as Otamahua meaning "place where children collected seabirds' eggs". From 1907 to 1925 it housed a small leper colony and in the early days of Antarctic

Mount Herbert Walkway

A good reason to cross Lyttelton Harbour is to tackle the **Mount Herbert Walkway** (14km loop; 6–8hr) which tops out at the summit of Mount Herbert, at 920m the highest point on Banks Peninsula. The views of the peninsula and across the plains to the Southern Alps are spectacular.

The track begins on the coastal road (Marine Drive) 600m west of Diamond Harbour and follows a grassy ridge straight towards Mount Herbert. It is a bit of a slog and quite exposed, so on a hot day take plenty of water and a hat. Near the top is a shelter where there is usually drinking water.

From near the summit it is possible to make a detour to the top of Mount Bradley and to the historic **Sign of the Packhorse** hut (see p.587).

Continuing clockwise, the track descends steeply across farmland and into the mostly bushy **Orton-Bradley Park**, where historic 1840s farm buildings recall pioneering times. The track brings you back to Marine Drive from where you'll need to walk (or hitch) 4km east along the road to get back to the start.

exploration Shackleton and Scott quarantined their dogs there before venturing to the South Pole. These days it's a venue for day-trips, swimming and walking: pack food, plenty of drinking water and rain gear. Two circular **walking tracks** (1hr & 2hr 30min), start from the island's wharf and visit safe swimming beaches along with several shipwrecks which can be seen at low tide. The island is reached with Black Cat Cruises (Oct–April daily 9.30am & 12.20pm with an additional boat Dec–March at 10.20am). Return services (Oct–March at 3.30pm, Dec–March at 12.30pm & 3.30pm).

Christchurch to Akaroa

With ample time on your hands and a taste for exploration consider approaching Banks Peninsula on the **Summit Road** (see box, p.587), winding around the crater rim of Lyttelton Harbour and the northern bays before finally delivering you down in Akaroa.

A much faster way of covering the 85km run **from Christchurch to Akaroa** is along SH75 that heads south from the city before curling along the southern shore of the peninsula, and over the hills to Akaroa: it takes around an hour and a half, though there are reasons to pause along the way.

Lake Ellesmere and Little River

Around 30km from Christchurch SH75 tracks the water's edge of **Lake Ellesmere** (Waihora), a vast expanse of fresh water separated from the Pacific Ocean by the 30km-long Kaitorete spit, jutting southeast from Banks Peninsula to rejoin the mainland. At the base of the spit is **Birdlings Flat**, a narrow shingle bank that has traditionally been a rich source of food for local Maori, who were granted protected fishing rights here in 1896; the accumulated shingle of the sheltering bank also provides a fossicking ground for greenstone and gems. Birdlings Flat separates the sea from **Lake Forsyth** (Wairewa), a long finger of water skirted by SH75 on the way to the tiny community of **Little River**, 53km from Christchurch, notable mainly for the *Little River Store Gallery* an excellent café, bar and bakery,

Barry's Bay

From Little River, SH75 climbs over the hills that separate Akaroa Harbour from the rest of Banks Peninsula and down to the tiny community of

BARRY'S BAY, home to the longstanding **Barry's Bay Cheese**, SH75 (daily 8.30am–5pm; ⓣ03/304 5809), where you can munch on free samples while watching cheese being made (Oct–April every second day).

There's **accommodation** nearby at *Rosslyn Estate*, just off SH75 (ⓣ03/304 5804, ⓔrosslyn@xtra.co.nz; ❹), with very comfortable en-suite B&B in a large 1860s country house set in extensive grounds. You'll be treated to home baking on arrival and evening meals on request ($35). For something cheaper, stay at *Halfmoon Cottage*, SH75 (ⓣ03/304 5050, ⓦwww.halfmoon.co.nz; shares $25, rooms ❷; closed June–Aug), a small and wonderfully relaxed hostel in a 1896 villa set in a pretty garden just across from the beach. There are free bikes and broadband, and kayaks for rent ($20 for 4hr).

Akaroa

The small waterside town of **AKAROA** ("Long Bay"), 85km southeast of Christchurch on the eastern shores of Akaroa Harbour, comes billed as New Zealand's **French settlement** Certainly the first settlers came from France, some of their architecture survives and the street names they chose have stuck, but that is about as French as it gets. Nonetheless, the town milks the connection with a couple of French-ish restaurants, some French-sounding boutique B&Bs and a tricolour fluttering over the spot where the first settlers landed.

Still, it is a pretty place with attractive scenery all around, a smattering of low-key activities including a unique dolphin swim, and easy access to the **Banks Peninsula Track** (see box, p.608). But Akaroa primarily pitches itself to those looking for gentle strolls followed by good food and wine before a comfy bed. These factors make the town a popular Kiwi holiday destination; a full two-thirds of its houses are *baches* (holiday homes), leaving only around 550 permanent residents.

The site of Akaroa was originally the domain of the Ngai Tahu paramount chief, Temaiharanui. In 1838, French Commander Jean Langlois purchased what he believed to be the entire peninsula for goods to the value of 1000 French francs, and returned to France to encourage settlers to populate a new French colony. However, while the French were making their way to New Zealand, the British sent Captain William Hobson to assume the role of lieutenant-governor over all the land that could be purchased; and just six days before Lavaud sailed into the harbour, the British flag was raised in Akaroa. Lavaud's passengers decided to stay, which meant that the first formal settlement under **British sovereignty** was comprised of 63 French and six Germans who had come along for the ride.

Although Akaroa can be seen in a day-trip from Christchurch, far better to spend a night or two in order to appreciate the town and its surrounds.

Arrival and information

Buses run by Akaroa Shuttle (Dec–March 3 daily; April–Nov 2 daily; $30 return; ⓣ0800/500 929, ⓦwww.akaroashuttle.co.nz) and Akaroa French Connection (2 daily; $30 return; ⓣ0800/800 575, ⓦwww.akaroabus.co.nz) leave the Christchurch visitor centre for the 90min run to Akaroa. They drop off outside the combined **post office** and **visitor centre**, 80 rue Lavaud (daily 9am–5pm; ⓣ03/304 8600, ⓦwww.akaroa.com) which has pack storage ($1 per hr, $5 a day). Opposite, you'll find a BNZ **bank** (Mon–Fri 9.30am–4.30pm) with ATM, and the *Turenne Coffee Shop* which has **Internet access.**

Accommodation

Akaroa's best **accommodation** caters to the weekend getaway set and there are some gorgeous B&Bs, lodges and high-quality hotels and motels. Staying in

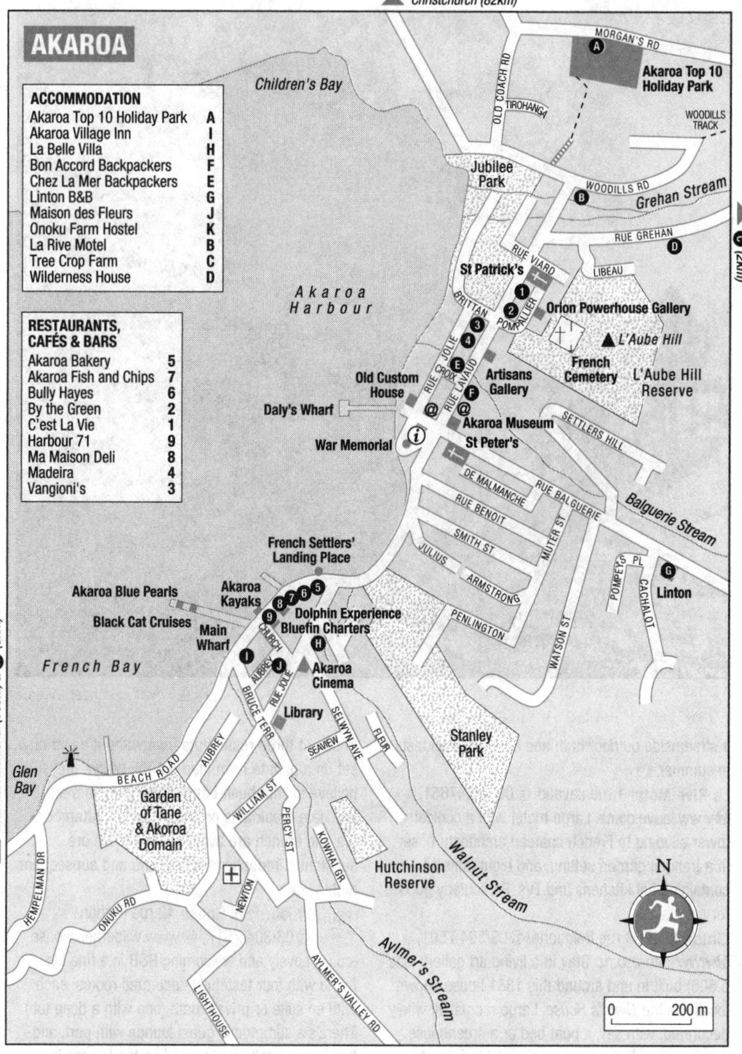

one of these seems to suit the spirit of Akaroa, and it is worth stretching the budget if you can. Otherwise, try some of the peninsula's superb backpacker hostels – a couple in town (see p.605), and several more scattered around the region in secluded bays.

B&Bs, lodges and hotels

Akaroa Village Inn 81 Beach Rd ⓣ0800/695 1111, ⓦwww.akaroavillageinn.co.nz. A rambling complex with probably the widest range of accommodation in town, based at the town's original 1842 hotel. Rooms are all tastefully decorated, self-catering and quite a few come with good harbour views. Studio units ⑤, apartments ⑥, luxury apartments ⑦

La Belle Villa 113 rue Jolie ⓣ03/304 7084, ⓦwww.labellevilla.co.nz. B&B in a lovely 1870s wooden house with spacious light en-suite rooms,

▲ Wharf at sunset, Akaroa

a streamside outdoor bath and alfresco breakfasts in summer. ❺

La Rive Motel 1 rue Lavaud ⓣ0800/247651, ⓦwww.larive.co.nz. Large motel with a conical tower alluding to French chateau architecture, set in a tranquil garden setting, and eight units all containing full kitchens and TVs. Particularly good for groups. ❹

Linton B&B 68 rue Balguerie ⓣ03/304 7501, ⓦwww.linton.co.nz. Stay in a living art gallery (see p.606) built in and around this 1881 house known locally as the *Giant's House*. Large rooms, all wildly decorated, with say, a boat bed or a greenhouse conservatory. A delicious continental breakfast is served. Shared bathroom ❽, en suite ❾

Maison des Fleurs 6 Church St ⓣ03/304 1111, ⓦwww.maisondesfleurs.co.nz. Boutique accommodation in a modern two-storey cottage (you get all of it), built from peninsula-milled timbers. It's superbly appointed with allergy-free linen, natural fibre beds and so on, plus there's a sunny balcony, wood stove for winter, and always a heap of fresh flowers, complimentary port and current magazines. ❽

Tree Crop Farm 2km up rue Grehan ⓣ03/304 7158 ⓦwww.treecropfarm.com. Romantic retreat in one of three rustic huts (two without electricity) set on a private farm (see p.606), where they believe in "hot bush baths under the stars and late, late breakfasts on the veranda". Afternoon tea and brunch are available and there are substantial reductions for second and subsequent nights. ❽

Wilderness House 42 rue Grehan ⓣ03/304 7517, ⓦwww.wildernesshouse.co.nz. Lovely and welcoming B&B in a fine old home with four tastefully decorated rooms, each with en suite or private bath (one with a deep tub). There's a sumptuous guest lounge with port, and breakfast is delicious, served on the terrace in good weather overlooking semi-formal grounds with English roses. They even have their own small vineyard. ❽

Hostels and campsites

Akaroa Top 10 Holiday Park Morgan's Rd, off the Old Coach Rd ⓣ03/304 7471, ⓦwww.akaroa-holidaypark.co.nz. Sprawling across a terraced hillside overlooking the harbour and the main street, this site has modern facilities, including a swimming pool. Camping $16, cabins ❷, s/c units ❹

Bon Accord Backpackers 57 rue Lavaud Ⓣ03/304 7782, Ⓦwww.bon-accord.co.nz. Small animal-friendly hostel (they have a dog and a cat) fashioned from two houses. Slippers and hot water bottles are provided and there's off-street parking. Dorms $25, rooms ❷

Chez La Mer Backpackers 50 rue Lavaud Ⓣ03/304 7024, Ⓦwww.chezlamer.co.nz. Historic building dating back to 1871, and offering high-quality budget accommodation in a homely environment with a nice garden out the back. The staff are helpful, and offer free use of bikes and fishing rods and useful hand-drawn maps of local walks and points of interest. Dorms $25, rooms ❷, en suites ❸

Onuku Farm Hostel 6km south of town on the Onuku road Ⓣ03/304 7066, Ⓦwww.onukufarm.co.nz. On a hill above a bay, this wonderfully secluded spot on a sheep farm centres on the cosy main house where there are doubles and dorms (including a 6-bunk en-suite girls' dorm with hairdryer). There's no TV, and Internet access is hidden away. Outside there's accommodation in a lovely brick cottage and a network of bush and farmland tracks some leading to the hammock-strung campsite equipped with outdoor kitchens and showers, and several huts and stargazers – kind of like wooden tents. The hostel also runs 3–4hr guided kayaking ($40), and dolphin-swimming trips ($90; max 6), and encourages fishing and mussel collecting. Free pick-up around 12.30pm from Akaroa. Cash only. Closed June–Aug. Camping $12, small campervans $15, dorms $25, rooms ❷

The Town

Akaroa is strung along the shore in a long ribbon easily seen on foot. For detailed exploration of the town's architectural and cultural gems, buy the *Akaroa Historic Village Walk* booklet ($9.50) or obtain an audio guide ($10) from the visitor centre.

Opposite the visitor centre, the **Akaroa Museum** (daily Oct–April 10.30am–4.30pm; May–Nov 10.30am–4pm; $4), stands head and shoulders above most small-town museums. Several interesting Maori artefacts and a twenty-minute film account of the remarkable and sometimes violent history of settlement on the peninsula are backed up by a display illustrating the differences between the English version of the Treaty of Waitangi and a literal English translation of the Maori-language document signed by Maori chiefs all over Aotearoa. Other exhibits deal with the peninsula's whaling history and settlement, and include fascinating albums full of photographs of the original French and German settlers and the British that followed them. Look, too, for displays on local son, **Frank Worsley**, who captained Shackleton's ship *Endurance* to Antarctica and, after disaster struck, the *James Caird* to South Georgia and safety.

The museum incorporates the early 1840s **Langlois-Eteveneaux Cottage**, thought to have been partly constructed in France before being shipped over, now filled with French nineteenth-century furniture. Also associated with the museum is the town's former **Court House**, with its original dock and bench peopled by unconvincing mannequins, and the tiny **Custom House**, across rue Lavaud next to Daly's Wharf, from which spy-glass-wielding officials once kept watch on the port below.

Continuing the Gallic theme, visit the **French Cemetery** at the northern end of town, reached by a footpath that leads from rue Pompallier into the L'Aube Hill Reserve. The first consecrated burial ground in Canterbury, the cemetery was sadly neglected until 1925, when the bodies were reinterred in a central plot marked by a single monument, shaded by weeping willows, said to have been grown from a cutting taken at Napoleon's grave in St Helena. Continue about 150m up L'Aube hill for even better views over the town and harbour. At the northern end of rue Pompallier, the 1864 French-inspired **Church of St Patrick** was built on the site of two earlier churches. Built from large slabs of unplaned totara, the rich colours of the black pine and kauri interior complement the bold stained glass in the east window, behind the altar.

Galleries and gardens

A former hydroelectric plant, also at the northern end of rue Pompallier, houses the **Orion Powerhouse Gallery** (Oct–April Mon–Fri 1.30–4.30pm, Sat & Sun 11am–4.30pm; donation requested), a venue for national and local exhibitions of arts and crafts, as well as for concerts of acoustic music on Sundays. Also worth a look is the **Artisans Gallery**, 45 rue Lavaud (daily 10am–5pm), a contemporary craft gallery selling pottery, weaving, silk, jewellery, knitwear, clothing and turned wood from an 1877 cottage.

Lastly, be sure not to miss **Linton**, 68 rue Balguerie (daily Christmas–March noon–4pm, April–Christmas 2–4pm; $12), home of sculptor Josie Martin and a working testament to her art. Every room, the garden and even the drive to the garage have become a canvas on which she can display her talents. Huge mosaics, concrete figures and sculpted seats tucked away in garden nooks all come with an overriding spirit of fun.

Drivers, and those who fancy more than just a gentle walk around town, can head out into the immediate surroundings of Akaroa. One destination that divides opinions is **Tree Crop Farm**, 2km up rue Grehan (daily 10am–5pm; closed in inclement weather; $10 including a drink and a nibble), a private lifestyle farm centred on a garden area with a kind of managed overgrown look. Fans love to amble along the farm tracks and through the gardens reading aphorisms written everywhere imaginable. They're initially entertaining – "the best plastic surgery is to cut up your credit cards", "old age isn't bad when you consider the alternative" – but soon become tiresome. A small café serves berry juices and exotic coffee drinks at relatively high prices, and there is accommodation (see p.604) in simple but nicely furnished huts.

Activities around Akaroa

If you want to do more than sip Pinot Gris and mooch around the galleries, there is no shortage of diversions, from waterfront strolls to dolphin swimming and kayaking. One good way of exploring is to join one of two rural delivery **mail runs** that follow the peninsula's narrow roads. There's really little to choose between the Akaroa Harbour Scenic Mail Run (Mon–Sat 9am; 4hr 30min; $50; ⓣ03/325 1334, ⓦwww.akaroamailrun.com) visiting the settlements around the western side of Akaroa Harbour, and the Eastern Bays Scenic Mail Run (Mon–Sat 9am; 4hr 30min; $50; ⓣ03/304 8526) which covers Okains and Le Bons Bay and more.

Harbour cruises and swimming with dolphins

At 1.2–1.4 metres in length the native Hector's dolphins are the world's smallest breed of dolphins. They are playful, and small pods are generally happy to approach customers on two-hour **dolphin-swimming** trips with Black Cat, Main Wharf, Beach Road (Oct–April 6am, 8.30am, 11.30am & 1.30pm; May–Sept 11.30am; $110, spectators $60; ⓣ0800/436 574, ⓦwww.blackcat.co.nz). There are partial refunds if you can't swim with the dolphins.

Black Cat also run two-hour **harbour cruises** (Nov–March at 11am & all year at 1.30pm; $55), visiting the mouth of the harbour and back via a beautiful high-walled volcanic sea cave, colonies of spotted shags and cormorants, and caves where blue penguins can sometimes be spotted.

Akaroa Dolphins, 65 Beach Rd (daily Nov–April 10.15am, 12.45pm & 3.15pm; May–Oct 12.45pm; ⓣ0800/990 102, ⓦwww.akaroadolphins.co.nz) also run a harbour cruise, including birdwatching ($60); and there are also trips from *Onuku Farm Hostel* (see p.605).

An atmospheric alternative is Fox II Sailing Adventures (Ⓣ0800/369 7245; mid-Dec to May daily 10.30am & 1.30pm; around $55, BBH backpackers $46), leaving from Daly's Wharf for **sailing** trips on a wooden 1922 ketch to the outer bays of Akaroa Harbour with an excellent chance of seeing dolphins.

Penguin and seal viewing

There are several opportunities to get out and see the local wildlife. Akaroa Seal Colony Safari (Ⓣ03/304 7255, Ⓦwww.sealtours.co.nz) run air-conditioned 4WD vehicles to **view fur seals**, from Goat Point on the eastern tip of the peninsula. Tours (daily 9.30am & 1pm; $70) last over 2hr 30min and are limited to six people.

Shireen and Francis Helps have been looking after white-flippered penguins (close relatives of little blues) on their farm at Flea Bay (on the Banks Peninsula Track; see p.608) for decades. You can see them close-up on tours run by Pohatu Penguins (Ⓣ03/304 8552, Ⓦwww.pohatu.co.nz) who offer **penguin viewing** (2–3hr; $55), 4WD nature tours ($70) and the chance to go **sea kayaking** around Flea Bay and the Pohatu Marine Reserve ($70). There are cheaper options if you can drive to the farm but the road is 4WD and steep. Anyone can join the daily wildlife-spotting **boat trips run by** Le Bons Bay Backpackers (see p.609), and kayaking and dolphin-swimming trips from *Onuku Farm Hostel* (see p.605).

Walks

For those who lack the time or inclination to tackle the **Banks Peninsula Track** (see box, p.608), there are equally rewarding shorter walks. The best is the **Round the Mountain Walk** (10km; 4hr return) circumnavigating the hills above Akaroa via the Purple Peak Road. The route is shown on a hand-drawn photocopied map available from the visitor centre.

For something easier, simply stroll along the waterfront Beach Road towards Glen Bay and the nineteenth-century red-and-white wooden **lighthouse** that used to stand at Akaroa Head to guide ships into the harbour, before being moved to its current location in 1980. Continuing towards Akaroa Head for about fifteen minutes, you'll come to **Red House Bay**, the scene of a bloody massacre in 1830, when the great northern chief Te Rauparaha bribed the captain of the British brig *Elizabeth* with flax to conceal Maori warriors about the vessel and then to invite Te Rauparaha's unsuspecting enemies (led by Temaiharanui) on board, where they were slaughtered. Te Rauparaha and his men then feasted on the victims on the beach.

You can also follow the inland **Onuku Road** (5km one way; 1hr 15min) which takes you to **ONUKU**, where you'll find the *Onuku Farm Hostel* (see p.605) and **Onuku Marae** with a pretty little nineteenth-century **church**.

Eating, drinking and entertainment

Akaroa is a good place to eat, and people from Christchurch think nothing of driving 85km here for their evening meal. **Expensive** establishments predominate, but there are also takeaways and cheaper cafés. Many places cut back their hours, or even close completely, during winter. For **movies**, check out the boutique Akaroa Cinema, corner of rue Jolie & Selwyn Ave (Ⓦwww.cinecafe.co.nz).

Akaroa Bakery 51 Beach Rd. Excellent fresh-baked bread, and a simple café serving sandwiches, pies, cakes, breakfasts and pizza. Daily 7am–5pm.

Akaroa Fish and Chips 59 Beach Rd. Outdoor seating, a good range of fish and all the usual extras – probably the best-quality cheap grub in the town.

Bully Hayes 57 Beach Rd Ⓣ03/304 7533. Named after a famous local con man, this place serves good-quality Kiwi fare, including roast

The Banks Peninsula Track

The private **Banks Peninsula Track** (35km; 2 or 4 days; Ⓦwww.bankstrack.co.nz; closed May–Sept), makes a wonderful alternative to DOC tracks and Great Walks. As well as a lovely combination of coastal cliff walking, volcanic landscapes, sandy swimming beaches, lush native bush and harbour views, you get to stay in some delightful, if fairly rustic accommodation and meet the locals. It is not a tramp for route-march aficionados, more a social hike best done over four days with friends keen to partake in a little botanising, some swimming and much lazing around.

You need to be reasonably fit, but because you're guaranteed a bunk each night you can walk at your own pace. The **fee** ($225 4-day option; $150 2-day option) includes transport to the start from Akaroa and accommodation along the way in lodging with showers, full kitchen, electricity and limited food supply.

You'll need to bring a good pair of boots, sleeping bag and all-weather gear. You should also carry provisions for at least the first two days, although it is possible to buy food at small shops at Stony Bay and Otanerito Beach, plus chocolate and alcohol at Flea Bay. There is limited scope for having your pack transported to your destination each night: see website for details.

Only twelve people are allowed to start the track each day on the 4-dayer, and four people on the 2-dayer, so **bookings** should be made well in advance, either online or through Banks Peninsula Track, PO Box 54, Akaroa (Ⓣ03/304 7612).

The route

The first evening you are driven 5km south of Akaroa to Onuku where you spend the night In **Onuku hut** or in one of the stargazer huts with a view of the heavens. A home-cooked meal ($20) is available. The track proper starts the next day. From **Onuku to Flea Bay** (11km, 3hr 30min), you climb steadily to 700m (great views) then descend past a series of small waterfalls, one of which you can walk behind. Accommodation at Flea Bay is in a charming 1850s cottage with a veranda overlooking the beach, and chocolate and alcohol on sale. Penguin colony viewing (free) and sea kayaking around the Pohatu Marine Reserve ($15) are available.

The short second day, from **Flea Bay to Stony Bay** (8km; 2hr 30min) is an exposed hike along coastal cliffs, with a seal colony providing lunchtime distraction around the halfway point. The night is spent in one of the gorgeous huts-cum-cottages in Stony Bay, where there's also a modest family museum, a fire bath under the stars, indoor/outdoor shower, a small shop selling bread, tinned food, beer and wine, and a few short tracks exploring the bay. Walkers on the 2-day option skip Flea Bay and stay here.

It is another short day from **Stony Bay to Otanerito Bay** (6km; 2hr), with comfortable overnight accommodation provided in a farmhouse just 50m from a great swimming beach, run by New Zealand author Fiona Farrell and her husband. The fourth and final day's walk heads inland, from **Otanerito Bay to Mount Vernon Lodge** (10km; 3hr; 600m ascent), through Hinewai Nature Reserve past several small waterfalls. Here you'll have the last glimpse of the ocean before hiking down to Mount Vernon Lodge on the outskirts of Akaroa, where some will have left their vehicle. It is another kilometre into Akaroa itself.

lamb, steaks and seafood (mostly $20–30) for lunch and dinner.

By the Green 37 rue Lavaud Ⓣ03/304 7717. Good modern café overlooking the town green, serving the town's best coffee, wines, light lunches and tempting cakes. Free Wi-Fi.

C'est La Vie 33 rue Lavaud Ⓣ03/304 7314. Lively and unconventional dinner-only French restaurant a small graffiti-covered room run by an over-the-top German woman. Everyone squeezes around a handful of tables to tuck into rich and traditional French dishes (mains $28–35) such as escargots, artichoke heart stuffed chicken breast and duck à l'orange. Booking is recommended, especially if you don't want to eat at the communal table. Closed May–Oct.

Harbour 71 71 Beach Rd Ⓣ03/304 7656. Superb quality dining in a relaxed setting overlooking the wharf. The fish is particularly fresh and they also do informal lunches and gourmet pizza. Closed Wed & Thurs.

Ma Maison Deli 69 Beach Rd. Great little deli with good coffee, pastries and breakfasts.

Madeira Rue Lavaud. Always jumping at weekends, this Kiwi pub offers big portions of cheapish food.

Vangioni's 40f rue Lavaud, entrance on rue Britain ⓣ03/304 7714. Casual bar and trattoria also specializing in delicious tapas and great pizza. Very reasonable. Open for dinner nightly and weekend lunches.

Around Akaroa

Unless you reached Akaroa via the Summit Road, you'll have missed some of the best scenery Banks Peninsula has to offer. Fortunately it is easy enough to drive over the hills to gems with deserted beaches like **Le Bons Bay** and **Okains Bay**, though getting around the twisty roads will take you longer than you'd think.

Le Bons Bay

Verdant **LE BONS BAY**, 20km northeast of Akaroa, is a small peaceful community with a number of holiday homes ranged behind a gorgeous sandy **beach**, framed on two sides by cliffs that provides safe swimming.

The place to stay is the wonderful family-run *Le Bons Bay* **backpackers** (ⓣ03/304 8582, ⓦwww.lebonsbay.co.nz; closed June–Sept; dorms $24, rooms ❷), a cosy 1875 house with spectacular views down to the beach 5km below. It is a little inconvenient without your own vehicle, but makes a great place to relax for a few days, lounging on the veranda or in the garden hammock, popping down to the beach to fish or gather shellfish which might be used in the communal evening dinner ($12, and well worth it). Breakfast is included, and you can call to arrange pick-up from Akaroa. The owners also run daily **boat trips** ($30) (open to all) to see penguins, dolphins, shags and seals.

Okains Bay

The next bay north from Le Bons Bay is **OKAINS BAY**, some 20km from Akaroa, which has a tiny permanent population but swells with Christchurch family holidaymakers in January. The beach and the placid lagoon formed by the **Opara Stream** are excellent for swimming and boating, but the real reason to visit is a the **Okains Bay Maori and Colonial Museum** (daily 10am–5pm; $6), a former cheese factory containing one of the most remarkable collections of Maori artefacts in the South Island.

Originally amassed by a local collector Murray Thacker, the collection includes a great collection of *hei tiki* (a pendant with a design based on the human form) in different styles from around Aotearoa, plus a valuable example returned here from an English collection. There's a "god stick" dating back to 1400, a war canoe from 1867 and greenstone adze heads. There's also a beautiful meeting house, with fine symbolic figures carved by master craftsman John Rua. Within the same compound, several outbuildings contain more traditional exhibitions relating to European settlement, including a "slab" stable and cottage – constructed from large slabs of totara wood.

Supplies are available at the wonderfully ancient Okains Bay Store and there's some scattered **accommodation** including **camping** by the beach at *Okains Bay Camping Ground* ($8), and *Double Dutch*, 32 Chorlton Rd (ⓣ03/304 7229, ⓦwww.doubledutch.co.nz; beds $25, room and en suite ❷; closed June–Aug) a wonderfully relaxing upscale hostel in a very spacious modern house with just seven beds that feels more like a shared house than a hostel. There's also the very welcoming *Kawatea Farmstay* (☎03/304 8621, ⓔkawatea@xtra.co.nz; ④, en suite ⑤), a century-year-old **homestead** set in lush gardens bordered by 5km of scenic coastline with three rooms decorated with native timbers and stained glass. Dinners available on request (around $40).

South to Otago

Heading south from Christchurch both the principal road, SH1, and the rail line forge straight across the **Canterbury Plains** connecting small farming service towns. Aside from the occasionally magnificent views of the snowcapped **Southern Alps** to the west, the drive south is through a monotonous landscape broken only by the broad gravel beds of braided rivers, usually little more than a trickle spanned by a kilometre-long bridge.

As the road passes the pottery town of **Temuka** and reaches the southern end of the Canterbury Plains, looming hills force it back to the shoreline at **Timaru**, a small city with a busy port. Timaru is also the point where SH8 strikes inland towards Fairlie, Lake Tekapo and Mount Cook. From here on, the trip south is a visual treat, with rolling hills inland and spectacular sea views.

The coastal highway continues south to the architecturally harmonious city of **Oamaru**, and the unique and fascinating **Moeraki Boulders**. This is also **penguin** country with several opportunities to stop off and spy blue and yellow-eyed penguins. From Moeraki there is little to delay you on your progress toward Dunedin, except maybe the small crossroads town of **Palmerston**, where SH85, "The Pigroot" to **Central Otago**, leaves SH1, providing another opportunity to forsake the coast and follow a historical pathway to the now defunct goldfields inland.

Rakaia, Ashburton and Temuka

Gradually leaving the suburbs of Christchurch behind, you soon hit **Dunsandel**, 40km south of the city centre, where the *Dunsandel Store*, on SH1, does excellent coffee, cakes and deli-style meals. Some 20km further south you cross the longest bridge in New Zealand, the 1.8km-long Rakaia River Bridge. It leads into the tiny salmon-fishing and sheep-shearing settlement of **Rakaia**, where a minor road called Thompson's Track heads inland towards Methven, Mount Hutt and Mount Somers (see p.645). A further 27km south is the larger though equally quiet farming town of **Ashburton**, where you might stop for a meal or a coffee at the starkly stylish *Lunch*, near the i-SITE at 264 Burnett St.

The first town of significance is **TEMUKA**, 150km south of Christchurch, which takes its name from the Maori for "fierce oven" -- indeed a large number of Maori earth ovens have been found in the area. It continues to live up to its reputation today with the presence of kilns for the ceramic factories built by immigrants from the "Potteries" area around Stoke-on-Trent in England. Within New Zealand, Temuka has become synonymous with **pottery**, and you can visit the Temuka Homeware shop (Mon–Fri 9am–5pm, Sat & Sun 9.30am–4pm;

Ⓦwww.temukahomeware.co.nz) on SH1 at the junction of Domain Avenue. Once a byword for dowdy patterns and colours, they've smartened their image in recent years and added the stylish *Brix* café (9.30am–4pm) an amiable spot to break your journey if you happen to hit town around lunchtime.

Timaru

The 28,000-strong port city of **TIMARU**, 18km south of Temuka, is at the end of a straight and flat two-hour drive from Christchurch. The city's gently rolling hills mark a subtle change and provide the setting for an austere streetscape that doesn't make it a vastly compelling place to stop, though the city is enlivened by the **Aigantighe Art Gallery** and the **South Canterbury Museum**.

The name Timaru comes from *Te Maru*, Maori for "place of shelter", as it provided the only haven for *waka* paddling between Banks Peninsula and Oamaru. In 1837 European settlement was initiated by Joseph Price, who set up a **whaling** station south of the present city at Patiti Point. A large part of today's commercial and pastoral development was initiated by Yorkshiremen **George and Robert Rhodes**, who established the first cattle station on the South Island in 1839 and effectively founded Timaru. Despite an influx of Europeans, it was some years before a safe harbour was established on the rocky coast. A welcome by-product of the land reclamation that created the harbour in 1877 was the fine sandy beach of Caroline Bay. For a time, Timaru became a popular seaside resort, and its annual **summer carnival**, starting on Boxing Day and running for over three weeks, is still well worth dropping in on.

The City

Timaru undulates over low hills, all roads eventually bringing you down to the reclaimed land of the harbour and the park-backed golden sweep of Caroline Bay, a good spot for the kids, even if the beach is overlooked by the port. Nearby, at the southern end of Stafford Street, is the central business district.

Beside the old train station the i-SITE (see p.613) nestles inside the 1870 Landing Service Building, a volcanic "bluestone" former store where goods were unloaded from the small boats that were winched up onto a shingle beach in front. By the time you read this, the i-SITE should contain the new **Maori Rock Art Centre** (Mon–Fri 8.30am–5pm, Sat & Sun 10am–3pm; small fee) containing displays on the **rock drawings** found in the vicinity (see box, p.613).

A couple of hundred metres uphill, the **South Canterbury Museum**, Perth Street (Tues–Fri 10am–4.30pm, Sat & Sun 1.30–4.30pm; donation appreciated; Ⓦwww.timaru.govt.nz), displays well-labelled local Maori artefacts, some good examples of **scrimshaw** (intricate etchings on whale teeth and bone) and other memorabilia from the whaling station that occupied Patiti Point in the late 1830s and early 1840s. Look out for sections of the wonderful **E.P. Seally collection** comprising hundreds of butterflies and moths from all over the world, including the *Morpho Cypris*, a beautiful blue from Brazil; the smaller electric-aquamarine *Morpho Adonis*; and the (now sadly silent) yodelling cicada. Hanging over the main hall of the museum is a reconstruction of the 1902 **aircraft** used by Temuka-lad **Richard Pearse** in his attempt to notch up the first powered flight in the world. Many hold him to have achieved powered flight in 1902, some months in advance of the Wright brothers. Pearse's plane was technically far ahead of that of his rivals, but he did not believe his first

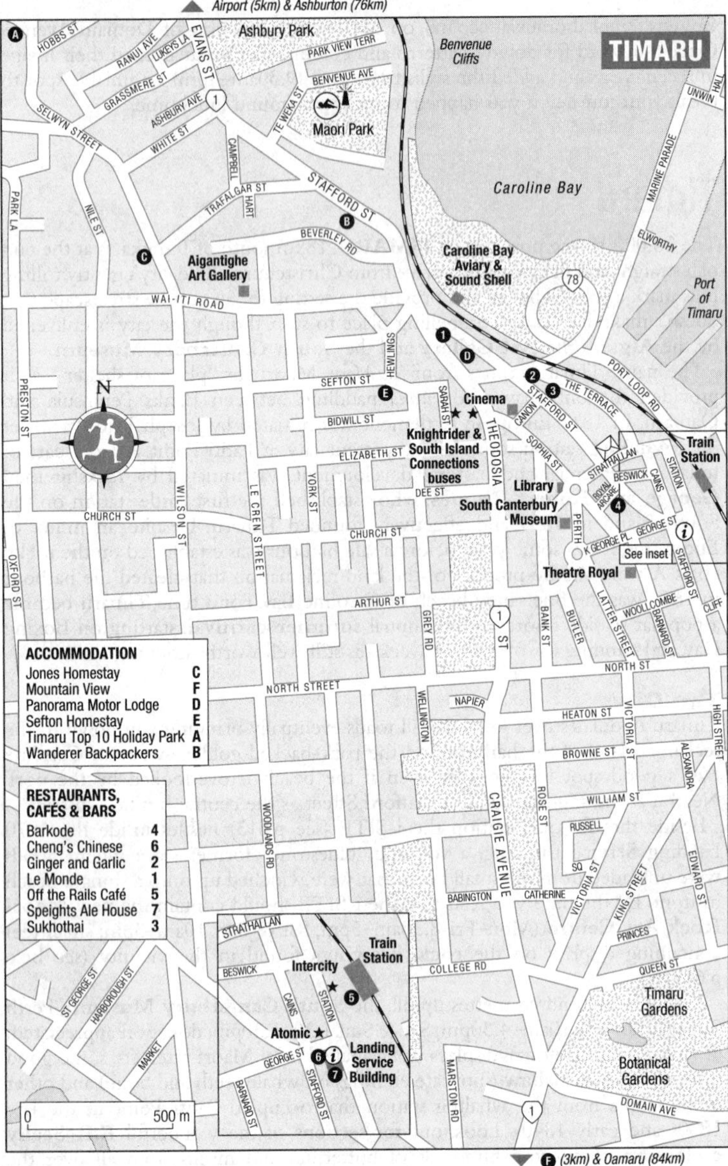

flight, a rather desperate 100m, followed by an ignominious plunge into gorse bushes, was sufficiently controlled or sustained to justify his townsfolk's claim. He was a lifelong tinkerer and inventor, the true gauge of his genius being his idea for an aircraft that could fly and hover like a modern Harrier jump jet. There's a memorial to Pearse at the site of the legendary flight, about 13km west of Temuka on the way to Waitohi.

Probably the best way to pass an afternoon is to visit the **Aigantighe Art Gallery**, 49 Wai-iti Rd (Tues–Fri 10am–4pm, Sat & Sun noon–4pm; donation appreciated; ⓣ03/687 7212, ⓦwww.timaru.govt.nz/artgallery.html), constructed around a venerable Timaru house known as Aigantighe (Gaelic for "at home"). Original features of the house have been preserved and provide a suitable setting for a rotating permanent collection – some of it dating back to the seventeenth century. A vigorous purchasing policy has produced an enviable collection of works by various artists, including five major works by native son Colin McCahon. Other artists to look out for are Frances Hodgkins, and the prolific Austen Deans.

In 1990 Kiwi, Japanese and Zimbabwean sculptors came here as part of a symposium and carved thirteen works from soft Mount Somers stone. These have weathered nicely and now sit harmoniously in the gallery's small but impressive **sculpture garden**. Look out particularly for *Baboon, nearest the house, carved with power tools* by a Zimbabwean who had only ever carved by hand. Check out also *Tu Terakiwhanoa*, by the internationally recognized Kiwi artist John Bevan Ford.

On a fine day, you could also spend a quiet hour ambling around the **Botanical Gardens**, Queen Street (daily 8am–dusk; free), or strolling along the low cliffs north of Caroline Bay past the wooden 1878 **Blackett's Lighthouse** to Dashing Rocks.

Practicalities

InterCity **buses** stop downtown outside the **train station**. Atomic buses stop a few steps away outside the **i-SITE visitor centre**, 2 George St (Mon–Fri 8.30am–5pm, Sat & Sun 10am–3pm; ⓣ03/688 6163 ext 1, ⓦwww.southisland.org.nz), which sells tickets. You probably won't need Timaru's Metro **bus service** (ⓣ03/688 5544, ⓦwww.metroinfo.org.nz), which has a flat rate of $1.50 for all journeys around the city, and $4 to Temuka. **Bikes** can be rented from The Cyclery, 106 Stafford St ($30 a day; ⓣ03/688 8892), or use Timaru **Taxis** (ⓣ03/688 8899).

The **post office**, inside Take Note, 19 Strathallan St (Mon–Fri 8am–5.30pm Sat 9am–12.30pm), has poste restante facilities. There's **Internet access** at *Off the Rail Café* (see p.614) and at *Danny's Internet Café*, 101 Stafford Ave (Mon–Fri 9am–5pm), and at the **library**, Sophia Street (Mon, Wed & Fri 9am–8pm, Tues & Thurs 9am–6pm, Sat 10am–1pm, Sun 1–4pm).

Accommodation is generally in good supply except for Christmas to mid-January when you should book well in advance. Motels line Evans Street to the north, B&Bs are more widely distributed and hotels and hostels are mostly central.

Rock art

Around five hundred years ago, Maori moa hunters visited the South Canterbury and North Otago coastal plain, leaving a record of their sojourn on the walls and ceilings of open-sided limestone rock shelters. There are more than three hundred **rock drawings** around Timaru, Geraldine and Fairlie: the faded charcoal and red ochre drawings depict a variety of stylized human, bird and mythological figures and patterns. The best of the cave drawings can be seen in the region's museums (notably the North Otago Museum in Oamaru, see p.617). Those remaining in situ are often hard to make out, and what is visible is often the misguided result of nineteenth-century repainting. If you're still keen to explore, pick up a map from the Timaru i-SITE and ask for directions. The best destination is Frenchman's Gully, where moa and a stylized birdman figure can be seen.

Timaru's **restaurants** offer decent range of eating options at reasonable prices, but nightlife is more limited. You can catch first-run Hollywood **movies** at Movie Max 5, corner of Canon and Sophia streets (ⓣ03/684 6987), and things hot up in Timaru for the three post-Christmas weeks of the **summer carnival** (ⓦwww.carolinebay.org.nz) when there's a circus, a fair and free concerts in Caroline Bay.

Accommodation

Jones Homestay 16 Selwyn St ⓣ03/688 1400, ⓔnevisjones@xtra.co.nz. Homestay in a lovely late-1920s house with lush gardens and its own grass tennis court. Rooms are en suite and it is only a 15min walk from town. ❹

Mountain View 23 Talbot Rd, off SH1 3km south of Timaru ⓣ03/688 1070, ⓦwww.bnb.co.nz/mtview.html. Small farm B&B offering homely rooms with private bathrooms and a cooked breakfast. Dinner by arrangement ($25). ❸

Panorama Motor Lodge 52 The Bay Hill ⓣ0800/103 310, ⓦwww.panorama.net.nz. Striking and hospitable motel with spacious units, all the usual facilities, as well as a sauna, spa baths, gym, off-street parking and great views over Caroline Bay. ❺

Sefton Homestay 32 Sefton St ⓣ03/688 0017, ⓦwww.seftonhomestay.co.nz. Comfortable and stylish homestay in a lovely 1920s house in leafy grounds. One en suite plus an equally attractive room with private guest bathroom fitted with a deep tub. ❹

Timaru Top 10 Holiday Park 154a Selwyn St ⓣ0800/242 121, ⓦwww.timaruholidaypark.co.nz. Well-kept, very high-standard holiday park offering a range of accommodation, close to the golf course and within walking distance of Maori Park. Camping $14, cabins & kitchen cabin ❷, s/c units ❸ motel units ❹

Wanderer Backpackers 24 Evans St ⓣ03/688 8795, ⓔwandererbackpackers@xtra.co.nz. Small roadside backpacker that's relatively close to town, off-street parking, a range of rooms and no check-out time. There are even occasional hunting trips. Camping $14, dorms $23, rooms ❷

Eating, drinking and entertainment

Barkode 8 Royal Arcade. Basement cocktail bar and club with DJs. Wed–Sat.

Cheng's Chinese 12 George St. Excellent set menus, good veggie dishes, and great chow mein, with main meals hovering in the $12–20 range. Sunday lunch buffet ($15).

Ginger and Garlic 335 Stafford St ⓣ03/688 3981. The best licensed restaurant in town with views over the bay, serving dishes such as roast vegetable tartlets with beetroot coulis and lamb backstrap in a smoked kelp crust. Mains around $30. Closed Sun.

Le Monde 64 Bay Hill ⓣ03/688 8550. Smart restaurant with views of Caroline Bay, serving the likes of confit of duck leg ($28) and rack of lamb ($32). Closed Sun & Mon.

Off the Rail Café 22 Station St, in the train station. The best and coolest café in town, housed in a 1967 former waiting room, with old booths, a jukebox with Sixties tunes, white leather sofa, a good selection of value-for-money food and zingy coffee. They also have Internet access and occasional alternative live music.

Speights Ale House 2 George St, in the Landing Service Building. Popular former brewpub offering generous pub-style lunches and dinners, plus occasional weekend live music in a cavernous bar that serves mostly Speight's ales.

Sukhothai 303 Stafford St ⓣ03/688 4843. Good Thai restaurant serving old favourites (mostly around $15–18) plus $10 lunch specials. Closed Mon.

Oamaru and around

The former port town of **OAMARU**, 85km south of Timaru on SH1, is one of New Zealand's more alluring provincial cities, and a relaxed place to spend a day or two. Perhaps the most immediate attraction is the presence of both blue and yellow-eyed **penguin colonies** on the outskirts of town, but the town itself has a well-preserved **Historic District**, a core of nineteenth-century buildings built of the distinctive cream-coloured local limestone that earned Oamaru the title "The Whitestone City". At the turn of the twentieth century it had a reputation as being the most attractive city in the South Island, and with

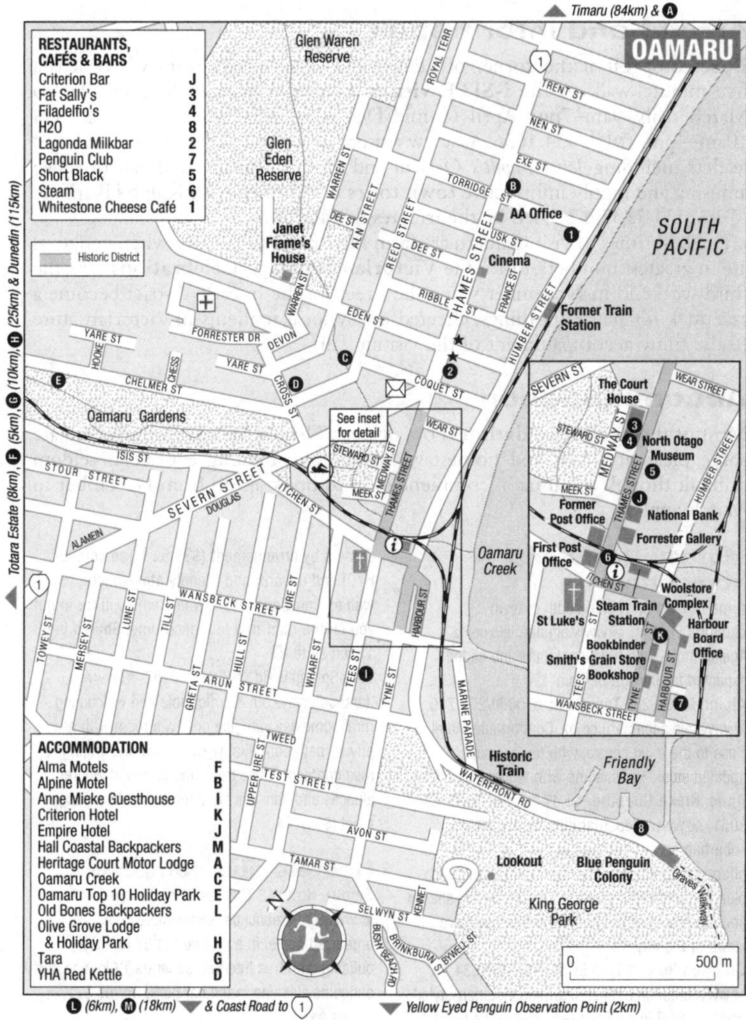

the ongoing restoration it is beginning to regain that status. A handful of the grand edifices have scrubbed up nicely and more are scheduled for treatment as cafés and niche business spread into the renovated buildings.

The limestone outcrops throughout the area once provided shelter for Maori and later the raw material for ambitious European builders. As a commercial centre for gold-rush prospectors, and shored up by quarrying, timber and farming industries, Oamaru grew prosperous. The port opened for **migration** in 1874, with three hundred ships arriving that year and a further four hundred between 1876 and 1878, although many foundered on the hostile coastline and in the late nineteenth century wrecks littered the shore. After this boom period Oamaru declined, times evocatively recorded in work by local lass, **Janet Frame**. It is only in recent years that the town has begun to come alive again.

Arrival and information

Buses drop off at the corner of Eden and Thames streets from where it is a five-minute walk to the **i-SITE visitor centre**, 1 Thames St (mid-Dec to March daily 9am–7pm; April to mid-Dec Mon–Fri 9am–5pm, Sat & Sun 10am–4pm; ⓣ03/434 1656, ⓦwww.visitoamaru.co.nz). They stock useful free leaflets including *Janet Frame's Oamaru* and *Historic Oamaru*, and can organize amusing and highly informative **town tours** of the town with Ralph's Rambles (ⓣ03/434 7337; $20), led by the irrepressible Ralph.

The best times to visit Oamaru are from November to January when penguins are in greatest numbers, or for the **Victorian Heritage Celebrations** over the third weekend in November when the streets of the historic district become a racetrack for penny-farthings, cheered on by local residents in Victorian attire to the tinny accompaniment of the visiting fair.

Accommodation

Most of the **accommodation** is on, or near, Thames Street, though there are some pleasant B&Bs and homestays further out. Finding a place is seldom difficult though the usual recommendation to book ahead from December to March applies.

Motels, B&Bs and homestays

Alma Motels SH1, 5km south of town ⓣ0800/000 644, ⓦwww.almamotels.co.nz. Ageing motel with functional units and all the expected facilities; a bargain. ❷

Alpine Motel 285 Thames St ⓣ0800/272 710, ⓦwww.alpineoamaru.co.nz. Comfortable motel close to the town centre, with ten spacious, updated studio units, some with full kitchens. ❸

Anne Mieke Guesthouse 47 Tees St ⓣ03/434 8051, ⓦwww.theoamarubnb.com. Large suburban house, perhaps in need of a little TLC, offering B&B close to the town centre and the blue penguin viewing area. Bathrooms are shared and the rooms at the back of the house have views of the bay. ❸

Criterion Hotel 3 Tyne St ⓣ0800/259 334, ⓦwww.criterion.net.nz. Charming Victorian-styled boutique B&B in an 1877 pub right in the heart of the historic district. A sizeable breakfast is included. Shared bath ❺, en suite ❻

Heritage Court Motor Lodge 346 Thames St ⓣ0800/732 200, ⓦwww.heritagecourtlodge.com. Newish, upmarket motel that's clean, quiet and spacious, and has comfortable units with cooking facilities, in-house video and several new units. ❹

Oamaru Creek 24 Reed St ⓣ03/434 1190, ⓦwww.oamarucreek.co.nz. An old nursing home that has been cleverly restored to provide the best B&B accommodation in town, with spacious, tastefully decorated rooms, fantastic home-produced organic breakfasts, dinners by arrangement ($35 for three courses, BYO) and a warm and friendly atmosphere, as well as knowledgeable owners who will try to put you on the right trail to a good time. Shared bath ❹, en suite ❺

Tara Springhill Rd ⓣ03/434 8187, ⓦwww.tarahomestay.com. Comfortable and welcoming rural homestay with just one twin room with a private bathroom 8km west of town set among rose gardens, native trees and farmland where alpacas and donkeys are kept, dinner by arrangement ($35). ❹

Hostels and campsites

Empire Hotel 13 Thames St ⓣ03/434 3446, ⓦwww.empirebackpackersoamaru.co.nz. Well-organized hostel in a restored 1867 heritage building with free Internet, separate TV lounge and penguins sleeping in the car park. Dorms $21, rooms ❷

The Hall Coastal Backpackers All Day Bay, 18km south of Oamaru ⓣ03/439 5411, ⓦwww.coastalbackpackers.co.nz. Relaxing rural backpackers, off the beaten track but within easy walk of a good beach and some coastal wetlands. Doubles and dorms are in a couple of separate buildings each with lounge and log-burning stove, and there's an on-site restaurant and bar. Closed June–Aug. Dorms $25, rooms ❷

Oamaru Top 10 Holiday Park Chelmer St ⓣ0800/280 202, ⓦwww.oamarutop10.co.nz. In a lovely sheltered setting close to Oamaru Gardens with a good range of accommodation. Camping $14, cabins ❷, kitchen cabins ❸, s/c units ❹

Protecting New Zealand's native wildlife

In 1769, on the first visit to New Zealand by James Cook, his botanist, Joseph Banks, declared the dawn chorus to be "the most melodious wild music I have heard". Sadly it is seldom heard today. Even before Cook's arrival, Maori had hunted the enormous moa to extinction, and the influx of Europeans and their animals resulted in the death of many more species. Most of those that remain – including the emblematic kiwi – cling on precariously, often surviving only with human help.

Tautara ▲

Moa and kiwi, from a nineteenth-century print ▼

An ark apart

New Zealand separated from other continental land masses 80 million years ago, leaving its flora and fauna to evolve in isolation. Maori found a place where land mammals were non-existent. Instead, they discovered the lizard-like **tuatara**, which had stayed much the same since the time of the dinosaurs, and carnivorous land snails with shells over 10cm in diameter. But the biggest oddity were the **birds** which, with no predators, had begun to occupy the evolutionary niches usually held by mammals. They became fearless, learning to walk amid the dense bush, gradually becoming flightless and growing in size. The largest sub-species of moa was heavier than an ostrich, while the kiwi developed skin as tough as leather, feathers like hair, a highly developed sense of smell, and a body temperature of 38°C, more akin to a mammal's than a bird's.

The end of isolation

With the arrival of Maori canoes, the highly specialised native birds had to contend with aggressive, fast-moving mammals. When Europeans started to settle in large numbers after 1840, they strove to turn New Zealand into a kind of British Isles in the South Pacific, creating a menagerie of **mammalian pests**. At the same time, **trappers** collected precious and colourful birds, and had them stuffed for museums around the world.

Mainland and island sanctuaries

The North and South islands got the full complement of pests, but some of the smaller islands were only infested with shipwrecked rats and mice. Early conservationists recognised that turning such islands into **sanctuaries** was the easiest way to preserve New Zealand's unique wildlife. Sawmiller-turned-conservationist **Richard Henry** made progress on Resolution Island from 1894, and three years later **Kapiti Island** (see p.290), north of Wellington, was designated a bird sanctuary.

Endangered birds were transferred to Kapiti but it was only after 1980 that active measures were taken to remove predators. There are now a couple of dozen such islands, though only a few are designated as **open sanctuaries**, where you get a chance to experience the glorious birdsong and appreciate just how fearless these birds can be (see p.475 for more).

It soon became difficult to find suitable islands, and conservationists started creating so-called **mainland islands**, reserves where intense trapping and poisoning of predators is used to give the birds a chance. Wellington's **Karori Sanctuary** (see p.475) took the idea one step further and pioneered the **predator-proof fence**, buried deep to keep out burrowing animals, equipped with smooth metal caps to deter agile possums and with a mesh fine enough to keep out baby mice.

▲ Tieke

▲ Stitchbird

Saving the kiwi

All six species of **kiwi**, New Zealand's national symbol, are considered "threatened", and two are "Nationally Critical", with only a couple of hundred birds apiece. Loss of suitable habitat is a substantial problem, but the major issue is **predation**. With their powerful legs and strong claws, adult kiwi are reasonably adept at defending themselves from possums, stoats and ferrets, but do less well against feral cats and escaped dogs. A single domestic dog is thought to have killed 500

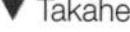

▼ Takahe

Predator-proof fence, Karori Sanctuary ▲

Pest Control ▲

Kea, Kapiti Island ▼

of the 900 birds in the Waitangi State forest over a six-week period in 1988. Kiwis don't actively look after their **chicks**, and it is estimated that where stoats are present (and that's just about everywhere on the North and South islands), the chicks have only a five percent chance of survival in the wild. Survival rates increase enormously over the first few months, and this critical period is the focus of **Operation Nest Egg** (Ⓦwww.savethekiwi.org.nz), in which eggs or newborn chicks are retrieved from nests, then reared in safe compounds or on predator-free islands until they are about six months of age. By then the one-kilo birds can fend for themselves and are set free in the wild.

Conservation in action

The following sanctuaries are some of the best places to see New Zealand's rare native birdlife.

North Island

Tiritiri Matangi, Auckland. Island sanctuary rich in birdlife. See p.161

Trounson Kauri Park, Northland. Nocturnal kiwi-spotting. See p.225

Bushy Park, Wanganui. North Island robins, kereru and more. p.271

Kapiti Island, near Wellington. Easily-accessible, and offering excellent bird-watching. See p.290

Pukaha Mount Bruce, Wairarapa. Award-winning wildlife centre. See p.445

Karori Sanctuary, Wellington. City sanctuary. See p.475

South Island

Motuara Island, Marlborough Sounds. Saddlebacks, South Island bush robins, kiwi and little blue penguins. See p.502

Ulva Island, off Stewart Island. One of the greatest concentrations of native birdlife in the country. See p.711

Mason Bay, Stewart Island. The best place to spot kiwi in the wild. See p.713

Olive Grove Lodge & Holiday Park SH1, 25km south of Oamaru ⓣ03/439 5830, ⓦwww.olivebranch.co.nz. Set close to the Moeraki Boulders, on a bend in a river with good swimming holes this hostel has a selection of brilliantly decorated doubles and twins and dorm bunks and plenty of space for camping and van hookups. Spa and sauna available. Closed mid-May to Sept. Camping $12, dorms $25, rooms ❷

Old Bones Backpackers Beach Rd, Kakanui ⓣ03/434-8115, ⓦwww.oldbones.co.nz. Gorgeous, purpose-built, upscale backpackers on the coast 6km south of town (follow Wharfe Rd) with just eight doubles and twins (no dorms) opening onto a spacious, comfortable and TV-free lounge/kitchen. Everything is to the highest standard, and there's free Internet, underfloor heating in the bedrooms and power hookups for campervans. Closed June–Aug. Beds $30, vans $15 per person, rooms ❷

YHA Red Kettle Corner of Reed & Cross sts ⓣ03/434 5008, ⓔyha.oamaru@yha.org.nz. Small and pleasant old-style hostel close to the town centre with five-bed dorms, a twin and a double rooms. Closed May–Sept. Dorms $25, rooms ❷

The Town

Thames Street and the knot of streets around Tyne, Itchen and Harbour streets define Oamaru's **Historic District**, a dense cluster of grand civic and mercantile buildings that sets the town centre apart from any other in the land. The key is Oamaru whitestone, a "free stone" which is easily worked with metal hand tools when freshly quarried but hardens with exposure to the elements. While keeping the prevailing Neoclassical fashion firmly in mind, the architects' imaginations ran riot, and the craftsmen were given free rein to produce deeply fluted pilasters, finely detailed pediments and elegant Corinthian pillars topped with veritable forests of acanthus leaves. Oamaru was given much of its character by architect R.A. Lawson and by the firm Forrester and Lemon who together produced most of the more accomplished buildings between 1871 and 1883.

Oamaru stone is still used in modern buildings – witness the Waitaki Aquatic Centre in Takaro Park – and enthusiasts can visit its source at the **Parkside Quarry**, 7km west of town, which has tours of both the quarry and lime works (by arrangement; $10; ⓣ03/433 9786, ⓦwww.oamarustone.co.nz).

Along Thames Street

The majority of civic buildings are along Thames Street. The first of the nineteenth-century edifices to command attention is the **Courthouse**, an elegant, classically proportioned Palladian building showing the same Forrester and Lemon hand as the adjacent Athenaeum building. This served as a subscription library before providing a home for the **North Otago Museum** (Mon–Fri 10.30am–4.30pm, Sat & Sun 1–4.30pm; donation), with its modest selection of displays on North Otago history, Maori digs and the life of local novelist Janet Frame.

The Former Post Office, a few steps further along Thames Street, originally came without the tower, which was added by the architect's son, Thomas Forrester, in 1903. This building replaced the adjacent 1864 First Post Office, an Italianate structure which predates all the other whitestone work and is the town's only remaining example of the work of W.H. Clayton. Directly opposite the one-time post offices are two of Lawson's buildings: the imposing **National Bank** has perhaps the purest Neoclassical facade in town; while its grander neighbour now operates as the **Forrester Gallery** (daily 10.30am–4.30pm; donations welcome). This features touring exhibitions of contemporary and traditional art, plus a basement of works by iconic Kiwi artist Colin McCahon and local painter Colin Wheeler, whose cityscapes are dominated by the colour of Oamaru stone.

Tyne-Harbour Street Historic District

Continuing towards the waterfront you enter Oamaru's original commercial quarter, full of whitestone flamboyance. Gentrification is taking its time, but this is gradually becoming the place to hang out, perhaps grabbing a coffee or a beer in between browsing the bookstore, art galleries and minor museums.

Follow Itchen Street east and as you round the corner into Tyne Street you'll spot the **Woolstore Complex**, 1 Tyne St, complete with the *Woolstore Café* and the **Oamaru Auto Collection** (daily 10am–4pm; $6), with its array of ancient and not-so-old vehicles. Upstairs, the **North Otago Electrical Museum** (Sun 10am–5pm; $3) contains a nostalgic mishmash of things containing fiddly wires, and a small **market** is held every Sunday (10am–4pm).

The old **Union Offices**, 7 Tyne St, is a traditional bookbinder's workshop (Mon–Fri 2–6pm; free; ⓣ03/434 9277), where you can watch fine book binding and repair work and see examples of old printing and letterpress machines. Next door is the elegant **Smiths Grain Store**, built in 1881 by stonemason James Johnson, while further along you'll find Slightly Foxed, 11 Tyne St, which offers a great array of secondhand and classic **books**. Harbour Street runs parallel to Tyne Street and is lined by more rejuvenated mercantile buildings. The 1876 Venetian Renaissance-style **Harbour Board Office** was one of the first public buildings designed by the prolific Forrester and Lemon. Also worth a look is the striking 1882 Loan and Mercantile Warehouse, 14 Harbour St, once the largest grain store in New Zealand. Grain sacks have recently been replaced by whiskey barrels and the **New Zealand Malt Whisky Company** offers tours of the beautifully restored premises and whiskey **tasting** (on demand; $15).

On weekends and public holidays you can gaze at the backs of some of these buildings from the **Oamaru Historic Steam Train** (every 45min 11am–4pm; $5 return; ⓣ03/434 5634), which runs a few hundred metres from the station behind the i-SITE.

The Oamaru Gardens and Janet Frame House

Five minutes' walk west of the Historic District, **Oamaru Gardens** (daily dawn–dusk, glasshouses 9am–4pm; free) offer manicured natural beauty in a streamside setting. The rhododendron dell, fragrant garden and Victorian summerhouse give a sense of the wealth the town once enjoyed.

About ten minutes stroll to the northwest, the **Janet Frame House**, 56 Eden St (Nov–April daily 2–4pm; $5), was the modest childhood home of one of New Zealand's greatest writers. She lived here from early school days to leaving for higher education: "I wanted an imagination that would inhabit a world of fact, descend like a shining light upon the ordinary life of Eden Street…" Since her death in 2004 the house has been restored to 1940s style; you can explore it, get some insight from custodian, Ralph, and listen to a marvellous recording of the author reading an extract from *Owls Do Cry*, about the very sofa you'll be sitting on.

Fans of her work may want to follow the **Janet Frame Trail** (leaflet available from the i-SITE) taking you to locations used in varying degrees of disguise in her books – the former subscription library in the Athenaeum that featured in *Faces In The Water*, or the rubbish dump that formed the symbolic centre of *Owls Do Cry*.

The penguin colonies

Oamaru is unique in having both yellow-eyed and blue **penguin colonies** within walking distance of the town centre. It is usually possible to see both

Blue penguins

Blue Penguins, the smallest of their kind, are found all around the coast of New Zealand, and along the shores of southern Australia, where they are known as little penguins. White on their chests and bellies, they have a thick head-to-tail streak along their back in iridescent indigo-blue. Breeding takes place from May to January, and the parents take it in turns to stay with the egg during the 36-day incubation period. The newly hatched chick is protected for the first two or three weeks before both parents go out to sea to meet the increasing demand for food, returning full of krill, squid and crustaceans, which they regurgitate into the chick's mouth. At eight weeks the chicks begin to fledge, but sixty percent die in their first year; the juveniles that do survive usually return to their birthplace. At the end of the breeding season the birds fatten up before coming ashore to moult: over the next three weeks their feathers are not waterproof enough for them to take to the sea and they lose up to half their bodyweight.

colonies in one evening, since the yellow-eyes tend to come ashore earlier than the blues. Penguins are timid creatures and easily distressed, so keep quiet and still, and do not encroach within ten metres of the birds. Once disturbed, the penguins may not return to their nests for several hours, even if they have chicks to feed.

The **Blue Penguin Colony**, (daily; best visited just before dusk; $22.50) is fifteen minutes' walk southeast of the town centre along Waterfront Road. In the visitor centre there's a chance to see an infra red 24-hour monitor in one of the nest boxes and videos on blue penguins before being deprived of your cameras and videos and led out to the 350-seat grandstand. Come during the breeding season (June–Dec) and you'll see chicks – and hear them calling to their parents out at sea, hunting for food. When the parents return around dusk, travelling in groups (known as rafts), they climb the steep harbour banks and cross in front of the grandstand to their nests. Outside the breeding season, penguins indulge in much less to-ing and fro-ing, but provide an engaging spectacle nevertheless. In the peak season (Nov–Jan) you might hope to see a hundred penguins in a night, though this might drop to a dozen or so in March, June and August. It can all seem a bit of a circus so, if you'd prefer a more intimate encounter, try the half-hour **Behind the Scenes** tour (daytime on request; $17.50; combo $35), which visits the breeding colony where you should see birds inside nesting boxes, maybe with chicks.

The much larger **yellow-eyed penguins** nest in smaller numbers but keep more sociable hours, usually coming ashore in late afternoon or early evening (best Oct–Feb). They mainly arrive on **Bushy Beach**, reached by road 2km along Bushy Beach Road, or on foot via the **Graves Walkway** that starts just past the blue penguin colony. The path curves round the headland at the end of Oamaru Harbour and onto a point overlooking the small cove of Boatman's Harbour. The walkway ends overlooking Bushy Beach, where a hide enables you to see the yellow-eyed penguins making their way across the beach in the morning and early evening.

To facilitate penguin watching you can use the door-to-door **Penguin Express** ($34, combining both yellow-eyed and blue colonies; ⓣ0800/256 565, ⓦwww.coastline-tours.co.nz), a bus tour that visits Bushy Beach and whips you around town with a bit of commentary, getting you to the blue penguins in time for their arrival.

Eating, drinking and entertainment

Oamaru isn't over-endowed with good places to **eat and drink**, though you'll do well enough for a night or two, and a range of pockets are catered for. You shouldn't have to stray too far from the central Thames Street to find what you want, though if you're planning an outing to Moeraki Boulders consider dining at *Fleur's Place* (see p.622).

Criterion Bar *Criterion Hotel*, 3 Tyne St. With the tenor of a Victorian English pub there's a long wooden bar, some good old-fashioned beer (notably London Porter and Emersons traditional ale), plus filling inexpensive food, including bangers and mash.

Fat Sally's 84 Thames St. A large and lively bar that's popular for big-screen sports, live music and plain old drinking, but also serves good pub food (mains $15–28), either in the bar or quieter rooms out back. Closed Mon.

Filadelfio's 70 Thames St. Casual spot with great pizzas, many of them vegetarian.

H2O Waterfront Road ⓣ 03/434 3400, ⓦ www.harbour2ocean.com. Stylish, modern café/restaurant by the blue penguin colony where the airy interior is a fine place to dine on the likes of ricotta, roast tomato and sage tart, or shaved chicken and baby pea lasagne ($18). Or just come for a sundowner on the deck overlooking the sea.

Lagonda Milkbar 193 Thames St corner of Eden St. Trad Kiwi tearoom, open for breakfast, lunch and early chips-with-everything dinner. Also operates as the InterCity booking office and has Internet access.

Penguin Club off Harbour St ⓣ 021/373 922 ⓦ www.thepenguinclub.co.nz. A legendary back-alley venue bar hosting Friday jam nights (from 8pm), poetry, theatre and gigs by Kiwi touring bands ($10–30 cover charge): almost everyone of note in the Kiwi music biz has played here. From the *Criterion Hotel*, walk down Harbour St, and turn left down an unprepossessing alley. Entry price is low, and if you pick up a programme of events from the visitor's centre you'll be let in at the members' price.

Short Black 45 Thames St. Cool daytime café serving excellent coffee, great snacks, salads and more substantial meals, including breakfast. Licensed.

Steam 7 Thames St. Daytime purveyors of the best coffee in town, plus delicious cakes, muffins and juices. Closed Sun.

Whitestone Cheese Café Corner of of Torridge and Humber sts. Small café associated with the Whitestone Cheese Company, and mainly a place for sampling their excellent cheeses with local wine. Particularly good are the Farmhouse, a semi-soft cheese with a lemongrass aroma and nutty taste, the Brie, which has a hint of mushroom, the strong Airedale and the Windsor Blue, a creamy soft cheese. They're all made on the premises: watch from the viewing gallery at the back (best before 3pm).

Listings

Car rental Smash Palace Rentals (ⓣ 03/434 1444) rents ten-year-old cars for as little as $30 a day. Courtyard Rentals (ⓣ 03/434 5222) have more modern vehicles and charge more like $60 a day.

Cinema Oamaru MovieWorld 3, 239 Thames St (ⓣ 03/434 1070), shows the latest movies.

Internet At the visitor centre and the *Lagonda Milkbar*.

Library Oamaru Public Library, next door to the North Otago Museum on Thames St (Mon–Fri 9.30am–5.30pm, Sat 10am–12.30pm).

Medical treatment Oamaru Hospital, 8 Stewart St ⓣ 03/433 0290).

Newspaper The Mon–Fri only *Oamaru Mail* has entertainment listings and emergency numbers.

Post office The post office, 2 Severn St (ⓣ 03/433 1190), has poste restante facilities.

Taxi Whitestone Taxis (ⓣ 0800/434 1234).

South of Oamaru to Moeraki and the Moeraki Boulders

South of Oamaru, most people make a beeline for the Moeraki Boulders and Dunedin, but it's worth taking half an hour or so to look around **Totara Estate**, SH1, 8km south of Oamaru (daily Nov–April 10am–5pm; May–Oct

9.30am–3.30pm; $7; ⓦ www.totaraestate.co.nz; 1hr tours; $15), the birthplace of the New Zealand meat industry. Until the early 1880s New Zealand was a major wool exporter and its flocks were becoming huge, but no one knew what to do with all the surplus meat. The country's small population certainly couldn't consume it all, no matter how meat-loving. Meanwhile, Britain's burgeoning industrial cities were on the brink of starvation. Shippers were just beginning to experiment with refrigeration, but New Zealand wasn't on the regular steamship routes and it fell to the Australian and New Zealand Land Company to pioneer refrigeration on a sailing ship. In 1882, the three-masted *Dunedin* was refitted with coke-driven freezers and filled with lamb from Totara Estate, one of the most fecund and productive sheep stations. The estate is now a grassy historic park built around solid whitestone buildings largely reconstructed with the original dressed stones. A small museum and video in the former workers' quarters sets the tone for the harness room, stables, granary barn and blacksmith's forge, all appropriately equipped. The foundations and partial remains of the original slaughterhouse and carcass shed form the basis of a modern reconstruction that gives an idea of what work was like here. If your imagination isn't vivid enough, half a dozen heritage breeds of sheep are kept nearby.

▲ Moeraki Boulders

Moeraki Boulders

Almost forty kilometres south of Oamaru on SH1 the large, grey and almost perfectly spherical **Moeraki Boulders** (some of which reach 2m in diameter) lie partially submerged in the sandy beach at the tide line. Their smooth skins hide honeycomb centres, which are revealed in some of the broken specimens. The boulders once lay deep in the mudstone cliffs behind the beach, as these were eroded, out fell the smooth boulders, and their distinctive surface pattern was formed as further erosion exposed a network of veins. The boulders were originally formed around a central core of carbonate of lime crystals that attracted minerals from their surroundings – a process that started sixty million years ago, when muddy sediment containing shell and plant fragments accumulated on the sea floor. The masses formed range in size from small pellets to large round rocks, some with a small void in the middle. There were a large number of these boulders in the area, but the smaller ones have all been carted off as souvenirs over the years, leaving only those too heavy to shift.

Access to this strangely compelling phenomenon is either by a 300m walk along the beach from a DOC parking area (often used for ad hoc camping), or more immediately via a restaurant/gift **shop** (daily Oct–April 8.30am–5.30pm; May–Nov 8.30am–4pm; ⓣ03/439 4827) which overlooks the beach, accessed on a short private trail ($2 in the honesty box at any hour).

Maori named the boulders Te Kaihinaki (food baskets), believing them to have been washed ashore from the wreck of a canoe whose occupants were seeking *pounamu*. The seaward reef near Shag Point (see p.623) was the hull of the canoe, and just beyond it stands a prominent rock, the vessel's petrified navigator. Some of the Moeraki Boulders were *hinaki* (baskets), the more spherical were water-carrying gourds and the irregular-shaped rocks farther down the beach were *kumara* from the canoe's food store. The survivors among the crew were transformed at daybreak into hills overlooking the beach.

Moeraki village

The picturesque fishing village of **MOERAKI**, 1km to the south along SH1 then 1.5km down a side road, makes a tranquil place to break your journey. Apart from easy access to the boulders, there's a chance to see yellow-eyed penguins up close. Follow signs to the white wooden lighthouse (1km off SH1 then 5km down an unsealed road). Alongside the lighthouse a path leads down to a hide, overlooking the beach at Katiki Point. Here yellow-eyed penguins emerge after a hard day's fishing (3.30pm–nightfall), and there are often seals visible on beaches nearby. The second path from the lighthouse heads off to the *pa* site, its importance explained on a panel nearby.

There's limited accommodation in these parts, but *Moeraki Motel* (ⓣ&ⓕ03/439 4862; ❸) has four units facing the bay, all with fully equipped kitchens and manages a number of holiday homes in the village (two-night minimum; ❹). There's also the *Moeraki Village Holiday Park* (ⓣ03/439 4759, ⓔmoerakivillageholidaypark@xtra.co.nz; tent sites $12, cabins ❶, flats ❸, motel units ❸), situated on a hill farther into the village, with cooking facilities (camp kitchens and outdoor barbecues). There's also the splendid *Olive Grove* (Oamaru, see p.617), 12km north on SH1.

The Moeraki Tavern does bar meals, but the best **eating** by far is at the marvellous: *Fleur's Place* (daily 7am–midnight; ⓣ03/439 4480, ⓦwww.fleursplace.com; licensed & BYO) which lures sophisticates from Dunedin (and Gwyneth Paltrow when she was filming nearby) to a characterful converted fishing shack for great seafood meals with fish straight off the boat (mains $24–32), a good wine selection or an excellent coffee.

Smaller **shuttle buses** will drop you in the village, although services run by the major companies merely drop off at the point where the side road into the village leaves SH1.

Shag Point and Palmerston

Just over 10km south of Moeraki Village, a side road runs 3km to **Matakaea Scenic Reserve**, where the rocks are often slathered with seals and a viewing platform allows distant views of yellow-eyed penguins.

A further 9km south, the lumber town of **PALMERSTON** marks the junction of two routes: SH1 running 55km south to Dunedin; and the "Pigroot" (SH85) inland to the Maniototo and the historic goldfield heartland of Central Otago. There's little reason to stop long in Palmerston, though on even the briefest visit you'll notice the hilltop **monument** dedicated to one-time local resident **John McKenzie**. As Minister of Lands, Agriculture and Immigration in the early 1890s he effectively laid the groundwork for modern farming by breaking up the vast holdings of absentee landlords and making them available to new immigrants.

The licensed *DeRail Café and Bar*, in the former station in the centre of town, offers the best **food** in town with gourmet pizza and the typically wide range of New Zealand café fare. Simple **accommodation** is available at *Pioneer Motels*, 56 Tiverton St (Ⓣ03/465 1234; ❸), but for something considerably more luxurious, call for directions to *Centrewood*, Bobby's Head Road (Ⓣ03/465 1977, Ⓦwww.ecostay.co.nz; ❽), a high-ceilinged 1904 homestead set amid English rose gardens well away from the road in the coastal hills and close to beaches frequented by seals and yellow-eyed penguins. The approach is low-key, but there is an effortless grace to the rooms let either separately or together, with use of a vast lounge with polished rimu floors and a small billiard table. Evening meals ($40–60) include wine and can be taken with the family who are descended from physicist Ernest Rutherford, and keep a small collection of mementoes relating to him.

South of Palmerston, it is 55km to Dunedin, though you might like to break the journey with a night or two at the *Asylum Lodge*, 36 Russell Rd, Seacliff (Ⓣ03/465 8123, ❷), a laid-back hostel sited in a former psychiatric hospital on the outskirts of Dunedin.

Travel details

Passenger trains run north of Christchurch to Kaikoura and Picton, and northwest to Arthur's Pass and Greymouth. Christchurch is the hub of the South Island's bus network: InterCity, Atomic Shuttle and Southern Link K Bus have the broadest networks. Only direct, non-stop flights are listed.

Trains

Christchurch to: Arthur's Pass (1 daily; 2hr 15min); Blenheim (1 daily; 4hr 45min); Greymouth (1 daily; 4hr 30min); Kaikoura (1 daily; 3hr); Picton (1 daily; 5hr 20min).

Buses

Christchurch to: Akaroa (4–5 daily; 1hr 30min); Aoraki Mount Cook (1 daily; 5hr 30min); Arthur's Pass (3 daily; 2hr 30min); Blenheim (11 daily; 4hr 45min–5hr 30min); Dunedin (9 daily; 5hr 30min–6hr 30min); Fairlie (5 daily; 2hr 30min); Geraldine (5 daily; 2hr); Greymouth (3 daily; 4hr 30min); Hanmer Springs (4 daily; 2hr); Hokitika (1 daily; 4hr 30min); Invercargill (2 daily; 9hr 30min); Kaikoura (11 daily; 2hr 30min); Lyttelton (every 15–30min; 35min); Maruia Springs (1 daily; 3hr 15min); Methven (2–4 daily; 1hr 10min); Nelson (4 daily; 7hr); Oamaru (9 daily; 4hr);

Picton (8 daily; 5hr–5hr 30min); Queenstown (5 daily; 7–8hr); Tekapo (5 daily; 3–4hr); Timaru (9 daily; 2hr 30min); Twizel (5 daily; 4–5hr); Wanaka (5 daily; 7–8hr).
Oamaru to: Aoraki Mount Cook (4 weekly; 3hr); Christchurch (9 daily; 4hr); Dunedin (9 daily; 2hr); Omarama (4 weekly; 1hr 45min); Tekapo (4 weekly; 3hr); Timaru (9 daily; 1hr); Twizel (4 weekly; 2hr).
Timaru to: Christchurch (8 daily; 2hr 30min); Dunedin (9 daily; 3hr 30min); Oamaru (9 daily; 1hr).

Flights

Christchurch to: Auckland (20–25 daily; 1hr 20min); Blenheim (2 daily; 50min); Dunedin (8 daily; 1hr); Hokitika (2–3 daily; 35min); Invercargill (5–6 daily; 1hr 15min); Napier/Hastings (2–3 daily; 1hr 20min); Nelson (5–8 daily; 50min); Palmerston North (4–5 daily; 1hr 10min); Queenstown (7 daily; 50min); Rotorua (3 daily; 1hr 15min–1hr 40min); Wanaka (1 daily; 1hr); Wellington (15 daily; 45min).
Timaru to: Wellington (4 daily; 1hr 10min).Raesto odolorem ilisit nosto odolor adit wisl il er si. Ilissit prat. Um dipit aliquam, consequis aliquis

10

The Central South Island

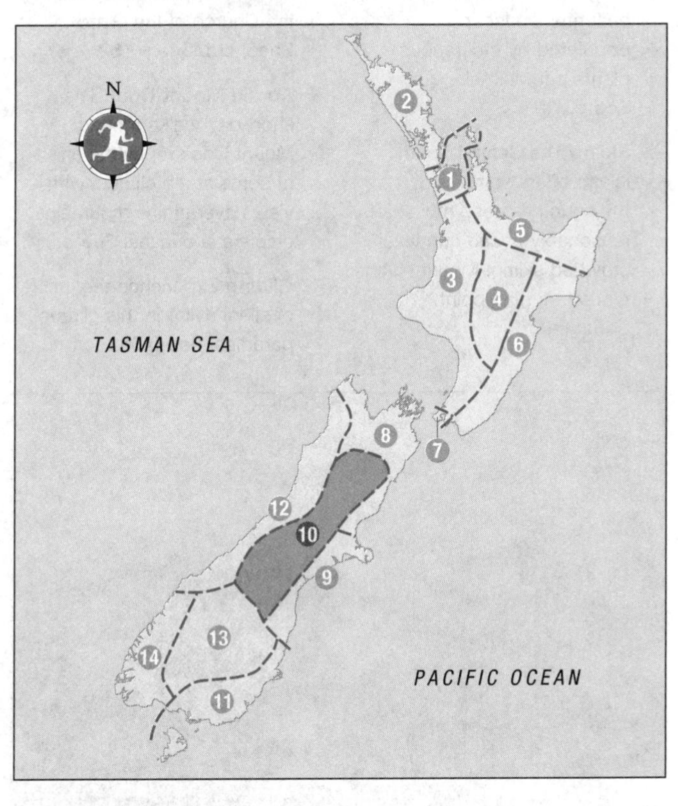

CHAPTER 10

Highlights

* **Hot springs** Soak your bones at the resort of Hanmer Springs, the more rustic Maruia Springs or the totally natural pool at Sylvia Flats. See pp.629–633

* **Arthur's Pass** Hiking here provides a jaw-dropping insight into a uniquely beautiful landscape populated by indigenous plants and animals. See p.633

* **Skiing** The Central South Island offers some of the country's best, most reasonably priced and least-crowded skiing. Mount Hutt is a great starting point. See p.640

* **Rafting the Rangitata** Raft some of the best and bounciest white water in the country on rafting trips from Peel Forest, or as a day-trip from Christchurch. See p.647

* **Lake Tekapo** These mountain-backed blue waters are best appreciated from the Church of the Good Shepherd. See p.652

* **Aoraki Mount Cook** The short day-walks around Mount Cook repay the effort of some steep climbs, with views over alpine mountains, glaciers and lakes. See p.652

* **Gliding** Experience the thrill of silent flying in this gliders' paradise. See p.662

▲ Church of the Good Shepherd, Tekapo

10

The Central South Island

The **Central South Island** is one of the most varied and visually stunning areas in New Zealand, with extensive pasturelands, dense native forests and a history rich in tales of human endeavour. The region's defining feature is the icy, white sawtooth ridge of the **Southern Alps** that forms the South Island's central north–south spine and peaks at New Zealand's loftiest summit, 3754-metre **Aoraki Mount Cook**. A logistical nightmare for Maori and European settlers, the region is typical pioneer country, and the communities themselves are simple places, tinged with the toughness and idiosyncrasies of the early settlers.

The mountains present an obstacle to travel between the east and west coasts, a barrier only breached in two places, both providing access to mountain scenery, walks and ski-fields. From Christchurch to Westport, the **Lewis Pass** road provides access to the tranquil, forested spa town of **Hanmer Springs** before passing the more low-key hot pools at **Maruia Springs**. Further south, both road and rail head through the more spectacular **Arthur's Pass**, historically an important trade route connecting the coalfields of the west coast with the port of Lyttelton. It lies at the heart of **Arthur's Pass National Park**, with its abundance of enthralling day-walks and longer trails.

South of Christchurch, roads lead across the Canterbury Plains towards the small foothill settlements of **Methven** and **Mount Somers**, a popular destination for **Mount Hutt**-bound skiers and summer adventurers after some stunning whitewater rafting, first-class tramping and accommodation with truly wonderful views.

The southern half of the region leaves behind the rolling hills for the sun-scorched grasslands of the **Mackenzie Country**, an area renowned for massive sheep runs and the beautiful blues of its glacier-fed lakes, **Tekapo** and **Pukaki**. The mightiest of the Southern Alps form an imperious backdrop and are most easily accessed at **Aoraki Mount Cook Village**, huddled at the foot of the mountain, and the starting point of numerous walks, unique glacial lake trips and truly memorable glacial landings by ski plane.

Some visitors base themselves at **Twizel**, an odd former construction town built to house workers building the complex Waitaki Valley Hydro Scheme. You'll see the dams, control gates and water channels everywhere. The hydro scheme eventually feeds all the water down the scenic **Waitaki Valley**, which

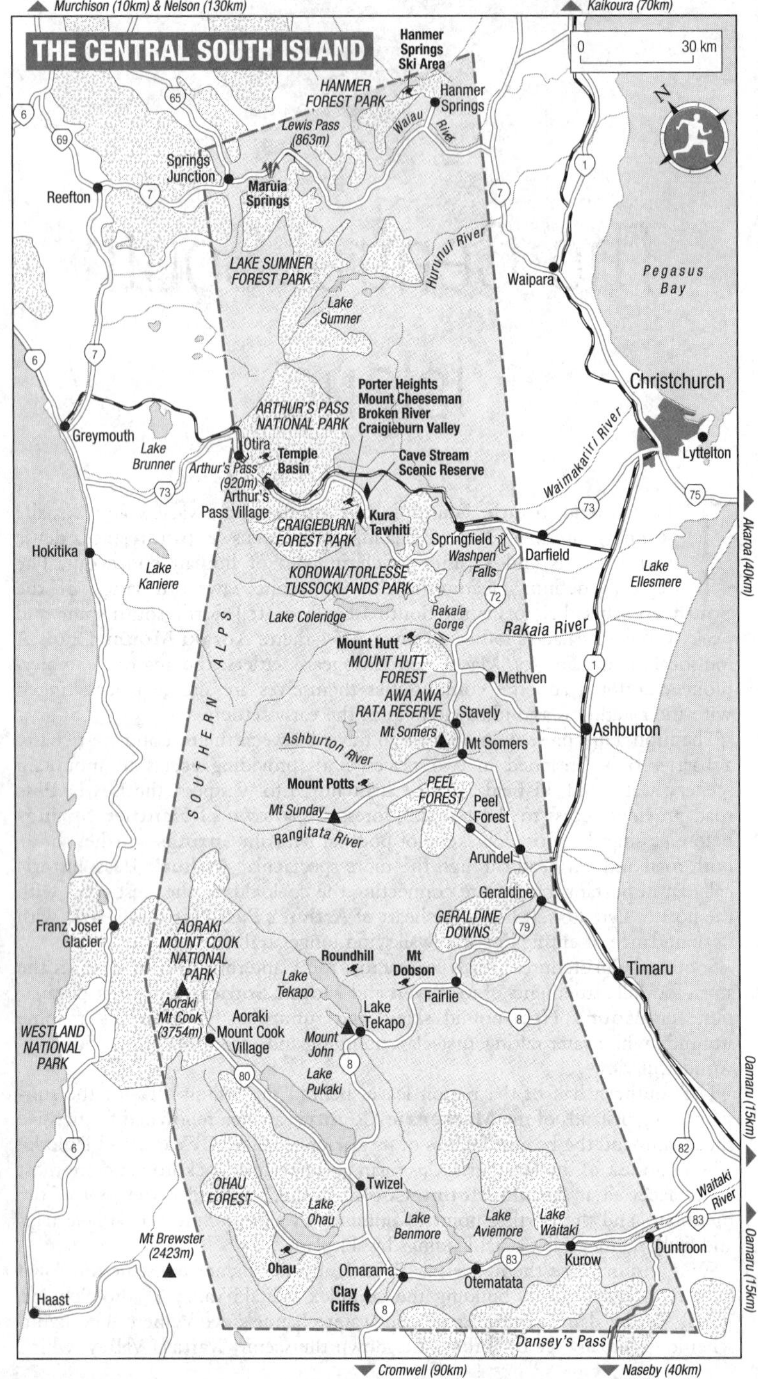

THE CENTRAL SOUTH ISLAND
Murchison (10km) & Nelson (130km)
Kaikoura (70km)
Hanmer Springs Ski Area
HANMER FOREST PARK
Hanmer Springs
Lewis Pass (863m)
Waiau River
Springs Junction
Maruia Springs
Reefton
LAKE SUMNER FOREST PARK
Hurunui River
Lake Sumner
Waipara
Pegasus Bay
Christchurch
Porter Heights
Mount Cheeseman
Broken River
Craigieburn Valley
ARTHUR'S PASS NATIONAL PARK
Greymouth
Lake Brunner
Otira
Temple Basin
Arthur's Pass (920m)
Arthur's Pass Village
Cave Stream Scenic Reserve
Kura Tawhiti
CRAIGIEBURN FOREST PARK
Springfield
Washpen Falls
Darfield
Waimakariri River
Lyttelton
Hokitika
Lake Kaniere
KOROWAI/TORLESSE TUSSOCKLANDS PARK
Lake Coleridge
Rakaia Gorge
Rakaia River
Lake Ellesmere
Akaroa (40km)
Mount Hutt
MOUNT HUTT FOREST
Methven
AWA AWA RATA RESERVE
Stavely
SOUTHERN ALPS
Mt Somers
Ashburton
Ashburton River
Mount Potts
PEEL FOREST
Peel Forest
Mt Sunday
Rangitata River
Arundel
Geraldine
GERALDINE DOWNS
Franz Josef Glacier
AORAKI MOUNT COOK NATIONAL PARK
Roundhill
Mt Dobson
Lake Tekapo
Timaru
Fairlie
Aoraki Mt Cook (3754m)
Aoraki Mount Cook Village
Mount John
WESTLAND NATIONAL PARK
Lake Pukaki
Oamaru (15km)
Twizel
OHAU FOREST
Lake Ohau
Lake Benmore
Lake Aviemore
Lake Waitaki
Waitaki River
Duntroon
Kurow
Mt Brewster (2423m)
Ohau
Omarama
Otematata
Clay Cliffs
Haast
Dansey's Pass
Cromwell (90km)
Naseby (40km)
0
30 km

threads its way to the east coast at Oamaru, though you may well be tempted to stay inland and forge south towards Wanaka and the bright lights of Queenstown.

The Central South Island **climate** is generally hot and dry in summer with long days that sear the grasslands a tinder-dry yellow-brown. In winter snow supplies numerous ski-fields. It is a climate that fosters unique alpine plants and wildlife, including the famous Mount Cook lily, the largest white mountain daisies in the world, and that most mischievous of birds, the kea – the world's only alpine parrot.

Hanmer Springs and the Lewis Pass

The most northerly of the cross-mountain routes, SH7 crosses the **Lewis Pass** following an ancient Maori and early Pakeha trade route. From the east, the route starts at Waipara, 80km north of Christchurch, then crosses the coastal plain and begins its gradual climb between the foothills of the Southern Alps. A side road spurs off to **Hanmer Springs**, a base for summer walks, hot pools and winter sports at the nearby **Hanmer Springs Ski Area**. Amid the exhilarating subalpine terrain and deep forest some 60km further west, you cross the **Lewis Pass** and drop down to the tiny resort of **Maruia Springs** with its soothing thermal waters. Several daily **buses** make the trip from Christchurch direct to Hanmer Springs, and other services head from Christchurch over the pass to Westport, on the west coast, and Nelson.

Hanmer Springs

About 140km north of Christchurch, a side road heads 9km north off SH7 to the spa town of **HANMER SPRINGS**, a place that's delightfully relaxing and has enough minor attractions and activities to fill the odd day. Pleasantly situated at the edge of a broad, fertile plain snuggled against the Southern Alps foothills, Hanmer has just 700 residents, but the place is awash with holiday homes and – in keeping with the holiday spirit – a preponderance of mini-golf courses.

While searching for stray cattle in 1859, one William Jones stumbled across the springs, fed by rainwater that seeps down through fractures in the rocks of the Hanmer Mountains and accumulates in an underground reservoir some 2km beneath the Hanmer Plain. After absorbing various minerals and being warmed by the earth's natural heat, the water rises to the surface via fissures in the greywacke rock. Word of Hanmer's waters spread at a time when the beneficial effects of mineral baths were much hyped and, by the 1870s, the town had become nationally famous for its waters' relaxing and curative properties.

The Town

The oak-lined Amuri Avenue runs past the visitor centre, most of the shops and the shady park that gives the town its quiet and sheltered feel. The park marks the entrance to the **Hanmer Springs Thermal Pools & Spa** (daily 10am–9pm; $12, two entries on same day $15; Ⓦ www.hanmersprings.co.nz). In the modernized pool complex, people lounge on the lawns around assorted landscaped pools full of light-blue water at a balmy 36°C. Artificial streams link the pools, providing great places to wallow, and there are faintly sulphurous springwater pools held at an enervating 41°C. Add in a standard chlorinated 25m swimming pool, a toddlers' pool, a waterslide ($5 extra), a series of more intimate private pools ($22 each for 30min, minimum of two, includes general entry for as long as you like),

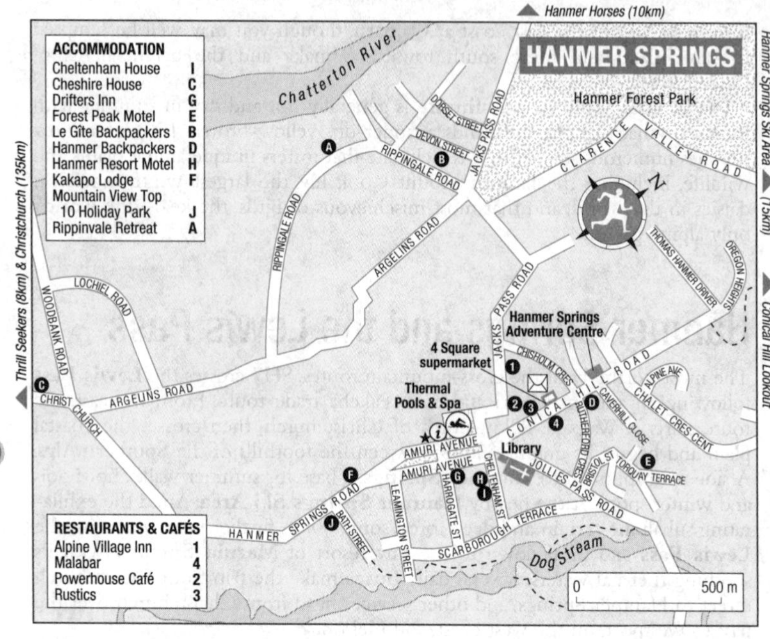

and the *Garden House Café* and you could stay all day. It is perhaps best in the evening when the crowds thin and you can relax as the sun sets. For further pampering, visit The Spa (☎03/315 0029), a new and stylish place to relax with a full-body **massage** (1hr; $80), Vichy pressured water exfoliation (1hr; $132) or all manner of other treatments.

Hiking and biking in Hanmer Forest Park

The Black pines, Norway spruce, Douglas firs and assorted deciduous trees of **Hanmer Forest Park**, on the northern and eastern fringes of town, make great territory for hiking. The excellent *Hanmer Springs Walks* leaflet maps out numerous **walks** (20min–6hr), notably the **Conical Hill Walk** (2km return; 1hr; 150m ascent), which climbs up to a good viewpoint over town; the **Woodland Walk** (2km; 45min; flat), with its stream, flax wetland and ponds teeming with birds; and the **Waterfall Track** (2.5km; 3hr; 400m ascent), leading to the 41m-high Dog Stream Waterfall.

Hanmer Forest is also renowned for **mountain biking**. Pick up the *Mountain Bike Tracks* leaflet ($2) and rent a bike ($45 a day) from Hanmer Adventure Centre, 20 Conical Hill Rd (☎0800/368 7386, Ⓦwww.hanmeradventure.co.nz), then go exploring the gravel roads and twisting singletrack. If you prefer riding downhill only, get the centre to transport you to the top of Jacks Pass for a self-guided ride back ($89, including a hot pools pass).

Adventure activities

Near the turn-off from SH7, 9km south of town, the Waiau Ferry Bridge is home to Thrillseekers (☎03/315 7046, Ⓦwww.thrillseeker.co.nz), an adventure centre enjoying a near-monopoly on local water-based activities. These include scenic two-hour-plus **rafting** trips through the Grade II Waiau River Canyon

(70–90min on the water; $145), **jetboat** rides through the steep-sided gorges of the Waiau River (40min; $99), **bungy jumps** ($135) from a 35m-platform midway across the Waiau Ferry Bridge and fun 4x4 **go-kart** trips in the backblocks ($129). For **quad biking**, visit Hanmer Adventure Centre (see p.630), who charge $129 for a fun-filled two hours riding specially developed tracks in the foothills.

For a different form of saddle, go **horse-riding** with Hanmer Horses, 187 Rogerson Rd (Ⓣ0800/873 546, Ⓦwww.hanmerhorses.co.nz; 1hr $45, half-day $90), whose trips are tailored to clients but usually involving stream crossings. They're a fifteen-minute drive northwest of town off Jacks Pass Road. **Serious riders** after multi-day trips should contact Alpine Horse Safaris (see p.67).

Hanmer Springs Ski Area

Intermediate boarders and skiers should have a fine time at the **Hanmer Springs Ski Area**, (generally open mid-July to Sept; tows $45; Ⓦwww.skihanmer.co.nz), a tiny place with just one rope tow and New Zealand's longest Poma-style lift. The ski-field (runs: one beginner; six intermediate; five advanced) is a forty-minute drive up the Clarence Valley Road (free for skiers, but sightseers have to pay a $10 toll). The road is dicey so take the **bus** operated by Hanmer Adventure Centre (see p.630; $30 return), where you can also rent ski gear. You'll find rentals, a day lodge with stoves, toasted sandwiches and tea and coffee, and comfortable backpacker accommodation ($25) in the ski area. The **Mount Lyford Ski-field** (see p.561), 60km to the northeast, is also accessible from Hanmer via SH70.

Practicalities

Bus transport to Hanmer is easiest with Hanmer Connection (Ⓣ0800/242 663, Ⓦwww.atsnz.com), who run here from Christchurch (3 daily) and Kaikoura (3 days a week). To continue over the Lewis Pass to Westport take Hanmer Connection to the highway junction and wait an hour for the East West (Ⓣ0800/142 622) service running between Christchurch and Westport. Southern Link K Bus also pass by on their run between Christchurch and Nelson, calling into Hanmer on request.

All buses stop outside the **i-SITE visitor centre** on Amuri Avenue, next to the hot pools (daily 10am–5pm; Ⓣ03/315 0020, Ⓦwww.hurunui.com), which contains a small **bank** (Mon–Fri 10am–2pm). There's also an 24hr **ATM** outside the small 4-square **supermarket** on Conical Hill Road.

Hanmer has a pretty good spread of **accommodation**, though since the place is very popular with holidaying Kiwis in summer it pays to book a few days ahead at the height of summer and during school holidays. Though it is small, Hanmer has over a dozen decent **places to eat**.

Accommodation

Cheltenham House 13 Cheltenham St Ⓣ03/315 7545, Ⓦwww.cheltenham.co.nz. The best B&B in town, with four large, gracious rooms set in a tastefully renovated 1930s house with a snooker room. There are also two cottages in the lovingly tended garden. Welcome drinks, spa and free Wi-Fi. ⑦

Cheshire House 164C Hanmer Springs Rd, Highway 7A, Hanmer Springs, Ⓣ03/315 5100, Ⓦwww.bnb.co.nz/cheshirehouse.html. Welcoming English-run B&B 3km south of town with three modern, en-suite rooms and great mountain views. ⑥

Drifters Inn 2 Harrogate St Ⓣ0800/374 383 Ⓦwww.driftersinn.co.nz. Centrally located motel-cum-lodge offering comfortable rooms (go for one that has been modernized), and use of several communal areas, including a kitchen. Prices include continental breakfast. Rooms ⑤, spa bath room ⑥

Forest Peak Motel 4 Torquay Terrace Ⓣ0508/224 678, Ⓦwww.forestpeak.co.nz. Motel with ten clean, if fairly spartan units and three attractive pine chalets, all set in attractive grounds close to town and the forest. ❸, chalets ❻

Le Gîte Backpackers 3 Devon St ⓣ03/315 5111, ⓦwww.legite.co.nz. The pick of the hostels, in a couple of converted houses plus a modern chalet , all 1km from the centre. There's plenty of room, including a nice deck, hammocks, tasteful decor and helpful staff. Share $25, rooms & en suites ❷

Hanmer Backpackers 41 Conical Hill Rd ⓣ03/315 7196, ⓔhanmerbackpackers@xtra.co.nz. Small, central chalet-style hostel, offering shared rooms and doubles plus a family room and a cosy lounge. Dorms $25, rooms ❷

Hanmer Resort Motel 7 Cheltenham St ⓣ0800/777 666, ⓦwww.hanmerresortmotel.co.nz. Old-fashioned central motel with a range of units kept to a very high standard and owners who can't do enough for you. Larger rooms have their own private garden and there's a kids' play area. Great value ❹

Kakapo Lodge 14 Amuri Ave ⓣ03/315 7472, ⓦwww.kakapolodge.co.nz. Large associate YHA that's central, welcoming and well appointed but a little stark. Dorms $26, rooms ❷, en suites & motel units ❸

Mountain View Top 10 Holiday Park Corner of Hanmer Springs Rd & Bath St ⓣ0800/904 545, ⓦwww.hanmerspringstop10.co.nz. Formal campervan-heavy park with a range of motel units, cabin accommodation and tent camping overlooking a riverside reserve. Bike rental $10 per hr. Camping $28 per site, cabins ❷, kitchen cabins ❸, s/c units ❹

Rippinvale Retreat 68 Rippingale Rd ⓣ0800/373 098, ⓦwww.hanmersprings.net.nz. Upmarket lodge on the edge of town with just two suites, both beautifully furnished and each with private courtyard and fresh flowers. Breakfast (with mostly home-grown and organic ingredients) is served in your room and there's a spa pool and outdoor fireplace in the spacious grounds. Doubles $350. ❾

Eating and drinking

Alpine Village Inn 10 Jacks Pass Rd. Middle-of-the-road locals' bar with a range of traditional fish, steak and chicken meals (mostly $18–22), plus $13 roast dinners.

Malabar 5 Conical Hill Rd ⓣ03/315 7754. Flashy Asian fusion restaurant with an adventurous menu putting a modern twist on dishes from South East and South Asia and Japan. Expect rack of Indian lamb, tandoori chicken and seafood tempura (mains $28–35), lovely desserts ($12), plus cocktails.

Powerhouse Café 6 Jacks Pass Rd. This funky modern café serves the best coffee and counter food in town for breakfast and lunch. Try their gluten-free muesli or Thai rice cakes perhaps followed by delicious orange-infused poppy seed cake.

Rustics 8 Conical Hill Rd ⓣ03/315 7274. Great little tapas restaurant with small plates of tasty treats such as pan-fried chorizo with roasted capsicum, battered monkfish or mini samosa (4 for $37). Larger plates of salad, pasta and risotto are also available along with delicious dessert tapas.

West to the Lewis Pass and Maruia Springs

West of the Hanmer Springs turn-off, SH7 continues its climb towards the 907-metre **Lewis Pass**, 65km to the west. Maori had long crossed through this high-country pass to trade, but it wasn't until 1860 that surveyors Christopher Maling and Henry Lewis stumbled upon it and so opened up a relatively easy route between the east and west coasts. In 1866 a bridle track linking Hanmer Plain with Murchison was finished, and by 1936 a spectacular highway was finally opened.

The countryside is initially low-yielding grassland with broom (blazing yellow in the summer), spiky matagouri, manuka and kanuka taking hold where farms failed. As you approach the pass, red and silver beech forest begins to predominate.

The only real reason to stop before the pass is for the unmarked **Sylvia Flats hot springs**, beside SH7, 49km west of the Hanmer Springs junction. Look for a sign announcing your entry into the Lewis Pass National Reserve, then, 500m on, turn into a rest area from where a small riverside track leads 100m upstream to some shallow pools. Here warm water bubbles up through the rocks, mixing with the cold river water to create refreshing thermal pools. Remember to bring something to deter some of the country's most ferocious sandflies, or come after dark when they've gone to bed.

The **Lewis Pass** itself is just 13km further on, and offers views along high-sided Cannibal Gorge towards the Spenser Mountains.

Maruia Springs

Over Lewis Pass it is a further 8km west to **MARUIA SPRINGS**, a Japanese-themed spa grouped around a bath complex with **hot pools** (daily 9am–8.30pm; communal pool areas $15, private baths $50 for 45min for up to 4 people) overlooking the Maruia River. Separate men's and women's bathhouses are supplemented by communal natural-rock outdoor pools whose steaming waters range from black to milky white, depending on the minerals they contain.

The hotel-style **accommodation** at the *Maruia Springs Resort* (Ⓣ03/523 8840, Ⓦwww.maruiasprings.co.nz; camping $25, en-suite rooms ❻) is nothing flash, but a continental breakfast is included and guests get free access to the springs. Within the complex is the *Hot Rocks* **café/bar** and the Japanese-style *Shuzan Restaurant*.

Arthur's Pass and around

The most dramatic of the three Southern Alps crossings links Christchurch with Greymouth, via **Arthur's Pass**. Traversed by a scenic rail line and the equally breathtaking SH73, the route is popular with city-based travellers eager for a taste of the high country and winter-sports enthusiasts wanting to take advantage of several ski-fields.

The pass gets its name from civil engineer **Arthur Dudley Dobson**, who "discovered" it after hearing about the route from local Maori who had traditionally used it as a highway for raiding parties and for trade, sometimes *pounamu* (greenstone). Dobson surveyed the pass in 1864, and by 1866 horse-drawn coaches were using it to serve the Westland goldfields. The railway was built in 1923, coinciding with the booming interest in alpine tourism worldwide.

From Christchurch to Arthur's Pass

Both road and rail routes from Christchurch to Arthur's Pass thread across the fertile Canterbury Plains beside the braided Waimakariri River before climbing up to Arthur's Pass Village at 735m above sea level. The 920-metre pass itself is 4km west of the village, marked by a large obelisk to Dobson.

From Christchurch the route is virtually flat to **Springfield**, 70km out of Christchurch, where the river and the rail line veer away to the northwest while the road ascends through the **Korowai/Torlesse Tussocklands Park** to **Porter's Pass**. The road then passes the otherworldly boulders of **Kura Tawhiti** and the fun tunnel walk at **Cave Stream**, while side roads wind steeply into the Craigieburn range to access some of the South Island's most entertaining small **ski-fields**.

Road and rail routes then rejoin to follow the Waimakariri River towards Arthur's Pass village, in the centre of the national park and wedged between the 2271-metre **Mount Rolleston** and the 1913-metre **Mount Temple**.

Just after Arthur's Pass Village, the railway dives through the long, glum **Otira Tunnel** while the road climbs to the pass then descends across the **Otira Viaduct**. This spectacular piece of engineering is best seen from a signed lookout point, where you can snap some spectacular photographs of the road and, in one spot, the roof that keeps the cascade of mountain water off its surface. Both road and rail then slip quickly down toward the pounding seas of the West Coast and dubious charms of Greymouth.

Springfield

Heading west out of Christchurch, consider a stop at **SPRINGFIELD**, especially if you fancy a high-speed boat trip down the **Waimakariri Gorge** to blow away the cobwebs. The gorge is narrow, and the river water clear as gin, with the many waterfalls making for a spectacular and beautiful ride. Waimak Alpine Jet, on Rubicon Road, off the Kowai Bush Road (30min $75, 1hr $105; ⓣ03/318 4881, ⓦwww.waimakalpinejet.co.nz), operate great trips in 22-seater jetboats: book ahead to be sure a trip is running.

In town, a **monument** beside SH73 remembers Springfield's best-loved son, **Rewi Alley**. Named after Rewi Maniapoto, the Maori leader who, at the battle of Orakau, shouted "*Kaore e manu te tongo. Ake! Ake!*" ("We will never make peace. Never! Never!"), Alley displayed similar resilience throughout his fascinating life. After World War I he worked as a missionary in China, later setting up small manufacturing co-operatives during the hazardous Japanese occupation. He went on to found schools, help with oil development, translate Chinese poetry, write poetry and prose of his own and act as an unofficial ambassador for China, despite his misgivings about the direction of the post-war communist regime and his increasing isolation within the country. The peaceful, Chinese-style garden memorial includes rock and water features, Rewi's abridged biography and a memorial to his remarkable mother, Clara, a leader in the New Zealand women's suffrage movement.

There's a small **visitor centre** and café on King Street (Mon–Fri 8.30am–4pm. Sat 8.30am–3pm, Sun 8.30am–2pm; ⓣ03/318 4000), in the train station, signposted 500m off SH73. Springfield also offers one of the friendliest and most comfortable associate YHA **hostels** on the South Island, the Japanese-run *Smylies*, SH73 (ⓣ03/318 4740, ⓦwww.smylies.co.nz; dorms $25, rooms ❷, motel units ❸). Busy with skiers in winter and climbers and mountain bikers in summer, it comes with Japanese baths (daily in winter; on request in summer), cosy rooms and Japanese meals (from $15). Breakfast ($10–15) comes continental, cooked, or Japanese-style. The *Springfield Hotel*, SH73, serves meals and takeaways and the *Shack Café* opposite is fine for coffee and snacks.

Porter's Pass and Kura Tawhiti (Castle Hill Reserve)

About 10km west of Springfield, the highway neatly bisects the 21,000-hectare **Korowai/Torlesse Tussocklands Park**, New Zealand's first conservation park designed to protect the unique and quickly disappearing tussock grasslands of the eastern South Island. As you crest the 932-metre **Porter's Pass**, consider stopping to hike up to the 1733-metre **Foggy Peak** (8km return; 3hr; 800m ascent). For more detail, consult the DOC leaflet on the area (available at the Christchurch and Arthur's Pass offices).

Beyond Porter's Pass, SH73 turns north and runs 10km to **Kura Tawhiti Scenic Reserve** (Castle Hill), a swathe of rolling grassland peppered by clusters of grey limestone outcrops ranging from the size of a sheep to something as big as, well, a castle. Since the mid-1990s, the place has gained an international reputation for the quantity and quality of its **bouldering**, an abbreviated rope-free form of rock climbing that doesn't generally get its adherents far off the ground, though experts might spend days perfecting their moves on a particularly hard problem. On fine days there are always boulderers out there, visible from a number of **paths** that wind among the rocks and tussock-covered hills.

▲ Rock formations at Kura Tawhiti Scenic Reserve

Maori once stopped here on trading missions and the place retains a spiritual significance. It is also a photogenic spot, with mountain daisies and Castle Hill buttercups blooming in summer.

Cave Stream Scenic Reserve

Some 6km westbound from Kura Tawhiti, **Cave Stream Scenic Reserve** nestles among limestone outcrops with views of the Craigieburn and Torlesse ranges. Here, there's a rare opportunity for the unguided exploration of a limestone cave (362m; 1hr). Cave art, signs of seasonal camps and the discovery of an ancient wooden-framed flax backpack and other artefacts over 500 years old (now in the Canterbury Museum, see p.580) indicate that Maori visited the area extensively. The cave contains bones as well as providing a home for large but harmless harvestman spiders and young eels that wriggle along the walls.

The **walk/wade** through the cave involves entering at the downstream end where you'll cross a deep pool before gradually hiking upstream. If the water near the entrance is above waist-high, fast-flowing, foaming and discoloured, do not attempt the walk. This is a wet and exciting underground adventure best done between December and April, but at any time dress warmly, take a companion, plus at least one torch each with spare batteries and make sure you have something dry to change into afterwards. There are only two major obstacles apart from the dark and cold: a 1.5m rockfall about halfway through that funnels the water and so is quite hard to climb, and a 3m waterfall at the very end. The latter is negotiated by climbing up a ladder of iron rungs embedded in the rock and crawling along a short, narrow ledge while holding onto an anchored chain.

Craigieburn Forest Park

The **Craigieburn Forest Park** lies on the eastern ranges of the Southern Alps, about 15km beyond Kura Tawhiti and 42km before Arthur's Pass Village. It is

Ski-fields around Arthur's Pass

There are five accessible ski-fields in the area around Arthur's Pass, each offering accommodation and equipment rental. Although the variety of runs isn't enormous, they are unusual and challenging, with some spectacular views, as well as reliable snow and quiet slopes. The **season** is generally July to September although October is often also good. For full details and information on snow conditions visit Ⓦwww.snow.co.nz. The fields are described from east to west, heading along SH73 from Christchurch. Many people choose to access the ski-fields from Christchurch, but if you want to cut down on travelling stay at *Smylie's* in Springfield (see p.634) or in Arthur's Pass Village.

Porter Heights 96km west of Christchurch, just off SH73 via a 6km unsealed road Ⓣ03/318 4002, Ⓦwww.skiporters.co.nz. The region's main commercial field and the longest single run in the southern hemisphere. Runs: 2 beginner; 3 intermediate; 9 advanced. Full lift pass $70/day; learners' pass $45.

Mount Cheeseman 112km from Christchurch along SH73 Ⓣ03/344 3247, Ⓦmtcheeseman.com. Well-appointed club field with good facilities, a friendly atmosphere and a wide variety of runs for intermediates, plus off-piste for those with greater experience. Runs: 2 beginner; 3 intermediate; 8 advanced. Lift passes are $60/day.

Broken River 120km out from Christchurch at the end of a 6km access road, off SH73 Ⓣ03/318 7270, Ⓦwww.brokenriver.co.nz. Field offering occasional night skiing and good snowboard terrain. Runs: 2 beginner; 7 intermediate; 10 advanced. Lift passes are $60/day, night pass $35. There are accommodation lodges (❸) and an instruction package is $44/hour. The ski area is only about 20-minute-walk from the car park and there's a free goods lift. It is possible to ski between Broken River and Craigieburn, with transferable lift passes.

Craigieburn Valley 120km out of Christchurch and another 6km up a side road Ⓣ03/318 8711, Ⓦwww.craigieburn.co.nz. One of the best-kept secrets in the southern hemisphere, this challenging field has just three rope tows giving a 500m rise and access to the mostly steep runs: 0 beginner; 6 intermediate; 15 advanced. Lift passes $60/day.

Temple Basin 4km west of Arthur's Pass Village Ⓣ03/377 7788, Ⓦwww.templebasin.co.nz. Right at the Arthur's Pass col, this field is superb for snowboarding, has a 430m drop, is floodlit for night skiing, and offers a variety of runs: 6 beginner; 10 intermediate; 8 advanced. There's a 1hr walk in and lift passes cost $60, dinner, bed and breakfast around $65.

chock-a-block with good walking tracks, longer tramps and mountaineering opportunities in the more rugged country further west. The park is dominated by alpine scrub, tussock grasslands and dense, moss-covered mountain beech forest peppered with scarlet native mistletoe flowers from December to February. A variety of native birds streak and squawk through the forest, including bellbird, rifleman, silver eye and kea and, between October and February, long-tailed and shining cuckoos join the throng. The nearby **Craigieburn Valley ski-field** (see box above), within the boundaries of the forest park, is one of the most exciting in the vicinity of Arthur's Pass.

In a signposted car park just off SH73 by Cave Stream are the **Craigieburn Picnic Area** (also a free DOC campsite) and a walkers' **shelter** with fixed maps of the local tramps. The *Craigieburn Forest Park Day Walks* leaflet (from local visitor centres) details eleven day-walks in the park. The best is the **Hut Creek Walk** (2km return; 1hr), which begins outside the Environmental Education Centre (closed to the public), some 3km along a dirt road which runs northwest from the picnic area. The track itself winds down to the creek and continues through mountain beeches, emerging onto a slope of native hebe, dracophyllum (whose leaves shade from green to a reddish-brown in spring and autumn), cassinia and matagouri. There are great views from the lookout, and kea (see box below) are often about. To tack on a pleasant extra twenty minutes try the nature trail that also begins at the centre. Rugged hikers might fancy the **Cass–Lagoon Saddle Track** (33km, 2 days, 1300m ascent), a lovely loop with an overnight stop at Hamilton Hut (20 bunks; $10) almost exactly halfway. It starts at the east end of Cass road bridge.

If you want to break your journey before the final assault on the pass, head for the *Flock Hill Lodge* (Ⓣ03/318 8196, Ⓦwww.flockhill.co.nz; dorms $25, linen $5 extra, rooms ❹), 10km west of Cave Stream, which has basic backpacker accommodation in shearers' quarters and a range of spacious units in beautiful grounds, plus a restaurant and bar for guests. A further 27km on, and 12km short of Arthur's Pass Village, the family-oriented *Bealey Hotel* (Ⓣ03/318 9277, Ⓦwww.bealeyhotel.co.nz; rooms ❷, motel units ❺), is wonderfully set on a knoll overlooking the broad expanse of the Waimakariri River. Even if you don't need to stay, call in for a drink or meal in the bar where there's heaps of information on the hotel's early role as a stop-off point for Cobb & Co coaches, which travelled to and from the West Coast, and its subsequent fleeting fame when the owner claimed to have seen moa hereabouts in 1993. It is widely accepted that these massive birds became extinct over 300 years ago, but scientists and TV crews still occasionally turn up to investigate the claims.

Arthur's Pass Village

ARTHUR'S PASS VILLAGE, 4km east of the pass itself, nestles at 735m in a steep-sided, forest-covered U-shaped valley. With only about fifty residents, it forms a thin straggle along the main road (SH73). The area receives over 4m of rainfall a year, and the village invariably hunches beneath mist or clouds: there's often a moody contrast between the white clouds that hover halfway up the valley wall and the rich green trees and vegetation of the valley floor and slopes.

Kea: New Zealand's alpine trickster

One of the most enduring memories of a visit to Arthur's Pass and many other alpine areas of the South Island is the sight of a bright green **kea** mischievously getting its beak into something, or simply posing for the camera. With their lolloping sideways gait, scavenging tendencies and inexhaustible curiosity, the world's only alpine parrots are so endearing you'll be tempted to try to feed them. Human food does them more harm than good, but these kleptomaniacs can be persistent and frequently grab sandwiches from inattentive lunching walkers. You'll hear the ruffle of feathers, see the flash of red beneath their wings and they'll be tearing at your lunch, just out of reach.

At backcountry huts you might find kea sliding down the corrugated iron roofing or pulling at the nails holding the roof on, and if they notice a carelessly abandoned pair of hiking boots they'll soon latch onto them. Trampers have been known to wake up to a pile of leather strips and shredded laces.

With these playful tendencies it is hardly surprising kea traditionally got the blame for attacking sheep, and for many years were routinely shot by farmers. Recent research seems to indicate kea only attack already weakened sheep, and shooting has long since stopped as the birds are now fully protected. Their numbers have stabilized at around 5000 birds.

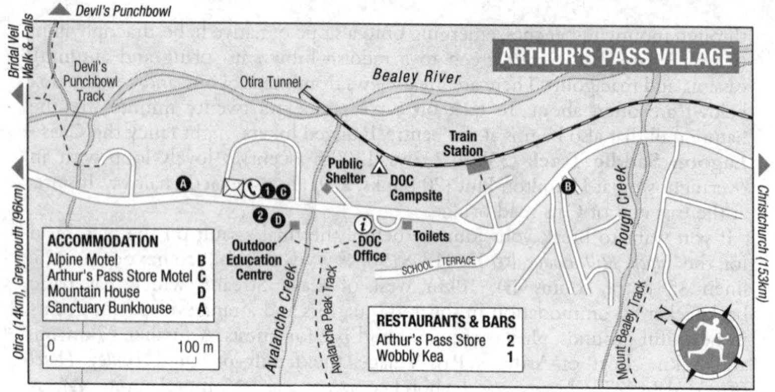

The kea (see box, p.637), don't seem to mind and are often around the village, especially in the early evening, toying with the tourists.

The Arthur's Pass settlement sprung up in the early 1900s to provide shelter for tunnel diggers and rail workers and nowadays ekes a living from the tourists visiting the surrounding **national park**. It's a superb base for walking and climbing, with nearby **Temple Basin ski-field** (see box, p.636) providing good skiing and snowboarding opportunities in winter.

Practicalities

Regular coast-to-coast **buses** (Coast to Coast ⓣ0800/800 847, West Coast Shuttle ⓣ07/768 0028 & Atomic Shuttles ⓣ03/349 0697) and the TranzAlpine **train** (see p.585) all stop in the centre of the settlement, a short walk from everything. There is an excellent **DOC office** and **visitor centre** on the main street (daily: Nov–April 8am–5pm; May–Oct 8.30am–4.30pm; ⓣ03/318 9211, ⓦwww.apinfo.co.nz) with extensive displays on wildlife, plants, geology and local history, and a video about the trail blazed by the stagecoaches and the railway is played on request ($1). The visitor centre also has a covered porch, open 24hrs, with a map of the village, weather information and search and rescue intentions cards. Other facilities are limited to a single **petrol pump** and meagre **groceries** at the *Arthur's Pass Store*.

There's a reasonable choice of good-value **accommodation** in the village, strung out along the main road, although places fill up quickly during the high season (Dec–March), when it's a good idea to book in advance. If there's no room at the inn, you could always try the *Historic Bealey Hotel*, 12km to the east, or the *Flock Hill Lodge*, 40km east, toward Christchurch. Only two establishments offer **meals**.

Accommodation

Alpine Motel SH73 ⓣ03/318 9233, ⓦwww.apam.co.nz. Basic but comfortable motel units with kitchens, satellite TV, DVD players and free Wi-Fi. There's also an outdoor spa pool. ❹

Arthur's Pass Store Motel SH73 ⓣ03/318 9235. Just two comfortable, modern studio units with kitchenette. ❺

DOC Campsite next to Arthur's Pass Public Shelter and backing onto the railway. Basic site with cold water and toilets. Camping $5 per person.

Klondyke Corner 8km east of the village. Free camping with long-drop toilet and river water, which should be treated.

Mountain House ⓣ03/318 9258, ⓦwww.trampers.co.nz. With dorms, double rooms and four two- and three-bedroom s/c houses high on the hill over the village (let by the room or whole house), this place offers by far the largest number and widest range of beds in the village. It is also an associate YHA and incorporates the first purpose-built YHA in the country, now being upgraded. Dorms $27, rooms ❸, cottage room ❸, whole cottage for up to six $200.

Sanctuary Bunkhouse SH73. Unstaffed dorm-style bunk accommodation with adequate shower and kitchen facilities. Great for recovering between tramps. No bookings; call the number on the door on arrival. $12

Eating and drinking

Arthur's Pass Store SH73. Serves breakfasts, pies, sandwiches and decent coffee, and has Internet access ($6 per hr) and a bottle store. Daily 8am–6pm, longer in summer.

Wobbly Kea SH73. Serves good coffee, gourmet pies, substantial and imaginative main meals ($19–28), pizzas ($24), and has a lively bar with occasional live music.

Arthur's Pass National Park

Despite the spectacular views you get from the pass itself, you really need to take one of the many day- (or longer) walks to get a feel for the remarkable alpine landscape of **Arthur's Pass National Park**, which spans the transition zone between the wet West Coast and the much drier east. Otira, just west of the pass, gets around 6m of rain a year while Bealey, 15km to the east, gets only 2m.

The 720 square kilometres surrounding the pass were designated the Arthur's Pass National Park in 1929, and have exerted a powerful attraction over walkers and mountaineers ever since. Explore a while and you'll see the rich crimson of the southern rata trees, the broad-leaved evergreen podocarp forest of the wetter regions and the tussock grasslands stretching east.

Although easily accessible, the park can still be a hazardous place and, apart from a few easy walks around Arthur's Pass Village, is a place for fairly experienced trampers: be prepared (see Basics, p.63), check the weather forecast and leave your intentions with DOC. The *Tramping in Arthur's Pass* leaflet assigns Route Guide numbers (RG) to the major tramps. You'll also need the 1:80,000 *Arthur's Pass National Park Parkmap*, or the 1:50,000 *Otira* topographic **map**, which covers most of the walks near the village. It is best to bring tramping supplies with you, though the *Arthur's Pass Store* has some groceries, and DOC sells gas canisters. The *Mountain House* operates a taxi-style Trampers Shuttle Service (☎027/419 2354) to the trailheads.

Tramps and walks

Avalanche Peak Track (5km return; 6–8hr; 1000m ascent). Strenuous day-hike that offers wonderful views of the surrounding mountains, though parts of the route are exposed and it should only be attempted in reasonable weather. The best way is going up the spectacular Avalanche Peak Track and then making a circuit of it by returning on the Scotts Track.

Bridal Veil Nature Walk (2.5km return; 1hr 30min; 50m ascent). Lovely walk that ascends a gentle gradient through mountain beeches then crosses the Bridal Veil Creek before returning along the road.

Casey Saddle to Binser Saddle (RG10: 40km; 2 days; 400m ascent). A fairly demanding tramp with great views as you cross easy saddles on well-defined tracks through open beech forest, staying overnight in Casey Hut (16 bunks; $10). It is a 30min walk back to your starting point.

Devil's Punch Bowl (2km return; 1hr; 100m ascent). The village's most popular short walk, following an all-weather climb and descent to the base of a 131-metre waterfall, crossing two footbridges and zigzagging up steps.

Mingha–Deception (RG6: 25km; 2 days; 400m ascent, 750m descent). A great overnighter which traces the route used for the mountain-run stage of the arduous Coast to Coast race (see p.742). Long sections are easy to follow, but there are unmarked areas requiring a little route finding, and some unbridged river crossings – so watch the water levels. If you're feeling particularly fit and travelling in the summer, add on a trip to Lake Mavis (500m ascent), a high mountain tarn with some lovely views. You can use either the Goat Pass Hut (20 bunks; $5) or the Upper Deception Hut (6 bunks; free) and ponder how mad you'd have to be to run the route competitively.

The South Canterbury foothills

The **South Canterbury foothills** mark the transition from the flat Canterbury Plains to the rugged and spectacular Southern Alps. It is a region frequently ignored by visitors hurrying out of Christchurch for the more obvious charms of Arthur's Pass in the west or Aoraki Mount Cook and Queenstown to the south, but warrants a little of your time. The area is primarily known for the winter resort town of **Methven**, which serves the ski slopes of **Mount Hutt**. Things are relatively quiet here in summer, but there's a wealth of natural attractions in the region, with the **Rakaia Gorge**, walks around **Mount Somers** and the pretty town of **Geraldine** rewarding travellers who make the effort to stop.

The main **route** through the area is SH72, dubbed the "Inland Scenic Route" – follow the brown signs. InterCity and Newmans **buses** running between Christchurch and Queenstown represent the main means of getting here by public transport, though services are limited to one or two per day.

Methven, Mount Hutt and around

A hundred kilometres west of Christchurch on SH77, **METHVEN** is Canterbury's winter-sports capital and the accommodation and refuelling centre for the **Mount Hutt** ski-field during the June to October **ski season**. In summer the town is quiet and uninspiring, but makes a good base for exploring the nearby Rakaia Gorge and Mount Somers and doing a handful of activities.

Scotsman Robert Patton bought land in the area in 1869 and named Methven after his home town. The place ticked by as a farming service town until the major development of the ski-field in the mid-1970s. About the only thing of sustaining interest from the early days is the **Anglican Church**, on the corner of Chapman and Alington streets, and even that is an interloper. Built in 1880 in the tiny settlement of Sherwood 75km south, the church was transported to Methven by two traction engines in 1884.

Practicalities

Buses stop on Main Street (SH77), outside the **i-SITE visitor centre**, 121 Main St (Oct–May Mon–Fri 9am–5pm, Sat & Sun 11am–4pm; June–Sept daily 7.30am–5.30pm; ⓣ03/302 8955, ⓦwww.amazingspace.co.nz), which has **Internet access** and books the Methven Travel shuttle to Christchurch ($35 one way). The town itself is easily explored on foot, and an array of companies offer minibus transport to the **ski-field**. The small shopping centre around the junction of Main Street and Forest Drive has banks, a post shop and several **ski shops** specializing in gear rental and repairs, the best of which are Big Al's (ⓣ03/302 8003) and Wombats (ⓣ03/302 8084).

In winter there's a huge range of **accommodation** in Methven, and most of it stays open for the summer season, when prices are often very reasonable. You can **eat** well enough, with some snug little cafés serving thick, steaming soups in winter and low-fat Italian salads and panini in summer, along with a smattering of pleasant if not overly lively bars, most open year-round.

Accommodation

Beluga 40 Allen St ⓣ03/302 8290, ⓦwww.beluga.co.nz. Luxurious and very welcoming en-suite B&B accommodation in a beautifully kept house that has retained its original charm and comes surrounded by tranquil gardens with an outdoor hot tub. There's also the popular, self-catering "garden suite", and a separate four-bedroom cottage (three-night minimum). Delicious breakfasts. Rooms ❻, garden suite ❼ cottage ❽

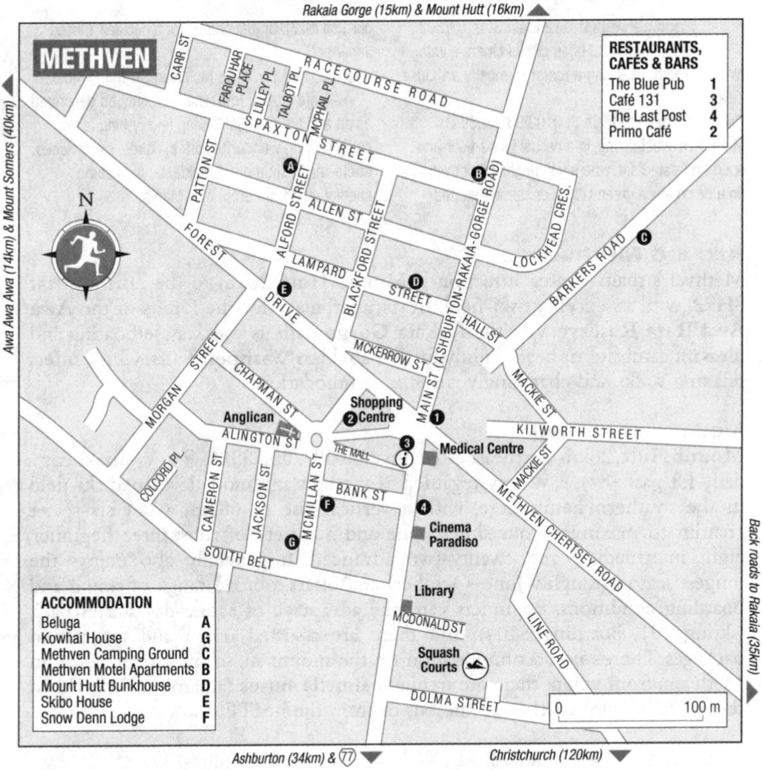

METHVEN

RESTAURANTS, CAFÉS & BARS

The Blue Pub	1
Café 131	3
The Last Post	4
Primo Café	2

ACCOMMODATION

Beluga	A
Kowhai House	G
Methven Camping Ground	C
Methven Motel Apartments	B
Mount Hutt Bunkhouse	D
Skibo House	E
Snow Denn Lodge	F

Kowhai House 17 McMillan St ⓣ03/302 8887, ⓦwww.kowhaihouse.co.nz. Comfortable, well set-up backpackers in a converted house, with fast Internet, free breakfast and an outdoor spa. Dorms $25, shares $27, rooms ❷, en suite ❸

Methven Camping Ground Barkers Rd ⓣ03/302 8005, ⓦwww.methvencampingground.co.nz. Simple site at the town showgrounds with powered sites, basic cabins and tourist cabins with TV, kettle and toaster. There's a separate games room and a well-equipped kitchen. Camping $12, basic cabins $17pp, tourist cabins ❷

Methven Motel Apartments 197 Main St ⓣ0800/468 488, ⓦwww.methvenmotels.co.nz. Sparkling new motel units, some of which are large, and have a big TV and spa bath. ❹

Mount Hutt Bunkhouse 8 Lampard St ⓣ03/302 8894, ⓔmthuttbunks@xtra.co.nz. Comfortable backpacker accommodation in the main house or a s/c house next door. Dorms $22, rooms ❷

Skibo House 82 Forest Drive ⓣ03/302 9493, ⓦwww.skibohouse.com. Wonderfully friendly B&B in a modern house. Most rooms have great mountain views, though they share a bathroom. There's an outdoor hot tub, and excellent breakfasts might include Bircher muesli and porridge. B&B ❹, s/c unit ❹

Snow Denn Lodge Corner of McMillan & Banks sts ⓣ03/302 8999, ⓦwww.yha.co.nz. Newish, purpose-built associate YHA hostel that's the best of the town's budget accommodation, with spacious lounges, well-equipped kitchens, free breakfast, free bikes, gear storage and an indoor hot tub ($5 per session). Dorms $27, rooms ❸, en suites ❸

Eating, drinking and entertainment

The Blue Pub *Methven Hotel*, corner of Kilworth St & Barkers Rd. This 1918 hotel popular with the après-ski crowd and locals has two sections, a casual restaurant and a lively bar. Hosts bands and weekend DJs.

Café 131 131 Main St. Spacious wood-floored café that's perfect for coffee, speciality teas and cakes (try the dreamy brandy cake with cream), but also serves a range of all-day breakfasts and tasty lunches ($5–16).

Cinema Paradiso 112 Main St ⓣ03/302 1957. Wonderful bijou digital cinema, with two tiny rooms showing a roster of mostly arthouse flicks.

The Last Post 116 Main St ⓣ03/302 8259. Methven's finest dining, in a casual wood-floor-and-open-fire restaurant, where you might expect yellow-fin tuna on Asian greens ($33) or salmon-stuffed chicken ($26). Or just drop in for a cocktail. Closed Jan–April.

Primo Caffe 38 McMillan St. Quirky little café stuffed into what can only be described as an antique-cum-junk shop (everything is for sale), serving wonderful coffee, cakes, sandwiches, home-made soup and breakfasts, plus some cheeky chat from proprietor Marya.

Around Methven

Methven's main winter attraction is **Mount Hutt**, 26km to the northeast off SH72, with its excellent ski-field. In summer, make for the forests of the **Awa Awa Rata Reserve**, visit the **Rakaia Gorge** with its walkway, jetboating and pleasant campsite, or head slightly further afield to **Washpen Falls**, which offers relaxing walks and charmingly rustic accommodation.

Mount Hutt ski-field

Mount Hutt, 26km northeast of Methven (ⓣ03/302 8811, ⓦwww.nzski.com; daily lift pass $84), is widely regarded as the best and most developed ski-field in the southern hemisphere, with a vertical rise of 683m, a fast six-seater chairlift to maximize your skiing time and a variety of runs: three beginner, eight intermediate and twenty-two advanced. It generally also enjoys the longest season (roughly June–October) and offers a broad range of skiing and boarding conditions. Beginners can take advantage of a one-day starter pack (skiing $91, boarding $104), and there are assorted rental and instruction packages. There's no accommodation on the mountain, so most people stay in Methven, from where there are frequent **shuttle buses** (all around $25; 1hr to the ski-field): buy a ticket on the bus or from the i-SITE.

Awa Awa Rata Reserve

Awa Awa Rata Reserve, 14km northwest of Methven, is a beautiful spot on the eastern flanks of the Southern Alps, home to tall mountain beech and snow tussock, which provides a home for a variety of native and introduced birds above the shrub line. It is all part of the Mount Hutt Conservation Area, covered by a DOC leaflet from the visitor centre that details several **walking tracks** (30min–2hr). Most are accessed from the McLennans Bush Road entrance, reached by heading north from Methven on SH77 and going straight ahead onto McLennans Bush Road at the base of Mount Hutt access road. It is worth taking a little extra time to examine the Mount Hutt flora during the spring and summer: of the **alpine plants** of New Zealand, 94 percent grow only in New Zealand, of which 130 species can only be found on Mount Hutt. One such is the unique vegetable sheep (*Raoulia eximia*), which forms huge grey mounds that look, from a distance, not unlike sheep lying down. There's also the *Ranunculus haastii*, a beautiful species of buttercup with blue-grey leaves and luminous yellow flowers, and ten species of mountain daisies, *Celmisias*, which form huge cushions of flowers.

Rakaia Gorge

Some 15km north of Methven, the Rakaia River emerges from the **Rakaia Gorge**, a steep-sided defile created by an ancient lava flow and now lined in many places with regenerating forest. **Maori history** tells how a *taniwha* (water spirit) lived nearby, hunting and eating moa and weka; his possessions, because of his status as a spirit, were *tapu*. One cold day he went to find a hot spring, and while he was away the northwest wind demon flattened his property. To prevent this happening again, the *taniwha* collected large boulders and stones from the mountains to block the course of the demon and so narrowed the Rakaia River, making it flow between the rocky walls. The spirit became so warm because of his exertions that the heat from his body melted the snow and ice on the mountains, and his perspiration fell on the rocks and formed crystals in the riverbed.

All this sweaty work can be seen from the **Rakaia Gorge Walkway** (15km; 3–4hr return), which starts where SH72 crosses the river. The path leads through several forest stands and spectacular geological areas, past hardened lava flows of rhyolite, pitchstone and andesite, to the upper gorge lookout. The less committed might fancy just walking as far as a fenced viewpoint high on a bluff above the river (1hr return).

Below the gorge, the river fans out into a classic example of the braided rivers so common on the eastern side of the South Island. Here you can board a **jetboat ride** with Rakaia Gorge Alpine Jet (Ⓣ03/318 6574, Ⓦwww.rivertours.co.nz), who run thrill trips and scenic tours (both 35min; $68), offer salmon fishing and hire rods. Perhaps the best bet is to let them take you to the top end of the **Rakaia Gorge** ($25, minimum two people) and then walk back. The gorge offers a delightful and easy walk – take a picnic and it's a great way to spend an afternoon.

On SH72, over on the south side of the river, the nicely sited *Rakaia Gorge* **campsite** ($6 per person) offers peaceful camping with coin-op hot showers (summer only) and toilets.

Washpen Falls

Just 17km south of SH73 and a 25min drive north of Methven is one of the more enjoyable **walks** in the area. The precious brainchild of landowner Tom McElrea and situated on his family farm, **Washpen Falls**, Washpen Road (Ⓣ03/318 6813, Ⓦwww.washpenfalls.co.nz, self-guided $10, guided $100 minimum of four, accommodation available in a romantic self-contained cottage ④), offers easy access to a stress-free, relatively easy-going meander through native bush and farmland. The basic walk (there are longer alternatives), heads up to a point, and offers spectacular views of the Canterbury Plains. Along the way are amazing rock formations, great examples of native-bush regeneration, incredible wooden stairs that seem to cling to the side of a cliff face – McElrea says they are perfectly safe and he should know, he built them – and of course the spectacular falls themselves.

Horse-riding and hot-air ballooning

One of the more unusual local activities is **horse trotting** with Horsepower Experience (daily by arrangement; $225 for 2hr 30min; Ⓣ03/302 4800), 20km north of Methven on Lauriston Barrhill Road, off SH77. This includes a tour and the opportunity to observe the usual preparations and participate in a race, riding tandem in one of the unstable-looking carts as it careers round the course behind a highly strung thoroughbred.

More traditional **horse-riding** is offered by High Country Horse Adventures (2hr for $90, half-day $140; Ⓣ0800/386 336, Ⓦwww.horsetrek.co.nz), who offer trips through spectacular mountain scenery. Pick the right day, and there's little to beat **hot-air ballooning** with Aoraki Balloon Safaris (Ⓣ0800/256 837, Ⓦwww.nzballooning.com), whose four-hour sunrise trip ($345) includes a champagne breakfast. The fine views of the patchwork quilt of the Canterbury Plains and the magnificent Southern Alps make this one of the best balloon flights on the South Island. They go any still clear morning, and winter is particularly good.

Mount Somers and around

The 1687-metre **Mount Somers** rises from the flatlands above the villages of **Mount Somers** and **Staveley**. It is not an especially striking sight, but is fully encircled by the **Mount Somers Track**, which is conveniently in the rain shadow of the mountains and is often above the bushline. When it is raining in Arthur's Pass and Mount Cook is clagged-in there's still a chance you'll be able to slip on your boots and get some hiking in here. The terrain is generally rugged, with patches of regenerating beech forest, and open tussock pocked by outcrops of rock. Large areas of low-fertility soil subject to heavy rainfall turn to bog, and as a result you'll find bog pine, snow totara, toatoa, mountain flax and maybe even the rare whio (blue duck).

Staveley

The northern access point for the walkway is tiny **Staveley**, 22km southwest of Methven, where the Staveley Village Store (daily 8am–6pm) stocks last-minute supplies (including espresso). Even if you have no intention of tackling a multi-day hike, at least drive the 2km to the northern trailhead at Sharplins car park and stroll to **Sharplins Falls** (1hr return).

There's lovely **accommodation** nearby at *Ross Cottage*, Flynns Road (④), a delightful 130-year-old self-catering cottage. It is operated by Tussock and Beech Ecotours (Ⓣ03/303 0880, Ⓦwww.nature.net.nz), who offer a self-guided **Mount Somers Track package** ($270) which includes two nights' dinner, bed and breakfast, DOC fees and self-guiding tips. They also run a range

▲ Woolshed Creek Hut, Mount Somers Track

of one- to three-day all-inclusive **eco-tours** ($290–$820), plus a two-night, one-day "Footsteps of Hobbits" trip ($405) visiting local *Lord of the Rings* sites.

Mount Somers

Access to the southern end of the walkway, near Woolshed Creek, is via the hamlet of **MOUNT SOMERS**, 8km south of Staveley. The Mount Somers Store sells hut tickets and a reasonable range of groceries, and the pleasant tree-filled *Mount Somers Holiday Park*, Hoods Road, 1km off SH72 (Ⓣ03/303 9719, Ⓦwww.mountsomers.co.nz; camping $11, cabins ❶, en suite ❷) offers **accommodation**. The only real **restaurant** is *Stronechrubie*, 1km south of Mount Somers on SH72 (dinner Wed–Sat, and Sun lunch; bookings essential Ⓣ03/303 9814, Ⓦwww.stronechrubie.co.nz), which serves high-country cuisine. Expect a choice of salmon, duck and rack of lamb (around $30) and an excellent wine selection. They also have rooms (❹) all with kitchens, wicker furniture and views of the mountain, and offer bed, breakfast and dinner packages ($220 for two).

Mount Somers Track

Moderately fit trampers should consider tackling the **Mount Somers Track** (25km loop; 2–3 days; 1000m ascent), a fairly strenuous subalpine loop round the mountain passing abandoned coal mines, volcanic formations and a deep river canyon. Roads meet the loop in the west at Woolshed Creek (accessed from Mount Somers) and in the east at Sharplins Falls car park (accessed from Staveley), so if you don't fancy the whole thing you can walk either half and organize a vehicle shuttle (see p.646).

If you are doing the whole loop, it is best done anticlockwise from the Staveley end.

Sharplins Falls Car Park to Pinnacles Hut (5km; 3hr 30min; 470m ascent). The route initially detours to the modest Sharplins Falls then climbs steadily through beech forest, reaching the tree line at Pinnacles Hut (14 bunks; $10), nestled below rock monoliths frequently used by climbers.

Pinnacles Hut to Woolshed Creek Hut (7km; 2hr 30min; 265m ascent). Climb towards the 1170-metre saddle, now through treeless tussock with wide views into the mountains and back to the plains. On the descent, take the 5min side trip to the Water Caves, where a stream courses below a rockfall of house-sized boulders. It is then only 10min to the new Woolshed Creek Hut (26 bunks; $10), a good place to stay a couple of nights, spending the intervening day exploring the little valleys and canyons hereabouts.

Woolshed Creek Hut to the Sharplins Falls car park (13.5km; 8hr; 400m ascent). The tramp follows the South Face Route around the mountain and feels quite different. There's a less isolated feel as you gaze across the Canterbury flatlands towards the distant coast. The terrain is a mix of high-country scrub (somewhat exposed at times) and beech forest. Soon after leaving the hut, the Howden Falls side track is worth a quick squiz. You then climb a ridge before traversing tussock-covered flats, passing a new day-shelter at about the halfway point. After a steep climb up through beech forest you begin the long descent, first on a ridge with great views then down into the bush to Sharplins Falls car park.

Track practicalities

Buy DOC **hut tickets** (two for each hut) before you start at the stores in Staveley or Mount Somers. You'll need to carry a cooking stove, pots and all your food, and may want to bring a map and compass. The rolling country on top of the hills is subject to disorientating fog, though marker poles point the way adequately in most conditions.

Those without a vehicle should base themselves in Methven, where Methven Travel operates a Mount Somers shuttle service on demand ($25 per person to Woolshed Creek car park, $15 to the Sharplins Falls car park; Ⓣ03/302 8106).

Searching for Edoras

Go searching for **Edoras** and you won't find it. Though the crew of the *Lord of the Rings: The Two Towers* spent the best part of a year erecting the set, everything was removed after filming. What you do get is Mount Sunday, a hundred-metre-high glacially levelled outcrop (**roche moutonée**) surrounded by open river flats a 48-kilometre drive west from the village of Mount Somers. Over half of the journey is on rough gravel but it is a beautiful drive, bounded by big, grassy, round-shouldered hills sheltering a flat valley, with the main icy backbone of the Southern Alps up ahead. Along the way you pass the exclusive Mount Potts Backcountry **ski area** (Ⓦwww.mtpotts.co.nz) and, opposite, Erewhon station, written about by English satirist Samuel Butler. *Erewhon* is initially set in the Canterbury high country but is increasingly devoted to a critique of mid-Victorian Britain.

Pick up the free and widely available *Journey to the Film Location of Edoras* leaflet and stop around 48km from Mount Somers. You should put an hour aside to wander across the fields (and cross a couple of streams) to get to Mount Sunday. Once you're standing on top surveying the grasslands all about, you can imagine the bleats of the sheep are the battle cries of ... well, maybe not.

Hassle-free Tours (Ⓣ0800/427 753, Ⓦwww.hasslefree.co.nz) run fun **day-trips** here ($175 from Methven; $199 from Christchurch) including a champagne picnic lunch in the hills.

Drivers not hiking the full circuit can organize a **vehicle shuttle** through the Staveley Village Store ($30; Ⓣ03/303 0859). After dropping you at the trailhead, they'll keep your vehicle safe and deliver it to the car park at your finishing spot in time for your emergence from the wilds.

Peel Forest and around

Peel Forest Park, 35km south of Mount Somers, encloses one of the last remaining patches of original native bush on the eastern side of the country, with alpine vegetation on the tops. The reserve is just outside the hamlet of **PEEL FOREST**, 12km west of SH72, where you'll find the **Peel Forest Store** (Ⓣ03/696 3567, Ⓦwww.peelforest.co.nz). This serves as a visitor centre, campsite booking office, post office, takeaway and bar, and stocks the DOC's *Peel Forest Park* leaflet outlining walking tracks ranging from thirty minutes to six hours.

Of these, the best are the **Acland Falls Walking Track** (1.5km; 1hr return), a steep climb followed by a short streamside walk to a 14m waterfall, and **Allan's Track** (4km; 2–3hr round-trip), a steady ascent past the head of Mills Stream and through podocarp forest, which can be extended by joining the **Deer Spur Track** (5km; 2hr return), a steep but well-defined route which climbs above the bushline to a mountain tarn at an altitude of about 900m. Take time to admire the huge, ancient totara trees, rata and ferns, and to watch the antics of the fantails and tomtits – these little birds often hover around, feeding on the insects disturbed by trampers and picnickers.

Entertaining **horse-riding** is offered by Peel Forest Horse Trekking ($55 for 1hr; Ⓣ0800/022 536, Ⓦwww.peelforesthorsetrekking.co.nz), either through forest or down to the river.

Pay fees at the Peel Forest Store if you want to stay at DOC's lovely, wooded Peel Forest Park **campsite** (camping $9, powered sites $11, cabins ❶), located almost 3km further on. There's also **accommodation** at the basic *Peel Forest Homestay*, 33 Rangitata Gorge Rd (Ⓣ03/696 3509, dorms $20, B&B ❸), adjacent to the Peel Forest Tracks

Rafting the Rangitata

Some of the best **whitewater rafting** in New Zealand is run by the very professional Rangitata Rafts (Ⓣ0800/251 251, Ⓦwww.rafts.co.nz), based 14km north of Peel Forest Store. They operate excellent trips on the Grade IV–V gorge section of the Rangitata River (Oct–May daily at 10.30am; $175), spending almost three hours on the river. Many people make it a day-trip from Christchurch, which adds two hours at either end and costs an extra $10.

After an early lunch, you kick off with an easy float where you learn to handle the raft and prepare for the challenging stuff ahead. Then it is a thrilling trip through the rapids of the high-sided Rangitata Gorge, with the option of walking round the two biggest rapids. There's also a nerve-testing optional ten-metre cliff jump before the final few rapids and a wrap-up shower and barbecue dinner. You can even **stay** at their backpacker-style *Lodge* (camping $8, bunks $20, rooms ❶) which has full cooking facilities.

Geraldine

The prosperous farming town of **GERALDINE**, 45km south of Mount Somers and 35km north of Timaru, is often full of bus passengers and other visitors browsing the smattering of craft shops, galleries and specialist food stores, though it also works as a base for the Rangitata **rafting trips** (see above).

In town, head straight for Giant Jersey, 10 Wilson St (Mon–Fri 9am–5pm, Sat & Sun 10am–4pm; free), where amongst the display of jumpers you'll find the *Guinness Book of Records*' **world's largest jersey** (weighing 5.5kg). More divertingly, there's also an array of heraldic mosaics and a 42-metre-long half-scale **tableau of the Bayeux Tapestry** (Ⓦwww.1066.co.nz), made entirely from tiny pieces of spring steel broken from knitting machines. The last eight metres are the artist's interpretation of how the missing final section of the original might have looked. Once you've finished staring yourself bug-eyed at the tapestries you can drive yourself batty by trying out a few of the owner's home-grown, cypher-like alphametics and magic-number cubes, after which you'll probably need some fresh air.

You might want to spend a few minutes in the tiny **Geraldine Historical Museum** (Mon–Sat 10am–noon & 1.30–3.30pm, Sun 1.30–3.30pm; donation), housed in a rather quaint blue and white stone building on Cox Street, or browse the old cars and tractors amassed in the **Geraldine Vintage Car and Machinery Museum**, 179 Talbot St, (mid-Sept–May daily 10am–4pm; June to mid-Sept Sat & Sun 10am–4pm; $7), 1km south of the i-SITE (see below).

To check out Geraldine's wealth of **artists, galleries and craft shops**, pick up the *Arts Trail* or the *Geraldine* leaflet (both free from the i-SITE). The most interesting **glasswork** is made at Denise Bélanger-Taylor Glassblower (Ⓣ03/693 9041), where this French-Canadian artist produces beautiful but extremely expensive bright plates, mosaics and jewellery. To get to the gallery head 5km along SH79 towards Fairlie, then 10km up Te Moana Road. Call ahead if you want to see Denise working and marvel at the home-made kiln; don't bother if you just want to browse the gallery.

Practicalities

Buses drop off at the junction of Talbot Street and SH79 (Cox) a few steps from Geraldine's **i-SITE visitor centre**, 32 Talbot St (Dec–March Mon–Fri 9am–5pm, Sat & Sun 10am–4pm; April–Nov Mon–Fri 9am–5pm, Sat & Sun 10am–2pm; Ⓣ03/693 1006, Ⓦwww.southisland.org.nz). There's a small concentration of **accommodation** in Geraldine, none of it too expensive, and it's rarely a problem getting a bed for the night. All the worthwhile **restaurants** and cafés are within a couple of hundred metres of each other along Talbot Street, where you'll also find gourmet cheese, pickle, fruit wine and chocolate stores selling excellent **picnic supplies**. If you decide to stay, be sure to catch a movie at the wonderful **Geraldine Cinema**, 84 Talbot St (typically open Thurs–Sun; $10; ⓣ03/693 8118), a casual sofas-and-beanbags affair where you can bring your own wine.

Accommodation

Geraldine Holiday Park Hislop St ⓣ03/693 8147, ⓦwww.geraldineholidaypark.co.nz. Well-tended, central site with bike rental, surrounded by sheltering trees. Camping $13, cabins ❶, s/c units ❸, motel units ❹

Geraldine Motels 97 Talbot St ⓣ0800/400 404, ⓦwww.geraldinemotels.co.nz. Comfortable, well-equipped motel units close to the town centre with a huge garden and play area backing on the river. Also has barbecue, an infrared sauna and a spa. Units ❸, new deluxe units ❹

Lilymay 29 Cox St ⓣ0800/545 9629, ⓔlilymay@xtra.co.nz. Hospitable B&B with shared bathrooms, a large garden and freshly baked cookies. ❸

Rawhiti Backpackers 27 Hewlings St ⓣ03/693 8252, ⓦwww.rawhitibackpackers.co.nz. With rooms decorated in different styles – French, Indian, Pacific, Kiwiana – this former maternity hospital has been transformed into a spacious and tasteful hostel. There are good communal areas, plenty of off-street parking and free bikes. There's a full kitchen, but excellent pizza dinners ($10), desserts ($5) and a range of breakfasts ($8–10) are served. Located almost 1km from the centre. Dorms $24, rooms ❷

The Springs 53 Kennedy St ⓣ03/693 7661 ⓔionajan@xtra.co.nz. The pick of the local accommodation is provided in this delightful converted outbuilding, separate and completely s/c but with friendly and helpful hosts who bake delicious fruit-muffin experiments and offer good local knowledge. It's located almost 2km south of the town centre in a pretty and quiet garden. ❹

Eating, drinking and entertainment

The Easy Way 76f Talbot St. Stylish café/bar with a wide range of imaginative food at moderate prices including tasty curries, good coffee and fine home-made cookies. It's the only real venue for live music.

Plums 44 Talbot St. Low-cost daytime café grub in a homely atmosphere – good for breakfasts and muffins.

Village Inn 41 Talbot St. Moderately priced restaurant with outdoor seating serving generous wholesome meals at decent rates. A sports-style bar is attached.

Verde Café Deli 45c Talbot St. Classy daytime café with a great selection of counter food, a tempting brunch menu and some outside seating.

Fairlie

Heading for the wilds of the Mackenzie Country, you first pass through the six-hundred-strong intersection town of **FAIRLIE**, 45km west of Geraldine. A statue of Mackenzie and his dog stands at the town's main intersection, but otherwise there's little reason to stop, except in winter when you might want to head for the small **Mount Dobson** ski-field (ⓣ03/685 8039, ⓦwww.dobson.co.nz), 26km towards Lake Tekapo. The mountain is known for its powder snow, long hours of sunshine, uncrowded fields and suitability for all levels of skiing and snowboarding, with five beginner runs, six intermediate and five advanced.

Aoraki Mount Cook and the Mackenzie Country

South of Fairlie SH8 shoots westward – bright-coloured lupin- and broom-flanked in the summer – through the sheep-grazed grasslands of the **Mackenzie Country** onto the Aoraki Mount Cook area, one of the most spectacular sections of the Southern Alps. The region is dominated by New Zealand's tallest mountain, the 3754-metre **Mount Cook**, increasingly known by its Maori name, **Aoraki**, meaning "cloud piercer". The two names are often run together as Aoraki Mount Cook.

Approaching from the north you cross the shallow **Burkes Pass** and burst out into the Mackenzie Country, an almost treeless region of rolling, dry tussock-lands divided into high-country sheep farms known as "stations" or "runs", often stocked with hardy Merino sheep that produce fine wool for premium suits and classy thermalwear.

Star billing goes to the glacier-fed **Lake Tekapo** and **Lake Pukaki**, opaque, pale-blue sheets backed by the glistening peaks of the Southern Alps. The main access to the mountainous terrain is provided by **Aoraki Mount Cook Village**, which grew at the base of the mountain to cater for nineteenth-century tourists brought by horse-drawn coaches. You can walk from Aoraki Mount Cook Village to the glaciers spilling out of the mountains, notably the 27km-long **Tasman Glacier**, fed by icefalls tumbling from the heavily glaciated surrounding peaks. The unexciting, modern town of **Twizel**, 70km to the south, makes a decent base for exploring the region and spying extremely rare **black stilts**, wading birds that are protected in a reserve nearby. From the gliding mecca of **Omarama** 30km south of Twizel, SH83 runs eastwards down the **Waitaki Gorge** to Oamaru, providing a quick link between the Aoraki Mount Cook area and the east coast.

Lake Tekapo and around

The small village of **LAKE TEKAPO**, 42km west of Fairlie, occupies the southern shore of **Lake Tekapo** and comprises little more than a roadside ribbon of cafés and expensive trinket shops surrounded by new housing developments. The name Tekapo derives from the Maori *taka* ("sleeping mat") and *po* ("night"), suggesting that this place has long been used as a stopover. Stay overnight to fully enjoy a sunset free of day-trippers and the wondrously clear night skies.

James McKenzie

A Kiwi folk hero, **James McKenzie** lends his name (well close enough anyway) to the **Mackenzie Country**, a 180km crescent of rolling dry grassland between Fairlie and Kurow (to the south on SH83). A Gaelic-speaking Scottish immigrant of uncertain background, McKenzie seems to have only spent a couple of years in New Zealand but his legend lives on. He was arrested in 1855 for stealing sheep on a grand scale, amassing over 1000 in all, most of them from the Rhodes brothers' Levels Run station near Timaru and grazing them in the basin of rich high-country pastureland which now bears his name. McKenzie escaped from prison three times during the first year of his five-year sentence and when holding him became too much trouble, he was given a free pardon, after which he quietly disappeared, some say to America, others say to Australia.

It is difficult to fathom exactly why McKenzie became such an important and popular figure in New Zealand lore. He was certainly a prodigious thief, somehow controlling his vast flock of rustled animals with the assistance of a single dog, Friday – a hound fondly remembered as the prototype for the many hard-working sheep dogs held in deep affection by South Islanders. McKenzie is also regarded as one of the great pioneers, opening up an area of hitherto undiscovered grazing land that contained some of the best sheep runs in the country. There is a poem in honour of the man and his dog in the visitor shelter at Lake Pukaki near the turn-off to Mount Cook.

How Aoraki Mount Cook came to be

Both the **sky father** (Raki) and the **earth mother** (Papa-tua-nuku) already had children by previous unions. After their marriage, some of the sky father's children came to inspect their father's new wife. Four brothers, Ao-raki, Raki-roa, Raki-rua and Raraki-roa, circled around her in a **canoe** called Te Waka-a-Aoraki, but once they left her shores disaster befell them. Running aground on a reef, the canoe was turned to stone. The four occupants climbed to the higher western side of the petrified canoe, where they too were transformed: **Aoraki** became Mount Cook, and his three younger brothers formed flanking peaks – Mount Dampier, Mount Teichelmann and Mount Tasman.

More prosaically, Mount Cook was named in honour of the English sea captain, by one Captain Stokes of HMS *Acheron* in 1851. Its summit was first reached in 1894 but, because of the peak's sacredness to Maori, climbers are asked not to step on the summit itself.

At an altitude of 710m, the area is reputed to have the clearest air in the southern hemisphere and on a good day views really do have sharp edges and vibrant colours, making this one of the best places from which to photograph the Southern Alps. The most striking thing about lakes Tekapo and Pukaki is their extraordinary colour: the light reflected from microscopic rock particles suspended in glacial meltwater lends the waters a vibrant turquoise hue. Fed by the **Godley** and **Cass** rivers, Lake Tekapo covers 83 square kilometres and spills into the **Tekapo River**, wending its way across the Mackenzie Basin.

The Village and Mount John

Everyone's first stop is the tiny lakeside **Church of the Good Shepherd**, Pioneer Drive (daily: Oct–May 9am–5pm; June–Sept 11am–3pm; donation appreciated), a little stone church built in 1935 as a memorial to the pioneers of the Mackenzie Country. Behind the rough-hewn Oamaru stone altar, a square window perfectly frames the lake and the surrounding hills and mountains. About 100m east of the church is the perky-looking **Collie Dog Monument**, erected in 1968 by the sheep farmers of the Mackenzie Country as a mark of their respect for the dogs that make it possible to graze this harsh terrain.

The air is astonishingly clear up here and the distance from towns keeps the light pollution to a minimum. This presents perfect conditions for observing the night skies and over the years the summit of **Mount John**, 9km northwest of Tekapo, has sprouted numerous telescope domes, mostly operated by the University of Canterbury, in conjunction with astronomical institutions around the world. You can drive to the summit, the site of *Astro Café* (see p.652), with its fabulous mountain views. This is the starting point for the hour-long **Observatory Tour** (daily 11am–3pm on request; $20; ⓣ03/680 6960, ⓦwww.earthandsky.co.nz), which tours the facilities as you learn about the scientific work conducted there. To look at the southern skies through a 16-inch telescope you'll need to join the two-hour **Stargazing Tour** (nightly: 8pm in winter, 10pm in summer; $68), which includes bus travel from Tekapo and an hour and a half on the cold mountain top taking turns to look at whatever's up: the Southern Cross, the Large Magellanic Cloud, nebulae, and perhaps the glorious Jewel Box.

The summit can also be reached on the **Mount John Lookout** walk (10km return; 3hr; 300m ascent), one of the best in the area. Start just past the motor camp on Lakeside Drive and climb through a larch forest full of birds to a loop track which circles the summit of Mount John. After soaking up views of the

Mackenzie Basin, Lake Tekapo and the Southern Alps, you can either return the way you came or continue on the longer loop path, eventually depositing you on the lakeshore at your starting point – well worth the extra hour it adds.

Activities

Determined sightseers short of time take a "Grand Traverse of Aoraki Mount Cook" **scenic flight** with Air Safaris, in the village on SH8 (50min; $280; ⓣ 0800/806 880, ⓦ www.airsafaris.co.nz). The flight swoops across the Main Divide to the West Coast, providing views of the Franz Josef and Fox glaciers, the Tasman and Muller glaciers and, of course, Aoraki Mount Cook. Tekapo Helicopters, a couple of doors along on SH8 (ⓣ 0800/359 835, ⓦ www.tekapohelicopters.co.nz), run trips from 25min to a 70min flight over Mount Cook ($190–500; minimum three people).

Staying closer to the ground, try guided **horse treks** through dramatic scenery with Mackenzie Alpine Trekking (Nov–April only; 1hr for $45, 3hr for $95; ⓣ 0800/628 269).

In winter, there's **ice skating** at Winter Park (ⓦ www.winterpark.co.nz), by the western lakeshore, while families flock to the **Roundhill** ski area (ⓣ 03/680 6977, ⓦ www.roundhill.co.nz) overlooking Lake Tekapo, 30km north of SH8. You'll find one long T-bar and a learner tow plus plenty of gentle slopes and undulating terrain incorporating two beginner and eight intermediate but no advanced runs. A lift pass costs $60 and there's the usual ski and board rental packages, plus tobogganing for $12 a day.

Practicalities

Intercity, Atomic & Southern Link **buses** running between Christchurch and Queenstown all stop outside the strip of businesses that constitute the town centre. The Kiwi Treasures souvenir shop also works as a small **visitor centre** (daily: Nov–March 8am–8pm; April–Oct 8am–6pm; ⓣ 03/680 6686) and post office, and supplies a free town map showing local walks. There is no **bank** or ATM. Most **accommodation** in this tourist-oriented village is on the expensive side, with the few budget options often oversubscribed, so it's a good idea to book ahead. On a fine day you can't do better than a picnic by the lake, but there are several decent cafés and **restaurants** – all within 200m along SH8.

Accommodation

The Chalet 14 Pioneer Drive ⓣ 0800/843 242, ⓦ www.thechalet.co.nz. A boutique motel with six individually decorated, s/c apartments, some overlooking the lake, well away from the highway. It's run by a friendly Swiss couple who also rent out holiday homes, do breakfasts and offer fully inclusive guided walks along the Cass River Valley ($250). ❻, family units ❼

Lake Tekapo Grandview B&B 32 Hamilton Drive ⓣ 03/680 6910, ⓦ www.laketekapograndview.co.nz. Four spacious and very comfortable en-suite rooms (three with great lake and mountain views and one with double spa bath) in a modern home, where you're served afternoon drinks and something from the cooked breakfast menu. ❽

Lake Tekapo Motels and Holiday Park 2 Lakeside Drive ⓣ 03/680 6825, ⓦ www.laketekapo-accommodation.co.nz. Situated at the southwestern end of Tekapo 1km from town, this large, well-equipped campsite overlooks the lake. Camping $15, cabins ❷, tourist cabins and motel ❸

Lakefront Lodge Backpackers Lakeside Drive ⓣ 0800/840 740. Pleasant, modern purpose-built hostel with lake views from the spacious lounge and some rooms. Also bike rental for $25 a day. Dorms $26, rooms ❷

Tailor-made-Tekapo Backpackers 9 Aorangi Crescent ⓣ 03/680 6700, ⓦ www.tailor-made-backpackers.co.nz. A 5min walk from the bus stop and shops, this hostel lacks a view but does have dorms and rooms with beds (no bunks) plus well-kept grounds with a vegetable garden. Dorm $25, rooms ❷, en suites ❸

YHA Lake Tekapo 3 Simpson Lane, just west of the village ⓣ 03/680 6857, ⓔ yha.laketekapo@yha.org.nz. Good hostel with a common room boasting a floor-to-ceiling lake view window. Book early in summer. Dorms $26, rooms ❸

Eating and drinking

Astro Café Mt John summit. They sell only cakes and stellar espresso, but the lake and mountain views from this café atop Mount John are stupendous.

Kohan SH8 ☎03/680 6688. Great view and great sashimi, without breaking the bank. The bento box will set you back $25.

Reflections ☎03/680 6234. Local salmon, lamb rump and peppered venison all get a run on the wide-ranging menu at this reliable restaurant with views. Mains $24–28.

Towards Lake Pukaki

From Tekapo, SH8 heads southwest towards **Lake Pukaki** some 47km away. The opaque, pale-blue waters of this 30km-long lake provide a perfect foreground for views north to Aoraki Mount Cook and its icy attendants. Linger a while, perhaps detouring along the paved Tekapo–Pukaki Canal road, which follows one of the canals of the Waitaki Hydro Scheme (see below).

The road then rejoins SH8 on the southern shores of Lake Pukaki. Skirting the shore of the lake brings you past an unsigned **free camping area**, known locally as *The Pines*. There are long-drop toilets, a water tap and fabulous lake and mountain views from spots along the waterfront. Around 1km further on there are similarly wonderful vistas from the **Lake Pukaki visitor centre** (daily: Nov–April 9am–6pm; May–Oct 10am–4.30pm; ☎03/435 3280), which stands beside a display showcasing the Waitaki Hydro Scheme (see box below).

Another kilometre on, SH80 branches north towards Aoraki Mount Cook Village, while SH8 continues 6km to Twizel (see p.659).

Aoraki Mount Cook Village

A good, fast road leads from the Lake Pukaki junction along the tussocklands of the western shore of Lake Pukaki to Aoraki Mount Cook Village, 55km distant. Twelve kilometres in you'll pass **Peters Lookout**, a popular viewing

The Waitaki Hydro Scheme

The **Waitaki Hydro Scheme** provides over a fifth of the nation's power from twelve power stations scattered along the Waitaki River and its headwaters around lakes Tekapo, Pukaki and Ohau. The scheme has its origins in the work of the engineer Peter Seton Hay, who in 1904 submitted a report to the New Zealand government indicating the extraordinary hydroelectric potential of the region. Construction began with the Waitaki power station in 1935 and continued through to 1985, when the commissioning of the Ohau C station completed one of the largest construction projects in New Zealand.

Throughout the region water is diverted along a confusing network of canals to fill a long sequence of storage lakes held back by impressive dams, particularly the 100m-high earth-built Benmore Dam.

National power demands continue to increase, and the government-owned Meridian Energy has tried to squeeze more power from the region with extra dams and channels. After much opposition from locals, boaters and environmentalists, projects have been cancelled and the country is fretting about how future energy needs will be met. The gas fields off the coast of Taranaki are running out, no one wants nuclear power and large hydro schemes are no longer popular. The government does little to encourage more energy-efficient living so energy managers are increasingly looking to new power stations exploiting New Zealand's abundant stocks of coal, though this seriously threatens the country's commitment to the Kyoto Protocol on greenhouse gases. For more on green issues, see box, p.912.

▲ Lake Pukaki, with Aoraki Mount Cook among the clouds

point on the lake side of the road, while at 33km the *Glentanner Park Centre* (see p.655) offers accommodation, meals and flights (see p.658).

On windy days, an atmospheric white dust rises from the plain at the base of the mountain as you approach the diffuse collection of buildings that make up **AORAKI MOUNT COOK VILLAGE**. It is a spectacular spot, at a height of 760m in an encircling horseshoe of mountains, and though the village is nothing special it blends in tolerably. It is dominated by **The Hermitage**, a swanky alpine-style hotel that owns almost everything in Aoraki Mount Cook and employs most of the summer population of 300. With a near-monopoly on services and an almost captive market, it should

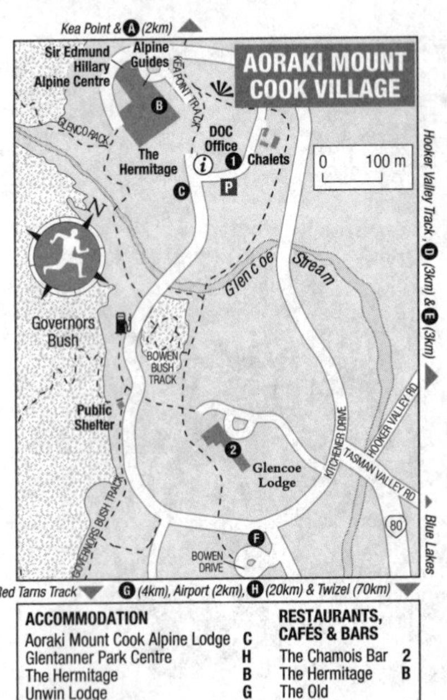

come as no surprise that prices are higher than elsewhere in the region. If you're watching the pennies, commute in from Twizel or Lake Tekapo, or stock up on groceries before you arrive and then camp or sleep in one of the self-catering lodges. If money is less of an issue, sit back and enjoy good food and comfortable lodgings in undeniably beautiful mountain surroundings.

Mostly you'll be wanting to get outside as much as possible, but it is worth spending some time in the brand-new **Sir Edmund Hillary Alpine Centre**, inside *The Hermitage* (daily 10am–5pm and later in summer), a suitable tribute to the man. It contains a **museum** ($12.50) showcasing the geology, mythology and development of the region, along with the history of the hotel and its place in Kiwi climbing history. There's also a state-of-the-art **3D theatre** ($25, including free museum entry) that whizzes you through the geographical, cultural and sporting evolution of the mountains hereabouts using a blend of authentic footage and computer graphics. With luck you'll see the real night sky while you're here, but it will mean much more after a visit to the **Planetarium** ($25, including free museum entry). Some of the profit from the centre goes to help fund Edmund Hillary's Himalayan Trust.

Practicalities

Most **bus** services on the Christchurch–Queenstown run stick to SH8, though one daily Newmans service comes direct to Aoraki Mount Cook Village. Alternatively, hop on The Cook Connection (ⓣ0800/266 526, ⓦwww.cookconnect.co.nz) which runs here from Twizel (2 daily; $35 return) and Tekapo (1 daily; $48 return). All buses call at *Glentanner Park Centre*, *Unwin Lodge* and the YHA on request, before dropping off at the car park near *The Hermitage*, from where everything is within walking distance.

The **DOC office and visitor centre** (daily: Dec–March 8.30am–6pm; April–Nov 8.30am–4.30pm; ⓣ03/435 1186, ⓔmtcookvc@doc.govt.nz) is the best place for information and advice on walks and activities. It stocks everything from leaflets to detailed maps, and has displays on the Aoraki Mount Cook area. Buy petrol before you get here, otherwise you'll have to cope with the single unstaffed **petrol pump** that requires a NZ credit card or EFTPOS card and PIN to use it, or phone the hotel desk and pay them $5 extra to do it for you. There is a **post office** in *The Hermitage* gift shop and **Internet access** at both *The Hermitage* coffee shop and *The Old Mountaineers*. Everyone accepts credit cards and EFTPOS since there is **no bank** or ATM.

Accommodation

Below we've listed all available accommodation. Book early from October to April – the village is quieter during the rest of the year and prices drop considerably, even at *The Hermitage*.

Aoraki Mount Cook Alpine Lodge Kitchener Drive ⓣ0800/680 680, ⓦwww.aorakialpinelodge.co.nz. Great accommodation at a realistic price, with comfy twins and doubles, a lounge with a fantastic view, a fully equipped kitchen and Internet access. ❺

Glentanner Park Centre 22km south on SH8 ⓣ03/435 1855, ⓦwww.glentanner.co.nz. Well-equipped site with camping, dorm-like accommodation (Oct–April only) and cabins with views of the mountains and the Tasman Valley. There's also a café. Camping $13, dorms $25, cabins ❸, s/c cabins ❹

The Hermitage ⓣ03/435 1809, ⓦwww.mount-cook.com. Large modernized complex of buildings approached through an impressive foyer. In the lounge you can sink into leather chairs with something from the bar and soak up the fabulous mountain views. Rooms in the main building vary in luxury ($610–900) and come with a balcony (though not necessarily a view) plus dinner and breakfast. The complex also includes s/c A-frame chalets offering B&B. ❽

Unwin Lodge near the airport turn-off, 4km from the village ⓣ03/435 1100, ⓔeureka@xtra.co.nz. An Alpine Club hut that gives priority to NZAC members and climbers but is open to all (handy if the YHA is full), offering basic bunkroom accommodation and the use of a massive common area with kitchen. Members $15, non-members $25.

White Horse Hill Campground Hooker Valley Rd. A serene and informal first-come-first-served DOC camping area with stony ground and running water in summer (which is not treated and should be boiled for 3min before use). The campsite is 2km north of *The Hermitage*, accessible by road or a 20min walk along the Kea Point Track. Camping $6.

Wyn Irwin Hut Hooker Valley Rd ⓣ03/357 4800, ⓦwww.cmc.net.nz. Basic hut with sixteen bunks, solar lighting, gas cooking and shower run by the Canterbury Mountaineering Club, who keep the place locked. You must book ahead and members get preference; $15.

YHA Mt Cook Corner of Bowen & Kitchener drives ⓣ03/435 1820, ⓔyha.mtcook@yha.co.nz. Excellent 74-bed hostel in a wooden building with modern, well-kept facilities. Free videos are shown in the evenings and there are free evening saunas, bargain pizzas, and a fairly well-stocked shop. It's nearly always full so book well in advance. Dorms $29, rooms ❸

Eating and drinking

Groceries don't come cheap here and the range is very limited, but *The Hermitage* has a small supply and the YHA a slightly wider selection: bring what you need from Twizel or further afield.

Sir Edmund Hillary

Until his death aged 88 in early 2008, surveys frequently voted **Sir Edmund Hillary** New Zealand's most admired citizen. His ascent, with Tenzing Norgay, of Mount Everest in 1953 was undoubtedly a noteworthy achievement, and his humanitarian work in the villages of Nepal was widely admired, but the root of the veneration lay more in his conduct. Hillary embodied the qualities Kiwis hold most dear: hard-working, straight-talking, honest and, most of all, modest. As he famously said on his return from the successful summit attempt, "Well George, we knocked the bastard off". That's what gets your face on every $5 note in the country.

Though he grew up near Auckland, Ed did much of his early climbing around Aoraki Mount Cook Village, where a **bronze statue** of a youthful Hillary stands outside *The Hermitage*. He returned less in later years, but was here in 2003 to officially open *The Old Mountaineers'* café and, but for failing health, would undoubtedly have returned to inaugurate the Sir Edmund Hillary Alpine Centre, which opened just a few days before his death.

The Chamois Bar *Glencoe Lodge*. Ordinary bar meals at modest prices and fairly cheap beer. Ideal if you just want to fill up after a day in the hills.

The Hermitage A wide range of cafés, restaurants and bars, mostly with great views and fairly high prices. There's the daytime *Coffee Shop* with a terrace; the buffet-style *Alpine Restaurant* serving all-you-can-eat breakfasts (continental $17; cooked $32), lunch ($26) and a buffet dinner ($53); and the swanky à la carte *Panorama Restaurant* (Ⓣ03/435 1809; mains $36–40), only open for dinner and with hotel guests having priority. The *Snowline Bar* has magic views and deep leather sofas.

The Old Mountaineers Ⓣ03/435 1890. Undoubtedly the best place to hang out, with a log fire, real mountain-lodge feel, comfy chairs with wonderful mountain views, a pool table, Internet access, café-style meals and great coffee, beer and wine. It is a little pricey, but it can't be beat.

Exploring the Aoraki Mount Cook National Park

The 700 square kilometres surrounding the peak and extending to the north and east form the **Aoraki Mount Cook National Park**, which was designated a **world heritage site** by UNESCO in 1986. With twenty-two peaks over 3000m, the park contains the lion's share of New Zealand's high mountains, mostly made of greywacke laid in an ocean trench 250–300 million years ago.

About 2 million years ago the Alpine Fault began to lift, progressively pushing the rock upwards and creating the Southern Alps. These days the process continues at about the same rate as erosion, ensuring that the mountains are at least holding their own, if not getting bigger. Aoraki Mount Cook is at the heart of a unique mountain area whose rock is easily shattered in the cold, leaving huge amounts of gravel in the valley floors. The tussock-cloaked foothills, where Mount Cook lilies, summer daisies and snow gentians thrive, contrast with the inhospitable ice fields of the upper slopes. The weather here is changeable, often with a pall of low-lying cloud liable to turn to rain, and the mountain air is lung-searingly fresh.

Almost everyone goes on a **walk** or two, but superb views are far more quickly attained on **scenic flights** over the glaciers and mountains. To get up close and personal with the ice take a **boat trip** or go **kayaking** on Tasman Lake, and in winter you can even **ski** down the glaciers.

Walking and guided trekking

Walks hereabouts cater to a wide range of abilities, with a variety of scenic trails from gentle day-hikes on the fringes of Aoraki Mount Cook Village to spectacular alpine treks. Walking as far as the Hooker and Tasman glaciers is well within the capability of the moderately fit.

Consult DOC for the latest information and get their *Walks in Aoraki/Mount Cook National Park* leaflet, listing ten excellent shorter walks (10min–5hr), all of which start in the village and can be extended by those with relevant experience. Don't walk on the surface of any of the glaciers unless you know what you're doing, or are in the company of someone qualified. Alpine Guides, inside *The Hermitage* (daily 8am–5pm; Ⓦwww.alpineguides.co.nz), offer experienced **climbing guides** and **rent equipment** such as walking poles ($5/day), boots ($15) crampons ($10) and axes ($10).

To experience high-altitude hiking (and spectacular views), go **guided trekking** with Alpine Recreation (Ⓣ0800/006 096, Ⓦwww.alpinerecreation.com) who run the Ball Pass Trek ($725), a three-day alpine crossing close to Aoraki Mount Cook and reaching 2130m at Ball Pass. Crampons may be required, but it is essentially just a very strenuous walk, staying in comfortable huts.

Tramps and walks

Blue Lakes and Tasman Glacier View (1km return; 40min; 100m ascent). A fairly gentle walk with good views of the lower sections of the Tasman Glacier, which is 600m deep at its thickest point, 3km across at its widest and moves at a rate of 20cm a day. One Harry Wigley landed an Auster aircraft on the glacier in 1955, paving the way for air access for mountaineers. The walk starts at the Blue Lakes car park, 8km drive up the Tasman Valley Road.

Governors Bush Walk (1hr return; 2km). Easy walk through a stand of silver beech with good views and abundant birdlife. Sheltered in poor weather.

Hooker Valley Track (9km return; 4hr; 200m ascent). Popular and superb hike which crosses a couple of swingbridges, passes pretty Mueller Lake, skirts the Alpine Memorial with views of the western side of Aoraki Mount Cook and ends at Hooker Lake. Starting at the *White Horse Hill* campsite saves 45min.

Kea Point Walk (2hr return; 7km; negligible ascent). Rewarding hike to a lookout over Mueller Lake with the hanging glaciers and icefalls of Mount Sefton above. Starting at the *White Horse Hill* campsite saves 45min.

Mueller Hut Route (10km return; 6–8hr; 1000m ascent). You'll need to be fairly fit for the slog up to the modern Mueller Hut. The route leaves the Kea Point Track just before its arrival at the glacier and climbs steeply westwards up the Sealy Tarns Track. From the tarns the route to the hut is marked by orange triangles which guide you up the final assault on loose gravel to a skyline ridge and the Mueller Hut (28 bunks; $35 summer, $30 winter; camping outside $15). At 1800 metres the views are quite startling and you are engulfed by almost perfect silence, interrupted

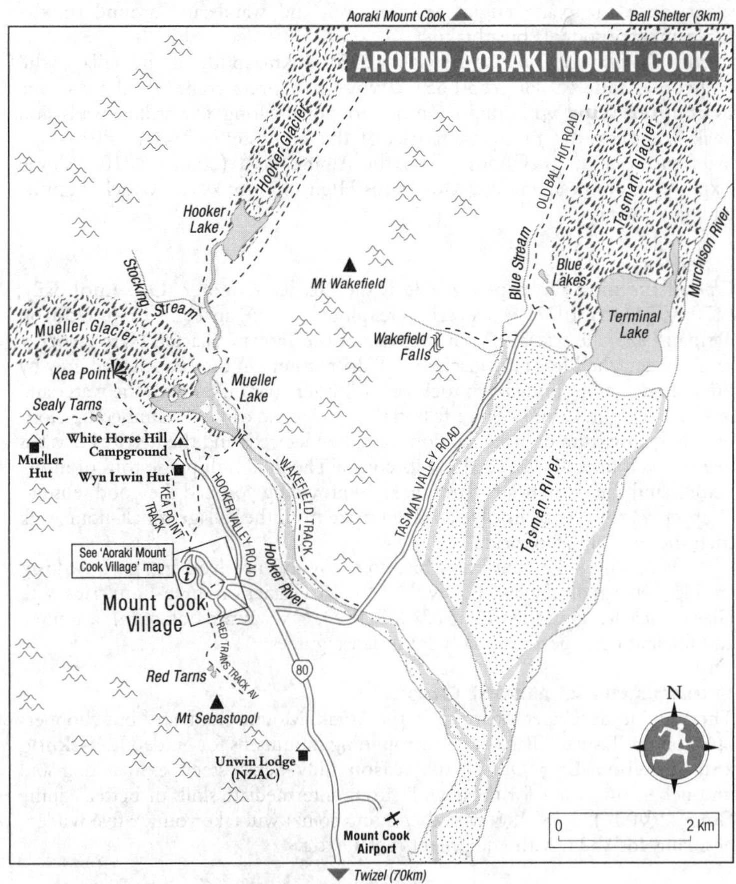

only by the murmur of running water and squawking kea. Crampons and ice axe will often be needed April to mid-Dec.

Red Tarns Track (4km return; 2hr; 300m ascent). This excellent and very achievable walk has one short, steep section but rewards with two tarns named after the red pondweed that grows in them. Uninterrupted views of Aoraki, the Village and along the Tasman Valley make it well worth the sweat.

Scenic flights

Scenic flights can provide you with glimpses of areas you could never dream of reaching on foot. Flying is extremely popular, so book a few days ahead and be prepared to be flexible as flights are cancelled in high winds or if visibility is poor. The peak season is from November to March, but in winter (June & July) the weather's often clearer, with better visibility.

Mount Cook Ski Planes (Ⓣ0800/800 702, Ⓦwww.mtcookskiplanes.com) have operated truly memorable fixed-wing flights from the Mount Cook Airfield for the last fifty years, and helped develop the technology for snow landings. They offer flights from as little as $230 (for 25min), ranging up to the mammoth Grand Circle (55min; $450), which loops around Aoraki, briefly crossing the Main Divide, hugging the immense valley walls and then landing on the Tasman Glacier, in a heart-stoppingly short distance. The glaciers are silent, once the plane engine splutters off, and wandering around on the footprint-free snow is breathtaking.

From *Glentanner Park Centre* (see p.655), 20km south of the village, the Helicopter Line (Ⓣ0800/650 651, Ⓦwww.helicopter.co.nz) fly three scenic **helicopter trips** with opportunities to hover along the valley walls and peaks, or view the tumbling blocks of the Hochstetter Icefall; all include brief snow landings. Choose from the Alpine Vista (20min; $210), Alpine Explorer (30min; $295) and Mountains High (45min; $415), which circumnavigates Aoraki.

Boating

One of the most fun trips available is the Glacier Explorer (Oct–April daily; $120; Ⓣ03/435 1077, Ⓦwww.glacierexplorers.co.nz), an eerie **boat ride** on Tasman Lake, the glacial lake at the base of the Tasman Glacier. Here icebergs, recently detached from the glacier itself, drift around in the lake, turned grey by the presence of ground-down rock, or rock flour, that mixes with the water and reflects the light. Chunks of ice fall off the glacier and can be examined up close, revealing a mixture of beautiful honeycombed ice cells and the detritus that has been picked up and carried along its course. The guides dispense tons of information and the three hours pass quickly – providing you had the good sense to wrap up warmly. Trips involve a fifteen drive from the Village, a half-hour walk then the one-hour boat ride.

For as much excitement but a bit more physical involvement, go **kayaking** among icebergs on the lake below the Mueller Glacier on three-hour trips with Glacier Sea Kayaking ($100; Ⓣ03/435 1890, Ⓦwww.mtcook.com), a unique and fascinating experience with enthusiastic guides.

Skiing Aoraki Mount Cook

There are no developed ski-fields in the Aoraki Mount Cook area but choppers open up the Tasman Glacier and surrounding mountains for guided **heli-skiing and snowboarding**. During the **season** (July–Sept), steep, exhilarating and untouched runs cater for those with strong intermediate skills or better. Alpine Guides (Ⓣ03/435 1834, Ⓦwww.heliskiing.co.nz) will take you for five wilderness runs for $825, with equipment rental extra.

▲ A (3km), Lake Pukaki (9km) & Mount Cook (70km)

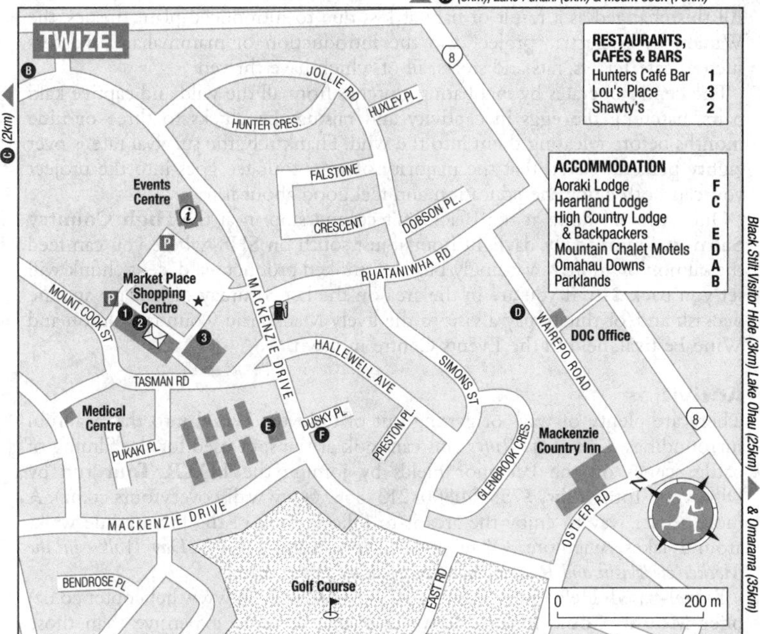

Twizel and around

Nine kilometres south of the junction of SH8 and SH80, you'll come upon the modest town of **TWIZEL** (rhymes with bridle), a leafy island surrounded by seas of pasture and backed by alpine scenery. It began life in 1966 as a construction village for people working on the Waitaki Hydro Scheme (see box, p.652). Twizel was due to be bulldozed flat after the project was finished in 1985 (some think this would have been a kinder fate) but enough residents wanted to stay that their wishes were granted. Long ridiculed as dull and featureless, this town of 1400 is now becoming a cheapish and more varied base for forays to the Mount Cook National Park (a 45min drive away), scenic Lake Ohau and the gliding operation at Omarama.

The town and the Black Stilt Visitor Hide

Twizel erupts into a frenzy in summertime, when tourists flock to visit Mount Cook and attend the various boat races on the surrounding lakes, before lapsing back into its moribund existence as an administrative centre.

The main sight is the **Kaki/Black Stilt Visitor Hide**, 3km south of Twizel on SH8. Access is solely on guided tours (Nov–March daily 9.30am & 4.30pm; 1hr; $12.50; book in advance ⓣ03/435 3124, ⓔinfo@twizel.com), which include the opportunity to sit in the hide, where you can watch the birds in their wetland habitat without disturbing them; binoculars are provided.

The colony is an attempt to preserve the world's rarest wading bird from extinction – an urgent task as only a hundred adults are left in the wild and 20 more in captivity. The long-red-legged kaki once thrived on the banks of braided rivers, feeding mainly on mayfly and exhibiting the endearing post-coital behaviour of walking cross-billed as if indulging in upright pillow talk.

All this changed as a result of habitat loss due to introduced plant species, the Waitaki hydroelectric project and the introduction of mammalian predators such as cats, ferrets, rats and stoats, all of which have thrived.

The centre operates by incubating clutches from all the wild and captive kaki pairs, hatching the eggs in captivity and raising the chicks to three or nine months before releasing them into the wild. Thankfully, the survival rate is over eighty percent. Given that the majority of your tour fee goes into the project you can both enjoy the education and feel good about it.

Once you are done at the Black Stilt colony, stop in at the **High Country Salmon Farm** (daily, daylight hours), just south on SH8, where you can feed the salmon or, more rewardingly, buy the smoked product – a decent chunk will set you back $15. If you are in the area on the last Saturday of January and are peckish and/or thirsty, pay a visit to the lively Mackenzie Country Salmon and Wine Festival, held in the Events Centre in town.

Activities

There are plenty of ways of getting out of unlovely Twizel into the beautiful surroundings. *Lord of the Rings* fans can look at the spot used for the filming of battle scenes on the Pelennor Fields by joining the **LOTR Tour** run by Discovery Tours (2hr; $75; ⓣ0800/213 868, ⓦwww.discoverytours.co.nz). A more sedate way to enjoy the area is to follow some of the picturesque walks around lakes Aviemore, Ohau and Tekapo, using DOC's *Day Walks in the Mackenzie Basin and Ruataniwha Conservation Park* leaflets.

Twizel-based Helicopters Line (ⓣ0800/650 652, ⓦwww.helicopter.co.nz) offer **Mount Cook flights** ($210–525): they're more expensive than those from Aoraki Mount Cook Village, but you get more time in the air.

Practicalities

The most convenient **bus** links are with Atomic and InterCity on their Queenstown–Christchurch runs. Both call in Twizel, from where The Cook Connection (ⓣ0800/266 526, ⓦwww.cookconnect.co.nz) runs to Mount Cook (2 daily; $35 return). Buses stop beside the **visitor centre** in the Events Centre, Mackenzie Drive (Nov–March daily 9am–6pm; April–Oct Tues–Sat 10am–4pm; ⓣ03/435 3124, ⓦwww.twizel.com), which has local info, stocks DOC leaflets and has fast Internet access. Across the road, Market Place Shopping Centre provides the town's focal point and contains a small supermarket, restaurants, a post shop and a **bank.**

Almost everything of interest is within walking distance from the Market Place; for exploring further afield, *Mackenzie Country Inn*, Warepo Road, offers **bike rental** ($10 a day).

Twizel's **accommodation** is reasonable value, but its proximity to Aoraki Mount Cook (45min drive) means it pays to **book ahead** from Christmas to the end of February. The selection of **eating places** is very limited.

Accommodation

Aoraki Lodge 32 Mackenzie Drive ⓣ03/435 0300, ⓦwww.aorakilodge.co.nz. Tasteful and welcoming B&B in the centre of town with four en-suite rooms, all with separate access. There's a large comfortable lounge, an attractive garden and cooked breakfasts. ❺

Heartland Lodge 19 North West Arch ⓣ0800/164 666, ⓦwww.heartland-lodge.co.nz. Spacious B&B, a couple of kilometres west of town, with mountain views, rooms with huge beds and underfloor heating and a separate s/c loft sleeping up to six. Loft ❹, B&B ❼

High Country Lodge & Backpackers 23 Mackenzie Drive ⓣ03/435 0671, ⓦwww.highcountrylodge.co.nz. This former hydro-electric workers' camp has retained some of its institutional character, with barrack-like bunkrooms: the hotel and motel rooms are a better bet. There's a communal kitchen on site. Dorms $25, budget rooms ❷, motel ❹

Mountain Chalet Motels Wairepo Rd ⓣ0800/629 999, ⓦwww.mountainchalets.co.nz. Twenty-five light-filled, s/c A-frame chalets along with an adjacent lodge section offering simple, comfortable backpacker accommodation in dorms. Good value. Dorms $25 ($20 with own linen), rooms ❷, chalets ❹

Omahau Downs SH8, 2km north of Twizel ⓣ03/435 0199, ⓦwww.omahau.co.nz. This wonderful hostel and B&B, in a rural setting just outside Twizel, has great views of Aoraki Mount Cook. Backpacker accommodation is in a farmhouse and there's a purpose-built s/c B&B lodge and separate cabin. All share access to an outdoor wood-fired bath ($10). Closed June–Aug. Dorms $22, rooms ❷, cabin ❹, B&B ❹

Parklands 122 Mackenzie Drive ⓣ03/435 0507, ⓔparklands1@xtra.co.nz. Large campsite with tent and powered sites plus some motel units and en-suite rooms which use a separate kitchen from campers. Camping $20 per site, room ❷, en-suite units ❸

Eating and drinking

Hunters Café Bar 2 Market Place ⓣ03/435 0303. Generous lunches (around $16) and dinners such as beer-battered fish and locally farmed salmon ($20–26). Occasional live music.

Lou's Place 25 Market Place. Low-cost basic dining on toasted sandwiches, nachos and the like.

Shawty's 4 Market Place ⓣ03/435 3155. The pick of the licensed cafés, doing good coffee, tasty breakfast and lunches and a fine line in gourmet pizzas, all served in the casual interior or outside. Wi-Fi hotspot.

Lake Ohau

A narrow road runs 25km west of Twizel to **Lake Ohau**, noted for its beech forest, river and **ski-field** (see below). It is a pretty area, and great if you have time to explore, but hardly competes with the lure of Aoraki Mount Cook. Renowned for the purity of its water, the lake surrounds boast some distinctive natural features, such as kettle lakes (small depressions left when blocks of glacial ice melt) and the terracing on its banks that reflects the light of summer sunsets. It is a popular fishing spot.

The **Ohau Forests** lie northwest from the lake, their stands of mountain beech and subalpine scrub crisscrossed by numerous tracks; DOC's *Ruataniwha Conservation Area* leaflet (from the Twizel visitor centre), details various walks (30min–4hr). The narrow, forested mountain ranges separate wide valleys cut by surging rivers, with short tussock grasslands predominating around the lakes and lowlands.

The community near the lake is made up almost entirely of holiday homes and has no amenities except for camping and the *Lake Ohau Lodge* (ⓣ03/438 9885, ⓦwww.ohau.co.nz/index.cfm/lodge; rooms ❸, deluxe ❺), which also offers breakfast ($12.50–18) and dinner ($37) from a set menu and access to a well-stocked bar.

Ohau snow fields

About 42km southwest of Twizel off SH8, **Ohau Snow Fields** (generally open July–Oct; ⓣ03/438 9885, ⓦwww.ohau.co.nz) is a small high-country ski-field with reliable powder snow and uncrowded slopes. The field has the longest T-bar in New Zealand and is especially good for intermediate skiers and boarders, with five beginner, eight intermediate and four advanced runs. **Equipment rental** is available at the field and lift passes cost $62 per day, with access provided by **bus** from the *Lake Ohau Lodge* ($17 return); otherwise, transport can be arranged by phoning the ski-field information number.

South from Twizel

South of Twizel, SH8 runs past the Kaki Visitor Hide (see p.659), the High Country Salmon Farm and a couple of water channels for the Waitaki Hydro

Scheme, then traverses tussock and sheep country to the junction settlement of **Omarama** – New Zealand's gliding capital – 30km on. The only other thing of interest is the **Clay Cliffs Scenic Reserve**, 5km north of Omarama.

Travelling south from Omarama towards Wanaka, Cromwell and Queenstown (see Chapter 13), SH8 crosses the **Lindis Pass**, a rewarding scenic drive through predominantly tussock and grassland, though in bad weather it can feel distinctly foreboding. Eastbound, you follow SH83 past the reservoirs of the Waitaki Valley (see p.663).

Clay Cliffs Scenic Reserve

Some 25km south of Twizel and 5km north of Omarama, a rough, signposted side road runs 10km west to **Clay Cliffs Scenic Reserve** ($5 per vehicle in the honesty box), which can be inaccessible after very wet weather. The braided Ahuriri River provides a picturesque backdrop to these eerie badlands, whose bare pinnacles and angular ridges are separated by narrow ravines and canyons. They were created when a 100-metre uplift caused by the Ostler Fault exposed gravels that responded individually to the weathering process.

The Maori name for the clay cliffs is Paritea, meaning white or light-coloured cliff, and they were so named by Araiteuru, who brought *kumara* (sweet potatoes) from Hawaiki. The cliffs provided natural shelter for moa hunters, with several surviving earth ovens indicative of early Maori settlement.

Omarama

Buses travelling through the Mackenzie Country all stop briefly at **Omarama** (Maori for "place of light"), little more than a road junction with a couple of petrol stations, a few cafés and some places to stay.

Prevailing westerly winds rise over the Southern Alps and create a unique air-wave across the flatlands of the Mackenzie Country, providing ideal **gliding** conditions. Omarama airfield was the one-time playground of Dick Georgeson, pioneer of New Zealand aviation and the South Island's first glider pilot, back in 1950. In the 1960s he held all manner of world gliding records, reaching a height of almost 11,000m in 1960. Southern Soaring (ⓣ0800/762 746, ⓦwww.soaring.co.nz) take advantage of the conditions to offer spectacular flights in two-seater gliders, with a chance to take the controls of amazingly responsive technological masterpieces (30min $285; 1hr $395; 90min – including a trip to Mount Cook – $595).

The land and rivers around Omarama are prime territory for hunting chamois and red deer and fly fishing for trout and salmon. The fish and the venison are delicious, but no one seems to know what to do with the chamois – except hang their heads on walls. Bookings for **fly fishing** can be made through the Sierra Motel and Tackle Shop, just north of the center on SH8 (ⓣ03/438 9785), who can sell you a fishing licence ($19 for 24hr) and put you in touch with fishing guides ($350 a half-day, $600 a day for two people).

The most relaxing **place to stay** is *Buscot Station*, 8km north of Omarama on SH8 (they'll arrange pick-ups if you book ahead; ⓣ03/438 9646, ⓔbuscotstn@xtra.co.nz; dorms $21, rooms ❷), a merino sheep farm where backpacker accommodation is provided in the old shearers' quarters, surrounded by a beautifully kept garden. Otherwise, there's the sheltered *Omarama Top 10 Holiday Park*, junction of SH8 and SH83 (ⓣ0800/662 726, ⓦwww.omaramatop10.co.nz; camping $15, cabins ❷, s/c units ❸), and the *Ahuriri Motel*, 700m east on SH83 (ⓣ0800/435 945. ⓦwww.ahuririmotels.co.nz; ❹), where backpackers get a basic room for their small group at $25 per bed.

There's good **eating** at *The Wrinkly Rams*, SH8, which does café fare and high-class pub meals. Alternatively, try *Clay Cliffs Estate*, 500m south on SH8 (Ⓣ03/438 9654, Ⓦwww.claycliffs.co.nz), a Tuscan-style **café/bar** (Tues–Sun 11am–late) offering lovingly cooked dishes (mains $25–32) in the grounds of New Zealand's highest **vineyard** (tasting $5).

The Waitaki Valley

The route from Omarama **east to Oamaru** follows SH83, passing through a string of small settlements evenly spaced along the **Waitaki Valley**, a region irrevocably changed by a mammoth hydroelectric scheme and the lakes it created (see box, p.652).

At **OTEMATATA**, 26km from Omarama, a side road runs 6km to the huge earth-built **Benmore Dam**, which you can walk or drive to the top of, or take a short loop track with distant views of Mount Cook. **Tours** of the power station (1hr; Oct–April daily 11am, 1pm & 3pm, May–Sept Sat & Sun only; $5; Ⓣ03/438 9212) leave from a small **visitor centre** (daily 10.30am–4.30pm) near the base of the dam, visiting the control room, generators and lots of gushing water. You can stay in town at the *Otematata Lakes Hotel* (Ⓣ03/438 7899, Ⓦwww.otematatalakeshotel.co.nz; ③), which has a dining room and bar and overlooks Lake Aviemore. Twenty kilometres further down SH83, by the Waitaki Dam lookout, *Café Hydro* is an excellent stopover for snacks, main meals, coffee or a glass of wine.

KUROW, 6km further along SH83, is regarded as a fisherman's paradise. Twin wooden bridges (dating from 1880) span the salmon- and trout-filled Waitaki River. There are a few limestone buildings of minor grandeur in the settlement itself, alongside the **Kurow Heritage Centre**, 57 Bledisloe St (Mon–Fri 9am–5pm), a museum/gallery of passing interest.

Another 19km on, at the side of the road, you'll see the rather unclear and shabby remains of some Maori **rock paintings** (see box, p.613) sheltered beneath a bird-infested rock overhang right beside the road and sadly the subject of some unwanted graffiti attention. Many of the best have been removed to museums for safekeeping and those that remain aren't that impressive to the untrained eye. **DUNTROON**, 4km on, is full of Gothic Revival architecture, and boasts the **Vanished World Centre**, 7 Campbell St (Nov–June daily 10am–4pm; July–Oct Sat & Sun 11am–3pm; Ⓣ03/431 2024, Ⓦwww.vanishedworld.co.nz; $5). Its primary exhibit tells the story of the fossilized whale skeleton discovered near Dansey's Pass, and provides the visitors with a chance to go and see it in the hills. The road continues over the hills towards **Naseby** in the Central Otago gold country.

Just off the highway, after about 1.5km, a winding narrow road climbs for 4km to the weird limestone formations of **Elephant Rocks**, popular with rock climbers of modest ability. The unmissable stand-alone rocks look like a small herd of elephants making their way through a grassy bowl.

Pressing on from Duntroon, the junction with the main east-coast highway (SH1) is just 35km away, and Oamaru is a further 8km south.

Travel details

The only **train** through the region is the TranzAlpine (see p.585) from Christchurch to Greymouth, stopping at Arthur's Pass. **Bus** routes centre on Christchurch going: north to Hanmer Springs, then over the Lewis Pass to

Nelson; and southwest towards Wanaka and Queenstown, passing Tekapo and Twizel. InterCity buses also visit Methven, and Newmans make a single daily run up to Aoraki Mount Cook. The Cook Connection links Aoraki Mount Cook with Twizel several times a day and also connects with Tekapo and Oamaru.

Trains

Arthur's Pass to: Christchurch (1 daily; 2hr 10min); Greymouth (1 daily; 2hr).

Buses

Aoraki Mount Cook to: Christchurch (1 daily; 5hr 30min); Oamaru (4 weekly; 3hr); Queenstown (1 daily; 4hr); Tekapo (1–2 daily; 1hr 30min); Twizel (4–5 daily; 1hr).
Arthur's Pass to: Christchurch (3 daily; 2hr 30min); Greymouth (3 daily; 1hr 30min); Hokitika (1 daily; 1hr 45min).
Christchurch to: Aoraki Mount Cook (1 daily; 5hr 30min); Arthur's Pass (3 daily; 2hr 30min); Fairlie (5 daily; 2hr 30min); Geraldine (5 daily; 2hr); Hanmer Springs (4 daily; 2hr); Maruia Springs (1 daily; 3hr 15min); Methven (2–4 daily; 1hr 10min); Tekapo (5 daily; 3–4hr); Twizel (5 daily; 4–5hr).
Fairlie to: Christchurch (5 daily; 2hr 30min); Tekapo (5 daily; 40min).
Geraldine to: Christchurch (5 daily; 2hr); Fairlie (5 daily; 30min); Methven (2 daily; 30min).
Hanmer Springs to: Christchurch (4 daily; 2hr); Kaikoura (3 weekly; 2hr).
Methven to: Christchurch (2–4 daily; 1hr 10min); Geraldine (2 daily; 30min).
Omarama to: Oamaru (4 weekly; 1hr 45min); Queenstown (5 daily; 2hr 15min); Twizel (5–6 daily; 30min).
Tekapo to: Aoraki Mount Cook (1–2 daily; 1hr 30min); Christchurch (5 daily; 3–4hr); Fairlie (5 daily; 40min); Oamaru (4 weekly; 2hr); Twizel (5 daily; 30min).
Twizel to: Aoraki Mount Cook (4–5 daily; 1hr); Christchurch (5 daily; 4–5hr); Oamaru (4 weekly; 3hr); Omarama (5–6 daily; 30min).

11

Dunedin to Stewart Island

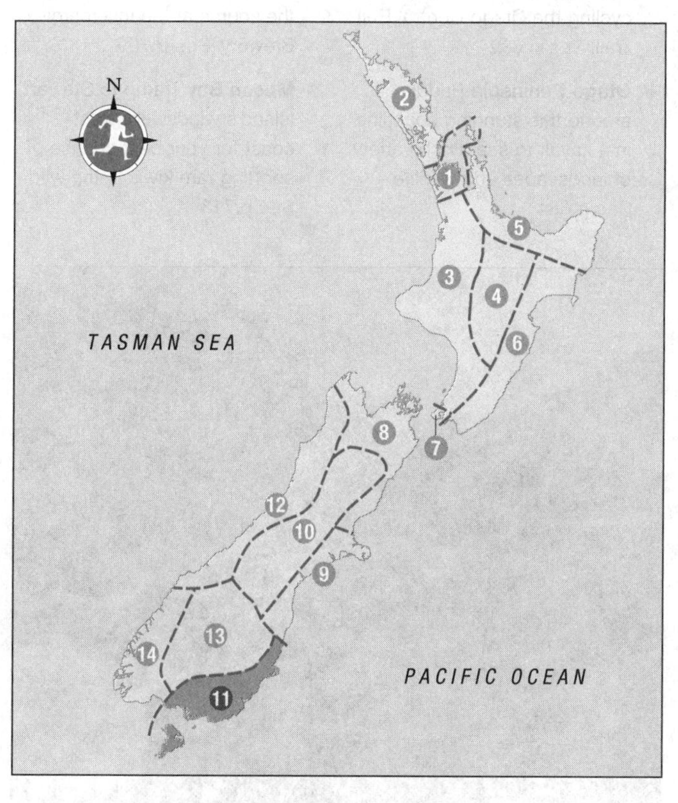

CHAPTER 11

Highlights

* **Dunedin** Dine on haggis and deliberate over 300 kinds of whisky inside the magnificent railway station of the country's Scottish city. See p.680

* **Taieri Gorge** Combine a train trip winding through the rugged Taieri Gorge with cycling the Otago Central Rail Trail. See p.682

* **Otago Peninsula** Paddle around this stunning coastline in a kayak to see a rich variety of landscapes and wildlife. See p.684

* **Curio Bay** Survey a fossilized forest, a yellow-eyed penguin colony and Hector's dolphins surfing the waves of the wild Catlins Coast. See p.697

* **Invercargill** Take a laid-back tour before taste-testing unique brews straight from the source at the Invercargill Brewery. See p.700

* **Mason Bay** Tramp to Stewart Island's windswept west coast for your best chance of spotting rare kiwis in the wild. See p.713

▲ Taieri Gorge Railway

11

Dunedin to Stewart Island

The southeastern corner of the South Island contains some of the least-visited parts of New Zealand, yet a couple of real gems are hidden away here. The darkly attractive harbourside city of **Dunedin**, some 400km south of Christchurch, is a seat of learning and culture, influenced by its university (the country's oldest) and its thriving Scottish traditions. From here south to Stewart Island, local accents are marked by a distinctive Scots "burr", the only true regional variation in the country. Within easy reach of the city is the windswept **Otago Peninsula**, an important wildlife haven where you can observe rare marine life and seabirds at close range. South of Dunedin, the wild **Catlins Coast** is a protected reserve. This magical, virtually forgotten region, home to several rare species, offers dramatically varied scenery, from hills covered with dense native forest to a shoreline indented with rocky bays, long sweeps of sand and intriguing geological formations.

On the South Island's southern tip lies **Invercargill**, bordered by the rich pastureland of Southland's farming communities. The city is the springboard to the country's third island, the comparatively small **Stewart Island**. Relatively few visit, but those who do are rewarded with virgin rainforest and extraordinary birdlife, particularly just offshore on **Ulva Island**.

To do the region justice you need to ease into the slower pace of life, allowing three days for Dunedin and the Otago Peninsula, two or more days in the Catlins and at least a couple on Stewart Island.

Kiwis from more northern parts delight in condemning the **climate** of the southern South Island, and it's true that the further south you go, the wetter it gets. Generally, the best time to come is November to April, when you're most likely to enjoy warmer, though changeable, weather, with midsummer temperatures averaging around 19°C. You'll also catch the best of the wildlife, coinciding with the breeding season of many species. The Catlins and Invercargill get their highest rainfall in the spring (Sept & Oct), while Stewart Island has showers most days in between bursts of sunshine.

Getting around is straightforward, with regular bus services as well as tour buses linking all the major towns and crossing the island to Queenstown and the West Coast along the dramatic Southern Scenic Route. Stewart Island is served by planes from Invercargill and ferries from the southern township of Bluff.

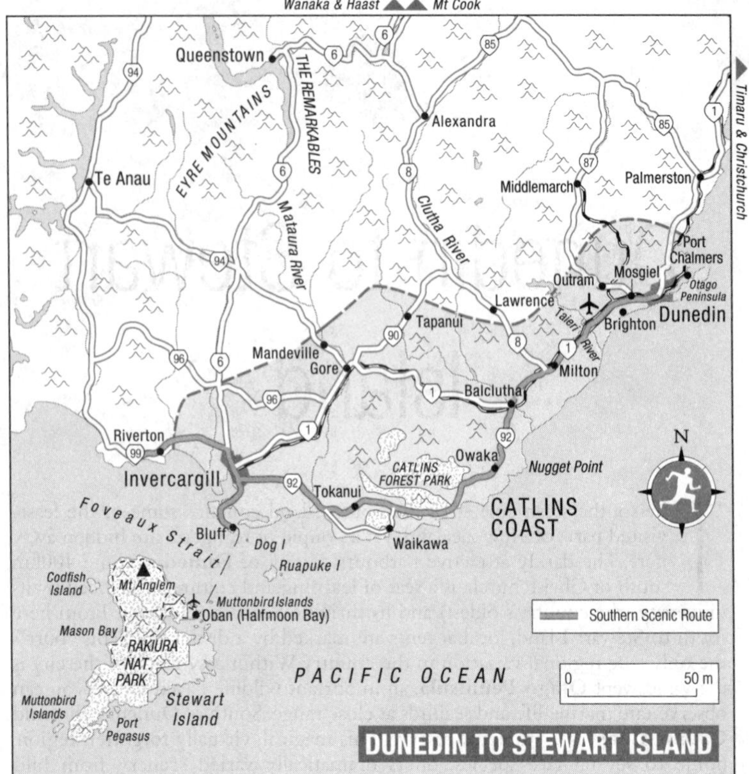

Dunedin

The "Edinburgh of the South", **DUNEDIN** (pronounced Dun-EEdin), takes its name from the Gaelic translation of its Scottish counterpart, with which it also shares street and suburb names (and rain). Founded by Scottish settlers, its heyday arrived when it became the commercial centre for the gold-rush towns of nearby Central Otago, leaving an enduring legacy of imposing **Gothic Revival architecture** fashioned from volcanic bluestone and creamy limestone, including grand villas that climb the hills around the town. Although its population of around 115,000 spreads beyond the hills and surf beaches, Dunedin's compact and manageable city centre is graced with flower-filled parks and gardens.

Some 25,000 students from the 1871-established **University of Otago** – New Zealand's oldest tertiary institution – contribute to a strong **arts scene**, as well as vibrant **nightlife** (during term time, at least).

Dunedin sits at the head of **Otago Harbour**, a long and sheltered body formed ten million years ago by volcanic eruptions and now virtually encircled by rugged hills. It is home to two working ports: a small one in the heart of Dunedin, and **Port Chalmers**, a container-port town whose main street is now sprinkled with antique shops.

Otago Harbour is protected from the Pacific Ocean by the **Otago Peninsula**, which teems with wildlife including rare penguins, seals and albatrosses. Just half an hour's drive from Dunedin, the peninsula is an easy day-trip, but also has some peaceful places to stay.

Some history

From around 1100 AD, **Maori** fished the rich coastal waters of nearby bays, travelling inland in search of moa, ducks and freshwater fish, and trading with other *iwi* further north. Eventually they formed a settlement around the harbour, calling it Otakou (pronounced "O-tar-go") and naming the headland at the harbour's entrance after their great chieftain, Taiaroa – today a well-developed *marae* occupies the Otakou site. By the 1820s European whalers and sealers were seeking shelter in what was the only safe anchorage along this stretch of coast, unwittingly introducing foreign diseases. The local population was decimated, dropping to a low of 110, but subsequent intermarriage bolstered numbers and formed a resilient cultural mix.

The New Zealand Company selected the Otago Harbour for a planned **Scottish settlement** as early as 1840 and purchased land from local Maori for a meagre sum, but it wasn't until 1848 that the first migrant ships arrived, led by Captain William Cargill and the Reverend Thomas Burns, nephew of the Scottish poet Robert Burns. With the arrival of English and Irish settlers the following year, the Scots were soon in the minority, but their fervour stamped a distinct character on the growing town.

In 1861, a lone Australian prospector discovered **gold** at a creek near present-day Lawrence, about 100km west of Dunedin. Within three months, diggers were pouring in from Australia, and as the main port of entry Dunedin found itself in the midst of a gold rush. The port was expanded, and the population doubled in six months, then trebled in the next three years, making the city New Zealand's most important. This new-found wealth spurred a building boom that resulted in many of the city's most iconic buildings, including the university.

By the 1870s gold mania had largely subsided, but the area sustained its economic primacy through **shipping**, railway development and farming. Decline set in during the early twentieth century, when the opening of the Panama Canal in 1914 made Auckland a more economic port for British shipping. In the 1980s, the improvement in world gold prices and the development of equipment enabling large-scale recovery of gold from low-yielding soils re-established **mining** in the hinterland. Today you can visit massive operations, including one at Macraes (see p.835), an hour's drive from Dunedin.

New Zealand's "liquid gold", Speight's Gold Medal Ale, is a full-strength lager (with grassy undertones for that "southern flavour") that has been brewed in Dunedin since the late 1880s, and remains the country's biggest-selling beer today.

Arrival, information and city transport

Dunedin **airport**, 5km off SH1 some 30km south of town, is served by domestic flights from Auckland, Christchurch and Wellington, as well as direct international flights from Sydney, Melbourne and Brisbane with Air New Zealand (see p.29). At the time of writing, a scheduled service between Dunedin, Alexandra and Queenstown was being trialled by local airline Mainland Air (Ⓦwww.mainlandair.com); check for updates. Shuttle buses including Super Shuttle (Ⓣ0800/748 885, Ⓦwww.supershuttle.co.nz; $28)

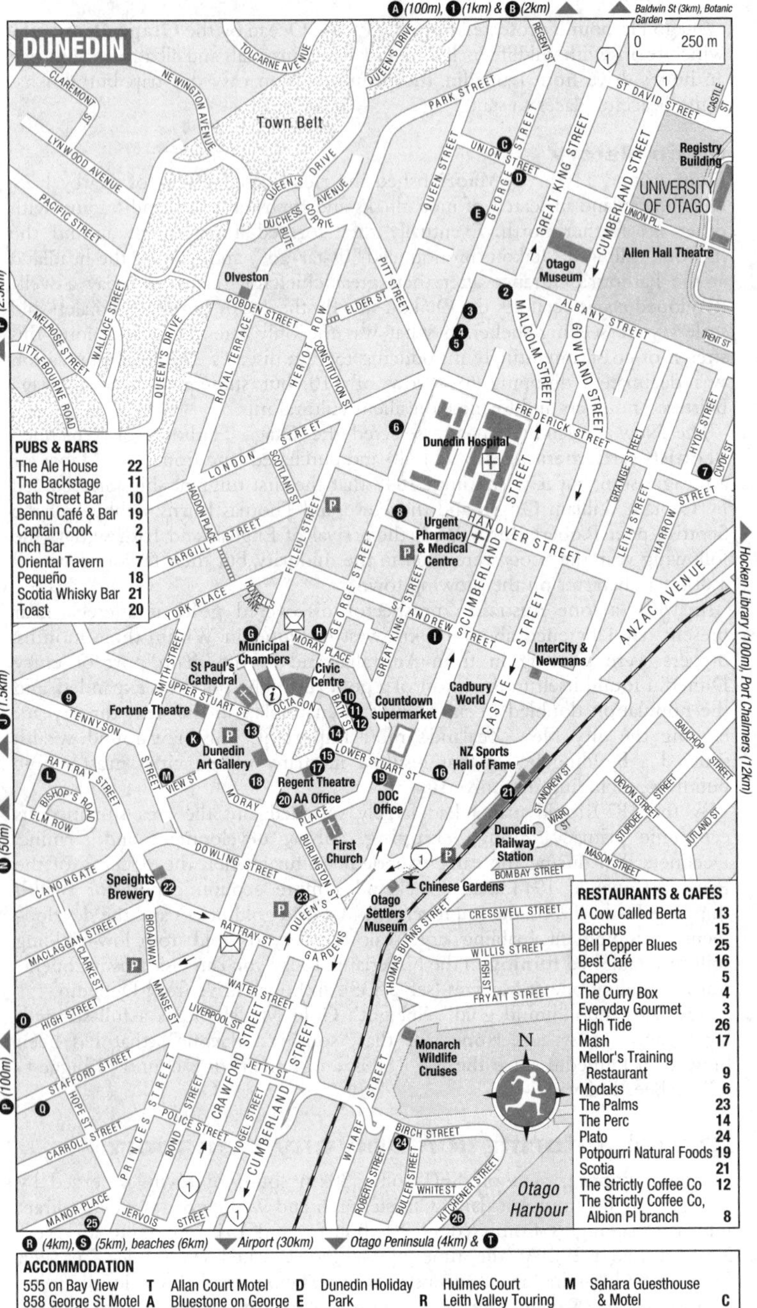

ACCOMMODATION

555 on Bay View	T	Allan Court Motel	D	Dunedin Holiday Park	R	Hulmes Court	M	Sahara Guesthouse & Motel	C
858 George St Motel	A	Bluestone on George	E	Elm Lodge	N	Leith Valley Touring Park	B	Victoria	I
97 Motel	K	The Brothers	L	Fletcher Lodge	O	Lisburn House	S	YHA Stafford Gables	Q
Aaron Lodge Top 10 Holiday Park	F	Central Backpackers	H	Gowrie House	J	On Top Backpackers	G		
		Chalet Backpackers	P						

connect each flight with the city centre ($28; cheaper for multiple passengers travelling together) dropping off at accommodation along the way; book ahead online or by phone. A taxi ride to the city centre will set you back about $60.

Dunedin has no mainline passenger **train** service, but tourist-oriented services along the Taieri Gorge Railway (see p.682) leave from the Dunedin Railway Station on Anzac Avenue. This is also the terminus for Atomic Shuttles. InterCity **buses** drop off in the city centre at 205 St Andrew St.

Information

In addition to handling transport, accommodation and trip bookings, Dunedin's **i-SITE visitor centre**, Municipal Chambers, The Octagon (Nov–March Mon–Fri 8.30am–6pm, Sat & Sun 8.45am–6pm; April–Oct Mon–Fri 8.30am–5pm, Sat & Sun 8.45am–5pm; ⓣ03/474 3300, ⓦwww.cityofdunedin.com) runs two-hour **guided walking tours** (11am daily; $20 including coffee). It also stocks walks leaflets including *Walk the City* ($2.50), detailing points of interest along a gentle stroll around central Dunedin, as well as *A Walking Guide to Dunedin* ($3.50) for **longer walks** in the Dunedin environs. You can also obtain factsheets for each walk from the **DOC** office, 77 Lower Stuart St (Mon–Fri 8.30am–5pm; ⓣ03/477 0677).

City transport

Dunedin's central sights, hostels, hotels and places to eat and drink are all easily accessible on foot. To get further out, the city has an efficient **bus** system orchestrated by the Otago Regional Council (ⓦwww.orc.govt.nz); check schedules at the visitor centre.

Most lines run Monday to Friday from around 7.30am to 11pm with more limited services on Saturday, and skeleton services on Sunday and public holidays. Buses are not numbered but are identified by their route: the most useful is the Normanby–St Clair run, which goes from the beach right through the city, past the Botanic Garden, to the foot of Baldwin Street and beyond. **Fares** are calculated according to the number of zones crossed: the central city is one zone ($1.20), to Baldwin Street is two zones ($1.60), to St Clair three zones ($2), and to Port Chalmers four zones ($2.30). On the Normanby–St Clair service there's a $7 **all-day pass**: buy it from the driver. All buses start from or pass through the centre of town, most stopping at different stands around The Octagon.

From March to October, you might also want to join the hop-on-hop-off **guided bus tour** with Dunedin City Explorer ($20; ⓣ0800/322 240) which makes an hour-long loop of the central city sights, Olveston, the Botanic Garden and Baldwin Street. Tickets are valid all day, including unlimited stops. Alternatively, try the **double-decker bus tour** with Citisights (1hr; $20; ⓣ03/477 5577), which departs from the visitor centre five times a day.

Drivers will soon discover the one-way system running north–south through the city and affecting Cumberland, Castle, Great King and Crawford streets. **Parking** is seldom a problem, with inexpensive meters and restricted zones in the centre but free long-term street parking a few hundred metres outside.

Accommodation

There's a broad choice of accommodation in Dunedin, most of it in or near the city centre. In summer, **booking ahead** is advisable, wherever you're staying. If you prefer something more rural, consider the nearby **Otago Peninsula** (see p.684).

Hotels and motels

555 on Bay View 555 Bayview Rd, corner of Anderson Rd ⓣ03/455 5779, ⓦwww.555onbayview.co.nz. Stylish, laid-back motel opposite the start of Portobello Rd and the Otago Peninsula, with chocolate-toned furnishings and thoughtful amenities including DVD players and coffee plungers, plus huge king-size beds in some rooms. Rooms ❹

858 George St Motel 858 George St ⓣ0800/858 999, ⓦwww.858georgestreetmotel.co.nz. An unusual and well-executed modern design by Dunedin architects, based on Victorian houses, divided into 13 big, luxurious units. Wi-Fi available. Studios ❺, suites ❻

97 Motel 97 Moray Place ⓣ0800/909 797, ⓔinfo@97motel.co.nz. Friendly and very central motel-style place with limited cooking facilities in cheerful rooms. Some also come with deep baths and there's plenty of off-street parking. ❺

Allan Court Motel 590 George St ⓣ0800/611 511, ⓔallan.court@earthlight.co.nz. Central, modern, upmarket and comfortable, with full kitchens in all units, guest laundry and a choice of breakfasts for an extra charge. ❺

Bluestone on George 571 George St ⓣ03/477 9201, ⓦwww.bluestonedunedin.co.nz. Classy apartments with minimalist furnishings, hard surfaces, and state-of-the-art kitchen and bathroom facilities, in-room laundries and high-speed Internet. ❺

Victoria 137 St Andrew St ⓣ0800/266 336, ⓦwww.victoriahoteldunedin.com. Elegantly refurbished in soothing neutral tones, this relaxed hotel in the heart of the city offers rooms, suites and a two-bedroom family apartment, plus an airy restaurant, a cosy bar and a café. ❺

B&Bs and homestays

The Brothers 295 Rattray St ⓣ03/477 0043, ⓦwww.brothershotel.co.nz. Stylish boutique hotel converted from a 1920s Christian Brothers' residence. Pared-down contemporary decor sets the tone for smallish rooms and larger "superior rooms" (including the former chapel), many opening to wide verandas. The spacious lounge has city views, Sky TV and broadband Internet; a continental breakfast is included, and parking free. ❻

Fletcher Lodge 276 High St ⓣ03/477 5552, ⓦwww.fletcherlodge.co.nz. Luxurious, central boutique lodge in an English baronial-style home with a secluded garden, built in 1924 for leading Kiwi industrialist Sir James Fletcher. The living room is richly oak-panelled, everything is kept spotless and all rooms are en suite, with underfloor heating. There's also a large suite ($550), off-street parking, a laundry service and a sumptuous breakfast. ❼

Gowrie House 7 Gowry Place, Roslyn ⓣ03/477 2103, ⓦwww.gowriehouse.co.nz. Rural and city views unfold from this cosy turn-of-the-twentieth-century house set on a hill 5min drive from the centre, on The Octagon to Maori Hill–Prospect Park bus route. One single, one double (opening to a cottage garden) and one twin room, all light and airy with shared facilities. ❻

Hulmes Court 52 Tennyson St ⓣ0800/448 563, ⓦwww.hulmes.co.nz. Well-priced pair of homes (one Edwardian, one a grand 1860 Victorian affair), just off The Octagon but quiet. Rooms are big and individually themed, several of them en suite, and there's off-street parking, mountain bikes and Internet access, all free. A continental breakfast is served in the sunny drawing room. Rooms ❺, en suites ❺

Lisburn House 15 Lisburn Ave, Caversham ⓣ03/455 8888, ⓦwww.lisburnhouse.co.nz. Luxurious and beautifully preserved Victorian-Gothic house with roaring open fires, 10min drive south of the city. Each of the three distinctly styled, spacious rooms has a canopied four-poster bed, fine linen, fresh flowers and a private bathroom. Not suitable for children. ❼

Sahara Guesthouse & Motel 619 George St ⓣ03/477 6662, ⓦwww.dunedin-accommodation.co.nz. Roomy 1863 guesthouse where most rooms have shared facilities. They also have a motel section with ten standard s/c units. There's a TV lounge and off-street parking, and light breakfast is included; cooked breakfasts are available for a small extra charge. ❹

Hostels

Central Backpackers 243 Moray Place ⓣ03/477 9985, ⓔduncb_nz@yahoo.co.nz. Efficiently run, recently renovated 40-bed hostel with well-laid-out dorms, backpack-size security lockers, and a surround-sound DVD lounge. Wi-Fi available; guests also get discounted rates at the adjacent Internet café. Dorms $24, shares $26, twins ❷, doubles ❸

Chalet Backpackers 296 High St ⓣ0800/242 538, ⓔkirsti@paradise.net.nz. Central, comfortable hostel with a great atmosphere and excellent kitchen and dining facilities. Four-shares have beds rather than bunks and there are nice single and double rooms plus a pool and piano room. Phone ahead in winter. Dorms $24, rooms ❷

Elm Lodge 74 Elm Row ⓣ0800/356 363, ⓦwww.elmwildlifetours.co.nz/elm_lodge.shtml. An atmospheric 1930s house on a hill warmed by a wood stove, with made-up beds, a free spa pool and BBQ. Walking distance to town, with free pick-up/drop-off. Dorms & shares $24, rooms ❷

On Top Backpackers Corner of Filleul St & Moray Place ⓣ03/477 6121, ⓦwww.ontopbackpackers.co.nz. Extremely hip, state-of-the-art new 100-bed hostel in the city centre, set above a pool hall and bar spinning dance beats, with a wraparound timber deck, BBQ terrace and light-filled open-plan kitchen/common room. Dorms $24, rooms ❷

YHA Stafford Gables 71 Stafford St ⓣ03/474 1919, ⓔyha.dunedin@yha.co.nz. Character-laden hostel in a rambling 1902 building with a rooftop garden overlooking the city and clued-in local staff. Dorms are three- to six-bed (some with balconies), doubles and twin rooms are generally large, and there are also family rooms. Office hours 7.30am–8.30pm. Dorms $27, rooms ❸

Campsites and motor parks

Aaron Lodge Top 10 Holiday Park 162 Kaikorai Valley Rd ⓣ0800/879 227, ⓦwww.aaronlodgetop10.co.nz. A sheltered, fairly spacious and well-tended site, in the hills 2.5km west of the city centre. Facilities include a heated pool and playground. Camping $29, cabins ❷, flats ❸, motel units ❺

Dunedin Holiday Park 41 Victoria Rd ⓣ0800/945 455, ⓦwww.dunedinholidaypark.co.nz. Lying alongside St Kilda Beach, this well-appointed park is 5min drive from the city centre and served by the Brockville–St Kilda bus: pick it up at The Octagon Stand 3. There's a seven-day camp store. Camping $14–18, cabins ❶, en-suite cabins ❸, motel units ❹

Leith Valley Touring Park 103 Malvern St ⓣ03/467 9936, ⓦwww.leithvalleytouringpark.co.nz. A small, pleasant campsite beside a creek at the foot of bush-clad hills, 3km north from the centre. It's served by The Octagon to Garden Village bus on weekdays and there's a 24hr grocery within walking distance. Camping $15–18, on-site vans ❶, flats ❸, motels ❹

The City

Dunedin's heart beats on the **The Octagon**, a green, tree-filled space in the heart of the city, bordered by historic buildings. Restaurants, offices, banks, bars, clubs and most of the sights concentrate around it, and the **shopping district** stretches immediately south along Princes Street and north along George Street. Further north lies the **university area** and the expansive **Botanic Garden**. To the east is the head of **Otago Harbour**, a sheltered inlet 22km long and no wider than a river in places. The waters are shared by windsurfers, yachts and sightseeing boats, and occasionally dolphins and whales. Two sandy **beaches** lie a short bus ride south from the city centre in the suburbs of St Clair and St Kilda.

The Octagon

Laid out in 1846, **The Octagon** blends together modern and beautifully preserved buildings overlooking grassland and trees. It's presided over by a statue of Robert Burns, symbolizing Dunedin's Scottish origins and literary associations. Every Friday (10am–4pm), the area spills over with **market** stalls selling locally-made crafts.

Dominating The Octagon is the 1880 **Municipal Chambers** building, a grand, classical structure with a clock tower, all constructed from limestone dramatically offset against volcanic bluestone. It's a fine example of the handiwork of Scottish architect **Robert A. Lawson**, whose hand can be seen in the design of many of Dunedin's public buildings. Beside the Municipal Chambers rise the twin white-stone spires of **St Paul's Cathedral**, one of Dunedin's finest buildings and the seat of Anglican worship in the city. This impressive Gothic Revival edifice, entirely constructed from Oamaru stone, was consecrated in 1919. Inside, the twenty-metre-high stone-vaulted ceiling is the only one of its kind in New Zealand, and much of the stained glass in the impressive windows is original; the stark chancel and altar were added in 1971.

Continuing anticlockwise around The Octagon, Dunedin City Council architects fashioned the gleaming **Dunedin Public Art Gallery**, 30 The

Octagon (daily 10am–5pm; gold coin donation, plus charges for special exhibitions) out of six Victorian buildings, all elegantly refurbished to create an airy, modern split-level space with several exhibition areas. The 1996-opened structure is a contrast to the original public art gallery, founded in 1884 and the oldest in the country. The foyer of polished wooden floors, ironwork and a hundred-year-old spiral staircase is worth a look in itself. The gallery's main strength is a rotated collection of early and contemporary New Zealand works, including William Goldie's well-known *All 'e same t'e Pakeha*, and a small gallery devoted to the works of Frances Hodgkins. There's also a collection of relatively minor works by Old Masters and more recent practitioners including Turner, Monet and Constable. The space regularly hosts temporary shows of international standard.

Further around, at 17 The Octagon, is the 1874 facade of the **Regent Theatre**, a one-time hotel that was transformed into a cinema then a theatre. Today it hosts international shows and the Royal New Zealand Ballet, as well as live music. Inside, elaborate nineteenth-century plasterwork and marble staircases are juxtaposed with 1920s stained-glass windows and geometric balustrades.

Behind the Regent Theatre on Moray Place stands the 54-metre stone spire of the **First Church of Otago**, visible throughout the city. The church, generally recognized as the most impressive of New Zealand's nineteenth-century churches, was designed in neo-Gothic style by Robert A. Lawson. Of particular interest inside are a wooden gabled ceiling and, above the pulpit, a brightly coloured rose window. Behind the altar is a small heritage centre (Sept–May Mon–Sat 10am–4pm; June–Aug Mon–Sat 10.30am–2.30pm).

South and east of The Octagon

Two hundred years of social history in Dunedin and Otago are catalogued at the **Otago Settlers Museum**, 31 Queens Gardens (daily 10am–5pm; gold coin donation), which draws from an exhaustive collection of artefacts, paintings and photographs. Highlights include the portrait gallery, whose walls are plastered with black-and-white photographs of the region's early settler families, and "Across the Ocean Waves", an insight into the rigours (and pleasures) of emigrating to Otago by sailing ship in the nineteenth century. Look too for the "Windows on a Chinese Past" display which provides an insight into the lives of the legions of Chinese who left their families behind to seek a fortune in the Otago Goldfields. Among the exhibits in the transport wing there's a beautifully appointed 1940s caravan, a restored double-ended Fairlie steam engine and the chance to sit astride a penny-farthing. Alongside the museum, work on Dunedin's new **Chinese Gardens** was underway at the time of research; the visitor centre can provide updates.

Impossible to miss, thanks to its towers, turrets and minarets, the resplendent **Dunedin Railway Station**, Anzac Avenue, was constructed on reclaimed swampland in 1906. The walls of its exquisitely preserved **foyer** glisten with green, yellow and cream majolica tiles made especially for New Zealand Rail by Royal Doulton, and the mosaic floor celebrates the steam engine and consists of more than 700,000 tiny squares of porcelain. Upstairs on the balcony, a stained-glass window at each end depicts an approaching train, whose headlights gleam from all angles. The station's upper floor houses the **New Zealand Sports Hall of Fame** (daily 10am–4pm; $5), a collection of memorabilia relating to 150-odd New Zealand inductees. Hagiographic displays are devoted to rugby loose forward Colin Meads, world record long jumper Yvette Williams, world champion sheep shearer Godfrey Bowen, mountaineer Edmund Hillary, fast bowler Richard Hadlee and many, many more.

▲ Dunedin Railway Station

Beyond the station is the extensive university research library, **Hocken Library**, 90 Anzac Ave (Mon–Fri 9.30am–5pm, Tues also 6–9pm, Sat 9am–noon; free). Its impressive collection of books, manuscripts, paintings and photographs relating to New Zealand and the Pacific was originally assembled by Dr Thomas Morland Hocken, a Dunedin physician and one of the country's first historians.

Cadbury World and Speight's Brewery

Stand downwind of Dunedin's downtown chocolate factory, just east of The Octagon, and it's hard to resist a visit to **Cadbury World**, 280 Cumberland St (tours daily: mid-Jan to Easter 9am–6.15pm, Easter to mid-Jan 9am–3.15pm;

tours around 1hr 15min; $16; ⓣ0800/223 287, ⓦwww.cadburyworld.co.nz). Enthusiastic guides clad in bright-purple overalls take you into the factory to see lines producing Crunchie, chocolate buttons, Easter eggs and dozens of other varieties, while showering you with free samples. Bookings are recommended any time of year, and essential during school holidays. **Reduced tours** (40min; $10) run on Sundays, public holidays and from Christmas to mid-January, when many of the lines shut down.

The **Speight's Brewery Tour**, 200 Rattray St (daily: 10am, noon, 2pm, plus Mon–Thurs 7pm and Sat & Sun 4pm; $17; ⓣ03/477 7697, ⓦwww.speights.co.nz), offers a similar experience inside one of New Zealand's oldest breweries, established in 1876 (now part of multinational conglomerate Lion Nathan). Its tall, brick chimney topped by a stone barrel, a few hundred metres southwest of The Octagon, is visible from across the city. Inside, hour-long tours (best booked in advance) take you on a light-hearted journey through the alchemy of traditional brewing. It's all burnished copper mash tuns and kauri gyles, concluding with six samples of the product, which you pour yourself from the taps. The entry is beside a **water spigot** fed by the same sweet-tasting artesian water that is used to brew the beer: you'll usually see locals filling water bottles and containers.

You can visit both factories on a **combined ticket** ($30), which includes discounts on merchandise (products are only available to non-tour visitors).

North of The Octagon

The star attraction of the absorbing **Otago Museum**, 419 Great King St (daily 10am–5pm; gold coin donation) is the fascinating "Southern Land, Southern People" gallery, which covers virtually all aspects of life and natural history in the southern half of the South Island and the sub-Antarctic islands. Large boulders give an idea of the rock that underlies the region in displays which also draw in a fossilized plesiosaur skeleton and the influence of Oamaru stone on the region's architecture. Everything is knitted neatly together, with a discussion on climate illustrated by a Maori flax rain cape, and coverage of the region's fish calling on the experience of whitebaiters.

Elsewhere in the building, look out for the Animal Attic, a deeply Victorian amalgamation of macabre skeletons and stuffed beasts. The special exhibitions gallery is usually worth a look, and **Discovery World**, an interactive science museum-within-a-museum (extra $6) is perfect for the six-to-elevens, who will be enchanted by its new **butterfly enclosure**.

Guided tours ($10) focusing on the museum's highlights take place at 11.30am, while at 3.30pm, the "Southern Land, Southern People" tour explores the relationship between the environment and its inhabitants.

Olveston

Dunedin's showpiece historic home is **Olveston**, 42 Royal Terrace (1hr guided tours only: daily 9.30am, 10.45am, noon, 1.30pm, 2.45pm & 4pm; $15; book a day ahead in summer ⓣ0800/100 880, ⓦwww.olveston.co.nz), ten minutes' walk northwest of The Octagon. Contained within the walls of this fine Edwardian house is a treasure-trove of art and antiques assembled by the Theomin family, who lived here from 1906 and were passionate about travel, art and music. On her death in 1966, the last-surviving family member, Dorothy, bequeathed the house and its contents to the city, and it remains just as she left it.

Built in 1904–06, the Jacobean-style building is reminiscent of the English Arts and Crafts Movement. A particularly striking piece of craftsmanship is the oak staircase in the Grand Hall, made in England and constructed without the use of nails. The house was a masterpiece of modernity for its time, with central heating, heated towel rails and a telephone system.

The University

New Zealand's oldest university, the **University of Otago** was founded by Scottish settlers in 1869. Based on the design of Glasgow University, it quickly expanded into a complex of imposing Gothic bluestone buildings, foremost among them the registry building with its Gothic **clock tower**. The visitor centre has free campus maps; a stroll through the campus from Union Street to Leith Street will take you past the key buildings.

The Botanic Garden and Signal Hill

Established in 1863, the serene **Dunedin Botanic Garden** (sunrise–sunset; free) lies at the foot of Signal Hill. The steep Upper Garden contains the expansive Rhododendron Dell, where well-established specimens grow among native bush, flowering trees and plants. It also has an arboretum, a native plant collection and an aviary, home to native birds such as kea and kaka, as well as exotic birds from all over the world. The flat Lower Garden features exotic trees, Winter Garden conservatories (daily 10am–4pm), an Alpine House (daily 9am–4pm), a rose garden and a playground. A volunteer-run information centre (daily 10am–4pm) lies between the tea kiosk and the Winter Garden. Access to the Lower Gardens car park is from Cumberland Street, while the Upper Gardens car park is on Lovelock Avenue. Tours of the gardens ($5) depart hourly from 10.30am to 1.30pm from October to March.

Just north of the Botanic Garden, Opoho Road leads up to the 393m summit of **Signal Hill**, a scenic reserve with a magnificent view over Dunedin, the upper harbour and the sea from the Centennial Memorial. Apparently the nation's only monument commemorating one hundred years of British sovereignty (1840–1940) following the signing of the Treaty of Waitangi, the memorial is flanked by two powerful bronze figures symbolizing the past and the future. Embedded in the podium is a tribute to Dunedin's namesake: a chunk of the rock upon which Edinburgh Castle was built.

If you're not driving you can ride the Opoho **bus** from The Octagon Stand 7 to within 1km of the summit (the route also stops at the north end of the Botanic Garden), or make the fairly gentle walk (6km return; 1hr 30min) from the Botanic Garden.

Baldwin Street

Dunedin rejoices in the world's steepest street, **Baldwin Street**, which, with a *Guinness Book of Records*-verified maximum gradient of 1 in 2.66, has a slope of almost 19 degrees. The views from the top of this cul-de-sac aren't bad, but the highlight is walking up, something achieved in about five minutes, under the bemused gaze of locals sitting out on their verandas. The honestly titled Baldwin Street Tourist Shop, 282 North Rd (daily 8.30am–6pm), near the bottom of the road, sells much-needed drinks as well as T-shirts and a certificate ($1.50) marking your achievement. During the annual "Gutbuster" event (generally held in late Feb as part of the Dunedin Summer Festival), contestants run to the top and back down again – the current record is one minute 56 seconds.

Baldwin Street is 5km north of the city centre: follow Great King Street until it becomes North Road then look for the tenth road on the right. The Normanby–St Clair bus from Stand 2 on Princes Street drops you at the foot of Baldwin Street.

Dunedin's beaches

Four kilometres south of the city centre, the suburbs of St Kilda and St Clair culminate in a long, wild sweep of sand enclosed by two volcanic headlands (served by frequent buses from the corner of The Octagon and Princes Street). **St Clair Beach** is excellent for surfing and is patrolled by lifeguards during the summer. For calmer waters, head to the western end and the **St Clair Hot Salt Water Pool**, The Esplanade (Oct–March Mon–Fri 6am–7pm, Sat & Sun 8am–7pm; $4.50; ⓣ03/471 9780), a large, outdoor, heated saltwater pool beside the rocky point. At the opposite end of The Esplanade, the *Esplanade Surf School* (ⓣ03/455 8655, ⓦwww.espsurfschool.co.nz), offers **surfing lessons** (1hr for $40, min three people, max six; 90min one-on-one lessons $70) with wetsuit and board supplied.

About halfway along the strip, St Clair merges with **St Kilda Beach**, which is reasonably safe for swimming as long as you keep between the flags; it is also patrolled in summer. At the beach's eastern end, a headland separates St Kilda from the smaller **Tomahawk Beach** (not safe for swimming), often dotted with horses and buggies preparing for trotting races at low tide. The best swimming beach in the area is the blend of sand and rocky outcrops at **Brighton**, 15km south of Dunedin: catch the Brighton bus from Stand 5 on Cumberland Street between Hanover and St Andrew streets ($4).

Eating

You'll find an excellent range of dining options throughout the **city centre** (especially around The Octagon and along George Street between Hanover and Albany streets), from classic espresso cafés to fine dining restaurants as well as dozens of cheap Cambodian, Korean and Filipino cafés alongside Thai, Indian and sushi. Hip cafés also cluster around St Clair's beachfront.

Quality spots for **stocking up** include the deli/café *Everyday Gourmet*, 466 George St (Mon–Fri 8am–5.30pm, Sat 9am–3pm, generally closed Sun), and the Saturday morning **farmers' market** in the Dunedin Railway Station car park. For staples, stop by the central 24hr Countdown supermarket at 309 Cumberland St.

Cafés

Best Café 30 Lower Stuart St. Part of Dunedin since the 1950s, this time-warp of a place (oilclothed tables, lino floors) dishes up old-school fish-and-chips meals served with sliced bread and curled butter (around $17), along with oysters (one dozen from $34) and whitebait patties (from $9 with salad) in season. Closed Sat & Sun.

Capers 412 George St. Woodsy café with a loyal following. Early birds flock for chunky sweet and savoury scones, chocolate pancakes and heaping serves of bacon and eggs ($6.50–14); late-risers can still get all-day breakfasts as well as ploughman's lunches, baked potatoes and filo parcels (all around $7.50). Daily 7am–2pm.

Mash 16 The Octagon. Hybrid café/restaurant serving everything from home-made museli ($8) to lemongrass and black-peppered beef salad with palm sugar and coriander vinaigrette ($13.50) depending on what time you're here. Breakfast and lunch daily, dinner Tues–Sat.

Modaks 318 George St. Down-to-earth daytime haunt with local pop art lining its red-brick walls. Outstanding coffee and healthy snacks such as spinach, brie and mushroom scones as well as vegan options like avocado, hummus and sundried tomato served with thick foccacia bread. DJs occasionally hit the decks on Friday nights.

The Perc 142 Lower Stuart St. Scrubbed-up Art Deco daytime digs serving scrumptious baked goods (go early before the cinnamon pinwheels sell out), sandwiches and smoothies. Switched-on staff, a cool collection of vinyl toys, and artwork by locals such as stencil artist Phil Frost.

Potpourri Natural Foods 97 Lower Stuart St. Established daytime vegetarian café, got up to look like a church with diamond-patterned stained glass and timber pews. Wholemeal baking, a big salad bar and enormous quiche slices. Closed Sun.

The Strictly Coffee Co 23 Bath St. The best coffee in town, sold by the cup or the kilo in an industrial-chic, cherry-red daytime café filled with chrome coffee grinders. Closed Sat & Sun. A second branch on Albion Place is open daily.

Restaurants

A Cow Called Berta 199 Upper Stuart St ☎03/477 2993. This venerable restaurant has been producing some of Dunedin's finest meals for years in the cosy ambience of a converted Victorian terrace house. Expect the likes of soy and honey marinated pork fillet with apple and brazil nut wontons ($35) followed by ginger and pear pudding with brandy sauce and home-made vanilla-bean ice cream ($13.50). Dinner only; closed Sun.

Bacchus 1st floor, 12 The Octagon ☎03/474 0824. Respected restaurant and wine bar with a great vantage point overlooking The Octagon. Over fifty wines, accompanied by moderately-priced seafood and meat dishes like porcini mushroom-crusted rack of lamb for lunch ($15.50–22.50) and dinner ($32.50–36.50). Lunch Mon–Fri; dinner Mon–Sat.

Bell Pepper Blues 474 Princes St ☎03/474 0973. Fine-dining restaurant incongruously situated next to a motorcycle showroom, where award-winning chef Michael Coughlin concocts adventurous modern Kiwi cuisine fused with Asian and Mediterranean flavours. Reserve ahead for both lunch (mains $15–18.50) and dinner (mains $29.50–37), or turn up for well-priced bar food. Lunch Wed–Fri; dinner Mon–Sat.

The Curry Box 442 George St ☎03/477 4713. Tandoori restaurant cooking up creamy curries, many in vegetarian versions (all $14–16). There's a weekday lunch special ($10) and an all-you-can-eat lunch buffet on Fri (noon–2.30pm; $13). Closed Sun lunch; BYO.

High Tide 29 Kitchener St ☎03/477 9784. Waterside hideaway with uninterrupted views over the harbour and peninsula. Consistently good seafood, vegetarian and meat dishes (mains $27–40), as well as home-made soups and desserts. Dinner Tues–Sun; licensed and BYO.

Mellor's Training Restaurant 1st floor, Otago Polytechnic, corner of York Place & Tennyson St ☎03/479 6172. Unbelievably cheap French/New Zealand cuisine prepared by world-class chefs and their students, with one of the best city views in Dunedin. Booking essential, ideally several days ahead. Open March–Oct Tues–Thurs for a set lunch (noon–2pm; $16) and dinner (6.30–9pm; $27). Licensed.

The Palms 18 Queens Gardens ☎03/477 6534. Semi-formal local favourite with picture windows overlooking Queens Gardens and a menu spanning dishes such as Angus beef fillet ($36) and leek-stuffed free-range chicken ($31). Lunch and dinner Mon–Sat; licensed and BYO.

Plato 2 Birch St ☎03/477 4235. Retro-styled restaurant in a former seafarers' crew-house. Fantastically kitsch 60s knick-knacks do their best to compete with four to five kinds of fresh-from-the-ocean fish each day as well as blasts-from-the-past like steak Diane (mains $22.50 to $30.50). Don't miss a pre- or post-dinner drink in the Brady Bunch-style den upstairs. Dinner daily; brunch 11am–2pm Sun.

Scotia Dunedin Railway Station, Anzac Ave ☎03/477 7704. Gastronomic Scottish restaurant grandly housed in Dunedin's historic train station, and masterfully run by kilt-wearing young Scottish maître d'/owner Craig Somerville. Starters like gorse-smoked rabbit paté ($12) are followed by wild venison with port-spiced cranberries ($29) and porridge gateau with marmalade ice cream and deep-fried Mars bars ($11); and a dram at the adjacent whisky bar (see p.680). Lunch Thurs–Sun, dinner Tues–Sat.

Drinking, nightlife and entertainment

Like all good university cities, drinking is taken seriously here. A number of the city's dozens of **pubs** and **bars** serve English- and German-style beers from Dunedin's premier micro-brewery, Emerson's. Local **bands** play often play at weekends, although once the students head home for the holidays some of the dancefloors can look pretty sad. For entertainment and events **listings**, pick up a copy of *Fink*, a free student-oriented weekly guide to music, exhibitions and movies available around town. The *Otago Daily Times* also has a listings section, best on Thursday.

To truly embrace the local culture, get along to a **rugby match** at Carisbrook Stadium (the "House of Pain") on Burns Street, 2.5km southwest of The Octagon. Games are usually held every second weekend during the season (roughly the end of Feb to end of Oct). The Champions of the World shop, 8 George St, has free schedules and also sells tickets.

The Dunedin Sound

In the late 1970s and early 1980s an idiosyncratic style of rock music, soon dubbed the **Dunedin Sound**, began to emerge from Dunedin's local pub scene. The bands writing and producing these jangly garage tracks were isolated from the commercial mainstream but were championed by indie Christchurch label Flying Nun (now based in Auckland; ⓦwww.flyingnun.co.nz) who put out early records by bands like The Chills, The Clean and The Verlaines. All saw some success in New Zealand and found a receptive (if underground) audience in Europe and the States.

As late as 1992, the *Chicago Tribune* called Dunedin the "Rock Capital of The World", but by then the scene had moved on. Some of the bands are still going (in one form or another), and in 2002 Flying Nun released its 21st birthday CD of Flying Nun covers called *Under The Influence*: ex-Pavement frontman Stephen Malkmus covered The Verlaines' wonderful *Death and the Maiden*.

The songs have certainly stood the test of time, and as the rock 'n' roll wheel turns, an updated version of the same kind of sound emanates from The Strokes and their imitators. To check out back catalogues and keep tabs on the latest bands breaking out of Dunedin, visit ⓦwww.dunedinmusic.com, which also has an online music store.

Pubs, bars and clubs

The Ale House 200 Rattray St ⓣ03/471 9050. Very popular and spacious Speight's-owned pub with excellent brews and top quality food in a wood and antique memorabilia setting. Daily from 11.30am.

The Backstage Bath St. Cosy, mellow live music venue featuring emerging and established Kiwi talent, from the Anji Sami Band to Liam Finn; check gig guides to see who's on. Cover charges vary.

Bath Street Bar 1 Bath St. Stylish nightclub behind a blank beige facade, where DJs play underground sounds. Usually $5 cover; closed Mon.

Bennu Café & Bar 12 Moray Place. Young professionals are drawn to this elegant venue in one of Dunedin's finest buildings, decorated with a skylight right over the bar, and palm trees. Beneath it, the nightclub *12 Below* has top DJs and bartenders who know their stuff.

Captain Cook 354 Great King St. Thanks to a constant stream of young students, who come for cheap food and cheap drinks in the raucous garden bar, "the Cook" reputedly has the highest beer consumption of any pub in New Zealand.

Inch Bar 8 Bank St. Intimate watering hole with specialty beers including Emerson's on tap, and a wide range of imported brands.

Oriental Tavern 155 Frederick St. Despite frequent name changes, "the Ori" remains a student stalwart (and pick-up joint), with a dancefloor and pool tables.

Pequeño Savoy Building, Princes St. All low lighting, leather sofas and banquettes around the fire. Excellent wine and cocktails and regular live jazz. Closed Sun.

Scotia Whisky Bar Dunedin Railway Station, Anzac Ave. Over 220 single-malt Scottish whiskies and another eighty-plus international varieties (and Irn Bru!), in a sophisticated, understated setting. Bar food includes haggis and oatcakes. Daily 9am–late.

Toast 53 Princes St. Cocktail bar mixing a mean Flaming Lamborghini ($16), with DJs hitting the decks Thurs–Sat. Mon–Fri 3pm–late, Sat 5pm–late, closed Sun.

Theatre, cinema and classical music

In addition to its **festivals**, Dunedin has a lively year-round **theatre** scene and several movie houses along with **classical music** and **opera** performances. Events can be **booked** through the venue or through the Ticketek office in the Regent Theatre in The Octagon, which takes bookings for a selection of national and local events (ⓣ03/477 8597, ⓦpremier.ticketek.co.nz; Mon–Fri 8.30am–5pm, Sat 10.30am–1pm).

Regular concerts are given by the New Zealand Symphony Orchestra, the Dunedin Sinfonia (a semi-professional orchestra), and chamber music groups at the Town Hall or the Glenroy Auditorium at the Dunedin Centre (Ⓣ03/474 3614). The Dunedin Opera Company stages two or three productions a year at the Mayfair Theatre, 100 King Edward St (Ⓣ03/455 3186), and public recitals are occasionally held by the music department of the University of Otago (see posters around town or check with the visitor centre).

Cinemas

Hoyts Octagon 33 The Octagon Ⓣ03/477 3250. Mainstream multiplex.

Rialto 11 Moray Place Ⓣ03/474 2200. Good for mainstream movies.

Metro Town Hall, Moray Place Ⓣ03/471 9635, Ⓦwww.nzcinema.co.nz. With only 56 seats this is one of the smallest public cinemas in New Zealand, and a delightful place to watch arthouse movies. Popcorn is out, but you're welcome to take your coffee in with you. Book ahead.

Theatres

Allen Hall Clyde St Ⓣ03/479 8896. Campus theatre that showcases the talents of the university's drama students. Shows are often of an alternative bent and don't cost much.

Fortune Theatre 231 Stuart St Ⓣ03/477 8323, Ⓦwww.fortunetheatre.co.nz. Converted from a neo-Gothic church, the Fortune divides its programme between new works by Kiwi playwrights, fringe theatre, popular Broadway-style plays and occasional musicals. Tickets around $30; closed Jan.

Globe 104 London St Ⓣ03/477 3274, Ⓦwww.globetheatre.org.nz. This small and intimate venue features contemporary plays, classical drama and experimental works.

Regent 17 The Octagon Ⓣ03/477 6481, Ⓦwww.regenttheatre.co.nz. The city's largest and most ornate theatre, hosting musicals, ballets, touring plays and performances by popular singers, comedians and groups.

Festivals

Dunedin Summer Festival All manner of local events, including a trolley derby, street races and the Baldwin St Gutbuster. Mid-Feb.

Scottish Week Daily concerts, pipe bands, Highland dancing enliven this celebration of the city's cultural roots in late Sept.

New Zealand International Film Festival, Dunedin Ⓦwww.enzedff.co.nz. The usual mix of oddball and pre-release mainstream movies. Late July to early Aug.

Fringe Festival Ⓦwww.dunedinfringe.org.nz. Ten-day arts and culture festival with street performers, short films, comedy and exhibitions, generally taking place in late Sept and early Oct every even year.

Otago Festival of the Arts Ⓦwww.otagofestival.co.nz. The Fringe Festival's high-end equivalent, held concurrently.

Rhododendron Festival Ⓦwww.rhododunedin.co.nz. Four-day celebration of Dunedin's myriad blooms, when the city's parks explode with colour and private gardens open to the public. End of Oct.

Listings

Automobile Association 450 Moray Place (Mon–Fri 8.30am–5pm; Ⓣ03/477 5945).

Banks and foreign exchange The major banks are clustered on George and Princes sts, all with ATMs. On Sat morning try the ANZ, corner of George & Hanover sts, which is open to 2pm.

Bike rental There's a handy cluster of bike shops around the junction of Lower Stuart & Cumberland Sts; try The Cycle Surgery, 67 Stuart St (Ⓣ03/477 7473, Ⓦwww.cyclesurgery.co.nz) who do repairs, rent bikes from $35 per day ($5 extra with panniers), and can help organize self-guided trips on the Otago Central Rail Trail, including accommodation.

Bookshops University Bookshop, 378 Great King St, opposite the Otago Museum (Ⓣ03/477 6976, Ⓦwww.unibooks.co.nz; Mon–Fri 8.30am–5.30pm, Sat 9.30am–3pm, Sun 11am–3pm), is a comprehensive independent bookshop on two floors, stocking a broad range of New Zealand and international fiction and non-fiction – bargains upstairs.

Buses Dunedin is a regional hub for bus services. Atomic Shuttles (Ⓣ03/322 8883, Ⓦwww.atomictravel.co.nz) operate Dunedin–Christchurch, Dunedin–Queenstown–Wanaka, Dunedin–Invercargill and Invercargill–Queenstown; InterCity/Newmans (Ⓦwww.intercitycoach.co.nz) operate Dunedin–Alexandra–Cromwell–Queenstown, Dunedin–Oamaru–Timaru–Christchurch, Dunedin–Gore–Invercargill, and Invercargill–Gore–Te Anau; and Wanaka Connexions (Ⓣ03/443 9122, Ⓦwww.wanakaconnexions.co.nz) run Dunedin–Alexandra–Cromwell–Wanaka/Queenstown and Invercargill–Lumsden–Queenstown–Wanaka. Catch-a-Bus (Ⓣ03/204 8183) links Dunedin and Invercargill.

Camping and outdoor equipment R & R Sport, 70 Lower Stuart St (☎03/474 1211), has the biggest range of camping, skiing, cycling and general sporting equipment. Bivouac, 171 George St (☎03/477 3679), has tramping, mountaineering, skiing and kayaking gear for rent and for sale.
Car rental As well as all the international and nationwide car rental agencies there are good local companies such as Rhodes, 124 St Andrew St (☎0800/746 337, Ⓦwww.rhodesrentals.co.nz) and Reliable Rentals (☎03/489 8929).
Horse-riding Hare Hill Horse Treks (☎0800/437 837, Ⓦwww.horseriding-dunedin.co.nz), some 15km northeast of Dunedin beyond Port Chalmers, do anything from a harbour trek (1hr 30min; $50) and a half-day trail ride ($80) to an overnight escape ($250 including dinner) staying in a romantic cottage.
Internet access Try The Common Room, 18 George St, right by The Octagon, which has a stack of fast machines.
Library Dunedin Public Library, corner of John & Stewart sts (☎03/474 3690; Mon–Fri 9.30am–8pm, Sat & Sun 11am–4pm), has excellent facilities, newspapers and slow but free Internet access.
Medical treatment Dunedin Hospital, 201 Great King St (☎03/474 0999). After-hours doctors are available at 95 Hanover St (☎03/479 2900).
Pharmacy After-hours service at Urgent Pharmacy, 95 Hanover St (☎03/477 6344; Mon–Fri 6–10pm, Sat & Sun 10am–10pm).
Post office The post shops (Mon–Fri 8.30am–5.30pm) at 243 Princes St and 233 Moray Place are most convenient. The former holds poste restante (☎03/477 3517).
Taxis The handiest taxi ranks are in The Octagon, between George & Stuart sts, or call United (☎0800/829 411), which also has wheelchair-accessible taxis.
Travel agents Brooker United Travel, 346 George St ☎03/477 3383; STA, 207 George St ☎03/474 0146 & 0508/782 872.

Around Dunedin

Scenic day-trips from Dunedin include a foray into the dry hill country aboard the **Taieri Gorge Railway**, and a trip to the dealer galleries and antique shops of Dunedin's harbourside acolyte, **Port Chalmers**. Set more time aside for the **Otago Peninsula**, where you can get incredibly close to animal and birdlife that is almost impossible to see anywhere else in the world. Tours by bus, boat and kayak all leave from Dunedin or you can stay overnight.

Taieri Gorge Railway

The **Taieri Gorge Railway** (services daily; ☎03/477 4449, Ⓦwww.taieri.co.nz) stretches 77km northwest from Dunedin through rugged mountains only accessible by train. Constructed between 1879 and 1921, the line once carried supplies the 235km from Dunedin to the old gold town of Cromwell, returning with farm produce, fruit and livestock bound for the port. Commercial traffic stopped in 1990, and much of the route was turned into the Otago Central Rail Trail (see box, p.831), but the most dramatic section – through the schist strata of the Taieri Gorge – continues to offer a rewarding journey at any time of year.

The air-conditioned train is made up of a mix of modern steel carriages with large panoramic windows and nostalgic refurbished 1920s wooden cars. Storage is available for backpacks and bicycles, and there's a licensed snack bar on board.

The most frequent trip is known as the Taieri Gorge Limited (4hr return; $46 one way, $69 return), which runs to **Pukerangi** – a peaceful spot 58km from the city near the highest point of the track (250m). Less frequently, the train continues a further 19km to the old gold town of **Middlemarch** (2hr 30min one way, 6hr return – trains stop for 1hr at Middlemarch; $51 one way, $77 return) in the fertile Strath Taieri Plains.

Apart from these day-trips, the Railway makes an excellent way to start your journey inland towards Wanaka and Queenstown. The Track and Trail bus service meets the train at Pukerangi or Middlemarch and heads through the Maniototo (see p.831) to Queenstown ($115): book through the Taieri Gorge Railway.

Cyclists can ride the train (bikes go free) then hop straight onto the Otago Central Rail Trail. If you don't have your own bike, look into the Rail-Trail-specific deals offered by Dunedin's bike rental companies (see "Listings", p.681).

A completely different but equally picturesque rail journey leaves Dunedin Railway Station and runs along the main northbound line 66km up the coast to Palmerston. Christchurch-bound passenger trains ceased to operate on this stretch in 2002 but you can now board the **Seasider** (Oct–March some Wed & Sun at 9.30am; $42.50 one way; $63 return), which takes four hours for the round trip.

Port Chalmers

If you've a few hours to spare, head 12km northeast of Dunedin along the winding western shore of Otago Harbour to **PORT CHALMERS**, a small historic town arranged around a contemporary container port. Its fine nineteenth-century buildings are undergoing gentrification on the back of a thriving artistic community headed by celebrated New Zealand painter and sculptor **Ralph Hotere**. Early in the week the galleries and antique/bric-a-brac emporia are deathly quiet, and though things pick up from Wednesday you should come at the weekend to see everything at its liveliest.

The site was chosen in 1844 as the port to serve the proposed Scottish settlement that would become Dunedin. Later, it served as the embarkation point for several **Antarctic expeditions**, including those of Captain Scott, who set out from here in 1901 and again for his ill-fated attempt on the pole in 1910. The first trial shipment of **frozen meat** to Britain was sent from Port Chalmers in 1882 and today the export of wool, meat and timber is its chief business.

The Town

Port Chalmers crawls up the hills on either side of **George Street**, which runs down a short hill to the port, where three container cranes loom over the town. Two late-Victorian churches dominate: the elegant stone-spired Presbyterian **Iona Church** on Mount Street, and the nuggety bluestone Anglican **Holy Trinity**, another Robert A. Lawson design.

George Street meets the port at its junction with Beach Street, where you'll find the small **museum** (Mon–Fri 9am–3pm, Sat & Sun 1.30–4.30pm; gold coin donation) in an 1877 former post office. Brimming with maritime artefacts and local settler history, museum highlights include a history of navigational equipment with splendid models and photographs. Look out for the working electric model of a **gold dredge**, built in 1900 by an apprentice boilermaker.

The rest of George Street is lined with **art galleries** and **craft shops** such as the Crafty Banker, 16 George St (Thurs–Sun), housed in an old bank. A further 12km north lies the small settlement of **Aramoana**, on a sand dune spit at the mouth of Otago Harbour, with wild, often deserted **beaches**.

Practicalities

By **car** from Dunedin, it's a ten-minute harbourside drive along SH88, or you can take the longer scenic route, following Mount Cargill and Upper Junction roads. From the north on SH1, take the road to Port Chalmers from Waitati. **Buses** from Dunedin to Port Chalmers leave from Stand 4 opposite the Countdown supermarket in Cumberland Street, dropping you off in George Street about 25 minutes later (sporadic service on Sun).

A small **information booth** sets up on the harbourfront in summer; if it's raining, you'll find it in the foyer of the **Port Chalmers Library**, 20 Beach St. The information booth and the library can both provide details of the port's more historically significant buildings and three road walks, the best being the **coastal walk** (4km; 1hr; mostly flat), which mostly follows gravel roads and offers great views of the harbour and Otago Peninsula beyond. Terns, oystercatchers, shags, gulls, herons and ducks can often be seen as you pass Back Beach.

Most people just make a day-trip from Dunedin, but you can **stay** at the quirkily designed *Billy Brown's*, 423 Aramoana Rd, Hamilton Bay, 5.5km north of Port Chalmers (Ⓣ03/472 8323, Ⓦwww.qualitydunedinbackpackers.co.nz; shares $25, rooms ❷) – it sleeps just eight, so book ahead.

For **eating** try *The Tall Poppy*, 36 George St, offering classics such as rib-eye steaks, scampi and pork loin, or go for takeaway pizza from the adjacent *Small Poppy* (opening hours can vary). Alternatively, you'll find scenic picnic spots dotted along Peninsula Beach Road, just around from the harbour. **Drinking** is best done at the 1876-built bluestone *Carey's Bay Historic Hotel*, 1km north.

The Otago Peninsula

A 35km-long crooked finger of land running northeast from Dunedin, the **OTAGO PENINSULA** divides Otago Harbour from the Pacific Ocean. This sparsely populated splinter offers outstanding **marine wildlife viewing** and affords sweeping views of the harbour on one side of the peninsula, the sea on the other, and the spread of Dunedin against its dramatic backdrop of hills.

The narrow and twisting (but smooth) harbourside road – Portobello Road and later Harington Point Road – from the city to the tip at Taiaroa Head takes less than an hour, passing a few places to stay and eat (the best covered on p.690) and stringing together most of the sights.

The chief reason for visiting the peninsula is the intriguing variety and abundance of **marine wildlife** that is drawn to its shores year round. At its tip is the small headland of **Taiaroa Head**, a protected area where several colonies of sea mammals and seabirds congregate. Unique among these is the majestic **royal albatross**, which breeds here in what is the only mainland albatross colony in the world. Also concentrated on the headland's shores are **penguins** (the little blue and the rare yellow-eyed) and **southern fur seals**, while the cliffs are home to other seabirds including three species of **shag**, **muttonbirds** (sooty shearwaters) and various species of gull. The peninsula's other beaches and inlets play host to a great variety of waders and waterfowl and, occasionally, New Zealand **sea lions**, while offshore, orca and other **whales** can sometimes be spotted.

Although there's ample opportunity to see much of the wildlife without having to pay, it's well worth forking out for one or more of the informative official **wildlife tours**, which take you up close while causing minimal disturbance to the animals.

On the way to Taiaroa Head, other worthwhile sights include the large woodland gardens and walks of **Glenfalloch**, renowned for their rhododendrons, azaleas and camellias; **Larnach Castle**, New Zealand's only castle, also set in flourishing gardens; **Fletcher House**, a delightfully restored small Edwardian villa; and the excellent Marine Studies Centre **aquarium**. A number of **scenic walks** cross both public and private land to spectacular views and unusual land formations created by lava flows.

Listings for **accommodation**, **restaurants**, **transport** and **tours** can be found under "Peninsula Practicalities" on p.690.

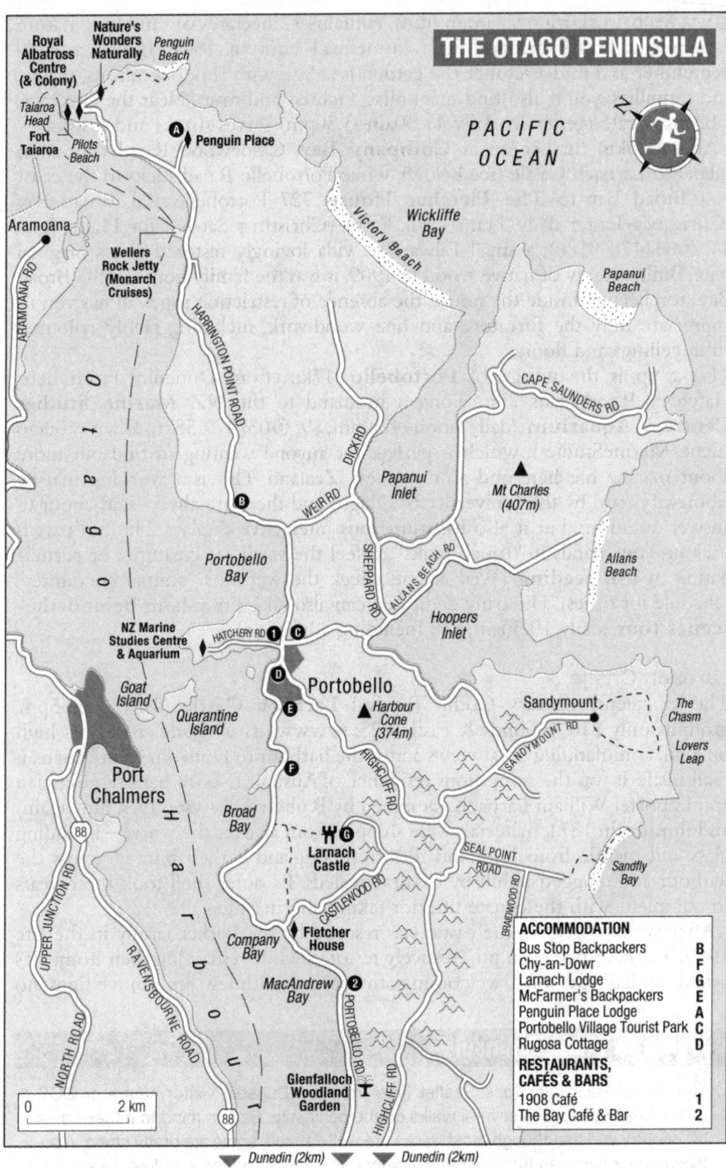

The road to Portobello

Around the head of Otago Harbour, **Portobello Road** shakes off Dunedin's scrappy southern suburbs and begins to weave its way along the harbour shoreline past little bays, many dotted with stilt-mounted boathouses in various states of disrepair.

Eleven kilometres from Dunedin, the peaceful **Glenfalloch Woodland Garden**, 430 Portobello Rd (daily dawn–dusk; $3; ⓣ03/476 1775;

Ⓦ www.albatross.org.nz/garden.htm), contains 12 hectares of rambling mature garden and bush, surrounding a homestead built in 1871. Between mid-September and mid-October the garden is ablaze with rhododendrons, azaleas and camellias; you'll also find magnolias, fuchsias and roses. Near the entrance, a licensed café (generally daily 11.30am–3.30pm) serves snacks and drinks.

Around 3km further on at **Company Bay**, Castlewood Road runs 4km inland to Larnach Castle (see below), while Portobello Road sticks to the coast past Broad Bay to **The Fletcher House**, 727 Portobello Rd, Broad Bay (Christmas–Easter daily 11am–4pm; Easter–Christmas Sat & Sun 11am–4pm; $4; Ⓣ03/478 0180), a small Edwardian villa lovingly restored to its original state. Built entirely of native wood in 1909, it was the family home of the Broad Bay storekeeper. Inside the house, the absence of restricting ropes allows you to appreciate fully the furniture and fine woodwork, including richly coloured rimu ceilings and floors.

Next up is the village of **Portobello**, 17km from Dunedin. From here, Hatchery Road leads 2km along a headland to the **NZ Marine Studies Centre & Aquarium** (daily noon–4.30pm; $9; Ⓣ03/479 5826, Ⓦ www.otago.ac.nz/MarineStudies), which is perfect for anyone wanting to find out more about marine life here and around New Zealand. This is a working marine laboratory (run by the University of Otago) and there are always staff about to answer questions, but it also has numerous interactive displays. The fun part is sticking your hands in "touch tanks" to feel the small sea creatures, or participating in **fish feeding** (Wed & Sat; check the website's "animal encounter" schedule for times). The truly dedicated can also take a one-hour **behind-the-scenes tour** (daily 10.30am; $18 including admission).

Larnach Castle

The nineteenth-century Gothic Revival **Larnach Castle** (daily 9am–5pm; grounds only $10, grounds & castle $25; Ⓦ www.larnachcastle.co.nz) sits high on a hill commanding great views across the harbour to Dunedin. More chateau than castle, it was the sumptuous residence of Australian-born banker, politician and importer William Larnach. Designed by Robert A. Lawson (yes, him again) and finished in 1871, materials were shipped from all over the world – including glass and marble from Italy and tiles from England – then punted across the harbour and dragged uphill by ox-drawn sleds. Its outer shell took three years to complete, with the ornate interior taking another nine.

After years of neglect the castle was rescued by the Barker family in the late 1960s and has since been progressively restored while remaining their home. It's grand but has a personal, welcoming atmosphere, with few prohibitive signs, no

Walks on Otago Peninsula

The *Otago Peninsula Tracks* leaflet (free from the Dunedin visitor centre or DOC office) briefly describes several walks on the peninsula. Bear in mind that they cover hill country and that though most tracks are well defined, some are pretty steep. Also, the weather here can turn cold or wet very quickly, even on the sunniest days.

One of the most accessible walks is the easy loop track to **Lovers Leap and the Chasm** (3km; 1hr; closed Aug–Oct), which crosses farmland to sheer cliffs dropping 200m to the sea, where you'll see collapsed sea caves and rock faces of layered volcanic lava flows.

The track begins from the end of Sandymount Road, a 25-minute drive from the centre of Dunedin.

The yellow-eyed penguin

Found only in southern New Zealand, the endangered **yellow-eyed penguin**, or *hoiho*, is considered the most ancient of all living penguins, but today numbers only around four thousand birds. It evolved in forests free of predators, but human disturbance, loss of habitat and the introduction of ferrets, stoats and cats have had a devastating effect. The small mainland population of just a few hundred occupies nesting areas dotted along the wild southeast coast of the South Island (from Oamaru to the Catlins), while other smaller colonies inhabit the coastal forest margins of Stewart Island and offshore islets, and New Zealand's sub-Antarctic islands of Auckland and Campbell.

Male and female adults are identical in colouring, with pink webbed feet and a bright yellow band that encircles the head, sweeping over their pale yellow eyes. Standing around 65cm high and weighing 5–6kg, they have a **life expectancy** of up to twenty years. Their **diet** consists of squid and small fish, and hunting takes them up to 40km offshore and to depths of 100m.

Maori named the bird **hoiho**, meaning "the noise shouter", because of the distinctive high-pitched calls (an exuberant trilling) it makes at night when greeting its mate at the nest. Unlike other penguins, the yellow-eyed does not migrate after its first year, but stays close to its home beach, making daily fishing trips and returning as daylight fails.

The penguins' **breeding season** lasts for 28 weeks, from mid-August to early March. Eggs are laid between mid-September and mid-October, and both parents share incubation duties for about 43 days. The eggs hatch in November and for the next six weeks the chicks are constantly guarded against predators. By the time the down-covered chicks are six or seven weeks old, their rapid growth gives them voracious appetites and both parents must fish daily to satisfy them. The fledglings enter the sea for the first time in late February or early March and journey up to 500km north to winter feeding grounds. Fewer than fifteen percent of fledged chicks reach breeding age, but those that do return to the colony of their birth.

audio tours, and intimate touches like photos on the sideboards. Look for the concealed spiral staircase in the corner of the third floor, which leads up to a terraced turret.

The castle's manicured **grounds** have also been brought back to life; keep an eye out for the handful of *Alice in Wonderland* statues, such as one of the Cheshire cat hiding in an ancient Atlas cedar tree.

Unless you have your own transport (or are on a tour), you'll have to take the Peninsula **bus** either to Company Bay, from where it's a five-kilometre (signposted) walk, uphill all the way, or to Broad Bay, from where you'll have an even steeper but shorter walk (2km). Once here, you can stop at the daytime café in the former ballroom, or **stay** overnight (see p.690).

Around Taiaroa Head

The peninsula's marine wildlife is mostly concentrated 10km east of Portobello around **Taiaroa Head**, 33km from Dunedin, where cold waters forced up by the continental shelf provide a rich and constant food source. Other than taking a tour, the best opportunities for seeing animals are on the beaches and inlets on either side of the headland. Southern fur seals can be seen at **Pilots Beach**, on the western side (follow the main road to the shore as it snakes past the Royal Albatross Centre) and from the **clifftops** on the eastern side of the headland. Pilots Beach is also home to a small colony of little blue penguins, which are best visited around dusk. A short signposted walk from the Royal

▲ Yellow-eyed penguin

Albatross Centre car park to a **cliff-edge viewing area** unfolds spectacular scenes of a spotted shag colony, while royal albatross in flight can be spied all year round from anywhere on the headland.

When **observing wildlife**, respect the animals by staying well away from them (at least 5m), and keeping quiet and still. **Penguins** are especially frightened by people and they may be reluctant to come ashore (even if they have chicks to feed) if you are on or near the beach and visible. In summer, keep to the track as they're extremely vulnerable to stress while nesting and moulting. Never get between a **seal** or **sea lion** and the sea; these animals can be aggressive and move surprisingly quickly.

The Penguin Place

For the rare privilege of entering a protected nesting area of around seventy yellow-eyed penguins, get along to the **Penguin Place**, Harington Point Road, an award-winning penguin-conservation project about 3km south of Taiaroa

Head. Carefully controlled and informative tours (Oct–early April 10.15am–dusk; early April–Sept 3.15–4.45pm; 90min; up to every 30min; $35; bookings essential on ⓣ03/478 0286, ⓦwww.penguin-place.co.nz) begin with a talk about penguins and their conservation, then a guide takes you to the beachside colony, where well-camouflaged trenches lead to several hides among the dunes. These allow extraordinary proximity to the penguins and excellent photo opportunities at pretty much any time of the day. Proceeds from the tours are used to fund the conservation work and unit that looks after injured penguins. You can **stay** overnight in budget accommodation on the farm (see p.691).

The Royal Albatross Centre and Historic Fort Taiaroa

The gateway to the only mainland colony of albatrosses in the world, the **Royal Albatross Centre** (daily: 24 Nov–April 8.30am–8pm; May–23 Nov 9am–5.30pm; free; ⓦwww.albatross.org.nz) contains galleries with interesting displays on local wildlife and history. You can buy tickets here for the centre's excellent **Royal Albatross Tour** (60min; 24 Nov–16 Sept $30; 17 Sept–23 Nov closed for breeding season; booking essential Dec–Feb and recommended at any time on ⓣ03/478 0499) which includes an introductory film and plenty of time to view the birds from an enclosed area in the reserve (binoculars provided). The **best months** for viewing are generally January and February, when the chicks hatch, and April to August, when parent birds feed their chicks. By September the chicks and adults are ready to depart and new breeding pairs start to arrive.

The Centre is also the starting point for visits to the **Historic Fort Taiaroa**, a warren of tunnels and gun emplacements originally built in 1885 when an attack from Tsarist Russia was feared, and rearmed during World War II. The main attraction is the restored Disappearing Gun (operated by hydraulics), visited on either the basic 30min tour (all year; $15) or the Unique Taiaroa Tour (24 Nov–16 Sept; 90min; $35), which combines with the Royal Albatross Tour. When the Royal Albatross Tour closes for the breeding season, the Centre offers an extended 75-minute Taiaroa Experience tour (24 Nov–16 Sept; $22) that takes you to the fort and gun, and gives you an insight into local Maori and European history in the area.

Breakfast, lunch (such as venison pies cooked in red wine) and evening meals ($12.50–25) are served at the Centre's glass-and-steel licensed café.

The royal albatross

The majestic and mysterious **albatross**, one of the world's largest seabirds, has long been the subject of reverence and superstition: the embodiment of a dead sea captain's soul, condemned to drift the oceans forever. A solitary creature, the albatross spends most of its life on the wing or at sea.

Second only in size to the wandering albatross, the mighty **royal albatross** has a wingspan of up to 3 metres. They can travel 190,000km a year at speeds of 120kph, and have a life expectancy of 45 years. The albatross mates for life, but male and female separate to fly in opposite directions around the world, returning to the same breeding grounds once every two years, and arriving within a couple of days of one another. The female lays one egg (weighing up to 500g) per breeding season, and the parents both incubate it over a period of eleven weeks.

Once the chick has hatched, the parents take turns feeding it and guarding it against stoats, ferrets, wild cats and rats. Almost a year from the start of the breeding cycle, the fledgling takes flight and the parents leave the colony and return to sea only to start the cycle again a year later.

Nature's Wonders Naturally

The road beyond the albatross colony continues through the car park a further 1.5km to **Nature's Wonders Naturally** (ⓣ0800/246 446, ⓦwww.natureswondersnaturally.com), who offer personalized adventure conservation tours around the head on specially constructed tracks in 8WD amphibious vehicles. The lively trips (daily; 1hr; $45) take in penguin-viewing areas, New Zealand fur seals, sea lions and old World War II relics. The panoramic café has sweeping views over the headland.

Peninsula practicalities

With your own transport, access to the peninsula from Dunedin is easy, either via **Portobello Road**, which snakes along the western shoreline, or the inland **Highcliff Road**, which winds up and over the hills. Dunedin visitor centre supplies the free *Visitor's Guide to the Otago Peninsula*. The public Peninsula **bus** (3–9 daily; $4) from Stand 5 on Cumberland Street in Dunedin runs halfway along the peninsula, as far as Portobello (35min), from where it's another 14km to Taiaroa Head. On weekdays a couple of services continue to Harrington Point, within 2km of Taiaroa Head.

Exploring the peninsula: cruises, tours and kayaking

Even if you have your own wheels there's a lot to be said for exploring the Otago Peninsula on an informative guided tour.

Elm Wildlife Tours ⓣ0800/356 563, ⓦwww.elmwildlifetours.co.nz. Ecologically minded guided bus tours with afternoon trips (5–6hr; $79) which visit the Albatross Centre. Trips can include an Albatross Centre tour ($112) or an hour-long Monarch Cruise ($119).

Monarch Wildlife Cruises & Tours Wharf St, Dunedin ⓣ03/477 4276 & 0800/666 272, ⓦwww.wildlife.co.nz. A comfy converted fishing boat with licensed galley is put to good use running one-hour cruises ($40) from the Wellers Rock jetty. These are worthwhile if you're driving out along the peninsula but it's worth considering their Peninsula Cruise (9am & 3.30pm; $80), which leaves from the wharf in Dunedin, cruises around Taiaroa Head then drops you at Wellers Rock (where you can visit the penguins or albatrosses; $40 extra) then returns to Dunedin by bus.

Wild Earth Adventures ⓣ03/473 6535, ⓦwww.wildearth.co.nz. For a different, often magical, perspective on the coast and its wildlife, take a sea-kayaking tour with this Dunedin-based company. Their 4hr trips ($79) go around Taiaroa Head, spending around 2hr on the water. Also assorted longer trips.

Accommodation and eating

There's more and more **accommodation** on the peninsula, though less in the way of **eating** options. You'll find a small supermarket in Portobello, along with a coffee shop. Several of the main sights – Glenfalloch, Larnach Castle, The Royal Albatross Centre and Nature's Wonders Naturally – also have excellent cafés.

Accommodation

Bus Stop Backpackers 252 Harington Point Rd, 3km north of Portobello. ⓣ03/478 0330, ⓔbackpacker@slingshot.co.nz. A retro-style beach house with harbour views and no dorms but singles, doubles and twins indoors or in a cute caravan or an old bus. If no one's about, just let yourself in and claim your bed. Rents bikes ($20 a day). Single $30, double $55, caravan $45. Breakfast available ($10).

Chy-an-Dowr 687 Portobello Rd, Broad Bay ⓣ03/478 0306, ⓦwww.chy-an-dowr.co.nz. A former general store, this big, timber two-storey property dating from 1905 sits right on the harbourfront. Three doubles (one en suite, two with separate but private bath); Wi-Fi available. ⑥

Larnach Lodge ⓣ03/476 1616, ⓦwww.larnachcastle.co.nz. In the grounds of Larnach Castle, cosy up in the rustic converted stables, containing six basic shared-bath rooms, or the individually decorated rooms in the grander *Lodge*, with twelve suite rooms such as the New Zealand room, with sheepskin rugs and unfurling peninsula views. All overnight guests get free castle admission and breakfast; you can also book a three-course dinner in the castle's elongated dining room ($54.50 per head plus wine). Stables ❺, lodge ❽

McFarmer's Backpackers 774 Portobello Rd ⓣ03/478 0389, ⓔmcfarmersbackpackers@hotmail.com. Overrun with animals and kids, and very family-friendly. No dorms, but cosy twins, doubles and a s/c cottage. Often closed in winter. Twins and doubles ❷, cottage ❸

Penguin Place Lodge Harington Point Rd ⓣ03/478 0286, ⓔpenguin.place@clear.net.nz. Simple but comfy backpackers at the Penguin Place, with great harbour views from many of the doubles and twins. $20 per person, linen hire $5. ❶

Portobello Village Tourist Park 27 Hereweka St, Portobello ⓣ03/478 0359, ⓔportobellopark@xtra.co.nz. Welcoming, well-managed campsite with a range of accommodation options and good facilities including coin-op Internet, a guest kitchen and laundry, and reams of local info. Camping $13, budget rooms ❶, s/c rooms and cabins ❸

Rugosa Cottage 1 Beconsfield Rd, Portobello ⓣ03/478 1076, ⓦ www.rugosa.co.nz. Large cottage surrounded by gorgeous gardens, offering sea and rural views. The Rose Room is a queen-size en suite, and the s/c Seafarers Cottage has a large en suite and a private garden. ❺

Eating

1908 Café 7 Harington Point Rd, Portobello ⓣ03/478 0801. Easily the finest restaurant on the peninsula, elegantly set in a 1908 house with an intimate interior and outdoor seating with views of the harbour. Updated twists on traditional New Zealand mains include chicken breast wrapped in Manuka-smoked bacon, locally caught fish, and lamb shanks braised in maple syrup and orange (all between $18–31). Open nightly plus weekend lunches.

The Bay Café & Bar 494 Portobello Rd, MacAndrew Bay ⓣ03/476 1357. Revamped dining spot with ringside views from its waterside terrace. Good steaks and unusual salads like walnut, pear and venison plus a decent wine list. Generally open for lunch and dinner daily from 11am.

South from Dunedin: Balclutha and the Catlins Coast

The rugged coastal route linking Dunedin and Invercargill is one of the least-travelled highways in New Zealand, and traverses some of the country's wildest scenery along the **Catlins Coast**. It is part of the **Southern Scenic Route** (ⓦwww.southernscenicroute.co.nz), which continues on to Te Anau in Fiordland.

The region is home to a vast tract of native forest, most of it protected as the **Catlins State Forest Park**, and consisting of rimu, rata, kamahi and silver beech. Roaring southeasterlies and the remorseless sea have shaped the coastline into plunging cliffs, windswept headlands, white-sand beaches, rocky bays and gaping caves, many of which are accessible on short bushwalks. **Wildlife** abounds, including several rare species of marine bird and mammal, and the whole region rings with birdsong most of the year, though the **birds** are at their most active during June to August when breeding.

Maori hunters once thrived in the region, one of the last refuges of the flightless moa, but by 1700 they had moved on, to be supplanted by European **whalers and sealers** in the 1830s. Two decades later, having decimated marine mammal stocks, they too moved on. Meanwhile, in 1840, Captain Edward Cattlin arrived to investigate the navigability of the river that bears his (misspelt) name, purchasing a tract of land from the chief of the Ngai Tahu. Boatloads of **loggers** soon followed, lured by the great podocarp forests. Cleared valleys were settled, bush millers supplied Dunedin with much of the wood needed for housing and, in 1872, more timber was exported from the Catlins than

The **western continuation** of the **Southern Scenic Route**, from Invercargill to Te Anau via Tuatapere, is covered in the Fiordland chapter, p.865.

anywhere else in New Zealand. From 1879, the rail line from Balclutha began to extend into the region, bringing sawmills, schools and farms with it. Milling continued into the 1930s, but gradually dwindled and today's tiny settlements are shrunken remnants of the once-prosperous logging industry.

The only stop-off point of any size between Dunedin and the Catlins Coast is **Balclutha**, which is a good place to stock up before entering the relative wilderness beyond. At Balclutha, SH1 turns inland, skirting the Catlins region before turning south to Invercargill at the town of **Gore**, a centre for brown-trout fishing. Alternatively, the SH92, a 126-kilometre stretch of road closer to the coast, is windy in places, so take it easy. While it's now sealed all the way, virtually all of the Catlin's attractions are accessed by gravel roads. Without your own transport, visit on one of several **guided tours** (see p.694).

Balclutha

The farming service town of **Balclutha**, 80km southwest of Dunedin on SH1, is cleaved in two by the **Clutha River**. There's little reason to stop longer than it takes to glean information on the Catlins or the approaches to Dunedin from the helpful **Clutha i-SITE visitor centre**, 4 Clyde St (mid-Oct to Easter Mon–Fri 8.30am–5pm, Sat & Sun 9.30am–3pm; Easter to mid-Oct Mon–Fri 8.30am–5pm, Sat & Sun 10am–2pm; ⓣ03/418 0388, ⓦwww.cluthacountry.co.nz), which has **Internet access**. **Buses** stop right outside and almost everything else is within a couple of blocks along Clyde Street.

Of the limited selection of **accommodation**, the best campsite is the small *Balclutha Motor Camp*, 56 Charlotte St (ⓣ03/418 0088, ⓔbalcluthacamp@xtra.co.nz; camping $12–14, cabins ❶), set five minutes' walk from the town centre in pleasant parkland with excellent modern facilities. You'll find both backpacker accommodation and fully self-contained motel units at the friendly *Helensborough Motor Inn*, 23 Essex St/SH1 (ⓣ0800/444 778, ⓦwww.helensboroughmotorinn.co.nz; dorms $25, units ❹).

For **eating**, the simple *Captain's Café*, 13 Clyde St, has reasonably priced lunches ($9–14) and dinners ($20–29.50), and is one of the few places in town open daily; your best bet for **drinking** is at the adjoining *Hotel South Otago*.

The Catlins Coast

The best way to enjoy the **Catlins Coast** is to absorb its unique atmosphere over at least a couple of days. From Nugget Point in South Otago (just southeast of Balclutha) to Waipapa Point in Southland (60km northeast of Invercargill), the wild scenery stretches unbroken, dense rainforest succumbing to open scrub as you cut through deep valleys and past rocky bays, inlets and estuaries. The coast is home to **penguins** (both little blue and yellow-eyed), **dolphins**, several types of seabird and, at certain times of year, migrating **whales**. Elephant **seals**, fur seals, and increasingly, the rare New Zealand **sea lion** are found on the sandy beaches and grassy areas, and **birds** – tui, resonant bellbirds, fantails, grey warblers and colourful tree-top dwellers such as kakariki and mohua – are abundant in the mossy depths of the forest.

The region is still little-travelled and outside the main settlement of Owaka you'll find a smattering of places to stay but very few places to eat or stock up. Numerous dining and accommodation business were up for sale

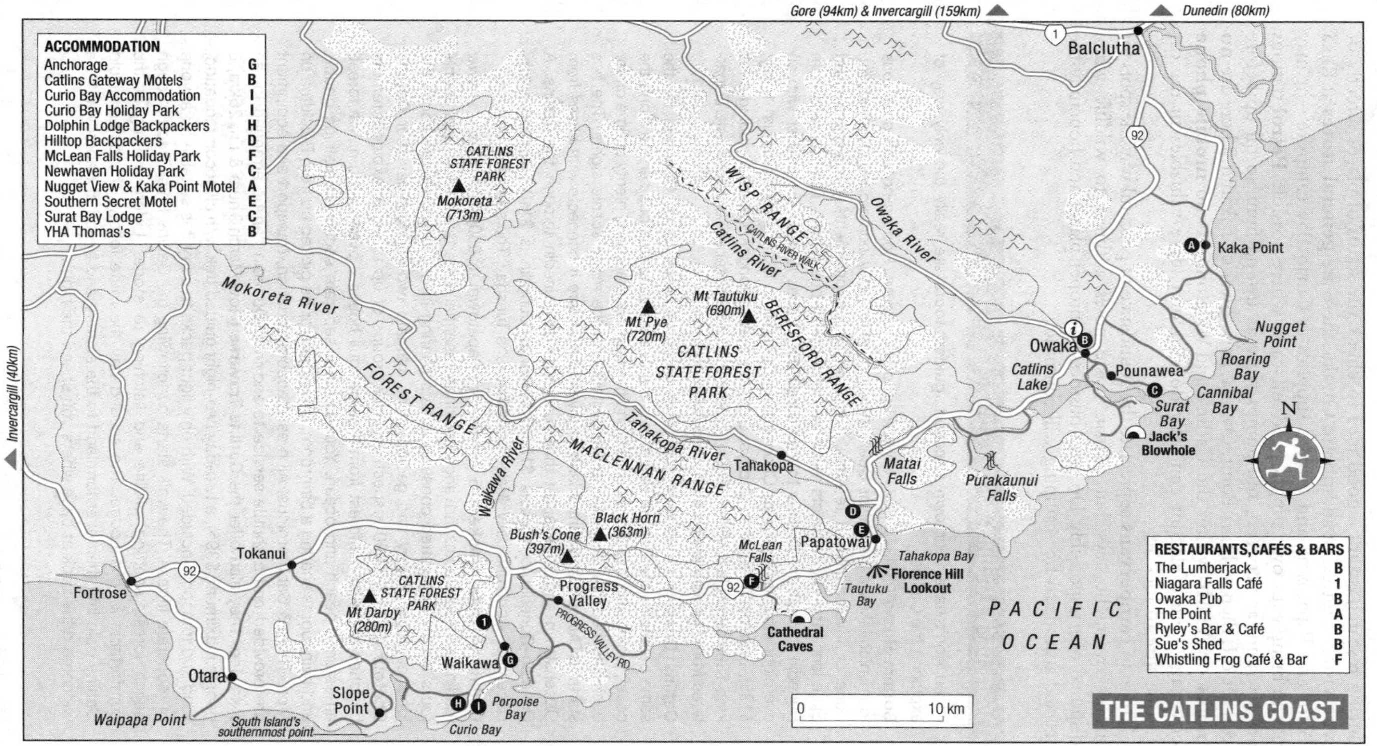

THE CATLINS COAST
ACCOMMODATION
Anchorage G
Catlins Gateway Motels B
Curio Bay Accommodation I
Curio Bay Holiday Park I
Dolphin Lodge Backpackers H
Hilltop Backpackers D
McLean Falls Holiday Park F
Newhaven Holiday Park C
Nugget View & Kaka Point Motel A
Southern Secret Motel E
Surat Bay Lodge C
YHA Thomas's B
RESTAURANTS,CAFÉS & BARS
The Lumberjack B
Niagara Falls Café 1
Owaka Pub B
The Point A
Ryley's Bar & Café B
Sue's Shed B
Whistling Frog Café & Bar F
Gore (94km) & Invercargill (159km)
Dunedin (80km)
Invercargill (40km)
Balclutha
Kaka Point
Nugget Point
Roaring Bay
Cannibal Bay
Surat Bay
Jack's Blowhole
Pounawea
Owaka
Catlins Lake
Owaka River
WISP RANGE
CATLINS RIVER WALK
Catlins River
Mt Tautuku (690m)
BERESFORD RANGE
Mt Pye (720m)
CATLINS STATE FOREST PARK
Mokoreta (713m)
Mokoreta River
FOREST RANGE
Tahakopa River
Tahakopa
MACLENNAN RANGE
Walkawa River
Black Horn (363m)
Bush's Cone (397m)
McLean Falls
Papatowai
Matai Falls
Purakaunui Falls
Tahakopa Bay
Florence Hill Lookout
Tautuku Bay
Cathedral Caves
PACIFIC OCEAN
Progress Valley
PROGRESS VALLEY RD
Tokanui
Fortrose
Mt Darby (280m)
Waikawa
Porpoise Bay
Curio Bay
Slope Point
Otara
Waipapa Point
South Island's southernmost point
0 10 km
N

during research, so it's a good idea to check the status of places directly or with visitor centres. In addition to Owaka, there are **general stores** at Kaka Point and Papatowai, and limited supplies at Curio Bay campsite – it may pay to bring your own supplies and self-cater where possible. **Petrol** stations are few and far between, and pumps close at around 5pm, so fill up before you set off, then at Kaka Point, Owaka, Papatowai or Tokanui. There are **no banks or ATMs** within the Catlins, and Vodafone has no **mobile phone coverage** here (Telecom generally does). Don't leave valuables in the car and be sure to lock it.

Those in **campervans** appreciate the abundance of peaceful wayside spots for sneaky overnight stays, but human waste poses a threat to wildlife when disposed of irresponsibly. Do your business in proper places and hopefully the relaxed attitude to free camping will continue.

Tours of the Catlins

If you don't have your own transport, **guided tours** are really the only way of exploring the Catlins.

Bottom Bus ⓣ03/4370 753, ⓦwww.bottombus.co.nz. Hop-on-hop-off small-bus tour which takes in the Catlins Coast as part of its four-day loop around Queenstown, Dunedin, Invercargill and Te Anau. It is used as a supplementary bus trip by Kiwi Experience though it attracts much less of a booze-bus crowd. The bus runs from Dunedin through the Catlins to Invercargill three times a week in summer with an overnight stop at Curio Bay. Choose from Dunedin to Invercargill (minimum 1 day; $135), Dunedin to Te Anau (2 days; $195), or several longer options including a full loop $385 taking in a Milford Sound cruise and underwater observatory visit. Departures from Dunedin are on Mon, Wed & Fri mornings.

Catlins Coaster ⓣ0800/304 333, ⓦwww.catlinscoaster.co.nz. Operated by the same people as the Bottom Bus, this is the closest thing to a bus service along the coast, picking up and dropping off along the way – and allowing plenty of time off for bush-and beach walks, wildlife encounters and the major scenic sights. The bus starts in Dunedin and runs inland to Invercargill where it connects with buses from Queenstown and Te Anau. It then runs back to Dunedin through the Catlins. A Dunedin–Dunedin loop costs $150, Invercargill–Dunedin is $140 including lunch. December–April runs daily; May–November runs Tuesday, Thursday and Sunday.

Catlins Wildlife Trackers 5 Mirren St, Papatowai ⓣ0800/228 5467, ⓦwww.catlins-ecotours.co.nz; advance bookings essential. Entertaining and inspirational tours led by committed conservationists sharing in-depth knowledge about the local ecology, history and geology. The intimate two- or four-day tour **Catlins Ecotour** ($345 & $690 respectively), for groups of up to eight, explores remote beaches and rich rainforest from their tranquil house – overlooking native forest, an estuary, beach and ocean. You stay in a separate section containing double and twin rooms sharing a bathroom. Drive there or be picked up from Balclutha on Mon, Thurs & Sat mornings. All meals, accommodation, transport and equipment are provided and a shuttle service to and from Dunedin can be arranged for an extra fee. They also offer the **Catlins Traverse** (Nov–March Thurs & Fri; 26km, 6 people maximum; $395), a two-day two-night guided trek with all accommodation, food and transport included. With only light packs to carry it is suitable for anyone of moderate fitness. The walk starts by following the Catlins River Track through beech forest, spotting wildlife and listening to stories before arriving at the comfortable *Mohua Lodge*. The second day the route follows the beautiful old Catlins train line then over farmland to the estuary and beach at Papatowai for a welcome drink back at base where you spend the night.

Kaka Point and Nugget Point

The first stop inside the Catlins is **Kaka Point**, 22km south of Balclutha, a tiny holiday community whose golden sands are patrolled by lifeguards in summer, making this a good swimming and surfing spot. Just behind the township a scenic reserve of native forest is accessible on an easy loop track (2.5km; 30min; signposted from the top of Marine Terrace).

The Point, a glass-and-wood landmark on the waterfront, is the spot to go for a coffee, a decent – and decently priced – meal or a beer by the fire; enter through the courtyard if the front door's locked. Among the handful of places to **stay** is the extremely well-appointed *Nugget View & Kaka Point Motels*, 11 Rata St (ⓣ0800/525 278, ⓦwww.catlins.co.nz; budget ❸, standard ❺, spa units ❻) which has a range of spacious units, almost all with decking and ocean views.

Nine kilometres south along the coast from Kaka Point, a car park marks the start of a fifteen-minute track to the dramatic **Nugget Point**, a steep-sided, windswept promontory rising 133m above the sea. Just offshore lie **The Nuggets**, jagged stacks of rock whose layers have been tilted vertical over time. The track ends at a still-functioning 1870 lighthouse from where you can gaze down on lively groups of honking southern fur seals. Gannets, spoonbills and three species of shag wheel overhead and nearby Roaring Bay has a hide from which you can watch **yellow-eyed penguins** (see p.687) as they leave their nests at sunrise and descend the steep grassy cliffs to the sea or as they return two hours before dark. Their progress is slow, so you need plenty of patience, and binoculars are handy.

You'll need to backtrack a few kilometres then head out to the coast again to reach the long crescent of sand known as **Cannibal Bay**, a haul-out spot for New Zealand sea lions which, from a distance, look like logs. Stroll along the beach for a closer look, but keep at least five metres away from them and back off quickly if they rear up and roar.

Owaka and Jack's Blowhole

The only settlement of any size within the Catlins is the farming town of **OWAKA**, 18km southwest of Kaka Point. Little more than a crossroads, it now harbours the whizz-bang new **Discover Destination Catlins** complex, corner of Campbell and Ryley streets (Mon–Fri 9.30am–4.30pm year-round, Sat & Sun 10am–4pm; ⓣ03/415 8371, ⓦwww.catlins-nz.com). The centre contains the **Owaka Library**, the well-curated new **Owaka Museum** (adults $5, couples $8), with evocative exhibits on local history, charting the town's fluctuating fortunes from the pioneer days to the present, and the **visitor centre**, which dispenses useful updates on eating and sleeping options, as well as DOC information. Staff here can also advise on practicalities, including a couple of farms offering **horse-riding**, plus trailhead transport for the **Catlins River Walk** (5hr one way), which traces the river through the rugged, remote high country several kilometres from town.

A gravel waterside drive runs 10km southeast from Owaka to Jack's Bay, from where a farmland track (20–30min each way; closed for lambing in Sept & Oct; $1 donation appreciated) leads to **Jack's Blowhole**, an impressive 55m-deep hole in the ground which connects though a 200m tunnel to the sea. Effectively the collapsed roof of a cave, the bottom of the hole is washed by surf at high tide, though few people seem to have ever seen it actually spout.

Opening hours for eating and sleeping options in the Catlins vary seasonally and from year to year; check with the visitor centre. Year-round, *Ryley's Bar & Café* at the *Catlins Inn*, 21 Ryley St (daily but meals usually only Thurs–Sat) has great-value pub grub. *Sue's Shed*, 3 Main Rd, serves wholesome muffins, cakes and salads through to seared cod, and also has **Internet access**; while slightly more upmarket, though still well-priced, meals are available at the central *The Lumberjack*, 3 Saunders St (mains around $25).

Accommodation

Catlins Gateway Motels Corner of Main Rd & Royal Terrace ⓣ0800/320 242, ⓔcatlinsgateway@xtra.co.nz. Spacious modern motel, and the only one in the area to offer Sky TV. ❹

Newhaven Holiday Park 325 Newhaven Rd, Surat Bay, 5km east of Owaka ⓣ03/415 8834, ⓦwww.newhavenholiday.com. Well-kept campsite with tent sites, van hookups, simple cabins and comfy tourist apartments all a 2min walk from beach and estuary. Camping $22–26 per site, cabins ❶, tourist apartments ❹

Surat Bay Lodge Surat Bay Rd, 5km east of Owaka ⓣ03/415 8099, ⓦwww.suratbay.co.nz. Backpackers tucked away in a peaceful spot where the Catlins Estuary meets the beach. There's free pick-up from Owaka, bike and kayak rental, and usually seals on the beach nearby. Dorms $25, rooms ❷

YHA Thomas's Corner of Clark & Ryley sts, Owaka ⓣ03/415 8333, ⓦwww.gaanz.co.nz. Wonderfully atmospheric hostel in a rambling early 1900s building with a slew of accommodation options, including plush en-suite rooms, as well as a pool table, two TV lounges and a well-equipped self-catering kitchen and laundry. Gay- and pet-friendly. Camping $8, powered sites $15, dorms $22, rooms ❶

Southwest to Papatowai

A couple of minor waterfalls lie to the southwest, both accessed along pleasant nature trails. The three-tiered **Purakaunui Falls** lie in a scenic reserve of silver beech and podocarp, signposted off the main road 14km from Owaka. There's a picnic area here and an easy track (10min) through the forest to a viewing platform.

Five kilometres south of the Purakaunui turn-off, the pretty **Matai Falls** (15min return) are reached along an easy trail through 10m-high native fuchsia trees, easily identified by their peeling pinkish bark and, in early summer, small red-and-blue trumpet flowers.

Across the estuary of the McLennan River, the small settlement of **PAPATOWAI** offers a general store, several forest and beach walks and an excellent **eco-tour** with the Catlins Wildlife Trackers (see box, p.697), plus the start of the **Catlins Top Track** (see box, p.697). In a cheerful old bus beside the main road, The **Lost Gypsy Gallery** (hours vary, generally closed Wed & June–Aug; free – cash only for purchases) makes a quirky stop, if only to play with the handmade automata built on site from recycled materials and old electrical components. Everything is for sale, from teabag dunkers to dancing penguins.

There are a few good **places to stay** including the small and delightful *Hilltop Backpackers*, 77 Tahakopa Valley Rd (ⓣ03/415 8028, ⓦwww.hilltopbackpackers.co.nz; dorms $25, rooms & en suite ❸), set on a farm signposted 1km inland from Papatowai, which occupies a pair of well-kept cottages with astounding views. Bring cash as they don't accept credit cards. Back on the main road, the *Southern Secret Motel* (ⓣ03/415 8600, ⓔsouthernsecret@xtra.co.nz; ❸), opposite the Papatowai general store, looks like an ordinary home on the outside but has four fabulously artistic rooms done out in Pacific colours, with mosquito net-draped wrought iron beds, sparkling new bathrooms and a free library of over 300 videos.

Porpoise Bay and Waikawa

On the main road 2.5km southeast of Papatowai, **Florence Hill Lookout** presents a fabulous panoramic view of Tautuku Bay, a magnificent crescent of pale sand backed by extensive forest. For a closer look, call in at the **Tautuku Boardwalk** (20–30min return), with a raised walkway nature trail over some lakeside marshes.

The Catlins Top Track

The longest and most varied walk in the region is the **Catlins Top Track** (22km loop), which begins and ends at Papatowai and crosses sweeping beaches, farmland and privately owned bush, delivering fascinating geology, a great variety of flora and fauna, and true tranquillity. It can be walked in a day (9–10hr; $15) but most people of moderate fitness walk it leisurely in two days ($35 including accommodation). The track is managed by Catlins Wildlife Trackers (ⓣ0800/228 5467, ⓦwww.catlins-ecotours.co.nz), who offer pack transfer for $30 per group. All walkers are given an excellent booklet that details each section of the walk accompanied by a map.

The first day takes about six hours, starting with a walk along one of the finest open beaches in the Catlins, before following an old coach road and climbing to weathered sandstone cliffs and the night's accommodation beyond. The second day takes half the time and is very different: you pass through bush containing ancient trees and emerge at the walk's highest point (just over 300m) to spectacular views before following a former railway line to the McLennan River and then continue to the pre-arranged pick-up point.

Numbers are limited to six overnight walkers, who stay in a converted 1960s trolley bus high up on a spectacular viewpoint, which has one double bed and four single bunks, electric lighting, a gas camping stove with cutlery and dishes, a gas heater in winter and its own water supply. There's even a separate loo with a view. Bring your own food, drinking water and sleeping bag.

Some 11km southeast of Papatowai a turn-off leads to **Cathedral Caves** ($3), the grandest and most accessible of the fifteen-or-so caves that punctuate this part of the coast. Its soaring walls were created by furious seas, and can only be entered two hours either side of low tide (they may also close at certain times of the year due to sand erosion): check with local visitor centres, or look at the entrance. Set aside an hour for the bush- and beach walk, more if you want to spend time exploring other caves in the area.

A kilometre or so further along the main road, Rewcastle Road runs 3km to the car park for the picturesque **McLean Falls** (30min return), reached along a rainforest walk. Easily the most impressive of the falls hereabouts, it is best in the late afternoon when sun strikes the main cascade. Just past the turn-off from the main road to the falls is the brand-new, eco-friendly *McLean Falls Holiday Park*, 29 Rewcastle Rd (ⓣ03/415 8338; ⓦwww.catlinsnz.com; camping $31, shares $25, cabins, rooms & cottages ❷–❺), whose state-of-the-art accommodation is built from materials that blend into the lush surroundings. The on-site *Whistling Frog Café & Bar* is a good spot for breakfast, lunch or dinner for guests and non-guests alike, with farm produce, strong espresso and genuinely friendly, personal service; chef-prepared mains like rosemary-braised lamb shanks cost around $32.50, with desserts including a tangy rhubarb crumble around $9.

About 20km on, off the SH92 en route to Waikawa, the *Niagara Falls Café* is a hidden culinary gem, serving sophisticated home-made café fare such as veggie burgers, fish and warming soups. Nearby, the fishing village of **WAIKAWA** is home to the small **Waikawa District Museum** (daily 10.30am–4.30pm; gold coin donation), with an interesting exhibition on seafarers and logging. The museum also doubles as the area's visitor centre. Limited **accommodation** in the area includes the waterfront *Anchorage*, 52 Antrim St (ⓣ03/246 8585, ⓔmccolgan@xtra.co.nz; ❹), whose comfortable units look out over the estuary.

Curio Bay and Slope Point

At the western end of Porpoise Bay, a headland is occupied by the *Curio Bay Holiday Park* (ⓣ03/246 8897; camping $15 per site, powered sites $25), a

The New Zealand sea lion and Hector's dolphin

Two extremely rare species – the New Zealand or **Hooker's sea lion** (*Phocarctos hookeri*) and **Hector's dolphin** (*Cephalarhynchus hectori*) – are found only in New Zealand waters.

Hooker's sea lions mostly live around the sub-Antarctic Auckland Islands, 460km south of the South Island, but some breeding also takes place on the Otago Peninsula, along the Catlins Coast and around Stewart Island. The large, adult male sea lions are black to dark brown, have a mane over their shoulders, weigh up to 400kg and reach lengths of over 3m. Adult females are buff to silvery grey and much smaller – less than half the weight and just under 2m. Barracuda, red cod, octopus, skate and, in spring, paddle crabs make up their diet, with Hooker's sea lions usually diving 200m or less for four or five minutes – although they are capable of achieving depths of up to 500m. Pups are born on the beach, then moved by the mother at about six weeks to grassy swards, shrubland or forest, and suckled for up to a year.

Sea lions prefer to haul out on sandy beaches and in summer spend much of the day flicking sand over themselves to keep cool. Unlike seals they don't fear people. If you encounter one on land, give it a wide berth of at least five metres (30m during the Dec–Feb breeding season) and if it rears up and roars, back off quickly – they can move surprisingly swiftly. Never antagonize or attempt to feed them.

The **Hector's dolphin**, with its distinctive black and white markings, is the smallest dolphin in the world and, with a population under 4000, is also one of the rarest. It's only found in New Zealand inshore waters – mostly around the coast of the South Island – with eastern concentrations around Banks Peninsula, Te Waewae Bay and Porpoise Bay, plus western communities between Farewell Spit and Haast. They roam up to 8km from shore in winter, but in summer prefer shallow waters within 1km of the coastline, catching mullet, arrowsquid, red cod, stargazers and crabs. Female dolphins are typically a little larger than the males, growing to 1.2–1.4m and weighing 40–50kg. They give birth from November to mid-February, and calves stay with their mothers for up to two years.

In summer and autumn, the tiny resident population at Porpoise Bay regularly enters the surf zone and even comes within 10m of the beach. Hector's Dolphins are shy and being disturbed can impact on feeding, which in turn affects their already low breeding rate. If you're spending time around them, be sure to follow DOC rules (posted locally), which essentially forbid, touching, feeding, surrounding and chasing dolphins and encourage you to keep a respectful distance. Swimming around pods with juveniles is also forbidden, and in summer most pods will have juveniles.

friendly year-round campsite with a tiny store, sites sheltered by flax, and wonderful views east along Porpoise Bay and west into **Curio Bay**. Hector's dolphins cavort in the surf of Porpoise Bay, while yellow-eyed penguins can be viewed (mostly at sunrise and at the end of the day) on the Curio Bay side, from the top of McColgan's Loop. As always, keep your distance from the animals.

A few hundred metres west along Curio Bay, a wave-cut platform reveals a fine **petrified forest** (1hr tours run by *Curio Bay Holiday Park* $20), its fossilised Jurassic trees clearly visible at low tide. Over 180 million years ago, when most of New Zealand still lay beneath the sea, this would have been a broad, forested floodplain. Today, the seashore, composed of several layers of forest buried under blankets of volcanic mud and ash, is littered with fossilized tree stumps and fallen logs.

Apart from the campsite, you can stay nearby at *Dolphin Lodge Backpackers*, 529 Curio Bay Rd (Ⓣ03/246 68 579, Ⓔdolphinsurf@extra.co.nz; dorms $22, linen hire $3, rooms ❶), a beautifully sited hostel on the dunes with a common room and veranda from where you can watch the waves roll in. Manager Nick Smart heads up the local **Catlins Surf School** (1hr 30min lesson $40 including wetsuit and board hire).

From Curio Bay it's 16km along unsealed roads to **Slope Point**, where a farmland walk (40min return; closed Sept & Oct for lambing) brings you to the South Island's southernmost point. Continuing west, a ten-minute drive takes you to **Waipapa Point**, 22km beyond Curio Bay, the site of New Zealand's worst civilian shipwreck, in 1881, when 131 lives were lost on SS *Tararua*. The lighthouse that now stands on the point was erected soon after and you may now see fur seals and sea lions on the golden beach and rocky platform at its foot.

Back on the main road, it is another 10km to the windswept trees of **Fortrose**, before a bland sixty-kilometre stretch of SH92 takes you to Invercargill.

Gore and around

The quiet Southland farming town of **GORE**, seventy-one kilometres west of Balclutha, is a pleasant enough transit point at the intersection of routes from Dunedin to Te Anau and Invercargill. Dominated by the Hokonui Hills, Gore spans the Mataura River ("reddish swirling water"), and claims to be the **brown trout capital** of the world – celebrated by an enormous fish statue in the town centre. During the fishing season (Oct–April) you can pit your wits against a brown trout with tackle rented from B&B Sports, 65 Main St (Ⓣ03/208 0801) and a license from the visitor centre ($18 per 24hr, $96 full season).

As New Zealand's home of **country music**, Gore comes alive for eight days in autumn for the Gold Guitar Awards (late May & early June; Ⓣ03/208 1978, Ⓦwww.goldguitars.co.nz), when hundreds of would-be country stars and a few established performers roll into town.

Stop by the **Hokonui Heritage Centre**, on the corner of Norfolk Street & Hokonui Drive (Mon–Fri 8.30am–5pm, Sat & Sun 9.30am–4pm), which contains the **i-SITE visitor centre** (same hours; Ⓣ03/203 9288, Ⓦwww.gorenz.com), a small local **history museum** (gold coin donation), and the entertaining **Hokonui Moonshine Museum** ($5), detailing decades of illicit whisky distillation deep in the local bush-covered hills, which began in 1836 and reached a peak during a regional fifty-year-long local Prohibition from 1903. The only people actually caught in the act were the Kirk brothers, whose cow shed and stills are on display.

Across the street, the **Eastern Southland Art Gallery** (Mon–Fri 10am–4.30pm, Sat & Sun 1–4pm; free) has a nationally significant collection of art bequeathed by expat Kiwi sexologist, Dr John Money, who amassed works including some majestic African carvings and career-spanning pieces from the private collection of Ralph Hotere.

Fans of vintage aircraft should head 17km west along the road to Queenstown (SH94) to the **Old Mandeville Airfield**, where you can take to the air on joyrides (from $70 for 10min to $185 for 30min; contact Croydon Aircraft Company Ⓣ03/208 9755) in a Tiger Moth, Fox Moth or Dragonfly. You're welcome to look around the hangar, where renovation is constantly in progress on all sorts of aircraft, and there's memorabilia-filled restaurant/bar (closed Mon).

Gore lies on the major bus route between Dunedin, Invercargill and Te Anau. Buses drop off at the visitor centre, where you can book **accommodation** and **transport** and pick up information on the area. Most **eating** options concentrate around Main Street, including *Howl at the Moon*, 2 Main St, an airy café/bar with a Kiwi cowboy feel, serving a good range of snacks and bigger meals for under $28. The bar hots up Friday and Saturday nights.

Invercargill and around

Many visitors pass straight through **INVERCARGILL**, regarding it as little more than a waystation en route to Stewart Island or the Catlins Coast. But this lively city, which was settled in the mid-1850s and sprawls over an exposed stretch of flat land at the head of the New River Estuary, is thriving. In 2000, community contributions allowed its main centre of learning, the Southern Institute of Technology (SIT), to offer free tuition for New Zealand and Australian residents (with lower-than-usual fees for international students) for all of its courses, including degrees in cutting-edge fields like Environmental Management and Fashion and Design Technology. As a result, Invercargill's population has swelled to 54,000, and its arts scene and nightlife continue to burgeon.

To the south, at the tip of a small peninsula, lies **Bluff**, the departure point for ferries to **Stewart Island** (see p.705).

Arrival, information and city transport

Direct domestic flights from Christchurch and Stewart Island land at Invercargill's **airport**, 2.5km southwest of the city centre. Blue Star taxis (Ⓣ03/218 6079; $15) provide transport into town; an airport shuttle service is provided by Executive Rental Cars (Ⓣ03/214 3434, $10 per passenger). Knightrider **buses** from Christchurch pull up at the corner of Tay and Jed streets, but all others stop outside the excellent **i-SITE visitor centre**, 108 Gala St (Dec–April Mon–Fri 8am–6pm Sat & Sun 8am–5pm; May–Nov daily 8am–5pm; Ⓣ03/214 6243, Ⓦwww.visitinvercargillnz.com), in the foyer of the Southland Museum, where you can pick up the *Event time in Southland* (good for local events listings) and get coin-operated **Internet access**. While here, pick up the Invercargill Bus Timetable outlining the city's dozen **bus** routes ($2, all-day pass $4.50; timetable information Ⓣ03/218 7170), which mostly make loops out from the centre. There are also a couple of free bus circuits; a notice board outside the library on Dee Street posts schedules.

The city's **DOC office**, on Level 7 of the State Insurance Building on Don Street (Mon–Fri 9am–4.30pm; Ⓣ03/214 4589), has information on walks and wildlife in the Catlins, Stewart Island and Fiordland.

Accommodation

Accommodation prices this far south are very reasonable, and there's a good choice in the centre close to the transport links, but note that Tuesday and Wednesday nights fill up quickly when business reps converge on the town.

295 on Tay 295 Tay St Ⓣ0800/295 295, Ⓦwww.295ontay.co.nz. Modern and palatial motel with all mod cons including broadband Internet access and full kitchens, some rooms have spa baths. ❺

Admiral Court Motor Lodge 327 Tay St Ⓣ0800/111 122, Ⓦwww.admiralcourt.co.nz. Ten spotless, fully s/c units with extras including breakfast delivered to your door, plungers with freshly ground coffee, Wi-Fi, and transport to and from the airport; a handful of units also have spa baths. ❺

Awa-Moa 110 Leet St Ⓣ03/214 3164, Ⓔmgmiller@southnet.co.nz. Extremely central B&B/homestay offering double rooms that share a guest bathroom. Good rates for singles. ❺

Burtonwood B&B Gala St Ⓣ03/218 8884, Ⓦwww.burtonwood.co.nz. Romantic B&B in a renovated Edwardian home overlooking Queens Park. Most of the olive- and rose-toned rooms have en-suite bathrooms, and a substantial continental breakfast is served (cooked breakfasts extra). Not suitable for kids under 12. ❻

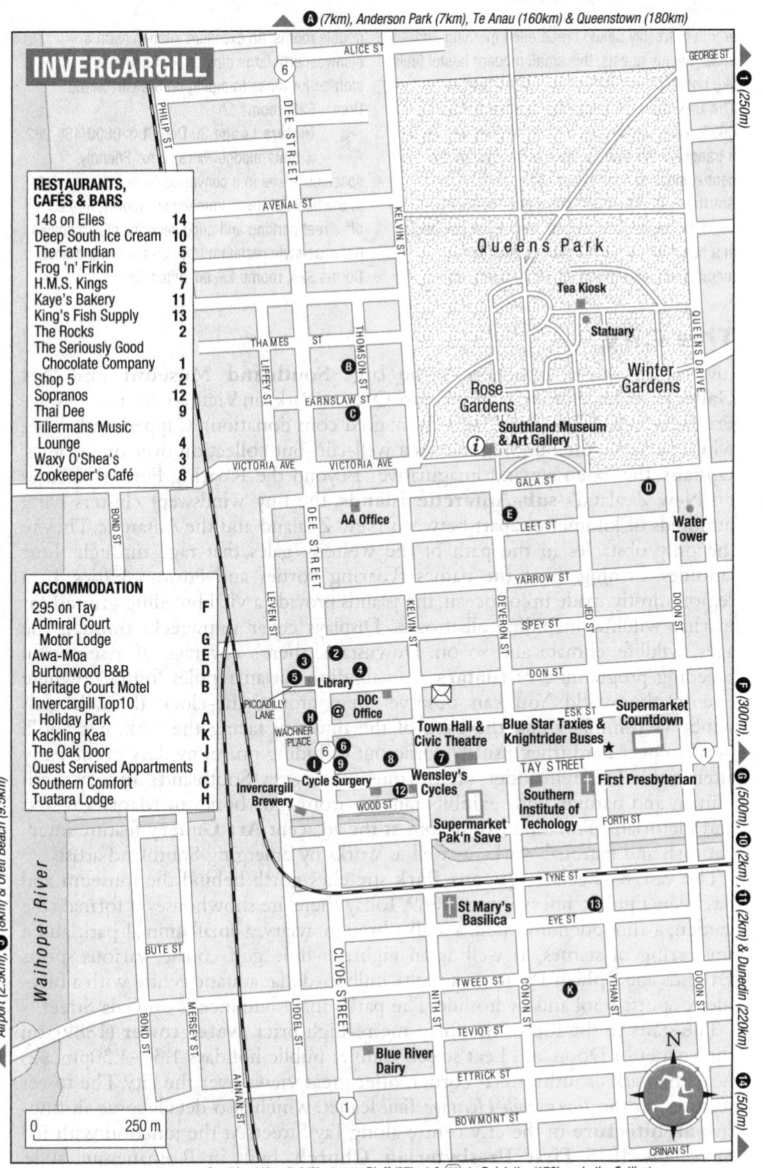

Heritage Court Motel 50 Thomson St ⓣ0800/243 748 & 03/214 7911, ⓦwww.heritagecourt.co.nz. The most reasonably priced motel just outside the centre in a quiet sunny spot near Queens Park and the visitor centre, with microwaves (sometimes full cooktops) in all units, as well as toasty electric blankets and a handy guest laundry. ❹

Invercargill Top 10 Holiday Park 77 McIvor Rd, 9km north of the city centre ⓣ0800/486 873, ⓦwww.invercargilltop10.co.nz. Upscale campsite with a high standard of facilities. Camping $28–30 per site, cabins ❸, tourist cabin ❸, unit ❹

Kackling Kea 225 Tweed St ⓣ03/214 7950 ⓦwww.kacklingkea.com. With thick duvets, the aroma of freshly baked bread each morning and under twenty guests, this small modern hostel feels like home. Dorms $23, shares $24, room ❷

The Oak Door 22 Taiepa Rd, Otatara ⓣ03/213 0633, ⓔblstuart@xtra.co.nz. A modern, airy B&B in a tranquil bush setting, 3min drive west of the centre, close to Oreti Beach. ❺

Southern Comfort 30 Thomson St ⓣ03/218 3838, ⓔcoupers@xtra.co.nz. Very good city hostel in a beautifully kept Victorian villa set among manicured lawns. Pleasant, clean dorms and double rooms, an excellent kitchen (with a dishwasher!), large dining room and free luggage storage for those tramping on Stewart Island. Dorms $23, rooms ❷

Tuatara Lodge 30 Dee St ⓣ0800/488 282, ⓔtuataralodge@xtra.co.nz. Friendly, spacious hostel in a converted bank building, right in the heart of town. Immaculate rooms, limited off-street parking and good security, plus a chilled Balinese-style restaurant/bar on the ground floor. Dorms $25, rooms ❸, en suites ❹

The City

Invercargill's chief attraction is the large **Southland Museum and Art Gallery**, at the southern entrance to Queens Park on Victoria Avenue (Mon–Fri 9am–5pm, Sat & Sun 10am–5pm; gold coin donation). Capped with a big white pyramid, the building houses a well-laid-out collection over two storeys. Upstairs, the extensive and imaginative "Beyond the Roaring Forties" focuses on New Zealand's **sub-Antarctic islands**, the tiny windswept clusters lying hundreds of kilometres apart between New Zealand and the Antarctic. They're the only obstacles in the path of the westerly gales that rage through these latitudes, earning them the names Roaring Forties and Furious Fifties. In a region mostly made up of ocean, the islands provide a vital breeding ground for marine wildlife, including albatrosses. Displays cover shipwrecks through the ages, wildlife, climate and so on. Downstairs, there's coverage of a successful breeding programme of **tuatara** – small, dinosaurian reptiles found nowhere else in the world. You can observe them around-the-clock through glass windows running along the back of the museum facing the park, but you'll need to peer hard (they usually come out of hiding on sunny days in the early afternoon). The remainder of the museum covers Southland's history, both human and natural, with exhibits ranging from moa bones to Maori artefacts and Victoriana. Rotating exhibitions at the adjacent **Art Gallery** feature international and national works, as well as works by emerging Southland artists.

The vast, 81-hectare **Queens Park** stretches north behind the museum and has been a public reserve since 1869. Today there are showhouses, a formal rose garden, a rhododendron dell, a walk-through aviary, a small animal park and a smattering of statues, as well as an eighteen-hole golf course, various sports grounds and **Splash Palace** – a multi-million-dollar aquatic centre with a fifty-metre sports pool and hydroslide. The park's main entrance is on Gala Street.

The stairs to the top of the forty-metre-high brick **water tower** (1889), on the corner of Doon and Leet streets (Sun & public holidays 1.30–4.30pm; $2) near the park's southeastern corner, offer great views over the city. The tower features on the *Invercargill Heritage Trail* leaflet, which also details some distinctive **architecture** in the city centre along Tay Street. At the junction with Jed Street the 1915 **First Presbyterian Church**, built in Romanesque style, displays impressive ornamental brickwork. It's usually closed apart from services but you can pop into the adjacent office during standard business hours and ask to peek inside.

Near the corner with Deveron Street stands the magnificent **Civic Theatre**, completed in 1906 in English Renaissance style with ornamental parapets carved from white Oamaru stone. The elegant copper dome of the Catholic **St Mary's Basilica**, two streets south, is visible for miles around, but you'll need to wait for a church service to see the sumptuous Oamaru stone interior.

Connoisseurs of fine beer won't want to miss a fun, very informal look around the **Invercargill Brewery**, 8 Wood St (Ⓣ03/214 5070; Ⓦwww.invercargillbrewery.co.nz; factory shop Mon–Thurs 11am–5.50pm, Fri 11am–6pm, Sat 11am–4pm, behind-the-scenes visits from 1pm; free), followed by a tasting session. Brewer Steve Nally makes half a dozen varieties, including Biman (pronounced BEE-man), specially created to pair with spiced curries, and Pitch Black, with coffee aromas, as well as limited seasonal productions like boysenberry or smoked beer.

Anderson Park, Oreti Beach and Tiwai Point

On the outskirts of Invercargill, 7km north of the city centre, the beautiful grounds of **Anderson Park** provide the setting for the atmospheric **Anderson Park Art Gallery** (daily 10.30am–5pm; gold coin donation during special exhibitions, otherwise free), housed in a 1925 neo-Georgian mansion built for a local businessman. Designed by Christchurch architect Cecil Wood, it was constructed from reinforced concrete and set against a backdrop of forest. During October, a spring exhibition of recent Kiwi art replaces the permanent collection of traditional and contemporary New Zealand art. Behind the gallery, **The Maori House**, built in the early 1920s and used for dances, has a doorway and porch decorated with carvings by Tene Waitere, a renowned Rotorua carver. There is no bus service out here; a taxi will cost about $20 one way.

Oreti Beach, 10km west of the city centre, is a beautiful broad expanse of fine sand, sweeping 30km right around to the seaside resort of Riverton to the west, and giving great views of Stewart Island and Bluff. Burt Munro of *The World's Fastest Indian* movie fame used the beach for many of his speed motorbike trials. In summer, it's popular for swimming (surf patrols operate when busy), yachting and water-skiing, but windy days cause violent sandstorms. There's no bus service to the beach, but if driving you can take your vehicle out onto the smooth, hard-packed sand (though chances are your vehicle insurance won't cover you if you get stuck).

Southland's biggest employer is the sprawling Tiwai Point **aluminium smelter**, 25km south of town. You can join a surprisingly interesting **free tour** (generally Mon, Wed & Fri at 10am; booking and safety briefing over the phone essential a day in advance, Ⓣ03/218 5440).

Eating and drinking

Invercargill has enough decent eateries to keep you sated, but the real treat here is the **artisan produce**. Pick up award-winning sheep's cheese from the *Blue River Dairy*, 111 Nith St (Ⓣ03/218 7367; Ⓦwww.blueriverdairy.co.nz); baked goods (including bargain-priced bags of broken biscuits) at *Kaye's Bakery*, 19 Onslow St (Ⓣ03/216 6065); creamy ices (including some made from the Invercargill Brewing Company's Pitch Black beer) from the factory/HQ of *Deep South Ice Cream*, 122 Rockdale Rd (Ⓣ03/216 5685); and fine handmade chocolates from *The Seriously Good Chocolate Company*, 20 Windsor St (Ⓣ03/217 5107; Ⓦwww.seriouslygoodchocolate.com), which has an attached tearoom.

Look out for local **seafood**, including excellent Bluff oysters (fresh April–Oct) and blue cod, as well as **muttonbird**, which you'll find on menus throughout town. You can buy the fresh seafood on display at *King's Fish Supply*, 59 Ythan St (Mon–Tue 8.30am–7.30pm, Wed–Sat 8.30am–8.30pm, Sun 4–8.30pm) to take away (priced by weight) or have it cooked to order while you wait (extra $1); they also do incredibly cheap, delicious fish and chips ($3.20) plus some landlubbers' meals such as burgers.

A number of the city's **bars** transform into dance venues as the evening wears on, though the town is usually quiet until Thursday night. Check *The Southland Times* for gigs by **local bands**. There are also a handful of **nightclubs**, which are at their liveliest during university term time. The five-screen Reading **cinema** at 29 Dee St (☎03/211 1555) has reduced ticket prices on Tuesday.

148 on Elles 148 Elles Rd, corner of Crinan St ☎03/216 1000. An elegant linen-and-candles dinner restaurant in a two-storey 1912 building 1km southeast of the centre. Reserve ahead for dishes like sirloin with cognac and field mushrooms, rack of lamb, or Mediterranean vegetable polenta (mains $20–33).

The Fat Indian Piccadilly Lane, 38 Dee St ☎03/218 9933. Open-kitchen curry house turning out a lengthy selection of aromatic Indian cuisine (mains $13.50–17.50), including daily blackboard specials. Lunch & dinner daily; licensed and BYO wine.

Frog 'n' Firkin 31 Dee St. Popular pub that's positively hopping after midnight late in the week when it turns into a fun dance venue.

H.M.S. Kings 80 Tay St ☎03/218 3443. Quality seafood restaurant stocked by King's Fish Supply where you can try fresh Bluff oysters in season and excellent local fish in a glossy timber nautical dining room. Lunch mains around $20, dinner mains around $30. Closed Sat & Sun lunch.

The Rocks Courtville Place, 101 Dee St ☎03/218 7597. The varied menu at this small, arty restaurant ranges from pork loin with apple sauce to "horse" (actually eye fillet of beef) plus plenty of pasta dishes. Lunch mains $16–17, dinner mains $28.50–32.50. Closed Sun.

Shop 5 Courtville Place, 101 Dee St. Attached to *The Rocks*, and one of the classier bars in town, though still casual and fun. Fri & Sat only from 5pm–late; bar menu available.

Sopranos 33 Tay St. Decently priced Mafia-themed gourmet pizza joint and buzzy early-evening bar. Closed Mon.

Thai Dee 9 Dee St ☎03/214 5112. Lime-infused Penang curry and stir-fried ginger root with vegetables are among the tangy dishes at this modern Thai restaurant. Closed Sat & Sun lunch.

Tillermans Music Lounge 16 Don St ☎03/218 9240. Popular bar with pool tables, and a focal point for (often fairly offbeat) live music on Sat nights.

Waxy O'Shea's 90 Dee St. Convivial and more convincing than average Irish bar with good music, occasionally live.

Zookeeper's Café 50 Tay St. Zany split-level bar/café easily identified by the corrugated iron elephant on the roof outside. Serves brunch, bar food, snacks (including an outstanding seafood chowder) and meals from $15–25, as well as local beers and wines.

Listings

Automobile Association 47 Gala St ☎03/218 9033.

Bike rental Cycle Surgery, 2l Tay St (☎03/218 8055) rents good-quality mountain bikes for $35 while Wensley's Cycles, corner of Tay & Nith sts (☎03/218 6206) rents from $20 a day.

Internet access At the visitor centre, the library and Comzone, 45 Dee St.

Left luggage At visitor centre ($2 a day).

Library Invercargill Public Library is at 50 Dee St (Mon–Fri 9am–8pm, Sat 10am–1pm, Sun 1–4pm; ☎03/218 7025).

Medical treatment Southland Hospital, on Kew Rd (☎03/218 1949), has a 24hr accident and emergency department. For illness and minor accidents outside surgery hours, contact the Urgent Doctor Service at 103 Don St (☎03/218 8821; Mon–Fri 5–10pm; Sat, Sun & public holidays 24hr).

Pharmacy Inside the Countdown supermarket (Mon–Thurs & Sat–Sun 8.30am–8pm, Fri 8.30am–9pm).

Police The central police station is at 117 Don St (☎03/211 0400).

Post office The main post office is at 51 Don St, near the junction with Kelvin St (Mon–Fri 8.30am–5pm, Sat 10am–12.30pm).

Bluff

Twenty-seven kilometres south of Invercargill, overlooking Foveaux Strait, is the small run-down fishing town of **BLUFF** and its man-made harbour. This is the departure point for ferries to **Stewart Island** (see p.705). You won't need more than a couple of hours to get a good look at the place, but without a car this will involve a good deal of walking, as the town spreads along the shoreline for about 6km.

Continuously settled since 1824, Bluff is the oldest European town in New Zealand. It's showing its age a little, but the busy **harbour** exports Southland's meat, timber, aluminium, fish and wool, and imports a variety of goods from overseas. In addition Foveaux Strait yields a highly sought-after delicacy – the sweet **Bluff oyster**. This deepwater shellfish is dredged from April until September then processed in local oyster sheds before being sent all over the country. Between June and August you can buy them direct at factory prices from several places on the waterfront including Johnson's Oysters (daily 8am–5pm; ⓣ03/212 8665). The annual **Bluff Oyster and Southland Seafood Festival** (ⓦwww.bluffoysterfest.co.nz) celebrates these slimy little bivalve molluscs on the third weekend in April at the Bluff Events Centre (tickets around $25) with cook-offs, oyster-opening competitions and street entertainment.

The Town

Doubling as the town's **visitor centre**, Bluff's small **Maritime Museum** (Mon–Fri 10am–4.30pm, Sat & Sun 1–5pm; $2), on Foreshore Road as you enter town from Invercargill, has historical displays focusing on whaling, the harbour development, oyster harvesting and shipwrecks. Pride of place is given to a triple-expansion steam engine, taken from a steam tug, *Monica*, which spent most of its life working the harbour.

Although Bluff isn't the South Island's most southerly point (that's Slope Point in the Catlins), at **Stirling Point** a multi-armed signpost balancing the one at the other end of the country at Cape Reinga marks the distance to major cities around the world, as well as the equator (5133km) and the South Pole (4810km). From the car park at the end of the road you can set out on a couple of easy walks: the **Foveaux Walkway** (6.6km; 2hr one way; mostly flat) which follows the coast back to town; and the **Topuni Track** (2km one way; 45min; 265m ascent) which climbs to **Bluff Hill Lookout**, with 360-degree views encompassing Stewart Island, 35km away. The lookout is also accessible by road from Bluff: follow Lee Street, opposite the ferry wharf for 3km.

Practicalities

Bluff is a twenty-minute drive down SH1 from central Invercargill. Stewart Island Experience (ⓣ0800/000 511) runs a regular bus service from Invercargill ($18 each way), to connect with the ferry. For details on ferry sailings to Stewart Island, see p.707.

Good **accommodation** in Bluff is limited. In town, try *The Lazy Fish*, 35 Burrows St (ⓣ03/212 7245, ⓦwww.thelazyfish.co.nz; room & cottage ❺), which has a double room, plus a self-contained cottage sleeping four with its own sunny courtyard. Alternatively, drive 2km south to *Land's End*, Stirling Point (ⓣ03/212 7575, ⓦwww.landsend.net.nz; ❺), seven well-cared-for en-suite rooms above the **café** of the same name. Breakfast (included) is served in the café, which is also the best place for lunch, or dinner by reservation (non-guests welcome): specialities include pan-fried blue cod, Stewart Island greenlip mussels and local cheese platters.

Stewart Island

New Zealand's third main island is the relatively unknown **STEWART ISLAND**, separated from the mainland by Foveaux Strait. Most of it is

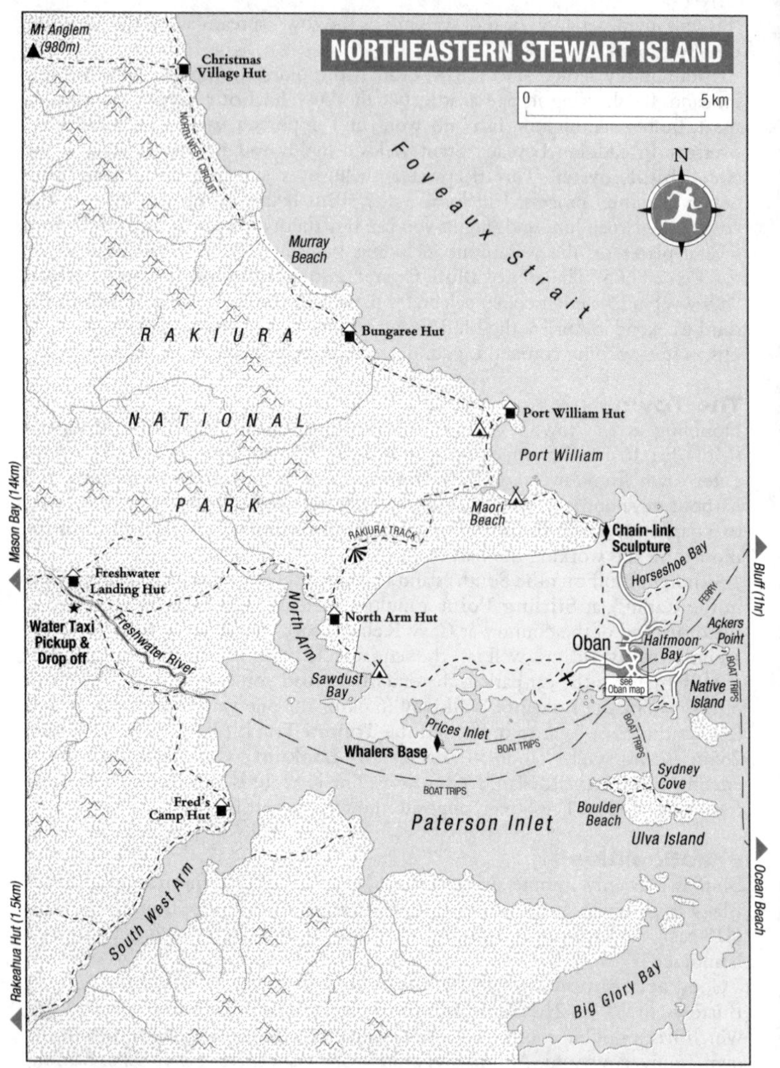

uninhabited and characterized by bush-fringed bays, sandy coves, windswept beaches and a rugged interior of tall rimu forest and granite outcrops. With the creation of **Rakiura National Park** in 2002 a full 85 percent of the island is now protected. Stewart Island's Maori name is Rakiura ("The Land of Glowing Skies"), although the jury is still out on whether this refers to the aurora australis – aka **southern lights** – occasionally seen in the night sky throughout the year, or the fabulous sunsets. Captain Cook came by in 1770 and erroneously marked a peninsula on his charts. The island was later named after William Stewart, the first officer on a sealing vessel that visited in 1809. With the arrival of Europeans, felling rimu became the island's economic mainstay, supporting three thousand people in the 1930s. Now almost all of Stewart Island's three hundred and sixty residents live in the sole town, **Oban**, surviving on **conservation** work, **fishing** (crayfish, blue cod and paua), **fish farming** (salmon and mussels) and tourism.

The slow island ways can quickly get into your blood and you may well want to stay longer than you had planned, especially if you're drawn to serious wilderness **tramping**, sea **kayaking**, and abundant **wildlife** in unspoilt surroundings.

While the island is never crowded (with only around 35,000 overnight visitors a year), if you head here between mid-December and mid-February you should book most things in advance. Year-round, come prepared for all weathers (often in the same day).

Getting to Stewart Island

Foveaux Strait has a reputation for trying the stomachs of even the hardiest sailors. Consequently, many people choose to **fly** from Invercargill (which can still be a bumpy ride) with Stewart Island Flights (3 daily; $95 one way, $165 return; ⓣ03/218 9129, ⓦwww.stewartislandflights.com), which offers small discounts for backpackers and seniors, as well as standby discounts (around $60 one way, $105 return). Getting out to Invercargill airport will cost $10–15 by taxi; the transfer between Oban's airfield and the centre of town is included in the price of your ticket. A strict **luggage allowance** of 15kg per person applies and camping gas canisters are not allowed. Airport parking costs $8 for the first twenty-four hours; cheaper for longer stays.

If you're bringing a lot of luggage, want to carry camping stove fuel or just need to save money, take one of the **ferries** run by Stewart Island Experience (2–4 daily; $55 each way ⓣ03/212 7660 or 0800/000 511; ⓦwww.stewartislandexperience.co.nz). They run a fast catamaran on the hour-long journey between Bluff and the wharf in Oban. Boats typically leave Bluff at 9.30am and in the late afternoon, with extra services in summer. A

▲ Boatshed near Oban, Stewart Island

connecting bus picks up from Invercargill city and airport, and costs $18 each way. From mid-October to late April, some buses continue from Bluff via Invercargill to Queenstown (4–5hr; $60) or Te Anau (3–4 hours; $60). There's secure parking at the Bluff terminal for $7.50 a night.

The dispersed nature of the sights on Stewart Island make it well suited to **guided walking trips**, such as those run by Kiwi Wilderness Walks (Ⓣ0800/486 774, Ⓦwww.nzwalk.com). Their Invercargill- or Te Anau-based four-night Stewart Island trips ($1495) incorporate a flight to Mason Bay with a walk along the beach to the Mason Bay hut, a hike to Freshwater Landing and water taxi to Oban for guided kayaking, a visit to Ulva Island and some free time. If you want to stay longer on the island that can easily be arranged. Several trips of similar scope are run by Ruggedy Range (Ⓣ03/219 1066, Ⓦwww.ruggedyrange.com).

Oban (Halfmoon Bay)

Scattered around Halfmoon Bay, **OBAN** (also commonly known as Halfmoon Bay) comprises little more than a few dozen houses, a visitor centre, a tiny museum, a couple of stores and cafés, and a hotel with a bar. More houses straggle away up the surrounding hills, surrounded by bush alive with native birds.

Coming from the South Island, you'll **arrive** at the downtown wharf or at the tarmac airstrip 3km west of town. If you're coming by water taxi, perhaps after visiting Mason Bay, you'll pull up at **Golden Bay** just over a kilometre to the southwest.

Information

The Stewart Island **DOC office/Rakiura National Park visitor centre**, Main Road (late Dec–March daily 8am–5pm; start April–late April Mon–Fri 8am–5pm, Sat & Sun 9am–4pm; late April–June Mon–Fri 8.30am–4.30pm, Sat & Sun 10am–noon; July–late Oct Mon–Fri 8.30am–5pm, Sat & Sun 10am–noon; late Oct–late Dec Mon–Fri 8.30am–5pm, Sat & Sun 9am–4pm; Ⓣ03/219 0009, Ⓦwww.doc.govt.nz), has excellent displays on the island's tracks and natural history, supplies local maps and information, and sells DOC hut passes, as well as screening free videos about the island. The centre also has **luggage lockers** (small $2.50, large $5; for as long as you like).

The best place to book trips and tours is the waterfront **i-SITE visitor centre**, 12 Elgin Terrace (generally daily 8.30am–5pm; Ⓣ03/219 1400, Ⓦwww.stewartisland.co.nz), which accepts credit cards.

Bear in mind that there are **no banks or ATMs** on Stewart Island. Many businesses take credit cards, and visitors with New Zealand bank accounts can use EFTPOS, but it is wise to bring plenty of cash. Note too that only Telecom has **mobile phone coverage** on parts of the island; Vodafone doesn't.

The **post office** is in the Stewart Island Flights depot, Elgin Street, on the waterfront near the junction with Ayr Street (Oct–March Mon–Fri 7.30am–6pm, Sat & Sun 8.30am–5pm; April–Sept daily 8.30am–5pm), where stamps are still cancelled by hand. For **Internet access** try *Justcafé* on Main Road, the *South Sea Hotel*, and *Stewart Island Backpackers*, all listed in this section.

Local transport

Oban is a pleasant place to **walk** around and unless you are staying in one of the more distant lodges you won't need any land transport. To get a feel for the lay of the land, join Stewart Island Experience's Village and Bays **tour** (1–3 daily; 1hr 30min; $35; Ⓣ03/219 0056; Ⓦwww.stewartislandexperience.co.nz). For independent transportation, rent a car ($80/day) or motor scooter ($40/2hr,

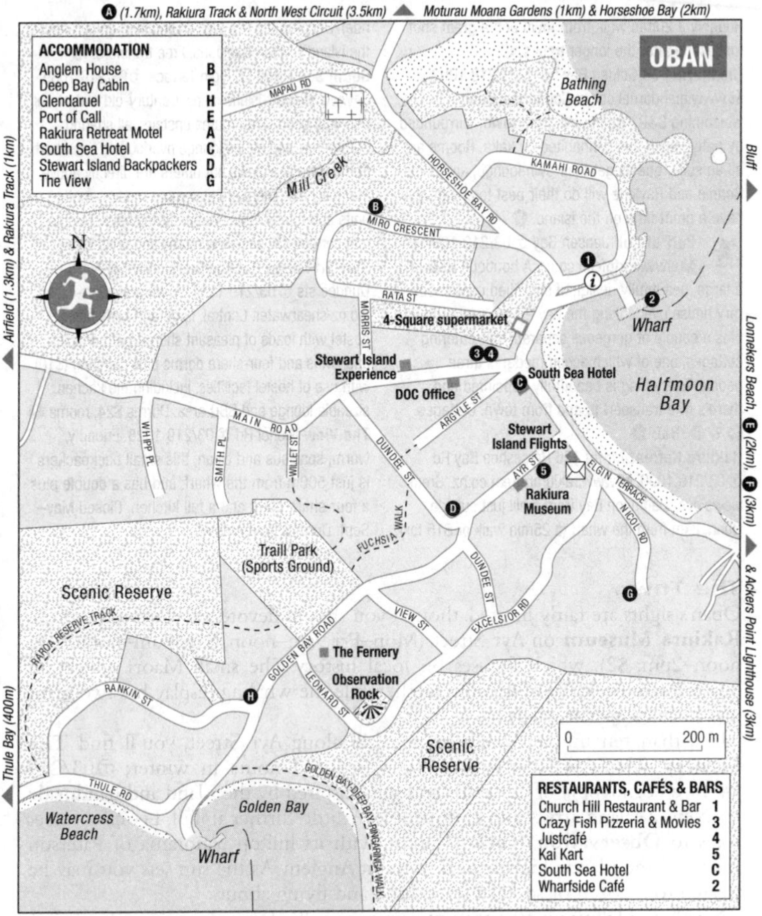

$60/8hr), all including fuel, from Stewart Island Experience. Once away from the small road system you'll need the aid of **water taxis**, typically speedboats with powerful outboard motors carrying six to ten. Four companies offer a broadly similar service (bookable through the i-SITE visitor centre), including Stewart Island Water Taxi (☎03/219 1394).

Accommodation

Despite its diminutive size and rural feel, Oban's range of **accommodation** is surprisingly broad, although finding a place in high season can be difficult: **book** before you arrive. If you fancy self-catering, enquire through the i-SITE visitor centre about **holiday cottages** for rent. A place with a couple of bedrooms will cost between $100 to $250 a night.

Anglem House 20 Miro Crescent ☎03/219 1552. Double-storey house associated with the YHA, divided into two comfortable, well-heated s/c apartments in a peaceful bush setting. ❷

Deep Bay Cabin Deep Bay ☎03/219 1219, ⓔwanjengell@xtra.co.nz. Snug s/c wooden cabin hidden in the bush with four bunks, kitchen and shower, and a year-round pot-bellied stove.

Roughly a 20min walk from town and a great spot for resting after the longer tracks. ❷

Glendaruel 38 Golden Bay Rd ⓣ03/219 1092, ⓦwww.glendaruel.co.nz. Comfortable and welcoming B&B 10min walk from town, surrounded by native bush that's inhabited by kaka. Rooms are all en suite, guests get their own lounge, and hosts Ronnie and Raylene will do their best to ensure you have a great time on the island. ❼

Port of Call Jensen Bay ⓣ03/219 1394, ⓦwww.portofcall.co.nz. A boutique B&B in a large, beautifully designed sun-filled contemporary house overlooking the bay 2.5km east of town, plus a couple of gorgeous separate self-catering cottages, one of which accommodates three people. Everything is beautifully appointed and there's free transport to and from town. Cottages ❻ & ❼, B&B ❽

Rakiura Retreat Motel 156 Horseshoe Bay Rd ⓣ03/219 1096, ⓦwww.rakiuraretreat.co.nz. Great views over Halfmoon Bay from a hill just outside Oban, 2km from the wharf (a 25min walk or $15 taxi ride). Decor in the five well-maintained units reflect the island's Maori traditions. Free transfers. ❻

South Sea Hotel 26 Elgin Terrace ⓣ03/219 1059, ⓦwww.stewart-island.co.nz. Century-old waterfront pub with good clean rooms upstairs, all sharing bathrooms, and a nice lounge overlooking the wharf. Some have sea views but others are directly above the noisy bar. There are also more modern motel units and rooms in a cottage out the back. Rooms and cottage ❹, sea-view rooms and units ❺

Stewart Island Backpackers corner of Ayr & Dundee sts ⓣ03/219 1114, ⓦwww.stewart-island.co.nz/shearwater. Central, large and fairly basic hostel with loads of pleasant shared-bath doubles and twins and four-share dorms plus camping ($10) with use of hostel facilities, including the kitchen, sizeable lounge and BBQ area. Dorms $24, rooms ❶

The View Nichol Rd ⓣ03/219 1328. Friendly, warm, spacious and clean, this small backpackers is just 500m from the wharf, and has a double plus a four-share dorm and a full kitchen. Closed May–Sept. Dorm $30, rooms ❸

The Town

Oban's sights are fairly limited, though you should devote a few minutes to the **Rakiura Museum** on Ayr Street (Mon–Fri 9am–noon, Sat 10am–noon, Sun noon–2pm; $2), which focuses on local history. The small Maori collection boasts a rare necklace of dolphin teeth, while the whaling display has two giant teeth from a sperm whale.

Less than ten minutes' walk up the hill along Ayr Street, you'll find **The Fernery** (Oct–April daily 10am–6pm; reduced hours in winter; ⓣ03/219 1453), a cornucopia of souvenirs and gifts inspired by the island and handmade by New Zealand artists and craftspeople. A little further uphill, Leonard Street leads to **Observation Rock** (15min), with its hilltop panorama of Paterson Inlet and the island's highest peak, Mount Anglem. As the sun sets you may be treated to a dozen or so kaka screeching and flying about.

North of Halfmoon Bay, twenty minutes' walk along Horseshoe Bay Road, are the secluded **Moturau Moana gardens**. Picnic tables, BBQS and a viewing platform looking out across the bay to Oban are set amid lawns, native plants and dense virgin forest.

Eating and drinking

Oban only has a few **places to eat**. Last dinner orders tend to be around 8.30pm – even earlier when the town is quiet. For self-caterers, grocery prices compare well with the mainland but fresh fish can be hard to come by as direct sales from the boats are illegal. Ask locals if this is what you're after. The small 4-Square **general store**, 20 Elgin Terrace, also sells prepared lunch boxes ($9–11). It closes around 7pm in summer, 6.30pm the rest of the year.

Church Hill Restaurant & Bar 36 Kamahi Rd ⓣ03/219 1323. Fine views of Halfmoon Bay from the deck of this century-old house help make this one of the best places to eat in town. Come for good-value lunches and dinners: perhaps an entrée of steamed mussels ($17.60) followed by stone-grilled rib-eye with mushroom sauce ($34), unsalted muttonbird (winter only) or crayfish.

Crazy Fish Pizzeria & Movies 10 Main Rd ⓣ03/219 1419. Gourmet pizzas, a good range of Dunedin- and Invercargill-brewed beers and a reasonable wine list. They also have a 50-seat cinema showing new releases (adults $18): take your dessert and coffee in with you. Open Oct–April 4pm–late.

Justcafé 6 Main Rd. Art-filled daytime café with great espresso, light meals, cakes, cookies and Internet access. The owners also operate a heavenly spa with a range of treatments like a "bush bath", hot stone massage and a seaweed body wrap (from $85), which can be booked here. Café and spa open Oct–April.

Kai Kart Ayr St. Billy Connolly stopped by this fabulously quirky old Pie Kart (aka glorified caravan), which has recently been decked out with leadlights and decoupaged tables. You can order superb blue cod fish and chips or burgers to eat inside or at the outdoor picnic tables, or take them to the adjacent beach. Mid-Oct to mid-April.

South Sea Hotel Elgin Terrace. The island's only pub, and very much its social centre. Also has a restaurant offering lunches and early evening meals such as grouper steak in a wine and caper sauce ($24).

Wharfside Café On the wharf ⓣ03/219 1470. Classy little café and restaurant above the ferry terminal with marvellous views over Halfmoon Bay. Seasonal opening hours change from year to year.

Paterson Inlet and Ulva Island

The birdlife in Oban is pretty special, but **Ulva Island** – an open wildlife sanctuary 2km south of Oban in the flooded valley of **Paterson Inlet** – goes one better with cacophonous birdsong and the chance to see endangered saddleback and rare red-crowned parakeets on a series of easy walks through dense rainforest to secluded beaches. The former Norwegian **Whalers Base** is another wildlife-rich destination, and can be included on guided **kayaking trips**.

Ulva Island

Tremendous local effort has rid the long, low **Ulva Island** (daylight hours; free) of introduced predators and it is now an **open sanctuary** where you'll see more native birdlife than almost anywhere else in New Zealand. The place is full of birdsong, its thick native vegetation alive with weka fowls, bellbirds, kaka, yellow- and red-crowned parakeets, tui, fantails, pigeons and many more, who approach visitors with fearless curiosity.

Access is mainly by **water taxi** (10min each way; $20–$25 return from Golden Bay). Armed with DOC's *Explore an Island Paradise: Ulva Island* booklet ($2), you can follow easy trails across a forest floor covered in mosses and liverworts, but the best way to appreciate this haven is on a **guided tour** such as that run by Ulva Goodwillie of Ulva's Guided Walks (ⓣ03/219 1216, ⓦwww.ulva.co.nz; approx 3hr; $95, including water taxi fees), who was named after the island and imparts local Maori stories.

Water taxis and cruises arrive at **Post Office Bay**, whose hundred-year-old former post office is a remnant from the days when the island was the hub of the local community. A web of trails crisscrossing the island leads first to nearby **Sydney Cove**, where there's a pleasant picnic shelter on the beach.

Whalers Base

On the shores of Paterson Inlet is **Whalers Base**, an over-wintering spot for Norwegian whalers near **Millars Beach**, about 7km west of Oban. It's only accessible by water taxi ($40 return), and most operators will leave you there for a few hours and pick you up later. From Millars Beach, an easy twenty-minute coastal walk heads north from the beachside picnic shelter through native bush to the whaling base. Several eerie relics remain from 1924–32 when a fleet of Antarctic whaling ships was repaired here, and the beach is littered with objects left behind: old drums, cables, giant iron propellers, a boiler out in the water and, at the far end, a wrecked sailing ship deliberately sunk by the whaling company to create a wharf.

Activities

Both Ulva Island and Whalers Base form part of various **tours** and kayak trips which take in Paterson Inlet and beyond. Adventurous visitors can explore more thoroughly by **sea kayaking** around the scattered inlets and islands. On extended trips you can even paddle out to the four water-accessible **DOC huts** around the inlet. Bottlenose dolphins and fur seals are frequent visitors, and the tidal flats attract wading birds including herons, oystercatchers, godwits and the New Zealand dotterel. Bear in mind that the waters around Stewart Island are changeable and May to August brings the most settled weather; only extremely experienced kayakers should venture into these waters unaccompanied.

There's also a chance to see **kiwi in the wild** without crossing the island to Mason Bay, and some great short **walks**. Longer hikes are covered on p.713.

Adventure trips and tours

Aurora Charters ⓣ03/219 1126, ⓔinfo@auroracharters.co.nz. Particularly good trips on a comfortable 25-passenger boat costing $70 for a half-day of fishing and scenic touring.

Bravo Adventure Cruises ⓣ03/219 1144, ⓔphilldismith@xtra.co.nz. Cruises geared around spotting the Stewart Island brown kiwi (a sub-species of the mainland birds) in remote areas around the shores of Paterson Inlet. Four-hour trips ($100) leave from the wharf in Halfmoon Bay around dusk, but are weather dependent and extremely popular, so it's essential to reserve well ahead of arriving on the island – even then a tour can't be guaranteed. You'll need warm clothing, sturdy footwear, a torch and a good level of fitness, as the outing entails a short boat trip and up to 2hrs walking, including some steep sections, in the dark to a windswept beach, where the kiwi feast on tiny crustaceans. Great care is taken to avoid disturbing these timid birds.

Seabuzzz ⓣ03/219 1282, ⓦwww.seabuzzz.co.nz. Water taxi operator running Aquacultural Tours ($60) to mussel and salmon farms.

Rakiura Kayaks ⓣ03/219 1160, ⓦwww.rakiura.co.nz. Excellent half-day ($55) and full-day ($80) guided trips, as well as overnight trips with the option of staying in a house on an offshore island (price negotiable), plus kayak rental ($45 per person per day).

Stewart Island Experience ⓣ03/219 0034, ⓦwww.stewartislandexperience.co.nz. Two trips, the first a leisurely Paterson Inlet Cruise (Oct–April 1–3 daily; 2hr 30min; $70) taking in the main sights including Whalers Base and a 45min guided walking tour of Ulva Island. Picnic lunch ($14.50) available if pre-ordered. The Underwater Explorer tour (Oct–April 1–3 daily; 45min: $35) in a semi-submersible takes you through forests of bladder kelp. You'll see butterfish, blue cod, banded wrasse, moki and sea tulips, curious, filter-feeding animals.

Short walks around Oban

Over a dozen short **walks** around Oban are covered in the DOC's *Day Walks* leaflet; a couple of the nicest are right in town.

Fuchsia Walk/ Raroa Track (2km one way; 30min). This little-used trail winds through fuchsia forest filled with tui, bellbirds and pigeons then comes out at Trail Park. Cross this and head down through rimu forest to the beach.

Golden Bay–Deep Bay–Ringaringa (6km loop; 1hr 30min–2hr). Skirting east from Golden Bay, the track follows the coast to Deep Bay and then over the hill to Ringaringa Beach. From here, follow the signs over a stile to Ringaringa Point and the graves of early missionaries Reverend Wohlers and his wife.

Harrold Bay and Ackers Point Lighthouse (3km return; 40min). Easy and well-graded coastal walk with a chance to see little blue penguins and muttonbirds returning to their nests at dusk (Nov–Feb). Near the start of the track, you can follow a brief diversion to Harrold Bay, the site of a simple stone house built in 1835, making it one of the oldest European buildings in New Zealand. The main track continues through coastal forest to a lighthouse and lookout point from where you can watch the penguins arduously climbing to their nests hidden in the bush. You'll need a torch to find your way around after dusk, but it's important to keep the beam pointed to the ground to avoid disturbing the birds, which are easily distressed. Follow the signs from Leask Bay, 2.5km east of town.

The rest of Stewart Island

There are no roads outside the immediate vicinity of Oban, so straying further afield requires some planning. Essentially you have to fly, take a water taxi or walk.

As ever, **trampers** need to be ready for whatever the New Zealand weather conjures up, doubly so on Stewart Island, which is exposed to winds coming straight across the southern ocean from Antarctica. Take several layers of clothing to cope with sun and rain (often at almost the same time), and don't forget sandfly repellent. Huts can be busy from November through to March, so it's a good idea to bring a tent.

Mason Bay

Stewart Island has become synonymous with **kiwi spotting** in the wild, something that is virtually impossible to do anywhere on mainland New Zealand. Tours from Oban include kiwi spotting, but most people are keen to get to **Mason Bay**, on the west coast, where they stay overnight in the 20-bunk DOC hut ($5; camping outside free) and head out after dark in the hope of finding these elusive creatures. You'll almost certainly hear them, and have a fair chance of seeing them provided you don't go crashing about in the bush: just pick a spot and wait for them to come to you. Take a torch, but again keep the beam pointed to the ground to avoid disturbing the birds.

For hardy visitors, the cheapest way to visit is to **walk** (37km one way; 13–15hr) along the southern leg of the North West Circuit (see p.714), probably staying overnight at Freshwater Landing Hut ($5). You can save a lot of time by catching a **water taxi** from Oban to Freshwater Landing Hut ($50 each way) then walking to Mason Bay (14km; 3–4hr; flat but often flooded – check conditions before you head out). Alternatively, Stewart Island Flights and one of the water taxi companies work together, allowing you to complete a "Coast to Coast" **loop**, flying from Oban to the beach at Mason Bay, staying a night or two there, walking to Freshwater Landing, then getting a water taxi back to Oban (or vice versa). It costs $185 for the flight and water taxi combo (hut accommodation extra), with a two-adult minimum. Flying direct to Mason Bay from Invercargill then completing the circuit to Oban costs $495 (three-adult minimum), not including transportation back to Invercargill.

Rakiura Track

Stewart Island's most popular overnight track is the relatively gentle **Rakiura Track** (36km loop; 2–3 days), one of New Zealand's Great Walks. This makes a circuit starting and finishing in Oban, though you can shave 7km off the route by getting someone to drop you off and pick you up at the road-ends. DOC's *Rakiura Track* leaflet is adequate for route finding, and you'll need to pre-purchase a **Great Walks Pass** from DOC for the two huts ($10 a night) and three campsites ($2.50) along the track. The huts are equipped with mattresses, wood stoves for heating only, running water and toilets, but you'll need your own stove. You can walk in either direction at any time of the year, and there is no limit on the number of nights you stay at each place.

The majority of people walk anticlockwise. Starting through bush, the track gets the best coastal walking in early around Maori Bay and Port William, site of the first hut. From Port William to the North Arm hut the track climbs over a three-hundred-metre forested ridge, where a viewpoint gives the only really long views of the tramp, across Paterson Inlet and beyond to the Tin Range. Beyond North Arm hut you only get glimpses of Paterson Inlet, but lots of bushland.

North West Circuit

It is a very big step up from the Rakiura Track to the **North West Circuit** (130km; 8–12 days) around the island's northern arm: only the hardiest (masochistic) trampers should consider attempting it. The boggy terrain quickly becomes energy sapping even in good weather: thigh-deep mud is not uncommon. And unless you organize a boat or charter flight to drop food at one of the coastal huts, you'll have to carry all your supplies.

The track itself alternates between open coast and forested hill country, offering a side trip (11km return; 6hr) to the 980-metre summit of Mount Anglem. DOC's *North West and Southern Circuit Tracks* leaflet gives a good overview, pinpointing the ten huts (mostly sited on the coast: there are no campsites). Most huts cost $5 a night (annual hut pass valid), but Port William and North Arm huts are both Great Walks huts ($10) so it will probably pay to buy a **North West Circuit Pass** ($45), which entitles you to a night in each hut on the circuit.

Travel details

There are no genuine passenger **train** services in the region, though the Taieri Gorge Railway can be useful for linking Dunedin with the Maniototo. Fairly frequent **buses** ply the main Christchurch–Dunedin–Invercargill route and the inland route from Dunedin to Queenstown, with a few other services plugging the gaps.

All **i-SITE** visitor centres throughout the region keep updated transport schedules.

Trains

Dunedin to: Middlemarch (summer Fri & Sun only 1 daily; 2hr 30min); Pukerangi (1 daily, 2hr).

Buses

Dunedin to: Alexandra (3 daily; 3hr); Balclutha (4–6 daily; 1hr 30min); Christchurch (5–7 daily; 5–6hr); Cromwell (3 daily; 3hr 15min); Gore (4–6 daily; 2hr 30min); Invercargill (4–6 daily; 3hr 30min); Lawrence (3 daily; 1hr 30min); Oamaru (5–7 daily; 2hr); Queenstown (3 daily; 4–5hr); Ranfurly (1 daily; 1hr 30min); Te Anau (1 daily; 4h 45min); Wanaka (2–3 daily; 4hr).

Invercargill to: Balclutha (3–5 daily; 2hr 30min); Dunedin (3–5 daily; 3hr 30min); Gore (3–5 daily; 1hr); Queenstown (2 daily; 2hr 30min); Te Anau (1 daily; 4hr); Wanaka (1 daily; 4hr).

Flights

Bluff to: Stewart Island (2–4 daily; 1hr).

Stewart Island to: Bluff (2–4 daily; 1hr).

Planes

Dunedin to: Auckland (1 daily; 1hr 50min); Christchurch (6–10 daily; 1hr); Wellington (3 daily; 1hr 10min).

Invercargill to: Christchurch (5–8 daily; 1hr 15min); Stewart Island (3 daily; 20min).

Stewart Island to: Invercargill (3 daily; 20min).

12

The West Coast

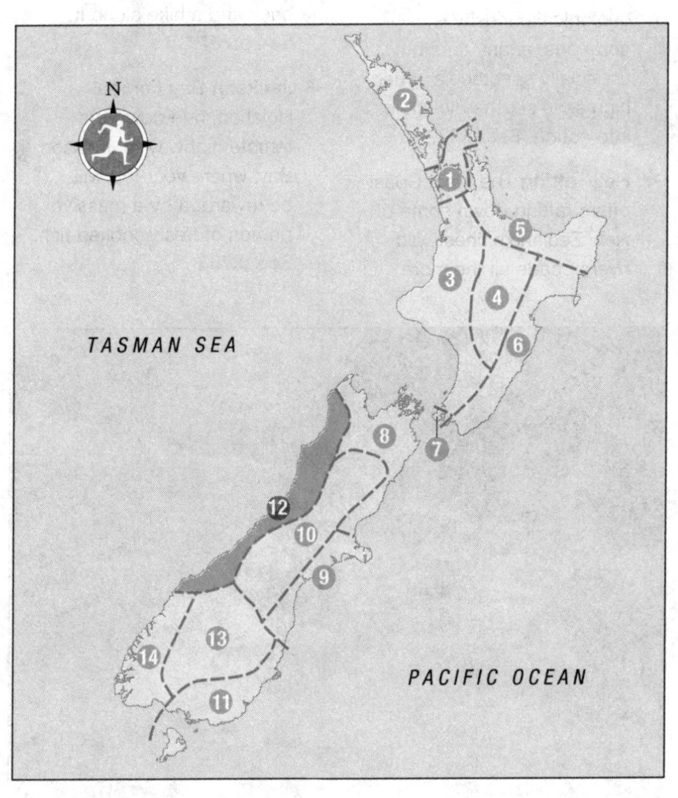

CHAPTER 12 **Highlights**

* **Oparara Basin** Set a day aside to explore caves harbouring moa bones, vast limestone arches and placid streams that are great for cooling off. See p.732

* **Pancake Rocks** This geological curiosity is gorgeous, at any time but especially spectacular when high seas set the blowholes into action. See p.737

* **Heli-rafting** The West Coast offers rafting down some of New Zealand's finest wild rivers, made all the more enticing by a helicopter flight into the headwaters. See p.749

* **Fox glacier** Hiking out onto the glacier is an awe-inspiring experience, surpassed only by a helicopter ride up to its back and a hike along it. See p.757

* **Jackson Bay** For real isolation, ride down the remote highway to Jackson Bay, where your trip will be rewarded by a massive portion of fresh-cooked fish. See p.763

▲ Glacier walking, Franz Josef Glacier

12

The West Coast

The Southern Alps run down the backbone of the South Island, both defining and isolating **the West Coast**. A narrow, rugged and largely untamed strip 400km long and barely 30km wide, it is home to just 32,000 people. Turbulent rivers cascade out of the mountains though lush bushland and past crystal lakes before spilling out into the Tasman Sea, its coastline fringed by astonishing surf-pounded beaches and backed by the odd tiny shack or, more frequently, nothing at all.

What really sets "the Coast" apart is the interaction of settlers with their environment. **Coasters**, many descended from early gold and coal miners, have long been proud of their ability to coexist with the landscape – a trait mythologized in their reputation for independent-mindedness and intemperate beer-drinking, perhaps fuelled by Irish migrants drawn to the 1860s gold rushes. Stories abound of late-night drinking sessions way past closing time, and your fondest memories of the West Coast might be chance encounters in the pub.

Cook sailed up this way in 1770, describing the Coast as "an inhospitable shore, unworthy of observation, except for its ridge of naked and barren rocks covered with snow. As far as the eye could reach the prospect was wild, craggy and desolate". Little here then for early **European explorers** such as Thomas Brunner and Charles Heaphy, who made forays in 1846–47, led by Kehu, a Maori guide. They returned without finding the cultivable land they sought, and after a shorter trip in 1861 Henry Harper, the first bishop of Christchurch, wrote, "I doubt if such a wilderness will ever be colonized except through the discovery of **gold**". Prophetic words: within two years reports were circulating of flecks in West Coast rivers and a year later Greymouth and Hokitika were experiencing full-on gold rushes. The boom was soon over, but mining continued into the twentieth century, with huge dredges littering the landscape, looking like beached galleons as they worked their way up the gravel riverbeds, scuttling through spent tailings.

As gold was worked out, longer-lasting **coal** took its place, laying the foundation for more permanent towns. The West Coast still produces half of the country's output. People taking advantage of the abundant open space and low land prices have nurtured a thriving **alternative culture** – you may well spot the smokestack of some purple bus sticking out from behind the trees. In the last twenty years, however, everything has been turned upside down by the challenge of increasing **tourism** and a greater awareness of the Coast's fragile **ecosystems**, a situation that gave rise to tension between the Coasters and the government, particularly regarding native timber felling and its impact on the area's unique environment.

No discussion of the West Coast would be complete without mention of the torrential **rainfall**, which falls with tropical intensity for days at a time; every

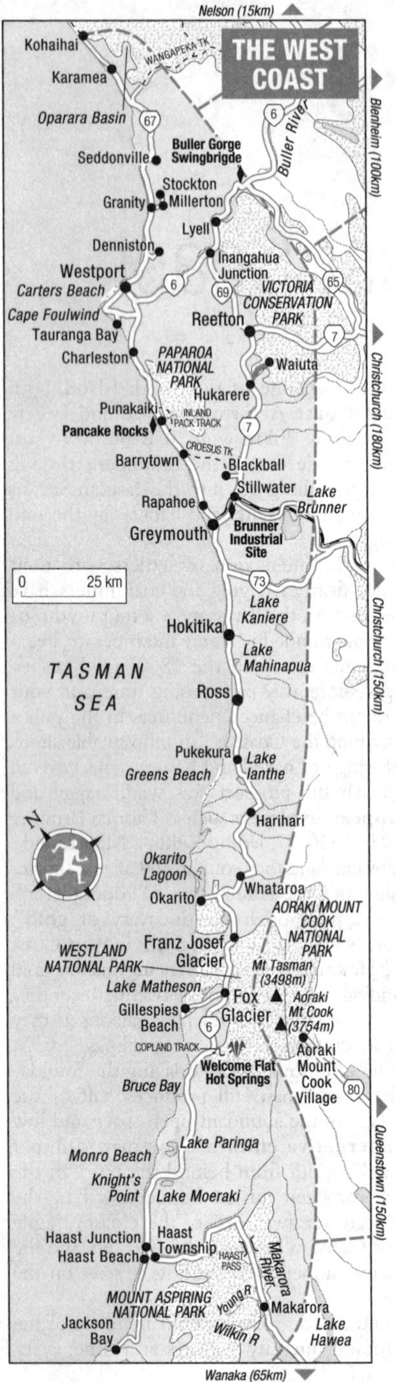

rock springs a waterfall and the bush becomes vibrant with colour. Such soakings have a detrimental effect on the soil, retarding decomposition and producing a peat-like top layer with all the minerals leached out. The result is **pakihi**, scrubby, impoverished and poor-looking paddocks that characterize much of the West Coast's cleared land. But the abundant sunshine that alternates with the downpours produces excellent conditions for **marijuana** cultivation, a significant component of the local economy. Enthusiasm for dope-growing is matched only by the springtime rush to catch **whitebait**, when fishers line the tidal riverbanks on rising tides trying to net this epicurean holy grail.

The boom-and-bust nature of the West Coast's mining past produced scores of ghost towns, but also spawned its three largest settlements – **Westport**, **Greymouth** and **Hokitika**. The real pleasure of the West Coast, though, lies in smaller places, where the Coasters' indomitable spirit shines through: places such as **Karamea**, on the southern limit of the Kahurangi National Park, the strike town of **Blackball** at the foot of the Croesus Track on the Paparoa Range, the gold town of **Ross** and windswept **Okarito**. With the exception of a couple of decent museums and a handful of sights, the West Coast's appeal is in its scenic beauty. The **Oparara Basin**, near Karamea, and the **Paparoa National Park**, south of Westport, exhibit some of the country's finest limestone formations, including huge arched spans and the famous Pancake Rocks, while in the Westland National Park the frosty white tongues of the **Franz Josef** and **Fox glaciers** career down the flanks of the Southern Alps into dense emerald bush.

Getting around

The simplest way to get around the West Coast is with your own **vehicle**. **Cycling** isn't such a chore: the coast road is undulating but the distances between towns aren't off-putting and you can always find somewhere to camp in between. Public transport, on the other hand, is fairly restrictive. **Trains** only penetrate as far as Greymouth; **bus services** are infrequent and, though they call at all the major towns, won't get you to most of the walks. Having said that, with patience and a degree of forward planning it is possible to see much of interest, especially if you are prepared to walk a little. For details of transport routes see "Travel Details" on p.767.

Since this is New Zealand, there's no lack of activities, particularly the matchless fly-in **rafting** trips down the West Coast's steep rivers. The limestone bedrock makes for some great adventure **caving**, and there's plenty of **hiking**, with the Heaphy Track in the north, the Inland Pack Track near Punakaiki and the stack of steep tramps around the glaciers.

Most people visit from November to April, but in **winter** temperatures are not as low as you might think and the greater number of clear days make for cloud-free viewing. Pesky **sandflies** are also less active in the winter. The West Coast never feels crowded but in the off season you'll have even more room to move and accommodation will be cheaper; the downside is that adventure trips and scenic **flights**, which require minimum numbers to operate, may be harder to arrange.

The northern approaches: along the Buller and Grey rivers

Stretching 169km from its source at Lake Rotoiti in the Nelson Lakes National Park to its mouth at Westport, the **Buller River**'s blue-green waters reflect sunlight dappled through riverside beech forests as they swirl and churn through one of the grandest of New Zealand's river gorges. The Maori name for the Buller is Kawatiri, meaning "deep and swift", qualities which lure rafters to several stretches. Gold was discovered along the Buller in 1858, sparking a gold rush centred on **Lyell**, now a ghost town whose outlying remains can be visited on the **Lyell Walkway**.

The Buller lies between the Lyell and Brunner ranges, and is traced by SH6 from Kawatiri Junction to Westport through Inangahua Junction, where Greymouth-bound travellers turn south towards **Reefton**. From Reefton, SH7 hugs the **Grey River**, a far less dramatic watercourse, as it flows through a wide valley to the east of the granite tops of the Paparoa Range past more evidence of long-dead gold and coal industries, principally at laid-back **Blackball** and the **Brunner Industrial Site**.

The Buller Gorge

SH6 from Nelson passes through Murchison (see p.546) and follows the Buller River 11km to **O'Sullivan's Bridge**, where you turn right to remain on SH6 as it enters the Upper Buller Scenic Reserve. After 6km, the road passes the **Buller Gorge Swingbridge** ($5; ⓣ03/523 9809, ⓦwww.bullergorge.co.nz), a kind of heritage park accessed by a 110-metre swingbridge, New Zealand's

▲ Flying fox, Buller Gorge

longest example of these swaying pedestrian footbridges. It crosses high above the Buller River parallel to a fun 160-metre-long **flying fox** (zipwire), on which you can ride sitting ($25), tandem ($25 each), or prone, Superman-style ($35). On the far side of the swift-flowing water, the heritage park has a variety of **bushwalks** (15min–2hr) taking in an earthquake fault line, gold mine workings and the Ariki Falls (1hr round trip). You can also pan for gold ($10).

Twenty kilometres on, the road passes the grassy site of **Lyell**, a former gold-mining town sat high above the Buller on flats beside Lyell Creek. In its 1890s heyday it supported five hotels, two banks, two churches and even its own newspaper, all serving a population of three thousand. Fires and the gradual decline in gold mining saw off the settlement, but the few remains can be visited via the short but fairly strenuous **Lyell Walkway**, which passes terraces where huts once stood, the sobering slabs that stand askew in the cemetery (15min return), and the ten-hammer Croesus quartz stamping battery (1hr 30min return). The roadside site of the former township itself is now a peaceful DOC **campsite** ($6).

At **Inangahua Junction**, 17km to the west, SH69 cuts south to Reefton, while SH6 continues west towards Westport through the **Lower Buller Gorge**, the narrowest and most dramatic section. The road hugs the cliff face in places, most notably at **Hawks Crag**, where the rock has been hewn to form a large overhang – the fact that the water level rose several metres above this carved-out section during a 1926 flood will give you some idea of the volume of water that can surge down the gorge. A few kilometres on you pass Buller Adventure Tours (see p.728) who run rafting trips on the river.

Reefton and around

Located beside the Inangahua River at the intersection of roads from Westport, Greymouth and Christchurch, **REEFTON**, as its name suggests, owes its existence to rich gold-bearing quartz reefs. These were exploited so heavily in the 1870s that Reefton was considered by some "the most brisk and business-like place in the colony". Reefton became the first place in New Zealand, and one of the first in the world, to install electric street lighting powered by a hydroelectric generator. Such forward-looking activity soon abated and Reefton weathered poorly though, with the reopening of an old gold mine on the outskirts of town, things are now looking up. Despite a couple of interesting galleries and a good café, after a couple of hours you'll probably want to head for Waiuta or press on down the Grey Valley.

Specific points of interest around town are linked by two walks, both the subject of brochures available from the visitor centre. The elegiac **Historic Walk** (40min) meanders around Reefton's grid of streets, visiting once-grand buildings – the Masonic Lodge, the School of Mines and the Court House – some ripe for preservation, others partway there. The pleasant **Powerhouse Walk** (40min) is slightly more uplifting in recalling an illustrious past, perhaps because of its course along the Inangahua River. In the centre of town, on the corner of Walsh and Broadway, the so-called "Bearded Miners" entertain visitors at an old **miner's cottage** and smithy (daily, pretty much when they feel like it; donation) and will fire up the forge and let you pan for gold.

The water for Reefton's original hydroelectric scheme was diverted 2km from Blacks Point, where the **Blacks Point Museum**, SH7 towards Springs Junction (Oct–April Wed–Fri & Sun 9am–noon & 1–4pm, Sat 1–4pm; $5), occupies a former Wesleyan Chapel. The museum charts the district's cultural and mining history through engaging photos and a large collection of lamps, moustache cups, clunky old typewriters and the like. Outside, an ancient five-hammer stamper battery is cranked into action on Sunday afternoons and during school holidays. The informative *Walks in the Murray Creek Goldfield* leaflet details nearby **walks** along mining trails.

Westland's endangered forest

If gold and coal built the West Coast's foundations, the **timber industry** supported the structure. Ever since timber was felled for sluicing flumes and pit props, Coasters relied on the seemingly limitless forests for their livelihood. Many miners became loggers, felling trees which take from three hundred to six hundred years to mature and which, according to fossil records of pollen, have been around for 100 million years.

Few expressed any concern for the plight of Westland's magnificent stands of **beech** and **podocarp** until the 1970s, when environmental groups rallied around a campaign to save the Maruia Valley, east of Reefton, which became a touchstone for forest conservation. It wasn't until the 1986 **West Coast Accord** between the government, local authorities, conservationists and the timber industry that some sort of truce prevailed. In the 1980s and 1990s most of the forests were selectively logged, often using helicopters to pluck out the mature trees without destroying those nearby. While it preserves the appearance of the forest, this is little comfort for New Zealand's endangered **birds** – particularly kaka, kakariki (yellow-crowned parakeet), morepork (native owl) and rifleman – and long-tailed **bats**, all of which nest in holes in older trees.

In 1999, Labour leader Helen Clark honoured her election pledge and banned the logging of beech forests by the State-owned Timberlands company. Precious West Coast jobs were lost and the government stepped in with the $100 million fund, which has helped kick-start the local economy. Thousands still feel betrayed in this traditionally Labour-voting part of the world, but with a strong farming sector, rampant property prices and booming tourism the future looks bright.

Practicalities

Buses all stop on Broadway, Reefton's main street, within sight of the helpful combined **i-SITE visitor centre** and **DOC office**, 67 Broadway (daily: Nov–March 8.30am–6pm; April–Oct 8.30am–4.30pm; ⓣ03/732 8391, ⓦwww.reefton.co.nz), which has **Internet access** and a small replica gold mine ($0.50), and rents out gold pans for $2 a day. For a small town there's a reasonable range of **places to stay** and **eat**.

Accommodation

Lantern Court Motel 63 Broadway ⓣ0800/526837, ⓔlanterncourt@xtra.co.nz. Central motel units, some well-worn in, others new and fancy. Older ❸, newer ❺

Old Bread Shop Backpackers 155 Buller Rd ⓣ03/732 8420. Small and simple but well-run hostel. Dorms $16, rooms ❶

Old Nurses Home 104 Shiel St ⓣ03/732 8881, ⓔreeftonretreat@hotmail.com. There's an old-fashioned feel to Reefton's former nurses' home, which now offers thirty twin and double rooms, all shared-bathroom, and many with little balconies overlooking the well-groomed gardens. Guests have access to a good kitchen and pool table. ❶

Reef Cottage B&B Inn 51–55 Broadway ⓣ0800/770 440, ⓦwww.reefcottage.co.nz. The best place in town, offering beautiful individually decorated Victorian- and 1920s-style en suites and a friendly welcome. B&B ❹

Reefton Domain Motor Camp 1 Ross St, at the top of Broadway ⓣ03/732 8477. Central campsite with hookups and good swimming in the Inangahua River. Camping $9, cabins ❶

Slab Hut Creek campsite Primitive DOC site ($6) 8km south on SH7 down the Grey Valley and 1km east.

Eating

Alfresco's 16 Broadway. Pleasant spot offering light meals, good coffee and decent pizza at lunch. Also open evenings during summer.

Reef Café 53 Broadway. Comfortable daytime café with some outdoor seating, serving muffins, sandwiches, pasta, soup and good coffee.

Hotel Reefton 71 Broadway. Straightforward bar meals, including great $14 roasts daily.

The Grey Valley

Southwest of Reefton, SH7 follows the Grey Valley, cut off from the Tasman Sea by the rugged Paparoa Range and hemmed in by the Southern Alps. From both sides, the bush is gradually reclaiming the mine workings that characterized the region for a century. Nothing has stepped in to replace them, and the small communities tick over, a few eking a living from inquisitive tourists keen to explore the former mining towns of **Waiuta** and **Blackball** and to walk the **Croesus Track**.

Waiuta

The first diversion of any consequence lies 21km south of Reefton, where **Hukarere** marks the junction for **WAIUTA**, a ghost town seventeen partly sealed kilometres east. This was the last of the West Coast's great gold towns, reaching a population of 6000 in the 1930s.

Its end came when a mine shaft collapsed in 1951, burying large deposits of gold-bearing reef-quartz almost 900m down, where it was uneconomic to extract them. Miners left for jobs on the coast, much of the equipment was bought by Australian mining companies and many houses were carted off, but the town wasn't completely abandoned; a few cottages are still occupied and there are several more buildings scattered around, including the original post office. The rolling country, pocked by waste heaps, is slowly being colonized by gorse and bramble, but the cypresses and poplars that once delineated gardens and the fruit trees that filled them remain; the rugby field, whippet track, croquet lawns and swimming pool are faring less well.

The whole place is wonderfully atmospheric for just mooching around, guided by the invaluable **Waiuta** leaflet (from Reefton) and strategically placed interpretive panels. You can see the lot in a couple of hours, but Waiuta is an ideal **place to stay** for well-equipped campers, who can pitch their tent just about anywhere. For the less hardy, the open-plan thirty-bunk **Waiuta Lodge** (book through the Reefton i-SITE; $15), has a fully equipped kitchen and a public phone. There's no other accommodation, no public transport and nowhere to buy food, so come prepared.

Blackball

Both the Grey River and SH7 meander through inconsequential small towns until they reach **Stillwater**, 11km short of Greymouth, where side roads lead to Blackball and Lake Brunner.

Refugees from the blistering pace of Greymouth gravitate to languid **blackball**, a former gold- and coal-mining village spread across a plateau at the foot of the Paparoa Range, 11km northeast of Stillwater. Here, commuters, neo-hippies and gnarled folk still hunting and prospecting in the bush seem to coexist fairly harmoniously. Blackball owes its existence to alluvial gold discovered in Blackball Creek in 1864, but gold returns diminished by the early twentieth century and it was left to coal to save the day. This supported Blackball until the mine's closure in 1964, along the way staking the town's place in New Zealand's history as the birthplace of the **labour movement**.

During the first three decades of the twentieth century, the whole of the Grey Valley was a hotbed of doctrinaire socialism, as organizers moved among the towns, pressing unbending mine managers to address the atrocious working conditions. Anger finally came to a head, resulting in the crippling 1908 "cribtime strike", when Pat Hickey, Bob Semple and Paddy Webb requested an extension of their "crib" (lunch) break from fifteen to thirty minutes. Management's refusal sparked an illegal ten-week strike – the longest in New Zealand's history – during which the workers' families were fined £75 for their action. None could pay and although the bailiffs tried to auction their possessions, the workers banded together, refusing to bid – one then bought all the goods for a fraction of their worth and redistributed them to their original owners. This spirit eventually won the day: the workers returned to the mine and crib time was extended, but the £75 was extracted from subsequent wages.

The struggle led to the formation of the Miners' Federation, which later transformed itself into the **Federation of Labour**, the country's principal trade union organization. Eric Beardsley's historical novel **Blackball 08** gives an accurate and passionate portrayal of the 1908 strike. These days Blackball's rustic tranquillity is the main draw, abetted by excellent walking through the gold workings of Blackball Creek and up onto the wind-blasted tops of the Paparoa Range along the **Croesus Track** (see p.724). Jane at the **Hilton** has a hatful of other suggestions including gold panning, evening possum shooting with Bob ($25) and even heli-hiking and heli-biking from the top of the range (around $100).

Practicalities

With no regular public transport, you'll have to find your own way to Blackball, where social life revolves around the welcoming and wonderfully low-key *Formerly The Blackball Hilton*, Hart Street (ⓣ0800/425 225, ⓦwww.blackballhilton.co.nz; camping $10, dorms $23, B&B ④). The last of the mining-era **hotels**, it opened as the *Dominion* in 1910 and subsequently operated as the *Hilton* – ostensibly named for the former mine manager remembered in Hilton Street nearby – until challenged by the international hotel chain of the same name. Apart from lively drinking with locals, the hotel offers accommodation in shared-bathroom double and twin rooms (and one six-bed dorm) all brightly decorated. The emphasis is on character rather than creature comforts, but guests have use of an indoor hot tub, small gym, table tennis table and a small kitchen. The restaurant is open for guests' breakfast, espresso, good lunches ($8–15) and dinners ($15–20) which might include Blackball salami antipasto.

For picnic supplies, call in at the excellent Blackball Salami *Co* up the street from the *Hilton* to feast on venison sausages, salami, delectable morsels; or pop across the road for fish and chips from the dairy.

Lake Brunner

From SH7 near Blackball, a good sealed road runs 55km south to link up with SH73 between Greymouth and Arthur's Pass. Along the way it passes Lake Brunner (Moana Kotuku), a filled glacial hollow celebrated for its trout fishing. The shoreline village of **MOANA** is popular with holidaying Kiwis but unless you have your own rod or aquatic playthings it is not brimming with things to do. By late summer the lake is surprisingly warm and makes for good **swimming**, or you can head out on foot along a couple of easy paths. At the end of town,

The Croesus Track

Prospectors seeking new claims gradually pushed their way up Blackball Creek. The scant remains of decades of toil now provide the principal interest on the **Croesus Track**, the first half of which is easily explored in a day from Blackball. The whole track over the 1200m Paparoa Range to Barrytown, on the coast 30km north of Greymouth, takes two relatively gentle days or one eight-hour slog. DOC's informative *Central West Coast* leaflet shows adequate detail for walkers, and the NZMS's 1:50,000 *Ahaura* Topomap is the one for map enthusiasts.

Access and accommodation

The track **starts** at Smoke-ho car park, at the end of a rough but passable road 7km north of Blackball, and **finishes** opposite the *All Nations Tavern* on SH6 in Barrytown, where buses pass twice daily in each direction. The most convenient approach is with Kea Tours (☎0800/532 868) who do a Blackball drop-off and Barrytown pick-up combo for $40 (minimum 2). The only hut is the first-come-first-served **Ces Clarke Hut** (24 bunks; $10), with panoramic views and a coal-burning stove.

The track

Much of the track was designed to accommodate tramways, so you get a gentle, steady grade as you wind through native podocarps interspersed with ferns, mosses and vines, gradually giving way to hardier silver beech and eventually alpine tussock and herbfields above the treeline. Sea mist commonly cloaks the tops during the middle of the day. Half an hour from the Smoke-ho car park, a side path (10min return) leads to the former site of the **Minerva Battery**. Immediately after the junction, the main path crosses Clarke Creek on a modern wire bridge above the remains of an old wooden bridge. Another half-hour on, a side track leads to two clearings that once contained **Perotti's Mill** (10min return) and the **Croesus Battery** (50min return). After almost an hour, another side path leads to the primitive **Garden Gully Hut** (5min return) and the **Garden Gully Battery** (40min return). The main track turns sharply west before reaching the **Ces Clarke Hut** on the treeline in around an hour: fill your water bottles here as there is no supply further on. The top of the ridge near Mount Ryall (1220m) lies two undulating hours beyond, a little more if you run off to climb **Croesus Knob** (1204m) along the way. If it isn't cloaked in cloud, the broad ridge offers wonderful views down to the coast, which is reached in under three hours by a steep but well-marked path that dives down into the bush.

beyond the motor camp a slender swingbridge over the fledgling Arthur River provides access to the riverside **Rakaitane Track** (30min return) and the **Lake Side Track** (20–60min return), which has good mountain views.

The TranzAlpine **train** makes a daily stop at Moana. Facilities here are limited, but there's **accommodation** at the *Lake Brunner Resort*, Ahau Street (ⓣ0800/525 327, ⓦwww.lakebrunnerresort.net.nz; ❻), which has a block of swanky modern units, some with great lake views. Two kilometres back towards Blackball, the *Lake Brunner Country Motel* (ⓣ03/738 0144, ⓦwww.lakebrunnermotel.co.nz; vans $28, cabins ❷, chalets ❹) offers motel-style chalets, a spa pool and fishing gear rental. The licensed *Station House Café*, Koe Street (ⓣ03/738 0158), offers the best **eating** around about, with lunches from $16, dinners from $25 and views across the lake.

Brunner Industrial Site

Back on SH7, a couple of kilometres past Stillwater, a tall chimney marks the **Brunner Industrial Site** (unrestricted access). Roadside information panels mark the path to a fine old suspension bridge (now strengthened and refurbished but still only open to foot traffic), which crosses the swirling river to the few remaining buildings and the largely intact ruins of distinctive beehive coking ovens.

On his explorations in the late 1840s, Thomas Brunner noted a seam of riverside coal, and by 1885 the site was producing twice as much coal as any other mine in the country and exporting firebricks throughout Australasia. In 1896 New Zealand's worst mining disaster (with 69 dead) heralded its decline. The site was finally abandoned in the 1940s, and only exhumed from dense bush in the early 1980s. Half an hour wandering around the foundations and the fifty-minute bushwalk to some of the old mine sites evoke a long-gone era.

Westport and around

While **WESTPORT** is gradually becoming more sophisticated, it remains defiantly old-fashioned. With limited diversions in town, most people spend their time in the surrounding area. Fresh walks to the seal colony at **Cape Foulwind** and the ghostly former coal towns of the **Rochford Plateau** compete with the lure of the limestone country and the Heaphy Track, accessed from Karamea 100km north. Besides, as this is a key transport interchange, you may well end up spending a night or two here, made tolerable by good-value accommodation, an interesting museum and a couple of adventure activities.

Westport was the first of the West Coast towns, established by one **Reuben Waite** in 1861 as a single store beside the mouth of the Buller River. He made his living provisioning the few Buller Gorge prospectors in return for gold, but when the miners moved on to richer pickings in Otago, Waite upped sticks and headed south to help found Greymouth. Westport turned to coal and, while the mining towns to the north were becoming established, engineers channelled the river to scour out a **port**, which fast became the largest coal port in the country but now lies idle. Westport battles on, with a respectable-sized fishing fleet and the odd ship laden with the produce of New Zealand's largest cement works at Cape Foulwind, which is fuelled by coal from open cast Stockton, the only large mine left.

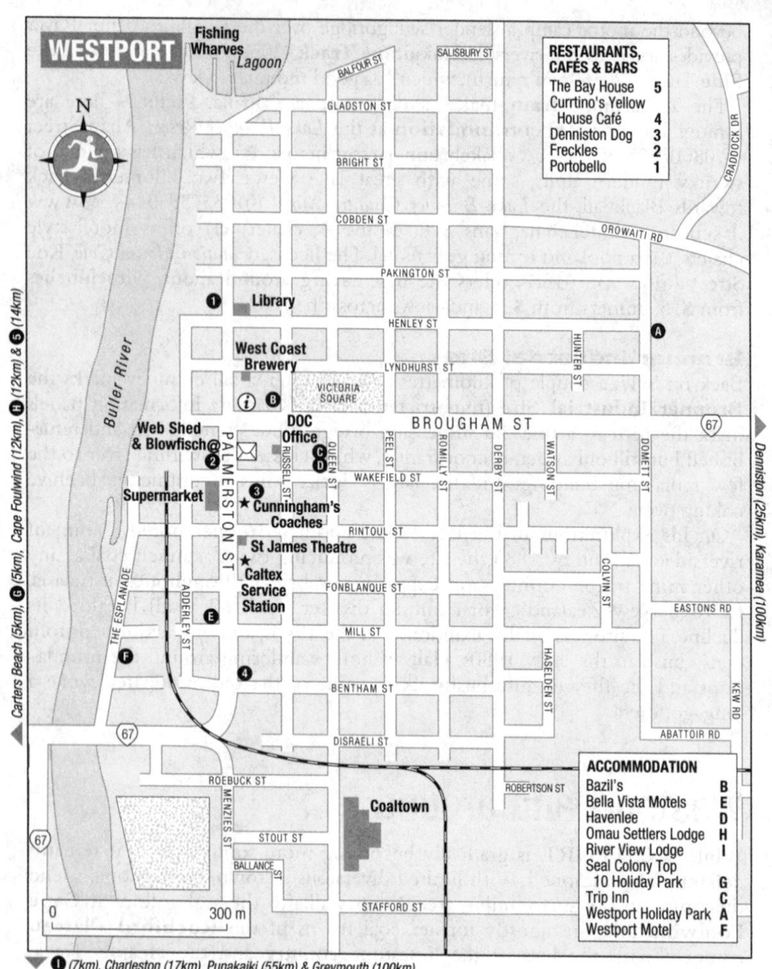

Arrival, information and transport

Almost everything of consequence in Westport happens around Palmerston Street. The helpful **i-SITE visitor centre**, 1 Brougham St (daily: Christmas–April 9am–7pm; May–Oct 9am–4pm; Nov–Christmas 9am–5pm; ⓣ03/789 6658, ⓦwww.westport.org.nz), is the place to go for general tramping information. Book your Heaphy Track hut tickets online, or let the visitor centre do it for a $5 supplement. For less-walked tracks consult the **DOC office**, 72 Russell St (Mon–Fri 8am–noon & 1–5pm; ⓣ03/788 8008). There's **Internet access** at the i-SITE and The Web Shed, 204 Palmerston St.

Bus stops are scattered around town. Southern Link K Bus and Karamea Express stop outside the i-SITE; Cunningham's Coaches from Karamea pull up at their depot at 179 Palmerston St; and InterCity and East–West stop outside the Caltex service station at 197 Palmerston St. Westport is compact enough for you to **get around** on foot, though to reach the nearby attractions you'll need your own transport or Buller Taxis (☎03/789 6900). **Bike rental** is available from Blowfisch, 204 Palmerston St ($35–45 a day; ☎03/788 8002).

Accommodation

Accommodation is fairly limited in Westport. **Backpackers** are reasonably well catered for, and there's a cluster of decent **motels** along Palmerston Street, though the choice of more luxurious places is limited. Discerning travellers might want to consider a couple of excellent places around 20km south towards Punakaiki (see p.735). **Book ahead** if you're going to be here on the weekend after February 6, when the Buller Marathon packs out the town.

Bazil's 54 Russell St ☎03/789 6410, Ⓔbazils.backpackers@xtra.co.nz. Two adjacent houses form this rambling associate YHA, which has some nice modern doubles and twins, a pleasant garden and bike rental for $5 a day. Popular with Kiwi Experience buses. Camping $10, dorms $25, rooms ②, en suite ③

Bella Vista Motels 314 Palmerston St ☎0800/235 528, Ⓔbvwestport@xtra.co.nz. Ugly but modern and well-appointed motel, with Sky TV. The studios are small and have limited cooking facilities, but larger ones are much more spacious and some have spa baths. Studios ④, spa units ⑤

Havenlee 76 Queen St ☎03/789 8543, Ⓦwww.havenlee.co.nz. One comfortable twin and two doubles, with private or shared facilities, in a very friendly homestay where you're plied with a continental breakfast and helpful information each morning. ④

Omau Settlers Lodge 1054 Cape Rd, 12km west of Westport ☎0800/466 287, Ⓔthecape@xtra.co.nz. Modern luxury units with beautiful recycled-wood-floored bathrooms, kettles and fridges, and continental breakfast included. A short drive from *The Bay House* restaurant (see p.728). ⑤

River View Lodge Buller Gorge Rd, 7km south of Westport ☎03/789 6037, Ⓦwww.rurallodge.co.nz. Attractive lodge overlooking the Buller River with four en-suite rooms, each with a veranda, and access to a tennis court. Dinner ($55) available by arrangement. ⑦

Seal Colony Top 10 Holiday Park Marine Parade, Carters Beach, 6km west ☎0508/937 876, Ⓦwww.top10westport.co.nz. Spacious, fully equipped site, with cabins ranging up to some very comfortable motel units, fronting onto a broad beach on the way to Cape Foulwind. Camping $15, cabins ②, motel units ④

Trip Inn 72 Queen St ☎03/789 7367, Ⓦwww.tripinn.co.nz. Six-bed dorms and an abundance of doubles and twins in a big old rambling backpackers that discourages the backpacker tour buses. There's a BBQ area and all the usual features, including plenty of videos, though no quiet lounge. Camping $14, dorms $25, rooms ②

Westport Holiday Park 31 Domett St ☎03/789 7043, Ⓦwww.westportholidaypark.co.nz. Smallish, low-key site partly hemmed in by native bush and with a Buller district-themed mini-golf course. Ten minutes' walk from the town centre. Camping $13, dorms $22, cabins ②, en-suite chalets ③, motels ③

Westport Motel 32 The Esplanade ☎0800/805 909, Ⓦwww.westportmotel.co.nz. These older motel units are all well appointed and come complete with modern kitchens. Cooked and continental breakfast available. ③

The Town

Anyone with even the vaguest interest in Westport's coal-mining past should visit **Coaltown**, Queen Street (daily 9am–4.30pm; $8), an imaginatively presented museum concentrating on the Buller coalfield. Scenes of the workings in their heyday pack an interesting video, which complements remnants salvaged from the site – a coal wagon on tracks angled as it was in situ, at an unsettling 45 degrees, and a huge braking drum – and a mock-up of a mine tunnel, complete with musty smells and clanking sound effects. Fascinating photos of the tramways in operation, a scale model of the plateau and a collection of miners' hats and lamps round out this engaging exhibition. The museum also tries to record the region's pioneer past, with less compelling exhibits on gold dredging, the Buller earthquakes, brewing and the town's maritime history.

Before leaving town, try the preservative- and chemical-free beers made by the co-operatively run **West Coast Brewery**, 10 Lyndhurst St (Mon–Fri 10am–5.30pm, Sat 11am–5.30pm; ⓣ03/789 6201), which distributes its beers throughout the northern half of the South Island, sponsors Hokitika's Wildfoods Festival and offers free tasting of their dark draught Pilsner and organic "Green Fern" lager.

Walks and activities

Once again we have Captain Cook, battling heavy weather in March 1770, to thank for the naming of Westport's most dramatic and evocatively titled stretch of coastline, **Cape Foulwind**, 12km west of town. The name also lends itself to the undulating four-kilometre **Cape Foulwind Walkway**, which runs over exposed headlands, airing superb coastal views. It is perfect for sunset ambling between the old lighthouse, a replica of Abel Tasman's astrolabe and the **Tauranga Bay Seal Colony**, where platforms overlook New Zealand's most northerly breeding colony of fur seals. The animals are at their most active and numerous from October to January, often numbering four hundred or more, a sign of the welcome recovery from the decimation of 150 years of sealing. The seals are at the southern end of the walkway, most easily reached from the sandy but treacherous beach of Tauranga Bay; a ten-minute walk.

For something wilder, go **rafting** with Buller Adventure Tours (ⓣ0800/697 286, ⓦwww.adventuretours.co.nz), located 8km east of Westport on SH6, heading into the Buller Gorge. Throughout the year they run the six major rapids of the Grade IV "Earthquake Slip" section of the **Buller River** around Lyell, spending over two and a half hours on the water for $110. They also offer **jetboat rides** through the Lower Buller Gorge (1hr 15min; $75), **horse trekking** through bush and along a river beach (from $75) and ninety-minute guided rides on sports quad bikes ($130).

Eating, drinking and nightlife

Westport's **eating** scene is picking up, though foodies still head out of town to **The Bay House**. **Pubs** are plentiful, most following the West Coast tradition, with those towards the northern end of Palmerston Street exhibiting a raw edge. **Nightlife** is limited to **movies** at the fine St James Theatre, 193 Palmerston St (ⓣ03/789 8936).

The Bay House Tauranga Bay ⓣ03/789 7133, ⓦwww.bayhousecafe.co.nz. Superb, if slightly overpriced, restaurant/café out towards the seal colony at the southern end of the Cape Foulwind Walkway. Coffee, lunch and excellent dinners (mains around $30) – such as fillet of beef with potato and parsnip rosti, locally caught turbot, at least one veggie option and mouth-watering desserts – are served in the cosy interior or on the terrace, where you can watch the surfers on the bay.

Currtino's Yellow House Café 243 Palmerston St ⓣ03/789 8765. The bright yellow and red walls of this converted house are surprisingly soothing as you tuck into the likes of artichoke dip ($12), bacon-wrapped chilli chicken ($26), herb-roasted salmon ($24) or their daily vegetarian dish. Come for lunch or dinner (all made to order on site and using local ingredients where possible), or just a coffee and hom0e-made cake. They even have a kid-friendly back garden. BYO and licensed.

Denniston Dog 18 Wakefield St ⓣ03/789 7640. Sophisticated (for Westport) café/bar with a good range of beers and excellent meals including Cajun fillets and green-lipped mussels (mostly $20–30).

Freckles 216 Palmerston St. Simple breakfasts, hearty sandwiches, quiches and cakes, and a few tasty treats such as Thai curry ($10). There's peaceful seating out the back. Closed Sun.

Portobello 62 Palmerston St ⓣ03/789 5670. Corinthian columns supporting the bar lend an over-the-top Italian tenor to this pizza restaurant. Steaks and salads are very reasonably priced and on Sun they dish up a $9 roast. There's often a DJ late Fri & Sat nights.

Around Westport

Westport historically thrived on supplying inhospitably sited coal-mining towns where fresh vegetables were hard to grow and sheep almost impossible to raise. Foremost among them was **Denniston**, located high on the Rochford Plateau. Since production stopped in the late 1960s, houses have been carted away and the bush is rapidly engulfing what remains of the mining machinery. It makes an intriguing place to explore for half a day, or longer if you want to tackle the **Denniston Incline Walk**. All the other deep mines have gone the same way, leaving a legacy of inclines, tramways and rusting machinery that can be visited on a number of walks, the **Charming Creek Walk** being the best.

Outwest Tours (ⓣ0800/688 937, ⓦwww.outwest.co.nz) run a couple of trips out this way from Westport. Their **Denniston Tour** (daily 9.30am–4pm; $95) visits the town and plateau, while the coal-company-sponsored **Stockton Mine Tour** (daily 10am–4pm; $15) gives an good insight into the operation of a working open cast mine.

Denniston

The Karamea Road runs north from Westport to Waimangaroa, 17km away, where a steep 9km road wends its way 600m up to the semi-ghost town of **DENNISTON**, the setting for Jenny Pattrick's 2003 bestselling historical novel *The Denniston Rose*.

The rich Coalbrookdale Seam was first discovered by one John Rochford in 1859, and the plateau was soon humming with activity, spurred on by the construction of the **Denniston Self-Acting Incline** in 1879. This impressive, gravity-powered tramway was the steepest rail-wagon incline in the world, lowering coal-filled wagons 518m over 1.7km, while hauling up empty wagons. Throughout its 88-year lifespan, over a thousand tonnes of coal a day would rattle at a prodigious 70km per hr down to Conn's Creek for the trip into Westport. Initially goods, machinery and even people came up the incline but after four unfortunates were flung to their death from careering wagons, a path was constructed in 1884, easing some of the hardship of living up on the plateau.

The region peaked at around 2500 inhabitants in 1910, but the accessible coal eventually played out and the incline closed in 1967. All that's left now is the post office, a fire station, half a dozen scattered houses, three or four of them occupied, and a treasure-trove of industrial archeology centred on a gaunt winding derrick. The views are great in fine weather, but a blanket of cloud and damp fog adds a suitably ethereal quality to this desolate landscape.

The old schoolhouse here has been turned into a small "Friends of the Hill" **museum** and **visitor centre** (Jan daily plus Sun all year 10am–3pm; free), containing historical photos and old mining machinery. It all comes alive when you talk to curator Gary James (ⓣ03/789 9755), who is usually happy to open up at any time.

At Conn's Creek, 2km inland from Waimangaroa, fit and ambitious visitors can tackle the **Denniston Walk** (2km one way; 2–3hr; 520m ascent), which follows the 1884 path roughly parallel to the incline.

North of Waimangaroa

North of Waimangaroa, SH67 runs 7km to **Granity**, where you can break your journey with a coffee from the *Drifters Café and Bar*, then continues 2km to **Ngakawau**. Here, a coal depot signals the start of the lovely **Charming Creek Walk** (5km one way; 2hr; 100m ascent), which follows an old railway that was used for timber and coal extraction between 1914 and 1958. The first half-hour is a bit dull, but things improve dramatically after the S-shaped Irishman's

Tunnel, which has great views of the boulder-strewn river below and, after a swingbridge river crossing, the Mangatini Falls. From here to the picnic stop by the remains of Watson's Mills is the most interesting section of the walk and is the furthest most people get (2–3hr return).

Ngakawau merges imperceptible with **Hector**, where you can grab a good espresso by the beach at the chilled-out *Imagine Café*, SH67, and stay comfortably at *The Old Slaughterhouse*, 2km north of the village on SH67 (Ⓣ03/782 8333, Ⓦwww.oldslaughterhouse.co.nz; dorms $27, rooms ❷). This small **hostel** in a lovely wooden house is perched on the hillside with vast ocean views and welcoming hosts. There are good bushwalks all about, and Hector's dolphins regularly play in the surf. Access is by a steep ten-minute walk off SH67, though the owners can carry your bags on a quad bike.

There's more accommodation 15km further north and 3km down a side road at the *Gentle Annie* (Ⓣ03/782 1826, Ⓦwww.gentleannie.co.nz; camping $10, dorms $20, rooms ❷, cottages sleeping six ❹), a very relaxed place beautifully sited near the mouth of the Mokihinui River, beside Gentle Annie Beach. Accommodation ranges from camping and a budget lodge to spacious and well-equipped self-catering cottages, all with either sea or river views; swimming, horse-riding and canoeing can all be organized.

Karamea and the Oparara Basin

The northwestern corner of the South Island competes with Fiordland as the least developed and most inaccessible region in the country, a distinction acknowledged by the formation of the **Kahurangi National Park** in 1996. The second-largest park in the country, it embraces a vast wilderness of spectacular hill country, supporting alpine meadows, the high Matiri ("Thousand Acre") Plateau, New Zealand's finest karst landscape, dramatic windswept beaches and a coastal strip warm enough to support extensive stands of nikau palms. Charles Heaphy and Thomas Brunner surveyed the region in 1846, paving the way for European and Chinese gold miners, who came a couple of decades later and took thin pickings as late as the 1930s. Pioneers established themselves at **Karamea**, now the base for visiting the fine limestone country of the **Oparara Basin** and the final straight of the **Heaphy Track**.

The road north from Westport initially runs parallel to the coast, pinched between the pounding Tasman breakers and bush-clad hills as it passes through meagre hamlets with barely a shop or a pub. The journey takes almost two hours if you don't stop, though there are plenty of opportunities to pause, not least at the coal towns around Westport (see p.729). North of the **Mokihinui River**, the road leaves the coastal strip, twisting and climbing over **Karamea Bluff** before descending again into a rich apron of dairying land. Rainfall begins to drop off and humidity picks up, promoting more subtropical vegetation characterized by marauding cabbage trees and coastal nikau palms. At the foot of the bluff, **Little Wanganui** marks the turn-off for the start of the **Wangapeka** and **Leslie–Karamea** tracks (jointly 52km; 3–5 days; see p.542 for details), which traverses the southern half of the Kahurangi National Park to Tasman Bay near Motueka.

Karamea

Diminutive **KARAMEA**, 100km north of Westport, is one of those places where doing nothing seems just right. This peaceful and isolated spot is virtually at the end of the road; to continue any distance north you'd have to go on foot along the Heaphy Track. At the same time there is no shortage of things to do in the vicinity, the southern section of the Kahurangi National Park easily justifying a day or two of exploration.

Back in 1874, this was very much **frontier territory**, with the Karamea River port providing the only link with the outside world. Settlers eked a living from **gold** and **flax**, but after a couple of fruitless years realized that the poorly drained *pakihi* soils would barely support them. They pushed on, opening up the first road to Westport just in time for the upheavals of the 1929 Murchison **earthquake**, which altered the river flow and permanently ruined the harbour. Logging finally ceased in 2000, leaving tourism, agriculture and burgeoning fruit-growing as the town's lifeblood.

Apart from **swimming** and **fishing** in the Karamea River there's not a great deal to do in town, and you'll soon want to head out to the Oparara Basin or the Heaphy Track.

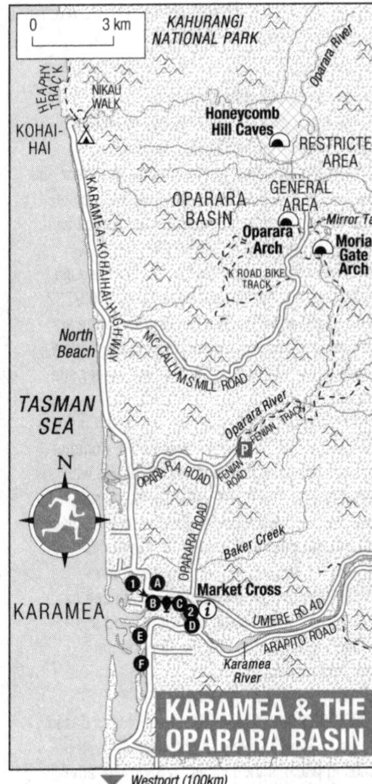

Practicalities

The **visitor centre** at Market Cross, 2km east of the centre (Jan–April daily 9am–5pm; May–Dec Mon–Fri 9am–5pm & Sat 9am–noon; ⓣ03/782 6652, ⓦwww.karameainfo.co.nz), has information about exploring the local area and **Internet access**. Use this to **book huts** for the Heaphy Track, or they'll do it for you for $5. The **Heaphy Track** is generally walked from north to south and is covered on p.541.

Two scheduled **bus** services ply the Westport–Karamea route: Cunningham's (Mon–Fri; $20; ⓣ03/789 7177) run up to Karamea in the late afternoon, returning to Westport in the early evening; Karamea Express (Nov–March Mon–Sat; April–Oct Mon–Fri; $27 each way; ⓣ03/782 6757) run south to Westport in the early morning and set off around 11.30am for the return journey. Both buses connect with ongoing services in Westport. Karamea Express also serve the **Heaphy Track** trailhead at Kohaihai (Nov–March daily around 2pm; $12; in winter on demand), and drop off at the Wangapeka trailhead on their Westport–Karamea run.

In recent years Karamea has begun to gear itself for tourism and there are now quite a few **places to stay**, and some good **camping** spots. **Eating** is limited to the three places mentioned below, plus a small **supermarket** at Market Cross.

Accommodation

Bridge Farm Motels SH67, 700m south of the visitor centre ⓣ0800/527 263, ⓦwww.karameamotels.co.nz. Modern motel on a deer and alpaca farm with spacious, well-appointed units, some with full kitchens and bathtubs, and all with continental breakfast included. ❹

Karamea Domain on SH67 between *The Last Resort* and the *Karamea Village Hotel* ⓣ03/782 6069. Fairly primitive site utilizing the showers and toilets of the town's sports field but with a good kitchen. Camping & hookups $14 per site, dorms $10.

Karamea Holiday Park SH67, 3km south of town ⓣ03/782 6758, ⓦwww.karamea.com. Commercial campsite on a neat and well-kept site with ageing cabins and motel units. They also rent bargain kayaks for mucking around on the adjacent estuary. Camping $10, cabins ❶, motels ❷

Karamea Lodge SH6, 5km south of town ⓣ03/782 6034, ⓦwww.karamealodge.co.nz. Luxury units with decks, sea views and a common kitchen and lounge. Continental breakfast included ❺

The Last Resort 71 Waverly St (SH67) ⓣ0800/505 042, ⓦwww.lastresort.co.nz. Based around an imaginatively styled main lodge, this rambling place is the biggest in town and after years of neglect is on the up again. There's good accommodation in dorms (no bunks but also no kitchen and no linen: bring a sleeping bag), simple but attractive lodge rooms (some en suite), motel-style studios and well-appointed "cottages" sleeping four. Shares $28, lodge ❸, studios ❹, cottages ❺

Rongo 130 Waverle St (SH67) ⓣ03/782 6667, ⓦwww.livinginpeace.com. Welcoming and comfortable rainbow-painted hostel in spacious grounds, with an organic veggie garden and comfy wood-floored rooms and dorms. Art and music play a bit part in the hostel's daily life, and they even run a community radio station (107.5FM). If you stay three nights you get the fourth free. Also ageing but comfy motel units off site. Dorms $30, rooms ❸, units ❸

Eating and drinking

Karamea Village Hotel Corner of Waverley St & Wharf Rd. Karamea's pub dishes up cheap takeaways, straightforward bar meals and a good selection of "Wild Food" dishes including renowned whitebait ($30).

The Last Resort (see above). Good semi-formal dining in the restaurant (mains around $25) in the main building, plus a more casual bar/bistro just across the car park.

Saracens Café Opposite the visitor centre. Relaxed spot which serves coffee, pies, enormous sausage rolls and sandwiches in a craft gallery. Outside seating.

The Oparara Basin and Kohaihai

Kahurangi's finest limestone formations lie east of the Karamea–Kohaihai Highway in the **Oparara Basin**, a compact area of **karst** topography characterized by numerous sinkholes, underground streams, caves and bridges created over millennia by the action of slightly acidic streams on the jointed rock. This is home to New Zealand's largest native **spider**, the harmless, 15cm-diameter gradungular spider (found only in caves in the Karamea and Collingwood area, where it feeds off blowflies and cave crickets), and to a rare species of ancient and primitive carnivorous **snail** that grows up to 70mm across and dines on earthworms. Tannin-stained rivers course gently over bleached-white boulders and, in faster-flowing sections, the rare whio (blue duck) swims for its supper. If your interest in geology is fleeting, the Oparara Basin still makes a superb place for an afternoon **walk** or a **picnic** by one of the rivers.

Ten kilometres north of Karamea, the steep, narrow and gravel McCallums Mill Road runs 14km east to the Oparara Basin, where the **Honeycomb Hill Caves** have become a valuable key to understanding New Zealand's fauna. The sediment on the cave floor has helped preserve the ancient skeletons of birds, most of them killed when they fell through holes in the cave roof. The bones of over fifty species have been found here including those of the Haast eagle, the largest eagle ever known with a wingspan of up to four metres.

▲ Nikau palms near Kohaihai

The cave system can only be visited on the excellent and educational **Honeycomb Hill Caves Tour** (daily 10am & 2pm on demand, min 2 persons; $75; ⓣ03/782 6652, ⓦwww.oparara.co.nz) which explores just some of the 15km of passages. Tours depart from the end of McCallums Mill car park, close to the cave, and take two and a half hours. If you don't have your own transport, a ride can be organized for $25 return. Cave trips can be combined with the **Honeycomb Hill Arch Kayak Tour** (mid-Dec to Aug; $75), a gorgeous paddle through bush and under a broad limestone arch.

As is common in limestone areas, the watercourses alter frequently, leaving behind dry caves such as the **Crazy Paving and Box Canyon caves** (about 10min return) near the Honeycomb Caves. Both are freely accessible along a five-minute track from the road-end car park and are good for spider- and fossil-spotting: take a torch each, and watch out for slippery floors.

The two most spectacular examples of limestone architecture lie at the end of beautiful, short bushwalks signposted from a car park 3km back down the road towards Karamea. The largest is the **Oparara Arch** (40min return), a vast two-tiered bridge 43m high, 40m wide and over 219m long, which appears magically out of the bush but defies any attempt at successful photography. The lovely **Moria Gate Arch** was named decades before *Lord of the Rings* movie fever swept the land. It is reached on a track (1hr return) through the untouched, high-canopy native forest then through a short cave (torch handy but not really needed). This can be combined with a visit to peaceful **Mirror Tarn** (90min for both).

Kohaihai

Visitors with no aspirations to tramp the full length of Heaphy Track can sample the final few coastal kilometres from the mouth of the Kohaihai River, 17km north of Karamea, where there is good river (but not sea) swimming, a beautifully sited toilets-and-water DOC **campsite** ($6) and an abundance of sandflies. In the heat of the day, you're much better off across the river in the cool of the **Nikau Walk** (30–40min loop), which winds through a shady grove dense with nikau palms, tree ferns and magnificent gnarled old rata trees dripping in epiphytes. When it cools off, either continue along the Heaphy to **Scott's Beach** (1hr 30min return), or stick to the southern side of the Kohaihai River and the **Zig-Zag Track** (35min return), which switchbacks up to an expansive lookout.

Paparoa National Park and around

South of Westport lies the Paparoa Range, a 1500m granite and gneiss ridge inlaid with limestone that separates the dramatic coastal strip from the valleys of the Grey and Inangahua rivers. In 1987, the coastal limestone country was designated the **Paparoa National Park**, one of the country's smallest and least-known parks. The highlight is undoubtedly the **Pancake Rocks**, where crashing waves have forced spectacular blowholes through a stratified stack of weathered limestone. But to skip the rest would be to miss out on a mysterious world of disappearing rivers, sinkholes, caves and limestone bluffs best seen on the **Inland Pack Track**, but also accessible on shorter walks close to Punakaiki.

Maori often stopped here while travelling the coast in search of *pounamu* (greenstone) and early **European explorers** followed suit seeking agricultural land. Charles Heaphy, Thomas Brunner and two Maori guides came

Paparoa walks and the Inland Pack Track

The best way to truly appreciate the dramatic limestone scenery of the Paparoa is on the **Inland Pack Track** (27km; 2–3 days; see map, p.736). Most of the terrain is easy going, but there are no bridges for river crossings, and while the water barely gets above your knees in dry periods, the rivers can become impassable after rain. With less time or greater demand for comfort, some of the best can be seen on two day-walks. The delightful **Punakaiki–Pororari Rivers Loop** (12km; 3hr 30min; 100m ascent) follows the initial stretch of the Inland Pack Track as far as the Pororari River, which is then followed downstream between some magnificent limestone cliffs to return to Punakaiki. The **Fox River Cave Walk** (10km; 2hr 30min; 100m ascent) traces the last few kilometres of the Inland Pack Track from the Fox Rivermouth as far as the caves and returns the same way.

Practicalities

DOC's *Inland Pack Track* leaflet provides enough information for the tramp, but you might also fancy the 1:50,000 *Paparoa National Park* map ($19).

The Inland Pack Track is best walked from south to north, which eliminates the risk of missing the critical turn-off up Fossil Creek. There are no huts along the way, just a massive rock **bivvy** known as the Ballroom Overhang at the end of a long first day. You're advised to carry a **tent** for protection from voracious sandflies, and to avoid a wet night in the open if the rivers flood. **Campfires** are permitted at the Ballroom Overhang, but DOC recommends carrying a stove as most of the usable wood has already been burned. Be sure to check the **weather forecast** with DOC and fill out an **intentions form**, remembering to check in on your return.

Drivers should leave their vehicle at the end of the walk and either hitch or catch one of the infrequent **buses** to get to the start (see p.737). Alternatively, base yourself in Punakaiki and call Green Kiwi Tours (ⓣ03/731 1843, ⓦwww.greenkiwitours.co.nz), who will drop off or pick up a vanload (1–8 people) at Fox River for $50: get a group together.

through in 1846, finding little to detain them, but within twenty years this stretch was alive with **gold** prospectors at work on the black sands at now-tiny **Charleston**.

Visitor interest is centred on **Punakaiki**, close by the Pancake Rocks, where bus passengers get a quick glimpse and others pause for the obligatory photos. A couple of days spent here will be well rewarded with a stack of wonderful walks, horse-riding, canoeing up delightful limestone gorges and just slobbing about.

Westport to Punakaiki

South of Westport, SH67 crosses the Buller River and picks up SH6, the main West Coast road. There's little specific reason to stop except for some lovely **places to stay**. Around 17km south of Westport, *Beaconstone*, Birds Ferry Road (T 027/431 0491, W www.beaconstone.co.nz; closed June–Sept; shares $28, rooms ❷, cottage ❷) is one of the best hostels on the coast, great value with a few doubles, one triple and a separate cottage with mountain views. Eco-friendly features include composting toilets and solar power, and it's set in 120 acres of native bush threaded by various trails. The adjacent *Birds Ferry Lodge*, Birds Ferry Road (T 0800/212 207, W www.birdsferrylodge.co.nz; rooms ❼, cottage ❽) offers considerably more luxurious accommodation with three rooms in the main house where excellent breakfasts and dinners ($65; mostly homegrown or locally sourced) are served with great views over the

The Inland Pack Track

The Inland Pack Track starts 1km south of the Punakaiki visitor centre beside the south bank of the Punakaiki River. From **Punakaiki River to Bullock Creek** (9.5km; 4hr; 220m ascent, 100m descent), the track gradually rises to a low saddle then descends to ford the Pororari River, continuing with views inland to the Paparoa Range before reaching Bullock Creek. This should be forded with some care – in flood conditions it can be impassable. From **Bullock Creek to Fox River** (10km; 3–4hr; 100m ascent, 150m descent), you skirt swampland then climb to a ridge before descending gradually to Fossil Creek, which is followed wading from pool to pool, occasionally clambering over fallen tree trunks. After half an hour of this, Fossil Creek meets the main tributary of the Fox River, Dilemma Creek, by a small sign – keep your eyes peeled. This is the most dramatic section of the trip but potentially the most dangerous, with 18 fords to cross between gravel banks in the bed of Dilemma Creek: if you have any doubts about the first crossing, turn back, as they only get worse. The lower river has carved out a deep canyon between gleaming white vertical cliffs and, if you can find a patch of sun, this makes a great place to rest awhile. The track resumes by a sign on the true left bank just above the confluence with the Fox River; a steep bluff on the right makes a useful landmark.

A signposted track crosses to the true right bank of the Fox River below the confluence, then crosses several more times to the vast limestone **Ballroom Overhang** (1km; 30min each way; negligible ascent) with its 100m-long lip. It could easily provide shelter for a hundred or more campers, and has a long-drop toilet. Return the same way to the confluence, from where the track runs to the **Fox Rivermouth** (5km; 2hr; 100m descent). A short distance along, a sign points across the river to the interesting **Fox River Cave** (30min). Meanwhile, the Inland Pack Track crosses to the car park by the Fox Rivermouth, some 12km by road from your starting point; southbound **buses** currently pass around 11.45am and 3.55pm.

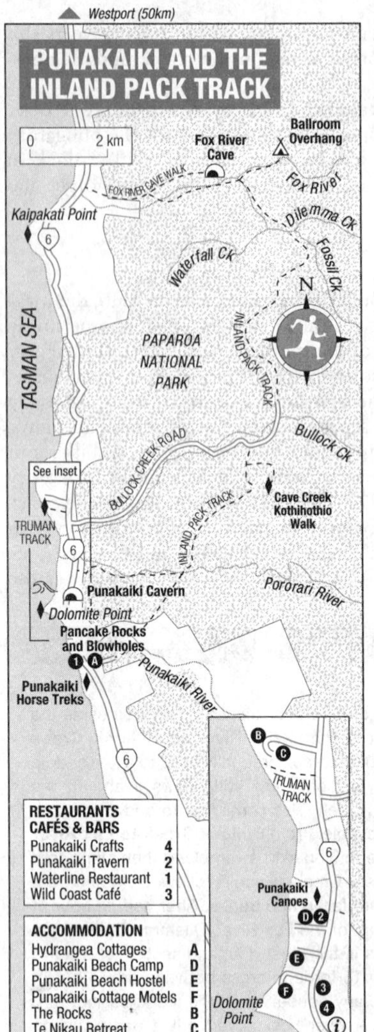

bushy valley. There's a fab spa pool and the option of staying in the separate two-bedroom *Fisherman's Cottage* with its bath under the stars. Stay two nights and owner André will throw in a fascinating guided tour of the area.

Continue 4km south to reach *Jack's Gasthof* (ⓣ03/789 6501, ⓔjack.schubert@xtra.co.nz; ❷), just a couple of colourful budget **rooms**, basic **camping** ($5) and a café and bar serving great pizza and the likes of Thai curry, Greek salad and fruit shakes: many of the ingredients are fresh from the garden and are organic. The whole set-up is pretty laid-back, with a sauna, swimming in the creek and loads of great bush-walking.

A couple of kilometres further along SH6 is **Mitchells Gully Gold Mine** (usually 9am–4pm; $5; ⓣ03/789 6553), a family-run mine working dating back to 1866, which has been reopened mainly to demonstrate the time-honoured methods used to extract fine gold held in a cement-like mass of oxidized ironsand. Along with a collection of mining paraphernalia, you can see a restored overshot wheel driving a stamping battery, and water races and tunnels that are still in use.

The most intensive mining went on 3km to the south at **CHARLESTON**, then a rollicking boomtown of around 18,000 people, but now with a mere thirty residents. From the **Charleston Tavern** Underworld Adventures (ⓣ0800/116 686, ⓦwww.caverafting.com) run the **Nile River Rainforest Train** (3–4 daily; $20) a 25-minute interpretive journey on a modern narrow-gauge train through some nice limestone country. The train journey forms part of Underworld Rafting (4hr; $135) a **caving trip** which also involves a bushwalk through a dramatic valley of limestone bluffs before delving underground decked out in wetsuit and caver's helmet and lugging a rubber inner tube. An informative guided walk through the Metro cave system finishes with a final drift down a flooded glow-worm cave and out through a gorgeous ravine into the Nile River. None of it is tremendously arduous; if you like caves and water, you'll like this. For the more timid there's the **Glow-Worm Cave Tour** (3hr; $80), while adrenalin seekers should opt for the full-on

Adventure Caving (5hr; $270) which explores the Te Tahi cave system by means of a thirty-metre abseil, plus numerous squeezes and climbs.

If they stay at all, many choose to **free camp** beside Constant Bay, where there are toilets and water. More formal alternatives cluster together on the main road: *Pounamu Backpackers* (ⓣ03/789 8011, ⓔpaulhoney@xtra.co.nz; shares $23, rooms ❷); the modest *Charleston Motel* (ⓣ03/789 7599, ⓦwww.charlestonmoel.co.nz; ❸); and the *Charleston Motor Camp* (ⓣ03/789 6773 ⓔcmcamp@xtra.co.nz; camping $10, cabins ❶). The *Charleston Tavern* dishes up suitably modern fare of nachos and grills and has a tiny shop for very basic supplies.

Some 20km south of Charleston rise the 50m cliffs of Te Miko – tagged Perpendicular Point by Charles Heaphy, who in 1846 recorded climbing the cliff on two stages of ladders constructed of shaky and rotten rata vines while his dog was hoisted on a rope. Te Miko remained an impenetrable barrier to pack animals until 1866, when a new Westport–Greymouth telegraph line prompted the forging of the **Inland Pack Track** (see p.735). The coast road, finally completed in 1927, now climbs over Te Miko, passing the **Iramahuwhero Point Lookout**, with stupendous views along the coast past the layered rocks of the Te Miko cliff.

Punakaiki and the Pancake Rocks

The **Pancake Rocks** and blowholes at **PUNAKAIKI** are often all visitors see of the Paparoa National Park, as they tumble off the bus outside the visitor centre opposite the twenty-minute paved loop track which leads to the rocks. Here layers of limestone have weathered to resemble an immense stack of giant pancakes, the result of **stylobedding**, a chemical process in which the pressure of overlying sediments creates alternating durable and weaker bands. Subsequent uplift and weathering has accentuated this effect to create wonderfully photogenic formations. The edifice is undermined by huge sea caverns where the surf surges in, sending spumes of brine spouting up through vast **blowholes**: high tide with a good swell from the south or southwest sees the blowholes at their best.

More shapely examples of Paparoa's karst landscape are on show on a number of walks. Inside the **Punakaiki Cavern**, 500m to the north, you'll find a few glow-worms (go after dark: torch essential) and, 2km beyond that, the **Truman Track** (30min return) runs down from the highway to a small beach hemmed in by wave-sculpted rock platforms.

There's good **river swimming** in the Pororari and Punakaiki rivers, and **sea bathing** at the southern end of Pororari Beach, a section also good for point-break **surfing**. Keeping with aquatic pursuits, Punakaiki Canoes (ⓣ03/731 1870, ⓦwww.riverkayaking.co.nz) rent out **kayaks** ($35 for 2hr, $55 per day) from their base beside the Pororari River and run guided trips from $70. There's also excellent **horse-riding** with Punakaiki Horse Treks (Oct–April; ⓣ03/731 1839), who charge $120 for two and a half hours trekking through bush, rivers and along the beach, and a range of **caving** and **environmental tours** with Green Kiwi Tours (ⓣ03/731 1843, ⓦwww.greenkiwitours.co.nz), costing $60 per hour for the whole group.

Practicalities

North- and south-bound **buses** run by InterCity and Southern Link K Bus stop for around half an hour outside the **Wild Coast Café**, giving enough time for a quick look at the Pancake Rocks across the road. DOC's **Paparoa National Park visitor centre** (daily: Dec–April 9am–6pm, May–Nov 9am–4.30pm;

(T)03/731 1895, (W)www.punakaiki.co.nz) has excellent displays on all aspects of the park, information on activities, walking maps and leaflets and extremely helpful staff.

Punakaiki is a tiny place, but its popularity is growing, spawning a slew of places to stay and a more limited supply of restaurants. There's no decent shop for buying supplies, so if you're self-catering, bring what you need.

Accommodation

Hydrangea Cottages SH6 (T)03/731 1839, (W)www.pancake-rocks.co.nz. Four gorgeous cottages set above the road, most with sea views. The real appeal, though, is the self-catering cottages themselves (studio, one- & two-bedroom), all constructed with native timbers and local stone and very tastefully decorated. Small discount for two-night stays. Studios 6, suites 8

Punakaiki Beach Camp SH6 (T)03/731 1894, (E)beachcamp@xtra.co.nz. Attractive, grassy campsite close to the beach and pub with campervan hookups. Camping $12, cabins 1, kitchen cabins 2

Punakaiki Beach Hostel 4 Webb St (T)03/731 1852, (W)www.punakaikibeachhostel.co.nz. There's a relaxed atmosphere to this vibrantly painted hostel where guests can buy freshly baked wholemeal bread, surf the Net and use the outdoor spa pool. Camping $18, dorms $24, rooms 2

Punakaiki Cottage Motels Mabel St (T)03/731 1008, (W)www.punakaikicottmotels.co.nz. Comfortable motel units with full kitchens, some overlooking the breakers. 5

The Rocks Hartmount Place (T)03/731 1141, (W)www.therockshomestay.com. Comfortable and welcoming homestay with three en-suite rooms, all with bush or sea views, and a lounge with a broad seascape. The same folk manage a couple of self-catering properties nearby: *Te Puna Bush Haven*, a well-appointed and nicely designed modern home surrounded by bush that sleeps four, and the luxurious *Flax Haven*, sleeping up to seven. B&B 6, *Te Puna* 6, *Flax Haven* 7

Te Nikau Retreat Hartmount Place, 200m north of the Truman Track and 3km north of the visitor centre (T)03/731 1111, (W)www.tenikauretreat.co.nz. Associate YHA hostel which must rank as one of the most relaxing backpackers in the country, carved out of bush that's peppered with nikau palms. The smattering of buildings includes small dorms, rooms, and rustic en-suite cabins for couples. Fresh bread, muffins and eggs are sold, and there's Internet access. Dorms $23, shares $25, rooms 2, en suites and cabins 3

Eating

Punakaiki Crafts SH6, by the visitor centre. The best espresso in town plus snacks and cakes served on the deck under nikau palms.

Punakaiki Tavern SH6, 1km north of the visitor centre. Straightforward pub with a pool table. Good value for simple bistro meals (mostly $18–25).

Waterline Restaurant *Punakaiki Rocks Hotel*, SH6, 700m south of the visitor centre (T)03/731 1167. Easily the fanciest place in Punakaiki, with classy à la carte dining in a room overlooking the sea. Open for lunch (11am–2pm; mains around $16) and dinner (from 6pm; mains around $30).

Wild Coast Café SH6, by the visitor centre. Popular with the buses, this place serves "West Coast" breakfasts (a mass of bacon, eggs and hash browns), bagels, panini and salads until sunset plus dinners several nights a week in summer.

Punakaiki to Greymouth

The road from Punakaiki to Greymouth is a spectacular drive, sometimes pushed onto the sea cliffs by the intrusive ramparts of the Paparoa Range, but there's little to stop for until you get close to Greymouth.

Tiny **RAPAHOE**, 30km south of Punakaiki, has about the safest bathing beach on the coast and a reputation for gemstones. Follow the track to the excellent vantage point of **Point Elizabeth** (2hr return) and perhaps **stay** at the basic *Rapahoe Beach Motor Camp*, 10 Hawken St ((T)0508/465 432, (E)rapahoebeach@actrix.co.nz; camping $12, on-site vans & cabins 1), which has a swimming pool and volleyball court and is only a short stagger from the local pub. From here it is just 10km to Greymouth.

Greymouth and around

The Grey River forces its way through a break in the coastal Rapahoe Range and over the treacherous sand bar to the sea at workaday **GREYMOUTH**, which ranks as the West Coast's largest town but still claims under ten thousand residents. Greymouth is hardly going to be a highlight on most visitors' itineraries, though there's some high-quality greenstone carving in evidence and a bunch of worthwhile **adventure activities**, while the kids will get a kick out of **Shantytown**, a replica gold town to the south. Best to do what you need to and move on, especially in winter when you might be plagued by **The Barber**, a razor-sharp cold wind that whistles down the Grey Valley and envelops the town in thick icy fog.

Greymouth began to take shape during the early years of the **gold rush** on land purchased in 1860 by James Mackay, who bought most of Westland from the Poutini Ngai Tahu people for 300 gold sovereigns. The town's defining feature is the river, which is deceptively calm and languid through most of the summer but awesome after heavy rains. Devastating **floods** swept through Greymouth in 1887, 1905, 1936, 1977 and 1988; since the last great flood, the Greymouth Flood Protection Scheme has successfully held back most of the waters.

Arrival, information and transport

The stylish way to arrive in Greymouth is on the daily TranzAlpine **train** from Christchurch (see p.585), which pulls in at the station on Mackay Street and is met by InterCity and Atomic **buses** (tickets from the visitor centre or the travel centre inside the station; ⓣ03/768 7080) running south to Hokitika and Franz Josef, and north to Westport and Nelson. Southern Link K Bus (ⓣ0508/458 835) also finish their daily run from Picton here, but don't synchronize with the train schedule. Greymouth's **airport** only has flights to Wellington with Air West Coast (ⓣ03/738 0524, ⓦwww.airwestcoast.co.nz).

The **i-SITE visitor centre**, inside the Regent Theatre on the corner of Mackay and Herbert streets (Nov–Easter Mon–Fri 8.30am–7pm, Sat 9am–6pm, Sun 10am–5pm; Easter–Oct Mon–Fri 8.30am–5.30pm, Sat & Sun 10am–4pm; ⓣ03/768 5101, ⓦwww.greydistrict.co.nz), has **Internet access** and will provide the *Grey District* visitor guide, which contains a good street map. You might want to check out **tours** to the Pancake Rocks (see p.737: 2.15pm; 2hr 30min; $85) and elsewhere run by Kea Tours (ⓣ0800/532 868, ⓦwww.keatours.co.nz).

Folk planning to **rent a car** in the South Island are increasingly riding the TranzAlpine train then picking up a rental in Greymouth. All the majors have **car rental** offices either at the train station or nearby, though you may find it cheaper to go with NZ Rent A Car (ⓣ03/768 0379) – who often charge little or no fee for long-term rentals dropped off in Queenstown or Christchurch. Short-term rental starts around $60 a day.

Accommodation

Greymouth has a reasonable selection of **places to stay**. Consider **booking** a couple of days ahead when local events pack out the town: the Kumara Races (second weekend in Jan), the Coast to Coast Race (second weekend in Feb; see p.742), Hokitika's Wildfoods Festival (second weekend in March) and the Around Brunner Cycle Race (3rd weekend in April).

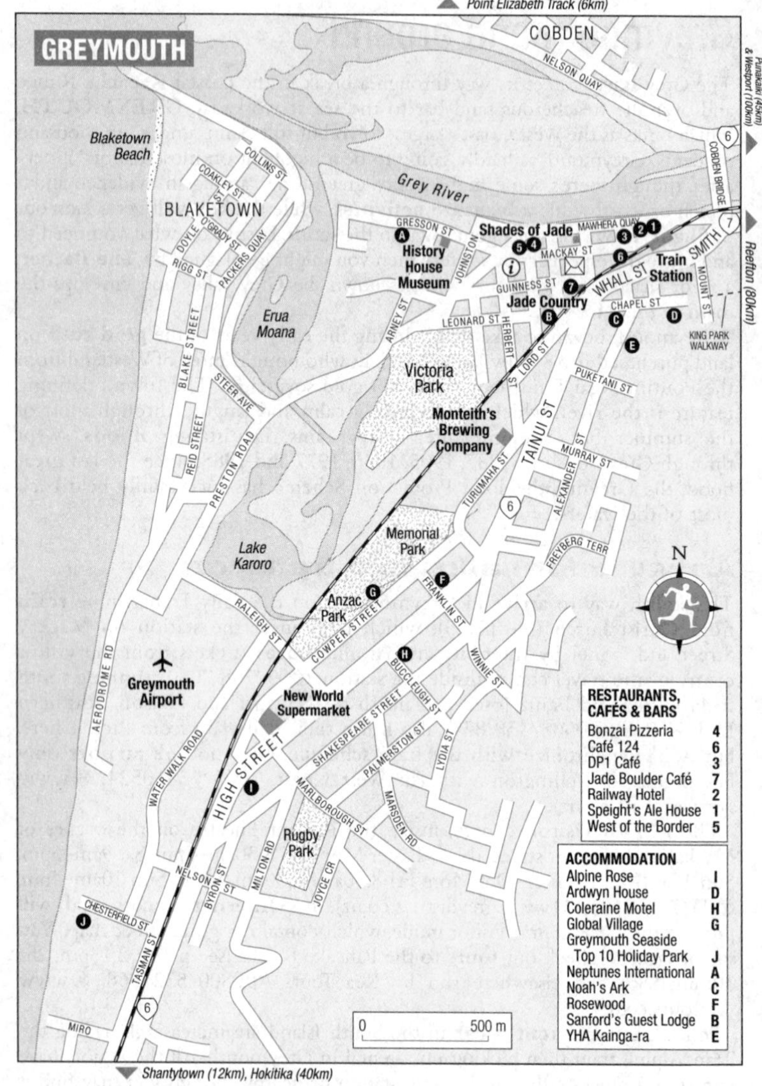

Alpine Rose 139 High St ⓣ0800/266 835, ⓦwww.alpinerose.co.nz. Comfortable and welcoming mid-range motel with whitebait breakfasts available all year ④

Ardwyn House 48 Chapel St ⓣ03/768 6107, ⓔardwynhouse@hotmail.com. Old-fashioned but appealing and very welcoming homestay in a 1920s house, surrounded by a quiet garden and close to the town centre. No en suites, but broad views across the town from many rooms. ④

Coleraine Motel 61 High St ⓣ0800/270 077, ⓦwww.colerainemotel.co.nz. Units in this sparkling new motel come with Sky TV, CD/DVD players and double glazing to keep the road noise down; some have spa baths. There are also swankier executive units and a comfy guests' lounge. Units ⑤, executive ⑤

Global Village 42 Cowper St ⓣ03/768 7272, ⓦwww.globalvillagebackpackers.co.nz. Light and spacious hostel backing onto parkland and a river. The rooms are imaginatively decorated in tribal themes with artefacts the owner has collected around the world and there's a range of tempting activities: free bikes and kayaks, low-cost sauna, spa and small gym, and a BBQ out back most fine evenings. All beds are made up and there are some single-sex dorms. Camping $14, dorms $23, rooms ❷

Greymouth Seaside Top 10 Holiday Park 2 Chesterfield St ⓣ0800/867 104, ⓦwww.top10greymouth.co.nz. The more central of the two motor parks, right by the beach and with very good facilities. Camping $17, cabins ❷, kitchen cabin ❷, motels ❸

Neptunes International 43 Gresson St ⓣ0800/003 768, ⓦwww.neptunesbackpackers.co.nz. Excellent hostel in a former pub with nautical decor, a free hot tub and two baths supplied with free bubble bath. Dorms and rooms all have made-up beds (no bunks) and there's a big-screen TV, pool and Internet access in the lounge. Free train pick-ups. Dorms $22, non-powered $10, powered sites $15, rooms ❷

Noah's Ark 16 Chapel St ⓣ0800/662 472, ⓦwww.noahsarkbackpackers.co.nz. Large and comfortable hostel occupying a two-storey villa originally built as a Catholic presbytery, with great verandas and a spacious lounge with Sky TV. Rooms and dorms are all lavishly decorated with animal themes, beds come made up and there are free bikes and a spa. Camping $17, dorms $23, rooms ❷

Rosewood 20 High St ⓣ0800/185 748, ⓦwww.rosewoodnz.co.nz. Appealing B&B in a characterful 1920s home – all wood panelling, lead-light windows and floral decor. Rooms are mostly en suite and a cooked breakfast is included. ❻

Sanford's Guest Lodge 62 Albert St ⓣ03/768 5605, ⓦww.sanfordsguestlodge.co.nz. Good-value small hotel with simple, airy shared-bathrooms, complete with colour TV and the option of a cooked breakfast ($5 extra per person). ❸

YHA Kainga-ra 15 Alexander St ⓣ03/768 4951, ⓔyha.greymouth@yha.co.nz. Former priest's residence, now a relaxed, central hostel with all the usual facilities, including a well-informed booking office, a selection of dorms, twins and doubles, and sea views over the town. Dorms $26, rooms ❷

The town and around

Greymouth has a long heritage of greenstone carving. Some of the finest pieces are found at the **Jade Country**, 1 Guinness St (Oct–April Mon–Fri 8am–7pm Sat & Sun 9am–7pm; May–Sept daily 8.30am–5pm; ⓦwww.jadenz.co.nz), including works by master carver Ian Boustridge. Even if you have no intention of buying, pop in to watch the cutting, grinding and polishing processes in the workshop, and to visit the **Jade Trail** (free), which tells the parallel stories of jade from a Maori mythological and geological perspective. Especially impressive five-tonne boulders of raw nephrite lead through to a room lined with ancient and modern carved pieces, put into a world context by the presence of Chinese and Meso-American works: look out for the Ming goddess figure and the grotesque eighth-century bat figurine from Copan in Honduras. Simple Maori adzes could hardly present greater contrast with the exquisite modern museum pieces.

Also poke your head into the tiny **Shades of Jade**, 16 Tainui St (Mon–Fri 8.30am–5pm, Sat 10am–2.30pm, Sun noon–2.30pm), a reasonably priced spot where the local carvers can keep the prices down because they own the shop and make their own stock only using New Zealand *pounamu*. There is live jade carving Monday to Friday.

Greymouth's **History House Museum**, Gresson Street (Mon–Fri 10am–4pm; ⓣ03/768 4028; $5), makes a good shot at relating the Grey District's history through piles of maritime memorabilia and a stack of photos depicting the town's heyday. The townspeople's long struggle to combat the floods is also given a thorough and diverting treatment.

Book ahead and be sure to wear closed footwear if you want to go on a **brewery tour** at Monteith's Brewing Company, corner of Turumaha and Herbert streets (ⓣ03/768 4149; daily 11.30am, 2pm, 4pm & 6pm; $15), where age-old recipes have been revived to produce some flavoursome brews popular all down the Coast. You can sample seven at the end of the 45-minute tour.

Choose a fine evening for a couple of pleasant walks. **King Park Walkway** (1hr return) starts on Mount Street near the Cobden Bridge and meanders through the bush to a panoramic viewpoint over the city and the Southern Alps. The coastal views are better from the **Point Elizabeth Track**, which starts 6km north of town and follows the coast through stands of nikau to a lookout (5km return, 90min). You can continue to Rapahoe (see p.738; another 3km) and pick up a bus from there back to town (2 daily).

Activities

Activities around Greymouth are predominantly aquatic, subterranean or both. Some of the best are run by Wild West Adventures (Ⓣ0508/286 877, Ⓦwww.fun-nz.com), notably their Taniwha Cave Rafting (5hr, 90–120min underground; $145), a challenging **caving** trip into the Taniwha system; wetsuits and cavers' lamps are the order of the day for scrambling down a fairly steep underground streambed, floating along deep sections on inner tubes with glow-worms above and, for the adventurous, squeezing through some tight sections. They also have the gentler **Jungle Boat Cruising** (3hr; $135), which plies placid waterways using rafts and pontoons made to look like jungle canoes.

Wild West also run a bunch of rafting and **heli-rafting** trips, as do Eco-Rafting (for both, see p.749). You might also want to try a little speculative **dolphin watching** (90min; $70) with Wild Cat Charters (Ⓣ03/762 6680, Ⓦwww.wildcatcharters.co.nz).

The Coast to Coast Race

Kiwis are mad on multisport and punch above their weight on the international circuit. Every weekend you'll see scores of people toning their muscles and honing their biking and paddling skills. The ultimate goal of all true multisporters is the gruelling 243km **Coast to Coast Race** (second weekend in Feb; Ⓦwww.coasttocoast.co.nz), which requires a pre-dawn start from the beach near Kumara Junction, 15km south of Greymouth. A 3km run leads to a 55km cycle uphill to Otira where jelly-kneed contenders tackle the most gruelling section, a 33km run up and down the boulder-strewn creek beds of the Southern Alps, before kayaking for several hours down Canterbury's braided Waimakariri River and then cycling the final stretch to Sumner.

From humble beginnings in 1983 – when it was the world's first major multisport event – the Coast to Coast has blossomed into a very professional affair with over a thousand competitors. Serious contenders engage a highly organized support crew and specialized gear; only the most high-tech of bikes will do and designers build racing kayaks especially for Waimakariri conditions. Most competitors take two days, but around 150 elite triathletes compete in "The Longest Day", the same course in under 24 hours. Mere mortals – though admittedly extremely fit ones – can also compete by forming two-person teams sharing the disciplines.

Women compete in increasingly large numbers, but the event remains largely a macho spectacle that draws considerable press interest and correspondingly generous sponsorship – a vehicle manufacturer is usually coaxed into offering a car or truck to the winner if they break a certain time. Several have gone to Kiwi super-athlete Steve Gurney, who won his ninth title (aged 39) in 2003, but failed to round out his tally in 2004 and has since retired. The course record is an astonishing 10hr 35min, set in 1994.

Eating and drinking

You'll soon exhaust Greymouth's scope for **eating and drinking**, but there are enough places serving tasty and hearty dishes to last the night or two you're likely to stay. For evening entertainment there are numerous pubs, plus mainstream **movies** at the Regent Theatre, on the corner of Herbert and Mackay streets.

Bonzai Pizzeria 31 Mackay St. Cheerful licensed restaurant with tearoom staples through the day, including some good pastries and quiches and a broad range of reasonably priced and tasty pizzas served daytime and evening.

Café 124 124 Mackay St. Modern licensed café offering a fine range of light meals, a good brunch menu, muffins and good coffee inside or at outdoor seating suitably sheltered from the West Coast weather. Evening meals ($18–28) could include chicken and coconut curry.

DP1 Café 108 Mawhera Quay. Greymouth's coolest café, serving snacks and excellent coffee, with Internet access and occasional gigs.

Jade Boulder Café 1 Guinness St. Licensed daytime café with a good range of brunch and lunch dishes including a tasty goat curry and whitebait sandwiches plus less rarefied fare. Great organic coffee and muffins.

Railway Hotel 120 Mawhera Quay. Basic pub chiefly notable for its nightly $5 all-the-sausages-you-can-eat BBQ, which can be upgraded to veggie patties ($8) or steak ($10).

Speight's Ale House 130 Mawhera Quay. Big and bustling restaurant/bar in a 1909 Edwardian Baroque former government building with a good menu of hearty dishes, perhaps including lamb shanks ($24), rump steak ($25) and sausage and mash ($17), mostly matched to beers from the Speight's range.

West of the Border 21 Mackay St. Loosely Western-themed restaurant serving groaning plates of BBQed chicken, buffalo wings and Texan BBQed pork ribs (all $23–28).

Shantytown

The replica 1880s West Coast gold-mining settlement of **Shantytown** (daily 8.30am–5pm; $16, entry plus gold panning $20; Ⓦwww.shantytown.co.nz), 8km south of Greymouth, then 4km off the main highway, is a good place to bring kids. Most of it has been constructed since the early 1970s, but the complex incorporates rescued older buildings, mostly fairly tastefully restored. Look out for the 1902 Coronation Hall from Ross, the 1865 church originally from No Town in the Grey Valley, and the hotel cobbled together from parts. Notice, too, the printing shop with its faded billboards advertising the latest films, and the wonderful 1837 Colombian Press, which found its way here from Philadelphia via London, Auckland and Napier. Your entry ticket entitles you to a short ride behind an 1887 steam engine, calling at a mine site and sawmill where boards are cut on summer days and, of course, sage prospectors will help you pan for "colour" in salted tanks.

No public **transport** runs to the site, but Greymouth Taxis (Ⓣ03/768 7078) charge $30 return, and Kea Tours (see p.739) finish their Goldstrike Tour (2 daily; 2hr 30min; $60) around various gold-rush sites at Shantytown.

Hokitika and around

South from Greymouth, SH6 hugs a desolate stretch of coast that's fine for long moody beachcombing walks, but there's little of abiding interest until **HOKITIKA**, 40km away. On initial acquaintance "Hoki", as it is known to its friends, appears only marginally more interesting than Greymouth – its jumble of mundane modern buildings interspersed with gussied up edifices from the town's golden days. Still, it is a long way to the next place of any size, and its proximity to the beach and good bushwalks, and a couple of quality restaurants, give it the edge.

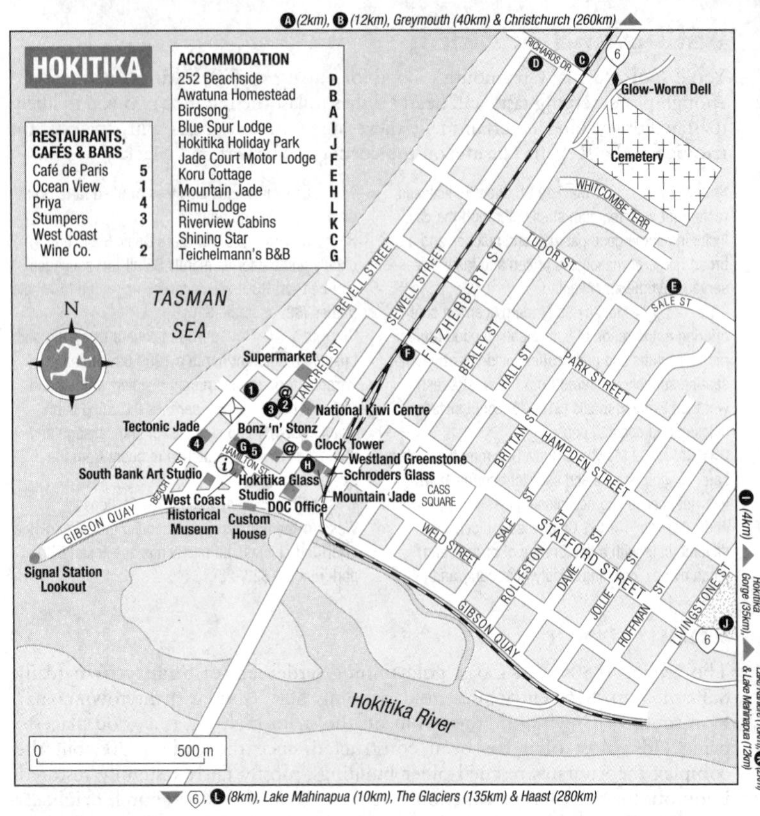

Like the other West Coast towns, Hokitika owes its existence to the **gold rushes** of the 1860s. Within months of the initial discoveries near Greymouth in 1864, fields had been opened up on the tributaries of the Hokitika River, and Australian diggers from Ballarat and Bendigo and Irish hopefuls all flogged over narrow passes from Canterbury to get their share. Within two years Hokitika had a population of 6000 (compared with today's 4000), streets packed with hotels, and a steady export of over a tonne of gold a month, mainly direct to Melbourne. Despite a treacherous bar at the Hokitika rivermouth, the **port** briefly became the country's busiest, with ships tied up four deep along Gibson Wharf. As gold became harder to find and more sluicing water was needed, the enterprise eventually became uneconomic and was replaced by dairying and the timber industry. The port closed in 1954, only to be smartened up in the 1990s as the focus for the town's Heritage Trail.

In the last decade or so, Hokitika has become synonymous with the annual **Wildfoods Festival** (second Sat in March; advance tickets $30; Ⓦwww.wildfoods.co.nz;), when the town quadruples its population for a celebration of bush tucker. Around fifty stalls around Cass Square sell such delicacies as stir-fried possum, golden-fried huhu grubs, marinated goat kebabs and smoked eel wontons, all washed down with home-brewed beer and South Island wine. The gorging is followed by an evening hoe-down, the Wildfoods Barn Dance ($15). Look out, too, for the annual **Wet West Film Festival** (Ⓦwww.wetwestfilmfest.com) which takes place in early October and celebrates all things watery, from moody art flicks to extreme kayaking. This is followed in mid-January by the **Driftwood and Sand Competition**, where entrants compete to produce the most original construction from detritus found on the wide driftwood-strewn beach.

Arrival and information

Air New Zealand **fly** daily to Hokitika from Christchurch, arriving 2km east of the centre. Buses from Christchurch and along the coast stop outside the National Kiwi Centre at 64 Tancred St (Ⓣ03/755 5251): Atomic buses also stop at the **i-SITE visitor centre**, on the corner of Hamilton and Tancred streets (Dec–March daily 8.30am–6pm; April–Nov Mon–Fri 8.30am–5pm, Sat & Sun 10am–4pm; Ⓣ03/755 6166, Ⓦwww.hokitika.org). Just a few paces away, the **DOC office**, on Sewell Street (Mon–Fri 8am–4.45pm; Ⓣ03/756 8282), is stocked with leaflets on local walks. **Internet access** is available at *Wong's Wok*, corner of Sewell and Weld streets by the clock tower. If you're heading south, there is an ATM at Franz Josef, but the **banks** here are the last before Wanaka, more than 400km away over the Haast Pass.

Accommodation

Accommodation in Hokitika is seldom hard to find, though you should book ahead during the Kumara Races (second weekend in Jan), for all of February including around the Coast to Coast race (second weekend in Feb) and during the Wildfoods Festival (second weekend in March). There are good options right in town, but many of the better places (at both ends of the scale) are some way out.

▲ Driftwood and Sand Competition, Hokitika

Greenstone

Maori revere **pounamu** (hard nephrite jade) and **tangiwai** (the softer, translucent bowenite), usually collectively known as **greenstone**. In Aotearoa's pre-European culture, it took the place of durable metals for practical, warfaring and decorative uses: adzes and chisels were used for carving, *mere* (clubs) for combat, and pendants were fashioned for jewellery. Charles Heaphy observed a group of Maori producing a *mere* in 1846, and noted the process by which they "saw the slab with a piece of mica slate, wet, and afterwards polish it with a fine sandy limestone which they obtain in the vicinity. The hole is drilled with a pointed stick with a piece of Pahutanui flint. The process does not appear so tedious as has been supposed; a month sufficing, apparently, for the completion."

In Maori, the entire South Island is known as **Te Wahi Pounamu**, "the place of greenstone", reflecting the importance of its sole sources, the belt from Greymouth through the rich Arahura River area near Hokitika south to Anita Bay on Milford Sound – where the beautifully dappled *tangiwai* occurs – and the Wakatipu region behind Queenstown. When the Poutini Ngai Tahu arranged to sell most of Westland to James Mackay in 1860, the Arahura River, their main source of *pounamu*, was specifically excluded.

Its value has barely diminished. Mineral claims are jealously guarded, the export of raw greenstone is prohibited and no extraction is allowed from national parks; penalties include fines of up to $200,000 and two years in jail. **Price** is heavily dependent on quality, but rates of $100,000 a tonne are not unknown in the raw state – and the sky's the limit when the stone is fashioned into sculpture and jewellery. Many of the cheaper specimens are quite crude, but pricier pieces (and we're talking a minimum of $100 for something aesthetically pleasing, and over $1000 for anything really classy) exhibit accomplished Maori designs executed to perfection; at the other end of the scale, simple pendants can be picked up for as little as $20.

Hokitika is the main venue for greenstone shoppers: bear in mind that the larger **shops** and **galleries** are firmly locked into the tour-bus circuit so prices (and standards) are high. They are fine for learning something about the quality of the stone and competence of the artwork, but smaller places often have more competitive deals. Buyers should also ask about the origins of the raw material – insiders suspect that ninety percent of all greenstone sold in NZ is cheaper jade sourced overseas. Specific shopping **recommendations** are given on p.747.

Hotels, motels and B&Bs

252 Beachside 252 Revell St ⓣ0800/252 252, ⓦwww.252beachside.co.nz. Spacious motel and campervan park offering a range of comfortable units 10min walk from the centre, plus swimming pool, spa, kids' playground, Internet access and campervan hookups. $30 per van, cabins ❷, units ❹

Awatuna Homestead SH6, 13km north of Hokitika ⓣ0800/006 888, ⓦwww.awatunahomestead.co.nz. Very welcoming B&B with three comfortable, tasteful rooms and one self-catering apartment. It is a place to relax, with canoes to paddle on the creek, assorted animals, plenty of books, outdoor bath and evening storytelling sessions; evening meals by arrangement. Rooms ❽, apartment ❼ plus $35 each extra person up to five.

Jade Court Motor Lodge 85 Fitzherbert St ⓣ0800/755 885, ⓦwww.jadecourt.co.nz. Modern and very well-equipped motel 5min walk from town with in-house video and pleasant gardens. Some rooms have private spa baths. Units ❹, spa units ❺

Koru Cottage 195 Sale St ⓣ03/755 7636, ⓦwww.korucottage.co.nz. Pretty self-catering cottage sleeping up to four that comes with TV/DVD, barbecue and full kitchen. They'll even loan you a whitebait net to try your hand during the season (Sept to mid-Nov). ❺

Rimu Lodge 33 Seddons Terrace Rd ⓣ03/755 5255, ⓦwww.rimulodge.co.nz. Luxury lodge situated on a ridge 9km south of town with long views over the Hokitika River from the guest lounge (with its big fire) and four tasteful rooms. ❼

Shining Star 16 Richards Drive ⓣ0800/744 646, ⓦwww.shiningstar.co.nz. Close to the beach with tent and campervan sites plus an extensive range of classy log cabins, most with good self-catering facilities. Also an infrared sauna and spa pool. Camping $12, cabins ❷, en-suite cabins ❸, s/c cabins ❸, motel units ❹

Teichelmann's B&B 20 Hamilton St ⓣ0800/743 742, ⓦwww.teichelmanns.co.nz. Comfortable and well appointed, if slightly twee, central B&B with friendly hosts, a range of en-suite rooms and a particularly nice garden cottage with double spa bath. A hearty cooked breakfast is served. ❼

Hostels and campsite

Birdsong 124 SH6, 3km north of town ⓣ03/755 7179, ⓦwww.birdsong.co.nz. Small, laid-back hostel, each brightly decorated room featuring a painting of the bird it is named after. All linen is supplied, everything is well looked after, and there's a pair of secluded bush baths ($4 per bath). Shares $26, rooms ❷, en suites ❸

Blue Spur Lodge Cement Lead Rd ⓣ03/755 8445, ⓔbluespur@paradise.net.nz, ⓦwww.bluespur.co.nz. Spacious, modern and airy pine house, plus lovely separate en-suite doubles, all in a tranquil setting 5km from town and close to bushwalks. There's bike and kayak rental at very reasonable rates and a restaurant and bar 10min walk down the road. Dorms $25, rooms ❷, en suites ❸

Hokitika Holiday Park 242 Stafford St ⓣ0800/465 436, ⓦwww.hokitika.com/holidaypark. Outwardly scruffy-looking but actually decent and well-priced campsite with clean and tidy cabins plus a good kids' playground. Camping $11, cabins ❶, kitchen cabin ❷, s/c units ❸, motels ❸

Mountain Jade 41 Weld St ⓣ03/755 8007, ⓔmtjade@minidata.co.nz. Nowhere near as nice as the out-of-town hostels, but it is at least central and cheap. Dorms $21, rooms ❷

Riverview Cabins 154 Kaniere Rd, 3.5km east of town ⓣ03/755 7440, ⓔriver-view@xtra.co.nz. Simple but quiet, welcoming and comfortable backpackers in four rooms, close to the Hokitika River. Free gold pans. Shares $27, rooms ❷

The Town

Hokitika's leading role in the West Coast gold rushes rightly occupies much of the **West Coast Historical Museum**, entered through the visitor centre (daily: Dec–Easter 9.30am–5pm; Easter–Nov Mon–Fri 9.30am–4pm, Sat & Sun 10am–2pm; $5). The photos depicting the dangers of crossing the Hokitika River bar and the pleasures of the hundred or so bars of another kind that once lined Tancred Street are highlights. Look out too for the *pounamu* room, with its fine pieces and discussion of the all-important Arahura River greenstone grounds.

With interest suitably kindled, grab the free **Hokitika Heritage Walk** leaflet, which details landmarks from the town's past, including the centrepiece **clock tower** commemorating the Boer War, and the Gibson Quay area. This restored former riverside dock makes a pleasant place for an evening stroll from the 1897 **Custom House**, past an ugly concrete memorial to ships lost on the bar, to the spit-end **Signal Station Lookout**, where coloured flags and raised balls used to help guide ships into the rivermouth.

Those with kids to entertain will welcome the **National Kiwi Centre**, 64 Tancred St (daily 9am–5pm; $14), a privately run aquarium and nocturnal house combo with the chance to see tuatara, huge fat eels (fed at 10am, noon & 3pm) and kiwi that are part of a captive breeding programme.

Arts and crafts

Hokitika is crafts mad. Everywhere you look is someone showing you how to carve wood, blow glass, weave wool or fashion a pendant. For those in buying mode, there are quality pieces to be found, and the southwestern end of Revell Street is becoming a bit of an artists' enclave. **Greenstone** (see p.746) is big business, with shops all over town. For some of the finest work, visit Tectonic Jade, 67 Revell St, or stroll down to the Traditional Jade Company, 2 Tancred St, for pendants at middling prices. If you want to work a piece for yourself, pop along to Bonz 'n' Stonz Carving Studio, 16 Hamilton St (Ⓣ0800/214 949, Ⓦwww.bonz-n-stonz.co.nz) the only place in the country where you can carve your own jade (5hr; $90): Steve Gwaliasi will guide you through the design and execution in greenstone.

Glass-blowing is another longstanding Hoki tradition, best seen at the Hokitika Glass Studio, 25 Tancred St. And don't miss the **copper art** at the South Bank Art Studio, 32 Revell St, where Ian Phillips creates wonderful hand-crafted sculptures out of heat-treated copper sheet.

Activities

Hokitika isn't just about watching glass being blown. Eco-rafting (see box, p.749) can take you **whitewater rafting** on some of the excellent local rivers, while Wilderness Wings, out at the airport (Ⓣ0800/755 8118), do a number of **scenic flights**, principally around Mount Cook and the glaciers (1hr 15min; $290), reached by flying past all the big, snowy peaks of the Southern Alps.

Eating and drinking and entertainment

Hokitika offers some of the best **eating** on the Coast, and it's reasonably priced too – reason enough to make this an overnight stop before heading south. The most pleasant places to **drink** are the restaurants, though Hokitika has its share of beer barns. For free evening entertainment, stroll to the attractive **Glow-Worm Dell** about a kilometre north of the centre beside SH6, or head along to the movies: mainstream at the Regent, 23 Weld St, and arthouse and alternative at the Crooked Mile Talking Movies, 36 Revell St (Ⓣ03/755 5309, Ⓦwww.crookedmile.co.nz), a **boutique cinema** with leather couches.

Café de Paris 19 Tancred St Ⓣ03/755 8933. Relaxed spot with an extensive selection of moderately priced breakfasts, café lunches and more formal evening dining with a French/Mediterranean theme (mains around $28). Sadly the service can be a bit clueless. Booking advisable in the evenings. Licensed & BYO.

Ocean View 111 Revell St Ⓣ03/755 8344. Classy à la carte evening dining, specializing in seafood and lamb (mains $28–32), served with great views over the sea from inside or out on their deck.

Priya 79 Revell St Ⓣ03/755 7225. Well-prepared, spicy dishes make this unpretentious curry restaurant one of the best on the coast. It serves all the usual suspects (around $16) and takeaways for a couple of dollars less.

Stumpers 2 Weld St, corner of of Weld Revell sts. Swish modern sports bar and daytime café with live bands and some passable meals.

West Coast Wine Co. 108 Revell St Ⓣ03/755 5417. They only do espresso coffee, wine, cocktails and the odd platter, but have a nice courtyard.

Around Hokitika

Some of the best bush scenery and the finest **walks** hereabouts lie 30km inland where the dairying hinterland meets the foothills of the Southern Alps. Minor roads (initially following Stafford Street out of town) make a good seventy-kilometre scenic drive, shown in detail on DOC's **Central West Coast: Hokitika** leaflet. The road initially passes the fishing, water-skiing and tramping territory of **Lake Kaniere**, a glacial lake 18km from Hokitika with several picnic sites and primitive camping ($6) along its eastern side. The most popular walk is the **Kaniere Water Race Walkway** (9km one way; 3hr; 100m ascent), which starts from the lake's northern end and follows a channel that used to supply water to the goldfields, through stands of regenerating rimu. The eastern-shore road passes the attractive **Dorothy Falls** and continues to a side road leading to the **Hokitika Gorge**, 35km from Hoki, where a short path leads to a swingbridge over the tranquil Hokitika River.

Rafting the wild West Coast rivers

The production-line rafting trips out of Rotorua and Queenstown are fun and don't cost that much, making them ideal for first-timers. But in recent years kayakers and rafters have realized that some of the most thrilling and scenic whitewater trips in the world are here on New Zealand's West Coast. Dramatically steep rivers spill out of the alpine wilderness, fed by the prodigious quantity of rain that guarantees solid flows most of the time. The steepness of the terrain means you're in Grade IV–V territory – constantly thrilling if not downright scary. If you've enjoyed rafting and want more, this is where to come.

Few of these rivers had been kayaked or rafted until the 1980s, when helicopters were co-opted to reach them. Most rafting trips still require **helicopter access**, so costs are relatively high, and what you pay will often depend on numbers. Getting, say, six people together will save you a packet.

Though their popularity is increasing, trips are still relatively infrequent and you should **book** as far in advance as possible. The main **season** is November to April, and you'll need to be at least 13 years old (15 or 16 for some of the more frightening runs).

The **most commonly run rivers** are (from north to south) the Karamea (Gd III+), the Mokihinui (Gd IV), the Arahura (Gd IV), the Whitcombe (Gd V), the Hokitika (Gd III–IV), the Wanganui (Gd III), the Perth (Gd V) and the Whataroa (Gd IV).

Eco-Rafting Hokitika ⓣ0508/669 675, ⓦwww.ecorafting.co.nz. A slightly different approach, using rafting to introduce customers to the nature and social history of the places visited. They do a half-day family rafting trip (4hr; $100) on the Grade II Arnold River, while the full-day offering ($130, including lunch) takes on Grade III sections of the Buller or Grey rivers. Check the website for heli-rafting deals.

Ultimate Descents 51 Fairfax St, Murchison ⓣ0800/748 377, ⓦwww.rivers.co.nz. Primarily concentrating on the Buller River (see p.547), but also offering one-day heli-rafting on the Karamea ($350), three-day trips on the same river ($995) and two-day trips on the Mokihinui ($650).

Wild West Adventures Greymouth ⓣ0508/286 877, ⓦwww.fun-nz.com. These guys offer a wide range of trips from hard-man descents of Whataroa ($525) and the Frisco Canyon on the Hokitika River ($200) to relatively gentle drive-in trips on the Arnold (Gd II; $145), and their so-called Love Adventure ($195) on the relatively tame Wanganui, involving hot pools and a bottle of bubbly. Look out for their half-price heli-raft specials.

Immediately south of Hokitika, SH6 runs 5km south to a landing where gentle paddle-boat **cruises** (ⓣ03/755 6166; Dec–April 2pm; 90min; excellent value at $30) take you along the Mahinapua Creek to the lake. A couple of kilometres on, the **Mahinapua Walkway** (16km return; 4hr; mainly flat; leaflet from DOC), offers easy walking with picnic opportunities at a lakeside beach. A further 2km south along SH6 the easy **Mananui Bush Walkway** (30min return) leads through coastal forest remnants to the dunes. There's a particularly nice basic **camping** spot at **Lake Mahinapua**, accessed off SH6 1km south ($6).

From Hokitika to the glaciers

The main highway leaves the coast **south of Hokitika** and snuggles in close to the Southern Alps for most of the 135km to the glacier at Franz Josef, the next town of any size. The journey through dairy farms and stands of selectively logged native bush is broken by a series of insignificant settlements such as **Ross**, **Pukekura** and **Harihari**, none of which warrant stopping long. There's more fun to be had visiting herons from Whataroa, and **Okarito** may just seduce you with the relaxed charms of its lagoon.

Ross

At the tiny village of **Ross**, 30km south of Hokitika, a lake-filled hole is all that remains of the rich opencast mine that sought alluvial **gold** until 2004. The mining company have moved to a new site nearby, but would dearly love to get at the gold-bearing gravels underneath the town. The government has given consent provided all the townspeople agree to move off the land: around half are adamant they'll stay.

Though Ross had over 3000 residents at its gold peak-rush, things had slowed considerably by 1909, when a couple of diggers prospecting less than 500m from the current visitor centre turned up the largest gold nugget ever found in New Zealand, the 3.1-kilo "**Honourable Roddy**", named after the then Minister of Mines. The nugget was bought by the government and given as a coronation gift in 1910 to Britain's George V, who melted it down to make royal tableware. A replica of the fist-sized lump of gold resides in the 1885 **Miner's Cottage**, Bold Street (daily: Dec–March 9am–4pm; April–Nov 9am–3pm; free), surrounded by gold-rush photos.

Leave time for the popular and well-signposted **Water Race Walk** (4km loop, 1hr 30min), which passes the remains of fluming designed to supply water for gravel washing. Before leaving the area, check out the Jade Studio at 23 St James St (daily noon–5pm), one of the best small **jade** galleries in the region.

The **visitor centre**, 4 Aylmer St (daily: Dec–March 9am–4pm; April–Nov 9am–3pm; ⓣ03/755 4077, ⓦwww.ross.org.nz), presents an interesting **video** (free) on the 1865 gold rush and subsequent sawmilling and farming history, and rents out gold pans ($10), giving you a chance to pan Jones's Creek where the "Honourable Roddy" was found. *Roddy Nugget Café*, on SH6, does **tearoom** staples and has what passes for a restaurant in this town. Being so close to Hokitika there's little reason to stay overnight, though backpackers might fancy *The Old Church*, SH6 17km south (ⓣ03/755 4000, ⓔstay@theoldchurch.co.nz; camping $13, dorms $23, rooms ❷, en suite ❸), a wonderfully relaxing little spot: bushwalks, kayaking, fishing and horse trekking can all be arranged.

Pukekura

A giant sandfly at the hamlet of **Pukekura**, 23km south of Ross, marks the **Bushman's Centre** (daily 9am–5.30pm; free; ⓣ03/755 4144, ⓦwww.pukekura.co.nz). The centre's **museum** ($4) takes a light-hearted approach to showing how people have made a living from the forest through timber milling, live deer capture, possum trapping and growing sphagnum moss for East Asian orchid growers. The centre's **restaurant** serves all manner of wild foods (wild boar sandwiches, rabbit, possum, hare and chamois), and you can **stay** across the road at the **Puke Pub and Lodge** (ⓣ03/755 4144; camping & powered sites $7.50–10, cabins ❶, safari tents ❸), where they have artificial hot pools out back.

The rest areas around beautiful (and often surprisingly warm) **Lake Ianthe**, 6km south, make good picnic stops. The **Lake Ianthe Recreation Reserve** has DOC **camping** ($6), though it's too close to the road to be truly peaceful.

Harihari

Some 17km further south, tiny **Harihari** was the marshy landing site of **Guy Menzies**, who flew from Sydney to New Zealand in 1931, becoming the first to do the trip solo. Menzies ended up strapped in upside down in the mud of La Fontaine swamp, 10km northwest of town, a site now marked by explanatory panels. A replica of Menzies' plane resides near the southern entrance to town in **Guy Menzies Park**. There's little else to see in town, but you might want to turn onto Whanganui Flat Road and drive 20km (partly gravel) coastwards past the Menzies' landing site to the lovely **Hari Hari Coastal Walkway** (8km loop; 2–3hr; negligible ascent), which runs past elaborate whitebaiting stands to the Doughboy Lookout (60m) with great views of the coast and the Southern Alps. After a short stretch of dramatic coastline you return though kahikatea forest and along the line of a tram track once used by loggers.

If you need to **stay**, try the old but pleasant and cycle-friendly *Flaxbush Motel*, SH6 (Ⓣ03/753 3116, Ⓔflaxbush123@xtra.co.nz; cabins ❷, motel rooms ❸), while the *Harihari Motor Inn* (Ⓣ0800/833 026, Ⓔhhmi@xtra.co.nz; dorms $19, rooms ❹) has space for camping ($10) and vans ($22 per site) and serves **bar meals**.

Whataroa

From October to late February, New Zealand's entire adult population of the graceful white heron (*kotuku*) arrives to breed at the Waitangiroto Nature Reserve near **Whataroa**, 30km south of Harihari. Sitting peacefully in a hide gazing across the river at forty-or-so nesting pairs of herons (plus a slightly larger numbers of royal spoonbills) going about their daily business of preening, fishing and mating is a wonderful experience. The only way to visit is with **White Heron Sanctuary Tours** (Oct–Feb 3–6 daily; 2.5hr; $95; booking advised Ⓣ0800/523 456, Ⓦwww.whiteherontours.co.nz), whose package includes a twenty-minute jetboat ride on the narrow Waitangiroto River and half an hour observing the birds from the hide.

Outside the heron season, their Rainforest Nature and Jetboating Tours ($95) follow essentially the same route but concentrate more on the flora, though you'll also see tui and bellbirds feeding on flowering kowhai from August to October for example. The White Heron Sanctuary Tours office on the main highway acts as the local **visitor centre** (no set hours; Ⓣ03/753 4120) and has **motel** units (❹) and cabins (❷), and the *Whataroa Hotel* serves evening **meals** and is the focal point of the town.

Okarito

In 1642, Abel Tasman became the first European to set eyes on Aotearoa at **Okarito**, a seductive hamlet scattered around the southern side of its eponymous lagoon and reached by a ten-kilometre side road, 15km south of Whataroa. Two centuries later, the discovery of gold sparked an eighteen-month boom that saw fifty stores and hotels spring up along the lagoon's shores. Timber milling and flax production stood in once the gold had gone but the community foundered, leaving a handful of holiday homes, a few dozen permanent residents and a lovely beach and lagoon, used as the setting for much of Keri Hulme's Booker Prize-winning novel, *The Bone People*.

Okarito Lagoon is hard to fully appreciate from the shore, but Okarito Nature Tours (Ⓣ03/753 4014, Ⓦwww.okarito.co.nz) run excellent-value guided **kayaking trips** (2hr; $65; minimum two) and rent double sea kayaks for half a day ($45) or overnight ($80), camping at a remote beach. Call first to check tide conditions, but plan to go out early in the morning when the water is calmest and the birds are most abundant.

If you don't want to paddle, opt for Experience Okarito Boat Tours (Nov–May daily; ⓣ03/753 4223, ⓦwww.okaritoboattours), who **cruise** leisurely through the lagoon and its feeder streams. Early tours (2–3hr; $75, $95 including lunch) concentrate on spotting birds while afternoon tours (1hr; $40) mainly focus on the gorgeous scenery.

Wildlife of a different feather can usually be seen with Okarito Kiwi Tours (ⓣ03/753 4330, ⓦwww.okaritokiwitours.co.nz), who'll take you into the bush **kiwi spotting** (2–4hr; $60), hoping to catch a glimpse of some of the 250 remaining Okarito brown kiwi. To maximize the already high success rate, wear quiet clothes.

The most popular walks are: the **Okarito Trig Walk** (1hr 30min return; 200m ascent) at the southern end of town, which climbs to a headland with fabulous mountain and coastal views; and the **Pakihi Walk**, 5.5km back towards SH6 (2km return; 20–30min; 50m ascent), a good gravel path leading to a lookout with long views of Okarito Lagoon.

Practicalities

Okarito only has one street, The Strand, and the community's limited **accommodation** is all on it: there is **no shop** or café, so bring provisions with you. The widest range of **accommodation** is at the **Okarito Beach House** (ⓣ03/753 4080, ⓦwww.okaritobeachhouse.com; dorms $23, doubles ❷, en suites ❷, cottage ❸) a huddle of buildings which includes comfy rooms and a romantic little self-contained cottage. A memorial commemorating Tasman's sighting stands next to the associate **YHA Okarito** (ⓣ03/753 4347, ⓔokaritoyha@yahoo.co.nz; $18; closed June–Aug), a simple two-room affair in an 1860 schoolhouse, with twelve made-up bunks. There is no shower so you'll need to wander across the street to the shady **campsite** ($7.50; no powered sites), where showers take $1 coins.

Some holiday houses are rented out, one of the best being *Cedar Cottage* (no phone; ⓔcedar.cottage.okarito@xtra.co.nz; ❹), a two-bedroom house with a log fire and a two-night minimum stay. Back on SH6, 4km south of the Okarito junction, DOC's fine *MacDonalds Creek* **campsite** ($6) is at Lake Mapourika.

The glaciers

Around 150km south of Hokitika, two blinding white rivers of ice force their way down towards the thick rainforest of the coastal plain – ample justification for the inclusion of this region in Te Wahipounamu, the South West New Zealand World Heritage Area. The glaciers form a palpable connection between the coast and the highest peaks of the Southern Alps. Within a handful of kilometres the terrain drops from over 3000m to near sea level, bringing with it **Franz Josef glacier** and **Fox glacier**, two of the largest and most impressive of the sixty-odd glaciers that creak off the South Island's icy backbone, together forming the centrepiece of the rugged **Westland National Park**. Legend tells of the beautiful Hinehukatere, who so loved the mountains that she encouraged her lover, Tawe, to climb alongside her. He fell to his death and Hinehukatere cried so copiously that her tears formed the glaciers, known to Maori as Ka Riomata o Hinehukatere – "The Tears of the Avalanche Girl".

The park is also characterized by the West Coast's prodigious **precipitation**, which here reaches its greatest expression, with five metres being the typical yearly dump. These conditions, combined with the rakish angle of the western slopes of the Southern Alps, produce some of the world's fastest-moving glaciers; stand at the foot for half an hour or so and you're bound to see a piece peel off. But these phenomenal speeds haven't been enough to completely counteract melting, and both glaciers have receded over 3km since Cook saw them at their greatest recent extent, soon after the Little Ice Age of 1750. Glaciers are receding worldwide, but the two here frequently buck the trend by advancing from time to time, typically around five years after a particularly big snowfall in the mountains.

The glaciers were already in full retreat when travellers started to battle their way down the coast to observe these wonders of nature. They were initially named "Victoria" and "Albert" respectively but, in 1865, geologist Julius von Haast renamed Franz Josef after the Austro-Hungarian emperor, and following a visit by prime minister William Fox in 1872, the other glacier was bestowed with his name.

Activity in the glaciers focuses on two small **villages**, which survive almost entirely on tourist traffic. Both lie close to the base of their respective glacier and offer excellent plane and helicopter **flights**, guided **glacier walks** and **heli-hiking**. With your own transport, it makes sense to base yourself in one of the two villages and explore both glaciers from there. If you have to choose one, Franz Josef has a wider range of accommodation, more restaurants, and offers the most comprehensive selection of trips, while Fox is quieter and more rural.

Franz Josef Glacier

FRANZ JOSEF GLACIER (Waiau) is the slightly larger of the two glacier villages, with a wider range of places to stay and an improving culinary scene. The Franz Josef glacier almost licks the fringes of the village, the Southern Alps

Glaciers for beginners

The existence of a **glacier** is a balancing act between competing forces: snowfall at the **névé**, high in the mountains, battles with rapid melting at the **terminal** lower down the valley, the victor determining whether the glacier will advance or retreat. Snowfall metres thick gradually compacts to form clear **blue ice**, which accumulates to the point when it starts to flow downhill under its own weight. Friction against the valley walls slows the sides while ice in the centre slips down the valley, giving the characteristic scalloped effect on the surface, which is especially pronounced on such vigorous glaciers as Franz Josef and Fox. Where a riverbed steepens, the river forms a rapid: under similar conditions, glaciers break up into an **ice fall**, full of towering blocks of ice known as **seracs**, separated by **crevasses**.

Visitors familiar with grubby glaciers in the European Alps or American Rockies will expect the surface to be mottled with **rock debris** which has fallen off the valley walls onto the surface; however, the glaciers here descend so steeply that the cover doesn't have time to build up and they remain pristine and white. Rock still gets carried down with the glacier though, and when the glacier retreats, this is deposited as **terminal moraine**. Occasionally retreating glaciers leave behind huge chunks of ice which, on melting, form **kettle lakes**.

The most telling evidence of past glacial movements is the location of the **trim line** on the valley wall, caused by the glacier stripping away all vegetation. At Fox and Franz Josef, the advance associated with the Little Ice Age around 1750 left a very visible trim line high up the valley wall, separating mature rata from scrub.

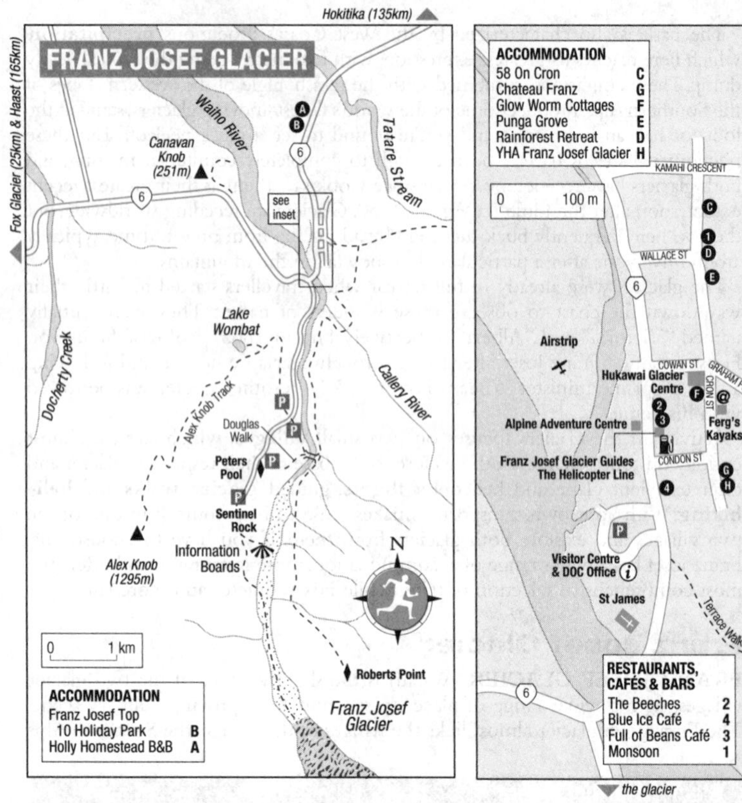

tower above and developers have done what they can to create an alpine character with steeply pitched roofs and pine panelling. It is an appealing place, and small enough to make you feel almost like a local if you stay for more than a night or two – something that's easily done, considering the number of fine walks and the proximity of the glaciers.

Arrival and information

First stop in Franz Josef should be the excellent combined **DOC office** and **visitor centre** on SH6 (daily: Nov–March 8.30am–6pm; April–Oct 8.30am–noon and 1–4.45pm; ⓣ03/752 0796, ⓔwestlandnpvc@doc.govt.nz), which has stacks of leaflets on walks in the area and first-class glacier and geology displays plus a diverting documentary (every 30min; $3) on the whole South West New Zealand World Heritage Area. The centre also gets **weather reports** at 3pm daily, so check with them before starting any serious walks.

There are no banks hereabouts, but there's an **ATM**, and fast and efficient **Internet access** at several places, including Ferg's Kayaks on Cron Street.

You can walk everywhere in town, but getting around the region without your own transport can be a pain. Glacier Valley Eco Tours (ⓣ0800/999 739, ⓦwww.glaciervalley.co.nz) offer a **shuttle service** to the glacier road-end ($12 return) and a series of local tours such as Lake Matheson (3hr; $65) and a Lake Matheson combo with Fox glacier ($95).

Accommodation

With the region's popularity and a bus schedule that forces many people to overnight here, accommodation in Franz Josef is tight throughout the summer. Between November and March (and particularly February), you should aim to make **reservations** at least a week in advance, more like six months for swankier places.

58 On Cron 58 Cron St ⓣ03/752 0627, ⓦwww.franz-josef-accommodation.co.nz. Franz's newest motel. Units are stylish, and some come with spa bath. ❻

Chateau Franz 8 Cron St ⓣ0800/728 372, ⓦwww.chateaufranz.co.nz. Heavily renovated hostel with a wide range of accommodation from budget dorms and smaller en-suite dorms to full-blown motel units. There's a free spa, free soup nightly and TVs and VCRs everywhere. Dorms $22, rooms ❷, en suites ❸

Franz Josef Top 10 Holiday Park SH6, 1km north of town ⓣ0800/467 897, ⓦwww.mountainview.co.nz. High-spec rural campsite with a good range of tent and powered sites, cabins and units. Camping $19, cabins ❷, kitchen cabins ❸, units ❹

Glow Worm Cottages 27 Cron St ⓣ0800/151 027, ⓦwww.glowwormcottages.co.nz. Small and homely hostel with a well-equipped kitchen, six-bed dorms and four-shares with their own bathrooms, plus comfy doubles and motel-style en suites. Free soup and spa. Dorms $23, rooms ❷, en suites ❹

Holly Homestead B&B SH6, 1.5km north of town ⓣ03/752 0299, ⓦwww.hollyhomestead.co.nz. Upmarket B&B in an attractive two-storey 1920s home just outside town with four en-suite rooms (one with bathtub), plus a new suite ($380). There's a nice deck with mountain views, and rates include a full communal breakfast. Only suitable for those 12 and over. ❼

Punga Grove 40 Cron St ⓣ0800/437 269, ⓦwww.pungagrove.co.nz. Stylish, modernized luxury motels, all nicely furnished and with Sky TV. Rainforest studios back onto the bush and come with gas log fire, underfloor heating and spa bath. Motel ❻, studios ❽

Rainforest Retreat 46 Cron St ⓣ0800/873 346, ⓦwww.rainforestretreat.co.nz. Large bush-girt lodge and campervan park with gravel pads (good for campervans; OK for tents) and access to a communal lodge. Also backpacker dorms and en-suite rooms, spacious studio motels, atmospheric log cabins on stilts, lovely luxurious lodges, a spa and sauna. Camping $13–17, dorms $25, en-suite four-shares $27, rooms ❷, motels ❺, log cabins ❻, lodges ❼

YHA Franz Josef Glacier 2–4 Cron St ⓣ03/752 0754, ⓔyha.franzjosef@yha.co.nz. Modernized and well-run hostel with a spacious kitchen, clean comfortable rooms, BBQ area and free sauna. Rooms in the newest wing overlook the rainforest. Dorms $25, rooms ❸, en suites ❸

The Town

Most people are eager to hike to the glacier, join a guided glacier walk or take a scenic flight. Glacier hikes go in most weathers, but on misty and wet days you may well find that scenic flights and heli-hikes are called off and alternatives are limited. At such times, the best bet is the **Hukawai Glacier Centre**, corner of Cowan and Cron streets (daily 10am–5pm or later; ⓣ03/752 0600, ⓦwww.hukawai.co.nz), a combined interpretive centre and indoor ice climbing wall. The Glacier Experience ($25) mimics a walk from the Tasman shore through the rainforest (filled with birdsong) and up the glaciers to the tops of the Southern Alps, with professionally executed displays on plate tectonics, geology, Maori legends and forest ecology. Highlights are the world rainfall comparison (300mm in LA; 600mm in London; 5100mm in Franz Josef), an excellent speeded-up sequence which compresses a year of glacier terminus movement into a few seconds, and screens which let you into the lives of local characters and guides. It's undoubtedly well done, but $25 does seem a bit steep.

Also steep, though in a good way, is the fun indoor **ice climbing wall** (90min; $90), where you're kitted out with warm clothing, crampons and a pair of ice axes and encouraged to tackle increasingly challenging faces (or even an overhanging bulge) while being safely belayed by a staff member or your suitably instructed mates. You should get in five to seven climbs in the time available, and non-participating friends or family can watch from the café.

Outside, a short walk follows SH6 for a couple of hundred metres south to the pretty half-timbered **St James Church** (always open), which once framed the glacier in the altar window. The ice retreated from view in 1953, and the church itself nearly did the same in 1995 when the flooded Waiho River scoured away the alluvial bank and left it precariously poised on a cliff. Opposite, the **Terrace Walk** (30min return; mostly flat) meanders through the bush to a pleasant viewpoint overlooking the Waiho River.

Glacier hiking, heli-hiking and ice climbing

It is possible to walk to the face of the Franz Josef glacier, but to walk on the ice you'll need to take a **glacier-walking** trip with Franz Josef Glacier Guides, SH6 (Ⓣ0800/484 337, Ⓦwww.franzjosefglacier.com). They offer a half-day trip (2–3 daily; $97) involving a trudge across the braided riverbed below the glacier, fitting your crampons, then a little over an hour on the ice, snaking up ample ice steps cut by your guide. For a more tangible sense of adventure, fork out for the full-day trip ($150) which gives around five hours on the ice, hopefully finding ice tunnels to explore. They also offer **heli-hiking** (1–2 daily; 3hr; $390), which combines a short helicopter flight with a couple of hours on a fascinating section of ice caves, pinnacles and seracs that you couldn't hope to reach on foot in a day: well worth saving up for. Try to be clear about your aspirations and abilities and you can be matched up with a party of like-minded folk. For an even more active day, go **ice climbing** (7–8hr; $250) – an instructional roped-up day in plastic boots with crampons and ice tools on steep ice.

Scenic flights

On any fine day the skies above Franz Josef are abuzz with choppers and light planes. Safety demands that specific flight paths must be followed, limiting what can be offered and forcing companies to compete on price; ask for youth, student, YHA, BBH, senior or just-for-the-sake-of-it discounts, most readily given if you can band together in a group of four to six and present yourselves as a ready-to-go plane or chopper load.

Most people go by **helicopter**, with all operators regularly landing on a snow-field high above the glacier where the rotors are left running – hardly a serene setting. The cheapest are Fox and Franz Josef Heliservices (Ⓣ0800/800 793, Ⓦwww.scenic-flights.co.nz), who offer one glacier (20min; $180), two glaciers (30min; $240), and two glaciers plus Mount Cook (40min; $340).

Planes give you a longer flight with greater range for less money, and a skiplane landing on a snowfield can be quite exciting. Mount Cook Ski Planes (Ⓣ0800/368 000, Ⓦwww.mtcookskiplanes.com) run overflights of both glaciers (25min with no landing; $230) and circuits of Mount Cook (40min; $340), the latter with ten minutes stopped on the Tasman glacier, where the silence is deafening. Air Safaris (Ⓣ0800/723 274, Ⓦwww.airsafaris.co.nz) are usually a smidgen cheaper but don't do landings: try their Grand Traverse (50min; $280).

Walks and activities around about

Top of everyone's list of **walks** is the one from the glacier car park, 5km south of the village, to the face of the Franz Josef glacier (6km return; 1hr 30min; flat), a roped-off and ever-changing wall of ice where the Waiho River issues from beneath the ice. The rough track crosses gravel beds left behind by past glacial retreats, giving you plenty of opportunity to observe small kettle lakes, the trim line high up the valley walls and a fault line cutting right across the valley (marked by deep gullies opposite each other). One of the best viewpoints is from the top of the glacier-scoured hump of **Sentinel Rock**, a ten-minute walk from the car park.

Worthwhile walks off the access road include the circular **Douglas Walk** (1hr) past Peter's Pool, a serene lake left by a retreat in the late eighteenth century, and the **Alex Knob Track** (12km return; 8hr; 1000m ascent), which climbs high above the glacier through several vegetation zones and offers fine views up the valley. The only way to actually walk on the glacier surface is with a guide (see p.756).

If you'd rather spend an active few hours sitting down, join a **guided kayaking** trip with Glacier Country, 20 Cron St (Ⓣ0800/423 262, Ⓦwww.glacierkayaks.com), who run relaxing and informative trips ($75) on the black waters of the kahikatea- and flax-fringed Lake Mapourika, 8km north of town. Trips run in the morning, afternoon and early evening, spend about three hours on the water and offer loads of photo opportunities. Great on a sunny day, they're also enjoyable in the rain.

Eating and drinking

Franz Josef has a surprisingly decent range of **places to eat** and drink. The relatively remote location keeps prices high though, and even if you are self-catering you can expect to pay over the odds for a limited stock of **groceries**.

The Beeches SH6. Quality café and restaurant good for coffee and lunches during the day and a broad range of reasonably priced dinners (mains around $27); all available indoors or out.

Blue Ice Café SH6. The modern and airy restaurant at street level serves imaginative and tasty mains for $25–30 and a range of gourmet pizzas from $20, which can also be ordered to take away or eaten in the upstairs bar, where the free pool table and rowdy music draws in a lively, sometimes backpacker-heavy, crowd nightly.

Full of Beans Café SH6. Cheerful and inexpensive café serving a middle-of-the-road selection of burgers, toasted sandwiches and the likes of Thai curry, venison hotpot and chicken salad.

Monsoon 46 Cron St. Convivial restaurant and bar offering the likes of burgers, fish 'n' chips, straightforward pizzas, and steaks for $12–25. Also open for breakfast.

Fox Glacier

Fox Glacier, 25km south of Franz Josef, lies scattered over an outwash plain of the Fox and Cook rivers, and supports the local farming community, as well as sightseers. Everything of interest is beside SH6 or Cook Flat Road, which passes the scenic Lake Matheson on the way to the former gold settlement and seal colony at Gillespies Beach. The foot of the Fox glacier is around 6km away.

Arrival, information and getting around

Fox experiences the same **bus** schedule as Franz Josef (see p.767) and consequently has similar shortages of accommodation through the summer months. If you come unstuck, seek help at the **DOC office**, SH6 (Mon–Fri 9am–noon & 1–4.30pm Ⓣ03/751 0807, Ⓔfoxglaciervcsouthwestlandao@doc.govt.nz), which also has displays concentrating on lowland forests and glaciation.

If you don't have your own **transport**, use Fox Glacier Shuttles & Tours (Ⓣ0800/369 287) to get to the glacier ($12 return), Lake Matheson ($12 return) and Copland Valley ($20 each way; min 2 people). They even run a tour along Gillespies Beach to the seal colony ($30–40 depending on numbers).

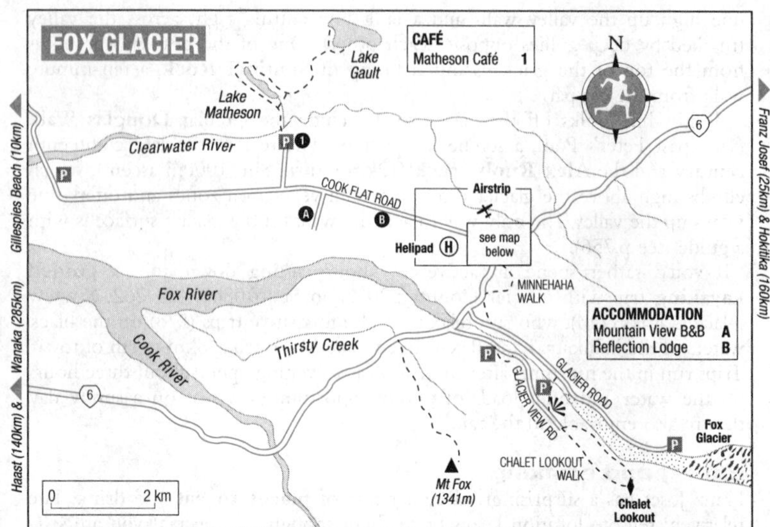

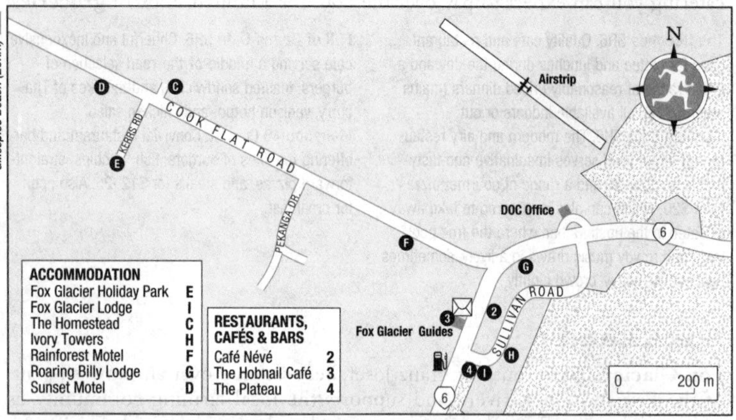

Accommodation

Fox's range of places to stay is more limited than Franz Josef's but is generally pretty good; **book** as far ahead as you can and be prepared for resort prices. The basic and free DOC **campsite** at Gillespies Beach (see p.760) is popular in summer.

Fox Glacier Holiday Park Kerrs Rd ⓣ0800/154 366, ⓦwww.foxglacierholidaypark.co.nz. Fairly basic campsite with tent sites, a bunkhouse, cabins and s/c units. Camping $15, cabins ❷, units ❹

Fox Glacier Lodge Sullivan Rd ⓣ0800/369 800, ⓦwww.foxglacierlodge.co.nz. A pine-lined alpine chalet with attractively furnished en-suite rooms (some with spa baths) sharing a communal kitchen. A buffet breakfast is included, and there are campervan hookups outside. Also self-catering apartments. Powered sites $15, rooms ❺, apartments ❼

The Homestead Cook Flat Rd, 700m off SH6 ⓣ03/751 0835, ⓔfoxhomestead@slingshot.co.nz. Friendly homestay in a pleasant old house within walking distance of town, with views of Mount Cook, pleasant en suites and a continental breakfast. ❺

Ivory Towers Sullivan Rd ⓣ03/751 0838, ⓦwww.ivorytowerslodge.co.nz. Fox's only genuine backpackers is a friendly, clean and colourfully decorated hostel. Most dorms have both beds and bunks, while doubles all have TV. The kitchen is spacious, there's a sauna ($8), a small cinema for those rainy afternoons and bikes can be rented for $24 a day. Dorms $26, rooms ②, en suites ③

Mountain View B&B 1 Williams Drive, 2km off SH6 ①03/751 0770, Ⓦwww.foxglaciermountainview.co.nz. Welcoming modern B&B with three en suites and a separate s/c cottage all on three hectares on the edge of town with great mountain views. You get tasteful decor in well-equipped rooms plus a full breakfast. ⑥

Rainforest Motel 15 Cook Flat Rd, 200m off SH6 ①0800/724 636, Ⓦwww.rainforestmotel.co.nz. Log cabins with attractive and well-priced studios and larger one-bedroom units. ⑤

Reflection Lodge Cook Flat Rd, 1.5km off SH6 ①03/751 0707, Ⓦwww.reflectionlodge.co.nz. So named because of the reflection of the mountains in the large garden pond, this neat homestay offers reasonably priced accommodation in comfortable, spacious and friendly surroundings. ⑥

Roaring Billy Lodge SH6 ①03/751 0815, Ⓔbilly@xtra.co.nz. Friendly homestay in the centre of Fox Glacier with simple rooms, a comfortable lounge area and a cooked vegetarian breakfast. ④

Sunset Motel Cook Flat Rd, 1km off SH6 ①0800/751 006, Ⓦwww.sunsetmotels.co.nz. The best of the upmarket motels, new, tastefully decorated and with great views of Mount Cook and Mount Tasman from all rooms. ⑥

Glacier hiking, heli-hiking and ice climbing

Trips on the Franz Josef glacier are very good, but **glacier walking** is generally more rewarding (and cheaper) on the Fox glacier, where entry is from the side, giving more immediate access to crevasses and seracs. Fox Glacier Guides (①0800/111 600, Ⓦwww.foxguides.co.nz) lead half-day walks (2–4 daily; $89) with around an hour on the ice, though it is worth stepping up to a full-day trip ($135), giving over three hours. They also offer **heli-hiking** ($380), with two and a half hours of icy hiking, and **ice climbing** (8–9hr; $225), which gives you the chance to get vertical for a few hours. To combine the two, try **heli-ice climbing** (8hr; $595), throwing in a scenic flight that gets you higher on the glacier.

Scenic flights

The Fox Glacier airport and helipad are slightly less busy than those at Franz Josef, but similar range of flights are on offer. Again, Fox and Franz Josef Heliservices (see p.756) are the cheapest **chopper flights** with the same deals as in Franz. The only company offering **plane flights** from Fox is Mt Cook Ski Planes (see p.756), which has flights for the same prices as from Franz Josef.

Walks and activities

It would be a shame to miss the Fox glacier just because you have already seen Franz Josef: the **approach walks** are quite different and their characters very distinct, the Fox valley being less sheer but with more impressive rock falls. The approach, imaginatively named Glacier Road, crosses the wide bed left by glacial retreats and is occasionally re-routed as "dead" ice under the roadway gradually melts. From the car park, 6km from the town, a track leads to the foot of the glacier in half an hour, crossing a couple of small streams en route. Partway back along Glacier Road, **River Walk** (2km; 30min) crosses a historic swingbridge to the Glacier Valley Viewpoint on Glacier View Road, which runs 3km along the south side of the Fox River. From here, the **Chalet Lookout Walk** (4km; 1hr 15min return; 150m ascent) climbs moderately for stupendous glacier and mountain views.

It's difficult to imagine a New Zealand calendar or picture book without a photo of Mount Cook and Mount Tasman mirrored in **Lake Matheson**, 5km west of town along Cook Flat Road. A well-signposted boardwalk through lovely native bush encircles the lake, which was formed by an iceberg left

▲ Matheson Café, Lake Matheson

behind when the Fox glacier retreated 14,000 years ago. It takes around an hour and gives everyone a chance for that perfect image, especially those who venture out before sunrise. The *Matheson Café*, by the Lake Matheson car park, is beautifully located.

About 5km beyond Lake Matheson, **Peak Viewpoint** is ideal for fabulous fine-day views of the top of the Fox glacier and the snowcapped mountains. Continue 10km further along Cook Flat Road to reach **Gillespies Beach**, a former gold-mining settlement with a small cemetery and a primitive DOC campsite (free). From the campsite an excellent **walk** threads north parallel to the beach, past the scant remains of an old gold dredge (30min return) to Gillespies Lagoon (1hr 15min return), a short Miners' Tunnel (1hr 40min return) and the Galway Beach Seal Colony (3hr 30min return).

Back in Fox, fill an empty half-hour with a stroll around the flat **Minnehaha Walk** (1km; 20min loop), which winds through lush bush that's cool and shady on a summer day, or dank and brooding in the rain. Come after dark to see **glow-worms**. If all this leaves you unruffled try a **tandem skydive** (Ⓣ0800/751 0080) from 12,000ft ($295).

Eating and drinking

For its diminutive size, Fox Glacier does a decent-enough job of catering to hungry walkers coming off the glacier-side paths, with a small selection of reasonably priced **cafés**, a restaurant and a couple of lively **bars**.

Café Névé SH6. Great café and bar serving excellent food and coffee throughout the day both inside and out. Try the venison ragout ($15), BLT on Turkish flatbread ($15) or the range of evening main courses (around $28), and something from their broad range of wines by the glass. The vegetarian gourmet pizza ($15–29) is particularly tasty.

The Hobnail Café SH6. Good café in alpine-chalet surroundings in the same building as Fox Glacier Guides, with a wide range of breakfasts, plus salads, sandwiches and more substantial lunches.

Matheson Café Cook Flat Rd. Good café at the start of the walk around Lake Matheson, made special by its mountain views through big picture windows. The breakfasts ($7–14) reward an early walk, or come later for lunch or coffee and cake as the afternoon sun catches the mountains.

The Plateau SH6. Newish café and bar serving classy lunches and dinners at what are quite modest prices for these parts. Try the herb-crusted chicken breast ($26) or one of the nightly special mains ($25–28). The desserts blackboard always has something tempting.

South Westland and Makarora

South from the glaciers, the West Coast feels remoter still. There wasn't even a road through here until 1965 and the final section of tarmac was not laid on the Haast Pass until 1995. SH6 mostly runs inland, passing the start of the hike to the **Welcome Flat Hot Springs** (see below) and through kahikatea and rimu forests as far as **Knight's Point**, where it returns to the coast along the edge of the Haast Coastal Plain, whose stunning **coastal dune systems** shelter lakes and some fine stands of kahikatea. The plain continues south past the scattered township of **Haast** to the site of the short-lived colonial settlement of **Jackson Bay**. From Haast, SH6 veers inland over the Haast Pass to the former timber town of **Makarora**, not strictly part of the West Coast but moist enough to share some of the same characteristics and a base for the excellent **Gillespie Pass** Tramp.

South to Haast

Many visitors do the run from the glaciers to Wanaka or Queenstown in one day, missing out on some fine country whose relative lack of comforts is balanced by its sheer remoteness. Facilities aren't completely absent: the majority of the accommodation and eating places are clustered around Haast, but there are a few pit stops along the way. One place you might like to break your journey is **Bruce Bay**, 45km south of Fox Glacier, where the road briefly parallels a long driftwood-strewn beach perfect for an atmospheric stroll.

Some 17km further south, the road crosses the **Paringa River**, where a plaque marks the southern limit ofThomas Brunner's 1846–48 explorations. He recorded in his diary the desire to "once more see the face of a white man, and hear my native tongue". Buses all stop nearby at the *Salmon Farm* for an

Welcome Flat Hot Springs

The most popular two-day hike in the region is the in-and-back jaunt to the **Welcome Flat Hot Springs**, a series of open-air pools where you're bound to find a spot that's just the right temperature for easing those bones. Almost everyone spends the night at DOC's adjacent **Welcome Flat Hut** (31 bunks; $15; no reservations; annual pass not valid). Be warned that during the summer the hut is very popular and you may just get a mattress on the floor or be forced to camp nearby ($5).

The track (detailed on DOC's *Copland Track* leaflet) starts by a car park on SH6, 26km south of Fox Glacier: Atomic and InterCity **buses** will drop off, and pick up pre-booked customers. From **SH6 to Welcome Flat** (17km; 6–7hr; 450m ascent) is a fairly tough tramp (far less defined than any of the Great Walks) following the true right bank all the way to Welcome Flat, crossing numerous creeks by hopping from rock to rock or wading. If the creeks are high, as they commonly are, you may have to use the flood bridges, which will add an hour or so. After heavy rain, the track becomes impassable: take plenty of extra supplies in case you get held up by a day or two.

overpriced snack or light lunch on a wooden deck overlooking salmon-rearing ponds. A better bet is to pick up some delicious hot- or cold-smoked salmon to take away and continue 8km south to the northern shores of **Lake Paringa** and DOC's simple but beautifully sited Lake Paringa **campsite** ($6).

Around 18km south of Lake Paringa, the **Monro Beach Walk** (5km; 1hr 30min return) leads through lovely forest to one of the best places for spotting rare **Fiordland crested penguins** – mainly during the breeding season (July–Dec), but also occasionally in February, when they come ashore to moult. Nature lovers with ample wallets can gain a deeper appreciation of the fragile ecosystems of south Westland by staying nearby at the exclusive *Wilderness Lodge Lake Moeraki* (ⓣ03/750 0881, ⓦwww.wildernesslodge.co.nz; ⑨) where, for around $360 per person per day, you get lodge **accommodation**, all meals, free canoe use and all manner of guided nature walks and safaris.

The highway finally returns to the coast 5km on at **Knight's Point**, where a roadside marker commemorates the linking of Westland and Otago by road in 1965. Ahead lies the **Haast Coastal Plain**, which kicks off at the tea-coloured **Ship Creek**, 10km on, where a picnic area and information panels by a beautiful long surf-pounded beach mark the start of two lovely walks: the twenty-minute **Kahikatea Swamp Forest Walk** up the river through kahikatea forest to a lookout and the **Mataketake Dune Lake Walk** (2km; 30min return) along the coast to the dune-trapped Lake Mataketake.

From Ship Creek it's only another 15km to the 700m-long Haast River Bridge, the longest single-lane bridge in the country, immediately before Haast Junction.

Haast

Haast is initially a confusing place, with three tiny communities all taking the name: Haast Junction, at the intersection of SH6 and the minor road to Jackson Bay, Haast Beach, 4km along the Jackson Bay Road (see p.763) and

▲ Haast Bridge

Haast Township, the largest settlement, 3km along SH6 towards the Haast Pass and Wanaka.

At Haast Junction, the distinctive **Haast Visitor Centre** (daily: early Nov to April 9am–6pm; rest of year 9am–4.30pm; ⓣ03/750 0809, ⓔhaastvc@doc.govt.nz) serves as the local visitor centre and has highly informative displays on all aspects of the local environment. The short *Edge of Wilderness* film is shown on demand ($3). To explore deeper, join a **jetboat safari** with Waiatoto River Safaris (daily on demand; ⓣ0800/538 723, ⓦwww.riversafaris.co.nz; $150), an excellent two-hour wilderness ride from the coast into the heart of the mountains with the emphasis firmly on appreciating history and scenery. Deep within Mount Aspiring National Park, you'll really get an appreciation of just how remote this area is.

Alternatively, try the extremely knowledgeable pilots at Heliventures (ⓣ03/750 0866, ⓦwww.heliventures.co.nz), who offer **flights** to the Lost Valley (30min; $260, min 3 people) and Mount Aspiring (1hr; $525, min 3 people), including a snow landing.

Even if you're just passing through you'll probably want to **eat**, but shouldn't expect too much. At Haast Township the **Fantail Café** does adequate teas, snacks and takeaways, while the *Frontier Bar* at the Haast World Heritage Hotel at Haast Junction does good pizza, lasagne and fish 'n' chips at modest prices. There's a small and fairly expensive supermarket for supplies.

Those wanting to **stay** have an increasing range of choices, but Haast gets busy from Christmas to the end of February and you should book ahead.

Accommodation

Collyer House Okuru, 13km south of Haast Junction ⓣ03/750 0022, ⓦwww.collyerhouse.co.nz. Very appealing luxury accommodation with four modern en suites decorated in a nice mixture of antique and modern furnishings, all with distant sea views. A sizeable cooked breakfast is served and there are evening meals by arrangement. ⑧

Haast Beach Holiday Park Okuru, 15km south of Haast Junction ⓣ03/750 0860. ⓔhaastpark@xtra.co.nz. Simple but comfortable holiday park close to the beach and the Hapuku Estuary Walk. Tents $15, dorms $25, cabins ①, kitchen cabins ②, motel units ④

Haast Lodge Haast Township ⓣ03/750 0703, ⓦwww.haastlodge.com. Reasonable hostel and motel that's handy for its campervan hookups. Also tent space, but only in dry weather. Camping $13, dorms $24, rooms ①, motel units ④

Heritage Park Lodge Haast Township ⓣ0800/526 252, ⓦwww.heritageparklodge.co.nz. Friendly motel offering probably the best-value rooms around: modern, comfortable studios with TV and video, and some units with self-catering facilities. ④

McGuires Lodge Haast Junction ⓣ0800/624 847, ⓦwww.mcguireslodge.co.nz. Modern upmarket lodge with attractive rooms, and a reasonable café/bar and fancier restaurant on site. ④

Wilderness Accommodation Haast Township ⓣ03/750 0029, ⓔwhitesnalex@xtra.co.nz. Comfortable and welcoming spot combining a backpacker hostel with four-shares and made-up doubles, and a series of motel studio units, all with access to a common area and kitchen. They also have scooter rental for $25 a half-day, ideal for trips to Jackson Bay. Dorms $25, backpacker rooms ②, units ③

The road to Jackson Bay

A modest number of inquisitive tourists make it 50km south of Haast to the fishing village of Jackson Bay, which is hanging on by its fingernails. Leaving Haast Junction, the canopies of windswept roadside trees bunch together like cauliflower heads down to and beyond **Haast Beach**, 4km south, where there's a small shop and petrol supplies.

Ten kilometres on, there's accommodation in the form of *Collyer House* (see above) and, a couple of kilometres beyond, *Haast Beach Holiday Park* (see above). Opposite, the **Hapuku Estuary Walk** (20min loop), follows a raised

Gillespie Pass: the Wilkin and Young valleys circuit

This tramp over the 1490m Gillespie Pass links the upper valley of the young river with that of the **Siberia Stream** and the **Wilkin River**. The scenery is superb, the match of any of the more celebrated valleys further south, but is tramped by a fraction of the folk on the Routeburn or the Greenstone tracks; perhaps the biggest gripe for the tramping purist is the disturbance caused by planes flying into the Siberia Valley. Be warned, however: the creation of a lake behind a potentially unstable landslip in late 2007 left the Young Valley **closed to trampers**, effectively making it impossible to do this walk. The valley is expected to reopen in late 2008, but check its status first with DOC.

The DOC's *Gillespie Pass, Wilkin Valley Tracks* leaflet has all the detail you need for this walk, though the 1:160,000 *Mount Aspiring Parkmap* and the 1:50,000 *Wilkin* **maps** are useful. The route can be divided up into smaller chunks, using Siberia Experience's planes and jetboats (see p.766), but the full circuit (58km) takes three days.

Access and accommodation

All the **huts** ($10; no advance booking) in the Wilkin and Young valleys are equipped with mattresses and heating (but not cooking) stoves; hut **tickets** and annual hut **passes** are available from the DOC office in Makarora (see p.766). The walk is typically done up the Young Valley and down the Wilkin – the way we've described it here. **Access** at both ends of the walk is a question of **wading** the broad, braided **Makarora River**, something not advised unless you have river-crossing experience. Someone dies almost every year. It is usually better to band together with other trampers and get a **jetboat** to drop you at the confluence of the Young and Makarora rivers ($25, min 3 people); it's also a good idea to arrange a **pick-up** by jetboat ($65) from Kerin Forks at the far end of the walk, unless you want to take your chances with river crossings or a stand-by backflight out of Siberia Valley ($65).

The route

After jetboating to the confluence of the Young and Makarora rivers, walk down the true right bank of the Makarora to the bush-side marker. From the **confluence to Young Hut** (20km; 6–7hr; 500m ascent), the easy-to-follow track traces the true left

boardwalk over a brackish lagoon and through kowhai forest that gleams brilliant yellow in October and November. Old sand dunes support rimu and kahikatea forest, and there are occasional views out to the **Open Bay Islands**, now a **wildlife sanctuary** and a major breeding colony for fur seals and Fiordland crested penguins.

The road continues 35km to **JACKSON BAY**, a former sealing station tucked in the curve of Jackson Head, which protects it from the worst of the westerlies. In 1875 it was chosen as the townsite to rival Greymouth and Hokitika. Assisted migrants – Scandinavians, Germans, Poles, Italians, English and Irish – were expected to carve a living from tiny land allocations, with limited and irregular supplies. Sodden by rain, crops rotted, and people were soon leaving in droves; a few stalwarts stayed, their descendants providing the core of today's residents, who eke out a meagre living from lobster and tuna fishing.

Try the **Wharekai Te Kou Walk** (40min return) across the low isthmus behind Jackson Head to a beach where Fiordland crested penguins can sometimes be seen from July to November. The **Smoothwater Track** (3hr return) has great coastal views on the way to the Smoothwater River.

There are no **facilities** in Jackson Bay except for *The Cray Pot*, a kind of diner on wheels where you can get fantastic fresh-cooked fish and chips, mugs of tea

bank through beech forest to Young Forks, where there is a campsite (free). After the fork, the track follows the South Branch, climbing steeply with some difficulty over a bad slip. It is then a steady climb up through forest to the new Young Hut (20 bunks).

Suitably rested, you've another fairly strenuous day ahead from **Young Hut to Siberia Hut** (12km; 6–8hr; 700m ascent, 1000m descent), first up to the treeline overlooked by the 2202m Mount Awful, apparently named in wonder rather than horror. Then it's over the Gillespie Pass, a steep and lengthy ascent eventually following snow poles to a saddle; it'll take three hours to reach this fabulous, barren spot with views across the snowcapped northern peaks of the Mount Aspiring National Park. Grassy slopes lead steeply down to Gillespie Stream, which is followed to its confluence with the Siberia Stream, from where it's a gentle, undulating hour downstream to Siberia Hut (20 bunks). Keen types might tag on a side trip to **Lake Crucible** (4–5hr return) before cantering down to the hut. Those with more modest aspirations can spend two nights at Siberia Hut and do the **Lake Crucible side trip** (13km; 6–7hr return; 500m ascent) on the spare day.

From the Siberia Hut, follow the true left bank of the Siberia Stream a short distance until you see Crucible Stream cascading in a deep gash on the far side. Ford Siberia Stream and ascend through the bush on the true right bank of the stream. It is hard going, and route-finding among the alpine meadows higher up can be difficult, but the deep alpine lake tucked under the skirts of Mount Alba and choked with small icebergs is ample reward. Planes fly in and out of the **Siberia Valley airstrip**, and you can take your chance on "backloading" **flights out** ($65). To continue tramping from **Siberia Hut to Kerin Forks** (8km; 2–3hr; 100m ascent, 300m descent), enter the bush at the southern end of Siberia Flats on the true left bank of Siberia Stream and descend away from the stream then zigzag steeply down to the Wilkin River and the **Kerin Forks Hut** (10 bunks), where many trampers arrange to be met by a jetboat. If it has rained heavily, fording the Makarora lower down will be impossible, so don't forgo the jetboat lightly. The alternative is to walk from **Kerin Forks to Makarora** (17km; 5–6hr; 100m ascent, 200m descent), following the Wilkin River's true left bank, then crossing the Makarora upstream of the confluence.

and various meat options, away from the sandflies, while gazing at the sea-tossed fishing boats through fake lead-light windows.

Haast Pass and Makarora

From Haast it is nearly 150km over the **Haast Pass** (at 563m, the lowest road crossing of the Southern Alps) to Wanaka – a journey from the verdant rain-soaked forests of the West Coast into the parched, rolling grasslands of Central Otago. Ngai Tahu used the pass as a greenstone trading route and probably introduced it to gold prospector Charles Cameron, who became the first Pakeha to cross in 1863; he was closely followed by the more influential **Julius Von Haast**, who modestly named it after himself. The pass was finally opened as a vehicular route in 1965.

The road starts beside the broad **Haast River** which, as the road climbs, narrows into a series of churning cascades. Numerous short and well-signposted walks, mostly to waterfalls on tributaries, spur off at intervals. The most celebrated include the **Thunder Creek Falls** (5min), the roadside **Fantail Falls**, and the **Blue Pools Walk** (30min return), where an aquamarine stream issues from a narrow, icy gorge: swim if you dare. Though there are few

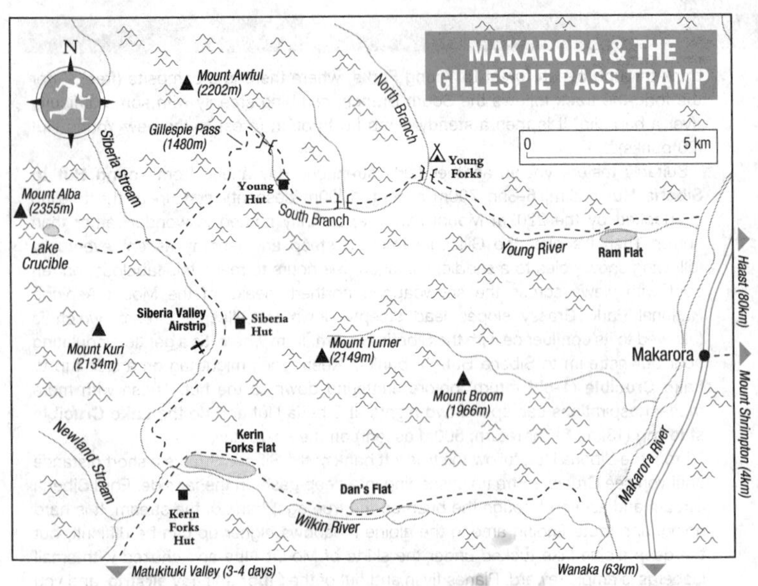

specific sights, it is a great area to linger a while, **camping** in one of the DOC's toilets-and-water sites (all \$6 per person) along the way: first up is Pleasant Flat, 45km from Haast, followed by Cameron Flat, 8km over the Pass and 10km short of Makarora.

Makarora

The hamlet of **Makarora** lies roughly midway between Haast and Wanaka, on the northern fringe of Mount Aspiring National Park. If you're aching for the comforts of Wanaka and Queenstown there's little reason to stop, but casual hikers, and keen trampers with a few days to spare, should consider tackling the local walks, some aided by flights and jetboat rides.

In the nineteenth century the dense **forests** all about and the proximity of Lake Wanaka made Makarora the perfect spot for marshalling cut logs across the lake and coaxing them down the Clutha River southeast to the fledgling North Otago **gold towns** of Clyde and Cromwell. The creation of the national park in 1964 paved the way for Makarora's increasing importance as the main northern access point to a region of majestic beauty, alpine vegetation and dense beech-filled valleys.

All you'll find here is a motor camp, a restaurant/bar, a shop and a **DOC office** (Dec–April daily 8am–5pm; May–Nov Mon–Fri occasionally staffed; ⓣ03/443 8365), the place to go for information and hut tickets for tramps. The main justification for stopping is to head out on the Gillespie Pass tramp (see p.764) or to join Southern Alps Air's excellent four-hour **Siberia Experience** (ⓣ0800/538 945, ⓦwww.siberiaexperience.co.nz; \$240), which includes a flight into the remote Siberia Valley, a three-hour tramp to the Wilkin River and a jetboat ride back to Makarora. The same deal but with a helicopter flight goes under the title **Siberia Wilderness Adventure** (\$290) and avoids a river crossing.

The same operator also offers flights around Mount Aspiring (around \$280, min 3 people). The **jetboating** section can also be tackled separately with

Wilkin River Jets (1hr; $90), as good value a jetboat ride as you'll find anywhere in New Zealand. Ask about their **Jumboland Wilderness Adventure** ($290), involving a helicopter flight, four hours of beech-forest walking along the Wilkin River and the jetboat out.

Finally, if the longer hikes seem a little daunting, there are a couple of **shorter walks** close to Makarora, the **Makarora Bush Nature Walk** (15min loop), which starts near the DOC office and, branching off this, the **Mount Shrimpton Track** (5km return, 4–5hr, 900m ascent), which climbs steeply up through silver beech to the bushline, then to a knob overlooking the Makarora Valley.

Almost everyone **stays** at the peaceful, pool-equipped *Makarora Wilderness Resort*, SH6 (Ⓣ03/443 8372, Ⓦwww.makarora.co.nz; camping $13, dorms $25, doubles ❷, kitchen cabins ❸, chalets ❹), a collection of self-catering and simple A-frame chalets in a clearing. The shop sells limited supplies and there's a modern wood-beamed restaurant and bar serving sandwiches and buffet lunches ($11–17) during the day, plus steak, chicken and veggie evening mains ($18–25). An alternative is *Larrivee Homestay*, SH6 (Ⓣ03/443 9177, Ⓦwww.larriveehomestay.co.nz; B&B ❺, cottage ❹), either in a lovely octagonal house hidden behind the DOC office or in a self-contained cottage.

Continuing towards Wanaka, a couple of lovely DOC **campsites** are the only real reasons to break your journey. Try *Boundary Creek* ($6) beside Lake Wanaka 10km south of Makarora, or *Kidds Bush* ($6) beside Lake Hawea, 6km down a side road off SH6 at The Neck, where lakes Wanaka and Hawea almost meet.

Travel details

The main West Coast bus route is InterCity/Newmans' service from Nelson to Fox Glacier via Westport, Greymouth, Hokitika and Franz Josef. A second service starts in Franz Josef and stops in Fox Glacier, Haast and Makarora on the way to Wanaka and Queenstown. This set-up enforces a night in either Franz Josef or Fox. To travel straight through, go with the faster Atomic (Ⓣ03/349 0697, Ⓦwww.atomictravel.co.nz), who run daily between Greymouth and Queenstown. Several other companies service smaller places.

Trains

The only passenger train service is the TranzAlpine, which runs from Christchurch to Greymouth in the morning then back again each afternoon.

Greymouth to: Arthur's Pass (1 daily; 2hr 15min); Christchurch (1 daily; 4hr 20min).

Buses

Fox Glacier to: Franz Josef (4 daily; 30min); Greymouth (4 daily; 3hr 45min–4hr 30min); Haast (3 daily; 2hr 40min–3hr); Hokitika (4 daily; 3hr); Makarora (3 daily; 4hr 30min); Queenstown (3 daily; 6hr–7hr 30min); Wanaka (3 daily; 5–6hr).

Franz Josef Glacier to: Fox Glacier (4 daily; 30min); Haast (3 daily; 3hr–3hr 30min); Greymouth (4 daily; 3hr–3hr 30min); Hokitika (4 daily; 2hr 30min); Makarora (3 daily; 4hr 20min–5hr); Queenstown (2 daily; 7–8hr); Wanaka (2 daily; 6–7hr).

Greymouth to: Arthur's Pass (3 daily; 1hr 30min); Christchurch (3 daily; 4hr 30min); Fox Glacier (4 daily; 3hr 45min–4hr 30min); Franz Josef (4 daily; 3hr–3hr 30min); Hokitika (4 daily; 30min); Murchison (1 daily; 2hr 15min); Picton (1 daily; 7hr); Punakaiki (3 daily; 30min); Queenstown (2 daily; 9–10hr); Wanaka (2 daily; 8hr–8hr 30min); Westport (3 daily; 1hr 30min–2hr 15min).

Hokitika to: Arthur's Pass (1 daily; 1hr 45min); Christchurch (1 daily; 4hr 30min); Fox Glacier (4

daily; 3hr); Franz Josef (4 daily; 2hr 30min); Greymouth (4 daily; 30min); Ross (4 daily; 25min); Whataroa (4 daily; 1hr 30min).
Westport to: Greymouth (3 daily; 1hr 30min–2hr 15min); Karamea (2 daily; 1hr 40min–2hr); Murchison (3 daily; 1hr 15min–1hr 45min); Nelson (3 daily; 3hr 30min–4hr); Punakaiki (3 daily; 1hr); St Arnaud (1 daily; 1hr 45min).

Flights

Greymouth to: Wellington (5 weekly; 1hr).
Hokitika to: Christchurch (2–3 daily; 35min).
Westport to: Wellington (1 daily Mon–Fri; 50min).

13

Queenstown, Wanaka and the Gold Country

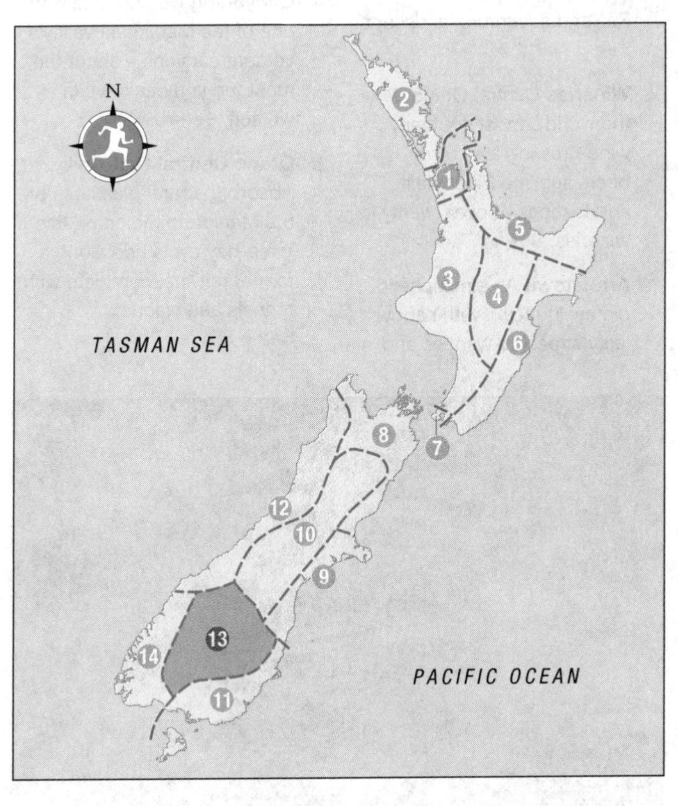

CHAPTER 13 Highlights

* **Nevis Highwire Bungy** Test your nerve on the Nevis; New Zealand's biggest elasticated leap is from a hut suspended harrowingly high above a plunging canyon. See p.785

* **Shotover River** Take a jetboat ride down through an iconic part of the New Zealand adventure landscape. See p.786

* **Wineries** Central Otago is the world's most southerly wine-growing area, and offers sublime Pinot Noir and tastings at over twenty wineries. See pp.793 & 828

* **Arrowtown** An atmospheric old mining town with narrow, leafy streets to wander, and good walks possible in the surrounding valleys. See p.794

* **The Routeburn Track** Lush bush, alpine scenery and the camaraderie of backcountry huts combine to make this one of New Zealand's best tramps. See p.803

* **Canyoning** Get intimate with one of the Matukituki Valley's verdant canyons – about the most fun you can have in a wetsuit. See p.815

* **Otago Central Rail Trail** Absorb the rural pleasures of the Maniototo region on this three-day cycle ride along a former rail line, complete with tunnels and viaducts. See p.831

▲ Jetboating on the Shotover River

13

Queenstown, Wanaka and the Gold Country

Wedged between the sodden beech forests of Fiordland, the fertile plains of south Canterbury, the city of Dunedin and the sheep country of Southland lies Central Otago, a region encompassing **Queenstown**, **Wanaka** and the surrounding **Gold Country**. Rolling, deserted hills to the east give way to the sharper profiles of the mountains around Queenstown and Wanaka, which rub shoulders with the final glaciated flourish of the Southern Alps. Meltwater and heavy rains course out of the mountains into the seventy-kilometre lightning bolt of **Lake Wakatipu**, which in turn drains east through the Kawarau River, carving a rapid-strewn path through the Kawarau Gorge. Along the way it picks up the waters of the Shotover River from the goldfields of Skippers and Arrowtown. To the north, the pristine, glassy lakes of Wanaka and Hawea feed the **Clutha River**, which joins forces with the Kawarau at Cromwell and high-tails it to the coast through the heartland of the Otago Gold Country.

Queenstown is undoubtedly the region's jewel, with a legendary setting looking across Lake Wakatipu to the craggy heights of the Remarkables range. New Zealand's self-proclaimed adventure capital, it can take on the atmosphere of a high-priced theme park, offering the chance to indulge in just about every adrenalin-fuelled activity imaginable: numerous competing operators have honed bungy jumping, jetboating, rafting, skydiving and paragliding into well-packaged, forcefully marketed products – although they're no less exciting for it. All this wonderful scenery and adventure has gained something of an international profile, providing some of the background for major feature films such as Martin Campbell's *The Vertical Limit*; *The Lion, The Witch and The Wardrobe*; and, if you include **Glenorchy** at the head of Lake Wakatipu, the highest concentration of locations from *The Lord of the Rings* trilogy.

For all Queenstown's appeal, you'll soon be looking for a break, something easily done in neighbouring **Arrowtown**, an extremely popular day-trip destination which wears its gold heritage well. Here it's possible to visit the intriguing remains of a former Chinese settlement and take a day-long walk to the defunct gold mines around the nearby ghost town of **Macetown**.

Perhaps the perfect antidote to the rigours and flash of Queenstown is the great outdoors, and some of the country's most exalted multi-day tramps start from the nearby town of Glenorchy. Well-organized track transport will drop

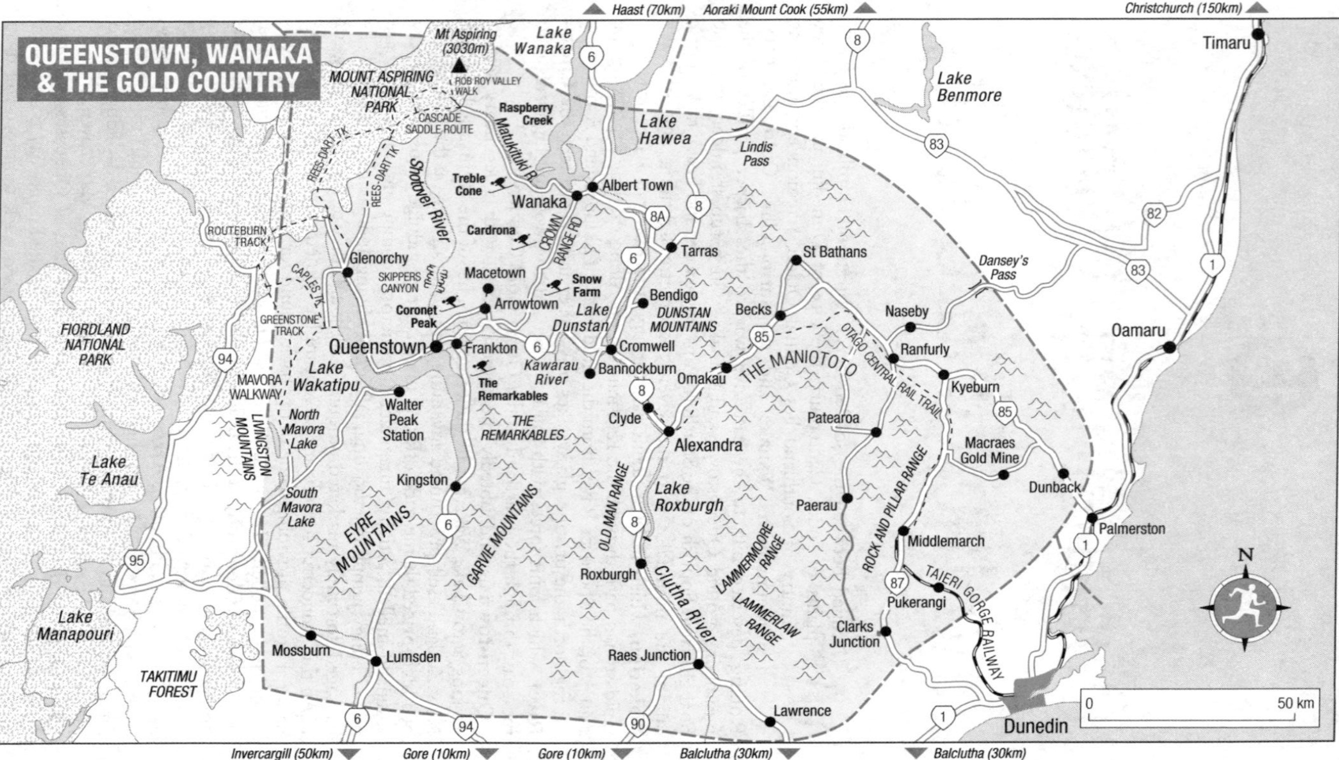
QUEENSTOWN, WANAKA & THE GOLD COUNTRY
Haast (70km)
Aoraki Mount Cook (55km)
Christchurch (150km)
Invercargill (50km)
Gore (10km)
Gore (10km)
Balclutha (30km)
Balclutha (30km)
Mt Aspiring (3030m)
Lake Wanaka
Lake Hawea
Lake Benmore
Timaru
MOUNT ASPIRING NATIONAL PARK
ROB ROY VALLEY WALK
CASCADE SADDLE ROUTE
Raspberry Creek
Matukituki R.
REES-DART TK
Shotover River
Treble Cone
Wanaka
Albert Town
Lindis Pass
ROUTEBURN TRACK
Cardrona
CROWN RANGE RD
Tarras
St Bathans
Dansey's Pass
Glenorchy
SKIPPERS CANYON
Macetown
Snow Farm
Bendigo
DUNSTAN MOUNTAINS
Becks
Naseby
Oamaru
CAPLES TK
GREENSTONE TRACK
Coronet Peak
Arrowtown
Lake Dunstan
FIORDLAND NATIONAL PARK
Queenstown
Frankton
Cromwell
OTAGO CENTRAL RAIL TRAIL
Ranfurly
THE MANIOTOTO
Lake Wakatipu
Kawarau River
Bannockburn
Omakau
Kyeburn
MAVORA WALKWAY
The Remarkables
Walter Peak Station
North Mavora Lake
LIVINGSTON MOUNTAINS
THE REMARKABLES
Clyde
Alexandra
Patearoa
Macraes Gold Mine
Lake Te Anau
Kingston
South Mavora Lake
Dunback
EYRE MOUNTAINS
GARVIE MOUNTAINS
OLD MAN RANGE
Lake Roxburgh
Paerau
ROCK AND PILLAR RANGE
Palmerston
Middlemarch
Roxburgh
LAMMERMOORE RANGE
TAIERI GORGE RAILWAY
Pukerangi
Lake Manapouri
Clutha River
LAMMERLAW RANGE
Clarks Junction
Mossburn
Lumsden
Raes Junction
TAKITIMU FOREST
Lawrence
Dunedin
N
0
50 km

you at the trailheads of the magnificent **Routeburn Track**, the match of any in the country; the less challenging **Caples** and **Greenstone** tracks, which can be combined with the Routeburn to make a satisfying five-day circuit; and the rugged **Rees–Dart Track**, which opens up the arduous Cascade Saddle Route towards Mount Aspiring.

The glacially scoured, three-sided pinnacle of "the Matterhorn of the South" forms the centrepiece of the **Mount Aspiring National Park**. This permanently snowcapped alpine high country is linked by the alluring Matukituki Valley to the small and expanding resort town of **Wanaka**, slung around the placid waters of its eponymous lake. Wanaka's laid-back atmosphere stands in marked contrast to the frenetic bustle of Queenstown, though there's no shortage of operators keen to take you canyoning, skydiving, jetboating, rock climbing or on any number of other pursuits.

Queenstown and Wanaka lie on the fringe of the **Otago Goldfields**, which stretch east towards the coast at Dunedin. Most of the gold has long since gone and the area is largely deserted, but there are numerous interesting reminders of New Zealand's gold-rush days, including old workings set amid rugged scenery. Queenstown and Arrowtown were two of the biggest gold towns, but to the east lie the more modest centres of **Cromwell**, **Alexandra** and **Roxburgh**, scattered along the banks of the Clutha River, which once provided Maori with the easiest route to the greenstone fields of the West Coast. Gold miners subsequently used the same paths, fanning out to found tiny towns such as **St Bathans** and **Naseby**, the most enjoyable places in which to idle among the mouldering boom-time remains.

From June to October the region's focus switches to **skiing**, with Queenstown acting as a base for the downhill resorts of **Coronet Peak** and **the Remarkables**, while Wanaka serves the **Cardrona** and **Treble Cone** fields, as well as the **Snow Farm** Nordic field.

Getting around the region is easily done: reasonably frequent buses link the main towns, and are supplemented by shuttle buses to trailheads, and by minibuses between hotels and the various adventure activities.

Queenstown

QUEENSTOWN is in many ways a victim of its own popularity. Kiwis and visitors seduced by New Zealand's tranquil rural beauty can often be overheard complaining that the country's main centre for adventure sports is getting overcrowded and too big for its boots. There is no doubt that it is one of New Zealand's most popular and commercialized year-round resorts, with haphazard development threatening to mar its beauty. But Queenstown remains an idyllic spot, attractively set beside the deep-blue Lake Wakatipu and hemmed in by craggy mountains. Furthermore, it offers the best selection of restaurants outside of the bigger cities, some of the flashiest (and most highly priced) accommodation in the country, and a nightlife that may suck you in for longer than you expect.

Queenstown is best taken in small doses, either as a base from which to plan lengthy forays into the surrounding countryside, or as a venue for sampling the many outdoor activities on offer. The most prominent of these is undoubtedly **bungy jumping**. The town's environs boast three of the world's most gloriously scenic bungy sites, visited either in isolation or as part of a package, perhaps including **whitewater rafting** and **jetboating** on the Shotover River.

Ring things

Queenstown and the surrounding area boast the country's highest concentration of **Lord of the Rings** film locations. Some spots are instantly recognizable, but others were digitally manipulated to the point where you really need to stand there with a still from the film to work out just what was and wasn't used.

An entire industry has been built up to show the visitors where it all happened. Just about anyone who runs adventure trips into the countryside will tag on "as seen in The Lord of the Rings" or "venturing into Middle-Earth" in their promotional material" but if you really want to stand where Frodo stood you need to join one of the **specialist tours**.

Locations

Arrow River, near Arrowtown. A spot around 200m upstream from the town centre was where Arwen helped Frodo across the Ford of Bruinen with the Nazgûl in pursuit.

The Deer Park, Kelvin Heights (aka Deer Park Heights; daily 9am–dark; $20 per vehicle). Signs here point to half a dozen locations from all three movies, including the site for Gandalf's ride towards Minas Tirith, the lakeshore where the Rohirrim were led to refuge and the rock Aragorn rolled off, seemingly to his death. Otherwise, this scenic hilltop park offers opportunities to feed the highland cattle, bison, llamas, miniature horses, etc.

Glenorchy. Orthanc, Saruman's tower, was digitally inserted into the plain at the head of Lake Wakatipu with the Dart Valley behind.

Kawarau River, beside the AJ Hackett bungy site. Stood in for the River Anduin in the first movie and the gorge walls here were digitally enhanced with the Argonath, the Pillars of the Kings.

Paradise, near Glenorchy. The beech-forest edge of Dan's Paddock, just north of the Arcadia Homestead, is where Gandalf rode to Isengard. The forests a little further north briefly stood in for Lothlórien.

The Remarkables. From the top of the ski-field road you can hike up to Lake Alta, where Aragorn, Frodo and co headed down Dimrill Dale toward Lothlórien.

Visitors after a more sedate time are equally spoilt for choice, with **lake cruises** on the elegant TSS *Earnslaw*, the last of the lake steamers; the **gondola ride** to Bob's Peak, which commands magnificent vistas from a cable car over Queenstown and the Remarkables range; and **wine tours** around some of the world's most southerly vineyards (see p.793). Formal lakeshore gardens and hillside viewpoints provide the focus for easy local **walks**, with heartier multi-day tramps starting at **Glenorchy** (see p.800) at the head of the lake. For details on visiting **Milford Sound** from Queenstown, see the box on p.856.

Even the frantic summers are nothing in comparison to winter, when Kiwi and international skiers descend on **Coronet Peak** and **the Remarkables**, two fine ski-fields within half an hour of Queenstown, which are at their peak during the annual **Queenstown Winter Festival** in late June and early July.

Arrival, information and city transport

Queenstown's main downtown area is concentrated around Rees Street, Shotover Street, Camp Street and the pedestrianized Mall, which runs from the Main Town Wharf northeast to Ballarat Street. **Buses** all arrive close to the junction of Camp and Shotover streets, from where it's less than fifteen minutes' walk to hotels and hostels. Just outside Frankton, 7km northeast of central

Skippers Canyon. Around 12km along the Skippers Road, the gravel riverbanks were used (along with the Arrow River, above) for shooting the Ford of Bruinen.

Twelve-Mile Delta, 11km west of Queenstown. DOC campsite that stood in for Ithilien in *The Fellowship of the Ring*.

Tours

Dart River Jet Safaris ⓣ0800/327 853, ⓦwww.dartriver.co.nz. Glenorchy-based jetboat trips with a significant LOTR component (see p.801).

Glenorchy Air ⓣ03/442 2207, ⓦwww.trilogytrail.com. This Queenstown Airport-based firm, which flew cast and crew doing filming, offers a One Ring Trilogytrail (3.5hr; $130), comprising a minibus tour of sites around Queenstown; a Two Ring Trilogytrail (2–3hr; $335) flying past locations around Arrowtown, Glenorchy and Mavora Lakes; and a Three Ring Trilogytrail (7hr including 2hr 30min of flying; $735), with landings at three more distant major locations, including Edoras (see p.646).

Heliworks ⓣ03/441 4011, ⓦwww.heliworks.co.nz. These folk did much of the flying for the cast and now run a wide range of LOTR scenic flights, starting at $385 for 45 minutes, including one landing.

Info&Track ⓣ03/442 9708, ⓦwww.infotrack.co.nz. Their budget 4WD Paradise Safari (4hr 30min; $99) includes Maori legends and gold-mining history as they uncover parts of Lothlórien, Isengard and so forth.

Nomad Safaris ⓣ0800/688 222, ⓦwww.nomadsafaris.co.nz. Specialist Safari of the Scenes tours in 4WD vehicles, with frequent stops to envisage scenes from LOTR being shot. The drivers, who were often involved as extras, can offer good background. The Wakatipu Basin trip (4hr; $140) focuses on the area immediately around Queenstown, while the Glenorchy trip (4hr; $140) heads up to the head of Lake Wakatipu.

Wanaka Sightseeing ⓣ03/338 0982, ⓦwww.lordoftheringstours.co.nz. This Wanaka-based company (Queenstown pick-ups available) have six LOTR tours, including helicopter options and the excellent Trails Of Middle Earth (full-day; $299), on which you get to visit twenty locations and pose for photos with swords and other props.

Queenstown is the city's **airport** (ⓦwww.queenstownairport.co.nz). Most flights are met by the door-to-door Super Shuttle (around $15 for one, $18 for two) and a few close competitors, and you can also get into town using the Connectabus (see "City transport", p.777). Taxis (ⓣ03/442 6666 or 442 7788) charge $25–35 for the ride into town. Most of the major car rental companies have offices at the airport.

The **i-SITE visitor centre**, corner of Camp and Shotover Streets (daily: Dec–April 7.30am–6.30pm; May–Nov 7.30am–6pm; ⓣ03/442 4100, ⓦwww.queenstown-nz.co.nz), can organize bookings and offers impartial advice. Shotover Street is awash with rival visitor centre-cum-booking offices for local and national activities as well as travel. Perhaps the most prominent is **The Station**, on the corner of Camp and Shotover streets, which acts as the nerve centre and the main pick-up spot for AJ Hackett bungy and the Shotover Jet. A few steps away, the **Info&Track Centre**, 37 Shotover St (daily 7am–9pm; ⓣ03/442 9708, ⓦwww.infotrack.co.nz) is a particularly handy backpacker-oriented booking office.

The **DOC visitor centre**, 36 Shotover St (Oct–April daily 8.30am–5pm; May–Sept Mon–Fri 8.30am–5pm; ⓣ03/442 7935, ⓔqueenstownvc@doc.govt.nz), inside the Outside Sports shop, comes stacked with leaflets on DOC activities and operates a Great Walks Booking Desk.

CENTRAL QUEENSTOWN

Arthurs Point (5km), A (6km), Coronet Peak (16km) & Skippers Road (16km)

Frankton (3km), Airport (5km), Arrowtown (20km) & Milford Sound (290km)

Fernhill (2km), R (10km), S (28km) & Glenorchy (50km)

RESTAURANTS, CAFÉS & BARS

@ Thai	15	Halo	14
Altitude	1	Kappa	7
Bardeaux	13	Patagonia Chocolates	12
Bombay Place	8	Pig and Whistle	4
Bunker	9	Póg Mahone's	6
The Cow	9	Solera Vino	3
Debajo	5	Vesta	19
Dux de Lux	18	Vudu	2
Finz	16	Wai	17
Habebes	10	Winnies	11

ACCOMMODATION

Adelaide St Guesthouse	U	The Lodges	K
Alpine Lodge	D	Pinewood	B
base Discovery Lodge	Y	Queenstown Lakeview Holiday Park	F
Black Sheep	P	Queenstown Motel Apartments	O
Browns Boutique Hotel	X	Scallywags	G
Bumbles	I	Shotover Top 10 Holiday Park	A
Butterfli Lodge	M	The Stable	T
Caples Court	H	St Moritz	L
Creeksyde	C	Twelve-Mile Delta Reserve	R
The Dairy	W	YHA Queenstown Lakefront	Q
Four Seasons Motel	J		
Hippo Lodge	E		
Hurley's	N		
The Last Resort	V		
Little Paradise Lodge	S		

Bob's Peak
Skyline Gondola
Ben Lomond Summit Track
Ben Lomond Track
Kiwi & Birdlife Park
Freshchoice
Library
Courthouse & Old Stone Library
Queenstown Hill (907m)
Queenstown Hill Track
Queenstown Bay
Queenstown Gardens
St Omer Park
Lake Wakatipu
Frankton Arm

See inset map for detail

Alpine Foodcenter
DOC Office
Wine Toastes
Eichardt's Hotel
Main Town Pier
Steamer Wharf

0 250 m
N

Tourist **publications** worth seeking out include the free *iTAG* guide (Ⓦwww.itag.co.nz) and *Kidz Go!* (Ⓦwww.kidzgo.co.nz), a free regional magazine with good guidance on how to keep the nippers entertained, and full listings of minimum ages for various activities. Also look out for the *Mountain Scene* newspaper for an insight into what's currently making Queenstown tick.

City transport

Pretty much everywhere you are likely to want to go in central Queenstown can be reached **on foot**. Most of the activities take place out of town, although all operators run courtesy buses from the centre of town to the site, usually picking up from accommodation en route. There are **taxi ranks** on Camp Street, at the top end of the Mall, and on Shotover Street; alternatively, book a taxi with Alpine Taxi (Ⓣ0800/442 6666) or Queenstown Taxis (Ⓣ0800/488 294).

The only useful bus service is Connectabus, from Camp Street outside McDonald's *McCafé* (daily departures every hour 7am–10pm; Ⓣ03/441 4471, Ⓦwww.connectabus.com), which runs out to Frankton ($5 each way), the airport ($5) and on to Arrowtown ($7; day pass $13).

Drivers will have no problem negotiating Queenstown's streets; although **parking** can be tight in the centre of town, you can usually search out a free all-day spot a few streets away.

Accommodation

Queenstown has the widest selection of **places to stay** in this corner of New Zealand, but such is the demand in the middle of summer and at the height of the ski season that rooms can be hard to come by, and prices are correspondingly high. Accommodation at both ends of the spectrum is excellent, but things can be a little tougher in the middle where there are few modestly priced, convenient **motels** and **B&Bs**. Boutique **lodges** are abundant and often superb, but prices are fairly high. Good deals are sometimes offered by the big **hotels** in what passes for Queenstown's off season (essentially April, May &

▲ Queenstown, with the Cecil Peak in the background

Nov) but in general you'll do better in smaller places. The best budget deals are to be found at the many **hostels**, which compete fiercely for trade, frequently offering high-standard rooms (some en suite) at modest prices. The Queenstown district also has a few compact **campsites** with attendant cabins.

With a few exceptions, all the accommodation is packed into a compact area less than fifteen minutes' walk from the centre of town. If a less frantic atmosphere – and lower prices – appeal, it's also worth considering **Arrowtown** (see p.796) as a base for exploring the Queenstown area or **Glenorchy** (see p.802).

Hotels

Browns Boutique Hotel 26 Isle St ⓣ03/441 2050, ⓦwww.brownshotel.co.nz. Very appealing downtown establishment with ten rooms, all comfortable, spacious and well appointed, with small balconies overlooking the town or the lake. There's also a luxurious guest lounge with an open fire, and continental breakfasts. 8

Hurley's Corner of Frankton Rd & Melbourne St ⓣ0800/589 879, ⓦwww.hurleys.co.nz. Tasteful, luxuriously appointed apartments and studios close to the centre, each equipped with a full kitchen, TV, CD player and spa baths and with free access to two saunas and a full gym. Studios 6, apartments 6

St Moritz 10 Brunswick St ⓣ03/442 4990, ⓦwww.stmoritz.co.nz. Large and recently refurbished modern hotel with spa pool, sauna and quality restaurant/bar with great views over the lake. It is worth going for the many rooms and spacious suites (all with bathtub) which come with similar vistas. Rooms 7, lakeview 8, suites 8

Motels and apartments

Caples Court 20 Stanley St ⓣ0800/282 275, ⓦwww.caplescourt.co.nz. Delightful, comfortable motel with more spirit to its decor than most, and each room done in a different style. Most have a kitchen and a balcony and seven of the nine units have views over the town and/or lake. The other two are tucked peacefully away beside a quiet garden. Garden units 4, lake view 6

Four Seasons Motel 12 Stanley St ⓣ03/442 8953, ⓦwww.queenstownmotel.com. Upgraded downtown motel with off-street parking, good kitchens, mountain views, an outdoor swimming pool (unfortunately beside the main road), a spa and a range of units. 5

The Lodges 8 Lake Esplanade ⓣ0800/284 356, ⓦwww.queenstownthelodges.co.nz. Slightly ageing but well-kept lakeside apartments with kitchen, laundry and parking. 6

Queenstown Motel Apartments 62 Frankton Rd ⓣ0800/661 668, ⓦwww.qma.co.nz. Good-value motel that's close to town. They have a few fairly functional older units and twelve very nice modern ones, all pale wood, bold colours and tasteful artworks. There's a strong environmental stance, with energy-saving light bulbs, and recycling bins in the kitchenettes. Old 4, new 5, new lake view 6

B&Bs, homestays and lodges

Adelaide St Guesthouse 27 Adelaide St ⓣ03/442 6207, ⓦwww.adelaidehouse.co.nz. Peaceful, basic seven-room B&B (one en suite) with plain but light and clean rooms and great lake views from the shared lounge, where a continental buffet breakfast is served. 3, en suite 4

The Dairy Corner of Brecon & Isle sts ⓣ03/442 5164, ⓦwww.thedairy.co.nz. An oasis of calm in the centre of Queenstown, this 13-room luxury hotel has delightful common areas hung with quality New Zealand artworks (several original) where you might sup something delightful from their extensive honesty bar. The rooms (some with bathtubs) aren't huge but all come well appointed and tastefully decorated in modern styles. Breakfast and afternoon tea are served in the original dairy (corner shop). Rates start at $430 but pay the extra $30 for a lake view. 9

Little Paradise Lodge Meilejohn Bay, 28km along Glenorchy Rd ⓣ03/442 6196, ⓦwww.littleparadise.co.nz. Eccentric but wonderful guesthouse in an idyllic setting close to the lake where almost everything is made from logs cut or stone hewn by the Swiss owner, Thomas, including the non-chlorinated swimming pool fed by its own stream and complete with water lilies. Accommodation is in standard rooms and a charming en-suite chalet. You can cook for yourself, and there is kayak rental ($10) and free fishing gear. Dorms $45, rooms 4

The Stable 17 Brisbane St ⓣ03/442 9251, ⓦwww.thestablebb.co.nz. Cosy and hospitable homestay stacked with books. There are just two rooms, the better of which is in a former stable, more than 130 years old with the bed on a mezzanine. Cooked or continental breakfasts are served. 7

Hostels

Alpine Lodge 13 Gorge Rd ⓣ03/442 7220, ⓦwww.alpinelodgebackpackers.co.nz. Small, welcoming and central hostel with separate movie and quiet lounges. They also operate the adjacent *Turner Lodge*, which has spacious en suites and its own lounge and cooking area that's less frenetic than the main hostel. Dorms $25, rooms ❷, lodge en suites ❸

base Discovery Lodge 47 Shotover St ⓣ03/441 1185, ⓦwww.basebackpackers.co.nz. Queenstown's largest (300+ beds) and liveliest hostel can feel a little cramped (especially in the kitchen) but is always bustling. All dorms have fridges, secure lockers and a toilet and shower and there's a range of en-suite doubles and twins with TV/DVD. Dorms $26, rooms ❸, en suites ❸

Black Sheep 13 Frankton Rd ⓣ03/442 7289, ⓦwww.blacksheepbackpackers.co.nz. Licensed backpackers converted from a motel, with three- to seven-bed dorms, BBQ near the spa pool, a bar (4–10pm), free light breakfast and 24hr reception. Dorms $25, rooms ❷

Bumbles 2 Brunswick St ⓣ03/442 6298, ⓦwww.bumblesbackpackers.co.nz. Popular hostel, well sited on the lakefront road, offering great views from most rooms and common areas, a spacious kitchen, a BBQ area and off-street parking. Dorms $27, ❷

Butterfli Lodge 62 Thompson St ⓣ03/442 6367, ⓦwww.butterfli.co.nz. A small house overlooking the lake, with a friendly atmosphere and cosy accommodation for a limited number of people. Book early; two-night minimum. Dorms $26, rooms ❷

Hippo Lodge 4 Anderson Heights ⓣ03/442 5785, ⓦwww.hippolodge.co.nz. A couple of suburban houses imaginatively converted into four sections, each with its own bathroom, kitchen and living area. Several of the rooms and lounges have fabulous views over Queenstown, and there are even a few cramped tent sites ($16). They're one of the few hostels to offer work (2–3hr a day) for accommodation. Dorms $26, rooms ❷, en suite ❸

The Last Resort 6 Memorial St ⓣ03/442 4320, ⓦwww.tlrqtn.com. Small hostel that's a bit rough around the edges but easily compensates with a homely atmosphere, free Internet, genial host and resident dog, Cocco the malemute. Female dorm available; two-night minimum. Dorms $27

Pinewood 48 Hamilton Rd ⓣ0800/746396, ⓦwww.pinewood.co.nz. An extensive collection of new and older renovated s/c buildings (all surrounded by lawns) jointly making up some of the best budget accommodation in Queenstown. Located a 10min walk from the centre, the facilities include a spa bath with views ($5 per half-hour), and some great new en suites which collectively have their own kitchen and lounge areas. Friendly staff too. Dorms $23, rooms ❷, en suite ❹

Scallywags 27 Lomond Crescent ⓣ03/442 7083. Pitched as an upmarket backpackers hostel, this suburban house is a steep 10min walk up from town. It has stupendous views and a very laid-back muck-in atmosphere, with use of a kitchen and free tea and coffee. Dorms $26, rooms ❷

YHA Queenstown Lakefront 88 Lake Esplanade ⓣ03/442 8413, ⓔyha.queenstownlakefront@yha.co.nz. One of New Zealand's flagship YHAs in an excellent, quiet location 7min walk from town. The feel is surprisingly homely and accommodation is in spacious, mostly four- to eight-bed dorms plus twins and doubles, many with good lake views. Dorms $24, rooms ❷

Campsites and motor parks

Creeksyde 54 Robins Rd ⓣ03/442 9447, ⓦwww.camp.co.nz. Highly organized and spotlessly clean Top 10 holiday park 10min walk from town with shaded sites, many of them used by campervans. A central building houses a spa bathroom and sauna (both $15/half-hour for two), a ski store and drying rooms. Camping $22, shared bath rooms ❷, en suites ❹, s/c units ❹

Queenstown Lakeview Holiday Park Brecon St ⓣ0800/482 735, ⓦwww.holidaypark.net.nz. Enormous site that sprawls over the base of Bob's Peak and seems to swallow just about all of Queenstown's campers. Accommodation runs from grassy, though not well-shaded, tent and van sites (showers $1) to kitchenless studios and fully s/c units sleeping up to five. Facilities are of a high standard. Camping $16, studios ❹, units ❹

Shotover Top 10 Holiday Park Close to the Shotover Jet site at Arthur's Point ⓣ0800/462 267, ⓦwww.shotoverholidaypark.co.nz. Smallish, quiet and fully equipped site. Camping $16, cabins ❷, s/c cabins ❹, motel units ❹

Twelve-Mile Delta Reserve 12km west of Queenstown towards Glenorchy. Lakeside DOC campsite with facilities limited to basic toilets and running water. Camping $7.

The Town

Central Queenstown has little to show for its gold-rush past. At the top of the Mall, Ballarat Street crosses a small stream spanned by an 1882 stone bridge to reach the **Courthouse** and **Old Stone Library** (now offices), both built in the mid-1870s and since dwarfed by century-old giant sequoias. At the opposite end of the Mall, the waterfront **Eichardt's Hotel** is a super-expensive affair dating partly from 1871. Around the corner on Marine Parade, the 1866 **Williams Cottage** retains many original features and now operates as a design store and café (see p.791). Marine Parade continues east to **Queenstown Gardens** (unrestricted entry), an attractive parkland retreat which covers the peninsula separating Queenstown Bay from the rest of Lake Wakatipu.

If you don't have time to head out to the wineries (see p.793) or just want some advance **wine tasting**, call in at Wine Tastes, 14 Beach St (daily 10am–10pm; Ⓣ03/409 2226, Ⓦwww.winetastes.com), a well-stocked shop with over eighty wines available from what are effectively sophisticated vending machines. Obtain a charge card and then sample what you fancy in either tasting, half-glass or glass quantities, then hang out on the leather chairs, perhaps with a cheeseboard. Samples range from $1.50 up to a $30 Grange Hermitage.

North of town, Brecon Street heads for Bob's Peak past Queenstown's **cemetery** – the final resting place of Queenstown pioneer Nicholas von Tunzelmann, as well as Henry Homer, discoverer of the Homer Saddle – on the Milford Road. Almost opposite, the **Kiwi & Birdlife Park** (daily: Nov–Feb 9am–7pm; March–Oct 9am–6pm; $30 including audio tour; Ⓣ03/442 8059, Ⓦwww.kiwibird.co.nz), is an expanse of ponds, lawns, native bush and aviaries that is home to some of New Zealand's rarest birds. The effect is more zoo than wildlife park, but it does a good job of presenting morepork, kea, kereru (native pigeons), kakariki (native parakeets) and black stilt (one of the world's ten most endangered bird species), alongside the products of captive breeding programmes for the North Island brown kiwi. Time your visit to coincide with the twenty-minute **Conservation Show** (daily 11am, 1pm & 3pm; free), when you get up close and personal with kereru, kea and tuatara, or the **Maori Performance** (11.15am & 3.15pm; free).

Bob's Peak

The best all-round views of Queenstown, Lake Wakatipu, the Remarkables and Cecil and Walter peaks are from **Bob's Peak**, which rises up immediately behind the town and can be reached on one of Queenstown's gentler rides. The **Skyline Gondola**, Brecon Street (daily from 9am, last entry 9.30pm; $21 return; Ⓦwww.skyline.co.nz), deposits you at the Skyline Complex, which can also be reached on foot in under an hour by following Lomond Crescent.

The conifer-clad slopes are the launch pad for **paragliders** throughout the day. The magnificent vistas may induce you to eat at the café or buffet restaurant (lunch $45, dinner $69, both including gondola ride), probably best left until after you've tried the Ledge bungy and swing (see pp.784–785), or the **Luge** (gondola plus one ride $28, plus five rides $40), a twisting concrete track negotiated on a wheeled plastic buggy with a primitive braking system – take it easy on your first run, then let rip once you've got the hang of it.

Cruising Lake Wakatipu

The coal-fired **TSS Earnslaw**, the last of the lake steamers, is one of Queenstown's most enduring images. Wherever you are, the encircling mountains echo the haunting sound of the steam whistle as this beautifully restored relic slogs manfully out from Steamer Wharf. Before the lakeside roads were built, almost all commerce in and out of Queenstown was conducted by boat.

Launched in 1912, the 51-metre-long craft was the largest steamer to ply the lake – and surely one of the most stately. Burnished brass and polished wood predominate even around the gleaming steam engine, which is open for inspection. Crowds usually cluster around the piano at the back of the boat for a surprisingly popular music-hall singsong that can make the return journey seem much longer.

The *Earnslaw* is operated by Real Journeys (☎0800/656 501, Ⓦwww.realjourneys.co.nz) and runs from Queenstown across the lake to **Walter Peak High Country Farm** (3–6 daily between 10am and 6pm; 1hr 30min; cruise only $45 return, $30 one way), a tourist enclave nestling in the southwestern crook of Lake Wakatipu. The Walter Peak homestead, a convincing replica of a building which burnt down in 1977, is beautifully sited among lawns that sweep down to the lakeshore, and plays host to a **farm tour** – an entertaining if sanitized vignette of farm life, with demonstrations of dog handling and sheep-shearing. The tour can be combined with tea and scones ($65 including cruise), a BBQ meal ($85) or a carvery buffet dinner (6pm; $110). The boat trip itself can be combined with a horse trek, tea and scones (3hr 30min; $105). There's also a Heritage Tour (4pm; $72) combining a cruise with a historic tour of the house and gardens and a little wine tasting.

By taking your own bike ($5) or motorbike ($20) with you on the boat, you can continue along the remote and unsealed 80km road up the Von River past Mavora Lakes to SH94 at Burwood, 27km east of Te Anau.

If you'd prefer to go by windpower, board a converted **America's Cup yacht** with Sail Queenstown ($150 for 2hr; ☎03/442 7517, Ⓦwww.sailqueenstown.co.nz), who take you out on the lake, conditions permitting, and give you a chance to help sail, or just sit back and relax.

The Shotover River and Skippers Canyon

The churning **Shotover River** is inextricably linked with Queenstown. The majority of the town's adventure-based trips – bungy jumping, rafting, jetboating, mountain biking and more (see "Activities", p.784) – take place on, in or around the river and, if you are prepared to drive the treacherous Skippers Road, there's also a stack of gold-rush relics to explore.

The Shotover rises in the Richardson Mountains north of Queenstown and picks up speed to surge through its deepest and narrowest section, **Skippers Canyon**, and into the Kawarau River downstream from Lake Wakatipu. Tributaries run off Mount Aurum, beneath which is the mother lode of the Shotover goldfields, first discovered when a couple of pioneer shearers, Thomas Arthur and Harry Redfern, found gold in 1862 at Arthur's Point, 5km north of Queenstown. Word spread that prospectors were extracting over ten kilos a day, and within months thousands were flocking from throughout New Zealand and Australia to work what was soon dubbed "The Richest River in the World". The river-edge gravels had been all but worked out by 1864, necessitating ever more sophisticated extraction techniques. With the introduction of gravity-fed water chutes, mechanical sieves and floating dredges, the construction of a decent road became crucial. From 1863, Chinese navvies spent over twenty years hacking away with pick and shovel at the Skippers Road; those who stuck out the harsh conditions began building quarters more substantial than the standard-issue canvas tents. Meanwhile, entrepreneurially minded pioneers began to exploit the boom, building 27 hotels along the 40km of road, and selling fresh fruit and vegetables at extortionate prices to miners often suffering from scurvy. By the turn of the century the river was worked out, though a few stayed on. Even today a couple of die-hards make a living from gold panning and sluicing, and in 1999, for a few days after flooding, happy hunters were panning up to $600 worth in a couple of hours.

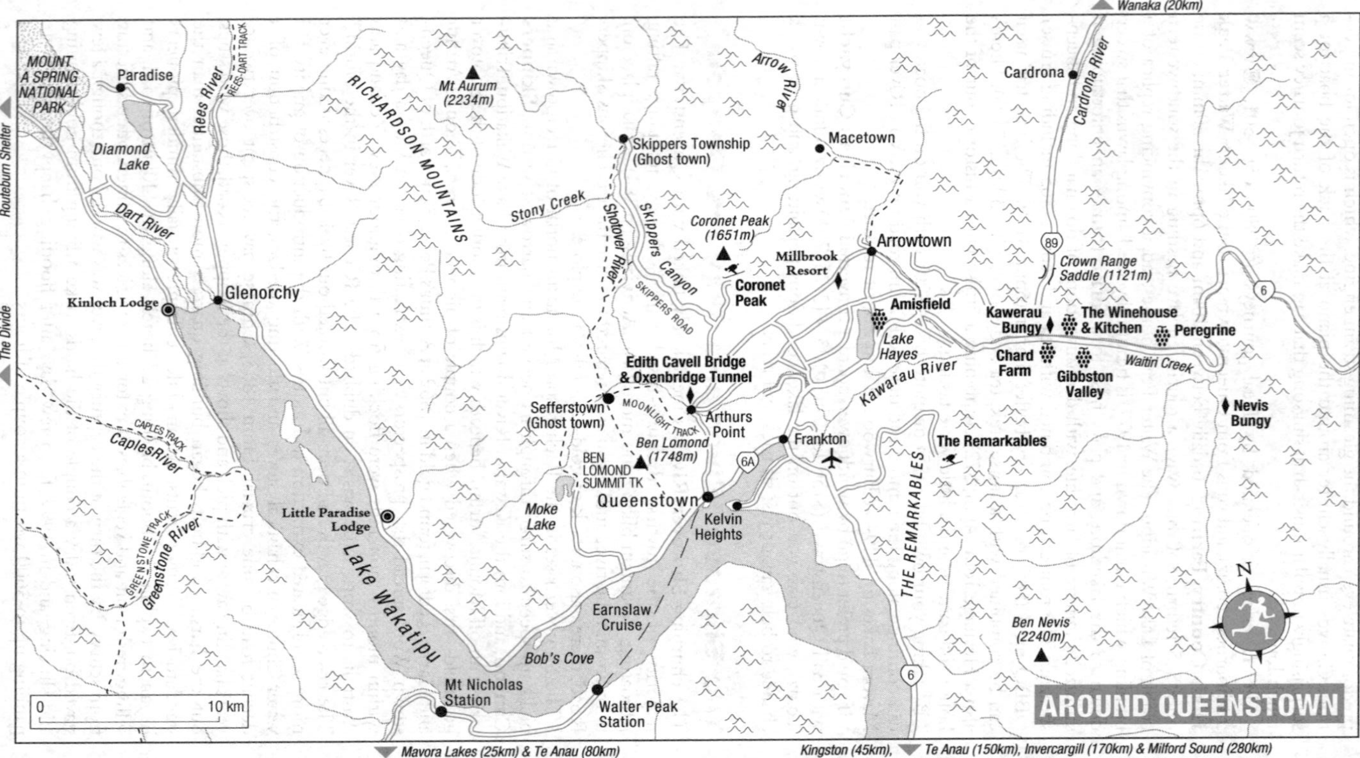
AROUND QUEENSTOWN
Wanaka (20km)
Cromwell (50km), Wanaka (110km) & 8
Routeburn Shelter
The Divide
Mavora Lakes (25km) & Te Anau (80km)
Kingston (45km), Te Anau (150km), Invercargill (170km) & Milford Sound (280km)
MOUNT ASPIRING NATIONAL PARK
Paradise
Diamond Lake
Rees River
REES-DART TRACK
Dart River
Glenorchy
Kinloch Lodge
RICHARDSON MOUNTAINS
Mt Aurum (2234m)
Stony Creek
Skippers Township (Ghost town)
Shotover River
Skippers Canyon
SKIPPERS ROAD
Arrow River
Macetown
Coronet Peak (1651m)
Coronet Peak
Millbrook Resort
Arrowtown
Amisfield
Lake Hayes
Cardrona
Cardrona River
89
Crown Range Saddle (1121m)
Kawerau Bungy
The Winehouse & Kitchen
Peregrine
Chard Farm
Gibbston Valley
Waitiri Creek
6
Kawarau River
Edith Cavell Bridge & Oxenbridge Tunnel
Sefferstown (Ghost town)
MOONLIGHT TRACK
Arthurs Point
Ben Lomond (1748m)
BEN LOMOND SUMMIT TK
Frankton
6A
Queenstown
Kelvin Heights
Moke Lake
The Remarkables
THE REMARKABLES
Nevis Bungy
CAPLES TRACK
CaplesRiver
GREENSTONE TRACK
Greenstone River
Little Paradise Lodge
Lake Wakatipu
Earnslaw Cruise
Bob's Cove
Mt Nicholas Station
Walter Peak Station
Ben Nevis (2240m)
N
0
10 km

The Skippers Road

The extremely narrow and winding **Skippers Road** is best left to experienced drivers. Locals who know the road like the back of their hand tend to hare around, leaving little space for oncoming traffic; besides, rental cars aren't insured for Skippers. Being driven to the start point for the Shotover rafting trips (see p.786) gives you a good chance to survey the area.

The Skippers Road, which follows the Shotover River only in its upper reaches, branches off Coronet Peak Road 12km north of Queenstown. It is approached along Malaghans Road through **Arthur's Point**, 5km north of Queenstown, marked by the historic but mundane *Arthur's Point Hotel*, the only one of the Skippers Road hotels still operating. Half a kilometre on, the Edith Cavell Bridge spans a gorge where the Shotover Jet (see p.786) performs its antics, its upstream progress limited by the Mother-in-Law rapid and the 1911 **Oxenbridge Tunnel**.

Skippers Road soon begins to shadow the river, negotiating Pinchers Bluff, where Chinese and European navvies cut the road from a near-vertical cliff face. Upstream, the 1901 **Skippers Bridge** was the first high-level one built – and consequently survived the winter floods, which had swept away all past efforts. For the first time, the township of Skippers had reliable access, though this did little to prevent the exodus that saw a population of 1500 dwindle to nothing once the gold ran out. The old schoolhouse has been restored and there are ruins of a few more buildings scattered around, but otherwise it is a bleak, haunted place. You can **camp** here at a toilets-and-water site for $7.

Walks around Queenstown

When the hard-sell on adventure activities in Queenstown gets a bit oppressive, a few hours away from town can be wonderfully therapeutic. The majority of the walks outlined below – listed in ascending order of difficulty – are well covered by DOC's *Queenstown walks and trails* leaflet. Serious multi-day tramps in the region are centred on Wanaka and Glenorchy (see p.822 and p.803, respectively).

One Mile Creek Walkway (6km return; 1hr 30min; 50m ascent). Fairly easy walk that heads through a gully filled with beech forest before following a 1924 pipeline from Queenstown's first hydroelectric scheme. The route starts on the lakefront by the Fernhill roundabout and offers a good opportunity to acquaint yourself with fuchsia, lancewood and native birds – principally fantails, bellbirds and tui.

Queenstown Hill Walk (5km return; 2–3hr; 500m ascent). Starting from the top of Belfast Street, this is a fairly steep climb through mostly exotic trees to panoramic views from the 907-metre Queenstown Hill.

Ben Lomond Summit Track (11km return; 6–8hr; 1400m ascent). A full-day, there-and-back tramp scaling Ben Lomond, one of the highest mountains in the region (1748m) and consequently subject to inclement weather, especially in winter when the track can be snow-covered. Start by the One Mile Creek Walk or use the Skyline Gondola and walk up past the paragliding launch site to join the track, which climbs through alpine tussock to reveal expansive views. Gentler slopes approach Ben Lomond Saddle, from where it's a steep final haul to the summit.

Ben Lomond–Moonlight Track (16km one way; 8–10hr; 1400m ascent). A demanding and difficult-to-follow route (especially in snow) which combines the ascent to Ben Lomond Saddle with a poled sub alpine route to the site of the former gold town of Sefferstown and the eastern section of the Moonlight Track to Arthur's Point. Organize someone to pick you up at Arthur's Point or be prepared for a five-kilometre slog back to Queenstown.

The best way to get up here is with Skippers Canyon Jet (ⓣ0800/226 966, ⓦwww.skipperscanyon.co.nz), who offer flexible packages with the added bonus of guides who have lived in the area for over twenty years. Either take their 4WD **tour** (4hr; $120) which explores the region and visits Winky's Museum (which the family own), or better still, combine it with their Skippers Canyon Jet (see p.786; 4hr 30min; $149): excellent value.

Activities

Many of Queenstown's activity companies are little more than a van and a mobile phone and don't operate an office, though most are directly associated with one of the **information** and **booking offices** that line Shotover Street. In practice, virtually every booking office will book any trip, or you could just book through your hotel or hostel. Prices don't usually vary, but it may be worth asking for backpacker discounts and so forth. Almost all the booking offices are open daily, usually to around 8pm.

With so much on offer, it's tempting to be frugal elsewhere and blow the lot when you reach Queenstown, but in reality most activities in Queenstown are more **expensive** than in other parts of the country. To get the most action for the least money here, check out one of the numerous **combination deals** knitting together two to five of the main activities. Worthwhile examples include the Shotover Trio (Shotover Jet, heli flight and Shotover raft trip; $309), and the Shotover Freefall (adding a tandem skydive; $549).

Bungy jumping

Even visitors who never had any intention of parting with a large wad of cash to dangle on the end of a thick strand of latex find themselves **bungy jumping** in Queenstown. A combination of peer pressure, magnificent scenery and avid promotion eventually gets to most people and, let's face it, historic bridges high above remote rivers beat a crane over a supermarket car park any day. AJ Hackett (ⓣ0800/286 495, ⓦwww.bungy.co.nz) operates three bungy sites around Queenstown, and all three can be combined in the "Thrillogy" ($425 including a T-shirt and transport) over several days. If you want a record of your fifteen minutes of hair-raising fame, you can pay an extra $45 per jump for three photos and two postcards or $45 for a DVD, or $80 for both.

AJ Hackett's original, most famous and most frequently jumped bungy site is **Kawarau Bungy** (43m; daily 9am–5pm; $160, including a certificate, T-shirt and transport from Queenstown if required), beside SH6, 23km east of Queenstown. It is the only place around Queenstown where you can get dunked in the river. At busy times the whole scene resembles a rather ghoulish production line, as bungy initiates are trundled out and tour buses disgorge spectators to fill several viewing platforms. The best views are from the Kawarau Bungy Centre (free entry), where you can learn more than you thought there was to know about bungy jumping on the Secrets Behind Bungy Tour ($20; 45min), an interactive leap through bungy history and the jump experience without your feet leaving the floor.

At the **Ledge Urban Bungy** (47m; summer generally 1–7pm; winter 4–9pm; $160, including T-shirt and gondola ride) at the top of the Skyline Gondola, it feels like you are diving out over Queenstown. Unlike at other sites, you're fitted with a body harness allowing you to do a running jump, and if they aren't too busy you may be able to jump with all manner of "toys" (surfboards, bikes and the like) to add that extra dimension. Night jumps in winter make for yet another variation for the committed.

Some say that with bungy jumping it is only the first metre that counts, but when it comes down to it, size does matter. AJ Hackett has pulled out all the stops with **Nevis Highwire Bungy** (134m; Queenstown departures daily at 8am, 10am, noon and 2pm; $220, including T-shirt), which gives around eight seconds of freefall. Jumpers launch from a partly glass-bottomed gondola strung way out over the Nevis River, a tributary of the Kawarau some 32km east of Queenstown. Access is by 4WD through private property so spectators will have to fork out $50 to watch their buddies, though this does give you a ride out to the launch gondola and a wonderful view.

Winter in Queenstown

Two ski-fields – **Coronet Peak** and the smaller **Remarkables** – within easy striking distance of numerous quality hotels, good restaurants and plenty of après-ski combine to make Queenstown New Zealand's premier **ski destination**. The highlight of the season is the ten-day **Queenstown Winter Festival** (Ⓦwww.winterfestival.co.nz), around the end of June or early July, which, as well as all the conventional ski/snowboard events, has snow sculpture, ski-golf and a great line-up of entertainment. Of the various other events, the family-oriented **Remarkables Spring Fling**, in the first week of the September school holidays, is one of the best.

Both ski areas (and Mount Hutt) are run by the same company, whose website (Ⓦwww.nzski.com) has snow reports and plenty of other practical information. One-day lift passes are specific to each area, but there are various **multi-day tickets** which are valid at all three fields (a three-day pass costs $228).

Neither ski area has **accommodation** on site, but frequent shuttle buses run to and from Queenstown (for around $25), where the supply is plentiful – except during school holidays. For **ski rental** visit the excellent (if pricey) Browns, corner of Shotover & Brecon streets, Ⓣ03/442 4003, Ⓦwww.brownsnz.com), who charge $40 a day for mid-range skis, boots and poles ($44 for a snowboard); or Outside Sports, 36 Shotover St (Ⓣ03/441 2111, Ⓦwww.outsidesports.co.nz), who offer similar deals.

Coronet Peak

When it opened in 1947, **Coronet Peak** (Ⓣ03/442 4640), 18km north of Queenstown, became New Zealand's first true ski destination. The most sophisticated snow-making equipment in Australasia extends its season into spring, when cobalt blue skies and stunning scenery earn it an enviable reputation. Its range of **runs** (three beginner, sixteen intermediate, twelve advanced) for skiers and riders of all abilities, and over 400 vertical metres of skiing, only add to its popularity. Throughout the season, which typically starts in early June and sometimes makes it into October, **buses** from Queenstown shuttle back and forth along the sealed access road (no toll). **Passes** for daytime skiing (9am–4pm) cost $89; floodlit skiing (July–Sept Fri & Sat 4–9pm) goes for $45.

The Remarkables

The Remarkables (Ⓣ03/442 4615), 28km east of Queenstown, occupies three mountain basins tucked in behind the wrinkled face of the Remarkables. It is best known for learner and intermediate terrain, but there are also good **runs** (three beginner, eight intermediate, eighteen advanced) for advanced skiers, and rapid access to some excellent country for off-piste ski touring. A **day pass** costs $84. Though the bottom of the lifts is 500m higher than at Coronet Peak, more snow is required to cover the tussock, giving a slightly shorter season (late June to early Oct). At 320m, the total vertical descent from the lifts is also less than at Coronet, but you gain an extra 120m by taking the Homeward Run – a long stretch of off-piste with sparkling scenery – to the fourteen-kilometre unsealed **access road** (no toll), where frequent free buses shuttle you back up to the chair lift.

Swinging

Swinging presents an alternative to bungy jumping that still involves launching yourself fearlessly into the void. Along with that stomach-in-your-mouth freefall sensation you get the bonus of a massive swoop through the air on the end of a rope. The 109-metre **Canyon Swing** (6–8 departures daily; $169, second swing $49; ⓣ0800/279 464, ⓦwww.canyonswing.co.nz) sweeps a huge arc over the Shotover River including 60m of freefall. If you time it right you'll have rafts full of spectators below on the river as you launch – forwards, backwards, cartwheel, seated in a chair or even with a bin over your head. This is currently the world's highest swing, though by late 2008 **AJ Hackett**'s planned 125-metre swing out at the Nevis bungy site should have grabbed that title. Until then, they make do with the 47-metre Ledge Sky Swing above Queenstown at the Ledge Bungy site (ⓣ0800/286 495, ⓦwww.bungy.co.nz; $120 including the ride to the top of the gondola).

Jetboating

Commercial **jetboating** kicked off in Queenstown way back in 1965 and remains high in the adrenalin hierarchy. There are strong arguments for spending your jetboating dollar on better-value wilderness trips elsewhere – the Wilkin River Jet, Waiatoto River Safaris and trips down the Wairaurahiri River spring to mind – but Queenstown does offer the most thrilling of these rides, the **Shotover Jet** (daily 8.30am–5pm; 30min; $109; ⓣ0800/746 868, ⓦwww.shotoverjet.com), which charges downstream along the Shotover Canyon from Arthur's Point, 5km north of Queenstown. With perilously close shaves with rocks and canyon walls plus several 360-degree turns and periodic dousings, you'll find your twenty-minute trip is quite enough. Courtesy minibuses take customers to Arthur's Point from The Station (see p.775) throughout the day.

There's no doubting the lure of the Shotover Jet, but you get better value for money with **Skippers Canyon Jet** (3 departures daily; $95; ⓣ0800/226 966, ⓦwww.skipperscanyonjet.com), who drive you out along the Skippers Road and take you jetboating among the ancient gold workings of the upper Shotover River. The thrills come with plenty of fascinating heritage, but the trip can also be combined with their 4WD trip (see p.784).

Rafting

The majority of jetboat operators stick to fairly flat water, leaving the rough stuff for **whitewater rafting** on the Kawarau and Shotover rivers. Although there appear to be three rafting companies, each with assorted packages and combo deals, all rafts are in fact operated by Queenstown Rafting (ⓣ0800/723 8464, ⓦwww.rafting.co.nz).

The more reliable of the two rivers is the large-volume **Kawarau River** (4hr with around 1hr on the water; $165) a seven-kilometre section of which negotiates four Grade III rapids (exciting but not truly frightening), ending with the potentially nasty Chinese Dog Leg, said to be the longest commercially rafted rapid in New Zealand. Being lake-fed, its flow is relatively steady, though it peaks in spring and drops substantially towards the end of summer.

In contrast, the **Shotover River** (5hr with almost 2hr on the water; $165; heli-rafting $239) is demanding: the rapids, revelling in names such as The Squeeze, The Anvil and The Toilet, reach their apotheosis in the Mother-in-Law rapid, usually bypassed at low water by diverting through the 170-metre Oxenbridge Tunnel (see p.783). The fourteen-kilometre rafted section of the river (Grade III–IV) flows straight out of the mountains and its level fluctuates considerably. In October and November, snow melt ensures good flows and a bumpy ride; by late summer low flows can make it a bit tame for hardened rafters, though it is still scenic and fun for first-timers. In winter the lack of sunlight reaching the depths of the canyon makes it too cold for most people, though you can elect to do a much shorter trip by accessing the rapids by helicopter. The same people also run three-day, fly-in wilderness trips on the **Landsborough River**.

Rafting is usually limited to those aged 13 or older, but by tackling an easier (Grade I–II) stretch of the Shotover, **Family Adventures** (Ⓣ0800/472 384, Ⓦwww.familyadventures.co.nz) can take all ages. Their trips (adults $150, kids $110) include a drive into the Skippers Canyon and around ninety minutes on the water, floating in rafts. You don't even need to paddle.

▲ Jet boating on the Shotover River

Family fun is also available on the Kawarau with **Flow** (adults $89, kids $50; ⓣ03/442 4922, ⓦwww.nzraft.co.nz), who offer a gentle combat with Grade I–II rapids in either a raft or an inflatable canoe, followed by a barbecue.

River surfing and whitewater sledging

From mid-October to April, two sections of the Kawarau River are used for the parallel sports of whitewater sledging and river surfing – the "Dog Leg" section by the rafters, and the "Roaring Meg" run, a few kilometres downstream, by the sledgers. For both sports small groups are equipped with a board or sledge, a wetsuit, a helmet and fins, then led downstream and encouraged to view their independence and freedom of movement as virtues rather than hazards. While rafters bob around high up on their inflatable perches, river surfers and sledgers get right in the thick of it: what look like ripples to rafters become huge waves and the serious rapids can be thoroughly daunting, as froth engulfs you on all sides: things work best if you are both confident in water and a decent swimmer.

River surfing involves floating downstream, grasping a foam boogie board and surfing as many as possible of the rapids' standing waves. Serious Fun ($149; ⓣ0800/737 468, ⓦwww.riversurfing.co.nz), run four-hour trips featuring ninety minutes' river surfing, usually doing two runs down either the "Dog Leg" or "Roaring Meg" sections, depending on the conditions. By the second run you're really getting the hang of surfing.

Mad Dog River Boarding ($139; ⓣ0508/623 364, ⓦwww.riverboarding.co.nz) just do one run on Roaring Meg, adding in a flat-water stretch with rope swings, rock jumps (up to 23m if you're really keen), waterslide and jet-skiing.

Largely the same techniques are used in **whitewater sledging**, which involves grasping the handles of a foam or plastic "sledge" and snuggling arms and upper body down into a streamlined shape. The extra buoyancy gives a better roller-coaster ride over the waves and greater manoeuvrability for catching eddies, though actually surfing waves is more difficult. Frogz ($135; ⓣ0800/437 649, ⓦwww.frogz.co.nz) offer double runs down the Roaring Meg section, with pick-ups in Queenstown and Wanaka.

Canyoning

Fans of river surfing and whitewater sledging may also be drawn to **canyoning**, in which small groups are led down verdant narrow canyons to walk in streams, swim across pools, slide down rocks and jump off cliffs. All participants are suitably protected by wetsuit, helmet and climbing harness. Canyoning.co.nz (Oct–April; ⓣ03/441 3003) run two trips. **Canyoning Queenstown** (3hr, 90min in the water; $145) involves morning and afternoon trips to Twelve Mile Delta just out of town; for a longer day out requiring a bit more commitment on your part, go **Canyoning Routeburn** (7hr with over 3hr in the water; $215), which involves walking the first twenty minutes of the Routeburn Track then launching yourself into a water-sculpted, narrow canyon full of jumps and slides. A Glenorchy pick-up saves you $20.

The Rung Way

If the mountains around Queenstown look tempting but you don't have the skills or equipment to go rock climbing, you can get a sense of the experience with **Rung Way** (ⓣ0800/786 4929, ⓦwww.rungway.co.nz). They run the southern hemisphere's only Via Ferrata, a system originally used in Europe to move troops quickly across mountainous terrain during the two world wars.

Suitably harnessed up, you make your own way up a trail of steel rungs drilled into a series of cliff faces just above Queenstown, clipping yourself into a long steel cable which runs beside the rungs. Previous experience isn't necessary, and more demanding routes are available for the gung-ho. Climbs take place daily at 9am and 1pm (4hr; $149).

Paragliding and hang-gliding

A fine day with a little breeze is all it needs to fill the skies above Queenstown with people **tandem paragliding** from Bob's Peak. Taking to the skies with Queenstown Tandem Paraglide (Ⓣ0800/759 688, Ⓦwww.paraglide.net.nz; $185, before 10am $150) works like a taxi rank, so if you want a go, simply pay your way up the Skyline Gondola then stand in line until it is your turn. How many acrobatic manoeuvres are executed during the ten to fifteen minutes you're airborne is largely down to you, your jump guide and the conditions. If you don't see anyone in the air during the main operating times (9am–5pm), don't bother with the gondola ride, as the weather's probably being uncooperative.

Three companies operate from just out of town, usually running off Coronet Peak. Extreme Air (Ⓣ0800/727 245, Ⓦwww.extremeair.co.nz) offer paragliding from 1300m ($195). If you want to fly with a three-time New Zealand champion and his crew, try Coronet Peak Tandems (from $175; Ⓣ0800/467 325, Ⓦwww.tandemparagliding.com). Both should give you around fifteen minutes in the air. And if all this pretending to be a bird feels like it might become addictive, Elevation (Ⓣ0800/359 444, Ⓦwww.elevation.co.nz) run a full-day session ($180) which will teach you controlled flight up to 20m above the ground and can lead on to full solo flights the following day.

Paragliding while being towed behind a boat goes by the name of **parasailing**, offered by Paraflights, Main Town Pier (Ⓣ0800/225 520, Ⓦwww.paraflights.co.nz). For $110 you are winched out on a rope until you reach a height of 100m above the lake surface and, after ten minutes admiring the scenery, you're winched back in again, still dry. Fly with a buddy and you pay $85 each.

There's notably more of a birdlike quality to **tandem hang-gliding**, where you and your instructor are harnessed in a prone position under the wing of a hang-glider and execute a number of progressively steeper turns as you soar down from Coronet Peak to the Flight Park on Malaghans Road 700m below. Skytrek (Ⓣ0800/759 873, Ⓦwww.skytrek.co.nz; $210 for 12–15min in the air) runs several flights a day throughout the year, sometimes launching from the Remarkables.

Skydiving and Fly By Wire

Queenstown is an expensive place to go **tandem skydiving**, but the scenery does partly compensate. NZone (Ⓣ0800/376 796, Ⓦwww.nzone.biz) run jumps from 12,000ft ($299; 45 seconds freefall) and 15,000ft ($399; 65 seconds), all taking place over Lake Wakatipu and landing by the foot of the Remarkables. Another airborne possibility includes a twenty-minute spin in a Pitt Special **stunt plane** with Actionflite (Ⓣ0800/478 866, Ⓦwww.actionflite.co.nz; $295).

Petrolheads keen to get airborne should try **Fly By Wire** (Ⓣ0800/359 299, Ⓦwww.flybywire.co.nz; $99 for 3.5min, $149 for 5min). This involves piloting a kind of miniature plane tethered by a hundred-metre leash to a fixed point on a wire strung between two hills. Loaded with a charge of fuel, there's free rein to circle around, gaining height (up to almost 100m) and swooping down, perhaps reaching 140km per hr. Once the fuel cuts out you drift back to earth.

Horse-riding

The scenery makes Queenstown a great place to go **horse-riding**. First-timers can visit Shotover Stables on Malaghans Road, 7km north of town (T03/442 7486), whose gentle treks ($65; 1hr 15min riding) emphasize local history and explore gold-mining relics down by the Shotover riverbed. With more experience (or just ambition), try Ben Lomond (T0800/236 566, Wwww.nzhorsetreks.co.nz), who head backcountry on trips such as Moke Lake (1.5hr; $85).

Mountain biking

Queenstown's exhilarating **mountain-biking** trips predominantly feature downhill riding. Fat Tyre Adventures (T0800/328 897, Wwww.fat-tyre.co.nz) has a variety of single-track mountain-biking packages with up to four hours in the saddle, including an excellent trip in the Dunstan Mountains above Cromwell (5hr; $195). The company also operates all-day trips to locations accessed by helicopter ($320–450), which are scenic, challenging and great fun. Gravity Action (T03/442 5277 1021, Wwww.gravityaction.com) offer relatively cheap thrills ($139 for over 2hr in the saddle) descending almost 600m down a narrow track which, until a better road was pushed through in 1888, was the only route into Skippers Canyon. Finally, Vertigo, 4 Brecon St (T0800/837 844, Wwww.vertigobikes.co.nz) offer a steep ride down from the top of the gondola in Queenstown (2hr 30min; $149) or helibiking from Ben Crauchan with 18km downhill with 1600 vertical drop (4hr; $329).

Off-road and four-wheel-drive tours

Guided **off-road driving** trips with Off Road Adventures (T03/442 7858, Wwww.offroad.co.nz) allow participants to learn to control quad bikes or motorbikes on a variety of terrains. Packages range from straightforward, family-oriented affairs (allow 3hr, 1hr riding; $129) to the tougher Adventure Tour (3hr, 1hr 55mins riding; $199), including steep trails on a high country station.

For those wishing to relinquish control, there are a number of **4WD** vehicles on offer where the driver/guide takes a gentler, more informative approach to the countryside, some focusing on LOTR locations. Easily the biggest operator is Nomad Safaris ($140; T0800/688 222, Wwww.nomadsafaris.co.nz), who do trips into Skippers Canyon (see p.783), cross the Arrow River over twenty times on the run into Macetown (see p.799), and offer a couple of "Safari of the Scenes" LOTR trips (see box, p.775). They'll also let you get behind the wheel for some real off-roading ($245).

Scenic flights and ballooning

To get high above Queenstown, enlist the services of Alpine Choppers (20min; $160; T03/451 0001, Wwww.alpinechoppers.co.nz), who run scenic flights with a landing at the top of the Remarkables (20min; $160), and fly to **Milford Sound** (2hr 30min; $590).

A more peaceful approach is in a **hot-air balloon** with Sunrise Balloons (3hr including around 1hr flight time; $345; T0800/468 247, Wwww.ballooningnz.com). After an early start, you climb as high as 2000m to gawp at the day's new sun and mountain scenery before landing for a champagne breakfast. On a clear day, Mount Cook can be seen more than 240km away.

Eating

Queenstown has stacks of restaurants, many of them very good and correspondingly expensive. They are increasingly making the most of Queenstown's summer climate, spilling out onto the pedestrianized streets or stretching out along the waterfront, where you can sit and watch the *Earnslaw* glide in. **Breakfast** and **snack** places generally close by 6pm, though some serve early **dinners**, while restaurants often double as bars as the evening wears on.

Cafés and snack bars

Habebes Wakatipu Arcade, Beach St. Hole-in-the-wall daytime Lebanese café serving Queenstown's best falafel, tabbouleh and Kiwi variations on Middle Eastern dishes, as well as juicy lamb and chicken kebabs. Most dishes $10–12.

Halo Camp St. Relaxed, licensed café with de rigeur good espresso and toothsome muffins plus a breakfast burrito ($14). Smoothies and gourmet burgers ($15) , many vegetarian, are served on sunny seating beside an old church. Evenings feature the likes of salmon, rib-eye and Moroccan chicken for $23–25.

Patagonia Chocolates 50 Beach St. Waterside café notable for its rich hot chocolate drinks (ginger, lavender, chilli) as well as luscious cakes, delectable gelato and handmade chocolates. Free Wi-Fi.

Vudu 23 Beach St. It has seen many a worthy challenger come and go, but this relaxed daytime and evening café remains the town's best. Comfy chairs and magazines set the tone for a place strong on inexpensive breakfasts, quiches, panini, scrumptious muffins and good coffee, plus more substantial fare like chicken wraps, steak sandwiches and pasta. The breakfast quesadilla is a local favourite ($15).

Vesta Marine Parade. Part gallery, part interior design shop, part tiny café, all in the delightfully cramped historic Williams Cottage. Come for dainty morsels, sweet treats and tea in the garden or tiny glasshouse.

Restaurants

@ Thai Church St ⓣ03/442 3683. The best of the town's Thai places and certainly authentic. The chicken satay is particularly scrumptious, the service is attentive and takeaways are available.

Bombay Place 68 Shotover St ⓣ03/441 2886. Authentic little Indian with Bollywood on the screen, serving the likes of shrimp masala ($20) and chicken sagwala ($17) plus some wonderful veggie options, with early-bird specials (daily 5–6.30pm). Takeaways available.

The Cow Cow Lane. Longstanding and popular pizzeria (be prepared to share a table) in a cosy stone house. The food's pretty good and reasonably priced ($20–25 a head). BYO & licensed.

Finz Steamer Wharf ⓣ503/442 7405. Perfectly sited restaurant beside the lake that's good value for seafood and serves classic bouillabaisse ($18) green-lipped mussels ($18) and crumbed calamari ($17).

Kappa 36a The Mall. Cheapish, no-nonsense Japanese place tucked away upstairs. Nip in for sushi ($4–7), a bowl of soba or udon noodles ($9–15), or one of their specials – perhaps nori-flavoured blue cod and asparagus tempura ($15).

Pig and Whistle 41 Ballarat St. Bustling English-style pub with a large beer garden, an open fire and good-value food, including ploughman's lunches and crumbed fish and chips (both $14).

Solera Vino 25 Beach St ⓣ03/442 6082. This small and elegant fine-dining restaurant offers delectable French Mediterranean dishes (mains around $30), and has a wine list as long as a baguette. Very popular, so booking is advisable. Dinner-only.

Wai Steamer Wharf ⓣ03/442 5969. Delightful fine-dining waterfront restaurant with outdoor seating right on the wharf. Mains ($38–45) might include roasted mahi mahi with scallops and sautéed bok choy, but it is worth considering setting the whole evening aside for their fabulous dégustation menu ($115, $175 with wine matches).

Winnies 7 The Mall. Popular for its pasta and its excellent and imaginative gourmet pizzas made from local ingredients. There's a good à la carte and blackboard menu, and prices are reasonable. The decent balcony seats and friendly service don't hurt either.

Drinking and nightlife

Despite its high profile and large number of visitors, Queenstown is still essentially a small town. Touring bands are relatively rare, there isn't much in the way of highbrow culture and some of the **clubs** border on being backpacker cattle markets. Still, they can be great fun (some have happy hours to get the evening rolling), and there is no shortage of chic hideaway **cocktail bars**. The free *Mountain Scene* newspaper, found all over town, has up-to-date **listings**, including the **movies** shown at the Reading Cinemas, 11 The Mall (ⓣ03/442 9990).

About the only regular entertainment is Kiwi Haka ($49; reservations essential ⓣ03/441 0101, ⓦwww.skyline.co.nz), a **Maori concert and hangi** performance including the *haka*, a *poi* display and the playing of traditional instruments. It takes place several times each evening up at the Skyline Gondola.

Bars and clubs

Altitude 47 Shotover St. The main backpacker party bar; boozy and with nightly adventure trip giveaways.

Bardeaux 5 Eureka Arcade. A funky little cocktail bar, with big sofas, a roaring fire and a broad selection of excellent whisky and wine. Relaxed early on, but picks up big time after 11pm and often stays open until 5am.

Bunker Cow Lane. A stylish upstairs cocktail bar with cool music – anything from jazz to ambient – open very late.

Debajo Cow Lane. Catholic-icon-filled late-night Spanish bar that likes to bill itself as Queenstown's "home of house". Killer cocktails too. Open until 5am.

Dux de Lux 14 Church St. The only brewpub in town, with half a dozen excellent beers and frequent (and good) Kiwi live music – mostly rock, reggae and blues – until late.

Póg Mahone's 14 Rees St. One of the better Irish bars you'll come across, typically crowded with folk clamouring for draught Guinness and loosely Irish bar meals (mains from $18–23) or warming themselves by the open fire. It's even fuller for the live Irish music on Thurs, Fri & Sat. Outdoor lakeside seating.

Winnies 7–9 The Mall. Lively pizza joint which progressively becomes less restauranty with thumping house and rock, pool table, occasional live bands and regular Latin and Beach Party nights.

Listings

Airlines Air New Zealand Travel Centre, Church St ⓣ03/441 1900.

Banks and exchange All major banks have a branch and ATM around the centre. Best bets for exchange services are in The Station, corner of Camp & Shotover sts (daily: Oct–May 8am–8pm; June–Sept 8am–7pm).

Bike rental Several places around town rent out low-spec bikes good for getting around town and the lakeside trails. Queenstown Bike Rentals, corner of Marine Parade and Church St (ⓣ0800/557 232, ⓦwww.discountrentals.co.nz), is among the cheapest ($10 per hr or $30/day), and has tandems ($20 per hr, $50/day). The company also rents out kayaks ($20/2hr) and scooters ($35/2hr, $55/day). For real off-road use, Dr Bike at Outside Sports, 36 Shotover St (ⓣ03/441 0074), rents out a variety of mountain bikes (from $30/half-day $50/full). Vertigo and Gravity Action also offer rentals (see mountain biking, p.790).

Buses Atomic Shuttles (ⓣ03/322 8883) runs to Christchurch, Dunedin and up the coast to Greymouth; InterCity (ⓣ03/474 9600) operates the most extensive services to all major destinations; Southern Link Shuttles (ⓣ03/358 8355) runs from Queenstown to Nelson via Wanaka and Christchurch, over two days; and Wanaka Connexions (ⓣ03/443 9122) runs the most direct service to Wanaka, plus Invercargill and Dunedin.

Camping and outdoor equipment At Small Planet, 17 Shotover St (ⓣ03/442 6393; daily 9am–8pm), you can pick up affordable new gear plus some used gear, including snowboards, ski gear, climbing, camping and tramping gear and books – all at good prices and with competitive buy-back deals. They also do rentals, and if you've got something to get rid of, they'll hawk it for 25 percent commission. Alpine Sports, 39 Shotover St (ⓣ03/442 7099, ⓦwww.alpinesports.co.nz), has heaps of rental camping gear.

Car rental Renting a car for a day to drive to Milford Sound is commonplace, but be prepared for a long and tiring drive. Numerous companies around town offer good deals: look for advertised rates.

Internet access Fierce competition along Shotover Street means good rates, fast connections and long opening hours, often until 10pm or later. Expect to pay around $3 per hr at places such as E Café, 50 Shotover St, and Internet Outpost, 27 Shotover St.

Library Corner of Shotover St & Gorge Rd (Mon–Sat 10am–5pm).

Medical treatment Queenstown Medical Centre, 9 Isle St (ⓣ03/441 0500), and Lakes District Hospital, 20 Douglas St, Frankton (ⓣ03/441 0015).

Pharmacy Wilkinsons Pharmacy, corner of The Mall & Rees St (daily 8.30am–10pm, ⓣ03/442 7313).

Police 11 Camp St (ⓣ03/441 1600).

Post office The main post office, 13 Camp St (Mon–Fri 8.30am–6pm, Sat 9am–4pm) has poste restante facilities.

Supermarket Fresh Choice, 64 Gorge Rd; Alpine Foodcentre, corner of Shotover and Stanley sts.

The Gibbston wineries

Grapes have only been grown commercially in the Central Otago district since the 1980s, but local winemakers have already garnered a shelf-full of awards. The vineyards of what is the world's most southerly wine-growing region lie close to the forty-fifth parallel in a landscape which detractors pooh-poohed as too cold for wine production, despite the fact that the Rhône Valley in France lies on a similar latitude. A continental climate of hot dry summers and long cold winters prevails, which tends to result in low yields and high production costs, forcing wineries to go for quality boutique wines sold at prices which might seem high ($20–30) until you taste them.

The steep schist and gravel slopes on the southern banks of the **Kawarau River** were first recognized as potential sites as early as 1864, when French miner Jean Désiré Feraud, bored of his gold claim at Frenchman's Point near Clyde, planted grapes from cuttings brought over from Australia. His wines won awards at shows in Australia (though standards were none too exacting at the time), but by the early 1880s he'd decamped to Dunedin. No more grapes were grown until 1976, when the Rippon vineyard was planted outside Wanaka (see p.814). It was another five years before the Kawarau Gorge was recognized as ideally suited to the cultivation of Pinot Gris, Riesling and particularly Pinot Noir grapes. As an added bonus, the dry conditions inhibit growth of fungus and mildew; the dreaded phylloxera has been kept at bay so far.

Altogether, over twenty wineries are open for tasting in Central Otago. There are concentrations around Bannockburn (see p.828) and Clyde (see p.828), but those closest to Queenstown are on the southern slopes above the Kawarau Gorge, around 20km to the northeast of the town along SH6.

You can drive to them all, but you'll learn a lot more if you join one of the **wine tours** that depart from Queenstown. For expert guidance and a chance to see a fair bit of the local area, Appellation Central Wine Tours (Ⓣ03/442 0246, Ⓦwww.appellationcentral.co.nz), runs informative small-group tours calling at wineries in Gibbston and around Bannockburn and Cromwell. The company's afternoon Boutique Wine Tour ($139) includes lunch at one of the four wineries, but enthusiasts will want to go for the more leisurely, full-day Gourmet Wine Tour ($185) taking in four vineyards, a mid-morning cheese tasting and a visit to The Big Picture (see p.828).

Wineries

The following are listed in increasing distance from Queenstown.

Amisfield 10 Lake Hayes Rd Ⓣ03/442 0556, Ⓦwww.amisfield.co.nz. Chic modern winery artfully combining local schist with big windows and recycled timbers. Tasting (daily 10am–6pm; $5) offers four wines usually including their renowned estate-grown Amisfield Pinot Noir. Put a few hours aside for lunch at their gorgeous bistro and courtyard (Tues–Sun 11am–8pm), perhaps going for the popular "trust the chef" option with seven dishes served over three courses ($45; with winematch and dessert $95). The Connectabus between Queenstown and Arrowtown passes right outside.

Chard Farm Chard Rd Ⓣ0800/843 327, Ⓦwww.chardfarm.co.nz. Free tasting of a wide range of wines, most notably the Chardonnay, Pinot Noir and Pinot Gris. It's reached down a precipitous 2km dirt road off SH6 opposite the Kawarau Bungy. Mon–Fri 10am–5pm, Sat & Sun 11am–5pm.

Gibbston Valley SH6 Ⓣ03/442 6910, Ⓦwww.gvwines.co.nz. The most highly evolved of the region's wineries, with tasting ($5), a popular daytime restaurant (the $24 Mediterranean platter is excellent) and an on-site cheesery selling a particularly toothsome wine-washed Monk's Gold, among others. The Winery & Cave Tour (hourly 10am–4pm; 30min; $9.50, $2 off if you eat lunch) explores not especially impressive cellars burrowed into the hillside, and includes an informed and generous tasting session.

The Winehouse & Kitchen SH6 ⓣ03/442 7310, ⓦwww.winehouse.co.nz. New winery and restaurant by the Kawarau bungy bridge owned by AJ Hackett Bungy co-founder Henry van Asch. Call in for extensive tastings ($5) or linger over lunch in a restaurant decorated with kitsch Kiwi icons or outside, where there's a big fireplace and a potager garden planted with things which influence the taste of their main wines – gooseberry, plum, lemon, etc.

Peregrine SH6 ⓣ03/442 4000, ⓦwww.peregrinewines.co.nz. Nestled under a huge steel and plastic structure designed to mimic both the peregrine's wing and the angled layering of the local schist, this stylish winery has free tasting with views of the elegantly industrial barrel room. Daily 10am–5pm.

Arrowtown and Macetown

ARROWTOWN, at the confluence of the Arrow River and Bush Creek 23km northeast of Queenstown, is a pretty place. It still has the feel of an old gold town, though on busy summer days any lingering authenticity can seem swamped by the tourists prowling the sheepskin, greenstone and gold of its souvenir shops. But the town still manages to retain the spirit of a living community, with grocers' shops, a pub and a post office coexisting alongside the gift-wrapped centre. Arrowtown has a permanent (and increasingly wealthy) population of around 2000, but in summer, when holiday homes are full and tourists arrive in force, it comes close to regaining the 7000-strong peak it attained during the **gold rush**.

Arrowtown's hidden Chinese history

The initial wave of miners who came to Arrowtown in the early 1860s were fortune-seekers intent on a fast buck. When gold was discovered on the West Coast, most of them hot-footed it to Greymouth or Hokitika, leaving a much-depleted community that lacked the economic wherewithal to support the businesses which had mushroomed around the mining communities.

The solution, as it had been ten years earlier on the goldfields of Bendigo and Ballarat in Australia, was to import **Chinese labour**. The first Chinese arrived in Otago in 1866, their number reaching 5000 by 1870. The community settled along Bush Creek, its **segregation** from the main settlement symptomatic of the inherent racism of the time – something which also manifested itself in working practices that forced the Chinese to pick over abandoned mining claims and work the tailings of European miners. Even Chinese employed on municipal projects such as the Presbyterian church got only half the wages paid to Europeans doing the same job.

A ray of light is cast amid the prevailing bigotry by contemporary newspaper reports, which suggest that many citizens found the Chinese business conduct "upright and straightforward" and their demeanour "orderly and sober" – perhaps surprisingly in what was an almost entirely male community. Most came with dreams of earning their fortune and returning home so, initially at least, few came with their families; a process of chain **migration** later brought wives, children and then members of the extended family. Few realized their dreams, but around ninety percent did return home, many in a box, driven into an early grave by overwork and poor living conditions. Many more were driven out in the early 1880s when recession brought racial jealousies to a head, resulting in the enactment of a punitive poll tax on foreign residents. There was little workable gold by this time and those Chinese who stayed mostly became market gardeners or merchants and drifted away, mainly to Auckland, though the Arrowtown community remained viable into the 1920s. Once the Chinese had left or died, the Bush Creek settlement was abandoned and largely destroyed by repeated flooding.

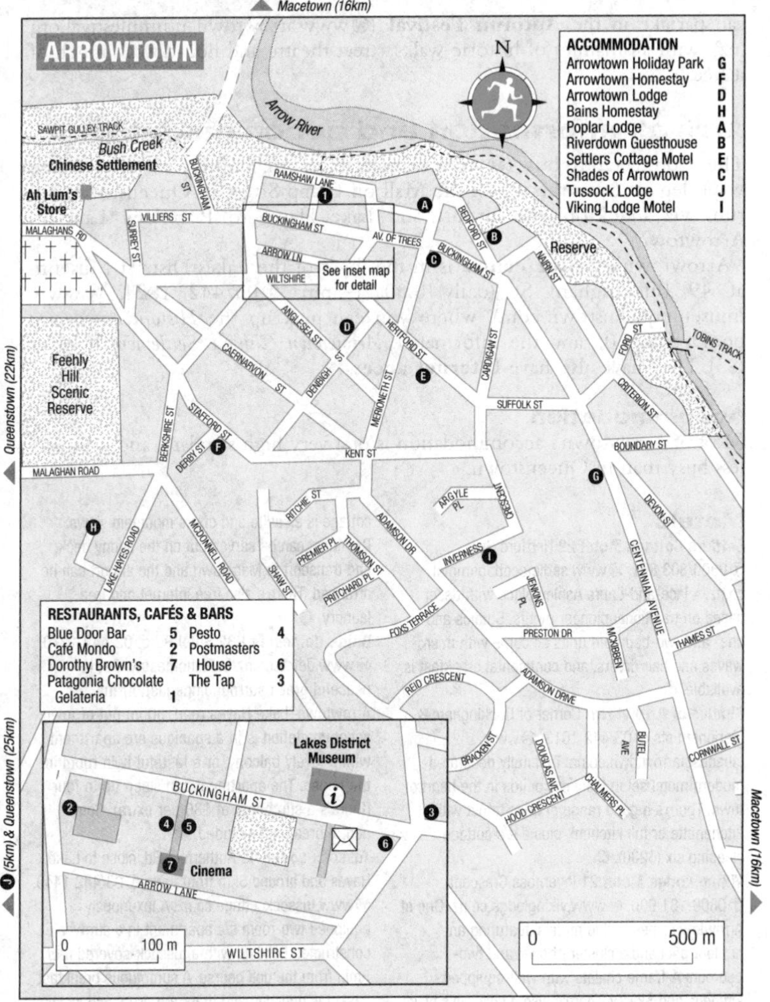

There is some debate as to whether American William Fox was actually the first to discover alluvial gold in the Arrow River in 1862, but he dominated proceedings, managing to keep the find secret while recovering over 100kg of gold. Jealous prospectors tried to follow him to the lode, but he gave them the slip, on one occasion leaving his tent and provisions behind in the middle of the night. The town subsequently bore his name until Foxes gave way to Arrowtown. The Arrow River became known as the richest for its size in the world – a reputation which drew scores of Chinese miners (see box, p.794), who lived in the now partly restored **Arrowtown Chinese Settlement**. Prospectors fanned out over the surrounding hills, where brothers Charley and John Mace set up **Macetown**, now an appealing ghost town.

The best way to appreciate Arrowtown itself is to linger on after the crowds have gone – there's plenty of accommodation. If your visit is in late April you can partake in the **Autumn Festival** (Ⓦwww.arrowtownautumnfestival.org.nz), with all manner of historic walks, street theatre and hoe-downs, much of it free.

Arrival, information and accommodation

The Connectabus **bus** (Ⓦwww.connectabus.com; hourly; 25min; $7 one way) departs from the top of the Mall on Camp Street in Queenstown and runs via Frankton, the airport and Lake Hayes to Ramshaw Lane in Arrowtown.

Arrowtown's **visitor centre** is in the foyer of the Lakes District Museum at 49 Buckingham St (daily 8.30am–5pm; Ⓣ03/442 1824, Ⓦwww.museumqueenstown.com), where you can pick up the *Historic Arrowtown* booklet ($2.50), and the informative *Arrowtown Chinese Settlement* booklet ($3). They have also have **Internet access**.

Accommodation

Most of Arrowtown's accommodation is of a very high standard, and is usually less busy than in Queenstown.

Motels

Settlers Cottage Motel 22 Hertford St Ⓣ0800/803 801, Ⓦwww.settlerscottagemotel.co.nz. A lace-and-Laura Ashley place with decor based on traditional pioneer motifs. Studios and one- and two-bedroom units all come with microwaves and hair dryers, and continental breakfast is available. ④

Shades of Arrowtown Corner of Buckingham & Merioneth sts Ⓣ03/442 1613, Ⓦwww.shadesofarrowtown.co.nz. Tastefully decorated modern motel set in leafy surrounds in the heart of town. There's a good range of units (most with kitchenette or full kitchen), plus a s/c cottage sleeping six ($200). ④

Viking Lodge Motel 21 Inverness Crescent Ⓣ0800/181 900, Ⓦwww.vikinglodge.co.nz. One of Arrowtown's best-value motels, featuring an outdoor pool and a cluster of one- and two-bedroom A-frame chalets with well-equipped kitchens and Sky TV. There's also a children's play area featuring a trampoline. ⑤

B&Bs and homestays

Arrowtown Homestay 18 Stafford St Ⓣ03/442 1747, Ⓦwww.arrowtownhomestay.co.nz. Two comfortable, simply decorated rooms in a spacious modern homestay 5min walk from the town centre. Has a solar-heated pool, lots of good books, table tennis, free Internet and long views over the Arrow Basin. ⑤

Arrowtown Lodge 7 Anglesea St Ⓣ0800/258 802, Ⓦwww.arrowtownlodge.co.nz. Four modern, comfortable and tastefully furnished cottages built from recycled nineteenth-century mud-bricks. Each cottage is en suite and offers mountain views. Breakfast can be served out on the sunny deck, and transport to Macetown and the airport can be arranged. There's also free Internet and free laundry. ⑥

Bains Homestay R32 Butel Rd Ⓣ03/442 1270, Ⓦwww.dotco.co.nz/bainshomestay. Set in peaceful green surroundings just off the Arrowtown–Lake Hayes road, 300m out of town, accommodation is in a spacious s/c apartment with a lovely balcony, or a tasteful twin room in the house. The apartment can sleep up to four (there's a surcharge of $30 per extra). Continental breakfast included. ⑤

Tussock Lodge 48 Rutherford Rd, close to Lake Hayes and around 5km from town Ⓣ03/442 1449, Ⓦwww.tussockcottage.co.nz. A luxuriously equipped two-room s/c apartment in a strawbale-constructed building with a tussock-covered roof, 5min from the golf course. A sumptuous breakfast basket is provided and there are bikes and kayaks for guests' use. ⑦

Hostels and campsites

Arrowtown Born of Gold Holiday Park 12 Centennial Ave Ⓣ03/442 1876, Ⓦwww.arrowtownholidaypark.co.nz. Arrowtown's only campsite: spacious, central, and with tennis court and swimming pool nearby. It has a modern kitchen and ablutions block (showers $1). Camping $15, studios ③, s/c flats ④

Poplar Lodge 4 Merioneth St Ⓣ03/442 1466, Ⓦwww.poplarlodge.co.nz. Extremely centrally located, basic but homely backpackers with small dorms, rooms and a separate en-suite unit. The owners are friendly, and the rose garden is a nice touch. Dorms $25, rooms ❷, unit ❸

Riverdown Guesthouse 7 Bedford St ⓣ03/409 8499, ⓔvalerie@southernlakes.co.nz. Delightful small boutique backpackers in a riverside location, close to the town centre. Double and en suites available plus one three-bed dorm with beds not made up. Closed May–Oct. Dorm $30, rooms ❸

The Town

Twin rows of sycamores and oaks, planted in 1867, have grown to overshadow the tiny miners' cottages along the photogenic **Avenue of Trees**, Arrowtown's most recognizable image. Most of the sixty or so cottages were built towards the end of the nineteenth century and they're unusually small and close together, the chronic lack of timber undoubtedly being a factor. The sheltering hills give Arrowtown parched summers and snowy winters, thrown into sharp relief by autumn, when the deciduous trees planted by the mining community cast golden shadows on a central knot of picturesque miners' cottages.

A visit to the informative Lakes District Museum (see below) is probably the best preparation for a stroll around the **Arrowtown Chinese Settlement** (unrestricted entry). This string of heavily restored buildings, hugging a narrow willow-draped section of Bush Creek at the western end of Buckingham Street, is easily the best-preserved of New Zealand's Chinese communities, and provides an insight into a fascinating, shameful episode in the country's history. Many of the buildings were originally built as temporary retreats – with tin, sod and timber the principal materials – only becoming permanent homes as miners aged. Little was left standing when an archeological dig began in 1983, and many of the dwellings languish in a state of graceful decay. Some schist, mortar and corrugated iron buildings fared rather better and several of these have been restored. The best is **Ah-Lum's Store**, built in typical Canton delta style in 1883 for Wong Hop Lee and leased from 1909 to 1927 to Ah-Lum, one of the pillars of the Chinese community in its later years. By this time integration was making inroads: Ah-Lum sold European as well as Chinese goods, and operated an opium den and bank. Many of the homes are fleetingly brought back to life by interpretation panels.

Artefacts found during the 1983 Chinese Settlement dig are displayed inside the **Lakes District Museum**, 49 Buckingham St (daily 8.30am–5pm; $6). Not surprisingly, it mainly covers the lives of the gold miners and their families, with a particular emphasis on the Chinese community. There's also a feature on opium smoking, which remained legal in New Zealand until 1901, some twenty years after games of chance – *fantan* and *pakapoo* – were proscribed. Technophiles also get a look in, with displays on the quartz-reef mining used at Macetown and on one of the country's earliest hydro schemes, which once supplied mining communities in Skippers and Macetown with power. Down in the basement are displays on the old brewery, a bakery, a print room and a school room.

Walks

Half a dozen good **walks**, listed in the free *Discover Arrowtown* leaflet available from the visitor centre, allow exploration of Arrowtown's history as well as its natural surroundings. Telltale poplar, rowan and willows in the valleys are relics of settlement by prospectors pushing further up Arrow and Bush creeks. Scattered communities sprang up along the banks, but were abandoned just as

▲ Buckingham Street, Arrowtown

suddenly; where settlers' cottages once stood, **fruit trees** have colonized the riverbanks, and in autumn apples, pears and plums weigh down the branches, and bushes of blackberry, blackcurrant, gooseberry, raspberry and elderberry become rampant. There are few specific sights, but you can easily spend a lazy afternoon gorging on fruit and trying to identify the overgrown sites of houses. The surrounding hills are speckled with **rose bushes**: according to folklore, these were planted by miners seeking vitamin C (rosehips are one of the richest sources); others contend that they were planted primarily for their root systems, which could be fashioned into briar pipes.

Of the walks, the **Sawpit Gully Trail** (7km loop; 2–3hr) is a local favourite; parts of it overlap with the eight-hour Macetown–Arrowtown circuit (see p.799), and it takes in a *Lord of the Rings* location (part of the "Ford of Bruinen"), gold-mining remains and some great views of the Remarkables and Lake Hayes.

Eating, drinking and entertainment

Arrowtown's small but booming **eating** scene has plenty to offer for a few days, and you're only 6km from *Amisfield* (see p.793), a great place for a long lunch. Just about the best entertainment venue is *Dorothy Brown*'s, off Buckingham Street (Ⓣ03/442 1964, Ⓦwww.dorothybrowns.com), a small-scale, high-quality **cinema** and bar that's almost too good to be true. Mainstream and more arty films can be seen from stupendously comfortable seats ($18) and you take your wine and snacks in with you.

Cafés, restaurants and bars

The Blue Door Bar Buckingham St, beside *Pesto*. Stylish, intimate and very cool (and therefore not particularly cheap) little bar in a 130-year-old cellar with a log fire. An informal affair, it puts on irregular live jazz, blues and folk.

Café Mondo Ballarat Arcade, 14 Buckingham St. Relaxed café with lots of outside seating and great muffins and cakes, plus breakfast and lunches – mostly around $15.

Pesto 18 Buckingham St ⓣ03/442 0885. Great gourmet pizza and pasta restaurant with just the right balance of casualness and formality. Most mains are under $20 and if they're busy they'll retrieve you from the *Blue Door Bar* (see p.798) when your table's ready. Daily 5pm–late.

Patagonia Chocolate Gelatteria Ramshaw Lane. Sumptuous ice creams. Try the rich passionfruit or rock melon sorbet.

The Postmasters House 54 Buckingham St ⓣ03/442 0991. Dinner-only fine dining in a lovely 1907 wooden house, with the option of taking your meal out on the veranda. The dishes makes good use of local produce, and often feature an Asian twist. Mains $30. Closed Mon–Tues & Sun.

The Tap 51 Buckingham St. The large leafy beer garden and English beers on tap understandably please a collection of locals and visitors, as do the lunch options, such as pie and mushy peas ($11). Dinner available most evenings.

Macetown

As gold fever swept through Otago in the early 1860s, prospectors fanned out, clawing their way up every creek and gully in search of a flash in the pan. In 1862, alluvial gold was found at Twelve Mile, sparking the rush to what later became known as **Macetown** (unrestricted entry), now a ghost town and a popular destination for mountain bikers, horse trekkers and trampers. The best way to experience the place's unique atmosphere is to arrive with tent and provisions and spend a day or two exploring the old mines and grubstake claims.

Macetown's story is one of boom and bust. At its peak, it boasted a couple of hotels, a post office and a school, but when the gold ran out, it couldn't fall back on farming in the way that Arrowtown and Queenstown did and, like Skippers, it died. All that remains of the town itself are a couple of stone buildings – the restored schoolmaster's house and the bakery – and a smattering of wooden

The Arrowtown–Macetown Circuit

The sixteen-kilometre 4WD road up the Arrow Creek from Arrowtown to Macetown is the district's premier biking and trekking route. Walkers can include the road as part of the fairly strenuous, full-day **Arrowtown–Macetown Circuit** (8hr loop; 32km; 700m ascent). The walk is best done in the months from **Christmas to Easter**, after the melting snows have subsided, making the 22 river crossings on the Arrow Creek a little easier – though even in summer, access can be problematic after rain. The *Macetown and the Arrow Gorge* booklet makes a good companion for the route, interpreting sights along the way.

The walk starts by the confluence of the Arrow River and Bush Creek, following the northern bank of the latter westwards, then skirting the base of German Hill and branching up Sawtooth Gully. The gully emerges through open hill country and leads on to Eichardt's Flat. (At this point, about an hour out of Arrowtown, you can pursue the **Sawpit Gully variation** east down Sawpit Gully to meet the Arrow River road and Arrowtown, making a 2–3hr circuit.)

From the Sawpit Gully junction, the Macetown path contours gradually around to the **Big Hill** saddle, with its expansive views back to Lake Hayes and **the Remarkables**. The route then drops steeply towards Eight Mile Creek, the path becoming indistinct – marked by infrequent poles – as it traverses soggy and potentially ankle-twisting country. After three or four hours, you stumble across the Arrow Creek road, just a couple of kilometres short of **Macetown**. When you've had your fill of Macetown, follow the Arrow Creek road back to Arrowtown; for respite from the dust, you can occasionally divert onto paths that run parallel to the road.

shacks. On first acquaintance, it isn't a massively exciting place, but the grassy plateau makes a great free camping spot, sheltered by low stone walls and willow, sycamore and apple trees. The only facilities are long-drop toilets and river water. The surrounding creeks and gullies are littered with the twisted and rusting remains of gold batteries, making a fruitful hunting ground for industrial archeology fans; the area is covered in some detail in the *Macetown and the Arrow Gorge* booklet ($3, available from the visitor centre in Arrowtown).

Macetown is a full-day (or overnight, if you want to camp) outing either on foot (see box, p.799), by **mountain bike** (you'll need to rent one from Queenstown), or on a **4WD** trip with Queenstown-based Nomad Safaris (Ⓣ0800/688 222; 4hr; $140), who will pick you up in Arrowtown on request.

Glenorchy and the major tramps

The tiny mountain-girt town of **GLENORCHY**, at the head of Lake Wakatipu 50km northwest of Queenstown, is quiet and supremely picturesque, making it a perfect retreat for a couple of days. For the majority of visitors, though, Glenorchy is simply a staging post en route to some of the finest **tramping** New Zealand has to offer – a circuit of the Rees and Dart rivers, the Routeburn Track and the Greenstone and Caples **tracks**. Even without the tramps, there's enough to do here to keep you for a couple of days.

The Glenorchy region's fantastic scenery owes a debt to beds of ancient sea-floor sediments laid down some 220–270 million years ago and metamorphosed into the grey-green schists and *pounamu* (greenstone) of the Forbes and Humboldt mountains. The western and northern flanks of the Forbes Mountains were shaped by the Dart Glacier, now a relatively short tongue of ice which, at its peak 18,000 years ago, formed the root of the huge glacial system that gouged out the floor of Lake Wakatipu. For a map of the area, see p.804.

In pre-European times the plain beside the combined delta of the Rees and Dart rivers was known as **Kotapahau**, "the place of revenge killing", a reference perhaps to fights between rival *hapu* over the esteemed *pounamu* which littered an area centred on the bed of the Dart River. There's still greenstone up there, but most is protected within the bounds of the Mount Aspiring National Park.

The first **Europeans** to penetrate the area were gold prospectors, government surveyors and nearby run-holders in search of fresh grazing. The fledgling community of Glenorchy served these disparate groups, along with teams of sawmillers and workers from a mine extracting scheelite, a tungsten ore used in armaments manufacture. Despite the lack of road access, **tourists** began to arrive early in the twentieth century, cruising across Lake Wakatipu on the TSS *Earnslaw* before being decanted into charabancs for the twenty-kilometre jolt north to the Arcadia homestead at **Paradise**. Paradise has been deemed stunning enough to act as movie backdrops for the Rockies, the European Alps and Middle Earth, though the jury is out on whether it draws its name from its idyllic qualities or the abundance of paradise ducks.

The **road from Queenstown** was eventually pushed through in 1962, opening up a fine lakeside drive that passes **Bob's Cove**, the best place to observe the lake's **seiche**, an ill-understood phenomenon which causes the lake level to fluctuate by around 150mm every five minutes. Yet Glenorchy has remained defiantly rural, and the few tourist-oriented ventures barely disturb the bucolic atmosphere. Most walkers base themselves at Glenorchy, from where there are convenient **buses** to the trailheads and to Queenstown.

The town and activities

While it is growing to meet the ever-increasing number of tourists, Glenorchy still doesn't amount to much – a petrol station, a post office, a couple of pubs and cafés, some accommodation and a grocery shop. Still, it is doing its best, with just about everyone plastering their promotional material with *Lord of the Rings* location imagery. If you need to see specific shooting sites, join the Queenstown-based Safari of the Scenes trips run by Nomad Safaris (see p.775). To get a feel for the area and its geography, follow the pleasant **Glenorchy Walkway** (2km loop; 30–40min; flat) from the wharf at the end of Islay Street along the edge of Lake Wakatipu and through the wetlands around the town's lagoon.

Almost all the **activities** in and around town are pitched at the Queenstown crowd, but you can link up with most groups when they arrive in Glenorchy. Durations and prices quoted here are from Glenorchy: most companies charge around $20 for transport to and from Queenstown and Queenstown-based trips will be two hours longer.

Jetboating

Busloads are transported from Queenstown for the excellent **jetboating** on the **Dart River**, which fully utilizes the vessel's shallow-water capabilities, picking routes through braided riverbeds amid grand snowcapped mountains on the edge of Mount Aspiring National Park. **Dart River Jet Safaris** (year-round; ⓣ0800/327 853, ⓦwww.dartriverjetsafaris.com) run three trips, all priced the same whether you join them in Glenorchy or Queenstown. Pure enthusiasts should go on the **Jetboat Safari** (2hr 30min–3hr; $229) which travels up to the national park boundary and back, jetboating all the way but with an optional (and delightful) walk up the Beansburn. Their combination **Wilderness Safari** (3hr; $199) involves a ninety-minute jetboat ride, a bushwalk and a ride in a 4WD coach through some magnificent scenery, including *Lord of the Rings* locations. Better still, you can combine an upstream jetboat ride with canoeing downstream in their **Funyaks** (7hr; $279), two- or three-person inflatable canoes. Suitable even for absolute beginners, this is a gentle trip with no rapids and very little likelihood of an enforced swim. The highlight is the brief stop to walk into **Rockburn Chasm**, where a small tributary of the Dart has carved out a narrow, twisting canyon filled with calm, clear water.

Other activities

Glenorchy has always been a horsey town, and you can have a go at Dart Stables (ⓣ0800/474 3464, ⓦwww.dartstables.com), which runs **horse-riding** trips (2hr for $115; all day $245; Ride of the Rings tours $155; overnight rides $525) through the surrounding countryside, often crossing rivers.

More of the local area can be seen with Mountainland Rovers (ⓣ0800/246 494, ⓦwww.mountainlandrovers.co.nz), whose **Land Rover tours** (3hr; $139) head up the Rees Valley to the spectacular Lennox Falls. The emphasis is on appreciating the scenery and history of the area, and driver Dick Watson spins a good yarn.

Out at the airstrip, 3km south on the road to Queenstown, NZ Skydive (ⓣ0800/586 749, ⓦwww.nzskydive.com) offers **skydiving** with some pretty special views. The best deal is the popular 12,000ft jump ($295). **Guided kayaking** trips on moody Lake Wakatipu are run from *Kinloch Lodge* (1hr/$35, 2hr/$75), who use sit-on-top kayaks and include some local history, in the form of a visit to a remote old sawmill, and delicious home baking, topped off with a dip in the outdoor hot tub.

Practicalities

Track Transport (Ⓣ03/442 9708, Ⓦwww.infotrack.co.nz) run **buses** between Queenstown and Glenorchy (Oct–April daily; 1hr; $18). Buckley Transport (Nov–April daily and on demand in winter; $20 one way; Ⓣ03/442 8215, Ⓦwww.buckleytransport.co.nz) have an early-bird Routeburn trip leaving Queenstown at 8am. They stop outside the Glenorchy **visitor centre**, 2 Oban St (Ⓣ03/441 0303, Ⓦwww.glenorchy-nz.co.nz), who have local information, handle DOC intentions forms, sell a limited supply of **groceries** and have **Internet access** and Wi-Fi. Look out too for the Trading Post, the check-in point for a daily boat to *Kinloch Lodge* (at 2.45pm; $10).

Considering its size, Glenorchy has a reasonable range of **accommodation** to suit most budgets. **Eating** is more limited, and if you need **groceries** for any of the tramps, stock up before leaving Queenstown.

Accommodation

Glenorchy Holiday Park & Backpackers 2 Oban St Ⓣ03/441 0303, Ⓦwww.glenorchynz.com. Well organized, with spacious tent sites and powered sites, plus cabins sleeping up to four. Non-residents can shower here for $5. Camping $15, dorms $25, cabins ❷

Glenorchy Hotel Corner of Mull & Argyll sts Ⓣ0800/453667, Ⓦwww.glenorchynz.com. Reasonable backpacker-style dorms, with communal kitchen and lounge, are hidden behind this hotel. Also plain double rooms (some en suite) with great views up the Dart Valley. Dorms $25, rooms ❸, en suite ❹

Glenorchy Lake House Mull St Ⓣ03/442 4900, Ⓦwww.glenorchylakehouse.co.nz. Central two-room lodge with sumptuous fittings and bedding, deep baths, a spacious lounge with mountain views and a big hot tub outside. Guests have the place to themselves but someone will miraculously appear to cook a delicious breakfast. Room with private bath ❽, en suite ❾

Kinloch Lodge 862 Kinloch Rd Ⓣ03/442 4900, Ⓦwww.kinlochlodge.co.nz. Located 26km from Glenorchy but close to the trailheads for the Greenstone, Caples and Routeburn tracks, this makes an excellent, peaceful retreat after some hard tramping, not least because of the free spa with great lake views ($10 for non-guests). Enthusiastically run, the original 1868 homestead houses small but very comfortable rooms with shared bathrooms, and there's a separate self-catering backpacker section with bunks and neat rooms (one en suite). Excellent meals are served (see below). They can arrange boat transport from Glenorchy ($10), plus bike rental, guided kayak trips and transport to the track ends. Dorms $27, backpacker rooms (one en suite for $110) ❸, backpacker en suite ❹, B&B rooms ❻

Kinloch DOC campsite A small affair tucked away in the trees by *Kinloch Lodge*, with a toilet, BBQ area, picnic table and stream water (not suitable for drinking without treatment). $7

Mount Earnslaw Motels 87 Oban St Ⓣ03/442 6993. Glenorchy's only motel has well-kept, spacious cabin style units with a homely feel and helpful management. ❹

Eating

Glenorchy Café & Bar in the former post office on Mull St. Excellent café serving breakfasts, soups, panini, gourmet pizzas and other home-made treats (check out the ludicrously large cookies), though you may have to share bench-space with Latte, the café cat. Open Fri & Sat evenings in summer.

Glenorchy Hotel Bar serving a good selection of Kiwi staples (mains from $17) and sunny beer garden.

Kinloch Lodge An excellent, cosy restaurant serving a range of breakfasts and espressos (8–9.30am), casual lunches (noon–3pm), and more formal dinners (6.30–8pm; reservations required in winter) with an à la carte menu (mains around $30) supplemented by a three-course table d'hôte ($40).

The major tramps

The fame of the **Routeburn Track** is eclipsed only by that of its westerly neighbour, the Milford Track (see p.857). Yet arguably the Routeburn is superior, with better-spaced huts, more varied scenery and a route that spends most of its time above the bushline and away from sandflies. The Routeburn is certainly one of New Zealand's finest walks, straddling the spine of the

Short hikes from Glenorchy

If you're not here for the major tramps but fancy a hike, consider a day-walk along the Routeburn Track. By using the first and last trailhead buses from Glenorchy, you get four hours to explore, either up to Routeburn Shelter, or tackling the **Lake Sylvan Walk** (5km loop; 1hr 30min; negligible ascent), which starts at a signposted car park 3km before Routeburn Shelter. It repeatedly crosses gravel river terraces supporting beech and totara forest then loops around Lake Sylvan, turned brown from its feeder streams leaching through the soil. You might even consider overnighting on the Routeburn at the Routeburn Flats hut ($40) which usually has space even when other huts are full, though booking is essential during the Great Walks Season (Nov–April).

Humboldt Mountains and providing access to many of the southwestern wilderness's most archetypal features: forested valleys rich with birdlife and plunging waterfalls are combined with river flats, lakes and spectacular mountain scenery. The nature of the terrain means that the Routeburn is usually promoted as a moderate tramp, though the short distance between huts eases the strain considerably. Fit hikers might consider doing it in two reasonably long days, though that doesn't leave much time for soaking up the scenery.

To return along SH94 and SH6 from the end of the Routeburn to the start is a journey approaching 300km, so to avoid a lot of backtracking, anyone with a day or two to spare should consider returning to Glenorchy by hiking either the **Greenstone** or **Caples tracks**. Both are easy tramps, following gently graded, parallel river valleys where the wilderness experience is moderated by grazing cattle from the high-country stations along the Lake Wakatipu shore. The Greenstone occupies the broader, U-shaped valley carved out by one arm of the huge Hollyford Glacier, but despite the grandeur of the surrounding mountain scenery, it's sometimes criticized for being dull. Its detractors prefer the Caples, which runs over the subalpine McKellar Saddle and down the Caples Valley, where the river is bigger and the narrow base of the valley forces the path closer to it.

The **Rees–Dart Track** is the toughest of the major tramps in the area, covering some fairly rugged terrain and requiring six to eight hours of effort each day. It follows the standard Kiwi tramp formula of ascending one river valley, crossing the pass and descending into another, but adds an excellent side trip to the Cascade Saddle.

In **winter** the Routeburn takes on a different character and becomes a much more serious undertaking. The track is often snowbound and extremely slippery, the risk of avalanche is high and the huts are unheated. Return day-trips from Routeburn Shelter to Routeburn Falls Hut and from The Divide to the Lake Mackenzie Hut are much better bets. The lower-level Greenstone and Caples tracks also make a less daunting prospect – not least because the huts are heated by wood-burning stoves which can be used throughout the year – though the McKellar Saddle is often snow-covered. The Rees–Dart Track in winter is really only for mountaineers.

Practicalities

Tramping **information** is best sought at the **DOC visitor centre** in Queenstown (see p.775), where you can fill in intentions forms (not required for the Routeburn), get the latest weather forecast, get the latest on track conditions and either rent ($5) or buy maps. DOC's *The Routeburn Track* and

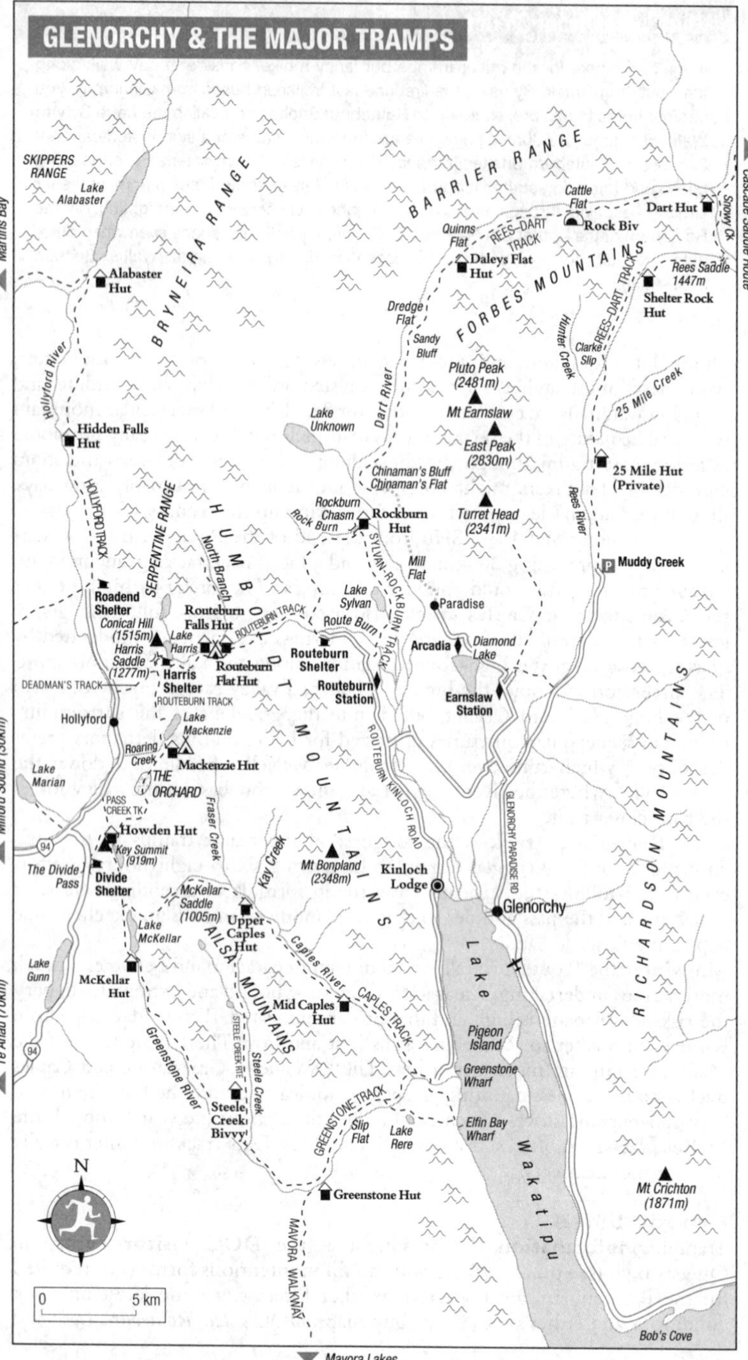
GLENORCHY & THE MAJOR TRAMPS
SKIPPERS RANGE
Lake Alabaster
Martins Bay
Alabaster Hut
BRYNEIRA RANGE
BARRIER RANGE
Cattle Flat
Dart Hut
Rock Biv
Snowy Ck
Cascade Saddle Route
Quinns Flat
REES–DART TRACK
Daleys Flat Hut
FORBES MOUNTAINS
Rees Saddle 1447m
Shelter Rock Hut
Dredge Flat
Sandy Bluff
Hunter Creek
Clarke Slip
REES–DART TRACK
Hollyford River
Pluto Peak (2481m)
Mt Earnslaw
25 Mile Creek
Dart River
Lake Unknown
East Peak (2830m)
Hidden Falls Hut
Chinaman's Bluff
Chinaman's Flat
25 Mile Hut (Private)
Rees River
HOLLYFORD TRACK
SERPENTINE RANGE
Rockburn Chasm
Rock Burn
Rockburn Hut
Turret Head (2341m)
HUMBOLDT MOUNTAINS
North Branch
SYLVAN–ROCKBURN TRACK
Mill Flat
Muddy Creek
Roadend Shelter
Lake Sylvan
Paradise
Conical Hill (1515m)
Lake Harris
Routeburn Falls Hut
ROUTEBURN TRACK
Route Burn
Routeburn Shelter
Arcadia
Diamond Lake
Harris Saddle (1277m)
Harris Shelter
Routeburn Flat Hut
Routeburn Station
Earnslaw Station
DEADMAN'S TRACK
ROUTEBURN TRACK
Hollyford
Lake Mackenzie
Roaring Creek
Mackenzie Hut
ROUTEBURN KINLOCH ROAD
GLENORCHY PARADISE RD
RICHARDSON MOUNTAINS
Lake Marian
THE ORCHARD
PASS CREEK TK
Milford Sound (30km)
Fraser Creek
Howden Hut
94
Key Summit (919m)
Mt Bonpland (2348m)
The Divide Pass
Divide Shelter
Kay Creek
Kinloch Lodge
McKellar Saddle (1005m)
Upper Caples Hut
Glenorchy
Lake McKellar
AILSA MOUNTAINS
Caples River
Lake Gunn
McKellar Hut
CAPLES TRACK
Lake
Mid Caples Hut
Te Anau (70km)
Pigeon Island
Greenstone River
STEELE CREEK RTE
Steele Creek
Greenstone Wharf
94
Steele Creek Bivvy
GREENSTONE TRACK
Slip Flat
Lake Rere
Elfin Bay Wharf
Wakatipu
N
Greenstone Hut
Mt Crichton (1871m)
MAVORA WALKWAY
0
5 km
Bob's Cove
Mavora Lakes

The Greenstone and Caples Tracks leaflets, together with the 1:65,000 *Routeburn, Caples & Greenstone Parkmap* ($19), cover these three walks. For the Rees–Dart Track, the *Dart and Rees Valleys* leaflet and *Mount Aspiring Parkmap* are good, but the more detailed 1:50,000 *Aspiring* and *Earnslaw* Topomaps are far better.

The information below assumes you're starting from Glenorchy, but it's also possible to hike the Greenstone/Caples and Routeburn combination from The Divide (north of Te Anau) with the luxury of *Kinloch Lodge* (see p.805) as your third night. The management runs transport from the Greenstone car park to the lodge ($20) then on to Routeburn Shelter ($18).

Trailhead transport

During the summer tramping season there's little difficulty in getting transport to or from either end of the tracks. Track Transport (Oct–April; ⓣ03/442 9708, ⓦwww.infotrack.co.nz) run a **bus service** to the trailheads, as follows: Queenstown to Glenorchy ($18) then on to the start of the Routeburn (another $18); Glenorchy to the Greenstone car park ($25); Glenorchy to the start of the Rees–Dart ($18); Glenorchy to Chinaman's Bluff (at the end of the Rees–Dart; $25). Trampers wanting to be dropped off or picked up at The Divide (the western end of the Routeburn) can hop on any of the buses running between Te Anau and Milford Sound (ask visitor centres or the companies on p.856 for schedules). Perhaps the most useful is Tracknet (ⓣ0800/483 262, ⓦwww.greatwalksnz.com), with Queenstown-bound buses ($67) passing The Divide at 10.15am and 3.15pm, plus one only going as far as Te Anau-bound buses ($32) at 5.45pm; Milford-bound buses ($27) pass at 8am, 10.55am and 2.30pm.

To save backtracking, trampers can arrange to have their **bags** sent from Queenstown to Te Anau ($10) and Milford Sound ($15) through the Info&Track Centre.

Hut and campsite bookings

The **Routeburn Track** is one of New Zealand's Great Walks and has a compulsory system for booking **accommodation passes** for the four huts and two campsites for the duration of its tramping season (late Oct–April). The system allows people to walk in either direction, retrace their steps and stay up to two nights in a particular hut. Numbers are limited, so book as far ahead as possible – three weeks if you can be adaptable, three months if you need a specific departure date or are part of a large group. This way you get a guaranteed bed in a hut equipped with flush toilets, running water (which must be treated), heaters and gas rings: you'll need to carry your own pans and plates. The cost is $40 per person per night.

It is easiest to **book** online (ⓦwww.doc.govt.nz) from July 1 for the following season, though it is also possible to book by mail and in person at DOC visitor centres. If the track is closed due to bad weather or track conditions, full refunds are given; however, new bookings can only be made if there is space. Changes can be made to existing bookings ($10 per alteration) before you start, again, if space allows. **Outside the season** the huts ($10) cannot be booked and annual hut passes are valid.

A limited number of simple **campsites** (with pit toilets and water; $10) exist close to the Routeburn Flats and Mackenzie huts; campers are not allowed to use hut facilities.

The **Greenstone and Caples tracks** are far less popular, and there is no booking system. Each trail has two $10 huts, but none of them has gas rings.

Note that all **times** and **distances** given in the following accounts are **one way**, unless otherwise stated.

Although it's better to buy hut tickets in advance (unless you have an annual hut pass), wardens may be able to sell you hut tickets. Free **camping** is allowed in both valleys along the fringes of the bush (though not on the open flats), but as ever you're encouraged to camp close to the huts and use their outside facilities. If you use the hut facilities but sleep outside you pay half the hut fee. Camp at least 50m away from the track if you're sleeping elsewhere.

The three **Rees–Dart** huts (each $10) cannot be booked in advance. Trampers should carry an annual hut pass or buy hut tickets in advance.

Guided walks

If you just want a **one-day hike** to sample the Routeburn and avoid the tyranny of shuttle buses, consider joining Info&Track's Routeburn Trail ($145), which includes transport from Queenstown and seven hours **guided walking** – maybe as far as Harris Saddle if the group is quick. Full Routeburn aspirants who aren't confident about their level of fitness or who prefer not to lug heavy backpacks can also join an organized group. The pace is fairly leisurely and walkers have to carry only their personal effects (no food or camping equipment); daily hikes are typically 5–6 hours, occasionally on rough terrain, so anyone unused to hillwalking should still do a good deal of preparatory hiking. **Accommodation** is in privately run huts, which are by no means luxurious, but do have hot showers and duvets on the bunks, and you'll be served cooked breakfasts and three-course dinners with wine.

There's a high **price** to pay for all this pampering: the **Routeburn Guided Walk** (Ⓣ0800/659 255, Ⓦwww.ultimatehikes.co.nz; Nov–April), including return transport from Queenstown and three days' walking, with two nights' accommodation in huts, costs $1190 (Nov & April $1050); the **Grand Traverse**, a five-day, six-night walk combining the Routeburn and Greenstone tracks, will set you back $1575 (Nov & April $1425). The Routeburn can also be combined with the Milford Track Guided Walk (see p.860).

The Routeburn Track

Most people walk the **Routeburn Track** (32km; 2–3 days) westwards from Glenorchy towards The Divide; it can also be combined with the Greenstone and Caples tracks to make three- to five-day loops. The Routeburn isn't for everyone, though, but anyone of moderate fitness who can carry a backpack for five or six hours a day should have little trouble. That said, the track passes through sub alpine country and snowfall and flooding can sometimes close it, even in summer.

Trailhead buses drop off at **Routeburn Shelter** mid-morning, mid- and late afternoon giving flexibility to hike to either Routeburn Flats hut or continue to Routeburn Falls huts, and even offering ample opportunity to explore the North Branch of Route Burn. The route from **Routeburn Shelter to Routeburn Flats Hut** (7km; 2–3hr; 250m ascent) follows Route Burn steadily uphill on a metre-wide track, though it's never strenuous and has an even shingle surface. Because Route Burn is a tributary of the Dart River, you are following a side valley and will have experienced a wide variety of scenery – river flats, waterfalls and open beech forest – by the time you reach the Routeburn Flats Hut (20 bunks). The nearby Routeburn Flats campsite is superbly sited on the edge of wide alluvial flats, at the end of a

▲ Crossing Sugar Loaf Stream on the Routeburn Track

short path a couple of hundred metres beyond the hut. Only a few tents are permitted so there is plenty of space to spread out, and campers can make use of an open fireplace and a small shelter, the run-off from which provides water for cooking. Hut users are better off making the first day a little longer and tackling the next leg, **Routeburn Flats Hut to Routeburn Falls Hut** (2km; 1hr–1hr 30min; 300m ascent), which is considerably steeper and rougher, the extra exertion rewarded by a stay at the modern and magnificently sited Routeburn Falls Hut (48 bunks), perched on the bushline above a precipice with eastward views looking back to Routeburn Flats and Sugar Loaf (1329m).

The stretch from **Routeburn Falls Hut to Mackenzie Hut** (11km; 4–6hr; 300m ascent, 350m descent) is the longest and covers the most exposed section of the track. Most of the day is spent above the bushline among the subalpine snow tussock of the Harris Saddle (1255m) and passing through bog country, where sundews, bladderworts and orchids thrive. You might even catch sight of chamois clambering on the rocks to either side of the saddle. The track climbs gradually enough to the Harris Saddle Shelter (2–3hr), which offers respite from the wind and has toilets; on a clear day, drop your pack here and climb up to the 1515-metre summit of **Conical Hill** (2km return; at least 1hr; 260m ascent) for superb views down into the Hollyford Valley and along it to Martin Bay and the Tasman Sea. Continuing from the Harris Saddle Shelter, you cross from the Mount Aspiring National Park into the Fiordland National Park and skirt high along the edge of the Hollyford Valley, before switchbacking down through silver beech, fuchsia and ribbonwood to Mackenzie Hut (50 bunks). The new **campsite** is a short way from the hut, near the lake.

From **Lake Mackenzie Hut to Howden Hut** (9km; 3–4hr; 250m descent), the track continues along the mountainside through a grassy patch of ribbonwood, known as The Orchard, and past the cascading Earland Falls to the Howden Hut (28 bunks) at the junction of three tracks. The Greenstone and Caples tracks (handy for turning the tramp into a five-day Glenorchy-based circuit) head south, while the Routeburn continues from **Howden Hut to The Divide** (3km; 1hr–1hr 30min; 50m net descent), initially climbing for fifteen minutes to a point where you can make a half-hour excursion to Key Summit for views of three major river systems – the Hollyford, the Eglinton and the Greenstone. From the **Key Summit** (919m) turn-off, the track descends through silver beech to the car park and shelter at The Divide.

The Greenstone Track

Trampers starting on the **Greenstone Track** (36km; 2–3 days) at The Divide first cover the short section to Howden Hut (described above), then walk south from **Howden Hut to McKellar Hut** (7km; 2hr–2hr 30min; 50m descent), passing (after 20min) the primitive but free Greenstone Saddle **campsite**. The Greenstone continues beside Lake McKellar to McKellar Hut ($10; 12 bunks), just outside the Fiordland National Park.

The easy track from **McKellar Hut to Greenstone Hut** (17km; 4hr 30min–6hr 30min; 100m descent) starts by crossing the Greenstone River and follows the true left bank down a broad, grazed valley mostly along river flats and through the lower slopes of the beech forests. A swingbridge then crosses Steele Creek, and the track continues for two more hours to the Greenstone Hut, a good base for exploring the gentle **Mavora Walkway** to the south. It will take you two to three days, passing through open tussock country and beech forest, to reach Mavora Lakes (see p.810); a couple of huts provide accommodation en route ($5).

From **Greenstone Hut to Greenstone car park** (10km; 3–5hr; 100m descent), the track follows the true left bank as the valley narrows and the river heads into a long gorge. The river soon meets the Caples River, an enticing series of deep pools that make great swimming holes. A swingbridge gives access to the left bank of the Caples River and the Caples Track; turn right to Greenstone Wharf (20–30min), or left to Mid Caples Hut (see p.809).

The Caples Track

The Caples Track (27km; 2 days) follows the Greenstone Track from **The Divide to Howden Hut** and then the first half of the section from Howden

Hut to McKellar Hut, turning off an hour south of Howden Hut and beginning the very steep bush-clad zigzag up the **McKellar Saddle** (1005m). Try to assess your capabilities beforehand as many find the walk from The Divide to Upper Caples Hut (17km; 7–9hr; 500m ascent, 550m descent) too much for one day, but are obliged to push on, as camping is neither pleasant nor permitted on the saddle's fragile bogland and open tussock. The descent mostly follows snow poles, crossing and recrossing the infant Caples River before regaining beech forest and the **Upper Caples Hut** ($10; 12 bunks).

Greenstone Wharf is within a day's walk of here, though you can break it into two sections: from **Upper Caples Hut to Mid Caples Hut** (7km; 2hr–2hr 30min; 50m descent) you mainly cross easy grassland to the hut ($10; 12 bunks). From **Mid Caples Hut to Greenstone Wharf** car park (7km; 2–3hr; 100m descent) the path reaches a short but dramatic gorge, crosses it and follows the true left bank, continuing alongside the bush edge and crossing grassy clearings before arriving at the junction with the Greenstone Track, from where it is only twenty minutes to Greenstone Wharf.

The Rees-Dart Track

Transport timetables make it most convenient to tackle the Rees–Dart Track by walking up the Rees and down the Dart. The track from **Muddy Creek car park to Shelter Rock Hut** (17km; 6–7hr; 400m ascent) follows a 4WD track across grass and gravel flats on the true left bank of the braided lower Rees and requires a couple of foot-soaking stream crossings. Press on past the Otago Tramping Club's Twenty-five Mile Hut (private), across Twenty-five Mile Creek and over more river flats for another hour or so, with Hunter Creek and the peaks of the Forbes Mountains straight ahead. Just past Hunter Creek, the Rees Valley steepens appreciably and becomes cloaked in beech forests, which continue sporadically until just below the treeline, where the path passes the site of the old Shelter Rock Hut. Head on for a kilometre until you hit tussock country, where one final crossing of the Rees River, now a large stream, takes you back to the left bank and the Shelter Rock Hut ($10; 22 bunks).

The second day, from **Shelter Rock Hut to Dart Hut** (9km; 4–6hr; 600m ascent, 450m descent), is the shortest but one of the toughest, scaling the 1447-metre Rees Saddle. Stick to the true left bank of the Rees, traversing subalpine scrub and gravel banks for a couple of kilometres, before crossing the river and gradually climbing up to a tussock basin and the saddle. Descend across snow grass beside Snowy Creek, which churns down a narrow gorge to your right. A kilometre or so later the track crosses a swingbridge to the true right bank, commencing a loose and rocky descent past a long series of cascades to another crossing of Snowy Creek, just above its confluence with the Dart River. There are camping spots in the grassy areas on the true right bank and accommodation in the form of the Dart Hut ($10; 32 bunks); many stay two nights here, giving time to explore the Cascade Saddle route (see "Walks in the Matukituki Valley" box on p.822).

The track from **Dart Hut to Daleys Flat Hut** (16km; 5–7hr; 450m descent) initially climbs high above the river and stays there for 3km, passing through beech forest before dropping to Cattle Flat, 5km of grassed alluvial ridges traced by a winding and energy-sapping but easy-to-follow route. At the end of Cattle Flat, the track returns to the bush and runs roughly parallel to the river until it reaches the beautiful grassy expanse of Quinns Flat (perfect in the late afternoon light), where the track turns inland. Within half an hour you reach the sandfly-ridden **Daleys Flat Hut** ($10; 20 bunks), redeemed by its pleasant location on the edge of a clearing.

From **Daleys Flat Hut to Chinaman's Bluff** (16km; 5hr–6hr; 100m ascent, 150m descent), the walk skips through the bush for around 4km until Dredge Flat, where you make your own track, looking for markers on the left that indicate where you re-enter the bush. The track then climbs steeply over Sandy Bluff before dropping down to river level for a fairly easy walk across the flats and along the river to Chinaman's Bluff. Track Transport pick up from here, though you can continue on foot from **Chinaman's Bluff to Paradise car park** (6km; 2hr; negligible descent) along the 4WD track.

Kingston and the road to Fiordland

The 170-kilometre road journey from Queenstown to Te Anau in Fiordland can be done in under three hours. It's an attractive if unspectacular route that follows the lakeshore road, hugging the foot of the Remarkables, then striking out west across open Southland farming country.

As the Dart Glacier retreated at the end of the last ice age, Lake Wakatipu formed behind the terminal moraine at what is now **KINGSTON**, a scattered community 46km south of Queenstown on SH6. Here you can board the **Kingston Flyer** (ⓣ0800/435 937, ⓦwww.kingstonflyer.co.nz; Oct–April only; departs Kingston 10am and 1.30pm; $33 one way, $44 return), a tourist train making a one hour there-and-back journey to the nowhere hamlet of **Fairlight**. Gleaming black steam engines haul creaky but sumptuous turn-of-the-century first-class carriages with embossed steel ceilings and brass gas lamps: arrive early to avoid being shunted down to the less exalted second-class seats, which are charged at the same rate.

Beyond Kingston there's little to delay your progress to Te Anau. Just short of the dull Southland farming town of **Lumsden**, a signposted short cut diverts you to **Mossburn** and SH94. Some 14km west of Mossburn, a narrow road heads north towards the popular summertime retreat of **Mavora Lakes**; the southern lake is reserved for pursuits like fishing and canoeing while the larger North Mavora Lake hosts rowdy boats. The trails through the surrounding beech forests are great for mountain biking, and trampers can head north along the Mavora Walkway and link up with the Greenstone Track (see p.808).

Back on SH94 you soon enter the Red Tussock Conservation Area, named for a type of grass essential to the livelihood of the takahe (see box, p.845), and before long you'll find yourself in Te Anau, perched on the brink of Fiordland (see p.838).

Wanaka

Wanaka (pronounced evenly as Wa-Na-Ka), only 55km northeast of Queenstown as the crow flies but an hour and a half by road, once languished in the shadow of its brasher southern sibling. Thanks to a similar combination of beautiful surroundings and robust adventure activities, it is now one of New Zealand's fastest-growing small towns, with extensive recent developments and new housing subdivisions popping up everywhere. Wanaka is situated at the point where the hummocky, poplar-studded hills of Central Otago rub up against the dramatic peaks of the Mount Aspiring National Park. It commands a wonderful spot on the shores of the willow-girt Lake Wanaka, with the jagged summits of the Southern Alps as often as not mirrored in its waters.

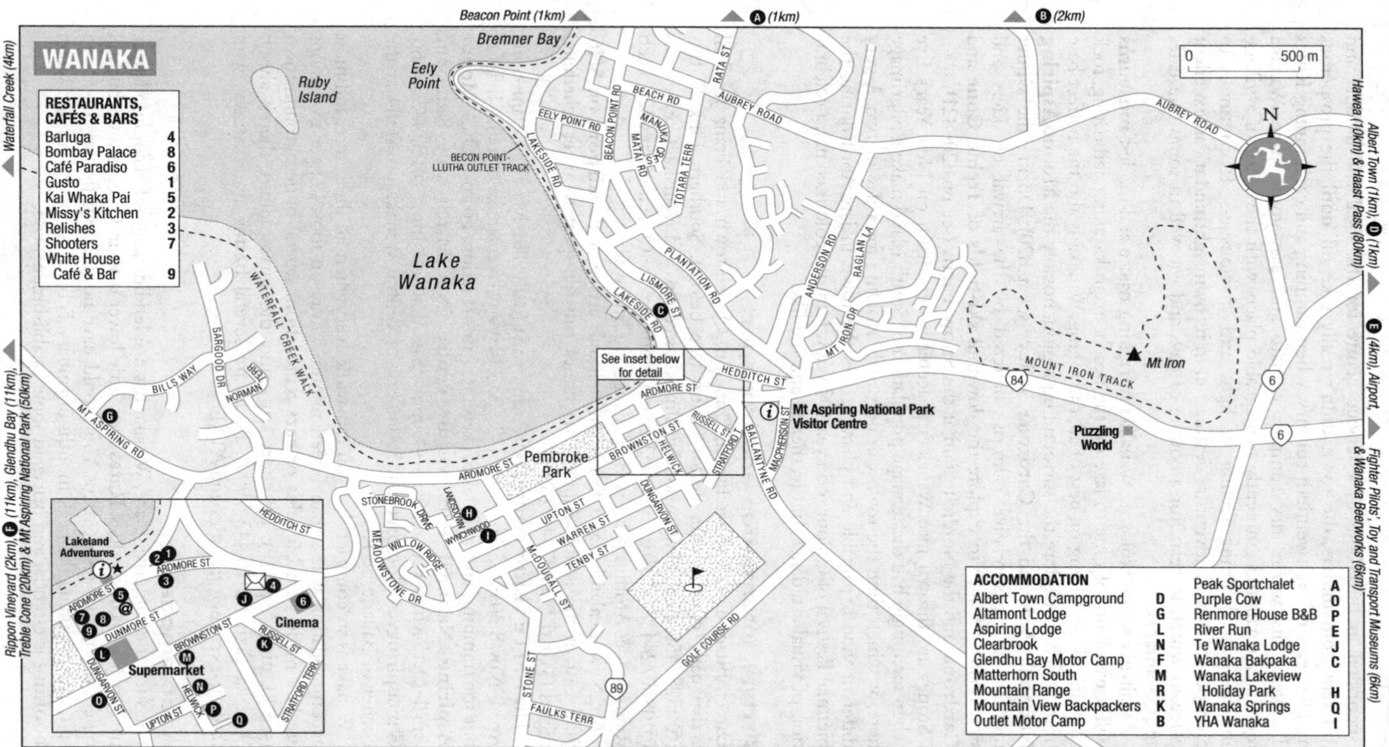
WANAKA
RESTAURANTS, CAFÉS & BARS
Barluga 4
Bombay Palace 8
Café Paradiso 6
Gusto 1
Kai Whaka Pai 5
Missy's Kitchen 2
Relishes 3
Shooters 7
White House Café & Bar 9
ACCOMMODATION
Albert Town Campground D
Altamont Lodge G
Aspiring Lodge L
Clearbrook N
Glendhu Bay Motor Camp F
Matterhorn South M
Mountain Range R
Mountain View Backpackers K
Outlet Motor Camp B
Peak Sportchalet A
Purple Cow O
Renmore House B&B P
River Run E
Te Wanaka Lodge J
Wanaka Bakpaka C
Wanaka Lakeview Holiday Park H
Wanaka Springs Q
YHA Wanaka I
Beacon Point (1km)
A (1km)
B (2km)
Albert Town (1km), D (1km) Hawea (10km) & Haast Pass (80km)
E (4km), Airport,
Fighter Pilots', Toy and Transport Museums (6km) & Wanaka Beerworks (6km)
R (200m), Base Camp Wanaka (200m), Cardrona (26km) & Queenstown (70km)
Rippon Vineyard (2km), F (11km), Glendhu Bay (11km), Treble Cone (20km) & Mt Aspiring National Park (50km)
Waterfall Creek (4km)
0 500 m
N
Lake Wanaka
Bremner Bay
Eely Point
Ruby Island
BECON POINT-LLUTHA OUTLET TRACK
WATERFALL CREEK WALK
See inset below for detail
Mt Aspiring National Park Visitor Centre
Mt Iron
MOUNT IRON TRACK
Puzzling World
Pembroke Park
Lakeland Adventures
Supermarket
Cinema
AUBREY ROAD
RATA ST
BEACH RD
EELY POINT RD
BEACON POINT RD
MANUKA CRES
MATAI RD
TOTARA TERR
LAKESIDE RD
PLANTATION RD
LISMORE ST
ANDERSON RD
RAGLAN LA
MT IRON DR
HEDDITCH ST
ARDMORE ST
RUSSELL ST
BROWNSTON ST
HELWICK
STRATFORD T
BALLANTYNE RD
MACPHERSON ST
DUNGARVON ST
UPTON ST
WARREN ST
TENBY ST
McDOUGALL ST
STONE ST
FAULKS TERR
GOLF COURSE RD
STONEBROOK DRIVE
LANDSDOWN
WYNCHWOOD
WILLOW RIDGE
MEADOWSTONE DR
SARGOOD DR
NORMAN TERR
BILLS WAY
MT ASPIRING RD
DUNMORE ST
STRATFORD TERR
84
6
89

Founded in the 1860s as a service centre for the local run-holders and itinerant gold miners, the town didn't really take off until the prosperous middle years of the twentieth century, when camping and caravanning Kiwis discovered its warm, dry summer climate and easy-going pace. Wanaka remains a small and eminently manageable place, with the tenor of a village and an overwhelming feeling of light and spaciousness. It continues to promote itself as an adventure destination in its own right, and it's an excellent place in which to relax for a couple of days and eat well in some fine cafés and restaurants.

A half-day spent exploring Wanaka's intriguing **maze** and modest **museums** will leave plenty of time to laze on the beach, or go kayaking, jetboating, rock climbing, horse-riding or, best of all, canyoning. Wanaka is also the perfect base from which to explore the surrounding region, notably the **Mount Aspiring National Park** and the **Cardrona Valley** (see p.820). During the winter months, Wanaka's relative calm is shattered by the arrival of skiers and snowboarders eager to explore the downhill **ski-fields** of **Treble Cone** and **Cardrona**, and the Nordic terrain at the **Snow Farm** (see pp.820–821).

Stones are thrown into Wanaka's peaceful waters again on New Year's Eve when seemingly half the teenage population of South Island make a pilgrimage here, at which time the town can be worth avoiding for a day or two. A very different vibe is palpable and characterizes the town in late April during the biennial Festival of Colour (odd years; Ⓦwww.festivalofcolour.co.nz), a celebration of visual art, dance, music, theatre and the like.

Arrival, information and transport

Direct **buses** from Christchurch, Dunedin, Queenstown and Franz Josef all arrive daily close to the visitor centre (see below). Southern Link K Bus (Ⓣ0508/458 835, Ⓦwww.southernlinkkbus.co.nz) and Wanaka Connexions (Ⓣ0800/244 844, Ⓦwww.time2.co.nz) both go to Queenstown ($25 each way), as does Atomic ($20) with a change at Cromwell.

Air New Zealand flights from Christchurch arrive at the **airport**, on SH6, 9km east of the centre. Alpine Coachlines run transport to meet scheduled flights ($10; Ⓣ0800/754 926).

The **i-SITE visitor centre**, 100 Ardmore St (daily: Jan–March 8.30am–6pm; April–Nov 8.30am–5pm; Ⓣ03/443 1233, Ⓦwww.lakewanaka.co.nz) is helpful, but for tramping and general backcountry information, go to DOC's **Mount Aspiring National Park visitor centre** (Nov–March daily 8am–5pm; April–Oct Mon–Fri 8.30am–4.30pm, Sat 9.30am–4pm; Ⓣ03/443 7660, Ⓔmtaspiringvc@doc.govt.nz), 500m east of central Wanaka on SH84 at the corner of Ballantyne Road.

Wanaka is so compact that you can **walk** everywhere in the centre, and most accommodation is less than fifteen minutes' away on foot. Longer excursions are best made with **bicycles** or **cars** rented from several outlets around town (see "Listings", p.819); for short trips into the surroundings, there's always Wanaka Taxis (Ⓣ03/443 7999). There are several **banks** around town, with foreign-exchange facilities and ATMs.

Accommodation

For such a diminutive place, Wanaka has a splendid range of accommodation, particularly luxury lodges. **Rates** are a little lower than in Queenstown, but still reflect the town's resort status. You should have no problem finding a place to suit, except during the peak months of January, February, July and August, when **booking** is essential and prices in some establishments rise.

Hotels and motels

Altamont Lodge 121 Mount Aspiring Rd, 2km west of Wanaka ⓣ03/443 8864, ⓦwww.altamontlodge.co.nz. The perfect tramper and ski lodge, with a pine-panelled alpine atmosphere, communal cooking and lounge areas, a spa pool, drying rooms and ski-tuning facilities. Rooms are functional but attractive, with shared bathrooms and good rates for singles. Bring your own bed linen or pay $5 extra per bed. ❷

Aspiring Lodge Corner of Dungarvon & Dunmore sts ⓣ0800/269 367, ⓦwww.aspiringlodge.co.nz. Spacious and attractive wood-panelled motel units (upstairs ones have partial lake views) with kitchenettes and a drying room. Continental breakfasts available. ❺

Clearbrook Corner of Helwick & Upton sts ⓣ0800/443 441, ⓦwww.clearbrook.co.nz. Classy, modern motel with tastefully decorated luxury units (studios, plus one- and two-bedroom apartments) ranged along the burbling Bullock Creek. All units have TV, stereo, full kitchen with dishwasher, laundry and balconies with mountain views. There are also separate three-bedroom houses sleeping six ($350). ❺

B&Bs and homestays

Mountain Range Heritage Park 2km along Cardrona Valley Rd ⓣ03/443 7400, ⓦwww.mountainrange.co.nz. Idyllic and peaceful seven-room luxury lodge amid tussock on the edge of town. The spacious rooms are simply but tastefully decorated with New Zealand artworks and there's an understated, informal air to the place. Hot tub, hammocks, welcome drinks and marvellous breakfasts round out a fine experience. ❽

Peak Sportchalet 36 Hunter Crescent, 2km north of town ⓣ03/443 6990, ⓦwww.peak-sportchalet.co.nz. Purpose-built s/c studio and two-bedroom chalet, run by a charming German couple who provide a buffet breakfast ($10 extra). Great for family or two couples. Studio ❹, chalet ❺

Renmore House B&B 44 Upton St ⓣ03/443 6566, ⓦwww.renmore-house.com. Large purpose-built house centrally located beside the burbling waters of Bullock Creek. The three plush en-suite rooms are all fitted out to a high standard. There are bikes for guests' use and the hosts are genial and welcoming. ❻

River Run Halliday Rd, 5km east of Wanaka ⓣ03/443 9049, ⓦwww.riverrun.co.nz. Stylish lodge gloriously sited on ancient river flats with trails leading down to the Clutha River. The modern house, built using lots of recycled timbers, was thoughtfully conceived by the owners and contains five beautifully appointed en-suite rooms as well as sunny verandas and a common dining area where most guests stay for three-course dinners ($85) that are the match of any restaurant in Wanaka. Rates ($345 & $525) include breakfast and pre-dinner drinks. ❾

Te Wanaka Lodge 23 Brownston St ⓣ0800/926252, ⓦwww.tewanaka.co.nz. One of the best B&Bs in town, with thirteen luxurious en-suite rooms all with private entrances and Sky TV. A cedar hot tub shares the peaceful garden with a delightful small cottage. There's a sumptuous buffet breakfast and even a house bar with a good wine selection. The owners are friendly and highly knowledgeable about all things outdoors. ❻

Wanaka Springs 21 Warren St ⓣ03/443 8421, ⓦwww.wanakasprings.com. Classy, purpose-built boutique lodge with smallish rooms, comfortable communal areas, sleekly decorated rooms, free liqueurs and a spa pool in a charming native garden. The hosts have good local knowledge. ❽

Hostels

Matterhorn South 56 Brownston St ⓣ03/443 1119, ⓦwww.matterhornsouth.co.nz. Combined hostel and budget lodge, with an appealing backpacker section featuring dorms of various sizes and a log fire surrounded by scatter cushions. The more upmarket section has modern, en-suite four-shares with TV and fridge, and access to an excellent kitchen and comfortable lounge area. Dorms $24, rooms ❷, four-shares taken as doubles ❸

Mountain View Backpackers 7 Russell St ⓣ03/443 9010, ⓦwww.mtnview.co.nz. Small and quite cosy hostel in a converted house with cheery dorms and doubles. Dorms $25, ❷

Purple Cow 94 Brownston St ⓣ03/443 1880, ⓦwww.purplecow.co.nz. Large and spacious hostel in a former hotel with dorms of up to six beds, many in separate blocks with their own lounge, bathroom and TV. Also en-suite doubles, some with lake view and TV/DVD. Sit and gaze at the fabulous lake view through the big picture windows or play pool in the large lounge. Bike rental ($9 per hr, $25/day). Dorms $26, rooms ❸

Wanaka Bakpaka 117 Lakeside Rd ⓣ03/443 7837, ⓦwww.wanakabakpaka.co.nz. Low-key hostel 5min walk from town and with great lake and mountain views, a peaceful atmosphere, summer BBQs and bike rental ($20 a day). Go for the nicer, newer rooms if you have a choice. Dorms $25, rooms ❷

YHA Wanaka 181 Upton St ⓣ03/443 7405, ⓔyha.wanaka@yha.co.nz. Ageing hostel set in peaceful grounds, though soon to be rebuilt on the same site. Call ahead to confirm it is open. Dorms $25, rooms ❷

Campsites and motor parks

Albert Town Campground 6km northeast of Wanaka on SH6. Open, informal camping area, with water and toilets, on the banks of the swift-flowing Clutha River. $7

Glendhu Bay Motor Camp Mount Aspiring Rd, 12km west of Wanaka ⓣ03/443 7243, ⓦwww.glendhubaymotorcamp.co.nz. Popular lakeshore family campsite with fabulous views across to Mount Aspiring, a boat-launching ramp, canoe rental ($10 per hr) and a motorboat ($70 per hr, plus fuel). Camping $12, bunks $17, cabins ❶

Outlet Motor Camp Lake Outlet Rd, 6km from Wanaka ⓣ03/443 7478. Very spacious and beautifully sited campsite at the point where Lake Wanaka becomes the Clutha River, in a great position for strolls along the lake or river frontage. Along with tent and powered sites there are on-site s/c tents with real beds. Camping $12, tents ❸

Wanaka Lakeview Holiday Park 212 Brownston St ⓣ03/443 7883, ⓦwww.wanakalakeview.kiwiholidayparks.com. The most convenient of the campsites, 10min walk from central Wanaka, with tent sites and all the usual facilities, including rooms in a lodge which has bathrooms and kitchen under the same roof and s/c tourist flats. Camping $15, dorms $18, standard cabins ❶, flats ❸

The Town

Though central Wanaka is a pleasant place to hang out, there are no sights as such. For attractions you'll either need to head east to Puzzling World and the museums around the airport or venture 3km west to the small **Rippon Vineyard**, Mount Aspiring Road (Dec–April daily 11am–5pm; July–Nov daily 1.30–4.30pm; ⓣ03/443 8084, ⓦwww.rippon.co.nz). There's free sampling (try the Pinot Noir and the rare Osteiner Riesling hybrid) and you'll struggle to find a more spectacular picnic spot, so pack a few sandwiches and sit back in the sun. The best approach to the vineyard from Wanaka is on foot, along the lakefront Waterfall Creek Walk (see box, p.816), though it is easy to go too far; to avoid this, turn up a track after the first block of vines. Every even year, in February, the vineyard plays host to the one-day Rippon **open-air music festival** (ⓦwww.ripponfestival.co.nz) with top Kiwi bands and a stonking after-party.

The solid lump of Mount Iron rises immediately east of town, pointing the way to **Stuart Landsborough's Puzzling World**, almost 2km away on SH84 (daily 8.30am–5.30pm; $10 for the Maze or the Illusion Rooms, or $12.50 for both; ⓣ03/443 7489, ⓦwww.puzzlingworld.co.nz). The star attraction is "The Great Maze", a complex wooden structure comprising 1500m of dead-end passageways packed into a dense labyrinth, with overhead bridges linking the two halves. Your mission is to reach all four corner towers, either in any order (30min–1hr) or in a specific sequence (at least 1hr), then find your way out again; if it all goes horribly wrong, you can cheat by using escape doors. The Illusion Rooms include: a dated room of holograms; the "Tilted House", which revels in tricks of perspective produced by the floor being fifteen degrees off the horizontal; and the "Hall of Following Faces", a large octagonal room with seven of the sides made up by arrays of moulded images of famous people – Churchill, Einstein, Van Gogh, Lincoln, etc. As you walk around the faces appear to turn towards you, aided by the lack of ears, which apparently hinder the illusion. Yet more fun can be had, and some of Peter Jackson's hobbit-realizing tricks understood, in the Ames Forced Perspective Room, which has been carefully manipulated to make you appear either ent- or hobbit-sized. Leave time to play with the frustrating puzzles in the café.

The airport area

Wanaka's airport is the base for a number of aerial activities (see p.817) and the **New Zealand Fighter Pilots Museum** (daily 9am–4pm; $10; ⓦwww.nzfpm.co.nz), which honours Kiwi pilots and ground crew who fought in the two world wars. This homage to the New Zealand contingent contains hagiographic profiles of the men and blow-by-blow descriptions of the major campaigns, all accompanied by rousing war anthems. The museum also features interactive story screens, plus two displays on the Battle of Britain and the Fall of Germany, as told by NZ pilots who survived them. Over Easter in even-numbered years the airport plays host to the three-day **Warbirds over Wanaka** air show (Ⓦwww.warbirdsoverwanaka.com; $140 for 3 days or $60 for Saturday, the main event), which sees over 100,000 people watch all manner of airborne craft take to the air.

A similar theme is explored in the adjacent **Wanaka Transport and Toy Museum** (daily 8.30am–5pm; $8), an astonishing four-hundred strong hoard of cars, trucks and bikes preserved by Wanaka's dry climate. Some machines are just well-kept examples of stuff still puttering around New Zealand roads, but there's also exotica such as a Centurion tank, Velocette and BSA bikes, a yellow-fur-covered Morris Minor and the Solar Kiwi Racer, an aluminium and glass-fibre bullet-shaped car powered by solar panels on its roof. Also on display are all manner of toys, including an impressive *Star Wars* collection, not to mention more than five hundred Barbies.

Next to the museum, the **Wanaka Beerworks** (daily 9am–4pm or later; Ⓣ03/443 1865, Ⓦwww.wanakabeerworks.co.nz) is an award-winning micro-brewery (simple tours daily at 2pm) which produces a golden malt, a pilsner and a dark ale, all three of which can be sampled for $5, and all of which are sold through bars and restaurants around Central Otago.

The perfect antidote to the museums lies across the road at **Have A Shot** (daily 9am–5.30pm), where you can, well, have a shot with a golf club, various guns or a bow at the archery range. Groups of more active combatants can join battle with spongy tennis balls in the battlefield (all $7–30).

Activities

Wanaka's relatively low profile and the absence of the hard sell and conveyor-belt style that characterizes some of Queenstown's slicker operations add up to a more relaxed approach – and frequently better value for money. Most accommodation and numerous agents around town handle **bookings**, or you can contact the activity operator direct.

Canyoning

If you like water and don't mind heights then the best activity around Wanaka is **canyoning** with Deep Canyon (Nov–March daily; Ⓣ03/443 7922, Ⓦwww.deepcanyon.co.nz) who take small groups into gorgeous narrow canyons following a creek downstream with heaps of jumps, slides and abseils. Warm, protective clothing helps ease the sense of vulnerability, and the day is rounded off with a fine picnic and strong coffee. First-timers are best opting for the **Niger Stream trip** (7–8hr; $215), down a pretty stream with plenty of jumping into deep pools. It helps if you've had some abseiling experience to get the best from **Big Nige** (7–8hr; $280) which kicks off with a big rappel down a waterfall. Plan ahead for less frequent trips such as the **Wilkin Wilderness** (12hr; $860), which combines a helicopter flight, a fabulous canyon and the Wilkin River Jet (see p.767).

Rock climbing and mountaineering

Wanaka's dry, sunny climate is ideal for **rock climbing**. An ideal starting point is Base Camp Wanaka, 50 Cardrona Valley Rd (daily 9am–6pm; Ⓣ03/443 1110, Ⓦwww.basecampwanaka.co.nz), 2km south of the town centre. For a bit of fun, try Clip 'N Climb ($15 for an hour, kids $5; bring trainers) where a totally safe top-rope system gives you the freedom to try all sorts of artificial climbs – against the clock, a face-to-face race, in the dark with UV-lit holds etc. To try something closer to the real thing, have a go on the indoor wall, or the superbly sculpted outdoor wall (both $15 for as long as you want), which is pretty close to climbing on real rock, and a great place to be in the afternoon sun. If you're new to the game they'll teach you how to belay safely and leave you to it. A good café aids recovery between climbs.

For **tuition** and guiding, try Wanaka Rock (ⓣ03/443 6411, ⓦwww.wanakarock.co.nz), which runs full-day introductory courses involving top-roping, seconding and abseiling for two to four people ($190 each; $110 for half-day). Alternatively, head out onto the Matukituki Valley schist and gneiss unsupervised with a copy of *Wanaka Rock* ($30, available from Good Sports – see p.819).

Professional **mountaineering** packages are offered by Adventure Consultants (ⓣ03/443 8711, ⓦwww.adventureconsultants.co.nz). They do five-day ascents

Walks around Wanaka

Visitors shy of the beard-and-Gore-tex walks in the Mount Aspiring National Park to the west might reap greater rewards from these more modest expeditions. No special gear is required, just robust shoes, wet-weather gear, sun protection and DOC's *Wanaka Walks and Trails* leaflet, which has a good map of most of the following walks.

Mount Iron Track (2km; 1–2hr; 240m ascent). The most accessible of Wanaka's hilltop walks climbs a 549-metre glacially sculpted outcrop, its western and northern slopes ground smooth by the glacier that scoured its southern face. The path through farmland and the bird-filled manuka woodland of the Mount Iron Scenic Reserve starts 1500m east of Wanaka on SH84, climbing the steep southern face to the summit. Here you can enjoy magnificent panoramic views of Wanaka and the nearby lakes, before following the path down the east face of Mount Iron towards the entrance to Puzzling World (see p.814).

Roy's Peak Track (16km; 4–6hr; 1100m ascent). A much more ambitious prospect, winding up to the summit (1578m) for wonderful views over Lake Wanaka and surrounding glaciers and mountains. The path starts 7km west of Wanaka on the Mount Aspiring Road, but is closed during the lambing season (1 Oct–10 Nov).

Diamond Lake Track (7km; 2hr 30min; 400m ascent). One of the finest local walks, with great lake and mountain views. From the car park 18km west of Wanaka on the Mount Aspiring Road there are a couple of short variations – but to get the views, you'll need to tackle the summit of Rocky Mountain (775m).

Beacon Point–Clutha Outlet Circuit (16km; 3–5hr; mostly flat). Long but undemanding riverbank and lakeside walk which starts from Wanaka and follows the shore to Eely Point (15min), a sheltered bay popular for boating and picnics. Beyond Eely Point is Bremner Bay and the continuation of the waterfront path to Beacon Point (a further 30min). Either return the same way or continue along Beacon Point Road to the *Outlet Motor Camp* and pick up the Outlet Track, which runs 4km to Alison Avenue, then down to SH6 not far from the Albert Town bridge. By following SH6 this can be turned into a loop back to Wanaka, passing Puzzling World (see p.814) and the base of Mount Iron.

Waterfall Creek Walk (3km one way; 35min; negligible ascent). The westbound equivalent of the Beacon Point–Clutha Outlet Circuit leaves Roy's Bay, heading through Wanaka Station Park and past Rippon Vineyard to a car park at Waterfall Creek. From here the path continues as the Millennium Walkway (5km each way; 1hr; 100m ascent), following lakeside terraces to Ironside's Hill. Both of these are open to bikers.

of Mount Aspiring (from $2490) as well as excellent seven-day mountaineering courses (Nov–April; $2450) which include ice climbing, snow-cave building and all the basic skills, plus several summit ascents.

Bike and horse-riding

Wanaka abounds with shops (see p.819) renting out all-terrain bikes and selling the *Lake Wanaka Cycling Map* ($2), which details excellent local off-road rides. The lakeside tracks (see box, p.816) are open to riders, and the "Sticky Forest" has a particularly dense knot of excellent single track. Alternatively get out to the Dirt Park (day pass $25; Ⓦwww.dirtparknz.com), right by the Snow Farm (see p.821), where there's chair-lift access to all manner of freestyle terrain.

Saddles of a different cut are employed by Backcountry Saddle Expeditions (Ⓣ03/443 8151, Ⓔbackcountry.saddle.expeditions@xtra.co.nz; 2hr $70, 4–6hr $210) from their stables 27km south of Wanaka in the Cardrona Valley; they'll pick you up from Wanaka if you book in advance.

Skydiving and paragliding

Magnificent scenery, clear skies and competitive prices make Wanaka an excellent place to get airborne. A ten-minute scenic flight can be combined with 45–60 seconds of freefall on a **tandem skydive** with Skydive Lake Wanaka, Wanaka Airport (Ⓣ0800/786 877, Ⓦwww.skydivenz.co.nz; $279 from 12,000ft, $369 from 15,000ft).

A less fraught approach to viewing the tremendous scenery is to go **tandem paragliding**. New Zealand's highest tandem flight takes off from the Treble Cone ski-field with Wanaka Paragliding (Ⓣ0800/359 754, Ⓦwww.wanakaparagliding.co.nz), who offer the Big Mountain Tandem (800m descent; 2hr with 15–25min in the air; $180). The cost includes transport and spectators can come along for the ride, for free.

Scenic flights

Scenic flights to Milford Sand (see p.853) from Wanaka tend to be a few dollars more expensive than those from Queenstown, but they do spend half an hour more flying over a wider range of stunning scenery, including Mount Aspiring, the Olivine Ice Plateau and the inaccessible lakes of Alabaster, McKerrow and Tutoko. Most local accommodation receives daily bulletins on Milford weather and flight conditions. Wanaka Flightseeing (Ⓣ0800/105 105, Ⓦwww.flightseeing.co.nz) offer a range of flights, including the wonderful journey over the Southern Alps to link up with a boat cruise on Milford Sound (4hr; $415). There's also a **helicopter** option with Aspiring Helicopters (2hr for $750; Ⓣ03/443 7152, Ⓦwww.aspiringhelicopters.co.nz). Alternatively, nip up to Makarora and check out the **Siberia Experience** (see p.766).

Cruises and boat activities

With a beautiful lake, a number of decent rivers and a friendly, low-key approach, there's plenty of opportunity for getting wet in style. Lakeland Adventures, in the i-SITE building (Ⓣ03/443 7495, Ⓦwww.lakelandadventures.co.nz), lays on all manner of waterborne activities, the most leisurely being **lake cruises**. The best are those to Stephensons Island (2hr; $70) where you take a short stroll, or to the Mou Waho Island (3hr; $99), where you can mingle with protected buff weka birds and walk to Arethusa Pool, a scenic lake within a lake.

From October to April, Alpine Kayak Guides (Ⓣ03/443 9023, Ⓦwww.alpinekayaks.co.nz) will take you on half-day **kayaking** trips on the Clutha

River (Grade II; 4hr; $135): they'll pick up in Wanaka or you can visit them at 150 Main Rd, Luggate, 12km east of Wanaka.

For thrills and spills, the best **jetboat ride** is with Wanaka River Journeys (3hr; $175; ⓣ0800/544 555, ⓦwww.wanakariverjourneys.co.nz), who thunder up the Mutukituki River, providing great views of Mount Aspiring, the Avalanche Glacier, Mount Avalanche and the rest, with a knowledgeable Maori guide and optional bushwalks.

A far cry from Queenstown's boisterous Kawarau and Shotover rivers are the **rafting trips** run by Pioneer Rafting (Sept–April daily; half-day $135, full-day $185; ⓣ03/443 1246, ⓦwww.ecoraft.co.nz). These are pitched at families, the emphasis being on appreciating the scenery, swimming and gold panning as you drift down the Upper Clutha (Grade II–III). No-holds-barred thrill-seekers need look no further than **whitewater sledging** on the Kawarau River with Frogz (see p.788).

Fishing

Lake Wanaka and nearby lakes and rivers are popular territory for quinnat salmon and brown and rainbow trout **fishing**. There's a maximum bag of six fish per day and you'll require the sport fishing licence ($19 a day, $96 for the season), obtainable from tackle shops. Unless you really know your bait, you'll have a better chance of catching your supper with Lakeland Adventures (see p.817), who can provide a knowledgeable fishing guide and a cabin cruiser holding six comfortably ($295 for 3hr for up to three people, plus $25 for each extra person). They can also rent out a rod, reel and lures for about $20 a day.

Eating and drinking

The sophisticated tastes and open wallets of Wanaka's skiers, combined with a healthy influx of summer tourists, have fostered an abundance of very good places to **eat and drink**. Unless you strike it lucky and catch a band passing through, though, the only entertainment is the wonderful Paradiso **cinema**, on the corner of Ardmore Street and Ballantyne Road (ⓣ03/443 1505, ⓦwww.paradiso.net.nz; $12), an offbeat place where you sit in sagging old sofas, armchairs, cushions or even the Morris Minor installed along one side. The films range from Hollywood to arthouse, and there's always an interval during which everyone tucks into cookies, ice cream, coffee or booze from the on-site café (see below).

Barluga Post Office Lane. Very cool little wine bar tucked away just off Ardmore St, with leather sofas and armchairs, trendy wallpaper, a log fire and a courtyard. Sit and watch the giant sideways clock tick by as you savour a quality local wine.

Bombay Palace Pembroke Mall ⓣ03/443 6086. Reliable curry restaurant with the usual range of north Indian favourites at modest prices. Takeaways available.

Café Paradiso Corner of Ardmore St & Ballantyne Rd. Groovy little licensed café attached to its cinema namesake, serving popcorn, cookies and cake, plus home-made ice cream that's free of additives and wondrously fruity ($3.20). Curry and pizzas (from $18) are available in the evening.

Gusto 1 Lakeside Rd. Casual café-style dining, friendly staff and a good location make this a fabulous lunch spot. There's good coffee, a wide range of fresh juices and some great food in generous portions, from salads and spicy chicken sandwiches to all-day breakfasts.

Kai Whaka Pai Corner of Ardmore & Helwick sts. Wanaka's essential daytime eating spot and a hot favourite with locals, who come here for Danish pastries and croissants for breakfast, fine coffee and fabulous meals through the day. In the evening the emphasis is on fresh uncomplicated meals, the most popular being the huge steaks ($30).

Missy's Kitchen 80 Ardmore St ⓣ03/443 5099. Probably Wanaka's finest dining, with a select menu and extensive wine list. Grab a seat on the balcony and perhaps tuck into polenta soufflé with caponata ($29) or venison osso buco in a bitter

▲ Cycling by Lake Wanaka

chocolate sauce ($33) followed by summer pudding with crème fraiche ($16).

Relishes 99 Ardmore St ☎03/443 9018. Pretension-free café/restaurant that's something of a local institution. Lunch ($14–18) might be a steak sandwich, roast pumpkin salad or a delicious antipasto plate for two ($26). Dinner mains go for around $30 and they also do mouth-watering desserts.

Shooters 145 Ardmore Rd. Big, modern drinkers' bar populated by a younger crowd, with sport on TV, pool tables, loud chart-oriented DJ-mixed tunes on Fri & Sat and airy seating out front, with lake views.

White House Café & Bar 33 Dunmore St ☎03/443 9595. At last visit the patio was sprouting weeds and the windows were none too clean, but it's hard to fault the food dished up by the eccentric owner. The menu is strong on vegetarian and seafood dishes with Mediterranean, north African and Middle Eastern leanings. The robust mains ($25–30) can be washed down with something from the extensive wine list (everything by the glass). Try the succulent baked eggplant and spicy tomato. The desserts are sensational and the coffee's strong.

Listings

Bike rental Numerous places around town rent bikes and many hostels and B&Bs have machines for guests' use. For more specialized needs visit Thunderbikes, 48 Helwick St (☎03/443 2558), who offer hardtails ($20/4hr, $40/day) and long-travel fully sprung models ($30/$55).

Camping and outdoor equipment Good Sports, 17 Dunmore St (☎03/443 7966), rent out fishing tackle ($10 a day), hiker tents (from $10 a day), sleeping bags ($7.50 a day) and just about everything else imaginable for use in the outdoors.

Car rental Aspiring Car Rentals (☎03/443 7883) have the cheapest cars in town, starting at around $45 a day, with unlimited kilometres and insurance.

Internet access All over town, including Wanaka Web, upstairs at 3 Helwick St (daily 10am–10pm).

Medical treatment Wanaka Medical Centre, 21 Russell St ☎03/443 7811.

Pharmacy Wanaka Pharmacy, 33 Helwick St ☎03/443 8000.

Police Helwick St ☎03/443 7272.

Post office 39 Ardmore St (Mon–Fri 8.30am–5.30pm, Sat 9am–noon).

Ski rental Racers Edge, 99 Ardmore St (☎03/443 7882, www.racersedge.co.nz), rent out skis ($36–47 per day) and snowboards ($42), and also run a ski-tuning and repair service – as does Good Sports on Dunmore St (☎03/443 7966).

Around Wanaka

Wanaka is the only town of any size within a huge area of western Central Otago, and the only resort with easy access to tramps in the **Mount Aspiring National Park**. Consequently, it's a popular base for exploring the surrounding countryside, principally the open and mountainous areas to the north and west, the Haast Pass road over to the West Coast, and the tortuous **Crown Range Road**, the most direct route to Queenstown, passing through the **Cardrona Valley**.

The Cardrona Valley

William Fox's unwitting discovery of gold at Arrowtown in 1862 quickly brought prospectors along the Crown Range and into the **Cardrona Valley**, where gold was discovered later that year. Five years on, the Europeans legged it to new fields on the West Coast, leaving the dregs to Chinese immigrants, who themselves had drifted away by 1870.

The paved **Crown Range Road** (SH89) through the valley is the most direct (though not necessarily the quickest) route from Wanaka to Queenstown. Reaching an altitude of 1120m, it is one of New Zealand's highest public roads

Winter in Wanaka

May signifies the end of the summer season, and Wanaka immediately starts gearing up for **winter**. Mountain-bike rental shops switch to ski rental (see "Listings", p.819), watersports instructors don their baggy boarder pants, pot-bellied stoves replace parasols at restaurants, and frequent shuttle buses run up to the ski-fields, calling at the hotels, hostels and sports shops along the way. If you plan to drive up to the ski-fields, you'll need tyre chains, which can be rented at petrol stations in Wanaka.

Cardrona

Cardrona Alpine Resort (open July to mid-Oct; ⓣ03/443 7411, ⓦwww.cardrona.com) sprawls over three basins on the southeastern slopes of the 1934-metre Mount Cardrona, the twelve-kilometre unsealed toll-free access road branching off 24km south of Wanaka and just short of the hamlet of Cardrona. Predominantly a family-oriented field, Cardrona is noted for dry snow and an abundance of gentle **runs** (five beginner, thirteen intermediate, nine advanced). Currently there are three quads and several learner tows, giving a maximum vertical descent of 390m and, though there is little extreme stuff, snowboarders have the run of three terrain parks. An adult **lift pass** costs $77.

You'll generally need snow chains to negotiate the access road to the base facilities halfway up the field. Non-drivers can get **buses** from Wanaka, and from Queenstown, an hour and a half away. The resort is unique in New Zealand in offering **accommodation** actually on the mountain – in luxury, fully self-contained studios for two (❼), or two- and three bedroom apartments which sleep up to eight ($345–600).

Treble Cone

More experienced skiers tend to frequent the excellent steep slopes of **Treble Cone** (late June to early Oct; ⓣ03/443 7443, ⓦwww.treblecone.co.nz), 22km west of Wanaka, accessed by a seven-kilometre toll-free access road. Its appeal lies in open uncrowded **runs** (four beginner, sixteen intermediate, nineteen advanced), spectacularly located high above Lake Wanaka, and a full 700 vertical metres of skiing with moguls, powder runs, gully runs and plenty of natural and created half-pipes. Three new groomed trails make it much better for beginners than previously and

and is windy enough in places that anyone towing a caravan or trailer is discouraged from using the road. Nonetheless, on a fine day the drive past the detritus of the valley's gold-mining heyday is a rewarding one, with views across the tussock high country.

Around 24km out of Wanaka lies a petrolhead's playground, the **Cardrona Adventure Park** (year-round, but call ahead outside the summer season; ⓣ0800/102 122, ⓦwww.adventurepark.co.nz). For a leisurely start, go quad biking across farmland with some wonderful views ($150/2hr). There's a more testosterone-fuelled appeal to **Monster Trucks**, where you can ride ($175) or drive ($250) a monster truck, negotiate an obstacle course in a monsterized school bus ($140 for a group of up to 12), or be aggressively driven around in a 8-wheel **Argo** ($90 for up to 3). The stunt drivers will scare the pants off you.

Two kilometres further on, tiny **Cardrona** comprises little more than a few cottages, a long-forgotten cemetery and the *Cardrona Hotel* (ⓣ03/443 8153, ⓦwww.cardronahotel.co.nz; B&B rooms ⑥), which stands in a state of arrested decay. Built in 1863, it survived the floods of 1878 that destroyed most of the old town, battling on until 1961. After years of neglect it was reopened in 1984, with its original facade and a completely renovated interior opening onto a great beer garden; it's now a popular watering hole for skiers

snowboarders will have a ball. Day **lift passes** go for $99; there's also a First Timer package ($99) including a lift pass, rental and two hours' instruction.

Morning **buses** leave from Wanaka, and a shuttle bus takes skiers from the start of the access road on Mount Aspiring Road up to the tows. Backcountry tours are also available from Treble Cone, with Aspiring Guides (ⓣ03/443 9422, ⓦwww.aspiringguides.com).

Snow Farm

With so many Kiwi skiers committed to downhill, it comes as a surprise to discover the **Snow Farm** (ⓣ03/443 0300, ⓦwww.snowfarmnz.com), a cross-country ski area across the valley from Cardrona, some 24km south of Wanaka, then 13km up a winding dirt road. At $30 for access to the field and $25 for ski rental, it's a relatively inexpensive way to get on the snow. From July to September, exponents negotiate the 55km of marked and groomed Nordic trails designed to cater to beginners and experts in both the Nordic and Telemark disciplines. The ski school caters to all levels, with improvers' clinics and children's programmes running throughout the season.

Heli-skiing

No one is going to fool you into believing that **heli-skiing** is cheap, but there's no other way of getting to runs of up to 1200 vertical metres across virgin snow on any of six mountain ranges. From June to October Harris Mountains Heli-Ski (ⓣ03/442 6722, ⓦwww.heliski.co.nz), New Zealand's biggest heli-skiing operator, offers almost 400 different runs on 150 peaks – mainly in the Harris Mountains between Queenstown's Crown Range and Wanaka's Mount Aspiring National Park.

Strong intermediate and **advanced skiers** generally get the most out of the experience. **Conditions** are more critical than at the ski-fields, but on average there's heli-skiing on seventy percent of days during winter, typically in four- to five-day weather windows separated by storms. Of the multitude of packages, the most popular are "The Classic" ($795), a four-run day, and "Maximum Vertical" ($975), comprising seven runs in one day, for advanced skiers only; **bookings** should be made well in advance.

in winter, and a good spot for bar and restaurant **meals** (mains such as pork, fish and mussel dishes $20–25). The comfortable, modern en-suite **rooms** have use of a spa pool.

South from here, the road twists and turns a further 26km through grassy flanks of bald, mica-studded hills to a great viewpoint overlooking Queenstown and Lake Wakatipu. It then steeply switchbacks down towards SH6 and Queenstown.

The Matukituki Valley and Mount Aspiring National Park

The **Matukituki Valley** is very much Wanaka's outdoor playground, a sixty-kilometre tentacle reaching from the parched Otago landscapes around Lake Wanaka to the steep alpine skirts of Mount Aspiring, which at 3030m is New

Walks in the Matukituki Valley

DOC's *Matukituki Valley Tracks* and *Rees–Dart Tracks* leaflets are recommended for these walks, along with the very detailed *Mount Aspiring National Park* map ($19). The routes can be tackled by relatively fit and experienced trampers, but the climatic differences in the park are extreme, and the half-metre of rain that falls each year in the Matukituki Valley is no indication of the six metres that fall on the western side of the park; as ever, go prepared.

Several huts in this area are owned by the New Zealand Alpine Club (NZAC) but are open to all: pay at the DOC visitor centre in Wanaka.

Raspberry Creek to Aspiring Hut

The popular and mostly pastoral day-walk from **Raspberry Creek to Aspiring Hut** (9km one way; 2hr 30min–3hr; 100m ascent) starts along a 4WD track which climbs gently from the Raspberry Creek car park beside the western branch of the Matukituki River, only heading away from the river to avoid bluffs en route to Downs Creek, from where you get fabulous views up to the Rob Roy Glacier and Mount Avalanche. Bridal Veil Falls is only a brief distraction before the historic Cascade Hut, followed twenty minutes later by the relatively luxurious stone-built **Aspiring Hut** (NZAC; 38 bunks; Nov–April $25 with gas; May–Oct $20 no gas), a common base camp for mountaineers off to the peaks around Mount Aspiring, which is wonderfully framed by the hut's picture windows. There's also **camping** ($5) near the hut.

Rob Roy Valley

The **Rob Roy Valley Walk** (6km one way; 2hr; 400m ascent) is shorter and steeper than the walk to Aspiring Hut and more spectacular, striking through beech forest to some magnificent alpine scenery, snowfields and glaciers. From the Raspberry Creek car park, follow the true right bank of the Matukituki for fifteen minutes to a swing-bridge; cross to the true left bank that leads on to the Rob Roy stream, which cuts through a small gorge into the beech forest. Gradually the woods give way to alpine vegetation – and the Rob Roy Glacier nosing down into the head of the valley.

Aspiring Hut to the head of the valley

An excellent day out from Aspiring Hut involves exploring the headwaters of the Matukituki River to the north. The **Aspiring Hut to Pearl Flat** (4km; 1hr 30min; 100m ascent) stretch follows the still-broad river as it weaves in and out of the bush to Pearl Flat. From **Pearl Flat to the head of the valley** (3.5km; 1hr 30min; 250m ascent) the path follows the right bank, crosses a huge avalanche chute off the side of Mount Barff and climbs high above the river through cottonwood and into open country.

Zealand's highest mountain outside the Mount Cook National Park. Extensive high-country stations run sheep on the riverside meadows, briefly glimpsed by skiers bound for Treble Cone, rock climbers making for the roadside crags, Matukituki-bound kayakers, and trampers and mountaineers hot-footing it to the **Mount Aspiring National Park**.

The park, first mooted in 1935 but not created until 1964, is one of the country's largest, extending from the Haast Pass (where there are tramps around Makarora; see p.766) in the north, to the head of Lake Wakatipu (where the Rees–Dart Track and parts of the Routeburn Track fall within its bounds) in the south. The pyramidal Mount Aspiring forms the centrepiece of the park, rising with classical beauty over the ice-smoothed broad valleys and creaking glaciers. It was first climbed in 1909 using heavy hemp rope and without the climbing hardware used by today's mountaineers, who still treat the mountain as one of the grails of Kiwi mountaineering ambition.

Scott Rock Bivvy, marked on some maps, is little more than a sheltering rock 50m east of the river and reached by a bridge.

An alternative, initially following the same route, goes very steeply from **Aspiring Hut to French Ridge Hut** (9km; 4hr; 1000m ascent); the hut (NZAC; 20 bunks; $20) has great mountain views but is usually only below the snowline from December to March.

Cascade Saddle Route

The most challenging and satisfying of the local tramps connects the Matukituki Valley to the Rees–Dart Circuit centred on Glenorchy (see p.800), via the arduous **Cascade Saddle Route** (4–5 days one way), a magnificent alpine crossing with fine panoramic views of the Dart Glacier and the Barrier Range. However, DOC warn this route should not be attempted in adverse weather and are adamant that parties need to be well prepared, preferably with alpine experience. Long stretches of exposed high country and a finishing point 150km (by road) from the start mean that the route is not one to be undertaken lightly, though it is usually possible to send your excess gear ahead to Queenstown with Wanaka Connexions (☎0800/244 844; around $10 per bag). Cascade Saddle can only be negotiated without specialized mountaineering equipment for around four months a year (typically Dec–March), and requires full waterproofs, while a tent gives you the option of breaking the longest day by spending a night just beyond the alpine meadows at the saddle.

The first part of the route follows the track from **Raspberry Creek to Aspiring Hut** (9km; 2hr 30min–3hr; 100m ascent – see description on p.822). From **Aspiring Hut to Dart Hut** (13km; 8–11hr; 1350m ascent), views of Mount Aspiring improve as you rise above the treeline onto the steep tussock and snowgrass ridge above. The route is marked by orange snow poles which lead you to a steel pylon (1835m) that marks the top of the ridge, down to Cascade Creek and across it before climbing gently to the meadows around Cascade Saddle (1500m; 4–6hr). Non-campers will have to press on another four or five hours to the Dart Hut, some 500m lower down, along the upper **Dart Valley**. The initial steep descent beside snow poles is treacherous when wet, but on a warm afternoon enjoys expansive views towards the mouth of the rubble-topped Dart Glacier, where chunks of ice periodically crash into the milky river that surges beneath it. In 1914, the terminus of the glacier had crept to within a kilometre of Dart Hut, but it is retreating an average of 50m a year and could all but disappear within eighty years. After following lateral moraine, rounding bluffs and fording streams, you eventually reach the new **Dart Hut** ($10; 32 bunks), from where it is two days to Glenorchy, following either the Dart or Rees river valleys.

Travelling along the unsealed section of the Mount Aspiring Road beside the Matukituki River, you don't get to see much of Aspiring, as Mount Avalanche and Avalanche Glacier get in the way. Still, craggy mountains remain tantalizingly present all the way to the **Raspberry Creek**, where a car park and public toilets mark the start of a number of magnificent tramps (see box, pp.822–823) into the heart of the park.

Buses operated by Mount Aspiring Express (Ⓣ0800/186 754; $30 one way, $50 return), and Alpine Coachlines (Ⓣ0800/754 926, Ⓦwww.good-sports.co.nz; same prices) run 55km along Mount Aspiring Road to the national park's main trailhead at Raspberry Creek. Transporting bikes costs $5 each way.

The Central Otago goldfields

Though Queenstown's gold-rush heritage has largely been swamped by adventure tourism, the mining past remains one of the main attractions of the **Central Otago goldfields**, a historically rich region east of Queenstown and Wanaka, centred on the middle reaches of the **Clutha River**. This barren, rugged and peculiarly beautiful high country is where, from the 1860s to the end of the century, gold was panned from the streambeds, dredged from the deeper rivers, and eventually mined and blasted from the land. Small-time panners still extract a little "colour" from the streams, but for the most part the gold has turned its back on the country it helped build. The landscape is now littered with abandoned mines, perilous shafts and scattered bits of mysterious-looking machinery.

Towns that boomed in the 1860s were mostly moribund by the early years of the twentieth century, but a few struggled on mostly growing **stonefruit**, and later grapes for what has become a burgeoning **wine region** full of unique flavours and enormous potential (see p.828).

The reconstructed nineteenth-century boom town at **Cromwell**, 50km east of Queenstown, probably won't delay you long, but is a good jumping-off point for the former mining settlement of **Bendigo** and the wineries of **Bannockburn**. The twin towns of **Clyde** and **Alexandra** have fashioned themselves as bases for the popular Otago Central Rail Trail, which penetrates the wild and open **Maniototo** region to the northeast. The dilapidated former gold towns of **St Bathans**, **Naseby** and **Ranfurly** are also quietly resurgent, while **Macreas Flat** still has a working mine. Back beside the Clutha River, SH8 dives southeast of Alexandra towards the coast through dull **Roxburgh** and **Lawrence**, where the gold rush initially started.

You need your own vehicle to really explore this region, but there is some **public transport**. The Taieri Gorge Railway (see p.682) runs from Dunedin to Middlemarch, where it is met by Track & Trail buses (Ⓣ03/477 5577, Ⓦwww.transportplace.co.nz) to Queenstown; Catch-A-Bus (Ⓣ03/479 9960) run a service (daily except Sat) between Wanaka and Dunedin through the Maniototo; and fairly frequent buses run along SH8 between Queenstown and Dunedin.

Some history

New Zealand's greatest gold rush kicked off in 1861 when Gabriel Read, an Australian, unearthed flakes of the precious metal beside the Tuapeka River, south of Lawrence. Within weeks Dunedin had all but emptied and thousands were camping out on the **Tuapeka goldfield** around **Gabriels Gully**. In the winter of 1862 Californian prospectors Horatio Hartley and Christopher Reilly teased their first flakes out of the Clutha River, bagging a 40kg haul in three months. This sparked off an even greater gold rush, this time centred on **Cromwell**, which mushroomed. Later in 1862, Thomas Arthur and Harry Redfern struck lucky at what is now Arthur's Point on the Shotover River, sparking a mass exodus for the fresh fields of what soon became known as "the richest river in the world". Miners flooded into **Skippers Canyon**, and later to **Arrowtown**, the last of the major gold towns and still the best preserved. Within a few years returns had dwindled and as traders saw their profits diminishing, **Chinese miners** were co-opted to pick over the tailings (discarded bits of rock and gravel) left behind by Europeans.

Though the boom-and-bust cycle was as rapid here as in gold country elsewhere, some form of mining continued for the best part of forty years, and the profits fuelled a South Island economy, which dominated New Zealand's exchequer. Dunedin's economy boomed, and the golden bounty funded the majority of the grand civic buildings there.

Many claims were eventually abandoned – not for lack of gold, but because of harsh winters, famine, war, a dip in the gold price, lack of sluicing water, or just disinterest. Although returns are far from spectacular, there are still people eking out a living from gold mining all over the province. There's very little appliance of science: instinct counts for much and fancy mining theories not at all. Bigger capital-intensive companies occasionally gauge the area's potential, and as one mining engineer pithily put it, "there's still a shitload of gold out there".

Gold from dirt

The classic image of the felt-hatted old-timer panning merrily beside a stream is only part of the story of gold extraction, but it's a true enough depiction of the first couple of years of the Otago gold rush. Initially all a miner needed was a pick and shovel, a pan, and preferably a special wooden box known as a "rocker" for washing the alluvial gravel. As the easily accessible gravel beds were worked out, all manner of ingenious schemes were devised to gain access to fresh paydirt. The most common technique was to divert the river, and some far-fetched schemes were hatched, especially on the Shotover River: steel sheets were driven into the riverbeds with some success, landslides induced to temporarily dam the flow, and a tunnel was bored through a bluff.

When pickings got thinner miners turned to **sluicing guns** that blasted the auriferous gravel free, ready for processing either by traditional hand-panning or its mechanical equivalent, where "riffle plates" caught the fine gravel and carpet-like matting trapped the fine flakes of gold. Eventually the scale of these operations put individual miners out of business and many pressed on to fresh fields.

To get at otherwise inaccessible gravel stock, larger companies began building **gold dredges**, great clanking behemoths anchored to the riverbanks but floating free on the river. Buckets scooped out the river bottom, then the dredge processed the gravel and spat the "tailings" out of the back to pile up along the riversides.

Otago's alluvial gold starts its life underground embedded in reefs of quartz, and when economic returns from the rivers waned, miners sought the mother lode. Reef quartz mining required a considerable investment in machinery and whole towns sprang up to tunnel, hack out the ore and haul it on sledges to the stamper batteries. Here, a series of water-driven (and later steam-powered) hammers would pulverize the rock, which was then passed over copper plates smeared with mercury, and onto gold-catching blankets, before the remains were washed into the berdan – a special kind of cast-iron bowl. Gold was then separated from the mercury, a process subsequently made more efficient with the use of cyanide.

Cromwell

East of Arrowtown, SH6 runs for 40km through the scenic Kawarau Gorge, past the Gibbston wineries (see p.793) to **CROMWELL**, a dull, flat little service town whose gold-mining roots are waterlogged below the shimmering surface of the **Lake Dunstan** reservoir. Formed by the Clyde Dam 20km downstream (see p.829), Lake Dunstan swamped much of Cromwell's historic core. The present-day town centre is uninspiringly modern, but the surrounding region is beginning to find its place on the tourist map thanks to its cluster of quality wineries, fruit orchards and old gold diggings.

Soon after Hartley and Reilly's 1862 discovery of **gold** beside the Clutha River, a settlement sprouted at "The Junction" at the fork of the Kawarau and Clutha rivers. Local stories tell that it was later renamed when a government survey party dubbed it Cromwell to spite local Irish immigrant workers. Miners low on provisions planted the first fruit trees in the region, little expecting that Cromwell would become the centre of the Otago **stonefruit** orchard belt.

The Town

On arrival, head straight for **Old Cromwell Town** (unrestricted entry), a kind of historic reserve on Melmore Terrace, where Lake Dunstan now laps the increasing number of restored old shopfronts, most of which would now be submerged had they not been dismantled and rebuilt on the water's edge. You can spend a pleasant half-hour browsing the art, craft and gourmet food shops before retiring for an espresso and cake at the *Grain & Seed Café*.

Aquatic activities are still in their infancy here, though you can join EcoExperience Lake Dunstan (ⓣ03/445 1745, ⓦwww.eco-tour.co.nz), who provide binoculars on their four-hour **bird-watching trips**, which explore the eerie and ensnaring waterlogged forest at the northeastern tip of Lake Dunstan ($350 for up to four people). The guide, Dick Marquand, also runs **fishing** trips (ⓦwww.troutfishingservices.co.nz); he's enthusiastic, knowledgeable and guarantees a trout on his fishing trips for up to three people ($190 for 2hr, with longer trips available).

▲ Old Cromwell Town

Practicalities

Queenstown- or Wanaka-bound **bus** travellers may well have to change in Cromwell, using the stop on Lode Lane right by The Mall. By early 2009, the **i-SITE visitor centre** (daily: Nov–March 9am–6pm; April–Oct 9am–5pm; ⓣ03/445 0212, ⓦwww.cromwell.org.nz) should have moved from its previous location in The Mall to a site on SH8B beside the fruit sculpture. It provides the free and comprehensive *Discover Cromwell* and *Walk Cromwell* leaflets and contains a small **museum** (donations welcome) packed full of gold-mining memorabilia, together with material on the construction of Clyde Dam.

Cromwell has a fairly limited range of accommodation and **places to eat**, but prices are low.

Accommodation

Cottage Gardens 80 Neplusultra St ⓣ03/445 0628, ⓦwww.fiordland.gen.nz/jill.htm. Welcoming and comfortable homestay with en-suite accommodation, a mature garden and dinner on request ($20). ④

Cromwell Motel Corner of Gair & Barry Aves ⓣ0508/445 0373, ⓦwww.cromwellmotel.co.nz. Ageing but pleasantly renovated motel in spacious grounds. ④

Cromwell Top 10 Holiday Park 1 Alpha St ⓣ0800/107 275, ⓦwww.cromwellholidaypark.co.nz. Large campsite on the edge of town with a wide range of accommodation. Very popular Christmas to late Jan. Camping $16, cabins ②, en-suite cabins ③, motel units ④

Quartz Reef Creek SH8, 4km north ⓣ03/445 0404, ⓦwww.quartzreefcreek.co.nz. Just two sunny rooms in a modern lakeside house. A bargain ④

Villa Amo SH6 ⓣ03/445 0788, ⓦwww.villaamo.co.nz. Two immaculate doubles in a large and airy house 8km north along SH6 and right on the lake foreshore, with highly sociable hosts. ⑥

Eating and drinking

The Big Picture SH6, 4km west of Cromwell. Very good daytime café that stays open on Fri and Sat evenings. Expect the likes of risotto ($18), warm roast veg salad ($14), fish of the day ($30) and plenty of classy wine.

Feast 26 The Mall ⓣ03/445 3020. Quality daytime café that's also one of the few reliable places open in the evening. Tues–Sat only.

Grain & Seed Café Old Cromwell Town. Good coffee and a range of light meals such as roast beef sandwich ($10) or Caesar salad ($13) served overlooking Lake Dunstan.

Juice Café on SH8B close to the bridge over Lake Dunstan. Excellent café specializing in fresh juices squeezed from their own orchards.

Around Cromwell

Big tour buses disgorge their load at the half-dozen **fruit stalls** that encircle Cromwell. Pick of the bunch is Jones' Fruit Orchards, 5km west on SH6, which is stacked with fresh and dried fruit, the former blended to form wonderful fruit ice creams, best consumed in the adjacent rose garden.

The only real tourist attraction around Cromwell is the **Goldfields Mining Centre** (daily 9am–5.30pm; ⓣ0800/111 038, ⓦwww.goldfieldsmining.co.nz), approached by footbridge over the brooding Kawarau 7km west of Cromwell on SH6. You can walk around by yourself in an hour or so ($15), but it is far more informative to join the fifty-minute guided tour (departs on the hour; $20) then wander at your leisure afterwards.

The extensive centre occupies a longstanding though not especially lucrative alluvial mining site, where ground-sluicing eventually gave way to Californian-style water jets. While this was an authentic mine, and is surrounded by engaging country, there is a staginess about the mining displays themselves. The stamper battery has been brought in, a turbine was recovered from the river before Lake Dunstan filled and the Chinese Village was constructed as a film set in the early 1990s. On the **guided tour** you get to handle some large gold nuggets, see the stamper battery cranked up using a water-powered Pelton wheel and try your hand at extracting a flake or two. A good **café** and leafy garden make this an especially pleasant stop for families.

The mining centre is also the base for **jetboat rides** with Goldfields Jet ($85 for 40min; ⓣ0800/111 038, ⓦwww.goldfieldsjet.co.nz), who run one of the few trips to actually negotiate rapids.

Dedicated ruin hounds can head out to remote clusters of cottage foundations such as those in the Carrick Range or the Nevis Valley (both south of Cromwell), or 15km north of Cromwell towards the Lindis Pass, where you'll find the quartz-mining district of **Bendigo** and its acolytes Logantown and Welshtown. None comprises much more than a few scattered remains and deep **mineshafts**, but a (careful) amble among the ruins is a fine way to pass a summer evening.

Bannockburn and the wineries

For goldfield aficionados the best bet is **BANNOCKBURN**, a scattered hamlet 9km southwest of Cromwell. Armed with the *Walk Cromwell* leaflet from the Cromwell visitor centre, you can make for the **Bannockburn Sluicings** (unrestricted entry), a tortured landscape that was once home to two thousand people desperately washing away the land to reveal the gold-rich seams below. A two-hour **self-guided trail** dotted with information boards starts 1500m along Felton Road and weaves around tail-races, sluicing and tunnelling operations up to Stewart Town, with its handful of dilapidated mud-brick huts and ageing pear and apricot trees that still fruit.

All this exploring is thirsty work, and you'll welcome the chance to sample the Bannockburn **wineries**. Since the early 1990s, the warm, north-facing hillsides around the sluicings have been increasingly planted in grape vines, and the vintages from them – primarily Pinot Noir and Pinot Gris – have garnered considerable praise. Eight wineries are open for tasting (call in advance to check times if you're visiting in winter), all listed on the free *Central Otago Wine Map*. For informed guidance, join Queenstown-based Appellation Central Wine Tours (see p.793).

A good starting point is **The Big Picture**, on SH6 4km west of Cromwell (Mon–Thurs & Sun 9am–6pm, Fri & Sat 9am–10pm; $20; ⓣ03/445 4052, ⓦwww.bigpicturewine.com) where the idea is to sniff all manner of aromas used to describe wine – citrus, clove, leather, truffle, liquorice, etc. You then venture into a small movie theatre where you find six wines waiting to be sampled. The film rolls and you are transported around Central Otago by helicopter as you are introduced to the landscape, the *terroir*, and lastly the winemakers themselves, who discuss the making and qualities of their wine as you sit there tasting it. There's also a good café/restaurant (see p.827).

One of the finer wineries is **Olssens**, 306 Felton Rd (summer daily 10am–5pm; ⓣ03/445 1716, ⓦwww.olssens.co.nz), which offers tasting ($4, refundable with purchase) and has a lovely sculpture garden that's perfect for whiling away the time as you tuck into one of their lunch platters (summer only; $10–25). For something a little more formal, visit **Carrick**, Cairnmuir Road (summer daily 11am–5pm; ⓣ03/445 3480, ⓦwww.carrick.co.nz), housed in a lovely modern building with art on the walls and views across Lake Dunstan to gold diggings. There's tasting ($4, refundable with purchase) and an excellent daytime restaurant, with most ingredients sourced locally.

Clyde

SH8 cuts southeast from Cromwell through 20km of the bleak and windswept **Cromwell Gorge**, hugging the banks of Lake Dunstan to peaceful **Clyde**. This former gold town contains a few nice places to stay and eat, mostly gearing themselves to people walking the Otago Central Rail Trail (see box, p.831).

Since the mid-1980s, the town has been dominated by the giant grey hydro-electric **Clyde Dam**, 1km north of town on SH8, which generates five percent of New Zealand's power and provides water for irrigation. Initially controversial, the dam is nevertheless considered something of an engineering marvel, with special "slip joints" providing the dam wall with flexibility in case of earthquakes.

The 1864 stone courthouse on Blyth Street now operates as the **Clyde Museum** (Tues–Sun 2–4pm; $3), worth a peek for its intriguing coverage of Clyde's botched Great Gold Robbery of 1870 when one George Rennie tried to make off with £13,000 in bullion and banknotes. The **Briar Herb Factory Complex**, corner of Fraser and Fache streets (Tues–Sun 2–4pm; $3), was established in the 1930s as New Zealand's first herb factory, and thrived for several decades, making use of the common thyme which still grows wild hereabouts, with entire hillsides flowering purple throughout November. The factory closed in the 1970s but lives on as an exhibition space; other parts of the factory are given over to horse-drawn vehicles, a rabbiter's hut and an early hospital full of ghoulish medical instruments.

Practicalities

Buses stop in Clyde on demand, pulling up on Sunderland Street, which is where you'll find the majority of the good places to stay and eat. Clyde is the northern terminus for the Otago Central Rail Trail (see box, p.831), and Trail Journeys, on the corner of SH8 and Springvale Road (ⓣ0800/724 587, ⓦwww.trailjourneys.co.nz), organize pretty much everything to do with riding the trail: they **rent bikes** and panniers (from $35/$5 a day respectively), can pick you and bike up from the far end, and book accommodation along the way. They also **rent kayaks** (single $35 a day, doubles $70) for use on Lake Dunstan and the Clutha River.

Accommodation

Hartley Arms 25 Sunderland St ⓣ03/449 2700, ⓔhartleyarms@xtra.co.nz. Small, cosy backpackers with two, four-bunk dorms and one double partly built into the original gold assay office. $30 per person; $35 including breakfast. ❸

Clyde Holiday and Sporting Complex Whitby St ⓣ03/449 2713, ⓔcrrc@ihug.co.nz. Campsite surrounding a sports ground, with fully s/c cabins and several on-site caravans, plus a pool. Camping $12, cabins ❶

Dunstan House 29 Sunderland St ⓣ03/449 2295, ⓦwww.dunstanhouse.co.nz. A comfy B&B in a former stagecoach waystop with bags of character. Rooms are imaginatively decorated (half en suite and some with clawfoot bath) some opening out onto a wraparound veranda on the first floor. Plenty of bike storage, and there's a piano in the lounge. Rooms ❺, en suites ❻

Eating and drinking

The Bank Café 31 Sunderland St. Good café in the heart of town, sometimes open in the evening.

Post Office Café Corner of Blyth and Matau sts. This 1865 former post office serves pub-style snacks and has a bar serving delicious Post Office Dark ale along with some excellent blackboard specials, inside or in the garden bar out the back. Two-course lunch specials for $13.

The Packing Shed 68 Boulton Rd, 4km south of Clyde ⓣ03/449 2757. Semi-formal rural café with lots of garden seating and delicious food such as salmon Caesar salad ($18). To get there, head across the river bridge opposite the *Post Office Café* and follow Earnscleugh Rd. Lunches plus early dinner Thurs–Sat.

Alexandra and around

A large white clockface – visible from as far away as 5km – looms out of the cliff which backs **ALEXANDRA** (affectionately known as Alex), 10km southeast of Clyde. Alexandra sprang up during the 1862 gold rush, and flourished for four frenzied years before turning into a prosperous service town for the fruit-growing heartland of Central Otago. Its stark rocky scenery may well persuade you to stop, particularly if your visit coincides with the longstanding **Alexandra Blossom Festival**, held on the fourth weekend in September.

A huge water wheel marks Alexandra's main point of interest, the **Alexandra Museum and Art Gallery** in Pioneer Park on Centennial Avenue (daily 9am–6pm; donation), which houses displays on the region's natural and social history, and coverage of the sorry tale of the rabbits which were introduced into the area in 1909, and did what rabbits do – so well that they soon became a major menace throughout the South Island. To combat the problem, the town holds an **Easter Bunny Shoot** every year, and hunters from all over New Zealand congregate on Good Friday to slaughter as many as they can.

In the early years, the only way across the Manuherikia River was by punt, but in 1879 the town built the **Shaky Bridge**, a suspension **footbridge**, which connects with the *Shaky Bridge Café* (see p.830) and a **lookout point** (2km one way; 40min) high above the town on Tucker Hill, affording great views of the whole area.

Activities

Its abundance of treeless hills makes Alex a good base for **mountain biking**. Head along to Altitude Adventures, 88 Centennial Ave (Ⓣ03/448 8917, Ⓦwww.altitudeadventures.co.nz), who specialize in guided single-track tours, from a half-day local trip (from $60) to a four-day grand tour of the area ($680, including bike rental and accommodation). They're also well set up for getting you on the Otago Central Rail Trail (see box, p.831) and rent bikes from around $30 a day (including helmet, tools and spares; $5 for panniers).

Practicalities

Buses all stop outside or close to the **i-SITE visitor centre**, 21 Centennial Ave in Pioneer Park (daily: Dec–March 9am–6pm; April–Nov 9am–5pm Ⓣ03/448 9515, Ⓦalexandra@centralotagonz.com) which has **Internet** access. There's a modest but adequate range of good-value **accommodation** and **places to eat**.

Accommodation

117 Avenue Motels 117 Centennial Ave Ⓣ0800/758 899, Ⓦwww.avenue-motel.co.nz. Sleek, brand-new motel with tastefully decorated units and suites (some with spa bath and Xbox). Units ❸, suites ❹

Alexandra Holiday Park 44 Manuherikia Rd/SH85 Ⓣ03/448 8297. Large and simple campsite 1km from the centre. Camping $14, cabins ❶, flats ❷

Marj's Place 5 Theyers St Ⓣ03/448 7098. Ⓦwww.marjsplace.co.nz. Very welcoming hostel-cum-homestay in two houses in a quiet street 1km from the centre. One house has three- and four-share rooms, backpacker doubles and a separate s/c cabin, while the other contains new rooms all with access to a spa bath and infrared sauna. Dorms $25, hostel rooms ❷, new rooms ❸

Rocky Range SH8, 2km southeast Ⓣ03/448 6150, Ⓦwww.rockyrange.co.nz. A French provincial-style lodge perched high and lonely on a hill amid schist outcrops with stunning panoramic views. Rooms (from $375 a night) are sumptuous and there's a great spa pool amid the rocks. Meals $65 (including wine). ❾

Eating and drinking

Monteith's Brewery Bar 26 Centennial Ave. Lively bar that serves good hearty meals, but most people come here to drink on the sunny terrace.

Oscar's 73 Centennial Ave Ⓣ03/448 5444. Cheery restaurant for tucking Into the likes of pork ribs ($20) and their Ultimate Kiwi Burger ($20).

Shaky Bridge Café Graveyard Gully Rd Ⓣ03/448 5111. For some modern sophistication wander across the Shaky Bridge to this appealing café. Come for a coffee and a muffin, stylish contemporary brunches ($13–17) or one of their sumptuous dinners (mains $28–30; Thurs–Sat only), which mix classic and Asian flavours. Closed Mon.

The Maniototo

The most interesting route to the east coast from Alexandra is through the **Maniototo**, a generic name for the flat high country shared by three shallow valleys – the Manuherikia River, the Ida Burn and the Taieri River – and the low, craggy ranges that separate them. Despite easy road access, the Maniototo seems a world apart, largely ignored by foreign visitors, though this is beginning to change with the upsurge in popularity of the **Otago Central Rail Trail** (see box, p.831).

Predictably, Europeans first came to the area in search of gold. They found it near **Naseby**, but returns quickly declined and farming on the plains became more rewarding. This was especially true when **railway** developers looking for the easiest route from Dunedin to Alexandra chose a way up the Taieri Gorge and across the Maniototo. In 1898, the line arrived in **Ranfurly**, which soon took over from Naseby as the area's main administrative centre.

Former gold-mining communities such as **St Bathans** and **Naseby** are worth a brief visit for their laid-back atmosphere, calm seclusion and subtle reminders of how greed transforms the land. In between you'll see dozens of small cottages, many abandoned – a testimony to the harsh life in these parts.

The main public **transport** is the Catch-a-Bus service (ⓣ03/479 9960; daily except Sat) between Dunedin and Wanaka, which leaves Dunedin at 8am (Mon–Thurs), arriving in Wanaka around noon and starting the return journey at 1pm. Friday's service leaves Dunedin at 4pm (arrive Wanaka 8pm) and Sunday's departure is 10am (arrive Wanaka 2pm). Visitors planning to use the

Otago Central Rail Trail

One of the finest ways to explore the Maniototo is on the **Otago Central Rail Trail** (ⓦwww.otagocentralrailtrail.co.nz), a largely flat 150-kilometre route from Clyde to Middlemarch that passes through all the main towns except for St Bathans and Naseby. Open to walkers, cyclists and horse-riders, it follows the trackbed of the former Otago Central Branch railway line and includes modified rail bridges and viaducts (several spanning over 100m), beautiful valleys and long agricultural plains. At Middlemarch it meets the Taieri Gorge Railway (see p.682), though unless you arrive on Friday or Sunday, you'll have to cycle 18km along the road to Pukerangi for the daily train.

Passenger trains ran through the Maniototo until 1990, but it wasn't until February 2000 that the trail opened, galvanizing a dying region. Most people **cycle**, and all sorts of accommodation has sprung up to cater to bikers' needs. Pubs and cafés located where the trail crosses roads aren't shy to advertise the opportunity to take a break.

The comprehensive and widely available *Otago Central Rail Trail* leaflet (free) outlines the route, with further context available in Gerald Cunningham's *Guide to the Otago Central Rail Trail* (Reed Outdoors; $25). The route is generally hard-packed earth and gravel, making it possible to ride most bikes, though fat tyres make for a more comfortable journey. The trail takes most people three days, but if you're just out to pick the choicest bits (or are walking and don't fancy the whole thing) aim for a couple of ten-kilometre stretches, both with tunnels, viaducts and interesting rock formations: Lauder–Auripo in the northern section, and Daisybank–Hyde in the east. A torch is handy (though not essential) for the tunnels.

Bikes and customized packages with **accommodation** can be organized through various agencies. The best bets are Cycle Surgery in Dunedin, *Blind Billy's Holiday Camp* in Middlemarch, Trail Journeys in Clyde and Altitude Adventures in Alexandra. A couple of commercial **websites**, ⓦwww.otagorailtrail.co.nz and ⓦwww.railtrail.co.nz, offer practical information on the trail.

Taieri Gorge Railway (see p.682) may appreciate the Track & Trail buses (Ⓣ03/477 5577, Ⓦwww.transportplace.co.nz) which meet the train and continue to Queenstown.

Omakau and Ophir

Heading northeast from Alexandra, you're immediately in the high-country plain, passing through inconsequential hamlets until you reach the twin settlements of **Omakau** (where the *Muddy Creek Café* does good coffee) and **Ophir**, 2km to the south. The latter was the original gold town hereabouts and still has its imposing still-operational 1886 **Post & Telegraph Office** (Mon–Fri 9am–noon) and the nice little **suspension bridge** across the Manuherikia River, 1km further south.

St Bathans

The first place with genuine appeal is the minute former gold town of **ST BATHANS**, 80km north of Alexandra and accessed 17km along St Bathans Loop Road from Becks. St Bathans boomed in 1863, but when the gold ran out in the 1930s everything went with it. These days it's virtually a ghost town, with just a handful of residents and an attractive straggle of ancient buildings along the single road. Some of the locals manage the atmospheric 1882 *Vulcan Hotel* (Ⓣ03/447 3629, Ⓔstbathans.vulcanhotel@xtra.co.nz; ❸), where local farmers and visitors prop up the wooden bar, which serves St Bathans Gold, a single malt bottled on the premises. With its garden bar and good café/restaurant, the pub makes a great place to stay; room 1 is reputed to be haunted. The hotel also manages **accommodation** in cottages around town, including the converted *Old Gaol* (❹) and the former *Constable's Cottage*, which sleeps six ($220). Just up the street from the hotel, the former post office is once again operating, as well as being a kind of mini-museum-cum-Victorian **gift shop**.

The prettiest thing about the area is the striking **Blue Lake** right beside the town, where mineral-rich water has flooded a crater left by the merciless sluicing of Kildare Hill, once 120m high but now entirely washed away. A short track leads from the *Vulcan* to a vantage point over the azure lake, now used for water-skiing, swimming and picnics.

Naseby

The small settlement of **NASEBY**, 25km east of St Bathans and 9km off SH85, clings to the Maniototo some 600m above sea level. At its 4000-strong peak in 1865, Naseby was the largest gold-mining town hereabouts, but today numbers have dropped to around 200 huddled in a collection of small houses (many of them originally built of sun-dried mud brick by miners), with a shop, a garage, a couple of pubs, a café and a great campsite.

Grahame Sydney

Many New Zealanders only know the Maniototo through the works of Dunedin-born realist painter **Grahame Sydney** (Ⓦwww.grahamesydney.com), who spends much of his time in the region. His broad, big-sky landscapes of goods sheds amid parched fields and letterboxes at lonely crossroads are universally accessible, and instantly recognizable to anyone visiting the region.

Prints and postcards of his work are found throughout the Maniototo and beyond, and originals hang in most of the country's major galleries. At first glance many of the works are unemotional renditions, but reflection reveals great poignancy. As he says, "I'm the long stare, not the quick glimpse".

The town's story is told through two tiny museums, both at the junction of Earne and Leven streets. The **Maniototo Early Settlers Museum** (Nov–May Tues–Sun 1.30–3.30pm) is packed with black-and-white photos of past residents' lives and also contains a small collection of items left by Chinese miners, while the **Jubilee Museum** (daily 10am–5pm; $1 token available from the general store across the street) houses the remains of an old watchmaker's shop together with displays on the local gold rush of the 1860s and 1870s.

Naseby's **visitor centre** (daily 11am–2pm; ⓣ03/444 9961) is in the former post office on Derwent Street. The most inexpensive place to stay is the pretty and tranquil *Naseby Larchview Holiday Park* (ⓣ03/444 9904, ⓦwww.nasebyholidaypark.co.nz; camping $12, cabins ❶, tourist flats ❷), in the forest about five minutes' walk along Swimming Dam Road. In town, the *Ancient Briton* pub in Leven Street (ⓣ03/444 9992 ⓔancientbriton@xtra.co.nz; ❹), has a number of rooms and a couple of self-contained units. For **B&B**, visit the comfortable shared-bath *Turnstone*, 13 Currowmore St (ⓣ03/444 9644, ⓔgrifford@xtra.co.nz; ❸), or the swisher, antique-filled *Old Doctor's Residence*, 58 Derwent St (ⓣ03/444 9775, ⓦwww.olddoctorsresidence.co.nz; ❽). The *Ancient Briton* and the nearby *Royal Hotel* both offer hearty **meals**, while the *Black Forest Café* on Derwent Street does reasonable meals and coffee.

In summer, visitors are either cooling off at the shaded **swimming dam**, ten minutes' walk up Swimming Dam Road, or exploring the surrounding **Naseby Forest**, which is one of New Zealand's best destinations for single-track **mountain biking**. You can rent bikes and obtain a trail map from Kilas Bike Shop, 20 Derwent St ($30 half-day, $50 full-day; ⓣ03/444 9088, ⓔkilasbikeshop@gmail.com). The best of the local **walks** is the **One Tree Hill Track** (1600m; 1hr return), which starts on Brooms Street in town and snakes uphill along the eastern side of Hogburn Gully, past dramatic honey-coloured cliffs entirely carved by water – leaflet available from the visitor centre.

Naseby is New Zealand's home of **curling** (a sort of lawn bowls on ice). This traditionally took place outdoors in winter but you can now try your hand at the indoor Naseby Curling International (daily 9am–5pm; $ 12 per hr). Instruction is usually available.

Dansey's Pass

The gravel Kyeburn Diggings Road runs east out of Naseby over **Dansey's Pass** (about 40km from Naseby), to Duntroon in the Waitaki Valley (see p.663). It is a narrow, barren and beautiful route that's reasonably well maintained but is sometimes closed in summer and often shut in winter: check in Naseby before setting out. Old gold workings are visible from the roadside, where water-jets from sluices have distorted the schist and tussock landscape, leaving rock dramatically exposed. Along the way you pass the charming **Dansey's Pass Coach Inn**, 16km east of Naseby (ⓣ03/444 9048, ⓦwww.danseyspass.co.nz; ❺), a comfortable lodge in the middle of nowhere. Built from local schist stone in 1862 (the stonemason was reputedly paid a pint of beer for each stone laid), it's the only relic of the once two-thousand-strong gold-rush community. The inn offers good beer, affordable lunches and fairly pricey dinners, as well as nicely modernized en-suite accommodation, which is booked up most weekends throughout the year.

Ranfurly

Back on SH85 and 5km southeast of the Naseby turn-off lies **RANFURLY**, the largest settlement on the Maniototo. It's a compact place enjoying a resurgence thanks to the popularity of the rail trail, and a rather desperate attempt to brand itself as New Zealand's **Rural Art Deco** centre (Ⓦwww.ruralartdeco.co.nz). In truth, there's only a handful of noteworthy buildings, but Ranfurly goes all out to make the best of what it has, particularly during the Rural Art Deco Weekend at the end of February. The **Art Deco Gallery**, 1 Charlemont St East (daily: Nov–April 10.30am–4.30pm; May–Oct 11am–4pm; $2 donation) contains all manner of Deco furnishings and houseware, but the star is the building itself, the 1948 Centennial Milk Bar. Opposite the visitor centre, the *Ranfurly Lion Hotel* and the Ranfurly Auto Repairs shop both exhibit a few Art Deco features, but elsewhere much is achieved with imaginative paint jobs and period signage.

In summer, anyone with a 4WD or high-clearance vehicle can set out from Ranfurly to explore part of the magnificent **Old Dunstan Road** (closed June–Sept), the original route to the Central Otago goldfields across the Rock and Pillar and Lammerlaw ranges. Ask for directions and current conditions.

Practicalities

The **visitor centre** is housed in the former train station on Charlemont Street East (Oct–May daily 9am–6pm; June–Sept Mon–Fri 10am–4pm; Ⓣ03/444 1005, Ⓦwww.maniototo.co.nz), which has a free audiovisual show on the region and pictorial displays tracing the history of the town and the Otago Central Railway. Ranfurly's range of **accommodation** is fairly limited but improving. **Eating** choices are even more restricted.

Accommodation

Komako 634 Waipiata-Naseby Rd, 3km south of Ranfurly Ⓣ03/444 9324, Ⓔgrant.heather@xtra.co.nz. Three gorgeous cabins right by the Rail Trail, surrounded by great views (plus blooming peonies Oct–Dec). ❼

Moyola 38 Charlemont St E Ⓣ03/444 9010 Ⓦwww.ruralartdeco.co.nz. For an extreme Deco experience, stay at this very comfortable self-serviced B&B jam-packed with assorted Deco furniture and fittings. ❺

Old Po Backpackers 11 Pery St Ⓣ03/444 9588, Ⓦwww.oldpobackpackers.co.nz. Central hostel with bargain accommodation and good facilities. Dorms $23, rooms ❷

Ranfurly Motels 1 Davis Ave, off Caulfield St Ⓣ0800/100 559 Ⓔranfurlymotels@xtra.co.nz. Quiet central motel units styled in Art Deco colours. ❹

Ranfurly Holiday Park Reade St Ⓣ0800/726387, Ⓦwww.ranfurlyholidaypark.co.nz. Central campsite with a range of facilities and accommodation. Camping $12, cabins ❶, motel units ❸

Eating and drinking

E-Central Café 14 Charlemont St E. Daytime café which does bikers' breakfasts, decent coffee and a range of light meals.

Ranfurly Lion Hotel 10 Charlemont St E. Good hotel restaurant in Art Deco surroundings. Expect lasagne ($20) steaks ($26) and fish and chips ($25).

Macraes Gold Mine, Middlemarch and south to Dunedin

At Kyeburn, 15km east of Ranfurly, the slow route to Dunedin (SH87) branches south off SH85 and twists through the eastern Maniototo, a barren yet scenic landscape squeezed between the towering Rock and Pillar Range and the Taieri River. Fifty kilometres south of Kyeburn you'll reach the tiny community of **Middlemarch**, the Friday- and Sunday-only terminus of the **Taieri Gorge Railway**, which makes a delightful two-hour run between here and Dunedin (see p.682 for details). Anyone planning to tackle the Otago Central Rail Trail from east to west should definitely consider starting by riding the railway either to Middlemarch or to **Pukerangi** (the weekday turn-around point), 18km to the south.

For useful visitor **information** on Middlemarch, check out Ⓦwww.middlemarch.co.nz. Most cyclists **stay** at *Blind Billy's Holiday Camp*, Mold St (Ⓣ03/464 3355, Ⓦwww.middlemarch-motels.co.nz; camping $11, dorms $22, on-site vans ❷, cabins ❷, s/c cabins ❸, motel units ❹), a campsite with cooking facilities in a converted railway carriage, a nice outdoor seating area and a wide range of cabins and motel units. Alternatively, try the comfortable *Middlemarch B&B*, Swansea Street/SH87 (Ⓣ03/464 3718, Ⓔlorna.williams@xtra.co.nz; ❹), with an indoor spa area and low-cost two-course evening meals on request.

Eating is limited to the daytime *Kissing Gate Café*, on SH85 at the southern end of town, weekend meals at the *Strath Taieri Hotel*, opposite the station on Snow Avenue, and takeaways.

The most renowned of Otago's operating gold mines, the huge opencast **Macraes Gold Mine**, lies on windswept hills between Ranfurly and Palmerston and can be visited on a two-hour **tour** (daily 10am & 2pm; $20; reservations essential on Ⓣ0800/465 386, Ⓦwww.oceanagoldtours.com), which also takes in a historic reserve and a fully operational stamper battery. Should you want to **eat or stay** in the area, try the historic *Stanley's Hotel* (Ⓣ03/465 2400, Ⓔstanleyshotel@xtra.co.nz; B&B ❹), a schist-stone construction with en-suite rooms, a restaurant and a garden bar. Rail-trail pick-ups and drop-offs are available.

Roxburgh and Lawrence

The fastest route from Alexandra to the coast is **SH8**, which follows the meandering course of the Clutha River, passing through rugged hill country between the Old Man and Lammerlaw ranges to the east, and the Knobby Blue Mountain range to the west. Along the way are a couple of mildly interesting gold towns, **Roxburgh** and **Lawrence**.

Roxburgh

Almost 30km south of Alexandra, a **viewpoint** overlooks the large, concrete **Roxburgh Dam** and the shimmering turquoise of Lake Roxburgh, which backs up for over 30km. Eight kilometres south of the dam, the bland former gold town of **ROXBURGH** sits hemmed in by vast orchards which yield bountiful crops of peaches, apricots, apples, raspberries and strawberries, all harvested by an annual influx of seasonal pickers. The season's surplus is sold from a phalanx of roadside stalls from early December through to May.

The central *Villa Rose Backpackers*, 79 Scotland St (Ⓣ03/446 8761, Ⓔinfo@villarose.co.nz; dorms $23, rooms ❷, studio ❸), a backpackers equipped with dorms, several doubles and new luxury studios, frequented by orchard workers; or *Lake Roxburgh Lodge*, SH8, 8km north (Ⓣ03/446 8220, Ⓦwww.lakeroxburghlodge.co.nz; ❹), which offers wonderful en-suite motel-style rooms and a very good licensed **restaurant**.

Lawrence

From Roxburgh, SH8 runs 32km south to **Raes Junction** (where SH90 spurs off southwest to Tapanui and Gore), and continues 26km to **LAWRENCE**, Otago's original gold town. It's hard to believe that this sleepy farming town, its population barely nudging 550, was once the scene of frenetic activity, as twelve thousand gold-seekers scrambled to try their luck in the gold-rich Gabriel's Gully. This short-lived boom (it was over in barely a year) is recalled in a smattering of Victorian buildings, hastily constructed in a variety of materials and styles. A few have now been converted into chi-chi **galleries** that provide some reason to linger.

The combined **visitor centre** and **Goldfields Museum** on Ross Place/SH8 (Oct–April Mon–Fri 9.30am–4.30pm, Sat & Sun 10am–4pm; May–Sept Mon–Fri 9.30am–3.30pm, Sat & Sun 11am–3pm; ⓣ03/485 9222, ⓦwww.lawrence.co.nz) brings something of those heady days to life through imaginative displays and sells gold pans for $7–12. From here, a 3.5-kilometre drive along Gabriel's Gully Road passes the **Pick and Shovel Monument** commemorating the pioneer miners, en route to **Gabriel's Gully Goldfield Park**, where a series of plaques explaining the old workings should take you an hour or so to explore. A climb up the steep rise of **Jacob's Ladder** gives a good view of the gully, long since filled with tailings that reach nearly 20m in depth. It is possible to visit Gabriel's Gully as part of a loop walk from town (8.5km loop; 2hr 30min) returning along a ridge.

After something to **eat** from one of the tearooms on Ross Place, or from the smart *Coffee Mine* café, at 26 Ross Place, you'll probably want to press on. If you decide **to stay**, try the fairly basic, creekside *Goldpark Motor Camp*, 1km south of the main road on Harrington Street (ⓣ03/485 9850, ⓔsouthernshearing@xtra.co.nz; camping $10, ❶). *The Ark*, 8 Harrington Place (ⓣ03/485 9328, ⓦwww.theark.co.nz; ❸) offers B&B in a fine old home with beautiful gardens.

Travel details

Buses

The following lists the direct scheduled bus services in summer and doesn't include the scores of tour buses which ply the Queenstown to Milford Sound route daily (see p.856 for details of these) or the buses from Glenorchy out to the tramping routes (see p.805). In winter services are cut back considerably.

Alexandra to: Dunedin (4 daily; 3hr); Lawrence (3 daily; 1hr 15min); Queenstown (3 daily; 1hr 30min); Ranfurly (daily except Sat; 1hr).

Arrowtown to: Queenstown (hourly; 30min).

Cromwell to: Alexandra (4 daily; 30min); Dunedin (4 daily; 3hr 40min); Lawrence (3 daily; 2hr); Queenstown (7–9 daily; 1hr); Wanaka (8–9 daily; 45–60min).

Glenorchy to: Queenstown (2–4 daily; 1hr).

Lawrence to: Alexandra (3 daily; 1hr 15min); Cromwell (3 daily; 2hr); Dunedin (3 daily; 1hr 20min).

Queenstown to: Alexandra (3 daily; 1hr 30min); Aoraki Mount Cook (2 daily; 4hr); Arrowtown (hourly; 30min); Christchurch (6 daily; 7hr–9hr); Cromwell (7–9 daily; 1hr); Dunedin (4 daily; 4–5hr); Franz Josef Glacier (2 daily; 7–8hr); Glenorchy (2–4 daily; 1hr); Greymouth (1 daily; 10hr); Kingston (3–4 daily; 1hr); Milford Sound (1 daily; 5hr 40min); Te Anau (3–4 daily; 2hr 15min); Wanaka (7–9 daily; 1hr 45min).

Wanaka to: Christchurch (6 daily; 7hr–9hr); Cromwell (8–9 daily; 45min–1hr); Dunedin (3 daily; 4hr–4hr 30min); Franz Josef Glacier (2 daily; 6–7hr); Queenstown (7–9 daily; 1hr 45min); Ranfurly (daily except Sat; 3hr).

Trains

Middlemarch to: Dunedin (summer Fri & Sun only 1 daily; 2hr 30min)

Pukerangi to: Dunedin (1 daily, 2hr).

Flights

Queenstown to: Auckland (6 daily; 1hr 45min); Christchurch (7 daily; 50min).

Wanaka to: Christchurch (1 daily; 1hr).

14

Fiordland

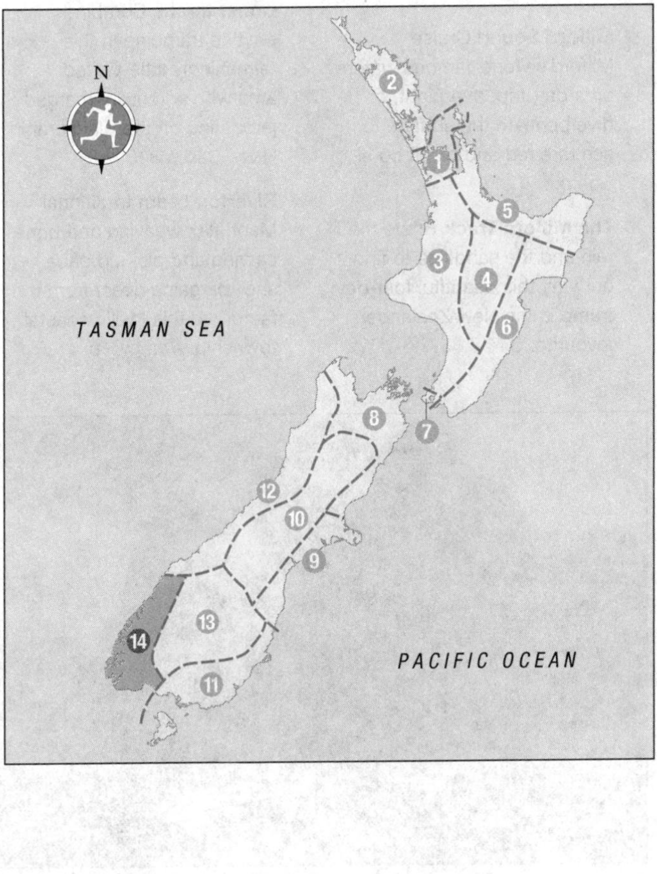
N
TASMAN SEA
PACIFIC OCEAN
1
2
3
4
5
6
7
8
9
10
11
12
13
14

CHAPTER 14

Highlights

* **Te Anau** Watch the inspirational film *Ata Whenua: Shadowlands*, shot from a helicopter above the region's landscapes, then book a heli-flight to see the bird's-eye views for yourself. See p.841

* **Milford Sound** Cruise Milford's world-famous waters on a day-trip, overnight, or dive beneath the surface to see rare red and black coral. See p.855

* **The Milford Track** Brave the rain and the sandflies to find out why this beautiful four-day tramp is the New Zealanders' favourite. See p.857

* **Doubtful Sound** Experience scenic grandeur and superb wildlife on a par with Milford Sound but without the bustle; even better when seen at sea level from a kayak. See p.864

* **Hump Ridge and South Coast tracks** Combine pristine tramping in this refreshingly little-visited area with adrenalin-charged jetboating on the Wairaurahiri River. See p.868

* **Riverton** Learn traditional Maori flax weaving and bone carving and pick up paua shell bargains direct from the factory at this idyllic coastal township. See p.870

▲ Kayaking Doubtful Sound

14

Fiordland

For all New Zealand's scenic grandeur, no other region can match the concentration of stupendous landscapes found in its southwestern corner. **Fiordland** is a place of superlatives, boasting New Zealand's two deepest lakes, its highest rainfall and some of the world's rarest birds. This hasn't gone unnoticed at the United Nations, which has gathered pretty much the whole area – along with the Mount Aspiring National Park and parts of south Westland and the Aoraki Mount Cook area – into the **Te Wahipounamu World Heritage Area**.

The **Fiordland National Park**, which incorporates almost the entire region, and thus most of the area covered in this chapter, is New Zealand's largest. It stretches from Martins Bay, once the site of New Zealand's remotest settlement, to the southern forests of Waitutu and Preservation Inlet, where early gold prospectors set up a couple of short-lived towns. Its 12,500 square kilometres embrace a raw and heroic landscape, with deep, icy and mountain-fringed lakes in the east and a western coastline of fifteen hairline fiords.

Maori legend tells how the **fiords** were formed at the hands of the great god Tu-to-Rakiwhanoa, while scientists point to a complex underlying geology, which evolved over the last 500 million years. When thick layers of seabed sediment were compressed and heated deep within the earth's crust, crystalline granite, gneiss and schist were formed. As the land and sea levels rose and fell, layers of softer sandstone and limestone were overlaid; during glacial periods, great ice sheets deepened the valleys and flattened their bases to create the classic U-shape, invaded by the sea lapping at their mouths.

After a few days in the inhospitable conditions created by Fiordland's copious rainfall and vicious **sandflies** (*namu*), you'll appreciate why there is little evidence of permanent Maori settlement in these parts, though they certainly spent summers hunting here and passed through in search of greenstone (*pounamu*). **Cook** was equally suspicious of Fiordland when, in 1770, he sailed up the coast on his first voyage to New Zealand: anchorages were hard to come by; the glowering sky put him off entering Dusky Sound; slight, shifting winds discouraged entry into what he dubbed Doubtful Harbour; and he missed Milford Sound altogether.

Paradoxically for a region that's now the preserve of hardy trampers and a few anglers, the southern fiords region was once the best-charted in the country. Cook returned in 1773, after four months battling the southern oceans, and spent five weeks in Dusky Sound. His midshipman, George Vancouver, returned in 1791, with the first bloodthirsty sealers and whalers hot on his heels. Over the mountains, **Europeans** seized, or paid a pittance for, land on the eastern shores of Lake Te Anau and Manapouri for the meagre grazing it offered, while

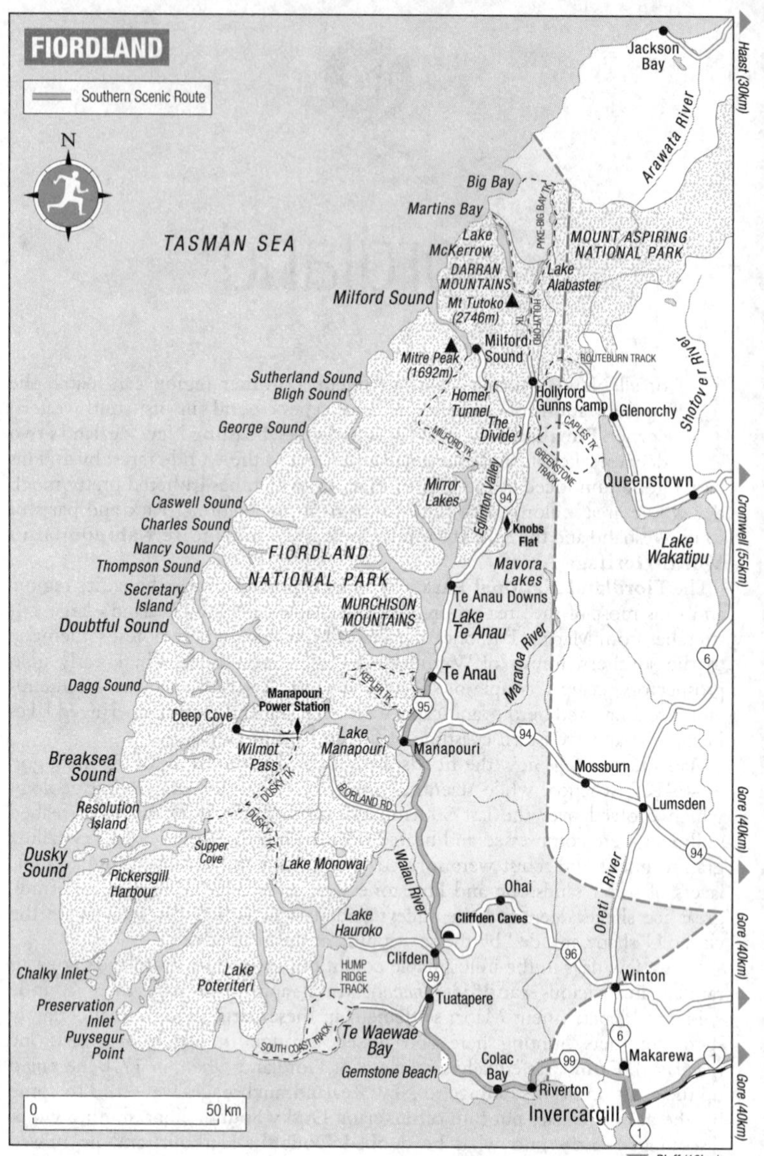

explorers headed for the interior, conferring their own names on the passes, waterfalls and valleys they came across – Donald Sutherland lent his name to New Zealand's highest waterfall and Quintin McKinnon scaled the Mackinnon Pass (but failed to persuade cartographers to spell his name correctly).

One persistent feature of Fiordland is the **rain**. Milford Sound is particularly favoured, being deluged with up to 7m of rainfall a year – the second-highest in the world (after the mountains of Tahiti). Fortunately the area's settlements are in a relative rain shadow and receive less than half the precipitation of the coast. Despite its frequent soakings, **Milford Sound** sees the greatest concentration of traveller activity. In fact, the Sound is particularly beautiful when it's raining, and ribbons of water plunge from hanging valleys directly into the fiords, where colonies of red and black coral grow and dolphins, fur seals and Fiordland crested penguins gambol. Many visitors on a flying visit from Queenstown see little else, but a greater sense of remoteness is gained by driving along the dramatically scenic **Milford Road** between the sound and the lakeside town of **Te Anau**. Better still, trudge here along the **Milford Track**, widely promoted as the "finest walk in the world", though others in the region – particularly the **Hollyford Track** and the **Kepler Track** – shouldn't be overlooked. A second lakeside town, **Manapouri**, is the springboard for trips to the West Arm hydroelectric power station, **Doubtful Sound** and the isolated fiords to the south. From Manapouri, the Southern Scenic Route winds through the western quarter of Southland through minor towns along the southwestern coast of the South Island.

Almost all **buses** in Fiordland ply the corridor from Queenstown through Te Anau to Milford Sound: most are tour buses (in various guises), stopping at scenic spots and regaling passengers with a jocular commentary, but others are scheduled services that disgorge trampers at the **trailheads**. Elsewhere, services are skeletal. The only **flights** you are likely to take are the scenic jaunts from Milford Sound to Te Anau or Queenstown, although others do exist.

Te Anau and around

Ringed by snowcapped peaks, the gateway town to Fiordland, **TE ANAU** (pronounced Teh AHN-ow), trickles along the shores of its eponymous lake, one of New Zealand's deepest and most beautiful. To the west, the lake's watery fingers claw deep into bush-cloaked mountains so remote that their most

Tu-to-Rakiwhanoa and Te Namu

Fiordland came into being when the great god **Tu-to-Rakiwhanoa** worked with his axe to carve the rough gashes of the southern fiords around Preservation Inlet and Dusky Sound, leaving Resolution and Secretary islands where his feet stood. His technique improved further north, where he formed the more sharply defined lines of Nancy Sound, Caswell Sound and Milford Sound (Piopiotahi), the acme of Tu's skill.

After creating this spectacular landscape, he was visited by Te-Hine-nui-to-po, the goddess of death, who feared that the vision created by Tu was so wonderful that people might wish to live in Piopiotahi for ever. To remind humans of their mortality, she freed *namu*, or **sandflies.** The place of this liberation, Te Namu-a-Te-Hine-nui-te-po, at the end of the Milford Track, is now known as Sandfly Point. And the pesky bugs have certainly had the desired effect. In 1773, when James Cook entered Dusky Sound, he was already familiar with the sandfly:

> **The most mischievous animal here is the small black sandfly which are exceedingly numerous and are so troublesome that they exceed everything of the kind I ever met with, wherever they light they cause swelling and such an intolerable itching that it is not possible to refrain from scratching and at last ends in ulcers like the small Pox. The almost continual rain may be reckoned another inconvenience attending this Bay.**

celebrated inhabitant, the takahe, was thought extinct for half a century. Civilization of sorts can be found on the lake's eastern side, home to a population of just 1500. The main way-station on the route to Milford Sound, Te Anau is an ideal base and recuperation spot for the numerous tramps, including several of the most famous and worthwhile in the country. Top of most people's list is the **Milford Track**, which is reached across the lake from here, as is the newer **Kepler Track**. To the north, the Milford Road passes The Divide, the western end of the Routeburn, Greenstone and Caples tracks (see p.808); beyond that is the Hollyford Valley and its tramp to the Tasman Sea, and at the southeastern end of the national park lies the new, privately run Hump Ridge Track.

Arrival, information and transport

Buses either drop off around town or stop on the town's main shopping and restaurant street, known as Town Centre. The best sources of information are the **i-SITE visitor centre**, at the junction of Town Centre and Lake Front Drive (daily 8.30am–5.30pm; ⓣ03/249 8900, ⓔfiordland-isite@realjourneys.co.nz), which shares space with the booking office for its owner, the area's largest tourism operator, Real Journeys, and DOC's **Fiordland National Park visitor centre**, 500m south along Lake Front Drive (daily: late Oct–late April 8.30am–6pm, rest of year 8.30am–4.30pm, ⓔfiordlandvc@doc.govt.nz). The latter contains a **Great Walks Booking Desk** (ⓣ03/249 8514, ⓔgreatwalksbooking@doc.govt.nz), as well as plenty of general information. From here, DOC run an excellent summer-visitor programme of hour-long evening talks (throughout Jan; $4) plus full-day, unhurried conservation-themed trips in the forests (mostly $60–90 but some as little as $10), all of which need to be booked in advance.

The **post office** and **banks** with ATMs are all found along Town Centre. While away on the tracks, trampers can usually **store gear** (free or for a small fee) at their accommodation, though it helps if you're staying there on your return. Tramping **gear rental** is available from several places, including Bev's Tramping Gear Hire, 16 Homer St (ⓣ03/249 7389, ⓦwww.bevs-hire.co.nz). Individual items are charged by the day (pack $7, sleeping bag $7 etc). The Great Walks Package Special ($120) contains everything you need – including food for up to four days – except boots.

Local transport

Getting around Te Anau is no problem: everywhere in town is easily walkable, and there's a plethora of transport to the various trailheads. **Bikes** can be rented from most backpackers and from Fiordland Mini Golf, Quadricycles & Bike Hire, 7 Mokonui St (ⓣ03/249 7211; $20 half-day, $25 per day). Scenic Shuttle (ⓣ0800/277 483) run to Manapouri in the morning, and Tracknet (ⓣ0800/483 2628, ⓦwww.tracknet.net) operate fairly frequent buses to Milford Sound, Queenstown and the Kepler and Routeburn trailheads. Taking an organized trip is generally cheaper, but you can rent a decent **car** from the unlikely sounding Rent-a-dent (ⓣ03/249 8576), at the Caltex station on Luxmore Drive.

Accommodation

Good motels string the length of Lake Front Drive and Quintin Drive, a block back. There are also a number of reasonable budget options and plenty of good B&Bs. At most motels and hotels, and some B&Bs, **rates** drop dramatically between June and August, and may be negotiable in the shoulder

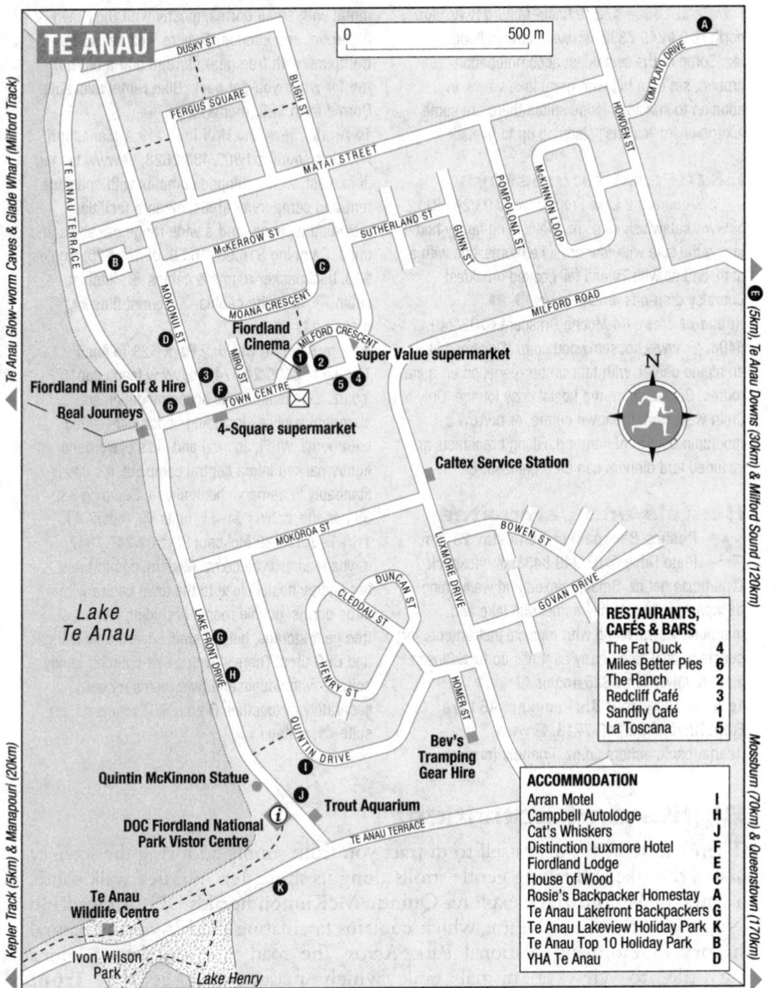

seasons (mid-April to May & Sept). We've listed central **camping** opportunities below, but many people head around 25km north to a couple of lakeside DOC campsites ($5) near Te Anau Downs.

Hotels and motels

Arran Motel 64 Quintin Drive ⓣ0800/666 911, ⓦwww.arranmotel.co.nz. Attractive en-suite rooms, some with cooking facilities and free Wi-Fi, plus courtesy car to and from the local transport options. Rates can vary, so it pays to check ahead to see what's on offer. ⑤

Campbell Autolodge 42 Lake Front Drive ⓣ0800/249 942, ⓦwww.cal.co.nz. Flower-bedecked place with lake views from all rooms, which all come with bath, shower and "mini kitchen" (hotplate, fridge and microwave), and free in-room broadband. ⑥

Distinction Luxmore Hotel Town Centre ⓣ0800/589 667, ⓦwww.luxmorehotel.co.nz. Large, central hotel with standard and (newer) superior doubles and twins with en suites, as well as a variety of eating options. Standard ⑦, deluxe ⑧

Fiordland Lodge 472 Te Anau–Milford Hwy, 5km north ⓣ 03/249 7832, ⓦ www.fiordlandlodge.co.nz. Some of the swankiest accommodation around, set on a hill with great lake views. In addition to spacious lodge suites there are some luxurious s/c "cabins" sleeping up to five. ⑨

B&Bs and homestays

Cat's Whiskers 2 Lake Front Drive ⓣ 03/249 8112, ⓦ www.catswhiskers.co.nz. Welcoming family home facing the lake with four en-suite rooms: one with a bath, and all with TV and full cooked breakfast. Courtesy drop-offs around town. ⑥–⑦

House of Wood 44 Moana Crescent ⓣ 03/249 8404, ⓦ www.houseofwood.co.nz. Designed like an alpine chalet, with four timber-panelled en-suite rooms. Guests share the hosts' cosy lounge. Only a 2min walk from the town centre, or borrow a mountain bike to get around. Filling breakfasts are included and dinners can be organized. ⑤

Hostels and campsites

Rosie's Backpacker Homestay 23 Tom Plato Drive ⓣ 03/249 8431, ⓔ backpack@paradise.net.nz. Small, relaxed and welcoming backpackers in a family home with lake and mountain views, along with musical instruments for guests to play. Book early as it fills up fast. Closed June & July. Dorms $25, rooms ②

Te Anau Lakefront Backpackers 48 Lake Front Drive ⓣ 03/249 7713, ⓦ www.teanaubackpackers.co.nz. Friendly former motel with small dorms, mostly with their own bathroom and kitchen. They're well set up for trampers, with free gear storage and a big hot tub for when you get back. Bike rental available. Dorms from $26, rooms ②

Te Anau Lakeview Holiday Park 1 Manapouri Rd, 1km south ⓣ 0800/483 2628, ⓦ www.teanau.info. Vast, well-equipped complex with spacious tent and campervan areas, modern facilities including a sauna, and a wide range of cabins and units. Camping $14.50–16.50, dorms $25, singles $30, backpacker rooms & cabins ②, kitchen cabin ③, en-suite cabins ④, tourist flats ④, motel units ⑤

Te Anau Top 10 Holiday Park 128 Te Anau Terrace ⓣ 0800/249 746, ⓦ www.teanautop10.co.nz. Excellent on-site accommodation and abundant facilities including underfloor-heated bathrooms, Wi-Fi, Jacuzzi and kid's playground, all tightly packed into a central campsite. It's understandably in demand: book ahead. Camping $32–38 per site, cabins ②–③, units ④, motels ⑤

YHA Te Anau 29 Mokonui St ⓣ 03/249 7847, ⓔ yha.teanau@yha.co.nz. Modern, comfortable two-storey hostel close to the town centre with large dorms, double rooms (including en suites), free gear storage, helpful staff, separate TV lounge and BBQ area. There's even a self-catering family cottage with double and twin rooms rented separately or together. Dorms $27, rooms ③, en suite ④, cottage ④

Sights and activities

There's little in Te Anau itself to distract you from simply admiring the scenery across the lake and taking gentle strolls along its shore. Ten minutes' walk south, a statue of Milford Track explorer Quintin McKinnon heralds DOC's Fiordland National Park visitors centre, which contains fascinating displays on the natural history of Fiordland National Park. Across the road you can drop $2 in a turnstile to view a dismal tank which masquerades as the **Trout Observatory**.

Nearby is DOC's **Te Anau Wildlife Centre** (unrestricted entry; $1 donation requested), where you can amble through the park-like setting and see injured or captive-bred native birds such as kakariki (parakeets), whio (blue duck), kea and kaka (indigenous parrots) and the celebrated takahe (see box, p.845).

Te Anau's main paying attraction is Real Journeys' **Te Anau Glow-worm Caves** (daily: Nov–March 2pm, 5.45pm, 7pm & 8.15pm; April–Sept 2pm, 7pm and some additional tours; around 2hr 15min; $56). The town's full Maori name, Te Ana-au, means "cave with a current of swirling water" and it was a search for the town's namesake which led to their rediscovery in 1948. It has been spruced up a little but remains a little old-fashioned in spirit, with a short underground boat ride, a glittering glow-worm grotto and a couple of splashing waterfalls.

Boats leave from the docks adjacent to the visitor centre and head to the western side of Lake Te Anau, where cave guides lead you underground in small groups on foot and by punt, spending thirty minutes in a 200-metre length of the Aurora cave system which tunnels under the Murchison Mountains.

Alternatives include a one-hour **jetboat ride** past *Lord of the Rings* locations on the placid Waiau River with Luxmore Jet ($85; ⓣ0800/253 826, ⓦwww.luxmorejet.co.nz), and **quad biking** with High Ride Four Wheeler Adventures (ⓣ03/249 8591, ⓦwww.highride.co.nz), who offer a three-hour ride ($145, including the shuttle from Te Anau) that takes in the high backcountry and includes some stunning views of lakes Manapouri and Te Anau. No prior experience is necessary. High Ride also have **horse-riding** ($80), again taking around three hours and including a shuttle from Te Anau.

Don't leave town without visiting the **Fiordland Cinema**, The Lane (ⓣ03/249 8812, ⓦwww.fiordlandcinema.co.nz), which presents the 32-minute *Ata Whenua: Shadowlands* (5–10 screenings daily 9am–10pm; $10). Filmed mostly from a helicopter, it shows Fiordland at its majestic best with wonderful cinematography, an original soundtrack and thankfully, no ponderous voiceover. You'll want to go straight out for a heli-flight (bookable at the cinema). Screenings are interspersed with a good selection of first-run movies. Armchairs are big and comfy, and you can take espresso or wine from the bar in with you.

Day-walks from Te Anau

If you're kicking around Te Anau wondering what to do before your big tramp, consider some **short walks** as training. Those not doing the Milford Track,

The takahe

For half a century the flightless blue-green **takahe** (*Notornis mantelli*) was thought to be extinct. These plump, turkey-like birds – close relatives of the ubiquitous pukeko – were once common throughout New Zealand. By the time Maori arrived, however, their territory had become restricted to the southern extremities of the South Island. When Europeans came, only a few were spotted by early settlers in Fiordland. No sightings were recorded after 1898; the few trampers and ornithologists who claimed to have seen its tracks or heard its call in remote Fiordland valleys were dismissed as cranks.

One keen birder, **Geoffrey Orbell**, pieced together the sketchy evidence and concentrated his search on the 500 square kilometres of the **Murchison Mountains**, a virtual island surrounded on three sides by the western arms of Lake Te Anau and on the fourth by the Main Divide. In 1948, he was rewarded with the first takahe sighting in fifty years. However, the few remaining birds seemed doomed: deer were merrily chomping their way through the grasses on which the takahe relied. Culling averted the immediate crisis and, despite periodic setbacks from harsh winters, management programmes have brought takahe numbers to about 250.

Meanwhile, studies at the **Burwood Bush** rearing facility (closed to the public), in the Red Tussock Conservation Area east of Te Anau, have shown that takahe often lay three eggs but seldom manage to raise more than one chick. DOC officers now enter the Murchison Mountains each November to manipulate the **egg quota** so that each pair has only one viable egg to hatch. Any "surplus" eggs are removed to Burwood Bush, where rearing techniques pioneered here are employed to raise takahe for release back into the wild. Taped takahe noises encourage the chicks to hatch; then, to prevent them imprinting on their carers, the chicks are fed using **hand puppets** designed to look like adult takahe.

Afraid of having all their eggs in one basket, DOC has established several populations on predator-free **sanctuary islands** – Maud Island in the Marlborough Sounds, Mana Island and Kapiti Island northwest of Wellington, and Tiritiri Matangi in Auckland's Hauraki Gulf – where the birds appear to be breeding well.

should consider joining one of the one-day guided walks at it southern end, though you can find better walks along the Milford Road (see box, p.851).

DOC visitor centre to Control Gates (4km one way; 50min; flat). Easy lakeside walk past the Te Anau Wildlife Centre to the point where the Waiau River leaves Lake Te Anau for Lake Manapouri. The Control Gates mark the start of the Kepler Track (see p.847).

Control Gates to Brod Bay (5km one way; 1hr 30min; gently undulating). The easy first section of the Kepler Track goes to Dock Bay (30min) where there's good swimming, and continues through mountain and silver beech forest past some limestone bluffs to the campsite at Brod Bay.

Control Gates to Rainbow Reach (9.5km one way; 2hr 30min–3hr 30min; mostly flat). Easy walking following the course of the Waiau River through red and mountain beech. By using the Tracknet buses to the Control Gates and back from Rainbow Reach (see "Kepler Track" account) you can spin this walk out over 5–7hr, perhaps going 3km beyond Rainbow Reach to a wetland viewing platform.

Milford Track Real Journeys (☎0800/656 501) and Trips 'n' Tramps (☎03/249 7081) jointly run easy day-walks (Nov to mid-April daily 9.15am; $165) beside the Clinton River at the start of the Milford Track. Trips involve a bus to Te Anau Downs, boat to Glade Wharf, 5–6hr hiking and relaxing including lunch at Clinton Hut and return.

Lake cruises and kayaking

A highlight of visiting Te Anau is **getting out on the lake**. If you're going tramping, this can be accomplished en route to the start of the Kepler or Milford tracks (see p.847 & p.857). The operators who provide trailhead transport also offer a number of other trips.

Cruise Te Anau ☎03/249 7593, Ⓦwww.cruiseteanau.co.nz. Scenic cruises aboard a restored kauri motor launch (summer daily 10am, 1pm & 5pm; 2hr 30min; $67) plus overnight cruises including dinner and breakfast (4pm–9.30am; $225). They also offer a guided day-walk up Mount Luxmore ($130), as well as summer track transport to Brod Bay at the start of the Kepler ($20 one way), and off-season transport to the start and end of the Milford (April–Nov only; $150).

Fiordland Wilderness Experiences ☎0800/200 434, Ⓦwww.fiordlandseakayak.co.nz. Rent a kayak to paddle on Lake Te Anau or Manapouri for $55 a day (no solo rentals).

Flights

Air Fiordland ☎03/249 7505, Ⓦwww.airfiordland.com. This company's wheeled planes are mostly used on flights to Milford Sound, the best deal involving a flight over the Milford Track to Milford Sound, a cruise and a bus back (7hr 30min; $380).

Southern Lakes Helicopters Lake Front Drive ☎0508/249 7167, Ⓦwww.southernlakeshelicopters.co.nz. Helicopter flights from a waterside helipad start at $170 for 25min and range up to a couple of hours including flights to Milford, Doubtful and Dusky sounds with landings in a narrow canyon or on snow high in the hills. They also do various flight/walk/cruise combinations and offer drop-offs for the tracks.

Wings & Water Lake Front Drive ☎03/249 7405, Ⓔwingsandwater@teanau.co.nz. Seaplane flights that are ideal for an aerial view of southern Fiordland. Local loops (10min; $75), Kepler Track overflights (20min; $175), Doubtful Sound overflights (40min; $265) and Milford Sound overflights (1hr; $395) are among the options. One worthwhile combo involves jetboating down the Waiau River to Lake Manapouri and then flying back to Te Anau via the hidden lakes (1hr; $205).

Eating and drinking

Eating options are constantly improving in Te Anau, over twenty informal restaurants and cafés in the small town. **Self-caterers** have two well-stocked supermarkets to choose from in the centre, as well as several bakeries. Given that most visitors are embarking on or coming off tramps, **drinking** is fairly low-key, and entertainment is mostly BYO.

The Fat Duck 124 Town Centre. Sophisticated bar/restaurant, great for breakfast and brunch, as well as meals like warm duck salad with raspberry dressing or twice-cooked pork belly (all $25–35), a wonderfully creamy seafood chowder ($13.50), and desserts such as pear, walnut and blue cheese pizza ($10.50). There's a top-notch selection of New Zealand beers and wines. Closed Mon & Tues in winter.

Miles Better Pies Corner of Milford Rd & Town Centre. Easily the best coffee in town (South Island-roasted Pomeroy's), along with gourmet pies and pasties to eat in or take to the lakefront, plus winter soups and fresh sushi. Open 6am–4.30pm daily.

The Ranch 111 Town Centre. Rambunctious locals' haunt with cheap, plentiful Kiwi grub (including an old-fashioned Sunday roast for $12.50) and drinks deals, plus lively DJ-run entertainment most nights and sometimes a band at weekends in summer.

Redcliff Café 12 Mokonui St ⓣ03/249 7431. Cosy timber cottage, good for a sundowner or late-night tipple, but primarily a casual restaurant serving a range of modern Kiwi dishes like Fiordland wild venison ($33), pan-seared chorizo with linguini and pumpkin-seed pesto ($24.50) and chocolate and hazelnut crème brûlée ($9.50). There's also a garden bar and occasional live bands. Daily from 4pm.

Sandfly Café 9 The Lane. Hip but laid-back daytime café with polished concrete floors and tables fashioned from tree branches, serving warming soups such as spicy Thai pumpkin ($8.50), and home-baked slices, sprout-stuffed bagels and cakes. Also Internet access and Wi-Fi. Closed Mon in winter.

La Toscana 108 Town Centre ⓣ03/249 7756. Rosé-pink-painted restaurant lined with wine bottles, serving Italian classics like pasta with vodka-flamed pancetta and good pizzas. Licensed & BYO wine, plus takeaway.

The Kepler Track

The **Kepler Track** (45–70km; 3–4 days), finished in 1988, was intended to take some of the load off the Milford and Routeburn tracks and its success in meeting this aim has, ironically, now made it equally popular. Tracing a wide loop through the Kepler Mountains on the western side of Lake Te Anau, the track takes in one full day of exposed subalpine ridge walking and some lovely virgin beech forest, and has the added advantage of being easily accessible (on foot if you are keen) from Te Anau. The track is typically walked anticlockwise, getting most of the climbing out of the way early, and ranges from as little as 45km – if you use boats and buses to the max – to 70km for the full Te Anau–Te Anau walk.

It is well graded and maintained throughout, to the extent that you barely need to look where you are treading for long sections. Still, its length and the long haul up to Luxmore Hut make this a reasonably strenuous tramp, and sections can be closed after snowfalls. DOC's *Kepler Track Independent Tramping* leaflet (free) is adequate, but for more detailed information consult the 1:60,000 *Kepler Track Trackmap* ($15).

Access and accommodation

The Kepler Track is one of New Zealand's Great Walks and through the summer season (late Oct to late April) its three main **huts** ($40 per night) – Luxmore (55 bunks), Iris Burn (50 bunks) and Moturau (40 bunks) – all come with a warden, gas rings and flush toilets. During this time it's essential to book in advance either online at ⓦwww.doc.govt.nz or through the Great Walks booking desks in Te Anau, Glenorchy or Queenstown. In winter, these huts lose their warden and their gas rings, go back to pit toilets, and revert to serviced hut status ($10). Trampers are discouraged from using the simple and very small Shallow Bay Hut, just off the track beside Lake Manapouri.

Camping ($10) is permitted at only two places, Brod Bay and Iris Burn, making for one very short and two very long days – assuming you walk the track anticlockwise – but getting the bulk of the climbing over with on the first long day.

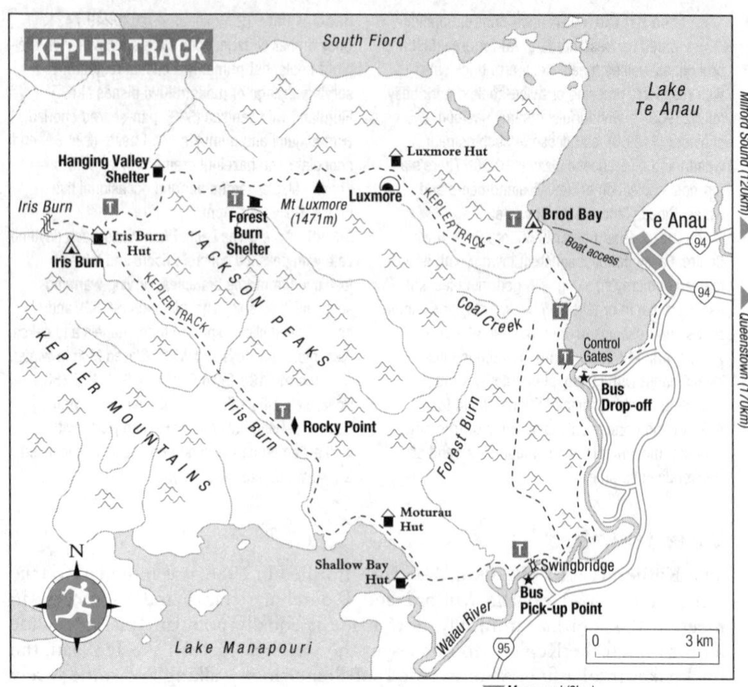

Trailhead transport

The Kepler Track starts at the Control Gates, 5km southwest of Te Anau. It is a pleasant enough walk around the southern end of the lake, but most people get the Tracknet **bus** (☎0800/483 262, Ⓦwww.tracknet.net; Oct– April only; $6), which picks up at accommodation around town at around 8.30am and 9.30am and drops off at the Control Gates. On the return leg, most trampers stop 11km short of the Control Gates at the swingbridge over the Waiau's Rainbow Reach. Tracknet pick up at Rainbow Reach at 10am, 3pm and 5pm and charge $9 back to Te Anau.

You can skip another 5km of lakeside walking (and make a relaxed start) by **boating** across Lake Te Anau from Te Anau wharf to Brod Bay with Kepler Water Taxi (8.30am & 9.30am or by arrangement; $20; ☎03/249 8364).

The route

If you're setting out from Te Anau, head south along Lake Front Drive, then right, following the lakeshore and taking the first right to the Control Gates.

Control Gates to Brod Bay (5.6km; 1hr–1hr 30min; flat). The track follows the lakeshore around Dock Bay and over Coal Creek, passing through predominantly beech and kamahi forests but with a fine stand of tree ferns. Brod Bay has good swimming off a sandy beach and makes a lovely place to camp.

Brod Bay to Luxmore Hut (8.2km; 3–4hr; 880m ascent). Non-campers must press on from Brod Bay, following a signpost midway along the beach. The path climbs fairly steeply; after a couple of hours you sidle below limestone bluffs, from where it is almost another hour to the bushline and fine views over Te Anau and Manapouri lakes and the surrounding mountains. The hut is almost one hour from the bushline. A 10min side trip from Luxmore Hut visits the short and fairly dull Luxmore Cave.

Luxmore Hut to Iris Burn Hut (14.6km; 5–6hr; 300m ascent, 900m descent). An exposed, high-level section where any hint of bad weather should be treated seriously. The track climbs to just below the summit of Mount Luxmore (from where you can hike up to the 1471m peak), then descends to Forest Burn Shelter before following a ridge to Hanging Valley Shelter and turning sharply south to trace another open ridge towards Iris Burn – reached by zigzagging west into the forested Hanging Valley then following the stream to the hut and campsite in a large tussock clearing. It's worth doing the easy walk to the Iris Burn waterfall (40min return).

Iris Burn Hut to Moturau Hut (16.2km; 4–6hr; 300m descent). The track from the Iris Burn Hut descends steadily through beech forest and riverside clearings. About halfway you pass toilets at Rocky Point, then enter a short gorge before hugging the river for several magical kilometres. Just before Iris Burn spills into Lake Manapouri, the track swings east and skirts Shallow Bay to the pleasant lakeside Moturau Hut. If you're doing the track in three days, press on to the bus pick-up at Rainbow Reach.

Moturau Hut to Rainbow Reach (6km; 1hr 30min; flat). Easy walk through gentle beech forest.

Rainbow Reach to the Control Gates (9.5km; 2–3hr; negligible ascent). Another easy walk for those who persevere with the final stretch, through mature lowland beech forest with opportunities for fishing and swimming. The river flows swiftly, so pick your spot carefully.

Milford Sound and around

Milford Sound is the most northerly and most celebrated of Fiordland's fifteen fiords, its vertical sides towering 1200m above the sea and waterfalls plunging from hanging valleys. While many of the other fiords approach Milford for their spectacular **beauty**, none come close for **accessibility**. Before the road was pushed through in 1952, visitors had to arrive by boat or walk the much-lauded **Milford Track** to reach the head of the fiord, but the opening of the Homer Tunnel paved the way for the phalanxes of buses that disgorge tourists onto fiord cruises. The tiny airport hardly seems to rest as planes buzz in and out, while the crowds – all day in the summer and around the middle of the day in spring and winter – can certainly detract from the grandeur of the spot. But don't let that put you off. Even torrential rain adds to the atmosphere of this magical place, as an ethereal mist descends, periodically lifting to reveal the waterfalls at their thunderous best.

Like the other sounds, Milford is a drowned glacial valley rather than a river valley, which is what technically makes it a fiord. Maori know it as **Piopiotahi** ("the single thrush"), and attribute its creation to the god Tu-to-Rakiwhanoa, who was called away before he could carve a route into the interior, leaving high rock walls. These precipitous routes are now known as the Homer and Mackinnon passes, but were probably first used by Maori who came here to collect *pounamu*. The first European known to have sailed into Piopiotahi was sealer John Grono who, in 1823, named the fiord Milford Haven after his home port in south Wales. The main river flowing into the Welsh Milford was the Cleddau, so naturally the river at the head of the fiord took that name too.

The earliest settler was Scot **Donald Sutherland**, who arrived with his dog, John O'Groat, in 1877; he promptly set a series of thatched huts beside the freshwater basin of what he called the "City of Milford", funding his explorations by guiding the small number of visitors who had heard tell of the scenic wonder hereabouts.

The predations of today's influx of visitors and the operation of a small fishing fleet have necessitated strategies to preserve the **fragile ecosystem**. Like all fiords, Milford Sound has an entrance sill at its mouth, in this case only 70m below the surface – by comparison, the deepest point is almost 450m. This

▲ Lady Bowen Falls, Milford Sound

effectively cuts off much of the natural recirculation of water and hinders the mixing of sea water and the vast quantities of fresh water that pour into the fiord. The less-dense tannin-stained fresh surface layer (up to 10m deep) builds up, further diminishing the penetration of light, which is already reduced by the all-day shadow cast by the fiord walls. The result is a relatively barren inter-tidal zone that protects a narrow – but wonderfully rich and extremely fragile – band of light-shy red and black **corals**; these normally grow only at much greater depths, but thrive here in the dark conditions. Unfortunately, Milford's fishing fleet use crayfish pots, which tend to shear off anything that grows on the fiord's walls. A marine reserve has been set up along the northeastern shore, where all such activity is prohibited, but really this is far too small and conservation groups are campaigning for its extension.

The road to Milford Sound

The 120-kilometre **Milford Road** (SH94), from Te Anau to Milford Sound, has to be one of the world's finest, though this hasn't stopped folk from hatching outlandish plans to circumvent it (including a proposed tunnel from Glenorchy to The Divide under discussion at the time of writing). As things stand now, this two-hour drive can easily take a day if you grab every photo opportunity, and longer still if you explore some of the excellent hiking trails outlined on the *Milford Road* leaflet, available free from the i-SITE visitor centre in Te Anau. Anywhere else the initial drive beside Lake Te Anau would be considered obscenely scenic, but it is nothing compared to the Eglinton Valley, where the road penetrates into steeper, bush-clad mountains and winds through a subalpine wonderland to the bare rock walls of the seemingly impassable head of the Hollyford River. The Homer Tunnel cuts through to the steep Cleddau Valley, then straight down to Milford Sound.

Maori parties must have long used this route on their way to seek *pounamu* at Anita Bay on Milford Sound, but no road existed until two hundred unemployment-relief workers with shovels and wheelbarrows were put on the job in 1929. The greatest challenge was to puncture the headwall of the Hollyford Valley: work on the 1200-metre-long **Homer Tunnel** began in 1935, but was badly planned from the start. Working at a one-in-ten downhill gradient, the builders soon hit water and were forced to pump out continuously; a pilot tunnel allowing the water to drain westwards was finished in 1948. After a concerted push, the road was completed in 1953, and officially inaugurated the following year, opening up Milford Sound to road traffic for the first time. Each April, uninhibited locals compete in a race through the tunnel completely naked (apart from running shoes).

Campers will want to spend a night in one of the dozen simple DOC **campsites** ($5) along the way, almost all with giardia-free stream water, long-drop toilets and fireplaces. Two are between Te Anau and Te Anau Downs, and the remaining ten pack into the next 50km, either on the grassy flats of the Eglinton Valley or in the bush nearby. Mackay Creek, Totara Creek and East Branch Eglinton, all around 50km north of Te Anau, are particularly good.

Milford Road safety

The subalpine section of the Milford Road is one of the world's most **avalanche-prone.** Since the last death on the road, in 1984, a sophisticated monitoring system has been put in place and explosives are dropped from helicopters to loosen dangerous accumulations of snow while the road is closed. This mostly happens between May and November, when motorists are required to carry chains (available from service stations in Te Anau for around $30); you'll be stopped at the small kiosk five minutes' drive out of Te Anau to make sure that you have them and know how to fit them – and sent back to Te Anau if you don't. It's not uncommon for people to be stuck in Milford overnight or longer if the road does close. Always check weather forecasts with the DOC office in Te Anau before you set out; weather reports are also regularly updated on ⓦwww.milfordroad.co.nz.

Whatever the season, drivers should bear in mind that there is heavy bus traffic, which tends to be Milford-bound from around 11am to noon and Te Anau-bound between 3 and 5pm. Apart from the store in the Hollyford Valley, 8km off your route, there is nowhere to buy food until you reach Milford, so go prepared. There is a pump in Milford, but it often runs out of petrol, so it's essential to fill up in Te Anau before you leave.

Driving to Milford Sound

Heading north from Te Anau, there's little reason to stop in the first 30km to the harbour at **Te Anau Downs**, where boats leave for the start of the Milford Track. It's home to the *Fiordland National Park Lodge* (ⓣ03/249 781, ⓦwww.teanau-milfordsoundco.nz; dorms $25, rooms & units ⑤), whose comfortable rooms, many with astounding lake views, are open year-round, although the backpackers section closes between May and September. There's a good restaurant on site, serving dinner (mains $28–30) in high season; it too often closes in the winter months.

The road then cuts east away from the lake, before veering north into the **Eglinton Valley** through occasional stands of silver, red and mountain beech interspersed with open flats of red tussock grass. Surprisingly in a national park, these plains are grazed, an anomaly resulting from longstanding leases which had to be honoured. The mountains that hem in the valley are, when the weather is calm, picturesquely reflected in the roadside **Mirror Lakes**, 56km north of Te Anau. There's basic but good self-catering **accommodation** in the valley at *Knobs Flat* (ⓣ03/249 9122, ⓦwww.knobsflat.co.nz; studio ④), with breakfast hampers available for $12.50. Half-day **guided walks** ($50) take you through the valley. Around 20km north, the *Cascade* campsite marks the start of the **Lake Gunn Nature Walk**.

As you get nearer to the head of the valley, the road steepens to **The Divide**, 84km north of Te Anau, at 532m the lowest east–west crossing of the Southern Alps. This is the start/finish of the Greenstone, Caples and Routeburn tracks, the last of which can be followed to Key Summit (see p.808). The car park has toilets and a walkers' shelter with a noticeboard advertising the times of passing buses, although it is far better for hikers to prearrange a pick-up.

Pressing on a couple of kilometres towards Milford, you descend into the valley of the Hollyford River, best seen from a popular viewpoint just before the Hollyford Road shoots off north. The Milford Road continues west towards the Hollyford's source, the huge glacial cirque of the Gertrude Valley.

A kilometre further on, the entrance to the **Homer Tunnel** is home to many curious **kea** (it's important not to feed them as it's resulted in fatalities). Despite recent improvements the tunnel remains rough-hewn, steep, narrow and dark. During peak periods in the summer months traffic lights dictate one-way traffic

Hikes from the Milford Road

Old-timers grumble about tourists wasting their time, effort and money on prize tramps like the Milford and the Routeburn when there are so many excellent walks easily accessible from the Milford Road. There are many challenging hikes off this road, but we've restricted ourselves to commonly tackled **day-walks**. For tougher stuff, the DOC office in Te Anau can suggest various alternatives.

Lake Gunn Nature Walk (3km loop; 45min; negligible ascent). Wheelchair-accessible nature walk with explanation of the area's forest and birdlife. Starts 74km north of Te Anau.

The Divide to Key Summit (5km return; 2–3hr; 400m ascent). Great panoramic views over three valley systems are the reward for this tramp along the western portion of the Routeburn Track. Starts 84km north of Te Anau.

Lake Marian (5km return; 2–3hr; 400m ascent). Excellent walk which ascends to a beautiful alpine lake, passing some wonderful cataracts (30–40min return) where boardwalks are cantilevered out from the rock wall. Starts 1km along Lower Hollyford Road, 88km north of Te Anau.

(expect a wait of up to 15min), but for the rest of the time you'll need to look out for oncoming vehicles.

The tunnel emerges at the top of a long switchback down to the Cleddau River. Almost 10km on from the tunnel all buses stop at **The Chasm**, while their passengers stroll (15min return) to the near-vertical rapids where the Cleddau has scoured out a deep, narrow channel. Tantalizing glimpses through the foliage reveal sculpted rocks hollowed out by churning stones or tortured into free-standing ribs that resemble flying buttresses. From here it is another 8km to Milford Sound.

The Hollyford Valley

The Milford Road drops down from The Divide into the **Hollyford Valley**, which runs 80km from its headwaters in the Darran Mountains north to the Tasman Sea at Martins Bay. The 16km gravel Lower Hollyford Road provides access to the Hollyford Track and the Lake Marian walk, plus a couple of other diversions.

The only habitation is 8km along the valley road at Hollyford *Gunns Camp* (no phone; Ⓔ gunnscamp@ruralinzone.net; camping & vans $10 per person, bunks $20, twin & double cabins ❶), a huddle of simple old 1930s cabins which served as married families' quarters for the long-suffering road-builders. Cabins generally have a double room and a four-berth bunk room, linked by a kitchen/lounge area equipped with a coal-burning range, and hot showers. Trampers' supplies (along with postcards, good books, maps, some rare bowenite greenstone pendants and souvenirs) are sold in the **shop** (daily 8.30am–8pm). There's also a **museum** (shop hours; $1, free to guests) containing photos, pioneer artefacts and some interesting paraphernalia relating to the one-time community at Martins Bay, the devastating floods that periodically afflict the region and the building of the Milford Road and the Homer Tunnel.

The road runs 8km beyond the camp to the Road End – the beginning of the Hollyford Track. It is also the start of a shorter walk to **Humboldt Falls** (20–30min return), a three-step cascade tumbling some 200m.

Milford Sound

For all the superlatives feted on Milford Sound, the smattering of buildings that comprise the small **settlement** are hardly in keeping with their magnificent surroundings, and the best of the fiord can only really be seen from the water. Nevertheless, the settlement looks out over the edge of a basin where the Cleddau and Arthur rivers surge into the fiord, and the whole scene is dominated by the triangular glaciated pinnacle of **Mitre Peak** (1694m), named for its resemblance to a bishop's mitre when viewed from this angle.

Arrival and getting around

The most worthwhile way to get to Milford Sound, and the one which conveys the greatest sense of place, is to **walk** the Milford Track (see p.857), though **drivers** and **cyclists** do get the freedom to stop, sightsee and camp at the numerous basic campsites along the dramatic road from Te Anau (see p.851). Failing either of those, you can fly, hop on a bus, or do a combination of both, often with a cruise on the fiord thrown in (see box on p.856 for a rundown).

There isn't much to the settlement at Milford Sound. The airstrip, fishing harbour, cruise terminal, post office, pub and café are scattered along the shore. Though they are not more than a few hundred metres apart, a sporadic free **shuttle bus** connects them all.

The Hollyford Track

The **Hollyford Track** (56 km; 3–4 days one way; DOC leaflet) is long but mostly flat, and open year round, though it can be muddy after rain. Running from the end of the Hollyford Valley road to Martins Bay, the track follows Fiordland's longest valley but suffers from being essentially a one-way tramp, requiring four days' backtracking – unless you're flash enough to fly out from the airstrip at Martins Bay or tough enough to continue around a long, difficult and remote loop known as the **Pyke–Big Bay Route** (9–10 days total; consult DOC's *Pyke–Big Bay Route* leaflet for details). The joy of the Hollyford is not in the sense of achievement that comes from scaling alpine passes, but in the appreciation of the dramatic mountain scenery and the kahikatea, rimu and matai **bush** with an understorey of wineberry, fuchsia and ferns. At Martins Bay, Long Reef has a resident **fur seal** colony, and from September to December you might spot rare Fiordland crested **penguins** (tawaki) nesting among the scrub and rocks.

Trampers who hate carrying a big pack and prefer more comfortable lodgings and having hearty meals cooked for them should consider a **guided walk** with Hollyford Track (Ⓣ0800/832 226, Ⓦwww.hollyfordtrack.com): small groups are led by knowledgeable guides, and nights are spent at the relatively luxurious *Martins Bay Lodge* and the *Pyke River Lodge* (3 days plus fly-out $1655).

Accommodation and access

The six DOC **huts** (mostly 12 bunks; $10) are each equipped with bunks, mattresses, water and toilets and do not need to be booked, though hut tickets or an annual hut pass should be bought in advance.

Buses on the Te Anau–Milford run will drop off at Marian Corner, where the Hollyford and Milford roads part company, and 16km from Road End, but it is best to go with Tracknet (Ⓣ0800/483 262) who run from Te Anau right to Road End (Nov–April; $40).

Hollyford Track also work in with local air companies to offer **flights** (which must be pre-booked) between Milford Sound and Martins Bay. Since most people choose to fly out from Martins Bay ($435 per plane for 1–4 people), it often works out cheaper to take a "backload" trip from Milford Sound to Martins Bay (around $110) and then walk the track in reverse.

Finally, you can avoid most of the long day's walk beside the attractive but samey Lake McKerrow with Hollyford Track's **jetboat service** between Martins Bay and the head of Lake McKerrow (Nov–April only; $85).

The route

Road End to Hidden Falls Hut (9km; 2–3hr; negligible ascent). The track follows a disused section of road which soon crumbles into a track with some riverbank walking to the Hidden Falls Hut.

Hidden Falls Hut to Alabaster Hut (10km; 3–4hr; 100m ascent). Keen walkers may want to push on from Hidden Falls Hut through ribbonwood and beech to Little Homer Saddle and past Little Homer Falls.

Alabaster Hut to Demon Trail Hut (15km; 3–4hr; negligible ascent). Leaving Alabaster Hut, you soon pass a side track to the nicely sited McKerrow Island Hut, before continuing beside Lake Alabaster to Demon Trail Hut.

Demon Trail Hut to Hokuri Hut (10km; 5–6hr; 100m ascent). Probably the toughest on the walk, following the shore of Lake McKerrow on rough ground with some tricky stream crossings, to the modern twelve-bunk Hokuri Hut.

Hokuri Hut to Martins Bay Hut (13km; 4–5hr; negligible ascent). Passing the scant remains of Jamestown, a cattle-ranching settlement that prospered briefly in the 1870s, and the small airstrip served by Hollyford Track's flights, you'll stumble across some of the dozen dwellings that comprise Martins Bay; whitebaiters and hunters stay here occasionally, although there are no permant residents. Continuing parallel to Martins Bay, and occasionally glimpsing the Hollyford River through wind-shorn trees, you reach the Martins Bay Hut.

Accommodation and eating and drinking

The prominent *Mitre Peak Lodge* is only open to Milford Track guided walkers. The only other **accommodation**, overnight cruises on the sound aside, is at the excellent *Milford Sound Lodge* (ⓣ03/249 8071, ⓦwww.milfordlodge.com; camping $15-18, dorms $28, rooms ❷), a well-run backpackers with spacious dorms, twins and doubles (with shared bathrooms), a comfortable lounge with Internet access, a piano, and a small pricey shop. It is almost 2km back from the wharf (linked by a courtesy bus).

The settlement's sole **place to eat** is the *Blue Duck Café & Bar* (daily 8.30am–late in summer, 9am–late in winter; ⓣ03/249 7982, ⓔblueduckcafe@xtra.co.nz) and attached **pub**, where you can dine on good sandwiches or full meals (most under $28) while watching the weather sweeping along the fiord. The duo also informally double as the **information office**.

Around Milford

You're pretty much surrounded by water here, and should waste little time getting out on it. However, if tales of his pioneering days have inspired you, pay homage at **Donald Sutherland's grave**, hidden among the staff accommodation behind the pub. Otherwise, there's a five-minute stroll up to a **lookout** behind *Mitre Peak Lodge*, or the **Piopiotahi Foreshore Walk**, which leads from the car park to the settlement along the edge of the fiord (5–10min; flat).

About a third of the way along the fiord is the **Milford Deep Underwater Observatory** (ⓣ03/249 9442, ⓦwww.milforddeep.co.nz), accessible on several of the major cruises (about a 20min stop; $24–28 more than the equivalent non-observatory cruise), such as Red Boat Cruises (ⓣ0800/264 536, ⓦwww.redboats.co.nz). The observatory consists of a floating platform moored to a sheer rock wall in Harrison Cove, part of the marine reserve. A spiral staircase takes you nine metres down through the relatively lifeless freshwater surface layer to a circular gallery where windows look out into the briny heart of the fiord. Sharks and seals have been known to swim by, but most of the action happens immediately outside in window-box "gardens", specially grown from locally gathered **coral** and plant species. Lights pick out colourful fish, tubeworms, sea fans, huge starfish and rare red and black coral. Unless you're an experienced diver this is the only chance you'll get to see these corals, which elsewhere in the world grow only at depths greater than forty metres.

Day cruises

The dramatic view from the shore of Milford Sound pales beside the incomparable spectacle from the water, with waterfalls plunging hundreds of metres into the fiord. It's difficult to grasp the heroic scale of the place, unless your visit coincides with that of one of the great cruise liners – even these formidable vessels are totally dwarfed by the cascades and cliff faces.

The majority of cruises explore the full 22km of Milford Sound, all calling at waterfalls, a seal colony and overhanging rock faces; at **Fairy Falls**, boats nose up to the base of the fall, while suitably attired passengers are encouraged to edge out onto the bowsprit and collect a cup of water. Longer trips sometimes anchor in **Anita Bay** (Te-Wahi-Takiwai, "the place of Takiwai"), a former greenstone-gathering place at the fiord's mouth, but still sheltered from the wrath of the Tasman Sea.

The simplest option is one of the twenty-odd two- to four-hour **day cruises** (best booked a few days in advance in summer) either on one of the large, fast and comfortable boats or one of the more intimate small boats. Trips cost from $60 to around $83 depending on the duration and size of the boat,

Trips to Milford Sound

As **Milford Sound** is on most visitors' itineraries, there's no shortage of operators willing to get you there from almost anywhere in the country. **From Queenstown**, a stream of luxury **buses** make the tiring four- to five-hour drive via Te Anau to Milford, complete with frequent photo-opportunity stops and a relentless commentary, decanting their passengers for a cruise on the fiord then running them back again – a hurried twelve hours in all. This so-called coach-cruise-coach format is too much for many people who opt for a fly-cruise-coach trip (which may mean you don't go if the weather is bad) or the coach-cruise-fly variation (which guarantees you get there, though if the weather comes in you may need to coach back).

Bus trips **from Te Anau** involve the middle (and most interesting) section of Queenstown-based trips and are appreciably shorter, generally taking a leisurely eight hours. Most tours also include a **cruise** on the sound once you get there – see p.855 for a rundown of the various vessels that ply its waters.

From Te Anau

The cheapest trips are those which don't include cruises – good value if you're going kayaking: try track-transport specialists Tracknet (Oct–April; 3 daily; ⓣ03/249 7777 ⓦwww.tracknet.net), who will get you there and back for $84, although you'll have to put up with detours to the trailheads. The big boys, such as Real Journeys (ⓣ0800/656 501), InterCity (ⓣ03/379 9020) and Great Sights (ⓣ0800/744 487), all run luxury **bus and cruise** packages from around $135, though there are small reductions for backpackers and substantial standby **discounts** outside the peak season.

The **most interesting** possibilities include full-day trips with Fiordland Wilderness Experiences (see p.846), which cost $130 round-trip from Te Anau including kayaking from October to May; or year-round with Trips 'n' Tramps (ⓣ03/249 7081, ⓦwww.milfordtourswalks.co.nz), whose nature guide-led trips ($140) concentrate on relaxed short bushwalks along the way before joining one of the Sound cruises.

From Queenstown

If you don't have the time to stay in Te Anau and visit Milford from there, you'll have to opt for a **coach-cruise-coach** day-trip from Queenstown, typically starting at 7am and returning just before 8pm. Of the numerous companies offering this, the best value is probably the backpacker-oriented BBQ Bus (ⓣ03/442 1045, ⓦwww.milford.net.nz; $169, $20 backpacker discount), which runs full-day trips with stops for short bushwalks and a BBQ in the Hollyford Valley.

More upmarket tours using air-conditioned vehicles, complete with multilingual commentary or interpretation material, are offered by several companies, including Real Journeys (ⓣ0800/656 503; $215), whose unusual wedge-profiled coaches give the best all-round views.

Many visitors shy away from such a long day and opt instead for a more expensive package involving the forty-minute **flight** to Milford's small airfield, a **cruise** and a **return flight**: Air Fiordland (ⓣ0800/103 404, ⓦwww.airfiordland.com) charge around $375. A good compromise, giving you a chance to see the scenery from the road in one direction, is a **fly-cruise-coach** combo. Most of the bigger bus and flight companies offer these including Air Fiordland, who charge $380 for the fly-cruise-coach or $510 to coach in and fly out, reflecting the greater demand for flights back from Milford.

Travellers locked into the Kiwi Experience circuit have to pay extra to do the Milford Sound leg; if you can get a group of four or five together, you can get here as cheaply, and with greater flexibility, by renting a car from Queenstown.

and there's little difference between them; operators include Mitre Peak Cruises (Ⓣ03/249 8110, Ⓦwww.mitrepeak.com), Real Journeys (Ⓣ0800/656 501, Ⓦwww.realjourneys.co.nz) and Red Boat Cruises (Ⓣ03/441 1137, Ⓦwww.redboats.co.nz).

Overnight cruises

Only Real Journeys run **overnight trips** on Milford Sound. Three of the vessels used for day cruises are equipped with beds, and each offers a slightly different experience, though all involve a leisurely cruise around, a chance to go kayaking, good meals and a night spent at anchor in some sheltered cove. The backpacker-orientated 61-berth *Milford Wanderer* (Oct–April daily 4.30pm–9.30am; Oct & late April $168, Nov to mid-April $210) is a motor-driven replica of a sailing scow, complete with cosmetic sails. On-board accommodation is somewhat institutional, with cramped four-bunk rooms equipped with sheets, duvets and towels, but a hearty three-course evening meal is served (drinks extra).

The more luxurious sixty-berth *Milford Mariner* (Sept–May daily 4.30pm–9am; Oct & late April $293, Nov to mid-April $390) has very comfortable private cabins with en suites and serves a higher class of meal; while their much smaller twelve-berth *Friendship* (Nov–March daily 4.30pm–9am; $210) is considerably more intimate with accommodation in six-bunked shared cabins: a very traditional nautical experience.

Kayaking and scuba-diving

The elemental nature of Milford Sound can best be appreciated without the throb of an engine, and **kayaking** here is sublime. If you'd rather go below surface (and are PADI or SSI certified), join a fascinating **scuba-diving** trip. The tannin-stained freshwater surface layer darkens the water quickly, making the flora and fauna think it's deeper than it really is. Consequently, black coral (white but with a black skeleton), brachiopods (ancient shellfish), purple and white nudribranchs, scarlet wrasse and telescope fish are all visible at surprisingly modest depths.

Fiordland Wilderness Experiences Ⓣ0800/200 434, Ⓦwww.fiordlandseakayak.co.nz. Ecologically oriented 4–5hr guided trips ($100 from Milford, $130 from Te Anau).

Rosco's Milford Sound Sea Kayaks Ⓣ03/249 8500, Ⓦwww.kayakmilford.co.nz. Extensive range of Milford Sound-based kayaking trips with expert guides, including a 7am Sunriser (3hr; $105, $135 from Te Anau), a 3.30pm Twilighter (4hr 30min; $149), a paddle and stroll along the Milford Track (4hr; $69) and various combos. Trips are mostly mid-Oct to mid-April, though the Sunriser runs all year.

Tawaki Dive Ⓣ03/249 9006, Ⓦwww.tawakidive.co.nz. Two guided dives cost $169 from Te Anau or $139 from Milford plus $99 for gear hire.

The Milford Track

More than any other Great Walk, the **Milford Track** has become a Kiwi icon and unlike other major tramps, where foreigners predominate, New Zealanders are in the majority here.

Its exalted reputation is partly accidental and partly historical. It seems likely that southern **Maori** paced the Arthur and Clinton valleys in search of *pounamu*, but there is little direct evidence. The first **Europeans** to explore this section of Fiordland were Scotsmen Donald Sutherland and John Mackay who, in 1880, blazed a trail up the Arthur Valley from Milford Sound. The story goes that while working their way up the valley they came upon the magnificent Mackay Falls and tossed a coin to decide who would name it, on

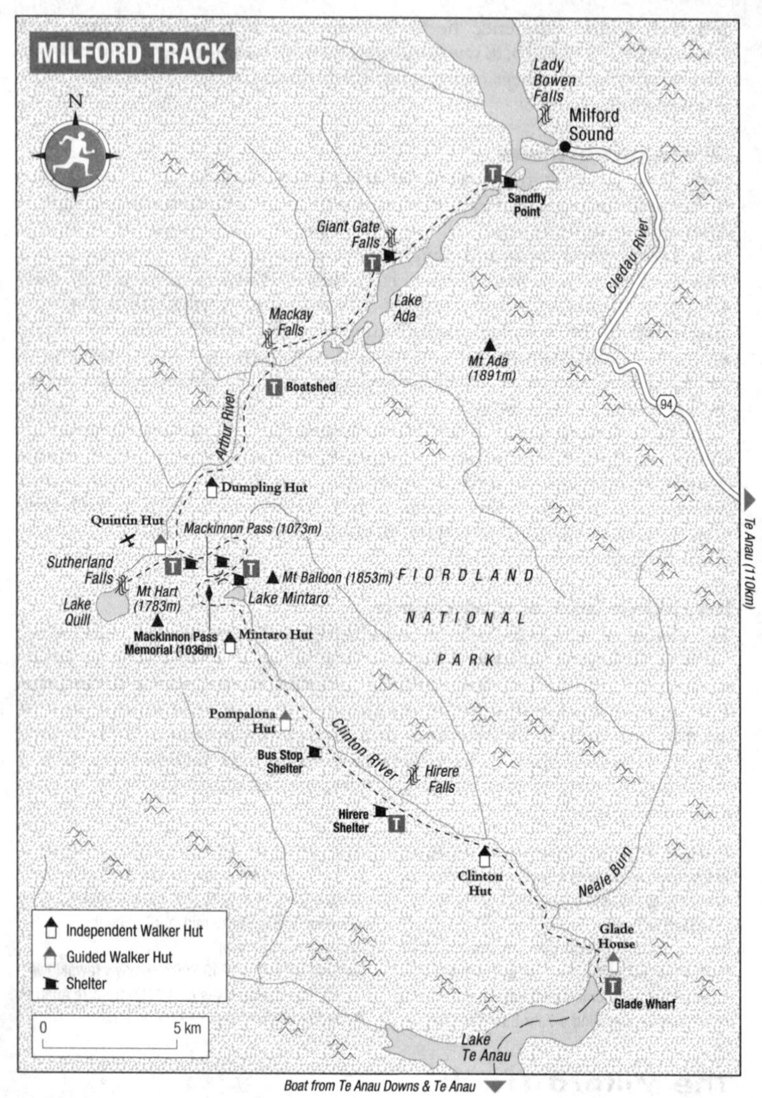

the understanding that the loser would name the next waterfall. Mackay won the toss but rued his good fortune when, days later, they stumbled across the much more famous and lofty Sutherland Falls. They may well have climbed the adjacent Mackinnon Pass, but the honour of naming it went to **Quintin McKinnon** who, with his companion Ernest Mitchell, reached it in 1888 after having been commissioned by the Otago Chief Surveyor, C. W. Adams, to cut a path up the Clinton Valley.

The route was finally pushed through in mid-October 1888 and the first **tourists** came through the next year, guided by McKinnon. The greatest fillip came in 1908 when a writer submitted her account of the Milford Track to the editor of London's *Spectator*. She had declared it "A Notable Walk" but, in a fit of editorial hyperbole, the editor retitled the piece "The Finest Walk in the World". From 1903 until 1966 the government held a monopoly on the track, allowing only guided walkers; the huts were supplied by a team of packhorses, which weren't finally retired until 1969.

Wider **public access** was only achieved after the Otago Tramping Club challenged the government's policy by tramping the Milford in 1964. Huts were built in 1966 and the first independent parties came through later that year.

Practicalities

There's no doubt that the Milford Track (54km; 4 days) is a wonderful route through some of Fiordland's finest scenery, but many trampers disparage it as over-regimented, expensive and not especially varied, while other complaints focus on the huts, which are badly spaced and lurk below the tree line among the sandflies. While these criticisms aren't unfounded – the tramp costs around $260 in hut and transport **fees** alone – the track is extremely well managed and maintained, the huts are clean and unobtrusive, and because everyone's going in the same direction you can go all day without seeing a soul. The Milford is also tougher than many people expect, packing the only hard climb and a dash for the boat at Milford Sound into the last two days. DOC's *Milford Track Independent Tramping* **leaflet** (free) is adequate for route-finding, though the 1:70,000 *Milford Track Trackmap* ($15) provides much more information.

Booking and accommodation

As with the Kepler and Routeburn tracks, **independent walkers** tackling the Milford Track during the late October to late April tramping season are subject to a rigid system of advance-booking **accommodation passes** for the three special category huts. You can only walk the track from south to north, spending the first night at Clinton Hut, the second at Mintaro Hut and the third at Dumpling Hut. No backtracking or second nights are allowed and there is strictly **no camping**. Numbers are limited to forty per day, so you'll need to book as far ahead as possible; a couple of months if you are adaptable, six months if you need a specific departure date or are part of a large group. This does have the huge advantage that you are guaranteed a bed.

Huts all have wardens and are equipped with flush toilets, running (but not drinking) water, heaters and gas rings, but not pans and plates; the **cost** is $120 for the three nights, and family discounts of twenty percent apply throughout the season. **Bookings** are taken for the following season from July 1 and can be made online at Ⓦwww.doc.govt.nz, or through the Great Walks Booking Desk, DOC (PO Box 29, Te Anau Ⓣ03/249 8514, Ⓔgreatwalksbooking@doc.govt.nz); pick up your accommodation passes from Te Anau before 11am on the day of departure. If the track is closed due to bad weather or track conditions full refunds are made, but new bookings can only be taken if there is space.

Outside the season the huts revert to serviced hut status ($10). They are unstaffed with no heating, clothes-drying or cooking facilities; bookings are not required and annual hut passes are valid. However, due to the presence of avalanche zones along the track, anyone walking out of season should check conditions with DOC before setting out, and fill out an intentions form with itinerary details.

Trailhead transport

Both ends of the Milford Track can only be realistically approached **by boat**, and arrangements must be made at the same time as accommodation passes are issued. Independent walkers need to catch the Tracknet bus (30min; $19) from Te Anau to the harbour at Te Anau Downs, 30km north of Te Anau, then the Real Journeys launch across Lake Te Anau to Glade Wharf (1hr; $59). There are early departures but since the first day's walk is very easy, it makes sense to make a late start using the 1.15pm bus and the 2pm launch.

At the Milford end of the track, catch either the 2pm or the 3.15pm launch from the aptly named Sandfly Point (Nov–April; $28.20) for the journey to Milford Sound (20min). Tracknet **buses** back to Te Anau can be picked up at 9.30am, 2.30pm and 5pm (3hr; $42).

Guided walks

For many years, the only way to walk the Milford Track was on a **guided walk**. Some would argue that this is still the best approach, with just your personal effects to carry and comfortable beds in clean, plain huts which aren't exactly luxurious, but do boast hot showers, duvets on the bunks, three-course dinners with wine and cooked breakfasts. Staff prepare the huts, cook the meals, make up the lunches and tidy up after you, but there's a price to pay for all this pampering. The **Milford Track Guided Walk** (Nov–April daily departures; ⓣ0800/659 255, ⓦwww.ultimatehikes.co.nz) is a four-night, five-day affair and costs $1850 ($1690 in Nov & April). For that you get a pre-track briefing in Queenstown, transport from there to the trailhead, accommodation and food on the track, a night at the *Mitre Peak Lodge*, a Milford Sound cruise and a return bus ride to Queenstown. Accommodation on the walk is in shared bunkrooms but for $2040 to $2200 you can upgrade to a private en-suite room, plus a $350 single supplement. The same company runs a variety of other guided walks including the Routeburn Track.

Anyone wanting a taste of the track without having to walk more than a couple of kilometres can join a Milford Track day-walk from Te Anau.

The route

The track starts at the head of Lake Te Anau and follows the Clinton River into the heart of the mountains, climbing over the spectacular Mackinnon Pass before tracing the Arthur River to Milford Sound.

Glade Wharf to Clinton Hut (5km; 1–2hr; 50m ascent). The first day is a doddle. It starts along a 2km 4WD track which serves Glade House (guided walkers only). The path then crosses a long swing-bridge to the right bank of the gentle, meandering Clinton River; keen anglers can spend an hour or two fishing for trout in the deep pools. The track runs through dense beech forest, only occasionally giving glimpses of the mountains ahead beyond Clinton Hut.

Clinton Hut to Mintaro Hut (16.5km; 4–6hr; 350m ascent). The track follows the true right bank of the Clinton River to its source, Lake Mintaro, right by the Mintaro Hut. Again this is easy going and, by the time you reach a short side track to Hidden Lake, Mackinnon Pass should be visible ahead. The track steepens a little to Bus Stop Shelter, then flattens out to Pompolona Hut (guided). From here it's a further hour to Mintaro Hut where, if it looks like it will be a good sunset, it pays to drop your pack and head up Mackinnon Pass.

Mintaro Hut to Dumpling Hut (14km; 5–6hr; 550m ascent, 1030m descent). The walk so far does little to prepare you for the third day. Though the surface of the broad path is firm and well graded, less experienced bushwalkers will find the haul up to Mackinnon Pass (1hr 30min–2hr) very strenuous. Long breath-catching pauses provide an opportunity to admire the wonderful alpine scenery, notably the headwall of the Clinton Valley, a sheer glacial cirque of grey granite. As the bush drops away behind you, the slope eases to the saddle at Mackinnon Pass, a great place to eat lunch, though you'll have the company of kea and the incessant buzzing of pleasure flights from Milford. A memorial to McKinnon and Mitchell marks the low-point of the saddle, from where the path turns east and climbs to a day shelter (with toilets and, in summer, a gas ring) just below the dramatic form of Mount

Balloon. From here it's all downhill, and steeply too, initially skirting the flank of Mount Balloon then following the path beside the picturesque Roaring Burn and down to the Arthur River. The confluence is marked by Quintin Hut (guided), which was originally built by the Union Steamship Company as an overnight shelter for sightseers from Milford visiting the Sutherland Falls. Though it remains a private hut, toilets and shelter are provided for independent walkers – who mostly dump their packs for the walk to the base of the 560m Sutherland Falls (4km return; 1hr–1hr 30min; 50m ascent), the highest in New Zealand. Dumpling Hut is another hour's walk from Quintin Hut.

Dumpling Hut to Sandfly Point (18km; 5–6hr; 125m descent). You're in for an early start and a steady walk to meet your launch or kayak at 2 or 3.15pm. After rain this can be a magnificent walk, the valley walls streaming with waterfalls and the Arthur River in spate. The track follows the tumbling river for a couple of hours to the Boatshed (toilets), before crossing the Arthur River on a swingbridge and cutting inland to the magnificent MacKay Falls. More a steep cascade than a waterfall, they are much smaller than the Sutherland Falls but equally impressive, particularly after rain. Don't miss Bell Rock, a water-hollowed boulder that you can crawl inside. The track subsequently follows Lake Ada, created by a landslip 900 years ago, and named by Sutherland after his Scottish girlfriend. A small lunch shelter midway along its shore heralds Giant Gate Falls, which are best viewed from the swingbridge that crosses the river at the foot of the falls. From here it is roughly an hour and a half to the shelter at Sandfly Point.

Manapouri, Doubtful Sound and the southern fiords

New Zealand has no shortage of beautiful lakes, but even among them, Lake Manapouri shines, its long, indented shoreline contorted into three distinct arms and clad with thick bushland tangled with ferns. The lake sits at 178m and has a vast catchment area, guzzling all the water that flows down the Upper Waiau River from Lake Te Anau and unwittingly creating a massive hydroelectric generating capacity – something which almost led to its downfall.

The one good thing to come from the hydroelectric project has been the opening up of **Doubtful Sound**, following the construction of the Wilmot Pass supply road. What was previously the preserve of the odd yacht and a few deerstalkers and trampers is now accessible to anyone prepared to take a boat across Lake Manapouri and a drive over the Wilmot Pass. Costs are unavoidably high and you need to be self-sufficient (no burger joints or corner shops here), but any inconvenience is easily outweighed by glorious isolation and pristine beauty. Wildlife is a major attraction, not least the resident pod of sixty-odd bottlenose dolphins, who frequently come to play around ships' bows and cavort near kayakers. Fur seals slather the outer islands, Fiordland crested penguins come to breed here in October and November, and the bush, which comes right down to the water's edge, is alive with kaka, kiwi and other rare bird species.

Cook spotted Doubtful Sound in 1770 but didn't enter as he was "doubtful" of his ability to sail out again in the face of winds buffeted by the steep-walled fiord. The breeze was more favourable for the joint leaders of a Spanish expedition, Malaspina and Bauza, who in February 1793 sailed in and named Febrero Point, Malaspina Reach and Bauza Island.

In fact, Cook seemed more interested in **Dusky Sound**, 40km south, where he spent five weeks on his second voyage in 1773, while his crew recovered from an arduous crossing of the Southern Ocean. On Astronomer's Point nearby, it is still possible to see where Cook's astronomer had trees felled so he could get an accurate fix on the stars; not far from here is the site where 1790s

Electricity, aluminium and brickbats

Lake Manapouri's **hydroelectric** potential had long been recognized, but nothing was done until the 1950s. Consolidated Zinc Pty of Australia wanted to smelt their Queensland bauxite into **aluminium** – a tremendously power-hungry process – as cheaply as possible, and alighted upon **Lake Manapouri**. They approached the New Zealand government, who agreed to build a power station on the lake, at taxpayers' expense, while Rio Tinto's subsidiary Comalco built a smelter at Tiwai Point, near Bluff, 170km to the southeast.

The scheme entailed blocking the lake's natural outlet into the Lower Waiau River and chiselling out a vast powerhouse 200m underground beside Lake Manapouri's West Arm, where the flow would be diverted down a 10km tailrace tunnel to Deep Cove on Doubtful Sound. By the time the fledgling **environmental movement** had rallied its supporters, the scheme was well under way, but the government underestimated the anger that would be unleashed by its secondary plan to boost water storage and power production by raising the water level in the lake by more than 8m. The threat to the natural beauty of the lake sparked **nationwide protests**, though the 265,000-signature petition prepared by the "Save Manapouri Campaign" failed to change the government's mind. It was only after the 1972 elections, when Labour unseated the National Party, that the policy was changed and the lake saved. The full saga is recounted in Neville Peat's *Manapouri Saved* (see "Books" in Contexts, p.920).

The **Manapouri Underground Power Station** took eight years to build. Completed in 1971, it remains one of the most ambitious projects ever carried out in New Zealand. Eighty percent of its output goes straight to the **smelter** – which consumes around fifteen percent of all the electricity used in the country, and it is widely perceived to be an unnecessary drain on the country's resources. Because of the unexpectedly high friction in the original tailrace tunnel the power station had always run below 85 percent capacity and to boost power production a second parallel tailrace tunnel was built in the late 1990s. Power companies are much more sensitive now, and the project was completed without major protest.

castaways built the first European-style house and boat in New Zealand. Marooned by the fiord's waters, Pigeon Island shelters the ruins of a house built by Richard Henry, who battled from 1894 to 1908 to save endangered native birds from introduced stoats and rats.

Manapouri

The scattered community of **MANAPOURI**, 20km south of Te Anau, wraps prettily around the shores of the lake of the same name which, in the 1960s, became a cause célèbre for conservationists (see box, above). Its contentious power station can be visited on day-trips.

Arrival and information

To get to Manapouri without your own transport, hop on the Te Anau–Invercargill Scenic Shuttle (ⓣ03/249 7654, ⓦwww.scenicshuttle.co.nz), which leaves Te Anau at 7.30am and returns from Manapouri to Te Anau mid-afternoon. Real Journeys buses connecting with boats to West Arm and Doubtful Sound may also take extras, but only if their cruise passengers don't fill the bus.

The road from Te Anau reaches Manapouri as Cathedral Drive and then becomes Waiau Street, passing almost everything of interest on the way to Pearl Harbour and the office of Real Journeys (daily: Nov–Feb 7.30am–8pm; March–Oct 8am–5.30pm; ⓣ0800/656 502, ⓦwww.realjourneys.co.nz), the closest thing the village has to an information centre, and the jumping-off point for lake cruises. The sole shop and the post office both occupy the same building as the *Cathedral Café* on Cathedral Drive – find one and you've found the lot.

Accommodation and eating

Though most people prefer to base themselves in Te Anau, Manapouri does offer a reasonable selection of **places to stay**. **Eating** is more limited, with only three choices. Far and away the best is the relocated weatherboard church of *Café 23*, 23 Waiau Street, which does great breakfasts from 7am, lunches, loads of home-made baked goods for mid-morning or afternoon snacks, and will stay open for dinner (meals all under $20) if you ring ahead. Otherwise try the *Cathedral Café*, Cathedral Drive, which serves light meals ($10–21) until around 6.30pm in summer, or venture to the *Lakeview Café*, 68 Cathedral Drive, at the *Manapouri Lakeview Motor Inn*, for slightly pricier bar meals until around 9pm.

The Cottage Waiau St ⓣ03/249 6838, ⓦwww.thecottagefiordland.co.nz. Attractive en suites, both with decks, in a cutesy house with a cottage garden close to the wharf. Continental breakfast is included, cooked is $10 extra. ❺

Freestone Backpackers SH99, 3km east of Manapouri ⓣ03/249 6893, ⓔfreestone@xtra.co.nz. Attractive backpackers in a series of comfy wooden chalets, each with great mountain and lake views from the veranda. All chalets come with one double bunk and three singles, plus a pot-belly stove and basic cooking facilities. Dorms $23, rooms ❷

Manapouri Lakeview Motor Park 50 Cathedral Drive, 1km from the wharf ⓣ03/249 6624, ⓔfjordland@xtra.co.nz. Fully equipped motor park with sauna, kids' play area and excellent vistas. Camping $12, cabins ❶, kitchen cabin ❷, motel units ❸

Possum Lodge 13 Murrell Ave ⓣ03/249 6623, ⓔpossumlodge@xtra.co.nz. Appealingly old-fashioned, peaceful and well-maintained campsite and hostel located right where the Waiau River meets the lake. Tent and powered sites $12–13, dorms $23, rooms & cabins ❷, motel units ❹

Around town

The several dozen houses that constitute Manapouri cluster at the outlet of the Waiau River, which the hydroelectric shenanigans have turned into a narrow arm of the lake now known as Pearl Harbour.

Apart from cruises and kayak trips, the only thing to do in Manapouri is to saunter along some of the **walking trails** detailed in the DOC's *Manapouri Tracks* leaflet (from the DOC in Te Anau and some local accommodation), such as the **Pearl Harbour to Fraser's Beach** trail (45min), which follows an easy track through lakeshore beech forest with fantails and silvereye flitting about the thin understorey. For all the other tracks, you'll need to row across the Waiau River in a boat rented from Adventure Kayak & Cruise, 33 Waiau St, next to the Mobil station (daily 8am–6pm; ⓣ03/249 6626, ⓦwww.fiordlandadventure.co.nz). Boats cost from $10 a day and you pay an extra charge to stay on the other side overnight, either camping or in one of the two DOC huts (each $5).

The most frequently walked route is the **Circle Track** (3hr loop; 7km; 330m ascent), which contours west around the lake before turning southeast to climb the ridge up to a point with stupendous views over the lake, then heads north back to the start.

The lake: cruises and kayaking

Most of the lake cruises are operated by Real Journeys (see p.862), who are the only operator to run trips across Lake Manapouri to the impressive, if controversial, **Manapouri Underground Power Station** (Oct–April 12.30pm daily; $61 from Manapouri, $80 from Te Anau). After crossing the lake, a bus takes you down a narrow, 2km-long tunnel to a viewing platform in the Machine Hall. All you can see are the exposed sections of seven turbines, but there's an interesting model of the whole system and some panels assaulting you with statistics before you're whisked back to the bus for the return to the surface. In addition to these three- to four-hour trips, Real Journey's Doubtful Sound day cruises include a visit to the power station.

For greater independence, you'll need **kayak rental**: Adventure Kayak & Cruise (see p.863) rent reasonable-quality single and double sea kayaks (1 day $45, 3 days $115); and Te Anau-based Fiordland Wilderness Experiences (see p.846), rent out better boats for a fraction more.

Doubtful Sound and the southern fiords

To fully appreciate the beauty and sense the isolation of the **southern fiords**, you really need to spend a few days among them, travelling by boat or kayak. If time is limited, plump for a full-day or overnight trip to **Doubtful Sound**; with more time to spare, spending a few days weaving between these mystical waterways is an unforgettable experience.

Real Journeys (Ⓣ0800/656 501, Ⓦwww.realjourneys.co.nz) run two trips to Doubtful Sound, the cheapest being the full-day **Wilderness Cruise** (1–2 daily; $230 from Manapouri, $264 from Te Anau, $312 from Queenstown; lunch $14.50 to $23 extra or bring your own), which includes a boat trip across Lake Manapouri and a bus ride for the 20km ride over Wilmot Pass – completely unconnected to any other road – to Deep Cove. Here you board a three-hour cruise out to the mouth of the fiord, where fur seals loll on the rocks, and into serene Hall Arm, where bottlenose dolphins often congregate. Most (but not all) trips then visit the power station before boating you back across the lake.

Spectacular though the day cruise is, it's no substitute for the **overnight cruise** on the *Fiordland Navigator* (Oct–April daily at 12.30pm, beginning to mid-May daily at noon; quad-share $335, twin-share $565, single $989), a comfortable modern cruiser designed to look like a traditional sailing scow. The trip doesn't visit the power station but you're away from Manapouri for a full 24 hours, time enough to immerse yourself in this extraordinary landscape by joining a nature walk, kayaking or even swimming. Food and accommodation are excellent and there are savings of around 20 percent in October and mid-April to mid-May, and a ten percent YHA discount throughout the summer. Transfers from Te Anau and Queenstown cost around $20 and $40 more respectively.

For a more in-depth encounter with the fiords, book up to several months in advance for one of the superb **multi-day trips** organized by Fiordland Ecology Holidays (see p.66). A similar ethical vein flavours the energetic **kayaking trips** with Fiordland Wilderness Experiences (Ⓣ0800/200 434, Ⓦwww.fiordlandseakayak.co.nz), who run popular two-day trips ($315) and longer explorations in remoter areas. From May to September, the *Milford Wanderer* also runs some outstanding multi-day trips – see p.66.

Other than overnight cruises and kayaking trips, the only way to **stay** by the Sound is at the isolated *Deep Cove Hostel*, Deep Cove, Doubtful Sound (Ⓣ03/216 1340, Ⓦwww.deepcoveoutdooredu.org.nz). Transport here is limited and it's only open mid-Dec to mid-Feb, but rental dinghies and appealing local walks let you explore the Sound at your own pace. Two- and four-bed bunkrooms come with mattresses, all eating and cooking utensils and good hot showers, but the nearest shop is at Manapouri, so bring a sleeping bag, food and everything else you'll need. Access is with Real Journeys, who offer a package ($285) including two nights at the hostel, transport and a Doubtful Sound cruise.

The Southern Scenic Route

Most visitors to Te Anau and Manapouri retrace their steps to Queenstown, missing out on the beautiful fringe country, where the fertile sheep paddocks of Southland butt up against the remote country of Fiordland National Park. The minor towns of the region are linked by the understated **Southern Scenic Route** (Ⓦwww.southernscenicroute.co.nz), a series of small roads where mobs of sheep are likely to be the biggest cause of traffic problems. From Te Anau it runs via Manapouri to SH99, following the valley of the Waiau River to the cave-pocked limestone country around **Clifden**. A minor road cuts west to Lake Hauroko, access point for the Dusky Track, while the Southern Scenic Route continues south through the small service town of **Tuatapere** (the most convenient base for hiking the Hump Ridge Track, and home to the track information office) to estuary-side little **Riverton** and on to Invercargill.

Scenic Shuttle **buses** (Ⓣ0800/277 483, Ⓔscenicshuttle@xtra.co.nz) do the trip from Te Anau through Manapouri, Tuatapere and Riverton to Invercargill and back daily (departing Te Anau 7.30am and Invercargill at 2pm in summer, 1pm in winter).

Clifden and Lake Hauroko

Back at the junction with the main highway, it is 32km further south to **CLIFDEN**, which is barely a town at all but is of some interest for the historic **Clifden Suspension Bridge**, one of the longest in the South Island, built over the Waiau River in 1899 and in use until the 1970s. Maori once camped on summer foraging trips at the **Clifden Caves** (unrestricted access), which are signposted both around 1km north of the bridge along SH96 and 1km down Clifden Gorge Road. With no one to guide you there's a palpable sense of adventure as you head into this 300m-long labyrinth lined with flowstone and stalactite formations and dotted with glow-worms. The passages are never tight but you'll need to do some crouching, scrambling and ladder-climbing as you follow a series of reflective strips. Let the Hump Ridge Track booking office and information centre (see p.867) know your intentions, and ideally go with at least one other person. Wear clothes you don't mind getting wet and muddy and take at least two torches between you.

Lake Hauroko, at the end of a dirt road, 30km west of Clifden, is New Zealand's deepest lake (462m), and far enough off the beaten track that you can skinny dip if you're keen. Low bush-clad hills surrounding the lake create the "sounding winds" immortalized in its name. There are no facilities at First Bay, the road end, though there is a primitive campsite midway between Clifden and Lake Hauroko. At the north end of the lake, the DOC Hauroko Burn Hut ($5) is accessible by boat, or on foot via the **Dusky Track** – one of the longest and most remote in New Zealand, and much tougher than any of the Great Walks. Experienced trampers considering tackling it should obtain information and condition reports from DOC offices in the region.

To explore this beautiful wilderness area, engage one of the companies running excellent wilderness **jetboating trips** on the lake and along the 27km of the Grade III **Wairaurahiri River** down to the coast. Hump Ridge Jet (Ⓣ0800/270 556, Ⓦwww.humpridgejet.com) run a one-day adventure

> The **eastern continuation** of the **Southern Scenic Route**, along the Catlins Coast to Dunedin, is covered in the Dunedin to Stewart Island chapter, p.691.

jetboating trip downriver ($180, $200 including BBQ lunch), allowing 4hr to relax or hike into the impressive Percy Burn viaduct then jetboating back. Wairaurahiri Jet (Ⓣ0800/376 174, Ⓦwww.wjet.co.nz) charge $199 for a similar trip, including a great BBQ lunch. Both companies can arrange transport from Tuatapere or Clifden.

Tuatapere and around

Two sawmills and one feeble stand of beech and podocarp forest is the only evidence that **TUATAPERE**, on the banks of the Waiau River 14km south of Clifden, could once have justified its epithet of "The Hole in the Forest". As the largest town in southwestern Southland, Tuatapere makes a good geographical base (though it is limited in terms of services) for exploring the southern limits of Fiordland. To fight the apparent stagnation, the community banded together to create the excellent **Hump Ridge Track**, to encourage travellers to the area. The South Coast Track visits come of the same area, and both can be combined with some great jetboating along the Wairaurahiri River, based nearby at Clifden.

The Town

Maori legend records the great war canoe Takitimu being wrecked on the Waiau River bar at Te Waewae Bay some six hundred years ago. Maori set up summer foraging camps along the river and used these as way-stations on the route to the *pounamu* fields around Milford Sound, but Tuatapere only came into being when European **pioneers** arrived around 1885. By 1909 the **railway** had arrived from Invercargill, bringing with it increasingly sophisticated steam-powered haulers that made short work of clearing the surrounding bushland. More recently, foresters' attention shifted west to the fringes of the Fiordland National Park where, in the 1970s, the Maori owners proposed clear felling stands of rimu. Environmentalists prevailed upon the Conservation

▲ Percy Burn Viaduct, Hump Ridge Track

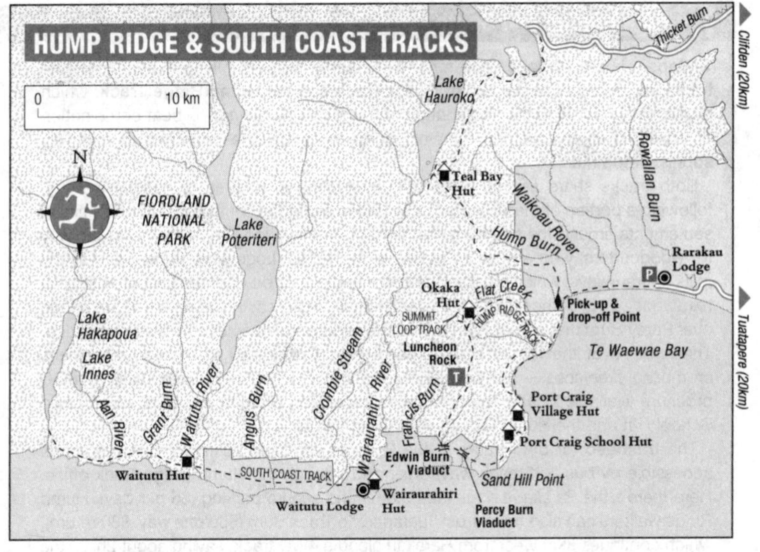

Minister who eventually, in 1996, agreed to pay compensation in return for a sustainable management policy. The bush makes a last stand at a riverside clump of beech, kahikatea and totara on The Domain – staff at the information centre will point the way. For a rose-tinted version of pioneer history, visit **Bushman's Museum**, accessed through the information centre (see below; same hours; gold coin donation appreciated).

Practicalities

Tuatapere is a small town thinly spread on both sides of the Waiau River. On the eastern side, the **Hump Ridge Track booking office and information centre**, 31 Orawia Rd (Nov–April daily 8.30am–5.30pm; May–Oct Wed–Sun 10.30am–3.30pm; ⓣ03/226 6399), is primarily set up for hikers heading off for the Hump Ridge Track. They can store valuables while you're on the tramp, but will also help with local accommodation, transport and the like.

Accommodation is limited but improving, with the comfortable *Tuatapere Motel*, 73 Main St (ⓣ0800/009 993; ❹) also operating the new and functional *Shooters Backpackers* (dorms $25, rooms ❷) next door. Across the road, the traditional *Waiau Hotel*, 49 Main St (ⓣ03/226 6409, ⓦwww.waiauhotel.co.nz; room only ❸, B&B ❹), has B&B and some en-suite rooms, while across the river a former forest workers' camp now operates as the fairly basic *Five Mountain Holiday Park*, 6 Clifden Rd ⓣ03/226 6667, ⓔbarrettz@xtra.co.nz; camping $10, rooms $22 per person), complete with grassy tent and powered sites and a row of twin and double rooms. On-site facilities include the *Cookhouse Café*, Internet access, and free vehicle storage for hikers.

Some 10km southeast of town, farmstay B&B is offered at *Hollyburn Lodge*, 415 Rowley Rd (ⓣ03/226 6765, ⓦwww.tuatapereaccommodation.com; ❹), and it is also worth considering staying at *Rarakau Lodge* (ⓣ03/225 8789; dorm $25), at the beginning of the Hump Ridge and South Coast tracks, which has three-bunk rooms, kitchen, lounge, and space for campervans and camping. Bring your own sleeping bag, pillow and food.

The Hump Ridge and South Coast tracks

Tuatapere is the obvious base for two markedly different hiking experiences: the traditional, mostly coastal **South Coast Track** and the **Hump Ridge Track**, which is gradually capturing the imagination of trampers for its hard-to-beat combination of coastal walking, historic remains, gorgeous subalpine country and relatively sophisticated huts.

Both tracks share several historically interesting kilometres of coastal walking, following a portion of the 1896 track cut 100km along the south coast to gold-mining settlements around the southernmost fiord of Preservation Inlet. This paved the way for woodcutters, who arrived en masse in the 1920s. Logs were transported to the mills on tramways, which crossed the burns and gullies on viaducts built of Australian hardwood – four of the finest have been faithfully restored, including the 125m bridge over Percy Burn that stands 35m high in the middle and has become a star attraction. The remains of the former mill village of **Port Craig** – wharf, rusting machinery, crumbling fireplaces – are equally fascinating and can be visited using a DOC brochure available locally. The only habitation at Port Craig now is DOC's Port Craig School Hut and the Hump Ridge's Port Craig Village Hut.

The **trailhead** for both tracks is the Rarakau car park, 20km west of Tuatapere, accessible by bus ($20 each way) organized through the Hump Ridge Track office. Here there's the *Rarakau Lodge* (see p.867) and secure parking ($5 per day). Hump Ridge walkers can also travel from Tuatapere to Track Burn ($50 one way, $80 return), which continues 8km west from Rarakau along a 4WD track, saving about 2hr at the beginning and end of the walk. The section from Rarakau to Track Burn costs $30 each way.

Various **jetboat** operators (see "Clifden and Lake Hauroko" account on p.865) will pick up and drop off at the Wairaurahiri rivermouth (around $140 per person one way), allowing you to walk sections of the tracks combined with a ride up or down the Wairaurahiri River.

The South Coast Track

The historic **South Coast Track** (covered on DOC's *Waitutu Tracks* leaflet) slices through the largest area of lowland rainforest in New Zealand. Although it is easy going and well graded it takes the best part of four days to reach Big River and you'll just have to turn around and walk back unless you prearrange a jetboat out of Wairaurahiri Hut with Wairaurahiri Jet or Hump Ridge Jet (see p.865). A popular alternative is to make a three-day excursion, staying at DOC's Port Craig School Hut ($10) for two nights and exploring the environs on the second day. Two more huts ($5 each) spaced four to seven hours' walk apart provide accommodation, and camping is free.

Walking the South Coast Track

Rarakau to Port Craig School Hut (17km; 5–7hr; negligible ascent). The first leg follows either the old logging road or, tide permitting, the beach – which should shave half an hour off your walking time.

Port Craig School Hut to Wairaurahiri Hut (16km; 4–6hr; 200m ascent). Here the track follows the old tramway, crossing all four of the restored viaducts, before dropping down to the Wairaurahiri River. There is alternative accommodation on the banks of the Wairaurahiri River in the form of the private *Waitutu Lodge* (book through the Tuatapere information centre; dorms $20): take sleeping bag and food.

Wairaurahiri Hut to Waitutu Hut (13km, 4–6hr, negligible ascent). This section of the path largely follows the coastal flats across Maori land. Fit trampers with camping equipment might want to continue from Waitutu Hut to Big River (12km; 5–7hr; negligible ascent), the end of the track; note that there are no facilities of any kind at Big River.

The Hump Ridge Track

The privately managed **Hump Ridge Track** (book in advance ⓣ0800/486 774, ⓦwww.humpridgetrack.co.nz or at the office in Tuatapere, see p.867) is done in three days with nights spent at two comfortable forty-bunk huts (each $45) equipped with lights, gas cookers, cooking pots and eating utensils, cold running water, six-bunk rooms, and ablution blocks with flush toilets and washbasins, and even porridge each morning cooked by the summer season hut manager. So-called **Freedom walkers** still need to bring a sleeping bag and food, and in the **winter season** (May to late Oct) when services are reduced (and huts cost just $22.50 a night) you'll need a cooking stove and all your pots and utensils. The tramp requires a good level of fitness and isn't a hike for beginners or kids under 10.

If this still sounds too difficult you can arrange for helicopter **bag transfer** (max 15kg) to the next hut. Either go for the full package ($140) or just have your stuff lifted up the steep climb to the first hut on the first day when the pack is heaviest ($50): everything, including empty bottles, must be carried out. Hikers can even upgrade to a double or twin room with sheets and duvet (add $50 per person).

In addition there's a **Freedom Plus** package ($445), which includes one night's backpacker accommodation in Tuatapere, full heli-packing, return transport to Track Burn, hot showers, a sleeping bag supplied at the huts and a souvenir T-shirt. Hot showers are not available to lowly Freedom walkers.

The trip can also be done as a **guided walk** with Kiwi Wilderness Walks (ⓣ0800/733 5494, ⓦwww.NZwalk.com), who run a four-day three-night trip ($1195) with everything Freedom Plus provides plus all meals, superior accommodation at the huts, hotel accommodation in Tuatapere and return transport from Te Anau or Invercargill.

The track must achieve some sort of record in having 8km of boardwalks, to protect the fragile alpine environment on the tops and preserve your feet from long stretches of mud. But you can still expect to encounter mud, and when off the boardwalks it feels like a real tramper's track, without the manicured surface of most Great Walks.

Walking the Hump Ridge Track

Everyone walks the track in the same direction either starting at Rarakau or catching transport to Track Burn.

Rarakau to Okaka Hut (18km; 6–9hr; 900m ascent). Starts along the coast but quickly turns inland along boardwalks through open forest with a thick understorey of crown ferns. It's hard work once you start climbing but you're rewarded with ever longer views though breaks in the beech forest until you finally burst out onto the open tops. You're soon at the Okaka Hut on the Hump Ridge, with fabulous views back the way you came. Allow time to explore the wonderful adjacent Summit Loop Track (1hr) along boardwalks past picturesque sandstone tors and some lovely alpine plants – gentians, orchids, bog pine, dracophyllum and much more.

Okaka Hut to Port Craig (19km; 6–9hr; 100m ascent, 900m descent). The track follows the Hump Ridge, staying high for several hours with magical views. Following lunch at a panoramic rock you descend along Edwin Burn to meet the South Coast Track. After crossing the Edwin Burn Viaduct, follow the old tramway (sleepers and spikes still intact) to the more majestic Percy Burn Viaduct then to the hut at Port Craig Village (or DOC's Port Craig School hut).

Port Craig to Rarakau (11km; 5–7hr; undulating). Wanders through towering coastal rimu and then down on to sandy beaches, and back to the Track Burn pick-up point (or on two more hours to Rarakau).

The best **eating** around is at the *Waiau Hotel*, 47 Main St, which is very much the social centre of town and has tasty home baking. Apart from that it's basically takeaways and self-catering. Don't leave town without trying the sausages (particularly venison) that made Tuatapere the "sausage capital of New Zealand" – either uncooked from the century-old Tuatapere Sausage Shop, 75 Main St or ready-to-eat from the well-stocked 4-Square supermarket on Main Street.

Colac Bay and Riverton

South of Tuatapere, SH99 follows the wind-ravaged cliffs behind the wide and moody Te Waewae Bay, where fierce southerlies have sculpted some much-photographed macrocarpa trees into compact forms. Beyond the small town of Orepuki, the road cuts inland, regaining the sea 45km southeast of Tuatapere, at the quiet community of **Colac Bay**, with a nationally renowned surf break.

For non-surfers, there's little reason to stop before **RIVERTON** (Aparima), a further 12km on and one of the country's oldest settlements. Frequented by whalers as early as the 1790s, the town was formally established in 1836 by another whaler, John Howell – who is also credited with kick-starting New Zealand's now formidable sheep-farming industry. Strung along a spit between the sea and the Jacob's River Estuary (actually the mouth of the Aparima and Pourakino rivers), where fishing boats still harbour, Riverton has a blissfully relaxed feel that might just lull you into staying for a day or so.

A 5m-high paua shell (made from concrete though lined with real paua, which some tourists occasionally mistake for a truly giant mollusc) greets you in town, and indeed the town is gaining a reputation as a paua capital, with several shops selling the polished **shells** by the score. The oldest and best of these is the Fiordland Gift Studio, 166 Palmerston St (ⓣ03/234 8153); you can also visit their factory on Bath Road for some great bargains.

A highlight of a visit to Riverton is the Maori Craft Studio at 130 Palmerston St (ⓣ03/234 9965, ⓔsolomon.whanau@xtra.co.nz), a quality craft shop offering the chance to learn **bone carving** (4–5hr; $65), probably producing an elegantly curved fish hook. Two days are needed to learn **flax weaving** ($90), right from cutting harakeke and preparing the fibres to weaving your *kete* (basket) or *pikau* (backpack); overnight accommodation in the owners' home is also possible on request for a small extra cost, allowing you to work on your weaving and experience warm local hospitality.

Many boat charters are available to take you out trout or saltwater **fishing**. Information is available from the **Riverton Heritage and Tourist Centre**, 172 Palmerston St (ⓣ03/234 8698), which is being expanded to explore both the Maori and European history of the region, and will also house a visitor centre; it should have reopened by the time you read this.

Surprisingly for such a pretty spot, Riverton is sorely lacking in **accommodation**. Easily the best place to stay is *Riverton Rock Guesthouse*, 136 Palmerston St (ⓣ03/234 8886, ⓦwww.rivertonrock.co.nz), where beautifully decorated rooms (❹–❺), including one with an open fire, occupy a tastefully renovated 1870s building. Breakfast is available ($12–20 per person), and you can use the well-equipped kitchen and comfortable lounge overlooking the estuary. If they're full, head next door to the *Globe Hotel Backpackers*, 144 Palmerston St (ⓣ03/234 8527, ⓦwww.theglobe.co.nz; dorms from $17, rooms ❶) with a good bar serving gourmet pizzas; alternatively ask about their self-catering cottages out by the beach. The well-run *Longwood Lodge Holiday Park*, 46 Richard St (ⓣ03/234 8132; camping $20–25, motel units ❸) has a games room that's ideal for wet days.

You'll find a limited range of simple **cafés** along Palmerston Street, and it's worth heading 2km west to the stylish but casual *Beach House Café*, 126 Rocks Hwy (ⓣ03/234 8274), which has sweeping views out to the sea and a cosy timber-lined dining room warmed by an open fire. It's great just for coffee and cake and even better for impeccably cooked fish and seafood (mains $24–29.50; lunch daily, dinner Thurs–Sun).

Beyond Riverton, SH99 heads into the hinterland of Invercargill, 40km away.

Travel details

Fiordland is off the main transport routes. There are no trains or scheduled flights from the main airlines, and even buses are relatively scarce. The i-SITE offices in the region keep updated transport schedules.

Bus companies

The main bus routes are Queenstown via Te Anau to Milford Sound, and Te Anau to Invercargill via Manapouri, Tuatapere and Riverton.

InterCity/Newmans ⓣ09/623 1504 ⓦwww.intercitycoach.co.nz: Queenstown–Te Anau–Milford and back daily; Te Anau–Gore–Balclutha–Dunedin daily.

Scenic Shuttle ⓣ0800/277 483, ⓔscenic-shuttle@xtra.co.nz: Te Anau–Manapouri–Tuatapere–Riverton–Invercargill daily both directions.

Tracknet ⓣ0800/483 2628 ⓦwww.tracknet.net: Queenstown–Te Anau–Milford and back three times daily plus Kepler Track shuttles from Te Anau.

Bus routes

The Divide to: Milford Sound (5 daily; 1hr 15min); Te Anau (5 daily; 1hr).

Manapouri to: Clifden (1 daily; 1hr 30min); Invercargill (1 daily; 3hr 30min); Riverton (1 daily; 3hr); Te Anau (2 daily; 20min); Tuatapere (1 daily; 2hr).

Milford Sound to: The Divide (5 daily; 1hr 15min); Queenstown (8 daily; 4hr 45min–5hr 30min); Te Anau (8 daily; 2hr 15min–2hr 45min).

Queenstown to: Milford Sound (8 daily; 4hr 45min–5hr 30min); Te Anau (8 daily; 2hr 15min).

Te Anau to: The Divide (2–5 daily; 1hr); Dunedin (1 daily; 4hr 45min); Invercargill (1 daily; 4hr); Manapouri (2 daily; 20min); Milford Sound (8 daily; 2hr 15min–2hr 45min); Queenstown (8 daily; 2hr 15min).

Tuatapere to: Invercargill (1 daily; 2hr 30min); Riverton (1 weekly; 1hr 30min).

Flights

Milford Sound to: Queenstown (at least 20 daily; 35min).

Te Anau to: Queenstown (3–5 daily; 30min).

Contexts

Contexts

History

White New Zealanders have long thought of their country as a model of **humanitarian colonization**. Most Maori take a different view, however, informed by the repeated theft of land and erosion of rights that were guaranteed by a treaty with the white man. Schoolroom histories have long been faithful to the European view, even to the point of influencing Maori mythology, but in the last couple of decades revisionist historians have largely discredited what many New Zealanders know as fact. Much that is presented as tradition turns out to be late nineteenth-century scholarship, often the product of historians who bent what they heard to fit their theories and, in the worst cases, even destroyed evidence. What follows is inextricably interwoven with Maori legend and can be understood more fully with reference to the section on Maoritanga (see p.893).

Pre-European history

It is thought that the ancestors of modern **Maori** arrived from Polynesia in double-hulled canoes between 1200 and 1300 AD. The was planned to the extent that they took with them the *kuri* (dog) and food plants such as taro (a starchy tuber), yam and *kumara* (sweet potato). The widely believed story of a legendary "**Great Fleet**" of seven canoes arriving in 1350 AD seems most likely to be the product of a fanciful Victorian adaptation of Maori oral history, which has been readopted into contemporary Maori legend.

The Polynesians found a land so much colder than their tropical home that many of the crops and plants they brought with them wouldn't grow. Fortunately there was an abundance of marine life and large flightless birds, particularly in the South Island, where most settled. The people of this **Archaic Period** are often misleadingly known as "Moa Hunters" and while some undoubtedly lived off these birds, the moa didn't exist in other areas. By around 1350 settlements had been established all around the coast, but it was only later that there is evidence of horticulture, possibly supporting the contention that there was a later migration bringing plants for cultivation. On the other hand, it may just signal the beginning of successful year-round food storage, allowing a settled living pattern rather than the short-lived campsites used by earlier hunters.

Polynesian migration

Modern scholarship suggests that humans from Southeast Asia first explored the South Pacific around five thousand years ago, gradually evolving a distinct culture as they filtered down through the Indonesian archipelago. A thousand years of progressive island hopping got them as far as Tonga and Samoa, where a distinctly **Polynesian** society continued to evolve, the people honing their seafaring skills to the point where lengthy sea journeys were possible. Around a thousand years ago, Polynesian culture reached its classical apotheosis in the **Society Islands**, a group west of Tahiti. This was almost certainly the hub for a series of migrations heading southwest across thousands of kilometres of open ocean, past the Cook Islands, eventually striking land in what is now known as New Zealand (Aotearoa).

Whichever is the case, this marks the beginning of the **Classic Period** when *kainga* (villages) grew up close to the *kumara* grounds, often supported by *pa* (fortified villages) where the people could retreat when under attack. As tasks became more specialized and hunting and horticulture began to take up less time, the arts – particularly carving and weaving (see p.897 & p.899) – began to flourish and warfare became endemic, digs revealing an armoury of *mere*, *patu* and *taiaha* (fighting clubs) not found earlier. The decline of easily caught birdlife and the relative ease of growing *kumara* in the warmer North Island marked the beginning of a northward population shift, to the extent that when the Europeans arrived, ninety-five percent of the population was located in the North Island, mostly in the northern reaches, with coastal settlements reaching down to Hawke's Bay and Wanganui.

European contact and the Maori response

Many **Europeans** were convinced of the existence of a *terra australia incognita*, an unknown southern land thought necessary to counterbalance the northern continents. In 1642, the Dutch East India Company, keen to dominate any trade with this new continent, sent Dutchman **Abel Tasman** to the southern oceans where he became the first European to catch sight of Aotearoa. He anchored in Golden Bay, where a small boat being rowed between Tasman's two ships was intercepted by a Maori war canoe and four sailors were killed. Without setting foot on land Tasman turned tail and fled up the west coast of the North Island, going on to add Tonga and Fiji to European maps. He named

▲ Statue of James Cook, Gisborne

James Cook

Yorkshireman Lieutenant (later Captain) **James Cook** was a meticulous **navigator** who sailed his barque *Endeavour* into the Pacific to observe the passage of Venus across the sun. Following Admiralty instructions he then continued west, arriving at "the Eastern side of the Land discover'd by Tasman" where he observed the "Genius, Temper, Disposition and Number of the Natives" and encouraged his botanists, Banks and Solander, to collect numerous samples.

On three voyages between 1769 and 1777 Cook spent a total of ten months around the coast of Aotearoa, leaving his mark with numerous place names. Some of his **charts** were in use well into the twentieth century, and his only significant errors were to show Banks Peninsula as an island and Stewart Island as a peninsula.

Aotearoa "Staten Landt", later renamed Nieuw Zeeland after the Dutch maritime province.

Nieuw Zeeland was ignored for over a century until 1769, when **James Cook** (see box, above) paid the first of three extensive visits. Cook and his crew found Maori a **sophisticated people** with a highly formalized social structure and an impressive ability to turn stone and wood into fabulously carved canoes, weapons and meeting houses – and yet they were tied to Stone Age technology, with no wheels, roads, metalwork, pottery or animal husbandry. Cook found them aggressive, surly and little inclined to trade, but after an initial unfortunate encounter near Gisborne (see p.414) and another off Cape Kidnappers, near Napier (see p.427), he managed to strike up friendly and constructive relations with the "Indians". These "Indians" now found that their tribal allegiance was not enough to differentiate them from the Europeans and subsequently began calling themselves **Maori** (meaning "normal" or "not distinctive") while referring to the newcomers as **Pakeha** ("foreign").

Offshore from the Coromandel Peninsula, Cook deviated from instructions and unfurled the British flag, claiming formal possession without the consent of Maori, but was still allowed to return twice in 1773 and 1777. The French were also interested, and on his 1769 voyage Cook had passed **Jean François Marie de Surville** in a storm without either knowing of the other's presence.

The establishment of the Botany Bay penal colony in neighbouring Australia aroused the first commercial interest in New Zealand and from the 1790s to the 1830s New Zealand was very much part of the Australian frontier. By 1830 the coast was dotted with semi-permanent **sealing** communities which, within thirty years, had almost clubbed the seals into extinction. The British navy was rapidly felling giant kauri trees for its ships' masts, while others were busy supplying Sydney shipbuilders. By the 1820s **whalers** had moved in, basing themselves at Kororareka (now Russell, in the Bay of Islands), where they could recruit Maori crew and provision their ships. This combination of rough whalers, escaped convicts from Australia and all manner of miscreants and adventurers combined to turn Russell into "the Hellhole of the Pacific", a lawless place populated by what Darwin, on his visit in 1835, found to be "the very refuse of Society".

Before long, the Maori way of life had been entirely disrupted. Maori were quick to understand the importance of guns and **inter-tribal fighting** soon broke out on a scale never seen before. Hongi Hika (see box, p.878) was the first off the mark, but the quest for new territory also fuelled the actions of Ngati Toa's **Te Rauparaha** (see p.290), who soon controlled the southern half of the North Island.

Hongi Hika

Hongi Hika from Ngapuhi *iwi* of the Bay of Islands was the first Maori chief to appreciate the value of firearms, and had already acquired several when missionary Thomas Kendall met him in 1814. By this time he was encouraging his people to grow crops that could be traded with Pakeha for guns.

In 1820 Hongi Hika travelled to England with Thomas Kendall to work on *A grammar and vocabulary of the language of New Zealand*. While he was there he briefly became the toast of London society and was presented to George IV as an "equal". Having little use for most of the gifts showered upon him, he traded them for 300 muskets. Eager to emulate the supreme power of the imperial king, Hongi Hika set about subduing much of the North Island, using the often badly maintained and inexpertly aimed guns to rattle the enemy, who were then slaughtered with the traditional *mere*. Warriors abandoned the old fighting season – the lulls between hunting and tending the crops – and set off to settle old scores, resulting in a massive loss of life.

The huge demand for firearms drove Maori to sell the best of their food, relocating to unhealthy areas close to flax swamps, where flax production could be increased. Even highly valued tribal treasures – *pounamu* (greenstone) clubs and the preserved heads of chiefs taken in battle – were traded. Poor living conditions allowed European **diseases** to sweep through the Maori population time and again, while alcohol and tobacco became widespread, Maori women were prostituted to Pakeha sailors, and the tribal structure began to crumble.

Into this scene stepped the **missionaries** in 1814, the brutal New South Wales magistrate **Samuel Marsden** arriving in the Bay of Islands a transformed man with a mission to bring Christianity and "civilization" to Maori, and to save the souls of the sealers and whalers. Subsequently Anglicans, Wesleyans and Catholics all set up missions throughout the North Island, playing a significant role in protecting Maori from the worst of the exploitation and campaigning in both London and Sydney for more policing of Pakeha actions. In exchange, they destroyed fine artworks considered too sexually explicit and demanded that Maori abandon cannibalism and slavery; in short Maori were expected to trade in their Maoritanga and become "**brown Europeans**". By the 1830s, self-confidence and the belief in Maori ways was in rapid decline: the *tohunga* (priest) was powerless over new European diseases which could often be cured by the missionaries, and Maori had started to believe the Pakeha, who were convinced that the Maori race was dying out. They felt they needed help.

The push for colonization

Despite Cook's discovery claim in 1769, imperial cartographers had never marked New Zealand as a British possession and it was with some reluctance – informed by the perception of an over-extended empire only marginally under control – that New South Wales law was nominally extended to New Zealand in 1817. The effect was minimal; the New South Wales governor had no official representation on this side of the Tasman and was powerless to act. Unimpressed, by 1831 a small group of northern Maori chiefs decided to petition the British monarch to become a "friend and the guardian of these islands", a letter that was later used to justify Britain's intervention.

Britain's response was to send the pompous and less-than-competent **James Busby** as British Resident in 1833, with a brief to encourage trade, stay on good terms with the missionaries and Maori, and apprehend escaped convicts for return to Sydney. Feeling that New Zealand was becoming a drain on the colony's economy, the New South Wales governor, Bourke, withheld guns and troops, and Busby was unable to enforce his will. Busby was also duped by the madness of Baron de Thierry, a Briton of French parents, who claimed he had bought most of the Hokianga district from Hongi Hika and styled himself the "sovereign chief of New Zealand", ostensibly to save Maori from the degradation he foresaw under British dominion. In a panic, Busby misguidedly persuaded 35 northern chiefs to proclaim themselves as the "**United Tribes of New Zealand**" in 1835. As far as the Foreign Office was concerned, this allowed Britain to disclaim responsibility for the actions of its subjects.

By the late 1830s there were around two thousand Pakeha in New Zealand, the largest concentration around Kororareka in the Bay of Islands. Most were British, but French Catholics were consolidating their tentative toehold, and in 1839 British-born James Clendon was appointed American consul. Meanwhile, **land speculators** and colonists were taking an interest for the first time. The

The Treaty of Waitangi: in English and Maori

The main points set out in the **English treaty** are as follows:

- The chiefs cede sovereignty of New Zealand to the Queen of England.
- The Queen guarantees the chiefs the "full exclusive and undisturbed possession of their Lands and Estates Forests Fisheries and other properties which they may collectively or individually possess".
- The Crown retains the right of pre-emption over Maori lands.
- The Queen extends the rights and privileges of British subjects to Maori.

However, the **Maori translation** presents numerous possibilities for misunderstanding, since Maori is a more idiomatic and metaphorical language, where words can take on several meanings. The main points of contention are as follows:

The preamble of the English version cites the main **objectives** of the treaty being to protect Maori interests, to provide for British settlement and to set up a government to maintain peace and order. On the other hand, the main thrust of the Maori version is that the all-important rank and status of the chiefs and tribes will be maintained.

In the Maori version, the concept of **sovereignty** is translated as *kawanatanga* (governorship), a word Maori linked to their experience of the toothless reign of British Resident James Busby. It seems unlikely that the chiefs realized just what they were giving away.

In the Maori text, the Crown guaranteed the *tangata whenua* (people of the land) the possession of their properties for as long as they wished to keep them. In English this was expressed in terms of **individual rights** over property. This is perhaps the most wilful mistranslation and, in practice, there were long periods when Maori were coerced into selling their **land**, and when they refused, lands were simply taken.

Pre-emption was translated as *hokonga* – a term simply meaning "buying and selling", with no explanation of the Crown's exclusive right to buy Maori land, which was clearly spelled out in the English version. This has resulted in considerable friction over Maori being unable to sell any land that the government didn't want, even if they had a buyer.

The implications of **British citizenship** may not have been well understood: it is not clear whether Maori realized they would be bound by British law.

Australian emancipationist, William Charles Wentworth, had "bought" the South Island and Stewart Island for a few hundred pounds (the largest private land deal in history, subsequently quashed by government order) and British settlers were already setting sail. The British admiralty finally began to take notice when it became apparent that the Australian convict settlements, originally intended simply as an out-of-sight, out-of-mind solution to their bulging prisons, looked set to become a valuable possession.

It was a combination of these pressures and Busby's continual exaggeration of the Maori inability to control their own affairs that goaded the British government into action. The result was the 1840 **Treaty of Waitangi** (see box, p.194, & p.879), a document that purported to guarantee continued Maori control of their lands, rights and possessions in return for their loss of sovereignty, a concept poorly understood by Maori. The annexed lands became a dependency of New South Wales until New Zealand was declared a separate colony a year later.

Settlement and the early pioneers

Even before the Treaty was signed, there were moves to found a settlement in Port Nicholson, the site of Wellington, on behalf of the New Zealand Company. This was the brainchild of **Edward Gibbon Wakefield**, who desperately wanted to stem American-style egalitarianism and hoped to use New Zealand as the proving ground for his theory of "scientific colonization". This aimed to preserve the English squire-and-yokel class structure by encouraging the settlement of a cross section of English society, though without the "dregs" at the bottom, but ended up encouraging absentee landordism.

Between 1839 and 1843 the New Zealand Company dispatched nearly 19,000 settlers and established them in "**planned settlements**" in Wellington, Wanganui, Nelson and New Plymouth. This was the core of Pakeha immigration, the only substantial non-Wakefield settlement being **Auckland**, a scruffy collection of waterside shacks which, to the horror of New Zealand Company officials, became the capital after the signing of the Treaty of Waitangi. Maori welfare and social justice had no place in all this, despite the precarious position of Pakeha settlements, which were nothing but tiny enclaves in a country still under Maori control.

The company couldn't buy land direct from Maori, but the government bought up huge tracts and sold it on, often for ten or twenty times what they paid for it. Maori must have been well aware that they were being swindled and could have negotiated better prices themselves, but sold almost the whole of the South Island in a number of large blocks. In 1850 the New Zealand Company foundered, leaving settlements which, subject to the hard realities of colonial life, had failed to conform to Wakefield's lofty theories and were filled with sturdy workers from labouring and lower-middle-class backgrounds.

In 1852 New Zealand achieved self-government and set about dividing the country into six **provinces** – Auckland, New Plymouth, Wellington, Nelson, Canterbury and Otago – which took over land sales and encouraged migrants with free passage, land grants and guaranteed employment on road construction schemes. The same people drawn to the Wakefield settlements heeded the call, hoping for a better life away from the drudgery of working-class Britain. At this point Maori still held the best land and were doing quite nicely growing potatoes and wheat for both local consumption and export to

Australia, where the Victorian gold rush had created a huge demand. Pakeha were barely able to compete, and with the slump in export prices in the mid-1850s, many looked to **pastoralism**. The Crown helped out by halving the price of land, allowing poorer settlers to become landowners but simultaneously paving the way for the creation of huge pastoral runs and putting further pressure on Maori land.

Maori discontent and the New Zealand Wars

The first five years after the signing of the Treaty were a disaster, first under governor Hobson then the ineffectual FitzRoy. Relations between Maori and Pakeha began to deteriorate immediately, as the capital was moved from Kororareka to Auckland and duties were imposed in the Bay of Islands. The consequent loss of trade from passing ships precipitated the first tangible expression of dissent, a famous series of incidents involving the Ngapuhi leader **Hone Heke**, who repeatedly felled the most fundamental symbol of British authority, the flagstaff at Russell. The situation was normalized to some degree by the appointment of **George Grey**, the most able of New Zealand's governors and a man who did more than anyone else to shape the country's early years. Soon Maori began to adapt their culture to accommodate Pakeha in a way that few other native peoples have – selling their crops, operating flour mills and running coastal shipping. Grey encouraged the process by establishing mission schools, erecting hospitals where Maori could get free treatment, and providing employment on public works. In short, he did what he could to uphold the spirit of the Treaty, thereby gaining enormous respect among Maori. Sadly, he failed to set up any mechanism to perpetuate his policies after he left for the governorship of Cape Town in 1853.

Under **New Zealand's constitution**, enacted in 1852, Maori were excluded from political decision-making and prevented from setting up their own form of government; although British subjects in name, they had few of the practical benefits and yet were increasingly expected to comply with British law. By now it was clear that Maori had been duped by the Treaty of Waitangi: one chief explained that they thought they were transferring the "shadow of the land" while "the substance of the land remains with us", and yet he now conceded "the substance of the land goes to the Europeans, the shadow only will be our portion". Growing **resistance** to land sales came at a time when settler communities were expanding and demanding to buy huge tracts of pastoral land. With improved communications Pakeha became more self-reliant and dismissive of Maori, who began to lose faith in the government and fell back on traditional methods of handling their affairs. Self-government had given landowners the vote, but since Maori didn't hold individual titles to their land they were denied suffrage. Maori and Pakeha aspirations seemed completely at odds and there was a growing **sense of betrayal**, which helped to replace tribal animosities with a tenuous unity. In 1854, a month before New Zealand's first parliament, Maori held inter-tribal meetings to discuss a response to the degradation of their culture and the rapid loss of their land. The eventual upshot was the 1858 election of the ageing **Te Wherowhero**, head chief of the Waikatos, as the Maori "King", the leader of the **King Movement** (see box, p.247) behind which Maori could rally to hold back the flood of Pakeha settlement. While some radical Maori wanted to completely rid the country of the white menace, most were moderates and made peaceful overtures that Pakeha chose to regard as rebellious.

By now, most settlers felt that the Treaty of Waitangi had no validity whatsoever and sided with the land sellers to drive the government to repress the Maori landholders. There had been minor skirmishes over land throughout the country, but matters came to a head in 1860, when the government used troops to enforce a bogus purchase of land at Waitara, near New Plymouth. The fighting was at first confined to Taranaki but soon spread to consume the whole of the North Island in the **New Zealand Wars**, once known by Pakeha as the Maori Wars and by Maori as *te riri Pakeha* (white man's anger). Maori were divided, with some settling old grievances by siding with the government against their traditional enemies. Through the early 1860s the number of Pakeha troops was tripled to around 3000, providing an effective force against Maori forces, who failed to adopt a co-ordinated strategy. Elsewhere Maori frequently faced off against ranked artillery and, though there were notable successes, the final result was inevitable. Fighting had abated by the end of the 1860s but peace wasn't finally declared until 1881.

British soldiers had been lured into service with offers of land and free passage and, in a further affront to defeated Maori, many of them were settled in the solidly Maori Waikato. Much of the most fertile land was **confiscated** – in the Waikato, the Bay of Plenty and Taranaki – with little regard to the owners' allegiances during the conflict. By 1862 the Crown had relinquished its right of pre-emption and individuals could buy land directly from Maori, who were forced to limit the stated ownership first to ten individuals and later to just one owner. With their collective power smashed, there was little resistance to voracious land agents luring Maori into debt then offering to buy their land to save them.

Between 1860 and 1881, the **non-Maori population** rose from 60,000 to 470,000, swamping and marginalizing Maori society. An Anglo-Saxon worldview came to dominate all aspects of New Zealand life, and by 1871 the Maori language was no longer used for teaching in schools. A defeated people were widely thought to be close to extinction: Anthony Trollope in 1872 wrote "There is scope for poetry in their past history. There is room for philanthropy as to their present condition. But in regard to their future – there is hardly a place for hope."

Meanwhile, as the New Zealand Wars raged in the North Island, **gold fever** had struck the South. Flakes had been found near Queenstown in 1861 and the initial rushes soon spread to later finds along the West Coast. For the best part of a decade, gold was New Zealand's major export, but the gold provinces never had a major influence on the rest of the country, nor does the gold era retain the legendary status it does in California and Victoria. The major effect was on population distribution: by 1858 the shrinking Maori population had been outstripped by the rapidly swelling horde of Pakeha settlers, most settling in the South Island where relations with Maori played a much smaller part.

Consolidation and social reform

The 1870s were dominated by the policies of Julius Vogel, an able Treasurer who started a **programme of public works** funded by borrowing on a massive scale. Within a decade what had previously been a land of scattered

▲ Sheep, long a mainstay of the economy, are herded down SH6

towns in separately governed provinces was transformed into a single country unified by improved roads, an expanding rail system, 7000 kilometres of telegraph wires and numerous public institutions. Almost all the remaining farmable land was bought up or leased from Maori and acclimatization societies sprang up with the express aim of Anglicizing the New Zealand countryside and improving **farming**. New Zealand quickly began to realize the agricultural expectation created by fertile soils, a temperate climate and relatively high rainfall. Arable farming was mostly abandoned and pastoralism was taking hold, particularly among those rich enough to afford to buy and ship the stock. With no extensive market close enough to make perishable produce profitable, **wool** became the main export, stimulated by the development of the Corriedale sheep, a Romney-Lincoln cross with a long fleece. Wool continued as the mainstay until 1882, when the first **refrigerated meat shipment** left for Britain, signalling a turning point in the economy and the establishment of New Zealand as Britain's offshore larder, a role it maintained until the 1970s.

From 1879 until 1896 New Zealand went into the "long depression", mostly overseen by the conservative "Continuous Ministry" – the last government composed of colonial gentry. During this time **trade unionism** began to influence the political scene and bolstered the Liberal Pact (a Liberal and Labour alliance), which, in 1890, wrested power from those who had controlled the country for two decades and ushered in an era of unprecedented social change. Its first leader, **John Ballance**, firmly believed in state intervention and installed **William Pember Reeves**, probably New Zealand's most radically socialist MP, as his Minister of Labour. Reeves was instrumental in pushing through sweeping reforms to working hours and factory conditions that were so progressive that no further changes were made to labour laws until 1936. He became too radical for most of his colleagues, however, and only remained in office until 1896. When Ballance died in 1892 he was replaced by **Richard "King Dick" Seddon**, a blunt Lancastrian who became, along with Grey, one of the country's greatest, if least democratic, leaders. He introduced a graduated

Accidental suffrage

In 1893, New Zealand became the first nation on earth to grant women the vote. Other territories (South Australia, Wyoming etc) had led the way with limited **women's suffrage**, but New Zealand threw the net wider. It is something New Zealanders are inordinately proud of even though it came about more by accident than any free-thinking principle.

The story goes that when a radical electoral reform bill was up for consideration, Prime Minister Seddon let an amendment pass on the mistaken assumption that it would be rejected by the Legislative Council (an upper house which survived until 1950), thus diverting the ill will of suffragists. Others contend that female suffrage was approved in response to the powerful quasi-religious temperance movement, which hoped to "purify and improve the tone of our politics", effectively giving married couples double the vote of the single man, who was often seen as a drunken layabout.

Whatever the rationale, New Zealand set a precedent and other major Western nations eventually followed suit – Finland in 1906, all Australian states by 1908, Britain in 1918, and the USA in 1920.

income tax and repealed property tax, hoping to break up some of the large estates. New Zealand was already being tagged the "social laboratory of the world", but more was to come.

In 1893, New Zealand was the first nation in the world to enact full **female suffrage**, undoubtedly in line with the liberal thinking of the time, but apparently an accident nonetheless (see box). In 1898 Seddon further astonished the world by weathering a ninety-hour continuous debate to squeeze through legislation guaranteeing an **old age pension**. Fabian Beatrice Webb, in New Zealand that same year, declared that "it is delightful to see a country with no millionaires and hardly any slums".

By the early twentieth century, the radical impetus had faded along with the memory of the 1880s depression, and Pakeha could rest easy in the knowledge that their standard of living was one of the highest in the world. But things were not so rosy for Maori, whose numbers had dropped from an estimated 200,000 at Cook's first visit to around 50,000 in 1896. However, as resistance to European diseases grew, numbers started rising, accompanied by a new confidence buoyed by the rise of Maori parliamentary leadership. **Apirana Ngata**, **Maui Pomare** and **Te Rangi Hiroa** (**Peter Buck**) were all products of Te Aute College, an Anglican school for Maori, and all were committed to working within the administrative and legislative framework of government, convinced that the survival of Maoritanga depended on shedding those aspects of the traditional lifestyle that impeded their acceptance of the modern world.

Seddon died in 1906 and the flame went out of the Liberal torch, though the party was to stay in power another six years. This era saw the rise of the "**Red Feds**", international socialists of the Red Federation who began to organize Kiwi labour. They rejected the arbitration system that had kept wage rises below the level of inflation for a decade, and encouraged **strikes**. The longest was at Blackball on the West Coast, where prime movers in the formation of the Federation of Miners, and subsequently the Federation of Labour, led a three-month stoppage.

The 1912 election was won by William Massey's Reform Party, with the support of the farmers or "cow cockies". Allegiances were now substantially polarized and 1912 and 1913 saw bitter fighting at a series of strikes at the gold mines of Waihi, the docks at Timaru and the wharves of Auckland. As workers opposed to the arbitration system withdrew their labour, the owners organized scab labour, while the hostile Farmers' Union recruited mounted "special constables" to help the government. Protected by naval and military forces, they decisively smashed the Red Feds. The Prime Minister even handed out medals to strike-breaking dairy farmers.

Coming of age

Though New Zealand had started off as an unwanted sibling of Mother England, it had soon transformed itself into a devoted daughter who could be relied upon in times of crisis. New Zealand had supported Britain in South Africa at the end of the nineteenth century and was now called upon to do the same in **World War I**. Locally born Pakeha now outnumbered immigrants and, in 1907, New Zealand had traded its self-governing colony status for that of a Dominion. This gave the country control over its foreign policy, but did not stop New Zealanders flocking to the war effort. Altogether ten percent of the population were involved, 100,000 fighting in the trenches of Gallipoli, Passchendaele and elsewhere. Seventeen thousand failed to return.

At home, the **Temperance Movement** was back in action, attempting to curb vice in the army brought on by the demon drink. Plebiscites in 1911, 1914 and 1919 narrowly averted national prohibition but the "wowsers" succeeded to the point that from 1917 pubs would close at 6pm (see box below) for the duration of the war.

The wartime boom economy continued until around 1920 as Britain's demand for food remained high. Things looked rosy, especially for Pakeha returned servicemen, who were rehabilitated on newly acquired farmland; in contrast, Maori returned servicemen got nothing. These highly mortgaged and inexperienced farmers began to suffer with the rapid drop in produce prices in the early 1920s, fostering a sense of insecurity. Despite weak political leadership, New Zealand continued to grow, with ongoing improvements in infrastructure – hydroelectric dams and roads – and enormous improvements in farming techniques, such as the application of superphosphate fertilizers, sophisticated milking machines and tractors. Yet it was ill-prepared for the **Great Depression**, when the Wall Street Crash sent shock waves through the country. The already high national debt skyrocketed as export income dropped and the Reform government cut pensions, health care and public works' expenditure. The budget was balanced at the cost of producing huge numbers of unemployed. Prime Minister Forbes dictated "no pay without work" and sent thousands of men to primitive rural relief camps for unnecessary tasks

The Six o'clock swill

Legislation requiring pubs to close at 6pm entered the statute books in 1917 and wasn't repealed until 1967. And so ended half a century of the **"Six o'clock swill"**, an hour or so of frenetic after-work consumption in which the ability to tank down as much beer as possible was raised to an art form. This probably did more to hinder New Zealand's social development than anything else: pubs began to look more like lavatories, which could be hosed down after closing, and the predilection for quantity over quality encouraged breweries to churn out dreadful watery brews.

such as planting trees and draining swamps. With the knowledge of the prosperous years to come it is hard to conjure the image of lines of ragged men awaiting their relief money, malnourished children in schools and former soldiers panhandling in the streets.

Throughout the 1920s the Labour Party had gradually watered down some of its socialist policies in an attempt to woo the middle-ground voter. In 1935 they were swept to power and ushered in New Zealand's second era of massive social change, picking up where Seddon left off. Labour's leader **Michael Joseph Savage** felt that "Social Justice must be the guiding principle and economic organization must adapt itself to social needs", a sentiment translated by a contemporary commentator as aiming "to turn capitalism quite painlessly into a nicer sort of capitalism which will eventually become indistinguishable from socialism". State socialism was out, but "Red Feds" still held half the cabinet posts. Salaries reduced during the depression were restored; public works programmes were rekindled, with workers on full pay rather than "relief"; income was redistributed through graduated taxation; and in two rapid bursts of legislation Labour built the model **Welfare State**, the first in the world and the most comprehensive and integrated. State houses were built and let at low rental, pensions were increased, a national health service provided free medicines and health care, and family benefits supplemented the income of those with children.

Maori welfare was also on the agenda and there were moves to raise their living standards to the Pakeha level, partly achieved by increasing pensions and unemployment payments. Much of the best land had by now been sold off but legal changes paved the way for Maori land to be farmed using Pakeha agricultural methods, while maintaining communal ownership. In return, the newly formed **Ratana Party**, who held all four of the Maori Parliamentary seats, supported Labour, keeping them in office until 1949.

New Zealand's perception of its world position changed dramatically in 1941 when the Japanese bombed Hawaii's Pearl Harbor. The country was forced to recognize its position half a globe away from Britain and in the military sphere of America. As in World War I, large numbers of troops were called up, amounting to a third of the male labour force, but casualties were fewer and on the home front the economy continued to boom. By the 1940s New Zealand was the world's most prosperous country, with a fabulous quality of life and the comfortable bed of the Welfare State to fall back on.

More years of prosperity

The Reform Party and the remnants of the Liberals eventually combined to form the National Party which, in 1949, wrested power from Labour. With McCarthyite rhetoric, National branded the more militant unionists as Communists and succeeded in breaking much of the power of the unions during the violent and emotional 1951 **Waterfront Lock-out**. From the late 1940s until the mid-1980s, **National** became New Zealand's party of government, disturbed only by two three-year stints with Labour in power. The conservatism always bubbling under had now found its expression. Most were happy with the government's strong-arm tactics, which emasculated the militant unions, and the country settled down to a prosperous life (see box opposite).

Such a life had huge appeal for Brits still suffering rationing after World War II, and between 1947 and 1975, 77,000 British men, women and children

The Kiwi ideal

Novelist C.K. Stead described the 1950s **Kiwi ideal** as "to live in a country with fresh air, an open landscape and plenty of sunshine; and to own a house, car, refrigerator, washing machine, bach, launch, fibre-glass rod, golf clubs, and so on". This ideal had a flipside. Historian Tony Simpson recalls "we used to run a smug little society in which all was forbidden unless it was specifically permitted, in which case it was compulsory".

became "**ten pound poms**", making use of the New Zealand government's assisted passage to fill Kiwi job vacancies.

While the egalitarian myth still perpetuated by many Kiwis may never have existed, by most measures New Zealand's wealth was evenly spread, with few truly rich and relatively few poor. The exception were Maori. Responding to the urban labour shortages and good wages after World War II many now took part in a **Maori migration** to the cities, especially Auckland. Yet by the 1970s, unemployment, unrest and a disproportionate prison population were exposing weaknesses in the Pakeha belief that the country's race relations were the best in the world. Pakeha took great pride in Maori bravery, skill, generosity, sporting prowess and good humour, but were unable to set aside the discrimination which kept Maori out of professional jobs.

On the economic front, major changes took place under **Walter Nash**'s 1957–60 Labour government, when New Zealand embarked on a programme designed to relieve the country's dependence on exports. A steel rolling mill, oil refinery, gin distillery and glass factory were all set up and an aluminium industry was encouraged by the prospect of cheap power from a hydroelectric project on Lake Manapouri (see box, p.862). When **Keith Holyoake** took over at the helm of the next National government, in 1960, Britain was still by far New Zealand's biggest export market but was making overtures to the economically isolationist European Common Market. Britain was no longer the guardian she once was and in the **military** sphere New Zealand began to court Pacific allies, mainly through the ANZUS pact, which provided for mutual defence of Australia, New Zealand and the US.

Dithering in the face of adversity

In 1972 Britain finally joined the Common Market. Some other export markets had been found but New Zealand still felt betrayed. Later the same year **oil prices** quadrupled in a few months and the treasury found itself with mounting fuel bills and decreasing export receipts. The Labour government borrowed heavily but couldn't avoid electoral defeat in 1975 by National's obstreperous and pugnacious **Robert "Piggy" Muldoon**, who denounced Labour's borrowing and then outdid them. In short order New Zealand had dreadful domestic and foreign debt, unemployment was the highest for decades, and the unthinkable was happening – the standard of living was falling. People began to leave in their thousands and the "brain drain" almost reached crisis point. Muldoon's solution was to "**Think Big**", a catch-all term for a number of capital-intensive petrochemical projects designed to utilize New Zealand's abundant natural gas to produce ammonia, urea fertilizer, methanol and synthetic petrol. It made little economic sense. Rather than use local technology and labour to convert vehicles to run on compressed natural gas (a system already up and running), Muldoon chose to pay international corporations to design huge prefabricated processing plants which were then shipped to New Zealand for assembly, mostly around New Plymouth.

Factory outfalls often jeopardized traditional Maori shellfish beds, and where once *iwi* would have accepted this as inevitable, a new **spirit of protest** saw them win significant concessions. Throughout the mid-1970s Maori began to question the philosophy of Pakeha life and looked to the Treaty of Waitangi (see box, p.879) to correct their grievances. These were aired at occupations of traditional land at Bastion Point in Auckland and at Raglan, and through a petition delivered to parliament after a march across the North Island.

Maori also found expression in the formation of **gangs** – particularly Black Power and the Mongrel Mob – along the lines graphically depicted in Lee Tamahori's film *Once Were Warriors*, which was originally written about South Auckland life in the 1970s. Fortified suburban homes still exist and such gangs continue to be influential among Maori youth.

Race relations were never Muldoon's strong suit and when large numbers of illegal **Polynesian immigrants** from south Pacific islands – particularly Tonga, Samoa and the Cook Islands – started arriving in Auckland he responded by instructing the police to conduct random "dawn raids" checking for "over-stayers", many of whom were deported. Muldoon opted for a completely hands-off approach when it came to sporting contacts with apartheid South Africa and in 1976 let pig-headed rugby administrators send an All Black team over to play racially selected South African teams. African nations responded by boycotting the Montreal Olympics, putting New Zealand in the unusual position of being an international pariah. New Zealand signed the 1977 Gleneagles Agreement requiring it to "vigorously combat the evil of apartheid" and yet in 1981 the New Zealand Rugby Union courted a **Springbok Tour**, which sparked New Zealand's greatest civil disturbance since the labour riots of the 1920s.

Economic and electoral reform

Muldoon's big-spending economic policies were widely perceived to be unsuccessful, and in 1984 Labour were returned to power under **David Lange**. Just as National had eschewed traditional right-wing economics in favour of a "managed economy", Labour now changed tactics, addressing the massive economic problems by grasping the baton of Thatcherite economics. Under Finance Minister Roger Douglas's **Rogernomics**, the dollar was devalued by twenty percent, exchange controls were abolished, tariffs slashed, the maximum income tax rate was halved, a Goods and Services Tax was introduced and state benefits were cut. Unemployment doubled to twelve percent, a quarter of manufacturing jobs were lost, and the moderately well-off benefited at the expense of the poor; nevertheless, **market forces** and enterprise culture had come to stay. As one of the world's most regulated economies became one of the most deregulated, the longstanding belief that the state should provide for those least able to help themselves was cast aside.

In other spheres Labour's views weren't so right-wing. One of Lange's first acts was to refuse US ships entry to New Zealand ports unless they declared that they were nuclear-free. The Americans would do nothing of the sort and

First-past-the-post, MMP and Maori seats

Ever since New Zealand achieved self-government from Britain in 1852, it had maintained a first-past-the-post Westminster-style of Parliament, with the exception of the scrapping of the upper house in 1950.

In the troubled economic times of 1993, when dissatisfaction with both major parties was running high, New Zealand voted for **electoral reform**. They chose Mixed Member Proportional representation (MMP), a system the country still struggles to fully understand. The debate as to how well it works continues, but it does give smaller parties an opportunity to have a greater influence, and New Zealand's Parliament has become all the more colourful for it.

Of the 120 MPs elected, around half represent their own area of the country ("electorate" or "seat") and half are elected from party lists. Voters get **two votes**. The first is for a person, who you hope will become your electorate MP. The second is for a party and is generally considered the more important as it determines the overall make-up of Parliament. A party's representation in Parliament is made up from the number of electorate seats they win plus a number of their list MPs determined by their percentage of the party vote.

To get any seats at all, small parties must exceed the threshold of five percent of the party vote, or win a constituency seat. If they win a seat, their representation is proportional to their party vote even if that is under five percent.

To further complicate matters, Maori voters can choose to vote either within the general system described above, or for one of the seven **Maori seats** which cover the country. All parties are entitled to field candidates in both general and Maori constituencies, though parties championing Maori concerns tend to win.

withdrew support for New Zealand's defence safety net, the **ANZUS** pact. Most of the country backed Lange on this but were less sure about his overtures towards Maori when, for the first time since the middle of the nineteenth century, he gave legal recognition to the Treaty of Waitangi. Now, Maori grievances dating back to 1840 could be addressed.

The rise in apparent income under Rogernomics created consumer confidence and the economy boomed until the **stock market crash** of 1987, which hit New Zealand especially hard. In 1990 National's **Jim Bolger** took the helm, and throughout the deep recession National continued Labour's free-market reforms, cutting welfare programmes and extracting teeth from the unions by passing the **Employment Contracts Act**, which established the pattern of individual workplaces coming to their own agreements on wages and conditions. By the middle of the 1990s the economy had improved dramatically and what for a time had been considered a foolhardy experiment was seen by monetarists as a model for open economies the world over. Meanwhile, the gap between the rich and the poor continued to widen and New Zealand's classless society was increasingly exposed for the myth it always was.

Modern New Zealand

In 1996, New Zealand experienced its first MMP election (see box above), which brought a new Maori spirit into parliament, with far more Maori MPs than ever before and maiden speeches received with a *waiata* (song) from their *whanau* (extended family group) in the public gallery. Unfortunately, most were political neophytes and few weathered the first term intact.

Bolger's poor handling of the first MMP coalition government saw his support wane, and he was replaced in a palace coup, in which **Jenny Shipley** became New Zealand's first female prime minister. In the 1999 election, the **Green Party** came out of left-field, long-sidelined but newly resurgent under MMP. They racked up six seats and helped form a government with Labour and the Alliance under **Helen Clark**. This brought New Zealand's first Rastafarian MP, **Nandor Tanczos**, resplendent in waist-length dreads and a hemp suit, and **Georgina Beyer**, the world's first transgender MP.

The Labour-led coalition stopped logging of beech forests on the West Coast and replaced the Employment Contracts Act with more worker-friendly legislation but failed to deliver on education and health care. Still, Labour were returned with an increased majority after the 2002 election.

Labour's popularity remained high until the 2003 **foreshore and seabed debate** in which Labour forced through legislation ostensibly guaranteeing beach-access to all. Maori perceived this high-handed action as an affront to their sovereignty, and traditionally Labour-supporting Maori voters turned to the new **Maori Party**, co-led by former Labour MP **Tariana Turia**. At the 2005 election the Maori Party won four of the seven Maori seats. Still, Labour were able to cobble together a coalition without Maori Party support, and continue in power though with a much reduced majority.

Meanwhile, the National opposition, now led by former currency trader **John Key**, are capitalizing on the public perception of a Labour government having outstayed its welcome. Opinion polls in the lead up to the next general election (due towards the end of 2008) give National a commanding lead, though it is still possible that a left-of-centre coalition could carry the day.

Chronology of New Zealand

1200–1300AD ▸ Arrival of first **Polynesians**.

c.1350 ▸ The traditional date of arrival of the "Great Fleet" from Hawaiki.

1642 ▸ Dutchman **Abel Tasman** sails past the West Coast but doesn't land.

1769 ▸ Englishman **James Cook** circumnavigates both main islands.

1772 ▸ French sailor **Marion du Fresne** and 26 of his men killed in the Bay of Islands.

1814 ▸ Arrival of **Samuel Marsden**, the first Christian missionary.

1830s ▸ Sealing and whaling stations dotted around the coast.

1833 ▸ James Busby installed as British Resident at Waitangi.

1835 ▸ Independence of the United Tribes of NZ proclaimed.

1840 ▸ **Treaty of Waitangi** Capital moved from Kororareka to Auckland.

1840s ▸ Cities of Auckland, Christchurch, Dunedin, Nelson, New Plymouth, Wanganui and Wellington established.

1852 ▸ NZ becomes a self-governing colony divided into six provinces.

1858 ▸ Settlers outnumber Maori.

1860–65 ▸ **Land Wars** between Pakeha and Maori.

1860s ▸ Major gold rushes in the South Island.

1865 ▸ Capital moved from Auckland to Wellington.

1867 ▸ Maori men given the vote.

1870s ▸ **Wool** established as the mainstay of the NZ economy.

1876 ▸ Abolition of provincial governments. Power centralized in Wellington.

1882 ▸ First **refrigerated meat shipment** to Europe. Lamb becomes increasingly important.

1890 ▸ NZ become "social laboratory" with introduction of compulsory arbitration and graduated income tax.

1893 ▸ Full **women's suffrage**; a world first.

1898 ▸ Old age pension introduced.

1910s ▸ Rise of organized labour under the socialist Red Federation. Strikes at Blackball, Waihi and Auckland.

1914–18 ▸ NZ takes part in WWI with terrible loss of life.

1917 ▸ **Temperance Movement** gets pubs closed after 6pm. Only repealed in 1967.

1920s ▸ Initial prosperity evaporates as the Great Depression takes hold.

1935 ▸ M.J. Savage's Labour government ushers in the world's first **Welfare State** with free health service, family benefits and increased pensions.

1941 ▸ Bombing of Pearl Harbor and WWII begins NZ's military realignment with the Pacific region.

1947 ▸ New Zealand becomes fully independent from Britain.

1950 ▸ Parliament's upper house abolished.

1951 ▸ NZ joins **ANZUS** military pact with the US and Australia.

1950s ▸ NZ comfortable as one of the world's most prosperous nations.

1957–60 ▸ Infrastructure improvements: steel mill, oil refinery, and numerous hydroelectric power stations built or planned.

1960s ▸ Start of **immigration from Pacific Islands**. Major **urbanization of Maori** population.

1972–75 ▸ NZ economy struggles to cope with huge oil price hikes and Britain's entry into the Common Market.

1975 ▸ **Waitangi Tribunal** established to consider Maori land claims.

1975–84 ▸ National's Robert "Piggy" Muldoon tries to borrow NZ out of trouble, investing heavily in ill-considered petrochemical projects.

1976 ▸ African nations boycott Montréal Olympics because of NZ's rugby contacts with South Africa.

1977 ▸ NZ signs Gleneagles Agreement banning sporting ties with South Africa.

1981 ▸ **Springbok Tour**. Massive protests as a racially selected South African rugby team tours NZ.

1984 ▸ The "Hikoi" land march brings Maori grievances into political focus.

1984 ▸ Labour regains power under David Lange. Widespread privatization and deregulation of NZ's protectionist economy. Refusal to allow American nuclear warships into NZ ports severely strains US–NZ relations.

1985 ▸ French secret service agents bomb Greenpeace flagship the **Rainbow Warrior** in Auckland Harbour.

1987 ▸ New Zealand becomes a **Nuclear-Free Zone**.

1987 ▸ Stock market crash devastates NZ economy.

1990–96 ▸ Jim Bolger leads National government, pressing on with Labour's free-market reforms and further dismantling the welfare state.

1996 ▸ First **MMP election** returns an alliance of National and NZ First.

1997 ▸ Jenny Shipley ousts Bolger to become NZ's **first woman Prime Minister**.

1999 ▸ **Labour** regain power under Helen Clark in coalition with the Alliance and the Green Party. The Greens' Nandor Tanczos installed as NZ's first Rastafarian MP and Labour's Georgina Beyer becomes the world's first transgender MP.

2000 ▸ British knighthoods replaced by NZ's own honours system.

2003 ▸ Privy Council in London replaced by a Supreme Court as NZ's highest legal body.

2003 ▸ Debate over the rights to the foreshore and seabed brings Maori grievances to a head.

2003 ▸ NZ population reaches four million. Continued immigration from East Asia brings the Asian population up to ten percent of the nation.

2005 ▸ Maori Party formed. Claims four Maori parliamentary seats.

Maoritanga

When the Pakeha first came to this Island, the first thing he taught the Maori was Christianity. They made parsons and priests of several members of the Maori race, and they taught these persons to look up and pray; and while they were looking up the Pakehas took away our land.

Mahuta, the son of the Maori King Tawhiao, addressing the New Zealand Legislative Council in 1903.

The term **Maoritanga** embodies Maori lifestyle – it is the Maori way of doing things, embracing social structure, ethics, customs, legends, art, and language (see p.927). In New Zealand's Anglo-European-dominated society, it is easy to see Maori culture as harping back to some fond-remembered idyll, but Maoritanga is contemporary and, in the last few decades, has seen a dramatic resurgence. Maori make up around fifteen percent of the population, but Maori–Pakeha marriage since the early nineteenth century has left a complex interracial pool. Many Pakeha claim Maori forebears and some contend that there are no full-blooded Maori remaining. Maori ancestry remains the foundation of Maoridom but a sense of belonging is increasingly important.

White New Zealanders have promoted the image of the two races living in harmony as one people, citing scenes of Maori and Pakeha elbow to elbow at the bar and Maori rugby players in the scrum alongside their Pakeha brothers. Pakeha boasted of successful integration, a world away from apartheid in South Africa or the virtual genocide exacted on North American and Australian peoples; Maori could claim all the benefits of Pakeha plus dedicated seats in parliament, extra university grants and various other concessions. Yet this ignored an undercurrent of Maori dissatisfaction over their treatment since the arrival of Europeans; the policy of **assimilation** relied on Maori conforming to the Pakeha way of doing things, making no concession to Maoritanga. Maori adapted quickly to European ways but were rewarded with the loss of their **land**. It is impossible to overestimate the importance of this: Maori spirituality invests every tree, hill and bay with a kind of supernatural life of its own, drawn from past events and the actions of the ancestors. It is by no means fanciful to equate the loss of land with the diminution of Maori life force.

It is only really since the 1980s that the paternal Pakeha view has been challenged, with the country reacting by adopting **biculturalism**. As Maori rediscover their heritage and Pakeha open their eyes to what has been around for generations, knowledge of Maoritanga and some understanding of the language is seen as desirable and advantageous. The government has increasingly channelled resources towards the "flax roots" of Maoridom, fostering a take-up in the learning of Maori language, resurgence in interest in Maori arts and crafts and a growing pride in being Maori. Customary rights to fisheries, resources, and parcels of land have been returned to Maori ownership but nonetheless, there is a sense that Maori are only getting as much as the Pakeha-dominated government is prepared to give back.

For many **Pakeha**, meanwhile, there is considerable unease over what is perceived as the government's soft stance on Treaty of Waitangi land claims (see box, p.879). Some envisage a future where Maori will own the land (including private land not currently up for redistribution under Treaty claims), will reclaim rights granted them by the Treaty, and will have more influence than

Pakeha. So far, reaction to the strengthening Maori hand in this climate of conciliation has only been voiced quietly but just how this scenario will pan out remains to be seen. True power-sharing and biculturalism seems a long way off, and Maori aspirations for "sovereignty" – a separate Maori government and judiciary – look far-fetched at present.

The sluggish pace of change, coupled with recent controversy over the foreshore law, enforced by the government to keep the country's coastline in Crown hands, has led to an increase in Maori activism. The foreshore law almost single-handedly led to the birth of the Maori party, which is growing in strength and influence and provides a voice for Maori discontent, but even this change is too little for some – as evidenced by the October 2007 raids of an alleged paramilitary training camp in the North Island. A group of mostly Maori activists led by Tame Iti were arrested as terrorists, although the charges were commuted to firearms offences. The government reaction, including the "lock-down" of the community at nearby Ruatoki, has set back race relations and left a bitter taste in Maori mouths, which has in turn heightened calls for greater self-determination, and may encourage a debate on the state of New Zealand biculturalism.

Maori legend

Maori culture remains primarily oral with chants, storytelling and oratory central to ceremonial and daily life. Different tribal groups had different sets of stories, or at least variations on common themes, but European historians with pet theories to promote often distorted the tales they heard and destroyed conflicting evidence, creating their own Maori folklore. Over time many of these stories have been taken back into Maori tradition, resulting in a patchwork of authentic and bowdlerized legends and helping create a common Maori identity.

Creation

From the primal nothingness of **Te Kore** sprang **Ranginui** the sky father and **Papatuanuku** the earth mother. They had numerous offspring, including: **Haumia Tiketike**, the god of the fern root and food from the forest; **Rongo**, the god of the kumara and cultivation; **Tu Matauenga**, the god of war; **Tangaroa**, the god of the oceans and sealife; **Tawhirimatea**, the god of the winds; and **Tane Mahuta**, the god of the forests. Through long centuries of darkness the brothers argued over whether to separate their parents and create light. Tawhirimatea opposed the idea and fled to the skies where his anger is manifested in thunder and lightning, while Tane Mahuta succeeded in parting the two and allowing life to flourish. Ranginui's tears filled the oceans and even now it is their grief that brings the dew, mist and rain.

Having created the creatures of the sea, the air and the land, the gods turned their attentions to humans and, realizing that they were all male, decided to create a female. They fashioned clay into a form resembling their mother and **Tane** breathed life into the nostrils of the Dawn Maiden, **Hinetitama**.

Maui the trickster and Kupe the navigator

Maori mythology is littered with demigods, none more celebrated than **Maui-Tikitiki-a-Taranga**, whose exploits are legend throughout Polynesia.

Maui fishes up the North Island

Maui's greatest work was the creation of **Aotearoa**. Because of his reputation for mischief, Maui's brothers often left him behind when they went fishing, but one morning he stowed away, revealing himself far out to sea and promising to improve their catch. Maui egged them on until they were beyond the normal fishing grounds before dropping anchor. In no time at all Maui's brothers filled the canoe with fish, but Maui still had some fishing to do. They scorned his hook (secretly armed with a chip of his grandmother's jawbone) and wouldn't lend him any bait, so Maui struck his own nose and smeared the hook with his blood. Soon he hooked a fabulous fish that, as it broke the surface, stretched into the distance all around them. Chanting an incantation, Maui got the fish to lie quietly and it became the North Island, Te ika a Maui, the fish of Maui. As Maui went to make an offering to the gods, his brothers began to cut up the fish and eat it, hacking mountains and valleys into the surface. To fit in with the legend, the South Island is often called Te waka a Maui, the canoe of Maui, and Stewart Island the anchor, Te punga o te waka a Maui.

With an armoury of spells, guile and boundless mischief, Maui gained a reputation as a trickster, using his abilities to turn situations to his advantage. Equipped with the powerful magic jawbone of his grandmother, he set about taming his world, believing himself invincible. He even took on **the sun**, which passed so swiftly through the heavens that people had no time to tend their fields. Maui vowed to solve the problem and, with the aid of his older brothers, he plaited strong ropes and tied them across the sun's pit before dawn. The sun rose into the net and Maui set upon the sun with his magic jawbone, beating the sun and imploring it not to go so fast. The sun weakened and agreed to Maui's request. Maui's legendary antics also extend to the creation of Aotearoa (see box above).

Maori trace their ancestry back to **Hawaiki**, the semi-legendary source of the Polynesian diaspora, for which the Society Islands and the Cook Islands are likely candidates. According to legend, the first visitor to Aotearoa was **Kupe**, the great Polynesian navigator. He was determined to kill a great octopus that kept stealing his bait; drawn ever further out to sea in pursuit, he finally reached landfall on the uninhabited shores of Aotearoa, the "land of the long white cloud". He named numerous features of the land before returning to Hawaiki with instructions on how to retrace his voyage.

Social structure and customs

Maori society is **tribal**, though the deracination resulting from the move from tribal homelands to cities has eroded many close ties. In urban situations the finer points of Maoritanga have been rediscovered and the basic tenets remain strong, with formal protocol ruling ceremonies from funeral wakes to meetings.

The most fundamental grouping in Maori society is the extended family or **whanau** (literally "birthing"), reaching from immediate relatives to cousins, uncles and nieces. A dozen or so *whanau* form localized sub-tribes or **hapu** (literally "gestation or pregnancy"), perhaps the most important group, comprising of extended families of common descent. *Hapu* were originally economically autonomous and today continue to conduct communal activities, typically through *marae* (see below). Neighbouring *hapu* are likely to belong to the same tribe or **iwi** (literally "bones"), a looser association of Maori spread over large geographical areas. The thirty-odd major *iwi* are tenuously linked by common ancestry, traced back to semi-legendary canoes, or *waka*. In troubled times, *iwi* from the same *waka* would band together for protection. Together these are the **tangata whenua**, "the people of the land", a term that may refer to Maori people as a whole, or just to one *hapu* if local concerns are being aired.

The literal meanings of *whanau*, *hapu* and *iwi* can be viewed as a metaphor for the Maori view of their relationship with their ancestors or **tupuna**, existing through their genetic inheritors, making the past a part of the present. Hence the respect accorded the **whakapapa**, an individual's genealogy tracing descent from the gods via one of the migratory *waka* and through the *tupuna*. The *whakapapa* is often recited on formal occasions such as **hui** (meetings).

Maori traditional life is informed by the parallel notions of **tapu** (taboo) and **noa** (mundane, not *tapu*). This belief system is designed to impose a code of conduct: transgressing *tapu* brings ostracism, ill fortune and sickness. Objects, places, actions and people can be *tapu*, demanding extra respect; the body parts of a chief, especially the head, menstruating women, sacred items, earrings, pendants, hair combs, burial sites, and the knowledge contained in the *whakapapa* are all *tapu*. There is a practical aspect too, with the productivity of fishing grounds and forests traditionally maintained by imposing *tapu* at critical times. The direct opposite of *tapu* is *noa*, a term applied to ordinary items that, by implication, are considered safe; a new building is *tapu* until a special ceremony renders it *noa*.

People, animals and artefacts, whether *tapu* or *noa*, possess **mauri** (life force), **wairua** (spirit) and **mana**, a term loosely translated as prestige but embodying wider concepts of power, influence and charisma. Birthright brings with it a degree of *mana* that can then be augmented through brave deeds or lost through inaction. Wartime cannibalism was partly ritual and by eating an enemy's heart a warrior absorbed his *mauri*; likewise personal effects gain *mana* from association with the *mana* of their owner, accruing more when passed to descendants. Any slight on the *mana* of an individual was felt by the *hapu*, who must then exact **utu** (a need to balance any action with an equal reaction), a compunction that often led to bloody feuds, sometimes escalating to war and further enhancing the *mana* of the victors. Pakeha found this a hard concept to grasp and deeds that they considered deceitful or treacherous could be considered correct in Maori terms.

The responsibility for determining *tapu* falls to the **tohunga** (priest or expert), the most exalted of many specialists in Maoritanga, conversant with tribal history, sacred lore and the *whakapapa*, and considered to be the earthly presence of the power of the gods.

Marae

The rituals of *hapu* life – *hui*, **tangi** (funeral wakes) and **powhiri** (formal welcomes) – are conducted on the **marae**, a combined community, cultural and drop-in centre where the cultural values, protocols, customs and vitality of Maoritanga find their fullest expression. Strictly, a *marae* is a courtyard, but the term is often applied to a whole complex, comprising the **whare runanga** (meeting house, or *whare nui*), *whare manuhiri* (house for visitors), *whare kai* (eating house) and an old-fashioned **pataka** (raised storehouse). *Marae* belonging to one or more *hapu* are found all over the country, while pan-tribal urban *marae* exist to help Maori who have lost their roots.

Visitors, whether Maori or Pakeha, may not enter *marae* uninvited, so unless you have Maori friends, you're most likely to visit on a commercially run **tour**. Invited guests are expected to provide some form of **koha** (donation) towards the upkeep of the *marae*, usually included in tour fees. Remember, the *marae* is sacred and due reverence must be accorded the **kawa** (protocols).

Following long tradition, **manuhiri** (visitors) approaching the *marae* are ritually challenged, to determine intent, by a **wero**, where a fearsome warrior bears down on you, with twirling **taiaha** (long club), flickering tongue and bulging eyes. The women then make the **karanga** (welcoming call), followed by the **powhiri** (sung welcome), breaking the *tapu* and acting as a prelude to touching noses, **hongi**, binding the *manuhiri* and the *tangata whenua* physically and spiritually. On commercial trips, the welcome ceremony is followed by a concert comprising songs, dances, chants, and a **hangi** (feast cooked in an earth oven).

Arts and crafts

The origins of **Maori art** lie in eastern Polynesia but half a millennium of isolated development has resulted in unique forms of expression. Eastern Polynesia has no suitable clay, so Maori forebears had no skills for pottery and focused on wood, stone and weaving, occasionally using naturalistic designs but more often the **stylized forms** that make Maori art unmistakable.

As with other *taonga* (treasures), many examples were taken by Victorian and later collectors, but there is determined effort by *iwi* and Te Puni Kokiri (the Ministry of Maori Development) to restore *taonga* to New Zealand, including severed heads scattered through museums around the world – some were recently returned by the Victoria & Albert Museum in London.

Woodcarving

Maori handiworks' greatest expression is **woodcarving**. The essence of great Maori woodcarving is that as much care is given to the production of a humble water bailer as to the pinnacle of Maori creativity, waka (canoes) and whare whakairo (carved houses). Early examples of wood carving feature the sparse, rectilinear styles of ancient eastern Polynesia, but by the fifteenth century these were replaced by the cursive style, employed by more traditional carvers today. In Northland, kauri wood was used, while elsewhere durable, easily worked totara was the material of choice. Carvers worked with shells and sharp stones in the earliest times, but the artist's scope increased with the invention of tools fashioned from **pounamu** (greenstone, a form of jade; see p.746). Some would say that the quality of the work declined with the coming

Whare

Originally the chief's residence, the *whare* gradually adopted the symbolism of the *waka* – some incorporated wood from *waka*. Each meeting house is a tangible manifestation of the *whakapapa*, usually representing a synthesis of the ancestors: the ridge-pole, the backbone; the rafters, the ribs; the interior, the belly; the gable, the head; and the barge-boards, the arms, often with finger-like decoration. Inside, all wooden surfaces are carved and the spaces filled with intricate woven-flax panels, *tukutuku*.

of the Europeans: not just through the demand for quickly executed "tourist art", but as a consequence of pressure to remove the phallic imagery found obscene by missionaries. As early as 1844, carving had been abandoned in areas with a strong missionary presence and it continued to decline into the early years of the twentieth century, when Maori pride was at its lowest ebb. By the end of the 1920s the situation had become so lamentable that Maori parliamentarian Apirana Ngata established Rotorua's pan-tribal **Maori Arts and Crafts Institute**; a foundation on which Maoritanga could be rebuilt.

The role of carver has always been highly respected, with seasoned and skilled exponents having the status of *tohunga* and travelling the country to carve and teach. The work is *tapu* and *noa* objects must be kept away – cooked food is not allowed near, and carvers have to brush away shavings rather than blow them – though women, previously banned, can now become carvers.

Maori carving exhibits a distinctive **style**. Relief forms are hewn from a single piece of wood with no concession to natural form, shapes or blemishes. There is no attempt to represent perspective, landscapes are symbolized not actually depicted and figures stand separately. Unadorned wood is rare, carvers creating a stylistic rather than symbolic bed of swirling spirals, curving organic forms based on fern fronds or seashells and interlocking latticework. Superimposed on this are key elements, often inlaid with paua shell.

The most common is the ancestor figure, the **hei tiki**, a grotesquely distorted human form, either male, female or of indeterminate gender, and often highly stylized. Almost as common is the mythical *manaia*, a beaked birdlike form with an almost human profile. Secondary motifs such as the *pakake* (whale) and *moko* (lizard) also occur.

While the same level of craftsmanship was applied to all manner of tools, weapons and ornaments, it reached its most exalted expression in *waka taua* (**war canoes**), the focus of community pride and endeavour. Gunwales, bailers and paddles are fabulously decorated but the most detailed work is reserved for the prow and sternpost, usually a matrix of spirals interwoven with *manaia* figures. As guns and the European presence altered the balance of tribal warfare in the 1860s, the *waka taua* was superseded in importance by the *whare whakairo* (carved meeting house).

Greenstone carving

Maori carvers also work in **pounamu** (greenstone), supplied by pre-European trade routes originating in the West Coast and Fiordland – indeed, the South Island became known as Te Wai Pounamu, the Greenstone Water. The stone was fashioned into adzes, chisels and clubs for hand-to-hand combat; tools that took on a ritual significance and demanded decoration. *Pounamu*'s hardness dictates a more restrained carving style and *mere* and *patu* tend to be only partly worked, leaving large sweeping surfaces ending in a flourish of delicate swirls. Ornamental pieces range from simple drop pendants worn as earrings or neck decoration to *hei tiki*, worn as a breast pendant. Like other personal items, especially those worn close to the body, an heirloom *tiki* possesses the *mana* of the ancestors and absorbs the wearer's *mana*, becoming *tapu*.

Tattooing

A stylistic extension of the carver's craft is exhibited in *moko*, ornamental and ceremonial **tattooing** that largely died out with European contact. Women had *moko* on the lips and chin, high-ranking men had their faces completely covered, along with their buttocks and thighs; the greater the extent and intricacy of the *moko*, the greater the status. A symmetrical pattern of traditional

▲ Moko, traditional Maori tattoos

elements, crescents, spirals, fern fronds and other organic forms, was gouged into the flesh with an *uhi* (chisel) and mallet, then soot rubbed into the wound. In the last couple of decades the tradition of full-face *moko* has been revived, as a symbol of Maoritanga and an art form in its own right; since 1999, *moko* artists have been eligible for government funding.

Weaving and clothing

While men carved, women dedicated themselves to weaving and producing clothing. When Polynesians arrived in these cool, damp islands their paper mulberry plants didn't thrive and they were forced to look for alternatives. They found *harakeke* (New Zealand **flax**), the foundation of Maori fibre-work. The strong and pliable fibres were used as fishing lines, as cordage for axe-heads and as floor matting. With the arrival of the Pakeha, Maori quickly adopted European clothes, but they continued to wear cloaks on formal occasions and today these constitute the basis for contemporary designs.

Flax grows on marshy land all over the country and so the long, spindly leaves were usually on hand. Used in something close to their raw form for *raranga* (plaiting) they made *kete*, handle-less baskets for collecting shellfish and *kumara*, triangular canoe sails, sandals and *whariki*, patterned floor mats still used in meeting houses. For finer work, trimming, soaking and beating flax, a laborious process, produced stronger and more pliable fibre.

Most flax was neutral but Maori design requires some **colouring**: black is achieved by soaking in a dilute extract of *hinau* tree bark then rubbing with a black swamp sediment, *paru*; red-brown ranges of colours require boiling in dyes derived from the tanekaha tree bark and fixing by rolling in hot ashes; while the less popular yellow tint is produced from the bark of the Coprosma species. These day synthetic dyes are used in an effort to be green.

Natural and coloured fibres are both used in *whatu kakahu* (**cloak-weaving**), the crowning achievement of Maori women's art, the finest cloaks ranking alongside prized *taonga*; the immense war canoe now in the Auckland Museum was once exchanged for a fine cloak. The technique is sometimes referred to as finger-weaving, no loom is used. The women work downwards from a base warp strung between two sticks. Complex weaving techniques are employed to produce a huge array of different textures, often decorated with *taniko* (coloured borders), cord tags tacked onto the cloth at intervals and, most impressively, **feathers**. Feather cloaks (*kahu huruhu*) don't appear to have been common before European contact, though heroic tales often feature key players in iridescent garments. The appeal of the bright yellow feathers of the huia probably saw to its demise, and most other brightly coloured birds are now too rare to use for cloaks, so new feather cloaks are rarely made.

Existing examples have become prestigious garments and you'll come across some fine examples in museums, the base cloth often completely covered by a dense layer of kiwi feathers bordered by zigzag patterns of tui, native pigeon and parakeet. More robust, *para* (rain capes) were made using the water-repellent leaves of the cabbage tree and a form of coarse canvas that could reportedly resist spear thrusts was used for *pukupuku* (war cloaks). Some *pukupuku* were turned into *kahu kuri* (dog-skin cloaks) with the addition of strips of dog skin, arranged vertically so that the natural fur colours produced distinctive patterns.

Weaving and plaiting have once again become popular; cloaks are an important element of formal occasions, whether on the *marae* for *hui* and *tangi*, or elsewhere for receiving academic or state honours. Old forms are reproduced directly or raided as inspiration for contemporary designs that interpret traditional elements in the light of modern fashion.

The haka and Maori dance

The All Blacks always perform the *haka*, a ferocious, thigh-slapping, foot-stomping, tongue-poking, eye-bulging chant taken from the Te Rauparaha *Haka* (see box, p.901). This is the best known of many posture dances (often wrongly referred to as war dances) designed to demonstrate the fitness and prowess of warriors. Its use by what are often predominantly Pakeha sides might seem inappropriate but it is entrenched in Kiwi culture; there was a considerable backlash in 1996 when the All Black coach suggested the *haka* should be changed to mollify those Maori *iwi* who had been decimated by Te Rauparaha. The new, specially written *Kapa O Pango haka* was unveiled in 2005 but it has not completely replaced the Te Rauparaha version.

At commercial **Maori concerts** (in Rotorua, Christchurch, Queenstown and elsewhere) there will always be a *haka*, usually the Te Rauparaha version,

The haka

Before every international rugby match, New Zealand's All Blacks put the wind up the opposition by performing an intimidating thigh-slapping, eye-bulging, tongue-poking chant. Traditionally this has been the Te Rauparaha *haka*, just one of many such Maori posture dances, designed to display fitness, agility and ferocity. The Te Rauparaha *haka* was reputedly composed early in the nineteenth century by the warrior Te Rauparaha, who was hiding from his enemies in the *kumara* pit of a friendly chief. Hearing noise above and then being blinded by light he thought his days were numbered, but as his eyes became accustomed to the sun he saw the hairy legs of his host and was so relieved he performed the *haka* on the spot.

Touring teams have performed the *haka* at least since the 1905 All Black tour of Britain, and since the 1987 World Cup for home matches as well. The performance is typically led by a player of Maori descent chanting:

Ringa pakia Slap the hands against the thighs
Uma tiraha Puff out the chest
Turi whatia Bend the knees
Hope whai ake Let the hip follow
Waewae takahia kia kino Stamp the feet as hard as you can

After a pause for effect the rest of the team join in with:
Ka Mate! Ka Mate! It is death! It is death!
Ka Ora! Ka Ora! It is life! It is life!
Tenei te ta ngata puhuru huru This is the hairy man
Nana nei i tiki mai Who caused the sun to shine
Whakawhiti te ra Keep abreast!
A upane ka upane! The rank! Hold fast!
A upane kaupane whiti te ra! Into the sun that shines!

usually performed by men. Though women aren't excluded, they normally concentrate on **poi dances**, where balls of *raupo* (bulrush) attached to the end of strings are swung around in rhythmic movements, designed to improve co-ordination and dexterity.

The drums of eastern Polynesia didn't make it to New Zealand, so both chants and the *haka* go unaccompanied. Along with the traditional bone flute, Pakeha added the guitar to accompany **waiata** (songs), relatively modern creations whose impact comes from tone, rhythm and lyrics. The impassioned delivery can seem at odds with music that's often based on Victorian hymns: perhaps the best known are *Pokarekare ana* and *Haere Ra*, both post-European-contact creations. Outside the tourist concert party, Maori music has developed enormously in recent years to the point where there are tribal and Maori-language music stations almost exclusively playing music written and performed by Maori, often with a hip-hop or R&B influence and a Pacific twist.

Landscapes and wildlife

Despite its diminutive size, New Zealand packs in an enormous diversity: pristine subtropical forest, rich volcanic basins, boiling mud pools and geysers, rugged white-silica and gold-sand fringed coastlines and spectacular alpine regions. Between them, these landscapes support an extraordinary variety of animals and plant life, with almost ninety percent of the flora not found anywhere else in the world. Many habitats, plants and wildlife are easily accessible, protected within national parks and scenic reserves.

The Shaky Isles

The earliest rocks found in the country are thought to have originated in the continental forelands of Australia and Antarctica, part of Gondwanaland, the massive supercontinent to which New Zealand belonged. Oceanic islands were created by continental drift, the movement of the large plates that form the earth's crust, which created a distinct island arc and oceanic trench about 100 million years ago.

Roughly 26 million years ago, the land that makes up New Zealand rose further from the sea, and the landscape you see today was formed by **volcanic** activity and continuous movement along fault lines, particularly the Alpine Fault of the South Island. New Zealand lies on the boundary between the Australian and Pacific tectonic plates, and in the North Island the two plates crash into one another, the Pacific plate sliding underneath the Australian to produce prolific volcanic activity. Under much of the South Island the Pacific plate is riding over the Australian, causing rapid **mountain building** and creating the Southern Alps. This gives New Zealand about four hundred **earthquakes** every year and, although only a quarter are big enough to be noticed, New Zealand has earned the moniker "the Shaky Isles" as a result. The volcanoes on the North Island periodically become impressively active: White Island (just off the coast of the Bay of Plenty) regularly blows off steam, while Mount Ruapehu erupted in 2006 and 2007.

Conservation and wildlife organizations and websites

Department of Conservation ⓦwww.doc.govt.nz. Government department charged with conserving New Zealand's natural and historic heritage. Their extensive website covers national parks, tramping, camping, conservation issues and much more.

Forest and Bird Protection Society ⓦwww.forestandbird.org.nz. New Zealand's leading independent conservation organization. Has plenty of info on biosecurity and at-risk species, plus a handy list of birding hotspots.

NZ Birds ⓦwww.nzbirds.com. Comprehensive site on everything feathery in New Zealand.

Save The Kiwi ⓦwww.savethekiwi.org.nz. Join the Department of Conservation and Bank of New Zealand effort to save this iconic bird from extinction.

The end of isolation

The first human didn't reach Aotearoa until around eight hundred years ago, and New Zealand's flora and fauna evolved untouched for aeons. Before the arrival of early Maori, the land was covered in thick **forest** composed of over a hundred species of tree, and the only mammals around New Zealand were the seals, whales and dolphins on the coast and a couple of species of **bat**. Land mammals were non-existent, a unique situation which allowed **birds** to fill the food chain; with no predators they gradually lost the ability to fly. When Maori introduced dogs and rats, the birds couldn't compete. Most of those that remain (see box, p.908) cling precariously to their existence.

Maori impact pales in comparison with the devastation wrecked by **Europeans**. Even Cook's first exploratory visits left a legacy of wild pigs, sheep and potatoes. In the early 1800s whalers and sealers bloodied the coastal waters, while logging campaigns cleared vast tracts of native trees for grazing cattle. Pioneers continued to tamper with the delicately balanced ecosystem in an attempt to turn New Zealand into a "New England". **Acclimatization societies** sprung up in the late 1800s to introduce familiar animals and plants from settlers' European homelands, and New Zealand would never have become the successful pastoral nation it is without grasses, pollinating birds, bees and butterflies or sheep and cattle. But many releases were much less successful, including blackberry, gorse, broom and numerous other weeds, and animals which either out-competed the native birds for food, killed their young or simply killed the adult birds.

The lowlands

You won't have to go far from the airport to see archetypal paddocks full of **sheep**, often backed by shelter belts of macrocarpa trees. The sheep population is around 40 million, roughly half of what it was thirty years ago, and much of the grazing land has been turned over to other uses. High prices for milk products in the last few years have encouraged a rise in dairying. Deer farming is also big business (with much of the meat exported to Germany) and you may even see farmed ostriches. Elsewhere, land has been turned over to horticulture. **Vineyards** continue to crop up, with the biggest concentrations around Gisborne, Hastings, Martinborough, Blenheim, Nelson, Waipara and Cromwell. Growers are toying with **olives** – with increasing success – and a few optimistic souls have planted oak and hazel trees in the hope of creating a truffle industry.

Throughout both farmed and forested New Zealand you'll see the native **cabbage tree** (*ti kouka*) with its thin grey trunk (up to 10m high) topped by spear-shaped leaves and clusters of hundreds of white flowers. The leaf shoots were eaten by Captain Cook and his men, who found them tolerably like cabbage.

Lowland forests

This rural picture is a far cry from the thick forest that greeted early settlers. Much was logged, burnt and cleared to carve out farms, but pockets of **native bush** survive. The forests of Northland, the Coromandel Peninsula, the west coasts of both islands, around Wellington and on Stewart Island contain a great variety of native trees. There are also sixty endemic native flowering plant

Wildlife-watching season

Location	Page ref.	Jan	Feb	Mar	Apr	May
Muriwai: gannets	141	•	•	•		
Tiritiri Matangi: blue penguins	161	◦	◦	•	◦	◦
Bay of Islands: dolphins	189	•	•	•	•	•
Bay of Islands: orca	189					•
Bay of Islands: minke whales	189	•				
Bay of Islands: Bryde's whales	189	•				
Trounson Kauri Park: kiwi spotting	225	•	•	•	•	•
Cape Kidnappers: gannets	436	•	•	•	•	•
Marlborough Sounds: Hector's dolphins	503	•	•	•	•	
Marlborough Sounds: dusky dolphins	503				•	•
Marlborough Sounds: bottlenose dolphins	503	◦	◦	◦	◦	◦
Abel Tasman: seal swimming	529	•	•	•	•	•
Kaikoura: sperm whales	559	•	•	•	•	•
Kaikoura: orca	559	•	•			
Kaikoura: dolphins	559	•	•	•	•	•
Kaikoura: humpback whales	559					
Kaikoura: seal swimming	559	•	•	•	•	•
Akaroa: Hector's dolphins	606	•	•	•	•	
Oamaru: blue penguins	617	•	◦		◦	◦
Oamaru: yellow-eyed penguins	619	•	•			
Otago Peninsula: royal albarosses	689	•	•	•	•	•
Catlins: Hector's dolphins	698	•	•	•	•	
Whataroa: white herons	751	•	•			
Whitebait season						

• Best months for viewing
◦ Present but in smaller numbers

species in lowland areas, whose blooms are almost all white or yellow. With no pollinating bees to attract there was little need for vibrant petals.

New Zealand's best-known tree, the **kauri**, is found in mixed lowland forest, particularly in Northland. With a lifespan of two to four thousand years, this magnificent king of the forest rises to thirty metres, two-thirds of its height being straight, branchless trunk. It was greatly revered by Maori canoe-builders who enacted solemn ceremonies before hacking them down. European shipbuilders used the trees for ships' masts and timbers, though many kauri were also turned into frames, cladding and floorboards for New Zealand's typical wooden houses. The tree is also the source of kauri gum, dug from ancient forests and exported in the late nineteenth and early twentieth century.

Open spaces along forest edges and riverbanks are often alive with tui (see p.909) sucking nectar from golden clusters of **kowhai**, the national flower. These hang from the kowhai tree, whose wood was once fashioned into Maori canoe paddles and adze handles.

Jun	Jul	Aug	Sep	Oct	Nov	Dec
			•	•	•	•
•	•	•	•	•	•	•
•	•	•	•	•	•	•
•	•	•	•	•		
		•	•	•	•	•
		•	•	•	•	•
•	•	•	•	•	•	•
					•	•
					•	•
•	•	•	•	•		
•	•	•	•	•	•	•
				•	•	•
•	•	•	•	•	•	•
						•
•	•	•	•	•	•	•
•	•					
				•	•	•
					•	•
			•	•	•	•
				•	•	•
•	•	•	•	•	•	•
					•	•
					•	•
			•	•		

The North Island and the top third of the South Island are home to New Zealand's only native palm, the **nikau**, whose slender branchless stem bears shiny leaves of up to 30cm, long pink spiky flowers and red fruit. Early European settlers used the berries as pellets in the absence of ammunition.

The **pohutukawa** is an irregularly branched 20m tree found as far south as Otago, seen in forests around the coast and at lake edges. It typically bears festive bright crimson blossoms around Christmas. Another well-known red-blooming tree is the gnarled **rata**, found in quantity in South Island forests and in ones and twos around the North Island.

New Zealand is also known for its unusual family of pine species, which are known as **podocarps** and don't resemble traditional pines. One such is the majestic **rimu** (red pine), which grows to 60m, with small green flowers, red cones and tiny green or black fruit. It was heavily milled for its timber (its charcoal was also mixed with oil and rubbed into tattoo incisions) and yet is still widespread throughout mixed forests. Other podocarps include **matai** (black pine), **miro** (brown pine), **kahikatea** (white pine), and **totara**, which usually lives for a thousand years and was also used by Maori to make war canoes. The tree's thick brown bark, meanwhile, was used for weaving baskets.

Below the canopy of these large trees you'll find an enormous variety of **tree ferns**, many of them hard to tell apart. The most famous, adopted as a national emblem, is the **ponga** (silver fern). Reaching about 10m in height, its long fronds are dull green on top and silvery white underneath.

The lowland forest is prime habitat for the bulk of New Zealand's endangered birds (see box, p.908).

Rivers, lakes and wetlands

High mountains and a good deal of rain mean that New Zealand is not short of rivers. Canterbury and the Waitaki specialize in distinctive **braided rivers**, their wide shingle beds and multiple channels providing a breeding ground for many birds, insects, fish and plants. Numerous lakes provide rich habitats for

The scourge of the bush: mammalian pests

Since human habitation began, 43 indigenous bird species have become extinct, and New Zealand now accounts for eleven percent of the world's endangered bird species. Direct human action is a factor, but arguably the worst damage inflicted by settlers on the country's unique ecosystem was through the introduction of non-native mammals.

Possums

Visitors to New Zealand soon become familiar with the nocturnal **possum**, if only as road-kill. To see a live specimen you'll probably need to go tramping, when their eyes reflect your torchlight around the hut at night. They may look cute, but they cause enormous damage to flora and fauna, stunting trees by munching on the new shoots, eating native birds' eggs and killing chicks. Consequently, New Zealanders have an almost pathological hatred of this introduced Australian marsupial; greenies who would never dream of wearing any other fur happily own possum-skin slippers.

Before the start of controlled European migration in 1840, enterprising individuals had started liberating **brushtail opossums** (*Trichosurus vulpecula*, more commonly known as **possums**) in New Zealand with the aim of establishing a fur industry. Releases only stopped around 1930, and control measures were finally introduced in 1951 when a bounty was to be paid on all killed possums from which skins had not been taken. Until the late 1980s possums were still killed for their fur, but successful anti-fur lobbying saw prices plummet. Hunting tailed off and possum numbers skyrocketed. Possums now number in excess of **seventy million**, and it is thought that they currently eat their way through 21,000 tonnes of vegetation every night. They are also carriers of bovine TB, endangering the dairy, beef and deer industries.

Possums are now so widespread that hunting barely has any effect and the government is forced to spend around $100 million a year on possum control. The most cost-effective is aerial drops of **1080 poison**, a controversial substance banned in almost every other country in the world. Farmers claim it kills their stock and the native birds it is designed to protect. Certainly native birds do die, but the decimation of the possum population allows such an increase in avian breeding success that bird numbers soon far exceed their pre-poisoning levels.

fish and birds; many of New Zealand's **wetlands**, on the other hand, have been drained for agriculture and property development, although some areas are preserved as national parks and scenic reserves. It's in low wetland areas that you're likely to come across the tallest of the native trees, the kahikatea (white pine), which reaches over 60m. There's a particularly fine stand in the central western North Island close to Te Awamutu.

One bird you're bound to see in the vicinity of a lake is the **pukeko** (swamp hen), a bird which is still in the process of losing the power of flight. Also found in parts of Australia, the pukeko is mostly dark and mid-blue with large feet and an orange beak, and lets out a high-pitched screech if disturbed.

New Zealand is renowned for its freshwater fishing, with massive brown and rainbow **trout** and **salmon** swarming through the fast-flowing streams. All introduced species, these fish have adapted so well to their conditions that they grow much larger here than most other places in the world; as a result, many native species have been driven out. Another delicacy found in New Zealand's waters are native **eels**. Curiously, despite spending most of their lives quietly in New Zealand rivers, they migrate over 2000km north to breed in the waters off Fiji.

Wild pigs, deer, thar and chamois

When James Cook sailed around New Zealand in the 1770s he released **pigs** so that on return voyages there might be something tasty to hunt and eat. These feral pigs (known as "Captain Cookers") are still out there rooting up the ground, although pig hunting keeps numbers down.

Seven **deer** species were successfully established for sport from 1851 up to the 1930s, and even today there are illegal releases of deer by hunters. Authorities are reluctant to advocate complete removal because of the political strength of the hunting lobby. In the first half of the twentieth century, the government also introduced the Himalayan **thar** and European **chamois**, both of which still inhabit the high country of the South Island.

Rabbits and mustelids

Rabbits were introduced to New Zealand from the 1840s and though they don't pose a particular threat to native wildlife, the means used to try to stem the population certainly do. In the 1880s **ferrets** were introduced, but instead of targeting rabbits, these members of the mustelid family found the flightless birdlife easy prey. **Stoats** were also introduced to combat the rabbit plague and have become the number one wildlife enemy in the land: hard to catch let alone kill. Smaller still are **weasels**, which particularly threaten smaller birds.

Dogs, cats, rats and mice

Uncontrolled **dogs** can't resist playing with any flightless birds they might come across and studies suggest they are responsible for 76 percent of adult brown kiwi deaths alone. There are an estimated 1.2 million **cats** in New Zealand, a quarter of them feral. Following their natural instincts they kill numerous birds and lizards, and some councils try to discourage pet ownership in suburbs bordering native bush, but enforcement is political suicide.

The *kiore* or Polynesian **rat** has been largely displaced by more aggressive Norway and ship rats. Rats live everywhere from the treetops to the leaf litter and ravage small bird and insect populations as well as devouring plant seeds, suppressing growth in the bush. **Mice** play a similarly devastating role.

New Zealand's rare and endangered wildlife

New Zealand now has 73 animal and plant species on the IUCN Red List of Globally Threatened Species compiled by Birdlife International (www.redlist.org). Among developed countries, only the United States (with 35 times the surface area) has more ranked species. Of the birds, some 22 percent of New Zealand species are regarded as globally threatened, including the following.

Birds

Bellbird (*korimako*). Relatively common in forest and shrub the length of the country, the shy, pale green bellbird is noted for its distinctive musical "mackmacko" call.

Black stilt (*kaki*). This thin black bird with round eyes and long red legs is incredibly shy – if you do see one in the wild, keep well away. It is one of the world's rarest wading birds. Usually found in swamps and beside riverbeds, the best place to see them is in the specially created reserve near Twizel.

Blue duck (*whio*). Uniquely among ducks, the whio (sometimes known as the torrent duck) spends most of its time in mountain streams, where it dives for its supper. One of four endemic species with no close relatives anywhere in the world, you can spot it by its blue-grey plumage, with chestnut on both breast and flanks. It also has an unusual bill with a black flexible membrane along each side, and beady yellow eyes (as seen on the $10 note). Its Maori name represents the male bird's call.

Fantail (*piwakawaka*). This relatively common forest dweller is more likely to be seen than heard, constantly opening and closing the tail that gives it its name. It often flies alongside walkers on trails, not out of a desire for company but to feed on the insects you disturb.

Kaka Large parrot closely related to the kea, though it does not venture from its favoured lowland forest environments. You can recognize the bird by its colour: bronze with a crimson belly and underside of the tail and wings.

Kakapo The world's only flightless parrot, kakapo were once so widespread they were kept as pets. Now there are less than a hundred birds left, all on a couple of predator-free islands off the coast of Fiordland (both off-limits to visitors).

Kakariki Bright green parakeets which come in yellow-crowned, red-crowned and the newly identified orange-crowned varieties. Found at most wildlife sanctuaries and on offshore Islands.

Kea The world's only truly alpine parrot. See box, p.637.

Kereru (aka *kukupa*). With adults weighing in around 650g, this is the world's second largest pigeon. Its metallic green, purple and bronze colouring and pure white breast is often seen flashing through low-lying forests with its distinctive noisy wing-slaps. It is a very ancient New Zealand species, which seems to have no relatives elsewhere.

Kiwi See box, p.912.

Kokako Rare slate-grey bird with distinctive blue wattles (patches of skin) on each cheek. An abysmal flyer, it lives mainly in protected forests and mainland islands where trapping keeps predator numbers low. Closely related to the saddleback (see p.909) and featured on the $50 note.

Keeping the fishermen company along the riverbanks of the Mackenzie country and Canterbury are the perilously rare **black stilts** (see box, p.908). The **common pied stilt**, a black-and-white bird, has been more successful in resisting introduced mammals.

Another inhabitant of the Canterbury braided riverbank is the **wrybill**. This small white and grey bird uses its unique bent bill to turn over stones or pull

Morepork (*ruru*). New Zealand's only native owl, this small brown bird is usually heard in the bush at night, and occasionally in town and city gardens. Both Maori and Pakeha names are supposed to represent its call.

NZ falcon (*karearea*). Seen sometimes in the north of the North Island and more often in the high country of the Southern Alps, Fiordland and the forests of Westland, New Zealand's only native raptor comes with a heavily flecked breast, chestnut thighs and a pointed head (as seen on the $20 note). Conservationists and winegrowers hope to reintroduce it to the Marlborough Plains where its natural hunting instincts may deter smaller nuisance birds.

Robin. There are three species of native robin, all occasionally glimpsed as they flit around the forest, often fearlessly pecking the dirt around your feet. They range from black with a cream or yellow breast to all black. Their prolonged and distinctive song lasts for up to thirty minutes, with only brief pauses for breath.

Saddleback (*tieke*). This rare but pretty thrush-sized bird is mostly black except for a tan-coloured saddle. Its chattering call welcomes you if you stumble into its patch of the forest.

Stitchbird (*hihi*). Small bird with a slightly curved beak and distinctive yellow and white patches on its sides. There are thought to be only 500–2000 left, some on Kapiti Island and Tiritirii Matangi where you can see them using the feeding stations.

Takahe Rare turkey-sized bird once thought extinct (see p.845).

Tui With its white throat and mostly green and purple velvet-like body, the tui is renowned for mimicking the calls of other birds and for its copious consumption of nectar and fruit. Its song has greater range than the bellbird and contains some rather unmusical squeaks, croaks and strangled utterances. Of all the threatened birds listed here, this is one of the most common.

Weka About the most common flightless native, the weka is a little like the kiwi but slimmer, far less shy, and is generally dark brown with marked golden flecks, especially on its heavily streaked breast. Like the kiwi, the weka grubs around at dusk but can be seen regularly during the day: many are bold enough to approach trampers and take titbits from their hands. The bird's whistle is a loud and distinctive "kooo-li". There are four subspecies found in a variety of habitats throughout the country.

Other endangered species

Tuatara This nocturnal lizard-like creature is a throwback to the age of dinosaurs and remains little changed over the last 260 million years. The tuatara lives on insects, small mammals and birds' eggs, a diet which sees them grow to sixty centimetres in length and keeps them alive for well over a hundred years. Your best chance of spotting one is in a zoo or kiwi house.

Weta A relatively common grasshopper-like insect that has lived in lowland forests for 190 million years. Several species live in the bush but they're hard to spot and you're most likely to see them in caves and in zoos. The most impressive species is the giant weta (*wetapunga*), which ranks as the heaviest insect in the world, weighing up to 71g. Although said to have been the model for Ridley Scott's *Alien*, they aren't poisonous.

out crustaceans from mud. The wrybill's close cousin, the **banded dotterel**, favours the sides of rivers, lakes, open land with sparse vegetation and coastal lagoons and beaches. It is a small brown and white bird with a dark or black band around its neck and breeds only in New Zealand, though it does briefly migrate to Australia. Around fast-flowing streams you might see (or at least hear) the increasingly rare **blue duck** (see box, p.908).

The highlands

With most of the lowland forests cleared for farming, you really need to get into the hills to really appreciate the picture that greeted first the Maori and then early European immigrants. Your best bets are the Tongariro, Whanganui, Taranaki, Nelson Lakes, Arthur's Pass and Aoraki Mount Cook national parks – all cloaked in highland forests, particularly New Zealand's native beech trees. Unlike most northern hemisphere beeches, the Kiwi varieties are evergreen. The 20m high **mountain beech** (tawhairauriki) grows close to the top of the treeline and has sharp dark leaves and little red flowers. Also at high altitudes, often in mixed stands, are **silver beech** (tawhai), whose grey trunks grow up to 30m. Slightly lower altitudes are favoured by black and red beech. Often mixed in with them, the thin, straggly **manuka** (tea tree) grows in both alpine regions and on seashores.

New Zealand has five hundred species of flowering alpine plant that grow nowhere else in the world. Most famous are the large white-flowered yellow-centred **Mount Cook lilies**, the world's largest buttercup. It flowers from November to January. On the high ground of the South Island is the **vegetable sheep**, a white hairy plant that grows low along the ground and, at a great distance, could just about be mistaken for a grazing animal.

Among alpine caves and rock crevices you might come across the black **alpine weta** (also known as the "Mount Cook flea"). Fewer species of birds inhabit the high country, but those that do exist are a fascinating bunch. In the Southern Alps you'll hear, then see, the raucous **kea** and perhaps the **New Zealand falcon** (for both see p.909). Subalpine areas host smaller birds like the yellow and green **rock wren** and the **rifleman**, a tiny green and blue bird with spiralling flight. Such areas are also the natural home of two of the country's rarest birds, the **takahe** and the **kakapo** (see p.908) though neither are seen outside a couple of tightly controlled areas.

The coast, islands and sea

New Zealand's indented coastline, battered by the Tasman Sea and the Pacific Ocean, is a meeting place of warm and cold currents, which makes for an environment suited to an enormous variety of fish. Tropical fish species such as barracuda, marlin, sharks and tuna are attracted by the warm currents, locally populated by hoki, kahawai, snapper, orange roughy and trevally. The cold Antarctic currents bring blue and red cod, blue and red moki, and fish that can tolerate a considerable range of water temperatures, such as the tarakihi, grouper and bass.

Marine mammals also grace the waters: the rare **humpback whale** is an occasional visitor to the shores of Kaikoura and Cook Strait, while **sperm whales** are common year-round in the deep sea trench near Kaikoura. **Orca** are seen regularly wherever there are dolphins, seals and other whales. One frequent visitor is the **pilot whale**: up to 200 pass by Farewell Spit each year; they're also seen in Cook Strait and the Bay of Plenty.

Common dolphins congregate all year round in the Bay of Plenty, Bay of Islands and around the Coromandel Peninsula. Of the three other species seen in New Zealand, **bottlenose dolphins** hang around Kaikoura and

▲Wind turbines near Palmerston North

Whakatane most of the year, while **dusky dolphins**, the most playful, can be spotted near the shore of the Marlborough Sounds, Fiordland and Kaikoura from October to May. At any time of year you might get small schools of tiny **Hector's dolphins** accompanying your boat around Banks Peninsula, the Catlins and Invercargill.

Until recently there were few opportunities to see the Hooker's (or "New Zealand") **sea lion** except on remote Antarctic islands, but these rare animals, with their round noses and deep, wet eyes are appearing once more around the Catlins and Otago Peninsula. The larger New Zealand **fur seal** is in much greater abundance around the coast. You're most likely to come across them in the Sugar Loaf Marine Reserve off New Plymouth, around the Northland coast, in the Bay of Plenty, near Kaikoura, around the Otago Peninsula and in the Abel Tasman National Park. Both seals and sea lions can become aggressive during the breeding season (Dec–Feb), so remember to keep your distance (at least 30m) at these times. **Elephant seals** still breed at Nuggets in the Catlins; more extensive colonies exist on the offshore islands.

Also drawn by the coast's fish-rich waters are a number of visiting and native seabirds, the most famous being the graceful and solitary **royal albatross**, found on the Otago Peninsula and, just offshore, the smaller **wandering albatross**. A far more common sight are **little blue penguins**, which you're almost guaranteed to see on any boat journey, all year round. The large **yellow-eyed penguin** is confined to parts of the east coast of the South Island, from Christchurch to the Catlins, while the **Fiordland crested penguin** with its thick yellow eyebrows is rarely seen outside Fiordland and Stewart Island. Other common seabirds include **gannets**, their yellow heads and white bodies unmistakable as they dive from great heights into shoals of fish; and **cormorants** and **shags** (mostly grey or black), usually congregating on cliffs and rocky shores. On and around islands you're also likely to see the **sooty shearwater**, **titi** (also known as "muttonbirds"), while the **black oystercatchers** and the black-and-white **variable oystercatchers**, both with orange cigar beaks and stooping gait, can be spotted searching in pairs for food on the foreshore almost everywhere.

Green issues

New Zealand comes with an enviable reputation for being **clean and green**, but this is more by accident than design. With a population of just over four million and a relatively short recorded history, you might expect human impact on the landscape to be limited. But in less than a thousand years (and mostly in the last 150) humans have managed to convert a full three-quarters of the land area to farming and commercial forestry, the latter essential to the national economy. These days, just ten percent of native forest remains. Meanwhile, generous winds and flushing rainfall conveniently dispose of much of the **pollution**, which dissipates unseen.

The kiwi

Flightless, dull brown in colour and not classically beautiful, **the kiwi** is nonetheless New Zealand's much-loved national symbol. Stout, muscular, shy and nocturnal, it is a member of the ratite family – which includes the ostrich, emu, rhea, cassowary and the long-extinct moa – and is one of the few birds in the world with a well-developed sense of **smell**. At night you might hear them snuffling around in the dark, using the nostrils at the end of their bill to detect earthworms, beetles, cicada larvae, spiders and also koura (freshwater crayfish), berries and the occasional frog. Armed with sensitive bristles at the base of its bill and a highly developed sense of hearing, the kiwi can detect other birds and animals on its territory and will readily attack them with its claws. The females are bigger than the males and lay huge eggs, weighing a fifth of their own body weight. After eighty days, the eggs hatch and the chicks live off the rich yolk; neither parent feeds them and they emerge from the nest totally independent. They sleep for up to twenty hours a day, which probably explains why they normally live to the age of 20 or 25.

Sadly there are probably fewer than 70,000 birds left in the country and numbers in the wild are dropping rapidly. Kiwi are most easily seen in nocturnal **kiwi houses** around the country in places such as Auckland Zoo, Otorohanga, Napier, Wellington and Hokitika. The best opportunities for seeing **kiwi in the wild** are:

Trounson Forest, Northland (see p.225).

Tiritiri Matangi, Auckland (see p.161).

Kapiti Island, near Wellington (p.290).

Mason Bay, Stewart island (see p.713).

Kiwi species

Kiwi have traditionally been divided into three species – Brown, Little Spotted and Great Spotted – but genetic research in the 1990s subdivided three new species off from the Brown Kiwi.

Great Spotted Kiwi Going by the Maori name *roa*, this is the largest kiwi species, with adults males averaging 2.4kg and females 3.3kg. They are the most rugged kiwi, and are happiest in subalpine regions with wet, mossy vegetation. Smaller birds range down

Land usage

With limited flat land, early European settlers and, later, returning WWI veterans spent years taming steep bush-covered hills. Only really suitable for raising sheep, these **farms** were profitable when wool and lamb prices were high, but in recent years farming such land has become uneconomic and some areas are being allowed to slowly revert to their natural state through the **tenure review** process, opening these lands up to the public as parks and reserves. Far more often, however, marginal lands are being planted with rows of introduced **pines** which get logged every 25 years, reducing them to unsightly fields of stumps. Meanwhile, the ever-growing need for housing, roads and associated infrastructure gobbles up productive farmland and threatens fragile wetland.

Pollution

In most parts of New Zealand you can inhale huge lungfuls of fresh air and lakes and rivers are frequently crystal-clear. But all is not as it seems. In large part due to poor public transport, New Zealand's **car ownership** rates are some of the highest in the world. New Zealand also imports huge numbers of secondhand cars from Japan that would not be allowed off the boat in

into lowland and coastal beech forests. European explorers told stories of kiwi the size of a turkey with powerful spurs on its legs, whose call was the loudest. Their harsh home has also helped keep them relatively safe from mammalian pests. Numbers seem fairly stable around 17,000 birds, mostly in the northern half of the South Island.

Little Spotted Kiwi Also known as Kiwi Pukupuku, this is the smallest of the kiwi, with adults weighing 1100 to 1300 grams. The main population (around 1000 birds) is on Kapiti Island. This species is mellow and docile by nature and pairs often share daytime shelter, going their separate ways to feed, grunting to one another as they pass. They rarely probe for food, instead finding prey on the ground or in the forest litter. The best time to hear them is just after dark from high points around an island. Listen carefully for the male's shrill whistle and the female's gentle purr.

Brown Kiwi These medium-sized kiwi are the most widespread, particularly in the central and northern North Island. They are famous for their big nose, bad temper and for being tough fighters against intruders on their territory. They live in a wide range of vegetation, including exotic forests and rough farmland on the North Island.

Rowi (aka Okarito Brown). Originally considered a subspecies of the Brown Kiwi, this is the rarest kiwi, with only around 250 surviving in the wild, all in the 10,000-hectare south Okarito Forest in South Westland. They're greyish in colour often with patches of white feathers on their face. Males and females share incubation – unlike most kiwi, where the male does the lion's share.

Haast Tokoeka These very rare birds only number around 300, unsurprisingly mostly around Haast in south Westland. They range from the shoreline to alpine tops but are most common around the bushline and in subalpine grasslands, even digging their burrows in snow when necessary.

Southern Tokoeka Totalling around 30,000, these are the most common kiwi, with a stable population on Stewart Island where there are no mustelids. Also found in Fiordland, they are one of the most primitive of all kiwi and the most communal, sometimes seen poking about along the tideline within a few metres of one another.

many other countries; there is no requirement for vehicles to be regularly emission tested.

Mountains streams and alpine tarns look so clean and fresh you'll be tempted to drink straight from them. In most cases this is probably fine, but the water might also harbour **giardia** (see p.79), an intestinal parasite that can easily ruin your holiday. It is best to treat all drinking water. Freshwater rivers have recently become prey to the **didymo** algae (*Didymoshenia geminata*); boaties, fishers and kayakers should thoroughly clean all their gear before moving to another river to prevent it spreading. Additionally, modern **farming** techniques are increasingly intensive, including the use of fertilisers which run off into rivers and streams. On the bright side, **industrial pollution** is a relatively minor issue, thanks to a relatively small manufacturing sector.

The search for power

With a growing power-hungry population and a lack of major investment over the last twenty or thirty years, New Zealand's power supplies are tightening. **Hydro** and **geothermal power** now only account for two-thirds of electricity supply, compared to eighty percent in the late 20th century. Even these are contentious: hydro reservoirs have destroyed numerous natural habitats, especially riverbanks, where threatened species of birds live, nest and feed. Geothermal stations are planned but over-extraction detrimentally affects geysers and boiling mud pools.

Building coal power stations (and converting oil and gas stations) could make New Zealand self-sufficient in electricity for over a hundred years, but at a considerable cost to the environment. Clean emission technologies are also strenuously debated. **Wind energy** continues to meet resistance from those complaining of noise and visual pollution, and installed capacity is still very low. For decades no one dared suggest New Zealand should invest in **nuclear power** but the power pinch and the need to follow Kyoto commitments is beginning to change long-held resistance.

The good news is that, despite government vacillation and the paramount interests of big business, an ever-increasing number of New Zealanders are actively working to preserve the country's unique environment – stay tuned.

Books

Kiwis are avid readers and almost equally keen writers, producing more glossy picture books and wildlife guides than their small population would seem to warrant. Modern writers, inheritors of an increasingly confident tradition, regularly produce excellent novels, poems and factual material. Almost all of the following titles can be found in bookstores or online. Books that are especially recommended are marked ★.

History, society and politics

James Belich *The New Zealand Wars* Well-researched, in-depth study from one of the country's more original thinkers, re-examining the Victorian and Maori interpretations of the colonial wars. A book for committed historians. *Paradise Reforged* is a history of New Zealanders from 1880 to 2000, concentrating on their relationship with the outside world.

Alistair Campbell *Maori Legends* A brief, accessible retelling of selected stories with some evocative illustrations.

R.D. Crosby *The Musket Wars* Account of the massive nineteenth-century upsurge in inter-*iwi* conflict, exacerbated by the introduction of the musket, which led to the death of 23 percent of the Maori population, a proportion greater even than that suffered by Russia in World War II.

Alan Duff *Out of the Mist and Steam* Duff, author of *Once Were Warriors* (see p.923), has created a vivid memoir of his life that falls short of autobiography but gives the reader a good idea where the material for his novels came from.

Duncan Fallowell *Going As Far As I Can* Modern NZ as seen through the eyes of an ageing, gay Englishman: there's no rugby, bungy jumping or *Lord of the Rings*. Kiwi noses were put out of joint by his acerbic jibes at their bad dress sense, ugly modern buildings and emotional constipation, but it is worth reading to find out why he loved Devonport but not Auckland and found Oamaru "one of the most majestic small towns south of the equator".

A.K. Grant *Corridors of Paua* A light-hearted look at the turbulent and fraught political history of the country from 1984 to the introduction of MMP in 1996.

Nick Hagar *The Hollow Men.* Written in 2006, this well-researched piece of extended journalism exposes, through leaked emails, the chicanery of the National Party in New Zealand under the leadership of Don Brash.

Tom Hewnham *By Batons and Barbed Wire* (o/p). A harrowing account of the 1981 Springbok Tour of New Zealand, which stirred up more social hatred than any other event and proved conclusively that there is more to New Zealand society than just a bunch of good blokes.

Hamish Keith *The Big Picture A History of New Zealand Art from 1642.* A fascinating and rewarding tome for anybody interested in the progression from early Maori art through European influence to today's fusion of styles.

★ **Michael King** *The Penguin History of New Zealand* Published in 2003, this is a highly readable and thoroughly up-to-date general history of New Zealand. Maori oral history gets good coverage and there's plenty on uneasy Maori–Pakeha relations, recent political changes and the Maori renaissance. *Death of the Rainbow Warrior* is a brilliant account of the farcical, and ultimately tragic, efforts of the French secret service to sabotage Greenpeace's campaign against French nuclear testing.

Hineani Melbourne *Maori Sovereignty: The Maori Perspective*; and its companion volume *Maori Sovereignty: The Pakeha Perspective* by Carol Archie. Everyone from grass-roots activists to statesmen gets a voice in these two volumes, one airing the widely divergent Maori visions of sovereignty, the other covering equally disparate Pakeha views. They assume a good understanding of Maori structures and recent New Zealand history but are highly instructive nonetheless.

Claudia Orange *The Story of the Treaty* A concise illustrated exploration of the history and myths behind what many believe to be the most important document in New Zealand history, the Treaty of Waitangi.

Margaret Orbell *A Concise Encyclopaedia of Maori Myth and Legend* A comprehensive rundown on many tales and their backgrounds that rewards perseverance, though it is a little dry.

Jock Phillips *A Man's Country? The Image of the Pakeha Male* Classic treatise on mateship and the Kiwi bloke. Thorough exploration through the formative pioneering years, rugby, wartime camaraderie, the family-man ideal and Nineties man.

Anne Salmond *Amiria: The Life Story of Maori Women* A reprint of an old classic, describing the traditional values passed on to the author, set against a background of tribal history and contemporary race relations.

D.C. Starzecka (ed) *Maori Art and Culture* A kind of Maori culture primer, with concise and interesting coverage of Maori history, culture, social structure, carving and weaving.

K. Taylor and P. Moloney *On the Left: Essays on Socialism in New Zealand* A comprehensive collection of political essays spanning over a century that shows why New Zealand society has such a strong egalitarian spine.

Chris Trotter *No Left Turn.* Wonderful episodic history of New Zealand, that convincingly argues that the country has been continuously shaped by "greed, bigotry and right-wing politics".

Dorothy Urlich *Cloher Hongi Hika* Compelling biography dealing with the foremost Maori leader at the time of the first contact between Maori and the Europeans, and his subsequent participation in the Musket Wars.

Mere Whaanga *A Carved Cloak for Tahu* Tells the story of the northern Hawke's Bay *hapu* of Ngai Tahu Mata Whaiti, including history, tradition and an overview of religions and the effects of those elements on modern development.

Fiction

Graeme Aitken *Fifty Ways of Saying Fabulous* Extremely funny book about burgeoning homosexuality in a young farm boy, who lives in a world where he is expected to clean up muck and play rugby.

Eric Beardsley *Blackball 08* Entertaining and fairly accurate historical novel set in the West Coast coal-mining town of Blackball during New Zealand's longest ever labour dispute.

Graham Billing *Forbrush and the Penguins* Described as the first serious novel to come out of Antarctica, this is a compelling description of one man's lonely vigil over a colony of penguins.

Samuel Butler *Erewhon* Initially set in the Canterbury high country (where Butler ran a sheep station), but increasingly devoted to a satirical critique of mid-Victorian Britain.

Nigel Cox *Tarzan Presley* Amusing reworking of the Tarzan myth where the hero grows up in New Zealand and then becomes the king of rock'n'roll – nothing if not ambitious.

Ian Cross *The God Boy* This first and only novel of note from Ian Cross is widely considered to be New Zealand's equivalent to *Catcher in The Rye*. It concerns a young boy trapped between two parents who hate each other and describes the violent consequences of the situation.

Barry Crump *A Good Keen Man; Hang on a Minute Mate; Bastards I Have Met; Forty Yarns, The Adventures of Sam Cash and a Song* Just a few of the many New Zealand bushman books by the Kiwi equivalent of Banjo Patterson, who writes with great humour, tenderness and style about the male-dominated world of hunting, shooting, fishing, drinking, and telling tall stories. Worth reading for a picture of a now-past New Zealand lifestyle.

Alan Duff *Once Were Warriors* Shocking and violent social realist book set in 1970s south Auckland and adapted in the 1990s for Lee Tamahori's film of the same name. Well-intentioned and passionate.

Janet Frame *An Angel at My Table* Though one of New Zealand's most accomplished novelists, Frame is perhaps best known for this three-volume autobiography, dramatized in Jane Campion's film which, with wit and a self-effacing honesty, gives a wonderful insight into both the author and her environment. Her superb novels and short stories use humour alongside highly disturbing combinations of events and characters to overthrow readers' preconceptions. For starters, try *Faces in the Water, Scented Gardens for the Blind, Towards Another Summer* and *Owls Do Cry*.

Maurice Gee *Crime Story; Going West; Prowlers; The Plumb Trilogy* Novels from an underrated but highly talented writer. Despite the misleadingly light titles, Gee's focus is social realism, taking an unflinching, powerful look at motivation and unravelling relationships.

Patricia Grace *Potiki* Poignant, poetic and exquisitely written tale of a Maori community redefining itself while its land is threatened by coastal development. *Baby No Eyes* is a magical weaving of real events with stories of family history told from four points of view. *Dogside Story*, shortlisted for the 2001 Booker Prize, is a wonderful story about the power of the land and the strength of *whanau* at the turn of the Millennium. *Tu* is an astonishing novel about the Maori Battalion fighting in Italy in WWII, drawn from the experiences of the author's father and other relatives.

Peter Hawes *Leapfrog with Unicorns* and *Tasman's Lay* Two from an unsung hero, cult figure and probably only member of the absurdist movement in New Zealand, who writes with great energy, wit and surprising discipline about almost anything that takes his fancy. Hawes has also written the not-to-be-missed *Inca Girls Aren't Easy*, a series of joyous, sad and slippery tales, under the name W.P. Hearst. A brilliant late addition to Hawes' eccentric canon, *Royce, Royce the People Choice,* is a sort of *Old Man and the Sea* mixed with *Moby Dick*.

Keri Hulme *The Bone People* The winner of the 1985 Booker Prize, and a wonderful first novel, set along the wild beaches of the South Island's West Coast. Mysticism, myth and earthy reality are transformed into a haunting tale peopled with richly drawn characters.

Witi Ihimaera *Bulibasha – King of the Gypsies* The best introduction to one of the country's finest Maori authors. A rollicking good read, energetically exploring the life of a rebellious teenager in 1950s rural New Zealand, it's an intense look at adolescence, cultural choices, family ties and the abuse of power, culminating in a masterful twist. Look out also for the excellent *The Matriarch* and *The Uncle Story*, the brilliant *Whale Rider* and *Star Dancer* by the same author.

Lloyd Jones *Mister Pip*. Intriguing, engaging Booker-shortlisted novel dealing with an unreported war on a remote South Pacific island where the schoolchildren's futures are entwined with a boy called Pip and a man named Dickens.

Shonagh Koea *The Grandiflora Tree* A savagely witty yet deeply moving study of the conventions of widowhood, with a peculiar love story thrown in. First novel from a journalist and short-story writer renowned for her astringent humour.

Katherine Mansfield *The Collected Stories of Katherine Mansfield* All 73 short stories sit alongside 15 unfinished fragments in this 780-page tome. Concise yet penetrating examinations of human behaviour in apparently trivial situations, often transmitting a painfully pessimistic view of the world, and startlingly modern for their time.

Ngaio Marsh *Opening Night; Artists in Crime; Vintage Murder* Just a selection from the doyenne of New Zealand crime fiction. Since 1934 she has been airing her Anglophile sensibilities and killing off innumerable individuals in the name of entertainment, before solving the crimes with Inspector Allen. Perfect mindless reading matter for planes, trains and buses.

Owen Marshall *Drybread* Sparingly written, poignant novel set between Christchurch and Central Otago which examines love and loss through its two protagonists: a mother returning to New Zealand to flee a court order from the US, and an emotionally scarred local journalist pursuing her story.

Ronald Hugh Morrieson *Came a Hot Friday* Superb account of the idiosyncrasies of country folk and the two smart spielers who enter their lives, in a visceral gothic comedy thriller focusing on crime and sex in a small town.

Frank Sargeson *The Stories of Frank Sargeson* Though not well known outside New Zealand, Sargeson is a giant of Kiwi literature. His writing, from the 1930s to the 1980s, is incisive and sharply observed, at its best in dialogue, which is always true to the metre of New Zealand speech. This work brings together some of his finest short stories. *Once is Enough, More than Enough* and *Never Enough!* make up the complete autobiography of a man sometimes even more colourful than his characters; Michael King wrote a fine biography, *Frank Sargeson: A Life*.

Maurice Shadbolt *Strangers and Journeys* On publication in

1972 this became a defining novel in New Zealand's literary ascendancy and its sense of nationhood, putting Shadbolt in the same league as Australia's Patrick White. A tale of two families, with finely wrought characters whose lives interweave through three generations. Very New Zealand, very human and not overly epic. Later works, which have consolidated Shadbolt's reputation, include *Monday's Warriors. Season of the Jew* and *The House of Strife*.

C.K. Stead *The Singing Whakapapa* Highly regarded author of many books and critical essays who is little known outside New Zealand and Australia. This powerful novel focuses on an early missionary and a dissatisfied modern descendant who is searching for meaning in his own life. His 1998 collection of short stories, *The Blonde with Candles in her Hair*, was less critically acclaimed, but still entertaining and readable. *All Visitors Ashore* is a masterpiece based around the harbourfront strike of 1951 and slyly alluding to Stead's literary contemporaries. Finally, *Mansfield* is an evocative fictional musing about New Zealand's most famous short- story writer.

Damien Wilkins *The Miserables* One of the best novels to come out of New Zealand, shorn of much of the colonial baggage of many writers. It is surprisingly mature for a first novel, sharply evoking middle-class New Zealand life from the 1960s to the 1980s through finely wrought characters.

Anthologies

Warwick Brown *100 New Zealand Artists* Companion to the *Picador Book of Contemporary New Zealand Fiction* but also allowing room for sculptors, printmakers, photographers and graphic artists.

James Burns (ed) *Novels and Novelists 1861–1979, a Bibliography* A sweeping and comprehensive introduction to the history of the New Zealand novel and the characters who have made it such a powerful art form.

Bill Manhire (ed) *100 New Zealand Poems* A very manageable selection that provides an excellent introduction to the poetry of the nation.

Owen Marshall (selected by) *Essential New ZealandShort Stories* A truly representative collection of fascinating tales by some of New Zealand's finest, including Frame, Ihimera, Mansfield, Shadbolt, Stead and Gee.

Ian Wedde and Harvey McQueen (eds) *The Penguin Book of New Zealand Verse* A comprehensive collection of verse from the earliest European settlers to contemporary poets, and an excellent introduction to Kiwi poetry; highlights are works by James K. Baxter, Janet Frame, C.K. Stead, Sam Hunt, Keri Hulme, Hirini Melbourne and Apirana Taylor.

Reference and specialist guides

Angie Errigo *Rough Guide to The Lord of the Rings* An essential companion for background on the whole J.R.R. Tolkien phenomenon with exhaustive detail about the man, the books, the films, fan websites and even the books' influence on Seventies prog rock.

Rosemary George *The Wines of New Zealand* Entertaining and informative look at New Zealand's most important wine regions, the history, the people and the product.

John Kent *North Island Trout Fishing Guide* and *South Island Trout Fishing Guide* Laden with information on access, seasons and fishing style, and illustrated with maps of the more important rivers.

Flora, fauna and the environment

D.H. Brathwaite *Native Birds of New Zealand* Brilliant colour photographs and lots of information pinpointing thirty rare birds that, with a little effort and some patience, you can observe while travelling around.

Andrew Crowe *Which Native Tree?* Great little book, ideal for identifying New Zealand's common native trees – though not tree ferns – with diagrams of tree shape, photos of leaves and fruit and an idea of geographic extent.

Susanne & John Hill *Richard Henry of Resolution Island* Comprehensive and very readable account of a man widely regarded as New Zealand's first conservationist. The book also serves as a potted history of this underpopulated area of Fiordland, peopled by many of the key explorers.

Geoff Moon *The Reed Field Guide to New Zealand Birds* Excellent colour reference book, with ample detail for species identification. *The Reed Field Guide to New Zealand Wildlife*, by the same author, is stuffed with colour photos.

Rod Morris & Hal Smith *Wild South: Saving New Zealand's Endangered Birds* A fascinating companion volume to a 1980s TV series following a band of dedicated individuals trying to preserve a dozen of New Zealand's wonderfully exotic bird species, including the kiwi, kakapo, takahe and kea.

Neville Peat *Manapouri Saved* Full and heartening coverage of one of New Zealand's earliest environmental battles when, in the 1960s, a petition signed by ten percent of the country succeeded in persuading the government to cancel its hydroelectric plans for Lake Manapouri.

Kerry-Jayne Wilson *Flight of the Huia* Focusing on Jurassic frogs and bizarre creatures such as the Alpine parrot, this book studies faunal change in New Zealand and current conservation issues.

Tramping

Pearl Hewson *New Zealand's Great Walks* Hewson is a no-nonsense DOC officer working out of the Wellington Office and what she doesn't know about the Great Walks isn't worth knowing. This is a practical, concise guide that concentrates her experiences into a useful aid to trampers.

Moir's Guide (NZ Alpine Club, NZ). Probably the most comprehensive guide to tramping in the South Island. It is divided into two volumes: North, covering hikes between Lake Ohau and Lake Wakatipu; and South, which concentrates on walks around the southern lakes and fjords including the Kepler Track, plus the less popular Dusky and George Sound tracks.

Cycling and adventure sports

Mike Bhana *New Zealand Surfing Guide* Pragmatic handbook to the prime surf spots around the New Zealand coast, with details on access, transport, the best wind and tide conditions and expected swells.

Graham Charles *New Zealand Whitewater: 120 Great Kayaking Runs* (Craig Potton, NZ). A comprehensive and entertaining guide to New Zealand's most important kayaking rivers. River maps and details on access are supplemented by quick reference panels with grades, timings, and handy tips like which rapids not to even think about running.

Bruce Ringer *New Zealand by Bike* (The Mountaineers, NZ). The definitive Kiwi cycle-touring guide, with 14 regional tours (with many side trips) which can all be knitted together into a greater whole. Plenty of maps and altitude profile diagrams.

Nigel Rushton *Pedallers' Paradise* (Paradise, NZ; ⓦwww.paradise-press.co.nz). Separate lightweight North Island and South Island volumes covering recommended routes.

Marty Sharp *A Guide to the Ski Areas of New Zealand* Exactly what you'd expect, with full descriptions of the fields complete with tow plans and information on access, local towns and ski rental.

Paul Simon and Jonathan Kennett *Classic New Zealand Mountain Bike Rides* (Kennett Bros, NZ). All you need to know about off-road biking in New Zealand, with details of over four hundred rides. Simon runs the ⓦwww.mountainbike.co.nz site.

Film

In the wake of *The Lord of the Rings* films, all shot in New Zealand, the Kiwi film industry enjoyed another of its intermittent revivals, previously most notable from 1988–1994 when *The Navigator, An Angel at my Table, The Piano, Once Were Warriors* and *Heavenly Creatures* all gained international recognition and success. Yet, while the directors involved went on to greater eminence, the renaissance faded away like a closing shot. Like most small countries, New Zealand lacks the resources, infrastructure and finances to sustain a large-scale film industry on a permanent basis. More often, the country is used as a relatively inexpensive backdrop for American TV series and for movies that need big outdoors scenes such as *The Chronicles of Narnia*. As a result the local film industry, with a few notable exceptions, is known mainly for technical back-up and providing extras.

An Angel at my Table Jane Campion, 1990. Winner of the Special Jury prize at the Venice Film Festival. One of the most inspiring films New Zealand has produced, based on the brilliant autobiographies of Janet Frame (see p.618).

Bad Blood Mike Newell, 1981. A New Zealand/British collaboration set in New Zealand in World War II that relates the true story of Stan Graham, a Hokitika man who breaks the law by refusing to hand in his rifle. The ensuing events give rise to a discussion of the Kiwi spirit.

Bad Taste Peter Jackson, 1988. Winner of the special jury prize at the Paris Film Festival. Aliens visit earth to pick up flesh for an inter-galactic fast-food chain and have a wild old time. A witty and irreverent spoof.

Broken English Gregor Nicholas, 1996. A tough, uncompromising movie about the relationship between a young Croatian girl and a Maori, with excellent performances and a powerful message about discrimination.

Came a Hot Friday Ian Mune, 1984. The best comedy ever to come out of New Zealand, concentrating on two incompetent confidence tricksters whose luck runs out in a sleepy country town.

Crush Alison Maclean, 1992. A competitor at Cannes. An offbeat, angst-ridden psychological drama set around Rotorua, where the boiling mud and gushing geysers underline the manipulative tensions and sexual chaos that arise when an American femme fatale enters the lives of a New Zealand family.

Desperate Remedies Peter Wells and Stewart Main, 1993. This winner of the Certain Regard Award at Cannes comments wryly on the intrigues and desires of a group of different people whose lives all somehow interconnect.

The Devil Dared Me To Chris Stapp, 2007. Lively, rude laddish film about becoming a stunt man; fun if you like that sort of thing and don't want to think too hard.

Eagle Versus Shark Taika Waititi, 2007. A low-key, well-realized love story starring Jemaine "Flight of the Conchords" Clement, with similar quirky humour.

Fifty Ways of Saying Fabulous Stewart Main, 2005. Clever adaptation of the book of the same name (see p.916) that grabs the spirit of the original and rings out lots of laughs as well as poignancy.

Forgotten Silver Peter Jackson, 2000. Jackson, at his

tongue-in-cheek best, constructs a fake documentary about a Kiwi movie pioneer, who invents film, sound, colour and the biblical epic, all in the bush of the West Coast.

Goodbye Pork Pie Geoff Murphy, 1980. A much loved comedy/road movie following the adventures of two young men in a yellow mini, the cops they infuriate, and the mixed bag of characters they encounter.

Heavenly Creatures Peter Jackson, 1994. Winner of the Silver Lion at Venice and an Oscar nominee. This account of the horrific Parker/Hulme matricide in the 1950s follows the increasingly self-obsessed life of two adolescent girls. An evocative and explosive film that brings all Jackson's subversive humour to bear on the strait-laced real world and, best of all, the girls' fantastic imaginary one. Kate Winslet's film debut.

In My Father's Den Brad McGann, 2004. Depicts an emotional rough ride for an exhausted war journalist (Matthew Macfadyen) who returns home and becomes involved in an unexpected and engrossing journey of discovery. From a novel by Maurice Gee (see p.917).

Kombi Nation Grant Lahood, 2003. Charming and clever low-budget road movie about the big OE (overseas experience), where young Kiwis head off to explore Europe in a VW van (hence the title).

The Navigator Vincent Ward, 1988. A well-received competitor at Cannes, this atmospheric and stylistically inventive venture employs all Ward's favourite themes and characters, including the innocent visionary, in this case a boy who leads five men through time from a fourteenth-century Cumbrian village to New Zealand in the twentieth century in a quest to save their homes.

Once Were Warriors Lee Tamahori, 1994. A surging fly-on-the-wall style comment on the economically challenged Maori situation in modern south Auckland, bringing to mind the British kitchen-sink dramas of the 1950s and 1960s. More a study of class than a full-blown racial statement, it revels in ordinary drudgery and despair, with a warts-and-all story about human weakness and strength of spirit against a background of urban decay. Based on the novel by Alan Duff (see p.917).

Out of the Blue Robert Sarkies, 2006. Based on the true events of the Aramouna Massacre, in which thirteen people lost their lives to a local unemployed gun collector. A dark tale concentrating on the heroism of the out-gunned seaside town police and inhabitants.

Patu Merata Mita, 1983. A powerful documentary recording the year of opposition to the 1981 Springbok rugby tour of New Zealand, which goes some way to showing the extraordinary passions ignited by the event.

The Piano Jane Campion, 1993. With Holly Hunter, Harvey Keitel, Sam Neill and Anna Paquin. This moody winner of the Cannes Palme d'Or (and three Oscars) made Campion bankable in Hollywood. Its mixture of grand scenes and personal trauma knowingly synthesizes paperback romance, erotica and Victorian melodrama – and includes Keitel's stab at the worst Scottish accent of all time.

River Queen Vincent Ward, 2005. Production problems on the Whanganui River saw Ward depart before the project was finished but what's left is a beautifully shot, over-simplified and uneven film worth a look just for the locations.

Scarfies Robert Sarkies, 2000. Surprise hit of the year in NZ and arthouses worldwide, a darkly funny story about students taking over a deserted house in Dunedin only to discover a massive dope crop in the basement. Things get progressively more unpleasant when the dope grower returns.

Sleeping Dogs Roger Donaldson, 1977. Perhaps the birth of the real New Zealand film industry, based on C.K. Stead's book *Smith's Dream*. Sam Neill plays a paranoid anti-hero hunted by repressive state forces. A slick thriller, it struggles to get beyond its fast-paced rush to a violent conclusion.

The Ugly Scott Reynold, 1996. Shown at the 1997 Cannes Film Festival, and winner of rave reviews in the US, this edgy comment on incarceration, reform and mistrust revolves around a serial killer who has been locked away and wants to convince the world he is cured.

Utu Geoff Murphy, 1983. One of the official selections at Cannes, this portrays a Maori warrior in the late 1800s who sets out to revenge himself on the conquerors of New Zealand, in the form of a Pakeha farmer. A tense, well-acted representation of many modern as well as historic issues.

Vigil Vincent Ward, 1984. A Cannes competitor, this dark, rain-soaked story portrays a young girl's coming of age and her negative reaction to a stranger who is trying to seduce her mother, adding to tension of her own sexual awakening.

Whakataratara Paneke Don C. Selwyn, 2001. The Maori *Merchant of Venice*, with English subtitles, an ambitious home-grown film that brings much local acting talent to the screen in an involved, if overly long, epic.

We're Here to Help Jonothan Cullinane, 2007. Inspiring film based on a true story about a man victimized by the Revenue Department who fought back and eventually won.

The World's Fastest Indian Roger Donaldson 2005. Feel-good movie about old codger Burt Munro, who in real life proved you don't have to be young to achieve your dreams – though being barmy helps. Anthony Hopkins in the lead role is marvellous and even does a passable Invercargill accent.

Language

Language

Language

English and *te reo Maori*, the Maori language, share joint status as New Zealand's official languages, but on a day-to-day basis all you'll need is English, or its colourful Kiwi variant. All Maori speak English fluently, often slipping in numerous Maori terms that in time become part of everyday Kiwi parlance. Mainstream TV and radio coverage of any event that has significance to Maori is likely to be littered with words totally alien to foreigners, but well understood by Anglophone Kiwis. It is initially confusing, but with the aid of our glossary (see p.930) you'll soon find yourself using Maori terms all the time.

A basic knowledge of Maori pronunciation will make you more comprehensible and some understanding of the roots of place names can be helpful. You'll need to become something of an expert to appreciate much of the wonderful oral history, and stories told through *waiata* (songs), but learning a few key terms will enhance any Maori cultural events you may attend.

To many Brits and North Americans, **Kiwi English** is barely distinguishable from its trans-Tasman cousin, "Strine", sharing much of the same lexicon of slang terms, but with a softer accent. Australians have no trouble distinguishing the two accents, repeatedly highlighting the vowel shift which turns "bat" into "bet", makes "yes" sound like "yis" and causes "fish" to come out as "fush". There is very little regional variation; only residents of Otago and Southland – the southern quarter of the South Island – distinguish themselves with a rolled "r", courtesy of their predominantly Scottish forebears. Throughout the land, Kiwis add an upward inflection to statements, making them sound like questions; most are not, and to highlight those that are, some add the interrogative "eh?" to the end of the sentence, a trait most evident in the North Island, especially among Maori.

Maori

For the 50–100,000 native speakers and additional 100,000 who speak it as a second tongue, **Maori** is very much a living language. It is gaining strength all the time as both Maori and Pakeha increasingly appreciate the cultural value of *te reo*, a language central to Maoritanga and forming the basis of a huge body of magnificent songs, chants and legends, lent a poetic quality by its hypnotic and lilting rhythms.

Maori is a member of the Polynesian group of languages and shares both grammar and vocabulary with those spoken throughout most of the South Pacific. Similarities are so pronounced that Tupaia, a Tahitian crew member on Captain Cook's first Pacific voyage in 1769, was able to communicate freely with the Aotearoa Maori they encountered. The Treaty of Waitangi was written in both English and Maori, but *te reo* soon began to lose ground to the point where, by the late nineteenth century, its use was proscribed in schools. Maori parents keen for their offspring to do well in the Pakeha world frequently promoted the use of English, and Maori declined further, exacerbated by the mid-twentieth-century migration to the cities. Though never on the brink of extinction, the language reached its nadir in the 1970s when perhaps only ten percent of Maori could speak their language fluently. The tide began to turn towards the end of the decade with the inception of *kohanga reo* **pre-schools** (literally "language nests") where Maoritanga is taught and activities are conducted in Maori. Originally a Maori initiative, it has now crossed over and progressive Pakeha parents are increasingly introducing their kids to biculturalism at an early age. Fortunate *kohanga reo* graduates can progress to the small number of state-funded Maori-language primary schools known as *kura kaupapa*. For decades, Maori has been taught as an option in secondary schools, and there are now state-funded tertiary institutions operated by Maori, offering graduate programmes in Maori studies.

The success of these programmes has bred a young generation of Maori speakers frequently far more fluent than their parents who, shamed by the loss of their heritage, are beginning to attend Maori evening classes. Legal parity means that Maori is now finding its way into officialdom too, with government departments all adopting Maori names and many government and council documents being printed in both languages. Maori-language **radio stations** are now commonplace in the northern half of the North Island where most Maori live, but the real boost came in 2004 with the launching of **Maori Television**. Substantially government funded, it still has relatively low ratings but is well worth tuning into for a very different take on what's going on. Partly in English, partly in Maori and occasionally a synthesis of the two, there's a wonderful cross-fertilization of styles. You can expect everything from movies and sitcoms to discussion panels on Maori issues and lifestyle programmes such as *Kai Time on the Road* (a cooking and Maori food show), and a *marae* makeover show.

In your day-to-day dealings you won't need **to speak Maori**, though both native speakers and Pakeha may well greet you with *kia ora* ("hi, hello"), or less commonly *haere mai* ("welcome"). On ceremonial occasions, such as *marae* visits, you'll hear the more formal greeting *tena koe* (said to one person) or *tena koutou katoa* (to a group).

Maori words used in place names are listed below, while those in common use are listed in the general glossary (see p.930). If you are interested in learning a little more, the best handy reference is Patricia Tauroa's *The Collins Maori Phrase Book*, which has helpful notes on pronunciation, handy phrases and a useful Maori–English and English–Maori vocabulary.

Maori place names

The following is a list of some of the most common words and elements you will see in **town and place names** throughout New Zealand. A.W. Reed's *Reed Dictionary of Maori Place Names* gives more detailed coverage of the same field.

Ao	Cloud
Ara	Road or path
Awa	River or valley
Hau	Wind
Ika	Fish
Iti	Small
Kai	Food, or eat
Kainga	Home, village
Kare	Rippling
Kino	Bad
Ma	White, clear
Manga	Stream
Manu	Bird
Mata	Headland
Maunga	Mountain
Mihi	Speeches
Moana	Sea, lake
Motu	Island or any thing isolated
Muri	End

Nui	Big	**Rua**	Hole, cave, pit, two
O	The place of	**Runga**	Top
One	Sand, beach	**Tahu**	Light
Pa	Fortified settlement	**Tai**	Sea
Pae	Ridge	**Tane**	Man
Papa	Flat, earth, floor	**Tapu**	Sacred
Patere	Chants	**Tara**	Peak
Puke	Hill	**Te**	The
Puna	Spring	**Tomo**	Cave
Raki	North	**Wai**	Water
Rangi	Sky	**Waka**	Canoe
Roa	Long, high	**Whanga**	Bay, body of water
Roto	Lake	**Whenua**	Land or country

Pronunciation

Laziness and arrogance have combined to give Pakeha – and consequently most visitors – a distorted impression of Maori pronunciation, which is usually mutated into an Anglicized form. Until the 1970s there was little attempt to get it right, but with the rise in Maori consciousness since the 1980s, coupled with a sense of political correctness, many Pakeha now make some attempt at Maori pronunciation. As a visitor you will probably get away with just about anything, but by sticking to a few simple rules and keeping your ears open, apparently unfathomable place names will soon trip off your tongue.

Maori was solely a spoken language before the arrival of British and French missionaries in the early nineteenth century, who transcribed it using only fifteen letters of the Roman alphabet. The eight **consonants**, **h**, **k**, **m**, **n**, **p**, **r**, **t** and **w**, are pronounced much as they are in English. The five **vowels** come in long and short forms; the long form is sometimes signified in print by a macron – a flat bar above the letter – but usually it is simply a case of learning by experience which sound to use. When two vowels appear together they are both pronounced, though substantially run together. For example, "Maori" should be written with a macron on the "a" and be pronounced with the first two vowels separate, turning the commonly used but incorrect "Mow-ree" into something more like "Maao-ri".

Here are a few **pronunciation** pointers to help you get it right:

- Long compound words can be split into syllables which all end in a vowel. Waikaremoana comes out as Wai-ka-re-mo-ana. Scanning our list of place name elements should help a great deal.
- All syllables are stressed evenly, so it is not **Wai**-ka-re-mo-ana or Wai-ka-re-**mo**-ana but a flat Wai-ka-re-mo-ana.
- Maori words don't take an "s" to form a plural, so you'll find many plural nouns in this book – kiwi, tui, kauri, Maori – in what appears to be a singular form; about the only exception is Kiwis (as people), a Maori word wholly adopted into English.
- **Ng** is pronounced much as in "sing".
- **Wh** sounds either like an aspirated "f" as in "off", or like the "wh" in "why", depending on who is saying what and in which part of the country.

Glossary

ANZAC Australian and New Zealand Army Corps; every town in New Zealand has a memorial to ANZAC casualties from both world wars.

Aotearoa Maori for New Zealand, the land of the long white cloud.

Ariki Supreme chief of an *iwi*.

Bach (pronounced "batch") Holiday home, originally a bachelor pad at work camps and now something of a Kiwi institution that can be anything from shack to palatial waterside residence.

Back-blocks Remote areas.

Bludger Someone who doesn't pull their weight or pay their way, a sponger.

Bro Brother, term of endearment widely used by Maori.

Captain Cooker Wild pig, probably descended from pigs released in the Marlborough Sounds on Cook's first voyage.

Chilly bin Insulated cool box for carrying picnic supplies.

Choice Fantastic.

Chook Chicken.

Chunder Vomit.

Coaster (Ex-) resident of the West Coast of the South Island.

Cocky Farmer, comes in "Cow" and "Sheep" variants.

Crib South Island name for a *bach*.

Cuz or **Cuzzy** Short for cousin, see "bro".

Dag Wag or entertaining character.

Dairy Corner shop selling just about everything, open seven days and sometimes 24 hours.

Dob in Reporting one's friends and neighbours to the police; there is currently a dobber's charter encouraging drivers to report one another for dangerous driving.

DOC Department of Conservation. Operators of the national parks, conservation policy, track administration and much more.

Docket Receipt.

Domain Grassy reserve, open to the public.

Eftpos Card-based debit system found in shops, bars and restaurants.

Feijoa Fleshy, tomato-sized fruit with melon-like flesh and a tangy, perfumed flavour.

Footie Rugby, usually union rather than league, never soccer.

Freezing works Slaughterhouse.

Godzone New Zealand, short for "God's own country".

Good as (gold) First rate, excellent.

Greasies Takeaway food, especially fish and chips.

Greenstone A type of nephrite jade known in Maori as *pounamu*.

Haka Maori dance performed in threatening fashion before All Black rugby games.

Handle Large glass of beer.

Hangi Maori feast cooked in an earth oven (see p.52).

Hapu Maori sub-tribal unit. Several make up an *iwi*.

Harakeke Flax.

Hard case See "dag".

Hogget The meat from a year-old sheep. Older and more tasty (though less succulent) than lamb, but not as tough as mutton.

Hollywood A faked or exaggerated sporting injury used to gain advantage.

Hongi Maori greeting, performed by pressing noses together.

Hoon Lout, yob or delinquent.

Hori Offensive word for a Maori.

Hot dog A battered sausage on a stick, dipped in tomato ketchup. What the rest of the world knows as a hot dog is known here as an American hot dog.

Hui Maori gathering or conference.

Iwi Largest of Maori tribal groupings.

Jafa Just Another Fucking Aucklander. Semi-derogatory term now (over)used as a noun. "He's a bloody Jafa".

Jandals Ubiquitous Kiwi footwear, thongs or flip-flops.

Jug Litre of beer.

Kiwifruit In New Zealand they are always called kiwifruit, never "kiwis". Golden-fleshed kiwifruit are also available, and less acidic than their green counterparts.

Lucked in In luck. What "Lucked out" means elsewhere in the world.

Lucked out Out of luck. The meaning completely reversed on its way across the Pacific.

Kai Maori word for food, used in general parlance.

Kaimoana Seafood.

Kainga Village.

Karanga Call for visitors to come forward on a *marae*.

Kaumatua Maori elders, old people.

Kawa-Marae Etiquette or protocol on a *marae*.

Kete Traditional basket made of plaited flax.

Kiore Polynesian rat.

kiwi The national bird and mascot of NZ, always set lower case.

Kiwi An alternative label for a New Zealander.

Koha Donation.

Kohanga Reo Pre-school Maori language immersion (literally "language nest").

Kumara Sweet potato.

Kuri Polynesian dog, now extinct.

Lay-by Practice of putting a deposit on goods until they can be fully paid for.

Mana Maori term indicating status, esteem, prestige or authority, and in wide use among all Kiwis.

Manaia Stylized bird or lizard forms used extensively in Maori carving.

Manuhiri Guest or visitor, particularly to a *marae*.

Maoritanga Maori culture and custom, the Maori way of doing things.

Marae Place for conducting ceremonies in front of a meeting house – literally "courtyard". Also a general term for a settlement centred on the meeting house.

Mauri Life force or life principle.

Mere War club, usually of greenstone.

Metalled Graded road surface of loose stones found all over rural New Zealand.

MMP Mixed Member Proportional representation – New Zealand's electoral system.

Moko Old form of tattooing on body and face that has seen a resurgence among Maori.

Muttonbird Gull-sized sooty shearwater that was a major component of the pre-European Maori diet and tastes like oily and slightly fishy mutton – hence the name.

Ngati Tribal prefix meaning "the descendants (or people) of". Also Ngai and Ati.

OE Overseas experience, usually a year spent abroad by Kiwis in their early twenties.

Pa Fortified village of yore, now usually an abandoned terraced hillside.

Paddock Field.

Pakeha A non-Maori, usually white and not usually expressed with derogatory intent. Literally "foreign" though it can also be translated as "flea" or "pest". It may also be a corruption of *pakepakeha*, which are mythical human-like beings with fair skins.

Pashing Kissing or snogging.

Patu Short fighting club.

Paua The muscular foot of the abalone, often minced and served as a fritter, while the wonderful iridescent shell is used for jewellery and decoration.

Pavlova Meringue dessert with a fruit and cream topping.

Pike out To chicken out or give up.

Piss Beer.

Pissed Drunk.

Podocarp Family of pine, native to New Zealand including rimu, kahikatea, matai, miro, totara etc.

Pohutukawa Gnarled native tree found around the coast of the upper North Island. Blooms bright red in mid-December and is sometimes known as New Zealand's Christmas Tree.

Poms Folk from Britain; not necessarily offensive.

Pounamu New Zealand greenstone, a unique type of jade.

Powhiri Traditional welcome onto a *marae*.

Puku Maori for stomach, often used as a term of endearment for someone amply endowed.

Puha Leafy plant traditionally gathered by Maori and eaten like spinach.

Rangatira General term for a Maori chief.

Rapt Well-pleased.

Rattle your dags Hurry up.

Root Vulgar term for sex.

Rooted To be very tired or beyond repair, as in "she's rooted, mate" – your car is irreparable.

Rough as guts Uncouth, roughly made or operating badly, as in "she's running rough as guts, mate".

Sealed road Bitumen-surfaced road.

Section Block of land usually surrounding a house.

She'll be right Everything will work out fine.

Shout To buy a round of drinks or generally to treat folk.

Skull To knock back beer quickly.

Smoko Tea break.

Snarler, snag Sausage.

Squiz A look, as in "Give us a squiz".

Stoked Very pleased.

Sweet Cool.

Taiaha Long-handled club.

Tall poppy Someone who excels. "Cutting down tall poppies" is to bring overachievers back to earth – every Kiwi's perceived duty.

Tamarillo Slightly bitter, deep-red fruit, often known as a tree tomato.

Tane Man.

Tangata whenua The people of the land, local or original inhabitants.

Tangi Mourning or funeral.

Taniwha Fearsome water spirit of Maori legend.

Taonga Treasures, prized possessions.

Tapu Forbidden or taboo. Frequently refers to sacred land.

Te reo Maori Maori language.

Tiki Maori pendant depicting a distorted human figure.

Tiki tour Guided tour.

Togs Swimming costume.

Tohunga Maori priests, experts in Maoritanga.

True Left On the left facing downstream.

True Right On the right when facing downstream.

Tukutuku Knotted latticework panels decorating the inside of a meeting house.

Tupuna Ancestors; of great spiritual importance to Maori.

Ute Car-sized pick-up truck, short for "utility".

Varsity University.

Vegemite or **Marmite** dark, savoury yeast-extract spreads. There's always debate between those that love Vegemite (Australian) and those that prefer Kiwi Marmite – sweeter and more appealing than its British equivalent – and of course those that loathe all the above.

Wahine Woman.

Waiata Maori action songs.

Wairua Spirit.

Waka Maori canoe.

Waratah Stake, a term used to describe snow poles on tramps.

Wero Challenge before entering a *marae*.

Whakapapa Family tree or genealogical relationship.

Whanau Extended family group.

Whare Maori for a house.

Whare runanga Meeting house.

Whare whakairo Carved house.

Wop-wops Remote areas.

Small print and Index

A Rough Guide to Rough Guides

Published in 1982, the first Rough Guide – to Greece – was a student scheme that became a publishing phenomenon. Mark Ellingham, a recent graduate in English from Bristol University, had been travelling in Greece the previous summer and couldn't find the right guidebook. With a small group of friends he wrote his own guide, combining a highly contemporary, journalistic style with a thoroughly practical approach to travellers' needs.

The immediate success of the book spawned a series that rapidly covered dozens of destinations. And, in addition to impecunious backpackers, Rough Guides soon acquired a much broader and older readership that relished the guides' wit and inquisitiveness as much as their enthusiastic, critical approach and value-for-money ethos.

These days, Rough Guides include recommendations from shoestring to luxury and cover more than 200 destinations around the globe, including almost every country in the Americas and Europe, more than half of Africa and most of Asia and Australasia. Our ever-growing team of authors and photographers is spread all over the world, particularly in Europe, the USA and Australia.

In the early 1990s, Rough Guides branched out of travel, with the publication of Rough Guides to World Music, Classical Music and the Internet. All three have become benchmark titles in their fields, spearheading the publication of a wide range of books under the Rough Guide name.

Including the travel series, Rough Guides now number more than 350 titles, covering: phrasebooks, waterproof maps, music guides from Opera to Heavy Metal, reference works as diverse as Conspiracy Theories and Shakespeare, and popular culture books from iPods to Poker. Rough Guides also produce a series of more than 120 World Music CDs in partnership with World Music Network.

Visit www.roughguides.com to see our latest publications.

Rough Guide travel images are available for commercial licensing at www.roughguidespictures.com

Rough Guide credits

Text editors: James Smart, Ros Belford, Ann-Marie Shaw
Layout: Sachin Tanwar
Cartography: Jasbir Sandhu
Picture editor: Sarah Cummins
Production: Rebecca Short
Proofreader: Karen Parker
Cover design: Chloë Roberts
Photographers: Jj Luck and Paul Whitfield
Editorial: London Ruth Blackmore, Alison Murchie, Andy Turner, Keith Drew, Edward Aves, Alice Park, Lucy White, Jo Kirby, Natasha Foges, Róisín Cameron, Emma Traynor, Emma Gibbs, James Rice, Kathryn Lane, Christina Valhouli, Monica Woods, Mani Ramaswamy, Joe Staines, Peter Buckley, Matthew Milton, Tracy Hopkins, Ruth Tidball; **New York** Andrew Rosenberg, Steven Horak, AnneLise Sorensen, April Isaacs, Ella Steim, Anna Owens, Sean Mahoney, Paula Neudorf, Courtney Miller; **Delhi** Madhavi Singh, Karen D'Souza
Design & Pictures: London Scott Stickland, Dan May, Diana Jarvis, Nicole Newman, Mark Thomas, Emily Taylor; **Delhi** Umesh Aggarwal, Ajay Verma, Jessica Subramanian, Ankur Guha, Pradeep Thapliyal, Anita Singh, Nikhil Agarwal
Production: Vicky Baldwin
Cartography: London Maxine Repath, Ed Wright, Katie Lloyd-Jones, Miles Irving; **Delhi** Jai Prakash Mishra, Rajesh Chhibber, Ashutosh Bharti, Rajesh Mishra, Animesh Pathak, Karobi Gogoi, Alakananda Bhattacharya, Swati Handoo
Online: Narender Kumar, Rakesh Kumar, Amit Verma, Rahul Kumar, Ganesh Sharma, Debojit Borah, Saurabh Sati, Ravi Yadav
Marketing & Publicity: London Liz Statham, Niki Hanmer, Louise Maher, Jess Carter, Vanessa Godden, Vivienne Watton, Anna Paynton, Rachel Sprackett, Libby Jellie, Jayne McPherson, Holly Dudley; **New York** Geoff Colquitt, Katy Ball; **Delhi** Ragini Govind
Manager India: Punita Singh
Reference Director: Andrew Lockett
Operations Manager: Helen Phillips
PA to Publishing Director: Nicola Henderson
Publishing Director: Martin Dunford
Commercial Manager: Gino Magnotta
Managing Director: John Duhigg

Publishing information

This sixth edition published September 2008 by **Rough Guides Ltd**,
80 Strand, London WC2R 0RL
345 Hudson St, 4th Floor,
New York, NY 10014, USA
14 Local Shopping Centre, Panchsheel Park,
New Delhi 110017, India
Distributed by the Penguin Group
Penguin Books Ltd,
80 Strand, London WC2R 0RL
Penguin Group (USA)
375 Hudson Street, NY 10014, USA
Penguin Group (Australia)
250 Camberwell Road, Camberwell,
Victoria 3124, Australia
Penguin Group (Canada)
195 Harry Walker Parkway N, Newmarket, ON,
L3Y 7B3 Canada
Penguin Group (NZ)
67 Apollo Drive, Mairangi Bay, Auckland 1310,
New Zealand
Cover concept by Peter Dyer.

Typeset in Bembo and Helvetica to an original design by Henry Iles.

Printed in Italy by L.E.G.O. S.p.A, Lavis (TN)

952pp includes index

A catalogue record for this book is available from the British Library

ISBN: 978-1-85828-661-7

1 3 5 7 9 8 6 4 2

Help us update

We've gone to a lot of effort to ensure that the sixth edition of **The Rough Guide to New Zealand** is accurate and up to date. However, things change – places get "discovered", opening hours are notoriously fickle, restaurants and rooms raise prices or lower standards. If you feel we've got it wrong or left something out, we'd like to know, and if you can remember the address, the price, the hours, the phone number, so much the better.

Please send your comments with the subject line "**Rough Guide New Zealand Update**" to ⓔ mail@roughguides.com. We'll credit all contributions and send a copy of the next edition (or any other Rough Guide if you prefer) for the very best emails.

Have your questions answered and tell others about your trip at ⓦ community.roughguides.com

Acknowledgements

Tony Thanks to all the operators I visited, people I stayed with and those that provided invaluable help along the way, particularly the dedicated staff of the NZ i-SITES. Special mention must be made of the hospitality of Gerry Hill at the Ponsonby Bed and Breakfast, the Matai Team (Don and Gavin), the YHA team, who always provide aid and a bed when necessary, and Tony Lyons of Ace Rentals. Much gratitude goes to editor James Smart, who has maintained enthusiasm and a good sense of humour throughout the process, all the other people at RG who have contributed and my fellow authors. Finally, the Oscar for "I couldn't have done it with out you" goes to Alison, while awards for best supporting roles go to Violet, Don, John, Anne, Clare, James and little Rob, Kate, John (the other), Stan, Rachel and all the usual suspects.

Paul would like to thank everyone met on research trips throughout the land, especially those who suggested great restaurants to check out, waxed lyrical about hotels and hostels and shared experiences. Special thanks go out to Wendy and Phil in Arrowtown, Richard and Raewyn in Wellington and Bruce for stretching his legs on the Mount Somers Circuit. Cheers too to Phil and Kozue for company around Lake Waikaremoana and my co-author Catherine for helping check out the bars in Christchurch. Lastly, huge gratitude is due to Marion for hanging in there through long absences.

Catherine Cheers to all the locals, fellow travellers and tourism professionals who provided insights, information and good times during my journey. In particular, thanks to Claire Allred at YHA HQ and the fantastic hostel managers throughout NZ; Tony Lyons and everyone at the aptly named Ace Rental Cars; Jan, Craig and friends in the Catlins; Kate in Martinborough; and Ulva on Stewart and Ulva islands. Cheers too to Carsten for awesome insider tips and for the surfboard loan; and to Paulie for the Fiordland debrief. At Rough Guides, major thanks to editor James Smart and fellow authors Paul and Tony for a smooth-sailing gig from start to finish and to Ros Belford for the Northland edits, as well as Kate Berens for getting me onboard. Above all, heartfelt thanks to my family and friends for support (and for the trans-Tasman visits). Lastly, cheers to Auckland airport's departure lounge for throwing a free Dave Dobbyn concert. Choice!

Readers' letters

Thanks to all the readers who have taken the time to write in with comments and suggestions (and apologies if we've inadvertently omitted or misspelt anyone's name):

Ralph & Sandra Allen, Manuel Garcia Angeles, C. & B. Arends, Graham Avery, Mrs R Batemen, Marilyn Bew, Christine Bock, Christine Chandler, Tomasz Cukiernik, Michael Cuningham, Helen Palmer Dale, Nigel Davenport, A.P Davies, June Dechant, Dr Lenka Drabkova, T.S Earnshaw, Margaret Ecclestone, Tim Ford, Mrs Foster, Eva & Wilfried Glawischnik, Michelle Gleadall, Sally Griffiths, James Grigg, Lee Gutcher, Richard M. Hanney, Keith & Angela Hanson, Margaret & Gil Harding, Nick Harry, Stephen Hayunak, Matt Heartman, Greg Krush, Sierra Jenkins, Jane Leigh, Louise Locock, Sally Lomax, Sally Madgwick, Natalie Maier, Sarah & Wayne Marston, Oscar & Margaret Merne, Ian & Jennifer Messerle, Peter & Diane McKinnon, Brian & Gill Mills, Penny Moore, Andrew Moth, Clive Paul, Charles Pochin, Andy Popperwell, Tia Renouf, Marion Richards, Róisín, Rose & Michel, Anna Sacra, Matt Sandland, Tanja Schimdt, Mike Scott, Richard Sedding, Bernie Shipp, Gavin Smyth, Jeff Southerton & Aileen McHarg, Jane Taylor, Vera Taylor, Simon & Maureen Tennent, Paul Thornton, Leen Van Butsel, Ivan Valencic, Alison Wardle, Anne Weeks, Ian Williams, Linda & Chuck Wills, Samantha Wilson, Sue & Ray Wiltshire, Donald Wood, Ann Woodward.

Photo credits

All photos © Rough Guides except the following:

Front cover

Boulders in surf, Moeraki, South Island © Kevin Schafer/ Getty

Back cover

Rafting, Shotover River, Queenstown © Paul Whitfield/Rough Guides

Title page

Kiwi on Lake Wakatipu © JTB/Drr.net

Introduction

New Zealand Rugby team doing the Haka © Associated Sports Photography/Alamy
Woman walking between hot springs © Steven Vilder/Eurasia Press/Corbis

Things not to miss

01 Milford Sound © Bruce Percy/Alamy
04 Bungy Jumping © AJ Hackett/Tourism New Zealand
07 Taieri Gorge © David Wall/Alamy
11 Maori Hangi © Dan Santillo/Alamy
15 Tree Ferns © Arco Images/Alamy
16 Whanganui river journey © Tourism New Zealand
17 Whale watching © Ben Crawford/Tourism New Zealand
22 Diving © Tourism New Zealand
25 Ninety Mile Beach © Chris McLennan/Tourism New Zealand
30 Caving in Waitomo © Imagestate/Alamy

Maori in the modern world colour section

Maori carving © David Wall/Danita Delimont Agency/Drr.net
Haka © James Heremaia/Tourism New Zealand
Hongi © James Heremaia/Tourism New Zealand
Warrior with Taiaha © Imagebroker/Alamy
Traditional Moko Tattoo © George Steinmetz/ Corbis
Maori paddlers on Waka © Richard Trillo

Adrenalin heaven colour section

Bungy Jumper © AJ Hackett/Tourism New Zealand
Heli-hikers on Franz Josef Glacier © David Wall/ Danita Delimont Agency/Drr.net
Skiing the Ragged Range © James Kay/Stock Collection/Drr.net

Protecting New Zealand's native wildlife colour section

Kiwi © Neil Farrin/JAI/Corbis
Tuatara © Andy Trowbridge/Drr.net
Moa and Kiwi, nineteenth-century print © Classic Image/Alamy
Saddleback bird © Dave Walsh/Drr.net
Male Stitchbird © Andy Trowbridge/Drr.net
Predator control, Kiwi conservation © Terry Whittaker/Alamy

Black and whites

p.166 Diver and Red Pigfish © Ross Armstrong/ Alamy
p.589 City Tram, Christchurch © Robert Harding/ Jupiter Images
p.666 View from train, Taieri Gorge © Ian Dagnall/Alamy
p.838 Sea Kayaking, Doubtful Sound © Suzanne Long/Alamy
p.899 Maori man © Anders Ryman/Alam

Index

Map entries are in colour.

B

C

D

E

F

G

L

M

INDEX

N

O

P

Q

R

S

U

V

W

Y

Map symbols

maps are listed in the full index using coloured text

- Chapter boundary
- International boundary
- Provincial boundary
- Motorway
- National highway
- Pedestrianized street
- Road
- Steps
- Underpass
- Unpaved road
- Path
- River
- Ferry route
- Railway
- Cable car
- Bridge/tunnel
- Mountain range
- Peak
- Waterfall
- Spring
- Surf/beach
- Cave
- Boat stop
- Bus stop
- International airport
- Domestic airport
- Fuel station
- Parking
- Hut
- Winery
- Point of interest
- Tourist office
- Gardens
- Lighthouse
- Hospital
- Post office
- Internet access
- Telephone
- Toilet
- Swimming pool
- Ski area
- Campsite
- Accommodation
- Restaurant
- Castle
- Golf course
- Viewpoint
- Ruins
- Museum
- Statue
- Church (regional maps)
- Church (town maps)
- Stadium
- Building
- Cemetery
- Park/forest
- Swamp
- Beach
- Glacier